Introduction to Advertising and Promotion Management

Introduction to Advertising and Promotion Management

George E. Belch

San Diego State University

Michael A. Belch

San Diego State University

Homewood, IL 60430
Boston, MA 02116

© RICHARD D. IRWIN, INC., 1990

Developmental editor: Ann M. Granacki
Project editor: Paula M. Buschman
Production manager: Carma W. Fazio
Compositor: Caliber Design Planning, Inc.
Typeface: 10/12 Clearface
Printer: Von Hoffmann Press, Inc.

Library of Congress Cataloging-in-Publication Data

Belch, George E. (George Edward)
    Introduction to advertising and promotion management/George E.
Belch, Michael A. Belch.
        p. cm.
    ISBN 0-256-07972-2   ISBN 0-256-09869-7 (International ed.)
    1. Advertising.   2. Sales promotion.   I. Belch, Michael A.
II. Title.
HF5823.B387   1990
659.1—dc20   89–27275
                                                CIP

Printed in the United States of America
2 3 4 5 6 7 8 9 0 VH 7 6 5 4 3 2 1 0

To Gayle, Derek, and Danny
GEB

To Renee and Jessica
MAB

and

To Mom and Dad
A special dedication from both of us
for being such great parents

Preface

There is probably no more dynamic and fascinating a field to either practice or study than that of advertising and promotion. In our increasingly complex world, organizations in both the private and public sector have learned that their ability to create and disseminate effective advertising and promotional messages to their target audiences is often critical to their success. Advertising messages are used to sell products and services as well as to promote causes, market political candidates, and deal with societal problems such as the AIDS crisis or drug abuse. Advertising has become a prestigious profession and a major course of study in many universities as more and more students are choosing careers in advertising or a related area of marketing and promotion.

This text serves as an introduction to the field of advertising and promotion management. It is important to note, however, that while advertising is its major focus, it is more than just a book on advertising. This is because there is more to an organization's marketing communications efforts than simply advertising. In recent years, the role of advertising and promotion in the overall marketing process has changed considerably. The audiences that marketers seek, along with the media and methods for reaching them, have become increasingly fragmented. Advertising and promotional efforts have become more regionalized and targeted to specific audiences. Spending on sales promotion activities targeted at both consumers and the trade has surpassed advertising media expenditures. Marketers are working to coordinate all of their communications efforts so they can send cohesive and effective messages to their customers. Many advertising agencies have acquired, started, or become affiliated with sales promotion, direct marketing, and public relations companies to better serve their clients' marketing communications and promotional needs.

This text takes a broad view in examining the field of advertising and promotion and the world of marketing communications. To fully understand advertising and its role in contemporary marketing, attention must be given to other promotional areas such as sales promotion, public relations, and personal selling. To effectively plan, implement, and evaluate advertising and promotional programs requires an understanding of the overall marketing process, consumer behavior, and communications theory.

We have attempted to present a balance of theoretical and practical perspectives and to integrate the two. We draw from the extensive research and theorizing in advertising, consumer behavior, communications, marketing, and other areas to provide the reader with a basis for understanding the marketing communications process and how it influences consumer decision making. The book also takes a promotional planning and strategy perspective and is built around a well-accepted model of the advertising and promotional planning process.

A particular strength of this text is the integration of the various concepts, theories, and ideas with practical application. Nearly every day an article or example of advertising and promotion in practice is reported in the media. We have used a variety of sources such as *The Wall Street Journal, Business Week, Fortune, Marketing & Media Decisions, Advertising Age, Adweek, Business Marketing,* and many others to find practical examples that are integrated throughout the text. Each chapter begins with a vignette that presents a practical example of effective, or sometimes ineffective, advertising and promotion or other interesting insights. Each chapter also contains a number of boxed items, Promotional Perspectives, that present in-depth discussions of particular issues related to the chapter material. There are more than 300 advertisements and illustrations, all of which were carefully chosen and keyed to the topic material to illustrate a particular idea, concept, theory, or practical application.

To the Student

As professors we were, of course, once students ourselves. In many ways we are perpetual students in that we are constantly striving to learn about, understand, and explain how advertising and promotion work. We share many of the interests and concerns that you do, and are often excited (and bored) by the same things. Having taught in the advertising and promotion area for a combined 25 plus years, we feel that we have developed an understanding of what makes a book in this field interesting to students.

In writing this book we tried to remember how we felt about the various texts we have used throughout the years. We have tried to incorporate the good things and minimize those we felt were of little use. We have strived not to make this a book of terms or overburden you with definitions, although we do call out those we feel are especially important to your understanding of the material. We also remember that, as students, we were often not really into theory—that was something for the professor to get excited about. It is our belief, however, that to fully understand how advertising and promotion works, it is necessary to establish some theoretical basis. The more you can understand about how things are supposed to work, the easier it will be for you to understand and explain why they do or do not work as planned.

Perhaps the one question that students most often ask is, "How do I use this in the 'real' world?" We did not forget to answer this question; we have provided numerous examples of how the various theories, concepts, principles, and so on can be used in practice. As you will see, these examples are from actual companies. Some are older, classic examples while most are current, and they cover a variety of products, services, markets, and topics. Please take time to read the chapter openings and Promotional Perspectives and study the diverse ads and illustrations. We think you will find that they stimulate your interest and are not far removed from those events with which you deal with in your daily life as a consumer and as a target of advertising and promotion.

To the Instructor

This text attempts to approach advertising and promotion from a broad perspective and to integrate theory with planning, management, and strategy. While we consider this an introductory text, we want to emphasize that we treat each topic in some depth. It is our belief that the marketing and advertising student of today needs a text that provides more than just an introduction to terms, definitions, and topics.

The book is positioned primarily for the introductory advertising, marketing communications, or promotions course as taught in the business/marketing curriculum. It can also be used in journalism/communications courses when there is an emphasis on a marketing and promotional planning perspective. In addition to its coverage of advertising, this text has chapters on consumer- and trade-oriented sales promotion, personal selling, and publicity/public relations. These chapter stress the integration of advertising with other promotional mix elements as well as the need to understand their role in the overall marketing program.

Organization of This Text

The first three chapters lay the foundation for understanding the various promotional mix elements, how advertising and promotion fit into the overall marketing process, how agencies operate and the functions they perform, and how a company organizes for advertising and promotion. Chapter 4 covers important perspectives on consumer behavior and their implications for advertising and promotion, while Chapters 5 and 6 present a detailed examination of communications theories and models and the individual communication elements such as source, message, channel, and receiver/response factors. Chapter 7 presents the important areas of market segmentation, target marketing, and positioning. It is our feeling that these first seven chapters provide the student with the background against which specific advertising and promotional planning decisions can be made and evaluated.

Chapter 8 focuses on setting goals and objectives for advertising and stresses the importance of knowing what to expect from advertising, the difference between sales versus communication objectives, characteristics of good objectives, and problems in setting objectives. The advertising and promotional budgets are discussed in Chapter 9 along with traditional methods for setting and allocating promotional expenditures.

Chapters 10 through 13 cover media strategy and planning as well as the various advertising media. Chapter 10 introduces the key concepts and principles of media planning, Chapter 11 discusses the broadcast media of television and radio, and Chapter 12 presents the organization, characteristics, strengths, and weaknesses of the print media. Chapter 13 examines the role of support media such as outdoor and transit advertising as well as some of the new media alternatives that are developing. The role and use of the rapidly growing area of direct marketing is also discussed in this chapter.

Chapter 14 examines creative strategy, focusing on the process that guides the creation of the advertising message, inputs to the creative process, and various creative approaches, appeals, and executions that are used by advertisers. Chapters 15 through 17 focus on nonadvertising areas of the promotional mix. Chapter 15 examines consumer-oriented sales promotion and its role in the marketing and promotional program while trade-oriented promotions and other aspects of reseller support are covered in Chapter 16. Basic issues regarding personal selling and its role in promotional strategy are also presented in Chapter 16. Chapter 17 covers publicity and public relations.

In Chapter 18 we turn our attention to evaluating and measuring the effectiveness of advertising and promotion. Various methods for pretesting and posttesting of advertising messages and campaigns are discussed. Chapters 19 and 20 focus on special markets for advertising and promotion. Chapter 19 deals with business-to-business marketing and examines how advertising and other forms of promotion are used to help one company sell its products or services to another firm. In Chapter 20 we examine the global marketplace and the role of advertising and promotions in international marketing.

The text concludes with a discussion of the regulatory, social, and economic environment. Chapter 21 examines the area of advertising regulation, including industry self-regulation and regulation by governmental agencies such as the Federal Trade

Commission. Advertising's role and influence in society is constantly changing and our discussion would not be complete without considering, in Chapter 22, the various criticisms regarding the social and economic effects of advertising.

Chapter Features

The following features are in each chapter to enhance students' learning and understanding of the material as well as their reading enjoyment.

Chapter Objectives   Provided at the beginning of each chapter to identify the main goals and indicate what should be learned from each chapter.

Opening Vignettes   Provide a practical example or application or discuss an interesting issue that is relevant to the chapter. These opening vignettes are designed to create interest in the material that is presented in the chapter.

Promotional Perspectives   Boxed items featuring in-depth discussions of interesting issues related to the chapter coverage. Each chapter contains several of these insights into the world of advertising and promotion.

Key Terms   Highlighted in boldface throughout the chapter, with a list at the end of each chapter. These terms help call students' attention to important ideas, concepts, and definitions.

Chapter Summaries   Written in detail to provide a synopsis and serve as a quick review of important topics covered.

Discussion Questions   Provided at the end of each chapter to give students an opportunity to test their understanding of the material and to apply it. These questions can also serve as a basis for class discussion as well as assignments.

Four-Color Visuals   Print advertisements, photoboards, and other material appear in many sections of the text. Numerous ads and illustrations in two colors and black and white are also presented. More than 300 ads and illustrations appear in the book.

Support Material

Instructor's Guide with Test Bank   A complete teaching resource that includes learning objectives, chapter outlines, lecture outlines, answers to discussion questions, teaching notes for transparency acetates, and additional references. A test bank of more than 1,200 questions including multiple choice, true-false, and essay questions for each chapter.

Four-Color Transparencies   Each adopter receives a set of 70 four-color acetate transparencies. These acetates present additional print advertisements and commercial photoboards that do not appear in the book as well as important charts and illustrations that enhance lectures and presentations.

Acknowledgments

The task of writing this text has proven to be an enormous one and has required much more time and effort than we ever anticipated. While this project represents a tremendous amount of work on our part, it would not have become a reality without the assistance and support of many other people.

Most authors probably begin a project thinking that they have the best ideas, approach, examples, organization, and the like for writing a great book. However, you quickly learn that despite how good your ideas and efforts may be, there is always room for them to be improved upon by others. A number of colleagues provided us with detailed, thoughtful reviews that were immensely helpful in making this a better book. We are very grateful to the following individuals for their constructive comments:

Lauranne Buchanan
University of Illinois

Lindell Chew
University of Missouri, St. Louis

Catherine Cole
University of Iowa

John Faier
Miami University

Raymond Fisk
Oklahoma State University

Donald Grambois
Indiana University

Stephen Grove
Clemson University

Ron Hill
American University

Paul Jackson
Ferris State College

Don Kirchner
California State University, Northridge

Paul Prabhaker
DePaul University, Chicago

Mary Ann Stutts
Southwest Texas State University

Terrence Witkowski
California State University, Long Beach

Robert Young
Northeastern University

We also would like to acknowledge the assistance and cooperation we received from many people in the business, advertising, and media communities. This book contains several hundred ads, illustrations, charts, and tables that have been provided by advertisers and/or their agencies, various publications, and other advertising and industry organizations. Many individuals took time from their busy schedules to provide us with requested materials. The numerous ads, charts, graphs, and other visuals they have given us permission to use are extremely valuable to an advertising text.

There are several advertising practitioners who helped make this book more practical and realistic by sharing their insights and experiences. We would like to acknowledge the assistance of Richard Brooks, president of Phillips-Ramsey, Inc., as well as the many individuals at Young & Rubicam—New York who provided tremendous insight into the advertising agency business. A special thanks goes to Susan Fournier for arranging the meetings with the Y&R people.

Obviously a manuscript does not become a book without a great deal of work on the part of a publisher. Various individuals at Richard D. Irwin and Times Mirror/Mosby have been involved with this project over the last several years. Beth Battram was instrumental in our working with Times Mirror/Mosby. In the early stages we received valuable guidance and assistance from Elizabeth Schilling. Alice Fugate carefully managed the review process for the first two drafts, providing useful comments on style and content. Ann Granacki has guided the final stages of this project, gracefully enduring our anxiety and trauma. Thanks also to Paula Buschman for managing the production process and helping keep track of all the artwork. We think we finally found it all!

We would also like to acknowledge the support we have received from the College of Business at San Diego State University. Dean Allan Bailey has provided us with an excellent working environment and has been very supportive. Tori McCoy and Althea Channell have been a tremendous help with their secretarial support.

On a more personal note, a great deal of thanks goes to our families for putting up with us over the past few years while we were writing this book. Renee, Jessica, Gayle, Danny, and Derek have had to endure the deviation from our usually pleasant personalities and dispositions. We look forward to returning to normal. Finally we would like to acknowledge each other for making it through this ordeal. Our mother will be happy to know that we still get along after all of this.

Contents

4

Perspectives on Consumer Behavior   90

5

The Communications Process   126

6

Source, Message, and Channel Factors   158

7

Market Segmentation and Positioning   198

8

Determining Advertising and Promotional Objectives   228

9

The Advertising and Promotions Budget   256

10

Media Planning and Strategy   278

11

Evaluation of Broadcast Media   328

12

Evaluation of Print Media: Magazines and Newspapers   376

13

Support Media and Direct Marketing   420

14

Creative Strategy   456

15

Consumer-Oriented Sales Promotion   504

16

The Role of Personal Selling and Reseller Support in the Promotional Program   548

17

Public Relations, Publicity, and Corporate Advertising   574

18

Measuring the Effectiveness of the Promotional Program 604

19

Business-to-Business Communications   636

20

International Advertising and Promotion   656

21

Advertising Regulation   700

22

Evaluating the Social and Economic Aspects of Advertising   726

Introduction to Advertising and Promotion Management

An Introduction to Advertising and Promotion

CHAPTER OBJECTIVES

1. To examine the promotional function and its role in an organization's marketing program

2. To introduce the various elements of the promotional mix and consider the advantages and limitations of each

3. To examine the various tasks and responsibilities involved in promotional management

4. To introduce a model of the promotional planning process and examine the various steps in this procedure

The Hot Cereal Wars

For years the Quaker Oats Company dominated the $600 million hot cereal market with its line of oatmeal products. However, in 1987 Quaker faced its first major challenge in years when General Mills introduced TOTAL Oatmeal. TOTAL Oatmeal's introduction was supported by a $20 million promotional campaign that included a $12 million budget for television advertising, print ads, direct-mail couponing, and cross couponing on other General Mills cereals. The advertising and promotional pieces emphasized that TOTAL Oatmeal had "more nutrition than Quick Quaker Oats" and used side-by-side nutritional comparisons with Quick Quaker Oats, as shown in Figure 1–1.

Quaker responded to TOTAL Oatmeal's assault on its brand by spending an unprecedented $45.6 million to defend its very high market share. Television advertising spending was increased 76 percent to $21.1 million during the peak season for hot cereals (fall and winter months). The ads featured actor Wilford Brimley as the grandfatherly spokesman for the product. The campaign theme, "Quaker Oats: It's the right thing to do," emphasized the nutritional value of the brand and health claims about cholesterol reduction (see Figure 1–2).

In addition to the advertising effort, Quaker's promotional campaign included the distribution of 12.5 million free samples of its instant oatmeal with the purchase of two boxes of other oatmeal flavors or other Quaker cereals, Thanksgiving and Christmas promotional tie-ins, and coupon inserts teaming the oatmeal products with ready-to-eat cereals and other products such as chocolate chips and Carnation Hot Cocoa Mix. To promote the fact that the product could be prepared in a microwave, game cards were placed in 11 million specially marked packages of Quick Quaker Oats with prizes including microwave ovens and 11-piece microwave cooking sets.

After the first year of battle, as the prime winter season for hot cereals ended, both sides were claiming victory. General Mills said that the new TOTAL Oatmeal brand was right on target, achieving 8 percent of hot cereal sales, whereas Quaker retained control of the market, as its share rose two percentage points to 67 percent. Indications were that smaller brands lost business as the two rivals battled but that the hot cereal market grew 24 percent, reversing a 30-year decline in sales.

For the 1988/89 winter season, General Mills raised its promotional spending to $35 million and added three new products to its line, including Oatmeal Swirlers, packets of instant oatmeal accompanied by a separate packet of fruit to add to the cereal. The Oatmeal Swirlers line was designed to enhance oatmeal's appeal to children. Quaker countered by raising its promotional budget to nearly $60 million and introduced Quaker Extra, an instant oatmeal fortified with 10 vitamins and minerals.

The popularity of oat-based cereal products continues to increase as a result of studies praising their health benefits. Thus, Quaker and General Mills, as well as several other companies, are likely to continue their aggressive advertising and promotional efforts as the hot cereal wars continue.[1,2,3,4]

Introduction

The battle between Quaker Oats and General Mills in the hot cereal market illustrates the significant role promotional strategy plays in modern marketing. When General Mills decided to declare Total war (pun intended) on Quaker Oats Company's dominant share of the hot cereal market, they turned to advertising and sales promotion techniques as their primary offensive weapons. Note how Quaker's strategy for defending its high market share also relied heavily on advertising and sales promotion tools. The promotional efforts of these companies, along with favorable market conditions created by consumers' feverish interest in oat-based cereals, have resulted in tremendous growth in a market that was stagnant for many years.

It will be interesting to see if Quaker and General Mills continue to increase their spending on advertising and promotion and whether the growth in this market will continue. What might happen to sales if they cut back on their promotional budgets and efforts? What steps might other competitors such as American Home Foods, Ralston Purina, and Nabisco take to promote their brands and make them more competitive? By the time you are reading this book, one of these companies may have altered their marketing and/or promotional program and experienced a significant change in its sales or market share. One thing that is unlikely to change, however, is the importance promotional strategy will play in the marketing programs of these firms, as well as thousands of others, as they attempt to communicate with and sell their products

Figure 1–1   TOTAL Oatmeal Used Direct Comparisons with Quaker Oats in Its Advertising and Promotions

Figure 1–2   Quaker Oats Used a Celebrity to Deliver Its Nutritional Message

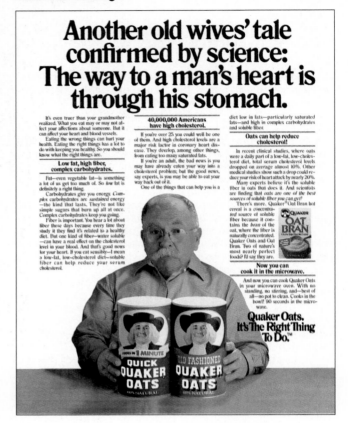

and services to consumers. Advertising and promotion have become integral parts of the marketing process in most organizations. To understand the role that promotion plays in this process better, let us first examine the marketing function itself.

What Is Marketing?

Before reading on, stop for a moment and think about how you would define what marketing is and what it entails. Chances are that each student reading this book would come up with a somewhat different answer to this question, as marketing is often viewed in terms of individual activities that constitute the overall marketing process. For example, one popular conception of marketing is that it primarily involves sales and the selling process. Other perspectives view marketing as consisting primarily of advertising or retailing activities. For some of you, activities such as market research, pricing, or product planning may have come to mind. While all these activities are a part of marketing, it is incorrect to limit your perspective to just these individual elements. The American Marketing Association, which is an organization representing marketing professions in the United States and Canada, defines **marketing** as

> the process of planning and executing the conception, pricing, promotion, and distribution of ideas, goods, and services to create exchanges that satisfy individual and organizational objectives.[5]

Consideration of this definition reveals that marketing involves more than just an individual activity such as sales or promotion. Actually, effective marketing requires that managers recognize the interdependence of these various activities and how they can be combined to develop a marketing program.

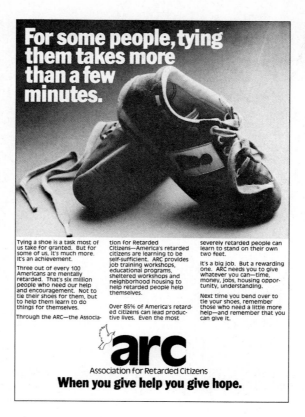

Marketing Focuses on Exchange

The definition presented above, along with most contemporary perspectives of marketing, recognizes that exchange is a central concept in marketing. In fact, it has been suggested that **exchange** constitutes the core phenomenon or basic domain for study in marketing.[6] For exchange to take place, there must be two or more parties with something of value to one another, a desire and ability to give up their something of value to the other party, and a way for the parties to communicate with each other. Advertising and promotion play an important role in the exchange process by informing consumers of an organization's product or service and convincing or persuading them of its ability to satisfy their needs or wants.

The exchange process generally involves consumers exchanging money for a company's product or service. However, not all marketing transactions involve the exchange of money for a tangible product or service. Nonprofit organizations such as charities, religious organizations, the arts, and colleges and universities (probably including the one you are attending) seek and receive millions of dollars in donations every year. Charitable organizations often use ads such as the one shown in Figure 1–3 to solicit contributions from the public. Donors generally do not receive any material benefits for their contributions but donate in exchange for intangible social and psychological satisfactions such as feelings of goodwill or altruism.

The Marketing Mix

The role of marketing is one of facilitating the exchange process by carefully examining the needs and wants of consumers, developing a product or service that satisfies these needs, offering it at a certain price, making it available through a particular place or channel of distribution, and developing a program of promotion or communication to create awareness and interest. These four *p's*—*product, price, place* (distribution), and *promotion*—are referred to as elements of the **marketing mix.** The basic task of

Figure 1—4   **A Distinctive Package and Brand Name Help Communicate a Quality Image for a Product**

marketing is one of combining these four elements into a marketing program to facilitate the potential for exchange with consumers in the marketplace.

Determination of the proper marketing mix does not just happen. Marketers must be knowledgeable of the issues and options that are involved in decisions regarding each element of the mix. They must also be aware of how these elements interact and how they can be combined to provide an effective marketing program. Developing a marketing program requires that the market be studied and analyzed through consumer research and that this information be utilized in developing an overall marketing strategy and mix.

The primary focus of this book is on one element of the marketing mix: the promotional variable. However, the promotional program must be part of a viable marketing strategy and coordinated with other marketing activities. A firm can spend large sums of money on advertising or sales promotion but stands little chance of success if the product is of poor quality, is priced improperly, or does not have adequate distribution and availability to consumers. The influence of other elements of the marketing program on promotion will be examined in more detail in Chapter 2, but first let us turn our attention to examining the role of promotion and its various components.

Role of Promotion in Marketing

Promotion has been defined as "the coordination of all seller initiated efforts to set up channels of information and persuasion to sell goods and services or promote an idea."[7] Promotion is best viewed as the communications function of marketing. In the broadest sense, all the marketing mix variables can be viewed as communicating with consumers. For example, a high price may symbolize and communicate quality to a customer, as may various aspects of the product itself such as its shape or design, packaging, or brand name. Vanderbilt perfume is an example of a product that uses a

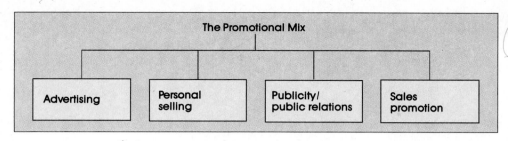

Figure 1–5   **Elements of the Promotional Mix**

distinctive package and brand name as well as a high price to connote a quality, upscale image that is reinforced by its advertising (see Figure 1–4).

While implicit communication does occur through the various elements of the marketing mix, most of an organization's communications with the marketplace take place through a carefully planned and controlled promotional program. The basic tools or elements that are used to accomplish an organization's communication objectives are often referred to as the **promotional mix** and include advertising, personal selling, publicity/public relations and sales promotion (see Figure 1–5). Each of the promotional mix elements plays a distinctive role in the marketing program and may take on a variety of forms, and each has certain advantages and limitations. Let us examine these elements in more detail.

The Promotional Mix

Advertising

Advertising is defined as any paid form of nonpersonal communication about an organization, product, service, or idea by an identified sponsor.[8] There are several aspects of this definition that should be noted. First, the *paid* aspect of this definition reflects the fact that the space or time for an advertising message generally must be bought. (An occasional exception to this is the public service announcement [PSA] where the advertising space or time is donated by the media.) The *nonpersonal* component indicates that advertising involves mass media (e.g., television, radio, magazines, newspapers) whereby a message can be transmitted to large groups of individuals, often at the same point in time. The nonpersonal nature of advertising means that there is generally no opportunity for immediate feedback from the message recipient (except in direct-response advertising). Therefore, before the message is sent, the advertiser must attempt to understand how the audience will interpret and respond to the message.

There are several advantages to the use of advertising in the firm's promotional mix. Since the company pays for the advertising space, it can *control* what it wants to say, when it wants to say it, and to some extent, to whom the message is sent. Advertising can also represent a cost-effective method for communicating with large audiences, and cost per contact through advertising is often quite low. For example, in the 1989 Super Bowl, the cost of a 30-second commercial spot was $675,000. However, the advertisers were potentially able to reach more than an estimated 120 million viewers with their message, resulting in an extremely low cost per exposure.

Advertising also can be used to create images and symbolic appeals for products and services, a capability that is very important to companies that are selling products and services that are very difficult to differentiate. For example, many consumers cannot distinguish one brand of beer or cigarettes from another on the basis of taste. Thus, the image or psychological associations that consumers have of a brand become a very important part of their purchase decisions. Marlboro cigarettes is an example of a product that became a market leader as a result of an advertising campaign that took a lackluster brand targeted toward women and repositioned it by creating a masculine image for the brand (Figure 1–6).

Figure 1—6   Marlboro Became a Leading Brand of Cigarettes by Developing a Masculine Image for the Product

Figure 1—7   Wendy's "Where's the Beef?" Ad Was Very Effective in Increasing Sales

Another advantage of advertising is its ability to strike a responsive chord with consumers when other elements of the marketing program have not been successful. For example, in 1984 Wendy's "Where's the Beef" advertising campaign, which featured the late Clara Peller, helped boost the fast-food chain's sales by 26 percent (Figure 1—7). The campaign slogan became a popular saying used by everyone from children to presidential candidates. Another example of the power of a creative ad campaign to impact a product's sales is discussed in Promotional Perspective 1—1.

Advertising does, of course, have some disadvantages. The costs of producing and placing advertising can be very high. One study indicated that the cost of producing a 30-second commercial for a national brand averages nearly $200,000 when all the costs, including those for development of material that is later rejected, are taken into account.[9] Media costs have also been increasing rapidly, particularly for television, as the cost of a 30-second spot on network TV during the evening averaged $104,000 in 1987 as compared with only $57,900 in 1980.[10] The lack of direct feedback of most advertising is also a drawback, as this makes it difficult for the advertiser to determine how well the message was received and whether it was effective.

Other problems with advertising include its credibility and the ease with which it can be tuned out or ignored. Advertising is often treated with skepticism by consumers, many of whom perceive it to be very biased and are concerned by its intent to persuade. Not only are consumers skeptical about many of the advertising messages they see and hear, but it is relatively easy for them to process selectively only those ads that are of interest or relevance to them. Actually, with so many messages competing for our attention every day, it is out of necessity that we must ignore the vast

Promotional Perspective 1—1

Putting Life into Life

Over 20 years ago the Quaker Oats Company introduced Life cereal, hailing the brand as a nutritional breakthrough because of its high protein content. Early advertising for the brand stressed its nutritional value and superior taste. However, Life was marketed for years with limited success because many mothers felt that children, the key market segment for ready-to-eat cereals, would not like the taste of a nutritious cereal.

The goal of the Doyle, Dane, Bernbach Agency when it took over the Life account was to convince mothers that Life was a nutritious cereal so good tasting that even kids would like it. In the early 1970s the agency created the now-famous "Mikey likes it" commercial depicting a cute three-year-old who hates everything but likes the taste of Life cereal when he tries it. (See Exhibit 1—1A.)

Consumer response to the Mikey ads was immediate. Although other elements of Life's marketing program were unchanged, sales increased substantially, and Life moved into the top 10 brands of ready-to-eat cereal in terms of market share. Only one other cereal introduced in the last 20 years had achieved such success. Other companion ads were developed, and the campaign was used successfully for over 10 years. A marketing manager at Quaker Oats indicated that the Mikey ads were probably the single most important contributor to the sales growth of Life cereal.

In 1987 Quaker ran a very successul promotion— "Whatever happened to Mikey?"—where consumers were asked to try and guess what the now-grown Mikey looked like (Exhibit 1—1B). Boxes of Life had 20 photos on the back and asked people to guess which one was the real Mikey. The contest received 750,000 entries, and Life's market share increased 20 percent during the promotion.

Sources: *The More Creative the Ad, the Better It Sells,* Film Series, American Association of Advertising Agencies, New York, 1983; William A. Robinson, "Best Promotions of 1986–1987 Robbie Award Winners," *Marketing Communications,* October 1987, p. 43.

Exhibit 1—1A   Life Cereal's "Mikey" Ad Was the Key to the Brand's Sales Growth

1. 1st BOY: What's this stuff?
   2nd BOY: Some cereal. Supposed to be good for you.

2. 1st BOY: Did you try it?

3. 2nd BOY: I'm not gonna try it. You try it. 1st BOY: I'm not gonna try it.

4. 2nd BOY: Let's get Mikey.

5. 1st BOY: Yeah. He won't eat it.

6. He hates everything.

7. 2nd BOY: He likes it. Hey Mikey.

8. ANNCR: There are two kinds of Life Cereals to please all kinds of kids. Regular Life and Cinnamon Life.

9. Make Life Cereals part of your nutritious breakfast.

Exhibit 1—1B   Life Used a Contest to Reintroduce Mikey in 1987 Successfully

majority of them. The extent to which the American consumer is bombarded with advertising and promotional messages is illustrated by the following:

> Every day, 12 billion display and 184 billion classified advertising messages pour forth from 1,710 daily newspapers, billions of others from 7,600 weekly newspapers, and 6 billion more each day from 430 general magazines and 10,500 other periodicals. There are 4,658 AM and 3,367 FM radio stations broadcasting an average of 330,000 commercials a day, redisseminated by 5,000 cable systems. Every day, millions of people are confronted with over 500,000 outdoor billboards and painted bulletins, with 1.5 million car cards and posters in buses, subways, and commuter trains, with 40 million direct mail pieces and leaflets, and with billions of display and promotion items.[11]

Personal Selling

A second major element of an organization's promotional mix is **personal selling,** which is a form of person-to-person communication in which a seller attempts to assist and/or persuade prospective buyers to purchase the company's product or service or to act upon an idea. Unlike advertising, personal selling involves direct contact between the buyer and seller, either face-to-face or through some form of telecommunications such as telephone sales. This interaction provides the marketer with communication flexibility, as the seller can see or hear the potential buyer's reactions to the message and modify the message accordingly. The personal, individualized communication that takes place through personal selling allows the seller to tailor and adapt the message to the specific needs or situation of the customer. Personal selling also involves more immediate and precise feedback because the impact of the sales presentation can generally be assessed by the reactions of the customer. If the feedback is unfavorable, the salesperson can modify the message. Personal selling efforts can also be targeted to specific markets and customer types who are the best prospects for the company's product or service.

Personal selling also has some disadvantages. A major problem with personal selling lies in the high cost per contact. In 1988 the cost of a sales call was estimated to range from $155 to $301, depending on the industry.[12] Thus, it can be very expensive to reach large audiences through this means. In addition, different salespeople may not deliver the same message, which makes it difficult to deliver a consistent and uniform message to all customers.

Publicity/Public Relations

Another important component of an organization's promotional mix is that of publicity/public relations. **Publicity** refers to nonpersonal communications regarding an organization, product, service, or idea that is not directly paid for nor run under identified sponsorship, usually coming in the form of a news story, editorial, or announcement about an organization and/or its products and services. Like advertising, publicity involves nonpersonal communication to a mass audience, but unlike advertising, publicity is not directly paid for by the company. The company or organization will attempt to get the media to provide coverage of or run a favorable story on a product, service, cause, or event to affect awareness, knowledge, opinions, and/or behavior. The various techniques used to gain publicity include news releases, press conferences, feature articles, photographs, films, and tapes.

An advantage of publicity over other forms of promotion is its credibility. Consumers generally tend to be less skeptical toward favorable information about a product or service when it comes from a source they perceive to be unbiased and objective. For example, the success (or failure) of a new movie is very often determined by the favorableness of the reviews it receives from film critics, who are viewed as objective evaluators by many moviegoers.

Another advantage of publicity is its low cost, as the company is not paying for

Promotional Perspective **1-2**

Suzuki Fights Negative Publicity

There are few things marketers fear as much as a wave of negative publicity concerning their products' safety. In recent years, few companies have had to deal with as much bad publicity as Suzuki, the Japanese company that manufactures the Samurai sports utility vehicle. The controversy began in June 1988 when Consumers Union, publisher of *Consumer Reports* magazine, held a press conference announcing that it would give the Samurai the first "not acceptable" rating it had issued for a car in a decade. Consumers Union argued that basic design flaws tended to make the Samurai prone to rolling over and dangerously unsafe. They also called on Suzuki to recall all 160,000 Samurais that had been sold in the United States, to take the vehicle off the market, and to give full refunds to Samurai owners.

The attack on the safety of the Samurai became front page stories in newspapers across the country and was featured on both national and local television news. The vehicle was quickly in danger of becoming somewhat of a national joke as comedians incorporated the Samurai rollover claims into their routines and consumers joked about it. Within a few weeks of the Consumers Union announcement, sales of the Samurai plummeted, dropping 71 percent in a one-month period.

Suzuki immediately began an advertising and public relations program to address the safety controversy and Consumers Union charges. The company held a press conference within a week criticizing Consumers Union for using shoddy and biased testing procedures and provided videotapes of the Samurai safely performing the turning maneuvers that led to the alleged rollover problem. In the 10 days following the Consumers Union press conference, Suzuki spent $1.5 million over and above its normal advertising budget to run ads quoting positive reviews of the Samurai from automotive trade publications. The company also provided dealers with materials disputing the charges to help them handle the controversy, and a toll-free number was set up for customers to call with any questions. In August Samurai sales set a one-month record of 12,208 vehicles. However, the sales were due in large part to a summer promotion that made it possible for dealers to slash up to 25 percent from the Samurai's base price.

In September the National Highway Traffic Safety Administration denied a petition by the Center for Auto Safety calling for a government recall of the Samurai. Suzuki officials felt that their aggressive, high-profile response to the charges helped them deal with the questions regarding the safety of the Samurai. The head of the public relations firm hired to help the company deal with the negative publicity stated that "Suzuki's strategy is going to go down in textbooks as a case of what a company does when falsely accused." Suzuki's strategy has now indeed made it into a textbook. However, it remains to be seen whether these efforts will be enough to overcome consumers' concerns over the safety of the Samurai and ensure its survival.

For the 1989 model year Suzuki introduced two new vehicles including the Swift subcompact car and Sidekick, a sport utility vehicle similar to the Samurai but with a wider wheelbase. The company planned to import only 2,000 Samurais a month and shift its marketing emphasis to the two new vehicles. However, for the first four months of 1989, combined sales of the Samurai and the Sidekick totaled only 9,068 vehicles compared with Samurai sales which alone were at 22,948 for the same period in 1988.

Sources: James Risen, "Suzuki Calls Consumer Group's Safety Test on Samurai 'Flawed,'" *Los Angeles Times,* June 10, 1988, pt. IV, p. 1; idem, "Suzuki Shifted into High Gear When Crisis Hit," *Los Angeles Times,* June 27, 1988, pt. IV, p. 1; Bradley A. Stertz, "Suzuki Takes Extraordinary Measures to Halt Sales Plunge of Samurai Model," *The Wall Street Journal,* July 15, 1988, p. 22; idem, "Suzuki Ending Its Dependence on Samurai, Plans 2 New Vehicles," *The Wall Street Journal,* September 22, 1988, p. 42; "Suzuki Sets Review for Its U.S. Account," *Advertising Age,* May 29, 1989, pp. 1, 8.

time or space in a mass medium such as television, radio, or newspaper. While an organization may incur some costs in developing publicity items or in maintaining a staff to execute this function, these expenses will be far less than for the other promotional programs.

While the low cost and credibility associated with publicity are advantages of this promotional element, a major disadvantage is the lack of control afforded the company. An organization can issue press releases or invite the media to preview its new, innovative product and hope for favorable coverage in the newspaper or on the evening news. However, there is no guarantee that a story about the product will appear in the paper or be aired when the company's key target audience is watching. Moreover, information about the product might be improperly presented or some critical details omitted. It should also be noted that publicity is not always favorable and can be very damaging to an organization. Promotional Perspective 1-2 discusses the problems American Suzuki Motor Corporation encountered as a result of negative publicity from allegations over the safety of the Suzuki Samurai.

Figure 1–8 Advertising Is Often Used by Companies to Enhance Their Corporate Image

Public Relations It is important that we recognize the distinction between publicity and public relations. When an organization systematically plans and distributes information in an attempt to control and manage the nature of the publicity it receives and its image, it is really engaging in a function known as public relations. **Public relations** (PR) is defined as "the management function which evaluates public attitudes, identifies the policies and procedures of an individual or organization with the public interest, and executes a program of action to earn public understanding and acceptance."[13] Public relations generally has a broader objective than publicity, as its purpose is to establish and maintain a positive image of the company among its various publics.

Publicity is one of the most important communication techniques used in public relations. However, the public relations function uses a variety of other tools to manage an organizations's image, including special publications, participation in community activities, fund-raising, sponsorship of special events, and various public affairs activities. Organizations also use advertising as a public relations tool to enhance their image. For example, Figure 1–8 shows an example of an award-winning corporate ad designed to show how the Du Pont company helps improve people's lives.

Traditionally publicity and public relations have been assigned more of a supportive role rather than considered a primary part of the marketing and promotional process. However, over the past five years, many firms have begun making public relations an integral part of their predetermined marketing and promotional strategies.[14] PR firms are increasingly touting public relations as a communications tool that can take over many of the functions of conventional advertising and marketing.

Sales Promotion

The fourth variable in the promotional mix is **sales promotion,** which is often defined as those marketing activities that provide extra value or incentives for purchasing a product and that can stimulate immediate sales from consumers or dealers. A variety of sales promotion tools are used to influence consumers including samples, coupons, rebates, contests, sweepstakes, premiums, and point-of-purchase materials. Sales promotion techniques are also targeted toward marketing intermediaries such as wholesalers, distributors, and retailers. Trade shows, merchandising allowances, price deals, and contests are examples of some of the sales promotional tools used with the middlemen.

Sales promotion expenditures in the United States exceeded $124 billion in 1988 and accounted for more promotional dollars than advertising.[15] A major reason why companies use sales promotion tools is that they can provide the marketing intermediaries with an extra incentive to stock and promote their brands and encourage consumers to buy them and thus can be useful in stimulating short-term sales. For example, coupons and price reductions can be used to induce a trial of a new brand or to maintain loyalty to an existing brand. Contests and sweepstakes are used to create interest or excitment in a company's product or service and as "insurance" to help increase the likelihood that an advertisement or promotional display gets notice and attention.

Many firms are reluctant to make sales promotions the sole basis of their promotional strategy because the sales gains resulting from these programs are often temporary, ending when the promotional period is over. Advertising support is viewed as necessary to convert the customer who tried the product because of a promotional deal into a regular, long-term user. However, some companies are switching the emphasis of their promotional strategy from advertising to sales promotion. For example, the Scott Paper Company reduced its advertising budget from $30 million in 1985 to only $6 million in 1987 so that more monies could be allocated to price promotions. Scott also terminated relationships with its two long-time advertising agencies in favor of a smaller agency with direct marketing and promotion expertise.[16]

Promotional Management

In the previous pages, we examined the four elements that constitute the promotional mix and considered the advantages and disadvantages associated with each. In the actual development of a promotional strategy, these promotional mix elements are not viewed separately but rather must be combined, balancing the strengths and weaknesses of each, to produce an effective promotional campaign. **Promotional management** involves the process of coordinating the four promotional mix elements to develop a controlled and integrated program of effective marketing communication.

In assembling the proper promotional mix, the marketer must consider which particular promotional tools to use and how to combine them to achieve the organization's marketing and promotional objectives. Advertising campaigns, sales promotion techniques, publicity and public relations, and personal selling efforts must be coordinated with one another and integrated into the overall marketing strategy to generate an effective communications program.

Companies also face the task of distributing the total promotional budget across the promotional mix elements. For example, a decision has to be made as to the roles of advertising, sales promotion, and personal selling and what percentage of the promotional budget to allocate to each. For most companies, the decision is not whether to use a promotional mix variable but rather how to combine variables to communicate with their target audience effectively.

Companies consider many factors in developing their promotional mix, including the type of product, the target market, the decision process of the buyer, the stage of the product life cycle, and its channels of distribution. For example, companies selling consumer products and services generally rely on advertising through mass media to communicate with ultimate consumers, whereas industrial marketers, who generally sell expensive, risky, and often complex products and services, more often tend to utilize personal selling. However, while advertising may receive less emphasis than personal selling in industrial marketing, it still is used to perform important functions such as building awareness of the company and its products, generating leads for the sales force, and reassuring customers about the purchase they have made. Conversely, personal selling also plays an important role in consumer product marketing. A consumer goods company retains a sales force to call on marketing intermediaries (wholesalers and retailers) who distribute and make available the product or service to the final consumer. While the company sales representative does not communicate with the ultimate consumer, she or he makes an important contribution to the marketing effort by gaining new distribution outlets for the company's product, securing shelf position and space for the brand, informing retailers about advertising and promotion efforts to ultimate users, and encouraging dealers to merchandise and promote the brand at the local market level.

While advertising and personal selling efforts may vary depending upon the type of market being sought, even firms in the same industry may differ in the allocation of their promotional efforts. For example, in the cosmetics industry, Avon and Mary Kay Cosmetics concentrate their promotional efforts on personal selling, whereas companies such as Revlon and Max Factor rely heavily on consumer advertising. Firms also differ in the relative emphasis they place on advertising and sales promotion. Companies selling high-quality brands will rely on advertising to convince consumers of their superiority, to justify their higher prices, and to maintain their "image" in the minds of consumers. On the other hand, brands of lower quality, or those that are difficult to differentiate, often compete more on a price or "value-for-the-money" basis rather than on image and may rely more on sales promotion to the trade and/or consumers.

The advertising and promotional program of an organization is generally developed with a specific purpose or objective in mind and is the end product of a detailed marketing and promotional planning process. We will now turn our attention to a model of the promotional planning process that presents the sequence of decisions that must be made in developing and implementing the promotional program.

Promotional Planning Process

As with any business function, planning plays a fundamental role in the development and implementation of an effective promotional program. It is the responsibility of those individuals involved in the promotional planning to develop a **promotional plan** that provides the framework for developing, implementing, and controlling the organization's promotional program and activities. Promotional planning is best viewed as a dynamic process, as it generally evolves over a period of time and involves interactions among company personnel as well as with external parties such as advertising agencies, public relations and marketing research firms, and consultants.

As was noted earlier, the goal of the promotional program is to develop an effective program of communication that will help an organization achieve its marketing objectives. To accomplish this, the promotional planners must make decisions regarding the role and function of the specific elements of the promotional mix, develop strategies for each element, and implement the plan. In planning and executing the promotional plan and strategies, it must be remembered that promotion is but one part of, and must be integrated into, the overall marketing plan and program.

A model of the promotional planning process is shown in Figure 1–9. The remainder of this chapter will present a brief overview of the various steps involved in the promotional planning process.

Figure 1–9   A Model of the Promotional Planning Process

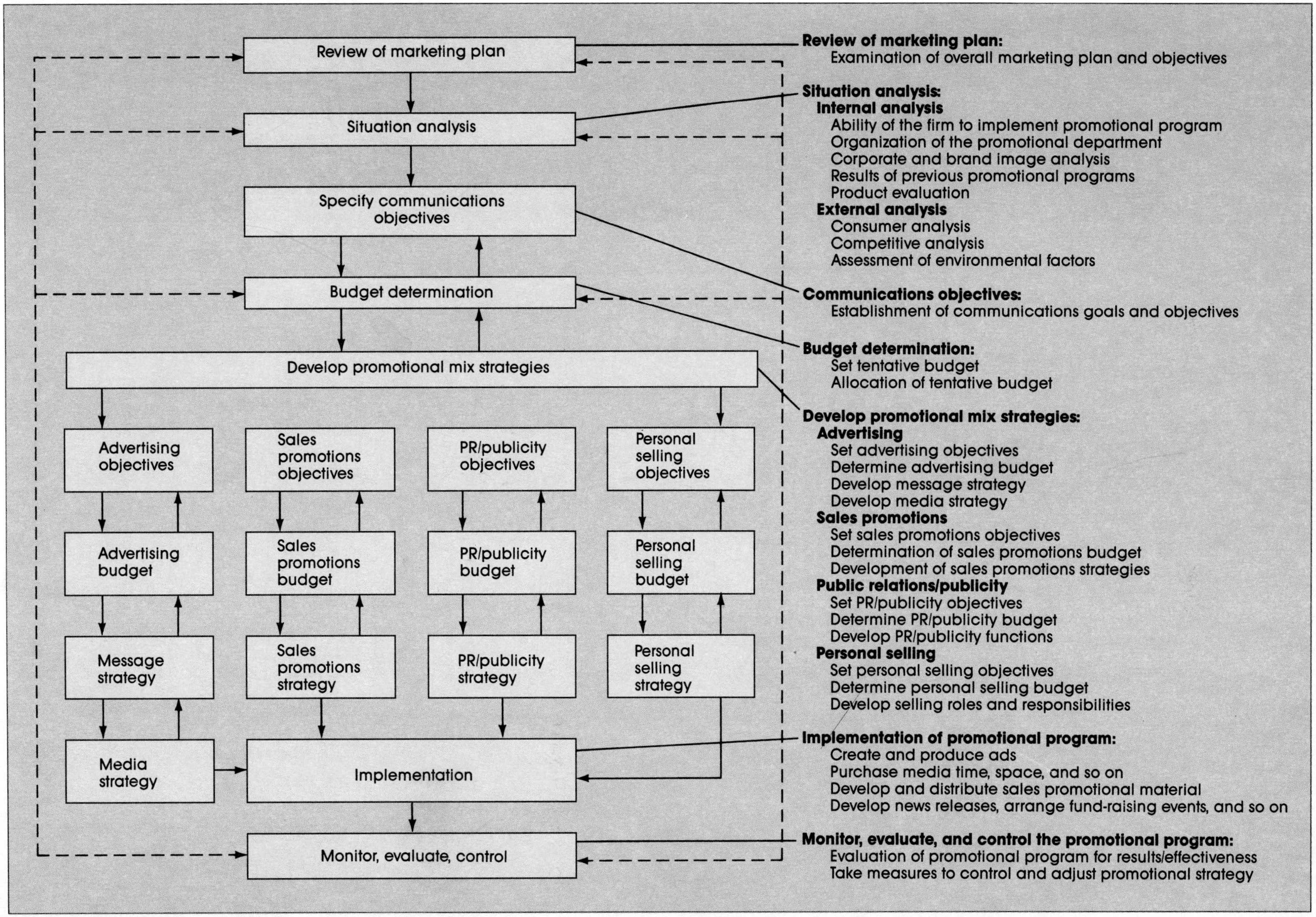

Review of marketing plan:
Examination of overall marketing plan and objectives

Situation analysis:
Internal analysis
Ability of the firm to implement promotional program
Organization of the promotional department
Corporate and brand image analysis
Results of previous promotional programs
Product evaluation
External analysis
Consumer analysis
Competitive analysis
Assessment of environmental factors

Communications objectives:
Establishment of communications goals and objectives

Budget determination:
Set tentative budget
Allocation of tentative budget

Develop promotional mix strategies:
Advertising
Set advertising objectives
Determine advertising budget
Develop message strategy
Develop media strategy
Sales promotions
Set sales promotions objectives
Determination of sales promotions budget
Development of sales promotions strategies
Public relations/publicity
Set PR/publicity objectives
Determine PR/publicity budget
Develop PR/publicity functions
Personal selling
Set personal selling objectives
Determine personal selling budget
Develop selling roles and responsibilities

Implementation of promotional program:
Create and produce ads
Purchase media time, space, and so on
Develop and distribute sales promotional material
Develop news releases, arrange fund-raising events, and so on

Monitor, evaluate, and control the promotional program:
Evaluation of promotional program for results/effectiveness
Take measures to control and adjust promotional strategy

Review of marketing plan
Situation analysis
Specify communications objectives
Budget determination
Develop promotional mix strategies

Advertising objectives → Advertising budget → Message strategy → Media strategy

Sales promotions objectives → Sales promotions budget → Sales promotions strategy

PR/publicity objectives → PR/publicity budget → PR/publicity strategy

Personal selling objectives → Personal selling budget → Personal selling strategy

Implementation

Monitor, evaluate, control

Source: Adapted from Michael L. Ray, "A Decision Sequence Analysis of Developments in Marketing Communications," *Journal of Marketing* 37 (January 1973), p. 31.

Review of the Marketing Plan

The first step in the promotional planning process is a review of the marketing plan and objectives. Before developing a promotional plan, it is important to understand where the company (or the brand) has been, its current position in the market, where it intends to go, and how it plans to get there. Most of this information should be contained in the **marketing plan,** which is a written document that describes the overall marketing strategy and programs developed for an organization, a particular product line, or a brand. Marketing plans can take a variety of forms but generally include five basic elements:

1. A detailed situation analysis that consists of an internal marketing audit and review and an external analysis of the market and environment
2. The establishment of specific marketing objectives that provide direction, a time frame for marketing activities, and a mechanism for measuring performance
3. The formulation of a marketing strategy and program that includes the selection of the target market(s) and decisions and plans for the four elements of the marketing mix
4. A program for implementing the marketing strategy into action, including a determination of specific tasks to be performed and responsibilities
5. A process for monitoring and evaluating performance and providing feedback so that proper control can be maintained and any necessary changes made in the overall marketing strategy or tactics

It is important for individuals involved in the promotional planning process to begin by carefully reviewing the marketing plan. For most firms the promotional plan is an integral part of their marketing strategy. Thus, it is important for the promotional planners to know the role advertising and other promotional mix elements will play in the overall marketing program. Also, the development of the promotional plan follows a procedure very similar to that used in the marketing plan and often makes use of the detailed information contained in this document. Promotional planners will want to focus on information in the marketing plan that is relevant to the development of the promotional strategy and its implementation.

Situation Analysis

Having reviewed the overall marketing plan, the next step in the development of a promotional plan is to conduct the situation analysis. The focus of the situation analysis in the promotional planning process is on those factors that influence or are relevant to the development of promotional strategy. Attention should be given to factors such as the company's (or brand's) current status in the market, the relevant target markets, specific marketing strengths and weaknesses that are relevant to promotion, marketing objectives, and decisions regarding market positioning and the marketing mix. The situation analysis performed for promotional planning purposes will include both an **internal analysis** and an **external analysis.**

Internal Analysis The internal analysis phase of the situation analysis assesses relevant areas concerning the firm and the product/service. Attention should be given to factors such as the capabilities of the firm and its ability to develop and implement a successful promotional program, the image of the company and/or the brand, an examination of past promotional strategies and their results, and an evaluation of the product or service itself. For example, the internal analysis may indicate that the firm is not capable of planning, implementing, and managing certain areas of the promotional program such as advertising or sales promotion. If this is the case, the firm will want to look externally for assistance from an advertising agency or some other promotional facilitator. In many situations the company may already be using an advertising agency, and the focus will be on the quality of the agency's work and the results achieved by past or current campaigns.

In this text we will examine advertising agencies and discuss the role they play, the functions they perform for their clients, the agency selection process, compensation, and considerations in evaluating agency performance. We will also discuss the role and function of other promotional facilitators such as sales promotion firms, public relations agencies, and marketing research firms.

Another aspect of the internal analysis is the assessment of the strengths and weaknesses of the firm or the brand from an image perspective. Quite often the image the firm brings to the market will have a significant impact on its promotional program. A firm with a strong corporate image, such as IBM, American Airlines, McDonald's, or Sony, is already a step ahead when it comes to marketing its products or services owing to its reputation for quality service, and so on. Companies or brands that are new to the market, and thus without an established image, or those with a negative image may have to concentrate on their image as well as on the benefits or attributes of the specific product. For example, the Adolph Coors Company is well known but not well liked by some groups who have made its products the target of numerous boycotts. Thus, the company has spent a considerable amount of money on corporate image advertising in addition to its basic product-oriented ads (Figure 1–10).[17]

Another aspect of the internal analysis is the assessment of the relative strengths and weaknesses of the product or service. Consideration must be given to the relative advantages and disadvantages of the product/service; any unique selling points or benefits it may have; its packaging, price, and design; and so on. This information is particularly important to the creative personnel who must develop the advertising message for the brand.

Table 1–1 shows a checklist of some of the areas that might be considered when performing an internal analysis for promotional planning purposes. However, addressing these areas may require some information that the company does not have available internally and must be gathered as part of the external analysis.

External Analysis The external analysis phase of the situation analysis focuses on factors such as characteristics of the firm's customers, competitors, and marketing environment, as shown in Table 1–1. An important part of the external analysis is a detailed consideration of the customers in terms of their characteristics and buying patterns, their decision processes, and factors influencing their purchase decisions. Attention must also be given to areas such as consumers' perceptions and attitudes, lifestyles, and criteria used in making purchase decisions. Often it is necessary to conduct marketing research studies to answer some of these questions, as shown in Promotional Perspective 1–3.

The external phase of the situation analysis will also include an examination of the competition, including both direct and indirect competitors. Particular attention will be focused on the firm's primary competitors with respect to their sales and market share, strengths and weaknesses, marketing and promotional strategies and budgets, image, and the like. The environmental analysis focuses on any relevant demographic, sociocultural, economic, technological, or legal/regulatory factors and how they might influence the firm's promotional strategy.

Specifying Communications Objectives

The next stage of the promotional planning process is the specification of communications objectives. In this text we stress the importance of making a distinction between communications and marketing objectives. **Marketing objectives** refer to what is to be accomplished by the overall marketing program and are often stated in terms of criteria such as sales, market share, or profitability. **Communications objectives** refer to what the firm seeks to accomplish with its promotional program and often are stated in terms of the nature of the message to be communicated or what is to be accomplished in terms of communications effects. Communications objectives may include creating awareness or knowledge about a product and its attributes or benefits,

Figure 1–10 This Ad for the Adolph Coors Company Was Designed to Improve the Company's Image

The four most dreaded words in the English language: "Mike Wallace is here."

It was a program that would interest anyone who likes good beer. And the truth.

When Mike Wallace and the "60 Minutes" crew showed up and said they wanted to do a story on Coors, I figured I had just two choices:
1. Tell them to go away (knowing they'd probably do a story on us anyway).
2. Throw open the entire brewery to them (and see what happened).

I chose the second course of action. I told Mike that he was free to go anywhere in our brewery and talk to anybody about anything.

If you saw the "60 Minutes" rerun last Sunday, you saw what happened.

You saw that Coors has an outstanding record for minority employment in many areas—including Hispanics, blacks and women.

You saw that every one of the hundreds of Coors employees polled by Mike Wallace denied the rumor that Coors pries into their personal lives. It's not surprising. We strongly believe in individuals' rights.

You saw that Coors employees enjoy abundant benefits. Because Coors is one of the highest paying employers in Colorado. We offer expansive health and medical programs, too. And programs to help employees continue their educations.

"60 Minutes" helped to set the record straight.

We didn't sponsor it. We had no say in what they said about us. But we think what Mike and his people found out about Coors is of interest to anyone who likes good beer.

And the truth.

Table 1–1   **Checklist of Areas Covered in the Situation Analysis**

Internal Factors
Assessment of firm's promotional organization and capabilities
   Organization of promotional department
   Capability of firm to develop and execute promotional programs
   Determination of role and function of advertising agency and other promotional facilitators
Review of firm's previous promotional programs and results
   Review previous promotional objectives
   Review previous promotional budgets and allocations
   Review previous promotional mix strategies and programs
   Review results of previous promotional programs
Assessment of firm or brand image and implications for promotion
Assessment of relative strengths and weaknesses of product/service
   What are the strengths and weaknesses of product or service?
   What are the product's/service's key benefits?
   Does the product/service have any unique selling points?
   Assessment of packaging/labeling/brand image?
   How does our product/service compare with competition?

External Factors
Customer analysis
   Who buys our product or service?
   Who makes the decision to buy the product?
   Who influences the decision to buy the product?
   How is the purchase decision made? Who assumes what role?
   What does the customer buy? What needs must be satisfied?
   Why do customers buy a particular brand?
   Where do they go or look to buy the product or service?
   When do they buy? Any seasonality factors?
   What are the customers' attitudes toward our product or service?
   What social factors might influence the purchase decision?
   Does the customers' lifestyle influence their decisions?
   How is our product/service perceived by the customers?
   How do demographic factors influence the purchase decision?
Competitive analysis
   Who are our direct and indirect competitors?
   What key benefits and positioning are used by our competitors?
   What is our position relative to the competition?
Environmental analysis
   Are there any current trends or developments that might impact the promotional program, including
      Demographic factors?
      Economic factors?
      Sociocultural factors?
      Technological factors?
      Legal/regulatory factors?

creating an image, or developing favorable attitudes, preferences, or purchase intentions. Communications objectives should be the guiding force for the development of the overall promotional strategy and will also guide the development of objectives for each of the promotional mix areas.

Budget Determination

After determining the specific communications objectives to be accomplished, attention turns to determining the promotional budget. The basic questions being asked at this point are: What will the promotional program cost? and How will these monies be allocated? The amount of money a firm needs to spend on promotion should be determined by what must be done to accomplish its communications objectives and what it will cost to perform these tasks. However, in reality, promotional budgets are often determined using a more simplistic approach such as determining how much money is available or basing promotional expenditures on a percentage of a company's or brand's sales revenue. It should be noted that at this stage the budget is often only tentative and may not be finalized until specific promotional mix strategies are developed.

Promotional Perspective 1–3

Determining the Image of a Bank

One of the first steps involved in the promotional planning process when an advertising agency acquires a new account is that of analyzing the market situation for the client's product or service. When a large West Coast ad agency resumed the advertising responsibility for the State Bank a few years ago, they immediately turned their attention to examining the marketing and competitive situation facing their client. The agency knew that there were three major competitors in the Arizona banking market including their client, Mesa Bank, and Canyon Bank. While they knew how their client's products and services compared with those of the competition, they did not know anything about consumers' perceptions of the three institutions and the image of each. To gain some insight into this area, the bank's marketing department conducted a research study among residents of Arizona to answer these questions. The goal of the research was to determine the types of bank products and services that were appealing to consumers, how the banks were perceived with respect to offering them, and the overall image of each bank.

The results showed that the State Bank fared very well with respect to factors such as speed of service and competitive interest rates, whereas competitors were more often perceived as being more conveniently located and more personable. With respect to image, some interesting discoveries were made. While all the banks were considered to be safe, secure, and competitive, the image of the banks themselves and the type of customers they were perceived as attracting were substantially different. The State Bank was considered a very conservative institution, well established, and ingrained in the history of the state—the kind of bank where the state's conservative Senator Barry Goldwater or Supreme Court Justice Sandra Day O'Connor might transact business. At the other extreme, Mesa was perceived as the "bank of the upwardly mobile" owing to its short term in existence, its large network of automatic teller machines, and its more decorative motif—the kind of bank where a movie star such as John Travolta or a baseball star such as Steve Garvey might bank. The final competitor, Canyon Bank, had no unique image in the mind of the consumers, as it was considered as neither conservative nor innovative. Commented one of the respondents, "They are just kind of there!"

Put yourself in the role of the advertising agency for each of these banks. What approach would you take in developing a promotional strategy for your client?

Developing Promotional Mix Strategies

This step of the promotional planning process is generally the most involved and detailed. As discussed earlier, each of the promotional mix elements has certain advantages and limitations and will assume a different role in the attainment of marketing and communications objectives. At this stage of the planning process, decisions have to be made regarding the role and importance of each promotional mix element and their coordination with one another. As can be seen in Figure 1–9, each promotional mix element will have its own set of objectives and a budget and strategy for meeting these objectives. Decisions must be made and activities performed to implement the promotional programs and procedures developed for monitoring and evaluating performance and making any necessary changes and adjustments.

Let us examine the advertising program as an example. This element of the promotional program will have its own set of objectives—usually involving the communication of some message or appeal to a target audience. A budget will be determined, providing the advertising manager and the agency with a sense of how much money is available for developing the advertising campaign and purchasing media to disseminate the advertising message. Two very important aspects of the advertising program are the development of the message and media strategy. Message development, often referred to as creative strategy, involves the determination of the basic appeal and message the advertiser wishes to convey to the target audience. This process, along with the advertisements that result from it, is to many students the most fascinating aspect of promotion. Media strategy involves determining the communications channels that will be used to deliver the advertising message to the target audience. Decisions must be made regarding the various types of media that will be used (e.g., newspapers, magazines, radio, television, direct mail, billboards) as well as determinations for specific media selections such as a particular magazine or TV program. This task requires care-

Table 1–2   **An Example of Promotional Mix Strategy Development**

Background

A number of years ago a large coffee company decided to introduce a freeze-dried version of their instant decaffeinated brand to the food services market, which consists of customers such as hotels, restaurants, hospitals, and colleges. Freeze-dried versions of instant coffees were making a major impact in the consumer market owing to their superior taste, and the company wanted to capitalize on this advantage in the food services segment of the market as well. The firm's introductory promotional plan included all elements of the promotional mix as described below.

Communications Objective

To create awareness of and interest in the new freeze-dried instant decaffeinated brand among all major accounts in the Eastern region during the second quarter.

Promotional Mix Strategies

Advertising

Objectives	Create awareness and interest among 80% of purchasing agents in food service accounts by end of second quarter
Budget	$1.1 million
Message strategy	Product presentation through full-page ads focusing on superior taste of freeze-dried product
Media strategy	One advertisement per month in each issue of major food service trade publications

Sales Promotion

Objectives	Support advertising program by helping create awareness and interest in product among purchasing agents and customers of food service accounts
Budget	$1 million
Strategy	Distribution of product dispensers and provision of promotional support materials such as table tents and menu stickers. Price-off promotions used to encourage trial by accounts

Publicity

Objectives	Make food service accounts aware of publicity and public relations efforts being made in consumer market, generate favorable publicity among doctors, dieticians, and other purchase influencers
Budget	n.a.
Strategy	Press releases and copies of reports of health benefits

Personal Selling

Objective	Introduce and demonstrate benefits of new product to all major accounts in Eastern region by end of second quarter
Budget	$3 million
Strategy	Sales calls by company salespeople to introduce product, explain benefits, and distribute samples and promotional materials

n.a. = not applicable
Note: All figures are hypothetical.

ful evaluation of the media options including their advantages and limitations, costs, and ability to deliver the message effectively to the target market.

Once the message and media strategy have been determined, steps must be taken to implement them. Most large companies hire advertising agencies to plan and produce their messages and to evaluate and purchase the media that will carry their advertisements. However, most agencies work very closely with their clients as they develop the ads and make media selection decisions, because it is the advertiser who must ultimately approve the creative work and media plan.

While we have used only advertising in our discussion, the example shown in Table 1–2 demonstrates how strategies would be developed for all four areas of the promotional mix.

Monitoring, Evaluation, and Control

The final stage of the promotional planning process shown is that of monitoring, evaluating, and controlling the promotional program. It is important that attention and effort be given to determining how well the promotional program is doing with respect to meeting communications objectives and helping the firm to accomplish its overall marketing goals and objectives. Not only does the promotional planner want to know how well the promotional program is doing but also why it is faring well or poorly. For example, problems with the advertising program may lie in the nature of the message or with a media plan that does not reach the target market effectively. By knowing the reasons for the results being achieved by the advertising strategy, the manager is in a position to take the appropriate steps to control or correct the program.

This final stage of the process is designed to provide managers with continual feedback concerning the effectiveness of the promotional program, which in turn can be used as input into the planning process. As shown by the feedback lines in Figure 1–9, information on the results or outcomes achieved by the promotional program serves as an input to subsequent promotional planning and strategy development.

Perspective of This Text

In the broadest sense *promotion* refers to a subset of the marketing mix and includes advertising, personal selling, publicity/public relations, and sales promotion. We will examine all four of these promotional mix elements in this text and their role in an organization's marketing and communications efforts. However, because advertising and sales promotion are generally more directly under the control of the promotions manager than are personal selling and publicity/public relations, the emphasis in this text will be on the former two areas. Personal selling in particular is typically a specialized marketing function outside the control of the advertising or promotional department. Furthermore, advertising or promotions managers generally do not plan strategy jointly with the sales department.[18] Likewise, publicity/public relations is often assigned to a separate department not under the direct control of the advertising or promotions manager. There should, however, be communication between these departments with advertising and sales promotion and a coordination of programs and efforts.

While our emphasis will be more on advertising and sales promotion, the importance of the remaining two areas and the need to integrate and coordinate all the promotional tools is well recognized in this text, and proper attention is devoted to each. However, many of the issues regarding the management and implementation of the sales and public relations programs of an organization are beyond the scope of this text.

The purpose of this book is to provide a thorough understanding of the field of advertising and promotion management. We believe that in order to plan, develop, and implement effective promotional programs, those involved in this process must have a strong foundation in and understanding of marketing, the communications process, and consumer behavior. Thus, the first part of this book is designed to provide this foundation by examining the role of advertising and promotion in the marketing process, consumer behavior, and the consumer decision-making process and various aspects of communications theory. We will also discuss the areas of market segmentation and positioning and how they relate to advertising and promotional strategy.

After laying the foundation for the development of the advertising and promotional strategy and program, this text will follow the promotional planning model presented in Figure 1–9. We will examine the various considerations in developing and specifying objectives and determining and allocating the budget. We will then turn our attention to the various aspects of advertising, including an overview of media strategy and issues in media planning and selection, an evaluation of the various types of media (print, broadcast, support media), and creative strategy and message development. The discussion then turns to the other elements of the promotional mix as sales promotion, personal selling and reseller support, and publicity/public relations are examined. Our examination of the promotional planning model is completed by discussing the procedures and considerations in measuring the effectiveness of the promotional program.

This text also gives attention to specialized areas of advertising and promotion that are becoming increasingly important, including business-to-business communications and international advertising and promotion. Finally, we will examine the environment in which advertising and promotion operates, including the regulatory, social, and economic factors that influence, and are in turn influenced by, a firm's promotional program.

Summary

Promotion is an integral part of the marketing process in most organizations. To understand the role of promotion in a marketing program, it is necessary to understand first what marketing's role and function are in an organization. The basic task of marketing is that of combining the four controllable decision elements, known as the marketing mix, into a comprehensive program that facilitates exchange with a target market. The elements of the marketing mix include the product or service, price, place of distribution, and promotion.

Promotion is best viewed as the communications function of marketing and is accomplished through a promotional mix that includes advertising, personal selling, publicity/public relations, and sales promotion. Each of these promotional mix variables has inherent advantages and disadvantages that influence the role they play in the overall marketing program. In developing the promotional program, the marketer must consider what particular tools to use and how to combine them to achieve the organization's marketing and communications objectives.

Promotional management involves the process of coordinating the four promotion elements to develop a controlled and integrated program of effective marketing communication. This program is organized through a promotional planning process that includes reviewing the marketing plan; conducting a situation analysis; specifying communications objectives; setting a budget; developing and implementing promotional mix strategies; and monitoring, evaluating, and controlling the promotional program.

Key Terms

Marketing	Sales promotion
Exchange	Promotional management
Marketing mix	Promotional plan
Promotion	Marketing plan
Promotional mix	Internal analysis
Advertising	External analysis
Personal selling	Marketing objectives
Publicity	Communications objectives
Public relations	

Discussion Questions

1. Discuss the role promotion plays in facilitating the exchange process between an organization and its customers. Choose a specific company and discuss how it uses marketing, and promotion in particular, in the development and maintenance of an exchange relationship with its customers.
2. Discuss the difference between a company's marketing mix and its promotional mix. How might the nature of the promotional mix be influenced by the marketing program?
3. Analyze the four basic elements of the promotional mix and their role in promotional strategy for each of the following:

- A manufacturer of consumer products such as Procter & Gamble
- A nonprofit organization such as a symphony orchestra in a major city
- A major league baseball or basketball franchise

4. What are the advantages and disadvantages of the four elements of the promotional mix? Identify the types of situations where a firm might rely heavily on a particular element.
5. Identify a product or service whose success or failure has been largely determined by the effectiveness of its advertising campaign. Discuss the reasons why the advertising played such an important role in determining its success or failure.
6. Identify a product, service, or cause that has been positively or negatively affected by publicity in recent years. Analyze any responses taken by the company to deal with the opportunity or problems created by the publicity.
7. Describe what is meant by promotional management and the various factors that must be considered in developing the promotional program.
8. Discuss the role that situation analysis plays in the promotional planning process. Why is the situation analysis so important to the promotional planner?
9. What is the difference between marketing objectives and communications objectives? Discuss the role each plays in the planning and development of promotional strategy.
10. Why is it so important for a firm to monitor and evaluate the effectiveness of and results achieved by its promotional programs? What are some ways of determining whether a promotional mix element is effective?

Notes

1. Beth Austin, "Quaker in $45.6 M Push," *Advertising Age,* July 13, 1987, p. 3.
2. Ron Alsop, "In the Oatmeal War, Rivals Claim Victory," *The Wall Street Journal,* March 21, 1988, p. 25.
3. Julie Liesse Erickson, "Cereal Makers Feel Their Oats," *Advertising Age,* August 15, 1988, p. 1.
4. Ibid., "Nabisco to Join Oat Bran Battle," *Advertising Age,* February 6, 1989, p. 4.
5. "AMA Board Approves New Marketing Definition," *Marketing News,* March 1, 1985, p. 1.
6. Richard P. Bagozzi, "Marketing as Exchange," *Journal of Marketing* 39 (October 1975), pp. 32–39.
7. Michael L. Ray, *Advertising and Communication Management* (Englewood Cliffs, N.J.: Prentice-Hall, 1982).
8. Ralph S. Alexander, ed., *Marketing Definitions* (Chicago: American Marketing Association, 1965), p. 9.
9. Margery L. Schwartz, "TV Commercials' Subliminal Costs," *PSA Magazine,* October 1985, p. 47.
10. "Trends in Media," Research Report by Television Bureau of Advertising, New York, New York, July 1988.
11. Leo Bogart, *Strategy in Advertising,* 2nd ed. (Chicago: Crain Books, 1984), p. 1.
12. Laboratory of Advertising Performance Study no. 8052–4, McGraw-Hill Research, 1988.
13. H. Frazier Moore and Bertrand R. Canfield, *Public Relations: Principles, Cases, and Problems,* 7th ed. (Homewood, Ill.: Richard D. Irwin, 1977), p. 5.
14. Art Kleiner, "The Public Relations Coup," *Adweek's Marketing Week,* January 16, 1989, pp. 20–23.
15. Russ Bowman, "Sales Promotion: Dollars Up But Cooling Down," *Marketing & Media Decisions,* July 1989, pp. 124–126.
16. David Kiley, "Scott Throws in Advertising Towel," *Adweek's Marketing Week,* March 7, 1988, p. 1.
17. Anne B. Fisher, "Spiffing Up the Corporate Image," *Fortune,* July 21, 1986, pp. 68–72.
18. A. J. Dubinsky, T. E. Barry, and R. A. Kerin, "The Sales-Advertising Interface in Promotional Planning," *Journal of Advertising* 10, no. 3 (1981), pp. 35–41.

2

The Role of Advertising and Promotion in the Marketing Process

CHAPTER OBJECTIVES

1. To examine the marketing process and the role of advertising and promotion in an organization's marketing program

2. To examine the various decision areas under each element of the marketing mix and how they influence and interact with advertising and promotional strategy

3. To examine classifications of various types of advertising targeted to both the consumer and business and professional markets

4. To examine the macroenvironment of marketing and the impact of various environmental influences on marketing and promotional strategy

Swatch the Watch

The Swiss have always been considered the finest watchmakers in the world. However, in the early 1980s, while they were making expensive mechanical watches, the industry was being inundated with cheap digital watches from the Far East. Moreover, overall demand for watches in the United States, the largest market for Swiss watches, was declining. The intense competition and decreasing demand brought the Swiss watch industry to near bankruptcy. In 1983, Swiss bankers took over the industry and forced the two largest manufacturing entities to merge into a consortium that would concentrate its effort on reviving high-price brands such as Longines, Omega, and Tissot. However, the industry was not saved by the traditional, expensive Swiss timepiece but rather by the Swatch—a $30 plastic fashion accessory that doubled as a stylish watch.

According to the president of Swatch USA, from the beginning the Swatch was viewed primarily as a fashion accessory and only secondarily as a watch (Figure 2–1). The marketing strategy for Swatch was designed to break into the U.S. market with a mass-appeal watch. The product concept was based on having four product lines: young and trendy, active and sporty, cool and clean, high style and classic. The advertising strategy for Swatch was consistent with the product concept, as the company always had four campaigns running simultaneously, each geared to a specific medium. A general fashion campaign would run on spot television on stations such as MTV, whereas a campaign for the Swatch family, using a new theme each month, would run in *Interview* magazine. A celebrity campaign was used in magazines such as *GQ, Rolling Stone,* and *Glamour,* whereas a fourth campaign was devoted to the trendy, short-lived items in the product mix. Swatch spent $4 million on advertising in 1984 and more than twice that in 1985 to reach its prime target audience of 12- to 24-year-olds, 60 percent of whom are female.

The Swatch distribution strategy complemented its fashion-oriented marketing approach. Most watchmakers sell expensive watches through fine-jewelry stores and lower-priced watches through drugstores and mass-merchandise outlets. However, Swatch chose a selective strategy whereby distribution was limited to department stores, which traditionally accounted for less than 10 percent of watch sales. Swatch guards its outlets closely and has been careful not to overdistribute. Thousands of stores interested in carrying Swatch watches have been turned down.

The Swatch watch has also been priced very attractively to the young target market. Low production costs were made possible by a revolutionary fully automated factory in Switzerland and a design calling for only 51 components, instead of the average of 91, which could be assembled on a single line by robots. The low production costs meant that the watch could be sold at retail in the United States for between $30 and $35, which was more than double the $15 wholesale price. Advanced technology and design resulted in a lightweight, waterproof, and shockproof watch that was nearly indestructible.

Many watch companies have been astounded by the success of Swatch's marketing strategy. Within a year of its introduction, the Swatch name had become synonymous with trendiness, and in 1985, U.S. orders reached 5 million, which was 1.5 million units more than the Swiss consortium had allotted for the U.S. market. By 1988 the company had sold nearly 25 million watches in the United States. The success of the Swatch has led to a broadening of the product line to include sunglasses, T-shirts, sweatshirts, and other fashion items. Some stores have even set up Swatch shops separate from the watch counter.

Success does, of course, breed imitation and competition. Timex, the leader in the mass market for watches, introduced Watercolors, a fashion line targeted at teens, whereas trendy apparel maker "Guess?" brought out fashion watches. Other watch companies such as Citizen, Bulova, and Casio have also introduced fashion watches. However, Swatch continues to dominate the U.S. market for fashionable watches and is now targeting European markets as well as South American and Asian countries.[1,2,3,4]

Figure 2–1 **Swatch Has Turned Watches into Fashion Accessories**

Figure 2—2 **Model of Marketing and Promotions Process**

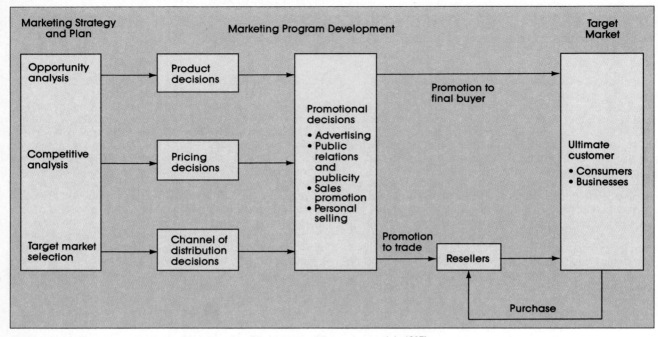

Source: Adapted from Fred C. Allvine, *Marketing* (San Diego: Harcourt Brace Jovanovich, 1987).

Introduction

The success of Swatch is the result of a carefully planned and well-executed marketing strategy and program. An environmental analysis revealed that the Swiss watch industry was facing a severe threat from the Japanese, but there was a marketing opportunity available in the U.S. market for a low-priced, fashion-oriented watch targeted toward young people. Swatch's strategy worked because it developed a distinctive and reliable product at a popular price, a promotional strategy that fit well with the product concept and made the product available through an overlooked, but appropriate, and well-controlled distribution system.

Promotion, as the communications tool of marketing, plays an important role in helping an organization sell its product, service, or idea to its target market. However, as can be seen in the Swatch example, promotion is only one part of the marketing program and is successful only when it is part of a sound marketing strategy and plan. As we saw in the promotional planning model in Chapter 1, a great deal of effort goes into the situation analysis and the planning and development of marketing strategy before any form of promotion can even be considered. In this chapter, we will take a closer look at how marketing influences the role of promotion and how promotional decisions must be coordinated with other areas of the marketing mix. We will use the model shown in Figure 2—2 as a framework for analyzing how promotion fits into an organization's marketing program.

This model consists of three major components—the organization's marketing strategy and plan, the marketing program development (which includes the promotional mix), and the target market. As can be seen in this model, the marketing process begins with the development of a marketing strategy whereby the company decides the product or service areas and particular markets in which it wants to compete. The company must then coordinate the various elements of the marketing mix into a cohesive marketing program that will reach the target market effectively. An important point to note in Figure 2—2 is that a firm's promotion program is directed not only to the final buyer but also to the channel or "trade" members who distribute its products to the ultimate consumer. These channel members must be convinced that there is a demand for the company's products so that they will carry them and will also aggressively merchandise and promote them to the consumer. Thus, we will consider promotion's role in the marketing program for building and maintaining demand not only among final consumers but among the trade as well.

The second part of this chapter will consider the environment in which marketing decisions are made, giving particular attention to how it affects a company's promotional strategies and programs. Marketing is a very dynamic field that must constantly monitor and react to changing environmental trends and conditions. These changes create marketing opportunities for some organizations but pose threats to other firms. They also have a direct influence on a firm's advertising and promotional strategy and programs.

Marketing Strategy and Plan

Any organization that wants to exchange its products or services in the marketplace successfully should have in place a strategic marketing plan to guide the allocation of its resources. A **strategic marketing plan** usually evolves from an organization's overall corporate strategy and serves as a guide for specific marketing programs and policies. As we noted in the first chapter, the development of marketing strategy is based on a situation analysis that is a detailed assessment of the current marketing conditions facing the company, its product lines, or its individual brands. From this situation analysis a firm develops an understanding of the market and the various opportunities it offers, the competition, and the market segments or target markets the company may wish to pursue. We will examine each step of the marketing strategy phase in more detail.

Opportunity Analysis

A careful analysis of the marketplace should lead to alternative market opportunities that the company might consider pursuing. **Market opportunities** represent areas where the company feels customer needs and wants are not being satisfied and where it could compete effectively. For example, over the past several years there has been a tremendous increase in the number of people who have taken up walking for exercise, and it is estimated that the market for walking shoes will reach $100 million by 1990.[5] Athletic shoe companies such as Nike and Reebok see the walking shoe market as an opportunity to broaden their traditionally younger consumer base to an older market. Nike has brought out a line of walking shoes to penetrate this market (Figure 2–3), whereas Reebok acquired Rockport Company, one of the largest manufacturers of walking shoes, to capitalize on this opportunity.

Market opportunities are generally identified by carefully examining the marketplace and identifying demand trends in various **market segments.** Marketers recognize that a market can rarely be viewed as a large, homogeneous group of customers but rather consists of many heterogeneous groups or segments. In the past few years, many companies have recognized the importance of tailoring their marketing programs to meet the needs and tastes of different groups.[6] For example, in the beer industry there are a number of product/market segments in which the various brands compete, including superpremium, premium, low-price, reduced-calorie, low-alcohol, no-alcohol, import, and most recently dry beer. Thus, a company deciding to bring out a new beer must decide in which particular segment it wishes to compete. This decision will obviously depend on the amount and nature of competition the brand will face in a particular market. A competitive analysis is an important part of marketing strategy development and warrants further consideration.

Figure 2–3   **Companies Such as Nike Are Pursuing a Market Opportunity in Walking Shoes**

THERE'S AIR IN OUR WALKING SHOES BECAUSE THERE'S NONE IN YOUR FEET.

You put Nike-Air walking shoes on. You walk in them. They feel terrific. They look terrific. You find yourself walking further, faster, more often. And what's behind it? A fancy-dance marketing idea? Nah. Just plain old science.

Competitive Analysis

In developing the firm's marketing strategies and plans for its products, the manager must carefully analyze the competition the brand will face in the marketplace. Every organization faces competition of one form or another, which may range from direct brand competition (which can also include its own brands) to more indirect forms of competition such as product substitutes. For example, General Foods markets Maxwell House coffee as its flagship brand in the regular ground coffee segment of the market. However, several years ago the company introduced Master Blend, a high-yield brand that gives more cups per pound than regular coffee. The new product ended up cannibalizing, or taking away, sales from Maxwell House. However, the combined sales of the two brands gave General Foods a net gain in its share of the ground market, as Master Blend helped slow the sales of competing brands such as Procter & Gamble's Folgers, Nestlé's Hills Brothers, and various regional brands.

In addition to these direct competitors, Maxwell House faces competition from other product forms such as instant and decaffeinated coffee. Also, many consumers have been switching to other beverages such as tea and soft drinks. Thus, competition is not only limited to directly competing brands but also comes from other products that satisfy consumers' needs for a beverage.

In the development of marketing programs, companies must be concerned with the ever-changing competitive environment they will be facing. Competitors' marketing programs will have a major impact on the firm's marketing strategy and must be carefully analyzed and monitored. The reactions of competitors to a company's marketing and promotional strategy are also very important. Competitors may cut price, increase promotional spending, develop new brands, or attack one another through comparative advertising. One of the more intense competitive rivalries is the battle the Coca-Cola and Pepsi-Cola companies have been waging against one another for more than a decade. The latest round of the "cola wars" is discussed in Promotional Perspective 2–1.

Promotional Perspective   **2–1**

Who's the Champ?

For more than a decade, the Coca-Cola Company and its arch rival, the Pepsi-Cola Company, have been battling for leadership of the soft drink market. The battle became very intense in 1975 when Pepsi launched its "Pepsi Challenge" advertising and promotional campaign, which showed consumers preferring the taste of Pepsi over Coke in blind taste tests. The Challenge campaign was effective in convincing many consumers that Pepsi had a superior taste and induced them to switch brands. By 1984, Pepsi had achieved a 2 percent market share lead over Coke in supermarket sales. Pepsi's success was a major factor in Coca-Cola's controversial decision to change the formula of its 99-year-old flagship brand and launch New Coke in April 1985. The introduction of New Coke resulted in a tremendous amount of protest from consumers loyal to the old formula and led to the subsequent reintroduction of original Coke as Coca-Cola Classic a few months later.

While Coke and Pepsi have continued to battle for leadership of the cola market, the soft drink wars have begun focusing on a new area—the sugar-free or diet market. By 1988 the sugar-free segment accounted for approximately 25 percent of the entire $40 billion soft drink market, and sales were increasing four to five times faster than those of sugared products. Coke's main diet drinks, Diet Coke and Caffeine Free Diet Coke had a 10.1 percent share of the take-home market in 1988, while Diet Pepsi and Caffeine Free Diet Pepsi held a 6.9 percent share.

In June 1988, Pepsi began a new round in the cola wars with a taste test challenge campaign claiming that "Americans preferred the taste of Diet Pepsi over Diet Coke 55 percent to 45 percent." The campaign started with a commercial featuring heavyweight boxing champion Mike Tyson that was aired on all three networks the night he defended his heavyweight championship by knocking out Michael Spinks in 91 seconds. The ad showed Tyson in a postfight interview telling reporters there was no question who was going to win the fight. Later in the commercial it becomes clear that he is talking about Diet Pepsi beating Diet Coke. Pepsi also developed radio and print ads promoting the taste test results to accompany the commercial.

Coke first countered the Pepsi punch by filing a protest with the television networks over Pepsi's test results, asking them not to air the commercial. Coke also produced its own, similar taste test commercials and print ads in just a few days to counter the Pepsi claims. As can be seen in Exhibit 2–1, not only were the claims similar, but the print ads even looked alike. The Coke ads also used a fight motif saying: "It was a mismatch from the opening . . . yet once again in taste tests, Diet Coke beats Diet Pepsi. Diet Coke, the winner and still champion." A Coke spokesperson indicated that the company was running the ads simply "to set the record straight" and would run the ads as long as appropriate.

A Pepsi spokesperson claimed that the Diet Coke challenge actually helped Diet Pepsi by bringing the battle to the forefront. However, Pepsi immediately filed

Exhibit 2–1   **Diet Coke and Diet Pepsi Both Claim Taste Superiority in Another Round of the Cola Wars**

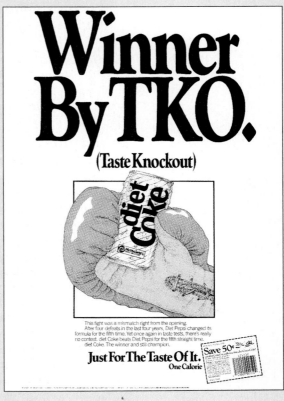

Promotional Perspective (concluded)

claims with the major networks charging that the Diet Coke ad was "misleading and factually inaccurate and should be withdrawn immediately." By August 1988 the three major networks had studied the two companies' research data and said they could not find any flaws or problems with the studies used as a basis for the superiority claims.

Thus, this round of the battle ended in a draw, as the networks ruled that they would air both firms' commercials, despite the conflicting claims over taste superiority.

As has traditionally been the case in the cola wars, it will ultimately be up to the consumer to determine the true champion.

Sources: Patricia Winters and Patrick McGeehan, "Cola Wars Return with a Diet Fight," *Advertising Age*, June 27, 1988, p. 1; Patricia Winters, "Heavyweight Bout," *Advertising Age*, July 4, 1988, p. 35; Ron Alsop, "Diet Coke or Pepsi? TV Cannot Decide So Both Are Picked," *The Wall Street Journal*, July 28, 1988, p. 26; "Coke and Pepsi Duke It Out Over Diet Drinks," *Marketing News*, August 1, 1988, p. 1.

A final aspect of competition that should be noted is the growing number of foreign companies that are successfully penetrating the U.S. market and taking business from domestic firms. In products ranging from electronics to automobiles to beer, imports are becoming an increasingly strong form of competition with which U.S. firms must contend. As we move from a national to a more global economy, U.S. companies must not only defend their domestic markets but also must learn how to compete effectively in the international marketplace. We will examine the role of advertising and promotion in international markets in Chapter 20.

Target Market Selection

After evaluating the marketing opportunities presented by the various segments, including a detailed competitive analysis, the company may select one or more as a target market for which it will develop a marketing program. This target market becomes the focus of the firm's marketing effort, and goals and objectives are set according to where the company wants to be and what it hopes to accomplish in this market. As noted in Chapter 1, these goals and objectives are set in terms of specific performance variables such as sales, market share, and profitability. The selection of the target market(s) in which the firm will compete not only is a very important part of its marketing strategy but also has direct implications for its advertising and promotional efforts. Considerations involved in segmenting a market, choosing target markets in which to compete, and positioning the product or service within the market are discussed in detail in Chapter 7.

Developing the Marketing Program

The development of the marketing strategy and selection of a target market(s) tell the marketing department which customers to focus on and what needs to attempt to satisfy. The next stage of the marketing process involves combining the various elements of the marketing mix into a cohesive and effective marketing program. The challenge facing the marketing manager at this point is somewhat analogous to that of a chef. In blending different combinations of ingredients together to produce the meal, the chef does not always follow a recipe but rather uses his or her own creativity or insight. In a similar manner the marketing manager must blend together the various elements of the marketing mix to develop an effective marketing program. In marketing, there is no standard formula to follow for a successful combination of marketing elements, as marketing mix strategies vary from company to company and across various situations. The experienced manager, like the expert chef, applies his or her skill, experience, and creativity to develop an effective and successful marketing program.

As was noted earlier, the development of a successful marketing program requires that all elements of the marketing mix be combined effectively. The product or service

Figure 2—4   **Advertising for Michelin Tires Stresses Security as Well as Performance**

must offer a benefit that satisfies a need at a price the customer is willing to pay and must be available in places where and when the consumer wants to purchase it. The role of promotion is to make the customer aware of the product, the benefits it offers, and where it can be purchased. In Chapter 1 we saw how promotion includes a number of elements such as advertising, personal selling, sales promotion, and publicity/public relations. Actually, each marketing mix element is multidimensional in nature and includes a number of decision areas. We will now turn our attention to examining these elements of the marketing mix, giving particular attention to how each influences and interacts with promotion.

Product

The basic reason for an organization's existence is that it has some product, service, or idea to offer consumers, generally in exchange for money. This offering may come in the form of a physical product (such as a soft drink, pair of jeans, automobile), a service (a bank, airline, or legal assistance), a cause (United Way, March of Dimes), or even a person (for example, a political candidate). Thus, in the broadest sense the product consists of anything that can be marketed and that, when used or supported, gives satisfaction to the individual.

It is important to recognize that a product is not just a physical object; rather, a product should be viewed as a bundle of benefits or values that satisfies the needs of consumers. The needs that are satisfied by a product may be functional and may include social and psychological benefits as well. For example, the ad for Michelin tires shown in Figure 2—4 stresses the security (psychological) that comes from driving on

Figure 2–5 **Advertising for Designer Jeans Helps Create Symbolism and Image to Consumers**

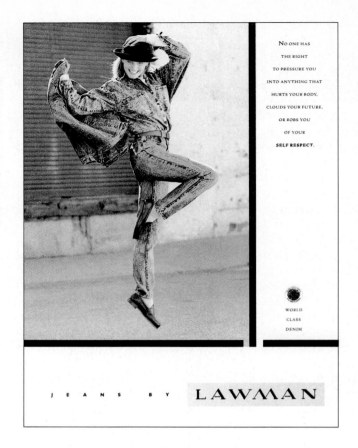

Michelins as well as their performance and durability (functional). The term **product symbolism** is used to refer to what a product or brand means to the consumer and what he or she experiences in purchasing and using it.[7] For many products, strong symbolic features and social and psychological meaning may be more important than functional utility.[8] For example, designer jeans such as Guess?, Calvin Klein, Jordache, and Lawman are often purchased on the basis of their symbolic meaning and image, particularly by teenagers and young adults. Advertising plays an important role in developing and maintaining the image of these brands (Figure 2–5).

Product planning involves decisions not only about the item itself, such as design and quality, but also other aspects such as service and warranties that go along with it, as well as the selection of a brand name and package design. The branding and packaging decisions are particularly important as communication devices and warrant further discussion.

Branding　Choosing a brand name for a product is important from a promotional perspective because of the role brand names play in communicating attributes and meaning. Marketers search for brand names that can effectively communicate product concepts and help position the product in the mind of the customer. Names such as Safeguard (soap), Easy Off (oven cleaner), Arrid (antiperspirant deodorant), and Spic and Span (floor cleaner) all clearly communicate the value and benefits of using these products.

Many companies use individual brand names for each of their products because they want each brand to have a unique and distinct image and not be influenced by association to a company, family, or product line name. However, promotional costs for new products are generally higher when individual brand names are used, as the company must create awareness among both consumers and retailers without the benefit of these same prior associations.

In recent years the high costs of establishing a brand identity have prompted many companies to use a **brand extension strategy** whereby a firm uses one of its existing brand names for a new or improved product that is usually in the same product category as the existing brand.[9] Examples of brand extensions include Diet Coke and Diet Pepsi soft drinks and Miller Lite, Coors Light, and Budweiser Light beers. Anheuser-Busch has also line extended the Michelob name to several brands including Michelob Light, Michelob Dark, and its newest brand, Michelob Dry (Figure 2–6).

Figure 2–6   **The Michelob Brand Name Has Been Extended to Light, Dark, and Dry Versions of Beer**

While often a successful strategy, the use of brand extensions has been criticized by some advertising experts on the grounds that excessive use of a brand name can erode brand image and create confusion among consumers.[10] Brand extensions can also be risky if a new product does not live up to consumer expectations, as this may have a negative impact on consumers' perceptions of other products using the name. It has been argued that the decision as to whether a firm should use a brand extension strategy is a compromise between dilution of brand image and possible consumer confusion, on one hand, and advertising efficiency, on the other.[11] As media costs escalate and shelf space becomes increasingly scarce, it is likely that companies with strong brand names will continue to use line extension strategies to reduce costs and increase awareness and, hopefully, acceptance of their new products among both consumers and retailers.

A strong brand name is a very important asset to a firm. Thus, companies generally take steps to protect their brand names by registering them as trademarks with the U.S. Patent Office. A **trademark** is a legal designation indicating that a firm has registered the brand name and thus has exclusive use of it. Companies are very careful about any infringement on their trademarks. A well-known trademark not only identifies a brand and prevents other firms from using that name but also can help a company in advertising its brands and creating and maintaining brand loyalty.

Packaging   Packaging is another aspect of product strategy that has become increasingly important. Traditionally, the role of the package was to provide functional benefits such as economy, protection, and storage. However, the role and function of the package have changed because of the self-service emphasis of many stores and the fact that more and more purchase decisions are being made at the actual point of purchase. One study estimated that as many as two thirds of all supermarket purchases are unplanned and made in the store.[12] Marketers have recognized that the package is often the consumer's first exposure to the product and must make a favorable first impression. For example, in a typical supermarket there are more than 10,000 items competing for a consumer's attention. Not only must a package attract and hold the consumer's attention, but it must also communicate information such as how to use the product, divulge its composition and content, and satisfy any legal requirements regarding disclosure. Moreover, many firms design a package to carry a sales promotion message such as a contest, sweepstakes, or premium offer.

Many companies view the package as an important way of both communicating with consumers and also of creating an impression of the brand in their minds. Design factors such as size, shape, color, and lettering all contribute to the appeal of a package and can be as important as a commercial in determining what goes from the store shelf to the consumer's shopping cart. Many products have used packaging to create a distinctive brand image and identity such as Michelob beer with its unusually shaped bottle and distinctive label (Figure 2–6). Packaging can also be used as a way of making a product more convenient to use. For example, Quaker State Motor Oil stressed the convenience of using its new plastic container, which was lighter and also eliminated the need for a separate pouring spout (Figure 2–7). General Foods recently introduced Maxwell House Filter Packs, which contain 10 premeasured packs of coffee, each producing five cups, in the hope that the new packaging concept will help revive declining sales (Figure 2–8).

Figure 2–7   **This Quaker State Motor Oil Ad Emphasized the Convenience of Its New Package**

Figure 2–8   **Maxwell House Coffee Uses a New Packaging Concept to Make the Product Easier to Use**

It is easy to see why packaging has become an important marketing and communications tool. Most consumer product companies have in-house package design directors whose job it is to consider how packages look in the store, how they are perceived by consumers, and how they hold up under use. However, for major revisions or new products, companies will often go to outside package design firms. For example, R. J. Reynolds commissioned fashion designer Yves St. Laurent to create the box for its Ritz cigarette brand, leading a spokesperson for the company to note, "this isn't a cigarette, this is a designer product."[13] The costs of developing a new package design vary with the product but can range from a few thousand dollars to several million. However, many firms feel that effective packaging can save them money by reducing the amount of advertising needed to introduce a new product or draw attention to modified brands.

Price

The *price variable* refers to what the consumer must give up to purchase a product or service. While price will be discussed in terms of the dollar amount exchanged for an item, it has also been argued that the cost of a product to the consumer includes time, mental or cognitive activity, and behavioral effort.[14] The marketing manager is usually concerned with establishing a price level, developing pricing policies, and monitoring competitors' and consumers' reactions to prices in the marketplace. There are a number of factors a firm must consider in determining the price it charges for its product or service, including costs, demand factors, competition, and perceived value.

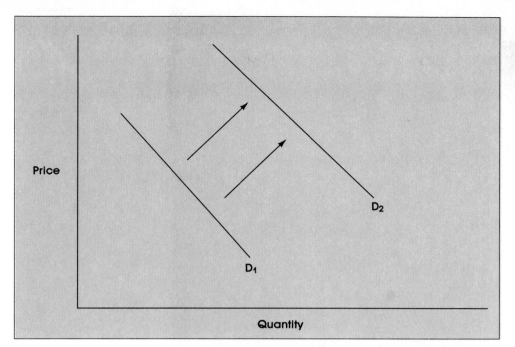

Costs Costs are a basic determinant of price, as the firm will generally set a price that covers all the costs of producing, distributing, and promoting its product or service and additionally includes a profit figure that yields a certain return on its investment. While promotional expenses such as advertising, personal selling, and sales promotion are costs that must be covered in a firm's pricing structure, they also can be ways to reduce costs by creating demand for the product that results in more sales and economies of scale in production and distribution.

Demand Factors Another important consideration in setting price is the demand for the product or service that will be generated at various price levels. The relationship between price and demand is generally an inverse one, meaning that as price declines, demand will increase, and vice versa. However, in some situations the relationship between price and demand may be positive if the consumer perceives price as an indicator of quality.[15] Thus, a higher price may result in more sales for a product (up to a point).

An important consideration in setting price is the concept of **price elasticity,** or the responsiveness of the market to changes in price. Elastic demand exists when the market is price sensitive such that a small decrease (increase) in price produces a larger increase (decrease) in demand. Inelastic demand exists when the market is price insensitive, and a small decrease (increase) in price results in a smaller increase (decrease) in demand. When a firm competes on the basis of price, a change in price will usually result in a change in demand, depending on the degree of elasticity. However, many firms try to increase demand through **nonprice competition** by using product differentiation, advertising, and other nonprice factors to influence demand. Under nonprice competition the goal of the firm is to shift its demand curve upward and to the right, as shown in Figure 2–9, which makes demand more inelastic and less price sensitive and results in greater sales at a given price. For example, many premium products such as Häagen-Dazs ice cream or Godiva chocolates are made from more expensive ingredients and perceived by consumers as being of superior quality and value. This perception is reinforced through their advertising, which helps these brands command premium prices from consumers willing to pay more for the best quality (Figure 2–10).

Figure 2–10 Some Products Compete on the Basis of Quality Rather Than Price

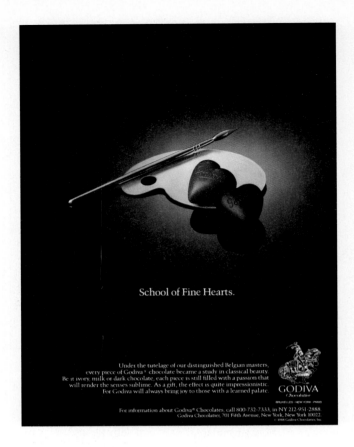

School of Fine Hearts.

Under the tutelage of our distinguished Belgian masters, every piece of Godiva® chocolate became a study in classical beauty. Be it ivory, milk or dark chocolate, each piece is still filled with a passion that will render the senses sublime. As a gift, the effect is quite impressionistic. For Godiva will always bring joy to those with a learned palate.

GODIVA
Chocolatier
BRUSSELS · LED · NEW YORK · PARIS

For information about Godiva® Chocolates, call 800-732-7333, in NY 212-951-2888. Godiva Chocolatier, 701 Fifth Avenue, New York, New York 10022.
© 1998 Godiva Chocolatier, Inc.

Competition   Another fundamental consideration in setting price is competition. Price is the one element of the marketing mix that is easiest to change, at least in the short run, and is often used as a competitive tool. Many companies use **competition-oriented pricing** whereby prices are set based primarily on what competitors are charging. Prices may be set to achieve competitive parity, or a firm may seek to keep its prices lower or higher than the competition. When competition-oriented pricing is used, prices are subject to rapid change and are often lowered to meet competition in specific markets. Competition-oriented pricing is very common in the retailing area, particularly among grocery stores, and in the marketing of services, such as in the airline industry. Extremely intense competition can sometimes lead to "price wars," such as in the airline industry where carriers are often forced to cut prices to remain competitive on certain routes.

Perceived Value   Most marketers recognize that price levels for a product or service must be in line with the perceived value of the offering. Consumers often use price as a basis for determining a product's value, suggesting a relationship between price and perceived quality. For example, Curtis Mathes has used the advertising slogan "The Most Expensive Television Sets Money Can Buy" for many years as a way of promoting its products as being of extremely high quality. Marketers often use non-price variables such as superior product quality, service, warranties, and brand image to build up perceived value in the consumer's mind and then price their products accordingly. The ad shown in Figure 2–11 shows how BMW uses price to convey an image of quality and value for its expensive automobiles.

Relating Price to Advertising   As we have seen in our discussion of the various considerations for price determination, factors such as product quality, competition,

Figure 2—11   **BMW Uses High Price to Suggest Quality and Value**

and advertising all interact in determining what price a firm can and should charge. The relationship between price, product quality, and advertising was examined in one study using information on 227 consumer businesses from the PIMS (Profit Impact of Marketing Strategies) project of the Strategic Planning Institute.[16] Several interesting findings concerning the interaction of these variables emerged from this study:

1. Brands with high relative advertising budgets were able to charge premium prices, whereas brands spending less than their competitors on advertising charged lower prices.

2. Companies with high-quality products charged high relative prices for the extra quality, but businesses with high quality *and* high advertising levels obtained the highest prices. Conversely, businesses with low quality and low advertising charged the lowest prices.

3. The positive relationship between high relative advertising and price levels was stronger for products in the late stage of the product life cycle, for market leaders, and low-cost products (under $10).

4. Companies with relatively high prices and high advertising expenditures showed a higher return on investment than companies with relatively low prices and high advertising budgets.

Another interesting finding of this study was that companies with high-quality products were hurt the most, in terms of return on investment, by inconsistent advertising and pricing strategies. The researchers concluded that pricing and advertising strategies go together, as high relative ad expenditures should accompany premium prices and low relative ad expenditures should be tailored to low prices.

Channels of Distribution

As consumers, we generally take for granted the role of marketing intermediaries or channel members. If we want a six pack of soda or a box of detergent, there are a variety of places we can go to buy them such as a supermarket, a convenience store, or even a drugstore. However, to the manufacturer of these products, the value and importance of these intermediaries are very much understood. Think for a moment what manufacturers of personal computers such as Compaq, IBM, or Apple would do if they could not sell their personal computers (PCs) through retail outlets such as Computerland or Sears? How would they make their products available so that millions of consumers and small businesses could examine and evaluate them?

One of the most important marketing decisions a firm must make involves the way its products and services are made available for purchase by the customer. A firm can have an excellent product at a great price, but it will be of little value unless it is available where the customer wants it, when the customer wants it, and with the proper support and service. **Marketing channels,** or the place element of the marketing mix, refers to "sets of interdependent organizations involved in the process of making a product or service available for use or consumption."[17]

Channel decisions involve the selection, management, and motivation of intermediaries such as wholesalers, distributors, brokers, retailers, and other parties who help a firm make a product or service available to its customers. These intermediaries are sometimes called **resellers** and are very critical to the success of a company's marketing program. Of course, a company can choose not to use any channel intermediaries and sell to its customers through **direct channels.** This type of channel arrangement is sometimes used in the consumer market by firms using direct-selling programs, such as Avon, Tupperware, or Fuller Brush, or those firms that use direct-response advertising or telemarketing to sell their products. Direct channels are also frequently used by manufacturers of industrial products and services, as they often are selling expensive and complex products that require extensive negotiations and sales efforts, as well as service and follow-up calls after a sale is made. Most consumer product companies distribute through **indirect channels** usually using a network of wholesalers or institutions that sell to other resellers and/or retailers—institutions that sell primarily to the final consumer.

The Role of Resellers in Promotional Strategy The resellers who distribute a company's products play a very important role in the promotional program. Channel members such as retailers are often relied on to participate in implementation of a firm's advertising and sales promotion program to the consumer market. It is important for a manufacturer to gain cooperation and support from retailers when they are running promotional programs. This may mean that the retailer agrees to such things as running an in-store sampling program, setting up a special promotional display, or agreeing to reduce prices during a promotion.

Resellers also make an important contribution to the manufacturer's marketing efforts through their own promotional programs. Most retailers have promotional programs that may include advertising and sales promotion and, in some instances, personal selling. The manufacturer will often work in conjunction with retailers so that the two parties' efforts complement one another. An important part of the advertising program of many retailers occurs through what is known as **cooperative advertising** whereby the manufacturer offers to pay for at least part of the retailer's cost of advertising for the manufacturer's specific brand(s). Under a co-op program, the manufacturer will share the cost of the local advertising the retailer does for his or her brand, up to a limit that is usually determined by a percentage of the retailer's purchase from the manufacturer. Cooperative advertising will be considered in more detail in Chapter 16.

Figure 2–12   **Trade Advertising Is Used to Interest Resellers in a Manufacturer's Product**

Developing Promotional Strategies—Push versus Pull

Most of you are aware of advertising and other forms of promotion directed toward ultimate consumers or business customers. We see these ads in the media and are often part of the target audience for the promotions. However, in addition to developing a consumer marketing mix, a company must also have a program to encourage the channel members to stock and promote its products. Programs designed to persuade the trade to stock, merchandise, and promote a manufacturer's products are part of what is known as a **promotional push strategy.** The goal of this type of strategy is to "push" the product through the channels of distribution by aggressively selling and promoting the item to the resellers or trade. As shown earlier in Figure 2–2, promotion to the trade includes all the elements of the promotional mix. Company sales representatives will call on resellers to explain the product, to discuss the firm's plans for building demand among ultimate consumers, and to describe special programs being offered to the trade, such as introductory discounts, promotional allowances, and cooperative ad programs. **Trade advertising** may be used by the company to interest wholesalers and retailers and motivate them to purchase its products for resale to their customers. Trade advertising usually appears in publications that serve the particular industry. For example, buyers in the grocery industry read *Progressive Grocer,* whereas a drugstore manager or buyer will read *Drug Store News.* An example of a trade ad for General Electric (GE) battery chargers and rechargeable batteries is shown in Figure 2–12.

The goal of a push strategy is to convince resellers that they can make a profit on a manufacturer's product and thus to encourage them to order the merchandise and push it through to their customers. However, in some situations manufacturers may face resistance from channel members because they may not want to take on an additional product line or brand. In these instances, companies may turn to a **promo-**

tional pull strategy whereby monies are spent on advertising and sales promotional efforts directed toward the ultimate consumer. The goal of a pull strategy is to create demand on the consumer end and encourage them to request the product from the retailer. Seeing the favorable demand from consumers, retailers will order the product from wholesalers (if they are used), who in turn will request it from the manufacturer. Thus, the product is "pulled" through the channels of distribution by the demand created on the consumer end.

Decisions as to whether to emphasize a push or a pull strategy will depend on a number of factors including the company's relations with the trade, its promotional budget, and demand for the firms' products. Companies that have very favorable channel relationships may prefer to use a push strategy and work closely with channel members to encourage them to stock and promote their products. A firm with a limited promotional budget may not have the funds for advertising and sales promotion that a pull strategy requires and may find it more cost-effective to build distribution and demand by working closely with resellers. When the demand outlook for a product is very favorable because it has unique benefits, is superior to competing brands, or is very popular among consumers, a pull strategy may be more appropriate. Actually, companies often use a combination of both push and pull strategies, with the emphasis changing as the product moves through the life cycle.

Promotion to the Final Buyer

As is shown in the marketing model in Figure 2–2, the marketing program includes promotion both to the trade or channel members and to the company's ultimate customers as well. Marketers use the various promotional mix elements—advertising, personal selling, sales promotion, and publicity/public relations—to inform consumers about their products, prices, and places where they are available. As was discussed in Chapter 1, each of these promotional mix variables plays a role in helping marketers achieve their promotional objectives. However, advertising is generally relied on for communicating information about products and services to the consumer market and and is becoming increasingly important in communicating with business customers as well. Thus, we will now turn our attention to examining the different forms of advertising used to communicate with the ultimate buyers of a product or service.

Classifications of Advertising

The nature and purpose of advertising differ from one industry to another and/or across situations. The target of an organization's advertising efforts often varies, as does its role and function in the marketing program. One advertiser may seek to generate immediate response or action from the customer, whereas another may be interested in developing awareness or a positive image for its products over a longer time period. To understand the nature and purpose of advertising to the final buyer better, it is useful to examine some classifications of the various types of advertising.

Advertising to the Consumer Market

National Advertising Advertising done by a company on a nationwide basis or in most regions of the country and targeted to the ultimate consumer market is known as **national advertising.** The companies that sponsor these ads are generally referred to as **national advertisers.** Most of the ads for well-known brands of products or services that we see on prime-time television or in other major national or regional media are examples of national advertising. This form of advertising is usually very general, as it rarely includes specific prices, directions for buying the product, or special services associated with the purchase. The purpose of this type of advertising is to make known or to remind consumers of the brand and its features, benefits, advantages, and

Figure 2–13 **This Ad for Sanka Is an Example of National Advertising**

uses or to reinforce its image so that consumers will be predisposed to purchasing it, wherever and whenever it is needed and convenient to do so. The ad for Sanka coffee shown in Figure 2–13 is an example of national advertising.

National advertising is the best-known and most widely discussed form of promotion, probably because of its pervasiveness. To understand better the scope of national advertising, it is helpful to look at the advertising expenditures of the 100 leading national advertisers for 1988, which are shown in Table 2–1. These figures reflect money spent in measured media as well as unmeasured media spending. Measured media include network and spot (local) television and radio, network cable TV, magazines, newspapers, and outdoor advertising. Unmeasured media spending represents money that went into support services such as direct-mail, sales promotion, and co-op advertising programs.

As can be seen in Table 2–1, the leader in advertising and promotional expenditures in 1988 was Philip Morris Companies, which spent over $2 billion advertising its tobacco products and the various brands of its two subsidiaries, Miller Brewing Company and General Foods Corporation. It is worth noting that 1988 marked only the second time in 24 years that Procter & Gamble was not the leader in ad spending. Further perusal of this table reveals that the vast majority of the top 100 advertisers are companies selling products and services to the consumer market.

Retail (Local) Advertising   Another prevalent type of advertising directed at the consumer market is classified as **retail/local advertising.** This type of advertising is done by retailers or local merchants to encourage consumers to shop at a specific store or to utilize a local service establishment such as a bank, fitness club, or restaurant. Whereas the national advertisers are concerned with selling their products at any lo-

Table 2–1   **100 Leading National Advertisers, 1988**

Rank	Advertiser	Ad Spending	Rank	Advertiser	Ad Spending	Rank	Advertiser	Ad Spending
1	Philip Morris Cos.	$2,058.2	35	Hershey Foods Corp.	$298.6	69	Kroger Co.	$144.1
2	Procter & Gamble Co.	1,506.9	36	U.S. Government	295.1	70	Seagram Co.	143.1
3	General Motors Corp. Co.	1,294.0	37	General Electric Co.	276.6	71	Volkwagen AG	140.3
4	Sears, Roebuck & Co.	1,045.2	38	Toyota Motor Corp.	272.9	72	Paramount Communications	139.2
5	RJR Nabisco	814.5	39	SmithKline Beecham	264.2	73	News Corp.	139.1
6	Grand Metropolitan PLC	773.9	40	Schering-Plough Corp.	262.2	74	CPC International	134.4
7	Eastman Kodak Co.	735.9	41	Campeau Corp.	260.5	75	Wm. Wrigley Jr. Co.	134.2
8	McDonald's Corp.	728.3	42	American Cyanamid Co.	256.2	76	Bayer AG	132.2
9	PepsiCo Inc.	712.3	43	American Stores Co.	250.5	77	E.I. du Pont de Nemours & Co.	131.4
10	Kellogg Co.	683.1	44	American Express Co.	247.2	78	Texas Air Corp.	128.8
11	Anheuser-Busch Cos.	634.5	45	Honda Motor Co.	243.3	79	Noxell Corp.	126.7
12	K mart Corp.	632.0	46	Tandy Corp.	232.0	80	American Dairy Farmers	126.6
13	Warner-Lambert Co.	609.2	47	Dayton Hudson Corp.	230.2	81	Sony Corp.	125.9
14	Unilever NV	607.5	48	Pfizer Inc.	230.1	82	Goodyear Tire & Rubber Co.	124.6
15	Nestlé SA	573.8	49	Nissan Motor Co.	224.9	83	Loews Corp.	123.8
16	Ford Motor Co.	569.8	50	IBM Corp.	214.4	84	Levi Strauss Associates	123.1
17	American Telephone & Telegraph	547.5	51	Hyundai Group	204.5	85	Columbia Pictures Entertainment	122.4
18	Chrysler Corp.	474.0	52	Campbell Soup Co.	202.5	86	Dr Pepper/Seven-Up Cos.	121.9
19	General Mills	470.1	53	Adolph Coors Co.	200.8	87	AMR Corp.	120.7
20	Johnson & Johnson	468.8	54	B.A.T. Industries PLC	184.1	88	Marriott Corp.	120.2
21	Bristol-Myers Squibb	430.7	55	BCI Holdings Corp.	180.2	89	UAL Corp.	120.2
22	J.C. Penney Co.	426.6	56	Revlon Group	177.3	90	Hallmark Cards	119.8
23	Quaker Oats Co.	423.4	57	American Brands	168.7	91	Citicorp	118.4
24	Ralston Purina Co.	421.0	58	Hasbro Inc.	164.5	92	ITT Corp.	115.9
25	Time Warner	409.7	59	Gillette Co.	160.5	93	Franklin Mint	114.8
26	May Department Stores Co.	399.7	60	Nynex Corp.	160.4	94	Wendy's International	114.2
27	American Home Products Corp.	393.2	61	Carter Hawley Hale Stores	159.8	95	Bell Atlantic Corp.	113.2
28	Coca-Cola Co.	385.1	62	Dow Chemical Co.	156.7	96	Delta Air Lines	112.6
29	H.J. Heinz Co.	340.1	63	Mobil Corp.	155.9	97	Whitman Corp.	111.7
30	Mars Inc.	339.7	64	Montgomery Ward & Co.	155.3	98	S.C. Johnson & Son	111.6
31	Sara Lee Corp.	326.9	65	MCA Inc.	153.7	99	Borden Inc.	110.5
32	Macy Acquiring Corp.	308.9	66	Clorox Co.	148.3	100	Subaru of America	108.0
33	Colgate-Palmolive Co.	306.6	67	Mazda Motor Corp.	146.7			
34	Walt Disney Co.	300.6	68	Philips NV	144.3			

Note: Dollars are in millions.

Source: Advertising Age, September 27, 1989, p. 1.

cation, retail or local advertisers must give the consumer a specific reason to patronize their establishment. Retail advertising tends to emphasize specific customer benefits such as store hours, credit policies, service, store atmosphere, merchandise assortments, or other distinguishing attributes. In addition, product availability and price are important advertising themes, often used in conjunction with a sale or special event. Retailers are concerned with building store traffic, and often their promotions take the form of **direct-action advertising** that is designed to produce immediate store traffic or sales. An example of a direct-action retail advertisement is shown in Figure 2–14.

In addition to their product- and price-oriented advertising, many retailers have turned to image advertising as well in an attempt to influence consumers' perceptions of their stores.[18] Figure 2–15 shows how K mart is using image advertising to influence consumers' perceptions of the image of its stores and the type of merchandise it carries.

Direct-Response Advertising   One of the fastest-growing sectors of the U.S. economy is that of direct marketing. **Direct-response advertising** is a method of direct marketing whereby a product is promoted through an advertisement that offers the customer the opportunity to purchase directly from the manufacturer. Traditionally, direct mail has been the primary medium for direct-response advertising, although television is becoming an increasingly important medium.

Direct-response advertising has become very popular in recent years owing primarily to changing lifestyles in this country, particularly the increase in two-income households. This has meant more discretionary income but much less time for in-store shopping. Thus, the convenience of shopping through the mail or by telephone has led to the tremendous increase in direct-response advertising. Credit cards and

Figure 2–14   Retail Advertising Often Encourages Consumers to Take Immediate Action

Figure 2–15   Retailers Attempt to Project Certain Images for Their Stores through Advertising

Figure 2—16   **This Ad by Market Leader Campbell's Is Designed to Stimulate Overall Demand for Soup**

"800" or toll-free numbers have also facilitated the purchase of products from direct-response advertisements.

This form of marketing and advertising is often used by small companies who lack the funds to promote their products to the consumer market on a large-scale basis or choose not to become involved in battles for retail shelf space. In recent years, however, a number of major corporations have expanded their marketing efforts to include direct-response advertising. Packaged goods companies such as General Foods, Procter & Gamble, Nestlé, and R. J. Reynolds are using direct-response advertising as a way of marketing their products to consumers, as are service companies such as American Express and Citibank.[19]

Primary and Selective Demand Advertising   Another way of viewing advertising to the ultimate customer is in terms of whether the message is designed to stimulate either primary or selective demand. **Primary demand advertising** is designed to stimulate demand for the general product class or entire industry, whereas **selective demand advertising** focuses on creating demand for a particular manufacturer's brands. Most of the advertising for various products and services is concerned with stimulating selective demand and emphasizes reasons for buying a particular brand. Advertisers generally assume that there is a favorable level of primary demand for the product class and focus attention on increasing their market share. Thus, their advertising attempts to give consumers a reason(s) to buy their brand.

There are several situations in which advertisers might concentrate on the stimulation of primary demand. When a company's brand (or brands) dominate a market, advertising may focus on creating demand for the product class, as it will benefit the

Figure 2–17 **The Beef Industry Sponsors Advertising Encouraging Consumers to Eat More Beef**

most from market growth. For example, Campbell Soup has over a 70 percent share of the condensed soup market, and the company's advertising objective is to encourage consumers to eat more soup. Notice that the "Campbell's soup is good food" ad (Figure 2–16) emphasizes the benefits of eating soup more than the brand itself.

Primary demand advertising is often used as a part of promotional strategy for a new product to help it gain acceptance among customers. Products in the introductory or growth stages of their life cycles often have primary demand stimulation as a promotional objective because the challenge is to sell customers on the product itself as much as it is to sell a particular brand. Of course, selective demand stimulation is not ignored, but the major concern is getting consumers to consider using the product. For example, when Sony introduced the video cassette recorder (VCR) to the market in the mid-1970s, much of its advertising stressed the benefits of video recorders in general. As competition entered the market, its advertising strategy shifted to a selective demand stimulation strategy whereby benefits of the Sony VCR over other brands was emphasized.

Stimulation of primary demand is also the objective sought for advertising conducted by industry trade associations such as the American Dairy Association, the Florida Citrus Growers, or the Potato Board. These associations will assess their members for funds to be used in promotional efforts to encourage the use of their product or services or to overcome declining primary demand trends. For example, the Beef Industry Council has been sponsoring an advertising campaign to help counter the decline in red meat consumption that has occurred in recent years. Ads such as the one shown in Figure 2–17 have been used to convince consumers that beef is not expensive, time-consuming to prepare, full of fat, and generally unhealthful. Sometimes major competitors may even join together to help stimulate sluggish or declining demand for their product class. Promotional Perspective 2–2 discusses how the coffee industry

Promotional Perspective 2-2

The New Coffee Generation?

In the 1960s U.S. consumers between the ages of 20 and 29 drank an average of 3.4 cups of coffee a day. In 1983, however, coffee consumption among this age group averaged only 1.3 cups daily. While concerns over caffeine were an important reason for coffee's decline, another major problem was that the drink had gone out of style among many young people. Coffee became associated with being old, whereas soft drinks were seen as more consistent with the young, dynamic lifestyle of the younger adult. Soft drink consumption among this "Pepsi Generation" had tripled over the past two decades.

To reverse the decline in sales among younger adults, the coffee industry decided to target a $20 million television advertising campaign at the 18- to 34-year-old age group. The campaign was financed by the 45 coffee-growing countries that belong to the International Coffee Organization and by the National Coffee Association, a trade group of coffee roasters and importers. Ironically, the association's two largest members, General Foods and Procter & Gamble, are also the two largest competitors in the U.S. market.

The actual campaign attempted to portray coffee as part of pursuing and achieving goals, as surveys among men and women in the target audience showed that they believed in self-development, hard work, and their ability to control their own destiny. The 30-second spots used quick cuts of famous people working at their jobs and, of course, enjoying a cup of coffee. Celebrities in the commercials included actress Cicely Tyson, author

Kurt Vonnegut, pro football quarterback Ken Anderson, rock star David Bowie, actress/comedienne Jane Curtin, and marathon runner Allison Rae. The ad theme was "You are the new American society, the movers and shakers. You are the new coffee generation. Join the coffee achievers." The ads also attempted to dispel the belief that coffee makes people nervous by stressing that "coffee calms you down and picks you up. Coffee gives you the serenity to dream and the vitality to do it. No other drink does that like coffee."

While follow-up research revealed that the campaign was effective in changing young adults' attitudes toward drinking coffee, consumption among this age group has remained low. In 1988 overall consumption of coffee remained relatively flat, as the proportion of consumers drinking coffee declined, but the amount consumed by those drinking the beverage increased slightly. The coffee industry continues to lose sales as more and more consumers make soft drinks their morning beverage instead of coffee. The coffee industry is now facing a new threat, as Coca-Cola has stepped up its efforts to tap the market with its "Coke in the morning" ad campaign, which is being test-marketed in several cities.

Sources: Kathleen A. Hughes "Coffee Makers Hope New Ads Will Reverse Declining Sales," *The Wall Street Journal*, September 1, 1983, p. 27; Jube Shiver, Jr., "Firms Try to Sweeten the Coffeepot," *Los Angeles Times*, November 1, 1984, p. 1; Patricia Winters, "Coffee Urged to Fight Soft Drinks," *Advertising Age*, February 29, 1988, p. 30; John C. Maxwell, Jr., "Coffee Consumption Continues to Cool Off," *Advertising Age*, June 13, 1988, p. 34.

used primary demand-oriented advertising to deal with the problem of declining coffee consumption among young adults.

Advertising to the Business and Professional Market

For many companies the ultimate customer is not the mass consumer market but rather another business, industry, or profession. **Business-to-business advertising** is used by one business to advertise its products or services to another. The target for business advertising is individuals who either use and/or are in a position to influence a firm's decision to purchase another company's product or service. There are three basic categories of business-to-business advertising, including industrial, professional, and trade advertising. (Trade advertising was discussed earlier in the chapter under promotional "Pull Strategies.")

Industrial Advertising   Advertising targeted at individuals in businesses who buy or influence the purchase of industrial goods or other services is known as **industrial advertising.** Industrial goods are those products that either become a physical part of another product (raw material, component parts), are used in the manufacture of other goods (machinery, equipment), or are used to help the manufacturer conduct business (office supplies, computers, copy machines, etc.). Business services, such as insurance, financial services, and health care, are also included in this category. Industrial advertising is usually found in general business publications (such as *Fortune*,

Figure 2—18   Television Commercials Are Being Used More Frequently to Advertise Business Products

Business Week, and *The Wall Street Journal*) or in publications targeted specifically to the particular industry. However, in recent years advertisements for industrial products and services have become more commonplace in mass media such as television. Figure 2–18 shows a storyboard of a commercial for Ricoh copiers that stresses the reliability of its products.

Industrial advertising is often not designed to sell a product or service directly, as the purchase of industrial goods is often a complex process involving a number of individuals. The role of an industrial ad is to help make the company and its product or service better known by the industrial customer, to assist in the development of an image for the firm, and perhaps most important, to open doors for the company's sales representatives when they call on these customers. Figure 2–19 shows an example of a classic advertisement run by McGraw-Hill Magazines for their business publications that addresses the reasons why a business-to-business marketer would want to advertise.

Professional Advertising Advertising that is targeted to professional groups—such as doctors, lawyers, dentists, engineers, or professors—to encourage them to use or specify the advertiser's product for others' use is known as **professional advertising.** Professional groups are important because they constitute a market for products and services they use in their business. Also, their advice, recommendation, or specification of a product or service is often a very important influence on many consumer's purchase decisions. For example, Vipont Pharmaceutical initially targeted advertising

Figure 2–19   This Ad Shows Why Industrial Marketers Need to Advertise

Figure 2–20   Vipont Uses Ads Targeted to Dentists to Encourage Them to Recommend Viadent Products to Their Patients

for Viadent plaque-fighting toothpaste and oral rinse to dentists to encourage them to recommend these products to their patients (Figure 2–20).

Professional advertising should not be confused with advertising done *by* professionals. In recent years advertising by professionals such as dentists, lawyers, and doctors has been increasing in popularity as legal restrictions have been removed and competition has increased.

These classifications of the various types of advertising demonstrate that this promotional element is used in a variety of ways and by a number of different organizations for promoting products and services to their target markets. Advertising is a very flexible promotional tool whose role in a marketing program will vary depending on the situation facing the organization and what information needs to be communicated.

Environmental Influences on Marketing and Promotion

The three components of the marketing model we have just examined represent "controllable factors" that are determined by the organization. A firm's marketing strategy, selection of a target market, and development, implementation, and control of its marketing program are all directed by management. However, there are a number of factors that cannot be controlled or directed by the firms or organization. These uncontrollable forces constitute what is often referred to as the **macroenvironment** of marketing and include demographic, economic, technological, natural/physical, socio-

Figure 2-21

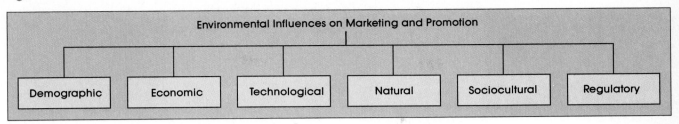

cultural, and regulatory factors (Figure 2–21). These environmental forces or influences can have a significant impact on a firm's marketing strategy and programs both in the short and long term and must be continually monitored and responded to. In this section, we will examine these environmental influences, giving particular attention to the impact each has on the promotional element of an organization's marketing program.

Demographic Environment

Demographics deals with the practice of analyzing and describing the distribution of the population according to selected characteristics such as age, sex, income, education, occupation, and geographic dispersion. Major demographic developments are occurring in the United States that are affecting firms' marketing and promotional programs. These include the aging of the U.S. population, the increasing number of women in the labor force, and changing ethnic compositions. Some of the effects of each of these are discussed in the following pages.

Aging of the Population
Perhaps one of the most notable characteristics of the U.S. population is the fact that it is aging as birthrates decline, life expectancies increase, and the baby boom generation gets older. A large reason for the graying of America is that the **baby boomers,** the 74 million Americans born between 1946 and 1964, are growing older. As this age cohort has grown older, they have represented a significant opportunity to marketers because of their size and purchasing power. In the 1970s the baby boomers made the 25- to 34-year-old age group the fastest-growing segment of the population. Between 1985 and 1995 the number of people aged 31 to 56 will grow by nearly 21 million, as the baby boom generation ages.[20] Also, as more of the original baby boomers reach childbearing age, they are creating a mini baby boom, which is creating a substantial market for infants' and childrens' products such as clothing, strollers, and toys.[21] Companies such as Oshkosh and Fisher-Price are experiencing strong sales growth as this market increases in size.

Baby boomers have a distinct profile compared with previous generations in terms of their education level, women's roles, tastes, buying habits, and for many, their affluence. One segment of the baby boom generation of particular interest to marketers in recent years has been that of the young, professional baby boomers, often referred to as "Yuppies." This segment represents the better-educated, more affluent, and according to many people, more materialistic group of baby boomers, as described in Promotional Perspective 2–3.

The baby boom generation has had, and will continue to have, a major impact on the market for consumer products. The aging of the population has resulted in tremendous opportunity for producers of goods and services that appeal to the baby boom market. However, it has also presented serious problems to companies whose primary target market consists of consumers in other age groups. For example, cereal companies prospered during the late 1960s and 1970s when the baby boom generation was at the prime cereal-consuming ages. However, as they grew older and birthrates declined, the number of children declined significantly. Cereal companies such as Kellogg, General Mills, and General Foods have had to refocus their marketing efforts

Promotional Perspective 2–3

Is the Yuppie Era Over?

Over the past decade, few market segments have received as much attention from marketers, advertisers, and the media in general as the "Yuppies," or young urban professionals. Yuppies represent the more affluent, mobile, and better-educated subsegment of the baby boom generation. Many of them are fast-track middle managers and professionals committed to their careers and making and spending money. They travel widely, eat out more often, and worship quality in their furniture, clothing, automobiles, and entertainment. They are generally characterized as being more self-indulgent and materialistic than other baby boomers, with insatiable appetites for designer clothing, espresso machines, personal computers, video and audio equipment, and foreign cars such as Saabs, Volvos, and BMWs. While it has been estimated that only one out of seven baby boomers qualifies as a genuine Yuppie, a study by Market Facts, Inc. suggests that nearly half the cohort consists of "psychographic yuppies"—individuals who think and act like yuppies.

Advertisers are interested in the Yuppie segment because of their higher income and their inclination to buy more and better things. For example, one study found Yuppies willing to pay an average of $2,000 more than non-Yuppies and $1,600 more than the general population for a new car. The percentage of Yuppies owning a foreign automobile is nearly twice that of other baby boomers or the general population.

While Yuppies would appear to be the ideal target for many advertisers, there are problems associated with marketing products and services to them. It has been argued that the characteristics that define the Yuppie are unclear and their purchase behavior, lifestyle, and media habits are not really understood. There is also the problem of "Yuppie backlash," as many who fit the demographic profile of the Yuppie do not like the label. As one marketing specialist put it, "You're talking about a class of people who put off having families so they can make payments on a BMW—to be a yuppie is to be a loathsome and undesirable creature!"

By the end of the 1980s, many advertisers' love affair with the Yuppie—and Yuppie values—had ended. Many people blamed the October 1987 stock market crash on Yuppies and their greediness and self-interest. Advertising executives argue that there were too many Yuppie commercials, and consumers simply became tired of them. Advertisers have become careful to avoid portraying Yuppie types in their ads or having their brands categorized as a "Yuppie product." Some have even taken to poking fun at or ridiculing Yuppies in their ads. One of the best-known Yuppie ad campaigns of the 1980s was Michelob's "Where you're going, it's Michelob" theme, which showed stereotypical Yuppies at work, play, and of course, enjoying Michelob. However, in 1987 Michelob abandoned the approach in favor of "The night belongs to Michelob" campaign. Instead of marketing itself as the beer of the Yuppie, the new ads are attempting to attract a much broader audience by repositioning Michelob as the beer that is synonymous with nighttime.

Sources: J. J. Burnett and A. J. Bush, "Profiling the Yuppies," *Journal of Advertising Research,* April/May 1986, pp. 27–36; "Yuppies: The Big Boom of the Baby Boom," *Marketing News,* June 7, 1986. Bruce Horowitz, "Where Have All the Yuppies Gone? Ads Have Dropped Them, Everyone Hates Them," *Los Angeles Times,* March 8, 1988, pt. IV, p. 6.

to persuade 25- to 40-year-olds to eat more cereal. They have been introducing more adult-oriented cereals such as the high-grain and -fiber products. In addition to introducing new products and changing their advertising appeals (Figure 2–22), the selection of media has also become more adult oriented. Cereal ads often appear on adult-oriented television programs and sporting events and in magazines that appeal to fitness- and nutrition-conscious consumers such as *Self, Runners World,* and *Sports Illustrated.*

The aging of the population will also lead marketers to put more emphasis on older consumers. In 1960 only 9 percent of the U.S. population was over 65 years of age, but by the year 2000 the number of people over 65 is expected to be close to 22 percent of the population.[22] Older Americans, variously referred to as the "Mature Market," "Welderly" (well-to-do elderly), and "Gray Powers," have become and will continue to be a prime target for marketers. The group of Americans over age 50 constitute 25 percent of the population but have 50 percent of the nation's disposable income, buying $800 million worth of goods and services each year.[23] Table 2–2 lists just a few of the programs firms have developed to target their marketing efforts toward older consumers. Figure 2–23 shows an advertisement for American Airlines Senior SAAvers Club, which offers a discount on air fares to anyone 65 or over.

The aging of the population is also resulting in an increased demand for media to reach older consumers. For example, *Modern Maturity,* which is provided as part of the American Association of Retired Persons's annual membership, became the largest

Figure 2–22   **Many Cereal Ads Are Now Targeted to Adults**

Figure 2–23   **American Airlines Targets Senior Citizens with Its Senior SAAvers Club**

paid circulation magazine in the United States in 1988, with 19.3 million subscribers.[24] This magazine has become a popular media vehicle for reaching active senior citizens (Figure 2–24).

Increase in Working Women   One of the most significant changes in American society over the last two decades has been the increase in the number of working women. The percentage of adult women in the labor force rose from 36.7 percent in 1965 to 55.4 percent in 1987, and projections are that by the year 2000 nearly two thirds of all women will be working outside the home.[25] The increase in working women has had a dramatic effect on the demand for a wide variety of products and services

Table 2–2   **Examples of Firms with Marketing Programs Targeted to Older Consumers**

Company	Program/Products
Sears	Mature Outlook Club (discounts to consumers over 50)
American and United airlines	Senior citizens discounts
Southwestern Bell	Silver pages (directories for senior citizens)
Eastern Airlines; Hilton Hotels	Get-up-and-go passport (reduced fares for those over 62)
Marriot Corporation	Housing projects for retired military officers
Campbell Soup	"Less sodium" products
Johnson & Johnson	Affinity Shampoo (targeted to those over 40)

Sources: "Last Year It Was the Yuppies—This Year It's Their Parents," *Business Week,* March 10, 1986, pp. 68, 72, 74; Peter Petjre, "Marketers Mine For Gold in the Old," *Fortune,* March 31, 1986, pp. 70–78.

Figure 2–24 *Modern Maturity* **Has the Largest Circulation of Any Magazine**

such as child-care services, microwave ovens, easy-to-prepare foods, restaurant meals, and women's clothing, to mention a few.

Another important effect of the increase in working women is the greater amount of disposable income brought about by the dual-earner household. In 1980 the median income of a family with a working wife was nearly $27,000, as compared with $19,000 for families with a nonworking wife. By 1985 the median income grew to $37,092 for households with working wives, compared with only $22,659 for those where the wife did not work.[26] This additional income affords the family greater opportunity to purchase more products and services, to take more trips and vacations, to eat out more often, and basically to enjoy a higher standard of living.

The increase in the number of working women has many implications for marketing and promotional strategy. Many marketers are directing more of their advertising to working women, as they not only constitute an important market segment but also are more likely to be involved in purchase decisions that have traditionally been the domain of men. A study by the Young and Rubicam advertising agency found that working women are more likely to be concerned with decisions regarding financial services, travel, and the selection of an automobile than are nonworking women.[27]

Advertisers have also had to change their media strategies to reach working women, as they are less likely to be around the house watching television or reading traditional women's magazines such as *Good Housekeeping* and *Ladies Home Journal.* Over the past decade a number of new magazines have been introduced to respond to the needs and interests of the working woman such as *Working Woman, Working Mother, Self, New Woman,* and *Savvy* (Figure 2–25).

Figure 2–25 Many Magazines Are Targeted to Working Women

Changing Ethnic and Racial Profile   The racial and ethnic profile of the U.S. population is changing rapidly. One in five Americans today is black, Hispanic, Asian, or a member of some other minority group. Blacks are the largest minority group, numbering nearly 28 million persons and having an estimated purchasing power of nearly $200 million. However, the fastest growing of all minority groups is the Hispanic, which is comprised of a number of different Spanish-speaking nationalities such as Mexican, Puerto Rican, and Cuban. Currently, there are more than 20 million Hispanics in the United States with an estimated purchasing power of nearly $100 billion. As a result of high immigration and birthrates, Hispanics are growing at a rate five times faster than the general population and will soon become our nation's largest minority group.[28] Some 90 percent of all Hispanics are concentrated in only 10 states, with 71 percent living in four major markets—New York, California, Florida, and Texas. Puerto Ricans are the predominant Hispanic group in New York; Cubans, in Florida; and Mexicans, in California, Texas, and the adjoining Southwest. The Asian population in this country has also burgeoned as the population of Chinese, Japanese, Filipino, Korean, and Vietnamese has increased over the past decade.

The size of these minority groups, as well as their diverse cultures, needs, and buying habits, makes them important market segments for many companies. However, advertisers are finding that the Hispanic and Asian minorities in particular cannot be reached effectively through the general media with traditional English language appeals. Thus, many companies are developing products and advertising appeals specifically for these markets. Advertising for ethnic subcultures is discussed in more detail in Chapter 4.

Other Trends   The demographic trends discussed above are some of the more notable and significant changes occurring among the U.S. population. Other demographic

Figure 2–26 **Advertising Often Encourages Consumers to Use Credit**

Figure 2–27 **Low Interest Rates Make It Possible for More Consumers to Purchase New Automobiles**

changes also taking place are geographic shifts in the population, rising education levels, and changes in the structure of American households, such as more one-parent families and the increase in single-person households. It is important for marketers to monitor changes in the demographic environment and identify their implications for their industry and individual products and services. Fortunately, demographic changes are the most predictable of all the forces that constitute the macroenvironment, as there is a wealth of demographic information available from both government and commercial sources.[29] Thus, companies should be well aware of relevant demographic trends and developments and how they might influence their marketing and promotional strategies.

Economic Environment

Marketing activity is influenced very heavily by the state of the economy. Thus, attention must be paid to economic conditions and trends and their potential impact on the demand for various products and services. Attention must be given to **macroeconomic conditions** that influence the state of the economy such as changes in gross national product (GNP), whether the economy is in an inflationary or recessionary period, interest rates, and unemployment levels. **Microeconomic trends** such as consumer income, savings, debt, and expenditure patterns are also important, as consumers' ability to buy is a function of many factors including changes in real income, disposable and discretionary income, savings, and debt levels. An interesting characteristic of the younger generation of American consumers is their willingness to use credit to finance many of their purchases (Figure 2–26). Consumers' liberal use of credit has been a major contributor to the growth of our economy; however, many critics argue that the high cost of credit is detrimental to the economic well-being of the consumer.

Changes in economic conditions may have a significant impact on marketing and advertising strategies. For example, in a recessionary period, activity in the economic environment slows down and even declines, as businesses decrease production, unemployment rises, and consumers have less money to spend. Companies will often cut back on marketing and advertising expenditures as a way of meeting budget forecasts. Advertising expenditures, in particular, may be a prime candidate for cutbacks since many executives question the need to spend huge sums of money in this area. As you will learn later in the text, this may not be an advisable strategy because it may compound the problems a company faces during a slow economic period.

Another example of how economic developments affect the marketplace can be seen in the impact of falling interest rates. During 1987/88, interest rates for home loans fell to as low as 8 percent. As a result the number of new housing starts increased considerably, and virtually everyone associated with the housing industry—including lenders, realtors, contractors, and suppliers—benefited. Furniture, carpeting, and major appliance manufacturers also enjoyed sales increases, as consumers purchased these products for their new homes. Lower interest rates on auto loans also helped sales of new cars, as consumers were able to obtain lower-rate financing for automobile purchases (Figure 2–27).

Technological Environment

Perhaps the most dramatic of the macroenvironmental forces that affect marketing is that of technology. Changes in scientific knowledge and technological advances have a pervasive influence not only on a particular industry but also on the way goods and services are marketed. Changes in technology can affect an industry in several ways. Technology can result in the emergence and development of a new industry. For example, the PC industry started in the 1970s and is already a multibillion dollar industry spending several hundred million dollars a year on advertising.

Technology can also radically alter or even destroy an existing industry. Consider the growth of the VCR industry. It is estimated that nearly two thirds of U.S. households will have a VCR by 1990.[30] This growth in the VCR market has created tremendous opportunities for manufacturers of the players and tapes, the movie industry, and the video stores who rent tapes to consumers. The growth of this industry, however, has also posed a threat to other markets such as movie theaters and pay-TV companies. Attendance at movie theaters declined in the late 1980s, as more people rented movies to watch at home. Likewise, fewer households were subscribing to pay television, such as Home Box Office (HBO), since they were able to rent the movies before they were shown on the pay channels.

Technology can also stimulate new markets in related industries. For example, the penetration of the microwave oven into nearly 70 percent of American homes has resulted in a resurgence of the frozen dinner market. Products such as Le Menu, Stouffer's Entrees, and Lean Cuisine have enjoyed tremendous growth, partly as a result of the microwave convenience of preparing these dishes as well as improvements in product quality (Figure 2–28).

Changes in technology are also having an impact on the marketing and advertising process. Computerized checkout lanes provide supermarkets with information concerning consumer demand for products on a daily basis. Home-shopping channels are already proving to be successful, whereas shopping through computers for banking services, airline tickets, stocks brokerage services, and even new cars is already a common practice in some areas.

Figure 2–28 **Microwave Dinners Have Become Very Popular**

Natural Environment

Perhaps the most difficult environmental influence to forecast or predict, yet very relevant to marketers, is change in the physical or natural environment. The natural environment includes the forces of nature as well as the availability of natural resources that influence a company's business and marketing strategy. Forces of nature such as weather patterns can influence demand for many products and services. For example, many ski resorts suffered severe losses in the early 1980s owing to a lack of snow. To respond to this problem, many resorts installed snowmaking equipment and began running ads guaranteeing consumers of skiable conditions, particularly in the early part of the season.

The natural environment also provides companies with the resources for producing goods and services. Changes in the availability and prices of raw materials have had a significant impact on the companies who use them and on consumers as well. For example, the drought of the summer of 1988 created havoc for farmers and their crops and resulted in a significant increase in the costs of many consumer products. Shortages in raw materials, increasing costs of energy, concern over increased levels of pollution, and increased intervention in resource management by governments and other agencies have resulted in both threats and opportunities to many companies.

Companies and consumers continually adapt to changes in the natural environment. For example, the Organization of Petroleum Exporting Countries (OPEC) oil embargoes led to spiraling gasoline prices in the 1970s and early 1980s and, in some areas, led to long lines at filling stations. As a result of the shortages, many oil companies changed their marketing approaches. Some changed completely to self-service stations, and most reduced services such as washing windows and checking oil. Little advertising was done for the companies' products because demand was exceeding supply. However, as oil prices began to fall and consumers switched to more fuel-efficient automobiles, supplies once again exceeded demand, and many oil companies found themselves in a position of needing to win back customers. Many of the services and marketing programs previously employed have now been reinstated by many companies. For example, Texaco instituted direct-mail campaigns to consumers, whereas Shell returned to the use of promotions to attract customers.

Sociocultural Environment

Marketing, and advertising in particular, is very much influenced by the basic beliefs, values, norms, customs, and lifestyle patterns that exist in a society. Marketers must take into account the core cultural beliefs and values that exist in the countries that compose their marketplace. Many U.S. firms are increasingly looking to international markets for their products and services as the domestic market becomes more saturated. While understanding the cultural values and customs of foreign markets is important to multinational companies, many marketers have their hands full tracking changes in the values, norms, and lifestyles of American consumers. Marketers must constantly monitor the sociocultural environment of the American public in order to spot new opportunities or to identify new threats. They must monitor social trends and changes in consumer values and respond to them through their marketing and promotional programs.

We should also recognize that marketing and advertising are often major contributors to social trends and changes in consumers' lifestyles and values. We will consider how sociocultural factors influence consumer behavior in more detail in Chapter 4, while the impact of advertising on society is discussed in Chapter 22.

Regulatory Environment

The final, and in many ways most frustrating, component of the external environment that an organization must consider is composed of the regulatory influences. Marketing decisions are constrained, directed, and influenced by the practices and policies of federal, state, and local governments. These policies are expressed through laws and regulations that are administered and enforced by various government agencies. Virtually every element of the marketing mix is influenced by some type of government regulation. Numerous laws exist to ensure product safety and to protect the health and well-being of consumers. The pricing variable is the focus of laws dealing with areas such as price fixing, price discrimination, discounts, and resale price maintenance. Distribution decisions and arrangements are also subject to a number of restrictions and regulations.

Of particular interest in this text are laws and regulations that affect advertising and promotion. Advertising and promotional practices are closely monitored at both the state and federal levels. The Federal Trade Commission (FTC) and numerous other federal agencies scrutinize advertising to protect consumers from false or misleading ads and to prevent a firm from gaining any competitive edge through unfair or deceptive advertising. Policing of the advertising industry is also undertaken by advertisers themselves and other groups such as the media through various self-regulatory programs. Chapter 21 will be devoted entirely to examining the regulatory environment of advertising and promotion.

Summary

Promotion plays an important role in an organization's efforts to market its product, service, or ideas to its customers. A model consisting of three components was presented for analyzing how promotion fits into a company's marketing program—the marketing strategy and plan, the marketing program development, and the target market. The marketing process begins with the determination of a marketing strategy that is based on a detailed situation analysis and serves as the guide for target market selection and the development of the firm's marketing program.

The various elements of the marketing mix must be coordinated to develop an effective and successful marketing program. Each marketing mix variable is multidimensional in nature and includes a number of decision areas. Product planning involves decisions regarding the basic product as well as selection of a brand name and packaging, all of which are important from a communications perspective. Price levels and pricing policies must consider cost and demand factors as well as competition and the consumers' perceived value of the product or service offering.

One of the most important marketing decisions a firm must make is the selection of marketing channels by which the product is made available to the customer for purchase. While some firms sell directly to the customer and forgo the use of any channel member, most use marketing intermediaries or resellers such as wholesalers and/or retailers. Marketing and promotional programs must be developed for these intermediaries to encourage them to stock, merchandise, and promote the manufacturer's product. Programs geared to the resellers or trade are part of a promotional push strategy, whereas monies spent on advertising and sales promotion to create demand among ultimate consumers constitutes a promotional pull strategy. Promotion to the final buyer occurs through the various promotional mix elements, although advertising is most often relied on to communicate information to both consumer and business markets. Various classifications of advertising to final customers were examined including national, retail or local, and business-to-business advertising, which includes industrial, trade, and professional advertising.

A number of factors cannot be controlled or directed by the organization and make up the macroenvironment of marketing, including demographic, economic, technological, natural/physical, sociocultural, and regulatory influences. These uncontrollable forces can have a significant impact on a firm's marketing strategy and programs, both in the short and long terms. Each of these environmental influences was examined, giving particular attention to its impact on promotional strategy.

Key Terms

Strategic marketing plan	Promotional pull strategy
Market opportunities	National advertising
Market segments	National advertisers
Product symbolism	Retail/local advertising
Brand extension strategy	Direct-action advertising
Trademark	Direct-response advertising
Price elasticity	Primary demand advertising
Nonprice competition	Selective demand advertising
Competition-oriented pricing	Business-to-business advertising
Marketing channels	Industrial advertising
Resellers	Professional advertising
Direct channels	Macroenvironment
Indirect channels	Demographics
Cooperative advertising	Baby boomers
Promotional push strategy	Macroeconomic conditions
Trade advertising	Microeconomic trends

Discussion Questions

1. What is meant by a market opportunity? Discuss several examples of market opportunities that companies have taken advantage of in recent years.
2. Assume that you are the advertising manager for a new, hot cereal product. Perform a competitive analysis for your brand, giving attention to the various forms of competition noted in the text.
3. Discuss the ways various aspects of product planning and strategy relate to advertising and promotion.
4. Find an example of a situation where a new product was recently introduced using a brand extension strategy. Discuss the advantages and disadvantages of using this strategy. Do you feel that the use of a line extension was appropriate in this situation? Why or why not?
5. Discuss the relationship of pricing strategies to advertising. What are some of the price-related factors that must be considered in developing the promotional program?
6. Discuss the differences between a promotional push strategy and a promotional pull strategy. What factors influence a firm's decision to use either a push or a pull strategy?
7. Discuss the differences between the following forms of advertising, giving attention to the objectives of each:
   - National versus local
   - Direct versus indirect
   - Primary versus selective demand
   - Industrial versus professional
8. Closely examine the expenditures of the 100 leading advertisers shown in Table 2–1. What are some of the common characteristics of these leading spenders? Does it make sense for companies to spend more than a billion dollars a year on advertising?

9. What are some of the conditions or situations in which a company might decide to concentrate its efforts on the stimulation of primary demand? Provide additional examples of primary demand advertising.

10. Discuss the role of advertising in industrial marketing firms. Given that industrial advertisers rely heavily on personal selling, why do they need to advertise?

11. Identify and discuss recent changes in the macroenvironment and how they have impacted the marketing and promotional strategies of a particular industry or individual companies.

Notes

1. Laura Konrad Jereski, "The Watch to Wear When You're Wearing More Than One," *Marketing & Media Decisions,* Spring 1985, pp. 121–28.

2. Matthew Heller, "Swatch Switches," *Forbes,* January 27, 1986, pp. 86–87.

3. John Grossman, "Plenty Up Their Sleeves at Swatch," *American Way Magazine* 5 (August 15, 1987), pp. 51, 102–105.

4. Alison Fahey, "Timex, Swatch Push Fashion," *Advertising Age,* July 18, 1988, p. 4.

5. "Walking Shoes May Open Gate to Big Profits," *Advertising Age,* July 7, 1986, p. 62.

6. "Marketing: The New Priority," *Business Week,* November 21, 1983, pp. 96–106.

7. J. Paul Peter and Jerry C. Olson, *Consumer Behavior* (Homewood, Ill.: Richard D. Irwin, 1987), p. 505.

8. Michael R. Solomon, "The Role of Products as Social Stimuli: A Symbolic Interactionism Perspective," *Journal of Consumer Research,* December 1983, pp. 319–29.

9. William M. Pride and O. C. Ferrel, *Marketing,* 6th ed. (Boston: Houghton Mifflin, 1989), p. 240.

10. Al Ries and Jack Trout, *Positioning: The Battle for Your Mind* (New York: McGraw-Hill, 1982).

11. Kenneth E. Runyon and David W. Stewart, *Consumer Behavior* (Columbus, Ohio: Merrill, 1987).

12. Elliot Young, "Judging a Product by Its Wrapper," *Progressive Grocer,* July 1985, pp. 10–11.

13. Kathleen Day, "Packaging Emerges as a Key Selling Tool," *Los Angeles Times,* March 17, 1985, pt. V, p. 1.

14. Peter and Olson, *Consumer Behavior,* p. 571.

15. David J. Curry, "Measuring Price and Quality Competition," *Journal of Marketing* 49 (Spring 1985), pp. 106–17.

16. Paul W. Farris and David J. Reibstein, "How Prices, Ad Expenditures and Profits Are Linked," *Harvard Business Review* 57, November/December 1979, pp. 173–84.

17. Philip Kotler, *Marketing Management,* 6th ed. (Englewood Cliffs, N.J.: Prentice-Hall, 1988).

18. Francine Schwadel, "Retailers Broaden Their Ad Campaigns to Promote Image as Well as Products," *The Wall Street Journal,* June 8, 1988, p. 28.

19. Edward Nash, "Adding a New Dimension to Mass Marketing," *Marketing Communications,* March 1988, pp. 62–68.

20. Bryand Robey and Cheryl Russell, "The Year of the Baby Boom," *American Demographics,* May 1984, p. 19.

21. "Bringing Up Baby: A New Kind of Marketing Boom," *Business Week,* April 22, 1985, p. 58.

22. "The Year 2000: A Demographic Profile of Consumer Market," *Marketing News,* May 25, 1984, pp. 8–10.

23. "Last Year It Was Yuppies—This Year It's Their Parents," *Business Week,* March 10, 1986, p. 68.

24. Ira Teinowitz, "'Modern Maturity'—No Signs of Gray," *Advertising Age,* February 20, 1989, p. 12.

25. U.S. Bureau of the Census, *Current Population Reports, 1988 Statistical Yearbook* (Washington, D.C.: Government Printing Office, 1988).

26. Ibid.

27. "Working Women More Attractive—Y&R," *Advertising Age,* January 11, 1982, p. 76.

28. Robert E. Mack, "Tapping the Hispanic Market: A Golden Growth Opportunity," *Marketing Communications,* March 1988, p. 54.

29. See "Business Guide to Demographic Products and Services," *American Demographics,* June 1985, pp. 23–33.

30. David Swanson and Bruce Klopfenstein, "How to Forecast VCR Penetration," *American Demographics,* December 1987, pp. 44–45.

3

The Structure of the Advertising and Promotions Industry

CHAPTER OBJECTIVES

1. To examine the structure of the advertising and promotions industry
2. To understand how companies organize for the advertising and promotions function
3. To explain the role and functions of each of the participants in the promotions process
4. To present methods for compensating and evaluating advertising agencies

A Revolution in the Advertising Agency Business?

"The problem in the auto industry right now is that there are too many cars and not enough people to buy them," said Jack Mayne, editor of *Automotive Age,* a trade magazine. "Consequently, the auto makers are looking at new things—including their advertising agencies."

The preceding quotation reflects a trend in other industries as well as the auto industry, but in 1988 a major coup was pulled off in the advertising industry business. General Motors (GM) awarded Hal Riney & Partners—a small (by New York standards) San Francisco–based advertising agency—a $100 million assignment to create advertising for its new Saturn car division. While the $100 million itself is a newsworthy enough story, the bigger story was that for the first time in years an auto manufacturer had gone outside New York and the largest ad agencies to select a relatively small firm to handle its account. "There has been an inbreeding between car advertisers and the big

agencies that has gone on for 60 years," noted one ad agency executive. And, indeed, American auto manufacturers have been a loyal group—Chevrolet has used agency Campbell Ewald for 74 years, whereas Oldsmobile has been handled by Leo Burnett for 54 years.

Why did GM break tradition? Creativity, the desire to use a smaller, more responsive agency, and the desire to use an agency organization similar to the competitors' have all been cited as reasons. (Honda had gone to a smaller agency, and Nissan followed shortly after GM.)

How will this event affect the advertising business? "If Riney is a success with Saturn," said Guy Day, retired co-founder of his own advertising agency, Chiat Day, "it will be one of the most significant events of this decade. . . . The chokehold that the big New York agencies have on these major ad budgets is disappearing. It's a whole new ballgame."[1]

Introduction

The development and implementation of a promotional program usually constitute a complex and detailed process involving the efforts of many persons. As consumers, we generally give little thought to the individuals or organizations who create the clever advertisements that capture our attention and interest or the contest or sweepstakes that we enter and hope to win. However, to those who are involved in marketing, it is important to have an understanding of the nature of the industry and the structure and functions of the organizations involved therein. As you can see in the opening to this chapter, the advertising and promotions business is a dynamic one, with large amounts of money, reputations, and jobs hinging on every agency decision.

The purpose of this chapter is to examine the structure of the promotions industry and the responsibilities of the participants involved. Attention will be focused on how the promotions function is organized and operates, as well as the roles of other participants in this process—particularly the role of the advertising agency.

Participants in the Promotions Process—An Overview

Before we discuss the specifics of the industry, it may be helpful to provide an overview of the entire system and to identify some of the players involved. As shown in Figure 3–1, there are four groups of participants in the industry, including the advertiser (or client), advertising agencies, media organizations, and collateral services. Each of these groups has specific roles to perform in the promotional process.

The advertisers, or **clients,** are the key participants in the process, as they have the products, services, or causes to be marketed, and they provide the funds that pay for the advertising and promotions efforts. The advertiser also assumes the major responsibility for developing the marketing program and for making the final decisions regarding the advertising and promotional program that will be employed. The organization itself may choose to perform most of these efforts, either through its own advertising department or by setting up an in-house agency. However, many organizations choose to use the services of an **advertising agency,** which is an outside firm that specializes in the creation, production, and/or placement of the communications

Figure 3–1

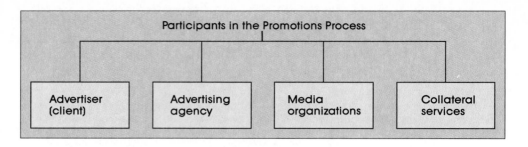

message and that may provide other services that facilitate the marketing and promotions process. Many large advertisers retain the services of a number of agencies, particularly when they market a number of products. For example, Procter & Gamble divides its approximately $1.5 billion in advertising among 17 different agencies, whereas companies such as Colgate-Palmolive utilize over 80 outside providers.

Media organizations are another major participant in the advertising and promotions process. The primary function of most media is to provide information or entertainment to its subscribers—the viewers or readers. However, from the perspective of the promotions planner, the purpose of the media is to provide an environment for the firm's marketing communications message. The media must have editorial or program content that attracts consumers so that, in return, the media vehicle can sell the advertisers and their agencies on the viability of buying time or space with them. An example of one attempt to convince buyers of the attractiveness of their medium is shown in Figure 3–2. While the media perform many other functions for advertisers that help them understand their markets and their customers, the primary objective of the medium is to sell itself as a way for companies to reach their target markets with their messages effectively.

Figure 3–2   The *Christian Science Monitor* Advertises the Value of Its Medium

The final participants shown in the promotions process of Figure 3–1 are those who provide **collateral services,** or the wide range of specialized functions used by advertisers, agencies, and media organizations. Collateral services include organizations such as package design firms, sales promotions firms, media buying services, research organizations, and production firms, among others. The function of these services varies depending on the specific need and situation of the advertiser. For example, a sales promotion firm may be utilized to develop a contest or sweepstakes that will be used as part of the firm's promotions campaign, whereas research organizations may provide input into, or evaluations of, the promotional program. Let us now turn our attention to the examination of the role of each of these participants in more detail.

Organizing for Advertising and Promotion in the Firm— the Role of the Client

Virtually every business organization uses some form of advertising and promotion. However, the way the firm organizes for these efforts depends on several factors including (1) the size of the company, (2) the number of products it markets, (3) the role of advertising and promotion in the company's marketing mix, (4) the advertising and promotions budget, and (5) the marketing organization structure of the firm. Many individuals throughout the organization may be involved in the promotions decision-making process. Marketing personnel have the most direct relationship with advertising and will often become involved in many aspects of the decision process, such as providing input to the campaign planning process, agency selection, and evaluation of proposed programs. Top management is usually interested in how the advertising program represents the firm, which may also mean that they become involved in the advertising decisions, even though these decisions may not be included in their day-to-day responsibilities.

While many people, both inside and outside the organization, are interested in, or have some input into, the advertising and promotions process, the direct responsibility for administering the program must be assumed by someone within the firm. For many companies this responsibility is assumed by an advertising department that is headed by an advertising or communications manager operating under a marketing director. An alternative, used by many large multiproduct firms, is to use a *decentralized marketing* or *brand management system.* Still a third option is to form a separate agency within the firm—or an *in-house agency.* Each of these alternatives is examined in more detail in the following sections.

The Centralized System

In many organizations marketing activities are divided along functional lines, with advertising placed alongside other marketing functions such as sales, marketing research, and product planning, as shown in Figure 3–3. Under this arrangement, the **advertising manager** is responsible for all promotions activities except sales, with all advertising and promotions matters channeled through this department. The most common example of a **centralized system** is the advertising department wherein the advertising manager controls the entire promotions operation, including budgeting, coordinating creation and production of advertisements, planning media schedules, and monitoring and administering the sales promotions programs for all the company's products or services.

The specific duties of the advertising manager will depend on the size of the firm and the importance placed on promotional programs. Some of the basic functions the manager and staff must perform include the following:

Figure 3–3 **The Advertising Department Under a Functional Organization**

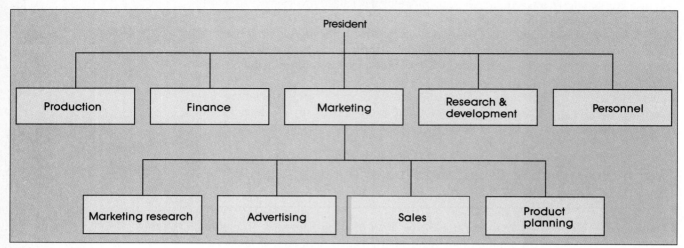

- *Planning and budgeting* The department is responsible for developing advertising and promotions plans that will be approved by management and recommending a promotions program based on the overall marketing plan, objectives, and budget. Formal plans will have to be submitted on an annual basis or when significant changes are being made in a program, such as the development of a new campaign. While the advertising department assumes the responsibility for developing the promotional budget, the final decision on the allocation of funds is usually made by top management.
- *Administration and execution* The manager must organize the advertising department and supervise and control its activities. He or she is also responsible for supervising the execution of the plan by subordinates and/or the advertising agency. This latter task requires working with various departments such as production, media, art, copy, and sales promotion. If an outside agency is used, the advertising department is relieved of much of the executional responsibilities; however, plans of the agency must be reviewed and approved.
- *Coordination with other departments* The manager must coordinate the advertising department's activities with those of other departments—particularly those involving other marketing functions. The advertising department must communicate with marketing research and/or sales to determine what product features are important to customers and should be emphasized in the company's communications. The department may also be responsible for preparing material that can be used by the sales force when calling on customers, such as sales promotions tools, advertising materials, and point-of-purchase displays.
- *Coordination with outside agencies and services* Many companies have an advertising department but still utilize many outside services. The department serves as liaison between the company and any outside service providers and also has the responsibility of determining which ones to use. Once outside services are retained, the manager will work with other marketing managers to coordinate their efforts and to evaluate their performances.

The Decentralized System

The centralized advertising department structure was the most commonly employed organization system used for many years. However, many firms began to develop problems with the traditional functional organization, particularly as the company grew in size and developed more products and brands. The major problem with the centralized structure concerns coordination and responsibility requirements. Under this arrangement, marketing decisions are made by several functional managers and must be co-

Figure 3–4   **The Product Manager Organizational Chart**

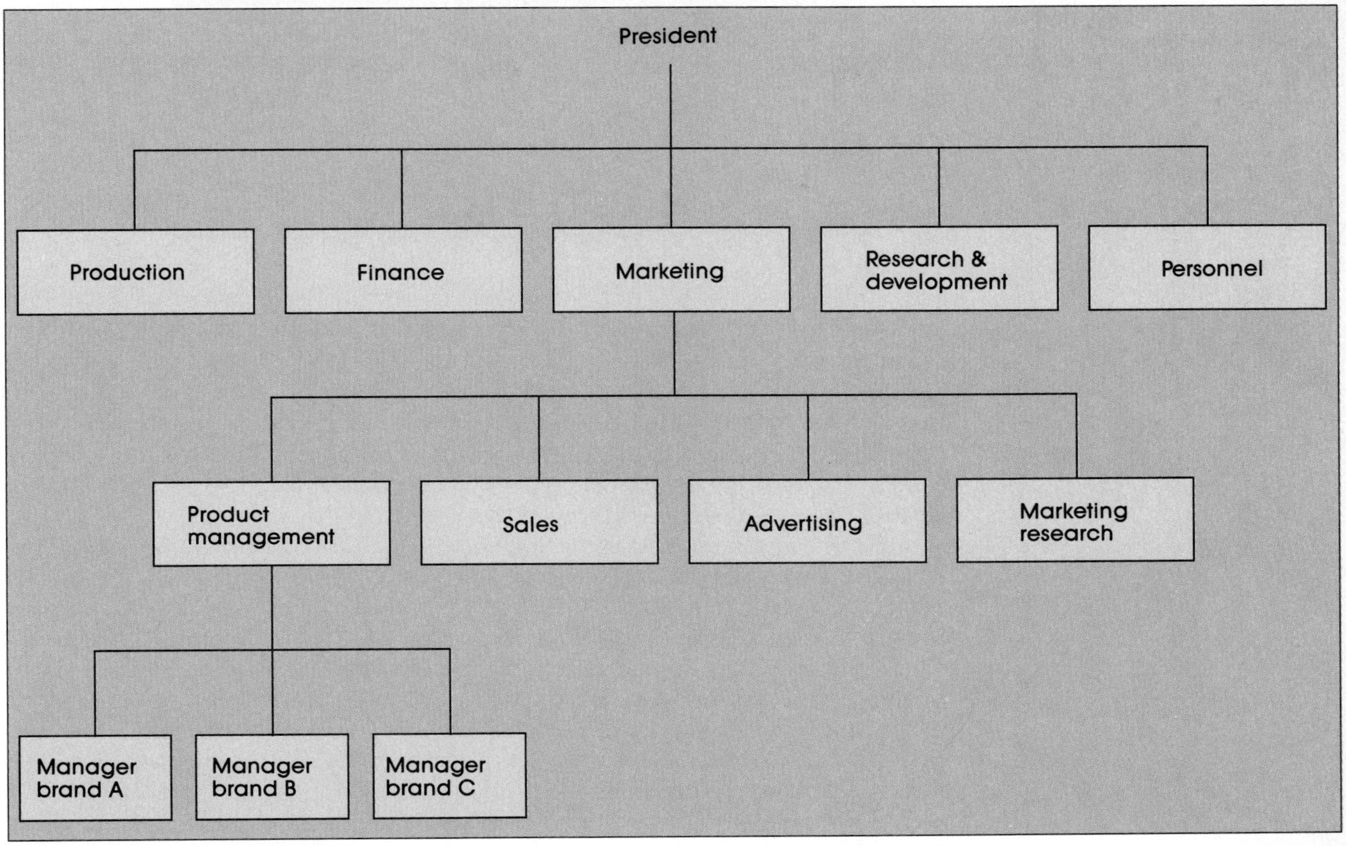

ordinated by someone in the marketing department. Moreover, no one department has specific responsibility for the welfare or problems of individual products or brands. Because of these problems, many companies developed **decentralized systems** such as the product or brand manager organization (in fact, this organizational system is now the most dominant structure in large consumer and industrial products companies).[2]

In this system, a **product manager,** or management team, has the responsibility for the planning, implementation, and control of the marketing program for an individual brand. The product manager(s) is also responsible for sales projections and profit performance of the brand and must develop and coordinate the budget. Companies utilizing this form of organization will generally support product managers with a structure of marketing services including sales, marketing research, and advertising departments, as shown in Figure 3–4. The product manager will utilize these services to assist in gathering information on customers, middlemen, competitors, product performance, and specific marketing problems and opportunities.

In a product management system, the responsibilities and functions associated with advertising and promotions are often transferred to the brand manager. The brand manager becomes the liaison between the outside service agencies and will be involved with the agency in the development of the promotional program. In a multiproduct firm, each brand may have its own advertising agency and may compete against other brands within the company as well as with outside competitors. For example, the brands shown in Figure 3–5 are all products of Procter & Gamble, with each competing for its own share of the market.

The role of the advertising department in a product management organization is to provide advertising and promotions support for the brand manager. The department may assist the manager in coordinating the advertising and sales promotions programs and may provide research and other support services. The advertising manager may review and evaluate the various parts of the program and serve as consultant and ad-

Figure 3–5 **Many of Procter & Gamble's Brands Compete Against Each Other**

viser. This person may have the authority to override the product manager's decisions that have been made relative to promotions. In some multiproduct firms in which many dollars are spent on advertising, the advertising manager may coordinate the work of the various agencies in order to obtain media discounts available as a result of the large volume of media purchases made by the firm. For example, companies such as Philip Morris, Procter & Gamble, and General Motors spend hundreds of millions of dollars on advertising their products and can save substantial sums of money by coordinating the media purchases through the advertising department.

Some companies, in an effort to reduce their costs and have greater control over agency activities, have set up their own advertising agencies internally. An **in-house agency** is an advertising agency that is set up, owned, and operated by the advertiser. Some in-house agencies are little more than an advertising department, whereas in other companies they may be given a separate identity and be responsible for the expenditure of large sums of advertising dollars. Many companies use in-house agencies exclusively, whereas others may combine in-house efforts with those of outside agencies. (The specific roles performed by in-house agencies will become more clear once we have discussed the functions of outside agencies. So as not to be redundant, and to keep you from throwing away this book, we will not discuss these responsibilities here.)

Evaluations of Advertising Organization Systems

Each of the organizational designs just discussed has its advantages and disadvantages, as are summarized in Table 3–1. We will consider these by first comparing the centralized system versus the decentralized system and then considering the merits of the in-house agency.

Table 3–1 **Comparison of Advertising Organizational Systems**

Organizational System	Advantages	Disadvantages
Centralized	• Facilitated communications • Less personnel required • Continuity in staff • Allows for more top-management involvement	• Less involvement with and understanding of overall marketing goals • Longer response time • Inability to handle multiple product lines
Decentralized	• Concentrated managerial attention • Rapid response to problems and opportunities • Increased flexibility	• Ineffective decision making • Internal conflicts • Misallocation of funds • Lack of authority
In-house agencies	• Cost savings • More control • Increased coordination	• Less experience • Less objectivity • Less flexibility

Centralized versus Decentralized Systems The advertising department organization is preferred by many companies, as it allows the advertising programs to be developed and coordinated from one central location. This provides an advantage to the firm in that communication and information regarding the promotions program will be facilitated, which will make it easier for top management to take part in the decision-making process. This arrangement can lead to greater efficiency in the advertising program by reducing the number of personnel who are needed, providing the opportunity for the development of trained professionals in specialized areas and building continuity.

At the same time, there are problems inherent in a centralized operation. First, it is difficult for the advertising department to become involved with, and to understand, the overall marketing strategy for the brand. The department may also be slow in responding to specific needs and problems of a product or brand. Moreover, as companies become larger and develop or acquire new products, brands, or even divisions, the centralized system may become impractical. This may force the company into the adoption of a decentralized system.

An advantage of the decentralized system is that each brand will receive concentrated managerial attention, resulting in a faster response to both problems and opportunities it faces. The product manager system allows for increased flexibility in the advertising program, which means that adjustments in the campaign may come more easily.

There are also drawbacks to the decentralized approach. Product managers often lack training and experience in advertising and promotion and sometimes cannot deal with decisions in these areas effectively. They may be concerned with short-run planning and administrative tasks rather than with the development of long-term programs. Also, individual product managers often end up competing for resources, which can lead to unproductive rivalries and a potential misallocation of funds. The persuasive manner of the manager, rather than the long-run profit potential of the individual brands, may be the critical factor determining the budgets. Finally, the product manager system has been criticized for failing to provide the brand manager with the authority over the functions that are needed to implement and control the plans they develop.[3] Some companies have dealt with this problem by expanding the role and responsibility of the advertising manager and his or her staff of specialists. The staff specialists counsel the individual product managers, with the advertising decision-making process involving the ad manager, the product manager, and the marketing director.

Those who argue against the product management system cite recent changes at Procter & Gamble to support their position. Perhaps the most renowned practitioner of the product management system, Procter & Gamble has decided to reorganize along entire product category lines (for example, all laundry detergents).[4] Procter & Gamble has called this change the major management decision in the company in the past 30 years and believes that the new organization will foster cooperation among the brand managers. Greater emphasis will be placed on how the products could work together— as opposed to having each compete for funding, plant capacity, and top managers' time and attention.

Evaluation of the In-House Agency One of the major reasons for using an in-house agency is to reduce advertising and promotions costs. Companies with very large advertising budgets pay a substantial amount of money to outside agencies in the form of media commissions. With an internal structure, these commissions would go to the in-house agency, resulting in substantial cost savings. An in-house agency can also provide related work such as preparing sales presentations and sales force materials, package design, and public relations efforts at a lower cost than outside agencies. Companies also prefer to have their advertising performed in-house so as to maintain tight control over the process, feeling that this arrangement makes it easier to coordinate the promotions with the firm's overall marketing program.

Promotional Perspective 3–1

Merger Mania Extends to Madison Avenue

The 1980s have clearly been the decade of "merger mania" in the business world as the number of mergers and acquisitions has grown from 2,326 in 1982 to more than 3,600 in 1987. Several "megacompanies" have evolved, with annual advertising and promotions budgets exceeding a billion dollars as Procter & Gamble acquired Richardson-Vicks, Philip Morris bought General Foods, and R. J. Reynolds acquired Nabisco. Merger mania has not been confined to the client side of the business, however, as advertising agencies have also entered into the act, with many of the top agencies in the country either merging with or acquiring another agency. In one case, three of the largest agencies—BBDO International, Doyle Dane Bernbach Group, and Needham Harper Worldwide—merged along with several other agencies to form Omnicom Group, a holding company with over $5 billion in billings.

The rash of mergers that have hit the advertising industry is due to several factors. First, the advertising business has become somewhat stagnant, as spending from network television advertising and magazines has decreased. Thus, agencies are turning to mergers and acquisitions as a way to seek growth. A second factor is the result of the increased merger and acquisition activity among name-brand consumer product companies. The resulting megacompanies with their strong, established brands and huge advertising and promotions budgets have the marketing clout to dominate and expand their presence in the various markets they serve. These companies generally seek agencies with top creative and marketing talent, which is often found at the largest and most sophisticated agencies. To meet these demands, agencies are also merging and acquiring other agencies.

Merger mania is not always viewed favorably, as not everyone believes that big companies need big agencies. In fact, many small- to midsized agencies have seized this trend as an opportunity to go after large accounts by offering them special attention that might not be available from the new superagencies. Problems have also resulted owing to agency conflicts, as mergers may mean that the new organization is handling accounts that may be in direct competition with one another—a practice previously considered unacceptable in the U.S. advertising community.

Source: "How Adversity Is Reshaping Madison Avenue," *Business Week,* September 15, 1986, pp. 142–150.

Opponents of the in-house system argue that they cannot provide the advertiser with the experience and objectivity of an outside agency, nor with the range of services. They argue that outside agencies have more highly skilled specialists and attract the best creative talent and that by using an external firm the company will have a more varied perspective to its advertising problems as well as greater flexibility. In-house personnel may become narrow or grow stale in their thinking while working on the same product line, but outside agencies may have different people with a variety of backgrounds and ideas working on the account. Flexibility is greater, as an outside agency can be more easily dismissed or replaced if the company is not satisfied, whereas changes in an in-house agency could be slower and more disruptive.

The cost savings of an in-house agency must be evaluated against these considerations. For many companies, high-quality advertising is critical to their marketing success and should be the major criterion in the determination as to whether to use in-house services.

The ultimate decision as to which advertising organization to use depends on which arrangement works best for the company. As you have seen, there are advantages and disadvantages to each system. Regardless of which system is chosen, an outside agency may still be useful. We now turn our attention to the functions of outside agencies and the roles they perform in the promotional process.

Advertising Agencies

Many major companies use the services of an advertising agency to assist them in the development, preparation, and execution of their promotional programs. An advertising agency is a service organization that specializes in the planning and execution of advertising programs for its clients. There are over 7,000 agencies listed in the *Standard Directory of Advertising Agencies;* however, the majority of the companies are

Table 3–2   **The Top 50 U.S. Advertising Agencies**

Rank	Agency, Headquarters	Worldwide Gross Income, 1988
1	Young & Rubicam, New York	$757.6
2	Saatchi & Saatchi Advertising Worldwide, New York	740.5
3	Backer Spielvogel Bates Worldwide, New York	689.8
4	McCann-Erickson Worldwide, New York	656.8
5	FCB-Publicis, Chicago/Paris	653.3
6	Ogilvy & Mather Worldwide, New York	635.2
7	BBDO Worldwide, New York	585.9
8	J. Walter Thompson Co., New York	559.3
9	Lintas: Worldwide, New York	537.6
10	Grey Advertising, New York	432.8
11	D'Arcy Masius Benton & Bowles, New York	428.7
12	Leo Burnett Co., Chicago	428.4
13	DDB Needham Worldwide, New York	399.9
14	HDM, New York (33% Y&R)	279.0
15	N W Ayer, New York	185.2
16	Bozell, Jacobs, Kenyon & Eckhardt, New York	179.2
17	Wells, Rich, Greene, New York	117.3
18	Scali McCabe Sloves, New York	107.0
19	Ketchum Communications, Pittsburgh	105.9
20	Campbell-Mithun-Esty, Minneapolis, Minn. (BSBW)	105.6
21	TBWA Advertising, New York	97.4
22	Ogilvy & Mather Direct Response, New York (O&M)	97.0
23	Ross Roy Group, Bloomfield Hills, Mich.	85.2
24	Della Femina, McNamee WCRS, New York	84.4
25	Wunderman Worldwide, New York (Y&R)	68.6
26	Chiat/Day, Venice, Calif.	65.0
27	Tracy-Locke, Dallas (BBDO)	54.5
28	Hill, Holliday, Connors, Cosmopulos, Boston	50.2
29	Lowe Marschalk, New York	45.6
30	AC&R Advertising, New York	44.2
31	Laurence, Charles, Free & Lawson, New York	43.3
32	McCaffrey & McCall, New York (S&SAW)	41.9
33	W.B. Doner & Co., Southfield, Mich./Baltimore	41.9
34	Admarketing Inc., Los Angeles	40.4
35	Jordan, McGrath, Case & Taylor, New York	38.5
36	Earle Palmer Brown Cos., Bethesda, Md.	36.2
37	Medicus Intercon International, New York (DMB&D)	35.5
38	Ally & Gargano, New York	34.4
39	Bernard Hodes Group, New York (DDB)	32.8
40	Levine, Huntley, Schmidt & Beaver, New York	32.1
41	Telephone Marketing Programs, New York	31.4
42	Sudler & Hennessey, New York (Y&R)	29.5
43	Ammirati & Puris, New York	28.0
44	Doremus & Co., New York (BBDO)	26.5
45	Direct Marketing Group, New York	26.1
46	Tatham-Laird & Kudner, Chicago	26.0
47	Kobs & Draft Advertising, Chicago (BSBW)	25.0
48	LGFE Inc., New York	24.6
49	Nationwide Advertising Service, Cleveland	24.1
50	Warwick Advertising, New York	24.0

Source: *Advertising Age*, March 29, 1989, p. 8.
Note: Dollars are in millions.

individually owned small businesses employing less than five people. The U.S. advertising agency business is highly concentrated, with 40 percent of the **billings** (the amount of client money agencies spend on media purchases and other activities) handled by less than 1 percent of the agencies, whereas the top 16 agencies in this country account for 18 percent of the total advertising income, as shown in Table 3–2. This business is also geographically concentrated, with 17 of the top 20 agencies headquartered in New York City.

In the 1980s there has been a trend toward even greater concentration in the advertising industry as large agencies merge to form **superagencies** that compete on a worldwide basis. These superagencies have been created through the mergers of advertising firms and/or companies providing other specialized services. Promotional Per-

Promotional Perspective 3-2

The Perils of Being a One-Client Agency

While one of the major advantages associated with using an outside advertising agency is that of objectivity and "fresh ideas," such is not always the case. In some instances the ad agency—while still a separate organization—begins to assume the identity of the client it represents.

Many agencies have set rules establishing a maximum amount that any single client may constitute in their overall income. A general rule in the industry is that this amount should not exceed 20 percent. For the largest agencies this may not pose a problem. But what about the small firm that has an opportunity to enter the "big time" by landing one major advertiser? (Consider, for example, the Hal Riney situation described at the beginning of this chapter.) Most agencies are going to forget this rule! For example, Honda accounts for 60 percent of Rubin Postaer & Associates' billings, whereas the West Coast offices of Chiat Day (80 percent, Nissan), Saatchi & Saatchi (90 percent, Toyota), and Ogilvy & Mather (80 percent, Mattel) have all been dominated by one client at one time or another.

What happens when one client so much dominates an agency? Many feel that the agency becomes little more than an extension of the client itself. Because so much of the agency employees' time is spent on the account, they devote less to other clients. In addition, efforts to attract new business are also reduced and are less effective, as prospective clients fear they will not receive their fair share of attention.

Perhaps the biggest problem of all is that the culture of the advertiser becomes the culture of the agency. The agency personnel start to think like the client, evaluating each decision wondering how the "boss" will respond and, in general, working very hard to ensure client satisfaction for fear of losing the account. Sometimes all independence and objectivity are lost, and as noted by Alan Gottesman, analyst at the New York office of Paine Webber, only two bad consequences can occur: "The client leaves, in which case the consequences are clear. Or, the client doesn't leave, in which case you sometimes wish it did!"

Source: Bruce Horowitz, "Thirtysomething Shows Peril of L.A. Agencies' Reliance on One Client," *Los Angeles Times*, February 14, 1989, pp. 8–9.

spective 3–1 discusses the "merger mania" that has been taking place in the U.S. advertising agency business. Later in this chapter we will go into more detail on the advantages and disadvantages associated with these arrangements.

The Role of the Advertising Agency

The functions performed by advertising agencies might possibly be conducted by the clients themselves through one of the designs discussed earlier in this chapter, yet most large companies choose to utilize the services of outside firms. This section will discuss some of the reasons why advertisers choose to use these external agencies.

Reasons for Using an Agency   Probably the main reason why outside agencies are used is that they provide the client with the services of highly skilled individuals who are specialists in their chosen fields. An advertising agency staff may include artists, writers, media analysts, researchers, and others with specific skills, knowledge, and experience that can be used to help market the client's products or services. Many agencies specialize in a particular type of business—for example, business-to-business advertising—and use their knowledge of the industry to assist their clients.

Another reason for using an advertising agency is that an outside agency can provide the advertiser with an objective viewpoint of the market and its business that is not subject to internal company policies, biases, or other limitations. (Although as shown in Promotional Perspective 3–2, there is no guarantee that this will always be the case!) The agency can also draw on the broad range of experience it has gained while working on a diverse set of marketing problems for its various clients. For example, an advertising agency that is handling a travel-related account may have on staff individuals who have worked with the airlines, cruise ship companies, travel agencies, hotels, and other travel-related industries, or the agency itself may have worked

Figure 3–6 Phillips-Ramsey Demonstrates the Variety of Clients It Serves

Figure 3—7 Full-Service Agency Organizational Chart

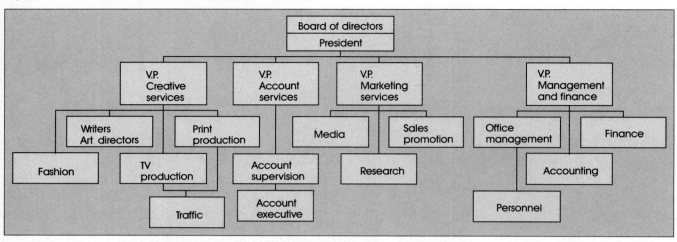

Source: Adapted from American Association of Advertising Agencies.

in this area. Thus, the agency can provide the client with experience and insight into the industry and apply these skills to the advertiser's communications. Figure 3—6 shows a poster used as a promotional piece for Phillips-Ramsey to demonstrate the variety of accounts the agency has served. As you can see, many of the clients may benefit from experiences of other products and services the agency has worked with.

Types of Advertising Agencies

As you learned earlier, advertising agencies can range in size from a one- or two-person operation to large organizations with over a thousand employees. Given this variation in size, the services offered and functions performed by an agency will vary. In this section, we will examine the different types of agencies, the services they perform for their clients, and how they are organized.

Full-Service Agencies Many companies employ what is known as a **full-service agency.** A full-service agency is one that offers its clients a full range of marketing, communications, and promotions services, including planning, creating, and producing the advertising, performing research, and selecting media. A full-service agency may also offer nonadvertising services such as strategic market planning, production of sales promotions, sales training and trade show materials, package design, and public relations and publicity.

Like the firm, the full-service agency must have an organizational structure. Agencies are made up of departments that provide the activities needed to perform the various advertising functions and serve the client, as shown in Figure 3—7 and discussed below.

Account services Account services, or account management, is the link between the advertising agency and its clients. Depending on the size of the client and its advertising budget, one or more account executives serve as a liaison between the two entities. The **account executive** is responsible for understanding the advertiser's marketing and promotions needs and interpreting them to agency personnel. He or she is responsible for working with the agency and coordinating efforts in planning, creating, and producing ads. The account executive must also present and obtain client approval for agency recommendations.

As the focal point of agency-client relationships, the account executive must know a great deal about the client's business and be able to communicate this to specialists in the agency working on the account. The ideal account executive has a strong marketing background as well as a thorough understanding of all the phases of the advertising process.

Marketing services   Over the past two decades, use of marketing services has increased dramatically. One of the services gaining increased attention is that of research, as agencies realize that to do an effective job of communicating with their clients' customers they must have a good understanding of the target audience. As was shown in Chapter 1, the advertising planning process begins with a thorough situation analysis, which is based on research and information about the target audience.

Most full-service agencies maintain a research department whose function is to gather, analyze, and interpret information that will be useful in developing advertising for their clients. This can be done through primary research—where a study is designed, executed, and interpreted by the research department—or through the use of secondary or existing sources of information previously published. In some situations the research department may acquire studies that were conducted by independent syndicated research firms or consultants. The research staff then interprets these reports and passes on the information to other agency personnel working on that account.

The research department may also be responsible for designing and carrying out research to test the effectiveness of advertising the agency is considering using—or pretesting. For example, copy testing is often conducted by the agency's research department to determine how messages developed by the creative specialists are likely to be interpreted by the receiving audience.

The **media department** of an agency has the responsibility of analyzing, selecting, and contracting for space or time in the media that will be used to deliver the client's advertising message. The media department is expected to develop a media plan that will reach the target market and effectively communicate the message. Since most of the client's ad budget is spent on media time and/or space, this department must develop a plan that both communicates with the right audience and is cost-effective.

Media specialists must be knowledgeable of all the alternative media including the audience they reach, their rates, and how well they match up with the client's target market. Media departments must review information on demographics, magazine and newspaper readership, radio listenership, and television viewing patterns of consumers in order to be able to develop an effective media plan.

Interestingly, the members of the media department also constitute a target market in and of themselves. As you can see by the ad in Figure 3–8, these individuals are the target of advertising, as well as sales promotions and personal selling efforts by representatives of various media who seek the placement of advertisements in their vehicles.

The departments discussed above perform most of the functions that full-service agencies need to plan and execute their client's advertising programs. Some agencies also offer additional marketing services to their clients to assist in other promotional areas. For example, an agency may have a **sales promotions department,** or merchandising department, that specializes in the development of contests, premiums, promotions, point-of-sale materials, and other sales materials. Agencies may also have direct-marketing specialists and package designers available to serve their clients if they have needs in these areas, whereas a number of firms may have public relations/ publicity departments as well. Generally, these services are not included as part of the regular advertising process and are available to clients on a separate-fee basis. However, the development of superagencies has led to an increase in *integrated marketing,* and many of these services are now being provided under one roof.[5]

Creative services   Perhaps the most important service that the agency offers to its clients is the ability to produce effective advertising messages. The creative services department is responsible for the creation and execution of the advertisements. The

Figure 3-8 **The Media Department Often Serves as a Target Market**

individuals who conceive the ideas for the ads and write the headlines, subheads, and body copy (the words constituting the message of the ad) are known as **copywriters.** Copywriters may also be involved in determining the basic appeal or theme of the ad campaign and often prepare a rough initial visual layout of the print ad or television commercial.

While copywriters are responsible for what the communication message says, the **art department** consists of art directors who are responsible for how the advertisement will look. For print ads, the art director and graphics designers prepare *layouts,* which are drawings that show what the ad will look like and from which the final artwork will be produced. In the case of television commercials, the layout is known as a **storyboard,** or a sequence of frames or panels that depict the commercial in still form.

Members of the creative department work together to develop advertisements that will communicate the key points that were determined to be the basis of the creative strategy for the client's product or service. Writers and artists generally work under the direction of the agency's creative director, who oversees all the advertising produced by the organization. The director sets the creative philosophy of the department and may even become directly involved in the creation of ads for the agency's largest clients.

Once the copy, layout, illustrations, and mechanical specifications of the advertisement have been completed and approved, the ad is turned over to the **production department.** Most agencies do not actually produce finished ads but rather maintain relationships with printers, engravers, photographers, typographers, and other suppliers whose services are needed to complete the finished product. For broadcast production the approved storyboard must be turned into a finished commercial. The production department's role may be to supervise the selection of people to appear in the ad and the setting for the scenes as well as to choose an independent production studio.

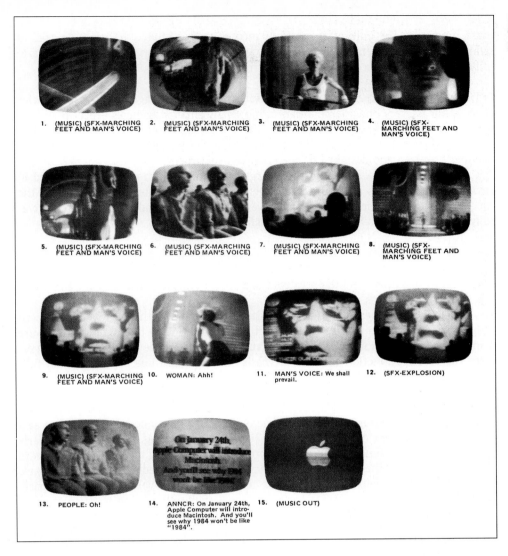

Figure 3–9   **The Famous "1984" Ad Was Directed by Ridley Scott**

The department may hire an outside director to turn the creative idea or concept into a commercial. For example, the famous "1984" ad for Apple Computer shown in Figure 3–9 was directed by Ridley Scott—the director of many movies including the science fiction film *Aliens*. Copywriters, art directors, account supervisors, and representatives from the client side may all participate in production decisions, particularly when large sums of money are involved in the ads.

As you may have deduced by now, the process of creating an advertisement often involves many people and may take several months. In large agencies with many clients, coordination of the creative and production processes can be a major problem. To ensure that the development of the advertising progresses properly, a **traffic department** is used in agencies to coordinate all phases of production, to see that the ads are completed on time and that all deadlines for submitting the ads to the media are met. The traffic department may be located in the creative services area of the agency or it may be separate.

Management and finance   Like any other business, an advertising agency must be managed and perform basic operating and administrative functions such as accounting, finance, and personnel management as well as attempt to generate new business.

A large agency will employ administrative, managerial, and clerical people to perform these functions. The bulk of an agency's income (approximately 64 percent) goes to salary and benefits for its employees. Thus, an agency must manage its personnel carefully and get maximum productivity from them.

Other Types of Agencies and Services   Not every agency is a full-service agency, nor is every one a large organization. Many smaller agencies expect their employees to handle a variety of jobs. For example, account executives may do their own research, work out their own media schedule, and coordinate the production of advertisements written and designed by the creative department.

Many advertisers, including some large companies, are not always interested in paying for the services of a full-service agency but may be interested in some of the specific services agencies have to offer. Over the past few decades several alternatives to full-service agencies have evolved, including the following.

Creative Boutiques   A **creative boutique** is an agency that specializes in and provides only creative services. These specialists have developed in response to some clients' desires to utilize only the creative talent of an outside provider while maintaining the other functions internally.

Creative boutiques are usually founded by members of the creative department of full-service agencies who have left the firm and taken with them clients who were primarily interested in maintaining their creative talents. These boutiques usually perform the creative function under a fee basis and are often less expensive than full-service agencies.

Media Buying Services   Another type of specialized service developed in the 1960s to provide assistance for smaller agencies and creative boutiques. **Media buying services** are independent companies that specialize in the buying of media, particularly radio and television time. As the task of purchasing advertising media has grown more complex—owing to the proliferation of specialized media—media buying services have found a niche by specializing in the analysis and purchase of advertising time and space. Both agencies and clients utilize their services, usually developing their own media strategies and using the buying service to execute them. Because media buying services purchase such large amounts of time and space, they receive large discounts and can save the small agency or client substantial amounts of money on media purchases. Media buying services are paid a fee or commission for their work.

Agency Compensation

As you have seen in the previous sections, the type and amount of services an agency performs can vary from one client to another. As a result agencies use a variety of methods to receive compensation for their services. Agencies are typically compensated in three ways: through commissions, through percentage charges or markups, and through fees. A discussion of each follows.

Commissions from Media

The traditional method of compensating agencies has been through a **commission system.** In this system the agency receives a 15 percent commission from the media on any advertising time or space it purchases for its client (outdoor advertising provides a 16⅔ percent commission). This system provides a very simple method of determining payments, as shown in the following example.

Assume that an agency prepares a full-page magazine ad and arranges to place the ad on the back cover of a magazine at a cost of $100,000. The agency will place

Table 3–3 **Example of Commission System Payment**

Media Bills Agency	
Costs for magazine space	$100,000
Less 15% commission	−15,000
Cost of media space	85,000
Less 2% cash discount	−1,700
Agency pays media	83,300
Agency Bills Advertiser	
Costs for magazine space	100,000
Less 2% cash discount	1,700
Advertiser Pays Agency	98,300
Agency income	15,000

the order for the space and deliver the ad to the magazine. Once the ad is run, the magazine will bill the agency for $100,000 less the 15 percent ($15,000) commission. The media will also offer a 2 percent cash discount for early payment, which the agency may also pass along to the client. The agency will bill the client $100,000 less the 2 percent cash discount on the net amount, or a total of $98,300, as shown in Table 3–3. The $15,000 commission represents the agency's compensation for its services.

Appraisal of the Commission System   Use of the commission system to compensate agencies has been the target of considerable controversy for many years, with a number of criticisms leveled. A major problem centers around whether the 15 percent commission represents equitable compensation for services performed. For example, two agencies may require the same amount of effort to create and produce an ad. However, one client may spend $200,000 in commissionable media, which results in $30,000 in agency income, whereas the other may spend $2 million, thus generating $300,000 in commissions. Critics argue that the commission system can encourage agencies to recommend high media expenditures so as to increase their commission level.

Another criticism of the commission system is that it ties agency compensation to media cost inflation, which has generally increased more rapidly than agency salaries and administrative costs. Over the past four years, media costs have increased over 5.7 percent, whereas the overall inflation level of the U.S. economy has averaged only 2 to 4 percent.[6] Thus, many advertisers feel that agency compensation costs have been disproportionately high.

The commission system has also been criticized for encouraging agencies to ignore cost accounting systems to justify the expenses attributable to work on a particular account. Still others charge that this system tempts the agency to avoid noncommissionable media such as direct-mail, sales promotions, or advertising specialties.

Defenders of the commission system argue that it should be retained because it is simple and easy to administer and because it keeps the emphasis in agency competition on nonprice factors such as the quality of the advertising developed. Proponents argue that agency services are proportional to the size of the commission, as more time and effort are devoted to the large accounts that generate the high revenue for the agency. It has also been argued that the system is more flexible than it appears because agencies can often perform other services for large clients at no extra charge, justifying such actions through the large commission to be received.

Overall the commission system has become a heated topic among advertisers. Opponents of the system have been designated as "traitors" and "public enemy number one" by their colleagues, who argue that their lack of support costs everyone in the agency business money and that their opposition is nothing more than a competitive strategy designed to gain accounts.[7] Those in support of an alternative system

Table 3–4 **Some Clients Who Do Not Always Pay 15 Percent**

Company	1987 Billings (in millions of dollars)	Agency Compensation
General Foods Corporation	n.a.	13–14% plus 3% on best campaigns
R. J. Reynolds	839.6	Less than 15% bonus to top agencies
Nissan	181.4	Negotiated fee based on costs
Scott Paper		Negotiated fee based on costs
Nabisco	n.a.	Sliding-scale bonus based on performance
Sears	886.5	Bonuses based on performance

n.a. = not available
Note: The R. J. Reynolds expenditures include Nabisco; General Foods is a subsidiary of Philip Morris, which spent $1.5 billion in 1987.

Sources: "A Word from the Sponsor: Get Results—or Else," *Business Week,* July 4, 1988, p. 66; "More Companies Offer Their Ad Agencies Bonus Plans That Reward Superior Work," *The Wall Street Journal,* July 26, 1988, p. 29.

contend that the old system is a "dead bird," estimating that only 43 percent of all accounts now pay a standard 15 percent fee.[8] As you can see in Table 3–4, some clients have gone to a **negotiated commission.** This commission structure can take the form of reduced percentage rates, variable commission rates, and commissions with minimum and maximum profit rates. Negotiated commissions are designed to take into account the needs of the client as well as the amount of time and effort exerted by the agency, thereby avoiding some of the problems inherent in the traditional system.

Percentage Charges

Another way that an agency is compensated is by adding a markup of **percentage charges** to various services that the agency purchases from other outside providers. These may include market research, artwork, printing, photography, and other services or materials. *Markup charges* usually range from 17.65 to 20 percent and are added to the client's overall bill. The logic of markups stems from the fact that the suppliers of these services do not allow the agency a commission, and the percentage charges cover administrative costs while allowing for a reasonable profit for the agency's efforts.

Fee- and Cost-Based Systems

As previously noted, many feel that the standard 15 percent commission system is not equitable to all parties. As a result, many agencies and their clients have developed fixed-fee arrangements or cost-plus agreements.

• *Fixed-fee arrangement*   Under this arrangement the agency and client agree on the specific work to be done and the amount of money the agency will be paid for its services. The arrangement requires the agency to make a careful assessment of its costs of serving the client for the specified time period, or for the project, plus determining a desired profit margin. **Fixed-fee agreements** should specify exactly what services the agency is expected to perform for the client to avoid any later disagreement.

• *Cost-plus agreement*   Under a **cost-plus system,** the client agrees to pay the agency a fee based on the costs of its work plus some agreed-upon profit margin (which is often a percentage of total costs). This system requires the agency to keep detailed records of the costs it incurs in working on the client's account. Direct costs (personnel time and out-of-pocket expenses) plus an allocation for overhead and a markup for profits determine the amount the agency bills the client.

In some situations, agencies are compensated through a fee–commission combination in which the media commissions received by the agency are credited against the fee. If the commissions received by the agency are less than the agreed-upon fee, the client must make up the difference to the agency. If the agency does much work for the client in noncommissionable media, the fee may be charged over and above the commissions received.

Fee agreements and cost-plus systems are commonly used in conjunction with a commission system arrangement. The fee-based system can be advantageous to both the client and the agency, depending on the size of the client, advertising budget, media used, and services required. Many clients prefer fee or cost-plus systems because they are provided with a detailed breakdown of where and how their advertising and promotions dollars are being spent. However, these arrangements can be difficult for the agency, as they require careful cost accounting and may also be difficult to estimate when bidding for an advertiser's business. Agencies are also reluctant to have clients involved in their internal cost figures.

As you can see from the preceding discussion of how agencies are compensated, there is no fixed method for making this determination to which everyone subscribes. Usually, an agreement will be established in which a combination of methods of payment is used—a trend that will likely be even more common in the future.

Evaluating Agencies

We are sure that it does not surprise you that given the substantial amounts of monies being spent on advertising and promotion, there has been an increased demand for accountability of the expenditures. This accountability must extend to the agency as well as the client itself, and regular reviews of the agency's performance are necessary.

The **agency evaluation process** usually involves two types of assessments, one of which is financial and operational in nature, whereas the other is more qualitative. The **financial audit** focuses on how the agency conducts its business. The financial audit is designed to verify costs and expenses, the number of personnel hours charged to an account, and analyses of payments to media and outside suppliers. The **qualitative audit** focuses on the agency's efforts in planning, developing, and implementing the client's advertising and promotions programs and considers the results achieved by the same.

In many situations, the agency evaluation process is done on a subjective, informal basis, particularly in smaller companies where advertising budgets are low or advertising is not seen as the most critical factor in the firm's marketing performance. In some companies formal systematic evaluation systems have been developed—particularly when budgets are large and the advertising function receives much emphasis. As advertising costs continue to rise, the top management of these companies wants to be sure that monies are being spent efficiently and effectively.

One example of a formal agency evaluation system is that used by Borden, Inc., a marketer of a variety of consumer products.[9] Borden's top executives meet twice a year with the company's various agencies to review their performances. Division presidents and other marketing executives complete the "Advertising Agency Performance Evaluation" report, part of which is shown in Figure 3–10. These reports are compiled and reviewed with the agency at each semiannual meeting. Borden's evaluations process consists of three areas of performance—share of market performance, creativity, and cooperation. Each area is weighted differently, with agency performance in achieving market share goals accounting for 60 percent of the total score and creativity and cooperation each constituting 20 percent.

While the assumption that the sales effectiveness of advertising can be quantified is questionable to many, Borden feels that the agencies are forewarned that the evaluation will be tied to market performance. Agencies that have not scored well after two semiannual evaluations have been dropped by the company.

Others more critical of the attempt to relate advertising effectiveness directly to sales have developed their own evaluation procedures. For example, R. J. Reynolds em-

Figure 3–10 Borden's Ad Agency Report Card

SECTION	PAGE
12.00.0	15 of 22
DATE ISSUED 4/85	DATE REVISED

Agency: ____________________
Product(s): ____________________

ACCOUNT REPRESENTATION AND SERVICE

	Excellent	Good	Average	Fair	Poor	Not Observed (Unknown)
1. Account Executives have *frequent personal contact* with product group.	( )	( )	( )	( )	( )	( )
2. Account persons act with *personal initiative.*	( )	( )	( )	( )	( )	( )
3. Account representatives *anticipate needs* in advance of direction by product group.	( )	( )	( )	( )	( )	( )
4. Account group *takes direction* well.	( )	( )	( )	( )	( )	( )
5. Agency readily *adapts to changes* in client's organization or needs.	( )	( )	( )	( )	( )	( )
6. Agency makes reasonable *recommendations* on allocation of budgets.	( )	( )	( )	( )	( )	( )
7. Account representatives function as *marketing advisors* rather than creative/media advisors only.	( )	( )	( )	( )	( )	( )
8. Account representatives *contribute effectively* to the development of new programs.	( )	( )	( )	( )	( )	( )
9. Account representatives respond to *client requests* in a timely fashion.	( )	( )	( )	( )	( )	( )
10. Agency recommendations are *founded on sound reasoning* and supported factually.	( )	( )	( )	( )	( )	( )
11. Account persons *submit alternative plans,* vs. a single plan/campaign/ad for brand review.	( )	( )	( )	( )	( )	( )
12. Account persons have a *firm point of view* and "sell" their recommendation.	( )	( )	( )	( )	( )	( )
13. Senior account management *is involved,* where appropriate.	( )	( )	( )	( )	( )	( )
14. Other areas not mentioned:						
____________________	( )	( )	( )	( )	( )	( )
____________________	( )	( )	( )	( )	( )	( )
____________________	( )	( )	( )	( )	( )	( )

	Excellent	Good	Average	Fair	Poor
Overall evaluation of Account Representation and Service	( )	( )	( )	( )	( )

General Comments on Account Representation and Service: ____________________

SECTION	PAGE
12.00.0	16 of 22
DATE ISSUED 4/85	DATE REVISED

Agency: ____________________
Product(s): ____________________

CREATIVE SERVICES

	Excellent	Good	Average	Fair	Poor	Not Observed (Unknown)
1. Agency produces *fresh ideas* and original approaches.	( )	( )	( )	( )	( )	( )
2. Agency *accurately interprets* facts, strategies and objectives into usable advertisements and plans.	( )	( )	( )	( )	( )	( )
3. Creative group is *knowledgeable* about Consumer Products Division's products, markets and strategies.	( )	( )	( )	( )	( )	( )
4. Creative personnel are concerned with *good advertising communications* and develops campaigns/ads that exhibit this concern.	( )	( )	( )	( )	( )	( )
5. Creative group *produces on time.*	( )	( )	( )	( )	( )	( )
6. Creative team *performs well* under pressure.	( )	( )	( )	( )	( )	( )
7. Agency presentations are well organized with sufficient *examples of proposed executions.*	( )	( )	( )	( )	( )	( )
8. Creative team *participates* in major campaign *presentations.*	( )	( )	( )	( )	( )	( )
9. Agency presents *ideas and executions* not requested but felt to be good *opportunities.*	( )	( )	( )	( )	( )	( )
10. Overall *quality of agency's television* creative ideas and executions.	( )	( )	( )	( )	( )	( )
11. Overall *quality of agency's radio* creative ideas and executions.	( )	( )	( )	( )	( )	( )
12. Overall *quality of agency's print* creative ideas and executions.	( )	( )	( )	( )	( )	( )
13. Other areas not mentioned:						
____________________	( )	( )	( )	( )	( )	( )
____________________	( )	( )	( )	( )	( )	( )
____________________	( )	( )	( )	( )	( )	( )

	Excellent	Good	Average	Fair	Poor
Overall evaluation of Creative Services:	( )	( )	( )	( )	( )

General Comments on Creative Services: ____________________

phasizes creative development and execution, marketing counsel and ideas, promotion support, and cost controls, without any mention of sales figures. Sears' approach focuses on the performance of the agency as a whole, arguing that a "partnership" between the agency and the client is established with this method.

The use of these forms of evaluation, as well as others employed by a variety of clients, is being adopted more regularly in the advertising community. As fiscal controls tighten, clients will increase the accountability requirements placed on their providers.

Gaining and Losing Clients

The evaluation process often results in outcomes that are not favorable to the agency. As you can see in Figure 3–11, the switching of agencies is not an uncommon practice. Because a number of reasons can be cited as causes for switching agencies, it is important to review these here, as understanding these potential problems decreases the likelihood that they will occur.[10,11] In addition, it is important to understand the process that agencies go through in their attempts to gain new clients. Let us first examine some of the most commonly cited reasons for losing clients.

Figure 3–10 **(concluded)**

Left form:

SECTION	PAGE
12.00.0	17 of 22
DATE ISSUED	DATE REVISED
4/85	

Agency: _____
Product(s): _____

PRODUCTION SERVICES

	Excellent	Good	Average	Fair	Poor	Not Observed (Unknown)
1. Account group, creative group and production team operate in a business-like manner to *control production costs* and other creative costs charges/services.	( )	( )	( )	( )	( )	( )
2. Agency obtains *three (3) bids on work* performed by *outside suppliers/vendors.*	( )	( )	( )	( )	( )	( )
3. Production personnel accurately *integrate creative plans and ideas* into usable finished advertising units.	( )	( )	( )	( )	( )	( )
4. Agency production group controls *mechanical production* (photographs, photostats, type-setting/proofs, engraving, electro-types, mats, printing and similar items) in a cost efficient manner.	( )	( )	( )	( )	( )	( )
5. Production group provides *cost efficient talent,* testimonial and residual services for television, radio and print commercial units.	( )	( )	( )	( )	( )	( )
6. *Jingles, musical arrangements and production,* recordings, etc. are completed in a cost efficient manner.	( )	( )	( )	( )	( )	( )
7. Other areas not mentioned: _____	( )	( )	( )	( )	( )	( )
_____	( )	( )	( )	( )	( )	( )
_____	( )	( )	( )	( )	( )	( )

	Excellent	Good	Average	Fair	Poor
Overall rating of production services	( )	( )	( )	( )	( )
Overall evaluation of agency's production cost controls (i.e. are advertising creative units being produced within generally accepted national cost ranges?)	( )	( )	( )	( )	( )

General comments on production services/costs: _____

Right form:

Agency: _____
Product(s): _____

SECTION	PAGE
12.00.0	18 of 22
DATE ISSUED	DATE REVISED
4/85	

MEDIA SERVICES

	PRODUCT GROUP EVALUATION						ADVERTISING SERVICES EVALUATION					
	Excellent	Good	Avg.	Fair	Poor	Not Observed (Unknown)	Excellent	Good	Avg.	Fair	Poor	Not Observed (Unknown)
1. Media group actively *explores creative uses* of the various media available.	( )	( )	( )	( )	( )	( )	( )	( )	( )	( )	( )	( )
2. *Senior media personnel* are appropriately involved in media planning/execution.	( )	( )	( )	( )	( )	( )	( )	( )	( )	( )	( )	( )
3. Agency media group presents alternative plans to the recommended plan.	( )	( )	( )	( )	( )	( )	( )	( )	( )	( )	( )	( )
4. Agency media recommendations reflect *sufficient knowledge* of Consumer Products Division's markets, audiences, products and objectives.	( )	( )	( )	( )	( )	( )	( )	( )	( )	( )	( )	( )
5. Agency keeps client up to date on *trends and developments* in the field of media.	( )	( )	( )	( )	( )	( )	( )	( )	( )	( )	( )	( )
6. Agency subscribes to and makes use of available and applicable *syndicated marketing and media* services.	( )	( )	( )	( )	( )	( )	( )	( )	( )	( )	( )	( )
7. Agency utilizes *marketing and media research* in relating to the selection and use of media.	( )	( )	( )	( )	( )	( )	( )	( )	( )	( )	( )	( )
8. Agency provides client with a regular review and analysis of *competition's media usage/spending.*	( )	( )	( )	( )	( )	( )	( )	( )	( )	( )	( )	( )
9. *Agency media administrative practices* are adequate, including coordination of media schedules, contracts, checking media to verify advertising has run, etc.	( )	( )	( )	( )	( )	( )	( )	( )	( )	( )	( )	( )
10. Agency is effective in media negotiations for *best possible position* for brand advertising.	( )	( )	( )	( )	( )	( )	( )	( )	( )	( )	( )	( )
11. Agency has proven to be an *"efficient bargainer"* in cases where negotiated purchases of media are possible.	( )	( )	( )	( )	( )	( )	( )	( )	( )	( )	( )	( )
12. Other areas not mentioned: _____	( )	( )	( )	( )	( )	( )	( )	( )	( )	( )	( )	( )
_____	( )	( )	( )	( )	( )	( )	( )	( )	( )	( )	( )	( )
_____	( )	( )	( )	( )	( )	( )	( )	( )	( )	( )	( )	( )

	Excellent	Good	Avg.	Fair	Poor		Excellent	Good	Avg.	Fair	Poor
Overall evaluation of Media Services.	( )	( )	( )	( )	( )		( )	( )	( )	( )	( )

General Comments on Media Services: _____

Why Agencies Lose Clients Some of the more well-known and cited reasons as to why agencies lose clients are:

• *Poor performance or service by the agency* The client becomes dissatisfied with the quality of the advertising provided by the agency and/or the service provided.

• *Poor communication* The client and agency personnel fail to develop or maintain a proper level of communication and exchange of information necessary to sustain a favorable working relationship.

• *Unrealistic demands by the client* The client places demands on the agency that exceed the amount of compensation received and reduces the profitability of the account.

• *Personality conflicts* Personnel working on the account on either the client or agency side do not have rapport or do not work well together.

• *Personnel changes* A change in personnel either at the agency or with the advertiser can create problems. New managers may wish to use an agency that they have previously used or with whom they have established previous ties. Agency personnel often take accounts with them when they switch agencies or start their own.

• *Changes in size of the client or agency* The client may outgrow the agency

Figure 3–11   A Rash of Advertisers Switch Agencies

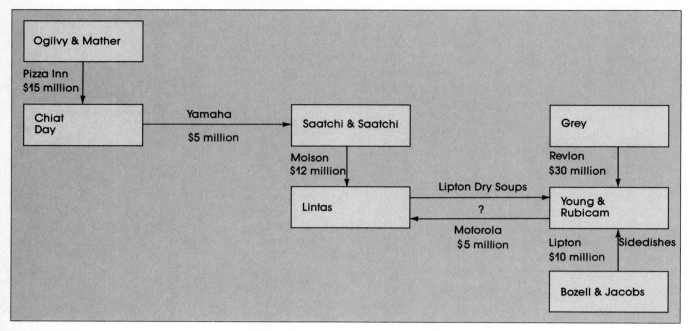

or decide that it needs a larger agency to handle its business. If the agency gets too large, the client may represent too small a percentage of the agency's business to command attention.

* *Conflicts of interest*   A conflict develops when an agency acquires a new account or merges with another agency or when an acquisition or merger takes place between two clients. In the United States it is a practice that an agency cannot handle two accounts that are in direct competition with each other. In some cases, even indirect competition will not be tolerated. (You can now probably imagine the problems being created by the mergers we discussed earlier!)

* *Changes in the client's marketing strategy*   A client may decide to switch agencies when a change in marketing strategy occurs and the advertiser feels that a new agency is needed to carry out the firm's marketing program.

* *Declining sales*   When sales of the client's product or service are stagnant or declining, advertising may be seen as contributing to the problem, and a new agency may be sought to seek a new approach.

* *Conflicting compensation philosophies*   When conflicting compensation philosophies emerge, disagreement develops over the level or method of compensation.

* *Changes in policies*   Changes in policies on either the agency or client side are often seen as reasons for change. Such policy changes may result from reevaluating the importance of the relationship, acquisition of a new (and larger) client by the agency, and/or mergers and acquisitions by either side.

If the agency recognizes these "warning signals," it will be more able to adapt its programs and policies to ensure that the client is satisfied. As you might guess, some of the situations discussed here are unavoidable, and others may be beyond the control of the agency. It is those that are within the agency's control that must be addressed to ensure maintenance of the account.

How Agencies Gain Clients   Competition for accounts in the agency business is intense, as most companies already have organized for the advertising function, and there are only a limited number of new businesses requiring such services each year. While small agencies may be willing to work with a new company, and grow along

TUMBLEWEEDS   **by TOM K. RYAN**

with it, larger agencies often do not become interested in these firms until they are able to spend a minimum of a million dollars per year on advertising. As you can imagine, once that expenditure level is reached, the competition for the account intensifies.

In large agencies, most new business results from clients who already have an agency but have (for some of the reasons cited earlier) decided to change their relationships. Thus, agencies must constantly search and compete for new clients. Some of the ways in which this is done are discussed below.

• *Referrals*   Many good agencies obtain new clients as a result of referrals from existing clients, media representatives, and even other agencies. These agencies must maintain good working relationships with their clients, the media, and outside parties who might provide potential business to them.

• *Solicitations*   One of the more common ways of gaining new business is through direct solicitation. In smaller agencies, principals such as the president may be responsible for soliciting new accounts. In most large agencies a new business development group will be assigned the task of searching for and establishing contact with new clients. The group is responsible for writing solicitation letters, conducting

Figure 3–12   Trade Media Such as *Advertising Age* Are Often Used as Sources of Information Regarding Potential Clients

Accounts up for grabs

BUDGET	CLIENT/BRAND	CONTENDERS	DECISION DATE	BUDGET	CLIENT/BRAND	CONTENDERS	DECISION DATE
$75 million	**E&J Gallo Winery Modesto, Calif.** Incumbents: N W Ayer Hal Riney & Partners	Altschiller Reitzfeld John Crawford Creative Dailey & Associates Della Femina, Travisano & Partners Levine, Huntley, Schmidt & Beaver John Noble Advertising Wieden & Kennedy	Undetermined	$15 million–$20 million	**Aetna Life & Casualty Hartford, Conn.** Incumbent: Jordan, McGrath, Case & Taylor	Undetermined	Unknown
				$17 million	**New York State Lottery Albany, N.Y.** Incumbent: McCaffrey & McCall	D'Arcy Masius Benton & Bowles DDB Needham Worldwide McCaffrey & McCall	June
$60 million	**Nissan's Infiniti Carson, Calif.** (New account)	Bloom Agency Hill, Holliday, Connors, Cosmopulos	June–July	$15 million (creative only)	**Jerrico's Long John Silver's Lexington, Ky.** Incumbent: Foote, Cone & Belding	Undetermined	Aug. 15
$40 million–$50 million	**Bell Atlantic Arlington, Va.** Incumbents: Ketchum Advertising Lewis, Gilman & Kynett Poppe Tyson	Undetermined	Unknown	$15 million	**Fuji Photo Film USA Elmsford, N.Y.** Incumbents: McCann-Erickson Lord, Geller, Federico, Einstein	D'Arcy Masius Benton & Bowles DDB Needham Worldwide McCann-Erickson Hal Riney & Partners	June
$40 million	**U.S. Postal Service Washington** Incumbent: Young & Rubicam	BBDO Worldwide Bozell, Jacobs, Kenyon & Eckhardt Campbell-Mithun DDB Needham Worldwide Earle Palmer Brown Cos. Grey Advertising Lintas:New York Ogilvy & Mather Young & Rubicam	Aug. 1	$10 million	**Schieffelin & Somerset New York** Incumbent: Lord, Geller, Federico, Einstein	N W Ayer David Deutsch Associates Lord, Geller, Federico, Einstein Hal Riney & Partners Smith/Greenland	June
						INTERNATIONAL	
$20 million	**Schering-Plough's Chlor-Trimeton, Fibre Trim and Ocu-Clear Madison, N.J.** Incumbent: Ogilvy & Mather	Altschiller Reitzfeld Berenter Greenhouse & Webster Levine, Huntley, Schmidt & Beaver Messner, Vetere, Berger, Carey	Unknown	$13.5 million	**International Wool Secretariat London** Incumbents: Davidson Pearce HDM Publicis Saatchi & Saatchi/RCP Others	Davidson Pearce CLM/BBDO	June
$20 million	**Austin Rover Cars of North America Miami** Incumbent: Hal Riney & Partners	Undetermined	June	$5 million–$10 million	**3M's Scotchgard in Europe Brussels** Incumbent: Grey Advertising in some countries	Backer Spielvogel Bates Worldwide Grey Advertising	Mid-July

"Accounts Up for Grabs" includes domestic accounts up for review that are at least $5 million and major international accounts.

Source: Advertising Age, June 6, 1989, p. 70.

Figure 3–13 Agencies Often Advertise Themselves to Gain New Business

"cold calling," and following up on leads that have been generated. In addition, the trade press is a good source of information on companies considering a change, as shown by Figure 3–12.

• *Presentations* One of the basic goals of the new business development group is to receive an invitation from a company to make a presentation. In this presentation, the agency has the opportunity to present information about itself, including its experience, personnel, capabilities, and operating procedures, as well as to demonstrate its previous work.

• In many situations the agency might be asked to make a speculative presentation, in which it is asked to examine the client's marketing situation and then propose a tentative communications campaign. Because speculative presentations may require a great deal of time and preparation, and may cost the agency money without a guarantee of gaining the business, many firms refuse to participate in what they consider to be "creative shootouts." They argue that agencies should be selected based on their experience and the services and programs they have provided for previous clients.[12,13] Nevertheless, most agencies do participate in this form of solicitation, either by choice or because they are required to do so to gain accounts.

• *Public relations* Agencies also seek business through publicity/public relations efforts. Executives often participate in civic and social groups and work with charitable organizations to help the agency become respected in the community. Participation in professional associations will also assist in the cultivation of new contacts. Successful agencies often receive free publicity for their work throughout the industry, as well as by the mass media.

• *Image and reputation*   Perhaps the most effective manner in which an agency can gain new business is through its reputation. Agencies that consistently develop excellent campaigns for their clients acquire favorable reputations and images and are often approached by clients. Agencies may enter their work in award competitions or advertise themselves in order to enhance their reputation and image in the marketing community (see Figure 3–13).

Collateral Services

For many companies the development and implementation of their promotional programs become the responsibility of an agency. However, there are several other types of providers whose specialized services are used to complement the efforts of ad agencies, including direct-marketing firms, sales promotions specialists, and marketing research companies and public relations/publicity agencies. Let us examine the role that these firms play and the functions they perform.

Direct-Marketing Companies

One of the fastest-growing areas in promotions is that of **direct marketing,** in which companies directly communicate with consumers through methods of telemarketing, direct-response advertising, and direct mail. As this industry has grown, numerous direct-marketing firms have evolved offering companies their specialized skills in both the consumer and business markets. These companies provide research, media services, and creative and production capabilities. A more extensive discussion of their role is reserved until Chapter 13.

Sales Promotions Specialists

The fastest-growing component of consumer products companies' promotional mix is that of sales promotions, with nearly $124 billion spent in this area in 1988. The development and management of sales promotions programs such as contests, sweepstakes, refund and rebate offers, and sampling and incentive programs constitute a very complex task. Thus, most companies utilize the services of a sales promotions agency to develop and administer these programs. Sales promotions specialists often work in conjunction with the company's advertising agency to coordinate their efforts with the advertising program and, as shown in Figure 3–14, tout their service offerings to these organizations. Some agencies have also created their own sales promotions subsidiaries or have acquired such a firm. Like direct marketing, much more insight into the roles and functions of these companies is provided later in this text.

Marketing Research Companies

Companies are increasingly turning to marketing research to assist them in understanding their target audiences and to gather information that will be of value in designing their advertising and promotions programs and evaluating these programs. While some advertisers have their own marketing research departments and the capabilities to conduct research, many do not. Moreover, even companies with marketing research departments will often use outside research agencies to perform some services. Many research companies are used because of the specialized services they offer and their capabilities to gather objective information that is valuable to the advertiser's promotional programs.

Public Relations/Publicity Agencies

Many large companies will use both an advertising agency and a public relations firm. The role of the public relations firm is to develop and implement programs to manage the organization's publicity and affairs with consumers and other relevant public. Pub-

Figure 3–14 **Advertising for a Collateral Services Agency**

lic relations and publicity activities should also be coordinated with the other elements of the promotional program. As we will discuss the public relations function in more detail in Chapter 17, we will just note here that such collateral services are offered.

Integrated Services

As mentioned earlier, one of the emerging trends in the advertising industry is that of **integrated marketing**, in which ad agencies offer a variety of promotional services under one roof. In addition to advertising, the agency may offer direct-marketing, public relations, sales promotions, and/or marketing research services through subsidiary organizations. For example, the J. Walter Thompson (JWT) ad agency has been reformulated into the JWT Group, consisting of JWT, Hill & Knowlton (public relations), another ad agency (Lord, Geller, Federico & Einstein), a market research company (MRB), and several sales promotion and specialist communication firms. The JWT company was in turn acquired by the WTT Group of London and made part of its global communications empire.

Proponents of the **one-stop services agency** argue that by maintaining control of the entire promotional process, greater synergy among each of the program elements is achieved, it is more convenient for the client, and the advertiser is assured of high-quality work in each area. Those opposed to the superagency concept contend that all the providers become involved in political wrangling over budgets, do not communicate with each other as well and as often as they should, and in reality do not achieve synergy. They claim that the efforts to control all aspects of the promotional program are nothing more than an attempt to hold on to business that might otherwise be lost to independent providers. As you can see in Promotional Perspective 3–3, both suc-

Promotional Perspective 3–3

The Pros and Cons of "One-Stop" Superagencies

In the late 1980s a major trend in the advertising world was the move to form superagencies. These superagencies usually combined a number of ad agencies, as well as other support organizations (public relations, sales promotions, etc.), into one large organization. The new agency was touted as a "one-stop supermarket" for promotional services, offering the client a number of advantages including convenience and a uniform program coordinated by one large group working together.

Some of the world's largest agencies became part of an even larger superagency, including Young & Rubicam, Ogilvy & Mather Worldwide, and the Omnicom Group (Needham Harper Worldwide, Doyle Dane Bernbach Group, and BBDO International). As noted by Chairman Alex Kroll of Young & Rubicam, "Integrated marketing is going to enhance the stature of companies like ours. We'll be more truly valuable and objective counselors to our clients."

Companies like Ryder System (truck rentals), Humana, and General Foods agreed, with the former two signing on with Ogilvy & Mather and Grey Advertising, respectively. Both companies reported a great deal of satisfaction with their decisions (Humana previously used 27 agencies at the same time!). In addition, the U.S. Army (a $100 million–plus account) uses Young & Rubicam as well as its subsidiaries to write solicitation letters, prepare brochures, create posters, and provide T-shirts and socks with the army logo on them. All 180 people from each of the units working on the account are housed in the same section of the agency's offices.

Not everyone is convinced that superagencies are the best way to go, however. Eastman Kodak uses WPP Group but rarely relies on any of WPP's 30 subsidiaries. Kodak believes that one-stop shopping is good in theory but does not believe that one agency can be the best in everything. Others such as Bristol-Myers have also been disappointed in the results, citing competition among the subsidiaries as a major problem. Even some agency executives are not quite willing to jump on the bandwagon. Victor Millar, the head of Saatchi & Saatchi's communications division, notes that "synergy has been very, very difficult to implement. Everybody talks about it, but nobody really gets it done." Jerry Della Femina, chairman of Della Femina McNamee WCRS, feels that "clients buy in because it's nice not to have to go out in the rain and shop for somebody else. It doesn't get him the best; it just gets him the most convenient."

The superagency concept is not yet accepted by all advertisers or advertising agencies. The fact is that a marketing effort will be needed to promote the agencies and the concept of one-stop shopping itself.

Sources:"Ad Firms Falter on One Stop Shopping," *The Wall Street Journal*, December 1, 1988, p. B1; "Do Your Ads Need a Superagency?" *Fortune*, April 27, 1987, pp. 84–89.

cesses and failures have been reported, and the verdict is still out regarding their effectiveness. One thing is certain, however: As companies continue to shift the promotional dollars away from advertising ($200 to $215 billion was spent in direct-marketing, promotions, and public relations activities in 1988, as opposed to $110 billion on advertising), agencies will continue to explore ways to keep these monies under "their roofs."[14]

Summary

The development, execution, and administration of an advertising and promotions program involve the efforts of many individuals, both within the company as well as outside the organization. A number of organizational designs may be considered for this purpose.

Centralized systems offer the advantages of facilitated communications, lower personnel requirements, continuity in staff, and more top management involvement. Disadvantages associated with this design include a lower involvement with overall marketing goals, longer response times, and difficulties in handling multiple product lines. Decentralized systems offer the advantages of concentrated managerial attention, more rapid responses to problems, and increased flexibility, though they may be limited by ineffective decision making, internal conflicts, misallocation of funds, and a lack of authority. In-house agencies, while offering the advantages of cost savings, control, and increased coordination, also have the disadvantage of less experience, objectivity, and flexibility.

Many firms use advertising agencies to assist them in the development and execution of their programs. These agencies may take on a variety of forms, including full-service agencies, creative boutiques, and media buying services. The first of these offers the client a full range of services including creative, account, marketing, and financial and management services, while the other two specialize in creative and media buying respectively. Agencies are compensated through commission systems, percentage charges, and fee- and cost-based systems.

Recently there has been an increase in the emphasis on agency evaluations. Agencies are being evaluated on both financial and qualitative aspects, and some clients are basing the agencies' compensations upon their performances.

Finally, a number of "superagencies" have developed. These large agencies are formed through the combination of separate agencies or agencies offering other marketing-related services such as direct marketing, sales promotions, marketing research, and public relations. These agencies offer one-stop marketing services and have been both supported and criticized by clients.

Key Terms

Clients	Storyboard
Advertising agency	Production department
Media organizations	Traffic department
Collateral services	Creative boutique
Advertising manager	Media buying services
Centralized system	Commission system
Decentralized systems	Negotiated commission
Product manager	Percentage charges
In-house agency	Fixed-fee agreements
Billings	Cost-plus system
Superagencies	Agency evaluation process
Full-service agency	Financial audit
Account executive	Qualitative audit
Media department	Direct marketing
Sales promotions department	Integrated marketing
Copywriters	One-stop services agency
Art department	

Discussion Questions

1. Discuss the role of the four participant groups in the advertising and promotions process.
2. What are some of the specific responsibilities and duties of the advertising manager under a centralized advertising department structure? Is an advertising manager needed if a company uses an outside agency?
3. What are the advantages of using a decentralized system? Discuss the responsibilities of a product manager with respect to advertising and promotions.
4. Discuss the pros and cons of using an in-house agency. When is a company likely to use this structure?
5. Discuss the reasons companies use outside agencies. Analyze the importance of the various services provided by a full-service agency.
6. What are the various ways agencies receive compensation for their services?
7. Discuss the pros and cons of the commission system. Do you think this system will survive? Explain your reasoning.

8. A number of companies have developed new systems in which agency compensation is based on brand performance in the marketplace. Do you feel this system is fair? Would you accept such a system if you were an agency?
9. What are some of the criteria that should be used by a client in evaluating its agency? Describe how the importance of these criteria might vary among different firms.
10. Discuss the role of superagencies and integrated services.

Notes

1. Adapted from Bruce Horowitz, "Small Agencies Beating Out Some Madison Avenue Giants— Here's Why," *Los Angeles Times,* June 7, 1988, pt. IV, p. 8.
2. Thomas J. Cosse and John E. Swan, "Strategic Marketing Planning by Product Managers— Room for Improvement?," *Journal of Marketing* 47 (Summer 1983), pp. 92–102.
3. Victor P. Buell, *Organizing for Marketing/Advertising Success* (New York: Association of National Advertisers, 1982).
4. "The Marketing Revolution at Procter and Gamble," *Business Week,* July 25, 1988, p. 72.
5. "Do Your Ads Need a Super Agency?" *Fortune,* April 27, 1987, p. 81.
6. "Media Costs '89: Easy Does It," *Marketing & Media Decisions,* August 1988, pp. 32–34.
7. "Achenbaum Puts His Cards on the Table," *Advertising Age,* May 9, 1988, p. 3.
8. "Achenbaum Fires Back at Critics," *Advertising Age,* May 30, 1988, p. 6.
9. Nancy Gijes, "Reviewing the Review: Borden Likes System of Agency Evaluation," *Advertising Age,* April 18, 1977, p. 3.
10. Peter Doyle, Marcel Corstiens, and Paul Michell, "Signals of Vulnerability in Agency-Client Relations," *Journal of Marketing* 44 (Fall 1980), pp. 18–23.
11. Daniel B. Wackman, Charles Salmon, and Caryn C. Salmon, "Developing an Advertising Agency-Client Relationship," *Journal of Advertising Research* 26, no. 6 (December 1986/ January 1987), pp. 21–29.
12. William Abrams, "Big Contest for Ad Accounts Forces Agencies to Go All Out," *The Wall Street Journal,* November 18, 1982, p. 33.
13. "Big Agencies Starting to Call for End to Costly Free Pitches," *The Wall Street Journal,* February 22, 1989, p. B7.
14. "Media Costs '89."

Perspectives on Consumer Behavior

CHAPTER OBJECTIVES

1. To examine the role that consumer behavior plays in the development and implementation of advertising and promotions programs

2. To examine various psychological approaches used to study consumer behavior and their implications for advertising and promotions

3. To examine the consumer decision-making process

4. To examine external factors such as culture, social class, and group influences and how these impact consumer behavior

Putting Consumers on the Couch

In 1988 researchers at the McCann-Erickson Ad Agency were baffled about how Southern women went about selecting a brand of insecticide. The women thought that a new brand that sold in little plastic trays was less messy and more effective than traditional bug sprays, yet they never switched over to the new product.

To find out why the women didn't change, the agency's researchers used a technique often used in psychological research. They had the women draw pictures of roaches and then write stories about them. Some of their drawings and accompanying explanations are shown here. As you can see the modern-day advertiser often puts consumers "on the couch" to understand their purchase motives.

The Mind of a Roach Killer

The McCann-Erickson ad agency asked women to draw and describe how they felt about roaches. The agency concluded from the drawings that the women identified the roaches with men who had abandoned them and thus enjoyed watching the roaches-men squirm and die. That's why, the agency figured, that women prefer spray roach killers to products that don't allow the user to see the roach die.

"ONE NIGHT I just couldn't take the horror of these bugs sneaking around in the dark. They are always crawling when you can't see them. I had to do something. I thought wouldn't it be wonderful if when I switched on the light the roaches would shrink up and die like vampires to sunlight. So I did, but they just all scattered. But I was ready with my spray so it wasn't a total loss. I got quite a few...continued tomorrow night when night time falls."

"I TIPTOED quietly into the kitchen perhaps he wasn't around. I stretched my arm up to the light. I hoped I'd be alone when the light went on. Perhaps he is sitting on the table I thought. You think that's impossible? Nothing is impossible with that guy. He might not even be alone. He'll run when the light goes on I thought. But what's worse is for him to slip out of sight. No, it would be better to confront him before he takes control and 'invites a companion'."

"A MAN LIKES a free meal you cook for him, as long as there is food he will stay."

Source: Ronald Alsop, "Advertisers Put Consumers on the Couch," *The Wall Street Journal*, May 13, 1988, p. 19.

Introduction

The "Mind of a Roach Killer" is just one example of how the advertiser uses knowledge of consumer behavior in the development of promotional campaigns. While this is certainly an interesting application, it is but one of many of the frequent attempts to borrow from disciplines outside marketing to develop promotional strategies designed to satisfy customers' needs and wants.

In previous chapters, we have discussed the importance of the situation analysis and the requirement of understanding the needs and wants of the consumer. In this chapter, we will consider in more detail the factors involved in the study of consumer behavior and the role of these factors in the design of an advertising and promotional program. As you can see from the "roach killer" example, such insights can provide substantial information.

Basic Considerations

Consumer behavior has been defined as the study of human behavior in a consumer role. Over the past two decades the emphasis placed on furthering our knowledge of the consumer has increased dramatically. Marketers have realized the necessity of understanding the reasons why consumers behave as they do, so that strategies and programs targeted to them might be more effectively designed. To acquire such knowledge, marketers have turned to other disciplines. A review of a basic consumer behavior text would reveal that anthropology, psychology, economics, and sociology are just a few of the many disciplines providing such insights. While it is beyond the scope of this text to provide you with an in-depth review of consumer behavior, it is important for the reader to have a basic understanding of the consumer's decision-making process, factors that impact this process, and the ways in which such knowledge is utilized in the development of promotional strategies. In the remainder of this chapter, we will examine some of the internal and external factors that have been shown to influence consumer behaviors and then consider a model of the decision-making process. We will also discuss how this information has been used in developing advertising and promotional strategies.

Psychological Perspectives of Consumer Behavior

If you were to take a few moments to examine texts in the area of social psychology, you would notice that a variety of theoretical approaches to understanding human behavior exist. While each of these theories might in itself contribute to our knowledge about how and why consumers behave as they do, many contributions have come from three psychological orientations—Freud's psychoanalytic theory, reinforcement theory, and cognitive theories. Without going into great depth in these areas, the basis of each theoretical orientation will be discussed, and some examples of how advertisers have applied this knowledge will follow.

Psychoanalytic Theory

One of the initial orientations considered by marketers in studying consumer behavior was **psychoanalytic theory.** Pioneered by Sigmund Freud, this orientation has been one of the more widely researched theoretical approaches studied in psychology and thus was a natural place to begin. Freud believed that the needs that motivate human behaviors are innate and based on two primary instincts—life (or self-preservation) instincts and death (or self-destruction) instincts. The life instincts were considered to be predominantly sexual in nature, whereas the death instincts were often manifested through self-destructive and/or aggressive behaviors. These instincts served as the bases for a variety of needs, mostly unconscious and many of which were too antisocial to be satisfied directly.[1] Freud considered the personality of the individual as having developed in an attempt to gratify these needs and consisting of three basic components: the id, the ego, and the superego. The **id** serves as the reservoir of all psychic energy and as the repository for all basic drives and motivations. Its function is to seek pleasure through the discharge of energy (tension). The **superego,** or moral arm of the personality, has as its function the repression of the drives of the id. Its role is to inhibit the impulses of the pleasure-seeking component, acting in accordance with the rules and regulations of society. These opposite desires lead to conflict, which necessitates the need for the third component, the **ego.** The ego serves as the mediator between the two by attempting to channel the drives of the id into behaviors acceptable to the superego. The methods employed for this purpose, known as **ego defenses,** are sometimes considered by marketers as motivational bases underlying purchase decisions. In a normal, healthy person the three components would be in balance, working together to satisfy needs. When one, or more, of the components was over- or underdeveloped, this balance would be upset, creating tension in the system.

Those who attempt to relate psychoanalytic theory to consumer behavior believe that consumers' motivations for purchasing are often very complex and would not be obvious to the casual observer—or for that matter, to the consumers themselves. Thus, many of the motives for purchase and/or consumption might be driven by deeply rooted sexual drives, and/or "death instincts," that could only be determined by probing the subconscious—an excellent example of which was provided in the "roach killer" example at the outset of this chapter.

Two of the first to conduct this type of research in marketing—Ernest Dichter and James Vicary—were employed by a number of major corporations to assist them in using psychoanalytic techniques to determine consumers' purchase motivations. The work of these researchers, and others who continue to use this approach, assumed the title of **motivation research.** Some of the findings of motivation researchers, and their applications of this discipline to marketing, follow.

Motivation Research in Marketing   As we stated earlier, motivation researchers are involved in attempting to ascertain the underlying motivations for consumer behavior, usually assuming that such motivations are not always conscious to the individual. Thus, a variety of methodologies are employed in an attempt to gain insight into the "true" underlying causes. Some of the methods employed include in-depth interviews, projective techniques, association tests, and focus groups (see Table 4–1) in which consumers are encouraged to bring out associations related to products and brands. As one might expect, such associations often lead to some interesting insights and conclusions as to why people purchase, for example:

- A man buys a convertible as a substitute mistress.
- Women like to bake cakes because they feel like they are giving birth to a baby.
- Women wear perfume to "attract a man" and to "glorify their existence."
- Men like frankfurters better than women because cooking them (frankfurters, not men!) makes women feel guilty—it's an admission of laziness.
- When people shower, their sins go down the drain with the soap as they rinse.[2,3,4]

As you can see from these examples, motivation research has led to some very interesting, albeit controversial, findings and to much skepticism in the minds of marketing managers. At the same time, however, major corporations have spent millions of dollars employing motivation research to help them market their products, as Promotional Perspective 4–1 illustrates.

Problems and Contributions of Psychoanalytic Theory and Motivation Research   Psychoanalytic theory has been criticized as (1) being too vague, (2) being unresponsive to the external environment, (3) being too reliant on the early development of the individual, and (4) using too small a sample for drawing conclusions. Because of the emphasis on the unconscious, verification of the results obtained is difficult, if not impossible, to establish, leading motivation research to be criticized both for the conclusions drawn as well as its lack of experimental validation. Since motivation research studies typically employ a small number of participants, there is

Table 4–1   Some of the Marketing Research Methods Employed to Probe the Mind of the Consumer

In-depth interviews	Face-to-face situations in which an interviewer asks a consumer to talk freely in an unstructured interview using specific questions designed to obtain insights into his or her motives, ideas, or opinions
Projective techniques	Efforts designed to gain insights into consumers' values, motives, attitudes, or needs that are difficult to express or identify by having them project these internal states upon some external object
Association tests	A technique in which an individual is asked to respond as to the first thing that comes to mind when he or she is presented with a stimulus; the stimulus may be a word, picture, ad, and so on
Focus groups	A small number of people with similar backgrounds and/or interests are brought together to discuss a particular product, idea, or issue

Promotional Perspective 4–1

Motivation Research at Work—Advertising Agency Applications

In an article appearing in *The Wall Street Journal*, a number of well-known advertising agencies revealed how they use motivation resesrach studies, and some of their results. You have already seen those of McCann-Erickson in the roach killer projections presented at the outset of this chapter. Here are a few more:

- N W Ayer asked consumers to draw shapes with their left hands in response to questions regarding new product ideas, in the belief that the right side of the brain (which controls the left side of the body) is more visual, symbolic, and emotional and therefore would be better for expressing images.
- Foote, Cone & Belding gave consumers stacks of photographs of people's faces, asking them to associate the faces with the kind of person who might use particular products.
- McCann-Erickson Worldwide had consumers draw stick figures of American Express gold and green card users. The gold card user was portrayed as more active than the "couch potato in front of a TV set" green card user.
- Saatchi & Saatchi Advertising WW used psychological probes to conclude that Ronald McDonald created a more nurturing mood than did the Burger King, who was perceived as "more aggressive, masculine and distant."

Source: Ronald Alsop, "Advertisers Put Consumers on the Couch," *The Wall Street Journal*, May 13, 1988, p. 19.

also concern that what is really being discovered are the idiosyncracies of a few individuals and that these findings are not generalizable to the population as a whole.

At the same time, it is difficult to ignore the contributions of the psychoanalytic approach in furthering our understanding of consumer behaviors. These insights can often be used as a basis for advertising messages aimed at the buyers' deeply rooted feelings, hopes, aspirations, and fears. In many instances these strategies may be more effective than rationally based appeals.

Figure 4–1 **Obsession Ads Employ the Use of Sex Appeals**

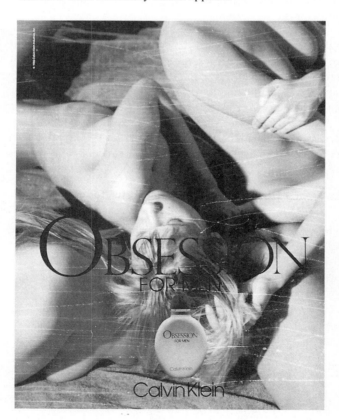

Figure 4–2   **Musk Has Often Been Promoted as a Sex-Appeal Product**

Figure 4–3   **After Six Uses Symbolism in Its Ad for Clothing**

While often criticized, motivation research has also contributed to the marketing discipline. The qualitative nature of the research is considered important to many marketers in their assessment of how and why consumers buy. Focus groups and in-depth interviews are valuable methods for gaining insights into consumers' feelings, whereas projective techniques are often the only means of getting around stereotypical or socially desirable responses. In addition, it is generally agreed that motivation research is the forerunner of "psychographics"—or lifestyle research—an often employed basis for segmenting markets and developing consumer profiles, which will be discussed in Chapter 7.

Finally, we know that buyers are sometimes motivated by symbolic as well as functional motives in their purchase decisions. Thus, the use of sexual appeals and symbols in ads such as those shown in Figures 4–1 through 4–3 are designed with this information in mind.

Reinforcement Theories

A second theoretical orientation assumed by many psychologists and adopted by consumer behavior researchers is the study of the acquisition of responses—or learning. Two major orientations of learning can be distinguished: *associative learning* (or *classical conditioning*) and *operant* (or *instrumental*) *conditioning*. While each elicits its own theory as to how people learn, the common basis for each of these approaches is traditionally referred to as **reinforcement theory** or **behaviorism.** (It should also be noted that cognitive theorists have developed their own conceptualization of learning,

Figure 4–4   **The Classical Conditioning Process**

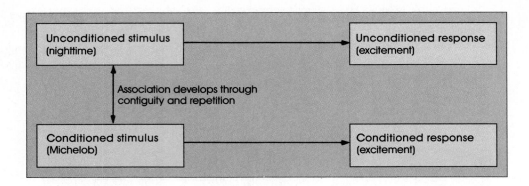

which has received wide acceptance and application in the study of consumer behavior. The cognitive approach will be discussed later in this chapter.)

The Basic Concept   The most traditional reinforcement theory approach to learning is characterized by the "S-R," or **stimulus-response orientation,** which emphasizes external factors while minimizing the significance of internal psychological processes. Stimulus-response theorists believe that for learning to occur all that is necessary is a time/space proximity between a stimulus and a response. Learning takes place through establishment of a connection between the stimulus and a response. Let us examine the basic principles of the two orientations mentioned earlier and their implications for promotional strategy.

Classical Conditioning   **Classical conditioning** assumes that learning is essentially an *associative process* with an already existing relationship between a stimulus and a response. Probably the best-known example of this type of learning comes from the well-known studies done with animals by the Russian psychologist Pavlov.[5] Pavlov noticed that at feeding times his dogs would salivate at the sight of food. The connection between food and salivation is not taught but is an innate reflex reaction. Because this relationship exists prior to the conditioning process, the food is referred to as an **unconditioned stimulus** and salivation is an **unconditioned response.** To see if salivation could be conditioned to occur in response to another neutral stimulus, Pavlov paired the ringing of a bell with the presentation of the food, and after a number of trials, the dogs learned to salivate at the sound of the bell alone. Thus, the bell became a **conditioned stimulus** that elicited a **conditioned response** resembling the original unconditioned reaction.

Two factors are important for learning to occur through the associative process. The first requirement is *contiguity*, which means that the unconditioned stimulus and conditioned stimulus must occur in close proximity in time and space. In Pavlov's experiment, the dog learns to associate the ringing of the bell with food because of the contiguous presentation of the two stimuli. The other important principle is *repetition*, or frequency, of the association. The more often the unconditioned and conditioned stimuli occur together, the stronger the association between them will be.

Applying classical conditioning   Learning through a classical conditioning process plays an important role in marketing, as buyers can be conditioned to form favorable impressions and images of various brands through the associative process. Advertisers strive to associate their products and services with certain perceptions, images, and emotions that are known to evoke positive reactions from consumers. Many products are promoted through image advertising in which the brand is shown with an unconditioned stimulus that is known to elicit pleasant and favorable feelings. Through the simultaneous presentation of the brand with this unconditioned stimulus, the brand itself becomes a conditioned stimulus that elicits the same favorable response. Figure 4–4 provides a diagram of this process, whereas the Michelob storyboard shown in

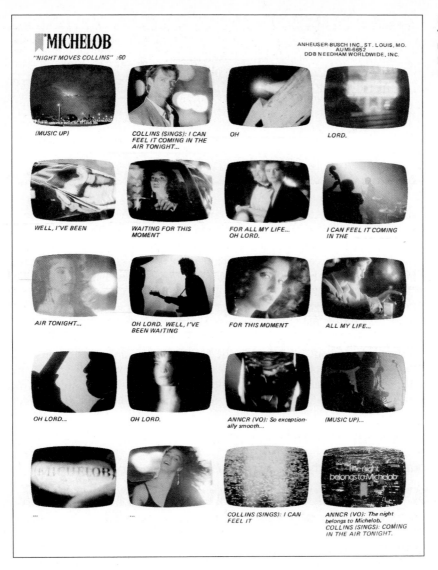

Figure 4–5
This Advertisement Employs the Use of Classical Conditioning by Associating Michelob with Nighttime Excitement

Figure 4–5 is an example of an application of this strategy. Notice how this ad associates Michelob with the excitement of nighttime.

Classical conditioning can also be used by associating a product or service with a favorable emotional state. A study by Gerald Gorn used this approach to examine how background music in advertisements influenced product choice.[6] He found that subjects were more likely to choose a product when it was presented against a background of music that they liked rather than music that they disliked. These results suggest that the emotions generated by a commercial are important because they may become associated with the advertised product through a classical conditioning process. Advertisers will often attempt to pair a previously neutral product or service stimulus with an event or situation that arouses positive feelings such as humor, an exciting sports event, or popular music.

Operant Conditioning Classical conditioning views the individual as a passive participant in the learning process who is simply a receiver of stimuli. Conditioning occurs as a result of exposure to a stimulus that occurs *prior* to the response. In the **operant conditioning** approach the individual must actively *operate* or act on some aspect of the environment for learning to occur. Operant conditioning is sometimes referred to as **instrumental conditioning** because the response of the individual is in-

Figure 4—6   Instrumental Conditioning in Marketing

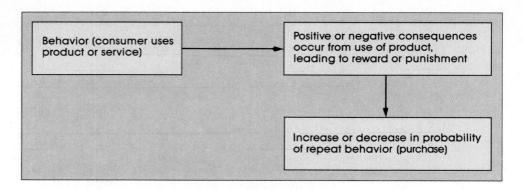

strumental in getting a positive reinforcement (reward) or negative reinforcement (punishment). Advocates of this type of learning argue that the *consequences* of the behavior of the individual are critical to the learning process. Behaviors that are rewarded or reinforced (positive consequences) will be continued, whereas those that are not rewarded or are punished (negative consequences) will be terminated.

The principles of operant conditioning can be applied to marketing, as shown by Figure 4—6. Companies will attempt to provide their customers with products and services that satisfy their needs and reward them so as to reinforce the likelihood of repeat purchase. Reinforcement can also play a role in advertising, as many ads use positive reinforcement by stressing the benefits or rewards that a consumer will receive for using a product or brand. Some ads even go beyond the basic reward of the product or service itself and stress additional benefits the consumer can receive from its use, as demonstrated by the ad for Security Pacific Bank shown in Figure 4—7.

Figure 4—7   Ad Demonstrating Additional Benefits from Using a Service

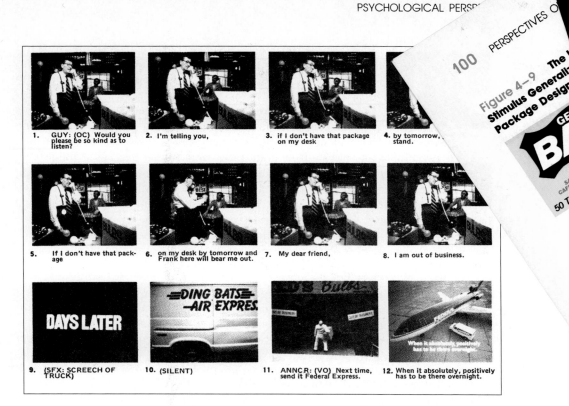

1. GUY: (OC) Would you please be so kind as to listen?
2. I'm telling you,
3. if I don't have that package on my desk
4. by tomorrow, stand.
5. If I don't have that package
6. on my desk by tomorrow and Frank here will bear me out.
7. My dear friend,
8. I am out of business.
9. (SFX: SCREECH OF TRUCK)
10. (SILENT)
11. ANNCR: (VO) Next time, send it Federal Express.
12. When it absolutely, positively has to be there overnight.

Reinforcement can also be implied in advertising by encouraging consumers to use a particular brand to avoid the unpleasant consequences of poor performance. The ad for Federal Express overnight delivery service shown in Figure 4–8 was one of a series in a campaign designed to warn consumers of the negative consequences of not having an important package arrive on time.

Elements of the Learning Process To understand better the learning process and how it can be used to influence consumer behavior, it is helpful to examine some basic elements of learning and their implications for advertising strategy.

Drives Learning is most likely to occur in the presence of a **drive,** which is an *internal* stimulus that impels action. Drives are generally the result of the activation of motives, which may include physiological needs such as hunger, thirst, pain avoidance, and sex or the learned, higher-order needs suggested by A. H. Maslow such as self-esteem, status, or self-actualization.[7]

Advertisers need to consider the drive state of the consumer in planning and developing their promotional programs. For example, commercials can be scheduled in an attempt to capitalize on situations where a drive exists—for example, advertising food products around the dinner hour, or sleeping pills late at night.

Cues **Cues** are *external* stimuli—or objects in the environment that have the potential to stimulate a drive or elicit other responses. Advertisements are often used as cues in an attempt to activate consumers' drives. In addition, the product itself, including the name and package design, may serve as a cue. Understanding how consumers perceive and react to these stimuli is particularly important to marketers in their efforts to design promotional strategies. Two principles involved in this process that will aid the marketer in this understanding are discussed next.

Stimulus generalization **Generalization** is the process whereby the same response is made to a new cue as was made to a previous, similar stimulus. In a marketing environment, consumers may make judgments about new products or brands based upon their beliefs, impressions, and past experiences with existing and/or similar products or brands. There are several ways marketers can use the stimulus generalization concept. For example, family branding strategies are often employed by companies with high-quality reputations, assuming that buyers will generalize their positive experiences and impressions from one of these products to another. Companies such as Heinz, Campbell, and General Electric brand and promote their products using a blanket company name. The principle of stimulus generalization is also utilized by smaller, lesser-known brands and private-label brands. By using similar packaging and promotions (designs, colors, art work, etc.) as the market leader, an attempt is made to get the consumer to generalize the image and quality of the well-known brand to its product. The Bayer aspirin package shown in Figure 4–9 is an example of the design that has often been copied. As a result Sterling Drug Inc. has had to institute action to prevent continued imitation of their valuable package design. While often effective, sometimes the use of this strategy may go too far, as demonstrated by the example presented in Promotional Perspective 4–2.

Stimulus discrimination   A learning process that is the opposite of generalization is that of **discrimination,** whereby the individual learns to discriminate one cue from another and make different responses to similar stimuli. It is important to the marketer that consumers learn to differentiate between various brands, particularly in product or service categories where the functional differences among various brands are not that great. Advertisers must find discriminating attributes or **unique selling propositions** that can be used to establish their brand as being different from competitors'. The ad shown in Figure 4–10 for Senco Fastening Systems is an example of an effort to differentiate its product based on superior service.

Mnemonic devices   Another way that marketers can influence the learning and retention of a stimulus cue is through the use of **mnemonics.** Mnemonics are memory-aiding devices such as symbols, rhymes, associations, and images that are used to assist in the learning and memory process. Advertisers often use mnemonics to assist the customer in learning and remembering information about the company or its products. For example, the "7/24" symbol shown in the San Diego Trust & Savings Bank ad in Figure 4–11 has been proven to be very effective in aiding consumers' recall that the bank's automatic teller system operates seven days a week, 24 hours a day. Advertisers utilize mnemonics in other ways such as telephone numbers spelling out the company name—for example, Evatone (382–8003)—or using catchy jingles—"Termites? Call Terminex, world's largest in termite control."

Response   A **response** is the behavior created by the stimulus. Reinforcement theorists attempt to measure learning in behavioral terms and prefer physically observable responses to determine if conditioning has occurred. The response of interest to marketers is usually the purchase of a product or service; however, marketers may also focus on responses that are short of actual purchase to gauge whether learning has occurred. Intermediate measures such as recall or recognition of an advertisement, image measures, or consumer inquiries can also be used to assess learning.

Reinforcement   **Reinforcement** refers to the *reward* associated with a particular response and is an important element of learning since it provides a rationale or reason for the individual to engage in a specific behavior. Behavior that is reinforced will strengthen the bond between a stimulus and a response. Thus, if a consumer buys a product in response to an advertisement and the consequences or outcomes resulting from the use of the product are positive, the likelihood of the consumer's using this product again is increased. Ideally, marketers want their customers to be satisfied (and thus their behavior reinforced) each time they use the product to encourage repeat purchases. Two techniques that are particularly relevant to marketers in their use of reinforcement in promotional strategies are *schedules of reinforcement* and *shaping.*

Promotional Perspective 4–2

Taking the Strategy of Stimulus Generalization Too Far

Muhammad Ali, the former world heavyweight boxing champion, was sued by Kiwi Shoe Polish for violating federal trade laws. It seems that when Ali's Champion Brands Industries decided to market a shoe polish, they packaged it too closely to the Kiwi brand—at least according to Kiwi. According to the plaintiff, Ali's product copied Kiwi's red, black, and gold colors and lifted the instructions word for word from the Kiwi cans. Kiwi argued that the "virtually identical" cans cost the company at least $1 million in damages to its trade, reputation, and goodwill and wanted the product taken off the market so that consumers would not be confused.

Ali claimed that there were differences in the packaging and contended that the size was different, that the name was Ali and not Kiwi, and that Kiwi did not have the right to claim the colors as their own. Further, Ali noted that his picture was on the can and added, "I hope I don't look like a kiwi bird."

Source: "Kiwi Picks Fight with Muhammad Ali," *Los Angeles Times*, June 11, 1986, pp. B1–B4.

Different **schedules of reinforcement** will result in varying patterns of learning and behavior. Learning will occur most rapidly under a *continuous* reinforcement schedule in which every response is rewarded. While learning occurs rapidly with continuous reinforcement, cessation of the behavior is very likely to occur when the reinforcement stops. Marketers must provide continuous reinforcement to consumers or risk having them switch to brands that will provide satisfaction.

Learning takes place more slowly, but is longer lasting when a *partial* or *intermittent* schedule is used and only some of the individual's responses are rewarded. An example of the use of partial reinforcement schedules can be seen in the designing of

Figure 4–10   Example of an Ad Employing the Stimulus Discrimination Principle

When you buy fasteners, is this all you get?

It is if you're not buying Senco. Only Senco® offers the extras that make your job easier and more profitable. Extras like:

Reliable delivery. When you order, we ship your materials within 36 hours or less.

Widest assortment. Whatever your needs, you will find that we have the biggest choice of fasteners in the industry.

Technical help. In-plant visits by your Senco representative offer you solutions and better ways to do your job.

New PowerPlus Tools. The SFN1 and SKS, plus the LS2, are state-of-the-art tools you can rely on for superior "pride-of-craftsmanship" finishes on every job.

Get *more* than just fasteners. Call the Senco office listed in the Yellow Pages under "Staples," or call toll-free 1-800-543-4596.

In Ohio, 1-800-582-1405.

SENCO®
FASTENING SYSTEMS

Preferred by Knowledgeable Craftsmen

Figure 4–11   The Use of a Symbol as a Mnemonic to Aid Recall

promotional programs. A firm may want to periodically offer consumers an incentive to use the company's product. However, the firm would not want to offer the incentive every time (continuous reinforcement) because consumers might become dependent on it and stop buying the brand when the incentive is withdrawn. An example of this approach examines the use of a continuous versus partial reinforcement on bus ridership.[8] It was found that discount coupons given as rewards for riding the bus were equally effective when given on a partial schedule as when given on a continuous schedule. The cost of giving the discount coupons under the partial schedule, however, was considerably less.

Reinforcement schedules can also be used to influence consumer learning and behavior through a process known as **shaping.** Shaping refers to the reinforcement of successive acts that lead to a desired behavior pattern or response. Rothschild and Gaidis argue that shaping is a very useful concept for marketers and provide the following rationale for its use.[9]

> Shaping is an essential process in deriving new and complex behavior because a behavior cannot be rewarded unless it first occurs; a stimulus can only reinforce acts that already occur. New, complex behaviors rarely occur by chance in nature. If the only behavior to be rewarded were the final complex sought behavior, one would probably have to wait a long time for this to occur by chance. Instead, one can reward simpler existing behaviors; over time, more complex patterns evolve and these are rewarded. Thus the shaping process occurs by a method of successive approximations. [P. 71]

In a promotional context, shaping procedures are used as part of the introductory program for new products. Figure 4–12 provides an example of how samples and discount coupons could be used to introduce a new product and take a consumer from trial to repeat purchase. Marketers must be careful in their use of shaping procedures because dropping the use of incentives too soon may result in the consumer failing to

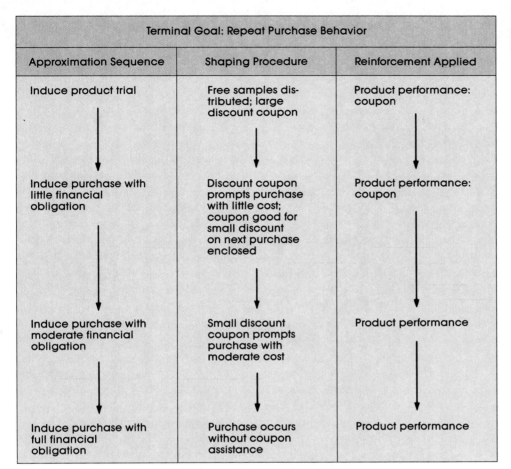

Figure 4—12 Application of Shaping Procedures in Marketing

Source: Michael L. Rothschild and William C. Gaidis, "Behavioral Learning Theory: Its Relevance to Marketing and Promotions," *Journal of Marketing Research* 45, no. 2 (Spring 1981).

establish the desired behavior, while overusing them may result in the consumer's purchase becoming contingent upon the presence of the promotional incentive rather than the product or service.

Problems and Contributions of Reinforcement Theory

The reinforcement theory approach emphasizes the role of *external factors*—as opposed to internal processing—as an explanation of learning and behavior. Rewarding or reinforcing behaviors results in a strengthening of a stimulus response association and an increase in the likelihood of the continuation of the response. Learning takes place either through direct reinforcement of a particular response or through an associative conditioning process. As we have seen in this examination of reinforcement theory, classical and instrumental conditioning have a number of implications for marketing and promotional strategies, and many of the principles discussed here can be of value in explaining and influencing a consumer's behavior.

While there are insights to be gained from the behaviorists' view of learning, this approach has been criticized for assuming a mechanistic view of the consumer. Internal psychological processes, such as motivations, thinking, and perceiving, are ignored, under the basic assumption that presentation of a stimulus will lead to a fairly

Figure 4–13 **The Cognitive Approach to Learning**

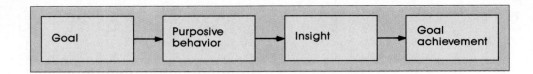

predictable response. Humans are considered to be similar to animals in the learning process. Because of this simplified approach to explaining behavior, many consumer researchers have become more interested in examining more complex mental processing. As a result the cognitive approach has dominated the field of consumer research in recent years.

Cognitive Theory

Over the past few decades the direction of mainstream psychology has shifted from a behaviorist to a cognitive orientation.[10] Likewise, the emphasis in consumer behavior has progressed from psychoanalytic to reinforcement to cognitive approaches. The final theoretical approach to be discussed here is that of the cognitive orientation and its applications to promotional management.

The Basic Concept
Cognitive theory has as its basis an information-processing, problem-solving, reasoning approach to human behavior. In contrast to the reinforcement perspective, cognitive orientations emphasize *internal processing*—or thinking. Cognitive processing concerns the individual's transformation of external information into meanings or patterns of thought and how these meanings are combined to form judgments about behavior.[11] This approach is quite different from the behaviorists' perspective, as can be seen in the following comparison:

> The basic concept contends that consumers do not respond simply to stimuli but instead act on beliefs, express attitudes and strive toward goals. The cognitivist is thus concerned with this entire range of conscious experience and not just objective behavior. . . . The human being is viewed as a highly complex sensory processing and data gathering organism . . . pulled to acts of choice by his goals and aspirations.[12]

While recognizing the behaviorists' perspective that some learning involves the simple process of association between stimulus and response, the cognitive orientation considers the consumer to be an adaptive problem solver who utilizes various processes in reasoning, forming concepts, and acquiring knowledge. As consumer behavior typically involves choices and decision making, this approach has a particular appeal to those studying this discipline. Figure 4–13 shows how the cognitive theorists would view the learning process.

We will continue our discussion of the cognitive orientation by examining several concepts that are important in understanding buyer behaviors. We will then examine a basic model of the consumer's purchase decision process based on this approach.

Cognitive Processes
Perception is the process by which the individual receives, selects, organizes, and interprets information in order to create a meaningful picture of the world.[13] As this definition suggests, perception is an individualized process as it depends on internal factors such as the individual's beliefs, experiences, needs, and moods as well as the external characteristics of the stimulus itself. Perception may also be considered a "filtering process" because these factors may influence what is received as well as how it is processed. For example, a person who has just finished exercising and is very thirsty may be more responsive to a soft drink ad and more likely to attend to and process the message than is someone who is not thirsty. Fur-

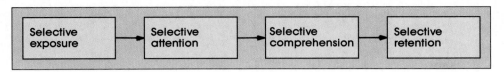

Figure 4–14   **The Selective Perception Process**

ther, the sheer number of stimuli that a person will be exposed to in any given day requires that this screening take place. This process, known as **selective perception,** may occur at a number of perceptual stages, as shown in Figure 4–14.

Selective exposure may occur as consumers choose whether or not to make themselves available to information. For example, a viewer of a television show may choose to change channels or leave the room during commercial breaks to avoid exposure to the advertisements. **Selective attention** occurs when the consumer chooses to focus attention on certain stimuli while excluding others. One study of selective attention estimates that the consumer is potentially exposed to nearly 1,500 ads per day yet perceives only 76 of these messages.[14] If this is true, it means that advertisers must take considerable effort to attract the consumer's attention and have their message noticed. To gain attention, advertisers have focused more efforts on the creative aspects of the ad, as demonstrated in the example in Promotional Perspective 4–3.

Even if the consumer does give attention to the advertiser's message, there is no guarantee that it will be interpreted in the intended manner. Consumers may engage in the process of **selective comprehension** in which they interpret information based on their own attitudes, beliefs, and experiences. In selective comprehension, consumers often interpret information in a manner that will support their own position. For example, an advertisement that disparages a consumer's favorite brand may be seen as biased or untruthful, and the claims may not be accepted.

The final screening process shown in Figure 4–14—**selective retention**—means that consumers do not remember all the information they see, read, or hear even after attending and comprehending it. The advertiser must attempt to ensure that information will be retained in the consumer's memory so as to be available when it is time to make a purchase. The use of mnemonics, which were discussed earlier, and advertising repetition are just two of the strategies used by advertisers in this endeavor.

Because advertisers know that consumers will engage in these processes of perception, they will attempt to use this knowledge in the development of their programs. One controversial strategy that some feel that advertisers pursue is that of appealing to the consumer subconsciously, as discussed in Promotional Perspective 4–4. As you can probably determine from reading this example, it is not a strategy that we believe in or recommend!

Attitudes   The perceptual process may lead to the formation of **attitudes.** As defined by Gordon Allport, "An attitude is a mental and neural state of readiness, organized through experience, exerting a directive or dynamic influence upon the individual's response to all objects and situations with which it is related."[15] As can be seen by this definition, attitudes are learned through past experiences and serve as a link between thoughts and behaviors. As such, attitudes will have an impact on the consumer's behavior toward a product or brand. The goal of the advertiser may be to create a positive attitude toward its product or brand and/or reinforce or change existing attitudes through marketing communications.

The process by which consumers form and change attitudes is of great importance to marketers and has been one of the more widely researched areas of consumer behavior. As indicated by the definition presented earlier, attitudes are thought to guide behavior. Thus, marketers would expect that the formation (or changing) of an attitude would likely be a necessary ingredient in acquiring a desired behavior.

Promotional Perspective 4–3

Using Color to Attract Attention to an Advertisement

In the recent introduction of Cherry 7-Up, the Seven-Up Company was concerned about how it might make the drink appear more appealing to its target market—teenagers. Borrowing from the creativity of MTV, in which black and white videos often utilized a "splash" of color on drumsticks, guitars, and other items, the company decided to try the same approach on its TV commercials. The result was to splash the color pink on the cans of soda, on a Cadillac, and on a boy's necktie in an otherwise black and white ad. Did it work? Seven-Up seems to think so. The new product became one of the most successful new products in soft drink history, helping Seven-Up to its first market share gain in the soft drink industry in over a decade.

Other companies have also employed this approach to attention getting by showing their products in color against a black and white background: Nuprin, with its yellow pills; Calvin Klein, with a colored perfume bottle; Pepto-Bismol, with its pink liquid; and—in print—Procter & Gamble, with its blue and white Sure deodorant. All employed this strategy in an attempt to have their product stand out.

Sources: "Public Drawn to Splash of Color Ads That Make Products Stand Out," *Los Angeles Times,* June 28, 1988, pt. IV, p. 6; Neal Santelmann, "Color That Yells 'Buy Me,'"*Forbes,* May 2, 1988, p. 110.

Exhibit 4–3 **Splash of Color Ads Help Attract Attention to the Product**

CONFIDENCE SHOWS.

Attitude structure The traditional approach to attitude structure considered attitudes as consisting of three components: cognitive, affective, and behavioral.[16] A brief description of each of these and some implications of each to marketing follow.

The **cognitive component** would consist of the consumer's knowledge and beliefs about the brand or product, free of emotions. Advertising strategies targeted at attitude formation through the cognitive component focus on the creation of beliefs about a product or brand (United is the friendly airline; Hertz is number one in auto rentals). Attitude change strategies would focus on changing beliefs (*Rolling Stone* magazine is not just a rock news magazine).

The evaluative or **affective component** refers to feelings about the product or brand. These feelings may be good or bad, pleasant or unpleasant. Consumers may show positive *affect* toward a brand ("I really like Pepsi") or negative affect ("I think the Yugo is not a good car"). Liking a product is generally thought to precede purchase.

As the action component, the **behavioral component** refers to the disposition to behave in a certain way toward the product or brand—or the readiness to respond. In consumer research the behavioral component is measured as a tendency to buy, or purchase intention. Advertisements are often designed to attempt to get the consumer in a state of mind to make a purchase (for example, "Buy now" ads).

Attitude models assume that the three components just discussed tend to be consistent with one another. For example, to have a favorable attitude toward a product is to suggest that beliefs about this product are positive, that one feels good about it, and that he or she is likely to behave in a manner consistent with his or her beliefs and feelings. Some researchers suggest that attitudes are formed through an *information integration* process in which these beliefs are combined to form an overall evaluation.[17] One approach to studying attitudes is the use of **multiattribute models.**

Promotional Perspective 4–4

Subliminal Perception—Fact or Fiction?

One of the most interesting and controversial topic areas in all of advertising is that of subliminal advertising. Rooted in psychoanalytic theory, subliminal advertising supposedly influences consumer behaviors by subconsciously altering perceptions or attitudes toward products without the knowledge—or consent—of the consumer.

The concept of subliminal advertising was introduced in 1957 when a marketing research group reported that they were able to increase the sales of popcorn and Coke by subliminally flashing "Eat popcorn" and "Drink Coca-Cola" across the screen during a movie in New Jersey. Since that time numerous books and research studies have been published regarding the existence and effectiveness of this advertising form. In 1982 Timothy Moore, publishing in the *Journal of Marketing,* reviewed the vast literature on subliminal perception. He concluded that

> while subliminal perception is a bona fide phenomenon, the effects obtained are subtle and obtaining them typically requires a carefully structured context. Subliminal stimuli are usually so weak that the recipient is not just unaware of the stimulus but is also oblivious to the fact that he/she is being stimulated. . . . These factors pose serious difficulties for any marketing application. . . .
>
> The point is simply that subliminal directives have not been shown to have the power ascribed to them by advocates of subliminal advertising. In general, the literature on subliminal

perception shows that the most clearly documented effects are obtained only in highly contrived and artificial situations. These effects, when present, are brief and of small magnitude. . . . These processes have no apparent relevance to the goals of advertising. [P. 46]

In 1988, after additional research in this area, Moore concluded that "there continues to be no evidence that subliminal messages can influence motivation or complex behavior." In addition to Moore's conclusions, a review of the literature by Joel Saegert and a study by Jack Haberstroh further discount this strategy. In the latter study, Haberstroh asked advertising agency executives if they had ever deliberately used subliminal advertising; 96 percent said no, 94 percent said they never supervised the use of implants, and 91 percent denied knowing anyone who had ever used this technique. Thus, it seems few people think subliminal advertising works and even fewer claim to use it.

Sources: Jack Haberstroh, "Can't Ignore Subliminal Ad Charges," *Advertising Age,* September 17, 1984, pp. 3, 42–44; Timothy Moore, "Subliminal Advertising: What You See Is What You Get," *Journal of Marketing* 46, no. 2 (Spring 1982), pp. 38–47; idem, "The Case against Subliminal Manipulation," *Psychology and Marketing* 5, no. 4 (Winter 1988), pp. 297–316; Joel Saegert, "Why Marketing Should Quit Giving Subliminal Advertising the Benefit of the Doubt," *Psychology and Marketing* 4, pp. 107–120.

In a multiattribute model, consumers are thought to have a number of beliefs about products' and/or brands' characteristics and performance on certain attributes and attach different levels of importance to these beliefs in determining overall evaluation. Using this approach, an attitude toward a particular brand could be represented as

$$A_B = \sum_{i=1}^{n} B_i \times E_i$$

where

A_B = attitude toward a brand
B_i = beliefs about the brand's performance on attribute i
E_i = importance attached to attribute i
n = number of attributes considered

For example, a consumer may have beliefs (B_i) about various brands of toothpaste on certain attributes. One brand may be perceived as having flouride and thus preventing cavities, tasting good, and helping control tartar buildup. Another brand may not be perceived as being good on these attributes, but consumers may believe that it freshens breath and whitens teeth.

To predict attitudes it is necessary to know just how much importance or value consumers attach to each of these attributes. For example, parents may prefer the cavity fighters for their children—leading to a more favorable attitude toward the first brand. Teenagers may prefer fresh breath and whitening ability and thus prefer the second.

Figure 4–15 Listerine Attempts to Influence Consumers' Attitudes by Adding a New Attribute for Consideration

The value of multiattribute models is that they allow marketers to understand and diagnose the underlying structure or reasons for consumers' attitudes better. By understanding the foundation of these attitudes, the marketer is better able to develop communications strategies for formulating, changing, or reinforcing them. For example, several attitude change strategies have been suggested, including

1. Changing an existing belief about a brand
2. Changing consumers' perceptions of the importance or value of an attribute
3. Adding a new attribute that was not previously considered
4. Changing the beliefs regarding a competing brand

Figure 4–15 demonstrates how Listerine has attempted to influence consumers' attitudes by showing how the product can be useful in helping prevent gingivitis. If successful, this ad will get consumers to consider a new attribute in evaluating and forming attitudes toward brands of mouthwash. The example in Promotional Perspective 4–5 demonstrates two additional strategies designed to alter attitudes.

Problems and Contributions of the Cognitive Orientation As noted earlier in this chapter, the cognitive orientation has evolved as the most popular approach for studying consumer behavior. While not all consumer behaviors are thought to be characterized by reasoning, information utilization, and problem solving, for the most part, the higher-level-processing approach has been used to explain many purchase deci-

Promotional Perspective 4—5

Changing Attitudes Toward Fuel Consumption

In 1981 the United States faced a fuel shortage. As a result gasoline stations were open for limited hours, efforts to lower consumption were promoted, and long lines of automobiles would form with drivers queuing up to wait for the gasoline stations to open so that they might purchase fuel. The strategies pursued by the automobile manufacturers in an attempt to create favorable attitudes toward their cars differed, as shown in the ads for Cadillac and Honda (see Exhibits 4—5A and 4—5B). While both were attempting to create favorable attitudes that would result in the desired behavior (sales) of their cars, the foreign companies emphasized the belief component of the model, whereas the U.S. manufacturers emphasized the evaluative component. Honda stressed miles per gallon (mpg) and promoted the fact that their cars would receive higher mpg figures than their U.S. counterparts. Realizing that the U.S. autos could not compete on this attribute, and

that an attempt to change this belief would be ineffective (and deceptive!), the U.S. auto advertisers attempted to change attitudes by emphasizing the importance of range—or the distance one could drive on a single tank of gas. Certainly gasoline lines were aversive to consumers, and if the automobile was able to help them avoid this undesirable consequence, attitudes toward the vehicle would be more positive.

Thus, two alternative strategies were employed to attempt to create and/or change consumers' attitudes—one by altering beliefs; the other by altering the importance attached to evaluating these beliefs. This example shows that both beliefs and evaluations are important in the formation and changing of attitudes and that advertisers may emphasize either or both in their campaign strategies.

Exhibit 4—5A   **This Cadillac Ad Stresses Range**

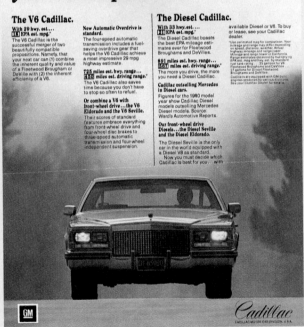

Exhibit 4—5B   **This Honda Civic Ad Stresses MPG**

sions. As a result this orientation now seems to constitute the "main stream" of research in consumer behavior and has served as the basis for a variety of models explaining the effects of advertising. In the next chapter we will discuss some of these models, but first let us examine a cognitive view of how consumers make purchase decisions.

Figure 4–16   **Stages in the Purchase Decision Process**

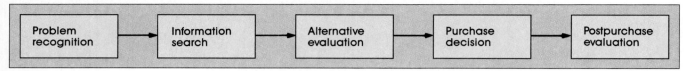

The Consumer Purchase Decision Process

While it is useful to examine the various concepts and how they influence buyer behavior, promotional planners must also understand the process that underlies the actual act of making a purchase. The consumer's purchase decision process is generally viewed as consisting of sequential steps or stages that the buyer passes through in making a purchase decision. This process consists of the five stages shown in Figure 4–16. A brief description of each stage follows.

Problem Recognition

Problem recognition, the first step in the process, occurs when there is a perceived *difference* between a person's ideal state of affairs and the actual situation. This difference may result from something as simple as a consumer's being out of stock of a product, to a more complex problem such as a consumer's perception that his or her clothing is not "in" or as desirable as he or she would like it to be. Advertisements may create problem recognition by instilling a belief that the existing state is not satisfactory. In some cases advertising is designed to help consumers recognize when they have a problem. For example, Figure 4–17 shows an example of an ad attempting to generate problem recognition by showing consumers how they can tell when they have clogged fuel injectors.

Sometimes marketers have trouble getting consumers to recognize or acknowledge that they have a problem. For example, one of the main reasons that consumers have been reluctant to purchase home computers is that most fail to see the problem or need that will be solved by owning one. In an example of one attempt to activate problem recognition, home computer manufacturers have stressed the benefits of having a computer for children to improve their skills. Certainly a problem would exist if your children were to fall behind their peers as a result of not having a computer!

Information Search

Once a consumer has recognized that a problem exists, he or she will begin to search for the information necessary to solve this problem. The initial search will consist of an attempt to scan memory to recall past experiences and knowledge regarding products or brands that may serve as potential solutions. This information retrieval is referred to as **internal search** and would involve the perceptual process and recall of beliefs and prior attitudes. Should the result of the internal search not be sufficient to solve the problem, the consumer will engage in **external search.** External sources of information include personal sources such as friends or relatives; commercial sources such as advertising, salespersons, or point-of-purchase displays; public sources including mass media articles and programs; and actually handling, examining, or testing the product. The determination as to which sources will be used is a function of the importance of the decision to be made. For example, the selection of a movie to see on a Friday night might entail talking to a friend or reviewing the movie guide in the daily newspaper. On the other hand, a more complex purchase—such as a stereo or new car—might entail the use of all the sources available. A review of *Road & Truck, Motortrend,* or *Consumer Reports,* discussions with family members and friends, and

Figure 4–17   **This Champion Ad Helps Encourage Problem Recognition**

Figure 4–18   **An Advertisement May Serve as an External Source of Product Information (see below)**

Figure 4-19   An Ad Stressing Objective Evaluative Criteria

test driving cars might all take place in an attempt to acquire information. At this point in the purchase decision the information-providing aspects of an ad such as the one shown in Figure 4–18 are extremely important.

Alternative Evaluation

One of the possible outcomes of the search stage is the derivation of a number of options for consideration. The brands or products considered as potential alternatives for solving the problem are referred to as the **evoked set.** The attributes used to determine which brands will constitute the evoked set are referred to as **evaluative criteria.** These attributes can be both objective—gas mileage, cost, and the like—and subjective—image, prestige, and so on—as is evidenced by the appeals utilized in the auto ads shown in Figures 4–19 and 4–20.

One of the keys to developing effective promotional strategies is to determine which attributes are most relevant to the consumer and will be used as evaluative criteria in the selection process. Marketers will also attempt to make a particular attribute *salient* or important in the consumer's alternative evaluation process through advertising. For example, Seven-Up made the absence of caffeine an important attribute for many soft drink consumers and forced its competitors also to develop caffeine-free sodas.

Purchase Decision

Having evaluated the various brands in the evoked set, the consumer may develop a *predisposition* or *intention* to buy. This decision will match purchase motives and evaluative criteria with attributes of brands in the evoked set and involves the processes of learning and attitude formation. As noted in our discussion of attitudes, purchase intentions may be formed, predisposing the consumer to a specific product or brand that

Figure 4—20   An Ad Stressing Subjective Evaluative Criteria

he or she intends to purchase. The purchase decision process may have occurred prior to the actual purchase act—that is, prior to ever leaving the home—or in other instances may take place less deliberately and may be more likely to be influenced at the point of purchase. You should be able to see at this point the different roles that the various promotional elements will assume. For example, shelf displays, point-of-purchase materials, and on-product coupons or premiums may be an important supplement to the advertising program at this stage.

Postpurchase Evaluation

The consumer decision process does not end once the product has been purchased. Information acquired from use of the product or brand will serve as feedback for future purchases. Think back a moment to the discussion of learning and attitudes. What we have learned about a product and the attitudes we form toward the same will be used in future decisions with favorable outcomes or consequences leading to retention in the evoked set, whereas unfavorable outcomes may result in elimination. Advertisers must continue to be concerned with this stage of the decision process, and must develop strategies beyond those of merely providing a good product or service. Follow-up letters designed to reinforce the consumer's decision, educational programs that provide realistic product expectations, and other forms of postpurchase promotions are frequently used to increase the likelihood of customer satisfaction.

Variations of Consumer Decision Making

The stages just presented serve as the foundation for consumer decision making. This does not mean, however, that the consumer will always engage in all of the stages presented, or in the sequence presented. As shown in Table 4—2, three variations are

Table 4–2   **Types of Problem-Solving Decisions**

Routine response behavior. For many products the decision process will consist of little more than problem recognition and a quick internal search. The consumer will spend little or no effort in the external search and/or product evaluation stages. This is particularly true when the purchase is habitual and involves frequently purchased products of low unit value. For example, think about your own decision-making process for milk, soda, or school supplies. How much time do you actually spend searching for alternative brands, evaluating alternatives, and so on? Marketers of products characterized by routine response behaviors should attempt to get and/or maintain their products in the consumers' evoked set and attempt to avoid anything that may result in their being removed from the products under consideration.

Limited problem solving. A somewhat more complicated process may occur when the consumer is only somewhat aware of the brands available and/or the criteria important in the selection process. A moderate amount of search and evaluation of criteria is likely to take place in such a situation. Think about your last purchase of clothing, a small appliance, or even the selection of a restaurant for a nice Saturday night dinner date. While you may not have become involved in a major decision process, you may have spent more time than usual in discussing alternatives, evaluating the prices and service, or considering the overall atmosphere of various places. When limited problem solving occurs, marketers will want to make information available to consumers through advertising or other forms of communication.

Extended problem solving. Along the same continuum, consider a situation in which you were about to invest a great deal of time and money in a purchase decision. For example, consider a purchase decision process for a stereo, automobile, or new home or in selecting a college to attend (assuming you had a choice!). You probably spent a great deal of time searching for information by talking to friends, reading catalogs, and/or exploring other forms of information available to you. The criteria used in making an alternative evaluation were more carefully considered, and the process was probably more time-consuming and involving. In these cases, you engaged in extensive problem solving. As with limited problem solving, marketers of products characterized by extended problem solving will want to provide a lot of information to consumers to assist them in their purchase decisions.

possible, including extended problem solving, limited problem solving, and routine response.[18]

The preceding discussion of the consumer decision-making process presents a very general view of the stages one may go through in selecting a product or brand. In fact, the procedure may vary depending on a number of factors, including the time available to make the decision, the perceived risk involved, and the consumer's level of involvement in the product. For example, one of the factors that will determine the level of problem solving to be employed will be the consumer's *involvement* with the product or brand. In Chapter 5 we will discuss the meaning of involvement, the differences between low- and high-involvement decision making, and the implications of each for designing advertising and marketing strategies.

Environmental Influences on Consumer Behavior

To this point we have discussed (1) a number of factors that must be considered in understanding the consumer's decision processes and (2) the different theoretical approaches for studying consumer behaviors. It is important to note at this point that the consumer does not operate in isolation. A number of external factors have been identified as having an influence on the purchase decision. Figure 4–21 portrays external factors that may influence the consumer's decision-making process. The remainder of this chapter will be devoted to examining some of these factors.

Culture

The need to understand the impact that culture will have on the decision-making process of consumers becomes increasingly important as marketers expand their interna-

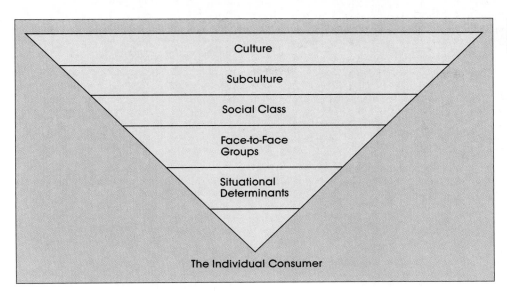

Figure 4–21 **External Influences on Consumer Behaviors**

tional efforts. At the same time, it is no less important that they understand the culture of their own countries and how it influences consumer behaviors.

Culture refers to the unique patterns of behavior and social relations that characterize a society and distinguish it from others. It refers to the norms, beliefs, and customs that are learned from society and that constitute its values. It is these values that, in turn, influence consumers' behavior. Because each culture has certain traditional values that differentiate it from others, it is necessary for the marketer to understand how these values might impact both the consumers' decision process as well as the marketing program.

Likewise, the marketer must be aware of changes that might be taking place in a particular culture and the implications these changes might have on the promotional program. For example, the American culture itself continues to be going through a number of changes, many of which will have direct implications for advertising. Marketing researchers are continually monitoring these changes and the impact that each will have for their products or services. In addition, these changes will have direct implications for advertising, as shown in Table 4–3.

While culture exerts a demonstrable influence on the consumer, the application of cultural values in an advertising context is not easily implemented. You must realize that advertisers must adapt promotional programs to these values rather than attempt to change them to meet their own objectives, as cultural values are deep-rooted and change very slowly. While advertising may contribute to cultural change over a long period of time, these changes are not likely to occur in the short run. Thus, the marketer must continually remain abreast of his or her market and attempt to adapt advertising and promotional strategies accordingly.

Subcultures

Within a given culture, one may find smaller segments that share distinguishing patterns of behavior. These groups are referred to as **subcultures** and may be defined by age, geography, race, religious, and/or ethnic differences. In the American culture, a number of subcultures have been identified.

Racial Subcultures Two major racial subcultures of interest to marketers in the United States are blacks and Orientals. Marketers have already recognized the importance of these segments as target markets. Products targeted to blacks (see Figure 4–22), black-oriented media (such as magazines, radio stations, and newspapers), and agencies specializing in advertising to this subculture already exist and are likely to

Table 4–3   Changes in the American Lifestyle and Advertising Implications

Lifestyle Change	Advertising Implications
An increased focus on "time control"	Emphasis on time-saving benefits of products and services
The origination of "component lifestyles" in which previous patterns of demographics and lifestyles become meaningless	More emphasis on individualism; less social group identification; more self-expression
"Convergence" in sex roles in which behaviors previously associated with one sex are now assumed by both	"Unisex" appeals; emphasis on convenience for women; more information needs by men
"Bifurcation of products"; that is, an increasing difference between high-priced goods and low-priced ones	The establishment of two distinct market segments; variations in appeals for each segment; variations in evaluating criteria
"Rebirth of the family"; an increased emphasis on family values and structure, public institutions	Changing perceptions of product values; changing roles in the decision-making process
"A new kind of conservatism"; the new generation will be politically conservative yet socially liberal	More pressure to "fit in," to dress appropriately, and to "belong" informally
A culture of convenience	Increased use of mail-order and other forms of direct marketing; more home shopping through television.

Source: "31 Major Trends Shaping the Future of American Business," *The Public Pulse* (Roper Organization) 2, no. 1 (January 1987).

increase in number. At the same time, the Oriental subculture is also continuing to increase in size. Orientals have their own media in many cities and constitute the target for numerous products and services, one of which is shown in Figure 4–23.

Figure 4–22   An Example of an Advertisement Targeted to Blacks

Figure 4–23   One of Many Products and Services Targeted to Orientals

Figure 4–24   **Some of the Magazines Targeted to the Hispanic Subculture**

Ethnic Subcultures   The United States has often been referred to as a "melting pot," meaning that people from all over the world have settled here and now live, work, and play together. Polish, Puerto Rican, Jewish, and Mexican-Americans (Hispanics) are just a few of the many ethnic groups existing in the United States today. Groups made up of persons from the same origin (race, religion, or nationality) who share a common heritage or environment are referred to as **ethnic subcultures.** As we discussed in Chapter 2, Hispanics represent one of the fastest-growing and increasingly important subcultures for marketing consideration. Like the black subculture, Hispanics have their own products, media, and advertising agencies, and as shown in Figure 4–24, a number of media are directly targeted to them.

Age Subcultures   In Chapter 2 we also discussed some of the implications of the aging of the U.S. population and noted the increase in marketing efforts targeted to the elderly. Along with this segment, a second frequently targeted age subculture is the young (mostly teenagers). Both groups have distinct values, interests, and patterns of behavior that distinguish them from the rest of the U.S. population. As such, they each have needs that marketers must address.

Like the elderly, teenagers have been targeted as an important market segment, owing in large part to their estimated spending power of over $70 billion.[19] Cosmetics companies such as Noxell, Maybelline, and Revlon and clothing companies such as Levi Strauss, Benetton, and Calvin Klein are just a few of the many companies targeting this group. The origination of MTV, which is primarily a teenage medium, is further evidence of these efforts, as are myriad magazines targeted to this group such as *Sassy, Just Seventeen*, and *Attitude*.

Geographic Subcultures   Differences in values, interests, and behaviors may also be demonstrated in different geographic locations throughout the country. The various values and lifestyles of these groups will likewise lead to differences in consumption behavior. In his book *Nine American Lifestyles,* Arnold Mitchell contends that the United States is really a grouping of nine different regions, and some of the differences between lifestyles of people in these areas are of significant importance to marketers.[20] The Roper Organization also recognizes nine geographic segments and regularly publishes information about their lifestyles and behaviors (see Figure 4–25).

Table 4−4   **Two Recent Views of the American Status Structure**

The Gilbert−Kahl New Synthesis Class Structure:[a] A situations model from political theory and sociological analysis	The Coleman−Rainwater Social Standing Class Hierarchy:[b] A reputational, behavioral view in the community study tradition

Upper Americans
    The Capitalist Class (1%)— Their investment decisions shape the national economy; income mostly from assets, earned/inherited; prestige university connections
    Upper Middle Class (14%)— Upper managers, professionals, medium businessmen; college educated; family income ideally runs nearly twice the national average
Middle Americans
    Middle Class (33%)— Middle-level white-collar, top-level blue-collar; education past high school typical; income somewhat above the national average
    Working Class (32%)— Middle-level blue-collar; lower-level white-collar; income runs slightly below the national average; education is also slightly below
Marginal and Lower Americans
    The Working Poor (11−12%)— Below mainstream America in living standard, but above the poverty line; low-paid service workers, operatives; some high school education
    The Underclass (8−9%)— Depend primarily on welfare system for sustenance; living standard below poverty line; not regularly employed; lack schooling
	Upper Americans
	    Upper-Upper (0.3%)— The "capital S society" world of inherited wealth, aristocratic names
	    Lower-Upper (1.2%)— The newer social elite, drawn from current professional, corporate leadership
	    Upper-Middle (12.5%)— The rest of college graduate managers and professionals; lifestyle centers on private clubs, causes, and the arts
	Middle Americans
	    Middle Class (32%)— Average-pay white-collar workers and their blue-collar friends; live on "the better side of town," try to "do the proper things"
	    Working Class (38%)— Average-pay blue-collar workers; lead "working class lifestyle" whatever the income, school background, and job
	Lower Americans
	    "A lower group of people but not the lowest" (9%)— Working, not on welfare; living standard is just above poverty; behavior judged "crude," "trashy"
	    "Real Lower-Lower" (7%)— On welfare, visibly poverty-stricken, usually out of work (or have "the dirtiest jobs"); "bums," "common criminals"

[a]Abstracted by Coleman from Dennis Gilbert and Joseph A. Kahl, "The American Class Structure: A Synthesis," chapter 11 in *The American Class Structure: A New Synthesis* (Homewood, Ill.: Dorsey Press, 1982).
[b]This condensation of the Coleman-Rainwater view is drawn from chapters 8, 9, and 10 of Richard P. Coleman and Lee P. Rainwater, with Kent A. McClelland, *Social Standing in America: New Dimensions of Class* (New York: Basic Books, 1978).
Source: Richard P. Coleman, "The Continuing Significance of Social Class to Marketing," *Journal of Consumer Research* 10, no. 3 (December 1983), pp. 265−80.

Social Class

Virtually all societies exhibit social stratification (even though the socialist and communist countries may claim that they do not) in which people are classified by others as having more power and prestige. This position of an individual or family on a social scale based on criteria valuable to society is referred to in the United States as **social class** and is of great importance to the marketer. While a number of methods for determining social class exist (see Table 4−4) in U.S. society, occupation, education, and source of income are typically used to classify people into three class rankings— upper, middle, and lower (working). Each stratum is considered as having its own characteristics, values, and consumer behaviors. The symbols used in advertising, the media strategies developed, and the promotional programs employed by marketers reflect the values, lifestyles, norms, and family roles of each social stratum. The Rolex ad shown in Figure 4−26 demonstrates a product that has been targeted to the upper social classes, with an attempt to incorporate some of the characteristics of this stratum into the copy and illustration.

Face-to-Face Groups

Think about the last time you attended a party. As you thought about dressing for the party, you probably asked yourself (or someone else) what others who were going to be there would be wearing. As a result, your selection of attire may have been influenced by those likely to be present. This simple example reflects one form of impact that groups may exert on your behavior. The rest of this section will detail others and demonstrate the importance of understanding group influences.

Types of Groups   A *group* has been defined as "two or more individuals who share a set of norms, values, or beliefs and have certain implicitly or explicitly defined relationships to one another such that their behavior is interdependent."[21] Groups are one

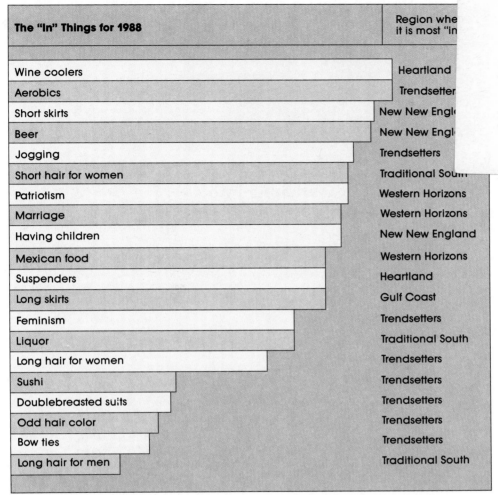

The "In" Things for 1988	Region whe it is most "in
Wine coolers	Heartland
Aerobics	Trendsetter
Short skirts	New New Engl
Beer	New New Engl
Jogging	Trendsetters
Short hair for women	Traditional Sou
Patriotism	Western Horizons
Marriage	Western Horizons
Having children	New New England
Mexican food	Western Horizons
Suspenders	Heartland
Long skirts	Gulf Coast
Feminism	Trendsetters
Liquor	Traditional South
Long hair for women	Trendsetters
Sushi	Trendsetters
Doublebreasted suits	Trendsetters
Odd hair color	Trendsetters
Bow ties	Trendsetters
Long hair for men	Traditional South

Note: USA's 9 nations: New New England—the New England area; Heartland—the Midwest; Atlantic Expanse—the Middle Atlantic states; New South—the Atlantic Coast from Virginia to Florida; Traditional South—Kentucky to Mississippi, west to Missouri; Gulf Coast—Louisiana, Texas, Oklahoma; Made in the USA—the Great Lakes states; Western Horizons—Alaska, the Dakotas south to Nebraska and west to Nevada; Multicultures—California, the Southwest to Texas.
Source: The 9 Nations of USA Weekend (Roper Organization) 1, no. 3 (1987).

of the primary factors influencing learning and socialization, and group situations constitute many of our purchase decisions. **Reference groups**—"a group whose presumed perspectives or values are being used by an individual as the basis for his or her judgments, opinions, and actions"—are used by consumers as a guide to specific behaviors, even though they might not be present at the time.[22] In the party example provided earlier, your peers—while not present at the time—provided a standard of dress that you referred to in your clothing selection. Likewise, your college classmates, family, coworkers, or even a group to which we might aspire might serve as a referent, and your consumption patterns will typically conform to the expectations of these groups.

Marketers utilize reference group influences in developing advertisements and promotional strategies. The ads shown in Figures 4–27 and 4–28 reflect examples of the use of **aspirational reference groups** (groups to which one might like to belong) and **disassociative groups** (groups to which we do not wish to belong or use as referents), respectively.

Family Decision Making—An Example of Group Influences   While the discussion to this point has focused on the individual consumer and the influences that

High-goal players. High-spirited ponies. High-style adventure. It's the United States Polo Association's Rolex Gold Cup.

A herald of the renaissance of American polo, The Cup has become one of the U.S.P.A.'s most highly regarded events.

Last year, more contenders galloped for The Gold than any other tournament in its class.

Sixteen teams and sixty-four players charged, jostled, swirled and swung their way through fifteen grueling matches.

They thundered over the turf of the Palm Beach Polo and Country Club, rotating six hundred thorough-bred horses in the course of the thirteen-day contest.

A competition aficionados consider one of the most prestigious, its renown has attracted the finest players from across the United States and as many as a dozen different nations.

The Rolex Gold Cup has also become a symbol of supreme sportsmanship, one whose reward is of a higher order—the pure honor of win-

The Rolex Gold Cup: Galloping into polo's new golden age.

ning, the true glory of victory.

It has added new lustre to a game so ancient, its history is lost in legend. Tamerlane is said to have been its patriarch. Darius's Persian cavalry, we're told, played it. It was the national sport of 16th-century India, Egypt, China and Japan. The British rediscovered and named it in 1857.

The linking of polo and Rolex is uniquely appropriate. Both sponsor and sport personify rugged grace. Each is an arbiter of the art of timing.

ROLEX

Datejust Oyster Perpetual Chronometer in stainless steel and 18kt gold with Jubilee bracelet.
Write for brochure. Rolex Watch U.S.A., Inc., Dept. 000, Rolex Building, 665 Fifth Avenue, New York, New York 10022-5383.
© 1986 Rolex Watch U.S.A., Inc.

Datejust, Oyster Perpetual, Jubilee are trademarks.

groups may have on his or her behavior, in some instances the group may be involved more directly than just as a referent. In the family group the family members may serve as referents to each other, or they may actually be involved in the purchase decision process itself—acting as an individual buying unit. As shown in Table 4–5, a variety of roles may be assumed in the family decision-making process, with each having implications for marketers.[23]

The implications of family decision making for advertising are many. First, the advertiser must determine who is responsible for the various roles in the decision-

Table 4–5 **Roles in the Family Decision-Making Process**

The initiator. The person responsible for initiating the purchase decision process; for example, the mother who determines that she needs a new car.

The information provider. The individual responsible for gathering information to be used in making the decision; the teenage "car buff" who knows where to find product information in specific magazines or collects it from dealers; and so on.

The influencer. The person who exerts influence as to what criteria will be used in the selection process. All members of the family may be involved. The wife may have her criteria, whereas others may each have their own input.

The decision maker(s). That person(s) who actually makes the decision. In our example, it may be the wife alone or in combination with another family member.

The purchasing agent. That individual who performs the physical act of making the purchase. In the case of an auto, both the husband and wife may decide to pick a car together and sign the purchase agreement.

The consumer. The actual user of the product. In the case of a family car, all family members are consumers. If a private auto, only the wife might be the consumer.

Figure 4—27   **Reference Groups May Be Those to Which We Aspire**

making process so that messages might be targeted at that person or persons. These roles will also dictate media strategies, as the appropriate magazine, newspaper, or television or radio stations must be used. Second, an understanding of the decision-making process and the use of information by individual family members are critical to the design of messages and choice of promotional program elements. In sum, an overall understanding of how the decision process works and the role that each family member plays is necessary for the development of an effective promotional program.

Situational Determinants

The final external factor is that of the purchase and usage situation. The specific situation in which consumers are to use the product or brand will directly affect their perceptions, preferences, and purchasing behaviors.[24] Three types of **situational determinants** may have an effect, including the specific *usage* situation, the *purchase* situation, and the *communications* situation. Usage refers to the situations in which the product will be used. For example, purchases made for private consumption may be thought of differently than those in which the purchase will be obvious to the public. The purchase situation more directly involves the environment operating at the time of the purchase. Time constraints, store environments, and other factors may all have an impact. The last of these—the conditions in which an advertising exposure occurs (in a car listening to the radio, with friends, etc.)—may be of the most relevance to the development of promotional strategies because the impact on the consumer will vary according to the particular situation. For example, the ability for a commercial to

Figure 4—28 **Reference Groups May Also Be Those to Which We Do Not Aspire**

be attended to may be greater when it is heard alone while driving in a car than it would in the presence of friends, at work, etc., where a number of distractions may be present, all competing for the listener's attention. If advertisers can isolate a particular period of time in which the listener is more likely to be attentive—for example driving time—they will be more likely to have the undivided attention of the listener.

In sum, situational determinants may either enhance or detract from the potential success of a message. To the degree that advertisers can assess situational influences that may be operating, they will increase the likelihood of successfully communicating with their target audiences.

Summary of External Factors

As shown in this section, a number of external factors may be influencing the consumer's purchase decision. To develop an effective promotional program, the marketer must be aware of these factors and the impact they bear. Plans may need to be developed to reach specific groups, and the values, norms, and lifestyles of each segment need to be incorporated to achieve the maximum impact.

Summary

The purpose of this chapter is to introduce you to the field of consumer behavior and its relevance to promotional strategies. The analysis of consumer behaviors takes place as a part of the situation analysis as the marketer attempts to better understand the purchase decision processes and factors which influence them.

We began our discussion with an overview of the three major orientations of psychology that have made major contributions to our understanding of consumer behavior, discussing the differences in perspectives and the various applications and implications of each for advertising and promotion. The psychoanalytic orientation approaches behavior by considering deeply rooted, subconscious motives, stressing primarily biological needs, and considering satisfaction as a reduction of tension created by conflicts between components of the personality. Purchase behaviors are thought to be based on sexual or self-destructive motives. Marketing implications would include the presentation of sexual advertisements, the use of symbols—particularly those relating to sex or death—and associating deep-seated motivations with product and/or brand purchases. The major weakness of this approach is the lack of reliability and validity of the research conducted in the marketing domain.

The second orientation, reinforcement theory, considers the basis of behavior to be drives, and views learning as occurring through the reinforcement of specific responses. Implications for marketing include the utilization of advertisements as cues, associating products with desirable situations, and the use of shaping techniques as well as others discussed in the chapter. The major criticism of this approach is the seemingly oversimplified perspective of human behavior.

Finally, cognitive theorists (including cognitive learning theorists) consider humans to be adaptive problem solvers and processors of information. The basis of motivations is considered to be a striving for consistency among elements of acquired information. Implications for advertising and promotion include the necessity to provide information content in ads, the development of strategies designed to affect attitude formation and change, and the need to understand the consumer as a problem solver and decision maker, constantly adapting to his or her environment.

While the three orientations discussed focus on internal views of consumer behaviors, it was noted that external factors may also impact the purchase decision. These external factors—culture, subculture, social class, group processes, and situational determinants—were discussed, as were the implications of each.

Key Terms

Consumer behavior
Psychoanalytic theory
Id
Superego
Ego
Ego defenses
Motivation research
Reinforcement theory
Behaviorism
Stimulus-response orientation
Classical conditioning
Unconditioned stimulus
Unconditioned response
Conditioned stimulus
Conditioned response
Operant conditioning
Instrumental conditioning
Drive

Cues
Generalization
Discrimination
Unique selling propositions
Mnemonics
Response
Reinforcement
Schedules of reinforcement
Shaping
Cognitive theory
Perception
Selective perception
Selective exposure
Selective attention
Selective comprehension
Selective retention
Attitudes
Cognitive component

Affective component
Behavioral component
Multiattribute models
Internal search
External search
Evoked set
Evaluative criteria
Culture

Subcultures
Ethnic subcultures
Social class
Reference groups
Aspirational reference groups
Disassociative groups
Situational determinants

Discussion Questions

1. Why is it important for advertisers to have some understanding of consumer behavior? What are some of the aspects of consumer behavior advertisers need to understand?
2. Discuss how psychoanalytic theory can be applied to marketing and advertising. Find three ads that you feel may be applying psychoanalytic theory techniques and explain why.
3. Michelob beer has been running an advertising campaign based on the theme "The night belongs to Michelob." The ads depict young men and women enjoying the exciting nightlife of the city. Evaluate this campaign from a classical conditioning theory perspective.
4. Discuss how promotional managers can use the principle of operant conditioning in the design of promotional strategies.
5. Discuss how stimulus generalization and discrimination can be used in marketing and advertising. Give an example of each.
6. Discuss how shaping procedures can be applied to assist a company in the introduction of a new brand of cereal.
7. Describe how cognitive learning theory differs from the reinforcement theory approach. For what type of products do you think a cognitive learning approach is likely? Why?
8. What problems does the selective perception process create for advertisers? How might they overcome some of these problems?
9. How might an advertising executive take advantage of consumers by using unethical methods such as subliminal advertising or by appealing to subconscious methods?
10. It has been suggested that attitudes constitute one of the most important concepts in all of consumer psychology. Discuss the importance and value of understanding consumer attitudes to promotional managers.

Notes

1. Morton Deutsch and Robert M. Krauss, *Theories in Social Psychology* (New York: Basic Books, 1965).
2. Jagdish N. Sheth, "The Role of Motivation Research in Consumer Psychology" (Faculty Working Paper, University of Illinois, Champaign, Ill., 1974).
3. Bill Abrams, "Charles of the Ritz Discovers What Women Want," *The Wall Street Journal,* August 20, 1981, p. 29.
4. Ernest Dichter, *Getting Motivated* (New York: Pergamon Press, 1979).
5. I. P. Pavlov, *The Work of the Digestive Glands,* 2nd ed., trans. W. N. Thompson (London, Griffin, 1910).
6. Gerald J. Gorn, "The Effects of Music in Advertising on Choice: A Classical Conditioning Approach," *Journal of Marketing* 46 (Winter 1982), pp. 94–101.
7. A. H. Maslow, "'Higher' and 'Lower' Needs," *Journal of Psychology* 25 (1948), pp. 433–436.

8. Brian C. Deslauries and Peter B. Everett, "The Effects of Intermittent and Continuous Token Reinforcement on Bus Ridership," *Journal of Applied Psychology* 62 (August 1977), pp. 369–75.

9. Michael L. Rothschild and William C. Gaidis, "Behavioral Learning Theory: Its Relevance to Marketing and Promotions," *Journal of Marketing Research* 45, no. 2 (Spring 1981), pp. 70–78.

10. William J. McGuire, "Some Internal Psychological Factors Influencing Consumer Behavior," *Journal of Consumer Research* 2, no. 4 (March 1976), pp. 302–19.

11. David E. Rumelhart, *Introduction to Human Information Processing* (New York: John Wiley & Sons, 1977).

12. Rom J. Markin, Jr., *Consumer Behavior: A Cognitive Orientation* (New York: Macmillan, 1974), p. 239.

13. Gilbert Harrell, *Consumer Behavior* (New York: Harcourt Brace Jovanovich, 1986), p. 66.

14. Raymond A. Bauer and Stephen A. Greyser, *Advertising in America: The Consumer View* (Boston: Harvard Business School, 1968).

15. Gordon W. Allport, "Attitudes," in *Handbook of Social Psychology,* ed. C. M. Murchison (Winchester, Mass.: Clark University Press, 1935), p. 810.

16. D. Krech, R. S. Crutchfield, and E. L. Ballachey, *Individual in Society: A Textbook of Social Psychology* (New York: McGraw-Hill, 1962).

17. Joel B. Cohen, Paul W. Minniard, and Peter R. Dickson, "Information Integration: An Information Processing Perspective," in *Advances in Consumer Research* 7, ed. Jerry C. Olson (Ann Arbor: Association for Consumer Research, 1980), pp. 161–70.

18. John A. Howard and Jagdish N. Sheth, *The Theory of Consumer Behavior* (New York: Wiley, 1969).

19. "Teenagers Are Often the Bread Buyers," *Marketing News* (February 13, 1987), p. 5.

20. Arnold Mitchell, *Nine American Lifestyles: Who We Are and Where We Are Going* (New York: Macmillan, 1983).

21. Lyman E. Ostlund, *Role Theory and Group Dynamics in Consumer Behavior: Theoretical Sources,* ed. Scott Ward and Thomas S. Robertson (Englewood Cliffs, N.J.: Prentice-Hall, 1973), pp. 230–75.

22. James Stafford and Benton Cocanougher, "Reference Group Theory," in *Perspective in Consumer Behavior,* ed. H. H. Kassarjian and T. S. Robertson (Glenview, Ill.: Scott, Foresman, 1981), pp. 329–343.

23. Jagdish N. Sheth, "A Theory of Family Buying Decisions," in *Models of Buying Behavior,* ed. Jagdish N. Sheth (New York: Harper & Row, 1974), pp. 17–33.

24. Russell Belk, "Situational Variables and Consumer Behavior," *Journal of Consumer Research* 2 (December 1975), pp. 157–164.

The Communications Process

CHAPTER OBJECTIVES

1. To examine the basic elements of the communications process and the role of communications in marketing

2. To examine various models of the communications process

3. To analyze the response processes of receivers of marketing

communications, including alternative response hierarchies and their implications for promotional planning and strategy

4. To examine the nature of consumers' cognitive processing of marketing communications

How Do Consumers Interpret Advertising?

A great deal of research goes into the determination of how consumers, or potential consumers, will interpret, react, and respond to an advertisement or television commercial. Some of the findings of this research are quite interesting and show how subtle and unpredictable consumers' reactions to advertising can be. Consider some of the findings of these studies:

- A study involving Head & Shoulders shampoo attempted to determine the emotional effects created by the ad. The study had subjects evaluate two Head & Shoulders ads that were identical and used the line: "I have something to tell you"—(obviously, that you have dandruff). However, in one ad the wife was delivering the line, whereas in the other the husband delivered it. The findings showed that the same ad was interpreted differently depending on who delivered the key line. The subjects felt fine when the wife said it, but when the husband delivered the line, he was perceived as judgmental, threatening, and irritating. (Beware guys!)
- Another study demonstrated that consumers are much more likely to forget advertisements if they are not in the market for the product or brand.
- Research also shows that effective communication is very difficult to accomplish, as 20 percent of all print ads were miscomprehended by readers. Television commercials are misunderstood at an even higher rate. The researcher suggests that advertisers keep the message simple and pretest their ads to be sure they are being understood.
- Finally, one study concludes that advertisers should not use faces in advertising because it makes it harder for receivers of the ad to imagine themselves in the ad. Advertisers who want to get consumers involved with their ads should use blurred images or avoid showing a full face, as consumers who can imagine themselves in the ad are more inclined to remember it and develop stronger attitudes toward the product.

The preceding represent but a small sampling of some of the many studies designed to determine how consumers respond to advertising. Researchers are using a variety of techniques such as "warmth monitors" to measure sentiment and irritation levels of ads. Interactive computer programs are being used to answer questions such as whether an ad should use humor or some other emotional appeal or whether another person should be present in the ad. All these studies and techniques are attempting to answer the most critical advertising question of all: "How will consumers respond to my ad?"[1]

Introduction

The basic commonality shared by all elements of promotional mix is that their function is to communicate. An organization's advertising and promotional strategy is implemented through the communications it sends to its current or prospective customers. Thus, it is important that advertising and promotional planners have an understanding of the communications process. As was noted in the introduction, the way consumers interpret, react, and respond to advertising can often be a very subtle and complex process. Creating an effective advertising and promotional campaign is far more complicated than just choosing a product feature or attribute to emphasize. Marketers must understand how their messages will be perceived and interpreted by consumers and how these reactions will shape their responses toward the product or service. The purpose of this chapter is to review the fundamentals of communications and to examine various perspectives regarding how consumers respond to promotional messages. Of course, our ultimate goal is to demonstrate how an understanding of the communications process can be of value in planning, implementing, and evaluating the promotional program.

The Nature of Communication

Communication has been variously defined as "the passing of information," "the exchange of ideas," or as the process of establishing a commonness or oneness of thought between a sender and a receiver.[2] These definitions suggest that for communications to occur there must be some common thinking between two parties and that this information must be passed on from one person to another (or from one group to another). As you will see in this chapter, the ability to establish this commonality in

Figure 5–1   A Model of the Communications Process

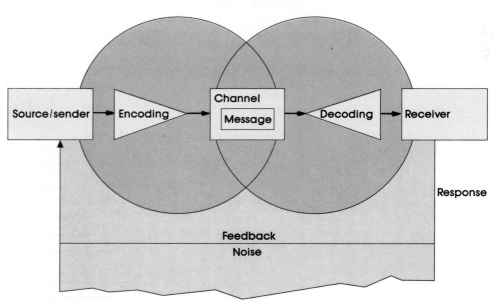

Fields of Experience

thinking is not always as easy as it might seem to be, as is certainly borne out by the fact that so many attempts to communicate are unsuccessful.

The communications process is often very complex, with success depending on many factors such as the nature of the message, the audience's interpretation of it, and the environment in which it is received. In addition, the receiver's perception of the source and the medium used to transmit the message may also impact the ability to communicate, as will many other factors. Words, pictures, sounds, and colors may have different meanings to different audiences, and people will vary in their perceptions and interpretations of them. For example, the word *soda* takes on different meanings in various parts of the country. If you were on the East Coast or West Coast and asked for a soda, you would receive a soft drink such as a Coke or Pepsi. However, in parts of the Midwest and South, a soft drink is referred to as a "pop." Asking for a soda may result in receiving a glass of pop with ice cream in it, as that is what is meant by a soda in these areas. It is very important that marketers understand the meanings that various words and symbols take on and how this might influence the consumers' interpretation of their products and messages.

A Basic Model of Communications

Over the years a basic model of communications has evolved that represents the various elements of the communications process, as shown in Figure 5–1. Two elements represent the major participants in the communications process—the sender and receiver; another two, the major communications tools—message and channel; and four others, major communications functions and processes—encoding, decoding, response, and feedback. The last element, noise, refers to any extraneous factors in the system that can interfere with the process and work against effective communication. Each of these elements will be examined in more detail.

Source/Encoding

The sender or **source** of a communication is the person or organization who has information to share with another person or group of people. The source may be an individual (for example, a salesperson or hired spokesperson—such as a celebrity—

Figure 5–2   **The Source of This Ad Is the NCR Corporation**

who appears in a company's advertisements) or a nonpersonal entity (such as the corporation or organization itself). The source of the ad shown in Figure 5–2 is the NCR Corporation, as no specific spokesperson or source is shown.

Because the receiver's perceptions of the source will influence the manner in which the communication is received, marketers must be careful to select a communicator that the receiver feels is knowledgeable and trustworthy or with whom he or she can identify or relate in some manner. (Further discussion of how these characteristics will influence the receiver's responses will be provided in Chapter 6.)

The communications process begins when the source selects words, symbols, pictures, and the like, to represent the message that will be delivered to the receiver(s). The process known as **encoding** refers to the putting together of thoughts, ideas, or information into a symbolic form. The sender's goal is to encode the message in such a way so as to ensure that it will be understood by the receiver. This means using words, signs, or symbols that are familiar to and understood by the target audience. For example, many symbols are developing universal meaning such as the familiar circle with a line through it that is used to denote no parking, no smoking, and so forth. Many companies also have highly recognizable universal symbols such as McDonald's golden arches or the Coca-Cola trademark.

Message

The encoding process leads to the development of a **message** that contains the information or meaning the source hopes to convey. The message may be verbal or nonverbal, an oral or written statement, or a symbolic form or sign. Messages must be put into a transmittable form that is appropriate for the channel of communication being used. In advertising this may range from simply writing some words or copy that will be read as a radio message to the expensive production of a television commercial. For many products it is not the actual words contained in the message that determine its communication effectiveness but rather the impression or image that the advertise-

Figure 5–3 **The Image Projected by an Advertisement Often Communicates More Than Words**

ment is able to create. Notice how the Calvin Klein ad shown in Figure 5–3 uses only a picture to deliver its message.

Channel

The **channel** is the method or medium by which the communication travels from the source or sender to the receiver. At the broadest level, channels of communication are of two types, personal and nonpersonal. **Personal channels** of communication are means of direct interpersonal (face-to-face) contact with target individuals or groups. Salespeople serve as personal channels of communication when delivering their sales message to a buyer or potential customer, whereas social channels of communication such as friends, neighbors, associates, coworkers, or family members are also examples. The latter groups or individuals often represent **word-of-mouth communications,** which are often a very powerful and influential source of information for consumers.[3]

Nonpersonal channels of communication are those that carry a message without involving interpersonal contact between sender and receiver. Nonpersonal channels are generally referred to as the **mass media** or mass communications, as the message is sent to many individuals at one time—for example, a television commercial broadcast on a prime-time evening show may be seen by 20 million households in a given evening. Nonpersonal channels of communication consist of two major types, print and broadcast, with several subtypes within each category. Print media include newspapers, magazines, direct mail, and billboards, whereas the broadcast media include radio and television.

Receiver/Decoding

The **receiver** is the person or persons with whom the sender shares thoughts or information. Generally the receivers are the consumers in the audience or market targeted by a company who read, hear, and/or see the marketer's message and decode it. **Decoding** is the process of transforming and interpreting the sender's message back into thought. This process is heavily influenced by the receiver's frame of reference or **field of experience,** which refers to the experiences, perceptions, attitudes, and values that are carried into the communications situation.

For effective communication to take place, it is necessary that the message decoding process of the receiver match the encoding of the sender. Simply put, this means that the receiver understands and correctly interprets what the source is trying to communicate. As can be seen in Figure 5–1, both the source and the receiver have a frame of reference or field of experience that they bring to the communications situation. Effective communication is more likely when there is some **common ground** between the two parties. (This is represented by the overlapping of the two circles representing the fields of experience.) The more knowledgeable the sender is of the receivers, the greater the likelihood of understanding their needs, empathizing with them, and communicating effectively.

While this notion of common ground between sender and receiver may sound very basic, it is often the cause of great difficulty in the advertising communications process. The reason is that marketing and advertising people very often have a very different background and field of experience than the consumers who constitute the mass markets with whom they must communicate. For example, most advertising and marketing people are college educated and work and/or reside in large urban areas such as New York, Chicago, or Los Angeles. However, these advertisers are attempting to develop commercials that will effectively communicate with millions of consumers who have never attended college, who work in blue-collar occupations, and who live in rural areas or small towns. Perhaps a single quote from the executive creative director of a large advertising agency, commenting on how advertising executives become isolated from the cultural mainstream, best describes this problem:

> We pull them in and work them to death. And then they begin moving in sushi circles and lose touch with Velveeta and the people who eat it.[4]

To avoid these problems, advertisers spend millions of dollars every year to research their target markets to understand better the frame of reference of the consumers who receive their messages. In addition, a great deal of time and money is spent pretesting messages to ensure that they are understood by the consumer and decoded in the manner in which the advertiser intended.

Noise

Throughout the communications process, the message is subject to the influence of extraneous factors that can distort or interfere with its reception. This unplanned distortion or interference in the communications process is known as **noise.** Errors or problems that occur in the encoding of the message, distortion in a radio or television signal, or distractions at the point of reception are examples of types of noise that might interfere with the communications process. A simple example of noise would be a situation where you are watching your favorite commercial on television and a problem occurs in the transmission of the signal. This would obviously interfere with your reception, and the impact of the commercial may be lessened.

Noise may also occur because the fields of experience of the sender and receiver have nothing in common. Lack of common ground may result in an improper encoding of the message such as using a sign, symbol, or words that are unfamiliar to the receiver or have different meaning. As noted earlier, the more common ground there is between the sender and the receiver, the less likely that this type of noise will occur.

An interesting example of how noise might affect the communications process is reflected in the debate that occurs every year over the value of advertising on the Super Bowl. Even though an estimated 120 million people tune into the game each year, and a number of good reasons for buying time on this event are offered (see Promotional Perspective 5–1), many advertisers do not feel it is money well spent. Why? Because much of the audience consists of people getting together to watch the big game in groups or "Super Bowl parties." During the commercials audience members may be talking to their friends, discussing the game, or getting something to eat or drink. Thus, the noise level is very high and the potential for effective communication is reduced.

Response/Feedback

The set of reactions the receiver has after seeing, hearing, or reading the message is known as a **response.** The responses of the receiver can range from nonobservable actions such as storing information in memory to taking immediate action such as dialing an 800 number to order a product advertised on television. Marketers are very interested in **feedback,** which is that part of the receiver's response that is communicated back to the sender. Feedback, which may take a variety of forms, closes the loop in the communications flow and provides the sender with a way of monitoring how the intended message is being decoded and received.

For example, in a personal selling situation, customers may pose questions, comments, or objections or indicate their reactions through nonverbal responses such as gestures and frowns.[5] While a salesperson has the advantage of receiving instantaneous feedback through the reactions of the customer, this is generally not the case when mass media are used. Because advertisers are not in direct contact with the customers, they must use other means of determining how their messages have been received. While the ultimate form of feedback occurs through sales, there are often problems in attempting to show a direct relationship between advertising and purchase behavior. Thus, marketers use other methods to obtain feedback, such as customer inquiries, store visits, coupon redemptions, and reply cards. Research-based feedback to analyze readership and recall of ads, message comprehension, attitude change, and other forms of response is also used. With this information the advertiser can analyze reasons for success or failure in the communications process and make corrections and adjustments as needed.

The 5-Ws Model of Communication

Another popular conceptualization of the communications process is the basic model developed by Lasswell a number of years ago.[6] This approach, which is often referred to as the **5-Ws model of communication,** says that a communications model must deal with five basic elements or questions. As can be seen below, each of these questions corresponds to an element in the basic communications model discussed earlier.

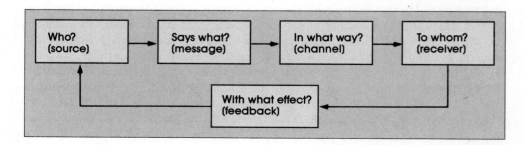

Promotional Perspective **5–1**

Super Spots—Advertising on the Super Bowl

In 1984 the cost of a 30-second commercial on the Super Bowl was $450,000. In 1986 it rose to $550,000, and in 1989 the cost was $675,000. No small piece of change for 30 seconds, right? Well, many advertisers think that it is a great bargain—perhaps the best media time advertisers can buy. So good, in fact, that the 50 or so spots available during the game are often sold out before Thanksgiving—long before anyone knows who will be playing in the game! Why is the Super Bowl considered such a good media buy? Here are just a few of the reasons offered:

1. *The hype.* The Super Bowl is not just a football game; it is an American "event." As one advertiser commented, "I'm surprised we don't send Super Bowl cards and write carols."
2. *The viewers.* Of the top 25 watched shows in history, 11 of them have been Super Bowls.
3. *The interest.* Many advertisers feel that the Super Bowl is one occasion where just as much attention is paid to the commercials as to the program content. Super

Bowl ads receive publicity and are often commented on by the game announcers.
4. *The showcase.* Ever since the Apple Macintosh 1984 commercial, advertisers have used the Super Bowl to show off their creative talents. Each year the commercials get more and more creative. For example, Coca-Cola used the 1989 game to sponsor a segment of the half-time show and run ads for Diet Coke in 3-D. This marked the first time 3-D commercials had ever been run on television.
5. *The "Big Time."* Some advertisers feel that being able to advertise on the Super Bowl is an indication that the company has made the "big leagues," demanding respect from consumers and competitors.

Despite the potential noise problem discussed in the text, the Super Bowl is a popular place to advertise and continues to command premium prices. Our guess is that it will remain that way for some time to come.

Source: "Super Spots," *San Diego Union*, January 31, 1988, D7–D8; Patricia Winters, "Coke Plans 3-D Look at Super Bowl," *Advertising Age*, December 19, 1988, p. 1.

The basis of this model is a **message flow** whereby the communication initiates with the source, is formulated into a message, and is transmitted through a medium or channel to receivers constituting a target audience. The impact or effects of the message are measured in terms of feedback, in which the receiver's reaction to the message is communicated back to the source. However, in the development of a communications plan, the marketer employs a **planning flow** in which this model is approached in reverse; that is, the receiver is the starting point since the success of a promotional program will be affected by the nature of the consumers who receive it. The medium, message, and source are selected based on the characteristics of the receiver or target audience. This process recognizes that promotional planning logically begins with the receivers who make up the firm's target market, as it is this desired audience that should influence decisions as to what is to be said; how, when, and where it is to be said; and who is best suited to say it.

The receivers of the communication are considered to be an uncontrollable variable in that the marketer cannot really control the actions of these persons. Marketers can choose a target audience of potential message recipients and attempt to influence their actions, but actual control of the receiver is beyond their capabilities. However, there are certain factors that the marketer is able to control and change. These controllable variables include the source, message, and channel or media that will be utilized.

Successful communications are accomplished when the marketer is able to select an appropriate source, develop an effective appeal, and then select the media that will best reach the target audience and effectively deliver the message. In Chapter 6 we will examine the various considerations involving the source, message, and channel decisions and see how promotional planners work with these controllable variables to develop communications strategies. However, decisions in these areas must take into consideration the target audience and how it will respond to the promotional message. Thus, in the remainder of this chapter we will examine the receiver in more detail and the process by which consumers respond to advertising and other promotional methods.

Analyzing the Receiver

To communicate effectively with their customers, marketers must have an understanding of who the target audience is, what (if anything) the market knows or feels about the company's product or service, and how the audience needs to be communicated with to influence its decision-making process. In addition, marketers need to know how the market is likely to respond to various sources of communications or different types of messages. Before decisions are made regarding source, message, and channel variables, promotional planners must have an understanding of the potential effects associated with each of these factors. In this section we will focus our attention on the receiver of the marketing communication and examine how the audience is identified and the process it may go through in responding to a promotional message. This information will serve as a foundation for evaluating the controllable communications variable decisions that are covered in the next chapter.

Identifying the Target Audience

The marketing communications process really begins with the identification of the audience that will be the focus of the firm's advertising and promotions efforts. One way of viewing the target audience is to recognize that it may consist of individuals, groups, or a general public or mass audience.

Individual and Group Audiences   The target market may consist of individuals having specific needs and for whom the communication must be specifically tailored. This often requires communication on a person-to-person basis and is generally accomplished through personal selling. Other forms of communication such as advertising may be used to attract the audience's interest and attention to the firm, but the detailed message is carried by a salesperson who can respond to the specific needs of the individual customer. Life insurance, financial services, and real estate are some examples of products and services that are promoted this way.

A second level of audience aggregation is represented by the group. Marketers often must communicate with a group of people who influence or make the purchase decision. For example, organizational purchasing often involves **buying centers** or committees that vary in size and composition. Companies marketing their products and services to industrial users or other organizations must have an understanding of various factors such as who is on the purchase committee, what aspect of the decision each individual influences, and the criteria that each member is using in evaluating a product. Advertising might be directed to each member of the buying center, and multilevel personal selling may be necessary to reach those individuals who influence the decision-making process or actually make the decision. Promotional Perspective 5–2 shows one example of how advertising and promotion might operate when a buying committee or group is involved.

As you may recall from Chapter 4, decision making in the consumer market can also include a group when various family members become involved in the purchase of a product or service such as an automobile, furniture, or the family vacation. Thus, to develop an effective communications program in either of these markets, advertisers need to know who is involved in the decision-making process, what role they play, and how best to reach them.

Mass Audiences   The situation that many advertisers are confronted with involves communicating with large numbers of consumers or mass audiences. Marketers of most consumer products attempt to attract the attention of large numbers of present

Promotional Perspective 5-2

Promoting to a Hospital

IVAC Corporation, one of the leading companies in the U.S. medical products industry, manufactures and sells a number of products including electronic thermometers, vital sign measurement systems, and intravenous (IV) infusion instruments and sets. To market these products to hospitals, IVAC must communicate with a variety of personnel who are involved in the decision-making process, including nurses, hospital pharmacists, purchasing agents, biomedical engineers, and administrators.

Each of these parties plays a different role in the purchase decision for IVAC products. For example, nurses are the actual users of the company's products and must be convinced that they are reliable, easy to use, and time saving. Their opinions and input are important not only because they are users but also because they often serve as strong influencers on the hospital's purchase decision. Pharmacists have the responsibility of preparing the medicines that are delivered through the IVAC systems and are interested in efficient and cost-effective ways to administer the drugs. Thus, they are both *users* and *influencers* in the decision-making process. Purchasing agents and hospital administrators are, of course, concerned with controlling expenses and keeping operating costs down. They serve as *deciders* who have the power to select or approve final suppliers and also as *buyers*

with formal authority for choosing the actual supplier and arranging the terms of purchase.

IVAC's promotional program is designed to reach all these hospital personnel. The company has a highly trained and specialized sales force who call on each of these parties to discuss their specific needs and concerns. The company also uses a variety of advertising appeals to address each group, as is shown in the Exhibits 5-2A through 5-2C.

The first ad is targeted to the nurses who use the IVAC vital signs measurement instrument. This ad appeared in publications read by nurses such as *Nursing Management* and *Nursing 89*. The second ad addresses issues relevant to hospital pharmacists and appears in publications read by this group such as the *American Journal of Hospital Pharmacy*. The third ad deals with costs and operating expenses, factors that concern purchasing agents and hospital administrators. This ad appeared in *Hospital Purchasing News* and *Hospitals*, publications that are targeted to these personnel.

As you can see from these examples, IVAC's promotional program must reach a number of different hospital personnel, each of whom have their own concerns, needs, and input into the decision-making process.

Exhibit 5-2A   IVAC Targets Advertising to the Nurses Who Use Its Products

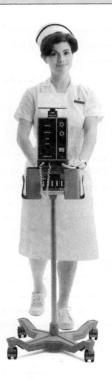

IVAC'S® VITAL·CHECK® Model 4000.
It gives you blood pressure, pulse, temperature and more time for each patient.

That's because the IVAC VITAL•CHECK–Model 4000 Multiple Vital Signs Measurement System takes all the vital signs at once. So you get readings faster than with the manual method.

And that adds up to increased productivity for you and more time for your patients.

Readings are consistent even when the staff varies.
The VITAL•CHECK System provides readings that are reliable. They're consistent from user to user, even when there's a change in shift.

Battery-powered and portable for making the rounds.
The VITAL•CHECK System is designed specifically for

the general floor. Everything is contained to take vital signs with ease and simplicity, and to move quickly from patient to patient.

Built-in versatility for continuous or periodic vital signs monitoring.
The VITAL•CHECK also contains an automatic mode, which monitors vital signs continuously and stores readings in the memory. So you get the readings you need with blood transfusions, vasoconstrictor medications or post-operative recovery without disturbing the patient.

Add it to your TEMP•PLUS Thermometer for a flexible cost-effective system.
Together, the VITAL•CHECK System and the IVAC TEMP•PLUS® Vital Signs

Measurement System–Model 2000 give you the versatility for all your vital signs needs throughout the hospital. In addition, both instruments are backed by IVAC's commitment to quality and service.

So call us today at 1-800-482-IVAC for more information on the VITAL•CHECK System. Then the next time you take vital signs, you could give something back. More of yourself.

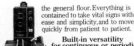

IVAC®
CORPORATION
VITAL SIGNS DIVISION

Bringing vital changes to health care.
10300 Campus Point Drive, San Diego, CA 92121-1579, 800-482-IVAC

Promotional Perspective (concluded)

Exhibit 5—2B　IVAC Promotes Time and Cost Savings to Hospital Pharmacists in This Ad

Savings are in the bag.

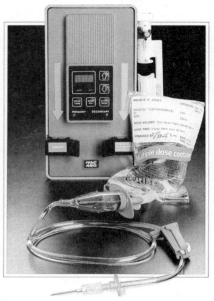

Cutting costs is one way to save. Increasing productivity is another. Increasing the efficiency of therapy a third. Now you can do all of these with the IVAC MultiDose System—Model 460. IV piggybacks with more than one dose can be efficiently prepared and hung. You get welcome savings; your patients receive reliable, accurate and effective therapy.

Save time.
The advantages start in the pharmacy where one container takes the place of four. You purchase fewer containers and spend less time preparing them. You can also pur-

chase medications in pharmacy bulk packages. Still more savings.

Save money.
Mathematical analyses show that a typical 350 bed hospital could save as much as $113,116.00 per year in operating costs alone using the MultiDose System. Over five years that same hospital could realize total dollar savings of more than $539,000.*

Save steps.
Increased efficiency on the floor makes the MultiDose System right for nurses too. For every drug delivered, nurses only spike one secondary drug container per day. Less opportunity for error and contamination. And there is no requirement to return to the infusion at the end of the secondary administration. The MultiDose System automatically

switches to the primary line, at the correct primary rate. Which brings us to a savings beyond measurement: the automatic and quiet transition back to the primary infusion saves your patients' sleep. And we all know the value of that, better care and fewer "sleeper" meds.

A companion to the accessory-compatible Volumetric Infusion Controller—Model 260, the MultiDose System can help you become more efficient and productive. Call us. Or write us, and we'll show you how cost containment and better patient care are in the bag. **IVAC** CORPORATION
1-800-482-IVAC

IVAC introduces the MultiDose System—Model 460

Exhibit 5—2C　IVAC Promotes Time Savings and Reduced Costs to Hospital Administrators and Purchasing Agents

"IVAC set the pace to reduce our operating expenses by nearly $300,000 a year."

Says A. Gary Muller, Administrator of Bay Medical Center in Panama City, Florida.

"By switching from an IVAC disposable-based program (IVSP) to one of IVAC's new acquisition programs (the Installment Purchase Program), we capitalized our equipment and reduced operating expenses by $298,304 a year.

Gary Muller meets with Ron Broadway

"It all happened because with the introduction of DRGs, hospitals have the incentive to be run more like businesses than ever before. And IVAC helped us meet our 8-point plan to control expenses and keep operating costs down."

Timesavings and reduced costs.

Ron Broadway, IVAC's District Manager for Bay Medical Center, completed a clinical needs analysis to identify the right number and type of instruments for each nursing area. Says Broadway, "I quantified the clinical benefits of a house-wide program, and showed significant timesavings for nurses and a potential reduction in IV related complications, patient related costs and length of hospital stay."

Clinical plus financial advice.

IVAC knows the financial aspects as well as the clinical needs of a hospital. In fact, a financial expert works with the sales force to customize acquisition plans to meet individual needs. So hospitals get new technology and standardization of Fluid Delivery Programs on a sound financial basis.

Get all the details on how IVAC helped Gary Muller meet his hospital's 8-point plan to handle DRGs. Call 1-800-482-IVAC and ask for a copy of the Bay Medical Center Case Study.

IVAC... helping hospitals be successful.

Bay Medical Center, Panama City, Florida

A. Gary Muller making his morning run along the white sand dunes of Panama City Beach.

IVAC CORPORATION

or potential customers through mass communications. Mass communications represents a one-way flow of information as the message flows from the marketer to the consumer, whereas feedback concerning the audience's reactions to the message is generally indirect and often difficult to measure.

Communicating with the general public or mass audiences generally requires that the marketer use some form of mass communication such as advertising or publicity. Using television advertising, for example, offers the marketer the opportunity to send a message to millions of consumers at the same time. However, this does not mean that effective communication has taken place, as this may be only one of several hundred messages that the consumer was exposed to that day. There is no guarantee that the information was attended to, processed, comprehended, or stored in memory for later retrieval. Even if the advertising message is processed, it may be misunderstood or misinterpreted by consumers or be of little interest to them. As noted in the opening vignette of this chapter, studies have shown that a significant percentage of both print and television advertising messages are miscomprehended.[7] Unlike the personal or face-to-face communication situation, the marketer has no opportunity to explain or clarify the message to make it more effective when mass communication is being used. Thus, the marketer must enter the communication situation with knowledge of the target audience and how it is likely to react and be influenced by the message. This means that the response process of the receiver must be understood along with its implications for promotional planning and strategy.

The Response Process

Perhaps the most important aspect of developing effective communications programs involves having an understanding of the **response process** the receiver may go through in moving toward a specific behavior (like purchasing a product) and how the promotional efforts of the marketer might influence these responses. In many instances the marketer may have only the objective of creating awareness of the company or brand name, as this may in itself trigger interest in the product. In other situations the marketer may want to convey detailed information so as to change consumers' level of knowledge and attitudes toward the brand and ultimately their behavior.

Traditional Response Hierarchy Models

A number of models have been developed to depict the response process or stages a consumer might pass through in moving from a state of not being aware of a company, product, or brand to actual purchase behavior. Figure 5–4 shows four of the best-known response hierarchy models. We will briefly discuss each of these and their implications.

The AIDA Model   The first of these hierarchical models was developed to represent the stages a salesperson must take a customer through in the personal selling process.[8] This model depicts the buyer as passing through successive stages of attention, interest, desire, and action **(AIDA model).** The salesperson must first get the attention of the customer and then arouse some level of interest in the company's product or service. This may be done by understanding the needs of the customer and showing the attributes or features of the product or service and emphasizing how they translate into benefits for the individual. Strong levels of interest will hopefully create desire by the customer to own or use the product. The action stage in the AIDA model involves getting the customer to make a purchase commitment and closing the sale. To the marketer, this is the most important stage in the selling process, but it can also be the most difficult. Companies train their sales representatives in a variety of closing techniques to help them complete the selling process.

Figure 5—4 **Models of the Response Process**

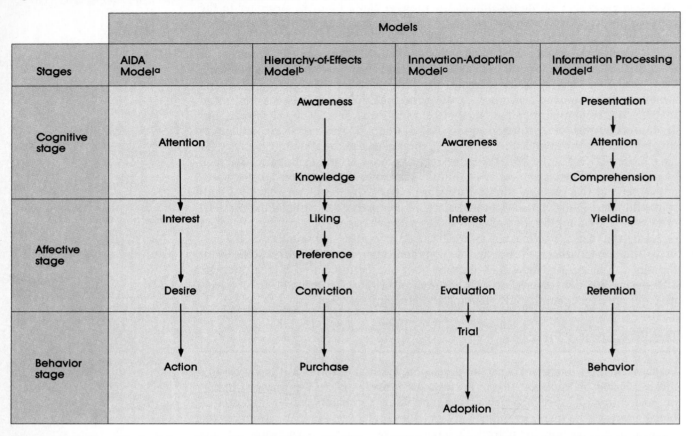

Stages	AIDA Model[a]	Hierarchy-of-Effects Model[b]	Innovation-Adoption Model[c]	Information Processing Model[d]
Cognitive stage	Attention	Awareness → Knowledge	Awareness	Presentation → Attention → Comprehension
Affective stage	Interest → Desire	Liking → Preference → Conviction	Interest → Evaluation	Yielding → Retention
Behavior stage	Action	Purchase	Trial → Adoption	Behavior

Sources: (a) E. K. Strong, *The Psychology of Selling* (New York: McGraw-Hill, 1925), p. 9; (b) Robert J. Lavidge and Gary A. Steiner, "A Model for Predictive Measurements of Advertising Effectiveness," *Journal of Marketing* (October 1961), p. 61; (c) Everett M. Rogers, Diffusion of Innovations (New York: Free Press, 1962), pp. 79–86; (d) William J. McGuire, "An Information Processing Model of Advertising Effectiveness," in *Behavioral and Management Science in Marketing,* ed. Harry L. Davis and Alvin J. Silk (New York: Ronald/Wiley, 1978), pp. 156–80; and Philip Kotler, *Marketing Management,* 5th ed. (Englewood Cliffs, N.J.: Prentice-Hall, 1984), p. 612.

The Hierarchy-of-Effects Model Perhaps the best known of these response hierarchies is the model developed by Robert Lavidge and Gary Steiner as a paradigm for setting and measuring advertising objectives.[9] Their **hierarchy-of-effects model** represents the process by which advertising works and assumes that there is a series of steps a consumer must pass through in sequential order from initial awareness of a product or service to actual purchase. A basic premise of this model is that advertising effects occur over a period of time, rather than being instantaneous. Thus, advertising communication may not lead to immediate behavioral response or action; rather, a series of effects must occur, with fulfillment of each step necessary before movement to the next stage in the hierarchy is possible.

As shown in Figure 5–4, the receiver must first become *aware* of the brand of product or service. Once awareness has occurred, the receiver must be provided with *knowledge* or information about the features, attributes, and so on, of the product. The information and knowledge the consumer acquires may lead to *liking*—a positive feeling or attitude toward the brand. These positive feelings may subsequently lead to *preference* whereby the brand is preferred over alternative brands. *Conviction* occurs when the consumer becomes convinced that he or she should buy the brand and forms a purchase intention. The final step that translates these feelings and convictions into behavior is *purchase*, which is, of course, the ultimate goal sought by the marketer.

As we will see in Chapter 8, the hierarchy-of-effects model has become the foundation for objective setting and measurement of advertising effects in many companies. However, this model has also been criticized, particularly for the assumption that a consumer must pass through all the stages before purchasing a product.[10] Since alternative models will be examined later in this section, we reserve our discussion of these criticisms until that time.

The Innovation-Adoption Model   The **innovation-adoption model** evolved from work in the area of the diffusion of innovations.[11] The innovation-adoption model represents the stages a consumer would pass through in the adoption of an innovation such as a new product. Like the other models, this model contends that potential adopters must be moved through a series of steps including awareness, interest, evaluation, and trial prior to adoption.

In the *awareness* stage, potential adopters become aware that the new product exists. At this stage they know very little else about it and may not be motivated to learn any more unless they feel the innovation is of interest to them. The marketer's next challenge is to move potential adopters to the *interest* stage, where they will learn more about the product such as its features, benefits, advantages, price, and availability. In the *evaluation* stage consumers will decide whether the new product meets their needs and satisfies specific purchase criteria and goals. The best way to evaluate a new product is through actual usage or trial, so that performance can be experienced and judged. Marketers often encourage trial through utilizing sales promotion techniques such as demonstrations, providing sampling programs, or making small sizes of a product available. After *trial*, consumers may move to the *adoption* stage if they decide to purchase the product or continue to use it. However, the outcome of trial may be rejection if the consumer decides against purchasing the new product or brand or using it in the future.

An excellent application of this model can be seen in the strategy used by Apple in the introduction of the Macintosh personal computer a few years ago. The stunning "1984" ad (which was discussed in Chapter 3, Figure 3–9) was used to introduce the "computer for the rest of us" on the Super Bowl in January 1984. This ad attracted a considerable amount of media attention also and helped create awareness and interest in the Macintosh. Subsequently, print ads providing extensive detail and information for evaluation appeared in a number of magazines (see Figure 5–5). In addition to the advertising campaign, a sales promotional program was subsequently implemented offering potential adopters the opportunity to "test drive" the Macintosh at a local dealership by taking it home overnight or for a weekend. As you can see, awareness, interest, evaluation, and trial were all created through a well-planned and -coordinated promotional program. The result was a very successful product introduction that resulted in the adoption of the Macintosh by millions of consumers and businesses.

The Information-Processing Model   The final of the four hierarchy models shown in Figure 5–4 is the **information-processing model** of advertising effects developed by William McGuire.[12] McGuire contends that the appropriate view of a receiver in a persuasive communication situation like advertising is as an *information processor* or *problem solver*. He suggests that the series of steps a receiver goes through in being persuaded constitute a **response hierarchy** consisting of a series of stages including (1) message presentation or exposure, (2) attention, (3) comprehension, (4) message acceptance or yielding, (5) retention, and (6) behavior. The stages of this model are similar to those of the hierarchy-of-effects sequence, as *attention* and *comprehension* are similar to *awareness* and *knowledge*, whereas *acceptance* or *yielding* is synonymous with *liking*. McGuire's model does include a stage not found in the other models: retention. The *retention* stage refers to the receiver's ability to retain that portion of the comprehended information that is accepted as valid or relevant. The retention stage is important since most promotional campaigns are not designed to motivate consumers to take immediate action but rather are providing information that will be used when a purchase decision is being made in some subsequent time period.

Each stage of the response hierarchy can be considered as a dependent variable that must be attained and that may serve as an objective of the communications pro-

Figure 5–5   Apple Used Detailed and Informative Ads to Explain the Features of the Macintosh

Source: William J. McGuire, "An Information Processing Model of Advertising Effectiveness," in *Behavioral and Management Science in Marketing*, ed. H. L. Davis and A. J. Silk (New York: Ronald/Wiley, 1978), p. 161.

Figure 5–6   Methods of Obtaining Feedback in the Response Hierarchy

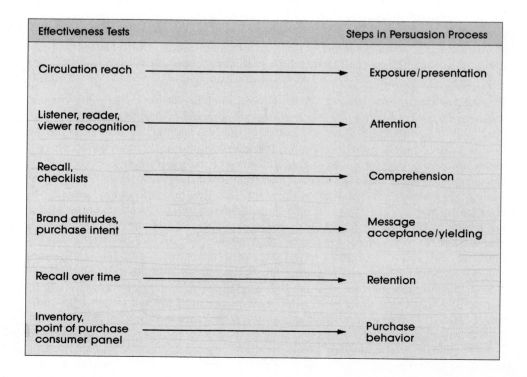

Effectiveness Tests	Steps in Persuasion Process
Circulation reach	Exposure/presentation
Listener, reader, viewer recognition	Attention
Recall, checklists	Comprehension
Brand attitudes, purchase intent	Message acceptance/yielding
Recall over time	Retention
Inventory, point of purchase consumer panel	Purchase behavior

cess. As shown in Figure 5–6, each of these stages is measurable and thus capable of providing the advertiser with feedback regarding the effectiveness of various strategies designed to move the consumer to purchase. As such, the model may serve as an effective framework for planning and evaluating the effects of a promotional campaign.

Implications of the Traditional Hierarchy Models

The hierarchy models of communication response that we have just examined are useful to promotional planners from several perspectives. First, they delineate the series of steps or stages that potential purchasers must be taken through in order to move them from a state where they are completely unaware of the existence of a product or service to the point where they are ready to purchase it. Second, potential buyers may be at different stages in the hierarchy, and thus the advertiser will face different sets of communication problems. For example, the marketer of an innovation, such as a compact disc player or camcorder, may need to devote considerable effort to making people aware of the product, explaining how it works and what its benefits are, and convincing consumers that they should consider purchasing it (Figure 5–7). On the other hand, marketers of a mature brand that enjoys a high level of customer loyalty may only need to engage in supportive or *reminder* advertising to reinforce positive perceptions and maintain the awareness level for the brand.

The hierarchy models can also be useful as "intermediate" measures of communication effectiveness. The marketer needs to know where audience members are with respect to the various stages of the response hierarchy. For example, research may reveal that one target segment has low awareness of the advertiser's brand, whereas another is aware of the brand and its various attributes but has a low level of liking or brand preference.

In the first segment the communications task would involve increasing the awareness level for the brand. The number of ads might be increased to gain exposure, or a

Figure 5–7   **Advertising for a New Product Explains Features and Benefits to Get Consumers' Interest**

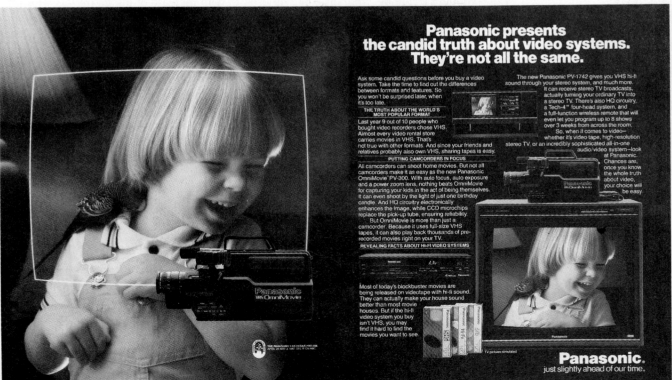

Figure 5—8   American Uses Its On-Time-Arrival Record to Create Positive Perceptions and Attitudes

The On-time Machine. It's more than an airplane. It's an entire airline. American Airlines. The airline with the best on-time arrival record of the five largest domestic airlines.*

At American Airlines, we know how important being on time is to you. And we're dedicated to making sure you get where you're going on time. Every time. That's why we spend more than $760 million a year on an exhaustive maintenance program to help reduce mechanical delays. Why we monitor our schedules daily to make sure the schedules we publish are accurate. And why we're constantly looking for new ways to provide even more dependable service.

That's the kind of commitment you've come to expect from American. And that's the kind of commitment it takes to be number one. Time and time again.

*Based upon Department of Transportation data and the cumulative percentage of nonstop domestic flights arriving within 15 minutes of schedule for all reported airports for the five largest airlines in terms of revenue passenger miles, September 1987 through February 1988.

American Airlines
Something special in the air.

product sampling program could be used to help increase brand awareness. However, in the second segment, where awareness is already high but liking and preference are low, the advertiser would have to determine the reason for the negative feelings and then attempt to address this problem in future advertising. For example, an airline may find itself in a position where business fliers are aware of the fact that they offer service between various cities but avoid flying the airline because they think that the flights rarely end up being on time. The airline would have to work to correct this perception, perhaps by using advertising stressing the company's on-time-arrival record (of course, assuming that it *is* good!).

In situations where research or other evidence reveals that a company is perceived favorably on a particular attribute or performance criterion, the company may want to take advantage of this in its advertising. For example, Figure 5—8 shows how American Airlines used the fact that it had the best on-time-arrival record as a basis for its advertising.

Evaluating Traditional Response Hierarchy Models

As can be seen in Figure 5—4, the four models presented all view the response process as consisting of movement through a sequence of three basic stages. The cognitive stage represents what the receiver knows or perceives about the particular product or brand. This state includes awareness that the brand exists and knowledge, information, or comprehension about specific aspects of it such as its attributes, characteristics, or benefits. The affective stage refers to the receiver's feeling or affect level (liking or disliking) for the particular brand. This stage also includes stronger levels of affect such as desire, preference, or conviction. The behavioral stage refers to the consumer's action toward the brand such as trial, purchase, or adoption.

Figure 5—9 **Alternative Response Hierarchies: The Three-Orders Model of Information Processing**

		Topical Involvement	
		High	*Low*
Perceived Product Differentiation	High	(Learning model) Cognitive *learn* ↓ Affective *feel* ↓ Conative *do*	(Low involvement model) Cognitive *learn* ↓ Conative *do* ↓ Affective *feel*
	Low	(Dissonance attribution model) Conative *do* ↓ Affective *feel* ↓ Cognitive *learn*	

Source: F. Stewart DeBruicker, "An Appraisal of Low-Involvement Consumer Information Processing," in *Attitude Research Plays for High Stakes,* ed. John C. Maloney and Bernard Silverman (Chicago: American Marketing Association, 1979), pp. 112–132.

These models are also similar in that they assume a similar ordering of these three stages whereby cognitive development precedes affective reactions, which in turn precede behavior. One might assume from the ordering shown in these models that consumers become aware and knowledgeable of a brand, develop interest and feelings toward it, form a desire or preference, and then make a purchase. While this is a logical progression that may be accurate in many situations, the response sequence may not always operate this way.

Over the past two decades, there has been considerable research in the marketing, social psychology, and communications areas that has resulted in a questioning of the traditional notion of a cognitive → affective → behavioral sequence of response. This has led to the development of several possible configurations of the response hierarchy. Michael Ray has developed a three-orders model of information processing that identifies three alternative orderings of these three stages based on perceived product differentiation and product involvement level.[13] (See Figure 5.9.) We will now turn our attention to examining these three models and their implications.

Alternative Response Hierarchies

The Standard Learning Hierarchy In many purchase situations it is reasonable to assume that the consumer will go through the response process in the sequence depicted by the communications models just reviewed. Ray has termed this a **standard learning model,** which consists of a "learn → feel → do" sequence or hierarchy. Information and knowledge acquired or *learned* about the various brands become the basis for the development of affect or *feelings* that guide what the consumer will *do* (e.g., actual trial or purchase). Under this hierarchy the consumer is viewed as an active participant in the communications process who actively seeks or gathers information through "active learning."

Ray suggests that the standard learning hierarchy is likely to occur when the consumer is highly involved in the purchase process and when there is a high amount of differentiation among competing brands. High-involvement purchase decisions such as those for industrial products and services and consumer durables such as personal computers, video cassette recorders, and automobiles are examples of areas where a standard learning hierarchy response process would be likely. Advertisements for products and services in these areas are usually very detailed and informative and attempt to provide the consumer with a great deal of information about the brand. Promotional Perspective 5–3 discusses how Peugeot appealed to this type of response hierarchy a few years ago with an educational ad campaign that featured extensive product information.

The Dissonance/Attribution Hierarchy A second response hierarchy proposed by Ray involves situations where behavior occurs first, followed by attitude change and then learning. This dissonance/attributional, or "do → feel → learn," may occur in situations where consumers must make a choice between two alternatives that are similar in quality but are complex and may have hidden or unknown attributes. The consumer may purchase the product based on the recommendation of some nonmedia source and may then attempt to support or rationalize the decision by developing a positive attitude toward the brand and perhaps even developing negative feelings toward the rejected alternative(s). This might be done as a way of reducing **postpurchase dissonance,** which refers to a state of psychological tension or anxiety the consumer may experience resulting from doubt or concern over the purchase. This dissonance reduction process involves **selective learning** whereby the consumer seeks information that supports the choice made and avoids information that fails to bolster the wisdom of the decision.

According to this model, marketers need to recognize that in some situations attitudes develop *after* purchase, as does learning from the mass media. Ray suggests that in these situations the main effect of the mass media is not so much in promoting original choice behavior and attitude change but rather in reducing dissonance by reinforcing the wisdom of the purchase or providing supportive information.

As with the standard learning model, this response hierarchy is likely to occur in situations where the consumer is involved in the purchase situation, and it is particularly relevant for postpurchase situations. For example, a consumer may purchase a life insurance policy through the recommendation of a general agent and then develop a favorable attitude toward the company and/or pay close attention to advertisements in order to reduce dissonance.

Perhaps the major problem with this view of the response hierarchy is accepting the notion of the mass media's not having any effect on the consumer's initial purchase decision. However, it should be noted that the rationale for this hierarchy is not that the mass media have no effect on the original choice decision but rather that the major impact of the mass media occurs *after* the purchase has been made. Thus, marketing communications planners must be aware of the need for advertising and promotions efforts both to encourage brand selection and to reinforce choices and ensure that a purchase pattern will continue into the future.

The Low-Involvement Hierarchy Perhaps the most intriguing of the three response hierarchies proposed by Ray is what has been termed the **low-involvement hierarchy** in which the receiver is viewed as passing from cognition to behavior to attitude change. This "learn → do → feel" sequence is thought to characterize situations of low consumer involvement in the purchase process. Ray suggests that this hierarchy tends to occur when involvement in the purchase decision is low, when there are minimal differences between brand alternatives, and when mass media advertising, particularly through broadcast media, is important.

Promotional Perspective 5—3

Treating Car Buyers as Intelligent Paid Off for Peugeot

Peugeot, S. A., the large French automaker, began marketing its cars in the United States in 1958. Although Peugeot's sales in the United States are small compared with those of its competitors', the company is the ninth largest automobile manufacturer in the world. In 1981, Peugeot Motors of America, Inc. (PMA), the company's U.S. subsidiary, took a major step toward increasing its share of the U.S. market with the introduction of the Peugeot 505 model and a new marketing and advertising campaign. The objectives of the campaign were to create interest in the 505 and draw potential buyers into dealer showrooms by providing consumers with detailed information that positioned the Peugeot 505 as a quality car that was comfortable, reliable, and well built.

The new advertising campaign consisted primarily of print ads and one 60-second television spot. Since Peugeot sales in the United States were not large, the company could not afford an extensive television ad campaign. Most of the ad budget was spent in print media with much of the money spent on ads in 10 major newspapers. All the ads featured long copy emphasizing quality and value. Suspension, steering, seats, and shock absorbers were dealt with at length in the ads, some of which included as much as a 2,305 word copy block. (See Exhibit 5–3A.)

Every national ad included a mail-in coupon that could be used to request additional information about the car, whereas regional ads substituted a list of local dealers in place of the coupon. The coupon was a very good response device for finding qualified buyers who might be giving serious consideration to the Peugeot. The television ad, which was filmed at Peugeot's automatic testing track in France, emphasized durability with attention to body welds and shock absorbers.

The results of Peugeot's new campaign were very successful. The company's 1981 U.S. sales were 16,725 in 1981 versus 12,807 in 1980, a 30% increase, despite the sluggish auto market that year. Peugeot continued the heavy information-oriented ad campaign and sales reached 20,000 in 1984—their best sales year ever in the United States. However, over the past few years Peugeot has run into increasing competition in the U.S. market, not only from other European car manufacturers but from Japanese and American companies who are targeting the

Exhibit 5—3A   **Ads for the Peugeot 505S Provided Consumers with Extensive and Detailed Information**

Promotional Perspective (concluded)

luxury sports sedan segment. Peugeot's U.S. sales slumped to only 9110 cars in 1988, which has led the company to launch a $50 million advertising and marketing campaign based primarily on the fact that its 405 model was European Car of the Year (Exhibit 5–3B). The new ads position the 405 as an affordable European sports sedan.

Sources: "Peugeot Marketing Campaign Treats Car Buyers as Intelligent; Sales Soar," *Marketing News* 15, no. 13 (December 25, 1981), pp. 1, 2; "Riding the Crest of the Raves," *Forbes,* October 17, 1988, pp. 140–41.

Exhibit 5–3B   Ads for the Peugeot 405 Position It as an Affordable High Performance European Sports Sedan

The notion of a low-involvement hierarchy is based in large part on the work of Herbert Krugman's theory explaining the effects of television advertising.[14] Krugman was interested in determining why television advertising was able to produce a strong effect on brand awareness and recall yet little change in consumers' attitudes toward the product. He hypothesized that television was basically a low-involvement medium and that the viewer's perceptual defenses are reduced or even absent when watching commercials. In a low-involvement situation the consumer does not compare the message with his or her previously acquired beliefs, needs, or past experiences as the individual might in a high-involvement situation. The commercial results in subtle changes in the consumer's knowledge structure, particularly with repeated exposure to the message. This change in the consumer's knowledge does not result in attitude change but is related to the learning of something about the advertised brand such as the ability to recall a brand name, ad theme, or slogan. According to Krugman, when the consumer enters a purchase situation, this information may actually be sufficient to trigger a purchase. The consumer will then form an attitude toward the purchased brand as a result of his or her experience with it. Thus, in the low-involvement situation the response sequence is as follows:

Message exposure under low involvement →
Shift in cognitive structure → Purchase →
Positive or negative experience → Attitude formation

Under the low-involvement hierarchy the consumer is viewed as engaging in *passive learning* and *random information catching* rather than active information seeking. Thus, if the consumer is passive and disinterested, the advertiser must recognize that he or she is less likely to give attention to actual message content but may focus more on nonmessage elements such as music, characters, symbols, and slogans or jingles. The advertiser might capitalize on this situation by developing advertising that uses a catchy slogan or jingle that is stored in the consumer's mind without any active cognitive processing and that becomes salient when he or she enters the actual purchase situation.

Examples of low-involvement advertising appeals are prevalent in much of the advertising we see for frequently purchased consumer products: Ads for Charmin toilet paper show Mr. Whipple imploring buyers, "Please, don't squeeze the Charmin!"; Bic disposable lighters are promoted by the theme "Flick my Bic"; Wrigley's Doublemint gum invites consumers to "Double your pleasure"; Bounty paper towels claim to be the "Quicker picker upper." Each of these appeals is designed to assist the consumer in making an association without really attempting to formulate an attitude or create attitude change.

Another popular creative strategy used by advertisers of low-involvement products is what advertising analyst Harry McMahan calls VIP, or visual image personality.[15] Advertisers often use symbols such as the Pillsbury Doughboy, Charlie the Tuna, Morris the Cat, Tony the Tiger, Speedy Alka-Selter, and Mr. Clean to develop visual images that will lead to identification and retention of advertisements. The campaign featuring Morris the Cat has helped make 9-Lives a leading brand of cat food, and the feline has become so popular that he even has his own fan club (Figure 5–10)!

Figure 5–10   Morris the Cat Has Been a Very Effective VIP for 9-Lives Cat Food

Implications of the Alternative Response Models

After reviewing these alternative models of the response process, it should be obvious that the traditional standard learning model may not always be applicable. The notion of a highly involved consumer who engages in active information processing and learning and acts on the basis of a well-formed attitude may in fact be inappropriate in many situations. In some situations consumers may make a purchase decision based on a general awareness resulting from repetitive exposure to advertising, and attitude development will occur after the purchase, if at all.

From a promotional planning perspective, what is important is that the marketer be able to examine the communications situation for its product or service and determine which type of response hierarchy is most likely to occur. This may be determined by analyzing involvement and product/service differentiation as well as consumers' use of various information sources and their levels of experience with the product or service. Once the manager has determined which response model is most likely to be in operation, the communications program can be designed so as to influence the response process in favor of the advertiser.

The FCB Planning Model   An interesting approach to analyzing the communications situation marketers may be facing comes from the work of Richard Vaughn of the Foote, Cone & Belding advertising agency. Vaughn and his associates developed an advertising planning model by building on traditional response theories such as the hierarchy-of-effects model and its variants and research on high and low involvement.[16] They also added the dimension of thinking versus feeling processing at each involvement level by bringing in theories regarding brain specialization. The right/left brain theory suggests that the left side of the brain is more capable of rational, cognitive thinking, whereas the right side is more visual and emotional and engages more in the affective or feeling functions. Their model, which became known as the "FCB grid," delineates four primary advertising planning strategies—informative, affective, habitual, and satisfaction—along with the most appropriate variant of the alternative response hierarchies (Figure 5–11).

Figure 5–11 **The Foote, Cone & Belding Grid**

	THINKING	FEELING
HIGH INVOLVEMENT	1. *INFORMATIVE (THINKER)* CAR–HOUSE–FURNISHINGS– NEW PRODUCTS MODEL: LEARN–FEEL–DO (Economic?) Possible Implications TEST: Recall Diagnostics MEDIA: Long Copy Format Reflective Vehicles CREATIVE: Specific Information Demonstration	2. *AFFECTIVE (FEELER)* JEWELRY–COSMETICS– FASHION APPAREL–MOTORCYCLES MODEL: FEEL–LEARN–DO (Psychological?) Possible Implications TEST: Attitude Change Emotional Arousal MEDIA: Large Space Image Specials CREATIVE: Executional Impact
LOW INVOLVEMENT	3. *HABIT FORMATION (DOER)* FOOD–HOUSEHOLD ITEMS MODEL: DO–LEARN–FEEL (Responsive?) Possible Implications TEST: Sales MEDIA: Small Space Ads 10 Second I.D.'s Radio; POS CREATIVE: Reminder	4. *SELF-SATISFACTION (REACTOR)* CIGARETTES–LIQUOR–CANDY MODEL: DO–FEEL–LEARN (Social?) Possible Implications TEST: Sales MEDIA: Billboards Newspapers POS CREATIVE: Attention

Source: Richard Vaughn, "How Advertising Works: A Planning Model," *Journal of Advertising Research* 20, no. 5 (October 1980), p. 31.

Vaughn suggests that the *informative strategy* is for highly involving products/ services where rational thinking and economic considerations prevail, and the standard learning hierarchy is the appropriate response model. The *affective strategy* is for highly involving and feeling purchases. For these types of products, psychological and emotional motives such as fulfilling self-esteem or enhancing one's ego or self-image would be stressed in the advertising. The ad for Lady Stetson cologne shown in Figure 5–12 appeals to these types of motives.

The *habitual strategy* is for low-involvement and thinking products with such routinized behavior patterns that learning occurs most often after a trial purchase. The response process for these products is consistent with a behavioristic learning-by-doing model (remember our discussion of instrumental conditioning in Chapter 4?). The *self-satisfaction strategy* is for low-involvement/feeling products where appeals to sensory pleasures and social motives would be important. Again, the "do" before "feel" or "learn" hierarchy is seen as operating, since product experience is an important part of the learning process. It should be noted that Vaughn acknowledges that some minimal level of awareness (passive learning) may precede purchase of both types of low-involvement products, although deeper, active learning is not necessary. This suggests that the low-involvement hierarchy discussed above (learn → do → feel) would be consistent with the FCB grid.

The FCB grid provides a useful way for those involved in the advertising planning process, such as creative specialists, to analyze consumer/product relationships and to develop appropriate promotional strategies. Consumer research can be used to determine how consumers perceive products or brands on the involvement and thinking/feeling dimensions.[17] This information can then be used to develop effective creative options such as using rational versus emotional appeals, increasing involvement levels, or even getting consumers to evaluate a think-type product more on the basis of feelings. The ad for Thermador appliances shown in Figure 5–13 is an example of this latter strategy, as it emphasizes psychological and emotional motives such as style, color, and sophistication. Appliances have traditionally been sold on the basis of more rational, functional motives.

Figure 5–12 **Cosmetic Ads Appeal to Psychological Motives**

Cognitive Processing of Communications

The hierarchical response models discussed above were for many years the primary focus of approaches to study the receivers' responses to marketing communications. Attention centered on an attempt to identify relationships between specific controllable variables—such as source and message factors—and outcome or response variables—such as attention, comprehension, attitudes, and purchase intentions. This approach has been criticized on a number of fronts and has been referred to as being "black box" in nature owing to its inability to explain what might be causing or determining these reactions.[18] In response to these concerns, researchers began turning their attention toward an attempt to understand the nature of cognitive processing better. **Cognitive processing** concerns how external information (such as an advertising message) is transformed into meanings or patterns of thought and how these meanings are combined to form judgments.[19] Several approaches and models have been developed to examine the nature of consumers' cognitive processing of advertising messages.

Figure 5–13 A Think-Type Product Is Advertised by Appealing to Feelings

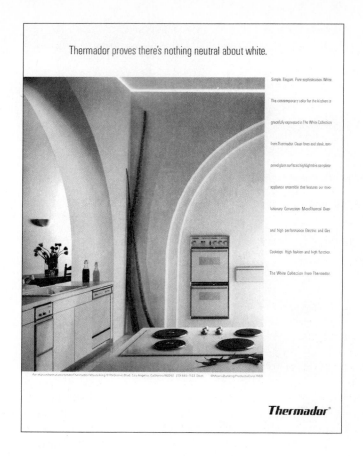

The Cognitive Response Approach

One of the most widely used methods for examining consumers' cognitive processing of advertising messages is through the assessment of their **cognitive responses** or the thoughts that occur to them while reading, viewing, and/or hearing a communication.[20,21] These thoughts are generally measured by having consumers write down or verbally report the thoughts they have in response to a message. The basic assumption is that these thoughts are a reflection of the recipient's cognitive processes or reactions and help shape and determine ultimate acceptance or rejection of the message. The cognitive response approach has been widely used in advertising research, both by academicians and advertising practitioners. The focus of this research has been to determine the types of thought processes or responses evoked by an advertising message and how these responses relate to measures such as attitudes toward the ad, brand attitudes, and purchase intentions. The model shown in Figure 5–14 depicts the three basic categories of cognitive responses researchers have identified and how they might relate to attitudes and intentions. We will briefly discuss each of these three types.

Product/Message Thoughts The first category of thoughts are those directed at the product or service itself and/or the claims being made in the communication. Much of the attention has focused on two particular types of responses—counterarguments and support arguments.

Counterarguments are thoughts that the recipient has that are counter or opposed to the position taken in the message. For example, a consumer may express disbelief or disapproval of a claim made in an ad ("I don't believe that any detergent could get that stain out!"). A **support argument** is a thought that supports or affirms

Figure 5–14   **A Model of Cognitive Response**

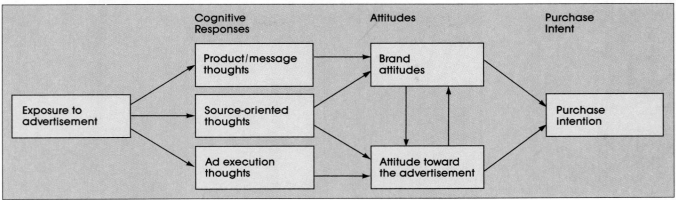

Source: Adapted from J. Lutz, Scott B. MacKenzie, and George E. Belch, "Attitude toward the Ad as a Mediator of Advertising Effectiveness," in *Advances in Consumer Research* X (Ann Arbor: Association for Consumer Research, 1983), p. 532.

the claims being made in the message ("That sounds like a really good product—I think I'll try it").

The likelihood of counterarguing is greater when the message makes claims that oppose the beliefs or perceptions held by the receiver. For example, a consumer viewing a commercial that attacks his or her favorite brand is likely to engage in counterarguing. Counterarguments have been shown to be strongly related to message acceptance, as the more the receiver counterargues, the less likely he or she is to accept the position advocated in the message.[22] Support arguments, on the other hand, are positively related to message acceptance. Thus, it is important for the marketer to develop advertisements or other promotional messages that minimize the likelihood of counterarguing and encourage the generation of support arguments.

Source-Oriented Thoughts   A second category of cognitive responses are those directed at the source of the communication. One of the most important responses in this category is that of **source derogations,** or negative thoughts about the spokesperson or organization making the claims, as it has been determined that such thoughts generally lead to a reduction in message acceptance. If consumers find a particular spokesperson annoying or distrustful, this may result in a lower likelihood of their accepting what it is these sources may have to say.

An example of this occurred a few years ago when Dreyer's ice cream developed an advertising campaign for their new Grand Light product, which centered around the use of spokespersons whose credibility was known to be suspect. The theme of the campaign was "An unbelievable spokesperson for an unbelievable product," which intended to be lighthearted and to acknowledge the dubious character of the spokespersons. However, many consumers became upset when convicted Watergate conspirator John Ehrlichman appeared in one of the commercials. Reactions against the company's use of Ehrlichman were so strong that the ad had to be withdrawn—obviously, a strong indication of the effects of source derogation.

Of course, source-related thoughts are not always negative. Receivers may react favorably to the source and generate favorable thoughts or **source bolsters.** As you would expect, most advertisers attempt to hire spokespersons to whom their target audience will react favorably so as to carry this effect over to the message.

Ad Execution Thoughts   The third category of cognitive responses shown in Figure 5–14 is thoughts the individual has toward the ad itself. Many of the thoughts receivers have when reading or viewing an ad do not directly concern the product and/or message claims per se but rather are affective reactions representing their feelings

Figure 5–15 Many Advertisements Are Using Emotional Appeals

toward the ad. These thoughts may include reactions to ad execution factors such as the creativity of the ad, the quality of the visual effects, colors, and voice tones. Execution-related thoughts can be either favorable or unfavorable and are important because of their effect on attitudes toward the advertisement as well as the brand.

In recent years much attention has been focused on consumers' affective reactions to advertisements—particularly television commercials.[23],[24] **Attitude toward the ad** (A → ad) represents the receivers' feelings of favorability or unfavorability toward the ad itself. Interest in consumers' reactions to the ad reflects the advertisers' acceptance of the fact that affective reactions are an important determinant of advertising effectiveness, as these reactions may be transformed to the brand itself, directly influencing purchase behaviors. For example, one study found that people who enjoy a commercial are two times more likely than those who are neutral toward the ad to be convinced that the brand is the best.[25]

The above discussion suggests that consumers' feelings toward the ad may be just as important as attitudes toward the brand (if not more so) in determining an advertisement's effectiveness.[26] However, the importance of affective reactions and feelings generated by the ad will depend on several factors such as the nature of the advertisement and the type of processing engaged in by the receiver.[27] As you will see in Chapter 6, many advertisers have begun to use emotional ads like the one shown in Figure 5–15 that are designed to evoke feelings and affective reactions, as the basis of their creative strategy. The success of this strategy will depend, in part, on the consumers' involvement with the brand and their likelihood of attending to and processing the message. We will end our analysis of the receiver by briefly examining a model that integrates some of the factors that may account for different types and levels of cognitive processing of a message.

The Elaboration Likelihood Model

Differences in the ways consumers process and respond to persuasive messages have been addressed in the elaboration likelihood model (ELM) developed by Richard Petty and John Cacioppo, shown in Figure 5–16.[28] According to the ELM, there are two basic processes through which persuasion occurs. Under the **central route to persua-**

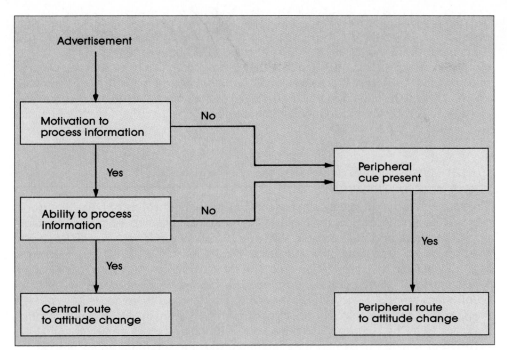

Figure 5–16   **An Abbreviated Version of the Elaboration Likelihood Model**

Source: David A. Aaker and John G. Myers, *Advertising Management,* 3rd ed. (Englewood Cliffs, N.J.: Prentice-Hall, 1987), p. 251.

sion the receiver is viewed as a very active and involved participant in the process whose ability and motivation to process a message are very high. When central processing occurs, the consumer will pay close attention to message content and will carefully scrutinize the communication. A high level of cognitive response should be generated, and the ability of the ad to persuade the receiver will depend primarily on the quality of the argument presented in the appeal rather than on executional factors.

Under the **peripheral route to persuasion** the receiver is viewed as lacking the ability or motivation to process information and is not likely to be engaging in detailed cognitive processing. Rather than thinking about and evaluating the information presented in the message, the receiver will rely on "peripheral cues" that may be incidental to the message content such as an attractive source or other executional factors. For example, in an interesting test of this model it was shown that the effectiveness of a celebrity depends on the receiver's involvement level.[29] When involvement was low, an advertisement with a celebrity endorser had a significant effect on attitudes. When the receiver's involvement level was high, however, the use of a celebrity had no effect on brand attitudes; rather, the *quality* of the arguments used in the ad was more important.

The explanation given for these findings was that a celebrity may serve as a peripheral cue in the low-involvement situation, which allows the receiver to develop favorable attitudes based on his or her feelings toward the source rather than engaging in extensive processing of the message. Under high involvement, however, the consumer will engage in more detailed central processing of the message content. Thus, the quality of the message claims becomes more important than the celebrity status of the endorser.

The ELM suggests that the type of message that will be most effective depends on the particular route to persuasion the consumer follows. Since low involvement may characterize many purchase situations, it should not be surprising that executional elements and affective reactions to ads are receiving more and more attention from advertisers.

As can be seen from our analysis of the receiver, the process consumers go through in responding to marketing communications can be viewed from a number of perspectives. Hopefully, the various approaches considered here will provide you with some insight into the response process of consumers and how they may react to promotional messages. It is important for the promotional planner to learn as much as possible about the target audience and how it might respond to the firm's promotional efforts. This will help the firm's advertising and promotional strategies to become more relevant to consumers and to increase the likelihood of generating favorable audience responses.

Summary

The common factor shared by all elements of the promotional mix is that their function is to communicate. It is important that promotional planners have an understanding of the communications process. This process can be very complex, with successful communication depending on a number of factors including the nature of the message, the audience's interpretation of it, and the environment in which it is received. A basic model of communication was presented showing the key elements of the communications process. For effective communication to occur, the sender must encode a message in a manner that will be decoded by the receiver in the intended manner. Feedback from the receiver helps the sender determine whether proper decoding has occurred or whether noise may have interfered with the communications process.

Promotional planning begins with the receiver or target audience, as marketers must understand how the audience is likely to respond to various sources of communication or types of messages. Various ways of analyzing the receiver for promotional planning purposes have been examined, both with respect to the composition of the target audience for the firm's promotional efforts (i.e., individual, group, or mass audiences) and the response process that the message recipient goes through. Various orderings of the traditional response hierarchy were examined including the standard learning, dissonance, and low-involvement models. The implications of these response models for promotional planning were discussed.

Attention was also given to the receiver's cognitive processing of marketing communications such as advertising. The cognitive response approach examines the thoughts message recipients have and how they shape and determine ultimate acceptance or rejection of a communication. The elaboration likelihood model recognizes two types of message processing or routes to persuasion, central and peripheral. A detailed analysis of the process by which consumers respond to advertising and other forms of promotion helps a firm develop more effective promotional strategies.

Key Terms

Communication	Common ground
Source	Noise
Encoding	Response
Message	Feedback
Channel	5-Ws model of communication
Personal channels	Message flow
Word-of-mouth communications	Planning flow
Nonpersonal channels	Buying center
Mass media	Response process
Receiver	AIDA model
Decoding	Hierarchy-of-effects model
Field of experience	Innovation-adoption model

Information-processing model
Response hierarchy
Cognitive stage
Affective stage
Behavioral stage
Standard learning model
Postpurchase dissonance
Selective learning
Low-involvement hierarchy

Cognitive processing
Cognitive responses
Counterarguments
Support argument
Source derogations
Source bolsters
Attitude toward the ad
Central route to persuasion
Peripheral route to persuasion

Discussion Questions

1. What is necessary for effective communication to occur? Discuss some of the barriers to effective communication in advertising.
2. Why are personal channels of communication often more effective than nonpersonal channels?
3. What is meant by *noise* in the communications process? What can be done to reduce noise in marketing communications?
4. Discuss the various forms feedback might take in the following situations:

   - An office copier salesperson has just made a sales presentation to a potential account.
   - A consumer has just seen a direct-response ad run on late-night television for an exercise machine.
   - Millions of consumers are exposed to an ad for a sports car during a Sunday afternoon football game.

5. Use the 5-Ws model to outline a promotional program for a company attempting to sell a new soft drink to the 18- to 24-year-old market.
6. Explain how the promotional process would differ for a personal computer company promoting its products to each of the following:

   - Individual consumers purchasing a computer for home use
   - A corporation who is considering buying a number of personal computers for use by its employees

7. Explain how the various response models discussed in this chapter would be useful in the following situations:

   - For a company introducing a new innovation such as a compact disc player
   - For a manufacturer of electronic components training new sales representatives
   - For a marketer of a consumer product such as paper towels

8. Discuss how the advertising and promotional implications differ for companies selling high- versus low-involvement products.
9. Discuss some of the ways a company selling a product such as instant coffee might be able to increase consumers' involvement level with its particular brand.
10. Have three friends read a print ad or watch a television commercial and write down their reactions to it. Use the cognitive response model discussed in this chapter to analyze their reactions. How do their responses relate to their overall evaluation of the ad as well as the product or service?
11. Compare the central and peripheral routes to persuasion. Provide examples of an ad that you think would be processed by a central route and one where you think peripheral processing would occur.

Notes

1. "Studying the Academic Studies," *Adweek's Marketing Week,* December 7, 1987, pp. F. K. 30–37.
2. Wilbur Schram, *The Process and Effects of Mass Communication* (Urbana: University of Illinois Press, 1955).
3. Barry L. Bayus, "Word of Mouth: The Indirect Effect of Marketing Efforts," *Journal of Advertising Research,* June–July 1985, pp. 31–39.
4. Quote by Gorden S. Bower in *Fortune,* October 14, 1985, p. 11.
5. Thomas V. Bonoma and Leonard C. Felder, "Nonverbal Communication in Marketing: Toward Communicational Analysis," *Journal of Marketing Research,* May 1977, pp. 169–80.
6. Harold D. Laswell, *Power and Personality* (New York: W. W. Norton, 1948), pp. 37–51.
7. Jacob Jacoby and Wayne D. Hoyer, "Viewer Miscomprehension of Televised Communication: Selected Findings," *Journal of Marketing,* Fall 1982, pp. 12–26; idem, "The Comprehension and Miscomprehension of Print Communications: An Investigation of Mass Media Magazines" (Advertising Education Foundation study, New York, 1987).
8. E. K. Strong, *The Psychology of Selling* (New York: McGraw-Hill, 1925), p. 9.
9. Robert J. Lavidge and Gary A. Steiner, "A Model for Predictive Measurements of Advertising Effectiveness," *Journal of Marketing* 24 (October 1961), pp. 59–62.
10. A summary review of problems with the hierarchy-of-effects model is offered by Kristin S. Palda, "The Hypothesis of a Hierarchy of Effects: A Partial Evaluation," *Journal of Marketing Research* 3 (February 1966), pp. 13–24.
11. Everett M. Rogers, *Diffusion of Innovations* (New York: Free Press, 1962), pp. 79–86.
12. William J. McGuire, "An Information Processing Model of Advertising Effectiveness, in *Behavioral and Management Science in Marketing,* ed. Harry J. Davis and Alvin J. Silk (New York: Ronald Press, 1978), pp. 156–80.
13. Michael L. Ray, "Communication and the Hierarchy of Effects," in *New Models for Mass Communication Research,* ed. P. Clarke (Beverly Hills, Calif.: Sage Publications, 1973), pp. 147–75.
14. Herbert E. Krugman, "The Impact of Television Advertising: Learning without Involvement," *Public Opinion Quarterly* 29 (Fall 1965), pp. 349–56.
15. Harry W. McMahan, "Do Your Ads Have VIP?" *Advertising Age,* July 14, 1980, pp. 50–51.
16. Richard Vaughn, "How Advertising Works: A Planning Model," *Journal of Advertising Research* 20, no. 5 (October 1980), pp. 27–33.
17. Ibid., "How Advertising Works: A Planning Model Revisited," *Journal of Advertising Research* 26, no. 1 (February/March 1986), pp. 57–66.
18. Jerry C. Olson, Daniel R. Toy, and Philip A. Dover, "Mediating Effects of Cognitive Responses to Advertising on Cognitive Structure," in *Advances in Consumer Research,* Volume V, ed. H. Keith Hunt (Ann Arbor: Association for Consumer Research, 1978), 5:72–78.
19. J. Paul Peter and Jerry C. Olson, *Consumer Behavior* (Homewood, Ill.: Richard D. Irwin, 1987), p. 45.
20. Anthony A. Greenwald, "Cognitive Learning, Cognitive Response to Persuasion and Attitude Change," in *Psychological Foundations of Attitudes,* ed. A. G. Greenwald, T. C. Brock, and T. W. Ostrom (New York: Academic Press, 1968).
21. Peter L. Wright, "The Cognitive Processes Mediating Acceptance of Advertising," *Journal of Marketing Research* 10 (February 1973), pp. 53–62.
22. Ibid., "Message Evoked Thoughts, Persuasion Research Using Thought Verbalizations," *Journal of Consumer Research* 7, no. 2 (September 1980), pp. 151–75.
23. Scott B. Mackenzie, Richard J. Lutz, and George E. Belch, "The Role of Attitude toward the Ad as a Mediator of Advertising Effectiveness: A Test of Competing Explanations," *Journal of Marketing Research* 23 (May 1986), pp. 130–43.
24. Rajeev Batra and Michael L. Ray, "Affective Responses Mediating Acceptance of Advertising," *Journal of Consumer Research* 13 (September 1986), pp. 234–49.
25. Ronald Alsop, "TV Ads That Are Likeable Get Plus Rating for Persuasiveness," *The Wall Street Journal,* February 20, 1986, p. 23.
26. Andrew A. Mitchell and Jerry C. Olson, "Are Product Attribute Beliefs the Only Mediator of Advertising Effects on Brand Attitude?" *Journal of Marketing Research* 18 (August 1981), pp. 318–32.
27. Julie Edell and Marian C. Burke, "The Power of Feelings in Understanding Advertising Effects," *Journal of Consumer Research* 14 (December 1987), pp. 421–33.

28. Richard E. Petty and John T. Cacioppo, "Central and Peripheral Routes to Persuasion: Application to Advertising," in *Advertising and Consumer Psychology,* ed. Larry Percy and Arch Woodside (Lexington, Mass: Lexington Books, 1983), pp. 3–23.

29. Richard E. Petty, John T. Cacioppo, and David Schumann, "Central and Peripheral Routes to Advertising Effectiveness: The Moderating Role of Involvement," *Journal of Consumer Research* 10 (September 1983), pp. 135–46.

Source, Message, and Channel Factors

CHAPTER OBJECTIVES

1. To examine the major variables in the communications system and how they influence consumers' processing of promotional messages

2. To examine the various options and considerations involved in the selection of a source or communicator of a promotional message

3. To examine various factors concerning the development of the promotional message including the effects of different types of message structures and appeals

4. To consider how the channel or medium used to deliver a promotional message influences the communications process

Irreverent But Effective Spokespeople

One of the most popular advertising spokespeople in recent years is not a well-known actor, sports figure, or entertainer but rather a sleazy pitchman with a creepy smile who feeds off the disbelief many consumers have about advertising claims. Joe Isuzu, who is really an actor named David Leisure, became one of the most popular figures in America by making humorously outrageous claims in commercials for the Japanese cars and trucks that bear his name. Isuzu began the "liar campaign" spots in 1986, and they have won numerous advertising awards including the 1987 Gold Lion at the International Advertising Film Festival in Cannes, France. For three consecutive years the Isuzu campaign has been rated one of the 10 most popular in Video Storyboard Tests Inc.'s annual survey, which asks 25,000 consumers which commercials they recall most readily and like the best.

The Isuzu spots initially appeared to be very effective, as not only were they attention getting, but Isuzu sales increased by 21 percent. However, by mid-1987 the company's sales began to decline, and for the first four months of 1988, they were down 24 percent. The sales decline prompted Isuzu to change its advertising strategy to focus more on its products and less on Joe Isuzu (Figure 6–1). As one automotive analyst noted, "Although the liar campaign is clever, it is not something that will solve Isuzu's biggest problem—its lack of an image. An image is the most important thing in the car market and right now, Isuzu doesn't have one."

Another irreverent, but effective, advertising spokesperson was Mark "Jacko" Jackson, the wacky, loud-mouthed, former Australian football player who replaced former Olympic gymnastics star Mary Lou Retton in ads for Energizer brand batteries in 1987 (Figure 6–2). Jacko was very effective at breaking through the advertising clutter shouting, "What's the longest-lasting battery you can buy? I'm gonna surprise ya. New Energizer." A reader of *Adweek* magazine summed up many consumers' reactions to the ad by writing, "Who is this guy and why is he shouting at me?" The reason Jacko was screaming at us was because he helped sell batteries. Consumer awareness of Energizer was up more than 20 percent within two months after he was introduced, and sales increased after a two-year decline.

Joe Isuzu continues to pitch cars and trucks for Isuzu and in April of 1989 awareness of the company's advertising reached an all-time high. However the Eveready Battery Company decided that consumers were getting tired of Jacko and ended his tenure as Energizer battery's spokesperson after two years. Eveready changed advertising agencies in early 1989 and indicated that Jacko would no longer be used in the United States.[1,2,3,4,5,6]

Introduction

The Isuzu and Energizer campaigns are examples of somewhat unusual approaches advertisers take in attempting to get their sales messages to consumers. In both campaigns, decisions had to be made regarding the source or spokesperson who would deliver the message as well as the appeal itself. The Isuzu ads rely on a humorous approach that is really a parody of the advertising process, whereas the Energizer campaign uses irritation to grab the consumers' attention and spark some interest in what to many people is a relatively dull and unexciting product. Both advertising approaches lend themselves to the channel or medium of television in order to communicate with the consumer effectively.

In this chapter we will analyze the major variables in the communications system—the source, the message, and the channel. We will examine the characteristics of sources of a message, explore how they impact cognitive processing, and consider some of the reasons why one type of communicator might be more effective than another. Attention will then be focused on the message itself and how structure and type of appeal might influence the effectiveness of the communication. Finally, we will consider how factors related to the channel or medium by which the message is sent will affect the communications process. Before examining each of these communications variables, let us examine how they interact with the receiver's response process.

Promotional Planning through the Persuasion Matrix

The development of an effective advertising and promotional campaign requires that the firm select the right spokespersons to deliver compelling messages through appro-

Figure 6–1 Joe Isuzu Is Entertaining, But Does He Sell Cars?

Figure 6–2 Jacko Was Irreverent But Helped Energizer Battery's Awareness and Sales

Dependent Variables: Steps in Being Persuaded	Independent Variables: The Communication Components				
	Source	Message	Channel	Receiver	Destination
Message presentation (p)			(2)		
Attention (a)		(3)			
Comprehension (c)				(1)	
Yielding (y)	(4)				
Retention (r)					
Behavior (b)					

Figure 6–3 **The Persuasion Matrix**

Source: William J. McGuire, "An Information–Processing Model of Advertising Effectiveness," in *Behavioral and Management Science in Marketing*, ed. Harry L. Davis and Alvin J. Silk (New York: Ronald/Wiley Press, 1978), pp. 156–180.

priate channels or media. Source, message, and channel factors were introduced in the previous chapter as controllable elements in a communications model. It was noted that in making decisions regarding each of these communications components, consideration must be given to how they interact with the response process. A useful approach combining the communications components and the stages of the response process has been suggested by William McGuire and is termed the **persuasion matrix** (Figure 6–3).[7]

In the persuasion matrix there are two sets of variables that are of interest— independent variables, which represent the components of the 5-Ws model of communication outlined in Chapter 5, and dependent variables, which represent the response hierarchy or the steps a receiver goes through in being persuaded. The independent variables represent the controllable components of the promotional program, as the marketer can choose the person who delivers the message, the type of appeal used, and the channel or medium. While marketers cannot really exert any control over the receiver, they can choose the target audience to whom their promotional messages will be directed. The destination variable is included to take into account the fact that the initial message recipient might pass information to others, such as friends or associates, through word-of-mouth communication.

A major consideration facing the promotional planner is how decisions regarding each independent variable will influence the various stages of the response hierarchy. For example, the use of a well-known celebrity or a sexy model as a spokesperson may enhance the attention given to the ad. However, consideration must also be given to the problem of enhancing one level of the hierarchy at the expense of another. A humorous message may be useful in gaining attention but may result in decreased comprehension if consumers fail to process its content. There are numerous cases in advertising where campaigns using techniques such as humor, explicit sexual appeals, or celebrities succeeded in capturing consumers' attention but resulted in poor recall of the brand name or copy points of the message.

McGuire suggests that the persuasion matrix can be of value in advertising planning by considering how each component of the campaign influences the steps in the response hierarchy. The following examples, which correspond to the numbers shown in the cells in Figure 6–3, reflect a few of the decisions that can be evaluated using the persuasion matrix.

Table 6–1 *Advertising Age* **Star Presenters**

1988	Wilford Brimley
1987	Michael J. Fox
1986	Paul Hogan
1985	William Perry
1984	Cliff Robertson
1983	John Cleese
1982	Rodney Dangerfield
1981	John Houseman
1980	Brooke Shields
1979	Robert Morley
1978	James Garner/ Mariette Hartley
1977	Bill Cosby
1976	O. J. Simpson

1. *Will the receiver be able to comprehend the ad?* Throughout the previous chapters, we have emphasized the importance of understanding the consumer. One important question to be addressed is, At what level is the consumer able to comprehend the message? For example, a less-educated person might have more difficulty than one with a higher education level interpreting a message. Jargon commonly referred to in one person's world may be unheard of in another's. Do you think everyone knows what a "BYTE" is? The more marketers know about the consumer, the more they will understand which words, symbols, expressions, and the like, they understand.

2. *Which media will increase presentation?* A top-rated television program in prime time will be seen by nearly 30 million households each week, whereas the 60th-rated program will reach approximately 5 million homes. *TV Guide* and *Readers Digest* are two of the leading magazines in terms of circulation, reaching nearly 16 million homes each week. The opportunity to have your ad presented to potential consumers is largely determined by the medium used. Of course, while the media noted above may be effective in reaching large numbers of consumers, the important issue is how well they reach members of the marketer's target audience. Weekly telecasts of golf tournaments reach only 3 to 4 million viewers, but this audience consists mostly of upscale businesspeople who are prime prospects for expensive cars, financial services, or business-related products.

3. *What message should be used?* A humorous message may be excellent for gaining attention, but how good is it for achieving comprehension? How well will the major selling points for the brand be remembered? There have been numerous situations in advertising where humorous commercials have won Clio awards (an award given each year in the advertising industry for creative advertising), yet the agency has lost the account. Why? Because while the humorous ads were effective in gaining attention, little else was communicated and sales of the client's product or service declined.

4. *Who can I use to get people to change their attitudes?* Marketers are constantly searching for a spokesperson who will be effective not only in getting consumers' attention but also in changing their attitudes and opinions about a product or service. Former President Ronald Reagan, because of his enormous popularity and the fact that he used to appear in commercials, received numerous offers from companies to appear as their spokesperson when he left the presidency. Each year *Advertising Age* gives a Star Presenter award to the individual who it feels has been most effective as an advertising spokesperson. The winners for the past 13 years are shown in Table 6–1.

Let us now turn our discussion to a more in-depth examination of the various considerations involved in making decisions regarding each of these communications components.

Source Factors

The source component of the marketing communications process can be viewed as a multifaceted concept since many types of sources can be involved in a promotional situation. For example, when Bill Cosby appears in a commercial as a spokesperson for Jell-O, is the source Cosby himself, the company (General Foods), or some combination of the two? When you read a favorable article on a new automobile in *Road & Track,* the magazine itself will probably be viewed as the source. As consumers, we often receive information from personal sources such as friends, relatives, or neighbors. These personal sources are often the most important influences on our purchase decisions.

While there are many alternative ways that the receiver may view the source of communications, for our purposes we will use the term **source** to mean the person who is involved in the communication of a marketing message in either a direct or an

Figure 6—4   Cliff Robertson Serves as a Spokesperson for AT&T

The more you hear the better we sound.

What would long distance service be
if it only served selected cities
at selected hours...
If there were no operator service...
no person-to-person or collect calling...
no immediate credit for wrong numbers...

We know one thing.
It wouldn't be AT&T.
Calling anywhere. Anytime.
Long distance operators.
And over a century of commitment.
That's AT&T.
The more you hear the better we sound.

AT&T
Reach out and touch someone

 AT&T

indirect manner. A direct source would be a spokesperson or endorser who delivers a message and/or demonstrates the product or service. For example, actor Cliff Robertson has been a very effective spokesperson for AT&T for many years (Figure 6—4). An example of an indirect source is one who does not actually deliver a message but rather appears as more of a "decorative model" whose role is to draw attention to and/or enhance the appearance of the ad. Most of the theory and research associated with the study of source factors deal with the characteristics of individuals as a message source and how they influence communication effectiveness. Our examination of source factors will follow this approach.

Source Characteristics

Companies are very careful in the selection of individuals who are used to deliver their selling messages. Many firms spend large sums of money to have certain individuals endorse their products, serve as spokespeople, or simply appear in their ads. In addition, companies spend millions of dollars on the recruitment, selection, and training of salespersons to represent them and deliver sales presentations for their products or services. The reason for all this concern is recognition by marketers that the characteristics of the source often have a significant impact on the effectiveness of their sales and advertising messages.

Marketers select as communicators individuals who have attributes or characteristics that will maximize message influence. The source's influence may stem from the fact that he or she is very knowledgeable and qualified in a particular area, that he or she is very popular and/or physically attractive, that the source typifies the target au-

Figure 6–5 **Source Attributes and Receiver Processing Modes**

Source Attribute	Process
Credibility ⟶	Internalization
Attractiveness ⟶	Identification
Power ⟶	Compliance

dience and is seen as similar to the receiver, or that the source can reward or punish the receiver in some manner.

A very useful framework for examining source attributes or characteristics is the classification scheme developed by Herbert Kelman.[8] According to this scheme, there are three basic categories of source attributes—credibility, attractiveness, and power. Each attribute involves a different "process" by which the source influences attitudinal or behavioral change in the message recipient. Figure 6–5 shows the three categories of source attributes and the psychological processes through which they operate. The following sections will examine these attributes and their importance in selecting the source of a marketing communication.

Source Credibility

Credibility refers to the extent to which the source is perceived as having knowledge, skill, or experience relevant to the communication topic and can be trusted to give an unbiased opinion or present objective information on the issue. There are two important dimensions to credibility—expertise and trustworthiness.

Expertise is a very important aspect of credibility, as a communicator who is perceived as being knowledgeable in a given area will be more persuasive than one with less expertise. **Trustworthiness** refers to the honesty, integrity, and believability of the source and is also an important aspect of credibility. A source may be perceived as being very knowledgeable, but his or her influence will be lessened if the audience members perceive the source as being biased or having underlying personal motives for advocating a particular position (such as being paid to endorse a product).

One of the most reliable effects found in communications research is that expert and/or trustworthy sources are more persuasive than sources who have less expertise or trustworthiness.[9] Information from a credible source can influence beliefs, opinions, attitudes, and/or behavior through a process known as **internalization.** Internalization occurs when the receiver is motivated to have an objectively correct or "right" position on an issue. The receiver will learn and adopt the opinion or attitude of the credible communicator since he or she feels that information from this source represents an accurate position on the issue. Once the receiver internalizes an opinion or attitude, it becomes integrated into his or her belief system and may be maintained even if the source of the message is forgotten.

The use of a highly credible communicator is particularly important when message recipients have a negative position toward the product, service, company, or issue being promoted, as the credible source is more likely to inhibit the generation of counterarguments than are those of moderate or low credibility. As discussed in Chapter 5, reduced counterarguing should result in greater message acceptance and persuasion.

Applying Expertise Because attitudes and opinions developed through an internalization process become part of the individual's belief system, it is desirable for mar-

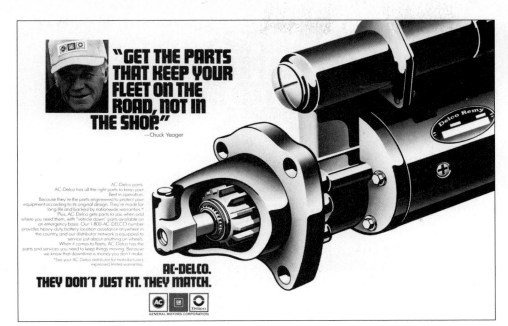

Figure 6–6   **Chuck Yeager's Expertise as a Famous Test Pilot Makes Him a Credible Spokesperson for Delco Auto Parts**

keters to use communicators who are high in credibility. Companies use a variety of techniques to convey source expertise. For example, millions of dollars are spent to train sales personnel to make them knowledgeable of the product line and thus increase their level of expertise in the eyes of the customer. Marketers of highly technical products will recruit sales representatives with specialized technical backgrounds in engineering, computer science, and other areas to ensure their expertise.

Advertisers also go to great lengths, and often great expense, to achieve source credibility. Spokespersons are often chosen because of their knowledge, experience, and expertise in a particular product or service area. For example, former test pilot Chuck Yeager appears in ads for Delco auto parts (Figure 6–6). Endorsements from individuals or groups recognized as experts are also commonplace in advertising. Procter & Gamble stresses the official acceptance of Ultra Pampers by pediatric nurses in the ad shown in Figure 6–7.

Applying Trustworthiness   While finding spokespersons who have expertise is important, it is also important that the message recipients find the source believable. Finding celebrities or other figures with a trustworthy image is often a difficult task. Many trustworthy public figures hesitate to endorse products because of the impact it could have on their reputation and image. It has been suggested that former CBS news anchorman Walter Cronkite, who has repeatedly been rated as one of the most trusted people in America, could command millions of dollars as a product spokesperson. Consumer advocate Ralph Nader is another person who has a very trustworthy image and would probably be a very credible endorser. However, it is unlikely that either would agree to appear in advertisements.

A problem that advertisers often encounter in using celebrities is that consumers recognize that they are endorsing a product or service because they are being paid to do so and thus become skeptical of the endorsement.[10] This problem can become very pronounced when a celebrity endorses more than one product, as is discussed in Promotional Perspective 6–1.

In addition to using public figures with a positive image, advertisers use other techniques to increase the trustworthiness of communicators in their messages. Hidden-camera techniques are often used in commercials to show that the consumer is

Figure 6–7 Ultra Pampers Promotes Its Acceptance from a Group of Medical Experts

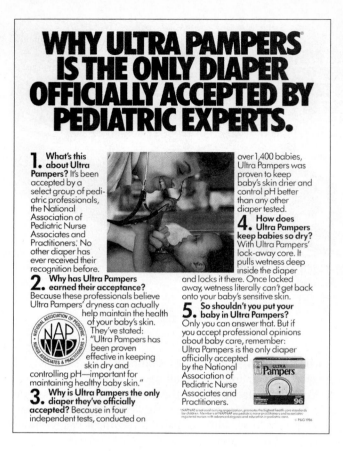

not a paid spokesperson and thus is making an objective evaluation of the product. Advertisers also use disguised comparisons in which their brand is compared with another by a consumer who is unaware of the brand identities. (Of course, the sponsor's brand *always* performs better than the consumer's regular brand, and he or she acts surprised upon learning this outcome!)

Using Corporate Leaders as Spokespersons   Another approach to enhancing source credibility that has become increasingly popular in recent years is the use of the company president or chief executive officer (CEO) as a spokesperson in the firm's advertising. Many companies feel that the use of a president or CEO is the ultimate expression of the company's commitment to meeting the needs of the customer. Numerous companies have used their leaders in advertising for their products and services, and in some cases the ads have not only been successful but have helped turn these individuals into celebrities.[11]

Frank Perdue, president of Perdue Farms, Inc., has become a folk hero in the Northeast for his ads for Perdue chickens (see Figure 6–8). Victor Kiam appears in commercials for Remington shavers, saying that he liked his electric shaver so much that he bought the company. The commercials helped sales of Remington electric razors grow from $43 million a year to more than $100 million over the past decade and resulted in celebrity status for Kiam.[12] Lee Iacocca, who became a national business hero for his turnaround of nearly bankrupt Chrysler Motors in the early 1980s, has been one of the most effective of the corporate spokespeople. Iacocca's appeals to the American consumer to give the new Chrysler's products a try were seen by many to be very instrumental in helping the company regain its position in the U.S. automobile market, and he continues to appear in the company's advertising (Figure 6–9).

There is some research evidence suggesting that the use of a company president or CEO can have a positive effect on attitudes and consumer likelihood of inquiring

Promotional Perspective **6—1**

Too Many Endorsements Hurt Celebrity Credibility

Two of the most popular celebrity endorsers of the 1980s were the late actor John Houseman and actor/comedian Bill Cosby. Houseman's popularity among advertisers stemmed from the serious, hard-working, and analytical image he projected and his commanding presence, which was perhaps most apparent in his role as a Harvard law professor in the movie *The Paper Chase*.

For several years Houseman was probably best known among television viewers as the spokesperson and compelling symbol for the investment firm of Smith Barney, Harris Upham & Co., which filmed nearly a dozen commercials using him to promote its financial services. The ad theme "We make money the old-fashioned way— we earn it" helped position the firm as a company for the serious investor. Houseman also used his success as a spokesperson for Smith Barney to sell his image to other companies. In addition to the Smith Barney campaign, he appeared in ads for Plymouth cars, Puritan vegetable oil, and McDonald's, leading many advertisers to become concerned about his becoming overexposed and losing his credibility. One agency executive reported watching a World Series game and seeing him in commercials for three different products.

Although Houseman was successful as a spokesperson for Smith Barney, this was not the case for some of the other campaigns that used him. Chrysler decided not to renew his contract after the first year because he was not perceived as effective in delivering its intended message. McDonald's used him for only a brief time period, as he was perceived as inappropriate for selling Big Macs and french fries.

There have been other situations where popular celebrities have extended themselves too far. In 1986 the E. F. Hutton Co. (now a part of Shearson-Lehman Hutton) hired Bill Cosby, hoping his popularity and good-guy image would help the financial services firm's reputation, which had been damaged by a check-kiting scheme. Cosby, one of the most popular figures in America, has been a successful pitchperson for a number of companies. However, the E. F. Hutton "Because it's my money" campaign, which cost an estimated $6 million, was dropped after nine months, even though his contract had three years remaining. As one executive noted: "When Bill Cosby speaks, who are you listening to? . . . Is it E. F. Hutton, Coca-Cola, Texas Instruments or any of the multiplicity of advertisers who have used him?" However, the company indicated that the decision to drop Cosby was not really his overexposure but rather a change in the direction of its advertising strategy.

Some advertisers protect themselves from celebrity overexposure by using an exclusivity clause that limits the number of products a celebrity can endorse. However, these clauses are usually quite expensive and thus are not used by many companies. Thus, the problem of celebrity overexposure will continue. Of course, the celebrity must also be aware of his or her own image and be careful not to damage it by endorsing too many products.

Sources: Barry H. Slinker, "Would You Buy a Burger from This Man? A Car? Some Stocks?" *Madison Avenue*, April 1984, pp. 52—58; Christy Marshall, "It Seemed Like a Good Idea at the Time," *Forbes*, February 28, 1987, p. 98.

Figure 6—8 **Frank Perdue Has Helped Convince Consumers of the Quality of Perdue Chickens**

Figure 6–9 **Lee Iacocca Has Been a Very Effective Corporate Spokesperson for Chrysler**

about the company's product or service.[13] While corporate leaders are often used as spokespeople in national advertising, it is also becoming commonplace to see local companies such as retailers use the owner or president in their ads. It is likely that many companies will continue to use their top executives in their advertising, particularly when they have celebrity value that helps enhance the firms' image.

Limitations of Credible Sources   While marketers generally seek to use credible sources to deliver their promotional messages, several studies have shown that a high-credibility source is not always an asset, nor is a low-credibility source a persuasive liability. For example, high- and low-credibility sources have been found to be about equal in effectiveness when the source is arguing for a position opposing his or her own best interest.[14] A high-credibility source is more effective when message recipients are not in favor of the position advocated in the message.[15] However, the use of a high-credibility source is less important when the audience has a neutral position and may even be less effective than a moderately credible source when the receiver has a favorable initial attitude or position.[16,17]

Another reason why a low-credibility source may be as effective as a high-credibility source is what is known as the **sleeper effect** phenomenon whereby the persuasiveness of a message increases with the passage of time. The immediate impact of a persuasive message may be inhibited because of its association with a low-credibility source. However, with the passage of time, the association of the message with the low-credibility source diminishes, and the receiver's attention focuses more on favorable information in the message, which results in more support arguing. There has been considerable debate over the existence of a sleeper effect, as many studies have failed to demonstrate its presence.[18] Many advertisers question the strategy of relying on the sleeper effect, suggesting that a more reliable strategy would be to use repeated exposure to a communication attributed to a credible source.[19]

Source Attractiveness

The source characteristic that is used the most by advertisers is probably that of **attractiveness.** When a source is considered to be attractive to a receiver, persuasion may occur through a process known as **identification.** Identification occurs when the receiver is motivated to seek some type of relationship with the source and thus adopts a similar position in terms of attitudes, opinions, preferences, or behavior. Maintaining this position depends on the source's continued support for the position as well as the receiver's continued identification with the source. If the source changes his or her position, the receiver may also change. An important point to keep in mind here is that unlike the process of internalization, information from an attractive source does not usually become integrated into the receiver's belief system. Thus, the receiver may only maintain the attitude or behavior as long as it is supported by the source or as long as the source remains attractive.

Advertisers have recognized for a long time the value of using highly attractive communicators to draw attention to and enhance the persuasiveness of their messages. Thus, they employ as spokespersons individuals who are well liked and often admired, such as sports or show business stars, and individuals who are very similar (in terms of lifestyle, personality, social status, education, etc.) to their target audience. Physically attractive models are also used to deliver their messages or just to embellish the advertisement. Just as there are several components to source credibility, source attractiveness also consists of various subcomponents including similarity, familiarity, and liking.[20]

Applying Similarity Most marketers recognize that people are more likely to be influenced by a persuasive appeal if it is perceived as coming from someone with whom they feel a sense of similarity.[21] If the receiver shares similar interests, lifestyles, opinions, and the like, with the communicator, he or she is more likely to share the same needs, desires, or goals, and the position advocated by the source would be better understood and received.

Similarity is utilized in various ways in marketing communications. For example, companies select salespersons who have characteristics that match well with their customers. A sales position for a particular region of the country may be staffed by someone from the local area to ensure that he or she has a common background and interest with the customers. You could imagine the problems a person from a large urban area such as New York City or Los Angeles might have in trying to sell to customers in rural areas such as Wyoming or Montana.

Companies may also try to recruit salespersons with a particular background to sell to customers to establish a common interest. Former athletes are often recruited to sell sporting goods equipment or to act as sales representatives for beer companies, since their customers usually have a strong interest in sports. Several studies have shown that when customers perceive a salesperson as similar to themselves, they are more likely to accept or be influenced by his or her message.[22,23]

Similarity is also used by advertisers who will try to create a situation whereby the consumer has empathy for the person shown in the commercial. For example, in a "slice-of-life" commercial, the advertiser usually starts out by presenting a predicament or problem situation with the hope of getting the consumer to the point of thinking: "I can see myself in that situation." This can help establish a bond of similarity between the communicator and the receiver and thus increase the source's level of persuasiveness. Figure 6–10 shows an example of a slice-of-life commercial for Dawn dishwashing detergent.

Using Celebrities The use of celebrities from the sports and entertainment fields to promote products and services has become a very popular strategy among advertisers. It is estimated that 20 percent of all commercials in 1986 featured celebrities, with advertisers spending more than $500 million for their services.[24] Singer Michael Jackson was paid more than $10 million to appear in four commercials for Pepsi-Cola in 1988.[25] Pepsi also paid pop singer Madonna an estimated $5 million to appear in several commercials in 1989, whereas Coca-Cola recruited rock star George Michael ($4 million), after previously signing the Pointer Sisters and Whitney Houston.[26]

Companies spend huge amounts of money to have celebrities appear in their commercials and endorse their products for several reasons. They view a celebrity as having "stopping power" and as a way of drawing attention to their messages in a very

Figure 6–10 **Slice-of-Life Commercials Show Situations Similar to Those Encountered by Consumers**

cluttered advertising and media environment.) Another reason is the expectation that the respect, popularity, and/or admiration that the celebrity enjoys will favorably influence consumers' attitudes and ultimately their purchase behavior.

Several studies support the attention-getting value of celebrities in advertising. A study by Gallup and Robinson of commercials used during the 1970s found that the use of a celebrity increased the likelihood that viewers would attend to the ads, whereas another study found that commercials using celebrities had a 22 percent higher level of recall.[27,28] However, other research has shown that only 40 percent of TV commercials using celebrities had better-than-average brand awareness scores and only half of these produced increases in brand attitudes.[29]

Issues in using celebrities   There are a number of factors that must be considered in the decision to use a celebrity as an endorser or spokesperson. First, consideration must be given to how the celebrity will affect the target audience's processing of the advertising message. While a celebrity may be effective in drawing attention to the ad, his or her impact on other response variables such as brand awareness and recall and brand attitudes must also be considered. A common concern in using celebrities is that consumers will focus their attention on the celebrity and fail to note the brand he or she is advertising. This problem reportedly occurred when comedian Rich Little was used in ads for Pizza Hut restaurants and Rodney Dangerfield as the spokesperson for Lo-Sal antacid tablets. Mazda dropped actor James Garner as its spokesperson after four years so that its ads could focus exclusively on the cars. Mazda's vice president of advertising stated, "We want the cars to be the stars."[30]

Attention must also be given to the audience toward whom the advertising campaign will be targeted. Consumers who are particularly knowledgeable about a product

CROCK By Bill Rechin and Don Wilder

cɪ service or have strongly established attitudes may be less impressed or influenced by a celebrity than those with little knowledge or neutral attitudes. For example, one study found that college-age consumers were more likely to have a positive attitude toward a product endorsed by a celebrity than were older consumers.[31]

One of the most important considerations in attempting to use a celebrity to influence brand attitudes is making sure that the image of the product and characteristics of the target market are carefully matched with the personality of the celebrity.[32] Examples of successful matching of celebrities with products include Joe Namath as a spokesperson for Brut cologne; Bill Cosby, for Jell-O; and numerous retired athletes, for Miller Lite beer. One way of determining effective celebrity matching is through marketing research. For example, research conducted by Sears showed that model Cheryl Tiegs has a very strong and favorable image among its female customers. Sears developed a clothing line bearing her name, which subsequently became one of the most successful product lines the company ever introduced.[33]

There have also been many campaigns where the celebrity matchup with the product was not very appropriate. For example, actor George C. Scott bombed as a spokesperson for Renault automobiles. Many consumers associated Scott with American patriotism as a result of his portrayal of the famous army general in the movie *Patton*. Thus, he was not seen as an appropriate pitchperson for French cars.[34]

Promotional Perspective 6–2 discusses some issues regarding athletes who capitalize on their celebrity status to become advertising spokespeople and why some are more effective than others.

A final consideration in the use of celebrities is whether there is any risk associated with having them represent your product because of their image or behavior. Several well-known entertainers and athletes have been arrested for drug abuse or have been involved in other activities that were potentially embarrassing to the companies whose products they were endorsing.[35] For example, Pepsi had to drop a television ad featuring pop singer Madonna and sponsorship of her concert tour when a controversy arose over one of her music videos. Several religious groups and many consumers found Madonna's "Like a Prayer" video objectionable on religious grounds and threatened a boycott of Pepsi products if the company continued to use her in its advertising.[36] Thus, companies often carefully research the personal life and background of celebrities before using them. Many firms include a moral clause in the contract, allowing them to terminate a celebrity should any controversy arise involving that individual.

Decorative and Physically Attractive Models A common technique employed by advertisers to draw attention to an advertisement and enhance its effectiveness is to use a physically attractive model. Often the attractive model is used as a passive or "decorative" model rather than as an active communicator. Research suggests that physically attractive communicators generally have a positive impact, as they

Promotional Perspective 6—2

Playing the Endorsement Game

It has become very common in the sports field for star athletes to expect to make almost as much money, or more, off the field or court than they do on it through product or service endorsements. However, the endorsement business is a very fickle one where on-the-field or -court performance is not always the key determinant of success as an endorser. Bob Uecker has used the antihero image that made him a folk hero in Miller Lite beer ads as a springboard to endorsements for a number of other products. William "The Refrigerator" Perry of the Chicago Bears became an overnight celebrity in 1985 when the 350-pound football tackle was used as a running back in goal-line situations and parlayed the nation's love affair for the "Frig" into some $2 million in endorsement contracts. However, many big-name athletes fail to earn much at all from endorsements.

The biggest endorsement money goes to basketball players, followed by golfers and tennis players. The reason is that the public buys the footwear, clubs, balls, racquets, and clothing that these highly visible athletes wear or use. Basketball star Michael Jordan makes nearly $4 million a year as the spokesperson for Nike's "Air Jordan" line of shoes and apparel, which totaled nearly $100 million in sales in its first year on the market.

In 1986 tennis star Boris Becker signed one of the sports world's most lucrative promotional deals when

1988 Ratings of Athletes' Appeal

When judged among all performers:
1. Michael Jordan (basketball)
2. Walter Payton (football, retired)
3. Julius Erving (basketball, retired)
4. Earvin "Magic" Johnson (basketball)
5. Doug Williams (football)
6. Mike Tyson (boxing)
7. Isiah Thomas (basketball)
8. Brian Boitano (skating)
9. Larry Bird (basketball)
10. Joe Montana (football)

When judged only among other athletes:
1. Greg Louganis (swimming)
2. Walter Payton (football, retired)
3. Florence Griffith Joyner (track)
4. Michael Jordan (basketball)
5. Julius Erving (basketball, retired)
6. Jackie Joyner-Kersee (track)
7. Willie Mays (baseball, retired)
8. John Madden (football, retired)
9. Earvin "Magic" Johnson (basketball)
10. Dorothy Hamill (skater)
    Mickey Mantle (baseball, retired)
    Merlin Olsen (football, retired)

Source: Marketing Evaluations/TVQ Inc.

Exhibit 6—2   Brian Bosworth's Flamboyant Personality Has Made Him a Popular Advertising Spokesperson

"Hey wimps, slugs and couch potatoes: Don't buy Avia® crosstrainers."

Avia 1360 crosstrainers: for athletic use only.

"No offense. But somehow, I don't think Avia® designed their Cantilever® sole to cushion the impact of rolling off a couch after a hard night of TV watching. Those special, wraparound support straps are kind of a waste if they aren't used to stabilize your feet during running, basketball, weightlifting, or tennis. But a few bozos seem to think they're for eating, drinking, snoozing, and lounging around.

"Not you, though, right? So do Avia and me a favor. If you see some slug-like individual checking out Avia crosstrainers in a store, tell him they're for hard-core athletes only. Suggest that he step over to some other shoe display. If that isn't too far to walk."   **AVIA**
FOR ATHLETIC USE ONLY.

Promotional Perspective (concluded)

Puma AG, the West German sporting goods company, agreed to pay him a reported $28.1 million over six years. However, just two years later Puma canceled the agreement as part of an austerity program to help the company cope with declining sales and mounting financial problems. The company also terminated its agreement with Argentine soccer star Diego Maradonna in an effort to cut its advertising budget by $27 million. A Puma spokesperson noted that costs of using top athletes had become too high and that it would no longer offer high fixed-rate endorsement salaries.

There are many factors that help make athletes popular as endorsers. Athletes who have made commercials before have a better chance of being noticed, as do those who play in the big media markets. Good media rapport is also important, as are good communication skills and personality. Former Chicago Bears quarterback Jim McMahon and Seattle linebacker Brian Bosworth have become popular spokespeople, not only because of their talent but because of their flamboyant personalities as well (Exhibit 6–2). Tennis star Ivan Lendel, on the other hand, is not very popular—a fact many at-

tribute to his craggy personality and tendency to frown during matches.

Advertisers often rely on surveys that measure a celebrity's appeal as a way of selecting athletes for endorsements. One of the more popular surveys used is Marketing Evaluations/TVQ Inc., which surveys more than 1,000 people every year to come up with its "Q" rating. The rating is obtained by dividing the number of people surveyed who describe a celebrity as "one of their favorites" by the number of people who know of him or her. Traditionally, Marketing Evaluations had just one annual list for all performers from athletes to actors to musicians. However, in 1988 the company came up with a separate rating that includes only athletes. The table shows the 10 most popular athletes when judged among all performers and when judged only among other athletes.

Sources: Roger Lowenstein, "Many Athletes Have a Tough Time Playing the Endorsement Game," *The Wall Street Journal,* August 29, 1986, p. 19; "Puma AG Scratches Promotional Pact with Boris Becker," *The Wall Street Journal,* July 27, 1988, p. 32; Joanne Lipman, "Retired-Athlete Factor Emerges as a Plus," *The Wall Street Journal,* March 14, 1989, p. B7.

result in more favorable evaluations of the ad and the product than do less attractive models.[37] However, it has also been shown that the gender appropriateness of the model for the product being advertised and the relevancy of the model to the product are also important considerations.[38] Products such as cosmetics or fashionable clothing are likely to benefit from the use of an attractive model, since physical appearance is very relevant in marketing these items.

When using an attractive model in an ad, consideration must also be given to whether he or she will draw attention to the ad but not to the product or message. The presence of an attractive or decorative model facilitates recognition of the ad but does not enhance copy readership or message recall.[39,40] Thus, advertisers must take steps to ensure that the consumer's attention will go beyond the model and get the individual to devote some attention to the product and advertising message.

Source Power

The final source characteristic in Kelman's classification scheme is that of **source power.** A source may have power when he or she can actually administer rewards and punishments to the receiver. As a result of this power, the source may be able to induce another person(s) to respond to the request or position he or she is advocating. However, the perceived power of the source depends on several factors. First, the source must be perceived as being able to administer positive or negative sanctions to the receiver *(perceived control).* Also, the receiver must feel that the source cares about whether or not the receiver conforms *(perceived concern).* Finally, the receiver's estimate of the source's ability to observe the source's conformity is important *(perceived scrutiny).*

When a source is perceived by the receiver as having power, the influence process occurs through a process known as **compliance.** Compliance results when the receiver accepts the persuasive influence of the source and acquiesces to his or her advocated position in hopes of obtaining favorable reaction or avoiding punishment. It should be noted that the receiver may show an outward or public acquiescence to the

Figure 6–11 *Actor Charles Bronson's Authoritative Personality Makes Him an Effective Communicator*

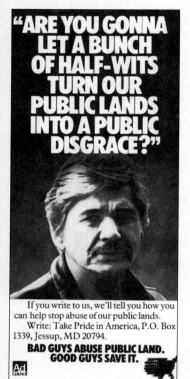

"ARE YOU GONNA LET A BUNCH OF HALF-WITS TURN OUR PUBLIC LANDS INTO A PUBLIC DISGRACE?"

If you write to us, we'll tell you how you can help stop abuse of our public lands. Write: Take Pride in America, P.O. Box 1339, Jessup, MD 20794.

BAD GUYS ABUSE PUBLIC LAND. GOOD GUYS SAVE IT.

source's position but may not have an internal or private commitment to this position. Thus, persuasion induced through the use of a communicator who relies on power may be superficial and last only as long as the receiver perceives that the source can administer some reward or punishment. This is quite different from the influence process, which occurs in reaction to a credible source, as previously discussed.

The use of power as a source characteristic is very difficult to apply through a nonpersonal influence situation such as that found in advertising. A communicator in an ad generally cannot apply any sanctions to the receiver or determine whether compliance actually occurs. An indirect way of using power may be to use an individual with a very authoritative personality or appearance as a spokesperson. For example, actor Charles Bronson, who typifies this type of image, has appeared in public service campaigns commanding people not to pollute or damage our natural parks (Figure 6–11).

The use of source power has greater applicability to situations involving personal communication and influence. For example, in a personal selling situation the sales representative may have some power over a buyer if the latter anticipates receiving special rewards or favors for complying with the salesperson's requests. Some companies provide their sales representatives with large expense accounts to spend on customers for this very purpose. Representatives of companies who are in a dominant position, where demand for their product exceeds supply, are often in a position of power, as buyers may comply with their requests to ensure an adequate supply of the seller's product.

Sales representatives must be very careful in their use of a power position, as long-term relationships with a customer may be damaged if a power base is abused to maximize short-term gains. For example, several years ago Procter & Gamble had developed a very negative image among retailers who felt that because of the strength the company had developed with its dominant brands, P&G and its sales force had become very rigid and arrogant in its procedures and policies toward the trade. However, many of the company's markets began to mature and become more competitive, and the major retailer's clout began to increase as a result of mergers and smaller stores going out of business. Thus, Procter & Gamble, and its sales reps, had to develop a much more conciliatory attitude and policies to maintain its sales growth.[41]

Message Factors

The manner in which marketing communications are presented is very important in determining their effectiveness. Promotional managers must consider not only what the content of their persuasive messages will be but also how this information will be structured for presentation and the type of message appeal that will be utilized. Advertising, in all media except radio, relies heavily on visual as well as verbal information in the presentation of a message. There are a considerable number of options available with respect to the design and presentation of a message. In this section, we will examine various issues that are of importance in designing the structure of a message and also consider what is known about the effects of different types of appeals that are often used in advertising.

Message Structure

Marketing communications usually consists of a number of elements or message points that the communicator wants to get across. An important aspect of message strategy is knowing the best way to communicate these points and overcome any opposing viewpoints or attitudes audience members might hold. Extensive research has been conducted on how the structure of a persuasive message can influence its effectiveness,

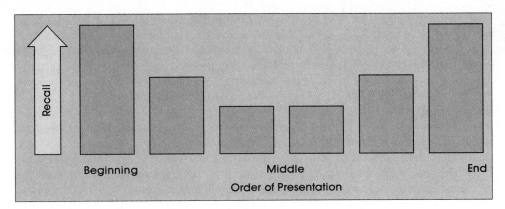

Figure 6—12 **Ad Message Recall as a Function of Order of Presentation**

including order of presentation, conclusion drawing, message sidedness, refutation, and verbal versus nonverbal message characteristics.

Order of Presentation   A basic consideration that has to be made in the design of a persuasive message concerns the order of presentation of the message arguments. Should the most important message points be placed at the beginning of the message, in the middle, or at the end? Research on learning and memory generally indicates that given a series of things to remember those presented first and last are remembered better than those presented in the middle (see Figure 6–12).[42] This would suggest that a communicator's strongest arguments should be presented early or late in the message but never in the middle.

Presenting the strongest arguments at the beginning of the message assumes that there is a **primacy effect** operating whereby information presented first is most effective. Putting the strong points at the end of the communication would assume that a **recency effect** will occur whereby the arguments presented at the end of the message are the most persuasive.

The decision as to whether to place the strongest selling points at the beginning or the end of the message will depend on several factors. If the target audience is opposed to the communicator's position, it may be necessary to present strong points first to reduce the amount of counterarguing the receiver would engage in. Putting weak arguments first might lead to such a high level of counterarguing that strong arguments will not be attended to or believed. Putting strong arguments at the beginning of the message may also be necessary if the audience has a low level of interest in the topic, as they may be needed to arouse attention and interest in the message. When the target audience is favorably predisposed toward the communicator's position or has a high level of interest in the issue or product, strong arguments can be saved for the end of the message. This should not only result in the audience members' leaving with a favorable opinion but should also result in better retention of the information.

The discussion above suggests that decisions regarding the order of presentation of message arguments depend on the situation facing the communicator. The order of presentation of message arguments can be particularly critical when a long, detailed message with many arguments is being presented, such as a sales presentation. Most effective sales presentations open and close with strong selling points, whereas weaker arguments are buried in the middle of the presentation. For short communications, such as a 15- or 30-second television or radio commercial, the order of argument presentation would appear to be less critical. However, it should be noted that many products and services are received by consumers with a low level of involvement, and consumer interest is minimal. Thus, an advertiser may want to present information such as the brand name and key selling points early in the message as well as at the end to enhance recall and retention.

Conclusion Drawing Another issue facing the marketing communicators is whether their messages should explicitly draw a firm conclusion for the audience or allow them to draw their own conclusions. Research suggests that, in general, messages with explicit conclusions are more easily understood and effective in influencing attitudes. However, other studies have shown that the effectiveness of conclusion drawing may depend on the target audience, the type of issue or topic, and the nature of the situation.[43]

For example, more highly educated people prefer to draw their own conclusions and may be annoyed at an attempt to explain the obvious or to draw an inference for them. However, a less educated audience may need to have the conclusion stated for them, as they may never draw a conclusion or may make an incorrect inference from the message. Marketers must also consider the audience's level of involvement in the topic or issue. For highly personal or ego-involving issues, message recipients may want to make up their own minds and may resent any attempts by the communicator to draw a conclusion.

The decision as to whether to draw a conclusion for the audience also depends on the complexity of the topic or issue. While a less intelligent audience may not understand the conclusions to be drawn on a complex issue, even a highly educated audience may need assistance if its knowledge level in a particular area is low. Consideration must also be given to whether the marketer wants the message to trigger immediate action or whether more of a long-term effect is desired. If immediate action is an objective, the message should draw a definitive conclusion for the target audience. This is a very common strategy in political advertising, particularly for ads run close to election day. When immediate impact is not the objective and repeated exposure will give the audience opportunities to draw a conclusion, an open-ended message might be used.

Drawing a conclusion in a message may be a way of ensuring that the target audience gets the point the marketer intended. However, assuming that the audience will do so, many advertisers feel that it is beneficial for customers to draw their own conclusions and thereby reinforce the points being made in the message. For example, a health services agency in Kentucky found that open-ended ads were more likely to be remembered and were more effective in getting consumers to use health services than ads stating a conclusion. Ads that posed questions about alcohol and drug abuse and left them unanswered resulted in more calls by teenagers to a help line for information than when a message offering a resolution to the problem was used.[44]

Some advertisers prefer to use a somewhat ambiguous message, hoping that consumers will become involved in interpreting the message in a manner that is personally relevant to them. Promotional Perspective 6–3 discusses how an ambiguous ad for Benson & Hedges cigarettes resulted in one of the most talked about ad campaigns in recent years.

Message Sidedness Another message structure decision facing the marketer is whether advertisements and sales presentations should use a **one-sided message,** and mention only positive attributes or benefits of a product or service, or a **two-sided message,** whereby good and bad points are presented. Research has shown that one-sided messages are most effective when the target audience already holds a favorable opinion toward the topic and will not hear opposing arguments. One-sided messages also have been found to work better than two-sided messages with a less educated audience.[45]

Two-sided messages have been shown to be more effective when the target audience's initial opinion opposes that of the communicator and when the audience is highly educated. Two-sided messages may be more effective because they enhance the credibility of the source and thus the message. By presenting both sides of an issue or acknowledging opposing viewpoints, the communicator is likely to be seen as less biased and more objective than when a one-sided message is used. Also, a better-edu-

Promotional Perspective 6—3

What's Going on in These Ads?

One of the most talked about cigarette advertising campaigns in recent years is a series of ads that the Philip Morris Company used for Benson & Hedges cigarettes in its "For people who like to smoke" campaign. The campaign consists of a series of ads showing people in various social settings enjoying a cigarette. According to the president of the agency that created the campaign, the appeal of the ads is that people create their own stories behind the pictures, and there is no strict interpretation to them.

The ad in the campaign that has drawn the most attention is one that shows a mysterious man in pajamas talking to a group consisting of five women and one man (Exhibit 6—3). The photographer and director who shot the picture said that his interpretation of the ad is that someone sick at home comes from his bedroom, curious about the noise in another room, and discovers his family and friends having brunch. However, the agency itself has vowed silence on what the ad is supposed to mean or what the jammie man is doing, leaving many people to come up with their own interpretation. *Advertising Age*, the ad industry's leading trade publication, asked its readers to send in their interpretation of the ad and got more than 400 responses, with many of them noting that "everyone in the office has been wondering about it, too."

The interest in the ad was so great that it prompted Philip Morris to run its own contest asking consumers to provide their opinion of what is going on in the ad. Entrants received a free coupon for Benson & Hedges, and the most original entries received a pair of designer pajamas—bottoms *and* tops.

The goal of the campaign, which consists of 35 different ads, was to attract attention to Benson & Hedges among younger, upscale smokers. The brand's sales had declined since 1986 owing to an image problem created by an aging consumer base and declining sales in the high-quality cigarette segment in which it competes. Although Philip Morris officials would not discuss the spe-

Exhibit 6—3 **What Is Your Explanation of What Is Going On in This Ad?**

cific results of the campaign, it is believed that it has helped meet this goal.

Sources: Judann Dagnoli, "B & H Ads to Change?" *Advertising Age*, April 25, 1988, p. 4; Lenore Skenazy, "B & H Bedtime Stories," *Advertising Age*, May 9, 1988, p. 102.

cated audience is more likely to know that there are opposing arguments to the issue. Thus, by acknowledging the other viewpoint or admitting a weakness in his or her position, the communicator can improve his or her credibility with this group.

Marketers generally present only favorable benefits of their products or services without mentioning any negative characteristics of their products or acknowledging an advantage a competitor might have. However, it has been shown that the use of a two-sided advertising message results in more positive perceptions of a source than does a one-sided message.[46,47]

The evidence noted above suggests that there are situations in which companies might benefit from the use of a two-sided message rather than the traditional one-sided appeal. However, most advertisers refuse to use two-sided messages, as they are concerned over negative effects of acknowledging a weakness in their brand or do not want to say anything positive about their competitors'. There are exceptions, however, as advertisers will sometimes compare brands on various attributes and do not always

Promotional Perspective 6—4

How the Opel Came in Second—and Won

Buick's Japanese-made Opel was in trouble. It was eleventh in sales among the twelve imported cars in its price class (Renault was last), and by the end of 1976, its U.S. sales had fallen by half. "We found ourselves with an inventory of about 20,000 cars, and were selling only 1,000 a month," says George Frink, director of marketing at Buick. "You could say we were headed for disaster."

Frink knew what had to be done—somehow he had to get people who were shopping for an import to take a look at the Opel. And the way to do it, he decided, was to run an ad campaign comparing the Opel with four leading imports—the Toyota Corolla, Datsun B-210, VW Rabbit, and Subaru DL—on the basis of measurable things, such as fuel economy and performance. Though a lot of supporting data from the Environmental Protection Agency was already available on some of these points, Buick bought ten models of each make that it was challenging in order to run tests of its own. This it did at the huge General Motors proving grounds in Mesa, Arizona.

It took time to devise tests that would clearly be both fair and meaningful. And once the tests got going, the necessity for absolute accuracy made things move slowly. By February, Frink was getting nervous. He wanted the ad campaign to run before summer, which experience has shown to be the best selling season for imports. Before the final tests were made—i.e., before he even knew how the Opel was going to finish—Frink slipped the first of five ads into newspapers nationwide, boldly announcing the "Five Car Showdown."

Judging by the results of the first showdown, Opel might just as well have stayed in the starting gate. The first tests were for quietness and roominess. And in these respects, "Opel finishes third to VW and Toyota," flashed the headline of the ad. It added: "Drats!"

By the end of the campaign in May, however, the Opel had placed a respectable second overall, behind VW's Rabbit. The folks at Buick were ecstatic, and so were the folks who bring out the Rabbit. Eager to spread the gospel according to Opel, VW ran its own ad—a "thank you" to Opel for proclaiming that the Rabbit was the best car tested.

Exhibit 6—4 **Opel Made Effective Use of a Two-Sided Message**

Buick spent about $4 million on the Opel Showdown, and it was worth it. Opel's share of the market more than doubled, to 1.9 percent, compared with 13 percent for VW. The percentage may seem slim, but Buick is now selling all the Opels that it gets, and that's a happier situation than the one it confronted just a year ago.

Source: Reproduced from "It Pays to Knock Your Competitor," *Fortune*, February 13, 1978, p. 106.

show their product as being the best on every one. Promotional Perspective 6—4 provides an interesting example of how General Motors used a two-sided advertisement for the Opel automobile very effectively a number of years ago.

Refutation A special type of two-sided message known as a **refutational appeal** is sometimes used whereby the communicator presents both sides of an issue and then offers arguments to refute the opposing viewpoint. Refutational appeals may be effective because they "inoculate" the target audience against potential counterclaims that might be raised by a competitor. Thus, the receiver will not be surprised by subsequent counterarguments he or she might be exposed to and might be better able to resist these claims by arguing against them. Several marketing studies have shown that two-sided refutational ads are more effective than one-sided messages in making consumers resistant to a message presenting an opposing viewpoint.[48,49]

Refutational messages may be useful in situations where marketers wish to build attitudes that are resistant to change and must defend against attacks or criticism of their products. Figure 6–13 shows an example of a refutational ad used by the Potato Board, an industry trade association, to refute arguments that potatoes are fattening. Market leaders, who are often the target of comparative messages, may find it advantageous to acknowledge the claims made by their competitors and then refute them to help build resistant attitudes and loyalty among their customers.

Verbal versus Nonverbal Messages   The various issues regarding message structure discussed thus far have focused primarily on the information or verbal component of the promotional message. Advertising copy is obviously an important component of an advertisement; however, the nonverbal or visual elements of an ad are also very important. Many advertisements provide very little product attribute information but rather rely on visual elements to portray the type of person who uses the brand or to evoke some type of emotional reaction from the receiver. In some cases the visual image supports the verbal appeal so as to generate a compelling impression in the consumer's mind. Notice how the ad for Ortega Taco Salsa uses visual elements to demonstrate its ingredients (Figure 6–14).

Both the verbal and visual portions of an advertisement influence the way an advertising message is processed.[50,51] Consumers may develop images or inferences about a brand based on the visual element of an ad such as a picture or illustration or the scenes in a television commercial. In some cases the visual portion of an ad may reduce the persuasiveness of the ad because the processing stimulated by the picture may be less controlled and consequently less favorable than that stimulated by words.[52]

Advertisers must be cognizant of the fact that both verbal and nonverbal components of an advertisement will impact its effectiveness. For products and services where

Figure 6—14 **Visual Images Are Often Designed to Support Verbal Appeals**

it is important to convey impressions of rationality and factualness, the use of a predominantly verbal message may be warranted.[53] For example, the financial services firm of Shearson-Lehman Hutton developed a very effective ad campaign that consisted simply of the verbal message being shown on the screen and read by the announcer (Figure 6–15). For products where emotional and image associations are important, the advertiser is likely to emphasize the visual portion of the ad.

Message Appeals

In the previous section, we considered how information might be structured in promotional messages to enhance effectiveness and persuasion. We will now turn our attention to another major aspect of message strategy that concerns the type of appeal the marketer will use to present the promotional message. One of the most important creative strategy decisions facing the advertiser involves the choice of an appropriate appeal. As was noted previously, some ads contain a great deal of information and are designed to appeal to the rational or logical aspect of the consumer's decision-making process, whereas others rely more on visual elements and appeal to feelings in an attempt to evoke some type of emotional reaction. Many feel that effective advertising combines the practical reasons for purchasing a product with emotional values.

Many promotional messages are based on **rational appeals,** which attempt to communicate directly information regarding the product or service such as its features and/or the benefits of owning or using it. The content of the rational appeal message is usually presented in a direct or logical manner and often relies on explanations and comparison such as the ad for the Volkswagen Jetta shown in Figure 6–16.

Rational appeals require a certain level of interest or involvement and information processing on the part of the message receiver to be effective. As was noted in the discussion of the elaboration likelihood model in Chapter 5, when motivation and ability to process the message are high, persuasion will occur through central processing of message content, and advertisements will be most effective if they contain strong and logical arguments for purchasing the product.

Figure 6–16   **This Jetta Advertisement Uses a Rational Appeal**

Figure 6–17 **This Ad for Bayer Stresses Its Effectiveness in Relieving Pain**

Rational appeals are often used for highly involving or complex consumer products, such as appliances, electronic products, or automobiles, where consumers have a high need for information and are likely to engage in evaluation and comparison of alternative brands. They are also very common in industrial marketing, both in advertising and in the development of sales presentations. Industrial buyers are usually very knowledgeable about the product or service they are purchasing and must be informed and convinced in a logical manner of the specifications, performance, value, quality, and so on, of an item before making a purchase.

Rational appeals are also used for many nondurable products, particularly when functional performance or efficacy is important to the consumer. The ad for Bayer aspirin shown in Figure 6–17 relies on a rational appeal to convince consumers of the product's ability to relieve pain. Many consumer products companies use a particular type of rational appeal known as comparative advertising as the basis for their advertising messages.

Comparative Advertising   **Comparative advertising** refers to the practice of either directly or indirectly naming one or more competitors in an ad and usually making a comparison on one or more specific attributes or characteristics (see Figure 6–16).[54] This form of advertising became a legitimate and popular practice after the Federal Trade Commission (FTC) began advocating its use in 1972. The FTC reasoned that the direct comparison of brands would provide more pertinent product information to consumers and thus a more rational basis for making purchase decisions. Television networks cooperated with the FTC by lifting their long-standing ban on comparative ads, and the result has been a flurry of comparative commercials. It has been estimated that nearly 35 percent of all television ads are comparative messages.

The decision to use a comparative message involves a number of considerations including consumers' response to the ad, perceptions of credibility, characteristics of the target audience, and the company's position in the market. An initial reason offered for using a comparative ad was that consumers would be more likely to pay attention to this type of message because of its novelty. However, since comparative ads have become so commonplace, their attention-getting value has probably declined.

It has been shown that viewers of comparative messages demonstrate higher recall of message content than viewers of noncomparative messages. However, comparative ads have generally not been shown to be more effective than noncomparative messages with respect to response variables such as brand attitudes or purchase intentions.[55] The advertiser must also consider how comparative messages might impact the credibility of the message. Consumers may perceive comparative ads as less believable and more offensive than noncomparative messages. Users of the brand that is attacked in the comparative message may be particularly skeptical about the credibility of the advertiser's claims.

One situation where comparative advertising may be particularly useful is for new brands attempting to enter the market. Comparative advertising allows a new market entrant to position itself directly against the more established brands and to promote its distinctive advantages relative to these competitors. Direct comparisons provide a new brand with a way of positioning itself in the "evoked" or choice set of brands the customer might be considering. For example, Ricoh Copiers used comparative messages when first introduced to position itself in the market with large companies such as IBM and Xerox.

Generally, comparative advertising is used the most by brands with the least to lose, which are those with the smallest market share. These brands will often compare themselves with the market leader, hoping to create an association with the established brand and to tap into the market segment that the leader has carved out. Market leaders, on the other hand, are often hesitant to use comparison ads, as most feel that they have little to gain by featuring competitors' products in their ads. There are exceptions, of course, such as when Coca-Cola resorted to comparative advertising in response to challenges made by Pepsi that were reducing Coke's market share.

Emotional Appeals

While rational appeals attempt to present useful information and influence consumers' logical, cognitive thought processes, advertisers often attempt to appeal to their feelings and emotions. The use of **emotional appeals** in advertising is really nothing new; companies such as AT&T, Hallmark, Kodak, and various life insurance companies have been utilizing this form of advertising for years. What is relatively new, however, is the number of companies in a variety of product/service areas that have turned to emotionally based advertising appeals. During the 1980s, many packaged-goods advertisers, who traditionally relied on rational arguments to sell their brands, began to recognize that emotional advertising can work effectively for them.[56] Marketers of products such as orange juice, toilet paper, bath towels, and coffee have turned to emotional appeals to differentiate their brands (Figure 6–18).

The increase in the use of emotional advertising appeals is due to several factors. First, the increased competition and similarity among brands that occur in the maturity stage of the product life cycle make it very difficult to differentiate a product using rational appeals. As one marketer noted:

> Many advertisers have turned to sentiment because they've run out of compelling appeals to logic. Their own sales pitches have lost their punch and for the increasing number of products that don't differ markedly from their competitors, new arguments are hard to find.[57]

A second reason for using emotional appeals is that they can have a positive effect on consumers' reactions to the ad. Emotional arousal can enhance communica-

Figure 6–18 **General Foods Uses an Emotional Appeal for Its International Coffees**

tion by increasing consumers' attention and their involvement with the ad and/or the brand. The feelings generated by an ad have been shown to influence the nature of message processing and affect attitudes toward the ad itself as well as brand attitudes.[58,59]

There are a number of emotion-based appeals that advertisers use, as will be seen later in the book in our discussion of creative strategy (Chapter 14). However, two of the more prevalent and interesting emotional appeals are those that use fear and humor.

Fear Appeals Marketers sometimes use **fear appeals** in their messages to create anxiety in the audience and arouse individuals to take action. Fear can be implemented in several ways. Some ads stress the physical danger or other negative consequences that can occur if attitudes or behaviors are not altered. For example, the American Cancer Society's anti-smoking ads stress that cigarette smoking is linked to lung cancer and other diseases and encourage consumers to stop smoking to protect their health. The negative consequences that can result from particular behaviors such as drunk driving or drug abuse are often shown in ads dealing with these problems (Figure 6–19). Fear appeals are also used to demonstrate negative consequences that may result if one does not engage in a particular behavior such as using a sunscreen or practicing regular dental hygiene.

A second way fear is used is through the threat of social disapproval or rejection that the individual might suffer if he or she does not use a particular product or service. Products such as deodorants, mouthwashes, and dandruff shampoos often appeal to the individual's need for approval and point out the embarrassment one might be saved from by using these products. The ad campaign for Dial soap—"Aren't you glad you use Dial? Don't you wish everybody did?"—is a good example of how mild fear appeals can be used in this manner.

How Fear Operates Before deciding to use a fear appeal–based message strategy, the advertiser should take into consideration how fear operates, what level to use, and

Figure 6–19   **Fear Appeals Are Used to Show the Dangers of Using Drugs**

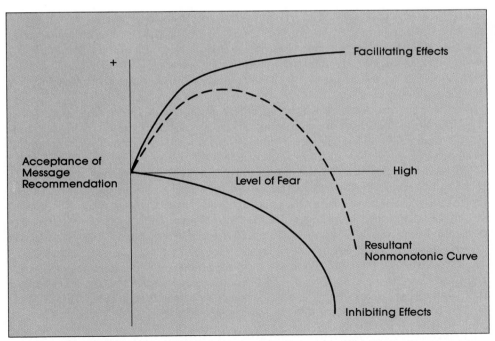

Figure 6–20   **Relationship Between Fear Levels and Message Acceptance**

Source: Michael L. Ray and William L. Wilkie, "Fear: The Potential of an Appeal Neglected by Marketing," *Journal of Marketing* 34 (January 1970), pp. 54–62.

how different target audiences might respond to it. The relationship between the level of fear in a message and acceptance or persuasion has been shown to be *nonmonotonic* or *curvilinear,* as shown in Figure 6–20. This means that with low levels of fear, message acceptance or persuasion increases as the amount of fear used rises. This increase in message acceptance does not continue, however, and beyond a certain point, acceptance or persuasion decreases as the level of fear rises.

This relationship between fear and persuasion can be explained by the fact that fear appeals have both facilitating and inhibiting effects.[60] A low level of fear can have *facilitating effects,* as it attracts attention and interest in the message and may motivate the receiver to take action to resolve the problem presented in the ad. Thus, increasing the level of fear in a message from low to moderate can result in increased persuasion. High levels of fear, however, can produce *inhibiting effects* whereby the receiver may emotionally block out the message by tuning it out, selectively perceiving it, or denying the message arguments outright. Figure 6–20 illustrates how these two countereffects operate to produce the curvilinear relationship between fear and persuasion. The implications of this relationship are that for fear appeals to be successful the level of fear utilized must be high enough to get the audience's interest and attention but not so high as to cause the consumer to reject or distort the message.

It is also important to consider the audience the message is targeted toward and how individuals might respond to fear appeals. Fear appeals are more effective when the message recipient is self-confident and less subject to anxieties and prefers to cope with dangers rather than avoid them.[61] They are also more effective among nonusers of a product than among users. Thus, a fear appeal may be more useful in refraining nonsmokers from starting than in convincing smokers to stop.

It has been suggested that fear appeals work best when the message provides the receiver with specific recommendations or actions to deal with the problem presented in the message. For example, ads for American Express Travelers Cheques show how a vacation can be ruined if you lose all your cash. However, the anxiety created is reduced by offering a solution to the problem—using the company's travelers checks and getting an immediate refund if they are lost or stolen.

Humor　At the opposite end of the emotional spectrum from fear appeals are messages that utilize humor. Humorous ads are often among the best known and remembered of all the advertising messages we see and/or hear and are also generally the most talked about. For example, the humorous commercials for Miller Lite beer have been the basis of one of the most effective and longest-running ad campaigns ever developed (Figure 6–21).

There are many reasons why an advertiser might choose to use a humorous message. Humorous messages are often more effective in attracting and holding consumers' attention and interest than are serious advertisements. This can be very important to advertisers, given the vast number of messages that compete for our attention every day. Humor can also enhance the effectiveness of a message by putting the consumer in a positive mood. Positive mood states not only may result in increased affect or liking of the ad itself but might also enhance the receiver's feeling toward the product or service. It has also been suggested that humorous commercials are effective because the humor can act as a distraction and thereby reduce the likelihood of the receiver's counterarguing against the message.[62]

While the factors noted above provide good reasons for using humor, not all marketing and advertising executives feel that humorous appeals are the best way to spend their advertising dollars. Many feel that while humor may be effective in drawing attention to the ad, it is often done at the expense of the message content. There is concern that humor can distract attention away from the brand and its attributes and toward the humorous situation or person depicted in the ad. Also, effective humor can

be very difficult to produce, and the end result is often a message that is too subtle to be understood by mass audiences. Thus, many advertisers prefer to use hard-sell, rational appeals that emphasize product attributes and key selling points rather than attempting to induce persuasion through a humorous appeal.

Obviously, there are valid reasons both for and against the use of humor in advertising, and not every product or service will lend itself to the use of a humorous appeal. An interesting study examined the viewpoints of advertising executives concerning the communication effectiveness of humor by surveying the research and creative directors of the top 150 advertising agencies. The directors were asked questions regarding which communications objectives are facilitated through the use of humor and the appropriate situational use of humor in terms of media, product, and audience factors. The general conclusions of this study are shown in Table 6–2.

Channel Factors

Thus far, our discussion of variables affecting the communications process has examined characteristics of the source or communicator and options regarding message structure and appeals. We have seen that effective communication often depends on the type of message employed and the person utilized to deliver this message. The final controllable variable of the communications process to be considered is the *channel* or *medium* actually used to deliver the message to the target audience. While there are a variety of methods available to transmit marketing communications, as noted in Chapter 5, they can be classified into two broad categories, *personal* and *nonpersonal* media. Let us consider some of the differences between these two communications modalities.

Table 6-2 **Summary of Study of Top Advertising Agency Research and Creative Directors' Opinions Regarding Use of Humor**

Humor does aid awareness and attention, which are the objectives best achieved by its use.
Humor may harm recall and comprehension in general.
  Humor may aid name and simple copy registration.
  Humor may harm complex copy registration.
  Humor may aid retention.
Persuasion in general is not aided by humor.
  Humor may aid persuasion to switch brands.
  Humor creates a positive mood that enhances persuasion.
Source credibility is not aided by humor.
Humor is generally not very effective in bringing about action/sales.
Creatives are more positive on the use of humor to fulfill all the above objectives than the
  research director.
Radio and TV are the best media to use humor, whereas direct mail and newspaper are
  least suited.
Consumer nondurables and business services are best suited to humor, whereas corporate
  advertising and industrial products are least suited.
Humor should be related to the product.
Humor should not be used with sensitive goods or services.
Audiences that are younger, better educated, upscale, male, and professional are best
  suited to humor; older, less educated, and downscale groups are least suited to humor
  appeals.

Source: Thomas J. Madden and Marc C. Weinberger, "Humor in Advertising: A Practitioner View," *Journal of Advertising Research* 24, no. 4 (August/September, 1984), pp. 23–26.

Personal versus Nonpersonal Channels

There are a number of basic differences between personal and nonpersonal communications channels. Information received from personal influence channels is generally more persuasive than is information received via the mass media. Reasons for the differences in the persuasive impact of personal versus mass media are summarized quite well in the following comparison of advertising versus personal selling:

> From the standpoint of persuasion, a sales message is far more flexible, personal and powerful than an advertisement. An advertisement is normally prepared by persons having minimal personal contact with customers. The message is designed to appeal to a large number of persons. By contrast, the message in a good sales presentation is not determined in advance. The salesman has a tremendous store of knowledge about his product or service and selects appropriate items as the interview progresses. Thus the salesman can adapt his to the thinking and needs of the customer or prospect at the time of the sales call. Furthermore, as objections arise and are voiced by the buyer, the salesman can treat the objections in an appropriate manner. This is not possible in advertising.[63]

Interface of Personal and Nonpersonal Channels While personal influence channels are generally recognized as being more flexible and powerful than nonpersonal channels, as noted earlier, many firms' promotional efforts involve nonpersonal communication through the mass media. However, it should also be recognized that in some situations the flow of information and influence can involve both personal and nonpersonal channels of communication through what is known as a **two-step flow** process. According to this model, in step one, information flows from the mass media to individuals actively involved with the media known as **opinion leaders.** The second step consists of a flow of information and influence from the opinion leaders to less active individuals known as opinion followers.[64]

A major implication of the two-step flow model is that the mass media do not have a direct and powerful influence on audience members; rather, mass media impact is mediated by opinion leaders who generally have greater exposure to the media. The primary function of the mass media is that of providing information, whereas personal sources exert more influence.

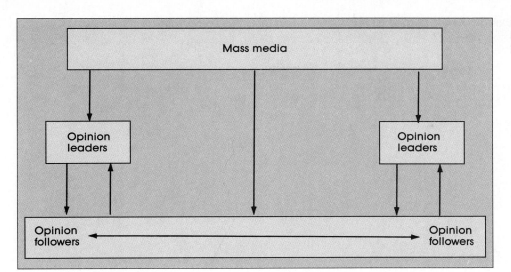

Figure 6–22 **Multistep Flow Model of the Communications Process**

The two-step model implies that marketers could communicate more effectively by identifying and reaching opinion leaders and letting them pass on information and influence others. However, this model may have limited applicability in today's communication environment. Opinion leaders are not the only individuals to receive information from the mass media. The explosion and prevalence of the mass media over the past several decades have resulted in a general public that is likely to receive information directly from the media as well as from opinion leaders. It is also likely that opinion leaders receive as well as give information, which suggests that word-of-mouth exchange involves a two-directional flow between opinion leaders and followers as well as with other opinion leaders rather than just a unidirectional flow.

It has also been suggested that the communications process is better represented as a **multistep flow** or process involving interaction among a number of parties rather than a basic two-step flow process, as shown in Figure 6–22.[65]

While there are problems with the original conception of the two-step flow model, marketers should give consideration to the implications of a multistep flow of influence. For example, marketers can target their efforts toward opinion leaders, in hopes that these individuals would pass the information on to opinion followers. Also, marketers may try to take advantage of opinion leadership by getting highly visible people to provide an endorsement or to use a product. For example, politicians often try to get celebrities to endorse their candidacy and to encourage others to vote for them. Sporting goods companies often provide free equipment to professionals who may be able to influence the opinions of the general public who sees them using or wearing a certain brand.

The notion of a two-step or a multistep flow model suggests that consideration must be given to the interface of personal and nonpersonal media to understand the communications process adequately. However, most promotional efforts do involve nonpersonal communication through mass media. Thus, in the remainder of this chapter we will examine factors relevant to the evaluation and selection of nonpersonal media, including general differences in alternative mass media and the effects of media context and environment.

Effects of Alternative Mass Media

The various mass media that advertisers use to transmit their persuasive messages differ in many ways including the number and type of people they reach, their costs, and their information-processing requirements and qualitative factors. Evaluation of mass

Figure 6–23   **Messages Containing a Great Deal of Information Are Best Suited to Print Media**

media in terms of how efficiently they expose a target audience to a communication is important, as we will see in the media chapters. However, we should also recognize that there are important differences in advertising media with respect to the effect they have on information processing and that communications are also influenced by the context or environment in which they appear.

Differences in Information Processing   Very basic differences among alternative mass media are the manner and rate at which information is transmitted and can be processed by the message recipient. Information from ads in print media, such as newspapers, magazines, or direct mail, is **self-paced media.** An individual reading a print ad processes the information at his or her own rate and can read or study the ad as long as is desired. In contrast, information from the broadcast media of radio and television is **externally paced media,** as the information transmission rate is controlled by the medium rather than by the message recipient.

The difference in the processing rate for print and broadcast media has some obvious implications for advertisers. Self-paced print media make it easier for the message recipient to process a long, complex message that may be difficult to understand. Thus, advertisers often use print ads when they want to present a detailed message with a lot of information. The ad for Apple computers shown in Figure 6–23 is an example. When broadcast media are used, however, the advertiser cannot use a detailed or complex message and must be careful to ensure that the information that is transmitted is understood. Thus, broadcast media may be more effective for transmitting shorter messages or, in the case of television, for presenting pictorial information along with a verbal message.

While there are limitations to the length and complexity that can be used in

Figure 6—24   **Print Ads Often Deliver the Same Message as Television Commercials**

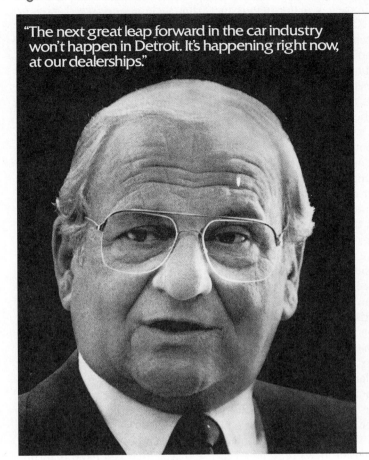

"The next great leap forward in the car industry won't happen in Detroit. It's happening right now, at our dealerships."

THE CAR BUYER'S BILL OF RIGHTS

"SERVICE IS YOUR RIGHT."

For the past two years, in overall dealer service and product quality, Chrysler has the highest customer satisfaction of any American car company.

At Chrysler, we understand that dealer service can make or break the relationship between car buyer and carmaker. That's why...just as we've made a commitment to stand behind the car buyer's rights...our more than 5,000 dealers have made an equally important commitment to deliver customer satisfaction.

And they're delivering. J.D. Power and Associates, one of the industry's most respected research organizations, surveyed over 25,000 owners of 1987 passenger cars. The results clearly showed that owners of Chrysler-built cars were happier with the overall service provided by their dealers, and with the quality of their cars,* than Ford or GM owners. That says a lot about the way our dealers treat your car, and the way they treat you.

Last year alone, our dealer technicians received more than 500,000 total hours of specialized training in the most advanced repair procedures. That's an increase of almost 200% from 1981. With this hands-on knowledge, and the most sophisticated equipment available, they're prepared to handle any problem.

You have a right to friendly treatment, honest service and competent repairs. Chrysler...and every Dodge, Chrysler, Plymouth, Jeep and Eagle dealer...intend to see that you get it.

"SERVICE IS YOUR RIGHT. AND WE INTEND TO SEE THAT YOU GET IT."

CHRYSLER MOTORS

CHRYSLER·PLYMOUTH·DODGE
DODGE TRUCKS·JEEP·EAGLE

*J.D. Power and Associates 1988 CSI Customer Satisfaction with Product Quality and Dealer Service for '86-'87 passenger cars. BUCKLE UP FOR SAFETY.

broadcast messages, advertisers do have ways of dealing with this problem. One strategy is to use a radio or television ad to get consumers' attention and direct them to specific print media for a more detailed message. For example, a real estate developer may use radio ads to draw attention to a housing development and direct the listener to the real estate section of the newspaper for more details. Another way that advertisers deal with this problem is to develop a broadcast and print version of the same message. The copy portion of the message will be similar in both media, but the print version of the ad can be processed at a rate that is comfortable to the individual receiver. Note that the ad for Chrysler Motors ("Service is your right") shown in Figure 6—24 is a print version of the television commercial presented earlier in this chapter (see Figure 6—9). Both were part of Chrysler's "Car Buyer Bill of Rights Campaign."

Effects of Context and Environment

Reactions to and interpretation of an advertising message can be a function of not only the message content but also the context or environment in which the ad appears. The famous communication theorist Marshall McLuhan's thesis "the medium is the message" implies that the medium communicates an image that is independent of any message it contains.[66] The notion of a **qualitative media effect** refers to the positive or negative influence the medium may contribute to the message. The medium may affect reactions to the message either through the image of the media vehicle itself or through the reception environment that is created.

For example, an advertisement for a high-quality men's clothing line might have more of a significant impact in a prestigious magazine such as *The New Yorker* or *Esquire* than in *Sports Afield* or *National Lampoon*. The former two magazines create a more appropriate reception environment for this type of advertising than the latter two. Advertisements can draw qualitative value from certain media because of the editorial content of the publication and the type of people who are attracted to it and the meaning or role the medium plays in the lives of consumers. An avid skier may respond very positively to an ad for ski boots in *Skiing* magazine partly because the articles, pictures, and other ads have gotten him or her excited over the upcoming ski season.

Media environments can also be created by the nature of the program in which a commercial appears. For example, a study of consumers' reactions to commercials shown during a happy-mood television program versus a sad-mood program found that the happy program not only created a more positive mood state but also resulted in greater perceived commercial effectiveness, more favorable cognitive responses, and better recall relative to the sad program.[67]

Advertisers may pay premium dollars to advertise on programs that are popular and create very positive moods. For example, the Olympics is a very popular media purchase among television advertisers as they seek to become a part of the excitement and festivities associated with the event. Christmas specials are another example of programs that can create favorable moods.

Sometimes advertisers avoid certain media environments if they feel the program might create a negative mood among viewers, or if they feel that association with a program may be detrimental to the company or its products. For example, many companies have ceased advertising on programs that have excessive violence or sex in them. A few years ago Chrysler withdrew its advertising from the ABC network miniseries *Amerika,* which was about life in the United States after a Soviet takeover. The company indicated that the subject matter and its portrayal were too intense and emotional and that its upbeat product commercials would be both inappropriate and of limited effectiveness in that viewing environment.[68] Coca-Cola has a corporate policy not to advertise on television news programs because it feels that bad news is inconsistent with the image of Coke as an upbeat, fun product. General Foods advertises coffee on news programs but not food products. A company spokesperson noted, "When a food commercial arrives after the reporting of hard news, you may have destroyed that feeling about food."[69]

Clutter Another aspect of the media environment that is important to advertisers is the problem of **clutter,** which refers to all the nonprogram material that appears in the broadcast environment, including commercials, promotional messages for shows, public service announcements, and the like. Clutter has become an increasing concern to advertisers, as there are simply too many messages competing for the consumer's attention, and it has become very difficult for the advertising for any one brand to get noticed.[70] The clutter problem has become compounded in television advertising by the trend toward shorter commercials. The 30-second commercial—which became the industry standard in the 1970s, replacing 60-second spots—is now giving way to 15-second commercials. Many advertisers are requesting 15-second spots, which is causing concern among the networks because of the clutter problem.

The advertising industry continues to express concern over the highly cluttered commercial viewing environment. Advertisers are increasingly turning to techniques such as humor, use of celebrity spokespersons, or other novel and/or unique, creative approaches as ways of breaking through the clutter and drawing attention to their messages.

Obviously, there are numerous other characteristics regarding source, message, and channel factors that must be considered in developing an advertising and promotional program.[71] Our goal in this chapter has been to provide a broad overview of some of the factors that must be taken into account regarding these communications variables and how they influence the response process of the message recipient. We will be considering these communications variables again later in the text. In Chapters 10 through 13, specific characteristics of the print and broadcast media are discussed along with media strategy, whereas in Chapter 14 we examine creative strategy and the development of advertising messages and campaigns.

Summary

This chapter has focused on the controllable variables that are part of the communications process, including source, message, and channel factors. Decisions regarding each of these variables should take into account the impact on the various stages or steps of the response hierarchy that the message receiver passes through. The persuasion matrix was presented for use in assessing the effect of controllable communication decisions on the response process.

Selection of the appropriate source or communicator to deliver a message is an important aspect of communication strategy. Three important attributes or characteristics were examined, including source credibility, attractiveness, and power, along with the process by which they might induce attitude or opinion change. Marketers utilize source characteristics to enhance message effectiveness by hiring communicators who are experts in a particular area and/or have a very trustworthy image. The use of attractive communicators such as celebrities to deliver advertising messages has become very popular; advertisers hope that they will catch the receivers' attention and influence their attitudes or behavior through an identification process.

The design of the advertising message is a critical part of the communications process. Attention was given to various options regarding message structure, including order of presentation of message arguments, conclusion drawing, message sidedness, and use of refutational appeals. The advantages and disadvantages of different message appeal strategies were considered including rational appeals, such as comparative messages, and emotional appeals, such as fear and humor.

Finally, attention was focused on the channel or medium used to deliver the message. Differences in personal and nonpersonal channels of communication were discussed along with the two-step flow model, which views the impact of the mass media as being mediated by the personal influence of opinion leaders. Differences in alternative mass media can have an information effect on the communications process as a result of information processing and qualitative factors. The context in which an ad appears and the reception environment are important factors to consider in the selection of mass media. Clutter has become a serious problem for advertisers, particularly on television where commercials become shorter and more numerous.

Key Terms

Persuasion matrix	Two-sided message
Source	Refutational appeal
Credibility	Rational appeals
Expertise	Comparative advertising
Trustworthiness	Emotional appeals
Internalization	Fear appeals
Sleeper effect	Two-step flow
Attractiveness	Opinion leaders
Identification	Multistep flow
Source power	Self-paced media
Compliance	Externally paced media
Primacy effect	Qualitative media effect
Recency effect	Clutter
One-sided message	

Discussion Questions

1. Choose a particular print ad or television commercial currently being used by a company and use the persuasion matrix to analyze how it might influence the consumer's response process.
2. What are the basic components of source credibility? Discuss how these credibility components are utilized in marketing communications.
3. Discuss some of the reasons why a highly credible communicator may not necessarily be more effective than one low in credibility.
4. Discuss the various components of source attractiveness. Provide examples of how attractiveness is used in advertising.
5. Discuss the pros and cons of using celebrities as advertising spokespersons. Provide examples of two celebrities that you feel are very appropriate (or inappropriate) for the brands they are endorsing and explain why.
6. Do you feel companies such as Coke and Pepsi can justify paying rock stars such as Michael Jackson or Madonna $10 million to appear in their commercials? Support your position.
7. Discuss the pros and cons of using the following types of message structures or appeals:

   • One- and two-sided messages
   • Messages that do or do not use a specific conclusion
   • Comparative advertisements
   • Fear appeals
   • Humorous advertisements

8. Analyze the use of fear appeal messages, such as the one shown in Figure 6–21, to deter drug abuse among teenagers and young adults. Do you feel these ads are effective? Why or why not?
9. Discuss how marketers can utilize the two-step or multistep flow of communications models in their promotional programs.
10. What is meant by a qualitative media effect? Choose several examples of media and analyze their qualitative factors.
11. What is meant by advertising clutter? What can advertisers and the media do to deal with the clutter problem?

Notes

1. "Terrific! I Hate It," *Forbes,* June 27, 1988, p. 130.
2. Barbara Lippert, "Lying with a Smile on Madison Avenue," *U.S. News & World Report,* February 23, 1987, p. 58.
3. Bruce Horowitz, "Isuzu's Ads Are Hot but Its Sales Are Not," *Los Angeles Times,* August 4, 1987, pt. IV, p. 1.
4. Bob Garfield, "Jacko Gives Jumpin' Jolt to Energizer's Campaign," *Advertising Age,* July 21, 1987, p. 1.
5. Julie Liesse Erickson, "Oy! Energizer Dumps DDB," *Advertising Age,* February 20, 1989, p. 4.
6. Scott Hume, "Isuzu Lies Its Way into Top 10," *Advertising Age,* May 29, 1989, p. 12.
7. William J. McGuire, "An Information Processing Model of Advertising Effectiveness," in *Behavioral and Management Science in Marketing,* ed. Harry J. Davis and Alvin J. Silk (New York: Ronald Press, 1978), pp. 156–80.
8. Herbert C. Kelman, "Processes of Opinion Change," *Public Opinion Quarterly* 25 (Spring 1961), pp. 57–78.
9. William J. McGuire, "The Nature of Attitudes and Attitude Change," in *Handbook of Social Psychology,* 2nd ed., ed. G. Lindzey and E. Aronson (Cambridge, Mass.: Addison-Wesley, 1969), pp. 135–214.

10. John C. Mowen and Stephen W. Brown, "On Explaining and Predicting the Effectiveness of Celebrity Endorsers," in *Advances in Consumer Research* 8 (Ann Arbor: Association for Consumer Research, 1981), pp. 437–441.

11. "Business Celebrities," *Business Week,* June 23, 1986, pp. 100–107.

12. "Terrific!"

13. Roger Kevin and Thomas E. Barry, "The CEO Spokesperson in Consumer Advertising: An Experimental Investigation," in *Current Issues in Research in Advertising,* ed. J. H. Leigh and C. R. Martin (Ann Arbor: University of Michigan, 1981), pp. 135–48.

14. A. Eagly and S. Chaiken, "An Attribution Analysis of the Effect of Communicator Characteristics on Opinion Change," *Journal of Personality and Social Psychology* 32 (1975), pp. 136–144.

15. For a review of these studies see Brian Sternthal, Lynn Phillips, and Ruby Dholakia, "The Persuasive Effect of Source Credibility: A Situational Analysis," *Public Opinion Quarterly* 42 (Fall 1978), pp. 285–314.

16. Brian Sternthal, Ruby Dholakia, and Clark Leavitt, "The Persuasive Effects of Source Credibility: Tests of Cognitive Response," *Journal of Consumer Research* 4, no. 4 (March 1978), pp. 252–260.

17. Robert R. Harmon and Kenneth A. Coney, "The Persuasive Effects of Source Credibility in Buy and Lease Situations," *Journal of Marketing Research* 19 (May 1982), pp. 255–60.

18. For a review see Noel Capon and James Hulbert, "The Sleeper Effect, An Awakening," *Public Opinion Quarterly* 37 (1973), pp. 333–58.

19. Darlene B. Hannah and Brian Sternthal, "Detecting and Explaining the Sleeper Effect," *Journal of Consumer Research* 11, no. 2 (September 1984), pp. 632–42.

20. H. C. Triandis, *Attitudes and Attitude Change* (New York: John Wiley & Sons, 1971).

21. J. Mills and J. Jellison, "Effect on Opinion Change of Similarity between the Communicator and the Audience He Addresses," *Journal of Personality and Social Psychology* 9, no. 2 (1969), pp. 153–56.

22. Arch G. Woodside and J. William Davenport, Jr., "The Effect of Salesman Similarity and Expertise on Consumer Purchasing Behavior," *Journal of Marketing Research* 11 (May 1974), pp. 198–202.

23. Paul Busch and David T. Wilson, "An Experimental Analysis of a Salesman's Expert and Referent Bases of Social Power in the Buyer-Seller Dyad," *Journal of Marketing Research* 13 (February 1976), pp. 3–11.

24. Aliza Laufer, "Hot Selling Properties," *Backstage,* June 5, 1987, p. 1.

25. Patricia Winters, "Pepsi to Use Jackson in 4-Part Spot," *Advertising Age,* September 14, 1987, p. 1.

26. "Singing for Their Soda," *Time,* February 6, 1989, p. 55.

27. Gallup-Robinson study results discussed in: Jane Sasseen, "Consumer: Sports, Jocks Run Faster, Jump Higher, and Sell Better," *Madison Avenue* (January 1984), pp. 92–98.

28. Cited in David Ogily and Joel Raphaelson, "Research on Advertising Techniques That Work—and Don't Work," *Harvard Business Review* 60 (1982), pp. 14–15.

29. Strafford P. Sherman, "When You Wish Upon a Star," *Fortune,* August 19, 1985, pp. 66–73.

30. Bruce Horowitz, "Mazda Drops Garner to Try New Route in Commercials," *Los Angeles Times,* February 10, 1989, pt. IV, p. 1.

31. Charles Atkin and M. Block, "Effectiveness of Celebrity Endorsers," *Journal of Advertising Research* 23, no. 1 (February/March 1983), pp. 57–61.

32. J. Forkan, "Product Matchup Key to Effective Star Presentations," *Advertising Age,* October 6, 1980, p. 42.

33. Donald R. Katz, "The Face That Revitalized Sears," *Advertising Age,* January 11, 1988, p. 32.

34. John Motavall, " Advertising Blunders of the Rich and Famous," *Adweek,* January 11, 1988, B.R. 18.

35. Alix M. Freedman, " Marriages Between Celebrity Spokesmen and Their Firms Can Be Risky Venture," *The Wall Street Journal,* January 22, 1988, p. 23.

36. James R. Schiffman, "PepsiCo Cans TV Ads with Madonna, Pointing Up Risks of Using Superstars," *The Wall Street Journal,* April 5, 1989, p. B-11.

37. For an excellent review of these studies see W. B. Joseph, "The Credibility of Physically Attractive Communicators," *Journal of Advertising* 11, no. 3 (1982), pp. 13–23.

38. M. J. Baker and Gilbert A. Churchill, Jr., "The Impact of Physically Attractive Models on Advertising Evaluations," *Journal of Marketing Research* 14 (November 1977), pp. 538–55.

39. Robert W. Chestnut, C. C. La Chance, and A. Lubitz, "The Decorative Female Model: Sexual Stimuli and the Recognition of the Advertisements," *Journal of Advertising* 6 (Fall 1977), pp. 11–14.
40. Leonard N. Reid and Lawrence C. Soley, "Decorative Models and Readership of Magazine Ads," *Journal of Advertising Research* 23, no. 2 (April/May 1983), pp. 27–32.
41. "Why P & G Wants a Mellower Image," *Business Week,* June 7, 1982, p. 60.
42. Herbert E. Krugman, "On Application of Learning Theory to TV Copy Testing," *Public Opinion Quarterly* 26 (1962), pp. 626–39.
43. C. I. Hovland and W. Mandell, "An Experimental Comparison of Conclusion Drawing by the Communicator and by the Audience," *Journal of Abnormal and Social Psychology* 47 (July 1952), pp. 581–88.
44. Paul Chance, "Ads without Answers Make Brain Itch," *Psychology Today* 9 (1975), p. 78.
45. C. I. Hovland, A. A. Lumsdaine, and F. D. Sheffield, *Experiments on Mass Communication* (Princeton, N.J.: Princeton University Press, 1949), 3: 201–27.
46. Robert E. Settle and Linda L. Golden, "Attribution Theory and Advertiser Credibility," *Journal of Marketing Research* 11 (May 1974), pp. 181–85.
47. Edmund J. Faison, "Effectiveness of One-Sided and Two-Sided Mass Communications in Advertising," *Public Opinion Quarterly* 25 (Fall 1961), pp. 468–69.
48. Alan G. Sawyer, "The Effects of Repetition of Refutational and Supportive Advertising Appeals," *Journal of Marketing Research* 10 (February 1973), pp. 23–37.
49. George J. Szybillo and Richard Heslin, "Resistance to Persuasion: Inoculation Theory in a Marketing Context," *Journal of Marketing Research* 10 (November 1973), pp. 396–403.
50. Andrew A. Mitchell, "The Effect of Verbal and Visual Components of Advertisements on Brand Attitudes and Attitude toward the Advertisement," *Journal of Consumer Research* 13 (June 1986), pp. 12–24.
51. Julie A. Edell and Richard Staelin, "The Information Processing of Pictures in Advertisements," *Journal of Consumer Research* 10, no. 1 (June 1983), pp. 45–60.
52. Jolita Kisielius and Brian Sternthal, "Detecting and Explaining Vividness Effects in Attitudinal Judgments," *Journal of Marketing Research* 21, no. 1 (1984), pp. 54–64.
53. Elizabeth C. Hirschmann, "The Effects of Verbal and Pictorial Advertising Stimuli on Aesthetic, Utilitarian and Familiarity Perceptions," *Journal of Advertising* 15, no. 2 (1986), pp. 27–34.
54. William L. Wilkie and Paul W. Farris, "Comparative Advertising: Problems and Potential," *Journal of Marketing* 39 (1975), pp. 7–15.
55. For a review of comparative advertising studies see Cornelia Pechmann and David W. Stewart, "Development of a Contingency Model of Comparative Advertising" (Working Paper, Graduate School of Management, University of California, Irvine, 1988).
56. "Emotion a Powerful Tool for Advertisers," *Advertising Age,* July 8, 1985, p. 28.
57. Bill Abrams, "If Logic Doesn't Sell, Try a Little Tug on the Heartstrings," *The Wall Street Journal,* April 8, 1982, p. 27.
58. Morris B. Holbrook and Rajeev Batra, "Assessing the Role of Emotions as Mediators of Consumer Responses to Advertising," *Journal of Consumer Research* 14, no. 3 (December 1987), pp. 404–420.
59. Julie A. Edell and Marian Chapman Burke, "The Power of Feelings in Understanding Advertising Effects," *Journal of Consumer Research* 14, no. 3 (December 1987), pp. 421–33.
60. Michael L. Ray and William L. Wilkie, "Fear: The Potential of an Appeal Neglected by Marketing," *Journal of Marketing* 34 (January 1970), pp. 54–62.
61. Brian Sternthal and C. Samuel Craig, "Fear Appeals Revisited and Revised," *Journal of Consumer Research* 1 (December 1974), pp. 22–34.
62. For a discussion of the use of humor in advertising see ibid., "Humor in Advertising," *Journal of Marketing* 37 (October 1973), pp. 12–18.
63. Harold C. Cash and W. J. E. Crissy, "Comparison of Advertising and Selling," *The Salesman's Role in Marketing, The Psychology of Selling* 12 (1965), pp. 56–75.
64. Paul F. Lazarsfeld, Bernard Berelson, and Hazel Gaudet, *The People's Choice* (New York: Columbia University Press, 1948).
65. Peter H. Reingen and Jerome B. Kernan, "Analysis of Referral Networks in Marketing," *Journal of Marketing Research* 23 (November 1986), pp. 370–78.
66. Marshall McLuhan, *Understanding Media: The Extensions of Man* (New York: McGraw-Hill, 1966).
67. Marvin E. Goldberg and Gerald J. Gorn, "Happy and Sad TV Programs: How They Affect

Reactions to Commercials," *Journal of Consumer Research* 14, no. 3 (December 1987), pp. 387–403.

68. Peter J. Boyle, "Chrysler Pulls Ads from Amerika," *New York Times,* January 28, 1987, p. C26.

69. *"GF, Coke Tell Why They Shun TV News," Advertising Age,* January 28, 1980, p. 39.

70. Peter H. Webb, "Consumer Initial Processing in a Difficult Media Environment," *Journal of Consumer Research* 6, no. 3 (December 1979), pp. 225–36.

71. For a review of marketing communications studies involving source, message, channel, and receiver factors, see George E. Belch, Michael A. Belch, and Angelina Villarreal, "Effects of Advertising Communications: Review of Research," in *Research in Marketing* (Greenwich, CT: JAI Press, 1987), 9: 59–117.

Market Segmentation and Positioning

7

CHAPTER OBJECTIVES

1. To review the strategies available to the marketer for selecting and entering a market

2. To provide an understanding of the concept of target marketing and its use in advertising and promotion

3. To provide an understanding of the concept of market segmentation and its use in advertising and promotion

4. To understand the use of positioning and repositioning strategies in advertising and promotion

5. To examine the factors to be considered in developing a positioning strategy

Japanese Automakers Target the U.S. Heartland

Mitsubishi Motors Corporation, a Japanese auto manufacturer, has been selling cars in the United States since 1982 but has never had an auto dealership in the state of Michigan—that is, until now. In 1989 Mitsubishi planned to open six dealerships in the Motor City (Detroit) itself. Why is this news important, you ask? It is important because Mitsubishi is now targeting a new market where they have not been successful in the past—the Midwest.

While Americans on the East and West coasts have adopted Japanese cars for quite sometime, the Midwest has been slow to purchase imports. For example, 50 percent of all autos sold in California are imports, whereas in Michigan only 15 percent are, and in Ohio more than 75 percent are American made. Because of the potential for sales in the Midwest market, Mitsubishi as well as other Japanese manufacturers (Toyota, Nissan, Subaru) are targeting the area with their marketing efforts. Besides opening dealerships, these companies are establishing manufacturing plants in the area, opening regional offices, and purchasing distributorships. In the advertising and promotions area, Nissan has increased its Midwestern region's advertising budget and is producing ads that reflect more Midwestern "sensitivities." Toyota has hired Detroit Pistons basketball star Isaah Thomas as its spokesperson and has increased its exhibit space at the Detroit Auto Show by 50 percent. As noted by auto analysts of the J. D. Power & Associates research firm, "The Japanese plan to wage war in the Midwest."[1]

Introduction

As the lead-in to this chapter demonstrates, companies often pursue a strategy of "targeting" a specific market or markets. In the case of the Japanese automakers, the Midwestern market was seen as offering strong market potential and thus became the focus for marketing (including advertising and promotions) efforts. Because of the diversity of consumers' needs and wants, and the increase in competitive offerings that has occurred in the past few decades, marketers have found it to be more advantageous to segment their markets and concentrate on the marketing of their products to specific groups rather than to the market as a whole. This means that specific advertising and promotions strategies will be developed for each of these markets, as was demonstrated by Nissan's plan to appeal to "Midwestern sensitivities" and Toyota's hiring of Isaah Thomas as its advertising spokesperson. In this chapter we will examine the concepts of market segmentation, target marketing, and market positioning and their relevance to the promotional planning process.

From our discussion of the decision process model you should remember that the situation analysis is conducted as the very first stage in the promotional planning process. You should also recall that the establishment of specific objectives—both marketing and communication—is derived from the situation analysis and that the promotional mix strategies are in turn developed in an effort to achieve these objectives. In this chapter you will discover that marketers rarely go after the entire market with one product, brand, or service offering; rather, a number of different strategies may be assumed, in which the market is broken down into *segments,* and one or more of these segments is targeted for marketing and promotional efforts. This means that different objectives may be established, different budgets may be used, and the promotional mix strategies may very well vary, depending on the market approach that is used. Focusing on one or more segments of the market involves a process referred to as *target marketing.* A discussion of this process follows.

The Concept of Target Marketing

Because few, if any, products can satisfy the needs of all consumers, companies often develop different marketing strategies to satisfy different consumer needs. The process by which marketers do this (presented in Figure 7–1) is referred to as *target marketing* and involves four basic steps—that is, identifying markets with unfulfilled needs,

Figure 7–1 **The Target Marketing Process**

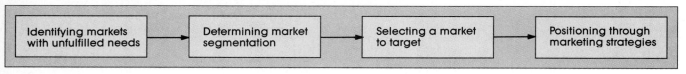

market segmentation, targeting specific segments, and positioning one's product or service through marketing strategies.

Identifying Markets

As noted, marketers develop various strategies in an attempt to satisfy the needs of consumers. One approach used for accomplishing this objective is **product differentiation,** whereby the manufacturer produces a variety of products from which the consumer can choose, as demonstrated by the Coca-Cola product line shown in Figure 7–2. A second approach is **target marketing,** in which the marketer identifies the specific needs of groups of people (or segments), selects one or more of these segments as a target, and develops marketing programs directed to each (remember the Japanese automakers?). This latter approach has found increased applicability in marketing for a number of reasons, including changes in the market itself (consumers are becoming much more diverse in their needs, attitudes, lifestyles, etc.); an increased utilization of the practice of segmentation by competitors; and the fact that more managers have been trained in the practice of segmentation, realizing the advantages associated with this strategy. Perhaps the best explanation, however, comes back to the basic premise that it is necessary to understand as much as possible about consumers in order to design marketing programs to meet their needs more effectively. In this regard, segmenting makes it possible to isolate consumers with similar lifestyles, needs, and the like, and increase our knowledge of their specific requirements. As we noted in earlier chapters, the more marketers are able to establish this "common ground" with consumers, the more effective they will be in addressing these requirements in their communications programs and informing and/or persuading potential consumers that the product or service offering will meet their needs.

Let us use the beer industry as an example. Many years ago one might have considered beer as beer—very little differentiation, many local distributors, very few truly national brands. The industry then began a period of consolidation, with many brands either being assumed by the larger brewers or ceasing to exist at all. As the number of competitors decreased, the competition among the major brewers increased. To compete more effectively, brewers began to look at different tastes, lifestyles, and so on, of beer drinkers and used this information as input into their marketing strategies. A direct result of this process was a segmentation of the marketplace.

As you can see by examining Figure 7–3, the beer market has now become quite segmented, with super premiums, premiums, populars (low price), imports, lights (low calorie), and malts being offered. Low-alcohol and non-alcoholic brands have also been introduced, as has draft beer in bottles and cans. And of course there are now imported lights, super premium drafts, dry beers, and on and on. Given that most of these product groups are thriving, it must be assumed that each has its own set of needs that it satisfies. While taste is certainly one factor being considered, others are also operating—some of which may include image, costs, and the size of one's waistline. A variety of reasons for purchasing are also operating, including social class, lifestyle, and economic considerations, any of which might be reflected in the brand's image.

The point of this discussion is that the market has been broken down— segmented—into a number of individual markets, each with its own specific characteristics and each requiring a separate marketing and promotions effort. The remainder of this chapter will discuss some of the ways of approaching this task.

Figure 7–2 **Coca-Cola's Approach to Product Differentiation**

Market Segmentation

Obviously, it is not possible to develop marketing strategies for each and every consumer. Rather, the marketer will attempt to identify broad classes of buyers who have the same needs and who will respond similarly to marketing actions. As noted by Eric N. Berkowitz, Roger A. Kerin, and William Rudelius, **market segmentation** is "dividing up a market into distinct groups that (1) have common needs and (2) will respond similarly to a marketing action."[2] The segmentation process involves five distinct steps:

1. Finding ways to group consumers according to their needs
2. Finding ways to group the marketing actions—usually the products offered—available to the organization

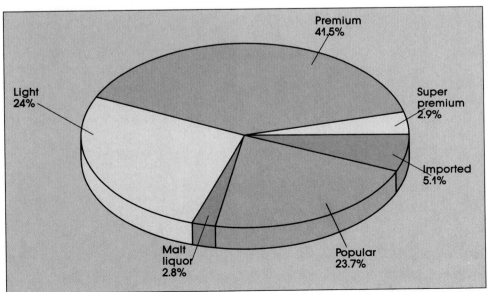

Figure 7–3 **Market Segments in the Beer Industry**

Premium
41.5%

Super premium
2.9%

Imported
5.1%

Popular
23.7%

Malt liquor
2.8%

Light
24%

Source: Adapted from "Beer Trends: Market Breakdown by Product," in *Beverage Industry Annual Manual 1989* (Cleveland: Edge, 1989), pp. 38–47.

3. Developing a market-product grid to relate the market segments to the firm's products or actions
4. Selecting the target segments toward which the firm directs its marketing actions
5. Taking those actions

The more the marketer segments the market, the more precise will be his or her understanding of it. At the same time, the more the market becomes divided, the less the number of consumers constituting each segment. Thus, a key decision to be made is, how far should one go in the segmentation process? That is, where does the process stop? As you can see by the strategy taken in the beer industry, it can go pretty far!

In planning the promotional effort, the manager must consider whether the target segment will support individualized strategies. More specifically, he or she must consider whether this group is *accessible* or can be reached with the communication.

Table 7–1   Bases For Market Segmentation

Main Dimension	Segmentation Variable	Typical Breakdown
	Customer Characteristics	
Geographic	Region	Pacific; Mountain; West North Central; West South Central; East North Central; East South Central; South Atlantic; Middle Atlantic; New England
	City or metropolitan statistical area (MSA) size	Under 5,000; 5,000 to 19,999; 20,000 to 49,999; 50,000 to 99,999; 100,000 to 249,999; 250,000 to 499,999; 500,000 to 999,999; 1,000,000 to 3,999,999; 4,000,000 or over
	Density	Urban; suburban; rural
	Climate	Northern; Southern
Demographic	Age	Infant, under 6; 6 to 11; 12 to 17; 18 to 24; 25 to 34; 35 to 49; 50 to 64; 65 or over
	Sex	Male; female
	Family size	1 to 2; 3 to 4; 5 or over
	Stage of family life cycle	Young single; young married, no children; young married, youngest child under 6; young married, youngest child 6 or older; older married, with children; older married, no children under 18; older single; other older married, no children under 18
	Ages of children	No child under 18; youngest child 6 to 17; youngest child under 6
	Children under 18	0; 1; more than 1
	Income	Under $5,000; $5,000 to $14,999; $15,000 to $24,999; $25,000 to $34,999; $35,000 to $49,999; $50,000 or over
	Occupation	Professional and technical; managers, official, and proprietors; clerical, sales; craftsmen, foremen; operatives; farmers; retired; students; homemakers; unemployed
	Education	Grade school or less; some high school; high school graduate; some college; college graduate
	Race	White; black; Hispanic; Asian; other
	Home ownership	Own home; rent home
	Dwelling	House (unattached); attached home or condominium; apartment; mobile home or trailer
Psychographic	Personality	Gregarious; compulsive; extroverted; aggressive; ambitious
	Lifestyle	Use of one's time; values and importance; beliefs

For example, you will see in a later chapter that in some instances there are no media that can be used to reach a targeted group. Or, in another situation, the promotions manager may identify a number of segments but will be unable to develop the required programs necessary to reach them. In this latter case the firm may have insufficient funds to develop the required advertising campaign, inadequate sales staff to cover all areas, or other promotional deficiencies. Having made the determination that a segmentation strategy is in order, the marketer must then establish the *basis* upon which the market will be addressed. The following section will discuss some of the bases for segmenting markets and demonstrate advertising and promotions applications.

Bases for Segmentation   As shown in Table 7–1, a variety of methods are available for segmenting markets. A marketer may use one of the segmentation variables shown in Table 7–1 as the sole basis of his or her strategy, or a combination of approaches may be required. For example, consider the market segmentation strategy

Table 7–1 **(concluded)**

Main Dimension	Segmentation Variable	Typical Breakdown
	Buying Situation	
Benefits offered	Product features	Situation specific; general
	Needs	Quality; service; economy
Usage	Rate of use	Light user; medium user; heavy user
	User states	Nonuser; ex-user, potential user; first-time user; regular user
Awareness and intentions	Readiness to buy	Unaware; aware; informed; interested; desirous; intending to buy
	Brand familiarity	Insistence; preference; recognition; nonrecognition; rejection
Buying condition	Type of buying activity	Minimum effort buying; comparison buying; special effort buying
	Kind of store	Convenience; wide breadth; specialty

Segmentation Variables and Breakdowns for Industrial Markets

	Customer Characteristics	
Geographic	Region	Pacific; Mountain; West North Central; West South Central; East North Central; East South Central; South Atlantic; Middle Atlantic; New England
	Location	In MSA; not in MSA
Demographic	SIC code	2-digit; 3-digit; 4-digit categories
	Number of employees	1 to 19; 20 to 99; 100 to 249; 250 or over
	Number of production workers	1 to 19; 20 to 99; 100 to 249; 250 or over
	Annual sales volume	Less than $1 million; $1 million to $10 million; $10 million to $100 million; over $100 million
	Number of establishments	With 1 to 19 employees; with 20 or more employees
	Buying Situation	
Nature of good	Kind	Product or service
	Where used	Installation; component of final product; supplies
	Application	Office use; limited production use; heavy production use
Buying condition	Purchase location	Centralized; decentralized
	Who buys	Individual buyer; group
	Type of buy	New buy; modified rebuy; straight rebuy

Source: Eric N. Berkowitz, Roger A. Kerin, and William Rudelius, *Marketing* (Homewood, Ill.: Richard D. Irwin, 1989), p. 202.

Figure 7—4 **Blue Cross Employs Geographic Segmentation**

that might be employed to market snow skis. While the consumer's lifestyle—that is, active, fun-loving, enjoys outdoor sports—would certainly be important, so too would other factors, such as age (participation in downhill skiing drops off significantly at about age 30) and/or income (Have you seen the price of a lift ticket lately?). Let us review the bases for segmentation and examine examples of promotional strategies employed in each.

Geographic segmentation   In the **geographic segmentation** approach, markets are divided into different geographic units. These units may include nations, states, counties, or even neighborhoods. For example, *USA Weekend,* the publication of the Roper Organization mentioned in Chapter 4, provides marketplace portraits of the "9 Nations of the USA," in which profiles of consumer habits in each area are discussed (see Promotional Perspective 7—1). Based on a number of economic and sociological factors, these reports have shown geographical differences with respect to

Perceptions of ads. There is a greater difference between Westerners and Northeasterners than there is between those of college education and those who have never completed high school in their perceptions of the credibility of ads.[3]
Credit card usage. Westerners and Northeasterners are more likely to have and use credit cards than are Southerners and Midwesterners.[4]
Use of print ads. Westerners, Multicultures, and Heartland are more likely to rely on print ads than are residents of the Traditional South.[5]
Zapping (erasing or fast forwarding through television commercials recorded on a VCR). Those in the Traditional South and Gulf Coast "zap" the least, whereas those in New England, Heartland, and Western Horizons do it most.[6]

In addition to those mentioned above, *USA Weekend* has reported on geographic differences with respect to the popularity of self-service, travel plans, personal interests, eating habits, and many other consumer behaviors.

While this segmentation profile involves regions of the country, others have employed geographic segmentation on smaller areas by developing programs targeted at specific states. The storyboard in Figure 7—4 is an excellent example of this latter ap-

Promotional Perspective 7–1

The 9 Nations of USA Weekend

The 9 Nations of USA Weekend is a newsletter published by the Roper Organization that reports on nine geographic segments of the United States. These geographic segments typically demonstrate differences with respect to attitudes, lifestyles, and consumer behaviors. These differences may have significant implications for marketers and advertisers and may serve as a basis for geographic segmentation strategies.

The nine USA nations—according to the Roper Organization—are characterized as follows:

- *New New England* Those living in New England comprise only 5 percent of the households in the *USA* marketplace yet rank first with respect to household income, percentage of married couples, proportion of working women, median age, and proportion of executives and professionals in the workplace.
- *The Heartland* The Heartland segment resides in the Midwestern "Bread Basket" and has a low household income, a lower level of education, and a high concentration of agricultural and blue-collar workers. The Heartland is the home of traditional American values.
- *Atlantic Expanse* Those living in the Mid-Atlantic states of New York south to Delaware and west to Pennsylvania and West Virginia constitute the largest of the nine nations. Their median age is just below the national norm, median income is slightly higher, and education levels are "smack in the middle." It has the largest proportion of full-time working persons and the highest level of white-collar workers.
- *New South and Traditional South* The New South is the area ranging along the Atlantic coast from Virginia to Florida, whereas the Traditional South is the center of the Cotton Belt—that is, Kentucky to Mississippi and west to Arkansas. The New South is characterized by slightly higher than median incomes, strong educational backgrounds, a work force

reflecting the national average, and a high proportion of widowed, divorced, or separated individuals. The Traditional South is characterized by a median income that is the lowest in the United States, the worst educational record, the lowest percentage of managerial and professional workers, and a higher-than-average married rate and family size.
- *Gulf Coast* The area including Louisiana, parts of Texas, and Oklahoma is considered the bridge between the South and the West. Education levels are high, although median income is below the national average. This area has the lowest level of full-time working persons, two-income households, and working women.
- *Made in the USA* The second largest of the nine nations comprises 17 percent of all households and is most closely a reflection of the norms of America with respect to median age and income. Located in the Great Lakes area, the residents are more likely to be married, have children, and have both spouses working than are other Americans.
- *Western Horizons* Physically the largest of the segments, this area ranges from Alaska to the Dakotas to Nebraska and Nevada. It has the least number of households, the most families with children under age 18, and lower household incomes. Only 17 percent of the population live in cities.
- *Multicultures* Extending from California to western Texas, this area has the second highest median income and is characterized by young, affluent, highly educated trendsetters. The number of marrieds is lowest, as is the number of families with children. The workers are very career minded.

Source: Adapted from *The 9 Nations of USA Weekend* (Roper Organization) 1, no. 7 (1987).

proach, as Blue Cross has seemingly determined that those living in California may require a different health care plan than those in other states—perhaps Nebraska. Still other companies have found that they may need to develop alternative strategies for areas as small as neighborhoods within a city, owing to differences in these areas.

Demographic segmentation   **Demographic segmentation** involves the division of the market on the basis of demographic variables such as age, sex, family size, income, and social class. In Chapter 5 we discussed some of these segments, such as the teenage and elderly markets, and those composed of a specific ethnic origin and/or race. The ad shown in Figure 7–5 is an example of a product that has met with a great deal of success by using yet another demographic variable—sex—as a basis for segmentation. Formerly, demographics was the principal segmentation criterion utilized by advertisers, and it may still be the most commonly used. Other examples of products that have successfully employed demographic segmentation include Virginia Slims cigarettes (sex), Affinity Shampoo (age), automobiles (income), prepackaged dinners (family size), and of course, many others. We are certain that if you stop and think for a moment, you can add many other products to this list.

Figure 7–5 **Secret Deodorant—Segmenting the Market by Sex**

Psychographic segmentation   Dividing the market on the basis of personality and/or lifestyles is referred to as **psychographic segmentation.** While there has been some disagreement as to whether or not personality is useful as a basis for segmentation, lifestyle factors have been proven to be used effectively. In fact, there are many who consider lifestyles as the most effective criterion for segmentation purposes.

The determination of lifestyles is usually based on an analysis of the activities, interests, and opinions (AIOs) of the consumer. These lifestyles are then correlated with the consumer's product, brand, and/or media usage. For many products and/or services, lifestyles may be the best discriminator between use and nonuse, accounting for differences in food consumption, clothing apparel, and automobile selections, among numerous other consumer behaviors.[7,8,9]

Psychographic segmentation has met with increasing acceptance and utilization with the advent of the **values and lifestyles program (VALS)** (although marketers employed lifestyle segmentation long before the popularity of VALS). Developed by the Stanford Research Institute (SRI), VALS has become one of the more popular and widely used methods for applying lifestyle segmentation. In the VALS typology, consumers are classified according to the values and lifestyles that they exhibit. VALS divides Americans into nine lifestyles, which are grouped in four categories based on their self-images, their aspirations, and the products they use. These classifications are shown in Table 7–2, whereas some of the advertising applications of VALS are demonstrated in Promotional Perspective 7–2.

While VALS has been widely adopted since its inception in 1978, SRI International reported in February 1989 that it has completely overhauled the system and introduced VALS 2.[10] According to SRI, the initial typology focused on the *differences* between inner-directed and outer-directed consumers, grouping people into nine clusters. In VALS 2, only three orientations are used, based on principle-oriented, status-oriented, and action-oriented characteristics (see Table 7–3). These groupings result in eight segments that exhibit distinctive attitudes, behaviors, and decision-making patterns. When combined with an estimate of the resources the consumer can draw upon

---

Promotional Perspective **7—2**

Applications of VALS

The values and lifestyles (VALS) program has been considered by many marketers to have revolutionized the art of segmentation. Both large and small companies have used the VALS program to develop advertising campaigns, as shown by the following examples:

- Dr Pepper's campaign "Hold out for the out of the ordinary—hold out for Dr Pepper" was targeted to Inner Directeds.
- Timex targeted three new health care products at the Achievers and Socially Conscious because it knew that these groups were more likely to adopt high-tech innovations and do a lot of gift buying.

- Jell-O's ad campaign featuring a mother telling her children that "she doesn't make dessert; she makes fun" was targeted to Belongers because of their roles as providers.
- Advertisers trying to appeal to an upscale audience will assume that Achievers, Experientials, and Societally Conscious are their target markets.
- *Penthouse* magazine believes its audience is mostly Inner-Directed Males; the *Atlantic Monthly* believes its is mostly the Societally Conscious.

Source: James Atlas, "Beyond Demographics," *Atlantic Monthly*, October 1984, pp. 49—58.

(education, income, health, energy level, self-confidence, and degree of consumerism), SRI feels that the new system is more current and a better predictor of consumer behaviors.

Since the system is just now being introduced, we cannot report on actual applications. We can tell you, however, that many of the current VALS customers—including Chevron, Mercedes-Benz, Eastman Kodak, Ogilvy & Mather Worldwide, and many others—are in the process of adopting the new VALS 2 typologies.

Behavioristic segmentation   **Behavioristic segmentation** divides consumers into groups according to their usage, loyalties, or buying responses to a product. For example, segmentation may be based on product or brand usage, degree (heavy versus light) of use, and/or brand loyalty. These characteristics are then combined with demographic and/or psychographic criteria to develop profiles of market segments. In the first case—usage—an assumption is made that nonpurchasers of a brand or product who have the same characteristics as purchasers will hold greater potential for adoption than those with different characteristics. A profile (demographic or psychographic) of the user is developed, which serves as the basis for the development of promotional strategies designed to attract new users. For example, it might be expected that Yuppies—who we demonstrated in an earlier chapter shared certain similarities in their consumption behaviors—who do not currently own a foreign car might be more likely to be potential buyers than those demonstrating different characteristics.

Degree of usage relates to the fact that a few consumers may account for a disproportionate amount of the share of purchase for many products or brands. For example, in industrial markets, many marketers refer to what they call the **80—20 rule,** meaning that 20 percent of their buyers account for 80 percent of their sales volume. Once again, upon identifying the characteristics of these users, targeting them would allow for a much greater concentration of efforts and much less wasted time and monies. The same "heavy-half" strategy is possible in the consumer market as well, as the majority of purchases of many products (for example, soaps and detergents, shampoos, cake mixes, beer, dog food, colas, bourbon, and toilet tissue—yes, toilet tissue!) is accounted for by a small proportion of the population (see Figure 7—6).[11] Perhaps you can think of some additional examples where this may be the case.

Benefit segmentation   In purchasing products, consumers are generally trying to satisfy specific needs and/or wants. As a result, these consumers are looking for specific benefits that products might provide in satisfying these needs. The grouping of con-

Table 7–2 **The VALS Typologies**

Percentage of Population	Consumer Type	Values and Lifestyles	Demographics	Buying Patterns	Spending Power
		Need-driven Consumers			
6	Survivors	Struggle for survival Distrustful Socially misfitted Ruled by appetites	Poverty-level income Little education Many minority members	Price dominant Focuses on basics Buy for immediate needs	$3 billion
10	Sustainers	Concern with safety, security Insecure, compulsive Dependent, following Want law and order	Low income Low education Much unemployment Live in country as well as cities	Price important Want warranty Cautious buyers	$32 billion
		Outer-directed Consumers			
32	Belongers	Conforming, conventional Unexperimental Traditional, formal Nostalgic	Low to middle income Low to average education Blue-collar jobs Tend toward noncity living	Family Home Fads Middle and lower market makers	$230 billion
10	Emulators	Ambitious, show-off Status-conscious Upwardly mobile Macho, competitive	Good to excellent income Youngish Highly urban Traditionally male, but changing	Conspicuous consumption "In" times Imitative Popular fashion	$120 billion
28	Achievers	Achievement, success, fame Materialism Leadership, efficiency Comfort	Excellent incomes Leaders in business, politics, etc. Good education Suburban and city living	Give evidence of success Top of the line Luxury and gift markets "New and improved" products	$500 billion

sumers on the basis of attributes sought in a product is known as **benefit segmentation**—a widely utilized basis for many firms. Perhaps a few examples would help increase your understanding of this strategy.

Consider the purchase of a wristwatch. While you might consider buying a watch for particular benefits such as accuracy, water resistance, or stylishness, others may be seeking an entirely different set of benefits. Watches are commonly given as gifts for birthdays, Christmas, and graduation. Certainly some of the same benefits are considered in the purchase of a gift, but at the same time, the benefits to be derived by the purchaser are quite different from those that will be obtained by the user. The appeals used in advertisements that portray watches as good gifts stress a different set of criteria to be considered in the purchase decision. The next time you see an advertisement or commercial for a watch, think about the basic appeal and the benefits offered in that ad.

Another example of benefit segmentation can be seen in the toothpaste market. In selecting a toothpaste, some consumers want a product with fluoride (Crest, Colgate), whereas others prefer one that freshens their breath (Close•Up, Aqua-fresh). More recent benefit segments are those offering tartar control (Crest) and assistance with plaque problems (Viadent). In the Viadent ad shown in Figure 7–7 the specific benefit

Table 7–2 **(concluded)**

Percentage of Population	Consumer Type	Values and Lifestyles	Demographics	Buying Patterns	Spending Power
		Inner-directed Consumers			
3	I-Am-Me	Fiercely individualistic Dramatic, impulsive Experimental Volatile	Young Many single Student or starting job Affluent backgrounds	Display one's taste Experimental fads Source of far-out fads Clique buying	$25 billion
5	Experimental	Drive to direct experience Active, participative Person-centered Artistic	Bimodal incomes Mostly under 40 Many young families Good education	Process over product Vigorous, outdoor sports "Making" home pursuits Crafts and introspection	$56 billion
4	Societally Conscious	Societal responsibility Simple living Smallness of scale Inner growth	Bimodal low and high incomes Excellent education Diverse ages and places of residence Largely white	Conservation emphasis Simplicity Frugality Environmental concerns	$50 billion
2	Integrated	Psychological maturity Sense of fittingness Tolerant, self-actualizing Word perspective	Good to excellent incomes Bimodal in age Excellent education Diverse jobs, residential patterns	Varied self-expression Esthetically oriented Ecologically aware One-of-a-kind items	$28 billion

Source: Arnold Mitchell, *Consumer Values: A Typology* (Menlo Park, Calif.: SRI, 1978); taken from Kenneth E. Runyon and David W. Stewart, *Consumer Behavior,* 3rd ed. (Columbus, Ohio: Merrill, 1987), pp. 362–63.

Figure 7–6   **Heavy and Light Users of Consumer Products**

Product (% Users)	Heavy half		Light half
Soaps and detergents (94%)	75%		25%
Toilet tissue (95%)	71%		29%
Shampoo (94%)	79%		21%
Paper towels (90%)	75%		25%
Cake mixes (74%)	83%		17%
Cola (67%)	83%		17%
Beer (41%)	87%		13%
Dog food (30%)	81%		19%
Bourbon (20%)	95%		5%

Source: Victor J. Cook and William A. Mindak, "A Search for Constants: The 'Heavy User' Revisited!" *Journal of Consumer Marketing* 1, no. 4 (Spring 1984), p. 80.

Table 7–3   **Lifestyle Characteristics of the VALS 2 Segments**

Actualizers
Value personal growth
Wide intellectual interests
Varied leisure activities
Well informed; concerned
with social issues
Highly social
Politically active

Fulfilleds
Moderately active
in community and politics
Leisure centers on home
Value education and travel
Health conscious
Politically moderate
and tolerant

Achievers
Lives center on
career and family
Have formal social relations
Avoid excess change
or stimulation
May emphasize work at
expense of recreation
Politically
conservative

Experiencers
Like the new,
offbeat, and risky
Like exercise, socializing,
sports, and outdoors
Concerned about image
Unconforming, but admire
wealth, power, and fame
Politically
apathetic

Believers
Respect rules and
trust authority figures
Enjoy settled, comfortable,
predictable existence
Socialize within family and
established groups
Politically conservative
Reasonably well
informed

Strivers
Narrow interests
Easily bored
Somewhat isolated
Look to peer group for
motivation and approval
Unconcerned about health
or nutrition
Politically apathetic

Makers
Enjoy outdoors
Prefer "hands on" activities
Spend leisure with family and
close friends
Avoid joining organizations,
except unions
Distrust politicians,
foreigners, and
big business

Strugglers
Limited interests
and activities
Prime concerns are safety
and security
Burdened with health problems
Conservative and traditional
Rely on organized
religion

Figure 7–7   **Viadent Stresses Specific Benefit of Plaque Control**

of plaque control is explicitly stated. A potential consumer seeking this benefit should have no trouble getting the message.

The Process of Segmenting a Market   It is important to keep in mind that the segmentation process is exactly that—a process. This process develops over time and is an integral part of the situation analysis. It is in this stage that marketers are attempting to determine as much as they can about the market—that is, what needs are not being fulfilled, what benefits are being sought, and what characteristics distinguish between the various groups in seeking these products and services. Thus, a number of alternative segmentation strategies may be considered and employed. Each time a specific segment is identified, additional information is gathered to assist in the understanding of this group.

For example, once a specific segment is identified based on benefits sought, lifestyle characteristics and demographics will be examined to help characterize this group and to further the marketer's understanding of this market. In addition, behavioristic segmentation criteria will also be examined. To take the skiing example cited earlier one step further, specific benefits may be sought in the product—flexibility or stiffness, for example—because of the type of skiing that is done. This information will be combined with that discussed earlier to provide a complete profile of the skier.

A number of companies now offer research services to assist marketing managers to define their markets and to develop strategies targeted to these groups. The VALS system offered by SRI is one example, as is the VISION System shown in Figure 7–8. As you can see by examining the clusters shown in this table, the VISION System uses demographic, psychographic, and geographic bases to break down the market into "microgeographic" units. These segments get as specific as postal carrier routes and census block groupings, each of which has specific identifiable demographic and lifestyle characteristics. Whether these microunits meet the criteria considered necessary for useful segmentation, of course, will be determined by the user of the system. While it may be too specific for a national company to attempt to define such small segments, it may be much more applicable for companies operating within one specific city or geographical area. The same data are often provided by smaller companies for organizations requiring such information on a countywide basis.

Having completed the segmentation analysis, the marketer now moves to the third phase shown in Figure 7–1: targeting a specific market to go after.

Selecting a Target Market

The outcome of the segmentation analysis will indicate to the firm the market opportunities available. The next phase in the target marketing process involves two steps: (1) determining how many segments to enter and (2) determining which segments will offer the most potential. Each of these will discussed in turn.

Determining How Many Segments to Enter   Three market coverage alternatives are available to the firm. **Undifferentiated marketing** would involve a decision to ignore the segment differences and to offer one product or service to the entire market. For example, many years ago when Henry Ford brought out the first assembly-line automobile, all potential consumers were offered the same basic product—a black Ford. For many years, Coca-Cola offered only one product version. While this standardized strategy allowed for cost savings to the company, it did not allow the opportunity to offer different versions of the product. **Differentiated marketing,** on the other hand, involves the decision to market in a number of segments, developing separate marketing strategies for each. The Dewar's ads shown in Figure 7–9 reflect a good example of this strategy, as the "profile" ad appears to be targeting a specific group (perhaps upwardly mobile, young to middle-aged?), whereas the second example might appeal more to older (perhaps more traditional?) individuals.

Figure 7–8   **VISION Uses Demographic, Psychographic, and Geographic Bases to Segment the Market**

Figure 7–9   **Dewar's Uses Different Appeals for the Same Product**

While an undifferentiated strategy offers the opportunity to reduce costs through increased production, it does not allow for variety or tailoring to specific needs. Through differentiation, products—or in the case of Dewar's, different advertising appeals—may be developed for the various segments, allowing for an increased opportunity to satisfy the needs and wants of various groups.

The third alternative, **concentrated marketing,** is used when the firm selects one specific segment and attempts to capture a large share of this market. An example of this strategy was that employed by Volkswagen in the 1950s when it was the only major automobile company competing in the economy car segment of the United States. While Volkswagen has now assumed a more differentiated strategy, other companies have found the concentrated strategy to be an effective one. For example, Perfection Sports Fashions, a company specializing in the selling of clothing to triathletes, has seen its business increase at an annual growth rate of more than 35 percent a year since 1984 (Figure 7–10).

Determining Which Segments Will Offer the Most Potential   The second step in the process of selecting a market involves the determination of the most attractive segment to approach. At this point the firm must examine the sales potential of the segment, the opportunities for growth, the competition, and its own ability to compete.

Having made the determination of the most attractive segment, the firm must then decide whether it has the capabilities to market to this group. Numerous stories abound of companies that have entered new markets only to find that their lack of resources or expertise would not allow them to compete successfully. For example, Royal Crown Cola (RC Cola) has often been quite successful in identifying new segment opportunities but because of limited resources has been less able to capitalize on them. RC has been credited with being first to bring to market diet colas and caffeine-free colas but has not been able to establish itself as a market leader in either market.

Having selected the segments to target, and having determined that it is able to compete, the firm now proceeds to the final step in Figure 7–1—the market positioning phase.

Market Positioning

Positioning has been defined as "the art and science of fitting the product or service to one or more segments of the broad market in such a way as to set it meaningfully apart from competition."[12] As you can see by this definition, the position of the product, service, or even store is the image that comes to the mind of the consumer and the attributes that he or she perceives as related to it. This communication takes place through the message itself—which explains these benefits—as well as the media strategy that is employed to reach the target group. Take a few moments to think about how some products are positioned and how this position is conveyed to you. For example, what comes to mind when we mention Mercedes, Dr Pepper, or United Airlines? What about department stores such as Niemann Marcus, Sears, and J. C. Penney? Now think of the advertisements, and when and where these ads are shown, for each of these products and companies. Are their approaches different from their competitors?

Approaches to Positioning   **Positioning strategies** generally assume one of two approaches—one focusing on the consumer, the other on the competition. While both approaches involve the association of product benefits with consumer needs, the former does so by specifically linking the product with the benefits to be derived by the consumer or creating a favorable brand image, as shown in Figures 7–11 and 7–12, respectively. The latter approach positions the product by comparing it, and the benefit

Figure 7–10 **Perfection Sports Fashions Pursues a Concentrated Marketing Strategy**

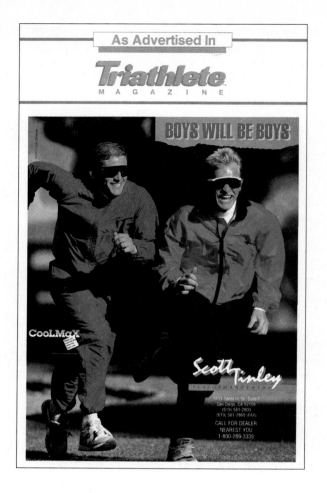

it offers, to the competition, as shown in the example provided in Figure 7–13. Other products such as Scope mouthwash (positioning itself as better tasting than Listerine) and Now cigarettes (comparing itself to a number of other cigarette brands on the amount of nicotene) have also employed this strategy successfully.

Market positioning has been considered by many advertising practitioners to be the most important factor in establishing a brand in the marketplace. As noted by David Aaker and John Myers, the term *position* or *positioning* has recently been used to indicate the brand's or product's image in the marketplace.[13] Jack Trout and Al Ries have suggested that to have a position in the marketplace, this brand image must be in respect to competitors'. In fact, these authors note that "in today's marketplace, the competitors' image is just as important as your own. Sometimes more important."[14] Thus, *positioning*—as used in this text—will relate to the image of the product and or brand relative to competitive products or brands. As noted in the examples previously provided, it is the position of the product or brand that is the key factor in communicating the benefits offered and in differentiating it from the competition. Let us now turn our attention to various strategies that might be employed to position a product.

Developing a Positioning Strategy   To create a position for a product or service, Trout and Ries suggest that managers ask themselves six basic questions:[15]

1. What position, if any, do we already have in the prospect's mind? (This information, of course, must come from the marketplace and not the managers' perceptions.)

Figure 7–11   **Timex Stresses Benefits to Position Its Product**

Figure 7–12   **Movado Effectively Creates a Brand Image**

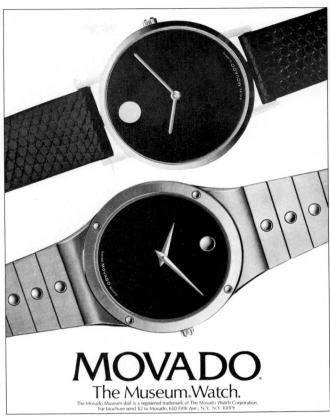

Figure 7–13   **Advil Positions Itself Relative to Its Competition**

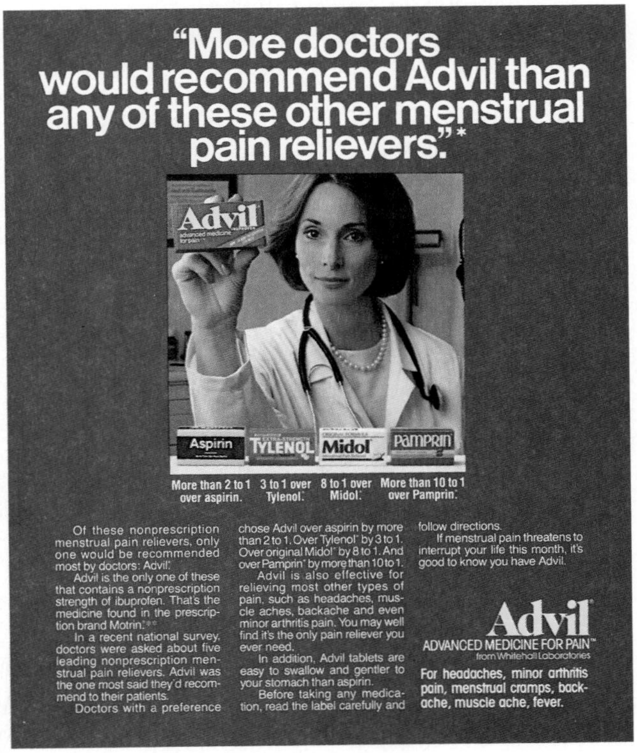

Figure 7–14 **An Example of Positioning on Numerous Product Benefits**

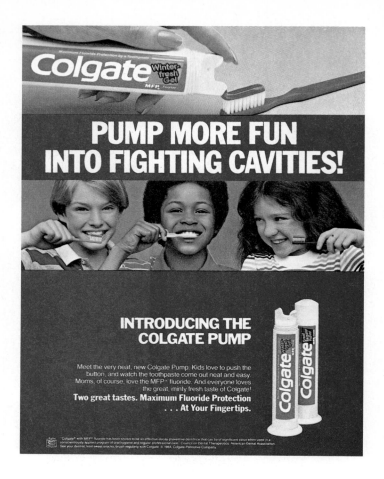

2. What position do we want to own?
3. What companies must be outgunned if we are to establish that position?
4. Do we have enough marketing money to occupy and hold the position?
5. Do we have the guts to stick with one consistent positioning strategy?
6. Does our creative approach match our positioning strategy?

There exist a number of positioning strategies that might be employed in the development of a promotional program. David Aaker and J. Gary Shansby[16] discuss six such strategies, whereas Aaker and Myers[17] add one additional approach. A discussion of each follows.

Using product attributes (characteristics) One of the more common approaches to positioning is that of setting the brand apart from competitors' based on specific characteristics or benefits offered. The mouthwash example cited earlier reflects an application of this strategy.

Sometimes a product may be positioned on more than one product benefit. A good example of this was demonstrated in our previous discussion of positioning in the toothpaste industry and in the advertisement shown in Figure 7–14. In addition to being a cavity fighter, Colgate introduces "fun" into brushing, as well as mentioning great taste and fluoride protection.

Positioning by price/quality Figures 7–15 and 7–16 reflect examples of brands that have been positioned on the price/quality dimension. The Technics approach reflects the image of a high-quality brand in which cost—while not irrelevant—should be considered secondary to the quality benefits to be derived. The Tyco ad demonstrates

Figure 7–15 **Technics Positions Its Brand as High Quality**

the wisdom of considering price as the key criterion. An important factor must be remembered in the latter approach and is demonstrated quite well by the ad in Figure 7–16: that is, that even if one attempts to position on the basis of price, quality is still important. Thus, while price may be the primary consideration, the product quality must be shown to be at least adequate—if not equal—to other competitive brands.

Positioning with respect to use or application   In this approach, the company will attempt to position the product with a specific *use* or *application*. For example, in the ads shown in Figure 7–17 for athletic shoes, the L. A. Gear positioning is for multiple uses including aerobics, exercising, body building, or just having fun. Nike is for cross training (useful for the court or running), and New Balance is positioned exclusively as a running shoe.

While this strategy is often used to enter a market based on a particular use, it has also been demonstrated to be an effective way to expand into different markets. The WD-40 ad shown in Figure 7–18 is an excellent example of a success story based on the ability of the product to satisfy a variety of needs. Likewise, Arm & Hammer Pure Baking Soda has been promoted as being effective for everything from baking to relieving heartburn to eliminating odors in carpets, ashtrays, and refrigerators.

Positioning by product class   Often the competition for a product may come from outside the product class as well as within. For example, those involved in the airline industry know that while they compete with other airline carriers, trains and buses also constitute viable alternatives. Amtrak has positioned itself as an alternative to taking the airplane, citing cost savings, enjoyment, and other advantages. Manufacturers

Figure 7–16 **Tyco Positions Its Brand on Quality for the Right Price**

Figure 7–17A **Alternative Positioning Strategies of Athletic Shoes**

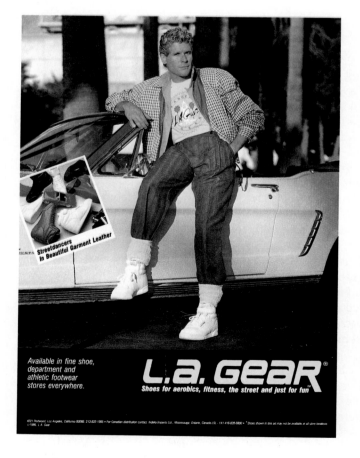

Figure 7—17B

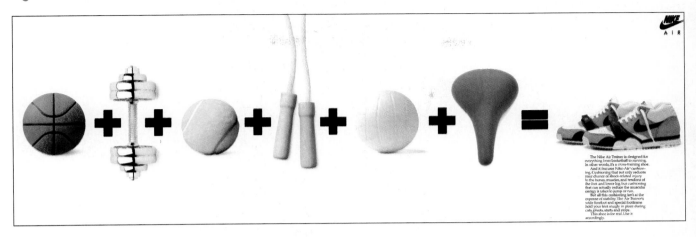

Figure 7— 17C

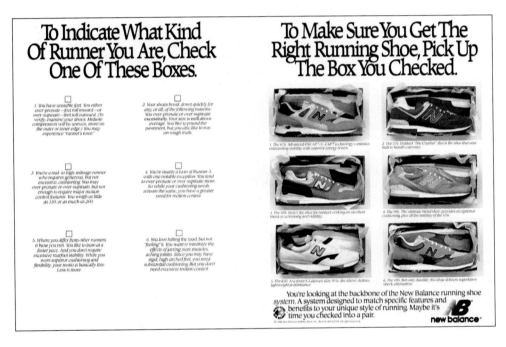

of record albums must compete with those in the cassette and compact disc industries, whereas many margarines position themselves against butter. Thus, rather than positioning against another brand, an alternative strategy would be to position oneself against another product category, as shown by the advertisement for potatoes in Figure 7—19.

Positioning by product user   Positioning a product by associating it with a particular user or group of users is yet another approach utilized by marketers. The Pontiac ad shown in Figure 7—20 is one such example of this approach (a car for those who are upwardly mobile), as were the Dewar's ads shown earlier. In both of these campaigns, identification or association with a specific group is evident.

Positioning by competitor   As we stated earlier in this chapter, competitors may be as important to one's positioning strategy as its own product or services offering. As

Figure 7–18   **WD-40 Demonstrates Numerous Product Uses**

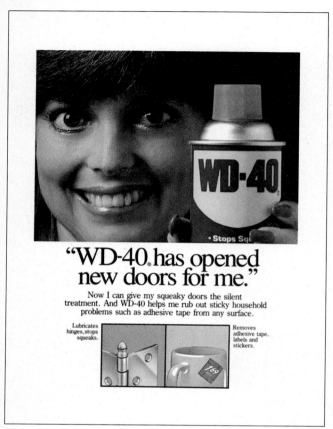

Figure 7–19   **An Example of Positioning by Product Class**

stated by Trout and Ries, the old strategy of ignoring one's competition will no longer work in today's marketplace.[18] (Advertisers used to think it was a cardinal sin to mention a competitor in their advertising!) In today's market, an effective positioning strategy for a product or brand may be derived by focusing on specific competitors. This approach is very similar to that discussed in positioning by product class, although in this case the competition is within the same product category. Perhaps the most well known example of this strategy is that assumed by Avis, who positioned itself against the leader Hertz by stating, "We're number two, so we try harder." The Sauza Tequila ad shown in Figure 7–21 is yet another variation of this approach where the competitors are not specifically named, yet the implications are obvious—they are not as good as Sauza.

In Chapter 6 we discussed the concept of comparative advertising. In comparative advertising, positioning by competitor is made very specifically. The Tyco ad (Figure 7–16) and the ad for Advil (Figure 7–13) are both examples of this approach while combining it with other positioning strategies (price/quality, product benefits). The point to be made here is that when positioning by competitor, it is often necessary to employ another positioning strategy as well to differentiate oneself.

Positioning by cultural symbols   As earlier noted, Aaker and Myers include one additional positioning strategy in which *cultural symbols* are utilized to differentiate brands; for example, the Jolly Green Giant, the Keebler Elves, Speedy Alka-Seltzer, Bud Man, Buster Brown, Ronald McDonald, Chiquita Banana, and Mr. Peanut. Each of these companies—as well as others—has successfully differentiated its product from competitors' by identifying symbols that represent it (Figure 7–22).

Figure 7—20   Pontiac Positions Itself as a Car for the Upwardly Mobile

Figure 7—21   Sauza Positions Itself Against Unnamed Competitors

Interestingly, the use of cultural symbols has become so common in our society that psychologists and sociologists have examined the mythological foundations underlying many of the characters and have expressed their own opinions as to the inherent meanings ascribed to them by consumers. In fact, a museum of modern mythology—featuring twentieth-century cultural symbols of advertising—has been started in San Francisco. Part of the attraction of this museum is its tracing of the evolution of the characters over time, taking into consideration the changing culture of the United States and the impact it has had on such symbols.

Repositioning   One final strategy involving positioning involves the altering or changing of a product's or brand's position. **Repositioning** a product usually occurs because of declining or stagnant sales or because of anticipated opportunities in other market positions. Repositioning is often difficult to accomplish because of previously entrenched perceptions about and attitudes toward the product or brand. Many companies' attempts to change their positions have met with little or no success. (For example, Sears attempted to reposition itself as a store of higher quality, appealing to more well-to-do customers. The strategy was unsuccessful and subsequently abandoned. In 1989, Sears once again attempted a repositioning strategy—this time to a "lower-price store.") One such effort at repositioning that has been extremely successful was that employed by *Rolling Stone* magazine. In an attempt to change the image held by advertisers of the type of person who reads *Rolling Stone*, the company embarked upon an extensive advertising campaign of its own essentially to reposition the

Figure 7—22   **Brands That Have Become Cultural Symbols**

magazine in the minds of potential advertisers. The advertisement shown in Figure 7–23 is just one example of how this strategy was successfully implemented.

Other companies have also been successful in attempts to reposition. For example, Pontiac effectively repositioned its product as a sportier car that adds "excitement" (as is reflected in the ad in Figure 7–20), whereas Dutch Boy paints was able to change its image to reach upscale, fashion-oriented consumers.

Determining and Developing the Positioning Strategy   Having explored the alternative positioning strategies available, the marketer must determine which strategy is best suited for his or her firm or product and begin the development of the positioning platform. As can be seen by referring to the promotional planning process shown in Chapter 1, the input into this stage will be derived from the situation analysis—more specifically, the marketing research conducted therein. Essentially, the development of a positioning platform can be broken down into a six-step process:[19]

1. *Identification of competitors* As previously mentioned, this process requires broad thinking. Competitors may not be just those products and/or brands that fall into your product class or with which you directly compete. Consider wine as an example. A red wine competes with other red wines of various positions. At the same time, competition may also include white wines, champagnes, and nonalcoholic wines. Likewise, wine coolers provide an alternative, as do beer and other alcoholic drinks. To take the case further, other nonalcoholic drinks may come into consideration at various times and/or situations. Thus, the marketer must consider any and all likely competitors, as well as the various effects that use and situations may have on the consumer.

2. *Assessing consumers' perceptions of competitors* Once we have been able to define the competition, it is necessary to determine how they are perceived and evaluated by consumers. This process involves the determination of which attributes are considered important to consumers in evaluating a product and/or brand. As you might expect, for many products a wide variety of attributes, or product benefits, may be considered—most, if not all, of which are important. Much of the research conducted by marketing firms is directed at making such determinations. Consumers are asked to take part in focus groups and/or complete surveys indicating which attributes are important to them in their purchase decisions. For example, attributes considered important in the selection of a bank may include convenience, friendliness of the tellers, financial security, and a host of other factors. This process establishes the basis for the determination of competitive positions, or step three.

3. *Determining competitors' positions* Having determined the relevant at-

Figure 7–23   One of a Series of Ads Designed to Create a New Image for *Rolling Stone* Magazine

Perception.

Reality.

If your idea of a Rolling Stone reader looks like a holdout from the 60's, welcome to the 80's. Rolling Stone ranks number one in reaching concentrations of 18-34 readers with household incomes exceeding $25,000. When you buy Rolling Stone, you buy an audience that sets the trends and shapes the buying patterns for the most affluent consumers in America. That's the kind of reality you can take to the bank.

tributes, and their relative importance to the consumer, the next step is to determine how each of the competitors (including your own entry) is positioned with respect to each attribute. This will also indicate how the competitors are positioned relative to each other. One such tool for making this determination is *multidimensional scaling* (MDS). As explained in Promotional Perspective 7–3, MDS leads to the development of a **perceptual map** of the positions of the various products and/or brands as perceived by the consumer.

4. *Analyzing the consumers' preferences* In our discussion of segmentation it was noted that there are various factors that may distinguish between groups of consumers, including lifestyles, purchase motivations, demographic differences, and so on. Each of these various segments may have different purchase motivations and different attribute importance ratings. As such, it becomes necessary to understand such differences. One method for making this determination is through the consideration of the "ideal" in the multidimensional scaling task. The *ideal* would be defined as the object that the consumer would prefer over all others, including objects that can be conceptualized but that do not actually exist. Identification of the ideal product may be useful for two purposes—either identifying different ideals among segments or identifying segments with similar or the same ideal points.

5. *Making the positioning decision* Having gone through the previous four steps should allow for the decision on which position to assume in the marketplace. Such a decision is not always clear and well defined, however, and conducting the research just described may provide only limited input. In that case, it becomes necessary for the marketing manager—or groups of managers—to make some subjective judgments. To make these judgments a number of questions should be raised:

- *Is the segmentation strategy appropriate?* Positioning usually entails a decision to segment the market. Consideration must be given as to whether the market seg-

Promotional Perspective 7–3

An Application of Perceptual Mapping

Multidimensional scaling (MDS) is a research technique employed by marketers to determine how consumers perceive products on various dimensions. The output of the MDS program yields a "perceptual map" of consumers' perceptions regarding how various products or brands are positioned on these dimensions. Exhibit 7–3A shows a perceptual map developed by researchers at the Pontiac division of General Motors. This map shows the position of Pontiac automobiles in relation to the perceived images of other General Motors divisions and other car manufacturers. In this particular perceptual map, the various autos are positioned on the dimensions of price (upscale luxurious or low price/practical) and image (conservative/family-oriented or expressive/sporty).

Identification of the positioning of Pontiac and its competitors is possible by studying the perceptual map. As you can see, the Japanese entries by Nissan, Toyota, Honda, and Mazda and the German-made VW were perceived by consumers as more sporty and practical,

whereas most of the General Motors automobiles were perceived as being more conservative and higher priced. The perceptual map allows the advertiser to determine copy points to emphasize should it decide that the current position is where it wishes to continue to be, and is also helpful in the identification of untapped segments for new products and/or repositioning strategies.

The arrow shown in this perceptual map indicates the direction Pontiac decided to move in its repositioning efforts. Pontiac management chose to pursue a more youthful, sporty image for its cars. An advertising strategy was developed to position Pontiacs as exciting automobiles with innovative styling and outstanding performance and road ability. The "We Build Excitement" advertising campaign theme was used to promote Pontiac's more stylish and sporty product line (Exhibit 7–3B).

Source: Peter Langenhorst, "Pontiac Division of General Motors (A)" (Charlottesville: Colgate Darden Graduate School of Business Administration, University of Virginia, 1987), 1–19.

Exhibit 7–3A   **Pontiac Division Perceptual Map, 1981**

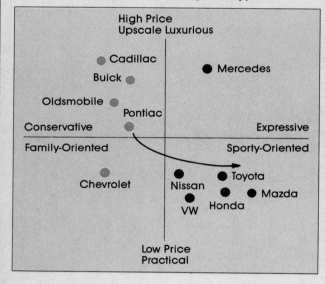

Exhibit 7–3B   **Pontiac Used the "We Build Excitement" Theme to Help Reposition Its Automobiles**

ment sought will support an entry and whether it is in the best interests of the company to deemphasize the remaining market. When a specific position is chosen, consumers may feel that this is what the product is for. As such, those not looking for that specific benefit may not consider the brand as their first choice, assuming it is for some other purpose. Should the marketer decide on an undifferentiated strategy, it may be possible to deemphasize a specific positioning approach, being much more general in the positioning platform. For example, Toyota's campaign of "You asked for it, you got it—Toyota" emphasizes a variety of product attributes and allows consumers to assume that they will get whatever they are looking for in the brand.

• *Are there sufficient resources available to communicate the position effectively?* It is very expensive to establish a position. One ad, or even a series of ads, is not likely to be enough to engrain the position. Thus, the marketer must commit to a long-range effort—in all aspects of the marketing campaign—to ensure that the objectives sought are obtained. All too often, the firm too quickly abandons a position and/or advertising campaign long before it has had an opportunity to establish a position successfully. The *Rolling Stone* campaign discussed earlier in this chapter is an excellent example of sticking with a campaign: The basic theme has now been running for a number of years. On the other hand, both Wendy's and Burger King have switched agencies and/or campaigns so often over the past few years that it has been impossible for them to establish a distinct position in the consumer's mind. Further, once a successful position has been attained, it is likely to attract competitors. Again, it may become expensive to ward off those attempting to become "me-too" brands—brands that attempt to assume the same position as the leader—and to continue to hold on to the brand distinction.

- *How strong is the competition?* The marketing manager must ask whether a position sought is likely to be maintained, given the strengths of the competition. For example, General Foods Corporation would often make it a practice not to be the first entry into a market, relying on the fact that it could make a better product. Thus, when competitors developed new markets with their entries. General Foods would simply improve on the product and capture a large percentage of the market share. This leads to two basic questions that must be answered: First, if our firm is first into the market, will we be able to maintain the position (quality wise, price wise, etc.)? Second, if someone else is already in the market position we seek, will we be able to demonstrate specific advantages allowing us to capture our share? This brings to consideration the issue as to whether the product can live up to its claims. If it is positioned as finest quality, it must be. If it is positioned as lowest cost, then it has to be. Otherwise, the position claimed is sure to be lost.

- *Is the current positioning strategy working?* There is an old saying, "If it ain't broke, don't fix it." If one's current efforts are not working, then it may be time to consider an alternative positioning strategy. If they are working, such a change is usually unnecessary and unwarranted. Sometimes executives become bored with a theme or grow tired of it and decide that it is time for a change. Often this change causes confusion in the marketplace, and weakens a previously established position as a result. Unless there is strong reason to believe that a change in positioning is necessary, one should stick with the current strategy.

6. *Can we monitor the position?* Once a position has been established it is necessary to monitor how well this position is being maintained in the marketplace. At the same time, the impact of competitors must be determined.

One method of monitoring is utilizing tracking studies. Tracking studies are designed to measure the image of the product or firm over time. Thus, changes in consumers' perceptions can be determined, with any slippage immediately noted and reacted to. At the same time, the impact of competitors can be determined.

Before leaving this chapter, you might stop to think for a moment about the positioning (and repositioning) strategies pursued by different companies. We are sure that you will quickly come to the realization that almost any successful product that comes to your mind occupies a distinct market position.

Summary

In the planning process the situation analysis requires the determination of the marketing strategy to be assumed. Of course, the promotional program will be developed with this strategy as a guide. One of the key decisions to be made is that of target marketing—a process involving market segmentation, market targeting, and market positioning strategies.

Market segmentation—or dividing the market into smaller groups—is a process that allows for the development of specifically targeted marketing strategies. A number of bases of segmentation were discussed, including geographic segmentation, demographic segmentation, psychographic segmentation, behavioristic segmentation, and benefit segmentation. More than one basis for segmentation may be employed at a time. For example, a market may be segmented on the lifestyles of consumers while at the same time considering the demographic groups or income groups engaging in such lifestyles.

Upon determination of the best segmentation strategy, market targeting is considered. Determination of the number of markets to enter and the most attractive segment—that is, the one with the greatest potential—is required. Having made these decisions, the next step is that of positioning, or creating an image of the product in the mind of the consumer. A number of positioning strategies were discussed—for example, positioning by product attributes, price/quality, use or application, product class, product user, competitor, and cultural symbol.

Sometimes it may be necessary to reposition—or change—the positioning of a product or brand. Sears, *Rolling Stone,* and Pontiac, among others, have at one time or another pursued a repositioning strategy.

Finally, it is important to remember that the process of target marketing is indeed that—a process. Market segmentation and target marketing and positioning do not just happen; rather, a series of steps are required, ultimately leading to a strategy to be pursued. Having gone through this process in the situation analysis, the manager is now ready to establish specific objectives to be sought.

Key Terms

Product differentiation	Benefit segmentation
Target marketing	Undifferentiated marketing
Market segmentation	Differentiated marketing
Geographic segmentation	Concentrated marketing
Demographic segmentation	Positioning
Psychographic segmentation	Positioning strategies
Values and lifestyles program (VALS)	Repositioning
Behavioristic segmentation	Perceptual map
80–20 rule	

Discussion Questions

1. Discuss the concept of target marketing. Why is target marketing important to the marketer?
2. Give examples of companies that are currently marketing their products or services through an undifferentiated strategy; a differentiated strategy; a concentrated strategy.
3. Discuss the process involved in segmenting a market. What are some of the factors that must be considered in determining whether or not to segment?
4. Identify the bases for segmentation. Give a current example of each.
5. Give examples of companies that might employ the VALS and/or VALS 2 programs. How might the VALS typologies relate to the purchase decision process for these products?
6. Define positioning. Identify companies and/or products that now hold a strong position in the market. Explain these positions.
7. Discuss the different approaches to positioning. Give examples of companies currently using each approach.

8. In the chapter, we discussed Sears' two different attempts to reposition the store in the minds of consumers. What is the position currently being promoted by Sears? Can you give other examples of companies that have recently pursued a repositioning strategy?

9. Discuss the six-step process involved in determining and developing a positioning strategy.

10. What are the questions that need to be asked when making the positioning decision?

Notes

1. Adapted from Gregory Witcher, "Japanese Auto Makers Target Midwest," *The Wall Street Journal,* December 19, 1988, p. B1.

2. Eric N. Berkowitz, Roger A. Kerin, and William Rudelius, *Marketing,* 2nd ed. (Homewood, Ill.: Richard D. Irwin, 1989).

3. *The 9 Nations of USA Weekend* (Roper Organization) 1, no. 4 (1987).

4. Ibid., no. 6.

5. Ibid., no. 5.

6. Ibid., no. 6.

7. Edward M. Tauber, "Research on Food Consumption Values Finds Four Market Segments; Good Taste Still Tops," *Marketing News,* May 15, 1981, p. 17.

8. Rebecca C. Quarles, "Shopping Centers Use Fashion Lifestyle Research to Make Marketing Decisions," *Marketing News,* January 22, 1982, p. 18.

9. "Our Autos, Ourselves," *Consumer Reports,* June 1985, p. 375.

10. Judith Graham, "New VALS 2 Takes Psychological Route," *Advertising Age,* February 13, 1989, p. 24.

11. Victor J. Cook and William A. Mindak, "A Search for Constants: The 'Heavy User' Revisited," *Journal of Consumer Marketing* 1, no. 4 (Spring 1984), p. 80.

12. *Ayer's Dictionary of Advertising Terms* (Philadelphia: Ayer Press, 1976).

13. David A. Aaker and John G. Myers, *Advertising Management,* 3rd ed. (Englewood Cliffs, N.J.: Prentice-Hall, 1987), p. 125.

14. Jack Trout and Al Ries, "Positioning Cuts Through Chaos in the Marketplace," *Advertising Age,* May 1, 1972, pp. 51–53.

15. Ibid.

16. David A. Aaker and J. Gary Shansby, "Positioning Your Product," *Business Horizons,* May–June 1982, pp. 56–62.

17. Aaker and Myers, *Advertising Management.*

18. Trout and Ries, "Positioning Cuts."

19. Aaker and Myers, *Advertising Management.*

Determining Advertising and Promotional Objectives

CHAPTER OBJECTIVES

1. To analyze the importance and value of setting specific objectives for advertising and promotion

2. To examine the role objectives play in the promotional planning process and the relationship of promotional objectives to marketing objectives

3. To consider the differences between sales and communications objectives and issues regarding the use of each

4. To examine the DAGMAR approach to setting advertising objectives and its value and limitations

5. To examine some problems advertisers encounter in setting objectives and measuring their accomplishment

An Effective Campaign

NCR Corporation sells business information systems to retail, financial, commercial, industrial, educational, medical, manufacturing, government, and distribution markets. In the mid-1980s the company decided to expand outside of its traditional markets and introduce its NCR Tower® (NCR Tower is a registered trademark of NCR Corporation) computer into two new, previously untapped areas: the data processing departments of Fortune 1000 companies and the small-business personal computer market. Although the company felt that it had a good product with a unique multiuser capability, it had met with only limited sales success one year after introduction. NCR found that the NCR Tower system was dwarfed by industry leaders IBM and Digital Equipment Corporation (DEC) and also found stiff competition from a variety of niche competitors. Computer trade publications that reached the target audience were full of competitive ads, making it difficult for NCR to establish a strong impression among data processing managers and others involved in the computer purchase decision, particularly given its budget limitations.

In 1984, NCR decided to develop an advertising program that would get the slow-selling NCR Tower noticed. Before developing its strategy, however, the company set four objectives for the campaign: to increase brand awareness by 50 percent among the target markets, to generate high-quality leads for its sales force, to improve the morale of the direct-sales force, and to increase sales by 10 percent within six months.

To help meet these objectives, NCR and its advertising agency decided to bypass the use of traditional print media and use television as a creative alternative, making it the first company to use television to promote a business-to-business computer product. A simple slice-of-entrepreneurial-life commercial that emphasized the NCR Tower's distinctive multiuser feature was one of the ads used for the small-business market (Figure 8–1). Media time was purchased on a regional basis around upscale programs such as "60 Minutes," "20/20," and major sporting events in 17 of NCR's targeted areas including New York, Los Angeles, Chicago, and other entrepreneurial centers.

Within 12 months after breaking the campaign, the following results were achieved:

- One month after introduction the company's sales offices were swamped with calls and walk-in customers asking for a demonstration of the $30,000 system. This led to a dramatic increase in sales force morale.
- An NCR tracking study conducted three months into the campaign indicated that brand awareness among both target audiences had increased 50 percent.

Figure 8–1 A Sound Advertising Strategy Helped NCR Meet Its Promotional Objectives for the NCR Tower Computer

- Within six months NCR Tower sales increased 25 percent, exceeding the target expectations by 15 percent. After 12 months, more than $30 million in added sales revenue had been generated for the NCR Tower computer, leading the company to double the ad budget for the next year.

NCR's promotional campaign for the NCR Tower computer won a Silver Effie, an annual award presented by the American Marketing Association of New York that is based on one measurable factor: the results achieved by an advertising campaign.[1]

Introduction

The success of NCR's advertising program for the NCR Tower computer was the result of a well-planned and -executed advertising strategy. However, the *development* of this campaign was guided by the company's marketing goals of penetrating two new markets with the NCR Tower system as well as by specific advertising objectives. Not only

Figure 8–2   The Objective of This Ad Is to Promote the Company as a Desirable Place to Work

did NCR set specific objectives before developing its strategy, but the company also had appropriate measures that helped in determining whether the campaign was successful in meeting these objectives. Unfortunately, many companies have considerable difficulty with what many view as the most critical step in the promotional planning process. Complex marketing situations, conflicting perspectives regarding the role and function of advertising and promotion and what they are expected to accomplish, and uncertainty over resources make the setting of marketing communications objectives, as one writer notes, "a job of creating order out of chaos."[2]

While the task of setting objectives can be complex and difficult, it is important that this be done properly, as specific goals and objectives are the foundation upon which all other promotional decisions are made. Budgeting for advertising and other promotional areas, as well as creative and media strategies and tactics, evolves from the objectives that have been set and what must be done to attain them. Clearly stated objectives also provide a goal or standard against which performance can be measured and evaluated.

While setting specific advertising and promotional objectives should be an integral part of the planning process, in reality many companies either fail to set objectives for their promotional program or set them in such a manner that they are inappropriate or inadequate for guiding the development of the promotional plan or guiding its effectiveness. Many marketers are uncertain as to what advertising and promotion can, or should be expected to, contribute to the marketing program. To many managers the goal of their company's advertising and promotional program is quite simple: to generate sales. They fail to recognize what is required in preparing customers to buy a particular product or service and the specific tasks that advertising and promotion must perform before a sale results.

Figure 8–3   What Do You Think the Objectives of This Ad Might Be?

BETA CAROTENE. JUST ANOTHER HEALTH FAD? OR DOES IT HELP REDUCE CANCER RISK?

You have probably been reading or hearing about a natural food substance called Beta Carotene. Newspapers, such as *The New York Times* and *U.S.A. Today* have been reporting on research findings published in leading professional publications on the association between Beta Carotene in the diet and lower incidence of certain cancers.

For example, *The New England Journal of Medicine** recently published a study done at Johns Hopkins University which showed a significantly lower occurrence of lung cancer in a group of people who had high blood levels of Beta Carotene. Based on these findings, it makes sense to eat foods rich in Beta Carotene. In fact, that is one of the recommendations made by the National Cancer Institute and the American Cancer Society.

Where can you find Beta Carotene? In dark green leafy vegetables like broccoli, spinach, kale, Swiss chard and greens from beets, collards and turnips. Also in yellow-orange vegetables like carrots, pumpkins, sweet potatoes. And fruits like apricots, peaches, papayas, cantaloupe and similar melons.

Including these foods in your diet isn't just another fad, it's a sound idea for anyone who is looking for ways to help reduce cancer risk. Remember, in addition to including plenty of fruits and vegetables in your diet, don't smoke and get regular medical check-ups.

*"Serum Beta-Carotene, Vitamins A and E, Selenium and the Risk of Lung Cancer" New England Journal of Medicine, Nov. 13, 1986.

ROCHE

A public service health message from Hoffmann-LaRoche Inc.

As we know, advertising and promotion are not the only marketing activities involved in the generation of sales. Moreover, it is not always possible to measure the effects of advertising in terms of sales. For example, the Dow Chemical ad shown in Figure 8–2 is designed to promote the company as a desirable place to work among prospective employees such as college students. Consider for a moment the ad shown in Figure 8–3 for beta carotene's ability to reduce cancer risks. What objectives might the sponsor, Hoffmann-LaRoche Inc., have for this ad and how might the company determine its effectiveness?

In this chapter, we will examine the nature and purpose of advertising and promotional objectives and the role they play in guiding and controlling promotional decision making. Attention will be given to the various types of objectives that are appropriate for different situations. We will also examine a specific model that has been used effectively for many years as a method for setting advertising objectives.

The Value of Objectives

Perhaps one of the reasons why many companies fail to set specific objectives for their advertising and promotional programs is that they fail to recognize the value of doing so. There are several reasons why advertising and promotional objectives are needed, including the functions they serve in communication, planning and decision making, and measurement and evaluation.

Communications

Two of the benefits of having specific objectives for the promotional program are that they serve as communications devices and facilitate the coordination of the various groups working on the campaign. Many people are involved in the planning and development of an advertising campaign on the side of both the client and the agency. All the parties involved in the promotional campaign development and approval process must have an understanding as to the roles advertising and other promotional mix elements are expected to play in the marketing plan and what is expected from these elements of the marketing program.

Coordination of the advertising and promotional program must take place within both the company and the agency, as well as between the two. Any other parties who are involved in the promotional campaign, such as public relations and/or sales promotion firms, research specialists, or media buying services, must also be aware of what the company hopes to accomplish through its marketing communications program. Many problems can be avoided if all parties involved have a set of written and approved objectives to guide their actions. The objectives can then serve as a common base for discussing issues related to the promotional program.

Planning and Decision Making

A second benefit of having specific promotional objectives is that they serve as a guide to the development of the advertising and promotional plan. As was noted earlier, all phases of a firm's promotional strategy will be developed and based on the established objectives, including budgeting, creative, and media decisions as well as the role of supportive programs such as public relations/publicity, sales promotion, and/or reseller support.

Specific and meaningful objectives can also be useful as a guide or criterion for decision making. Promotional planners are often faced with a number of strategy and tactic options in terms of choosing among various creative options, media selection, and allocation of the budget among various elements of the promotional mix. Choices among these options should be made on the basis of how well a particular strategy matches the firm's promotional objectives.

Measurement and Evaluation of Results

A very important reason for setting specific objectives is that they provide a benchmark or standard against which the success or failure of the promotional campaign can be measured. If specific objectives have not been set, it becomes extremely difficult to determine what was accomplished by the firm's advertising and promotion efforts. As we will see later in this chapter, one of the characteristics of good objectives is that they are *measurable;* that is, they include a specification of a method and criteria for determining how well the promotional program worked. By setting specific and meaningful objectives, the promotional planner is essentially providing a measure(s) that can be used to evaluate the effectiveness of the advertising campaign. Most organizations are concerned over the returns they get for their promotional investment, and a comparison of actual performance against measurable objectives is the best way to determine if the return on the advertising and promotion investment justifies the expense.

Determining Promotional Objectives

The determination of objectives for advertising and promotion occurs after a thorough situation analysis has been conducted and the marketing and promotional issues facing the company or a brand have been identified. A thorough situation analysis is critical to the marketing and promotional planning process, as this review becomes the foundation upon which marketing objectives are determined and the marketing plan is developed. Promotional objectives evolve from the company's overall marketing plan and are rooted in the firm's marketing objectives. While advertising and promotion objectives are not the same as marketing objectives, in many firms there is a tendency to treat the two as synonymous. Thus, a discussion of the differences between the two is in order.

Marketing versus Communications Objectives

Marketing objectives are generally stated in the firm's marketing plan and are statements of what is to be accomplished by the overall marketing program within a given time period. Marketing objectives are usually defined in terms of specific, measurable outcomes such as sales volume, market share, profits, or return on investment. Good marketing objectives should be quantified, include a delineation of the target market, and note the time frame for accomplishing the goal (often this is one year since this is the planning period used by most marketers). For example, a personal computer company may have as its marketing objective: "to increase sales by 10 percent in the small-business segment of the market during the next 12 months."

A company with a very high market share may seek to increase its sales volume by stimulating growth in the product category. This might be accomplished by increasing consumption by current users or encouraging nonusers to use the product. Some firms have as their marketing objectives increasing sales by expanding distribution of their product in certain market areas. Companies often have secondary marketing objectives that are related to actions they must take to solve specific problems and thus achieve their primary objectives. For example, ways to increase sales or market share may be to enhance product quality, improve trade relations, lower prices, or increase advertising.

As was noted earlier, objectives for advertising and promotion are derived from marketing objectives, as the planning of promotional strategy must take into account what the firm hopes to achieve in terms of sales volume, market share, or other criteria and the secondary objectives related to these goals. Once the advertising or promotional manager has reviewed the marketing plan, he or she should have an understanding of where the company hopes to go with its marketing program, how it intends to get there, and the role advertising and promotion will play.

It should be recognized, however, that marketing goals defined in terms of criteria such as sales, profit, or market share increases are usually not appropriate as promotional objectives. These are objectives for the entire marketing program, and their achievement will depend on having the proper coordination and execution of all the marketing mix elements including product planning and production, pricing, and distribution, in addition to promotion.

Advertising objectives should be based on the particular communications tasks that are required to deliver the appropriate message to the target audience. This requires that the advertising manager be able to translate general marketing goals into communications goals and specific promotional objectives. Some guidance in doing this may be available from the marketing plan, as the situation analysis should provide the promotional planner with important information on factors such as

- The market segments the firm wants to target and information on the target audience such as demographics, psychographics, and purchase motives
- Information on the product and its main features, advantages, benefits, uses, and applications
- Information on the company's as well as competitors' brands such as sales and market share in various segments, positioning, competitive strategies, promotional expenditures, creative and media strategies, and tactics
- Ideas on how the brand should be positioned and specific behavioral responses being sought such as trial, repurchase, brand switching, and increased usage

In some situations the company may not have a formal marketing plan, and the information noted above may not be readily available. If this is the case, the promotional planner must attempt to gather as much information as possible about the product and its markets from sources both in and outside the company.

After reviewing the information in the marketing plan or that gathered on his or her own, the promotional planner should have an understanding of how promotion fits into the marketing program and what the firm hopes to achieve through advertising and other promotional elements. The next step is to set specific objectives for advertising and other promotional mix variables in terms of communications goals or tasks.

Many promotional planners do indeed approach promotion from a communications perspective and agree that the objective of advertising in particular is usually to communicate information or a selling message about a product or service. However, many managers view their promotional programs from a sales perspective and argue that sales or some related measure, such as market share, is the only meaningful goal for advertising and promotion and thus should be the basis for setting objectives. These two perspectives have been the topic of considerable debate and are worth examining further.

Sales versus Communications Objectives

Sales-Oriented Objectives

To many managers the only meaningful objective for their promotional program is sales. They take the position that the basic reason a firm spends money on advertising and promotion is to sell its product or service. Spending on advertising and promotion represents an investment and allocation of a firm's scarce resources that require an economic justification. Rational managers generally evaluate and compare investment options on a common financial basis such as return on investment (ROI). As will be discussed in Chapter 9, determining the specific return on advertising and promotional dollars is often quite difficult. However, many managers feel that monies spent on advertising and promotion should produce measurable results such as increasing sales volume by a certain percentage or dollar amount or increasing the brand's market share. Thus, they argue that objectives (as well as the success or failure of the campaign) should be based on the achievement of sales results.

Some managers also prefer **sales-oriented objectives** since they feel that this makes the individuals involved in the advertising and promotional process think in terms of how the promotional program will influence sales. Another reason is that managers often tend to confuse marketing objectives with advertising and promotion objectives. For example, a firm's marketing goal may be to increase its sales level to $200 million. This goal not only becomes the basis of the marketing plan but also carries over as the primary objective of the promotional program as well. Thus, when the advertising and promotional campaign is being planned, the only guiding objective is the $200 million sales goal figure, and the success of the campaign is judged against attainment of this target.

Problems with Sales Objectives   Think about the situation described above for a moment. If the company failed to achieve its target sales level of $200 million, does this mean that the advertising and promotional program was ineffective? Before answering this question, it might be helpful to compare this situation to that of a football game and think of the role of advertising as being similar to that of a quarterback. The quarterback is often one of the most important players on the team but is only effective if the individual gets support from the other players. If the team loses, is it fair to blame the loss entirely on the quarterback? The answer to both questions is, of course, no, as just as the quarterback is but one of the players on the football team, promotion is but one element of the marketing program and there are many other

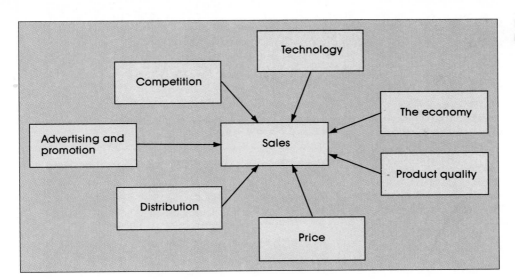

Figure 8–4   **Factors Influencing Sales**

explanations as to why the targeted sales level was not reached. In the football game the quarterback is going to lead the team to victory only if the linemen block, the receivers catch the quarterback's passes, and the running backs help the offense establish a balanced attack of running and passing. The quarterback can play an outstanding game and the team can still lose if the defense gives up too many points.

In the business world problems in achieving sales results could lie with any of the other marketing mix variables, including product design or quality, packaging, distribution, or pricing. The advertising program can be effective in making consumers aware of and interested in the brand, but this does not mean that they will buy it, particularly if it is not readily available or is priced higher than a competing brand. As shown in Figure 8–4, sales are a function of many factors, not just advertising and promotion. Promotional Perspective 8–1 discusses the Oldsmobile division of General Motors' problems in generating sales despite a very effective advertising campaign.

Another problem with sales objectives is that the effects of advertising are not always immediate and often occur over an extended time period. Many experts recognize that advertising has a lagged or **carryover effect** such that monies spent on advertising do not necessarily have an immediate impact on sales.[3] Advertising may create awareness, interest, and/or favorable attitudes toward a brand, but these feelings may not result in an actual purchase until the consumer enters the market for the product, which may occur in a later time period.

When sales are used as a measure of promotional effectiveness, consideration must be given to the fact that the influence of advertising may not be evident during the time period when it actually occurs. Thus, sales results gathered either during or immediately after an advertising campaign will not always reflect its full impact. Models have been developed to account for the carryover effect of advertising and to help determine the long-term effect of advertising on sales.[4] However, the carryover effect adds to the difficulty of determining the precise relationship between advertising and sales.

Yet another problem with using sales objectives is that they offer little guidance or direction to those individuals who are responsible for planning and developing the promotional program. The creative and media people working on the account need some direction as to the nature of the advertising message the company hopes to communicate, the intended audience, and the particular effect or response that is being sought. As we will see later in this chapter, communications objectives are recommended because they provide operational guidelines for those involved in planning, developing, and executing the advertising and promotional program.

Promotional Perspective 8—1

Great Advertising Alone Can't Sell Cars

It has often been noted in marketing that even the best advertising cannot sell a product if consumers are not interested in it. In 1989, the Oldsmobile division of General Motors became yet another company that had to deal with the problem of declining sales despite a great advertising campaign. During the 1960s and 1970s Oldsmobile was positioned as the performance car division of GM. However, during the 1980s most of the Oldsmobile division's products, such as the Cutlass Ciera and 88 Royale, were conventional looking cars that appealed primarily to people in their mid-50s looking for a traditional American car.

In 1988, General Motors decided to reposition the Oldsmobile division to appeal to baby boomers in their late 30s and early 40s. After years of safe, staid advertising, a new campaign was developed to appeal to younger consumers and create a new image for Oldsmobile. For the 1989 model year the "New Generation" advertising campaign was launched, built around the slogan "This is not your father's Oldsmobile—this is a new generation of Olds." The "New Generation" television ads featured celebrities of the 1950s and 1960s being introduced to the new Oldsmobile cars by their children (Exhibit 8–1).

The new campaign received critical acclaim in the automobile industry and in January of 1989 the campaign scored seventh in *Advertising Age* magazine's monthly poll of best remembered ads, which was the first time Oldsmobile ads had ever made the top 10. Moreover, the *Advertising Age* survey found that the awareness levels were strongest among the 35 to 44 age group that Oldsmobile was targeting. However, despite a great ad campaign and an estimated $120 million in spending, the Oldsmobile division's sales in the first five months of 1989 were down 13 percent from 1988's already low levels and 15 percent below the same period in 1987.

Why did sales decline despite a solid advertising campaign? Several theories were offered by Oldsmobile dealers, including an overall decline in GM sales, a generally soft automobile market in 1989, and prices that were too high for many younger buyers. However, the major problem appeared to be that most of the Oldsmobile cars were too bland and did not appeal to the younger automobile buyer targeted in the ads. Oldsmobile hopes to remedy this problem in the early 1990s by introducing several new sportier vehicles that should fit better with the "New Generation" image. Oldsmobile marketing officials

Exhibit 8—1   The "New Generation" Campaign Is Helping Change Oldsmobile's Image

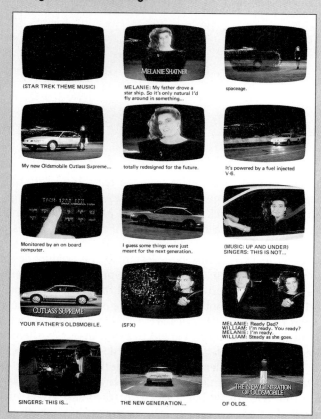

feel that the new ad campaign has already helped by moving the division's image in the desired direction. One Oldsmobile executive commented on the image being created by noting that "if you stick with it and pound on it, it'll work." However, Oldsmobile, like many other companies has learned that great advertising will only work if the consumer is interested in your product.

Source: Joseph B. White, "New Ads Give a Boost to the Olds Image But Don't Help the Old Sales Woes Much," *The Wall Street Journal*, June 19, 1989, p. B1.

Where Sales Objectives Are Appropriate   As the preceding discussion reveals, there can be many problems in attempting to use sales as objectives for a promotional campaign. However, there are situations where sales objectives are appropriate. Certain types of advertising and promotion efforts are *direct action* in nature, as they attempt to induce the prospective customer to take immediate action in the form of some overt behavioral response. Direct-response advertising is an example of a type of

Figure 8–5   **Sales Results Are an Appropriate Objective for Direct-Response Advertising**

advertising that evaluates its effectiveness on the basis of sales. Under this form of advertising, merchandise is advertised in material mailed to customers, in newspapers and magazines, or on television. The consumer purchases the merchandise through the mail or by calling an 800 number. The ad for the Escort radar detector shown in Figure 8–5 is an example of a product that is sold through direct-response advertising.

The direct-response advertiser generally sets objectives and measures success in terms of the level of sales response generated by the ad. For example, objectives for and the evaluation of, a direct-response ad run on television are based on the number of orders received each time a station broadcasts one of the commercials. Because advertising is really the only form of communication and promotion used in this situation and response is generally immediate, setting objectives in terms of sales is appropriate.

Retail advertising, which accounts for a significant percentage of all advertising expenditures, is another area where the advertiser is often seeking a direct response, particularly when sales or special events are being promoted. The ad for the preseason ski sales at Pat's Ski & Sport Shop shown in Figure 8–6 is designed to attract consumers to their stores during the four-day sales period (and of course to generate sales volume). Pat's management can determine the effectiveness of its promotional effort by analyzing store traffic and sales volume during these four days and comparing them to figures for normal, nonsale days. Of course, as we saw in Chapter 2, retailers may also want to allocate advertising and promotional dollars to "image building" campaigns that are designed to create and enhance favorable impressions and perceptions about their stores. In this case, sales-oriented objectives would not be appropriate because the effectiveness of the campaign would be based on its ability to create or change consumers' perceptions or images of the store.

Sales-oriented objectives are also used in situations where advertising plays a dominant role in a firm's marketing program and where other factors are relatively stable. For example, many packaged-goods products compete in mature markets with

Figure 8–6   Retail Advertising Often Has as an Objective the Generation of Immediate Sales

established channels of distribution, stable competitive prices, and promotional budgets and sell products of similar quality. In this situation, advertising and promotion are viewed as the key determinants of a brand's sales or market share, and thus it may be possible to isolate the effects of advertising or sales promotion.[5] Many companies have accumulated enough market knowledge and experience with their advertising and promotional programs so as to have considerable insight into the sales levels that should be expected to result from their promotional efforts. Thus, they feel that it is reasonable to set objectives and to evaluate the success of their promotional efforts in terms of sales results. The repositioning of established brands, which was discussed in Chapter 7, is often done with the goal of improving their sales or relative market share.

It is important to recognize that advertising and promotional programs are prone to be evaluated in terms of sales, particularly when expectations are not being met. Marketing and brand managers are often under pressure to show sales results and often take a short-term perspective in their evaluation of advertising and promotional programs. They are often looking for an explanation or a "quick fix" for declining sales or loss of market share, and advertising and/or sales promotion are often the first areas examined. The problems of making direct links between advertising and sales are ignored, and campaigns, as well as advertising agencies, may be changed if sales expectations are not being met. As was discussed in Chapter 3, many companies are asking their agencies to accept incentive-based compensation systems that are tied to actual sales performance. Thus, while sales may not be an appropriate objective in many advertising and promotional situations, many managers are inclined to keep a close eye to sales and market share figures and make changes in the promotional program when these numbers become stagnant or begin to decline.

Communications Objectives

While some marketers argue that promotional objectives should be based on sales, many recognize the problems associated with attempting to use sales-oriented objectives. Moreover, there are certain situations where the goal of advertising is not really sales oriented but rather is designed to enhance the image or reputation of the company or achieve some other nonbehavioral effect.

Given the problems inherent in the use of sales-oriented objectives, many marketers take the perspective that the primary role of promotional elements such as advertising is to communicate and thus efforts should be based on **communications objectives.** Advertising and other promotional efforts are viewed as being designed to accomplish various communications tasks such as creating awareness, brand knowledge and interest, favorable attitudes and image, and purchase intentions. The consumer is generally not expected to respond immediately after seeing an ad; rather, there is a realization that advertisers often have to provide the consumer with relevant information and create favorable predispositions toward the brand before purchase behavior will occur.

For example, the ad for RCA ColorTrak Monitor-Receivers shown in Figure 8—7 is designed to convince consumers of the product's technological superiority and create favorable attitudes toward the brand. While there is no call for immediate action in the ad, it is designed to create favorable impressions about the product such that consumers will consider this brand when they enter the market for video equipment.

Advocates of communications-based objectives generally use some form of the

Figure 8—8 Effect of Advertising on Consumers: Movement from Awareness to Action

Related Behavioral Dimensions	Movement toward Purchase	Example of Types of Promotion or Advertising Relevant to Various Steps
Conative: The realm of motives. Ads stimulate or direct desires.	Purchase ↑	Point-of-purchase Retail store ads Deals "Last-chance" offers Price appeals Testimonials
	Conviction ↑	
Affective: The realm of emotions. Ads change attitudes and feelings.	Preference ↑	Competitive ads Argumentative copy
	Liking ↑	"Image" copy Status, glamour appeals
Cognitive: The realm of thoughts. Ads provide information and facts.	Knowledge ↑	Announcements Descriptive copy Classified ads Slogans Jingles Skywriting
	Awareness ↑	Teaser Campaigns

Source: Robert J. Lavidge and Gary A. Steiner, *Journal of Marketing* 25 (1961), pp. 59–62.

hierarchical models discussed in Chapter 5 as a basis for setting advertising and promotion objectives. As you may recall, these hierarchy models vary somewhat in terms of the intermediate steps they use but essentially view the consumer as having to pass through three successive stages including a cognitive, affective, and conative sequence. The underlying logic of these models is that as consumers proceed through the successive stages, they move closer to making a purchase. Figure 8–8 shows the various steps in the Robert Lavidge and Gary Steiner hierarchy-of-effects model that the consumer passes through in moving from awareness to purchase, along with examples of types of advertising or promotion relevant to each step.

Communications Effects Pyramid A way of understanding communications tasks to be performed by advertising and promotion is to view them as being analogous to building a pyramid by accomplishing lower level objectives such as awareness and knowledge or comprehension.[6] Subsequent tasks involve moving consumers who are aware of or knowledgeable about the product or service to higher levels in the pyramid. Of course, the initial stages, at the base of the pyramid, will be easier to accomplish than those toward the top, such as trial and repurchase or regular use. Thus, the percentage of prospective customers moved to each level will decline as they move up the pyramid. We will use the communications effects pyramid presented in Figure

Figure 8—9   **Communication Effects Pyramid**

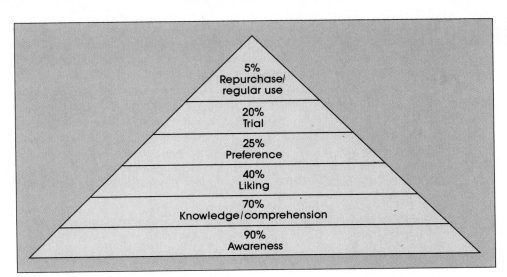

8—9 to show how a company introducing a new brand of shampoo targeted at 18- to 34-year-old females might set its advertising and promotion objectives.

The first task of the promotional program for a new product is to create a broad level of awareness among the target audience. This can be done through repetitive advertising in a variety of media that reach 18- to 34-year-old females such as magazines, television, and radio. Thus, the specific objective would be:

> To create a 90 percent awareness of Backstage shampoo among 18- to 34-year-old females during the first six weeks of the campaign

The next step in the pyramid process is to communicate information so that a certain percentage of the target audience will not only be aware of the new product but will also understand its features and benefits. Let us assume that the new Backstage brand is being positioned as a milder shampoo that does not contain soap as an ingredient and improves the texture and shine of the hair. The specific objective for the second stage would be as follows:

> To communicate the specific benefits of Backstage shampoo—that it contains no soap and improves the texture and shine of the hair—among 70 percent of the target audience to make them interested in the brand

At the next level, the promotional campaign is designed to create positive feelings toward the new Backstage brand. A certain percentage of the consumers who have been made aware of the new brand must be moved to the affective stages of liking and preference. To accomplish this objective the advertising must effectively communicate the benefits so as to create favorable attitudes toward the product. Of course, only a certain percentage of the target audience will develop a liking or positive feelings for the brand, and an even smaller number will be moved to the preference block. The specific objective at this stage would be:

> To create positive feelings toward Backstage shampoo among 40 percent of the target audience and a preference for the brand among 25 percent

Once the preceding steps have been accomplished, a certain percentage of the target audience will move to the action stage at the top of the pyramid. The promotional plan may be designed to create trial among consumers that will be influenced not only by advertising but also by sales promotion techniques such as couponing and sampling. The objective at this stage might be:

> To use sampling and cents-off coupons, along with advertising, to elicit trial of Backstage shampoo among 20 percent of 18- to 34-year-old females during the first three months

The ultimate goal of the promotional program is to make consumers loyal to the new brand so that they will repurchase it. Repurchase and regular use of Backstage shampoo will, of course, depend on the consumers' evaluations and feelings after using it. However, the promotional program may call for continued advertising and periodic sales promotions not only to retain those consumers who have tried Backstage shampoo but also to take new consumers through the pyramid and get them to try the brand. The shampoo market is extremely competitive, with only a few brands having more than a 10 percent market share. Thus, the ultimate goal may be to get a percentage of women who try the brand to become regular users and to continue to attract new customers. Keeping in mind the aforementioned problems of attempting to use sales objectives for advertising and promotion, the final objective would be as follows:

> To develop and maintain regular use of Backstage shampoo among 5 percent of the 18- to 34-year-old females

While we have used the communications pyramid to show how objectives would be set for a new brand, this model could also be used to determine promotional objectives for an established brand. The promotional planner must determine where the target audience lies with respect to the various blocks in the pyramid, as this will provide insight into what communications tasks need to be accomplished. For example, if awareness levels for a brand and knowledge of its features and benefits are low, the communications objective should be to increase them. On the other hand, these blocks of the pyramid may already be in place, but liking or preference may be low. In this situation the advertising goal may be to change the target markets' attitudes or image of the brand to make them more favorable and move them through to purchase.

Problems with Communications Objectives   Not all marketing and advertising managers accept the idea of using communications objectives. Accomplishing communications objectives is seen as being of value only if this results in sales for the product, and they argue that it is too difficult to translate a sales goal into a specific communications objective. However, it should be recognized that at some point a sales goal must be transformed into a communications objective. For example, if the marketing plan for an established brand has as an objective increasing sales by 10 percent, the promotional planner will eventually have to think in terms of the message that will be communicated to the target audience to achieve this. Possible objectives in this situation might include the following:

- Increasing the percentage of consumers in the target market that associate specific features, benefits, or advantages with our brand
- Increasing the number of consumers in the target audience who prefer our product over the competition's
- Encouraging current users of the product to use the product more frequently or in more situations

One of the problems promotional planners encounter in attempting to translate sales goals into specific communications objectives is that they are not sure of what constitutes adequate levels of awareness, knowledge, liking, preference, or conviction. There are no formulas, books, or specific sources that can provide this information. The promotional manager will have to use his or her personal experience along with that of others such as the brand or product managers as well as the marketing history of this and similar brands. Consideration should be given to norms or average scores that have been achieved in the past on various communications measures for this or similar products, as well as the levels achieved by competitor's products. This information can be related to the amount of money and time spent building these levels as well as the resulting sales or market share figures. Promotional Perspective 8–2 dis-

Promotional Perspective **8-2**

Making Successful Commercials for New Products

Every year, thousands of new products are introduced to the consumer market, many of which are supported by multimillion-dollar television advertising campaigns. Unfortunately, nearly 80 percent of these products will fail for various reasons, including poor product quality, bad timing, lack of a significant difference from competing products, or poor execution of the marketing program—including advertising. With respect to advertising, the basic issue is whether these new products are being backed by commercials that help or hurt their chances for success. Some insight into this question was provided in a year-long study conducted by Evalucom, Inc., a commercial testing company, in conjunction with major advertisers involved in new product introductions.

Evalucom evaluated 50 commercials used to introduce new products in 10 broad product categories. For each commercial, the advertiser had previously determined whether or not it had succeeded or failed in stimulating anticipated levels of trial, using ad tracking and sales results. Of the 50 commercials studied, 27 were judged to have been successful and 23 were deemed unsuccessful. Attempts were also made to control for problems from other areas of the marketing program such as promotion, pricing, distribution, and media spending.

The Evalucom analysis used a procedure whereby a diagnostic evaluation of the commercial is made using a procedure that identifies communications building blocks or "meaning segments." Trained analysts, assisted by a computer, systematically search each ad for the presence or absence of more than 2,000 criteria relating directly to the content, structure, and manner of presentation. Evalucom has found five basic advertising communications objectives that are critical to the success of any commercial. These include

- Capturing attention at the beginning of the commercial
- Building interest and involvement
- Communicating clearly
- Creating awareness of the brand name
- Meeting the advertiser's communications strategy

The new product study, however, went beyond these basic communications requirements and considered factors that were related to the success or failure of commercials for new product. Evalucom's study pointed to the existence of four factors that made a difference as to whether a new product commercial was successful in generating sales. These included the following:

1. *Communicating that something is different about the product.* All the successful introductory commercials in the study communicated some point of difference for the new product.
2. *Positioning the brand difference in relation to the product category.* All 27 successful commercials positioned their brand's difference within a specific product category. For example, a new breakfast product was positioned as the "crispiest cereal" or a new beverage as the "smoothest soft drink."
3. *Communicating that the product difference is beneficial to consumers.* Some 93 percent of the successful commercials linked a benefit directly to the new product's difference.
4. *Supporting the idea that something about the product is different and/or beneficial to the consumer.* All the successful commercials communicated support for the product's difference claim or its relevance to consumers. Support took the form of demonstrations of performance, information supporting a uniqueness claim, endorsements, or testimonials.

The results of this study suggest that advertisers and their agencies can increase their odds of developing sales-effective new product commercials by incorporating these communications imperatives into their messages.

Source: Kirby Andrews, "Communications Imperatives for New Products," *Journal of Advertising Research* 26, no. 5 (October/November, 1986), pp. 29–32.

cusses an interesting study that identified five basic advertising communications objectives that are critical to the success of a commercial for a new product.

At some point sales-oriented objectives must be translated into what it is the company hopes to communicate and to whom they hope to communicate it in order for the planning and implementation of the promotional strategy to proceed. Many marketing and promotional managers recognize the value of setting specific communications objectives and the important role they play as operational guidelines to the planning, execution, and evaluation of the promotional program. Communications objectives are the criteria used in the DAGMAR approach to setting advertising goals and objectives, which has become one of the best known and most influential approaches to the advertising planning process. We will now turn our attention to the DAGMAR model and the role communications objectives play in this approach.

DAGMAR—An Approach to Setting Objectives

In 1961, Russell Colley prepared a report for the Association of National Advertisers entitled *Defining Advertising Goals for Measured Advertising Results.*[7] In this report Colley developed a model (that became known by the acronym **DAGMAR**) for setting advertising objectives and measuring the results of an advertising campaign against these objectives. The major thesis of the DAGMAR model is that communications effects are the logical basis for advertising goals and objectives and against which success or failure should be measured. Colley's rationale for communications-based objectives was as follows:

> Advertising's job, purely and simply, is to communicate to a defined audience information and a frame-of-mind that stimulates action. Advertising succeeds or fails depending on how well it communicates the desired information and attitudes to the right people at the right time and at the right cost.[8]

Under the DAGMAR approach, an advertising goal involves a communications task that is specific and measurable. A **communications task,** as opposed to a marketing task, involves something that can be performed by, and attributed to, advertising rather than requiring a combination of several marketing factors. Colley proposed that the communications task be based on a hierarchical model of the communications process. The four stages of commercial communication suggested by Colley include:

- *Awareness*   Making the consumer aware of the existence of the brand or company
- *Comprehension*   Developing an understanding of what the product is and what it will do for the consumer
- *Conviction*   Developing a mental disposition or conviction in the consumer to buy the product
- *Action*   Getting the consumer to take some action and purchase the product

As discussed previously, there are other hierarchical-type models of advertising effects that can be used as a basis for analyzing the communications response process. In fact, some advertising theorists have advocated using the Lavidge and Steiner hierarchy-of-effects model since it is more specific and provides a better method of establishing and measuring results.[9]

While the hierarchical model of advertising effects was the basic model of the communications response process used in DAGMAR, Colley also gave attention to other specific tasks that advertising might be expected to perform in leading to the ultimate objective of a sale. He developed an "advertising task checklist," shown in Table 8–1, that consists of 52 tasks that might characterize the purpose and contribution of advertising. Colley advocated that all those individuals concerned with advertising go through this or a similar checklist and thoughtfully consider each item. The result would be the establishment of realistic and agreed-upon goals. While Colley did not suggest that this list was complete, it does provide a number of considerations for campaign planners who are attempting to develop advertising objectives.

Characteristics of Objectives

A second major contribution of DAGMAR to the advertising planning process was Colley's specification of what constitutes a *good objective*. Colley argued that advertising objectives should be stated in terms of concrete and measurable communications tasks, specify a target audience, indicate a benchmark starting point and the degree of change sought, and specify a time period for accomplishing the objective(s). Each of these requirements is examined more closely.

Concrete and Measurable   The communications task specified in the objective should be a precise statement of what appeal or message the advertiser wants to com-

Table 8–1 **Advertising Task Checklist**

This checklist is a "thought starter" in developing specific advertising objectives. It can be applied to a single ad, a year's campaign for each product, or it can aid in developing a company's entire advertising philosophy among all those who create and approve advertising.

	Scale of Importance					
	Not Important				Very Important	
	0	1	2	3	4	5

To what extent does the advertising aim at closing an *immediate sale*?

1. Perform the complete selling function (take the product through all the necessary steps toward a sale)
2. Close sales to prospects already partly sold through past advertising efforts ("Ask for the order" or "clincher" advertising)
3. Announce a special reason for "buying now" (price, premium, etc.)
4. Remind people to buy
5. Tie in with some special buying event
6. Stimulate impulse sales

Does the advertising aim at *near-term* sales by moving the prospect, step by step, closer to a sale (so that when confronted with a buying situation the customer will ask for, reach for, or accept the advertised brand)?

7. Create awareness of existence of product or brand
8. Create "brand image" or favorable emotional disposition toward the brand
9. Implant information or attitude regarding benefits and superior features of the brand
10. Combat or offset competitive claims
11. Correct false impressions, misinformation, and other obstacles to sales
12. Build familiarity and easy recognition of package or trademark

Does the advertising aim at building a "long-range consumer franchise"?

13. Build confidence in company and brand that is expected to pay off in years to come
14. Build customer demand, which places company in stronger position in relation to its distribution (not at the "mercy" of the marketplace)
15. Place advertiser in position to select preferred distributors and dealers
16. Secure universal distribution
17. Establish a "reputation platform" for launching new brands or product lines
18. Establish brand recognition and acceptance, which will enable the company to open up new markets (geographic, price, age, sex)

Specifically, how can advertising contribute toward increased sales?

19. Hold present customers against the inroads of competition
20. Convert competitive users to advertiser's brand
21. Cause people to specify advertiser's brand instead of asking for product by generic name
22. Convert nonusers of the product type to users of product and brand
23. Make steady customers out of occasional or sporadic customers
24. Advertising new uses of the product
25. Persuading customers to buy larger sizes or multiple units
26. Reminding users to buy
27. Encouraging greater frequency or quantity of use

Table 8–1 (concluded)

	Scale of Importance				
	Not Important 0	1	2	3	Very Important 4	5

Does the advertising aim at some specific step that leads to a sale?
28. Persuade prospect to write for descriptive literature, return a coupon, enter a contest
29. Persuade prospect to visit a showroom, ask for a demonstration
30. Induce prospect to sample the product (trial offer)

How important are "supplementary benefits" of end-use advertising?
31. Aid salespeople in opening new accounts
32. Aid salespeople in getting larger orders from wholesalers and retailers
33. Aid salespeople in getting preferred display space
34. Give salespeople an entree
35. Build morale of company sales force
36. Impress the trade (causing recommendation to their customers and favorable treatment to salespeople)

Is it a task of advertising to impart information needed to consummate sales and build customer satisfaction?
37. "Where to buy it" advertising
38. "How to use it" advertising
39. New models, features, package
40. New prices
41. Special terms, trade-in offers, etcetera
42. New policies (guarantees, etc.)

To what extent does the advertising aim at building confidence and goodwill for the corporation among:
43. Customers and potential customers?
44. The trade (distributors, dealers, retailer people)?
45. Employees and potential employees?
46. The financial community?
47. The public at large?

Specifically what kind of images does the company wish to build?
48. Product quality, dependability
49. Service
50. Family resemblance of diversified products
51. Corporate citizenship
52. Growth, progressiveness, technical leadership

Source: Russell H. Colley, *Defining Advertising Goals for Measured Advertising Results* (New York: Association of National Advertisers, 1961), pp. 62–68.

municate to the target audience. Advertisers generally use a copy platform to describe the basic message they hope to communicate to their target audience. The objective or copy platform statement should be specific and clear enough to provide guidance and direction to creative specialists who must develop the actual advertising message. For example, the objective of the ad shown in Figure 8–10 was to "get the facts out and neutralize the junk-food misconceptions about McDonald's good food." This ad and several others were part of a campaign by McDonald's to respond to concerns and criticisms about the nutritional value of its food.[10]

According to DAGMAR, it is also important that the objective be measurable and that attention be given to the method and criteria that can be used to determine if the intended message has been properly communicated. In the case of the McDonald's campaign discussed above, consumers' perceptions of the quality and nutritional value of its food could be used to determine if the communications objectives were being met.

Figure 8–10   **The Objective of This Ad Was to Neutralize Junk-Food Misconceptions about McDonald's Food**

Target Audience   Another important characteristic of good objectives is that they include a well-defined target audience. Generally, the primary target audience for a company's product or service is identified and described in the situation analysis and may be based on descriptive variables such as geography, demographics, and psychographics as well as on behavioral variables such as usage rate or benefits sought. When variables such as usage rate or benefits sought are the basis for target audience selection, attention must still be given to describing their demographic and, if possible, psychographic characteristics since advertising media selection decisions are based on these variables.

Benchmark and Degree of Change Sought   An important part of setting objectives is knowing the target audience's present status concerning response hierarchy variables such as awareness, knowledge, image, attitudes, and intentions and then determining the degree to which the consumers must be changed or moved by the advertising campaign. The determination of the target market's present position regarding the various response stages requires that **benchmark measures** be taken. This often requires that a marketing research study be conducted to determine prevailing levels of the response hierarchy. In the case of a new product or service, the starting conditions are generally at or near zero for all the variables, and no initial research would be needed.

The establishment of benchmark measures is important, as this gives the promotional planner a basis for determining what communications tasks need to be accomplished and for specifying particular objectives. For example, a preliminary study for a brand may reveal that awareness is high, but knowledge of its specific benefits is low, as are consumer attitudes. Thus, the objective for the advertising campaign would not be concerned with increasing awareness but rather with improving the target audience's knowledge level of the brand and improving attitudes toward it.

The use of quantitative benchmarks not only is valuable in establishing communications goals and objectives but also is a prerequisite to determining if the campaign was successful. As noted earlier in this chapter, objectives provide the standard against which the success or failure of a campaign is measured. An advertising campaign that results in a 90 percent awareness level for a brand among its target audience cannot really be judged to be effective unless one knows what percentage of the consumers were aware of the brand before the campaign began. A 70 percent precampaign awareness level would lead to a different interpretation of the campaign's success than would a 30 percent level.

Specified Time Period   A final consideration in setting advertising objectives is the specification of the time period in which the objectives are to be accomplished. Appropriate time periods can range anywhere from a few days to a year or more. Most advertising campaigns specify time periods ranging from a few months to a year. The length of the time period depends on the situation facing the advertiser and the type of response being sought. For example, creating or increasing awareness levels for a brand can be accomplished fairly quickly through an intensive media schedule, which results in widespread and repetitive advertising to the target audience. On the other hand, the repositioning of a product requires a change in consumers' perceptions regarding the image of the brand and will require much more time. For example, the repositioning of Marlboro cigarettes from a feminine brand to one with a masculine image took several years to accomplish. As was discussed in Promotional Perspective 8–1, marketing executives at Oldsmobile recognized that the repositioning of the image of its automobiles would take more than one year.

Assessment of DAGMAR

The DAGMAR approach to setting advertising objectives has definitely had a tremendous amount of influence on the field of advertising. Many promotional planners have turned to this model as a basis for setting objectives and assessing the effectiveness of their promotional campaigns. DAGMAR also focused advertisers' attention on the value of using communications-based objectives, rather than sales-based, as measures of advertising effectiveness and encouraged the measurement of stages in the response hierarchy as a way of assessing a campaign's impact. Colley's work has led to improvements in the advertising and promotional planning process by providing those involved with a better understanding of the goals and objectives toward which their efforts should be directed. This usually results in less subjectivity and also leads to better communication and relationships between the client and its agency.

While DAGMAR has made contributions to the advertising planning process, this approach has not been totally accepted by everyone in the advertising field. A number of problems have been noted with the DAGMAR model that have led to questions regarding its value as an advertising planning technique.[11,12] These problems are both conceptual and practical in nature and merit consideration.

Problems with the Response Hierarchy   A major criticism of the DAGMAR approach centers on the hierarchy-of-effects model upon which it is based. You may recall that Colley proposed that the communications task be based on a hierarchical-type response model and suggested that movement through the sequential steps such as awareness, comprehension, attitude, and conviction will ultimately lead to purchase. As discussed in Chapter 5, critics of the hierarchy-of-effects model argue that consumers do not always go through this sequence of communications effects before making a purchase. For example, a consumer may pass directly from awareness to purchase

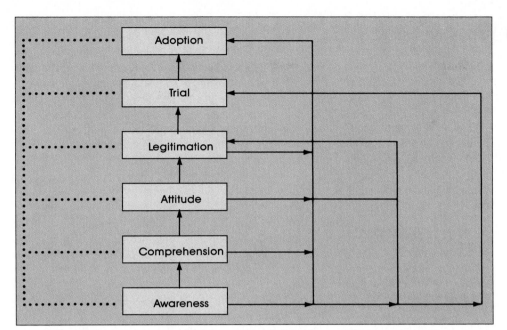

Figure 8–11 Modified Hierarchy Model

Source: Richard Vaughn, "How Advertising Works: A Planning Model," *Journal of Advertising Research* 20, no. 5 (October 1980), p. 29.

without learning about the product, forming an attitude toward it, or developing a conviction to buy it.

The problem concerning the assumption that consumers always proceed through the various levels of the response hierarchy in the specified order has been recognized, and alternative response models have been developed.[13] For example, an updated version of DAGMAR, known as DAGMAR MOD II, was developed.[14] This version recognizes that the appropriate response model will depend on the particular situation and emphasizes the identification of the sequence of decision-making steps that are applicable in a buying situation.

In developing the Foote, Cone & Belding grid, "FCB grid," which was discussed in Chapter 5, Richard Vaughn proposed using Thomas Robertson's adoption process model[15] as a modified hierarchy model. Vaughn's model, which is shown in Figure 8–11, proposes that

> some consumers, under some conditions, for some products, might follow a sequential path. The dotted lines [in Figure 8–11] are feedbacks which can alter outcomes. Other decision patterns on the right track consumers as they violate the formal sequence of the hierarchy. Thus, consumers can learn from previous experience and swerve from the awareness to purchase pattern.[16]

Vaughn suggests that this modified model preserves the "learn → feel → do" sequence of most hierarchy models but also adds more flexibility. Close examination of this model shows that it offers a way of integrating the three response hierarchies discussed in Chapter 5. This promotional manager must determine which response sequence is relevant in the purchase process for the product or service being advertised and what role advertising and other promotional mix elements play in moving consumers through the applicable hierarchy. Appropriate objectives can then be set to guide the promotional program.

Problems with the Attitude-Behavior Relationship   Another problem implicit in the DAGMAR model concerns the relationship between attitudes and behavior. Many critics contend that attitude change does not necessarily lead to a change in behavior.[17,18] Thus, even if advertising efforts do lead to the development of favorable affective states, there is no guarantee that consumers will make a purchase on the basis of their attitude.

The argument that attitude change does not lead to behavior is not really damaging to DAGMAR. Problems with the attitude-behavior relationship often results from the fact that general attitudes are often used to attempt to measure specific behaviors. By using specific measures such as attitude toward purchasing or using a particular brand or intentions to buy a specific brand, the attitude-behavior relationship can be improved.[19] In extensive study of the relationship between attitudes and purchase behavior for consumer products, a clear relationship was shown between the two.[20] Thus, while the relationship between attitudes and purchase behavior may not always be high, attitude change is generally considered a valid advertising objective, particularly in high-involvement purchase situations.

Sales Objectives   Another objection to DAGMAR comes from those who argue that the only relevant measure of advertising objectives is sales. Communications objectives are viewed as a "cop-out" and as ignoring the basic reason why a firm spends money on advertising—which is to generate sales. They point out the fact that advertising can accomplish communications objectives yet have little or no impact on sales and that advertising is effective only to the extent that it induces consumers to make a purchase.[21] Thus, since a communications variable is only of interest if it can be shown to be related to sales, why not measure sales directly? The fallacy in this logic has been addressed in our discussion of reasons for using communications objectives and need not be repeated here.

Practicality and Costs   A fourth problem often noted with DAGMAR concerns the difficulties involved in implementing this approach. A manager attempting to utilize DAGMAR has to determine what constructs or variables are relevant and how they should be measured. The establishment of quantitative benchmarks and the ultimate measurement of communications results require that money be spent on research. Not only is this costly, but it can also be time-consuming and can lead to considerable disagreement over method, criteria, measures, and so forth. As a result, many critics argue that DAGMAR is viable only for large companies with big advertising and research budgets and the capabilities of conducting the research needed to establish benchmarks and measure changes in the communications response hierarchy. Many firms do not want to spend the money on research that is needed to utilize the DAGMAR approach effectively or feel that they cannot afford to do so.

Inhibits Creativity   A final criticism of DAGMAR is that it inhibits advertising creativity by imposing too much influence and structure on the creative people responsible for developing the advertising. Creative people in advertising are often searching for the "great idea" that will result in a unique and, hopefully, effective campaign. Many creative personnel feel that having to adhere to the rational and planned DAGMAR approach makes the creative department overly concerned with numbers and quantitative assessment of a campaign's impact in terms of measures such as awareness, brand-name recall, or specific persuasion measures. The net effect is that the emphasis is on "passing the numbers test" rather than developing a message that is truly creative and adds to or enhances the product. The problems associated with the quantification of advertising and overresearching its effectiveness will be examined in greater detail in Chapter 18.

There is little question that the DAGMAR approach makes the creative personnel more accountable and may inhibit their freedom to search for the great creative idea. On the other hand, spectacular advertising ideas are not easy to come by, and many advertisers are more concerned with avoiding ineffective advertising. Well-planned campaigns using a DAGMAR approach are viewed by many advertising and marketing managers as a way of avoiding the problem of developing ads with no specific direction or purpose, even if the result is some restriction on the creative department.

Promotional Perspective 8–3

Ad Campaigns Do Something Right, But What?

An interesting study was conducted some years ago by an advertising researcher in which the campaign objectives and "proofs of success" for 135 supposedly successful ad campaigns created by 40 agencies were analyzed. Two specific questions addressed in this study included:

1. Did the agency set specific objectives for the campaign, that is, objectives specific enough to be measured?
2. Did the agency attempt to measure the effectiveness of the campaign by clearly stating how the campaign fulfilled the previously set objectives?

As a basis for analysis relative to the first question, a *specific objective* was defined as one that made clear the four criteria set forth in DAGMAR: (1) what message was to be delivered (2) to what audience and (3) with what intended effect(s) and (4) what specific criteria were going to be used to measure the success of the campaign.

The analysis of the stated campaign objectives showed that 64 percent fulfilled the first three criteria, but only 2 of the 135, or less than 1 percent, met all four criteria. The major problems found in the objectives included a failure to state objectives in quantifiable terms, a failure to realize that the results of advertising could not be measured in sales, and a failure to specify the target audience. Relative to the first question, only 2 of the 135 campaigns used a quantified objective, which is needed to establish benchmarks and measurement criteria. Twenty-four percent of the campaigns stated objectives in terms of sales, thus ignoring the other factors that may have influenced sales results during the campaign; 16 percent of the objectives failed to specify a target audience.

In regard to the second question concerning evidence of how the campaign fulfilled the objectives, the study found that only in 31 percent of the campaigns were proofs of success related directly to the objectives the agency set. The major problems found were the following:

1. With an objective of awareness, success was stated in sales.
2. With an objective of new image, success was stated in terms of readership or inquiries.
3. With more than one objective set forth, success was stated only in relation to one of them.

An example of a campaign where the proof of success did not logically relate to the statement of campaign objectives was that for Welch's Grape Juice:

Objectives: To convince mothers that Welch's Grape Juice is the best fruit drink they can serve for their children:

- Because it is good for them
- Because it is the best tasting of all fruit drinks

Proof of success: Despite the aggressive competition from scores of competitive brands of fruit drinks, Welch's not only has held its position but has shown consistent improvement in sales year after year.

The objective of this campaign was to convince mothers that this product was the best fruit drink for their children because of its nutritional value and good taste. However, the proof of success or advertising effectiveness was cited in terms of sales, and no mention was made of mothers' awareness or image of the brand's taste or nutritional value.

Source: Stewart H. Britt, "Are So-Called Successful Advertising Campaigns Really Successful?" *Journal of Advertising Research* 9, no. 2 (1969), pp. 3–9.

Problems in Setting Objectives

The DAGMAR approach specifies that advertising goals and objectives should include a statement of the basic message to be delivered, the target audience, the intended effect, and specific criteria that will be used to measure the success of the campaign. Thus, when the time comes to determine whether the campaign was successful, the advertiser can evaluate it by comparing actual performance against intended results that were specified in the original objectives. The logic underlying DAGMAR is that the advertising or promotional manager should decide what the advertising and promotions campaign is expected to achieve and then make plans to test and determine how successful the outcome was, relative to expected results.

While this may sound like a logical process to the advertising and promotion planning process, most advertisers and their agencies fail to follow these basic principles. They often fail to set specific objectives for their campaigns and/or usually do not have the proper evidence to determine the success of their promotional programs. Promotional Perspective 8–3 discusses a classic study that examined the problems with how advertisers set objectives and measure their accomplishment.

The results of the study discussed in Promotional Perspective 8–3 suggest that most advertising agencies did not state appropriate objectives for determining success and thus could not really demonstrate whether a supposedly successful campaign was indeed a success. Even though these campaigns may have been doing something right, they generally were not aware of what it was. Although this study was conducted in 1969, the same problems may still be prevalent in advertising today.

A recent study examined the advertising practices of business-to-business marketers to determine whether their advertisements used advertising objectives that met the four DAGMAR criteria specified by Colley.[22] Entries from the annual Business/Professional Advertising Association Gold Key Awards competition, which solicits the best marketing communications efforts from business-to-business advertisers, were evaluated with respect to their statements of objectives and summary of results of their campaigns. The results of this study indicated these advertisers did not utilize the four components of good advertising objectives, specify objective tasks or measure results in terms of stages of a communications hierarchy-of-effects strategy, or match objectives to evaluation measures. The authors concluded that

> advertising practitioners have only partially adopted the concepts and standards of objective setting and evaluation set forth over 25 years ago.[23]

Improving Promotional Planners' Use of Objectives

As the foregoing discussion has stressed, it is very important that advertisers and their agencies pay close attention to the objectives they set for their campaigns. They should strive to set specific and measurable objectives that not only serve as a guide to promotional planning and decision making but also can be used as a standard against which advertising and promotional performance can be evaluated. Unfortunately, as we have seen, many companies either do not understand how to set appropriate objectives for their advertising and promotional programs or fail to do so for some other reason.

In many companies, there is a lack of understanding of what the role and function of advertising are because top management has only an abstract idea of what the firm's advertising is supposed to be doing. A study by the American Business Press, which measured the attitudes of chairmen, presidents, and other senior managers of business-to-business advertising companies, found that more than 50 percent of the 427 respondents said that they did not know whether their advertising was working, and less than 10 percent said that they thought their advertising was working well.[24] This study showed overwhelmingly that top management did not even know what their company's advertising was supposed to do, much less how to measure it.

It is unlikely that most firms are going to set objectives meeting all the criteria set forth in DAGMAR. However, it is important that promotional planners set objectives that are specific and measurable and go beyond basic sales goals. Even if steps are not always taken to measure specific communications response elements, meeting the other criteria will sharpen the focus and improve the quality of the advertising and promotions planning process.

Objectives for Other Promotional Elements

While the goal of this chapter has been to discuss and consider various issues regarding the determination of objectives for an organization's overall promotional program and strategy, much of the attention has focused on setting objectives for advertising. For example, DAGMAR is basically a model for setting objectives and planning the advertising program. One of the reasons so much attention is given to advertising objectives is that it is often the lead element in the promotional mix, particularly in consumer products marketing, and thus receives most of the attention in the planning process. Elements such as sales promotion and/or publicity/public relations often are used on an intermittent basis to support and complement the advertising program.

However, advertising is used on a continual basis and is viewed as the key element in the firm's promotional strategy and its ability to meet communications objectives.

Of course, there are some situations where advertising will play a subservient role to other elements of the promotional mix, such as in business-to-business marketing where personal selling is the major promotional element. However, as shown in the NCR example at the beginning of the chapter, advertising can also play an important role in the promotional programs of these firms as well.

Many of the considerations discussed in determining advertising objectives are relevant when setting goals for other elements of the promotional mix. The promotional planner should determine what role elements such as various sales promotion techniques, publicity and public relations, and personal selling will play in the overall marketing program and how they will interact with advertising, as well as with one another. When setting objectives for these other promotional elements, consideration must be given to what it is the firm hopes to communicate or accomplish through the use of this element, among what target audience, and during what time period. As with advertising, results should be measured and evaluated against the original objectives, and attempts should be made to isolate the effects that each promotional element played. A more thorough discussion of objectives for other promotional elements is provided in the chapters devoted to each later in the text.

Summary

This chapter has examined the role of objectives in the planning and evaluation of the advertising and promotional program. Specific objectives are needed to guide the development of the promotional program as well as to provide a benchmark or standard against which performance can be measured and evaluated. Objectives serve important functions as communications devices, as a guide planning the promotional program and making decisions regarding various alternatives, and for the measurement and evaluation of the promotional program.

Advertising and promotional objectives evolve from the organization's overall marketing plan, and objectives are based on the role these elements play in the marketing program. The determination of promotional objectives occurs after a thorough situation analysis has been conducted and the marketing and promotional issues have been identified. Many managers view their advertising and promotional programs from a sales perspective and use sales or a related measure such as market share as the basis for setting objectives. However, because of the various problems associated with sales-based objectives, many promotional planners take the perspective that the role of advertising is to communicate. Thus, communications-based objectives such as those in the response hierarchy are used as the basis for setting advertising goals. A communication effects pyramid was discussed and used to illustrate what appropriate objectives might be for the various stages in the hierarchy.

The DAGMAR approach to setting objectives was examined in detail, along with the characteristics of good objectives specified by this advertising planning process. Good advertising objectives meet four basic criteria: They are set in concrete and measurable communications terms; they specify a target audience; they contain a benchmark and indicate the degree of change being sought; and they specify a time period for accomplishing the objectives. Many companies fail to meet these criteria in setting objectives for their advertising and promotional programs. Many of the principles used in setting advertising objectives can also be applied to other elements in the promotional mix.

Key Terms

Marketing objectives	Communications objectives	Benchmark measures
Sales-oriented objectives	DAGMAR	
Carryover effect	Communications task	

Discussion Questions

1. Discuss the importance and value of setting advertising and promotion objectives and the role they play in the promotional planning process.
2. What are the differences between marketing objectives and communications objectives? Why do so many managers confuse the two?
3. Choose a particular product or service and provide examples of what its marketing objectives might be as well as the communications objectives.
4. One of the more controversial areas of marketing and promotion is whether sales are the most appropriate criteria for measuring advertising effectiveness or whether communications objectives should be used. Discuss the use of sales versus communications objectives, giving attention to the problems and advantages of each.
5. Discuss how the communications effects pyramid can be used in developing communications objectives for a new brand as well as an established brand.
6. Find three examples of commercials used to introduce new products to the consumer market. Evaluate these commercials using the four communications imperatives for new products discussed in Promotional Perspective 8–2.
7. What are the four characteristics of good objectives suggested by DAGMAR? Do you think most advertisers set objectives that meet these criteria?
8. A criticism of DAGMAR is that it limits advertising creativity by imposing too much influence and structure on the creative specialists. Do you agree or disagree? Evaluate this criticism.
9. It has been suggested that most top managers of business-to-business firms are not aware of whether their advertising is working and what it is supposed to be doing. How would you explain the role and function of advertising to these managers?

Notes

1. David Perry, "Award Winning Marketing That Sells," *Business Marketing,* March 1987, pp. 122–131.
2. Robert A. Kriegel, "How to Choose the Right Communications Objectives," *Business Marketing,* April 1986, pp. 94–106.
3. Donald S. Tull, "The Carry-over Effect of Advertising," *Journal of Marketing,* April 1965, pp. 46–53.
4. Philip Kotler, *Marketing Decision Making: A Model Building Approach* (New York: Holt, Rinehart and Winston, 1971), chap. 5.
5. For a more detailed discussion of this, see William M. Weilbacher, *Advertising,* 2nd ed. (New York: Macmillan, 1984), p. 112.
6. Courtland I. Bovee and William F. Arens, *Advertising,* 3rd ed. (Homewood, Ill.: Richard D. Irwin, 1989).
7. Russell H. Colley, *Defining Advertising Goals for Measured Advertising Results* (New York: Association of National Advertisers, 1961).
8. Ibid., p. 21.
9. Don E. Shultz, Dennis Martin, and William Brown, *Strategic Advertising Campaigns,* 2nd ed. (Lincolnwood, Ill.: Crain Books, 1984).
10. Scott Hume, "McDonald's Heavy in Print for Nutrition," *Advertising Age,* January 19, 1987, p. 2.
11. Michael L. Ray, "Consumer Initial Processing: Definitions, Issues, Applications," in *Buyer/Consumer Information Processing,* ed. G. David Hughes (Chapel Hill: University of North Carolina Press, 1974).
12. David A. Aaker and John G. Myers, *Advertising Management,* 2nd ed. (Englewood Cliffs, N.J.: Prentice-Hall, 1982), pp. 122–23.
13. Sandra Ernst Moriarty, "Beyond the Hierarchy of Effects: A Conceptual Framework," in *Current Issues and Research in Advertising,* ed. Claude R. Martin, Jr., and James H. Leigh (Ann Arbor: University of Michigan, 1983), pp. 45–55.

14. Aaker and Myers, *Advertising Management.*
15. Thomas S. Robertson, *Innovative Behavior and Communication* (New York: Holt, Rinehart and Winston, 1971).
16. Richard Vaughn, "How Advertising Works: A Planning Model," *Journal of Advertising Research* 20, no. 5 (October 1980), p. 29.
17. A. W. Wicker, "Attitudes vs. Action: The Relationship of Verbal and Overt Behavioral Responses to Attitude Objects," *Journal of Social Issues* 25, no. 4 (1969), pp. 41–78.
18. Icek Ajzen and Martin Fishbein, "Attitude-Behavior Relations: A Theoretical Analysis and Review of Empirical Research," *Psychological Bulletin,* September 1977, pp. 888–918.
19. Icek Ajzen and Martin Fishbein, *Understanding Attitudes and Predicting Social Behavior* (Englewood Cliffs, N.J.: Prentice-Hall, 1980).
20. Alvin A. Achenbaum, "Advertising Doesn't Manipulate Consumers," *Journal of Advertising Research* 12 (April 1972), pp. 3–13.
21. Kristian S. Palda, "The Hypothesis of a Hierarchy of Effects: A Partial Evaluation," *Journal of Marketing Research* 3 (February 1966), pp. 13–24.
22. Steven W. Hartley and Charles H. Patti, "Evaluating Business-to-Business Advertising: A Comparison of Objectives and Results," *Journal of Advertising Research* 28 (April/May 1988), pp. 21–27.
23. Ibid., p. 25.
24. Study cited in Robert F. Lauterborn, "How to Know If Your Advertising Is Working," *Journal of Advertising Research* 25 (February/March 1985), pp. RC 9–11.

The Advertising and Promotions Budget

CHAPTER OBJECTIVES

1. To understand the process of advertising and promotions budget setting

2. To understand theoretical issues involved in budget setting

3. To examine the various methods for establishing an advertising budget

4. To examine factors influencing the size and process of allocating the advertising and promotions budget

Poor Budgeting Dooms a Printer

In 1987, Pacific Printing decided that it wanted to enter the photocopying business. The company's interest in entering this market was motivated by a proliferation of copy services that had sprung up in the city, giving the owner of the printing company the impression that there was money to be made in this business. After clearing out a back room in the print shop , the owner's next move was to purchase the top-of-the-line Xerox copy machine—for cash. Upon taking delivery of the copier, this same owner called in an advertising consultant to help him embark on an advertising and promotional strategy that would position him among the leaders. He explained his goals to the consultant and asked for a proposal for a promotional plan, including the figure that the consultant felt was necessary to make the program work.

When the consultant returned a week later and presented the advertising and promotional budget he was proposing, the print shop owner was shocked. He explained to the consultant that he had never dreamed of spending anywhere near that amount and, in fact, only had about a tenth of the proposed budget available. The consultant—himself now a bit shocked—asked the owner how he had arrived at the figure he had established. His answer was, "After I purchased the copy machine, and cleared out the back room, this was all that I felt that I could afford." The consultant left without the contract, and Pacific Printing never got off the ground in the photocopying business.

Introduction

The preceding story may seem slightly incredible to you and create a disbelief that any business could attempt to utilize such a method for establishing a budget. Or you may believe that this particular owner was not a very astute businessperson. While the latter may be true to a point, the budgeting approach described is not that uncommon, particularly in small companies. The purpose of this chapter is to provide you with insight into some underlying theory with respect to budget setting, to discuss how companies budget for promotional efforts, and to demonstrate the inherent strengths and weaknesses associated with these approaches. Essentially, this chapter will focus on two primary budgeting decisions—the establishment of a budget amount and the budget allocation decision.

Establishing the Budget

The size of a firm's advertising and promotions budget can vary from a few thousand dollars to more than a billion. Regardless of its size, the budgeting decision is not a trivial matter. When companies like Procter & Gamble and Philip Morris spend over a billion dollars per year to promote their products, they are expecting that such expenditures are going to lead to the accomplishment of their stated objectives. The budget decision is no less critical to a firm who may be spending only thousands of dollars, as their ultimate success or failure may often depend on the monies spent. Thus, one of the most critical decisions facing the marketing manager is that of how much to spend on the promotional effort. Moreover, this decision is not a one-time responsibility, as a new budget is formulated every year, each time a new product is introduced, or when either internal or external factors may necessitate a change to maintain competitiveness.

While one of the most critical decisions to be made, the budgeting area has perhaps been the most resistant to change, with new insights and/or methods occurring very infrequently. A comparison of advertising and promotional texts over the past 10 years would reveal that the same methods for establishing budgets are discussed, and the theoretical basis for this process remains rooted in economic theory and marginal analysis. (Advertisers also use an approach based on **contribution margin**—the differ-

Figure 9–1   Marginal Analysis

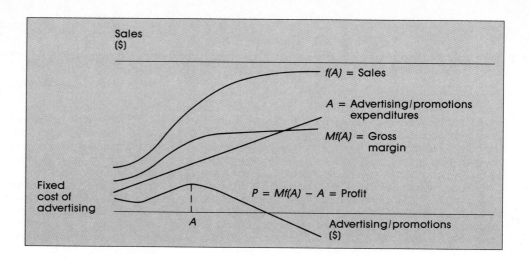

ence between the total revenue generated by a brand and its total variable costs—but, as noted by Robert Steiner, *marginal analysis* and *contribution margin* are essentially synonymous terms.)[1] We will begin our discussion of budgeting with an examination of these theoretical approaches.

Theoretical Issues in Budget Setting

Most of the models used to establish advertising budgets can be categorized as taking an economic or a sales response perspective. A discussion of each of these approaches follows.

Marginal Analysis   Figure 9–1 graphically represents the concept of **marginal analysis.** In this figure it can be seen that as advertising/promotional expenditures increase, sales and gross margins will also increase to a point and level off. Profits are shown to be a result of the gross margin minus advertising expenditures. Utilizing this theory to establish its budget, a firm would continue to spend advertising/promotional dollars so long as the marginal revenues created by these expenditures exceed the incremental advertising/promotional costs. As shown on the graph, the optimal expenditure level would be established at that point where marginal costs were equal to the marginal revenues that they generate (Point *A*). If the sum of the advertising/promotional expenditures exceeded the revenues these efforts generated, one would conclude that the appropriations were too high, and scale down the budget. If revenues were higher, a higher budget might be in order. (We will see later in this chapter that this approach might also be applied to the allocation decision.)

While marginal analysis seems logical intuitively, there are certain weaknesses with this approach that limit its usefulness. These weaknesses include the assumptions (1) that sales are a direct result of advertising and promotional expenditures and that this effect can be measured and (2) that advertising and promotion are solely responsible for sales. Let us examine each of these assumptions in more detail.

1. *Assumption that sales are a direct measure of advertising and promotions efforts*   In Chapter 8 we discussed the fact that the advertiser needs to set communications objectives that contribute to the accomplishment of overall marketing objectives but at the same time are separate and distinct. One of the reasons cited for this strategy is that it is often difficult, if not impossible, to demonstrate the effects of advertising and promotions on sales. In studies using sales as a direct measure, it has been almost impossible to establish the contribution of advertising and promotion. As noted by Frank Bass, "There is no more difficult, complex, or controversial problem in mar-

keting than measuring the influence of advertising on sales."[2] Or, in the words of David Aaker and James Carman, "Looking for the relationship between advertising and sales is somewhat worse than looking for a needle in a haystack."[3] Thus, to try to show that the size of the budget will lead to an impact directly on the sales of the product is misleading. A more logical approach would be to examine the impact of various budgets on the attainment of communications objectives.

2. *The assumption that sales are determined solely by advertising and promotion* Under this assumption, the remaining elements of the marketing mix (price, product, and distribution) are ignored. The promotional function is considered to be the one factor impacting sales. As has been noted in previous chapters, the effects of poor product quality, inaccurate pricing, and/or inadequate distribution cannot be overcome by exceptional advertising and/or promotions. In addition, environmental factors may impact the effectiveness of the promotional program—leading the marketing manager to assume the advertising was not effective when in fact some other factor may have hindered the accomplishment of the desired objectives.

Finally, as we saw in the discussion of communications objectives, sales are not the only goal to be attained through the promotional effort. Awareness, interest, attitude change, and other communications objectives are often sought, and while the bottom line may often be to sell the product, these objectives may serve as the basis upon which the promotional program is developed.

Overall, then, you can see that while the economic approach is a logical one that applies one perspective to the budgeting process, the difficulties associated with determining the effects of the promotional effort on sales and revenues limit its applicability in practice. The actual application of marginal analysis as a basis for budgeting is, as a result, seldom used (with the exception of direct-response advertising).

Sales Response Models   While examining Figure 9–1, you may have wondered why the sales curve was drawn in such a way as to show sales leveling off even though advertising and promotions efforts continued to increase. It should be noted at this point that the relationship between advertising and sales has been the topic of much research and discussion designed to determine the shape of the response curve.

Almost all advertisers subscribe to one of two models of the advertising/sales response function. These two response curves, the **concave-downward function** and **the S-shaped response curve,** are described below.

The concave-downward function   After reviewing over 100 studies of the effects of advertising on sales, Julian Simon and Johan Arndt concluded that the effects of advertising budgets follow the microeconomic law of diminishing returns.[4] That is, as the amount of advertising increases, its incremental value decreases. The logic is that those with the greatest potential to buy will likely act on the first (or earliest) exposures, whereas those less likely to buy are not likely to change as a result of the advertising. Of those who may be potential buyers, each additional advertisement will supply little or no new information that will affect their decision. Thus, according to this model, the effects of advertising would almost immediately begin to diminish, as shown in Figure 9–2. Budgeting under this model would indicate that less advertising dollars may be necessary to create the optimal influence on sales.

The S-shaped response function   A second model that is assumed by many advertising managers is the sales response model shown in Figure 9–3. As can be seen, this model projects an S-shaped response function to the budget outlay, with the response again being measured in sales.

According to the S-shaped response model, initial outlays of the advertising budget have very little impact—as indicated by the essentially flat sales curve in range A.

Figure 9-2 **The Concave-Downward Response Curve**

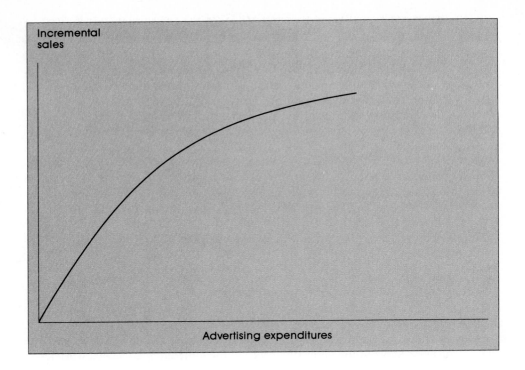

After a certain budget level has been reached (the beginning of range B), advertising and promotional efforts begin to have an effect, as additional increments of expenditures result in an increased sales level. This incremental gain continues only to a point, however, because at the beginning of range C the impact of additional expenditures begins to return little or nothing at all in the way of sales. This model suggests that a small advertising budget is likely to have no impact at all beyond the sales that may have been generated through other means (word of mouth, etc.). At the other extreme, more does not necessarily mean better, as additional dollars spent beyond range B have no additional impact on sales and for the most part can be considered wasted. As with marginal analysis, one would attempt to operate at that point on the curve in area B where the maximum return for the money is attained.

As with marginal analysis, weaknesses in these sales response models render the models academic—that is, of limited use to practitioners for direct applications. Many of the same problems seen earlier—the use of sales as a dependent variable, measurement problems, and so on—limit the usefulness of these models. At the same time, you should keep in mind the purpose of discussing such models. Even though marginal analysis and the sales response curves may not be directly applicable, their value lies in providing the manager with some insight into a theoretical basis of how the budgeting process should work. There has been some empirical evidence established that indicates that the models may have validity. For example, one manager, based on his industry experience, has provided support for the S-shaped response curve; his results indicate that a minimum amount of advertising dollars must be spent before a noticeable effect on sales will take place.[5] The studies discussed in earlier chapters on learning and the hierarchy of effects also demonstrate the importance of repetition on gaining awareness and on subsequent higher-order objectives such as adoption. Thus, while we may not be able to say that these models provide a tool for setting the advertising and promotional budget directly, we can be fairly comfortable in using them to guide our appropriations strategy from a theoretical basis. As you will see later in this chapter, having a theoretical basis offers an advantage over many of the methods currently being utilized for budget setting and allocation.

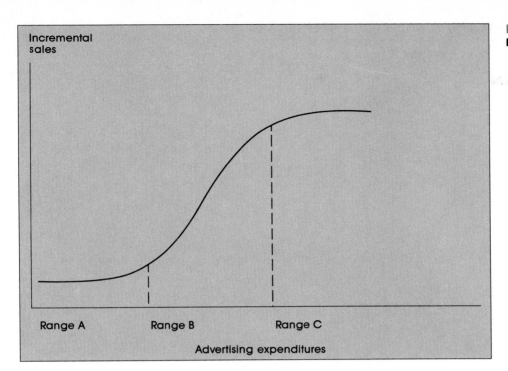

Figure 9–3 **The S-Shaped Response Function**

Additional Factors Considered in Budget Setting

While the theoretical bases just discussed should be considered in establishing the budget appropriation, a number of other issues have also been shown to be necessary for consideration. Some of these are discussed here.

Situational Factors Influencing the Budget   As we stated earlier, a weakness in attempting to use sales as a *direct* measure of response to advertising is the fact that various situational factors may be having an effect. In one very comprehensive study 24 different variables were shown to have an impact on the advertising-sales ratio. Table 9–1 lists these factors, and their relationships.[6] For example, a product characterized by emotional buying motives, hidden product qualities, and/or a strong basis for differentiation would see a noticeable impact of advertising on sales, whereas those characterized as large dollar purchases would be less likely to benefit. Other factors involving the market, customer, costs, and strategies employed were also shown to have different effects.

The results of this study are indeed interesting although limited. The factors presented here relate primarily to the percentage of sales dollars allocated to advertising and the factors influencing these ratios. As we will see later in this chapter, the percentage-of-sales method of budgeting has inherent weaknesses in that the advertising and sales effects may be reversed. Thus, in the case of these factors we cannot be sure whether the situation actually led to the advertising sales relationship or vice versa. Thus, while these factors should be considered in the budget appropriation decision, they should not be used as the sole determination as to where and when to increase or decrease expenditures.

Keys to Budget Setting   A 1986 survey of The *Advertising Age* Editorial Sounding Board (92 executives of the top 200 advertising companies in the United States—representing the client side—and 130 executives of the 200 largest advertising agencies and 11 advertising consultants—representing the agency side) yielded the results

Table 9–1   **Factors Influencing Advertising Budgets**

Factor	Relationship of Advertising/Sales
Product factors	
Basis for differentiation	+
Hidden product qualities	+
Emotional buying motives	+
Durability	−
Large dollar purchase	−
Purchase frequency	Curvilinear
Market factors	
Stage of product life cycle	
Introductory	+
Growth	+
Maturity	−
Decline	−
Inelastic demand	+
Market share	−
Competition	
Active	+
Concentrated	+
"Pioneer" in market	−
Customer factors	
Industrial products users	−
Concentration of users	+
Strategy factors	
Regional markets	−
Early stage of brand life cycle	+
High margins in channels	−
Long channels of distribution	+
High prices	+
High quality	+
Cost factors	
High profit margins	+

Note: + relationship means that the factor leads to a positive effect of advertising on sales; − relationship indicates little or no effect of advertising on sales.
Source: Paul W. Farris, "Determinants of Advertising Intensity: A Review of the Marketing Literature" (Report no. 77–109, Marketing Science Institute, Cambridge, Massachusetts, 1977).

shown in Table 9–2 regarding factors gaining and losing in importance in budget setting. As can be seen in this table, there is some lack of consensus as to what is becoming more or less important in the determination of the size of the budget. While clients—referring to their own companies—most commonly cite intended changes in advertising strategy and/or creative approaches as important in setting the ad budget, those on the agency side are more likely to cite *profit contribution goals* or other financial targets of the client as growing in importance. Some disagreement is seen in respect to which factors are decreasing in importance also, as only the level of the previous year's spending appears as a key factor to both groups.

Overall, the responses of these two groups reflect, in part, their perceptions as to how budgets are set. To understand fully why differences in the relative importance of these factors might be indicated, it is important to understand the approaches currently employed in budget setting. The next section of this chapter examines these.

Budgeting Approaches

As just discussed, the theoretical approaches to establishing the promotional budget are seldom employed. In fact, in smaller firms they may never be used. Rather, a number of different methods developed through practice and experience are implemented. This section will review some of the more traditional methods employed for setting budgets and the relative advantages and disadvantages of each. However, before dis-

Table 9-2   Importance of Factors in Budget Setting

Advertisers—Referring to Own Companies	
Growing in Importance	
Intended changes in advertising strategy and/or creative approach	51%
Competitive activity and/or spending levels	47
Profit contribution goal or other financial target	43
Decreasing in Importance	
Level of previous year's spending, with adjustment	17
Senior management dollar allocation or set limit	11
Volume share projections	8
Agencies—Referring to Client Companies	
Increasing in Importance	
Profit contribution goal or other financial target	56%
Competitive activity and/or spending levels	43
Intended changes in advertising strategy and/or creative approach	37
Decreasing in Importance	
Projections/assumptions on media cost increases	25
Level of previous year's spending, with adjustment	24
Modifications in media strategy and/or buying techniques	17

Source: Herbert Zeltner, "Strategy, Creative Shaping Ad Budgets," *Advertising Age,* January 20, 1986, p. 2.

cussing each of these methods, it is important for you to understand two things: First, it is very common for a firm to employ more than one method; and second, the budgeting approaches utilized by firms vary according to the size and sophistication of the organization. Let us proceed with a discussion of each of the more commonly employed methods and then return to a discussion of these two points.

Top-Down Approaches

The approaches discussed in this section may be referred to as **top-down approaches** owing to the fact that a budgetary amount is established (usually at an executive level), and then the monies are passed down to the various departments (as shown in Figure 9–4). As you will see, these budgets are essentially predetermined and have no true theoretical basis. Top-down methods include the affordable method, arbitrary allocation, percentage of sales, competitive parity, and return on investment (ROI).

The Affordable Method   In the Pacific Printing example provided at the outset of this chapter, it was stated that the owner of the company allocated his money to various sources such as equipment, and remodeling, leaving very little for advertising and promotion. When asked how he arrived at the budget that was set, the owner said, "This is all that I could afford after my expenses." As noted at that time, this approach is not uncommon among small firms. Unfortunately, it is also not uncommon in large firms either—particularly those that are not marketing driven and who either do not understand or do not believe in the role and function of advertising and promotion. For example, many high-tech firms will focus their emphasis on new product development and engineering, assuming that the product—if good enough—will sell itself. In many of these companies, little monies are left for performing the advertising and promotions tasks.

In the **affordable method** (often referred to as the all-you-can-afford method) the firm determines the amount of monies to be spent in various areas such as production and operations and, having done so, allocates remaining dollars to advertising and promotion, considering this to be the amount that they can afford. As should be obvious, there is no consideration of the task to be performed by the advertising/promotions function, and the likelihood of under- or overspending is high, as no guidelines for measuring the effects of various budgets are established.

Figure 9–4 Top-Down versus Bottom-Up Approaches to Budget Setting

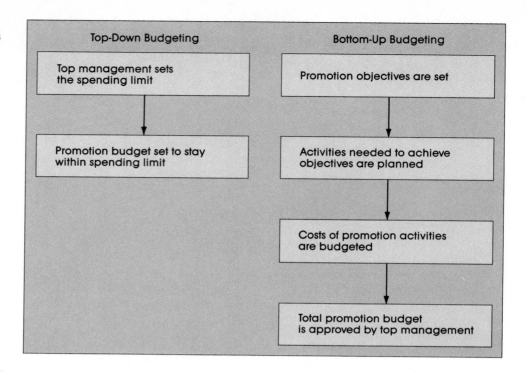

The logic for utilizing this approach stems from a "We can't be hurt with this method" thinking. That is, if we know what we can afford, and we do not exceed it, we will not get into financial problems. While this may be true in a strictly accounting sense, this method does not reflect sound managerial decision making from a marketing perspective. Often, using this method does not result in enough money being allocated to get the product off the ground and into the market. In terms of the S-shaped sales response model discussed earlier, the firm is operating in range A. In other instances, once the market gets tough and sales and/or profits begin to fall, this method would surely lead to budget cuts at a time when they very well might need to be increased.

Arbitrary Allocation Perhaps an even weaker method than the affordable method for establishing a budget is that of **arbitrary allocation.** While the previous method at least gave some thought to economic considerations, in this approach virtually no theoretical basis is considered, and often the budgetary amount is set by fiat. In a discussion of how managers set advertising budgets, Melvin Salveson reported that often these decisions may reflect "as much upon the managers' psychological profile as they do economic criteria."[7] While Salveson was referring to larger corporations in this regard, the approach is no less common in small firms and nonprofit organizations.

In the arbitrary allocation approach, no advantages are obvious. No systematic thinking has occurred, no objectives have been budgeted for, and the concept and purpose of advertising and promotion have been largely ignored. Other than the fact that the manager feels that some monies must be spent on advertising and promotion and then picks a number, there is no good explanation as to why this approach continues to be used. At the same time, budgets continue to be set this way, and our purpose in discussing it is to point out that this method is employed—not recommended.

Percentage of Sales Perhaps the most commonly used method for budget setting (particularly in large firms) is the **percentage of sales method.** In this method the

Table 9–3   Alternative Methods for Computing Percentage of Sales for Entree Cologne

Method 1: Straight % of sales	
1989 Total dollar sales of Entree Cologne	$1,000,000
Straight % of sales at 10%	$100,000
1990 Advertising budget for Entree Cologne	$100,000
Method 2: % of unit cost	
1989 Cost per bottle of cologne to manufacturer	$4.00
Per unit cost allocated to advertising	1.00
1990 Forecasted sales of 100,000 units	
1990 Advertising budget (100,000 × $1.00)	$100,000

advertising and promotions budget is based on the sales of the product, with the amount to be determined in either of two ways: (1) taking a percentage of the sales dollars or (2) assigning a fixed amount of the unit product cost to promotion and multiplying this amount by the number of units sold. These two methods are shown in the examples in Table 9–3.

A second variation of the percentage of sales method is offered by using a **percentage of projected future sales** as a base. (This is reflected in method 2 provided in Table 9–3.) Again, this method may use either a straight percentage of projected sales method or a unit cost projection, as shown above.

Examination of the budgets of the different industries shown in Table 9–4 will reveal that the percentage allocated will vary from one industry to the next, with some firms budgeting a very small percentage (for example, 0.6 in the food store industry), whereas others spend a much higher proportional amount (for example, 18.4 percent in games and toys). (It must be kept in mind, however, that the actual dollar amounts spent may vary quite markedly according to the company's total sales figure. Thus, a smaller percentage of sales in the food industry may actually result in significantly more advertising dollars being spent!)

Proponents of the percentage of sales method cite a number of advantages to this approach. First, they argue that it is financially safe and keeps ad spending within reasonable limits, as it bases spending on the past year's sales or what the firm expects to sell in the upcoming year. Thus, there will be sufficient monies to cover this budget, with increases in sales leading to budget increases, and decreases resulting in decreases accordingly. Second, the percentage of sales method is simple, straightforward, and easy to implement. Regardless of which basis—past or future sales—is employed, the calculations necessary to arrive at a budget are not very difficult. Finally, this budgeting approach is generally stable. While the budget may vary with increases and decreases in sales, for the most part, as long as these changes are not drastic, the manager will have a fairly reasonable idea of the parameters of the budget.

At the same time, the percentage of sales method has some serious disadvantages that render it less than an optimal budgeting strategy. Perhaps the most serious of these weaknesses is the basic premise upon which the budget is established: *sales.* Using sales as the basis for setting the advertising appropriation is analogous to putting the cart before the horse. Rather than considering advertising as the cause of sales, the roles are reversed, with sales determining the amount of advertising and promotions. The result is a reversal of the cause and effect relationship between advertising and sales.

A second problem with this approach is actually one of the characteristics cited as an advantage earlier: stability. The position of proponents is that if all firms use a similar percentage, then stability will be brought to the marketplace. What happens if someone varies from this standard percentage? The problem here is that this method does not allow for changes in strategy either internally or from competitors. A firm wishing to be aggressive may wish to allocate more monies to the advertising and pro-

Table 9—4 Advertising-to-Sales Ratios (by Industry), 1989

Industry	SIC no.	Ad dollars as percent of sales	Ad dollars as percent of margin	Annual growth rate (%)	Industry	SIC no.	Ad dollars as percent of sales	Ad dollars as percent of margin	Annual growth rate (%)
Abrasive, asbestos, misc minerals	3290	1.3	3.8	(1.0)	Lawn, garden tractors, equip	3524	4.0	11.3	13.6
Adhesives & sealants	2891	4.4	9.5	11.3	Lumber & other bldg matl-retl	5211	1.8	6.9	6.8
Agriculture chemicals	2870	1.2	4.3	26.1	Machine tools, metal cutting	3541	1.3	5.2	0.5
Agriculture production-crops	100	2.1	6.0	7.8	Magnetic/optic recording media	3695	3.6	9.7	13.7
Air cond, heating, refrig equip	3585	1.5	5.8	13.3	Malt beverages	2082	8.4	21.7	7.7
Air courier services	4513	1.5	8.4	9.3	Manifold business forms	2761	0.8	2.1	7.2
Air transport, scheduled	4512	1.8	16.0	12.7	Meatpacking plants	2011	1.2	9.4	15.3
Aircraft parts, aux equip, NEC	3728	0.8	3.5	9.4	Membership sport & rec clubs	7997	11.0	13.5	18.8
Apparel & other finished prods	2300	2.9	8.0	7.2	Men, youth, boys frnsh, wrk clthg	2320	2.7	9.0	12.8
Apparel & accessory stores	5600	2.4	5.9	11.6	Metal forgings & stampings	3460	1.6	6.0	7.5
Auto & home supply stores	5531	2.3	7.0	18.5	Metalworking machinery & equip	3540	5.5	14.0	12.9
Auto rent & lease, no drivers	7510	2.8	4.0	7.7	Misc amusement & rec services	7990	6.5	18.0	15.9
Automatic regulating controls	3822	8.2	31.7	7.9	Misc chemical products	2890	6.1	17.2	7.8
Bakery products	2050	1.7	3.7	4.8	Misc elec machy, equip, supplies	3690	3.1	8.9	(12.1)
Beverages	2080	9.5	17.0	11.3	Misc fabricated metal prods	3490	0.7	2.7	12.4
Bldg matl, hardware, garden-retl	5200	4.0	8.5	(8.7)	Misc food preps, kindred prods	2090	2.9	7.8	10.9
Bolt nut screw rivets washers	3452	0.9	2.9	6.0	Misc general mdse stores	5399	3.1	11.6	3.7
Books-publishing & printing	2731	3.3	8.1	10.8	Misc industl coml machy & equip	3590	2.4	7.2	(2.9)
Brdwoven fabric mill cotton	2211	2.8	11.7	6.9	Misc manufacturing industries	3990	3.0	6.5	10.5
Btld & canned soft drinks, water	2086	2.9	6.2	15.5	Misc plastics products	3080	1.9	10.9	5.1
Business services, NEC	7389	6.6	13.2	5.0	Misc shopping goods stores	5940	3.7	9.5	5.2
Cable & other pay tv services	4841	2.2	3.9	20.3	Motion pic, videotape production	7812	9.8	18.7	13.2
Can fruit, veg, presrv, jam, jel	2033	2.2	6.9	7.4	Motion pic, videotape distrib	7822	13.0	15.1	26.8
Can/frozen presrv, fruit, veg	2030	6.9	17.1	7.3	Motion picture theaters	7830	4.3	20.6	17.5
Carpets & rugs	2273	0.7	2.8	13.0	Motor homes	3716	1.7	11.2	10.6
Catalog, mail-order houses	5961	5.7	15.8	11.0	Motor veh parts, supply-whsl	5010	2.8	20.6	23.6
Chemicals & allied prods	2800	2.7	6.7	13.8	Motor vehicle parts, accessory	3714	1.6	6.4	27.5
Child daycare services	8351	1.6	3.5	19.9	Motor vehicles & car bodies	3711	1.7	7.3	12.6
Cigarettes	2111	5.7	12.9	9.1	Motorcycles, bicycles & parts	3751	1.6	6.5	21.5
Computer & software stores	5734	0.9	3.4	8.7	Motors & generators	3621	0.9	2.7	4.5
Computer integrated sys design	7373	1.8	3.9	12.0	Newspaper-publishing & print	2711	3.6	10.2	12.9
Comp processing, data prep svc	7374	0.7	2.0	7.4	Office furniture	2520	1.2	3.7	9.9
Commercial printing	2750	1.9	6.8	15.4	Office furniture, ex wood	2522	2.0	6.0	9.6
Communications equip, NEC	3669	2.1	5.6	10.1	Office machines, NEC	3579	1.4	4.3	5.6
Computer & office equipment	3570	1.2	2.7	9.7	Operative builders	1531	1.2	4.2	21.0
Computer peripheral eq, NEC	3577	2.0	4.7	12.0	Operators-nonres bldgs	6512	3.7	8.0	8.2
Computer storage devices	3572	1.1	4.1	14.2	Ophthalmic goods	3851	10.5	18.5	19.7
Computer terminals	3575	2.7	8.3	5.9	Ortho, prosth, surg appl suply	3842	1.8	4.2	12.5
Construction machinery & equip	3531	0.9	3.3	14.7	Paints, varnishes, lacquers	2851	3.7	9.6	9.5
Convrt paper paprbrd, except box	2670	1.9	4.3	11.1	Paper mills	2621	3.6	11.1	2.0
Cookies & crackers	2052	4.8	9.1	2.7	Patent owners & lessors	6794	3.0	7.1	6.8
Cutlery hand tools, gen hrdwr	3420	10.9	21.6	10.9	Pens, pencils, other office matl	3950	5.4	11.1	9.2
Dairy products	2020	4.7	14.6	9.9	Perfume, cosmetic, toilet prep	2844	10.4	16.1	24.6
Dental equipment & supplies	3843	3.2	7.7	80.3	Periodical-publishing, printing	2721	3.7	6.7	5.4
Department stores	5311	2.9	14.3	5.5	Personal credit institutions	6141	1.5	2.6	5.8
Drug & proprietary stores	5912	1.5	5.6	9.9	Personal services	7200	5.7	16.0	3.4
Eating places	5812	3.3	16.5	7.6	Petroleum refining	2911	2.7	9.0	14.3
Educational services	8200	5.0	9.4	17.6	Pharmaceutical preparations	2834	6.8	10.1	9.8
Elec meas & test instruments	3825	2.5	4.8	8.6	Phone comm, ex radiotelephone	4813	2.2	4.5	2.8
Electr, other elec eqp, ex comp	3600	3.1	9.2	10.7	Phono records, audio tape disc	3652	8.3	23.2	13.3
Electric housewares & fans	3634	4.0	15.4	(10.9)	Photofinishing laboratories	7384	4.0	10.9	9.7
Electric lighting, wiring equip	3640	3.2	9.6	10.0	Photographic equip & suppl	3861	3.6	9.9	14.0
Electrical work	1731	1.2	12.6	28.1	Plastic matl, synthetic resin	2820	1.2	6.2	18.8
Electromedical apparatus	3845	1.3	2.2	16.2	Plastics products, NEC	3089	1.9	5.1	12.5
Electronic comp, accessories	3670	0.9	2.6	3.2	Plastics, resins, elastomers	2821	1.6	4.3	(20.7)
Electronic components, NEC	3679	1.4	4.7	10.6	Pottery & related products	3260	5.7	12.2	64.3
Electronic computers	3571	5.1	10.3	14.4	Poultry slaughter & process	2015	3.1	20.7	12.1
Electronic connectors	3678	1.6	3.8	15.4	Prepackaged software	7372	4.8	9.2	19.2
Electronic parts, equip-whsl, NEC	5065	1.6	5.5	12.0	Printing trades machy, equip	3555	1.1	2.8	4.7
Employment agencies	7361	5.7	17.8	21.3	Prof & coml equip & supply-whsl	5040	3.0	8.6	9.6
Engines & turbines	3510	1.7	6.3	7.5	Pumps & pumping equipment	3561	1.1	3.1	7.9
Engr acc resh mgmt rel svcs	8700	1.8	7.7	1.2	Radio broadcasting stations	4832	8.6	22.4	21.2
Equip rental & leasing, NEC	7359	3.7	5.7	3.9	Radio, tv broadcast comm equip	3663	1.0	3.3	4.6
Fabricated rubber prods, NEC	3060	0.4	1.5	52.2	Radio, tv consumer elec stores	5731	5.3	23.8	16.9
Facilities, support mgmt svcs	8744	2.4	34.3	23.8	Radiotelephone communication	4812	4.2	8.1	28.7
Family clothing stores	5651	1.9	5.9	9.8	Real estate investment trust	6798	1.5	2.3	6.8
Farm machinery & equipment	3523	1.4	7.6	(4.5)	Record & tape stores	5735	1.4	3.3	13.5
Finance-services	6199	0.6	3.7	4.1	Refrig & service ind machine	3580	2.3	6.8	7.8
Food & kindred products	2000	7.8	18.7	13.0	Retail stores	5990	5.8	12.7	14.6
Footwear, except rubber	3140	3.4	9.9	5.9	Rubber & plastics footwear	3021	5.2	14.2	15.4
Furniture stores	5712	7.1	15.7	7.0	Sausage, other prepared meat pd	2013	6.9	21.0	8.7
Games, toys, child veh ex dolls	3944	14.2	29.3	8.1	Savings instn, not fed chart	6036	0.9	2.4	(1.5)
Gen med & surgical hospitals	8062	0.8	4.5	(2.5)	Savings instn, fed chartered	6035	0.8	1.8	7.8
Glass, glassware-pressed, blown	3220	2.7	6.7	7.9	Security brokers & dealers	6211	3.1	7.3	13.6
Grain mill products	2040	9.4	20.6	8.8	Semiconductor, related devices	3674	1.0	2.4	10.3
Greeting cards	2771	5.1	10.3	11.7	Shoe stores	5661	2.8	7.4	(7.6)
Groceries & related pds-whsl	5140	1.5	10.7	10.6	Short-term bus credit, ex ag	6153	1.2	2.4	11.5
Grocery stores	5411	1.3	5.5	5.6	Skilled nursing care facil	8051	2.3	21.1	(5.1)
Guided missiles & space vehc	3760	5.3	170.1	6.4	Soap, detergent, toilet preps	2840	7.7	17.4	8.7
Hardware, plumb, heat eqp-whsl	5070	1.4	12.4	9.5	Special clean, polish preps	2842	14.5	24.8	8.0
Help supply services	7363	1.3	5.3	2.9	Special industry machinery	3550	7.9	33.4	17.5
Hobby, toy & game shops	5945	1.6	5.0	11.6	Special industry machy, NEC	3559	1.4	3.3	14.9
Home furniture & equip stores	5700	5.0	10.3	10.5	Sporting & athletic gds, NEC	3949	5.5	15.8	13.9
Hospital & medical svc plans	6324	0.7	14.9	26.1	Search det nav guide aero sys	3812	0.2	0.7	1.3
Hospitals	8060	5.0	29.7	24.9	Subdivid develop, ex cemetery	6552	1.3	6.1	6.0
Hotels, motels, tourist courts	7011	3.4	10.7	5.0	Sugar & confectionery prods	2060	10.6	28.9	10.8
Household appliances	3630	4.2	14.0	77.8	Surgical, med instr apparatus	3841	2.4	4.5	11.9
Household audio & video eqp	3651	2.8	9.8	10.6	Svcs to dwellings, other bldgs	7340	1.8	6.2	4.9
Household furniture	2510	4.8	14.8	12.1	Switchgear & switchboard app	3613	1.1	3.3	7.7
Ice cream & frozen desserts	2024	6.9	25.6	16.6	Tele & telegraph apparatus	3661	1.6	3.6	9.2
Industl inorganic chemicals	2810	16.5	34.4	19.8	Telegraph & oth message comm	4822	3.3	53.6	2.2
Indl trucks, tractors, trailers	3537	1.4	5.4	4.5	Television broadcast stations	4833	2.5	6.2	1.8
Industrial measurement instr	3823	1.6	3.7	10.7	Tires & inner tubes	3011	2.0	7.5	6.7
Investment advice	6282	8.6	19.8	11.3	Unsupp plastics film & sheet	3081	5.3	20.3	3.0
Iron & steel foundries	3320	1.2	4.2	12.0	Variety stores	5331	1.9	7.5	8.6
Jewelry & watches-whsl	5094	3.9	25.0	10.6	Water transportation	4400	5.4	14.4	6.2
Jewelry stores	5944	3.3	6.9	(5.8)	Wmns, miss, chld infnt undgrmt	2340	3.4	8.5	11.4
Knitting mills	2250	1.9	6.8	10.0	Women's clothing stores	5621	2.7	7.5	8.6
Lab analytical instruments	3826	1.7	3.3	7.9	Womens, misses, jrs outerwear	2330	1.7	6.3	18.5
Lab apparatus & furniture	3821	1.2	2.7	16.3	Wood hshld furn, ex upholsrd	2511	2.9	8.8	18.9

Source: Schonfeld & Associates, 1 Sherwood Drive, Lincolnshire, Ill. 60069 (312) 948-8080. Legend: SIC - Standard Industrial Classifica-tion. NEC - Not elsewhere classified. Ad dollars as percent of sales - Ad expenditures/net sales. Ad dollars as percent of margin - Ad ex-penditures/(net sales - cost of goods sold). Annual growth rate of advertising dollars.

Source: Advertising Age, November 13, 1989, p. 32.

motions budget—a strategy that would not be possible with a percentage of sales method.

As seen in Promotional Perspective 9–1, this method of budgeting may result in severe misappropriation of funds. If one believes that advertising and promotion have a role to perform in marketing a product, then they should believe that allocating more monies to advertising will, as shown in the S-shaped curve, generate incremental sales (to a point). Products with low sales will have smaller promotions budgets, which in turn will hinder their sales progress. At the other extreme, very successful products may have an excess budget—some of which may be better appropriated elsewhere.

The percentage of sales method is also difficult to employ for new product introductions. If no past sales histories are available, there may exist no basis for establishing the budget. Projections of future sales may be difficult, particularly if the product is highly innovative and/or may have fluctuating sales patterns.

Finally, if the budget is contingent upon sales, decreases in sales will lead to decreases in budgets when they may need to be increased. To continue to cut the advertising and promotions budgets may add impetus to the downward sales trend. On the other hand, some of the more successful companies have been those who have allocated additional funds during hard times or downturns in the cycle of sales. For example, Sunkist Growers can attribute at least some of its success in establishing and maintaining its strong image to the fact that it has maintained consistent levels of advertising expenditures over 80 years—despite recessions.[8]

While the percentage of future sales method has been proposed as a remedy for some of the problems discussed here, the reality is that problems with forecasting, cyclical growth, and uncontrollable factors have limited the effectiveness of this approach as well.

Competitive Parity   If you asked marketing managers if they ever set their advertising and promotions budgets based on what their competitors allocated, they probably would deny it. Yet if you examined the advertising expenditures of these companies, both as a percentage of sales and in respect to the media in which they are being allocated, you would see very little variation in the percentage of sales figure for firms within a given industry. Such results are not likely to have happened by chance alone, as the expenditures of competitors are available from a variety of sources, including companies that provide competitive advertising information, trade associations, and other advertising industry periodically.

In the **competitive parity method,** budget amounts are established by matching the percentage sales expenditures of the competition. The argument here is that to set budgets in this fashion would be to take advantage of the collective wisdom of the industry—that is, to utilize the knowledge of others as well as oneself. A second advantage offered is that this method specifically takes the competition into consideration, which leads to stability in the marketplace by minimizing marketing warfare. If the competition knows that others are thought to be less likely to match their increases in promotional spending, they are less likely to take an aggressive posture to attempt to gain market share. Thus, the likelihood of unusual or unrealistic ad expenditures is minimized.

The competitive parity method has a number of disadvantages however. For one, the method ignores the fact that advertising and promotions are designed to accomplish specific objectives by addressing certain problems and opportunities. Second, it assumes that because firms have equal, or nearly equal, expenditures, their programs will be equally effective. Such an assumption ignores the contributions of creative executions and/or media allocations as well as the success or lack thereof of various promotions. Further, it ignores possible advantages of the firm itself; for example, some firms simply make better products than others.

In addition to the disadvantages cited above, there is no guarantee that the competition will continue to pursue their existing strategies. Given that competitive parity figures must be determined by examination of competitors' previous years promotional

Promotional Perspective 9–1

A Tale Of Misappropriation

Once upon a time there was a company that manufactured a very broad line of products. (The company name cannot be disclosed for proprietary reasons but we will tell you that this is a true story about a top U.S. corporation.) This company was considered by many to be one of the more successful marketing companies of its time, and indeed, it had the leading selling brand in most of the consumer product categories in which it competed. This story is about one of these successful products—and its stepsister, a not-so-lucky brand.

The successful brand was by far the leader in its product class. At one time, this brand controlled over 90 percent of the market and showed no signs of slowing its growth. The stepsister brand, on the other hand, while an excellent product, was consistently not among the leaders.

The parent company of these two brands employed a percentage of sales method of establishing the advertising and promotional budget. As you might expect, the successful brand received much more monies allocated to it than did the brand with the flat sales curve and constant (though small) market share. In fact, the suc-

cessful brand had so much money allocated to it that it literally did not know what to do with it all. The brand managers' biggest challenge was how to figure out where they might spend their promotional dollars so that they would use it all and continue to get more in succeeding years. Some of the promotions that they developed were so silly that the sales force never let them out of the trunk of their cars.

Meanwhile, the not-so-successful brand was going nowhere. The brand manager constantly asked for more funding but was consistently turned down because of a lack of sales. The company just could not see spending any additional promotional monies on a brand with so little sales and market share.

Unfortunately, there is no happy ending to this story. The successful brand continues to be successful and continues to develop effective advertising and promotions as well as some that will never be used. The stepsister brand manager is still seeking budget increases so that he may increase his advertising and promotions, which in turn he feels will increase his sales and market share. The percentage of sales budgeting method curse continues.

---

expenditures (short of corporate espionage), changes in market emphasis and/or spending may not be recognized until the competition has already established an advantage. Further, there is no guarantee that the competition will not increase or decrease their own expenditures, regardless of what other companies do. Finally, promotional wars may not be avoided. In Promotional Perspective 9–2 you can see that two very close competitors did engage in exactly such warfare in the past—and may have been fortunate to have survived!

In summary, it is very unlikely that a firm will employ the competitive parity method as a sole means of establishing the promotional budget. This method is typically used in conjunction with the percentage of sales or other methods. In fact, it is not a very wise strategy to ignore the competition. Managers must always be aware of what competitors are doing; they should not just emulate them in setting their own goals and developing their own strategies.

Return on Investment (ROI) As previously noted, in employing the percentage of sales method, sales become the cause of advertising. At that time we stated that this relationship is backward and that advertising should be seen as a contributor to sales. In the marginal analysis and S-shaped curve approaches, it is expected that incremental investments in advertising and promotions dollars should lead to increases in sales. The key word here is *investment*.

In the **ROI budgeting method,** advertising and promotions are considered as investments, just as plant and equipment, and the like, are in other areas of the firm. Thus, the budgetary appropriation (investment) should then lead to certain returns. As with other aspects of the firm's efforts, advertising and promotion are expected to meet a certain level of return.

While the ROI method appears to be good on paper, the reality is that it is almost never possible to assess the returns provided by the promotional effort—at least

Promotional Perspective 9–2

Advertising Spending Wars

Spending wars in the advertising industry are most common when two leaders are going head to head for the top spot. Coke versus Pepsi, 7-Up versus the colas, and the wine cooler wars of the late 1980s are just a few of the more publicized examples. However, no spending competition has received as much attention as the battle between Miller Brewing Company and Anheuser-Busch (AB), which has continued over a decade or so.

In 1977, Miller—then the seventh ranked brewer in the country—decided to use its marketing expertise and power provided by its new parent company, Philip Morris, to attempt to increase its sales and market share. One of the strategies was to substantially increase advertising spending.

To meet this challenge, AB also decided to increase its ad budgets—by 67 percent the first year, 47 percent and 38 percent in the two subsequent years, and no less than 19 percent throughout the period 1977 to 1984.

The result of this substantial increase in ad expenditures by AB was an increase in sales that correlated very highly with the amount of advertising dollars spent. Thus, this example has often been cited as an example of the power of advertising, of successful budgeting, and of sound marketing strategy.

One researcher who disagrees with the success attributed to the AB strategy is Michael Stankey. According to Stankey, the increase in AB's budget placed it in an unattractive debt/equity position and resulted in lowered dividend payouts during the same period. In other words, according to Stankey, "The funds generated from operations were insufficient to support the assets required by the push for growth. . . . AB was forced to take on debt in order to sustain the rapid rate of sales growth." While this strategy placed AB moderately above average in risk, such a three-fold increase in debt/equity could have spelled disaster for other companies.

For many companies engaging in advertising spending wars, the story does not end as happily as it did for AB and Miller—both are the beer industry leaders at this time. Other companies have spent substantial sums of money to achieve little or no sales or market share gains. Others have been "shaken out" of the industry owing to their inability to maintain such expenditures. The bottom line is that a strategy of "keeping up with the Joneses" in ad spending had better be given a lot of thought!

Source: Michael J. Stankey, "How Advertising Impacts Sustainable Growth," *Business,* July-September 1987, pp. 12–22.

---

as long as sales continue to be the basis for evaluation. Thus, while managers are certain to pose the question as to how much return they are getting for such expenditures, the bottom line is that it still remains a question, and ROI remains a virtually unused method of budgeting.

Summary of Top-Down Budgeting Methods

Having just read this section, you are probably asking yourself why we even discussed this material. The budgeting methods examined are either not recommended for use or, when they are used, have severe disadvantages that limit their effectiveness. While this may be true, it is nevertheless necessary to understand the various methods considered and used so that you might recognize their limitations. This is particularly true since, in reality, these are the methods most commonly employed by marketers, as demonstrated by the research studies cited in Table 9–5.

As shown in Table 9–5, the use of percentage of sales methods remains high, particularly that based on anticipated sales. Fortunately, both the affordable and arbitrary methods appear to be on the decrease, as is the use of quantitative methods. On the increase is the use of a method not yet discussed—the objective and task method. Let us now turn our discussion to this method, reserving our discussion of quantitative models until later.

Build-up Approaches

The major flaw associated with the top-down methods is that they are judgmental approaches that lead to predetermined budget appropriations that are often not linked to objectives and the strategies designed to accomplish them. A more effective budgeting

Table 9–5   **Comparison of General Methods Used by Consumer Advertisers to Set Advertising Budgets**

Method	Percentage of Respondents Using Each Method		
	San Augustine and Foley (1975)	Patti and Blasko (1981)	Lancaster and Stern (1983)
Quantitative methods	4	51	20
Objective and task	12	63	80
Percentage anticipated sales	52	53	53
Unit anticipated sales	12	22	28
Percentage past sales	16	20	20
Unit past sales	12	n.a.	15
Affordable	28	20	13
Arbitrary	16	4	n.a.
Match competitors	n.a.	24	25
Outspend competitors	n.a.	n.a.	8
Share of voice/market	n.a.	n.a.	5
Previous budget	n.a.	n.a.	3
Others	20	n.a.	12

n.a. = not applicable
Note: Totals exceed 100% due to multiple responses and rounding.
Source: Kent M. Lancaster and Judith Stern, "Computer Based Advertising Budgeting Practices of Leading U.S. Advertisers," *Journal of Advertising* 12, no. 4 (1983), p. 6.

strategy would be to consider the communications objectives established and budget according to what is deemed necessary to attain these goals. Examination of the decision process model established in Chapter 1 would indicate that the budget decision is an interactive process with the communications objectives, on the one hand, and the promotional mix alternatives, on the other. The idea is to budget so that these promotional mix strategies can be implemented to achieve the stated objectives. Methods for budget setting utilizing this approach will now be considered.

Objective and Task Method   As previously noted, it is important that objectives setting and budgeting go hand in hand rather than in a sequential step fashion. It is difficult to establish a budget with no specific objectives in mind, and likewise setting objectives without regard to the budget available makes no sense. For example, the objective of Pacific Printing may have been to create awareness of the availability of his copy services throughout the southern California market. With the minimal budget he had established, it is obvious that attainment of this goal was impossible.

The **objective and task method of budget setting** utilizes a **build-up approach,** employing a three-step process: (1) defining the communications objectives to be accomplished, (2) determining the specific strategies and tasks that will be required to attain these objectives, and (3) estimating the costs associated with the performance of these strategies and tasks. The total budget is based on the accumulation of these costs.

The actual process of implementing the objective and task approach is somewhat more involved, as the following discussion indicates. In using this method, the manager is required to monitor and evaluate this process throughout and change existing strategies according to the attainment and/or nonattainment of objectives. As shown in Figure 9–5, this process involves several steps. Let us examine these in more detail:

1. *Isolation of objectives* Upon presentation of the promotional planning model, a company will have two sets of objectives to be accomplished—the marketing objectives for the product and the communications objectives. Upon establishing the former, the task now involves determination of the specific communications objectives that will be designed to accomplish these goals. As in any objective setting process, communications objectives must be specific, attainable, and measurable as well as time constrained.

Figure 9–5 **The Objective and Task Method**

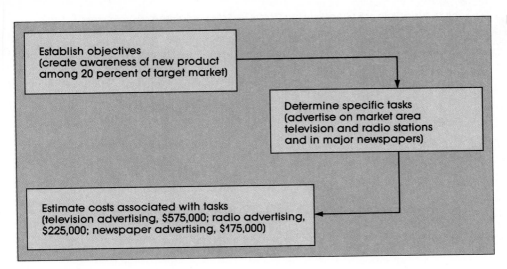

2. *Determination of tasks required* Again referring to the promotional planning process, a number of elements are involved in the strategic plan designed to attain the objectives established (these strategies will constitute the remaining chapters in this text and may involve all the elements of the promotional mix). These tasks may include advertising in various media, sales promotions, and/or other elements of the promotional mix, each with its own role to perform.

3. *Estimation of required expenditures* Build-up analysis requires a determination of the estimated costs associated with the tasks developed in the previous step. For example, this would involve costs for developing awareness through advertising, trial through sampling, and so forth.

4. *Monitoring* As will be seen in the chapter on measuring effectiveness, there are methods that can be applied to determine how well one is doing with respect to attainment of the established objectives. Performance in this regard should be monitored and evaluated in light of the budget appropriated.

5. *Reevaluation of objectives* Once specific objectives have been obtained, monies might be better spent on new goals. Thus, if one has achieved the level of awareness sought, the budget should be altered to stress a higher-order objective such as evaluation or trial.

The major advantage of the objective and task method is that the budget is driven by the objectives to be attained. Thus, rather than being established at the top and passed down, the managers closest to the marketing effort will have input and specific strategies that will be considered in the budget setting process.

The major disadvantage of this method is that of making the determination as to which tasks will be required as well as the costs that will be associated with each. In many cases these determinations are not easily made. For example, specifically what tasks would be necessary to attain awareness among 50 percent of the target market? How much will it cost to perform these tasks? While these decisions may be easier to determine for certain objectives—for example, estimating the costs of sampling required to stimulate trial in a defined market area—it is not always possible to know exactly what is required and/or how much it will cost to complete the job. While this process becomes easier if one has had past experience to use as a guide—either with the existing product or a similar one in the same product category—it is especially difficult for new product introductions. As a result the budget setting process using this method is not as easy to perform or as stable as some of the methods discussed earlier. Given this disadvantage, many marketing managers have not adopted the objective and task method for allocating the budget. However, they have stayed with some of the top-down approaches discussed earlier for setting the total expenditure amount.

Figure 9–6 Share of Advertising/Sales Relationship

Two-Year Summary. Share of Advertising–Share of Sales Relationships for New Brands of Food Products

	Attained share of sales	Average share of advertising	Ratio of share of advertising to share of sales
Brand 101	12.6%	34%	2.7
102	10.0	16	1.6
103	7.6	8	1.1
104	2.6	4	1.5
105	2.1	3	1.4

Two-Year Summary. Share of Advertising–Share of Sales Relationships for New Brands of Toiletry Products

	Attained share of sales	Average share of advertising	Ratio of share of advertising to share of sales
Brand 401	19.5%	30%	1.5
402	16.5	25	1.5
403	16.2	20	1.2
404	9.4	12	1.3
405	8.7	16	1.8
406	7.3	19	2.6
407	7.2	14	1.9
408	6.0	10	1.7
409	6.0	7	1.2
410	5.9	6	1.0
411	5.9	10	1.7
412	5.2	6	1.2

Source: James O. Peckham, *The Wheel of Marketing* (Chicago: A. C. Neilsen Company, 1975).

The objective and task method—while preferred over others previously discussed—is more difficult to implement when there is no track record for the product. Thus, budgeting for new product introductions tends to be a special case in and of itself. The following section addresses this problem.

Payout Planning   The first months of a new product's introduction typically require heavier-than-normal advertising and promotions appropriations to stimulate higher levels of awareness and subsequently trial. After studying more than 40 years of Nielsen figures, James O. Peckham has estimated that the average share of advertising to share of sales ratio necessary to launch a new product successfully is approximately 1.5:2.0.[9] Translated, this means that with respect to promotions a new entry should be spending at approximately twice the desired market share, as shown in the two examples in Figure 9–6. For example, in the food industry, brand 101 was able to gain a 12.6 percent market share by spending 34 percent of the total advertising dollars in this category. Likewise, brand 401 in the toiletry industry had a 30 percent share of advertising dollars to gain a 19.5 percent share of sales.

To make the determination as to how much to spend, marketers will often develop a **payout plan.** The purpose of this plan is to determine the investment value of the advertising and promotions appropriation. The basic idea is to project the revenues that the product will generate over a period of two to three years, as well as the costs that will be incurred. Based on an expected rate of return, the payout plan will assist in the determination of what advertising and promotions expenditures will be

Table 9–6   **Example of Three-Year Payout Plan (in millions of dollars)**

	Year 1	Year 2	Year 3
Product sales	15	35.5	60.75
Profit contribution (@ $0.50/case)	7.5	17.75	30.38
Advertising/promotions	15	10.5	8.5
Profit (loss)	(7.5)	7.25	21.88
Cumulative profit (loss)	(7.5)	(0.25)	21.63

necessary and at what period of time this return might be expected. An example of a three-year payout plan is shown in Table 9–6. As can be seen by examining this table, the product would lose money in year 1, almost break even in year 2, and finally begin to show substantial profits by the end of year 3.

It is important to note that the advertising and promotions figures are higher in year 1, declining in years 2 and 3. This appropriation is consistent with that suggested earlier by Peckham and reflects the additional outlays necessary to make as rapid an impact as possible. (Keep in mind that shelf space is limited, and a store owner is not likely to wait around for a product to become successful!) In addition, it must reflect the companies' guidelines for new product expenditures, as companies generally have established time periods in which the product must begin to show a profit. Finally, it should be kept in mind that building market share may be more difficult than maintaining it—thus, the substantial drop-off in expenditures in the later years.

In summary, while the payout plan is in itself not always perfect, it does guide the manager in the establishment of the budget. When used in conjunction with the objective and task method, it provides a much more logical approach to budget setting than the top-down approaches previously discussed.

Quantitative Models   Attempts to apply *quantitative models* to budgeting have met with limited success. For the most part, these methods have employed **computer simulation models** involving regression analysis to determine the relative contribution that the size of the budget has on the sales response to advertising. Because of problems associated with these methods, their acceptance and use have been limited—as is demonstrated in the figures reported earlier in Table 9–5. At the same time, as is evident in this same table, some advertisers have found the quantitative approach to be satisfactory and continue to employ this method. Unfortunately, the value of quantitative models has yet to reach the promised potential. Perhaps as computers continue to find their way into the advertising domain, better models may be forthcoming. The specific discussion of these models is beyond the scope of this text, however, and we will limit our discussion to noting that such methods do have merit but may need more refinement prior to achieving widespread success.

Summary of Budgeting Methods

The preceding discussion of budgeting approaches indicates that there is no universally accepted method of setting a budget figure. Weaknesses in each method may make them unfeasible or inappropriate for use. At the same time, as is indicated in Table 9–5, the use of the objective and task method continues to increase, whereas less sophisticated methods are declining in favor. In addition to the increased use of the objective and task method, more advertisers are employing the payout planning approach. By using these approaches in combination with the percentage of sales methods, these advertisers are more likely to arrive at a useful and more sophisticated method of budget setting. For example, many firms now start the budgeting process by establishing the objectives they need to accomplish and budget for them. However, the budget may be constrained by the application of a percentage of sales, or other method, when considering whether or not it is affordable. In addition, competitors' budgets may also influence this decision.

Figure 9–7 **Split of Advertising versus Promotions Budgets**

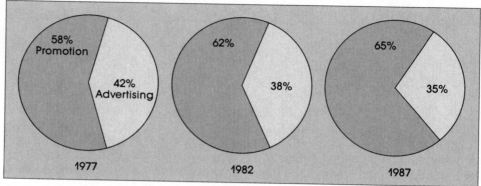

Source: Nathaniel Frey, "Ninth Annual Advertising and Sales Promotion Report," *Marketing Communications* (August 1988), p. 11.

Allocating the Budget

Once the budget has been appropriated, the next step is to allocate it. The allocation decision involves the determination as to which markets, products, and/or promotional elements will receive the funds appropriated. In this section, we will discuss the factors influencing this decision.

Allocating to Advertising and Promotions Elements

In recent years advertisers have begun to shift some of their budget dollars away from traditional advertising media and into sales promotions targeted at both the consumer and the trade (Figure 9–7).

In citing the reasons for such changes, marketers have noted that rapidly rising media costs, the ability of sales promotions to motivate trial, maturing of the product and/or brand, and the need for more aggressive promotional tools have led to the shifts in strategy.[10] (We will discuss both consumer and trade promotions and the reasons for some of these changes in Chapters 15 and 16.)

Client/Agency Policies

Another factor that may influence the allocation of the budget is the individual policy of the company or the advertising agency. The advertising agency may discourage the allocation of monies to sales promotions, preferring to spend them on the advertising area. While the agency position is that promotional monies are harder to track in terms of effectiveness, and that they may be used improperly if not under its control, it has also been noted that in many cases commissions are not made on this area and that this fact might contribute to the agency's reluctance.[11]

The orientation of the agency or firm may also directly influence where monies are spent. Many ad agencies are managed by top officers who have ascended through the creative ranks and as a result are more willing and inclined to emphasize the creative budget. Others may have preferences for specific media. For example, in 1985, BBDO Worldwide—one of the largest advertising agencies in the United States—began to position itself as an expert in cable television programming and as a result began to spend more of the clients' monies in this medium. Other agencies have also acquired reputations as being more inclined to prefer one advertising medium over others. All in all, both the agency and the client may have specific preferences and favor certain aspects of the promotional program, perhaps based on past successes, that will influence to a very large degree where the dollars are spent.

Market Size

While the budget should be allocated according to the specific promotional tools necessary to accomplish the stated objectives, it must be kept in mind that the *size* of the market will have an impact on the decision. In smaller markets it is often easier and less expensive to reach the target market. Too much of an expenditure in these markets will lead to saturation and a lack of effective spending. In larger markets the target group may be more dispersed and thus more expensive to reach. Think, for example, about the cost of purchasing media in Chicago or New York City versus a smaller market like Columbus, Ohio, or Birmingham, Alabama. As you might easily imagine, the former would be much more costly and as such would necessitate a higher budget appropriation.

Market Potential

For a variety of reasons some markets hold more potential than do others. Marketers of snow skis would find greater returns on their expenditures in Denver, Colorado, than they would in Ft. Lauderdale, Florida. Imported Mexican beers sell better in the border states (Texas, Arizona, California) than they do in the Midwest. A disproportionate number of imported cars are sold in California and New England, relative to the rest of the United States. In those instances that particular markets hold higher potential, the marketing manager might decide to allocate additional monies to them. (Keep in mind, however, that just because a market does not have high sales does not mean that it is to be ignored. The key here is *potential*—and a market with low sales but high potential may be a candidate for additional appropriations.)

Economies of Scale in Advertising

Some studies have presented evidence that firms and/or brands maintaining a large share of the market have an advantage over smaller competitors and thus can spend less money on advertising and realize a better return.[12] The logic of this is that larger advertisers can maintain advertising shares that are smaller than their market shares, owing to the fact that they may get better advertising rates, have declining average costs of production, and may accrue the advantages of advertising several products jointly. In addition, more favorable time and space positions, cooperation of middle people, and favorable publicity are seen as more likely to accrue. Reviewing the studies in support of this position, and then conducting research over a variety of small-package products, Kent Lancaster found that this situation did not hold true and that in fact larger brand share products might actually be at a disadvantage in this regard.[13] His results indicated that firms with leading brands are not maintaining their brand shares with lower advertising shares; the leading brands spend an average of 2.5 percentage points more than their brand share on advertising. More specifically, this study concluded the following:

1. There is no evidence to support the position that larger firms can support their brands with lower relative advertising costs than smaller firms.
2. There is no evidence that the leading brand in a product group enjoys lower advertising costs per sales dollar than do other brands.
3. There is no evidence of a static relationship between advertising costs per dollar of sales and the size of the advertiser.

The results of this study, and other that have shown similar results, would indicate that there are really no **economies of scale** to be accrued as a result of the size of the firm or the market share of the brand.[14,15]

   In sum, it seems obvious that a number of considerations must be taken into account in the budget allocation decision. Factors such as the market size and potential, the specific objectives sought, as well as previous company and/or agency policies and preferences may all influence this decision.

Summary

As you have probably concluded upon reading this chapter, the budget decision is not typically based on supporting experiences or strong theoretical foundations. Nor is it one of the more soundly established elements of the promotional program.

The major problem associated with the budgeting methods now employed is that they are not based on the sound theoretical approach—economic models are limited, they often try to demonstrate the effects on sales directly, and they ignore other elements of the marketing mix. Some of the methods discussed have no theoretical basis whatsoever and for all intents and purposes ignore the actual role that advertising and promotions are meant to perform.

One possible suggestion for improving the budget appropriation is to tie the measures of effectiveness to communications objectives rather than to the broader-based marketing objectives. As noted in this chapter, one method for doing this would be to employ the objective and task approach, with communications objectives. While this approach may not be the ultimate solution to the budgeting problem, it would be an improvement over those methods currently being employed.

In other instances, marketers have found it advantageous to employ a combination of methods. For example, some companies establish the dollar amount of the budget by using a percentage of sales method, then allocate these monies by employing an objective and task approach. Others may consider combining payout planning and objective and task approaches.

As in the budget determination decision, a number of factors must be taken into consideration when allocating advertising and promotions dollars. Market size and potential, agency policies and preferences, and those of management itself may influence the allocation decision.

Key Terms

Contribution margin
Marginal analysis
Concave-downward function
S-shaped response curve
Top-down approaches
Affordable method
Arbitrary allocation
Percentage of sales method
Percentage of projected future sales

Competitive parity method
ROI budgeting method
Objective and task method of budget
  setting
Build-up approach
Payout plan
Computer simulation models
Economies of scale

Discussion Questions

1. Discuss the marginal analysis approach to budget setting. What are some of the weaknesses that limit its application?
2. Compare the S-shaped response curve and the concave-downward sales response models. What types of products and/or services would be most likely to be characterized by each?
3. Discuss how you would explain to a small-business owner the reasons why it

would be necessary to budget a larger amount to advertising and promotion, basing your argument on the S-shaped response function.

4. What are some of the situational factors that might influence the budget setting process? Give examples of each.

5. Compare top-down and build-up approaches to budget setting. What are some of the reasons why managers might employ each?

6. In the percentage of sales approach to budget setting, a large difference may exist between percentages set by different companies. Give examples of companies setting a low figure. A high figure. Why are these figures so different?

7. Discuss the objective and task approach to budget setting. What are the advantages and disadvantages associated with this approach?

8. What factors may influence the budget allocation decision? Give an example of each of these.

9. Some advertisers believe that there are economies of scale that are accrued in the advertising process. Discuss their reasons for taking this position. Does research evidence support this position?

10. What are some of the possible reasons that the use of quantitative models in the budgeting process is declining?

Notes

1. Robert L. Steiner, "The Paradox of Increasing Returns to Advertising," *Journal of Advertising Research,* February/March 1987, pp. 45–53.

2. Frank M. Bass, "A Simultaneous Equation Regression Study of Advertising and Sales of Cigarettes," *Journal of Marketing Research* 6, no. 3 (August 1969), p. 291.

3. David A. Aaker and James M. Carman, "Are You Overadvertising?" *Journal Of Advertising Research* 22, no. 4 (August/September 1982), pp. 57–70.

4. Julian A. Simon and Johan Arndt, "The Shape of the Advertising Response Function," *Journal of Advertising Research* 20, no. 4 (1980), pp. 11–28.

5. Paul B. Luchsinger, Vernan S. Mullen, and Paul T. Jannuzzo, "How Many Advertising Dollars Are Enough?," *Media Decisions* 12 (1977), p. 59.

6. Paul W. Farris, "Determinants of Advertising Intensity: A Review of the Marketing Literature" (Report no. 77–109, Marketing Science Institute, Cambridge, Massachusetts, 1977).

7. Melvin E. Salveson, "Management's Criteria for Advertising Effectiveness" (Proceedings 5th Annual Conference, Advertising Research Foundation, New York, 1959), p. 25.

8. Robert Settle and Pamela Alreck, "Positive Moves for Negative Times," *Marketing Communications,* January 1988, pp. 19–23.

9. James O. Peckham, "Can We Relate Advertising Dollars to Market Share Objectives?" in *How Much to Spend for Advertising,* ed. M. A. McNiven (New York: Association of National Advertisers, 1969), p. 30.

10. "Marketers Fuel Promotion Budgets," *Marketing and Media Decisions,* September 1984, p. 130.

11. Ibid.

12. Randall S. Brown, "Estimating Advantages to Large Scale Advertising," *Review of Economics and Statistics* 60 (August 1978), pp. 428–437.

13. Kent M. Lancaster, "Are There Scale Economies in Advertising?" *Journal of Business* 59, no. 3 (1986), pp. 509–526.

14. Johan Arndt and Julian Simon, "Advertising and Economies of Scale: Critical Comments on the Evidence," *Journal of Industrial Economics* 32, no. 2 (December 1983), pp. 229–41.

15. Aaker and Carman, "Are You Overadvertising?"

10

Media Planning and Strategy

CHAPTER OBJECTIVES

1. To introduce the key terminology necessary to understand media planning

2. To provide an understanding of the development of a media plan

3. To provide an understanding of the process of developing and implementing media strategies

4. To introduce sources of media information and characteristics of media

Saab Builds Media Presence on a Small Budget[1,2]

When Peter Berla took over the job of managing Saab's advertising in the United States in 1980, the car had the image of being an "imported oddity for liberal academics," and sales were suffering (except, perhaps, among liberal academics!). Since taking over nine years ago, Berla has seen the image of the Saab change to a status symbol of upward mobility and has watched as sales increased 250 percent during the same period. What is even more amazing is that these results were obtained using only one advertising medium—print—and on a relatively small advertising budget by auto industry standards (approximately $25 million in 1989). Another creative success story, you say? Well, perhaps the most interesting facet of this story is that neither Berla's background nor Saab's success is due to creative. Both can be attributed to a successful media strategy.

While economics dictates to some degree the Saab media strategy (the budget does not allow for a large number of ads on TV), Berla feels that print offers a lot of advantages over television, particularly for the target group he seeks. Until 1989, 100 percent of the advertising was placed in print, with 95 percent in magazines and 5 percent in newspapers. The emphasis was on national print media, using national magazines and newspapers such as *The Wall Street Journal* and *USA Today,* with very little local advertising outside of cooperative ads. Classified advertising was discouraged.

In 1989 Saab ventured into a regional marketing strategy, focusing its efforts in the Pacific, southeastern, and south central states. While major national newsweeklies were still the prime medium, regional spot television ads and direct-mail campaigns were also introduced.

What does this 39-year veteran of media strategy look for in a print medium? Editorial honesty, style of writing, layout, and a feeling of compatibility that he cannot define. In addition, the medium must have a broad reach—usually with a circulation minimum of 50,000. What does he look for in broadcast? Not much!

Introduction

The Saab media strategy presented at the outset of this chapter reflects an excellent example of some of the decisions involved in the media strategy and planning process and also demonstrates the importance of media to the attainment of marketing and communications goals. The primary objective of the media plan is to develop a framework that will allow for delivery of the message to the target audience(s) in the most effective and cost-efficient manner possible. The purpose of this chapter is to present the various methods of message delivery available to the marketer, to examine some key considerations used in making media decisions, and to discuss the process of developing media strategy and plans. In the succeeding chapters we will explore the relative advantages and disadvantages of the various media and examine each in more detail.

An Overview of Media Planning

The media planning process is not an easy one, as a number of options are available to the planner. These options include mass media such as television, newspapers, radio, and magazines (and the choices available within each of these categories) as well as out-of-the-home media such as outdoor advertising, transit advertising, and electronic billboards. In addition, a variety of support media such as direct marketing, specialty advertising, and in-store point-of-purchase options must also be considered.

While at first glance it might seem that the choice between these alternatives is relatively straightforward, you will see as this chapter progresses that this is often not the case. Part of the reason media selection becomes so involved is due to the nature of the media themselves. For example, television provides the opportunity to combine both sight and sound—an advantage not offered by other media. On the other hand, magazines may be able to convey more information and may keep the message available to the potential buyer for a much longer period of time. Newspapers also offer their own specific advantages, as do outdoor, direct media, and each of the others.

Table 10–1 **Expenditures of Top Advertisers in Various Media**

AD $ SUMMARY
COMPANY RANKINGS

BAR/LNA MULTI-MEDIA SERVICE

January - December 1988

RANK	COMPANY	9-MEDIA TOTAL	LNA MAGAZINES	LNA NEWSPAPER SUPPLEMENTS	MEDIA RECORDS NEWSPAPERS	LNA OUTDOOR	BAR NETWORK TELEVISION	BAR SPOT TELEVISION	BAR SYNDICATED TELEVISION	BAR CABLE TV NETWORKS	BAR NETWORK RADIO
		TOP 1000 COMPANIES RANKED BY 9 MEDIA DOLLARS (000)									
1	PHILIP MORRIS COMPANIES INC	1,091,799.8	270,250.9	16,868.4	76,710.6	61,424.8	388,601.8	157,577.9	88,592.1	23,075.1	8,698.2
2	GENERAL MOTORS CORP	905,061.2	190,798.7	12,233.0	86,834.8	2,996.6	443,402.3	115,286.2	6,053.9	9,200.8	38,254.9
3	PROCTER & GAMBLE CO	813,014.2	79,279.4	1,383.9	21,976.7	682.1	370,174.7	222,883.1	60,899.1	30,201.5	25,533.7
4	RJR NABISCO INC	457,735.3	131,462.7	4,153.3	37,704.2	57,366.4	174,002.4	18,907.3	15,145.8	14,251.9	4,741.3
5	PEPSICO INC	431,248.8	1,752.6	94.8	7,577.4	3,080.1	145,047.9	257,956.9	7,089.9	4,707.0	3,942.2
6	FORD MOTOR CO	420,540.0	125,531.6	155.1	25,271.8	2,156.5	175,687.8	68,884.5	4,543.1	6,267.1	12,042.5
7	KELLOGG CO	401,816.3	5,978.9	157.5	17,198.6	70.4	297,739.8	53,286.7	23,376.4	4,008.0	- -
8	MCDONALDS CORP	401,003.0	6,371.3	- -	527.9	6,305.7	245,388.5	128,102.2	12,516.2	1,791.2	- -
9	SEARS ROEBUCK & CO	392,654.4	33,372.7	1,601.8	160,968.6	804.1	97,361.2	24,541.8	1,741.1	4,650.7	67,612.4
10	ANHEUSER-BUSCH COS INC	369,735.8	10,563.0	964.7	10,192.3	6,707.5	207,277.9	87,485.9	9,756.5	21,396.7	15,391.3
	TOP 10 TOTAL	5,684,608.8	855,361.8	37,612.5	444,962.9	141,594.2	2,544,684.3	1,134,912.5	229,714.1	119,550.0	176,216.5
11	UNILEVER NV	362,948.2	59,448.7	218.4	15,917.4	714.6	189,651.5	49,944.0	26,959.1	8,278.5	11,816.0
12	GENERAL MILLS INC	358,846.1	18,404.1	530.0	24,688.8	294.8	137,450.1	145,944.5	5,714.5	20,010.6	5,808.7
13	CHRYSLER CORP	349,510.5	104,526.7	2,050.7	11,653.4	939.6	163,020.8	45,535.2	890.8	9,699.9	11,193.4
14	AMERICAN TELEPHONE & TELEGRAPH CO	341,320.4	66,192.7	5,138.7	32,689.7	361.4	173,912.3	36,752.7	6,189.5	7,772.7	12,310.7
15	NESTLE SA	299,929.1	63,476.6	3,318.9	16,363.3	788.9	109,495.6	69,152.4	26,643.8	5,023.2	5,666.4
16	MAY DEPARTMENT STORES CO	258,763.1	2,447.0	1,931.4	224,282.1	120.3	4,166.9	25,815.4	- -	- -	- -
17	EASTMAN KODAK CO	242,218.7	31,942.9	3,125.2	7,546.4	557.0	144,751.1	21,239.2	16,945.9	11,386.5	4,724.5
18	JOHNSON & JOHNSON	234,797.6	30,635.6	2,679.0	5,078.4	77.4	167,275.7	10,902.7	12,810.1	4,274.0	1,064.7
19	PILLSBURY CO	229,637.2	7,414.9	76.4	8,076.6	2,398.2	90,478.2	99,425.3	19,156.6	2,611.0	- -
20	AMERICAN HOME PRODUCTS CORP	223,893.8	13,516.0	74.8	7,998.4	- -	163,362.8	22,550.5	3,894.6	8,173.5	4,323.2
21	BRISTOL-MYERS CO	222,634.2	43,186.6	597.0	6,627.0	- -	119,140.2	9,983.6	32,646.9	6,861.5	3,591.4
22	GENERAL MOTORS CORP DEALERS ASSN	220,596.1	- -	- -	23,656.1	5.3	196,920.7	- -	14.0		
23	QUAKER OATS CO	216,402.1	30,214.6	1,005.0	14,207.7	455.9	123,327.1	24,327.4	18,413.8	4,031.9	418.7
24	COCA-COLA CO	215,699.0	4,082.4	407.4	9,503.5	2,538.4	119,090.7	56,126.3	18,952.1	4,589.0	409.2
25	WARNER-LAMBERT CO	209,552.5	18,883.1	1,442.8	3,637.0	203.8	111,071.7	34,497.9	19,564.6	3,340.2	16,911.4
	TOP 25 TOTAL	9,671,357.4	1,349,733.7	60,208.2	856,888.7	151,049.8	4,360,879.0	1,984,030.3	438,496.4	215,616.5	254,454.8
26	K MART CORP	203,353.7	25,035.4	733.9	73,072.6	123.0	56,291.7	28,951.1	4,124.3	3,230.0	11,791.7
27	MACY ACQUIRING CORP	200,490.6	2,166.1	85.5	182,211.5	376.4		15,651.1		- -	- -
28	MARS INC	184,904.3	9,860.3	512.0	5,358.6	23.0	91,365.8	38,289.6	23,779.6	9,994.7	5,720.7
29	TOYOTA MOTOR CORP	184,491.5	36,476.1	712.3	5,011.4	821.7	64,193.1	68,581.5	5,944.8	2,749.8	0.8

Thus, the characteristics of each alternative must be taken into consideration, along with many other factors. This process becomes even more complicated when the manager has to choose between alternatives within the same medium—for example, choosing between *Time* and *Newsweek* or between the "Cosby Show" and "The Wonder Years."

In addition to the nature of the media, the potential for achieving effective communications through a well-designed media strategy warrants the added attention. An example of the power of an effective media strategy was demonstrated by an innovative and somewhat controversial media program employed by Pioneer Electronics in the late 1970s. This strategy involved placement of ads in male-oriented general interest magazines such as *Playboy*, *Penthouse*, and *Rolling Stone*. Stereo manufacturers had previously advertised only in magazines targeted to audiophiles such as *Stereo Review* and *Hi Fidelity*. This broadening of media use to general interest consumer magazines contributed to their doubling of sales every year for a period of six years and changed the nature of stereo advertising for an entire industry.

Finally, the product and/or service being advertised will impact the media planning process. As demonstrated in Table 10–1, firms have found that some media are more useful to them in conveying their messages than are others. For example, Procter & Gamble tends to rely more heavily on television advertising, whereas General Motors prefers print media. The result is placement of advertising dollars in these preferred media—and significantly different media strategies.

Some Basic Terms and Concepts

Prior to beginning our discussion of media planning, we will review some basic terms and concepts that are used in the media planning and strategy process.

Media planning consists of the series of decisions involved in the delivery of the promotional message to the prospective purchasers and/or users of the product or brand. Media planning is a process, meaning that a number of decisions are made, and each of these may be altered or even abandoned as the plan develops.

The **media plan** will require the development of specific **media objectives** and specific **media strategies**—or plans of action—designed to attain these objectives. Once the decisions have been made, and the objectives and strategies formulated, this information is organized into the media plan—the guide for media selection.

The **medium** is the general category of available delivery systems, which includes broadcast media such as television and radio, print media such as newspapers and magazines, direct mail, outdoor advertising, and other support media. The **media vehicle** is the specific carrier within a medium category. For example, *Time* and *Newsweek* are print vehicles, whereas specific television programs such as the "Cosby Show" and "60 minutes" are broadcast vehicles. As you will see in succeeding chapters, each vehicle has its own characteristics as well as its own relative advantages and disadvantages. Specific decisions must be made as to the value of each in delivering the message.

Reach is a measure of the number of different audience members exposed at least once to a media vehicle (or vehicles) in a given period of time. **Coverage** refers to the potential audience that might receive the message through a vehicle. (It is important to distinguish between *coverage* and *reach,* as the former relates to potential audience, whereas the latter refers to the actual audience delivered. (The importance of this distinction will become more obvious to you later in this chapter.) Finally, **frequency** refers to the number of times the receiver is exposed to the media vehicle in a specified time period. Later in this chapter you will be introduced to additional terms and concepts. At this point, however, we have established enough common ground to begin our discussion of the process of media planning.

The Media Plan

The purpose of the media plan is to determine the best way to get the advertiser's message to the market. In a very basic sense, the goal of the media plan is to find that combination of media that will enable the marketer to communicate the message in the most effective manner to the largest number of potential customers at the minimum cost.

The activities involved in the development of this plan and the purposes of each are presented in Figure 10–1. As you can see, a number of decisions must be made throughout this process. These decisions are not set in stone, however. As the plan evolves, events may occur that necessitate that changes be made. As a result, many advertisers will find it necessary to frequently alter and update their objectives and strategies.

In addition to the difficulties associated with frequently making revisions, the media planning process is further complicated by a number of other problems. Let us review some of these.

Problems in Media Planning

Unfortunately, the media strategy decision has not become a standardized task. A number of problems exist, each of which contributes to the difficulty involved in establishing the plan and at the same time reduces its effectiveness. Some of these problems are described next.

Figure 10—1   Activities Involved in Developing the Media Plan

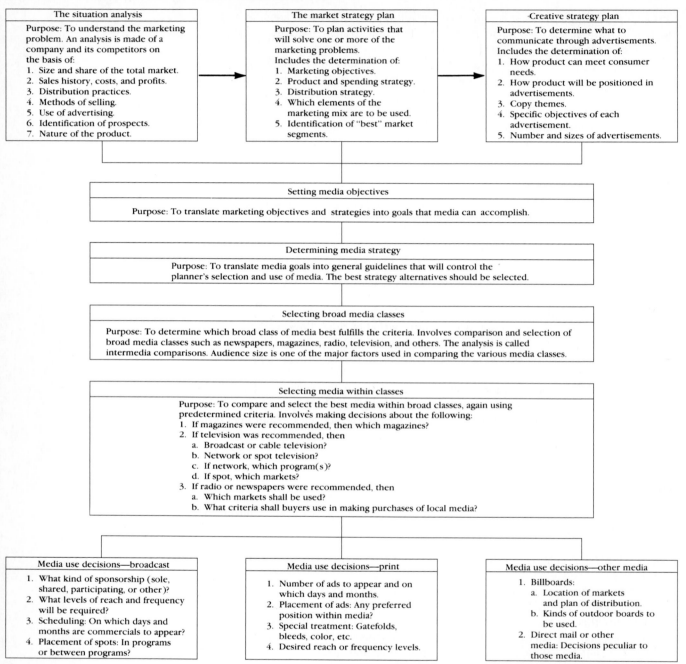

Source: C. Bovee and W. F. Arens, *Contemporary Advertising*, 3rd ed. (Homewood, Ill.: Richard D. Irwin, 1989), p. 377.

Insufficient Information   While a great deal of information about markets and the media exists, media planners often require more than is available. Some information may not be available for a variety of reasons, whereas other information may be of limited value as a direct result of measurement problems. Some data are just not measured, either because they cannot be or because to do so would be too expensive. For example, no continuous measures of radio listenership exist, as only periodic listenership studies taking place at specified periods of time throughout the year are performed. Second, there are problems with some of the measures in respect to the methods that they employ. (We will discuss this problem in more detail later in the chapter.)

A third measurement problem may occur as a result of the timeliness of the measurements, as some audience measures are taken only at specific times of the year (for example, **sweeps periods**—February, May, November—that are used for measuring television audiences and setting advertising rates). This information is then generalized to succeeding months, so that future planning decisions must be made on past data that may not reflect current behaviors. Think about planning for television advertising for the fall season. There are no data on the audiences of new shows, and audience information, if taken on existing programs during the summer months, may not be an accurate indicator of how these programs will do in the fall. For example, in the summer of 1988, a writers' strike delayed and caused changes in the fall program schedule, leaving the networks as well as potential advertisers with severe planning headaches. While the strike was eventually settled, it was not until well into the summer, which left little time for plan development. Contingency plans had to be developed, many of which involved switching advertising monies to other media.

The lack of available information is an even more pronounced problem with small advertisers. Because of their limited budgets, many of these advertisers may not be able to afford to purchase the information they require. As a result, their decisions are made on limited or out-of-date data or no data at all.

Inconsistent Terminologies Problems arise owing to the fact that the cost bases used by different media often vary. In addition, the standards of measurement used to establish these costs are not always consistent. For example, print media may present cost data in terms of the cost to reach a thousand people (cost per thousand—CPM), whereas broadcast media may refer to cost per ratings point (CPRP), and outdoor refers to the number of "showings." Audience information that is used as a basis for these costs has also been collected by different methods. Finally, terms that actually mean something different (such as *reach* and *coverage*) may be used synonymously, adding to the confusion.

Time Pressures It seems that advertisers are always in a hurry—sometimes because they need to be, other times because they *think* they need to be. In the former case, actions by a competitor may require rapid response. For example, the cutting of airfares by one carrier will require immediate response by others. In the latter case a false sense of urgency may be dictating time pressures. In either situation, media selection decisions may be made without proper planning and analyses of the markets and/or media. In other instances, there may just not be enough time to analyze all the information that is available.

Measures of Effectiveness Because it is so hard to measure the effectiveness of advertising and promotions in general, it is also difficult to determine the relative effectiveness of various media or media vehicles. While progress is being made in this regard (particularly in the area of direct-response advertising), in many situations the media planner is forced to assume the impact of these alternatives.

Because of these problems, not all media decisions are quantitatively determined. Sometimes managers may have to assume the image of a medium in a market in which they are not familiar, anticipate the impact that recent events may cause, or make judgments without full knowledge of all the available alternatives.

While the problems just discussed may complicate the media decision process, they by no means render it an entirely subjective exercise. In the remainder of this chapter, we will explore in more detail how media strategies are developed and ways of increasing their effectiveness.

Developing the Media Plan

In the promotional planning model presented in Chapter 1, we discussed the process of identifying target markets, establishing objectives, and formulating strategies for attaining these objectives. The development of the media plan and strategies follows a

Figure 10–2 **Developing the Media Plan**

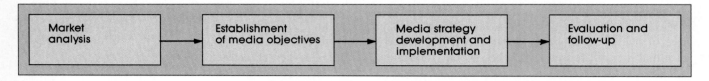

similar path—the primary difference being that the focus is more specifically keyed to determination of the *best* way to deliver the message. Otherwise, the process—shown in Figure 10–2 —is very similar, involving a series of stages including (1) market analysis, (2) establishment of media objectives, (3) media strategy development and implementation, and (4) evaluation and follow-up. Each of these will be discussed in turn, with specific examples provided. In addition, an example of an actual media plan is included in Appendix B to Chapter 10 and we will refer to this plan throughout the remainder of this chapter to exemplify each phase further.

Market Analysis and Target Market Identification

While an extensive examination of the market has already been performed in the situation analysis stage of the overall promotional planning process, this initial analysis is broader in that it involves a complete review of internal and external factors, competitive strategies, and the like. In the development of media strategy, a market analysis is again performed, although this time the specific focus is on the media and delivering the message. The key questions to be asked at this stage are:

- To whom shall we advertise (who is the target market)?
- What internal and external factors may have an influence on the media plan?
- Where (geographically) and when should we focus our efforts?

To Whom Shall We Advertise?

While a number of target markets might be derived as a result of the situation analysis, the decision as to which specific groups to go after may involve the media planner working as a team with the client, account representative, marketing department, and creative directors. A variety of factors may be used to assist the media planners in this decision—some of which will require primary research, whereas others will be available from published sources (secondary sources) of information.

One example of secondary information is that provided by the *Simmons Market Research Bureau (SMRB)*. SMRB provides syndicated data on audience size and composition for approximately 100 publications, as well as broadcast exposure and data on usage of consumer products. This information is provided in the form of raw numbers, percentages, and indexes. As can be seen in Table 10–2, information is given on (1) the number of adults in the United States by each category under consideration; (2) the number of users, (3) the percentage of users falling into each category (for example, the percentage of users that are female); (4) the percentage of each category that uses the product (for example, the percentage of all females using); (5) an index number; and (6) the same information (as 2 through 5) classified by heavy, medium, and light users. (While not shown here, both Simmons and its major competitor, *Mediamark Research, Inc. [MRI]*, also provide lifestyle information as well as media usage characteristics of the population.)

In many instances, media planners are more concerned with the percentage figures and the index numbers than they are with the raw numbers. The reasons for this vary, but it is primarily due to the fact that they may have their own data from other

Table 10—2　**Market Research Profile of Cola Users**

	TOTAL U.S. '000	ALL USERS A '000	B % DOWN	C ACROSS %	D INDX	HEAVY USERS SEVEN OR MORE A '000	B % DOWN	C ACROSS %	D INDX	MEDIUM USERS THREE-SIX A '000	B % DOWN	C ACROSS %	D INDX	LIGHT USERS TWO OR LESS A '000	B % DOWN	C ACROSS %	D INDX
TOTAL ADULTS	176250	95744	100.0	54.3	100	34903	100.0	19.8	100	30334	100.0	17.2	100	30507	100.0	17.3	100
MALES	84066	49530	51.7	58.9	108	18964	54.3	22.6	114	16142	53.2	19.2	112	14423	47.3	17.2	99
FEMALES	92184	46214	48.3	50.1	92	15938	45.7	17.3	87	14192	46.8	15.4	89	16084	52.7	17.4	101
18 - 24	26535	17376	18.1	65.5	121	7555	21.6	28.5	144	5623	18.5	21.2	123	4198	13.8	15.8	91
25 - 34	42634	26414	27.6	62.0	114	9960	28.5	23.4	118	8889	29.3	20.8	121	7565	24.8	17.7	103
35 - 44	33688	19208	20.1	57.0	105	6647	19.0	19.7	100	5749	19.0	17.1	99	6812	22.3	20.2	117
45 - 54	23361	12028	12.6	51.5	95	4159	11.9	17.8	90	3777	12.5	16.2	94	4092	13.4	17.5	101
55 - 64	22021	10141	10.6	46.1	85	3512	10.1	15.9	81	2964	9.8	13.5	78	3664	12.0	16.6	96
65 OR OLDER	28011	10577	11.0	37.8	70	3069	8.8	11.0	55	3333	11.0	11.9	69	4176	13.7	14.9	86
18 - 34	69169	43790	45.7	63.3	117	17515	50.2	25.3	128	14512	47.8	21.0	122	11763	38.6	17.0	98
18 - 49	115355	69463	72.6	60.2	111	26312	75.4	22.8	115	22288	73.5	19.3	112	20863	68.4	18.1	104
25 - 54	99683	57649	60.2	57.8	106	20766	59.5	20.8	105	18414	60.7	18.5	107	18469	60.5	18.5	107
35 - 49	46186	25673	26.8	55.6	102	8797	25.2	19.0	96	7776	25.6	16.8	98	9100	29.8	19.7	114
50 OR OLDER	60895	26280	27.4	43.2	79	8591	24.6	14.1	71	8046	26.5	13.2	77	9644	31.6	15.8	91
GRADUATED COLLEGE	31644	16222	16.9	51.3	94	4704	13.5	14.9	75	5026	16.6	15.9	92	6492	21.3	20.5	119
ATTENDED COLLEGE	32702	18397	19.2	56.3	104	6088	17.4	18.6	94	5729	18.9	17.5	102	6579	21.6	20.1	116
GRADUATED HIGH SCHOOL	69681	38622	40.3	55.4	102	14657	42.0	21.0	106	12608	41.6	18.1	105	11357	37.2	16.3	94
DID NOT GRADUATE HIGH SCHOOL	42223	22503	23.5	53.3	98	9453	27.1	22.4	113	6971	23.0	16.5	96	6079	19.9	14.4	83
EMPLOYED MALES	60414	37042	38.7	61.3	113	14394	41.2	23.8	120	12049	39.7	19.9	116	10598	34.7	17.5	101
EMPLOYED FEMALES	51321	27352	28.6	53.3	98	9111	26.1	17.8	90	8460	27.9	16.5	96	9781	32.1	19.1	110
EMPLOYED FULL-TIME	97700	56518	59.0	57.8	106	20873	59.8	21.4	108	17759	58.5	18.2	106	17886	58.6	18.3	106
EMPLOYED PART-TIME	14034	7876	8.2	56.1	103	2632	7.5	18.8	95	2751	9.1	19.6	114	2493	8.2	17.8	103
NOT EMPLOYED	64516	31350	32.7	48.6	89	11397	32.7	17.7	89	9824	32.4	15.2	88	10128	33.2	15.7	91
PROFESSIONAL/MANAGER	28104	15040	15.7	53.5	99	4231	12.1	15.1	76	4969	16.4	17.7	103	5840	19.1	20.8	120
TECH/CLERICAL/SALES	35802	20856	21.8	58.3	107	7127	20.4	19.9	101	6603	21.8	18.4	107	7126	23.4	19.9	115
PRECISION/CRAFT	14098	8697	9.1	61.7	114	3647	10.4	25.9	131	2832	9.3	20.1	117	2218	7.3	15.7	91
OTHER EMPLOYED	33730	19800	20.7	58.7	108	8500	24.4	25.2	127	6105	20.1	18.1	105	5194	17.0	15.4	89
SINGLE	37865	22960	24.0	60.6	112	9155	26.2	24.2	122	7594	25.0	20.1	117	6211	20.4	16.4	95
MARRIED	106963	57825	60.4	54.1	100	20239	58.0	18.9	96	18194	60.0	17.0	99	19392	63.6	18.1	105
DIVORCED/SEPARATED/WIDOWED	31422	14958	15.6	47.6	88	5508	15.8	17.5	89	4546	15.0	14.5	84	4904	16.1	15.6	90
PARENTS	67328	41891	43.8	62.2	115	15697	45.0	23.3	118	13254	43.7	19.7	114	12941	42.4	19.2	111
WHITE	152234	81240	84.9	53.4	98	28834	82.6	18.9	96	25457	83.9	16.7	97	26950	88.3	17.7	102
BLACK	19434	11634	12.2	59.9	110	5044	14.5	26.0	131	3727	12.3	19.2	111	2863	9.4	14.7	85
OTHER	4582	2869	3.0	62.6	115	1024	2.9	22.3	113	1150	3.8	25.1	146	*695	2.3	15.2	88
NORTHEAST—CENSUS	37366	19474	20.3	52.1	96	7160	20.5	19.2	97	5960	19.6	16.0	93	6354	20.8	17.0	98
MIDWEST	43426	23589	24.6	54.3	100	7805	22.4	18.0	91	7389	24.4	17.0	99	8396	27.5	19.3	112
SOUTH	60402	34244	35.8	56.7	104	14286	40.9	23.7	119	11135	36.7	18.4	107	8823	28.9	14.6	84
WEST	35057	18437	19.3	52.6	97	5651	16.2	16.1	81	5850	19.3	16.7	97	6935	22.7	19.8	114
NORTHEAST—MKTG.	39212	20134	21.0	51.3	95	7687	22.0	19.6	99	6299	20.8	16.1	93	6148	20.2	15.7	91
EAST CENTRAL	25018	14008	14.6	56.0	103	5270	15.1	21.1	106	4168	13.7	16.7	97	4570	15.0	18.3	106
WEST CENTRAL	29430	15741	16.4	53.6	99	4992	14.3	17.0	86	4689	15.5	16.0	93	6059	19.9	20.6	119
SOUTH	52142	29950	31.3	57.4	106	12210	35.0	23.4	118	10024	33.0	19.2	112	7716	25.3	14.8	85
PACIFIC	30528	15912	16.6	52.1	96	4743	13.6	15.5	78	5155	17.0	16.9	98	6014	19.7	19.7	114
COUNTY SIZE A	73211	39343	41.1	53.7	99	14093	40.4	19.2	97	12259	40.4	16.7	97	12991	42.6	17.7	103
COUNTY SIZE B	52831	29042	30.3	55.0	101	10716	30.7	20.3	102	9546	31.5	18.1	105	8779	28.8	16.6	96
COUNTY SIZE C	26575	14335	15.0	53.9	99	5520	15.8	20.8	105	4405	14.5	16.6	96	4410	14.5	16.6	96
COUNTY SIZE D	23633	13024	13.6	55.1	101	4574	13.1	19.4	98	4124	13.6	17.5	101	4326	14.2	18.3	106
METRO CENTRAL CITY	53736	29860	31.2	55.6	102	11694	33.5	21.8	110	9450	31.2	17.6	102	8716	28.6	16.2	94
METRO SUBURBAN	81523	43613	45.6	53.5	99	15257	43.7	18.7	95	13606	44.9	16.7	97	14750	48.3	18.1	105
NON METRO	40991	22270	23.3	54.3	100	7951	22.8	19.4	98	7278	24.0	17.8	103	7041	23.1	17.2	99
TOP 5 ADI'S	40121	21835	22.8	54.4	100	7220	20.7	18.0	91	6924	22.8	17.3	100	7691	25.2	19.2	111
TOP 10 ADI'S	55858	29861	31.2	53.5	98	10654	30.5	19.1	96	9468	31.2	17.0	98	9738	31.9	17.4	101
TOP 20 ADI'S	80357	42970	44.9	53.5	98	15051	43.1	18.7	95	13475	44.4	16.8	97	14444	47.3	18.0	104
HSHLD INC. $60,000 OR MORE	20289	10973	11.5	54.1	100	3475	10.0	17.1	86	3475	11.5	17.1	100	4023	13.2	19.8	115
$50,000 OR MORE	31340	17061	17.8	54.4	100	5573	16.0	17.8	90	5453	18.0	17.4	101	6035	19.8	19.3	111
$40,000 OR MORE	53108	29320	30.6	55.2	102	9666	27.7	18.2	92	9340	30.8	17.6	102	10314	33.8	19.4	112
$30,000 OR MORE	82233	45660	47.7	55.5	102	15183	43.5	18.5	93	14597	48.1	17.8	103	15880	52.1	19.3	112
$30,000 - $39,999	29126	16340	17.1	56.1	103	5516	15.8	18.9	96	5258	17.3	18.1	105	5566	18.2	19.1	110
$20,000 - $29,999	34891	18403	19.2	52.7	97	7162	20.5	20.5	104	5586	18.4	16.0	93	5655	18.5	16.2	94
$10,000 - $19,999	37097	20020	20.9	54.0	99	7770	22.3	20.9	106	6334	20.9	17.1	99	5916	19.4	15.9	92
UNDER $10,000	22029	11661	12.2	52.9	97	4788	13.7	21.7	110	3816	12.6	17.3	101	3057	10.0	13.9	80
HOUSEHOLD OF 1 PERSON	21267	9231	9.6	43.4	80	3146	9.0	14.8	75	3081	10.2	14.5	84	3004	9.8	14.1	82
2 PEOPLE	55771	26653	27.8	47.8	88	9134	26.2	16.4	83	8386	27.6	15.0	87	9134	29.9	16.4	95
3 OR 4 PEOPLE	71810	41676	43.5	58.0	107	15187	43.5	21.1	107	13170	43.4	18.3	107	13319	43.7	18.5	107
5 OR MORE PEOPLE	27402	18184	19.0	66.4	122	7436	21.3	27.1	137	5697	18.8	20.8	121	5051	16.6	18.4	106
NO CHILD IN HSHLD	104468	50922	53.2	48.7	90	18017	51.6	17.2	87	16080	53.0	15.4	89	16826	55.2	16.1	93
CHILD(REN) UNDER 2 YRS	14095	9185	9.6	65.2	120	3703	10.6	26.3	133	2914	9.6	20.7	120	2568	8.4	18.2	105
2 - 5 YEARS	25865	16449	17.2	63.6	117	5953	17.1	23.0	116	5630	18.6	21.8	126	4866	16.0	18.8	109
6 - 11 YEARS	33171	20687	21.6	62.4	115	7835	22.4	23.6	119	6760	22.3	20.4	118	6093	20.0	18.4	106
12 - 17 YEARS	33224	20514	21.4	61.7	114	7807	22.4	23.5	119	6195	20.4	18.6	108	6512	21.3	19.6	113
RESIDENCE OWNED	123262	65009	67.9	52.7	97	22176	63.5	18.0	91	20179	66.5	16.4	95	22654	74.3	18.4	106
VALUE: $60,000 OR MORE	70282	36812	38.4	52.4	96	11872	34.0	16.9	85	11699	38.6	16.6	97	13241	43.4	18.8	109
VALUE: UNDER $60,000	52980	28196	29.4	53.2	98	10304	29.5	19.4	98	8479	28.0	16.0	93	9413	30.9	17.8	103

Source: Simmons Market Research Bureau, Inc., 1988.

sources—both primary and secondary—with which they feel more comfortable; the numbers provided may not be specific enough for their needs; or because of the methods by which the data were collected, they feel that the numbers provided may be ques-

Table 10–3   **Lipstick and Lip Gloss Usage—Women**

Lipstick and Lip Gloss	Base: Women*		
Used lipstick and/or lip gloss in last six months	79.9%		
Number of times used in last seven days	Base: Lipstick/Lip Gloss Users*		
Heavy—more than 10 times	30.5%		
Medium—7 to 10 times	35.5%		
Light—less than 7 times	34.0%		

Base: Women*	Lipstick and Lip Gloss Usage		
	Heavy Users	Medium Users	Light Users
	Index	Index	Index
Age: 18–34	67	89	120
35–44	122	99	94
45–54	141	121	76
55–64	136	101	89
65 or over	94	109	87
Employment:			
Professional	118	109	81
Executive, administrative, managerial	148	109	65
Clerical, sales, technical	133	104	81
Precision, crafts	128	63	79
Other employed	84	100	110
Household income:			
$50,000 or more	134	112	84
$40,000–$49.9	130	102	77
$35,000–$39.9	123	98	90
$25,000–$34.9	95	103	107
$15,000–$24.9	87	105	108
Less than $15,000	67	85	115

*Mediamark Research, Spring 1986.

Source: "Winning the Marketing Game—How Syndicated Consumer Research Helps Improve the Odds," New York, Mediamark Research, Inc., 1986, p. 14.

tionable. The total (raw) numbers provided by Simmons and MRI are then used in combination with, or as a supplement to, their own figures.

On the other hand, the **index number** is quite often relied on as a good indicator of the potential of the market. This index number is derived from the formula:

$$\text{Index number} = \frac{\text{Percentage of users in a demographic segment}}{\text{Percentage of population in the same segment}} \times 100$$

This number serves as a guide as to the use of a product by a particular segment. An index number over 100 means that use of the product is proportionately greater in that segment than one that is average (100) or less than 100. For example, in the MRI data shown in Table 10–3 it can be seen that the age groups 35–44, 45–54, and 55–64 are more likely to be heavy users of lipstick and lip gloss than are those in the other age segments, as are those with a household income of $35,000+. All occupation groups are heavy users, with the exception of those in the category "other employed." Thus, marketers—depending on their overall strategy—may wish to use this information to determine which groups are now using the product and to target this group, or they may wish to identify a group that is currently using the product less in an attempt to develop that segment.

While the index is a useful aid, it should not be used alone. Rather, percentages and product usage figures must also be considered to get an accurate picture of the market. While the index for a particular segment of the population may be very high,

Table 10–4   How High Indexes Can Be Misleading

Age Segment	Population in Segment (percent)	Product Use in Segment (percent)	Index
18–24	15.1	18.0	119
25–34	25.1	25.0	100
35–44	20.6	21.0	102
45+	39.3	36.0	91

leading one to believe that this is an attractive segment to target, this may be a result of a low denominator—that is, a very small proportion of the population in this segment. An example of how this might occur is provided in Table 10–4. While the 18- to 24-year-old age segment has the highest index, it also has both the lowest product usage and the lowest population percentage of any segment. If the marketer relies solely on the index, while ignoring product use, he or she would be ignoring a full 82 percent of product users.

Further, keep in mind that Simmons and MRI provide only demographic and limited geographic and lifestyle information. As you learned in the chapter on segmentation, demographics are but one way to segment a market. Other factors may also be important—and in fact may be more useful in defining specific markets.

What Internal and External Factors May Be Operating?

Media strategies will be influenced by both *internal* and *external* factors operating at any given time. Internal factors may involve the size of the media budget, managerial and administrative capabilities, or the organization of the agency, as demonstrated in Promotional Perspective 10–1. External factors may include the economy (the rising costs of media), changes in technology (the availability of new media), competitive factors, and the like. While some of this information may require primary research to determine, a substantial volume of information is also available through secondary sources including magazines, syndicated services, or even the daily newspaper.

Table 10–5 presents one such example of a service that provides competitive information. As shown, the BAR/LNA Multi-Media Service provides media spending figures for various brands competing in the same market. Competitive information is also available from a variety of other sources, as shown in Appendix A to Chapter 10.

Where to Promote?

The question of where to promote relates to geographical considerations. As noted in Chapter 9, companies often find that sales are stronger in one area of the country than another and may allocate advertising expenditures according to the market potential of an area. For example, for years Maxwell House coffee has had a much more substantial brand share in the East than it has had in the West. The question that needs to be asked is, Where will the advertising be more wisely spent? Should General Foods allocate additional promotional dollars to those markets where the brand is already the leader so as to maintain market share, or does more potential exist in those markets in which the firm is not doing as well—that is, in areas in which there is more room to grow? Perhaps the best answer to this question is that the firm should spend advertising and promotions dollars where they will be the most effective, that is, in those markets where they will generate the most response. Unfortunately, as we have seen so often, it is not always possible to measure directly the impact of promotional efforts. At the same time, there are certain tactics that can be employed to assist the planner in making this determination. Some of these will now be discussed.

Promotional Perspective 10–1

Organizing the Media Buying Department

While various firms and advertising agencies may have different ways of organizing the media buying department, three seem to be the most common. The first form employs a product/media focus, whereas the second places more emphasis on the market itself. The third organizes around media classes alone.

Form 1 In this organizational arrangement, the media buyers and assistant media buyers are responsible for a product or group of products and/or brands. Their responsibilities include the media selection and buying for these products/brands in whichever geographic areas they are marketed. For example, if the agency were responsible for the advertising of Hart skis, the media planners would determine the appropriate media in each area for placing advertisements for these skis. The logic underlying this approach is that the planner knows the product and will identify the best media and vehicles for promoting the same.

Form 2 In this approach, the market is the focal point of attention. Media planners become "experts" in a particular market area and are responsible for all products/brands that the firm and/or agency markets in those areas. For example, a planner may have responsibility for the Memphis, Tennessee, market. If the agency has more than one client who wishes to market in this area, the media selection for all of the brands/products is the responsibility of the same person—in this case, the logic being that his or her knowledge of the media and vehicles in the area allows for a more informed media choice. The nonquantitative characteristics of the media would get more attention under this approach.

Form 3 Organizing around a specific class of media—for example, print or broadcast—is a third alternative. In this case, the purchasing and development unit will handle all the agency print or broadcast business. Members of the media department become specialists who are brought in very early in the promotional planning process. Their knowledge of the media and the audience each serves is considered a major benefit. In addition, by handling all the media buys, their ability to negotiate better deals is stronger.

As to which strategy works best, who is to say? Each has been in use for some time, and proponents have reasons for their organization. Discussions with media personnel in ad agencies tend to indicate that the second approach discussed here requires that the agency be of substantial size and have enough clients to support the geographical assignment, whereas the first alternative seems to be the most common design.

Using Indexes to Determine Where to Promote As was stated previously, media planners will often use indexes to guide their efforts. In addition to those provided by Simmons and MRI, three additional indexes may also be found to be useful:

1. *The Survey of Buying Power Index* One very commonly used source of information is the **Survey of Buying Power Index,** published annually by *Sales and Marketing Management* magazine. The Survey of Buying Power is conducted for every major metropolitan market in the United States and is based on a number of factors, including population, effective buying income, and total retail sales in the area. Each of these factors is individually weighted and a "buying power index" is derived that charts the potential of a particular metro area, county, or city relative to the United States as a whole. The resulting index provides the media planner with insight into the relative value of that market, as shown in Table 10–6. When used in combination with other market information, the Survey of Buying Power is quite useful to the marketer in determining which geographic areas should be targeted.

2. *The Brand Development Index* The rate of product usage by geographical area is an additional factor that could be integrated into the decision process through the use of the **Brand Development Index (BDI).** This index is represented as follows:

$$\text{BDI} = \frac{\text{Percentage brand total U.S. sales in the market}}{\text{Percentage of total U.S. population in the market}} \times 100$$

The BDI considers the percentage of the brand's total U.S. sales that occur in a given market area as compared with the percentage of the total population in the market.

Table 10—5

BAR/LNA MULTI-MEDIA SERVICE
CLASS/BRAND $

January - December 1988
QUARTERLY AND YEAR-TO-DATE ADVERTISING DOLLARS (000)

CLASS/COMPANY/BRAND	CLASS CODE	9-MEDIA TOTAL	LNA MAGAZINES	LNA NEWSPAPER SUPPLEMENTS	MEDIA RECORDS NEWSPAPERS	LNA OUTDOOR	BAR NETWORK TELEVISION	BAR SPOT TELEVISION	BAR SYNDICATED TELEVISION	BAR CABLE TV NETWORKS	BAR NETWORK RADIO
H313 CAR ELECTRONIC ENTERTAINMENT EQUIPMENT -------- CONTINUED --------											
FORD MOTOR CO											
FORD CAR STEREO SYSTEMS	H313										
Q2		2,326.8	--	--	--	--	--	--	--	--	2,326.8
Q4		2,114.2	--	--	--	--	--	--	--	--	2,114.2
88 YTD		4,441.0	--	--	--	--	--	--	--	--	4,441.0
87 YTD		3,955.0	--	--	--	--	--	--	--	--	3,955.0
FORD JBL AUDIO SYSTEMS	H313										
Q1		128.8	128.8	--	--	--	--	--	--	--	--
Q4		1,204.3	1,204.3	--	--	--	--	--	--	--	--
88 YTD		1,333.1	1,333.1	--	--	--	--	--	--	--	--
COMPANY TOTAL											
Q1		128.8	128.8	--	--	--	--	--	--	--	--
Q2		2,326.8	--	--	--	--	--	--	--	--	2,326.8
Q4		3,318.5	1,204.3	--	--	--	--	--	--	--	2,114.2
88 YTD		5,774.1	1,333.1	--	--	--	--	--	--	--	4,441.0
87 YTD		3,955.0	--	--	--	--	--	--	--	--	3,955.0
GENERAL MOTORS CORP											
DELCO CAR CD SYSTEM	H313										
Q4		39.3	39.3	--	--	--	--	--	--	--	--
88 YTD		39.3	39.3	--	--	--	--	--	--	--	--
87 YTD		624.8	624.8	--	--	--	--	--	--	--	--
DELCO GM/BOSE CAR STEREO SYSTEMS	H313										
Q4		37.9	37.9	--	--	--	--	--	--	--	--
88 YTD		37.9	37.9	--	--	--	--	--	--	--	--
87 YTD		254.8	254.8	--	--	--	--	--	--	--	--
DELCO STEREO CAR SYSTEMS	H313										
Q1		2,059.7	--	--	--	--	2,059.7	--	--	--	--
Q2		661.3	83.0	--	--	--	578.3	--	--	--	--
Q4		2,450.5	89.8	--	--	--	2,279.9	--	--	80.8	--
88 YTD		5,171.5	172.8	--	--	--	4,917.9	--	--	80.8	--
87 YTD		4,320.0	317.2	--	--	--	2,300.1	1,340.9	--	--	361.8
COMPANY TOTAL											
Q1		2,059.7	--	--	--	--	2,059.7	--	--	--	--
Q2		661.3	83.0	--	--	--	578.3	--	--	--	--
Q4		2,527.7	167.0	--	--	--	2,279.9	--	--	80.8	--
88 YTD		5,248.7	250.0	--	--	--	4,917.9	--	--	80.8	--
87 YTD		5,199.6	1,196.8	--	--	--	2,300.1	1,340.9	--	--	361.8
HARMAN INTERNATIONAL INDUSTRIES INC											
INFINITY CAR SPEAKERS	H313										
Q4		34.3	34.3	--	--	--	--	--	--	--	--
88 YTD		34.3	34.3	--	--	--	--	--	--	--	--
87 YTD		27.0	27.0	--	--	--	--	--	--	--	--
HITACHI LTD											
HITACHI CAR STEREO SYSTEM	H313										
Q4		40.8	40.8	--	--	--	--	--	--	--	--
88 YTD		40.8	40.8	--	--	--	--	--	--	--	--
INTERNATIONAL JENSEN INC											
JENSEN CAR STEREO SPEAKERS	H313										
Q1		35.1	35.1	--	--	--	--	--	--	--	--
Q4		129.7	129.7	--	--	--	--	--	--	--	--
88 YTD		164.8	164.8	--	--	--	--	--	--	--	--
87 YTD		244.4	244.4	--	--	--	--	--	--	--	--
JENSEN CAR STEREO SYSTEMS	H313										
Q1		36.7	36.7	--	--	--	--	--	--	--	--
Q3		201.0	201.0	--	--	--	--	--	--	--	--
Q4		114.6	114.6	--	--	--	--	--	--	--	--
88 YTD		352.3	352.3	--	--	--	--	--	--	--	--
87 YTD		311.6	311.6	--	--	--	--	--	--	--	--
JENSEN TRUCK STEREO SPEAKERS	H313										
Q2		17.6	17.6	--	--	--	--	--	--	--	--
Q3		11.4	11.4	--	--	--	--	--	--	--	--
Q4		20.7	20.7	--	--	--	--	--	--	--	--
---- CONTINUED ----											

FOOTNOTE: 1987 YTD EXPENDITURES INCLUDE ONLY THOSE BRANDS ACTIVE IN 1988.

The resulting BDI is an indication of the sales potential that exists for that brand in that market area. An example of this calculation is shown in Table 10–7. As with the index previously discussed, the higher the index number, the more market potential that exists. In this case the index number of 312 would indicate that this market has high potential for brand development.

3. *The Category Development Index* The **Category Development Index (CDI)** is computed in the same manner as the BDI, the only difference being that the CDI uses information regarding the product category (as opposed to the brand) in the numerator, as is represented in the following formula:

$$CDI = \frac{\text{Percentage of product category total sales in market}}{\text{Percentage of total U.S. population in market}} \times 100$$

The CDI then provides information with respect to potential for development of the total product category, rather than specific brands. When this information is combined with the BDI, a much more insightful promotional strategy may be developed. For example, consider the market potential for coffee in the United States. One might first look at how well the product category does in a specific market area, finding that in some areas such as Utah and Idaho the category potential is lower (see Table 10–8). In analyzing the BDI the company may find that relative to other brands in this area it may be doing very well or very poorly. This information can then be used in determin-

Table 10-6　**Survey of Buying Power Index**

Rhode Island

POPULATION—12/31/88

S&MM ESTIMATES

METRO AREA County City	Total Population (Thousands)	% Of U.S.	Median Age Of Pop.	% of Population by Age Group 18-24 Years	25-34 Years	35-49 Years	50 & Over	Households (Thousands)	Total Retail Sales ($000)	Food ($000)	Eating & Drinking Places ($000)	General Mdse. ($000)	Furniture/ Furnish/ Appliance ($000)	Auto-motive ($000)	Drug ($000)
PROVIDENCE–PAWTUCKET– WOONSOCKET	908.7	.3665	34.6	11.3	16.3	18.8	30.6	335.5	6,377,299	1,293,726	671,378	712,039	299,587	1,278,861	281,800
Bristol	48.3	.0195	35.8	10.8	14.8	20.5	30.5	16.4	218,371	51,025	27,548	6,355	4,441	57,307	9,427
Kent	164.7	.0664	34.4	9.4	17.1	20.6	28.3	59.7	1,468,544	235,913	126,681	317,843	64,208	311,936	52,130
Warwick	88.5	.0357	35.7	9.1	16.4	20.2	30.9	32.4	1,027,984	133,601	81,757	305,685	49,695	176,717	27,203
Providence	589.0	.2376	35.4	11.4	15.8	18.2	32.4	222.0	3,837,187	829,791	422,904	347,968	193,774	743,202	196,756
Cranston	74.5	.0300	38.9	9.6	15.5	18.7	36.4	27.8	501,721	103,405	57,104	22,945	28,719	93,190	39,640
East Providence	51.1	.0206	37.0	10.0	15.4	18.5	34.2	19.2	410,703	81,974	36,246	23,409	24,258	123,648	21,502
• Pawtucket	73.3	.0296	36.8	10.6	15.4	17.3	34.9	29.8	501,817	105,450	34,120	67,067	19,879	90,029	24,803
• Providence	159.8	.0645	33.3	15.2	16.5	15.6	31.5	63.1	1,014,724	196,812	132,818	91,301	71,721	194,121	37,384
• Woonsocket	45.4	.0183	34.6	9.9	15.7	16.7	32.6	17.6	349,453	73,686	27,450	42,400	17,761	76,730	16,690
Washington	106.7	.0430	31.3	13.7	18.7	19.3	23.8	37.4	853,197	176,997	94,245	39,873	37,164	165,416	23,487
SUBURBAN TOTAL	630.2	.2541	34.8	10.5	16.4	20.0	29.7	225.0	4,511,305	917,778	476,990	511,271	190,226	917,981	202,923
OTHER COUNTIES															
Newport	86.6	.0349	32.4	11.7	19.1	19.9	25.2	31.0	708,341	105,673	119,958	40,789	23,195	203,732	24,715
TOTAL METRO COUNTIES	908.7	.3665	34.6	11.3	16.3	18.8	30.6	335.5	6,377,299	1,293,726	671,378	712,039	299,587	1,278,861	281,800
TOTAL STATE	995.3	.4014	34.4	11.3	16.6	18.9	30.1	366.5	7,085,640	1,399,399	791,336	752,828	322,782	1,482,593	306,515

RETAIL SALES BY STORE GROUP—1988

EFFECTIVE BUYING INCOME—1988

METRO AREA County City	Total EBI ($000)	Median Hsld. EBI	% of Hslds. by EBI Group: (A) $10,000-$19,999 (B) $20,000-$34,999 (C) $35,000-$49,999 (D) $50,000 & Over A	B	C	D	Buying Power Index
PROVIDENCE–PAWTUCKET– WOONSOCKET	11,664,156	26,087	20.7	27.0	17.6	17.1	.3805
Bristol	629,280	28,115	20.5	28.2	16.7	20.6	.0182
Kent	2,218,539	29,549	17.8	29.0	20.6	19.0	.0764
Warwick	1,220,378	30,168	17.2	29.0	20.7	19.7	.0459
Providence	7,457,886	24,584	21.6	25.7	16.8	16.2	.2395
Cranston	1,056,928	28,790	19.3	26.8	18.9	20.5	.0325
East Providence	676,243	27,882	20.3	27.0	20.6	17.3	.0227
• Pawtucket	901,629	22,998	23.0	27.2	16.1	12.7	.0298

EFFECTIVE BUYING INCOME—1988

METRO AREA County City	Total EBI ($000)	Median Hsld. EBI	% of Hslds. by EBI Group: (A) $10,000-$19,999 (B) $20,000-$34,999 (C) $35,000-$49,999 (D) $50,000 & Over A	B	C	D	Buying Power Index
• Providence	1,862,333	18,850	25.2	23.5	12.2	11.9	.0619
• Woonsocket	510,946	21,582	23.3	25.4	15.3	12.0	.0184
Washington	1,358,451	27,774	20.3	30.3	18.1	18.0	.0464
SUBURBAN TOTAL	8,389,248	28,933	18.9	28.1	19.5	19.5	.2704
OTHER COUNTIES							
Newport	1,263,843	30,006	18.6	25.7	19.2	23.0	.0406
TOTAL METRO COUNTIES	11,664,156	26,087	20.7	27.0	17.6	17.1	.3805
TOTAL STATE	12,927,999	26,388	20.6	26.8	17.7	17.6	.4211

Source: *Sales & Marketing Management*, August 7, 1989.

ing how well a particular product category and a particular brand are performing and in determining what media weight (or quantity of advertising) would be required to gain additional market share, as shown in Table 10–9.

While the indexes just discussed provide important insights into the market potential for the firm's products and/or brands, it must be remembered that this infor-

Table 10-7　**Calculating BDI**

$$BDI = \frac{\text{Percentage of brand sales in South Atlantic Region}}{\text{Percentage of U.S. population in South Atlantic Region}} \times 100$$

$$= \frac{50}{16} \times 100$$

$$= 312$$

Table 10-8　**Combining CDI and BDI**

$$CDI = \frac{\text{Percentage of product category sales in Utah/Idaho}}{\text{Percentage of total U.S. population in Utah/Idaho}} \times 100$$

$$= \frac{1\%}{1\%} \times 100$$

$$= 100$$

$$BDI = \frac{\text{Percentage of total brand sales in Utah/Idaho}}{\text{Percentage of total U.S. population in Utah}} \times 100$$

$$= \frac{2\%}{1\%} \times 100$$

$$= 200$$

Table 10−9   Using BDI and CDI Indexes

	High BDI	Low BDI
High CDI	High market share Good market potential	Low market share Good market potential
Low CDI	High market share Monitor for sales decline	Low market share Poor market potential
High BDI and high CDI	This market usually represents good sales potential for both the product category and the brand.	
High BDI and low CDI	The category is not selling well, but the brand is; probably a good market to advertise in, but should be monitored for declining sales.	
Low BDI and high CDI	The product category shows high potential but the brand is not doing well; a determination as to reasons why is necessary.	
Low BDI and low CDI	Both the product category and the brand are not doing well; not likely to be a good place for advertising.	

Source: Adapted from Jack C. Sissors and Lincoln Bumba, *Advertising Media Planning*, 3rd ed. (Lincolnwood, Ill.: NTC Business Books, 1989), p. 155.

mation is supplemental to the overall strategy determined earlier in the promotional decision-making process. In fact, much of this information may have already been provided to the media planner. At the same time, it may be used more specifically by the media department in the determination of the media weights to assign to each particular area. This decision will ultimately affect the budget allocated to each area as well as other factors such as reach, frequency, and scheduling.

Establishing Media Objectives

Just as the situation analysis leads to the establishment of marketing and communications objectives, the media situation analysis should lead to the determination of specific media objectives. Keep in mind that the media objectives are not ends in themselves. Rather, they are designed for the purpose of leading to the attainment of communications and marketing objectives. As such, media objectives are the goals to be attained by the media program and should be limited to those that can be accomplished through media strategies. Examples of media objectives may include:

1. Use broadcast media to provide coverage of 80 percent of the target market over a six-month period
2. Reach 60 percent of the target audience at least three times over the same six-month period
3. Concentrate heaviest advertising in winter and spring, with lighter emphasis in summer and fall

Developing and Implementing Media Strategy

Having determined what is to be accomplished, efforts turn to consideration of *how* to achieve these objectives—that is, the development and implementation of media strategies. As noted, media strategies evolve directly from the actions required to meet objectives and involve the criteria presented in Table 10−10.

Developing a Media Mix

A wide variety of media and media vehicles are available to the advertiser. While it is possible that only one medium and/or vehicle might be employed, it is much more likely that a number of alternatives will be used. The objectives sought, the characteristics of the product or service, the size of the budget, and individual preferences are just some of the factors that might be taken into consideration in determining what combination of media will be used.

As an example, consider a promotional situation in which a product requires a visual demonstration to be communicated effectively. In this case, television might be the most effective medium. If, on the other hand, the promotional strategy calls for the use of coupons to stimulate trial, print media will be necessary.

By employing a media mix, advertisers are usually able to add more versatility to their media strategies, as each of the various media contributes its own distinct advantages (as will be demonstrated in succeeding chapters of this text). By combining media, it may be possible to increase coverage, reach, and frequency levels while also improving the likelihood of achieving overall communications and marketing goals.

Determining Target Market Coverage

The media planner will assume the responsibility for determining which target markets should receive the most media emphasis. (In the Denny's plan, this was determined to be adults ages 25 to 54 in Chicago, Houston, and Los Angeles—see "Media Objectives," Appendix B, pp. 315–16.) Developing media strategies involves a matching of the most appropriate media to this market by asking the question, "Through which media and media vehicles can I best get my message to prospective buyers?" The issue here is to get coverage of the market, as represented in Figure 10–3. As can be seen in this figure, the optimal goal would be to achieve coverage *b*—that is, to attain full market coverage.

The truth is that this is a very unlikely and overly optimistic scenario. In more realistic situations, conditions *c* or *d* are most likely to occur. In the former (*c*) the coverage of the media does not allow for coverage of the entire market, leaving some potential customers without exposure to the message. In the latter situation the marketer is faced with a problem of overexposure—defined as **waste circulation**—in which the coverage of the media exceeds the targeted audience. Waste circulation refers to the shaded area extending beyond the target audience. If this coverage reaches persons who are not sought as buyers, and who are not potential users, then this coverage is "wasted." (Keep in mind that this term is used to explain the coverage that reaches nonpotential buyers and/or users. One may not be part of the intended target market but for various other reasons may still be considered as potential—for example, those who may be buying the product as a gift for someone else.)

The goal of the media planner is to attempt to extend the coverage of the media to as many of the members of the target audience as possible while at the same time minimizing the amount of waste circulation. The typical situation usually involves trade-offs. Sometimes one will have to live with less coverage than is desired, whereas at other times coverage will have to include members not specifically targeted, as the media most likely to be effective may also expose others not sought. In this latter instance, waste circulation is justified based on the fact that the media employed are likely to be the most effective means of delivery available and that the cost of the waste circulation is exceeded by the value gained from the use of these media. (Notice in the Denny's plan, while not directly discussing waste circulation, the benefit of the coverage provided by network and spot television is addressed under "Plan Development," see Appendix B, p. 316.)

If you have ever watched a professional football game on television, you may have a good idea as to what it is we are referring to. When watching these games, you may have noticed a number of commercials for stock brokerage firms such as Dean Witter Reynolds and Shearson Lehman Hutton. It is obvious that not all viewers are candidates for stock market services and might constitute waste circulation. At the same time, a very high percentage of potential customers can be reached with this strategy, and the program is considered a good media buy because the ability to generate market coverage outweighs the disadvantages of high waste circulation.

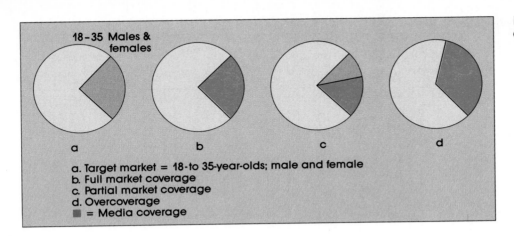

Figure 10–3   **Marketing Coverage Possibilities**

18–35 Males & females

a   b   c   d

a. Target market = 18-to 35-year-olds; male and female
b. Full market coverage
c. Partial market coverage
d. Overcoverage
■ = Media coverage

Table 10–11 represents an example of how information provided by Simmons can be used to match media to target markets. A profile of magazines read and television shows watched by skiers is shown. (You can practice the use of index numbers here!) From Table 10–11 you can see that *Ski, Skiing,* and *Tennis* magazines would likely be wise selections, whereas *Reader's Digest* and *Woman's Day* magazine or *True Story* would be less likely to lead to the desired exposures.

Determining Geographic Coverage

It probably comes as no surprise to you that snow skiing is much more popular in some areas of the country than in others. Thus, it would not be the wisest of strategies to promote skis in those areas where interest is not as high—unless, of course, it would be possible to generate an increase in interest. In our example, it may be possible to promote an interest in skiing in the Southeast. However, the likelihood that we would experience a notable increase in sales of ski equipment is not very high, given the market's distance from snow. As a result the objective of weighting certain geographic areas—known as **geographical weighting**—more than others makes sense, and the strategy of exerting more promotional efforts and dollars in these areas naturally follows. (See Denny's "Media Objectives," Appendix B, p. 316.)

Scheduling

Obviously, companies would like to keep their advertising in front of the consumer at all times as a constant reminder of the product and/or brand name. In reality, this is not possible for a variety of reasons (not the least of which is the budget!), nor may it always be necessary. The primary objective of *scheduling* is to time the promotional efforts so that they will coincide with the highest potential buying times. While for some products these times may not be easily identifiable, for others they are very obvious. Three scheduling methods available to the media planner are represented in Figure 10–4.

Continuity refers to a continuous pattern of advertising. Continuous may mean advertising every day, every week, or every month—the *key* is that a regular (continuous) pattern is developed with no gaps or no-advertising periods. Examples of such strategies might include advertising for food products, laundry detergents, or other products consumed on an ongoing basis without regard for seasonality.

A second method, **flighting,** employs a less regular schedule, with intermittent periods of advertising and nonadvertising. At some time periods, there may be heavier promotional expenditures, and at others there may be no advertising at all. Many banks, for example, spend no monies on advertising in the summer months, while maintaining advertising throughout the rest of the year. Snow skis are another example of a

Table 10–11 **Media Characteristics of Roller Skaters and Downhill Skiers**

	TOTAL U.S. '000	ROLLER SKATING A '000	B % DOWN	C ACROSS %	D INDX	5 OR MORE DAYS A '000	B % DOWN	C ACROSS %	D INDX	DOWNHILL SNOW SKIING A '000	B % DOWN	C ACROSS %	D INDX	5 OR MORE DAYS A '000	B % DOWN	C ACROSS %	D INDX
TOTAL	176250	7768	100.0	4.4	100	2421	100.0	1.4	100	7212	100.0	4.1	100	3126	100.0	1.8	100
OMNI	2779	**153	2.0	5.5	125	**67	2.8	2.4	176	*254	3.5	9.1	223	**82	2.6	3.0	166
1,001 HOME IDEAS	3799	*222	2.9	5.8	133	**43	1.8	1.1	82	**145	2.0	3.8	93	*72	2.3	1.9	107
OUTDOOR LIFE	7899	400	5.1	5.1	115	**95	3.9	1.2	88	360	5.0	4.6	111	*144	4.6	1.8	103
PARADE MAGAZINE	62303	2613	33.6	4.2	95	947	39.1	1.5	111	2800	38.8	4.5	110	1133	36.2	1.8	103
PARENTS	5799	376	4.8	6.5	147	*157	6.5	2.7	197	*361	5.0	6.2	152	**128	4.1	2.2	124
PEOPLE	26170	1598	20.6	6.1	139	533	22.0	2.0	148	1337	18.5	5.1	125	559	17.9	2.1	120
PERSONAL MEDIA GROUP (GROSS)	7577	336	4.3	4.4	101	**119	4.9	1.6	114	700	9.7	9.2	226	*220	7.0	2.9	164
PLAYBOY	9055	436	5.6	4.8	109	*107	4.4	1.2	86	488	6.8	5.4	132	*208	6.7	2.3	130
POPULAR MECHANICS	5548	**222	2.9	4.0	91	**100	4.1	1.8	131	*329	4.6	5.9	145	*199	6.4	3.6	202
POPULAR SCIENCE	4334	*298	3.8	6.9	156	**138	5.7	3.2	232	294	4.1	6.8	166	**111	3.6	2.6	144
PREVENTION	6251	*193	2.5	3.1	70	**40	1.7	0.6	47	*269	3.7	4.3	105	**125	4.0	2.0	113
PSYCHOLOGY TODAY	3117	*117	1.5	3.8	85	**53	2.2	1.7	124	309	4.3	9.9	242	**87	2.8	2.8	157
READER'S DIGEST	37829	1578	20.3	4.2	95	549	22.7	1.5	106	1408	19.5	3.7	91	624	20.0	1.6	93
REDBOOK	9847	639	8.2	6.5	147	*235	9.7	2.4	174	401	5.6	4.1	100	*157	5.0	1.6	90
ROAD & TRACK	3457	*196	2.5	5.7	129	**86	3.6	2.5	181	292	4.0	8.4	206	**110	3.5	3.2	179
RODALE'S ORGANIC GARDENING	1921	**42	0.5	2.2	50	**21	0.9	1.1	80	**29	0.4	1.5	37	**9	0.3	0.5	26
ROLLING STONE	5183	*228	2.9	4.4	100	**120	5.0	2.3	169	454	6.3	8.8	214	*194	6.2	3.7	211
SCIENTIFIC AMERICAN	1476	*69	0.9	4.7	106	**32	1.3	2.2	158	*161	2.2	10.9	267	**79	2.5	5.4	302
SELF	2880	*231	3.0	8.0	182	**75	3.1	2.6	190	*247	3.4	8.6	210	**74	2.4	2.6	145
SEVENTEEN	3901	*410	5.3	10.5	238	**166	6.9	4.3	310	*156	2.2	4.0	98	**68	2.2	1.7	98
SHAPE	1670	**143	1.8	8.6	194	**35	1.4	2.1	153	*165	2.3	9.9	241	*20	0.6	1.2	68
SKI	1377	**82	1.1	6.0	135	**3	0.1	0.2	16	664	9.2	48.2	+++	*286	9.1	20.8	+++
SKIING	1616	**119	1.5	7.4	167	**18	0.7	1.1	81	797	11.1	49.3	+++	*212	6.8	13.1	740
SMITHSONIAN	5515	*182	2.3	3.3	75	**54	2.2	1.0	71	525	7.3	9.5	233	*209	6.7	3.8	214
SOAP OPERA DIGEST	4481	*344	4.4	7.7	174	**93	3.8	2.1	151	**154	2.1	3.4	84	**80	2.6	1.8	101
SOUTHERN LIVING	6828	*343	4.4	5.0	114	**88	3.6	1.3	94	*234	3.2	3.4	84	**43	1.4	0.6	36
SPORT	2950	*201	2.6	6.8	155	**33	1.4	1.1	81	*173	2.4	5.9	143	**84	2.7	2.8	161
THE SPORTING NEWS	3144	**173	2.2	5.5	125	**18	0.7	0.6	42	*191	2.6	6.1	148	**81	2.6	2.6	145
SPORTS AFIELD	3852	**179	2.3	4.6	105	**68	2.8	1.8	129	*204	2.8	5.3	129	**91	2.9	2.4	133
SPORTS ILLUSTRATED	19029	1009	13.0	5.3	120	234	9.7	1.2	90	1231	17.1	6.5	158	470	15.0	2.5	139
STAR	11067	543	7.0	4.9	111	*203	8.4	1.8	134	*316	4.4	2.9	70	**115	3.7	1.0	59
SUNDAY MAGAZINE NETWORK	42840	1788	23.0	4.2	95	489	20.2	1.1	83	2104	29.2	4.9	120	852	27.3	2.0	112
SUNSET	3183	**136	1.8	4.3	97	**47	1.9	1.5	107	*147	2.0	4.6	113	*50	1.6	1.6	89
TV GUIDE	42061	1859	23.9	4.4	100	565	23.3	1.3	98	1609	22.3	3.8	93	623	19.9	1.5	84
TENNIS	1354	**47	0.6	3.5	79	**11	0.5	0.8	59	*208	2.9	15.4	375	**147	4.7	10.9	612
TIME	23476	1159	14.9	4.9	112	359	14.8	1.5	111	1598	22.2	6.8	166	712	22.8	3.0	171
TRAVEL & LEISURE	2059	**47	0.6	2.3	52	**14	0.6	0.7	50	**168	2.3	8.2	199	**95	3.0	4.6	260
TRUE STORY	3858	*194	2.5	5.0	114	**78	3.2	2.0	147	**61	0.8	1.6	39	**6	0.2	0.2	9
USA TODAY	5253	334	4.3	6.4	144	**87	3.6	1.7	121	379	5.3	7.2	176	*189	6.0	3.6	203
USA WEEKEND	26292	1135	14.6	4.3	98	277	11.4	1.1	77	1300	18.0	4.9	121	585	18.7	2.2	125
U.S. NEWS & WORLD REPORT	10831	413	5.3	3.8	87	**95	3.9	0.9	64	657	9.1	6.1	148	339	10.8	3.1	176
US	4398	328	4.2	7.5	169	**116	4.8	2.6	192	*290	4.0	6.6	161	**64	2.0	1.5	82
VANITY FAIR	1417	**41	0.5	2.9	66	**23	1.0	1.6	118	**143	2.0	10.1	247	**52	1.7	3.7	207
VOGUE	4969	*221	2.8	4.4	101	**113	4.7	2.3	166	449	6.2	9.0	221	*180	5.8	3.6	204
WALL STREET JOURNAL	4603	*188	2.4	4.1	93	**37	1.5	0.8	59	401	5.6	8.7	213	*224	7.2	4.9	274
WEIGHT WATCHERS	2520	**117	1.5	4.6	105	**49	2.0	1.9	142	**51	0.7	2.0	49	**31	1.0	1.2	69
WOMAN'S DAY	14953	846	10.9	5.7	128	295	12.2	2.0	144	485	6.7	3.2	79	*208	6.7	1.4	78
WOMAN'S WORLD	5148	*256	3.3	5.0	113	**48	2.0	0.9	68	**154	2.1	3.0	73	**75	2.4	1.5	82
THE WORKBASKET	2438	**73	0.9	3.0	68	**24	1.0	1.0	72	**84	1.2	3.4	84	**0	0.0	0.0	0
WORKBENCH	1792	**104	1.3	5.8	132	**32	1.3	1.8	130	**88	1.2	4.9	120	**28	0.9	1.6	88
WORKING MOTHER	1731	**153	2.0	8.8	201	**43	1.8	2.5	181	**90	1.2	5.2	127	**26	0.8	1.5	85
WORKING WOMAN	2536	**174	2.2	6.9	156	**31	1.3	1.2	89	**116	1.6	4.6	112	**46	1.5	1.8	102
WRK MOTHER/WRK WOMAN (GROSS)	4268	*327	4.2	7.7	174	**74	3.1	1.7	126	*206	2.9	4.8	118	**72	2.3	1.7	95
DAILY NEWSPAPERS																	
NET ONE DAY REACH	113178	4621	59.5	4.1	93	1386	57.2	1.2	89	5064	70.2	4.5	109	2200	70.4	1.9	110
READ ONLY ONE	88945	3628	46.7	4.1	93	1089	45.0	1.2	89	3659	50.7	4.1	101	1496	47.9	1.7	95
READ TWO OR MORE	24233	993	12.8	4.1	93	297	12.3	1.2	89	1405	19.5	5.8	142	703	22.5	2.9	164
WEEKEND/SUNDAY NEWSPAPERS																	
NET ONE DAY REACH	112825	4966	63.9	4.4	100	1467	60.6	1.3	95	5432	75.3	4.8	118	2277	72.8	2.0	114
READ ONLY ONE	98987	4332	55.8	4.4	99	1213	50.1	1.2	89	4543	63.0	4.6	112	1897	60.7	1.9	108
READ TWO OR MORE	13838	635	8.2	4.6	104	*254	10.5	1.8	134	889	12.3	6.4	157	381	12.2	2.8	155
OUTDOOR																	
100 SHWG – 30 DAY AV FREQ	28.52	33.79				32.23				29.99				27.62			
30 DAY REACH	154720	7263	93.5	4.7	107	2257	93.2	1.5	106	6506	90.2	4.2	103	2858	91.4	1.8	104
50 SHWG – 30 DAY AV FREQ	15.03	17.78				16.77				15.88				14.45			
30 DAY REACH	147029	6912	89.0	4.7	107	2177	89.9	1.5	108	6164	85.5	4.2	102	2743	87.7	1.9	105
25 SHWG – 30 DAY AV FREQ	8.17	9.48				8.88				8.52				7.65			
30 DAY REACH	135300	6499	83.7	4.8	109	2062	85.2	1.5	111	5766	80.0	4.3	104	2599	83.1	1.9	108
CABLE TV: HOME WIRED	78395	3558	45.8	4.5	103	1005	41.5	1.3	93	3671	50.9	4.7	114	1585	50.7	2.0	114
HOME NOT WIRED	97855	4210	54.2	4.3	98	1415	58.4	1.4	105	3541	49.1	3.6	88	1541	49.3	1.6	89
HAVE PAY CABLE	40491	2203	28.4	5.4	123	676	27.9	1.7	122	2075	28.8	5.1	125	835	26.7	2.1	116

*Projection relatively unstable because of sample base—use with caution.
**Number of cases too small for reliability—shown for consistency only.
†††The symbol used when there is a four-digit index.

Source: Simmons Market Research Bureau, Inc., 1988.

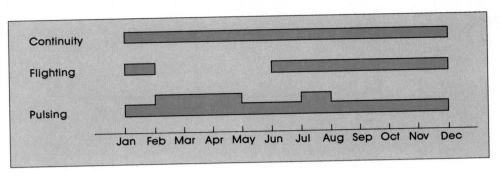

Figure 10–4 **Three Methods of Promotional Scheduling**

seasonal product that might be advertised very heavily between October and April; less in May, August, and September; and not at all in June or July.

The final method, **pulsing,** is actually a combination of the first two. In a pulsing strategy, continuity is maintained, but at certain times a heavier emphasis on promotional efforts is required. An example of a pulsing strategy is that used in the automobile industry, where advertising continues throughout the year but may increase at certain times like April (income tax refund check time), September (new models being brought out), and the end of the model year. Again, the scheduling strategy will depend on the objectives, buying cycles, and the budget, among other factors. It should also be understood that there are certain advantages and disadvantages to each scheduling method, as shown in Table 10–12. (Notice that in the Denny's media plan, flighting is recommended as the best strategy; again, see Appendix B, p. 322.)

Determining Reach versus Frequency

You probably noticed that the topic heading for this section included the word *versus.* There is a reason for this: Given that advertisers face a variety of objectives, and given that they have budget constraints, the decision is usually one of having to trade off reach and frequency. The issue becomes one of determining whether to advertise to have the message be seen or heard by more persons or by a smaller number of persons more often. The information necessary to make this decision becomes one of how much reach and frequency are needed, respectively. Let us explore these issues.

Table 10–12 **Characteristics of Scheduling Methods**

Method	Characteristics
Continuity	
Advantages	Serves as a constant reminder to the consumer Covers the entire buying cycle Allows for media priorities (quantity discounts, preferred locations, etc.)
Disadvantages	Higher costs Potential for overexposure Limited media allocation possible
Flighting	
Advantages	Cost efficiency of advertising only during purchase cycles May allow for inclusion of more than one medium or vehicle with limited budgets Weighting may offer more exposure and advantage over competitors
Disadvantages	Increased likelihood of wearout Lack of awareness, interest, retention of promotional message during nonscheduled times Vulnerability to competitive efforts during nonscheduled periods
Pulsing	
Advantages	All of the same as the previous two methods
Disadvantages	Not required for seasonal products (or other cyclical products)

Figure 10–5 **Who's Still There to Watch the Ads?**

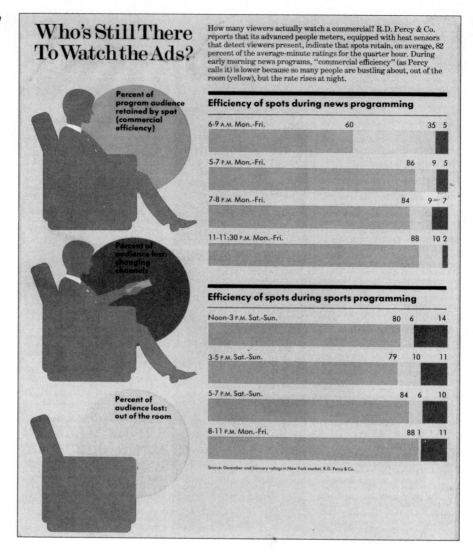

Who's Still There To Watch the Ads?

How many viewers actually watch a commercial? R.D. Percy & Co. reports that its advanced people meters, equipped with heat sensors that detect viewers present, indicate that spots retain, on average, 82 percent of the average-minute ratings for the quarter hour. During early morning news programs, "commercial efficiency" (as Percy calls it) is lower because so many people are bustling about, out of the room (yellow), but the rate rises at night.

Percent of program audience retained by spot (commercial efficiency)

Percent of audience lost: changing channels

Percent of audience lost: out of the room

Efficiency of spots during news programming

6-9 A.M. Mon.-Fri.	60	35	5
5-7 P.M. Mon.-Fri.	86	9	5
7-8 P.M. Mon.-Fri.	84	9	7
11-11:30 P.M. Mon.-Fri.	88	10	2

Efficiency of spots during sports programming

Noon-3 P.M. Sat.-Sun.	80	6	14
3-5 P.M. Sat.-Sun.	79	10	11
5-7 P.M. Sat.-Sun.	84	6	10
8-11 P.M. Mon.-Fri.	88	1	11

Source: December and January ratings in New York market, R.D. Percy & Co.

How Much Reach Is Necessary?   Thinking back to the hierarchies discussed in Chapter 5, you will recall that the first stage of each of the models requires awareness of the product and/or brand. As a hierarchy, the more persons aware, the more persons likely to be at each of the subsequent stages. Achieving awareness requires reach— that is, exposing potential buyers to the message. For new brands or products, a very high level of reach is to be sought, as the objective is to have as many persons as are potential buyers aware of the new entry. At the same time, high reach is also desired at later stages of the hierarchy. For example, at the trial stage of the adoption hierarchy, a promotions strategy employing cents-off coupons or free samples might be employed. An objective of the marketer will be to reach a large number of people with these samples, in an attempt to make consumers aware of the product, get them to try it and develop favorable attitudes toward it. (In turn, these attitudes might lead to purchase.)

The problem arises in the fact that there is no known way of determining how much reach is required to achieve levels of awareness, attitude change, or buying intentions, nor can we be sure that an advertisement placed in a vehicle will actually reach the intended audience. (There has been some research with respect to the former of these problems, and we will allude to this research shortly when we discuss effective reach.)

For example, if you were to buy advertising time on the TV program *60 Minutes,* does this mean that everyone who is tuned to this program will see the ad? The answer is, of course, no, as many will leave the room, be distracted during the commercial, and so on, as shown in Figure 10–5. (The figure also provides a good example of the difference between reach and coverage.) Likewise, if I expose everyone in my target group to the message one time, will this be sufficient to create a 100 percent level of awareness? The answer again is no, as research indicates that one exposure is not likely to be enough. This then leads us to the next question: What *frequency* of exposure is necessary for the ad to be seen and to have an impact?

What Frequency Level Is Needed?   Frequency of exposure was discussed in Chapter 4 when it was indicated that the number of times a person would need to be exposed to a message before that message would have an effect was approximately three.[3] With respect to its use in media planning, *frequency* carries a slightly different meaning. (Remember when we said that one of the problems in media planning was that often terms take on different meanings?) In the latter instance, *frequency* refers to the number of times one is exposed to the media vehicle and not necessarily the ad itself. While one study has estimated that the actual audience to the commercial may be as much as 30 percent lower than that exposed to the program, all researchers are not in agreement on this figure.[4] For example, Figure 10–5 demonstrated that depending on the program this number may range from a low of 12 percent to as high as 40 percent. At the same time, most advertisers do agree that a 1:1 exposure ratio does not exist. So, for example, while your ad may be placed in a certain vehicle, the fact that someone has been exposed to that vehicle does not ensure that your ad has been seen. As a result the frequency level expressed in the media plan is not the same as that of actual ad exposure and, in fact, is an overstatement of the actual level of exposure to the ad that might be expected. This overstatement has led some media buyers to refer to the reach of the media vehicle as "opportunities to see" an ad rather than actual exposure to the ad itself.

Because the advertiser has no sure way of knowing whether exposure to a vehicle results in exposure to the ad, the media and advertisers have adopted a compromise position and agree that one exposure to the vehicle will constitute reach, given that this exposure must take place for the viewer even to have an "opportunity to see" the ad. Thus, it is this figure that is used in the calculation of reach and frequency levels. This compromise does not, however, provide an answer to the question that is raised in respect to the level of frequency that is required to make an impact. And, as has been stated, the exact number is not known. The creativity of the ad, the involvement of the receiver, noise, and a variety of other intervening factors confound any attempts to make this precise a determination.

At this point we are fairly certain that the question in your mind must be: "If nobody knows this stuff, how do they make these decisions?" It is a very good question, and the truth is that the decisions are not always made on hard data—remember, we said that there is some creativity to media planning. Or, as noted by Joseph Ostrow, executive vice president–director, Communications Services with Young and Rubicam, "Establishing frequency goals for an advertising campaign is a mix of art and science but with a definite bias toward art."[5] Let us first examine the process involved in setting reach and frequency objectives and then discuss the logic of each.

The Process of Establishing Reach and Frequency Objectives   As you might expect, it is possible to be exposed to more than one media vehicle with an ad, resulting in repetition (frequency). For example, if one ad is placed on one television show one time, the number of persons exposed would be the reach. Now let us assume that the ad was placed on two shows. The total number exposed once is **unduplicated reach.** At the same time, some people would see the ad twice. Thus, the reach of the two shows, as depicted in Figure 10–6, would include a number of persons who were reached by each show *(C).* This overlap in reach is referred to as **duplicated reach.**

Both unduplicated and duplicated reach figures are important. In respect to the

Figure 10–6 **Representation of Reach and Frequency**

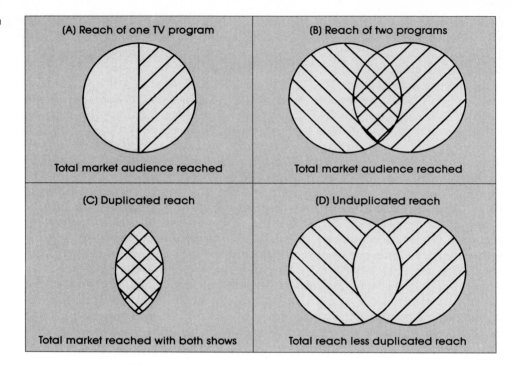

former, an indication of potential new exposures is provided, whereas duplicated reach provides an estimate of frequency. Most media buys are likely to include both forms of reach. Let us consider an example.

A measure of potential reach in the broadcast industry is the television (or radio) **program rating.** While this number is expressed as a percentage figure, an estimate of the total number of homes reached could easily be calculated by taking this percentage number times the number of homes with television sets. For example, if there are 90.4 million homes with television sets in the United States and the program has a rating of 30, then the calculation would be 0.30 × 90.4, or 27.12 million homes. (We will go into much more detail on ratings and other broadcast terms in Chapter 11.)

To estimate the reach obtained through a media buy, the media buyer will typically use a numerical indicator determined by gross ratings points (GRPs). A discussion of the concept of gross ratings points and an example of its use follows.

Using Gross Ratings Points   When the marketer wants to know how many potential audience members might be exposed to a series of commercials, he or she uses the program rating described earlier. The average number of times that the home is reached during this period of time is the frequency of exposure. A summary measure can be used that combines these two figures and provides the media buyer with an indication of the weight that the schedule will deliver. This number is a commonly used reference point known as **gross ratings points,** or **GRPs.** The formula used in calculating GRPs is

$$GRP = Reach \times frequency$$

GRPs are based on the total audience that might be reached by an advertising buy and uses a duplicated reach estimate.*

*A figure found to be more useful by advertisers is that of **target ratings points (TRPs).** TRPs refer to the number of persons in the primary target audience that the media buy will reach—and the number of times. This figure is more useful in determining the efficiency of the advertising in that it does not include waste circulation. However, it is calculated in the same manner as GRPs and is still subject to the same limitations. In the remainder of this chapter we will use only the term *GRPs,* except in specific instances where the distinction is necessary.

Figure 10–7 **Estimates of Reach for Network TRPs**

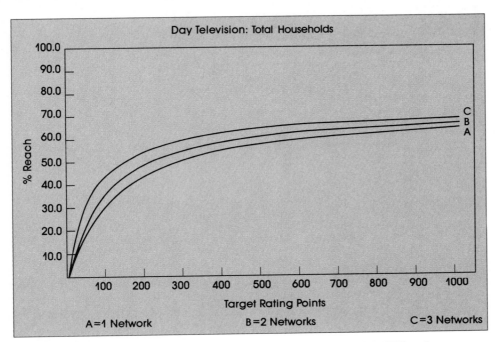

Source: Foote, Cone & Belding, *TV Reach/Frequency Reference Manual* (New York, 1985), p. 4.

Given that GRPs are not a direct measure of actual reach, the questions that must be asked by the advertiser are, How many GRPs are needed to attain a certain reach? and How do these GRPs translate into effective reach? For example, how many GRPs must one purchase to attain an unduplicated reach of 50 percent, and what is the frequency of exposure this schedule will deliver? The following example may help you to understand how this process works.

First, it is necessary to understand what these ratings points represent. A purchase of 100 GRPs might mean 100 percent of the market is exposed once or 50 percent of the market is exposed twice or 25 percent of the market is exposed four times, and so on. As you can see, this information must be more specific for the marketer to use effectively. In respect to the first question (How many GRPs are necessary?), the manager needs to know how many members of his or her intended audience the schedule actually reaches. The chart shown in Figure 10–7 is useful in making this determination.

In referring to Figure 10–7, you can see that a purchase of 100 TRPs on one network would yield an estimated reach of 32 percent of the total households in the target market. This figure would climb to 37.2 percent if two networks were used, and 44.5 percent on three. Working backward through the formula for GRPs (TRPs), the estimate of frequency of exposure—3.125, 2.688, and 2.247, respectively—demonstrates the trade-off between reach and frequency levels that would be attained.

In February 1987, Seven-Up purchased 1,400 GRPs in a four-week period to introduce a new advertising campaign. This purchase employed 189 separate TV spots and was estimated to reach 96 percent of the target audience an average of 14 times. To determine if this was a wise media buy, we need to know the answer to the second question—was this an effective reach figure? Certainly, reaching 96 percent of the target market is attractive. But what about the frequency level? Why was this number so high? And was it likely to be effective? In other words, does this level of GRPs affect awareness, attitudes, and purchase intentions?

A number of researchers have explored this issue. David Berger, vice president and director of research at the Foote, Cone & Belding advertising agency, has determined that 2,500 GRPs are likely to lead to approximately a 70 percent probability of high awareness, whereas 1,000 to 2,500 would be approximately 33 percent likely, and

Table 10–13   **The Effects of Reach and Frequency**

1. One exposure of an advertisement to a target group within a purchase cycle has little or no effect in all but a minority of circumstances.
2. Since one exposure is usually ineffective, the central goal of productive media planning should be to place emphasis on enhancing frequency rather than reach.
3. The weight of evidence suggests strongly that an exposure frequency of two within a purchase cycle is an effective level.
4. Beyond three exposures within a brand purchase cycle or over a period of four or even eight weeks, increasing frequency continues to build advertising effectiveness at a decreasing rate but with no evidence of decline.
5. Although there are general principles with respect to frequency of exposure and its relationship to advertising effectiveness, differential effects by brand are equally important.
6. Nothing we have seen suggests that frequency response principles or generalizations vary by medium.
7. The frequency of exposure data from this review strongly suggest that wearout is not a function of too much frequency per se; it is more of a creative or copy problem.

Source: Adapted from Michael J. Naples, *Effective Frequency: The Relationship between Frequency and Advertising Effectiveness* (New York: Association of National Advertisers, 1979).

less than 1,000 would result in almost no likelihood.[6] David Olson obtained similar results and further showed that as awareness increased, trial of the product would also increase, although at a significantly slower rate.[7] In both cases it was evident that a high number of GRPs would be required to make an impact.

Table 10–13 presents a summary of the effects than can be expected at different levels of exposure, based on a review of research in this area. As this table shows, there are a number of factors that may be operating, and direct relationships may be difficult to establish.[8]

In addition to those results shown in Table 10–13, Ostrow has shown that while the number of repetitions increases awareness rapidly, much less of an impact is likely for attitudinal and behavioral responses.[9]

Getting back to our Seven-Up example, you can imagine how expensive it had to be to purchase 1,400 gross ratings points on television. Now that you have additional information, we will ask again, "Was this a good buy?"

Determining Effective Reach   Given that the marketer is faced with a budget constraint, he or she must decide whether it is in the best interest to increase reach at the expense of frequency or vice versa, that is, increase the frequency of exposure but to a smaller audience. As shown, there are a number of factors that will influence this decision. For example, a new product or brand introduction would attempt to maximize reach—particularly unduplicated reach—to create awareness in as many persons as possible as quickly as possible. At the same time, if the product were a high-involvement product, or one whose benefits may not be very obvious, a certain level of frequency will be necessary to achieve effective reach.

Effective reach represents the percent of a vehicle's audience reached at each effective frequency increment. This concept is based on the assumption that one exposure to an ad may not be sufficient to convey the desired message. As we saw earlier, the exact number of exposures necessary for the ad to make an impact is not known with certainty, although advertisers have settled on a minimum of three as the required number. Thus, effective reach is shown in the shaded area in Figure 10–8 in the range of 3 to 10 expsures. Below 3 exposures is considered insufficient reach while beyond 10 is considered excessive exposure and thus ineffective reach.

Since they do not know precisely the number of times the viewer will actually be exposed, advertisers will typically purchase GRPs that lead to a frequency of exposure greater than three in an attempt to ensure the likelihood of effective reach. (This use of effective reach is demonstrated very well in Denny's "Television Daypart Mix Analysis"; see Appendix B, pp. 317–18.)

Determining effective reach is further compounded by the fact that when calculating GRPs, advertisers use a figure that they refer to as **average frequency.** *Average*

Figure 10–8 **Graph of Effective Reach**

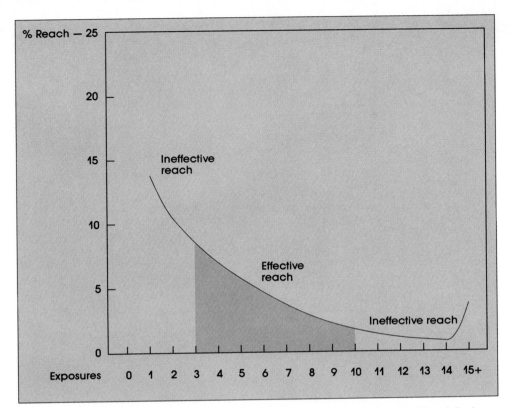

Note: The audience in the 3 to 10 exposure (shaded) areas would be the effective reach. Although the 1 exposure reach was 14.3 percent, the effective reach (3 to 10 exposures) would range from 9.4 to 2.2 percent, noncumulatively, or 9.4 to 40.6 percent cumulatively (9.4 plus 7.7 plus 6.2, etc., equals 40.6).
Source: J. Walter Thompson, *The Concept of Effective Reach* (New York, November 6, 1973), p. 6.

frequency refers to the number of times the average household reached by a media schedule is exposed to the vehicle over a specified period of time. The problem with using this figure can easily be seen by examining the scenario below:

Consider the following media buy in which:

50 percent of audience is reached 1 time
30 percent of audience is reached 5 times
20 percent of audience is reached 10 times

Average frequency = 4.0

In this media buy the average frequency is 4.0, which is slightly over the number established as effective. Yet at the same time a full 50 percent of the audience had only a one-time exposure. Thus, the average frequency number can be misleading, and including this number in calculations of GRPs might result in underexposing the audience.

Even though the use of GRPs has its problems, this does not mean that it cannot provide useful information to the marketer. It has been established that a certain level of GRPs is necessary to achieve awareness and that increases in GRPs are likely to lead to more exposures and/or to more repetitions—both of which are necessary to have an effect on higher-order objectives. Perhaps the best advice for purchasing GRPs is offered by Ostrow. He recommends the following strategies.[10]

1. Instead of using average frequency, the marketer should decide what minimum frequency goal is needed to reach the advertising objectives effectively and then maximize reach at that frequency level.
2. To determine effective frequency one must consider three elements including marketing factors, message factors, and media factors.

Table 10—14   **Factors Important in Determining Frequency Levels**

Marketing Factors

- *Brand history* Is the brand a new brand or an established one? New brands generally require higher frequency levels than do established brands.
- *Brand share* An inverse relationship exists between brand share and frequency. The higher the brand share, the lower the frequency levels required.
- *Brand loyalty* An inverse relationship exists between loyalty and frequency levels, as the higher the loyalty, the lower the level of frequency required.
- *Purchase cycles* Shorter purchasing cycles require higher frequency levels to maintain top-of-mind awareness.
- *Usage cycle* Products used on a daily basis (or more) will quickly be used and need to be replaced. A higher level of frequency is desired.
- *Competitive share of voice* Higher frequency levels are required when a high level of competitive noise exists and when the goal is to meet or beat competitors.
- *Target group* The ability of the target group to learn and to retain messages has a direct effect on frequency.

Message or Creative Factors

- *Message complexity* The more simple the message, the less frequency required.
- *Message uniqueness* The more unique the message, the lower the frequency level required.
- *New versus continuing campaigns* New campaigns require higher levels of frequency to register the message.
- *Image versus product sell* Creating image requires higher levels of frequency than does a specific product sell.
- *Message variation* Single messages require less frequency, whereas a variety of messages will require more.
- *Wearout* Higher frequency may lead to wearout. This effect must be tracked and used to evaluate frequency levels.
- *Advertising units* Larger units of advertising require less frequency than smaller ones to get the message across.

Media Factors

- *Clutter* The more advertising that appears in the media used, the more the need for frequency to break through the clutter.
- *Editorial environment* An ad that is consistent with the editorial environment will require lower levels of frequency to communicate.
- *Attentiveness* The higher the level of attention achieved by the media vehicle, the less frequency is required. Low attention—getting media will require more repetitions.
- *Scheduling* Continuous scheduling requires less frequency than does flighting or pulsing.
- *Number of media used* The lower the number of media used, the lower the level of frequency required.
- *Repeat exposures* Media that allow for more repeat exposures—for example, monthly magazines—require less frequency.

Source: Joseph W. Ostrow, ''Setting Frequency Levels: An Art or a Science?'' *Marketing and Media Decisions,* 1987, pp. 9–11.

A summary of the factors cited in the second recommendation are shown in Table 10–14.

In summary, you can see that the reach versus frequency decision—while extremely critical—is a very difficult one to make. A number of factors must be taken into consideration, and concrete rules do not always apply. The result is a decision that many times is ''more of an art than a science.''

Considering Creative Aspects and Mood

The context of the medium in which the advertisement is to be placed may also affect viewers' perceptions. Given a specific creative strategy, certain media may be required to operationalize that creativity. For example, television—because it provides both sight and sound—may be more effective in generating emotions than other media, and magazines may create different perceptions than will newspapers. In developing a

Promotional Perspective   10-2

Creativity Through Clay

In 1986 the California Raisin Advisory Board reviewed its research on consumers' perceptions of raisins. Their results demonstrated that while people liked raisins and knew that they were good for you, their feelings toward the dried grapes smacked of ambivalence. The advisory board told its ad agency that it needed to "bring life" to the raisins.

The ad agency—Foote, Cone & Belding—hired Will Vinton Productions, Inc. from Portland, Oregon, to help them. Vinton's firm was responsible for the origination of Gumby, a cartoon character made of clay that was popular on television in the 1960s.

Vinton used his obviously vivid imagination to construct clay raisins, place them in a conga line with sneakers, and have them dance to the tune "I Heard It Through the Grapevine." How successful was he? Well, consider this:

- The telephones were flooded with calls from TV viewers to find out when the next commercial would be aired—they did not want to miss it.
- Magazines, newspapers, and news programs carried features about the campaign.

- One lady wrote in to say it was the best thing she had ever seen on television.
- Another wrote in to say that it was the only commercial on television that he did not fast forward—and that he was a raisin-eater again.
- Kids all over the country were doing the "Raisin Shuffle."
- A raisin fan club was started and still going strong two years later.

In addition to the raisin account, Vinton's claymation landed Kentucky Fried Chicken, Domino's Pizza, Alka-Seltzer, Nike, and Cap'n Crunch and increased his business to $3 million a year. Domino's research indicates that the clay "NOID" has dramatically improved its image, and ad recall is up significantly.

The ability to generate emotion is the key ingredient to the clay characters and obviously leads to some effective advertising. None of this would have been possible in any other medium but television.

Sources: "You've Come a Long Way, Gumby," *Business Week*, December 4, 1986, p. 74; "Cue the Raisins," *San Diego Union*, November 9, 1986, sec. 1, p. 1.

media strategy, both *creativity and mood factors* must be considered. Let us examine each in more detail.

Creative Aspects   A number of cases exist that demonstrate that it is possible to increase significantly the success of a product through a strong creative campaign. At the same time, to implement this creativity it is necessary to employ a medium that will support such a strategy. For example, the use of claymation, discussed in Promotional Perspective 10–2, required television as a vehicle to be successful. Likewise, the print campaign of Obsession cologne, an ad for which was shown as Figure 4–1, used print media to communicate its desired message effectively.

Mood   Certain media are more or less effective in enhancing the creativity of a message because these media create a mood that carries over to the communication itself. For example, think about the mood created by the following magazines: *Gourmet, Skiing, Travel,* and *House Beautiful.* Each of these special interest vehicles brings the reader into a particular mood. The promotion of fine wines, ski boots, luggage, and home products are enhanced by this mood. As a further example, think about the different image that might be created for your product if you advertised it in these media:

The New York Times versus *The National Enquirer*
Architectural Digest versus *Reader's Digest*
A highly rated prime-time TV show versus an old rerun

As noted, the message may require a specific medium and a certain media vehicle to achieve its objectives. Likewise, certain media and vehicles themselves have images that in turn may carry over to the perceptions of messages placed within them.

Flexibility

To have an effective media strategy a degree of *flexibility* must be included. Because of the rapidly changing marketing environment, strategies may need to be modified. If the plan has not built in some flexibility, opportunities may be lost and/or the company may not be able to address adequately threats that develop. This need for flexibility may result from

1. *Market opportunities* Sometimes a market opportunity may arise that the advertiser may wish to take advantage of. For example, the development of a new advertising medium may offer an opportunity that was not previously available for communicating information about a product or service.

2. *Market threats* Occasions may arise in which internal or external factors may pose a threat to the firm, and a change in media strategy is dictated. For example, a competitor may alter its media strategy to gain an edge. Failure to respond to this challenge may create problems for the firm.

3. *Availability of media* Sometimes a desired medium (or vehicle) is not available to the marketer. This may occur owing to the fact that the medium does not reach a particular target segment or because there is no longer any time or space available in that medium. For example, in the former instance, there are still some areas of this country where certain media do not reach. In the latter, while the media may be available, limited advertising time or space may have already been sold or cutoff dates for entry may have passed. Alternative vehicles or media may then have to be considered.

4. *Changes in media or media vehicles* A change in the medium or in a particular vehicle may necessitate change in the media strategy employed. For example, the advent of cable television opened a new opportunity for message delivery. Likewise, a drop in ratings or a change in editorial format may lead the advertiser to use different programs or print alternatives.

Each of these factors requires that the media strategy be developed with a degree of flexibility that allows the manager to adapt to specific market situations.

Budget Considerations

It is obvious that one of the more important decisions in the development of media strategy is that of cost estimating. The value of any strategy can be determined by how well it is able to deliver the message to the audience with the lowest cost and the least amount of waste. We have already explored a number of other factors—such as reach, frequency, and availability—that will impact this decision. Given these factors, it is the goal of the marketer to arrive at the optimal delivery by balancing cost with each of these. (Once again, Denny's "Television Cost Analysis" demonstrates how this issue is addressed; see Appendix B, pp. 318–20.) As will be seen in the following discussion, understanding and using cost figures may not be as easy as it first seems.

Cost Bases Advertising and promotional costs can be categorized in two ways. The **absolute cost** of the medium or vehicle is the actual total cost that would be required to place the message. For example, a full-page color advertisement in *Newsweek* magazine would cost approximately $91,500.00. **Relative cost** refers to the relationship between the price paid for advertising time or space and the size of the audience delivered and is used to compare media vehicles. Relative costs are important because the manager must try to optimize audience delivery within the constraints of the budget. Thus, given that a number of alternatives are available for delivering the message, an evaluation of the relative costs associated with these choices must be made. The way that media costs are provided and problems in comparing these costs across media often make such evaluations difficult. Let us examine these in more detail.

Table 10–15   Cost per Thousand Computations—*Time* versus *Newsweek*

	Time	*Newsweek*
Per page cost	$98,500	$91,500
Circulation	4 million	3.5 million
Calculation of CPM	$\dfrac{\$98,500 \times 1,000}{4,000,000}$	$\dfrac{\$91,500 \times 1,000}{3,500,000}$
CPM	$24.62	$26.14

Determining relative costs of media   To evaluate alternatives, advertisers must compare the relative costs of media as well as vehicles within these media. Unfortunately, the broadcast, print, and out-of-home media do not always provide the same cost breakdowns, nor necessarily do vehicles within the print media. Following are the cost bases used.

1. *Cost per thousand* For years the magazine industry has provided cost breakdowns on the basis of **cost per thousand** (CPM) people reached. The formula used for making this computation is

$$\text{Cost per thousand (CPM)} = \frac{\text{Cost of ad space (absolute cost)} \times 1,000}{\text{Circulation}}$$

Table 10–15 provides an example of this computation for two alternative vehicles within the same medium—*Time* and *Newsweek*—and shows that (all other things being equal) *Time* is a more cost-effective buy, even though the absolute cost is higher. (We will come back to that "all other things being equal" in a moment.)

2. *Cost per ratings point* The broadcast media provide a different comparative cost figure, referred to as **cost per ratings point (CPRP),** based on the following formula:

$$\text{Cost per ratings point (CPRP)} = \frac{\text{Cost of commercial time}}{\text{Program rating}}$$

An example of this calculation is shown in Table 10–16, which indicates that "Murder She Wrote" would be more cost-effective.

3. *Milline rate* For newspapers the cost-efficiency formula is based on the **milline rate,** which is the cost per line of space per million circulation. As shown in Table 10–17, the cost of advertising in the *Pittsburgh Post Gazette* is significantly higher than that of the *Philadelphia Inquirer* (again, all things being equal).

As you can see, it is difficult to make the comparisons across various media. For example, what is the broadcast equivalent of cost per thousand, or the milline rate? In an attempt to provide some standardization of relative costing procedures, the broadcast and newspaper media have begun to provide their cost-efficiency measures in terms of cost/000 utilizing the following formulas:

$$\text{Television:} \quad \frac{\text{Cost of 1 unit of time} \times 1,000}{\text{Program rating}}$$

$$\text{Newspapers:} \quad \frac{\text{Cost of ad space} \times 1,000}{\text{Circulation}}$$

While the comparison of media on a cost per thousand basis is important, intermedia comparisons can be misleading if the numbers used are taken at face value. The ability of television to provide both sight and sound, the longevity of magazines, and other characteristics of each medium make it difficult to make direct comparisons based on cost/000 alone. Thus, the media planner should use these numbers but must also

Table 10–16 **Comparison of Cost per Ratings Point—"Family Ties" versus "Murder She Wrote"**

	"Family Ties"	"Murder She Wrote"
Cost per spot ad	$5,100.00	$4,300.00
Rating	32	30
Reach (total persons)	560,000	525,000
Calculation	$5,100/32	$4,300/30
CPRP	$159	$143

consider the specific characteristics of each of the media and media vehicles in the decision.

Some other factors must also be considered when evaluating the cost efficiency utilizing cost/000. It is possible that the cost/000 figure may be either an *overestimation* or an *underestimation* of the actual cost efficiency. Consider, for example, a situation when a certain degree of waste circulation is inevitable. In this case the circulation figure (using the *Time* magazine figures to demonstrate our point) exceeds the target market. As noted earlier, if these persons reached by this message are not potential buyers of the product, then having to pay to reach them results in a cost/000 figure that reflects a lower cost than is true, as shown in scenario A of Table 10–18.

Given the figures in scenario A, it is necessary to use the potential reach to the target market—the destination sought—rather than the overall circulation figure, as those not in the target market are not of interest. In using the target market audience, you may find that a medium with a much higher cost/000 figure is a wiser buy if it is reaching more potential receivers.

CPM may also be an underestimate of cost efficiency. Magazine advertising space sellers have argued for years that because of the fact that more than one person may read an issue, that the actual reach is underestimated. They have argued for making comparisons using a **readers per copy** figure in calculating cost/000. This new cost-efficiency determination would include a **pass-on rate,** estimating the number of persons to whom the magazine has been "passed on to" as the true circulation figure. Referring to scenario B in Table 10–18, you can see how this might lower the cost-efficiency estimates. Consider, as an example, a family in which the father, mother, and two teenage children all read each issue of *Time* magazine. Assume that such families constituted 25 percent of *Time*'s circulation base. While the circulation figure includes only one magazine, in reality there are four potential exposures in these households, increasing the total reach to 7 million. As a result, the companies argue that magazines are being judged unfairly if cost/000 figures are used alone.

While the readers per copy figure seems to make sense intuitively, in reality it has the potential to be extremely inaccurate owing to the use of the pass-on rate, as

Table 10–17 **Milline Rate Comparisons—*Pittsburgh Post Gazette* versus *Philadelphia Inquirer***

	Pittsburgh Post Gazette	*Philadelphia Inquirer*
Cost per page	$13,000.00	$9,150.00
Cost per line	$7.20/line	$9.25/line
Circulation	168,500	984,000
Calculation	$\text{Milline rate} = \dfrac{\text{Line rate} \times 1,000,000}{\text{Circulation}}$	
Milline rate	$\dfrac{\$7.20 \times 1,000,000}{168,500}$	$\dfrac{\$9.25 \times 1,000,000}{984,000}$
	$42.73	$9.40

Table 10–18   **Cost per Thousand Estimates**

Scenario A: Overestimation of Efficiency

Target market: 18–49
Magazine circulation: 4,000,000
Circulation to target market: 65% (2,600,000)
Cost per page: $98,500

$$\text{CPM} = \frac{\$98,500 \times 1,000}{4,000,000} = \$24.62$$

$$\text{CPM (actual target audience)} = \frac{\$98,500 \times 1,000}{2,600,000} = \$37.88$$

Scenario B: Underestimation of Efficiency

Target market: all age groups, male and female
Magazine circulation: 4,000,000
Cost per page: $98,500
Pass-on rate: 3* (25% of households)

$$\text{CPM (based on readers per copy):} = \frac{\text{Page cost} \times 1,000}{\text{Circulation} + 3(1,000,000)} = \frac{\$98,500 \times 1,000}{7,000,000} = \$14.07$$

*Assuming pass-on was valid.

discussed in Promotional Perspective 10–3. While the scenario of the family reading *Time* was easy enough to understand and estimate the readership, consider these occasions: How many persons in a fraternity read each issue of *Sports Illustrated* or *Playboy* that is delivered? How many members of a sorority or on a dorm floor read each issue of *Cosmopolitan* or *Self?* How many of either group read each issue of *Business Week?* While research is conducted to make these determinations, obtaining the estimates of pass-on is very subjective, and using these figures to estimate reach is highly speculative. Thus, while these figures are regularly provided by the media, managers are very careful in using them directly. At the same time—and once again—the art (versus science) of media buying enters, for many magazines' managers may have a pretty good idea that the reach is greater than the circulation figure provided. In these cases the circulation figure is treated as a conservative estimate of reach.

In addition to the potential for over- and/or underestimation of cost efficiencies, CPM's are limited in that they describe only *quantitative* estimates of the value of media. Thus, while they may be good for comparing very similar vehicles (such as *Time* and *Newsweek*), they are less valuable in making intermedia comparisons. We have already noted some differences between the various media that prohibit making direct comparisons, and in the next section, we will discuss other characteristics of media that must be taken into consideration.

In looking back at what you have just read, you can see that the development of media strategy involves a number of factors that must be considered. As you can now see, Ostrow may not be that far off when he calls this process an art rather than a science, as so much of this process requires going beyond the numbers.

Evaluation and Follow-up

All plans require some evaluation to assess their performance. The media plan is no exception.

In outlining the planning process, we stated that objectives are established and strategies are developed for the purpose of attaining them. Having implemented these strategies, marketers need to know whether or not they were successful. Measures of effectiveness must consider two factors: (1) How well did these strategies perform the media objectives established? and (2) How well did this media plan contribute to the attainment of the overall marketing and communications objectives? If the strategies

Promotional Perspective   10—3

Readership Figures Stir Controversy

Although the rates that magazines charge for their advertising space are determined primarily by circulation figures, decisions by media planners as to where to place ads are often based on readership figures supplied by two research firms: Mediamark Research, Inc. (MRI) and Simmons Market Research Bureau. These companies provide total readership figures (which are generally higher than circulation figures because of multiple readership of magazines) for magazines and national newspapers. These figures are also broken down to examine readership by various demographic groups based on sex, age, and income. Media planners use these figures to determine which publications are best for reaching specific types of consumers that comprise the advertiser's target market. Because of the importance media planners place on these figures, they have become crucial to the individual publication. As the vice president of one top agency noted, "If the readership numbers shift just a hair, there is a big shift in the number of ad pages."

Since the readership figures are often used as the basis for placing more than 5 billion dollars of print advertising every year and can mean life or death for an individual publication, their accuracy is an obvious concern among advertisers, agencies, and the publications themselves. However, Simmons and MRI rarely agree in their readership results and the validity of these figures has become the source of considerable controversy. The table shows the top five magazines based on total adult readership as estimated by each firm in 1987. As can be seen in this table, differences in readership estimates for the four publications common to each list range from just over 3 million to more than 13 million readers (for Reader's Digest)!

Despite these differences executives at both Simmons and MRI stand by their numbers while publishers and advertising people are left trying to determine which figures are more accurate. The problem stems from differences in the two firms' research methods. Simmons shows specific issues of magazines to people and counts as readers those who have read or glanced through those issues. MRI shows people flash cards with magazine logos printed on them and counts as readers anyone who says they have read a weekly within the last 7 days or a monthly within the last 30 days. Both firms interview about 20,000 people for their study.

Numerous criticisms have been made of the procedures used by each firm. Simmons' methods have been challenged because the researchers use stripped-down versions of each issue to show respondents that include only nine or so articles and no ads. MRI's technique has been criticized for overinflating readership figures because people get confused by magazines with similar names and are likely to say they read publications they really do not. Concern has also been expressed over the small samples used to estimate readership for small circulation publications. Both services note, however, that their reports point out numbers that may be based on samples too small to be considered reliable and list a margin of error for each magazine's results.

Many advertising agencies acknowledge the inconsistencies in the numbers and try to work with the raw data and other information in deciding where to place a client's ad. A committee of advertising and research executives is working to resolve the problem by attempting to generate accurate results by counting as readers only those people in the population who say they read a publication the day before. However, measuring readership of the more than 250 magazines covered in the readership studies could prove to be a formidable and expensive proposition. Thus publishers are likely to continue to challenge unfavorable figures, and advertisers and their agencies still must decide which figures are more reliable.

Source: Adapted from "Readership Figures for Periodicals Stir Debate in Publishing Industry," *The Wall Street Journal*, September 2, 1987, p. 25.

Study in Contrasts

(Top five magazines based on total adult readership, in millions)	
The Simmons List	
1. *TV Guide*	43.2
2. *Reader's Digest*	37.5
3. *People*	24.6
4. *National Geographic*	23.6
5. *Time*	23.2
The MRI List	
1. *Reader's Digest*	50.9
2. *TV Guide*	46.8
3. *Better Homes and Gardens*	35.5
4. *People*	30.4
5. *National Geographic*	30.3

Note: Excludes Sunday magazines.

Source: Joanne Lipman, "Readership Figures for Periodicals Stir Debate in Publishing Industry," *The Wall Street Journal*, September 2, 1987.

employed were successful, they should be used in the future plans; if not, then some analysis as to why they were not should be undertaken.

The problem with measuring the effectiveness of the media strategies is probably obvious to you at this point. At the very outset of this chapter we suggested that the planning process was limited by problems with measurements and lack of consistent terminology (among others). While these problems limit the degree to which we can assess the relative effectiveness of various strategies, that does not mean that it is impossible to make such determinations. As indicated in the Pioneer example, sometimes it is quite possible to show that a plan has worked. Even if the evaluation procedure is not 100 percent foolproof, it will be better than no attempt at all.

The Use of Computers in Media Planning

In this age it should not be surprising that attempts to improve on the media buying process through the use of computers has received a great deal of attention. While advanced planning models have been around since at least 1963, for the most part these models have met with limited success. Programs based on linear programming, simulation, and iteration have been adopted by only a relatively small number of agencies.

Where computers have been employed, however, is in the automation of the process we have just reviewed in this chapter—that is, in each of the four steps involved in planning and strategy development. While the art of media strategy has not been mechanized, advances in the quantitative side have significantly improved the managers' decision-making capabilities while also saving substantial time and effort. Let us briefly examine some of these methods.

The Use of Computers in Market Analysis

Earlier in this chapter we discussed the use of Simmons and MRI data and provided examples of each. In Chapter 7 we reviewed the information provided in PRIZM, VALS, and VISION. All these data have now been computerized and are available for access either through an interactive system or on the agency's own PC. For example, MRI offers its clients interactive capabilities with its mainframe or its MEMRI software data base that can be used on a personal computer for cross tabulation of media and demographic data, reach and frequency estimates, and cost rankings, in addition to numerous other applications. The interactive capabilities also allow for an interface with PRIZM, VALS, and VISION data.

In addition to customer analyses, other information used in the analysis stage is available. Table 10–19 is an example of the BAR/LNA data that were reviewed earlier that are also available through computer access.

The analyses of these data would assist in determining which markets and which groups should be targeted for advertising and promotions. By using this information, along with other data, the marketer can also readily define media objectives.

The Use of Computers in Media Strategy Development

In the strategy development phase, we discussed the need to make decisions regarding coverage, scheduling, costs, and the trade-off between reach and frequency, among others. Perhaps one of the primary benefits to media planners to accrue from computers is the development of programs to assist in the development of these strategies. While there are far too many of these programs to review in this text, we would like to provide you with a very small sampling just to demonstrate our point.

Reach and Frequency Analyses on the Computer Table 10–20 demonstrates one example of how software programs are now being used to determine reach and frequency levels and are also assisting in the decision as to which alternative is best. As shown in Table 10–20 various media mixes for television and radio at different TRPs are computed, with reach and frequency estimates, the number of persons

Table 10–19

BAR/LNA MULTI-MEDIA SERVICE
COMPANY/BRAND $

January - December 1988

PARENT COMPANY/BRAND	CLASS CODE	9-MEDIA TOTAL	LNA MAGAZINES	LNA NEWSPAPER SUPPLEMENTS	MEDIA RECORDS NEWSPAPERS	LNA OUTDOOR	BAR NETWORK TELEVISION	BAR SPOT TELEVISION	BAR SYNDICATED TELEVISION	BAR CABLE TV NETWORKS	BAR NETWORK RADIO
FOODMAKER INC											
CHI-CHIS MEXICAN RESTAURANTS	G330	6,496.5	--	--	136.5	151.6	--	6,208.4	--	--	--
JACK IN THE BOX BUSINESS PROPOSITION	B710	62.0	--	--	62.0	--	--	--	--	--	--
JACK IN THE BOX RESTAURANTS	G330	22,946.6	--	--	37.8	259.3	--	22,649.5	--	--	--
COMPANY TOTAL		29,505.1	--	--	236.3	410.9	--	28,857.9	--	--	--
FOOTWEAR UNLIMITED											
TRUFFLES CASUAL SHOES WOMEN	A131-2	38.8	38.8	--	--	--	--	--	--	--	--
FORALL CONFEZIONI SPA											
PAL ZILERI SPORTSWEAR MEN	A115-1	20.2	20.2	--	--	--	--	--	--	--	--
PAL ZILERI SUITS MEN	A114-1	9.6	9.6	--	--	--	--	--	--	--	--
PAL ZILERI WEARING APPAREL MEN	A119-1	30.8	30.8	--	--	--	--	--	--	--	--
COMPANY TOTAL		60.6	60.6	--	--	--	--	--	--	--	--
FORBES INC											
AMERICAN HERITAGE BOOKS	G618	228.3	196.7	--	--	--	--	31.6	--	--	--
AMERICAN HERITAGE MAGAZINE	B420	23.9	23.9	--	--	--	--	--	--	--	--
AMERICAN HERITAGE MAGAZINE SUBS	G618	412.5	102.1	--	--	--	93.2	112.0	--	105.2	--
FORBES BOOKS	B410	997.5	997.5	--	--	--	--	--	--	--	--
FORBES MAGAZINE	B420	146.0	146.0	--	--	--	--	--	--	--	--
FORBES MAGAZINE SUBS	G618	1,417.6	--	--	692.0	--	--	30.9	12.8	681.9	--
FORBES SOFTWARE	G615	26.4	26.4	--	--	--	--	--	--	--	--
FORBES STOCK MARKET COURSE	G61C	211.0	211.0	--	--	--	--	--	--	--	--
FORBES TRINCHERA RANCH FORT GARLAND	T431	45.3	45.3	--	--	--	--	--	--	--	--
LAUCALA RESORT FIJI ISLANDS	T431	404.7	404.7	--	--	--	--	--	--	--	--
SANGRE DE CRISTO RANCHES INC REAL ESTATE	B230	1,849.6	1,849.6	--	--	--	--	--	--	--	--
COMPANY TOTAL		5,762.8	4,003.2	--	692.0	--	93.2	174.5	12.8	787.1	--
FORBES/COHEN PROPERTIES											
GARDENS SHOPPING CENTER	G719	53.2	53.2	--	--	--	--	--	--	--	--
FORCE E											
FORCE E SPORTING GOODS	G717	47.6	47.6	--	--	--	--	--	--	--	--
FORD AUTO DEALERS ASSOCIATION											
FORD DEALERS ASSN LEASING	T113-9	507.6	--	--	55.9	--	--	451.7	--	--	--
FORD DEALERS ASSOCIATION	T113-9	110,625.7	--	--	24,962.5	900.0	42.1	84,721.1	--	--	--
FORD DLRS ASSN PARTS & SERVICE	T113-9	0.3	--	--	--	--	--	0.3	--	--	--
LINCOLN-MERCURY DEALERS ASSN LEASING	T113-9	601.0	--	--	601.0	--	--	--	--	--	--
LINCOLN-MERCURY DEALERS ASSOCIATION	T113-9	28,381.0	--	--	13,045.5	333.9	--	15,001.6	--	--	--
COMPANY TOTAL		140,115.6	--	--	38,664.9	1,233.9	42.1	100,174.7	--	--	--
FORD MOTOR CO											
ASTON MARTIN LAGONDA	T112	114.0	114.0	--	--	--	--	--	--	--	--
BDM CORP RECRUITMENT	B720-8	7.2	7.2	--	--	--	--	--	--	--	--
BDM INTERNATIONAL INC RECRUITMENT	B720-8	19.2	19.2	--	--	--	--	--	--	--	--
FIRST NATIONWIDE BANKING NETWORK	B154	9,214.5	3,603.9	--	2,375.2	9.1	3,040.1	21.6	--	164.6	--
FIRST NATIONWIDE SAVINGS ASSOCIATION	B154	2,525.8	--	--	--	--	--	2,525.8	--	--	--
FORD AEROSPACE & COMMUNICATIONS CORP GP	B190-8	505.4	66.8	--	438.6	--	--	--	--	--	--
FORD AEROSPACE COMMUNICATIONS CORP REC	B720-8	26.9	26.9	--	--	--	--	--	--	--	--
FORD AEROSTAR	T121	12,541.3	6,113.8	--	--	--	5,332.1	789.4	25.0	281.0	--
FORD AUTHORIZED LEASING SYSTEM	T114-7	1,967.1	191.3	--	1,713.2	--	--	62.6	--	--	--
FORD BACKHOE LOADER	T661	8.8	--	--	--	--	--	8.8	--	--	--
FORD BALER	T661	3.4	--	--	--	--	--	3.4	--	--	--
FORD BRONCO	T121	7,071.0	3,105.5	--	--	4.1	2,816.0	1,016.0	30.8	98.6	--
FORD BRONCO & F150	T121	1.9	--	--	--	--	--	1.9	--	--	--
FORD CAR STEREO SYSTEMS	H313	4,441.0	--	--	--	--	--	--	--	--	4,441.0
FORD CARGO TRUCKS	T121	4,699.2	368.3	--	160.8	44.8	2,223.0	1,628.5	135.3	138.5	--
FORD ESCORT	T111	29,484.6	7,050.0	--	--	38.1	15,961.1	5,465.9	518.9	450.6	--
FORD ESCORT & IMPORT FESTIVA	T111	819.8	--	--	--	--	--	819.8	--	--	--
FORD ESCORT & MUSTANG	T111	0.4	--	--	--	--	--	0.4	--	--	--
FORD ESCORT & THUNDERBIRD	T111	106.7	--	--	--	--	--	106.7	--	--	--
FORD ESCORT WAGONS	T111	509.6	509.6	--	--	--	--	--	--	--	--
FORD F-150	T121	3,417.6	2,491.2	--	--	0.2	--	926.2	--	--	--
FORD F-SERIES LIGHT TRUCKS	T121	1,021.2	1,021.2	--	--	--	--	--	--	--	--
FORD F150 & F250	T121	18.4	--	--	--	--	--	--	--	18.4	--
FORD FESTIVA	T111	244.4	--	--	220.3	24.1	--	--	--	--	--
FORD FESTIVA & TAURUS	T112	67.7	--	--	--	--	--	67.7	--	--	--
FORD IMPORT FESTIVA	T112	12,692.2	1,173.7	--	--	--	8,532.6	2,699.1	63.6	223.2	--
---- CONTINUED ----											

Table 10–20   **San Diego Trust & Savings Bank Reach and Frequency Analyses**

Product Message

Media Mix (A 25–54)	Reach/Frequency (% / X)	3+ Level (%)	1st Quarter Weekly Cost
TV (125)	84 / 4.5	51	$21,480
TV (125) R (125)	91 / 8.2	71	29,450
TV (125) R (150)*	92 / 9.0	73	31,045
TV (150)	86 / 5.2	57	25,660
TV (150) R (125)	92 / 9.0	73	33,625
TV (150) R (150)	92 / 9.8	74	35,220
TV (175)	89 / 5.9	61	29,930
TV (175) R (125)	93 / 9.7	75	37,900
TV (175) R (150)	93 / 10.5	76	39,490
TV (200)	90 / 6.7	65	34,255
TV (200) R (125)	93 / 10.5	76	42,225
TV (200) R (150)	93 / 11.3	78	43,820

(Based on a three-week flight.)
*Recommended.

Source: San Diego Trust and Savings Bank.

reached three or more times, and the costs provided. The program also has determined—based on the combination of reach, frequency levels, frequency of exposures three or more times, and cost/000—that a mix of 125 TRPs on television and 150 TRPs on radio would result in the best buy. Keep in mind that this recommendation only considers the most efficient combination of these factors and does not allow for the "art" of media buying.

The preceding is just one of the many examples of how computer programs—in this case, the Telmar system—are now being used in the media strategy development phase. Many others, again available for PC use, are also available.

The one area in which computers have not yet provided a direct benefit is in the evaluation stage of the media plan. While these programs do generate what they consider to be optimal solutions to the use of TRPs, GRPs, and media mixes, the true test is what happens when the plan is implemented. We will reserve our discussion of the evaluation process until the chapter on measuring effectiveness.

Characteristics of Media

To this point, we have discussed the elements involved in the development of media strategy. One of the most basic elements in this process was said to be the matching of media to markets. In the following chapters, you will see that each medium has its

Table 10—21   Media Characteristics

Media	Advantages	Disadvantages
Television	Mass coverage High reach Impact of sight, sound, and motion High prestige Low cost per exposure Attention getting Favorable image	Low selectivity Short message life High absolute cost High production costs Clutter
Radio	Local coverage Low cost High frequency Flexible Low production costs Well-segmented audiences	Audio only Clutter Low attention getting Fleeting message
Magazines	Segmentation potential Quality reproduction High information content Longevity Multiple readers	Long lead time for ad placement Visual only Lack of flexibility
Newspapers	High coverage Low cost Short lead time for placing ads Ads can be placed in interest sections Timely (current ads) Reader controls exposure Can be used for coupons	Short life Clutter Low attention-getting capabilities Poor reproduction quality Selective reader exposure
Outdoor	Location specific High repetition Easily noticed	Short exposure time requires short ad Poor image Local restrictions
Direct mail	High selectivity Reader controls exposure High information content Opportunities for repeat exposures	High cost/contact Poor image (junk mail) Clutter

own characteristics that make it more or less advantageous for the attainment of specific objectives. Prior to examining these media specifically, it will be helpful to establish an overall framework in which some of these characteristics are defined and compared.

Table 10–21 represents an overall comparison of media and some of the characteristics by which they are evaluated. This is a very general comparison and an analysis of the various media options must be undertaken for each situation. However, as an overview, it does provide you with a good starting point from which to make comparisons. The following chapters in this text discuss in more depth the characteristics of various media and their relative advantages and disadvantages with respect to the accomplishment of advertising and promotions objectives.

Summary

This chapter has presented an overview of the determination of media objectives, development of the media strategy, and the formalization of these in the form of a media plan. In addition, sources of media information, characteristics of media, and an actual plan were provided.

The media strategy must be designed to supplement and support the overall marketing and communications objectives. As such, the objectives of this plan are designed to provide delivery of the message that the program has developed.

The basic task involved in the development of media strategy is to determine the best matching of media to the target market, given the constraints of the budget. The media planner will attempt to balance reach and frequency and to deliver the message to the intended audience with a minimum of waste circulation. At the same time, a number of additional factors must be considered, all of which will impact the media decision.

Media strategy development has been referred to by one well-known practitioner as an art rather than a science. The reason for this assessment was based on the fact that while much quantitative data are available to the planner, there is also a reliance on creativity and/or nonquantifiable factors.

This chapter was designed to provide you with an overview of the media planning and strategy development process. A number of factors were considered, including the development of a proper media mix, determining target market and geographic coverage, scheduling, balancing reach and frequency, and creative aspects. In addition, budget considerations and the need for flexibility in the schedule were discussed. Finally, the use of computers in the media planning process was considered.

Key Terms

Media planning
Media plan
Media objectives
Media strategies
Medium
Media vehicle
Reach
Coverage
Frequency
Sweeps periods
Index number
Survey of Buying Power Index
Brand Development Index (BDI)

Category Development Index (CDI)
Waste circulation
Geographical weighting
Continuity
Flighting
Pulsing
Unduplicated reach
Duplicated reach
Program rating
Gross ratings points (GRPs)
Target ratings points (TRPs)
Effective reach
Average frequency

Absolute cost   Milline rate
Relative cost   Readers per copy
Cost per thousand (CPM)   Pass-on rate
Cost per ratings point (CPRP)

Discussion Questions

1. Discuss some of the problems inherent in the media planning process. Give an example of each.
2. Describe each step involved in developing the media plan. Discuss some of the decisions that must be made at each stage.
3. What type of information is provided by Simmons Market Research Bureau? By MRI? How is this information used in the media planning process?
4. How do advertisers use index numbers? Explain how these numbers can be used erroneously.
5. In the text it was stated that marketers usually will find it advantageous to use a media mix. Describe what this means and give examples of companies currently pursuing this strategy.
6. It has been said that there is an inverse relationship between reach and frequency. Discuss the meaning of this and give examples when each should be the primary objective.
7. Discuss the three methods of media scheduling. When should each be used? What types of products might employ each strategy?
8. Describe some of the bases used for determining relative media costs. Discuss some of the problems inherent in using these to make cross-media comparisons.
9. How are computers being used in media planning? Describe some of the tasks that computer programs can perform.
10. Discuss the meaning of reach. How is reach measured? What is meant by the term *effective reach?*

Notes

1. "Saab's Peter Berla: Building a Presence on a (Relatively) Small Budget," *Inside Print*, February 1987, pp. 32–40.
2. Laura Clark, "Saab Maps Out Regional Approach," *Advertising Age*, December 5, 1988, p. 53.
3. Herbert E. Krugman, "Why Three Exposures May Be Enough," *Journal of Advertising Research,* December 1972, pp. 11–14.
4. Michael J. Naples, *Effective Frequency: The Relationship between Frequency and Advertising Effectiveness* (New York: Association of National Advertisers, 1979).
5. Joseph W. Ostrow, "Setting Frequency Levels: An Art or a Science?" *Market and Media Decisions,* 1987, p. 19.
6. David Berger, "How Much to Spend" (Foote, Cone & Belding Internal Report), in Michael L. Rothschild, *Advertising* (Lexington, Mass.: D. C. Heath, 1987), p. 468.
7. David W. Olson, "Real World Measures of Advertising Effectiveness for New Products" (Speech to the 26th Annual Conference of the Advertising Research Foundation, New York, March 18, 1980).
8. Naples, *Effective Frequency.*
9. Joseph W. Ostrow, "What Level Frequency?" *Advertising Age,* November 1981, pp.13–18.
10. Ibid.

Sources of Media Information

Cross-Reference Guide to Advertising Media Sources

	General Information	Competitive Activities	Market Information (geographic)	Audience Information (target groups)	Advertising Rates
Nonmedia information (general marketing)	1, 11, 18, 19, 26, 28, 29	1, 23	11, 12, 18, 19, 21, 24, 26, 30	18, 19, 26	
Multimedia or intermedia	1, 18, 19, 26	1, 15	21	2, 14, 31	2
Daily newspapers		17		5, 18, 19, 25, 26	2, 30
Weekly newspapers					30
Consumer magazines	16	15		18, 19, 26	2, 30
Farm publications				5, 32	2, 30
Business publications			7, 9	7, 32	2, 30
Network television		8, 15		4, 18, 19, 20, 26	2
Spot television		8, 15		4, 18, 19, 20, 26	2, 30
Network radio		8, 22		13, 18, 19, 20, 26, 27	2
Spot radio		22		4, 6, 13, 20, 26	2, 30
Direct mail					2, 30
Outdoor		15			2, 10
Transit					2

1. *Advertising Age*
2. Advertising agency media estimating guides
3. American Business Press, Inc. (ABP)
4. Arbitron Ratings Company
5. Audit Bureau of Circulations (ABC)
6. Birch Radio, Inc.
7. Business/Professional Advertising Association (B/PAA) Media Data
8. Broadcast Advertisers Reports (BAR)
9. Business Publications Audit of Circulation (BPA)
10. *Buyer's Guide to Outdoor Advertising*
11. *State and Metropolitan Area Data Book*
12. *Editor & Publisher Market Guide*
13. C. E. Hooper, Inc., "Hooperatings"
14. Interactive Market Systems (IMS)
15. Leading National Advertisers (LNA), Inc.
16. Magazine Publishers Association, Inc. (MPA)
17. Media Records, Inc.
18. Mediamark Research, Inc. (MRI)
19. Mendelsohn Media Research, Inc. (MMR)
20. Nielsen Media Research Company
21. PRIZM
22. Radio Expenditure Reports
23. SAMI Burke, Inc.
24. *Sales and Marketing Management Survey of Buying Power*
25. Scarborough's Newspaper Ratings Company, Ltd.
26. Simmons Market Research Bureau: *Study of Media and Markets*
27. Sindlinger Report
28. *Standard Directory of Advertisers*
29. *Standard Directory of Advertising Agencies*
30. Standard Rate and Data Service
31. Telmar
32. Verified Audit Circulation Corporation (VAC)

Source: Arnold M. Bantam, Donald W. Jugenheimer, and Peter B. Turk, *Advertising Media Sourcebook*, 3rd ed. (Lincolnwood, Ill.: NTC Business Books, 1989), pp. 8–9.

Media Plan for Denny's

(Courtesy of Denny's Inc.)

FY85 Media Spending Principles

For this fiscal year, the development of Spending Principles began at a strategy retreat at La Quinta in November 1983. At that conference, representatives from Denny's operations, research and development, field marketing, and national marketing—as well as FCB and WIMC—identified the *key marketing issues* facing Denny's in the months ahead. From these issues, which ranged from operational to creative/positioning concerns, the FCB/WIMC team developed the Spending Principles that would serve as the overall guidelines for media plan direction.

The original list of Spending Principles as discussed on February 14, 1984, was divided into seven categories. After reviewing these issues and evaluating them in light of budgets and priorities, we agreed to the following actions:

1. *Strategies* Network versus spot will continue to be evaluated on a month-to-month basis, even if it means that we could go several consecutive quarters without a spot month to use for testing. The reach versus frequency issue will be explored via a media test that restructures our daypart mix to build frequency against women.
2. *Target audience* Although the current target of adults 25–54 was confirmed for this year's plan, it was agreed that adults 55+ was the most important secondary target—and that a specific marketing plan would be developed to address them separately at a later date.
3. *Other media* Apart from Key Priority Market and Field Marketing plans—which will include radio, newspaper, transit, outdoor, direct-mail, and free-standing inserts—network and spot TV were the recommended vehicles for national support in FY85.
4. *Competitive recognition* This too was applied as a Key Priority spending principle, particularly when evaluating competitive spending as a percentage of sales versus Denny's spending-to-sales ratio.
5. *Tested programs* Because of the importance and implications of the simultaneous promotion test, Denny's requested that this test be redesigned in more representative/readable markets and replicated in FY85.
6. *Budgeting* Rather than establish budgets for Key Priority and testing plans up front, it was agreed that preliminary plans for each would be developed and the budgets would be task-driven and payout-evaluated.
7. *Tactics/buying procedures* It was generally agreed that syndication opportunities would be evaluated and that flighting patterns would vary by promotion. It was also recommended and approved that movies continue to be a strong programming consideration despite controversial subject matter concerns.

In summary, most of the "new thinking" springing from the Spending Principles discussion is applied in the incremental plans (Key Priority markets, testing, and special projects) rather than the FY85 national plan itself. The FY85 plan is an evolutionary one distinguished by fewer, longer promotional events as well as the incremental efforts; its guiding principles are, however, very similar to those used in the 1984 planning process.

Media Objectives

The FY85 media recommendation is based on the following objectives:

- Continue to build high awareness of Denny's superior price/value relationship via promotion of new/existing menu items.

- Provide broad national reach against Heavy Users, defined as those persons who frequent a family restaurant four or more times over a 30-day period. Demographically defined as

  Adults 25–54

Primary	Men 25–54
Secondary	Women 25–54

- Provide advertising support for all national promotional items.
- Provide advertising support for all Denny's markets, as affordable.
- Continue to build advertising awareness in Key Priority markets, as affordable, including:

  1. Chicago
  2. Houston
  3. Los Angeles

- Provide advertising support for specialized field marketing efforts.
- Test at least two key media strategies as a means of building incremental sales.

Media Strategies

- Utilize media vehicles that will selectively and efficiently deliver key prospects, adults 25–54.

  Television is recommended because it provides the greatest opportunity for appetite appeal through visual presentation of Denny's preparation message.

  Network Provides national support for all Denny's markets for nationally promoted items.
  Spot Provides flexibility to advertise and/or test various promoted items in payout/selected/Key Priority markets.

- Flight advertising to coincide with each promoted item.

  One-month promotions will receive three weeks of advertising, beginning the first day of the month.
  Two-month promotions will receive four weeks of advertising flighted over five weeks, beginning the first day of month 1.
  An extended promoted item, that is, Grand Slam Breakfast, will be supported beyond the initial flight as justified through payout analysis.

Plan Development

Television continues to be the key media vehicle for Denny's offering the most complete advertising communication to the consumer. Several elements must be addressed to ensure that Denny's will receive the most cost-effective media support affordable, including: the payout analysis, a daypart mix analysis, and a comparison of the efficiencies of network television versus spot television.

From an overall perspective, network television is demonstrably more efficient than spot television. More important, it offers these advantages over spot television:

- Coverage of *all* markets
- In-program commercial placement
- Lays groundwork for entry into new markets
- Opportunity to purchase on an up-front basis, which allows for greater cost efficiency

Spot television, however, also has specific advantages for Denny's. Specifically, spot has the ability to

- Provide coverage for selected markets
- Test various promotions for possible national rollout (at a lower out-of-pocket cost as compared with network)
- Tailor promotions on a market-by-market basis to satisfy local DMA operational needs

Television Daypart Mix Analyses

A daypart mix analysis demonstrates the relationship of out-of-pocket cost to Denny's target audience after adjustment for noticing. It is done to ensure that the most cost-effective media schedules will be implemented for Denny's in each quarter. Six daypart mixes were selected for analysis and were evaluated on the following criteria.

- Equal delivery of men and women.
- Cost effectiveness after adjustment for noticing opportunity. Specifically, adjustment for noticing opportunity more closely reflects *true commercial target audience delivery*. Foote, Cone & Belding has established a set of media weights that reduces the number who will be exposed to the commercial to the estimated number who can be expected to notice the commercial. For example, not everyone who watches television will see a commercial when it is aired, just as not everyone who reads a given publication sees every page containing an advertisement. Further, of those who *do* have the opportunity to notice the commercial, noticing weights calculate what percentage of men, women, and adults will be viewing during a particular daypart.
- Inventory availabilities in each daypart. (That is, if the most cost-efficient daypart mix is 100 percent early news, can Denny's target rating point goal be achieved in this daypart?)

While the selected daypart mix for each quarter is the most cost-effective in terms of cost per effective reach point (CPERP), which is the cost divided by the effective reach points, it does not necessarily have the lowest out-of-pocket cost of the six daypart mixes analyzed. For example, in First Quarter FY85:

Daypart Mix	Cost per Effective Reach Point	Out-of-Pocket Cost for 100 TRPs
#1	$37,091	$771,500
#2	38,753	744,065

Daypart Mix #1 is *more cost-effective* with a lower CPERP but requires a larger total expenditure than Daypart Mix #2, $771,500 versus $744,065 for Daypart Mix #2.

The most cost-effective daypart mix for network television in FY85/FY86 by quarter includes:

Quarter	Daypart Mix
First FY85	100% Prime
Second FY85	100% Prime
Third FY85	85% Prime, 15% Late night
Fourth FY85	100% Prime
First FY86	100% Prime

Please note, in order to establish the network budget that was negotiated during the up-front network television marketplace (which includes the new season '84/'85 through mid-September 1985), First Quarter FY86 has been included in this analysis.

Appendix B Table 10–1 **Denny's FY85 Television Cost Analysis: Network versus Spot First Quarter FY85, August 1984 Demo: Adults 25–54**

Media Vehicle	# DMAs	% Denny's TV HHs[1]	% Sales[2]	Cost per Flight		Cost: Sales	Efficiency Index[3]
				TRPs	$		
Network							
Most cost-effective daypart mix[4]							
W/o New York	125	90.99	98.64	265	2,228,385[5]	22,591	100
Inc. New York	126	100.00	100.00	265	2,422,365[5]	24,224	93
Spot							
Payout markets							
Most cost-eff. DPM w/o New York	52	49.52	76.83	295	1,312,160	17,094	132
100% prime w/o New York	52	49.52	76.83	295	2,091,550	27,248	83
Payout plus selected markets							
Most cost-eff. DPM w/o New York	60	61.65	84.77	295	1,659,580	19,596	115
100% prime w/o New York	60	61.65	84.77	295	2,552,340	30,137	75
All Denny's markets							
Most cost-eff. DPM w/o New York	125	90.99	98.64	295	2,397,465	24,305	93
100% prime w/o New York	125	90.99	98.64	295	3,438,225	34,856	65

[1]Denny's DMAs constitute 85.475% of U.S. TV households.
[2]Payout analysis as of 3/21/84.
[3]Efficiency index: comparisons made to network without New York, based on the most cost-effective daypart mix.
[4]100% prime.
[5]Includes time, compensation, cut-ins, and integration.

Appendix B Table 10–2 **Denny's FY85 Television Cost Analysis: Network versus Spot Second Quarter FY85, November 1984 Demo: Adults 25–54**

Media Vehicle	#DMAs	% Denny's TV HHs[1]	% Sales[2]	Cost per Flight		Cost: Sales	Efficiency Index[3]
				TRPs	$		
Network							
Most cost-effective daypart mix[4]							
W/o New York	125	90.99	98.67	265	2,312,920[5]	23,441	100
Inc. New York	126	100.00	100.00	265	2,505,840[5]	25,058	94
Spot							
Payout markets							
Most cost-eff. DPM w/o New York	33	32.63	58.97	295	936,330	15,878	148
100% prime w/o New York	33	32.63	58.97	295	1,493,290	25,323	93
Payout plus selected markets							
Most cost-eff. DPM w/o New York	47	56.44	80.32	295	1,753,775	21,835	107
100% prime w/o New York	47	56.44	80.32	295	2,634,735	32,803	72
All Denny's markets							
Most cost-eff. DPM w/o New York	125	90.99	98.67	295	2,720,195	27,569	85
100% prime w/o New York	125	90.99	98.67	295	3,879,250	39,315	60

[1]Denny's DMAs constitute 85.475% of U.S. TV households.
[2]Payout analysis as of 3/21/84.
[3]Efficiency index: comparisons made to network without New York, based on the most cost-effective daypart mix.
[4]100% prime.
[5]Includes time, compensation, cut-ins, and integration.

Further, daypart mix analyses (DMAs) were completed for spot television for each quarter. Selected daypart mixes were evaluated for all Denny's DMAs. The spot analysis for each quarter can be found immediately following the daypart mix analysis for network. [See Appendix B Tables 10–1 through 10–4.]

Television Cost Analysis—Network versus Spot

As discussed earlier, network television offers some significant advantages for a national company such as Denny's. One of the most compelling advantages is the greater cost efficiencies of network television as compared with spot television in generating incremental sales.

Apppendix B Table 10—3   Denny's FY85 Television Cost Analysis: Network versus Spot Third Quarter FY85, March 1985
Demo: Adults 25—54

Media Vehicle	# DMAs	% Denny's TV HHs[1]	% Sales[2]	Cost per Flight		Cost: Sales	Efficiency Index[3]
				TRPs	$		
Network							
Most cost-effective daypart mix[4]							
W/o New York	125	90.99	98.73	265	2,063,785[5]	20,903	100
Inc. New York	126	100.00	100.00	265	2,271,845[5]	22,718	92
Spot							
Payout markets							
Most cost-eff. DPM w/o New York	63	55.33	80.22	295	1,366,635	17,036	123
85% prime, 15% LF w/o New York	63	55.33	80.22	295	1,859,975	23,186	90
Payout plus selected markets							
Most cost-eff. DPM w/o New York	69	66.45	88.72	295	1,736,270	19,570	107
85% prime, 15% LF w/o New York	69	66.45	88.72	295	2,320,765	26,158	80
All Denny's markets							
Most cost-eff. DPM w/o New York	125	90.99	98.73	295	2,460,595	24,922	84
85% prime, 15% LF w/o New York	125	90.99	100.00	295	3,044,695	30,447	69

[1]Denny's DMAs constitute 85.475% of U.S. TV households.
[2]Payout analysis as of 3/21/84.
[3]Efficiency index: comparisons made to network without New York, based on the most cost-effective daypart mix.
[4]85% prime, 15% late fringe (LF).
[5]Includes time, compensation, cut-ins, and integration.

Appendix B Table 10—4   Denny's FY85 Television Cost Analysis: Network versus Spot Fourth Quarter FY85, May 1985
Demo: Adults 25—54

Media Vehicle	# DMAs	% Denny's TV HHs[1]	% Sales[2]	Cost per Flight		Cost: Sales	Efficiency Index[3]
				TRPs	$		
Network							
Most cost-effective daypart mix[4]							
W/o New York	125	90.99	98.64	265	2,879,225[5]	29,189	100
Inc. New York	126	100.00	100.00	265	3,119,315[5]	31,193	94
Spot							
Payout markets							
Most cost-eff. DPM w/o New York	33	35.27	62.03	295	1,083,760	17,480	165
100% prime w/o New York	33	35.27	62.03	295	1,686,810	27,207	107
Payout plus selected markets							
Most cost-eff. DPM w/o New York	46	56.65	80.67	295	1,877,310	23,280	125
100% prime w/o New York	46	56.65	80.67	295	2,794,240	34,651	84
All Denny's markets							
Most cost-eff. DPM w/o New York	125	90.99	98.64	295	2,899,850	29,398	99
100% prime w/o New York	125	90.99	100.00	295	4,035,010	40,350	72

[1]Denny's DMAs constitute 85.475% of U.S. TV households.
[2]Payout analysis as of 3/21/84.
[3]Efficiency index: comparisons made to network without New York, based on the most cost-effective daypart mix.
[4]100% prime.
[5]Includes time, compensation, cut-ins, and integration.

The charts on the following pages have been developed to demonstrate the relative efficiencies of network and spot television for Denny's. As costs change significantly by quarter, an analysis is provided for each quarter in FY85. Comparisons are based on the cost to generate 1 percent of sales (cost:sales) for an average flight:

- Network—@ 265 TRPs
- Most cost-effective daypart mix (DPM) excluding and including New York City
- Spot—@ 295 TRPs

  Most cost-effective daypart mix (DPM)
  Same DPM as network DPM excluding New York

  - Payout markets

- Payout plus selected markets
- All Denny's markets

The cost:sales ratio is derived by dividing the cost per flight for each market group level by the respective percentage of sales the advertising expenditure will cover. For example:

$$\text{Cost per flight:} \atop \text{Percentage Denny's sales covered:} \quad \frac{\$2,228,385}{98.64} = \$22,591$$

The cost:sales data are then compared via an efficiency index. The efficiency index is derived by dividing the cost:sales data for each market group level into the most cost-effective DPM excluding New York. For example:

Market Group	Cost:Sales	Efficiency Index
Network—most cost-effective DPM excluding New York	$22,591	100
Payout		
Most cost-effective DPM	17,094	132
Same DPM as network	27,248	83

Thus, it is 32 percent more efficient to cover sales in the payout markets when utilizing the most cost-effective DPM as compared with network (most cost-effective DPM excluding New York). On the other hand, it is 17 percent more efficient to cover sales via network—most cost-effective DPM excluding New York than payout markets when utilizing the same DPM as network.

When evaluated on a cost:sales basis, network television (purchased on an upfront basis) is clearly a stronger media investment than spot television for the first three quarters in FY85. This includes all three groups of Denny's markets evaluated—payout markets, payout plus selected markets, and all Denny's markets. In terms of sales, network television affords the opportunity to cover virtually 100 percent of Denny's sales as compared with 80 to 89 percent for payout plus selected markets via spot television. Therefore, we believe a premium of 7 to 15 percent for network over spot is not unreasonable, as it ensures coverage of all Denny's markets (except New York) as compared with spot television for payout plus selected markets (47 to 69 markets). When comparisons are made based on the same daypart mix, network is a clear winner over spot for all market groups.

The Fourth Quarter is the only time of the fiscal year when spot is more efficient than network. Given current budget parameters, a premium of 25 percent cannot be justified at this time. It is recommended that television activity in this quarter be limited to spot television.

Market Group Payout Analyses

The market group payout analyses included on the following pages [see Appendix B Tables 10–5 through 10–8] further demonstrate the viability of network television during the first three quarters of FY85. For example, in Third Quarter FY85, the total media investment is $2,309,785 for network versus $1,736,270 for spot television in the payout plus selected market group. On balance, spot television in payout plus selected markets looks like a better investment with a significantly lower out-of-pocket (total) cost than network. However, payout projections are estimated to be approximately $20,000 greater for network television. The payout estimate for network at $1,369,702 is approximately $20,000 more than the payout estimate for the payout plus selected market group at $1,349,213.

Appendix B Table 10—5   **Denny's FY85 Market Group Payout Analysis First Quarter, August 1984**

Market Group	# DMAs	Monthly Food Sales	% Sales	Media Cost	% Payout	Payout $
All: Network* @ 265 TRPs	125	93,683,897*	98.64*	2,228,385	6.9	+680,500
Payout: Spot @ 295 TRPs	52	72,907,621	76.83	1,312,160	6.9	+951,622
Payout plus: Spot @ 295 TRPs	60	80,434,961	84.77	1,659,580	6.9	+837,926
Base network alternatives						
A. Payout plus network base						
Payout: Spot @145 TRPs	52	72,907,621	76.83	1,269,581	6.9	+994,201
Net* @ 150 TRPs						
Balance: Net* @ 150 TRPs	73	20,776,276	21.81	636,729	4.5**	−216,009
				1,906,310		+778,192
B. Payout plus selected plus net						
Payout plus: Spot @ 145 TRPs	60	80,434,961	84.77	1,593,392	6.9	+904,114
Net* @ 150 TRPs						
Balance: Net* @ 150 TRPs	65	13,248,936	13.87	483,728	4.5**	−215,437
				2,077,120		+688,677

*Excluding New York; including time, compensation, cut-ins, and integration.
**Estimated.
Note: All comparisons based on most cost-effective daypart mix.

Appendix B Table 10—6   **Denny's FY85 Market Group Payout Analysis Second Quarter, November 1984**

Market Group	# DMAs	Monthly Food Sales	% Sales	Media Cost	% Payout	Payout $
All: Network* 265 TRPs	125	84,987,372*	98.67*	2,305,235	6.9	+333,623
Payout: Spot @ 295 TRPs	33	51,727,985	58.97	957,275	6.9	+648,879
Payout plus: Spot @ 295 TRPs	47	69,783,314	80.32	1,774,720	6.9	+392,052
Base network alternatives						
A. Payout plus network base						
Payout: Spot @ 145 TRPs	33	51,727,985	58.97	900,473	6.9	+705,681
Net* @ 150 TRPs						
Balance: Net* @ 150 TRPs	92	33,259,387	39.70	874,902	4.5**	−201,399
				1,775,375		+504,282
B. Payout plus selected plus net						
Payout plus: Spot @ 145 TRPs	47	69,783,314	80.32	1,612,953	6.9	+553,819
Net* @ 150 TRPs						
Balance: Net* @ 150 TRPs	78	15,204,058	18.35	564,217	4.5**	−256,335
				2,177,170		+297,484

*Excluding New York; including time, compensation, cut-ins, and integration.
**Estimated.
Note: All comparisons based on most cost-effective daypart mix.

Appendix B Table 10—7   **Denny's FY85 Market Group Payout Analysis Third Quarter, March 1985**

Market Group	# DMAs	Monthly Food Sales	% Sales	Media Cost	% Payout	Payout $
All: Network* @ 265 TRPs	125	110,579,282*	98.73*	2,063,785	6.9	+1,369,702
Payout: Spot @ 295 TRPs	63	89,856,331	80.22	1,366,635	6.9	+1,423,404
Payout plus: Spot @ 295 TRPs	69	99,371,418	88.72	1,736,270	6.9	+1,349,213
Base network alternatives						
A. Payout plus network base						
Payout: Spot @ 145 TRPs	63	89,856,331	80.22	1,318,150	6.9	+1,471,889
Net* @ 150 TRPs						
Balance: Net* @ 150 TRPs	62	20,722,951	18.51	521,835	4.5**	−102,195
				1,839,985		+1,369,694
B. Payout plus selected plus net						
Payout plus: Spot @ 145 TRPs	69	99,371,418	88.72	1,629,739	6.9	+1,455,744
Net* @ 150 TRPs						
Balance: Net* @ 150 TRPs	56	11,207,864	10.01	391,931	4.5**	−164,972
				2,021,670		+1,290,772

*Excluding New York; including time, compensation, cut-ins, and integration.
**Estimated.
Note: All comparisons based on most cost-effective daypart mix.

Appendix B Table 10–8   **Denny's FY85 Market Group Payout Analysis Fourth Quarter, May 1985**

Market Group	# DMAs	Monthly Food Sales	% Sales	Media Cost	Payout % Payout	Payout $
All: Network* @ 265 TRPs	125	88,098,419*	98.64*	2,879,225	6.9	−143,769
Payout: Spot @ 295 TRPs	33	55,375,850	62.03	1,083,760	6.9	+635,660
Payout plus: Spot @ 295 TRPs	46	72,023,500	80.67	1,877,310	6.9	+359,020
Base network alternatives						
A. Payout Plus Network Base						
Payout: Spot @ 145 TRPs	33	55,375,850	62.03	1,107,543	6.9	+611,877
Net* @ 150 TRPs						
Balance: Net* @ 150 TRPs	92	32,722,569	36.61	1,054,937	4.5**	−392,305
				2,162,480		+219,572
B. Payout plus selected plus net						
Payout plus: Spot @ 145 TRPs	46	72,023,500	80.67	1,846,033	6.9	+390,297
Net* @ 150 TRPs						
Balance: Net* @ 150 TRPs	79	16,074,919	17.97	706,497	4.5**	−380,980
				2,552,530		−9,317

*Excluding New York; including time, compensation, cut-ins, and integration.
**Estimated.
Note: All comparisons based on most cost-effective daypart mix.

Recommendation

Highlights of media activity recommended for FY85 include the following:

- Eight promotional cycles are planned over 12 months.
- Payout markets will receive eight flights of television support for a total of 2,510 TRPs over the year, including network, syndication, and spot television. The balance of Denny's markets will receive a minimum of 1,625 TRPs flighted to provide support for five national promotions scheduled over nine months.
- Two-month promotions will receive four weeks of media activity flighted over the two months to achieve maximum reach, awareness, and commercial message reinforcement within current budget parameters.
- Selected syndicated television programs were added to the media mix in FY85, as they offered the opportunity to provide national coverage of Denny's key prospects with cost efficiencies significantly greater than for network alternatives. Syndication provides an efficient complement to planned network activity and is flighted as such.
- Marketing considerations and, more important, payout and media efficiency analyses dictate that advertising support be limited to spot television in the Fourth Quarter.
- Special attention is being paid to business-building tactics via key priority markets and media testing. These opportunities have been addressed in detail in separate sections of this document.

    See the flowchart of scheduled media activity and the current budget summary on the following pages [see Appendix B Tables 10–9 and 10–10, respectively].

Implementation

The 1984/85 network up-front marketplace was led by bullish daytime demand, sparking dramatic cost increases as high as 30 percent and spilling over into double-digit prime cost hikes. In startling contrast, Denny's was very successful in holding the line, purchasing 149 units from the three major networks at an overall target cost per point (CPP) just 4.7 percent above last year.

    To further improve television cost efficiency, Denny's will allocate approximately 11.8 percent of its national broadcast expenditures (15.5 percent of TRPs) to syndi-

Appendix B Table 10—9   **Media Flowchart**

DENNY'S FY85
REVISED OPTION II
MEDIA SCHEDULE

■ Payout Market Only
▥ Payout Plus Selected Markets

8/16/84

MEDIA	JULY	AUGUST	SEPT	OCTOBER	NOV	DEC	JANUARY	FEBRUARY	MARCH	APRIL	MAY	JUNE	JULY	AUGUST	SEPTEMBER
PROMOTIONAL CYCLE	BAB	VARIOUS		GSB		DINNER		DINNER		BREAKFAST	VARIOUS		DINNER	VARIOUS	BREAKFAST
Important Dates	1)	2) 3)			4)										
Goal:	265		265	75	265	75	265	75	265	75			150		265
Network TV															
TRPs/week															
TRPs/flight	265		265	61.6	224.2	61.6	221.2	60.4	221.2	60.4			128.4		232.6
Syndicated TV															
TRPs/week															
TRPs/flight				13.4	40.8	13.4	43.8	14.6	43.8	14.6			21.6		32.4
Spot TV															
TRPs/week															
TRPs/flight		295									295		295	295	
Testing															
Key Priority:															
Los Angeles															
Chicago															
Houston															
% Sales Covered	98.64	75.25	98.62	98.64	98.67	98.73	98.79	98.76	98.73		62.03	84.38			

1984 MONDAY DATES

1985 MONDAY DATES

cated programming. This will reduce the overall network/syndication CPP to less than that of 1983/84. Late night fine-tuning will comprise 19.4 percent of the buy in Third Fiscal Quarter 1985. See the previously distributed *Syndicated Television Recommendation* prepared by Western International Media Corp. (WIMC) dated May 18, 1984. This recommendation includes a complete explanation/summary of syndicated television and its importance to Denny's in FY85.

Total FY85 network/syndication expenditures (excluding compensation, cut-ins, integration, and New York) amount to $10,953,210. These were based on the buy authorization immediately following, dated June 26, 1984.

Following the buy authorization and Western's buying trip to New York each year, WIMC distributes a summary of the planned and recommended prime-time, syndication, and fine-tuning expenditures for the 1984/85 season. Please refer to this document titled *Denny's 1984–1985 Network Television Recommendation,* June 27, 1984, for details of the recommendation.

Spot television flights are authorized on a per flight basis. To date, the only spot flight authorized and bought is August. Please refer to the FY85 Spot Market List, which shows those markets that received advertising in August and their actual expenditure to date. The May and June columns reflect payout and payout plus selected markets with budgets based on the most cost-effective daypart mix in that quarter. Note that boldface type denotes payout markets and regular type denotes selected markets. For additional details of daypart mix and promotion by market, see the August Spot Buy Authorization dated June 19, 1984, previously distributed. [See Appendix B Table 10–11, an example of a Denny's authorization Form.]

The remaining activity will be implemented as planning is finalized (key priority, field marketing, testing, etc.).

Appendix B Table 10–10   **Denny's FV66 Budget Summary**

Promotional Cycles	BAB	Various	GSB	GSB	Dinner	Dinner	Dinner
National #9200	July	August	September	October	November	December	January
Network television							
Network (time only)	2,177,200	—	2,087,550[1]	543,000[1]	1,776,083	488,917	1,431,164
Compensation	69,670	—	86,521	24,979	115,000	20,000	110,000
Cut-ins	—	—	—	—	41,220	13,740	41,220
Integration	24,520	—	19,206	3,500	15,000	—	17,000
Total network TV	2,271,390	—	2,193,277	571,479	1,947,303	522,657	1,599,384
Syndicated television							
Syndication (time only)	—	—	—	72,790	218,370	72,790	224,370
Cut-ins	—	—	—	—	18,000	6,000	18,000
Total syndication	—	—	—	72,790	236,370	78,790	242,370
Testing (Incremental)							
Simul/continuity	—	—	—	112,100	50,065	112,100	24,845
Increased frequency	—	—	47,074	47,074	47,074	47,074	47,074
Copy test	—	—	20,835	20,835	20,835	20,835	20,835
(we take care)							
Total testing (incremental)	—	—	67,909	180,009	117,974	180,009	92,754
Hispanic testing	—	—	—	—	—	56,366	—
Shipping charges (estimates)							
Total	1,500	2,000	2,100	500	1,500	500	1,500
Contingency							
Total	30,769	30,769	38,462	30,769	30,769	38,462	24,315
Total national #9200	2,303,669	32,769	2,301,748	855,547	2,333,916	876,784	1,960,323
Nonnational #9203							
Spot television	—	1,086,746	—	—	—	—	—
Nonnational media (fld.mkg)	38,462	38,462	48,077	38,462	38,462	48,077	38,462
Contingency	7,692	7,692	9,615	7,692	7,692	9,615	7,692
Total nonnational #9203	46,154	1,132,900	57,692	46,154	46,154	57,692	46,154
Key priority #9213							
Total key priority #9213	—	63,462	177,963	142,371	142,371	177,963	142,371
Total media	$2,349,813	$1,229,131	$2,537,403	$1,044,072	$2,522,441	$1,112,439	2,148,848

[1]Sept/Oct—GSB includes LN $110,000.

Appendix B Table 10–11   **FCB/Denny's Buy Authorization**

Activity:	National
Promotion:	FY85/86 Up front
	Late night (Jan/Feb/Mar)
	Syndication (Oct–Sept)
Medium:	Network television
	Syndication
Flight dates:	10/1/84–9/22/85
Goals:	

	Budget	TRPs
Up-front prime	$ 9,143,603	1,175.0
Late night (Jan, Feb, Mar)	602,010	96.6
Syndication (Oct–Sept)	1,301,211	238.4
	$11,046,824	1,510.0

Comments: Budget figures are for *time only*. Compensation budget to be authorized on a per flight basis.

Client signature _____ Date_____

Dinner February	Breakfast March	Breakfast April	Various May	Dinner June	FY85 Planned Total	Total Budget	Difference
390,788	1,995,000	—	—	—	10,889,702		
20,000	110,000	—	—	—	556,170		
13,740	—	—	—	—	109,920		
—	13,500	—	—	—	92,726		
424,528	2,118,500	—	—	—	$ 11,648,518	$ 11,674,718	−26,200
74,790	299,160	—	—	—	962,270		
6,000	—	—	—	—	48,000		
80,790	299,160	—	—	—	$ 1,010,270	$ 1,010,270	-0-
86,227	24,845	—	—	—	410,182		
47,074	—	—	—	—	282,444		
20,825	—	—	—	—	125,000		
154,126	24,845	—	—	—	$ 817,626	$ 789,093	+28,533
—	—	—	—	56,366	$ 112,732	$ 112,732	-0-
500	2,000	—	2,100	2,100	$ 16,300	$ 16,300	-0-
24,315	30,394	30,769	30,769	38,462	$ 379,024	$ 379,024	-0-
684,259	2,474,899	30,769	32,869	96,928	$13,984,470	$ 13,982,137	+2,333
—	—	—	1,054,035	1,691,165	3,831,946	4,057,360	−225,414
			Payout	Payout			
38,462	48,077	38,462	38,462	48,073	500,000	500,000	-0-
7,692	9,615	7,692	7,692	9,619	100,000	100,000	-0-
46,154	57,692	46,154	1,100,189	1,748,857	$ 4,431,946	$ 4,657,360	$ −225,414
142,371	177,963	142,371	142,371	177,961	$ 1,629,538	$ 1,693,000	−63,462
$872,784	$ 2,710,554	$ 219,294	1,275,429	$2,023,746	$20,045,954	$20,332,497	$ −286,543

Evaluation of Broadcast Media

CHAPTER OBJECTIVES

1. To examine the structure of the television and radio industries and the role of each medium in the advertising program

2. To examine the advantages and limitations of television and radio as advertising media

3. To examine the various issues, concepts, and considerations of relevance in using television and radio in the media program

4. To explain how advertising time is purchased for the broadcast media, how audiences are measured, and how rates are determined

5. To consider future trends and developments regarding television and radio and how they will influence the use of these media in advertising

Bring Back the Good Old Days

Life used to be fairly simple for advertisers who wanted to use television as part of their media mix. In the 1960s and 1970s television was dominated by the three major networks. In 1965 only 8 percent of U.S. television households could receive nine or more TV stations on their primarily black and white sets, and the networks had nearly 95 percent of the prime-time viewing audiences. Nearly 80 percent of the commercials shown in 1965 were 60 seconds in length, which meant that consumers saw only 12 to 15 ads per hour. In most households the man was the breadwinner, whereas the woman stayed home and raised the children. Thus, the daytime game shows and soap operas became very popular as advertising media vehicles. In the evening the family could be reached by network programs such as the *Ed Sullivan Show, The Beverly Hillbillies,* or *Star Trek.*

During the 1970s things began to change. The number of U.S. households with televisions increased from 54.8 million in 1965 to nearly 70 million in 1975, with three quarters of the homes having color TVs and 43 percent having two or more sets. The percentage of TV households able to receive nine or more stations increased to 31 percent; however, the network share of the prime-time audience was still over 90 percent in 1975. One important trend that did develop in the 1970s was the emergence of the 30-second commercial, as 93 percent of the network spots in 1975 were 30 seconds in length. With this trend toward shorter commercials, many advertisers began to become concerned about getting consumers' attention and the problem of advertising clutter. However, the size of the TV viewing audience and popularity of the medium continued throughout the last half of this decade and into the 1980s. During this period advertisers were increasingly turning to television, as it was generally regarded as the most effective advertising medium for products and services targeted to mass markets. The competition for the limited amount of network time, along with an inflationary economy, led to a dramatic increase in television advertising rates. One ad agency estimated that the cost of a prime-time spot in-creased 230 percent from 1970 to 1982—a figure far greater than any other advertising medium and the general inflation rate.

Throughout the decade of the 1980s there have been dramatic changes in the dynamics of television in general and particularly in TV advertising. Cable television has become a major industry, as more than half of U.S. homes are now wired for cable, which greatly expands their viewing options. In 1987 the A. C. Nielsen Company estimated that 86 percent of U.S. TV households could receive 9 or more stations, whereas 31 percent could receive 30+. The network share of the TV viewing audience has been steadily declining as their share of the prime-time viewers dropped below 70 percent in cable households in 1989. Thirty-second commercials were the standard in 1985, accounting for 84 percent of the network spots. The number of ads on network TV has nearly tripled over the past two decades to more than 6,000 per week. The problem of commercial clutter promises only to get worse as 15-second commercials are expected to become the standard advertising unit by 1990.

As if all this were not enough to give most media planners headaches, zapping, or remote control channel changing, is becoming a major problem, as is zipping, or fast forwarding, through the commercial breaks on programs recorded on video cassette recorders (VCRs). VCRs are now in more than 60 percent of American homes, and penetration is particularly high among baby boomers—one of Madison Avenue's most coveted audiences. Just for good measure, throw in a well-educated audience (many of whom find television shows and commercials boring or even irritating), dual-income households with little time for TV viewing, and very few new ads that are captivating or original, and you get a sense of the problems facing the television advertiser. No wonder so many people in agencies, companies, and the television industry yearn for the good old days![1,2,3]

Introduction

The Changing Role of the Broadcast Media

For nearly 70 years the **broadcast media** of radio and television have been a dominant part of the lives of most Americans. Radio was a major news, information, and entertainment medium from the 1920s to the early 1950s. During this era, advertisers embraced radio not only by developing and placing messages for the new medium but also by creating and producing programs that would attract audiences and serve as a vehicle for their commercials. However, the golden era of radio came to an abrupt halt beginning in 1950 with the introduction of television as a national medium. As can be seen in Figure 11–1, the number of households in the United States with television sets increased from 4.6 million in 1950 to 32 million in 1955. Radio stations saw many of their listeners become television viewers, and the major networks turned most of their attention to developing programs for the new medium. Advertisers be-

Figure 11–1 The Growth of Television Ownership in the United States

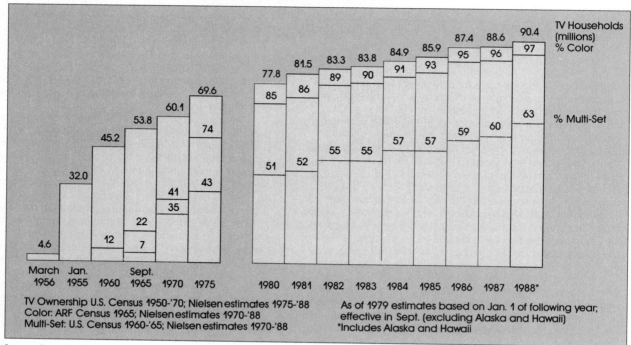

TV Ownership U.S. Census 1950-'70; Nielsen estimates 1975-'88
Color: ARF Census 1965; Nielsen estimates 1970-'88
Multi-Set: U.S. Census 1960-'65; Nielsen estimates 1970-'88

As of 1979 estimates based on Jan. 1 of following year;
effective in Sept. (excluding Alaska and Hawaii)
*Includes Alaska and Hawaii

Source: *Report on Television 1989,* Nielsen Media Research (Northbrook, Ill.: A. C. Nielsen, Co., 1989).

gan turning their attention to television as well, recognizing that it was the best medium for reaching the increasing number of families that were developing as the "baby boom" moved into full gear. Of course, advertisers were also attracted to television because of the creative opportunities it offered for presenting and demonstrating their products. Radio went through a very difficult period in the 1960s and 1970s, as many advertisers neglected the medium in favor of television. However, during the 1980s many advertisers rediscovered the advantages and opportunities available through radio advertising, and it has once again become a very popular medium.

Television has seen unprecedented growth over the past three decades, both in terms of increases in households owning a set and also with respect to advertisers' use of the medium. However, just as radio faced challenges in the 1960s and 1970s, many feel that television is now entering a period of transition. As noted at the beginning of the chapter, the limited availability of network television time, a greater number of viewing options due to cable and VCRs, as well as increasing clutter and dislike for commercials have many advertising and television executives very concerned. Two of the three major networks have been acquired by larger companies (NBC by RCA, which was in turn bought by General Electric; and ABC by Capital Cities Communications), whereas CBS made massive cuts and layoffs to remain a private company. As we enter the 1990s, the role and nature of television as an advertising medium are clearly in a state of transition and change.

An Overview of Radio and Television

Radio and television are probably the most pervasive media in the lives of most American consumers. Think for a moment about the number of television sets and radios in your home. Some 98 percent of the 92 million U.S. households own a television set (97 percent of which are color), and 63 percent own two or more sets (Figure 11–1). The typical person spends an average of three and a half hours a day watching television.[4] Radio is clearly the most ubiquitous of all the media, as there are more than 500 million radios in the United States, or over five per household.[5] This total

includes the more than 120 million automobile radios that entertain, inform, and present commercials to us as we drive in our cars every day. Obviously, advertisers recognize the value of the broadcast media for reaching the consumer, as nearly $23 billion was spent on television advertising and over $7 billion on radio in 1988.[6]

Radio and television have certain similarities as broadcast media. Unlike the print media, radio and television are *time-* rather than space-oriented and are sold in segments ranging from a few seconds to as much as an hour. Both radio and television are organized similarly, as some stations belong to a network or nationwide system of programming, whereas others are independent producers and buyers of programming. Time on both media is sold on a network or nationwide basis as well as on a local market basis. Radio and television both rely on the public airways to broadcast their programs, must be licensed to operate, and are regulated by the Federal Communications Commission (FCC). Both media use similar methods for gathering information on the size and composition of their audiences. Finally, both are often referred to as low- or passive-involvement media since the consumer can pick up messages and be influenced by either radio or television commercials without actively attending to them. Think about how often you turn on the radio or even the television for "background" entertainment while doing something else (such as reading this book!).

While radio and television do share these characteristics, it should be obvious that as advertising media vehicles they differ in many ways. Because radio offers only an audio message, it is more limited in its ability to communicate and present the advertiser's appeal. Radio is also a relatively low cost medium and more adaptable to changing conditions and situations but lacks the prestige of television. However, as the ad in Figure 11–2 shows, radio and television often compete with one another for advertisers' media dollars.

In this chapter we will examine the broadcast media of radio and television including the general characteristics of each as well as specific strengths and weaknesses. We will examine how advertisers use radio and television as part of their advertising and media strategy, how they buy television and radio time, and how audiences are

Figure 11–3 **This Television Commercial Helps Demonstrate the Sensation of Driving a Sports Car**

measured and evaluated for each medium. We will also consider how various factors and developments are likely to change the role of television and radio as advertising media vehicles in the future.

Television

It has often been said that television represents the ideal advertising medium. The ability of television to combine visual images, sound, motion, and color present the advertiser with the opportunity to develop creative and imaginative appeals unlike any other medium. However, television does have certain problems or limitations that limit or even prevent its use by many advertisers. Let us examine some of the specific advantages and limitations of television as an advertising medium.

Advantages of Television

Creativity and Impact   Perhaps the greatest advantage of television is the opportunity it provides for presenting the advertising message. The interaction of sight and sound offers tremendous creative opportunity and flexibility in developing the message and makes it possible to create dramatic and life-like representations of products and services. Television commercials can be used to convey a mood or image for a brand as well as to develop emotional or entertaining appeals that may help make an otherwise dull product appear exciting or interesting.

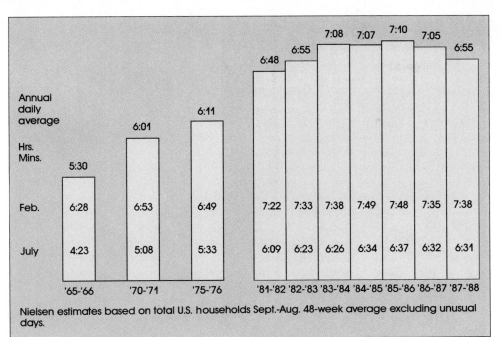

Source: *Report on Television 1989,* Nielsen Media Research (Northbrook, Ill.: A. C. Nielsen Co., 1989).

Television is also an excellent medium for demonstrating a product or service. For example, print ads are effective for showing a sports car and communicating information regarding its features, but only a TV commercial can put you in the driver's seat and give you the sense of actually driving through high-speed turns, and winding roads, as shown by the Mazda RX-7 Turbo commercial in Figure 11–3.

Coverage and Cost Effectiveness   Another advantage of television advertising is that it makes it possible to reach large audiences. As noted earlier, television sets have virtually saturated American households and become an important source of news and entertainment. Nearly everyone, regardless of age, sex, income, or education level watches at least some television on a regular basis. As can be seen in Figure 11–4, the average hours of household viewing TV usage per day has risen from five and a half hours in 1965, leveling off at around seven hours in the mid- to late-1980s.

Marketers who sell products that appeal to broad target audiences find not only that television gives them an opportunity to reach their market but also that television offers very good cost efficiencies. For example, a 30-second advertisement on a top-rated network program such as the "Cosby Show" may cost $380,000, but it will be exposed to nearly 30 million households. Thus, the cost of reaching a thousand consumers by advertising on this program will be less than $13.00 (if you cannot perform this calculation, you should refer back to Chapter 10). In 1988 the average cost per thousand (CPM) was $8.22 for network evening shows and only $2.26 for daytime weekday shows.[7]

Because of its ability to reach large audiences and the cost efficiencies it offers, television is a particularly popular medium among companies selling mass-consumption products. Companies with widespread distribution and availability of their products and services use television to reach the mass market and deliver their advertising messages at a very low cost per thousand. Television has become a highly dominant and indispensable medium to large consumer packaged–goods companies who devote a large percentage of their media budgets to television advertising. In 1988 the top 100 national advertisers (many of whom are consumer packaged-goods companies) accounted for nearly 75 percent of all monies spent on network television advertising.

Figure 11–5 MTV Promotes Its Ability to Reach the Youth Market

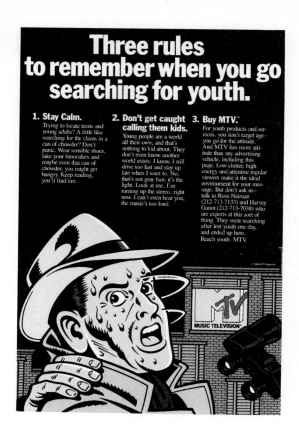

Captivity and Attention   Television is basically intrusive in that commercials impose themselves on viewers as they watch their favorite programs. Unless a special effort is made to avoid commercials, most of us will end up being exposed to thousands of them each year. Of course, the increase in viewing options and the penetration of VCRs, remote controls, and other automatic devices have made it easier for TV viewers to avoid commercial messages. For example, a recent study of consumers' viewing habits found that the audience for commercials declines an average of 17 percent from that of the program (an issue that is discussed later in this chapter).[8] However, the remaining viewers are likely to be exposed and devote some attention to many advertising messages. As discussed in Chapter 5, the low-involvement nature of consumer learning and response processes may mean that television advertising has the potential to have an effect on consumers simply through heavy repetition and exposure to catchy slogans, jingles, and the like.

Selectivity and Flexibility   Television has often been criticized for being a nonselective medium since it is difficult to reach a precisely defined and small market segment through the use of television advertising. While this is true to some extent, selectivity is possible since there are variations in the composition of television audiences as a result of program content, broadcast time, and geographic coverage. Audiences may vary by time of the day or night when they watch television, the programs watched, and even the day of the week. For example, Saturday morning television caters to children, Saturday and Sunday afternoon programs are geared to the sports-oriented male, and weekday, daytime shows appeal heavily to housewives. With the growth of cable television, advertisers are able to refine their television coverage further by appealing to groups with specific interests such as sports, news, or music. The ad for MTV shown in Figure 11–5 promotes the value of the network for reaching the youth market.

Flexibility is also possible through television advertising, as advertisers can adjust their media strategies to take advantage of potential that may exist in different geographic markets through local or spot advertisements in specific market areas. Ads can also be scheduled to be seen repeatedly or to take advantage of special occasions. For example, Gillette has traditionally been a major sponsor during the baseball World Series Classic every fall, which allows it to advertise heavily to men who constitute the primary market for many of the company's products.

Limitations of Television

Although television has many advantages and is unsurpassed from a creative perspective, the medium has several disadvantages that limit or preclude its use by many advertisers. These problems include high costs, the lack of selectivity, the fleeting nature of a television message, commercial clutter, and distrust of TV ads.

Costs Despite the efficiency of television in reaching large audiences, the fact remains that it is an expensive medium in which to advertise. The high cost of using television stems not only from the expense of buying airtime but also from the costs of producing a quality commercial. In a survey of 1987 commercial production costs, the American Association of Advertising Agencies found that the average national brand 30-second spot cost $156,000 to produce.[9] Even local ads can be very expensive to produce and often are not of high quality. The high costs of producing and airing commercials may be less of a problem for major advertisers with large budgets. However, high costs often price small- and medium-sized advertisers out of the television market, as they cannot afford to develop and run a television advertising program.

Lack of Selectivity As discussed in the previous section, some selectivity is available in television through variations in programs and with the growth of cable TV. Many advertisers, however, are seeking a very specific, and often small, target audience and find the coverage of television often extends beyond their market, thus reducing its cost effectiveness, as was discussed in Chapter 10. Geographic selectivity can be a problem to local advertisers such as a retailer since a station bases its rates on the total market area it reaches. For example, television stations in Pittsburgh, Pennsylvania, reach viewers in western Pennsylvania, eastern Ohio, northern West Virginia, and even parts of Maryland. The small company or retailer whose market is limited to the immediate Pittsburgh area may find television to be an inefficient media buy since the stations cover a geographic area that is larger than the merchant's trade area.

The audience selectivity of television is improving as advertisers are able to target certain groups of consumers through the type of program or day and/or time when they choose to advertise. However, television still does not offer the advertiser the same audience selectivity as other media such as radio, magazines, newspapers, or direct mail for reaching precise segments of the market.

Fleeting Message A concern that many advertisers have with television is that commercials usually last for a very short time and generally leave nothing tangible for the viewer to examine or to consider. As was discussed in Chapter 6, television commercials have become shorter and shorter as the demand for a limited amount of broadcast time intensifies and advertisers seek to get more message impressions from their media budgets (Figure 11–6). As can be seen in Table 11–1, 30-second commercials

Table 11–1　Changes in Percentage of Network Commercials by Length

Commercial Length	1965	1975	1980	1985	1987	1988
15	—	—	—	10	31	36
30	23	93	96	84	65	61
60	77	6	2	2	2	2
All others	—	1	2	4	2	1

Source: Television Advertising Bureau from *Broadcast Advertisers Reports.*

Figure 11–6 **The Use of Shorter Commercials Is Increasing**

1. BOSS: Dorsel,

2. BOSS (VO): you did remember to send the document to Denver? DORSEL: Denver?

3. BOSS (VO): You know the deadline's tomorrow. DORSEL: Tomorrow...

4. ANNCR (VO): Next time you blow it, remember, there's always Federal Express.

have been produced since the mid-1970s. However, in September 1986 the three networks began accepting 15-second spots across their full schedules (except during children's viewing time), and after just three years, these shorter ads are accounting for more than a third of all network spots.

The trend toward shorter commercials means that advertisers must be able to get consumers' attention and present an idea or selling proposition during a very short time period. While this may be possible with very simple, single-minded messages, it is very difficult to communicate a more detailed or complex message in a 15-second spot. However, it appears that the lower costs of 15-second spots is appealing to advertisers, and the trend toward shorter commercials will continue, as discussed in Promotional Perspective 11–1.

Clutter The problems of fleeting messages and shorter commercials are compounded by the fact that the advertiser's message is only one of many that is seen during a commercial break and as a result may have trouble being noticed amid all the "clutter." Perhaps the greatest concern advertisers have expressed recently with regard to television advertising is the potential decline in its effectiveness owing to the problem of clutter.[10] The next time you watch television, take a moment to count the number of commercials and other items, such as promotions for the news or upcoming programs, that appear during a station break, and you will appreciate why clutter is a concern.

The major cause of clutter has been the shift among advertisers to the use of shorter commercials, as discussed above. However, the clutter problem could also increase if television networks and individual stations make more time available for commercials. For many years the amount of time available for commercials was restricted by the Code Authority of the National Association of Broadcasters and was limited to 9.5 minutes per hour during prime time and 12 minutes during non–prime time. However, the code was suspended in 1982 on the grounds that it violates antitrust law. While initially the networks did not alter their time standards, over the past several years they have increased the number of commercial minutes in their time schedules to control the cost of advertising time and increase their revenues.[11] As the size of the networks' viewing audience continues to decline, it is likely that they will seek to increase the amount of time available for commercials.

Distrust and Negative Evaluation To many critics of advertising, the television commercial personifies everything that is wrong with the industry. Critics of advertising often single out television ads because of their pervasiveness as well as the intrusive nature of the medium. Consumers are seen as defenseless against the barrage of television ads since they are not able to control the transmission of the message. In addition, studies have shown that distrust of the various forms of advertising is generally the highest for television commercials.[12] Particular concern has been raised over the effect of advertising on specific groups such as children or the elderly.

Promotional Perspective **11—1**

Does Anyone Remember the 60-Second Commercial?

The time it takes you to read this first paragraph is roughly the length of time advertisers have to deliver their message in a typical commercial. There was a time, which most of us do not remember, when the 60-second TV commercial was prevalent. However, the standard 60-second commercial of the 1960s became a 30-second spot in the 1970s and 1980s, and many advertising media experts predict that 15-second commercials will replace 30-second spots as the standard length by the early 1990s.

An important factor behind the decline in commercial length has been the spiraling inflation in media costs over the past decade. With the average costs of a prime-time spot reaching over $100,000, many advertisers see shorter commercials as the only way to keep their media costs in line. By using 30- or even 15-second commercials, they can run additional spots and reinforce the message or reach a larger audience.

Another reason is that many advertisers feel that the shorter commercials can deliver a message just as effectively as longer spots and, of course, for much less money. A large-scale study compared the performance of 15- and 30-second spots and found that using an index, where the average 30-second spot scored a 100 for communication performance, the typical 15-second spot scored a 76. The 15-second spots also scored well on another performance measure, which was the average number of ideas played back per viewer—2.6 for the 15 versus 2.9 for the 30. Finally, the 30- and 15-second spots were rated about equally with regard to viewers' sense of the importance of the main idea created by the commercial.

The booming demand for 15-second spots by advertisers has created a number of problems for the three major TV networks, who are concerned about clutter and product protection—not having two commercials for the same product in the same commercial cluster or pod. For example, CBS policy limits two 15-second spots or one "split 30" (which is a 30-second spot where the advertiser promotes two different products with separate messages) to both a 90-second and a 120-second pod, so there are never more than five commercial messages during a break. The networks indicated that they had reached saturation levels for 15-second spots during the 1988/89 television season and were expected to begin charging premiums for these spots to help lessen demand. Originally the networks priced the 15-second spots at half the cost of a 30-second spot. While the networks' intentions were to attract smaller advertisers, many large packaged-goods marketers began using the shorter format, since they found them to be nearly as effective yet at half the costs, which allowed them to use more prime-time advertising.

It is expected that some large TV advertisers will battle any network attempts to charge premiums for the 15-second spots and that the networks will change their policies to add more 15-second spots to the commercial pods. However, many feel that the networks, along with some major advertisers, want limits on the number of shorter spots so that commercial clutter does not get worse. For example, in June of 1989 ABC announced that it was reducing by 20 percent the number of 15-second spots in news shows, its "Good Morning America" program, and in prime time in an effort to deal with the clutter problem.

Sources: Robert Parcher, "15-Second TV Commercials Appear to Work 'Quite Well,'" *Marketing News*, January 3, 1986, p. 1; Verne Gay, "Price Hikes Loom for TV's Hot :15s," *Advertising Age*, August 29, 1988, p. 1; Joanne Lipman, "ABC to Cut 20% of 15 Second Ads in Bid to End Commercial Clutter," *The Wall Street Journal*, June 20, 1989, p. B8.

When to Use Television Advertising

The various advantages of television, particularly its powerful impact and ability to reach large audiences, make it a very important medium for many advertisers. For these companies the decision is not *whether* to use this form of advertising but rather *how* they can use it most effectively. However, as we have discussed in the preceding pages, television does have its limitations as an advertising medium. Thus, companies considering whether or not to use this form of television must take several factors into consideration including the following[13]:

• Do we have a large enough budget to finance the production of quality commercials? This is particularly important for large companies competing on a national or regional level since they want to protect the image of their brands as well as that of their company. Many local companies do produce commercials for a fraction of the cost of national ads (and it is often evident), but they are not attempting to compete on a national level against firms with high-quality commercials.

• Do we have a large enough media budget to sustain a continuous schedule and generate the exposures needed to have an impact on the target audience? Television advertising may be a very efficient media buy for many companies, but the absolute costs of buying commercial time and sustaining a TV schedule can be very expensive, particularly on a national level.

• Is there a large market for our product or service, and can this market be reached efficiently through a specific network, station, or program? Because of the costs of TV advertising, a firm selling to a specialized market must consider whether there is a way to target this audience through television effectively. Many companies are taking advantage of the specialized audiences reached through cable and independent stations and are making television part of their media mix.

• Is it necessary to make a strong impact on the market through the use of a creative advertising campaign? Television is a very powerful medium, and many companies have used it to create messages that focus attention on their products or services and effectively differentiate them from competitors'. Television is the best medium for making a strong impact on consumers and adding a dimension of prestige to a company and/or its brands.

Buying Television Time

There are a number of options available to advertisers who choose to utilize television as part of their media mix. Advertisers can purchase time in a variety of program formats that appeal to various type and sizes of audiences. Commercial time can be purchased on a national, regional, or local basis. An advertiser can choose to sponsor an entire program, participate in the sponsorship, or use spot announcements during or between programs.

The purchase of television advertising time is a highly specialized phase of the advertising business, particularly for large companies spending huge sums of money. The large advertiser who makes extensive use of television advertising generally utilizes agency media specialists or specialized media buying services to arrange their media schedule and purchase television time. Decisions have to be made regarding national or network versus local or spot purchases, selection of specific stations, sponsorship versus participation, different classes of time, and of course appropriate programs. Local advertisers may not have to deal with the first decision but do face all the others if they choose to utilize television advertising. In this section we will examine some of the considerations involved in the purchase of television time.

Network versus Spot

A basic decision that faces all advertisers is the allocation of their television media budget among network versus local or spot announcements. Most national advertisers that are heavy users of television use network schedules to provide national coverage and supplement this with regional or local spot purchases to reach markets where additional coverage is desired or needed. Each of these types of television advertising purchases is examined in more detail below.

Network Advertising   A common way by which advertisers disseminate their messages is the purchase of airtime from a **television network.** A network assembles a series of affiliated local television stations or **affiliates** to which it supplies programming and services. These affiliates, most of which are independently owned, contractually agree to preempt time during specified hours for programming provided by the networks and to carry the national advertising within the program. The networks share the advertising revenue they receive during these time periods with the affiliates. The affiliates are also free to sell commercial time in nonnetwork periods and during station breaks in the preempted periods to both national and local advertisers.

Table 11-2 **Primetime Network Television 30-Second Price List 1989/90**

Time	SUN ABC	SUN CBS	SUN NBC	SUN FOX	MON ABC	MON CBS	MON NBC	MON FOX	TUE ABC	TUE CBS	TUE NBC	WED ABC	WED CBS	WED NBC	THU ABC	THU CBS	THU NBC	FRI ABC	FRI CBS	FRI NBC	SAT ABC	SAT CBS	SAT NBC	SAT FOX
7:00	Life Goes On* 55K	60 Minutes 215K	Disney 110K	Booker* 80K																				
8:00	Free Spirit* 65K	Murder She Wrote 240K	Sister Kate* 150K	America's Most Wanted 140K	MacGyver 95K	Major Dad* 115K	ALF 200K	21 Jump Street** 85K	Who's the Boss? 260K	Rescue 911* 95K	Matlock 125K	Growing Pains 200K	Peaceable Kingdom* 75K	Unsolved Mysteries 155K	Mission Impossible** 60K	48 Hours 95K	Cosby 300K	Full House** 150K	Snoops* 105K	Baywatch* 90K	Mr. Belvedere** 95K	Paradise 60K	227 115K	Cops** 55K
8:30	Homeroom* 55K		My Two Dads** 160K	Hidden Video* 115K		People Next Door* 125K	Hogan Family 180K		Wonder Years 250K			Head of the Class 175K					Different World 280K	*Family Matters 125K			Living Dolls* 60K		Amen 135K	**The Reporters 50K
9:00	Movie 140K	Movie 175K	Movie 180K	Married With Children** 140K	Football 235K	Murphy Brown 195K	Movie 160K	Alien Nation* 55K	Rosanne 375K	Wolf* 100K	Heat of the Night 145K	Anything But Love** 150K	Jake and the Fatman 100K	Night Court 195K	The Young Riders 90K	Top of the Hill* 105K	Cheers 330K	**Perfect Strangers 145K	Dallas 100K	Hardball* 120K	Mystery Movie 80K	Tour of Duty** 70K	Golden Girls 210K	
9:30				Open House* 80K		Famous Teddy Z 159K			Chicken Soup* 230K			Doogie Howser, M.D.* 115K		Nutt House* 130K			Dear John 250K	Just the Ten of Us 115K					Empty Nest 200K	Beyond Tomorrow* 45K
10:00				Tracy Ullman Show** 60K		Designing Women** 180K		Movie 75K	thirty-something 200K	Island Son 65K	Midnight Caller 140K	China Beach 150K	Wiseguy 145K	Quantum Leap 110K	Prime Time Live* 110K	Knots Landing 155K	L.A. Law 260K	20/20 140K	Falcon Crest 95K	Mancuso FBI* 125K	Saturday Night with Connie Chung 70K		Hunter 160K	Local
10:30				Gary Shandling 55K		Newhart** 135K																		

*New program **Time period change

Source: Verne Gay, "Unit Costs Soar 25–30% for November Prime," *Variety,* August 30–September 5, 1989, pp. 73–74.

The three major television networks—NBC, ABC, CBS—each have affiliates throughout the nation such that they have almost complete national coverage. Thus, when an advertiser purchases airtime from one of these three national networks, the commercial is transmitted across the nation through the affiliate station network. Network advertising truly represents a mass medium, as the advertiser can broadcast its message simultaneously throughout the country with a network commercial.

A major advantage of network advertising is the simplification of the purchase process, as the advertiser only has to deal with one party or media representative to air a commercial nationwide. The networks also offer the most popular programs and generally control prime-time programming, which is when the large audiences are available. According to the A. C. Nielsen Company, a typical prime-time program reaches approximately 13 million households. Thus, advertisers interested in reaching the huge nationwide audiences will generally buy network time during the prime viewing hours of 8 to 11 P.M.

There are some problems associated with network advertising that limits its attractiveness to some companies. The major drawback is the high cost of network time. Table 11–2 shows estimates of costs for a 30-second spot on the three networks' prime-time shows during the 1989/90 television season. The average costs of a 30-second spot on a prime-time show ranged from $122,273 on CBS to $158,750 on ABC to $165,341 on NBC. Thus, only advertisers with large budgets can afford to use network advertising on a regular basis.

Availability of time can also be a problem as more advertisers turn to network advertising to reach mass markets. Over the past several years a large portion of the prime-time commercial spots, particularly on the popular shows, has been sold during the up-front market. The **up-front market** is a buying period that takes place prior to the upcoming television season when the networks sell a large part of their commercial time. Thus, advertisers hoping to use prime-time network advertising must plan

Promotional Perspective 11–2

Buying Time in the Up-front Market

Every spring, representatives of advertising agencies, media buying services, and the major television networks get together to kick off what has become known as the "up-front market" for network television advertising time. The networks sell a large part of their commercial time as much as 52 weeks in advance during this period. National advertisers buy anywhere from a third to three quarters of their network TV time for the upcoming broadcast year in the up-front market to secure guarantees or assurances that purchased ratings levels will be met and to get lower prices that they could get in the short-term or "scatter market" after the season begins.

The process begins in April or May when advertisers release their network TV budget guidelines to their agencies. Media planners set rough buying goals in terms of audience targets and gross ratings points and decide how much money will go to each network daypart. Once the networks announce their new prime-time schedules, the negotiating process begins. Actual rates paid for commercial time in the up-front market depend on a number of factors including the ratings from the previous season as well as those predicted for the upcoming year and demand—which depends on the number of advertisers who choose to enter the up-front market. Up-front sales for the 1988/89 season were 15 percent lower than the previous season, as many advertisers began allocating more of their media budgets to cable TV. However, up-front sales for the 1989/90 network season

reached a record level of $3.7 billion, fueled by a heavy demand for commercial time by automobile manufacturers. Media planners fine-tune their network mix depending on prices and availabilities they encounter during the negotiating process.

During the buying process, network account executives and agency media buyers negotiate a package of programs. While the advertisers may prefer to buy a package consisting of all top-rated shows, the networks rarely sell these shows without including a few new or struggling series in the deal. Once the package is set, negotiation over price begins, with actual rates depending on rating guarantees, cancellation options, and other points. Buyers willing to make deals without guarantees or cancellation options can usually win other concessions such as lower prices. Once the deal is set, the network puts it on hold and allows the agency a week or so to go over the buy with its client before making a commitment. Billions of dollars in network time are purchased during the up-front market with a handshake and a smile, as signed contracts are almost unheard of in the business. No money actually changes hands until the commercial time airs and the networks invoice the order.

Sources: Joe Mandese, "Let the Season Begin," *Marketing & Media Decisions*, May 1988, pp. 36–44; Wayne Wally, "Cable Steals Upfront Show from TV Nets," *Advertising Age*, June 13, 1988, p. 1; Verne Gay, "Upfront Market Draws Bleak Forecast for Nets," *Advertising Age*, June 6, 1988, p. 1; Wayne Walley, "Red-hot Upfront Market Could Hit $3.7B," *Advertising Age*, June 19, 1989, pp. 1, 76.

their media schedules and purchase time very early. The up-front market buying process is discussed in more detail in Promotional Perspective 11–2.

A final problem with network advertising is that companies often have variations in the market potential for their products and may not want to pay for nationwide advertising. For example, Coors beer did not have a distribution network in a number of states including New York, New Jersey, and Pennsylvania until 1987. Thus, the company did not want to make heavy use of network advertising and reach consumers who could not purchase the product in their areas. Consequently, much of Coors' television media budget was spent on spot advertising rather than network until distribution was established in most of the states.

While the majority of network advertising dollars go to the three major networks, several other types of networks have evolved in recent years, including the Fox Broadcasting Company, which broadcasts its programs over a group of affiliated independent stations. Cable television networks also have developed to provide programming to local cable systems in cities throughout the country (cable television is discussed later in the chapter). Network television can also be purchased on a regional basis, making it possible for an advertiser's message to be aired in certain sections of the country with one media purchase.

Regional networks were created by the major TV networks in the early 1970s in response to complaints by smaller companies that access to network TV gave national companies an unfair competitive advantage. Facing legal action if they did not offer regional advertising packages, the networks agreed to do so. However, the networks agreed to make regional buys available only under the conditions that they could find advertisers interested in reaching remaining parts of the country during the time slot such that the network ultimately ended up with a national sale. An advertiser who makes a regional network purchase generally pays in proportion to the percentage of the country receiving the message plus a nominal fee for splitting the feed. The amount of money spent for regional network advertising represents less than 5 percent of network advertising revenue.[14] However, the increasing use of regional marketing by national advertisers is likely to result in increased regional network advertising.[15] For example, in 1988 American Airlines began using a regionalized advertising strategy that used separate creative campaigns in various areas of the country such as the East and West coasts.[16]

Spot and Local Advertising **Spot advertising** refers to commercials shown on local television stations, with the negotiation and purchase of time being made directly from the individual stations. All nonnetwork advertising done by a national advertiser is known as **national spot** advertising, whereas airtime sold to local firms such as retailers, restaurants, banks, and auto dealers is known as **local advertising.** Local advertisers desire media whose coverage is limited to the geographic markets in which they do business. As discussed earlier, this may be difficult to accomplish with television as the broadcast area covered by a local station may extend beyond the retailer's trade area. However, many local businesses are large enough to make efficient use of television advertising.

Spot advertising offers the national advertiser greater flexibility in adjusting to local market conditions. The advertiser can concentrate commercials in areas where market potential is the greatest or where additional support is needed. This is obviously appealing to advertisers with uneven distribution or limited advertising budgets, as well as those interested in test-marketing or introducing a product in limited market areas. National advertisers also often use spot television advertising through local retailers or dealers as a part of their cooperative advertising programs and as a way of providing local dealer support.

A major problem to the national advertiser in using spot advertising is that it can be more difficult to purchase since the time must be purchased from a number of local stations. Moreover, there are more variations in the pricing policies and discount structure of the individual stations than with the networks. However, this problem has been reduced somewhat by the use of **station reps** or individuals who act as sales representatives for a number of local stations and represent them in dealings with national advertisers.

Spot advertisements also are subject to more commercial clutter since local stations can only sell time on network-originated shows during station breaks between programs, except when network advertisers have not purchased all the available time. As discussed earlier, the abundance of ads and other nonprogram material during these station breaks or adjacencies means more clutter and can result in lower recall of the advertising. Viewership also generally declines during station breaks, as people may leave the room, zap to another channel, attend to other tasks, or cease watching television.

While spot advertising is mostly confined to station breaks between programs on network-originated shows, local stations sell time on their own programs, which consist of news, movies, syndicated shows, or locally originated programs such as the "P.M. Magazine" shows broadcast in many cities. There are also independent stations in most cities that can be used by spot advertisers. Local advertisers find the independent stations particularly attractive because they generally have lower rates than the major network affiliates. Figure 11–7 shows an ad for a local television station in Chicago promoting its programming.

The decision facing most national advertisers is not whether to use either network or spot advertising but rather how to combine the two to make effective use of

Figure 11—7   An Independent Station Promotes Itself

39 YEARS OF COMEDY, TRAGEDY, DRAMA, THRILLERS, SPECTACLE AND CLIFFHANGERS.

BUT ENOUGH ABOUT THE CUBS.

Sometimes, we're our own worst competition. Our strong sports reputation overshadows our blockbuster movies, first run comedies, television classics and syndicated specials. So while we're leading the league with our spectacular sports coverage, it's our combination of movies, entertainment and news that puts us in a league by ourselves. It's how we've ended up with 39 perfect seasons.

WGN-TV CHICAGO 9
A Tribune Broadcasting Station

WGN IS PROUD TO SALUTE KTLA ON ITS 40TH ANNIVERSARY OF BROADCASTING.

their television advertising budget. Tables 11–3 and 11–4 show the top 25 advertisers for both network and spot television, respectively, and the percentage of their advertising budgets devoted to each.

Methods of Buying Time

In addition to deciding whether to use network versus spot advertising, television advertisers must decide whether to sponsor an entire program, participate in a program, or use spot announcements between programs. Sponsorship of a program and participations are available on either a network or a local market basis, whereas spot announcements are only available from local stations.

Sponsorship   Under a **sponsorship** arrangement, an advertiser assumes responsibility for the production and usually the content of the program as well as the advertising that appears within it. In the early days of television most programs were produced and sponsored by corporations and were identified by their name such as the "Texaco Theater," the "Bell Telephone Hour," and the "Armstrong Circle Theater." Today most shows are produced either by the networks themselves or through independent production companies who sell the program to the network.

Several major companies have been sponsoring special programs for many years such as the "Hallmark Hall of Fame" dramatic series and the "Kraft Masterpiece Theater." However, sole sponsorship of programs, which is usually limited to specials, has been declining steadily since the mid-1970s. In the 1974/75 television season, 31 advertisers sponsored a total of 91 prime-time specials. However, by the 1986/87 season only 10 companies sponsored 21 specials.[17] There is some indication that sole sponsorships may be making a comeback, however, as several companies including AT&T, General Electric, Clorox, and Chrysler have begun program sponsorships.

Table 11–3 **Top 25 Network TV Advertisers**

| Rank | Advertiser | Network TV Expenditures | | | As % of Co.'s '88 Ad Total |
		1988	1987	% Chg	
1	General Motors Corp.	$443,402	$272,953	62.4	34.3
2	Philip Morris Cos.	388,602	376,628	3.2	18.9
3	Procter & Gamble Co.	370,175	377,552	(2.0)	24.6
4	Kellogg Co.	297,740	237,985	25.1	43.6
5	McDonald's Corp.	245,389	216,067	13.6	33.7
6	Anheuser-Busch Cos.	207,278	186,948	10.9	32.7
7	Unilever NV	189,652	213,481	(11.2)	31.2
8	Ford Motor Co.	175,688	161,177	9.0	30.8
9	RJR Nabisco	174,002	209,777	(17.1)	21.4
10	American Telephone & Telegraph	173,912	146,418	18.8	31.8
11	Johnson & Johnson	167,276	181,999	(8.1)	35.7
12	American Home Products Corp.	163,363	182,057	(10.3)	41.5
13	Chrysler Corp.	163,021	151,569	7.6	34.4
14	Pepsico Inc.	145,048	140,342	3.4	20.4
15	Eastman Kodak Co.	144,751	145,961	(0.8)	19.7
16	General Mills	137,450	133,724	2.8	29.2
17	Quaker Oats Co.	123,327	104,107	18.5	29.1
18	Bristol-Myers Squibb	121,265	137,519	(11.8)	28.2
19	Coca-Cola Co.	119,091	92,360	28.9	30.9
20	Warner-Lambert Co.	111,072	102,472	8.4	18.2
21	Nestle SA	109,496	115,403	(5.1)	19.1
22	Grand Metropolitan PLC	102,009	122,205	(16.5)	13.2
23	Sears, Roebuck & Co.	97,361	89,973	8.2	9.3
24	SmithKline Beecham	93,651	81,756	14.5	35.4
25	Honda Motor Co.	91,884	78,065	17.7	37.8

Note: Dollars are in thousands.
Source: Broadcast Advertisers Reports as reported in BAR/LNA reports, *Advertising Age,* September 27, 1989, p. 54.

Table 11–4 **Top 25 Spot TV Advertisers**

| Rank | Advertiser | Spot TV Expenditures | | | As % of Co.'s '88 Ad Total |
		1988	1987	% Chg	
1	PepsiCo. Inc.	$257,957	$271,069	(4.8)	36.2
2	Procter & Gamble Co.	222,883	238,049	(6.4)	14.8
3	Philip Morris Cos.	157,578	176,159	(10.5)	7.7
4	General Mills	145,945	135,805	7.5	31.0
5	Grand Metropolitan PLC	130,339	142,005	(8.2)	16.8
6	McDonald's Corp.	128,102	129,010	(0.7)	17.6
7	General Motors Corp.	115,286	103,522	11.4	8.9
8	Anheuser-Busch Cos.	87,486	83,750	4.5	13.8
9	Hasbro Inc.	78,681	72,148	9.1	47.8
10	Time Warner	78,368	79,345	(1.2)	19.1
11	Hyundai Group	73,305	76,487	(4.2)	35.8
12	Nestle SA	69,152	62,743	10.2	12.1
13	Ford Motor Co.	68,885	50,292	37.0	12.1
14	Toyota Motor Corp.	68,582	66,294	3.5	25.1
15	Nissan Motor Co.	64,147	43,593	47.2	28.5
16	Walt Disney Co.	62,955	54,415	15.7	20.9
17	Coca-Cola Co.	56,126	65,847	(14.8)	14.6
18	Kellogg Co.	53,287	61,925	(13.9)	7.8
19	American Stores Co.	51,416	46,228	11.2	20.5
20	Adolph Coors Co.	50,533	23,770	112.6	25.2
21	Unilever NV	49,944	58,555	(14.7)	8.2
22	Chrysler Corp.	45,535	45,300	0.5	9.6
23	News Corp.	45,355	47,529	(4.6)	32.6
24	Imasco Ltd.	43,828	43,346	1.1	48.3
25	Nynex Corp.	42,412	33,783	25.5	2.4

Note: Dollars are in thousands.
Source: Broadcast Advertisers Reports as reported in BAR/LNA reports, *Advertising Age,* September 27, 1989, p. 58.

There are several reasons why a company might choose to sponsor a program. Sponsorship allows the firm to capitalized on the prestige of a high-quality program (such as those noted above) and thus enhance the image of the company and its products. A second reason for sponsorship is that the sponsor has control over the placement and content of its commercials. The commercials can be placed wherever the advertiser wants them in the program and can be of any length as long as the total amount of commercial time does not exceed network or station regulations. Advertisers introducing a new product line often will sponsor a program and run commercials that are several minutes in length to introduce and explain the product. For example, IBM used this strategy to introduce its new generation of personal computers. Promotional Perspective 11–3 discusses the reasons behind Procter & Gamble's long-standing sponsorship of afternoon soap operas.

While these factors make sponsorship attractive to some companies, the high costs of sole sponsorship limit this option to only large firms. For example, a network sponsorship in 1986/87 was estimated to cost an average of $2.1 million, compared with an average of $626,000 in 1974/75.[18] Some advertisers share the cost of sponsoring a program with other advertisers and sponsor the program on alternate weeks or divide the program into segments for advertising purposes. However, most commercial time is purchased through other methods such as participations.

Participations   Most advertisers either cannot afford the costs of sponsorship or want greater flexibility than that which results from sponsoring a program. Thus, nearly 90 percent of network television advertising time is sold as **participations,** with several advertisers buying commercial time or spots on a particular program. An advertiser can participate in a particular program once or several times on a regular or irregular basis. Participating advertisers have no involvement or financial responsibility for the production of the program, as this is assumed by the network or individual station that sells and controls the commercial time.

There are several advantages to participation. First, the advertiser has no long-term commitment to a program, and television advertising expenditures can be adjusted to buy any number of participation spots that fit within the budget. This is particularly important to small advertisers with a limited budget. The second advantage of participation is that the television budget can be spread over a number of programs, which provides for greater reach in the media schedule. This can be particularly important when introducing a new product or advertising campaign.

The disadvantage of participations is that the advertiser has very little control over the placements of advertisements, and there may also be problems with availability. Preference is given to advertisers who are willing to commit to numerous spots, and the firm trying to buy single spots in more than one program may find that time is unavailable in certain shows, particularly during prime time.

Spot Announcements   As discussed earlier, spot announcements are bought from the local television stations and generally appear during the adjacent time periods of network programs (hence the term **adjacencies**), rather than within them. The spot announcements are most often used by purely local advertisers but are also utilized by companies with no network schedule (because of spotty or limited distribution) or by large advertisers who make dual use of network and spot advertising.

Selecting Time Periods and Programs

Another consideration in buying television time is selecting the particular time period and program for the advertiser's commercial messages. The cost of television advertising time varies depending on the time of day and, of course, the particular program, since audience size varies as a function of these two factors. Television time periods are divided into **dayparts,** which are specific segments of a broadcast day. The time

Promotional Perspective 11-3

Sponsoring Soaps to Sell Soap

Although the Procter & Gamble (P & G) Company is widely recognized as one of the nation's largest advertisers, a less well-known fact about the Cincinnati-based company is that it is also the biggest supplier of daytime television programs. Through its subsidiary, Procter & Gamble Productions, P & G produces more than 780 hours of daytime programming a year. P & G has been involved in the production of radio and television programs for over 50 years, and program sponsorship has been an integral part of the firm's successful media strategy. By producing the daytime programs on which it advertises, P & G has been able to enjoy cost efficiencies as much as 75 percent lower than its competitors. Since Procter & Gamble spent $253.8 million in daytime network commercials in 1986 (a figure that does not include the costs of producing shows), the importance of cost efficiencies is obvious.

The exact cost per thousand (CPM) efficiencies P & G enjoys from advertising on its own programs are known only to the company. However, while the cost per thousand for women on P & G's "As the World Turns" was listed as $4.00 in a 1985 Nielsen report, some media experts contend that P & G's CPMs are only around $1.00.

The efficiency of P & G's soap sponsorship has come into question recently, as the company canceled several shows including "Texas," "The Edge of Night," and after a 35-year run on NBC, "Search for Tomorrow." The low ratings (less than 3.0) for these shows and increasing production costs made it more efficient for P & G to buy advertising time on non–P & G–produced shows.

Procter & Gamble is the only major advertiser that also produces network programming. In addition to its daytime soap operas, P & G produces numerous TV specials and miniseries and has begun to develop regular series such as sitcoms and drama serials. The company's production of television programs and specials is likely to continue as long as it proves cost-effective and provides P & G with favorable commercial positions.

Source: "Soaper Slide Hits P & G TV Strategy," *Advertising Age*, November 10, 1986, p. 1.

---

segments that make up the television programming day often vary from station to station. However, a typical classification of dayparts for a weekday is shown in Table 11-5.

The various daypart segments will attract different audiences both in size and nature, and thus advertising rates will vary accordingly. Prime-time draws the largest audiences, with 8:30 to 9:00 P.M. being the most watched half-hour time period and Sunday being the most popular night for television.[19] As noted earlier, firms wanting to advertise during prime time must pay premium rates. Thus, the prime-time daypart is dominated by the large national advertisers.

The various dayparts are important to advertisers since they attract different demographic groups. For example, daytime television generally attracts women, whereas early morning attracts women and children. In recent years, daytime ratings have been declining as more and more of the traditional female viewers join the work force. With nearly 65 percent of women in the work force, many advertisers are turning to other dayparts such as early morning to reach them. The top early morning advertisers have increased their spending in this daypart in recent years to reach working women. The late fringe (sometimes called late night) daypart segment has become particularly popular among advertisers trying to reach young adults who tune into shows such as "The Tonight Show," "Late Night with David Letterman," and ABC's "Nightline."

Table 11-5 **Common Television Dayparts**

Morning	7:00 A.M.–9:00 A.M., Monday through Friday
Daytime	9:00 A.M.–4:30 P.M., Monday through Friday
Early fringe	4:30 A.M.–7:30 P.M., Monday through Friday
Prime-time access	7:30 P.M.–8:00 P.M., Sunday through Saturday
Prime time	8:00 P.M.–11:00 P.M., Monday through Saturday and 7:00 P.M.–11:00 P.M. on Sunday
Late news	11:00 P.M.–11:30 P.M., Monday through Friday
Late fringe	11:30 P.M.–1:00 A.M., Monday through Friday

Audience size and demographic composition will also vary depending on the type of program. In recent years situation comedies attracted the largest prime-time audiences, with women 18 to 34 comprising the greatest segment of the audience.[20] Feature films ranked second, followed by general drama shows. Women 55+ were the largest audience segment for these programs.[21] The audience for particular programs is discussed in the following section.

Measuring the Television Audience

One of the most important considerations in using television advertising concerns the size and composition of the television viewing audience. Audience measurement is very critical to the advertiser as well as the networks and stations. From the advertisers' perspective the viewing audience is very important because they want to know the size and characteristics of the audience they are reaching when they purchase time on a particular program. Also, the rates they pay are a function of audience size; so the advertiser wants to be sure that audience measurements are accurate.

Audience size and composition are also important to the network or station, as these are what determine the amount they can charge for their commercial time. As you are probably well aware, television shows are frequently canceled because they fail to attract enough viewers to make their commercial time attractive to potential advertisers. The determination of television audience size is not an exact science and has been the subject of considerable controversy through the years. In this section we will examine how television audiences are measured and how advertisers use this information in planning their media schedules.

Audience Measures

The measurement of the size and composition of television audiences is performed by television rating services. The standard source of national or network television audience information is the A. C. Nielsen Company, whereas local audience information is available from Nielsen and the Arbitron Company. For information on the demographic composition of television audiences, advertisers also use the Simmons reports and Mediamark Research (MRI), as discussed in Chapter 10.

Both Nielsen and Arbitron gather viewership information from a sample of television homes and then project this information to the total viewing area. The various techniques used to gather audience measurement information include diaries, electronic meters or recorders, and personal interviews. There are various types of information that the rating services provide that are used in measurement and evaluation of a television station's viewing audience. These are important to the media planner in making decisions regarding the value of buying commercial time on a program and are discussed before examining the rating services.

Television Households   This figure refers to the number of households in the market that own a television set. The A. C. Nielsen Company estimates that 90.4 million U.S. households owned at least one television set as of January 1989. Since over 98 percent of U.S. households own a TV set, television households generally correspond to the number of households in a given market.

Program Rating   Probably the best known of all the audience measurement figures is the **program rating.** This number represents the percentage of TV households in an area that are tuned to a specific program during a specific time period. The program rating is calculated by dividing the number of households tuned to a particular show by the total number of households in the area. For example, if 12 million households (HH) watched a program such as the "CBS Evening News," the national rating would be 13.3, which is calculated as follows:

Table 11-6   Nielsen Ratings for Top 15 Regularly Scheduled Network Programs in November 1988

Total U.S. TV Households	AA%
1. Bill Cosby Show	27.9
2. A Different World	23.4
3. Cheers	22.8
4. Roseanne	22.3
4. Golden Girls	22.3
6. 60 Minutes	22.2
7. Who's the Boss?	20.8
8. Growing Pains	20.2
9. Empty Nest	19.8
10. Murder, She Wrote	19.3
11. Dear John	18.3
12. Head of the Class	18.2
13. Hogan Family	17.9
14. L.A. Law	17.8
15. Alf	17.5

Men 18 +	AA%
1. 60 Minutes	16.4
2. NFL Mon. Night Football	15.7
3. CBS NFL Football Gm. 1	15.0
4. Bill Cosby Show	14.3
5. Cheers	12.8
6. NFL Game 2	12.6
7. Murder, She Wrote	11.9
8. CBS NFL Football Gm. 2	11.5
9. A Different World	11.4
9. Golden Girls	11.4
11. L.A. Law	11.2
11. NBC Sun. Night Movie	11.2
13. ABC Sun. Night Movie	11.0
14. Roseanne	10.7
15. NFL Single Game	10.6

Children 2-11	AA%
1. Bill Cosby Show	21.8
2. A Different World	18.2
3. Hogan Family	17.7
4. Alf	17.3
5. Roseanne	15.8
6. Who's the Boss?	15.5
7. Growing Pains	15.2
8. Family Ties	15.0
9. Magical World of Disney	14.5
10. Head of the Class	14.2
11. Garfield & Friends	13.0
12. Muppet Babies II	12.9
13. Pee Wee's Playhouse	12.8
14. Golden Girls	11.5
14. Cheers	11.5

Women 18 +	AA%
1. Bill Cosby Show	21.7
2. Golden Girls	18.8
3. A Different World	17.4
4. Roseanne	17.1
5. Cheers	16.8
6. 60 Minutes	16.6
6. Murder, She Wrote	16.6
6. Empty Nest	16.6
9. Who's the Boss?	15.4
10. Knots Landing	14.5
11. Growing Pains	14.4
12. Dear John	13.7
12. Dallas	13.7
12. Hunter	13.7
15. L.A. Law	13.2

Teens 12-17	AA%
1. Bill Cosby Show	21.3
2. A Different World	19.7
3. Hogan Family	17.2
4. Roseanne	16.9
5. Growing Pains	16.6
6. Head of the Class	16.1
7. Cheers	15.4
8. Alf	14.9
9. Who's the Boss?	14.8
10. Family Ties	13.3
11. Wonder Years	13.0
12. Golden Girls	12.6
13. ABC Sun. Night Movie	12.5
14. NBC Sun. Night Movie	12.2
15. Day By Day	11.2

Note: Nielsen average audience (AA) estimates; two or more telecasts (15 mins. or longer).
Source: Nielsen Report on Television 1989, Nielsen Media Research (Northbrook, Ill.: A. C. Nielsen Co., 1989), p. 15.

$$\text{Rating} = \frac{\text{HH tuned to show}}{\text{Total U.S. HH}} = \frac{12,000,000}{90,400,000} = 13.3$$

A **ratings point** represents 1 percent of all the television households in a particular area tuned to a specific program. On a national level one ratings point represents 904,000 households. Thus, a top-rated program such as the "Cosby Show," which had an average rating of 27.9 in November 1988, would reach 25.2 million households each week (27.9 × 904,000).

The program rating is the key number to the stations since the amount of money they can charge for commercial time is based on this figure. Ratings points are very important to the networks, as well as individual stations, as a 1 percent change in a program's ratings over the course of a viewing season can mean millions of dollars in gains or losses in advertising revenue. Table 11-6 shows the Nielsen ratings for the top 15 regularly scheduled programs for all U.S. households and for selected demographic groups during November 1988.

Households Using Television   The percentage of homes in a given area that are watching television during a specific time period is referred to as **households using television (HUT).** This figure is sometimes referred to as *sets in use* and is always expressed as a percentage. For example, if 50 million of the U.S. TV households have their television sets turned on at 10 P.M. on a Wednesday night, the HUT figure would be 55 percent (50 million ÷ 90.4 million). As Figure 11-8 shows, there are wide variations in television usage depending on the time of day and season of the year.

Figure 11–8 **Percentage of Households Using Television at Various Times**

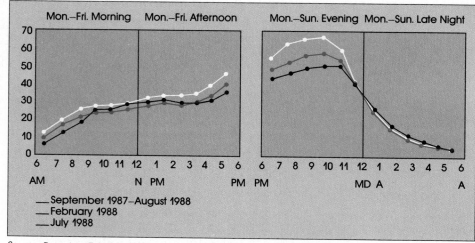

Source: Report on Television 1989, Nielsen Media Research (Northbrook, Ill.: A. C. Nielsen Co., 1989).

Share of Audience   Another important audience measurement figure is the **share of audience,** which refers to the percentage of households using television in a specified time period that are tuned to a specific program. This figure takes into account variation in the number of sets in use and the total size of the potential audience, since it is based only on those households that have their sets turned on. Share of audience is calculated by dividing the number of households (HH) tuned to a show by the number of households using television (HUT). Thus, for the "CBS Evening News" example, if 55 percent (or 50 million) of U.S. households had their sets turned on, the share of audience would be 24, which is calculated as follows:

$$\text{Share} = \frac{\text{HH tuned to show}}{\text{U.S. households using TV}} = \frac{12 \text{ million}}{50 \text{ million}} = 24$$

It should be noted that the share of audience figure will always be higher than the program rating unless all the households had their sets turned on (in which case, they would be equal). Share figures are important since they reveal how well a program does with the available viewing audience. For example, during late night television the size of the viewing audience drops substantially, so the best way of assessing the popularity of a program is to examine the share of the available audience that it attracts relative to competing programs.

In addition to these figures, rating services will also provide an audience statistic known as **total audience.** This figure represents the total number of homes viewing any five-minute part of a telecast. This number can also be broken down to provide audience composition figures that are based on the distribution of the audience into demographic categories.

Network Audience Information

The primary source of national and network television audience information is the A. C. Nielsen Company's Nielsen Television Index (NTI), which provides daily and weekly estimates of television viewing and national sponsored network program audiences. For more than 20 years Nielsen provided this information using a two-pronged system consisting of a national sample of metered households along with a separate sample of diary households. In the 1,700 metered households, an electronic measurement device known as the **audimeter** (audience meter) was hooked up to the TV set to conduct a continuous measurement of the channels to which the set is tuned. Net-

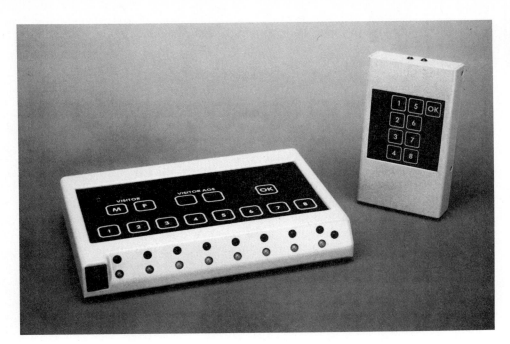

Figure 11−9 **The People Meter Is Now Used by Nielsen for Measuring National TV Audiences**

work viewing for the country—or the famous "Nielsen ratings"—was based on the results provided by audimeters placed in a national sample of homes carefully selected to be representative of the population of U.S. households. The metered households were also supported by a separate panel of 2,600 households that recorded viewing information in diaries. Since the audimeter could only measure the channel to which the set was tuned, the diary panel was used to gather demographic data on the viewing audience.

For many years considerable concern was expressed in the television and advertising industry over the audimeter/diary system. In particular, several problems were noted with the diary method. First, the information from diaries was not available to the network and advertising analysts for several weeks. Then studies indicated that the method was overstating the size of some key demographic audiences. Problems were noted in that the cooperation rates among diary keepers were going down, and many of the women who kept a household's diary were not noting what the man in the home was watching when he was alone. The complex new video environment and explosion in viewing options were also making it difficult for diary keepers to maintain accurate viewing records.

As a result of these problems, and in response to competitive pressure from another audience measurement company from England, AGB, in fall 1987 the A. C. Nielsen Company made a major change in its method of audience measurement by making the *people meter* the sole basis of its national rating system and eliminating the use of the diary panel.

The People Meter   The **people meter** is an electronic measuring device that incorporates the technology of the old-style audimeter in a system that records not only what is being watched but also by whom in 4,000 homes. The actual device is a small box with eight buttons—six for the family and two for visitors—which can be placed on the top of the TV set (Figure 11−9). An accompanying remote control unit also makes it possible to make electronic entries from anywhere in the room. Each member of the sample household is provided a personal button on the system that is used to indicate his or her presence as viewer. The device is also equipped with a sonar sensor to alert the viewers entering or leaving the room to punch in or log out on the meter.

The viewership information the people meter collects from the household is stored in the home system until it is retrieved by Nielsen's computers. The data collected by the system include when the set is turned on, which channel is viewed, when the channel is changed, and when the set is off, in addition to the information on who is viewing. The demographic characteristics of the viewers are also in the system, and viewership can be matched to these characteristics. The Nielsen's operation center processes all this information each week for release to the television and advertising industry. Nielsen uses a sample of metered households in the nation's largest markets (New York, Los Angeles, and Chicago) to provide overnight viewing results.

Nielsen's switch to people meters has generally been viewed as an improvement over the diary panel system, and the company plans to expand them to more markets over the next several years. However, initial reaction to the system was not all positive, particularly by some of the networks who saw estimates of their audience sizes by the new system coming out lower than under the old system. Promotional Perspective 11–4 discusses some of the background and controversy brought on by the use of people meters.

Local Audience Information

Information on local television audiences is important to both local advertisers and those firms making national spot buys. The two major sources of local audience information are again the A. C. Nielsen Company and the Arbitron Company. To measure television viewership in local markets, Nielsen provides the Nielsen Station Index (NSI). The NSI measures television station audiences in over 200 local markets known as **designated market areas (DMAs).** DMAs are nonoverlapping areas used for planning, buying, and evaluating television audiences and are generally a group of counties in which stations located in a metropolitan or central area achieve the largest audience share. Nielsen uses audimeters for several of the larger markets such as New York, Chicago, and Los Angeles, whereas other markets are measured by diaries only. NSI reports information on viewing by time periods and programs and includes audience size and estimates of viewing over a range of demographic categories.

The Arbitron Company provides audience measurement information for the 214 or so largest television markets. Like Nielsen, Arbitron uses electronic meters and diaries for measuring audiences in the 13 largest markets, whereas only diaries are used in the other markets. Arbitron also defines its markets in terms of nonoverlapping geographic areas, each area known as an **area of dominant influence (ADI).** Each county in the nation is assigned to an ADI, which is an exclusive geographic area consisting of all counties in which the home market stations receive a preponderance of viewing. Each ADI is also part of a greater unit called the *total survey area,* which includes counties outside the ADI where there is an audience for stations broadcasting from within the ADI. Arbitron also reports information for a *metro rating area (MRA),* which is an area within the ADI that generally corresponds to the U.S. government's metropolitan statistical areas. Figure 11–10 provides a sample page from Arbitron showing how a television market is measured, whereas Table 11–7 shows the television household and population estimates for the top 70 ADIs.

Using Audience Measurement Data

The national and local audience data provided by Nielsen and Arbitron are important to the media planner. Both services provide detailed audience estimates by daypart, time period, and program, as shown in the sample page from Arbitron (Figure 11–11). This information is valuable in determining the appropriate combination of television programs needed to provide various levels of coverage or reach of the advertiser's target audience as well as for determining frequency levels.

Promotional Perspective **11—4**

People Meter Raises Controversy

For more than 30 years television networks relied exclusively on the A. C. Nielsen Company to provide national audience rating information. Nielsen used a sample of 1,700 homes wired with audimeters to measure whether a set was turned on and the channel to which it was tuned. This method, however, could not determine who, if anyone, was watching, so Nielsen used a different set of 2,600 homes to maintain viewing diaries that were mailed in every four weeks. The diary method was always a topic of considerable controversy, as some diary keepers waited until the end of the four-week period to complete them and therefore did not provide accurate reports of the shows they actually watched. One of the major complaints against diaries was that they inflated network viewing, as people were more likely to fill in the diary pages with well-known and popular network shows that they may not have even watched. The confusion of diary keeping was compounded by the rise of cable and independent stations. In the 1960s and 1970s the three networks dominated television, and recall of programs watched was relatively easy. However, today households choose from as many as 30 or more channels, and diary keeping has become very confusing.

The concern over the accuracy of viewing diaries led many advertisers and agencies to challenge their use. In 1984, 16 of the 20 largest agencies became the first to sign with a new Nielsen competitor, AGB Television Research, the U.S. affiliate of an English company that had been providing ratings in Europe and Asia for years. AGB was the first company to commercialize the "people meter." In response to the competitive threat from AGB, Nielsen began installing its own people meter method in 1985 and in 1987 announced that the system would replace the National Audience Composition diary system used to record audience characteristic information. Nielsen started its people meter system with a sample of 2,000 households and expanded to 4,000 in 1988 when the company announced that it would rely solely on the system for its national ratings.

Nielsen's change to the people meter system has put the networks on the defensive, as the meters have shown that some network prime-time shows are drawing audiences that are as much as 15 percent smaller than when measured by the diary method. This means, of course, that advertisers and their agencies expect to pay less money for television commercial time on these shows. The networks responded by denouncing the accuracy of the people meter system, the sample composition, and its ability to produce statistically reliable results. Several networks even threatened to cancel their audience measurement contracts with the A. C. Nielsen Company. However, Nielsen researchers have argued that the people meter represents the state of the art in electronic measuring equipment and is a more accurate technique for measuring audience composition than the diaries.

For now, the networks have very little choice but to accept Nielsen's people meter system, as in August 1988, AGB announced that it was suspending its U.S. TV-rating operations, stating that it had underestimated the costs of competing with Nielsen. Thus, the company that was credited (or blamed) with accelerating the use of people meters in the United States is now gone, leaving Nielsen with a monopoly in the national audience measurement market. However, most television and advertising analysts do expect there to be future developments in this area, from Nielsen as well as from other media research firms.

Sources: "Who's Gyping Whom in TV Ads?" *Fortune,* July 6, 1987, p. 78; "People Meter to Be Sole Tool for '87 Nielsen TV Ratings," *Marketing News,* January 30, 1987, p. 1; "AGB Suspends Its U.S. TV-Ratings Operation," *Marketing News,* August 29, 1988, p. 1.

Television time is often bought on the basis of gross ratings points (GRPs), which were discussed in Chapter 10. Media planners will evaluate a television schedule to determine how many GRPs it will deliver. For example, a media plan may call for five advertisements on a weekly network prime-time show with an average rating of 22. In the five-week period this schedule will deliver 110 gross ratings points ($22 \times 5 = 110$).

Audience measurement data are also important for making cost comparisons among commercial options on different television programs. For example, the media buyer must determine which program is most cost efficient in reaching the advertiser's target audience. This may be done by applying the cost per thousand (CPM) and cost per ratings point (CPRP) formulas discussed in Chapter 10 to each program option. For example, the CPRP formula can be used to determine the efficiency of a television media schedule by adding up the total cost of the programs purchased and dividing by the number of ratings points delivered.

The lower the cost per thousand and the cost per ratings point figures, the more efficient a program is in reaching the advertiser's target audience. The audience information needed to make these calculations is available in the NTI report for network

Figure 11–10 **Sample Page of Arbitron ADI**

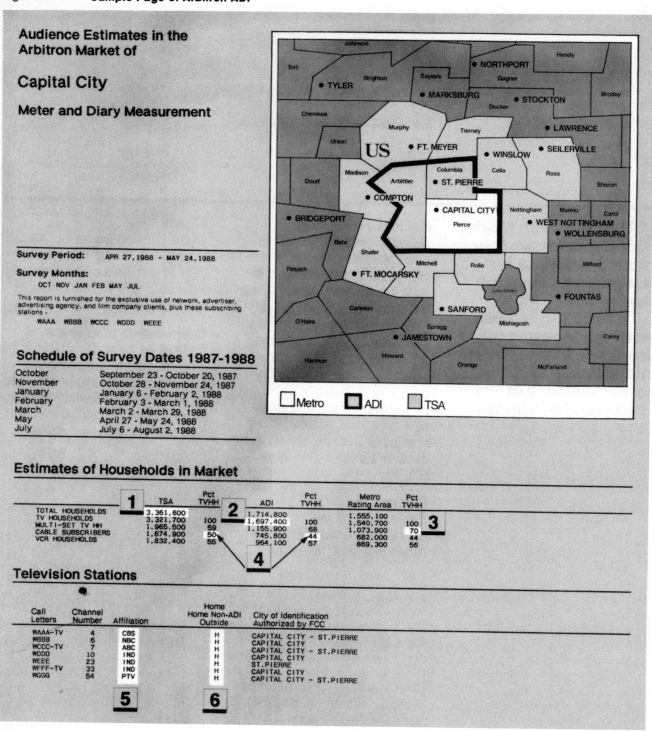

commercial time, whereas for spot or local announcements the figures would come from the NSI or Arbitron ratings.

Cost information for local stations may be available from a source such as *Standard Rate and Data Service,* although the actual cost of commercial time varies depending on the outcome of the negotiation process between the station and media buyer. For network time cost, figures are generally based on the price the buyer ne-

Table 11–7 **Top 70 ADIs Ranked by Size**

Rank	Market	ADI TV Households	ADI % of U.S. TV Households	ABC % of U.S.	ABC Index	CBS % of U.S.	CBS Index	NBC % of U.S.	NBC Index
1.	New York	6,876,000	7.74	7.97	103	6.42	83	6.65	86
2.	Los Angeles	4,663,900	5.25	5.28	100	4.04	77	4.39	84
3.	Chicago	3,084,400	3.47	4.03	116	2.83	82	3.51	101
4.	Philadelphia	2,643,700	2.98	3.75	126	2.97	100	3.14	106
5.	San Francisco	2,141,100	2.41	2.37	98	1.90	79	1.95	81
6.	Boston	2,050,700	2.31	2.52	109	2.04	88	2.32	100
7.	Detroit	1,697,400	1.91	2.18	114	1.72	90	2.14	112
8.	Dallas–Ft. Worth	1,647,700	1.86	2.05	111	1.93	104	1.54	83
9.	Washington, D.C.	1,592,800	1.79	1.75	97	1.62	90	1.60	89
10.	Houston	1,466,500	1.65	1.90	115	1.29	78	1.26	76
	Markets 1–10	27,864,200	31.37	33.80	108	26.76	85	28.50	91
	Cumulative total	27,864,200	31.37	33.80	108	26.76	85	28.50	91
11.	Cleveland	1,414,900	1.59	2.07	130	1.62	101	1.66	104
12.	Minneapolis–St. Paul	1,297,600	1.46	1.15	79	1.39	95	1.05	72
13.	Atlanta	1,273,000	1.43	1.42	99	1.49	104	1.71	119
14.	Tampa–St. Petersburg	1,237,400	1.39	1.49	107	1.68	121	1.55	111
15.	Seattle–Tacoma	1,224,200	1.38	1.32	96	1.05	76	1.18	86
16.	Miami	1,213,200	1.37	1.19	87	1.13	83	1.36	99
17.	Pittsburgh	1,192,200	1.34	1.44	107	1.41	105	1.54	115
18.	St. Louis	1,084,200	1.22	1.07	88	1.28	105	1.49	122
19.	Denver	1,021,600	1.15	1.03	89	.96	84	1.03	89
20.	Sacramento–Stockton	929,000	1.05	1.03	98	1.01	97	1.00	95
	Markets 11–20	11,887,300	13.38	13.21	99	13.02	97	13.57	101
	Cumulative total	39,751,500	44.75	47.01	105	39.78	89	42.07	94
21.	Phoenix	927,000	1.04	.97	93	1.04	100	.95	91
22.	Baltimore	902,800	1.02	1.02	100	1.13	111	.93	91
23.	Hartford–New Haven	868,100	.98	.93	95	1.08	110	.70	72
24.	Indianapolis	813,000	.92	.80	87	1.03	113	.94	103
25.	San Diego	805,400	.91	.78	86	.88	97	.66	73
26.	Portland, Ore.	795,100	.90	.80	89	.82	92	.72	81
27.	Orlando–Daytona Beach	782,400	.88	.94	107	.96	109	.93	106
28.	Kansas City	720,400	.81	.88	108	.80	98	.59	73
29.	Cincinnati	716,000	.81	.73	90	.99	122	.58	72
30.	Milwaukee	701,900	.79	.82	104	.76	96	.80	101
	Markets 21–30	8,032,100	9.06	8.67	96	9.49	105	7.80	86
	Cumulative total	47,783,600	53.81	55.68	103	49.27	92	49.87	93
31.	Charlotte	688,300	.78	.79	102	.97	126	.59	76
32.	Nashville	686,500	.77	.73	94	.92	119	.94	121
33.	Columbus, Ohio	658,400	.74	.65	87	.84	114	.89	121
34.	New Orleans	645,900	.73	.74	102	.96	132	.85	117
35.	Raleigh–Durham	621,000	.70	.84	121	.77	110	.60	86
36.	Greenville–Spartanburg–Asheville	616,700	.69	.66	95	.82	118	.91	132
37.	Oklahoma City	616,200	.69	.58	84	.76	110	.66	94
38.	Buffalo	609,500	.69	.71	104	.74	108	.82	119
39.	Grand Rapids–Kalamazoo–Battle Creek	595,800	.67	.63	93	.58	87	.67	100
40.	Salt Lake City	589,800	.66	.62	93	.58	87	.62	93
	Markets 31–40	6,328,100	7.12	6.95	98	7.94	112	7.55	106
	Cumulative total	54,111,700	60.93	62.63	103	57.21	94	57.42	94
41.	Memphis	583,700	.66	.72	109	.66	101	.91	139
42.	San Antonio	549,300	.62	.56	91	.56	91	.59	95
43.	Norfolk–Portsmouth–Newport News–Hampton	544,100	.61	.59	97	.70	113	.73	120
44.	Providence–New Bedford	542,300	.61	.67	111	.52	85	.72	119
45.	Harrisburg–York–Lancaster–Lebanon	531,300	.60	.51	85	.61	102	.71	118
46.	Charleston–Huntington	517,700	.58	.52	89	.56	96	.73	126
47.	Louisville	514,700	.58	.51	88	.68	117	.65	112
48.	Dayton	510,700	.58	.44	76	.65	113	.56	98
49.	Birmingham	503,700	.57	.50	87	.43	75	.77	136
50.	Greensboro–Winston Salem–High Point	502,600	.57	.57	100	.70	123	.58	103
	Markets 41–50	5,300,100	5.98	5.59	93	6.07	102	6.95	116
	Cumulative total	59,411,800	66.91	68.22	102	63.28	95	64.37	96

Table 11-7 (concluded)

Rank	Market	ADI TV Households	ADI % of U.S. TV Households	ABC		CBS		NBC	
				% of U.S.	Index	% of U.S.	Index	% of U.S.	Index
51.	Wilkes Barre-Scranton	483,800	.54	.65	120	.58	106	.60	110
52.	Albany-Schenectady-Troy	481,600	.54	.47	86	.65	119	.60	110
53.	West Palm Beach	462,500	.52	.47	91	.48	93	.56	108
54.	Tulsa	461,600	.52	.50	97	.61	118	.50	95
55.	Little Rock	455,700	.51	.57	111	.56	108	.64	124
56.	Albuquerque	445,300	.50	.53	105	.42	84	.50	99
57.	Jacksonville	442,400	.50	.40	79	.68	136	.48	97
58.	Mobile-Pensacola	440,800	.50	.54	109	.62	124	.58	116
59.	Flint-Saginaw-Bay City	429,400	.48	.45	94	.45	93	.67	138
60.	Wichita-Hutchinson	427,400	.48	.41	85	.50	103	.41	85
	Markets 51-60	4,530,500	5.09	4.99	98	5.55	109	5.54	109
	Cumulative total	63,942,300	72.00	73.21	102	68.83	96	69.91	97
61.	Knoxville	423,000	.48	.51	106	.64	135	.42	89
62.	Richmond	419,100	.47	.46	97	.56	118	.49	105
63.	Fresno-Visalia	412,600	.46	.49	105	.45	97	.42	89
64.	Shreveport-Texarkana	407,600	.46	.55	119	.52	113	.50	109
65.	Toledo	400,500	.45	.39	86	.52	116	.61	135
66.	Des Moines	375,800	.42	.40	95	.44	103	.44	103
67.	Syracuse	370,000	.42	.39	93	.44	106	.44	105
68.	Green Bay-Appleton	369,600	.42	.48	115	.45	109	.44	106
69.	Portland-Poland Spring	362,100	.41	.40	99	.42	103	.40	98
70.	Omaha	351,100	.40	.35	89	.41	103	.35	89
	Markets 61-70	3,891,400	4.39	4.42	101	4.85	110	4.51	103
	Cumulative total	67,833,700	76.39	77.63	102	73.68	96	74.42	97

Source: Broadcasting/Cable Yearbook 1989, Broadcast Publications, Inc., Washington D.C., 1989.

gotiates with the network and will vary depending on time of the season, availability, unsold time, and other factors. For example, a few years ago the networks had a considerable amount of unsold prime-time and daytime commercial spots owing to a sluggish national advertising market. Many agencies would wait until within 24 hours of airtime to purchase spots and command discounts as high as 50 percent on some programs.[22]

The Future of Television

The traditional structure of television has changed significantly in recent years with developments such as cable TV, the formation of superstations, and the penetration of VCRs into American households. Each of these developments has had an influence on audience viewing trends and has led to changes in the nature of television advertising and media scheduling. The significance of these developments is examined in this section, along with a discussion of what may lie ahead in terms of audience measurement.

Cable Television

Perhaps the most significant development in the broadcast media has been the growth and expansion of **cable television.** Cable, or CATV (community antenna television), which delivers television signals through wire rather than the airways, was initially developed to provide reception to remote areas unable to pick up broadcast signals. Cable then expanded to metropolitan areas and grew rapidly owing to the improved reception it offered and because it provided subscribers a wider selection of stations. In 1988 there were approximately 8,000 operating cable systems in the United States with 43.2 million subscribers, representing over 120 million people or over 50 percent

Figure 11–11   Sample Page from Arbitron TV Ratings

Daypart Estimates

The Daypart Summary gives you a general picture of television viewing in the market: overall ratings and shares, household deliveries and viewing levels according to audience characteristics.

HOW TO READ

Daypart Estimates

1 WCCC's average ADI household audience Mon.-Fri., 7AM-9AM was a 5 rating and a 22 share. This means that 5% of the ADI television households were watching WCCC, which represents 22% of the households viewing television at that time.

2 WCCC's audience share is down for this survey period to 22%, from 26% one year ago.

3 24% of all households in the ADI were viewing television during the daypart.

4 In the Metro area, WCCC had a 5 household rating, which constituted a 21% share.

5 WCCC reached 7% of the Women 18-34 in an average quarter-hour of this daypart.

6 6% of all Men 18-34 in the ADI viewed television in this daypart.

7 88% of the TSA's total television households are in the Metro. 95% are in the Home ADI.

8 2% of WCCC's TSA television households reside in Adjacent ADI #2.

9 During an average quarter-hour, WCCC was viewed by 1% of the television households in Adjacent ADI #2. (For television household estimates in Adjacent ADIs, see "Counties Included in Survey Area" in the Market Data section.)

APPLICATIONS

Has the station improved its performance over the last four surveys?
Check the HUT totals of survey-to-survey changes and compare these to the station's estimates to see if the share of the total audience has gone up or down.

When are people watching television?
Evaluate the viewing audience of the station by daypart. Demographic breakdowns allow you to determine the best time to reach your target audience.

Table 11−8 **Top 10 Cable TV Advertisers**

Rank	Advertiser	Cable TV Expenditures			As % of Co.'s '88 Ad Total
		1988	1987	% Chg	
1	Procter & Gamble Co.	$30,202	$23,713	27.4	2.0
2	Time Warner	23,891	19,415	23.1	5.8
3	Philip Morris Cos.	23,075	21,024	9.8	1.1
4	Anheuser-Busch Cos.	21,397	22,943	(6.7)	3.4
5	General Mills	20,011	17,991	11.2	4.3
6	RJR Nabisco	14,252	14,667	(2.8)	1.7
7	Eastman Kodak Co.	11,387	7,989	42.5	1.5
8	Clorox Co.	10,126	6,894	46.9	6.8
9	Mars Inc.	9,995	14,877	(32.8)	2.9
10	Chrysler Corp.	9,700	6,684	45.1	2.0

Note: Dollars are in thousands.

Source: Broadcast Advertisers Reports as reported in BAR/LNA reports, *Advertising Age,* September 27,1989, p. 70.

of the nation's television households.[23] Advertising revenue from cable exceeded $1 billion from national advertising alone in 1988. Table 11−8 shows the cable television advertising expenditures of the top 10 cable advertisers in 1988.

Cable television broadens the program options available to the television viewer, as well as the advertiser, by offering specialty channels such as ESPN (sports), CNN (news), Nashville Network (country music), MTV (music videos), and many others, as listed in Table 11−9. While these stations are supported by both subscriber fee and advertising revenue, cable operators also offer programming that is not available to commercial sponsorship and is available only to households willing to pay a separate fee beyond the monthly subscription charge. These pay channels include HBO, Showtime, and the Movie Channel. Since these stations do not show advertising, they are not of interest to advertisers, except as competitors for the viewing audience of commercial television.

Cable television has had considerable influence on the nature of television as an advertising medium. First, the expanded viewing options available through cable have led to considerable audience fragmentation. This has resulted in a reduction of the share of audience for the three major networks. For example, the combined audience shares of CBS, NBC, and ABC for prime-time programming fell to 68 percent during the 1988/89 television season from a high of 94 percent a decade earlier.[24] Many cable stations have become very popular among consumers and have led television advertisers to reevaluate their media plans and the prices they are willing to pay for network and spot commercials on network affiliate stations.

Advantages of Cable In addition to considering the impact of cable on network audiences, media planners have also been giving increasing attention to cable stations as media options. Many advertisers have turned to cable programs because of the opportunities they present for **narrow casting** or advertising to specialized markets. For example, ESPN (Figure 11−12) is very popular among advertisers whose primary target audience is the male sports enthusiast, whereas MTV is used by advertisers interested in reaching teenagers and young adults. Gillette has been purchasing more time on cable stations such as TBS, CNN, USA, and MTV to reach 18- to 34-year-olds. Nabisco advertises over 30 products on cable using the medium to target children, teenagers, and women with greater efficiency. For several years Anheuser-Busch has had exclusivity as a beer advertiser on most ESPN sports programs, thus avoiding "beer advertising clutter."[25]

Another reason advertisers are interested in cable is because of its lower cost and its flexibility. Many advertisers have found that the cost of producing a program for

Table 11–9   **Cable Programming Status Report**

Cable Service	Number of Systems	August 1988 Subs.
Basic Cable Services		
ESPN	19,500*	47,800,000
CNN	8,298	46,869,000
WTBS	9,171	45,718,000
USA	10,100*	45,200,000
MTV	5,010	42,700,000
CBN	8,215	41,642,000
Nickelodeon	6,195	41,200,000
Nashville Net	7,335	41,051,392
Lifetime	3,800	39,800,000
C-Span	3,014	39,200,000
Nick at Nite	3,285	36,900,000
Weather Channel	3,200	36,000,000
Arts & Entertainment	2,600	34,200,000
Discovery Channel	3,567	33,800,000
Headline News	3,228	32,693,000
Financial News Network	3,500	30,500,000
V-HI	2,140	27,900,000
WGN-TV	9,781*	24,653,463
Score	1,150	20,000,000
Cable Value Network	1,600	20,000,000
Black Entertainment TV	1,200	20,000,000
Home Shopping Network I	1,342	15,700,000
C-Span II	539	15,700,000
Learning Channel	930	12,800,000
QVC Network	931	12,600,000
WWOR	2,499	12,302,073
Telshop	850	12,000,000
Silent Network	350	10,300,000
Eternal Word TV	461	10,100,000
Fashion Channel	600	10,000,000
Inspirational Network (PTL)	950	10,000,000
WPIX	858	9,678,474
Travel Channel	260	9,300,000
Trinity	260	8,000,000
Tempo TV	700	8,000,000
Country Music TV	830	8,000,000
Movietime	273	7,000,000
Acts	358	6,600,000
Home Shopping Network II	302	5,500,000
KTLA(TV)	182	4,929,355
Shop TV	119	4,400,000
Nostalgia	325	4,000,000
KTVT	417	3,588,270
Galavision	290	3,000,000
Mind Extension University	70	1,700,000
Family TV Network	50	1,100,000
America's Shopping Channel	—	1,000,000
Pay Services		
HBO	7,400	15,900,000
American Movie Classics	1,500	12,000,000
Showtime	6,000	6,300,000
Cinemax	4,200	5,100,000
Disney	5,000	3,810,000
Movie Channel	6,000	2,600,000
Bravo	320	1,100,000
Playboy	500	490,000
Pay-per-View Services		
Viewer's Choice I & II	181	3,500,000
Request TV	190	4,500,000
Home Premiere Television	—	1,200,000
Cable Video Store	65	175,000
Zap Movies	7	66,000

*Affiliates include noncable system distributors.
Showtime/The Movie Channel does not break out individual system counts. PPV subs. are addressable homes.
Figures for WGN–TV, WPIX(TV), KTLA(TV), and KTVT(TV) include TVRO and SMATV affiliates.

Source: Broadcasting/Cable Yearbook 1989, Broadcast Publications, Inc., Washington, D.C., 1989.

Figure 11—12   ESPN Promotes Its Ability to Reach Men

cable television is substantially lower than for a network show. A two-hour network program may cost about $2.5 million, whereas a half-hour cable show can be produced for anywhere from $3,000 to $15,000. Even if the advertiser does not produce the program, spot announcements on cable are considerably lower on most cable stations. This makes television a much more viable media option to smaller advertisers with limited budgets or those firms interested in targeting their commercials to a very well defined target audience. Also, with cable, advertisers generally do not have to make large up-front commitments, which may be as much as a year in advance, required by the networks.

In addition to the lower costs, cable affords the advertiser much greater flexibility in the type of commercials that can be used. As noted earlier in the chapter, the typical network commercial has been reduced to 30 seconds or less in length. However, cable stations are willing to accept much longer ads, and many advertisers will use two- and three-minute commercials on cable programs. Some cable advertisers have used **infomercials,** which are commercials that are longer in format, ranging from three to eight minutes in length. This longer format is used to communicate detailed information about a product or service, to demonstrate how to use it, or to discuss special features or advantages. For example, Procter & Gamble has used infomercials on Nickelodeon to teach children how to care for their teeth and to advertise Crest toothpaste. Direct-response advertisers often use these longer ads to describe their products to consumers and to encourage them to call in their order during the commercial.

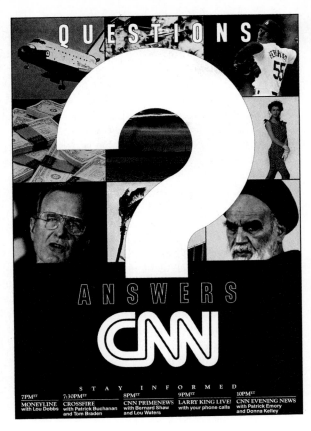

Figure 11–13   **CNN Is Hailed as Equal to the Networks in News Coverage**

Limitations of Cable   While cable is becoming increasingly popular, many advertisers have avoided using it for a number of reasons. One of the major problems facing this medium is that it is still overshadowed by the major networks, as households with basic cable service still watch considerably more network programming per week than cable shows. This stems from the fact that cable generally has less desirable programming and poorer production quality than broadcast TV. Also, the large number of cable stations has resulted in audience fragmentation and has made buying procedures more difficult, since numerous stations must be contacted to reach the majority of the cable audience in a particular market. There are also problems with the quality and availability of local ratings for cable stations.

Another problem with cable is its lack of penetration, particularly in the top 10 major markets. In the three major metropolitan areas of New York, Chicago, and Los Angeles less than 50 percent of the households have CATV. Many areas of the country still do not have cable, and even in markets where it is available, its penetration is often under 50 percent. Thus, advertisers using cable may not be reaching more than half of the consumers in many areas.

The Future of Cable   The future of CATV as an advertising medium will ultimately depend on the size and characteristics of the audience the cable stations can reach with their programs. This in turn will depend on the ability of cable to offer programs that attract subscribers and viewers. Although cable has long been a stepchild in terms of program development and acquisition, this has begun to change. For example, Cable News Network (CNN) has become widely recognized for the quality of its news programming and is viewed by many as the equal of the major networks in news coverage (Figure 11–13). ESPN's landmark deal for exclusive Sunday night coverage of National Football League games, and its new contract to televise major league baseball, proved that a cable network could compete with the major networks in a sports bidding war.[26]

Cable stations also have begun competing against broadcast stations in the syndication market for reruns of popular shows. Better programming will lead to higher ratings, and higher ratings will lead to more advertising dollars, which will in turn fund better programs for cable.

Cable is becoming particularly popular as a source of sports programming. It is predicted that every sizable city in the country will have its own regional sports network within a few years and that many professional sporting events will be available only on cable.[27] This will change the media strategy of many companies trying to reach the young male consumer. As cable penetration increases, as programming improves, and as advertisers discover its efficiency, cable's popularity as an advertising medium will grow. Many advertising agencies have developed specialists to examine and plan for the use of cable in their clients' television advertising schedules.

Superstations

Another television alternative that evolved from cable is that of the superstation. Superstations are independent network stations that send their signals via satellite to cable operators to make them available to their subscribers. There are currently three superstations in the United States—WOR (New York), WGN (Chicago), and the best known WTBS, Channel 17 in Atlanta (which like CNN is part of the Turner Broadcasting System, Inc.). Programming on superstations generally consists of sports, movies, and reruns of network shows. The superstations present advertisers with another relatively inexpensive option for reaching large numbers of households and are another source of competition for the major networks as their audiences increase in size.

Video Cassette Recorders

An important development that has influenced the television viewing patterns of American households and caused concern to advertisers is the increasing penetration of video cassette recorders (VCRs) into American homes. In 1988 penetration level of video cassette recorders in American homes reached 60 percent, and this figure is expected to surpass the 70 percent level in the early 1990s.[28] The size of television programs' viewing audiences will be reduced as consumers turn to prerecorded tapes of movies and other programs. VCRs have also made possible **time shifting,** whereby a program can be recorded during its regularly scheduled period but viewed at some other time. Movies and daytime soap operas are the most commonly recorded programs, whereas game shows, sitcoms, sporting events, and the news are the least recorded.

A concern among advertisers is that many viewers of prerecorded programs engage in **zipping** or fast-forwarding through the commercials while watching the show, thus reducing the viewership of the messages. Advertisers are obviously concerned about VCRs and their potential effect on viewing audiences as well as the **zapping** problem that results from channel changing via remote control. These problems are discussed in Promotional Perspective 11–5. As will be discussed in Chapter 13, some advertisers have begun to place commercials in video cassette versions of movies.[29]

Developments in Audience Measurement

Another area where the advertising industry is likely to see changes over the next several years is in audience measurement. Technological developments and a very competitive research marketplace will continue to drive companies toward the never-ending quest for the ideal TV rating system. Many people feel that people meters are only the first step in improving the way television viewing audiences are measured. However, while they are seen as an improvement over the diary method, they still require cooperation on an ongoing basis by people in the metered homes and thus suffer from potential cooperation biases. Work will continue on developing passive measurement sys-

Promotional Perspective 11–5

Zapping: A Potential Problem for Advertisers

When advertisers buy time on a television station or network program, they are not purchasing guaranteed exposure but rather the opportunity to communicate a message to the station's or network's viewing audience. While advertisers continue to pay more and more money for these communication opportunities, there is increasing concern that the size of these commercial viewing audiences may be reduced because of the "zapping" problem.

Zapping can be viewed in two separate ways, including time shifting or the "fast-forwarding" over commercials during playback of a program previously recorded on a VCR, and channel switching or using a remote control device to switch away from commercials. The first, which is sometimes referred to as *zipping,* has become an increasing concern to advertisers as the penetration of video cassette recorders increases. As VCR penetration grows to 70 percent or more of U.S. television homes, as predicted, a significant number of these households may cease watching live television in favor of recording their program choices. The viewing of prerecorded shows enables the viewer to zap over commercials. A study by Nielsen revealed that while 80 percent of recorded shows are actually played back, viewers zap past more than half of the commercials.

With regard to channel switching, a study of 1,000 TV homes in the New York City area found that the average household zaps once every 3 minutes and 26 seconds. A Nielsen study found that most commercial zapping occurs at the beginning and, to a somewhat lesser extent, at the end of the program, with little occurring with the body of the show. However, since many programs are of a half-hour length and have a greater portion of their commercials at the beginning and end, they are more affected by zapping. Zapping at these points is likely to occur because commercial gaps are so long and predictable. Also, the emergence of 24-hour continuous format programs such as CNN or MTV means that the viewer can switch over for a few news headlines or videos and then back to the program.

Research attempting to profile zappers has found that young adults zap more than older adults, and men are more likely to zap commercials than are women. Zappers are more likely to have remote control channel selectors available, which facilitates the changing of stations, and are less likely to know what shows they are going to watch before they sit down to watch television. Zappers are also less likely to watch a show from start to finish and are more likely to change channels between shows, during shows, and at commercials. It has also been shown that the highest-income households, those that advertisers most want to reach, are the heaviest zappers.

The obvious issue facing advertisers is how to inhibit zapping. Hard-core zappers simply may zap everything and may have a television viewing style that will prove difficult to change. The networks can use certain tactics to hold viewers' attention such as previews of the next week's show or short closing scenes at the end of programs. Some programs start with action sequences before opening credits and commercials to hold the viewers' attention. Anheuser-Busch recently began using the "Bud Frame" during sports programming in which the Budweiser spot frames the live coverage of a sporting event. There is also evidence that ads that attract viewers' interest are less likely to be zapped. For example, during the 1988 Grammy awards, most ads lost 10 percent of viewers, but Pepsi spots featuring singer Michael Jackson lost only 1 percent to 2 percent. However, as more viewers gain access to VCRs and remote control capability, the zapping problem is likely to increase.

Sources: Barry M. Kaplan, "Zapping—The Real Issue Is Communication," *Journal of Advertising Research* 25, April/May 1985, pp. 9–12; Carrie Heeter and Bradley S. Greenberg, "Profiling the Zappers," *Journal of Advertising Research* 25, April/May 1985, pp. 15–19; Dennis Kneale, "Zapping of TV Ads Appears Pervasive," *The Wall Street Journal,* April 25, 1988, p. 27.

---

tems such as sonar, thermal infrared, and ultrasonic counters that can correctly count viewing audiences and can be used as an adjunct to the people meter system.[30] However, the problem of uniquely identifying members of the viewing audience is likely to remain.

Attention is also being focused on developing *commercial rating* systems rather than just program ratings. Problems created by technological advances in video equipment such as zipping, zapping, and flipping channels have focused more attention on the need to develop accurate ratings of more than just program audience viewing.[31] If advertisers know the rating of a commercial versus the program rating, they then might force the networks into pricing their time based on these figures, which could result in lower rates.

In 1988 a media research firm, the R. D. Percy Company, developed a heat sensor system that could determine the rating of a commercial on a second-by-second basis and announced plans to launch a full-scale commercial ratings service.[32] However, the company suspended operations owing to financial problems, and it is uncertain at the time this book is being written as to whether it will resume operations.[33] It is likely, however, that the A. C. Nielsen Company will begin to develop a commercial ratings system as advertisers become more interested in pinpointing the ratings of commercials than of the programs.

Another important development is the tying together of television audience viewership information with the purchase behavior of the household through the use of **single-source data.** A number of companies including Information Resources, Nielsen, and Arbitron have developed single-source systems that are being tested in various markets.[34] These systems monitor the television shows a household watches as well as the brands it purchases, coupon usage, magazine and newspaper readership, and demographics. We will discuss the use of single-source data in more detail in the chapter on measuring effectiveness (Chapter 18).

It appears that the 1990s will see a considerable amount of change and developments in terms of viewing options, video technology, and audience measurement. These trends and developments must be carefully monitored by advertisers and media planners as well as by people in the television industry, as they can have a profound impact on audience size, composition, and the way advertisers use, and pay for the use of, television as an advertising medium.

Radio

Television has often been referred to as the ideal advertising medium and to many people personifies the glamour and excitement of the industry. Radio, on the other hand, has been called the "Rodney Dangerfield of media" in reference to the lack of respect many advertisers have for the medium and the fact that it is often taken for granted by many advertisers.[35] As noted at the beginning of this chapter, the role of radio as both an advertising medium and an entertainment medium changed dramatically with television's rapid growth in popularity during the 1950s, 1960s, and 1970s. However, radio did survive and has become a very healthy, although somewhat different, medium. Radio has evolved into a primarily local advertising medium, whereas it was dominated by network programming and national advertisers prior to the growth of television. In 1987, network advertising accounted for less than 6 percent of radio's revenue.[36] Radio has also become a medium characterized by highly specialized programming appealing to very narrow segments of the population.

The survival of radio is perhaps best demonstrated by the numbers. The number of radio stations in this country has grown to more than 10,000, including 4,902 commercial AM stations and 4,041 commercial FM stations. In 1987 there were over 500 million radios in use, or an average of 5.7 per household (including 123 million in automobiles and another 8 million "walkman"-type radios). Radio has grown into a ubiquitous medium that is background to many activities such as reading, driving, running, walking, working, and interacting. The pervasiveness of this medium has obviously not gone unnoticed by advertisers, as radio advertising revenue has grown from $693 million in 1960 to more than $7.8 billion in 1988 (Figure 11–14).

Radio has survived and flourished as an advertising medium because it offers advertisers certain advantages for communicating messages to their potential customers. However, radio does have inherent limitations and thus plays a somewhat different role as an advertising medium. In this section we will examine the characteristics of radio and the role it plays in the advertiser's media strategy.

Advantages of Radio

Cost and Efficiency One of the main strengths of radio as an advertising medium is its low cost. Radio commercials are very inexpensive to produce, as they require only a script of the commercial to be read by the radio announcer or a copy of a

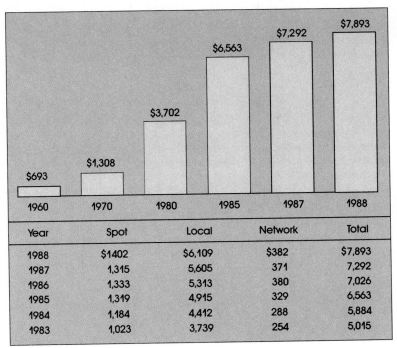

Figure 11–14   **Radio Revenue Growth**

Year	Spot	Local	Network	Total
1988	$1402	$6,109	$382	$7,893
1987	1,315	5,605	371	7,292
1986	1,333	5,313	380	7,026
1985	1,319	4,915	329	6,563
1984	1,184	4,412	288	5,884
1983	1,023	3,739	254	5,015

Note: Numbers are in millions of dollars.
Source: Radio Advertising Bureau.

prerecorded message that can be broadcast by the station. The cost for radio time is also low, as radio spots can be purchased very inexpensively. Even a minute on network radio can cost only $5,000, which translates into a cost per thousand figure of only $3 to $4. The low relative cost of radio makes it one of the most efficient of all advertising media, whereas the low absolute or actual cost means that the budget needed for an effective radio campaign is often lower than for other media.

The low cost of radio also means that advertisers can build more reach and frequency into their media schedules, given a certain budget. Advertisers can use different stations to broaden the reach of their messages and multiple spots to ensure an adequate frequency level. Many national advertisers have begun to recognize the cost efficiency of radio. For example, a few years ago Miles Laboratories spent its entire advertising budget of $600,000 for Bactine first-aid spray in this medium. While the media budget was too small to allow for much impact with television ads, radio proved very effective in reaching its target audience of young mothers, which included working women as well as mothers staying at home. The effects of the radio campaign on Bactine sales was so favorable that Miles decided to allot 15 percent of its total ad budget to radio for other brands such as Alka-Seltzer and Flintstones vitamins.[37] Promotional Perspective 11–6 discusses how Motel 6 used radio advertising to help turn around the company.

Selectivity   Another major advantage of radio is the high degree of audience selectivity that is available through the various program formats and geographic coverage of the numerous stations. Radio enables companies to focus their advertising on specialized audiences such as certain demographic and lifestyle groups. Most areas have radio stations with formats such as rock and roll, easy listening, classical music, country western, talk shows, and all news, to name a few. Hard-to-reach consumers such as teenagers, college students, or working adults can be reached more easily through radio than most other media. Light television viewers spend nearly twice as much time with radio as with television and are generally an upscale market in terms of income

Promotional Perspective **11—6**

A Successful Radio Campaign Has Motel 6 Leaving a Lot of Lights On

One of the largest portions of the 2.8 million room lodging industry is the economy or budget segment, which is dominated by the Motel 6 chain (the "6" originally stood for $6 a night when the company was founded in 1962). Although Motel 6 is the nation's largest chain of budget motels, prior to 1986 they had no marketing department, never had an advertising campaign, charged guests $1.49 to have their televisions connected, and did not even provide telephones in the motel rooms.

In 1986 Motel 6 hit bottom as it lost $18.7 million and its occupancy rate dropped to 66.7 percent. This prompted the investment company that had bought the chain to take steps to help turn it around. Phones were installed in every room, the TV hookup charge was dropped, rooms were refurbished, and a number of new motels were built, bringing the total number of Motel 6s to over 500. By 1988 Motel 6 had earnings of $5.3 million, and occupancy was up to 73.8 percent. While these changes were important in Motel 6's turnaround, the company's top executives agree that such a rapid reversal would not have been possible without its pervasive radio campaign featuring Tom Bodett, a 33-year-old-contractor-turned-writer, as spokesperson for the company.

Motel 6 originally went with radio in 1986 because it had a limited ad budget of just over $1 million and because it felt that radio was the best way to reach travelers, most of whom arrived by car or truck and without a reservation. In the radio spots developed by the chain's ad agency, Bodett delivers a down-home, humorous message that tells travelers that is it okay to be cheap and ends with the campaign slogan: "We'll leave the light on for you" (Exhibit 11—6). Much of the success of the campaign comes from Bodett's country-style voice and delivery. It has also been suggested that Bodett is so effective because on radio his "real-folk" voice takes on a variety of faces. Older people envision him as a road-weary traveler, younger people see him as one of them, and businesspeople hear a harried salesperson.

While the exact reason is difficult to determine, there is little doubt that Bodett has been effective and has become very popular in the process. He has his own national radio show and even has his own fan club. Although he receives mountains of mail addressing him as the head of the chain, Motel 6's real president does not mind, noting that "he can be chairman of the board if he wants! . . . He's contributed that much to the turnaround of this company." Bodett is heard in more than 70 different executions of Motel 6 spots, and in 1989 the company spent over $8 million on network and radio advertising. The success of the Motel 6 ads has led other motel chains such as Econ Lodges and Red Roof Inns to develop radio campaigns using celebrity spokespeople. However, none has been as successful as Bodett's folksy appeal.

Source: "King of the Road," *Marketing and Media Decisions,* March 1989, pp. 80—86.

Exhibit 11—6 **Example of Motel 6 Radio Spot**

"Hi. Tom Bodett for Motel 6 with a plan for anyone whose kids are on their own now. Take a drive, see some of the country and visit a few relatives. Like your sister Helen and her husband Bob. They're wonderful folks and always happy to pull the hide-a-bed out for you, but somehow the smell of mothballs just isn't conducive to gettin' a good night's sleep. And since Bob gets up at 5:30, well that means you do too. So here's the plan. Check into Motel 6. 'Cause for around 22 bucks, the lowest prices of any national chain, you'll get a clean, comfortable room, and Helen and Bob'll think you're mighty considerate. Well you are, but maybe more important, you can sleep late and not have to wonder if the towels in their bathroom are just for decoration. My rule of thumb is, if they match the tank and seat cover, you better leave 'em alone. Just call 505-891-6161 for reservations. I'm Tom Bodett for Motel 6. Give my best to Helen and Bob and we'll leave the light on for you."

One of the 70-plus radio spots for Motel 6 created by The Richards Group.

and education level.[38] Radio has also become a popular way to reach specific non–English-speaking ethnic markets. For example, Los Angeles, New York City, and Miami have several radio stations that broadcast in Spanish and reach these areas' large Hispanic markets. As mass marketing declines and gives way to market segmentation and regional marketing, radio will continue to grow in importance.

Flexibility Radio is probably the most flexible of all the advertising media, as it has a very short closing period, which means that advertisers can change their message almost up to the time it goes on the air. Radio commercials can usually be produced and scheduled on very short notice. Advertisers can also adjust their messages to local market conditions and marketing situations very easily through radio.

Mental Imagery Another potential advantage of radio that is often overlooked is that it allows listeners to use their imagination when processing a commercial mes-

sage. While the creative options of radio are limited, many advertisers have taken advantage of the absence of a visual element to let consumers create their own picture or image of what is happening in a radio message. The Radio Advertising Bureau ran an "I saw it on the radio" campaign contending that advertisers can create a "theater of the mind" with listeners if they use creative and imaginative commercials (Figure 11–15).

For example, a radio campaign for Molson Golden beer used a series of man-meets-woman vignettes as part of its advertising program for the brand in the United States. These spots took advantage of listeners' opportunity to fantasize and develop their own images of the characters in the scenes developed in the commercials. An example of one of the Molson radio spots is shown in Figure 11–16.

It has also been suggested that radio can be used to reinforce television messages through a technique called **image transfer** whereby the images of a TV commercial are implanted into a radio spot.[39] This involves establishing the video image of a TV commercial, then using the audio portion (spoken words and/or jingle) as the basis for the radio campaign. The idea is that when consumers hear the radio message, they will make the connection to the television commercial, which reinforces its video images. Image transfer offers advertisers a way of combining radio and television ads and making them work together by reinforcing one another.

Merchandising Value and Support   Radio stations often become an integral part of many communities, and the radio personalities may become popular figures. Advertisers often use radio stations and personalities to enhance their involvement with a local market and to gain influence with local middlemen such as retailers.

Limitations of Radio

There are several factors that limit the effectiveness of radio as an advertising medium that must be considered by the media planner in determining the role the medium will play in the advertising program.

Figure 11–16   Molson Beer Made Effective Use of Radio by Letting Listeners Use Their Imaginations

FEMALE:	Excuse me, is this stool taken?
MALE:	Uh, no.
FEMALE:	Mind if I sit here?
MALE:	Help yourself.
FEMALE:	Thanks.
MALE:	Would you, uh, pass me the peanuts?
FEMALE:	Sure—(sound of a glass being knocked over)—oh, oh, I'm terribly sorry. Oh, I've ruined that tie, and it's so beautiful too. Let me wipe it up.
MALE:	(softly) That's okay.
FEMALE:	Um, that's a very interesting cologne you're wearing.
MALE:	Huh? It's beer!
FEMALE:	(Chuckle) Oh, no, I'm sorry. Let me buy you another one, please.
MALE:	No, that's all right—I'll just suck my tie.
FEMALE:	(Chuckle) Let me make it up to you. How about a Molson Golden?
MALE:	Molson Golden?
FEMALE:	Yah, imported from Canada. It's excellent. Crisp, clear, smooth—you'll really love it.
MALE:	Uh, yah, yah . . .
FEMALE:	You will?
MALE:	Are you trying to pick me up?
FEMALE:	(Chuckle) The thought never entered my mind.
MALE:	Well, think.
FEMALE:	(Chuckle)
ANNOUNCER:	Molson Golden beer, from North America's oldest brewery. Since 1786, Molson makes it golden. Imported by Martlet, Great Neck, New York.
MALE:	Well, you're not doing a very good job of this.
FEMALE:	I know, let me start over: Is this stool taken?
MALE:	(Shouts) Hold the peanuts!

Creative Limitations   A major drawback of radio as an advertising medium is, of course, the absence of a visual image. The radio advertiser cannot show the product, demonstrate it, or use any type of visual appeal or information. A radio commercial is, like a television ad, a short-lived and fleeting message that is externally paced, which does not allow the receiver to control the rate at which the message is processed. Because of the creative limitations of radio, many companies tend to ignore it, and agencies often assign junior people to the development of radio commercial messages.

Fragmentation   Another problem with radio is the high level of audience fragmentation that occurs because of the large number of stations. Radio listeners can choose from a large number of stations, and the percentage of the market tuned to any particular station is usually very small. For example, the top-rated radio station in many major metropolitan areas with a number of AM and FM stations may attract less than 10 percent of the total listening audience. Thus, advertisers who want to have broad reach in their radio advertising media schedule will have to buy time on a number of stations to cover even a local market.

Chaotic Buying Procedures   It should be readily apparent how chaotic the media planning and purchasing process can become for the advertiser who wants to use radio on a nationwide spot basis. Acquiring information and evaluating and contracting for time with even a fraction of the 8,000 commercial stations that operate across the country can be very difficult and time-consuming. This problem has been diminished somewhat in recent years as the number of radio networks increases and the growth in syndicated programs offering a package of several hundred stations expands.

Limited Research Data   Audience research data on radio are often limited, particularly as compared with television, magazines, or newspapers. Most radio stations are not large operations and lack the revenue to support detailed studies of their audiences. Also, most users of radio are local companies who are not able to support research on radio listenership in their markets. Thus, media planners do not have a great deal of audience information available to guide them in their purchase of radio time.

Buying Radio Time

The purchase of radio time is similar to that of television, as advertisers can make either network, spot, or local buys. Since these options were reviewed in examining ways of buying television time, they will only be discussed here briefly.

Network versus Spot Radio

Network Radio   Advertising time on radio can be purchased on a network basis using one of the national networks. In 1987 the Westwood One Network purchased Mutual Broadcasting Network and NBC Radio Network, leaving four major networks: ABC, CBS, Westwood, and United Stations. There are also more than 100 regional radio networks across the country. The advantage of using networks is that the advertiser can minimize the amount of negotiation and administrative work needed to get national or regional coverage, and the costs will be lower than if individual stations were used. However, there can be considerable variation in the number of affiliated stations on the network roster and the type of audience they reach. Thus, the use of network radio results in less flexibility in selecting stations. Table 11–10 shows the top 25 network radio advertisers for 1987.

Spot Radio   National advertisers can also use spot radio to purchase airtime on individual stations in various markets. The purchase of spot radio provides advertisers greater flexibility in selecting markets, individual stations, and airtime and making any

Table 11–10   **Top 25 Network Radio Advertisers**

| Rank | Advertiser | Network Radio Expenditures | | | As % of Co.'s '88 Ad Total |
		1988	1987	% Chg	
1	Sears, Roebuck & Co.	$67,612	$52,701	28.3	6.5
2	General Motors Corp.	38,255	18,906	102.3	3.0
3	Procter & Gamble Co.	25,534	23,665	7.9	1.7
4	Bayer AG	18,701	20,221	(7.5)	14.1
5	Campbell Soup Co.	18,572	14,763	25.8	9.2
6	Cotter & Co.	18,284	12,488	46.4	20.8
7	Warner-Lambert Co.	16,911	24,614	(31.3)	2.8
8	Anheuser-Busch Cos.	15,391	23,456	(34.4)	2.4
9	American Telephone & Telegraph	12,311	15,004	(17.9)	2.2
10	Ford Motor Co.	12,043	19,766	(39.1)	2.1
11	Unilever NV	11,816	8,627	37.0	1.9
12	K Mart Corp.	11,792	6,824	72.8	1.9
13	U.S. Government	11,788	10,124	16.4	4.0
14	City Investing Co.	11,549	NA	NA	NA
15	Schering-Plough Corp.	11,256	10,641	5.8	4.3
16	Chrysler Corp.	11,193	4,874	129.7	2.4
17	Dow Jones & Co.	10,218	8,951	14.1	NA
18	News Corp.	9,734	4,899	98.7	7.0
19	Philip Morris Cos.	8,698	9,611	(9.5)	0.4
20	Teledisc USA	8,591	15,758	(45.5)	NA
21	Black & Decker Manufacturing Co.	7,485	2,106	255.4	11.8
22	Hershey Foods Corp.	5,952	3,332	78.6	2.0
23	General Mills	5,809	2,473	134.9	1.2
24	State Farm Mutual Auto. Insurance	5,801	NA	NA	NA
25	Mars Inc.	5,721	8,569	(33.2)	1.7

NA= not applicable
Note: Dollars are in thousands.

Source: Broadcast Advertisers Report as reported by BAR/LNA reports, *Advertising Age,* September 27, 1989, p. 74.

Table 11–11   **Top 25 Spot Radio Advertisers**

| Rank | Advertiser | Spot Radio Expenditures | | | As % of Co.'s '88 Ad Total |
		1988	1987	% Chg	
1	Anheuser-Busch Cos.	$42,696	$43,550	(2.0)	6.7
2	General Motors Corp.	40,185	34,829	15.4	3.1
3	Philip Morris Cos.	40,092	29,489	36.0	1.9
4	Pepsico Inc.	28,198	19,766	42.7	4.0
5	Sears, Roebuck & Co.	25,431	21,211	19.9	2.4
6	Southland Corp.	22,108	18,317	20.7	30.5
7	Grand Metropolitan PLC	21,090	16,366	28.9	2.7
8	Delta Air Lines	19,948	19,671	1.4	17.7
9	Chrysler Corp.	19,412	17,345	11.9	4.1
10	Procter & Gamble Co.	15,777	7,906	99.6	1.0
11	BellSouth Corp.	15,771	13,291	18.7	18.6
12	Adolph Coors Co.	15,442	10,073	53.3	7.7
13	Coca-Cola Co.	15,286	13,051	17.1	4.0
14	Melville Corp.	14,607	13,777	6.0	18.0
15	News Corp.	13,360	3,960	237.4	9.6
16	Ford Motor Co.	11,827	14,861	(20.4)	2.1
17	Hondo Motor Co.	11,531	4,661	147.4	4.7
18	Bond Corp. Holdings	11,408	10,756	6.1	15.9
19	AMR Corp.	10,662	16,106	(33.8)	8.8
20	U.S. Government	10,352	8,844	17.1	3.5
21	Montgomery Ward & Co.	10,232	NA	NA	6.6
22	Volkswagen AG	10,162	4,472	127.2	7.2
23	Geo. A. Hormel & Co.	9,891	8,119	21.8	13.9
24	U.S. West	9,522	8,639	10.2	15.7
25	GTE Corp.	9,265	7,357	25.9	12.9

Note: Dollars are in thousands.
Source: Radio Expenditure Reports, *Advertising Age,* September 27, 1989, p. 90.

adjustments in the message for local market conditions. Spot radio accounts for approximately 20 percent of radio time sold. The top 25 spot radio advertisers for 1987 are shown in Table 11–11.

Local Radio   By far the heaviest user of radio is the local advertiser, as nearly 75 percent of radio advertising time is purchased from individual stations by local companies. Auto dealers, retailing operations, restaurants, and financial institutions are among the heaviest users of local radio advertising.

Time Classifications

As with television, the broadcast day for radio is divided into various time periods or dayparts, as shown in Table 11–12. The size of the radio listening audience will vary widely across the various dayparts, and advertising rates will follow accordingly. The largest radio audiences (and thus the highest rates) occur during the early morning and late afternoon drive times. Radio rates also vary according to the number of spots or type of audience plan purchased. Variation in radio rates is common depending on the supply and demand of time available in the local market and the ratings of the individual station. Rate information is available directly from the stations on their rate

Table 11–12   **Dayparts for Radio**

Morning drive time	6:00 A.M.–10:00 A.M.
Daytime	10:00 A.M.–3:00 P.M.
Afternoon/evening drive time	3:00 P.M.–7:00 P.M.
Nighttime	7:00 P.M.–12:00 A.M.
All night	12:00 A.M.–6:00 A.M.

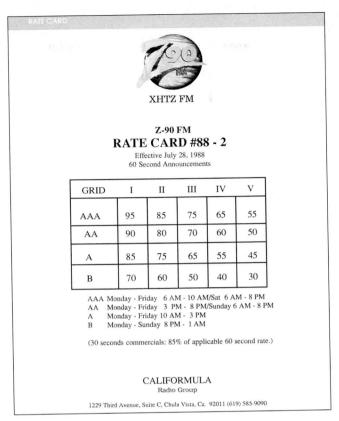

Figure 11—17 **Sample Radio Rate Card**

cards (see Figure 11–17) and is summarized in Standard Rate and Data Service's (SRDS) Spot Radio Rates and Data for both local stations and radio networks. A sample page from SRDS is shown in Figure 11–18 for the Denver, Colorado, market. However, it should be noted that many stations do not adhere strictly to rate cards and the rates published in SRDS. Radio rates will vary according to market demand and time availability.

Audience Information

As noted earlier, one problem with radio is the lack of audience information. Because there are so many radio stations and thus many small, fragmented audiences, the stations themselves cannot support the expense of detailed audience measurement. Also, owing to the nature of radio as incidental or background entertainment, it becomes very difficult to develop precise measures of radio listenership in terms of who listens at various time periods and for how long. There are three major radio ratings services, with Arbitron and Birch Radio being the primary suppliers of audience information for local stations and the RADAR (radio's all-dimension audience research) studies, which supply information on network audiences.

Arbitron Arbitron covers 260 local radio markets with one to four ratings reports per year. Arbitron uses a sample of representative listeners in each market and has them maintain a diary of their radio listening for a seven-day period. Audience estimates for the market are based on these diary records and reported by time period and selected demographics in the *Arbitron Ratings/Radio* book to which clients subscribe. Figure 11–19 provides a sample page from the Arbitron Ratings Report for persons in the 18 to 49 age target audience across the various dayparts. The three basic estimates in the Arbitron report include:

Figure 11—18 **Page from Standard Rate and Data Service Spot Radio Rates and Data**

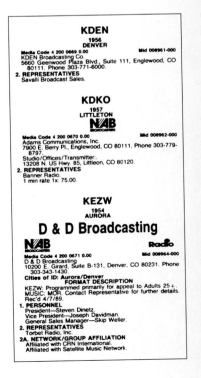

Figure 11–19 **Page from Arbitron Radio Ratings Report**

Target Audience
PERSONS 18-49

	MONDAY-FRIDAY 6AM-10AM				MONDAY-FRIDAY 10AM-3PM				MONDAY-FRIDAY 3PM-7PM				MONDAY-FRIDAY 7PM-MID				WEEKEND 10AM-7PM			
	AQH (00)	CUME (00)	AQH RTG	AQH SHR	AQH (00)	CUME (00)	AQH RTG	AQH SHR	AQH (00)	CUME (00)	AQH RTG	AQH SHR	AQH (00)	CUME (00)	AQH RTG	AQH SHR	AQH (00)	CUME (00)	AQH RTG	AQH SHR
KEZY METRO	25	410	.2	.8	22	372	.2	.7	28	389	.2	1.0	12	265	.1	1.3	34	399	.3	1.8
TSA	25	410			22	372			28	389			12	265			34	399		
KIKF METRO	55	298	.5	1.8	65	287	.5	2.2	27	259	.2	1.0	12	108	.1	1.3	19	200	.2	1.0
TSA	55	298			65	287			27	259			12	108			19	200		
KOCM METRO	25	280	.2	.8	45	218	.4	1.5	31	266	.3	1.1	8	93	.1	.9	10	96	.1	.5
TSA	25	280			45	218			31	266			8	93			10	96		
KWIZ METRO	17	129	.1	.6	9	93	.1	.3	26	150	.2	1.0	5	104		.6	15	123	.1	.8
TSA	17	129			9	93			26	150			5	104			15	123		
KWIZ-FM METRO	18	195	.1	.6	42	269	.3	1.4	26	302	.2	1.0	7	111	.1	.8	22	193	.2	1.2
TSA	18	195			42	269			26	302			7	111			22	193		
KWVE METRO	23	299	.2	.8	26	240	.2	.9	21	267	.2	.8	13	158	.1	1.4	24	240	.2	1.3
TSA	23	299			26	240			21	267			13	158			24	240		
KYMS METRO	43	254	.4	1.4	31	248	.3	1.0	36	301	.3	1.3	14	167	.1	1.5	43	239	.4	2.3
TSA	43	254			31	248			36	301			14	167			43	239		
KABC METRO	113	553	.9	3.7	107	452	.9	3.6	79	514	.6	2.9	32	347	.3	3.5	21	199	.2	1.1
TSA	113	553			107	452			79	514			32	347			21	199		

Footnote Symbols: * Audience estimates adjusted for actual broadcast schedule. + Station(s) changed call letters since the prior survey - see Page 5B.

- Person estimates—the number of persons listening
- Rating—the percentage of listeners in the survey area population
- Share—the percentage of the total estimated listening audience

These three estimates are further defined by using quarter-hour and cume figures.

The **average quarter-hour (AQH) figure** identifies the average number of persons estimated to have listened to a station during any 15-minute period of any given daypart. For example, station KEZY has an average quarter-hour listenership of 2,500 during the weekday 6 A.M. to 10 A.M. daypart. This means that any weekday, for any 15-minute period during this time period, an average of 2,500 people between the ages of 18 and 49 are tuned to this station. This figure helps to determine the audience and cost of a spot schedule within a particular time period.

Cume is a term used for *cumulative audience,* which is the estimated total number of different people who listened to a station for a minimum of five minutes in a quarter-hour period within a reported daypart. In Figure 11–19 the cumulative audience of persons 18 to 49 for station KEZY during the weekday morning daypart is 41,000. Cume provides an estimate of the reach potential of a radio station.

The **average quarter-hour rating (AQH RTG)** expresses the estimated number of listeners as a percentage of the survey area population. The **average quarter-hour share (AQH SHR)** is the percentage of the total listening audience tuned to each station and shows the share of listeners each station captures out of the total listening audience in the survey area.

Birch Radio   A second radio ratings service is Birch Radio, which measures station listenership in the 130 or so major radio markets and in a number of smaller markets when specifically requested. Birch uses telephone surveys rather than diaries and publishes its reports on a monthly basis, with quarterly summaries.

RADAR   In the RADAR studies, which are sponsored by the major radio networks, audience estimates are collected twice a year and are based on daily telephone interviews covering seven days of radio listening behavior. Each listener is called daily for a week and asked about radio usage from the day before until that moment. Network audience measures are provided by RADAR along with estimates of audience size for all stations and various segments. The audience estimates are time-period measurements for the various dayparts. RADAR also supplies reports that provide estimates of network audiences to all commercials and to commercials within various programs. The research is conducted year round and is published annually in *Radio Usage and Network Radio Audiences.*

As is the case with television, media planners must use the audience measurement information to evaluate the value of various radio stations in reaching the advertiser's target audience and their relative cost. The media buyer responsible for the purchase of radio time works with information on target audience coverage, rates, time schedules, and availability to try to optimize the advertiser's radio media budget.

Future of Radio

Radio managed to survive the threat it encountered from television by becoming a more localized medium that could focus on specialized segments. As the number of commercial radio stations increases, the specialization and fragmentation of the radio audience will continue. Particularly noteworthy is the growth of FM stations, which have a more limited range but have the advantage of broadcasting in stereo. Most radios sold today have both AM and FM capability, and 75 percent of radio listening is on FM stations.[40] This figure is even higher for young adults (18–34), where nearly 80 percent of listening occurs on FM because of the more youth-oriented format of FM stations and the superior fidelity of stereo.[41] AM radio stations have begun to respond to the challenge of FM by changing the format of their programs and getting permission from the FCC to broadcast in stereo. The aging of the population may be of benefit to AM stations, as older consumers are less likely to listen to music and tune into more talk shows, local information programs, news, and sports. Although AM stations still account for more than half of the $7 billion in radio advertising revenue, this percentage is down from the 90 percent of radio revenue AM stations attracted in 1970.

Another important trend in radio is the increasing number of radio networks and syndicated programs that offer advertisers a package of several hundred stations. This reduces the fragmentation and purchasing problems associated with radio and increases the appeal of the medium to national advertisers.

Advertisers continue to discover ways to make effective use of radio in their media plans, and the increases in radio advertising revenue should continue. Radio will remain a popular medium among local advertisers and is growing in popularity among national advertisers as well. In the mid-1980s a number of large companies, including Procter & Gamble, AT&T, and Warner-Lambert, increased their network radio advertising budgets considerably.[42] However, by the end of the 1980s a number of firms reduced their advertising budgets and reduced their spending on radio advertising significantly.

It has been noted that local radio stations may begin to see more competition from cable television. A number of radio advertisers are switching their advertising dollars to local cable because the rates are comparable with those of radio and there is the added advantage of TV's visual impact.[43] Concern has also been expressed over the continuing growth in the number of radio stations competing for a stagnant listener market with similar programming. Thus, there are a number of challenges facing radio in its quest to continue to gain audiences and attract advertising revenue. While radio is no longer likely to be taken for granted by advertisers, the medium must deal with these problems if it is to sustain its growth.

Summary

Television and radio, or the broadcast media, are the most pervasive media in most consumers' daily lives and offer advertisers the opportunity to reach vast audiences. Both broadcast media are time-, rather than space-, oriented and are organized similarly in that they utilize a system of affiliated stations belonging to a network, as well as individual stations, to broadcast their programs and commercial messages. Advertising on radio or television can be done on national or regional network programs or may be purchased on a spot basis from local stations.

Television has grown faster than any other advertising medium in history and has become the leading medium for national advertisers. No other medium offers the creative capabilities of television, as the combination of sight, sound, and movement present the advertiser with a vast number of options for presenting a commercial message with high impact. Television also is a medium that offers advertisers mass coverage at a low relative cost. Variations in programming and audience composition, along with the growth of cable television, are helping television offer more audience selectivity to advertisers. While television is often viewed as the ultimate advertising medium, it does have several limitations, including the high cost of producing and airing commercials, a lack of selectivity relative to other media, the fleeting nature of the message, and the problem of commercial clutter. The latter two problems have been compounded in recent years by the trend toward shorter commercials.

Information regarding the size and composition of television audiences is provided on a national level by the A. C. Nielsen Company, whereas local audience information is provided by Nielsen along with the Arbitron Ratings Company. The amount of money networks or stations can charge for commercial time on their programs is based on these audience measurement figures. This information is also important to media planners, as it is used to determine the combination of shows needed to attain specific levels of reach and frequency with the advertiser's target market.

Future trends in television include the continued growth of cable television and the resulting increase in available channels to cable households. The continued penetration of video cassette recorders poses a potential threat to traditional television viewing patterns as consumers record shows to watch at their own leisure and fast-forward through the commercials and as they watch more prerecorded programs such as movies. Developments and changes are likely to occur in the measurement of television viewing audiences, with greater emphasis placed on measuring the number of people watching the commercial as well as the program.

The role of radio as an entertainment and advertising medium has changed with the rapid growth of television. Radio has evolved into a primarily local advertising medium that offers highly specialized programming appealing to very narrow segments of the market. Radio offers advertisers the opportunity to build high reach and frequency into their media schedules and the ability to reach selective audiences at a very efficient cost.

The major drawback of radio is its creative limitations owing to the absence of a visual image. The short and fleeting nature of the radio commercial along with the highly fragmented nature of the radio audience are also problems. As with television, the rate structure for radio advertising time varies with the size of the audience delivered. Information regarding radio audiences is provided by Arbitron and Birch Radio for local markets and by the RADAR studies for network audiences.

A major trend in radio is the continued specialization and fragmentation of radio audiences. FM radio has begun to dominate the listening audience, although AM stations are responding to this challenge with changes in program formats and the addition of stereo broadcasting capabilities. Radio may face challenges in the future from cable television.

Key Terms

Broadcast media
Television network
Affiliates
Up-front market
Regional networks
Spot advertising
National spot
Local advertising
Station reps
Sponsorship
Participations
Adjacencies
Dayparts
Program rating
Ratings point
Households using television (HUT)
Share of audience
Total audience

Audimeter
People meter
Designated market areas (DMAs)
Area of dominant influence (ADI)
Cable television
Narrow casting
Infomercials
Time shifting
Zipping
Zapping
Single-source data
Image transfer
Average quarter-hour (AQH) figure
Cume
Average quarter-hour rating
  (AQH RTG)
Average quarter-hour share (AQH SHR)

Discussion Questions

1. Discuss how the changes that have been occurring in the television industry over the past two decades have affected the use of TV as an advertising medium.

2. It has been suggested that radio became a forgotten medium during the 1960s and 1970s that was rediscovered by advertisers in the 1980s. Discuss the reasons radio was neglected by many advertisers and why it has become popular again.

3. Discuss the specific advantages and disadvantages of television as an advertising medium.

4. Evaluate the trend in television advertising toward the use of shorter commercials. Do you feel that 15-second TV spots can be as effective as 30-second spots? Why or why not?

5. Choose a particular television daypart other than evening prime time and analyze the products or services being advertised during this period. Why do you think these firms have chosen to advertise during this daypart?

6. Discuss the methods used to measure network television viewing audiences and local audiences. Do you feel that the measurement methods being used for each are yielding valid estimates of program audiences? Why or why not?

7. What are the advantages and limitations of advertising on cable television networks or stations? Choose a cable station and evaluate the firms that are advertising during a particular program.

8. What are the advantages and limitations of advertising on radio? What types of advertisers are most likely to use radio?

9. Discuss how the concept of image transfer can be used in radio advertising. Provide an example of a radio campaign that is using this concept and evaluate it.

10. Discuss the future of radio as an advertising medium. Do you think it will become more or less popular during the 1990s? Why?

Notes

1. *Report on Television 1988,* Nielsen Media Research (Northbrook, Ill.: A. C. Nielsen Co., 1988).
2. William Myers, "Why Americans Are Turning Off to TV," *Adweek,* January 1986, pp. 4–6.
3. Bill Abrams, "Advertisers Growing Restless Over Rising Cost of TV Time," *The Wall Street Journal,* January 27, 1983, p. 20.
4. "Trends in Viewing," Television Bureau of Advertising, Inc., July 1988.
5. *Broadcasting/Cable Yearbook 1988* (Washington, D.C.: Broadcast Publications, Inc.).
6. "Trends in Advertising Volume," Television Bureau of Advertising, Inc., New York, May 1988.
7. "Trends in Media: Audience, Costs, CPM's," Television Bureau of Advertising, Inc., July 1988.
8. Dennis Kneale, "Zapping of TV Ads Appears Pervasive," *The Wall Street Journal,* April 25, 1988, p. 27.
9. Janet Meyers and Laurie Freeman, "Marketers Police TV Commercial Costs," *Advertising Age,* April 3, 1989, p. 51.
10. Robert H. Bolte and Pier Mapas, "Clutter Clatter," *Marketing & Media Decisions,* March 1988, p. 144.
11. "CBS Adds 3½ Minutes of Ad Time," *Advertising Age,* March 16, 1987, p. 2.
12. Ernest F. Larkin, "Consumer Perceptions of the Media and Their Advertising Content," *Journal of Advertising* 8, 1979, pp. 5–7.
13. Adapted from Charles H. Patti and Charles F. Frazier, *Advertising* (New York: Dryden Press, 1988).
14. "Zeroing in with a Network Buy," *Marketing & Media Decisions,* February 1987, p. 31.
15. "Marketing's New Look," *Business Week,* January 26, 1987, pp. 64–69.
16. Jennifer Lawrence, "American Air Books New Regionalized Ad Strategy," *Advertising Age,* September 12, 1988, p. 1.
17. Ron Alsop, "TV Advertisers See Gain in Being Sole Sponsor," *The Wall Street Journal,* February 9, 1988, p. 33.
18. Ibid.
19. *Report on Television 1989,* Nielsen Media Research (Northbrook, Ill.: A. C. Nielsen Co., 1989), p. 9.
20. Ibid., p. 10.
21. Ibid.
22. "Advertisers Cut Bargain Deals in Sluggish Media Marketplace," *Advertising Age,* March 26, 1987, p. 35.
23. *Broadcasting/Cable Yearbook 1989* (Washington, D.C.: Broadcast Publications, Inc.).
24. Judith Graham, "Net TV Declines to Affect Upfront," *Advertising Age,* April 24, 1989, p. 3.
25. Rich Zahradnik, "The Winning Circle," *Marketing & Media Decisions,* April 1988, pp. 70–81.
26. William Smith, "ESPN's New Game Plan," *Marketing & Media Decisions,* March 1989, p. 26.
27. "Sports on TV: Cable Is the Team to Watch," *Business Week,* August 22, 1988, pp. 66–69.
28. Steve Sternberg, "VCRs: A New Medium, A New Message," *Marketing & Media Decisions,* January 1989, pp. 81–84.
29. David Kalish, "On Media's Doorstep," *Marketing & Media Decisions,* July 1988, pp. 39–42.
30. Daozheng Lu and David A. Kiewit, "Passive Peoplemeters: A First Step," *Journal of Advertising Research,* June/July 1987, pp. 9–14.
31. Joe Mandese, "A Dream Come True," *Marketing & Media Decisions,* July 1988, pp. 30–37.
32. Verne Gay, "Rating TV Spots," *Advertising Age,* April 18, 1988, p. 2.
33. Joanne Lipman, "R. D. Percy & Son Suspend Operations: Nielsen Is Left with a Virtual Monopoly," *The Wall Street Journal,* August 8, 1988, p. 18.
34. Joanne Lipman, "Single-Source Ad Research Heralds Detailed Look at Household Habits," *The Wall Street Journal,* February 16, 1988, p. 35.
35. Quote by William Staklein, head of Radio Advertising Bureau, cited in "More Firms Tune Into Radio to Stretch Their Ad Budgets," *The Wall Street Journal,* July 17, 1986, p. 27.
36. "Trends in Advertising Volume."
37. "More Firms Tune Into Radio," p. 27.
38. "Radio Takes Upbeat Approach to Upscale Ad Market," *San Diego Union,* February 20, 1983, p. I-1.

39. Verne Gay, "Image Transfer: Radio Ads Make Aural History," *Advertising Age,* January 24, 1985, p. 1.
40. "Broadcast Beat," *Marketing & Media Decisions,* July 1988, pp. 143–44.
41. "AM Radio Fights to Win Listeners With Stereo and Format Changes," *The Wall Street Journal,* October 21, 1985, p. 27.
42. "More Firms Tune Into Radio."
43. David Kalish, "Bad Reception," *Marketing & Media Decisions,"* August 1988, pp. 63–65.

12

Evaluation of Print Media: Magazines and Newspapers

CHAPTER OBJECTIVES

1. To examine the structure of the magazine and newspaper industries and the role of each medium in the advertising program

2. To examine the advantages and limitations of magazines and newspapers as advertising media

3. To examine the various types of magazines and newspapers and the value of each as an advertising medium

4. To examine how advertising space is purchased in magazines and newspapers, how readership is measured, and how rates are determined

5. To consider future trends and developments regarding magazines and newspapers and how they will influence their use as advertising media

It's What's Up Front That Counts

Over the past decade the magazine publishing business has become extremely competitive, with hundreds of new publications appearing each year and more money being invested in existing titles to make them more attractive to both readers and advertisers. Millions of dollars are being spent on luxurious photography, sophisticated graphics, higher-quality paper, and other techniques to entice readers. However, in the business of selling magazines, nothing is more important than the cover.

Although the large majority of the more than 11,000 magazines sold in the United States are through subscription, editors are very concerned about choosing covers that will attract the attention and interest of the newsstand purchaser as well. Single-copy sales are important to publishers, as they not only help them achieve the circulation guarantees they make to advertisers but also tell editors what interests the reading public.

Choosing a successful cover is more of an art than a science, and there are numerous factors for editors to consider. Certain themes such as sex, how to make money, losing weight, and stories on celebrities are very popular, whereas political themes, particularly foreign politics, are considered a sure loser. *Time* magazine's worst-selling cover of 1988 was a feature on John Sasso and James Baker III, the managers of the Dukakis and Bush presidential campaigns. Its best-selling cover featured a story entitled "Who Was Jesus?" which coincided with the release of the controversial movie *The Last Temptation of Christ*. Figure 12–1 shows the best- and worst-selling covers of 1988 for several other popular magazines.

Many magazines have found that issues based on an annual theme are among their best sellers such as *Esquire*'s "Dubious Achievement" issue, *Fortune*'s survey of the top 500 corporations, and of course, *Sports Illustrated*'s annual swimsuit issue. While *Business Week* usually does very well with its annual issue exploring the best mutual funds, its best seller in 1988 was the issue on the best business schools.

While finding the right cover can be difficult, many publications have turned to celebrities to attract readers, including movie stars, athletes, business stars, and—as one article noted—perhaps best of all, fallen stars. In *Advertising Age*'s 1988 survey, Cher was the runaway winner for appearing on the most magazine covers, followed by Britain's Sarah Ferguson, who was popular because of her pregnancy and a weight problem. Oprah Winfrey placed fourth, apparently because she lost 65 pounds, and an edition of *Ebony* with her on the cover was the magazine's best seller in five years. Other popular cover celebrities included Princess Diana, boxer Mike Tyson, and actors Eddie Murphy and Tom Cruise. Several politicians including George Bush, Michael Dukakis, and Jessie Jackson were also in the top 10, but probably because of civic-minded editors rather than for their ability to sell magazines.

Many observers wonder how long the American consumers' insatiable appetite for stories on celebrities can continue. However, as the magazine marketplace becomes more competitive, look for more publications to use celebrities to attract readers.[1,2]

Introduction

Magazines and newspapers have been in existence as advertising media for more than two centuries and for many years were the only major media available to advertisers. However, with the growth of the broadcast media, particularly television, reading habits declined as more consumers turned to TV viewing not only as their primary source of entertainment but also as a source of news and information. Despite the competition from the broadcast media, newspapers and magazines have remained important media vehicles, both to consumers and to advertisers.

There are thousands of different magazines published in this country appealing to nearly every specific consumer interest and lifestyle, as well as to the thousands of different businesses and occupations. By becoming a highly specialized medium that reaches a specific target audience, the magazine industry has grown and prospered. Newspapers are still the primary advertising medium in terms of both ad revenue and number of advertisers. Newspapers are particularly important as a local advertising medium for the hundreds of thousands of retail businesses and are often used by large, national advertisers as well.

The print media of magazines and newspapers are an important part of our lives. For many consumers newspapers are their primary source of product information, as they would not even think of going shopping without checking to see who is having a sale or clipping coupons from the weekly food section or Sunday inserts. Many people subscribe to and/or read a number of different magazines each week or month to be-

Figure 12–1 **The Best- and Worst-Selling Covers of 1988**

Best Publication	Subject	Date of Issue
Business Week	The Best B-Schools	Nov. 28
Ebony	At Home With Oprah Winfrey	October
Essence	Spike and Joie Lee	February
Life	The Year in Pictures	January
Los Angeles	Ted Danson (also annual restaurant guide)	August
Money	Where to invest in 1988	Jan. 28
Ms.	★Meryl Streep	December
Newsweek	The Search for Adam & Eve	Jan. 11
People	Burt & Loni's wedding	May 16
Time	Who Was Jesus?	Aug. 15

Worst Publication	Subject	Date of Issue
Business Week	Coup at Alcoa	June 27
Ebony	Sidney Poitier	May
Essence	Jody Watley	May
Life	Paul Newman's children's camp	September
Los Angeles	Dabney Coleman	February
Money	15 sure ways to cut your taxes	Aug. 15
Ms.	Teen abortions	April
Newsweek	Organ transplants	Sept. 12
People	American hostages in Lebanon	July 18
Time	Sasso & Baker	Oct. 3

Best and worst categories represents comparative sales of different issues of the same publication.
★estimate

Source: Los Angeles Times, January 29, 1989, pt. IV, p. 6. Copyright, 1989, Los Angeles Times. Reprinted by permission.

come better informed or simply to be entertained. Individuals employed in various occupations rely on business magazines to keep them informed and updated on current trends and developments in their industries as well as in business in general.

While most of us are very involved with the print media, it is important to keep in mind that very few, if any, newspapers or magazines can survive without the support of advertising revenue. For example, consumer magazines generated an average of 50 percent of their revenues from advertising in 1987, whereas business publications received nearly 73 percent.[3,4] In many cities the number of daily newspapers has declined because they could not attract enough advertising revenue to support their operations. Thus, the print media must be able to attract large numbers of readers or a very specialized audience to be of interest to advertisers.

The Role of Magazines and Newspapers

The role of magazines and newspapers in the advertiser's media plan differs from the broadcast media in that they allow the presentation of detailed information that can be leisurely processed at the reader's own pace. On the other hand, the print media are not intrusive like radio and television and generally require some attention and effort on the part of the reader for the advertising message to have an impact. For this reason newspapers and magazines are often referred to as being **high-involvement media.**[5] Newspapers are a mass medium in that they are received in nearly 70 percent of American households on a daily basis. Magazines, however, reach a very selective audience and, like radio, can be valuable in reaching specific types of consumers and market segments. While both magazines and newspapers are print media, the advantages and disadvantages of the two are quite different, as are the types of advertising each attracts. In this chapter we will focus our attention on these two major forms of print media. The specific advantages and limitations of each medium will be examined along with factors that are important to the media planner in determining when and how to use newspapers and magazines in the media plan.

Magazines

Over the past several decades, magazines have been a rapidly growing medium that serves the educational, informational, and entertainment needs and interests of a wide range of readers in both the consumer and business markets. The number of consumer magazines has nearly doubled since 1970 as 100 to 200 new magazines were introduced each year during the 1980s. The American public's interest and involvement in magazines has led many advertisers to invest their media dollars in magazine advertising. The amount of money spent on advertising in consumer magazines has grown from slightly over $1 billion in 1970 to $5.9 billion in 1988.[6] Magazines rank second only to television as a medium for national advertisers. There has also been a tremendous growth in business publications, which serve the interests of various industries, businesses, and professions. The number of business publications has grown to more than 4,000, and advertising revenue in these magazines has increased from $836 million in 1970 to $3.5 billion in 1987.[7]

Magazines are the most specialized of all advertising media. While some magazines such as *Reader's Digest, Time,* or *TV Guide* are general mass-appeal publications, most are targeted to a very specific type of audience. There is a magazine designed to appeal to nearly every type of consumer in terms of demographics, lifestyle, activities, interests, or fascination. There are also numerous magazines targeted toward specific businesses and industries as well as toward individuals engaged in various professions.

The wide variety of magazines available makes this an appealing medium to a vast number of advertisers. Although television accounts for the largest amount of advertising expenditures among national advertisers, more companies advertise in magazines than any other medium. Users of magazines range from large consumer products companies such as the Philip Morris Companies, R. J. Reynolds/Nabisco, and General Motors Corporation that spend well over $100 million a year on magazine advertising to a small company advertising scuba equipment in *Skin Diver* magazine.

Classifications of Magazines

To gain some perspective on the various types of magazines available, and the advertisers who use them, it is useful to consider the way magazines are generally classified. Standard Rate and Data Service (SRDS), which is the primary reference source on magazines for media planners, divides magazines into three broad categories or classes based on the audience to which they are directed, including consumer, farm, and business publications. Each of these broad categories is then further classified according to the editorial content and audience appeal of the magazine.

Consumer Magazines Consumer magazines are those that are bought by the general public for information and/or entertainment. Standard Rate and Data Service divides consumer magazines into 51 classification groupings such as general interest, sports, travel, and women's. Another way of classifying consumer magazines is on the basis of distribution, as they can be sold through subscription or circulation, store distribution, or both. For example, *Time* and *Newsweek* are sold both through subscription and in stores, whereas *Woman's Day* is sold only through stores. *People* maga-

Table 12–1   **Top Magazines**

By Subscriptions*	
1. *Modern Maturity*	20,314,462**
2. *Reader's Digest*	15,505,421
3. *National Geographic*	10,761,406**
4. *TV Guide*	9,007,037
5. *Better Homes & Garden*	7,446,343
6. *McCall's*	4,589,316
7. *GuidePosts*	4,239,396
8. *Time*	4,172,148
9. *Ladies' Home Journal*	4,110,612
10. *Good Housekeeping*	3,676,674
In Single-Copy Sales*	
1. *TV Guide*	7,323,014
2. *Woman's Day*	4,283,525
3. *National Enquirer*	3,765,857
4. *Family Circle*	3,697,907
5. *Star*	3,184,869
6. *Cosmopolitan*	2,344,033
7. *Penthouse*	1,837,181
8. *People Weekly*	1,800,996
9. *Woman's World*	1,529,503
10. *Glamour*	1,505,117

*Excludes comics, publisher packages, and bulletins.
**Membership associations.
Source: Audit Bureau of Circulations' FAS-FAX report for six months ended June 30, 1989.

zine was originally sold only through stores but then added subscription sales as the magazine gained in popularity. Table 12–1 shows the top 10 magazines in terms of subscriptions and single-copy sales, respectively. Magazines can also be classified by issue frequency, with categories including weekly, monthly, and bimonthly being the most common.

Consumer magazines represent the major portion of the magazine industry, accounting for nearly two thirds of all advertising dollars spent in magazines. Moreover, the distribution of advertising revenue in consumer magazines is highly concentrated, as the top 25 magazines account for more than 70 percent of total consumer magazine advertising. Table 12–2 shows the 50 leading consumer magazines and their advertising revenue in 1988.

Consumer magazines are obviously best suited for marketers interested in reaching general consumers of products and services as well as for companies trying to reach a specific target market. The most frequently advertised product categories in consumer magazines are tobacco products, alcoholic beverages, automobiles, food, and household products. Marketers of tobacco products and hard liquor spend a large amount of their media budgets in magazines since they are prohibited from advertising in the broadcast media. The top 25 advertisers in consumer magazines are shown in Table 12–3.

While large national advertisers tend to dominate consumer magazine advertising in terms of expenditures, it should be noted that the nearly 2,000 different consumer magazines are also very important to smaller companies selling products that appeal to specialized markets. Special-interest magazines are very effective at assembling consumers with similar lifestyles or interests and offer marketers an efficient way to reach these people with a minimal amount of wasted coverage or circulation. For example, a manufacturer of high-quality, expensive running shoes such as New Balance or Saucony might find *Runner's World* the best vehicle for advertising to the serious runner (Figure 12–2).

Not only are these specialty magazines of value to firms interested in reaching a specific market segment; in addition, the editorial content of many of these magazines creates a very favorable advertising environment in which to advertise relevant prod-

Table 12—2   **Magazines Ranked by 1988 Ad Revenue, with Rankings by Total Ad Pages**

	1988 Ad Revenue		1987 Ad Revenue		1988 Ad Pages		1987 Ad Pages	
	Million $	Rank	Million $	Rank	Pages	Rank	Pages	Rank
Time	349.7	1	328.7	2	2,506	11	2,367	14
TV Guide	335.4	2	331.2	1	3,507	4	3,626	3
Sports Illustrated	323.9	3	263.2	4	2,978	9	2,652	10
People Weekly	305.3	4	266.2	3	3,826	3	3,582	5
Parade	266.5	5	223.6	6	665	104	615	107
Newsweek	241.7	6	239.3	5	2,479	12	2,564	11
Business Week	227.3	7	217.5	7	4,586	1	4,709	1
Better Homes & Gardens	152.8	8	142.2	8	1,469	33	1,434	36
Fortune	137.4	9	122.0	12	3,237	7	3,018	8
Family Circle	134.4	10	124.0	11	1,856	21	1,650	27
Good Housekeeping	129.3	11	132.5	9	1,621	29	1,707	22
Forbes	128.7	12	128.5	10	3,459	5	3,625	4
U.S. News & World Report	128.1	13	106.1	17	1,873	20	1,700	24
New York Times Magazine	120.4	14	111.7	14	4,114	2	4,110	2
Woman's Day	115.6	15	115.5	13	1,686	27	1,696	25
Cosmopolitan	114.6	16	111.5	15	2,361	13	2,387	13
Reader's Digest	114.0	17	107.2	16	1,221	50	1,192	49
Vogue	87.5	18	79.5	19	3,331	6	3,295	6
Glamour	87.0	19	87.6	18	2,056	19	2,213	16
Ladies' Home Journal	83.8	20	76.7	21	1,366	42	1,287	41
USA Weekend	79.8	21	64.9	23	553	112	468	123
Money	79.8	22	78.6	20	1,406	38	1,571	30
Redbook	68.6	23	64.9	24	1,213	51	1,224	44
McCall's	62.6	24	67.7	22	1,035	66	1,146	53
Rolling Stone	62.1	25	55.2	26	1,848	22	1,749	21
Southern Living	61.7	26	58.2	25	1,477	32	1,408	38
Elle	55.4	27	39.0	37	2,215	16	2,080	17
Golf Digest	55.3	28	45.2	30	1,266	46	1,161	51
Parents	53.1	29	50.0	28	1,431	36	1,409	37
Life	48.7	30	34.9	45	770	92	583	110
Mademoiselle	48.6	31	45.4	29	1,794	24	1,775	20
The New Yorker	47.8	32	50.9	27	2,292	15	2,703	9
Sunset	46.3	33	44.7	31	1,586	30	1,569	31
Car & Driver	44.9	34	40.4	34	1,225	49	1,201	46
Travel & Leisure	44.8	35	39.5	35	1,413	37	1,227	43
New York Magazine	44.1	36	43.4	32	3,052	8	3,132	7
Gentlemen's Quarterly	44.1	37	36.7	43	2,178	17	1,933	19
Bride's	43.8	38	35.0	44	2,867	10	2,477	12
Inc.	42.2	39	38.8	39	1,233	48	1,170	50
Architectural Digest	42.2	40	33.9	46	1,843	23	1,589	29
Smithsonian	41.4	41	38.9	38	1,069	62	1,056	59
Playboy	40.7	42	37.6	41	688	99	663	100
Modern Maturity	40.0	43	42.1	33	230	153	261	148
Seventeen	38.7	44	39.4	36	1,394	39	1,457	35
Ebony	38.0	45	37.1	42	1,201	52	1,126	55
Country Living	37.3	46	31.5	49	1,120	57	1,066	58
Field & Stream	36.9	47	38.4	40	965	71	971	64
National Geographic	35.7	48	28.8	53	259	149	222	151
Self	34.8	49	30.3	50	1,244	47	1,195	47
Road & Track	33.0	50	31.8	48	1,179	55	1,194	48

Source: Adweek, Special Report—Magazine World 1989, February 13, 1989, p. 28.

ucts and services. For example, the avid skier often cannot wait for the first snowfall after reading the season's first editions of *Skiing* and *Ski* magazine and may be particularly receptive to ads for skiing products while reading these publications.

Farm Publications   The second major SRDS category consists of all the magazines directed to farmers and their families. There are approximately 270 publications tailored to nearly every possible type of farming or agricultural interest. Standard Rate and Data Service breaks farm publications into 11 classification groupings ranging from general-interest magazines aimed at all types of farmers (e.g., *Farm Journal, Successful Farmer, Progressive Farmer*) to those in specialized agricultural areas such as poul-

Table 12–3   **Top 25 Magazine Advertisers**

| Rank | Advertiser | Magazine Expenditures | | | As % of Co.'s '88 Ad Total |
		1988	1987	% Chg	
1	Philip Morris Cos.	$270,251	$271,178	(0.3)	13.1
2	General Motors Corp.	190,799	153,926	24.0	9.3
3	RJR Nabisco	131,463	105,674	24.4	6.4
4	Ford Motor Co.	125,532	125,529	0.0	6.1
5	Chrysler Corp.	104,527	100,433	4.1	5.1
6	Procter & Gamble Co.	79,279	79,501	(0.3)	3.9
7	American Telephone & Telegraph	66,193	76,270	(13.2)	3.2
8	Time Warner	64,989	53,029	22.6	3.2
9	Nestle SA	63,477	56,616	12.1	3.1
10	Grand Metropolitan PLC	59,545	54,948	8.4	2.9
11	Unilever NV	59,449	58,259	2.0	2.9
12	Franklin Mint	48,981	31,733	54.4	2.4
13	Honda Motor Co.	47,159	42,701	10.4	2.3
14	Bristol-Myers Squibb	43,616	40,154	8.6	2.1
15	Revlon Group	42,488	36,562	16.2	2.1
16	Sony Corp.	41,771	31,862	31.1	2.0
17	General Electric Co.	36,747	37,727	(2.6)	1.8
18	Schering-Plough Corp.	36,617	29,202	25.4	1.8
19	Toyota Motor Corp.	36,476	27,105	34.6	1.8
20	American Brands	35,888	38,545	(6.9)	1.7
21	Nissan Motor Co.	35,826	19,361	85.0	1.7
22	E.I. du Pont de Nemours & Co.	34,676	41,676	(16.8)	1.7
23	Sara Lee Corp.	34,107	24,268	40.5	1.7
24	U.S. Government	33,436	44,164	(24.3)	1.6
25	Sears, Roebuck & Co.	33,373	21,608	54.4	1.6

Note: Dollars are in thousands.

Source: Leading National Advertisers reports, *Advertising Age,* September 27, 1989, p. 48.

try *(Gobbles),* hog farming *(Hog Farm Management),* or cattle raising *(Beef*—see Figure 12–3). There are also a number of farm publications that are directed at farmers in specific states or regions such as *Nebraska Farmer* or *Montana Farmer Stockman.* It should be noted that farm publications are not classified under business publications because historically farms were not perceived as businesses.

Business Publications   Business publications are those magazines or trade journals that are published for specific businesses, industries, or occupations. Standard Rate and Data Service has a separate edition for business publications in which approximately 4,600 magazines and trade journals are listed and broken into 140 categories. The major categories include:

1. Magazines directed at specific professional groups such as *National Law Review* for lawyers or *Architectural Forum* for architects
2. Industrial magazines that are directed to businesspeople in various manufacturing and production industries such as *Iron Age, Chemical Week,* or *Industrial Engineering*
3. Trade magazines targeted to wholesalers, dealers, distributors, and retailers such as *Progressive Grocer, Drug Store News, Women's Wear Daily,* or *Restaurant Business*
4. General-business magazines aimed at executives in all areas of business such as *Forbes, Fortune,* or *Business Week* (general-business publications are also included in SRDS's consumer publications edition).

The numerous business publications reach specific types of professional people with particular interests and needs and provide them with important information relevant to their industry, occupation, and/or careers. Business publications are important to advertisers because they provide an efficient way of reaching the specific types of individuals who constitute their target market. A great deal of marketing occurs

Figure 12–2   Runner's World Is an Excellent Medium for Reaching the Serious Runner

Figure 12–3   *Beef* Magazine Is Read by Many Cattlemen

at the trade and business-to-business level where one company sells its products or services directly to another. We will examine the role of advertising in business-to-business marketing in greater detail in Chapter 19.

Advantages of Magazines

Magazines have a number of characteristics and qualities that make them particularly attractive as an advertising medium. The specific strengths of magazines include their selectivity, excellent reproduction quality, flexibility, permanence, prestige, readers' high receptivity to magazine advertising and involvement with the publication, and services they offer to advertisers.

Selectivity   One of the main advantages of using magazines as an advertising medium is their **selectivity** or ability to reach a specific target audience. Magazines are the most selective of all media with the exception of direct mail. The high degree of selectivity of magazines stems from the fact that most magazines are published for special-interest groups. The thousands of magazines published in the United States reach all types of consumers and businesses and allow advertisers to target their advertising to segments of the population that are of the most interest to them. For ex-

Figure 12–4 *Newsweek*
Special Editions Descriptions

Newsweek Business subscribers are 100% individually questionnaire-qualified by professional/managerial job title. The edition is managed to yield higher income subscribers through both subscriber questionnaire and zip code match.

The rates below are effective with the premier issue of Newsweek Business, January 9, 1989, and also apply to Management Digest Quarterly:

Newsweek Woman is the only demographic edition of a newsweekly targeted exclusively to today's affluent and influential women. Advertisers find it efficient in reaching successful women who don't have the time to read the traditional women's books.

FALL LOOKS '89

September 18 Issue: Talk to America's most active, intelligent and well-heeled women in Fall Looks '89. This very special section in Newsweek Woman will provide our readers with the last word on fashion and fitness. Under the direction of Lois Perschetz, best-selling author and former editor of Women's Wear Daily and W, fashion and beauty experts will write articles devoted to "total looks" covering the season's news for today's busy women.

ample, *Modern Photography* is targeted toward photography buffs, *Stereo Review* reaches those with an avid interest in music, *American Baby* reaches new mothers, and *Ebony* focuses in on the upscale black market. Promotional Perspective 12–1 discusses the various magazines available for reaching the affluent market.

In addition to selectivity based on interests, magazines also can provide the advertiser with high demographic and geographic selectivity. *Demographic selectivity,* or the ability of a medium to reach specific demographic groups, is available through magazines in two ways. First, most magazines are, as a result of editorial content, aimed at fairly well defined demographic segments. For example, *Ladies' Home Journal, MS, Self,* and *Cosmopolitan* are read predominately by women; *Esquire, Playboy,* and *Sports Illustrated* are read mostly by men; and teenage girls can be reached through *Seventeen* or *Sassy.*

A second way magazines offer demographic selectivity is through special editions. Even magazines that appeal to broader audiences such as *Reader's Digest, Time,* or *Newsweek* can provide a high degree of demographic selectivity through their special demographic editions. Most of the top consumer magazines offer different editions targeted at different demographic markets. Figure 12–4 provides a description of two specific demographic editions offered by *Newsweek* magazine.

Geographic selectivity, whereby an advertiser can focus advertisements in certain cities or regions of the country, is also possible through magazines. One way of achieving geographic selectivity is by using a magazine that is edited for, and targeted toward, particular areas. There are numerous magazines devoted to regional interests such as *Yankee* (New England), *Southern Living* (South), *Sunset* (West), and *Texas Monthly* (guess where?). One of the more successful media developments of recent years has been the growth of "city magazines" in most major American cities. Publications such as *Los Angeles Magazine, Philadelphia, Pittsburgh, Denver,* and *San Diego Magazine,* to name a few, provide residents of these areas with articles concerning lifestyle, happenings, events, and the like, in these cities and their surrounding metropolitan areas.[8] These magazines offer very high geographic selectivity and also tend

Promotional Perspective 12-1

Reaching the Affluent Consumer

Many companies are interested in selling their products or services to affluent consumers who have the lifestyle, and the income, that encourages them to spend freely and often lavishly. A problem these firms must deal with, however, is just how to reach the growing ranks of big spenders who might be in their target market. Many advertisers dismiss television as an efficient way to reach the well-to-do consumer since they typically are not heavy viewers of television, and few shows are watched solely by affluent consumers. Radio and newspapers also lack the ability to focus specifically on the affluent consumer and thus are not cost-effective ways of reaching this market.

Given the limitations of these media, many magazines have been promoting their ability to deliver the upscale consumer to advertisers. Even mass circulation publications such as *TV Guide* have begun boasting about the affluence of their readers.

Many advertisers are interested in more than just high income levels and consider other factors such as the magazine audiences' median age level, occupation, and their inclination to spend or invest their money. For example, *Architectural Digest* is an excellent medium for reaching upscale consumers (see Exhibit 12-1). Some publications have also emerged that are designed to

reach the very affluent market. In 1986 American Airlines began publishing *Private Clubs* magazine, which is sold only to consumers with enough money to belong to city clubs or country clubs. The publication is expected to attract readers with an average household income of $144,000 or "the sort of people who don't bother reading menu prices." Other publications aimed at the very affluent include *European Travel* and *Life* magazines for the sophisticated American traveler; *View,* a leisure magazine for physicians; *Avenue,* a high-society magazine delivered free to residents of Manhattan's posh Upper East Side; and *Millionaire,* a publication for those with a net worth exceeding the magic figure. One entrepreneur even tried marketing a magazine that would have been placed in the back seats of limousines. The idea received a cool reception by many ad agencies, figuring that if limousine riders do read anything, it will be from their briefcase.

As the number of affluent consumers in the United States increases, there will undoubtedly be new magazines emerging that promise to deliver these big spenders to advertisers eager to pitch their products and services to them.

Source: "Wealth of Affluent Magazines Vie for Advertisers' Attention," *The Wall Street Journal,* January 9, 1986, p. 23.

Exhibit 12-1   *Architectural Digest* **Touts Its Affluent Readers**

In the pattern of Schumacher . . .

In the manner of The Boston Company . . .

The fabrics and wallcoverings of F. Schumacher & Co. and the banking and financial services of The Boston Company project totally different styles. Yet they share the same atmosphere in Architectural Digest.

Unlike a magazine of fleeting interest, Architectural Digest engages the minds of the most discerning readers, many of whom never part with a single issue.

The interior designs in this magazine can be found nowhere else.

The writers, from Christopher Buckley to Kurt Vonnegut, are a constant source of wit and insight.

And our three million affluent readers possess attributes that go far beyond the realm of demographics.

Their interests range far and wide from exquisite jewelry and watches to luxurious cruises and resorts.

And from Bulgari and Rolex to Holland America and Trump Plaza of the Palm Beaches, all of our advertisers have the same objective: to set themselves apart from the ordinary in the most extraordinary way.

If your products are as uncommon as theirs, Architectural Digest may be all your advertising is missing.

Architectural Digest is an advertiser's dream.

Figure 12—5 **The** *San Diego* *Magazine* **Reader Is Very Upscale**

SAN DIEGO MAGAZINE
1989-1990 DEMOGRAPHICS

READER PROFILE

Sex		Household Income	
Women	54.1%	$30,000 +	88.6%
Men	45.9%	$50,000 +	70.4%
		$75,000 +	49.3%
		$100,000 +	32.2%
Age		Median HHI	$74,202
		Average HHI	$113,600
18-24	5.3%		
25-49	51.1%		
50-59	16.0%	**Net Worth**	
60 +	27.6%		
Median Age	46.3	$100,000 +	82.8%
		$250,000 +	62.0%
		$500,000 +	40.0%
Marital Status		$1 Million +	21.8%
		$5 Million +	2.6%
Married	74.0%	Median	$386,029
Single	13.4%	Average	$836,150
Divorced/Widowed	12.6%		
		Head Of Household Occupation	
Education			
		Chairman/Pres./CEO/VP	13.6%
Attended College	81.3%	Top Management	29.4%
Graduated College	53.2%	Middle Management	12.2%
Post-Graduate Degree	22.2%	Total Management	41.6%
		Professional/Technical	16.2%
Home Ownership		Business/Industry	50.1%
		Total Prof./Business	66.3%
Own Home	80.8%		
Median Value	$245,455		
Average Value	$332,710	**Professional Activities**	
		(Purchase Or Approve Purchase)	
Number People In Home		Computers & Services	59.2%
		Communications Systems	50.3%
		Advertising	32.1%
One	18.6%	Office Furniture	28.5%
Two	49.3%	Insurance	24.3%
Three	15.2%	Business Gifts/Premiums	24.6%
Four Or More	16.9%	Company Cars	20.4%
Average	2.4	Plant Or Office Space	16.8%

Source: "The Readers Of San Diego Magazine — 1989" By Don Bowdren Associates

P.O. BOX 85409, SAN DIEGO, CALIFORNIA 92138 (619) 225-8953

to be read by a very upscale audience, as shown by the profile in Figure 12—5 of the *San Diego Magazine* reader.

Another way of achieving geographic selectivity in magazines is through the purchase of specific geographic editions of national or regional magazines. A number of publications divide their circulation into specific geographic groupings based on regions or major metropolitan areas and offer advertisers the option of concentrating their advertisements in these editions. For example, *Newsweek* breaks the United States into 11 geographic areas and offers regional editions for each, as shown in Figure 12—6. In addition to these geographic regions, *Newsweek* offers advertisers their choice of editions directed to the top 40, 20, or 10 metropolitan areas. Many magazines allow advertisers to combine regional or metropolitan editions to best match the geographic market of interest to them.

In 1989, Standard Rate and Data Service listed 226 consumer magazines offering geographic and/or demographic editions. These editions are particularly attractive to regional and national advertisers. Regional advertisers can purchase space in editions that only reach areas where they have distribution, yet still enjoy the prestige of advertising in a major, national magazine. National advertisers can use the geographic editions to focus their advertising on particular areas of the country with the greatest potential or those needing more promotional support. They also can use regional editions to test-market products or alternative promotional campaigns in various regions of the country.

Ads in regional editions can also list the names of retailers or distributors in various markets, thus encouraging greater local support from the trade. As noted in previous chapters, the trend toward regional marketing is increasing the importance of having regional media available to marketers. The availability of regional and demographic editions can also enhance the cost efficiency of magazines, as they result in a lower cost per thousand for reaching desired audiences.

Figure 12—6 **Geographic Editions of *Newsweek* Magazine**

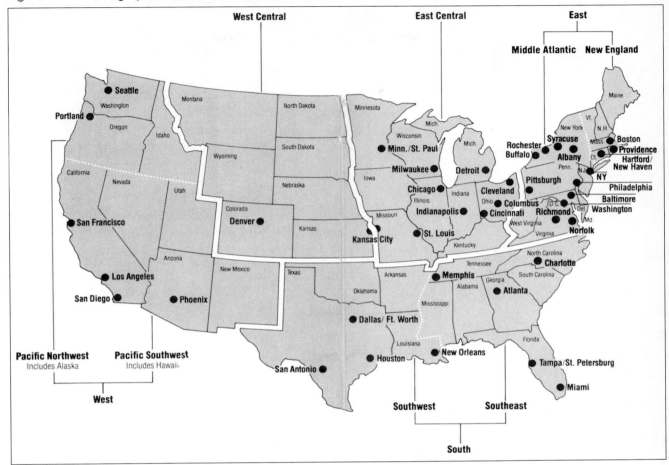

Reproduction Quality   One of the most valued attributes of magazine advertising is the reproduction quality that is possible for the ads. Magazines are generally printed on a high-quality paper stock and use printing processes that provide excellent reproduction in black and white or color. Since magazines are a very visual medium where illustrations are often a dominant and critical part of an advertisement, this is a very important property. The reproduction quality of most magazines is far superior to that offered by the other major print medium of newspapers, particularly when color is needed. The use of color has become a virtual necessity in most product categories, and more than two thirds of all magazine ads now use color.

Creative Flexibility   In addition to their excellent reproduction capabilities, magazines also offer advertisers a great deal of flexibility in terms of the type, size, and placement of the advertising material. Some magazines offer (often at an extra charge) a variety of special options that can be used to enhance the creative appeal of the ad and usually increase attention and readership of the ad. Examples of such options include gatefolds, bleed pages, inserts, and creative space buys.

   Gatefolds enable an advertiser to make a striking presentation by using a third page that folds out and gives the ad an extralarge–sized spread. Gatefolds are often found at the inside cover of most large consumer magazines or on some inside pages. Advertisers utilize gatefolds to make a very strong impression, and they are often used on special occasions such as the introduction of a new product or brand. For example, automobile advertisers often use gatefolds to introduce new versions of their cars each model year. Not all magazines offer gatefolds, however, and they usually must be reserved well in advance and are always sold at a premium.

Figure 12–7   **This Award-Winning Ad Helped Consumers Discover the McD.L.T.**

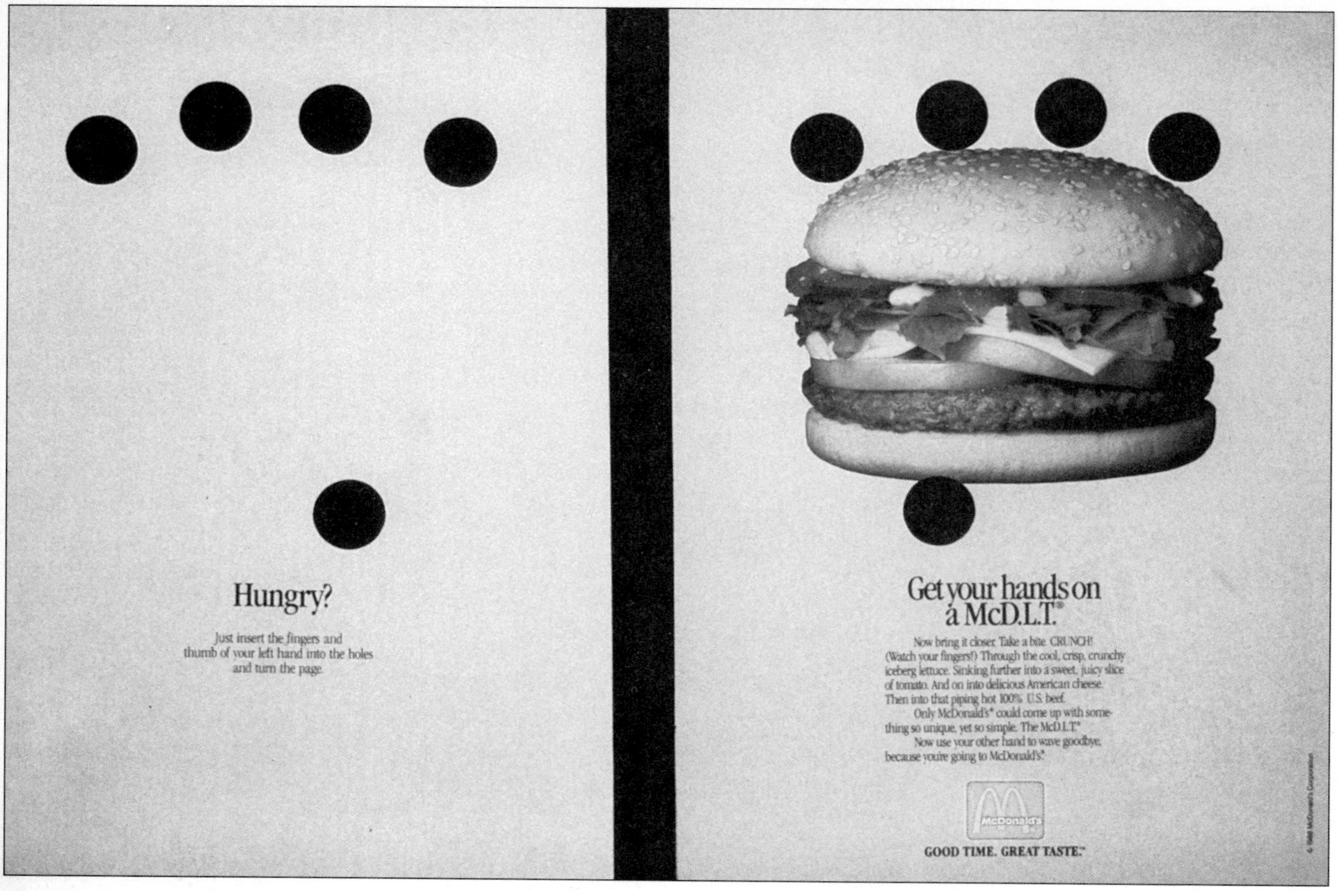

Hungry?

Just insert the fingers and
thumb of your left hand into the holes
and turn the page.

Get your hands on
à McD.L.T.®

Now bring it closer. Take a bite. CRUNCH!
(Watch your fingers!) Through the cool, crisp, crunchy
iceberg lettuce. Sinking further into a sweet, juicy slice
of tomato. And on into delicious American cheese.
Then into that piping hot 100% U.S. beef.
    Only McDonald's® could come up with some-
thing so unique, yet so simple. The McD.L.T.®
    Now use your other hand to wave goodbye,
because you're going to McDonald's®.

GOOD TIME. GREAT TASTE.™

Bleed pages are those where the advertisement extends all the way to the end of the page, rather than leaving a margin around the ad. Bleed pages are used to give the advertisement an impression of being larger and to make a more dramatic impact in presenting the ad. Many magazines charge an extra 10 to 20 percent for bleed pages.

In addition to gatefolds and bleed pages, other types of creative options are available through magazines including unusual page sizes and shapes and other techniques. For example, consumers following the instructions in the McDonald's ad shown in Figure 12–7 discovered a McD.L.T. in their hand. This clever execution was voted one of the best print ads of 1988 by *Adweek*. Promotional Perspective 12–2 discusses how several companies have used "pop-ups" and 3-D inserts to develop attention-getting print messages.

Inserts of various forms can also be used in many magazines. These include return cards, recipe booklets, coupons, records, and even product samples. Cosmetic companies use "scratch and sniff" inserts as a way of introducing new cologne or perfume scents, whereas some companies use them to promote deodorants, laundry detergents, or other products where the smell of the product is important. Inserts are often used in conjunction with direct-response ads and as part of sales promotion strategies.

Creative-space buys are another option made available by magazines. Some magazines allow advertisers to purchase space units in certain combinations so as to increase the impact of their media budget. For example, WD-40, an all-purpose lubrication product, used quarter-page ads on four consecutive pages of several magazines with a different use for the product mentioned on each page (see Figure 12–8). This strategy allowed the company to get greater impact for its media dollars and was helpful in promoting the variety of uses for the product.

Promotional Perspective **12—2**

Using a 3-D Sales Pitch

Getting the magazine reader's attention is becoming increasingly difficult as the number of ads appearing in most publications increases. Some advertisers, however, have grabbed the eye of magazine readers by developing ads that literally jump off the page at them through the use of three dimensional pop-up ads. Honeywell developed a pop-up ad to catch the eye of potential clients that showed a state-of-the-art corporate park in which all the buildings are equipped with the company's 24-hour fire and burglar alarms and other automated systems (Exhibit 12—2A). The cost of producing the ad and running it one time in *Business Week* magazine was estimated to be $1 million.

Transamerica Corporation also used a 3-D pop-up construction to develop a corporate ad depicting the city of San Francisco and the company's corporate symbol— the Transamerica pyramid tower (Exhibit 12—2B). The purpose of the ad was to promote the Transamerica Insurance Companies as leaders in providing innovative insurance coverage. The ad was run in *Time* in September 1986 at a cost of nearly a million dollars and was rated one of the best ads of the year by *Adweek*, a leading advertising industry publication.

In 1987 Toyota took the concept of 3-D advertising a step further by inserting nearly 14 million pairs of three-dimensional glasses—made of cardboard and plastic— in issues of *Time, People,* and *Cosmopolitan* magazines. The glasses were provided so that readers could look at a three-dimensional image of a Toyota Corolla set against the San Francisco skyline. According to Toyota, the company decided to use the 3-D campaign, which had an estimated cost of $1.5 million, because it wanted "a blockbuster ad that would get people to notice Toyota." The Corolla subcompact was Toyota's best-selling car for many years, but sales had dropped nearly 10 percent. The company redesigned the 1988 Corollas and used the 3-D ad as part of a print campaign designed to rehaul its image.

An important question is, of course, whether the pop-up and 3-D ads are effective enough to justify their high costs. Research studies by Starch INRA Hooper indicate that pop-up inserts outperform ordinary four-color spread ads nearly 2:1 in attention value. Both the Honeywell and Transamerica ads attained record-setting Starch "Noted" scores (percentage of readers who remembered seeing the ad). Similarly, the "Seen/Associated" scores (percentage of readers who could associate the ads with the company) for both inserts more than doubled those of ordinary four-color ads (see Exhibit 12—2C).

It is likely that magazine readers will see more 3-D ads "pop up" and other creative techniques as advertisers look for ways to break through the clutter and capture the consumer's attention and interest. Intervisual Communications Incorporated, the company that produced the Transamerica and Honeywell ads, has recently begun a new program called AdVoice that uses a microchip and speaker system to add a full range of spoken words and sounds to print ads.

Source: Bruce Horowitz, "Toyota Sets Sights on New Dimension in Ads to Bolster Sales of Corolla," *Los Angeles Times,* October 6, 1987, pt. IV, p. 8.

Exhibit 12—2A   **Honeywell's Million Dollar Pop-Up Ad**

Exhibit 12—2B   **Transamerica's Pop-Up Featured the Transamerica Tower Against the City of San Francisco**

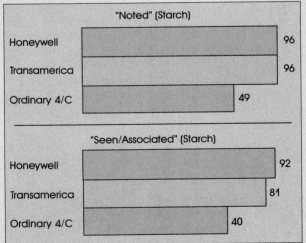

Exhibit 12-2C   **Starch Scores for Pop-Up Ads versus Ordinary Four-Color Ads**

"Noted" (Starch)	
Honeywell	96
Transamerica	96
Ordinary 4/C	49

"Seen/Associated" (Starch)	
Honeywell	92
Transamerica	81
Ordinary 4/C	40

Source: Intervisual Communications, Inc.

Figure 12—8   WD—40 Used Quarter-Page Ads to Get Greater Impact from Its Media Budget

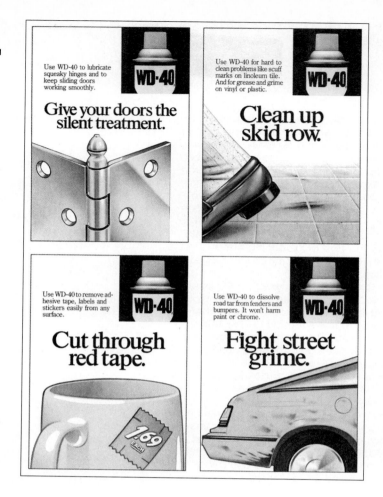

Permanence   Another distinctive advantage offered by magazines is their permanence or long life span. As mentioned in the previous chapter, television and radio are characterized by fleeting messages that have a very short life span, whereas newspapers are generally discarded soon after being read. Magazines, however, are generally read over a several-day time period and are often kept for reference. Thus, they are retained in the home longer than any other medium and are generally read or referred to on several occasions. A study of magazine audience readership found that readers devote an hour or more over a period of two to three days reading an average magazine.[9] Studies have also found that nearly 75 percent of consumers retain magazines for future reference.[10] One benefit of the longer life of magazines is that readership occurs at a less hurried pace, and there is more opportunity to examine and appraise ads in considerable detail. This means that ads can use longer and more detailed copy, which can be very important for high-involvement and complex products or services. The permanence of magazines also means that readers can be exposed to ads on multiple occasions, which can enhance readership, and the opportunity to pass magazines along to other readers is increased.

Prestige   Another positive feature of magazine advertising is the prestige the product or service may gain from advertising in publications with a favorable image. Companies whose products rely very heavily on perceived quality, reputation, and/or image will often buy space in prestigious publications with high quality and involving editorial content and for which consumers have a high level of interest in the advertising pages. For example, *Esquire* and *Gentlemen's Quarterly* provide a very favorable envi-

Figure 12–9   The *Good Housekeeping* Seal of Approval Is Used to Increase Consumer Confidence in Products

THE NEW TRADITIONALIST.

A NEW KIND OF WOMAN WITH DEEP-ROOTED VALUES
IS CHANGING THE WAY WE LIVE.

There's a rebirth in America.
There's a renewal, a reaffirmation
of values, a return to quality and
quality of life.
   We have seen it approaching, we
have felt it happening, it has begun
to affect our lives.
   And now, suddenly, it is upon us
in full force.
   Market researchers call it "neo-
traditionalism."
   To us it's a woman who has
found her identity in herself, her
home, her family. She is the
contemporary woman whose
values are rooted in tradition.
   The quality of life she has chosen
is the embodiment of everything
Good Housekeeping has always
stood for. The values she is
committed to are the values we
represent — the Magazine, the
Seal, the Institute.
   Who else can speak to the New
Traditionalist with that kind of
authority and trust?
   That's why there's never been a
better time for Good Housekeeping.

AMERICA IS COMING HOME TO
GOOD HOUSEKEEPING

ronment for advertising men's fashions, and a clothing manufacturer may advertise its products in these magazines to enhance the prestige or image of its lines. *Architectural Digest* provides a very impressive editorial environment that includes high-quality photography and artwork. The upscale readers of the magazine are likely to have a very favorable image of the publication that may transcend to the products advertising on its pages. *Good Housekeeping* provides a unique consumer's refund or replacement policy for products that bear the limited warranty seal or that advertise in the magazine (Figure 12–9). This can increase the level of confidence a consumer has in a particular brand and reduce the amount of perceived risk associated with a purchase.

While most media planners recognize that the environment created by a publication is important, it can be difficult to determine the degree of prestige a magazine provides. Subjective estimates based on media planners' knowledge or experience may be used to assess a magazine's prestige as can objective measures such as reader opinion surveys.[11]

Consumer Receptivity and Involvement With the exception of newspapers, consumers are more receptive to advertising in magazines than in any other medium. Magazines are generally purchased because the information they contain is relevant and interesting to the reader, and advertisements represent additional information that may be of value. For example, the consumer in the market for a new automobile may purchase *Road & Track* or *Motor Trend* to read reviews of cars he or she is considering. The automobile ads contained in the publication are also likely to be of interest to

Figure 12–10 **This Ad by the Magazine Publishers of America Promotes Consumers' Receptivity to Magazine Advertising**

the consumer, particularly those for cars being considered for purchase. The ad shown in Figure 12–10, which was part of a campaign by the Magazine Publishers of America (MPA), stresses the high level of receptivity of magazine readers to automotive advertising.

Studies of magazine readers have shown that the majority of them welcome advertisements in magazines, whereas only a small percentage rate them unfavorably.[12] In addition to their interest or relevance, magazine ads are likely to be received favorably by consumers since, unlike broadcast ads, they are nonintrusive and can easily be ignored by the reader.

Not only are consumers more receptive to advertising in magazines, but they are also generally more involved with magazines than other media. Consumers generally pay for magazines, and the amount they must lay out has nearly doubled over the past 10 years. In 1988 the average single-copy price of a magazine was $2.30, whereas the average yearly subscription rate was $24.85.[13] Some publications such as *Unique Homes* have single-copy prices as high as $7.00. The readers' high level of involvement with a magazine may make them more attentive and likely to recall the ads contained in it. The Magazine Publishers Association has conducted studies showing that magazine readers are more likely to attend to and recall advertisements than are television viewers.[14]

Services A final advantage of magazines is the special services some publications offer advertisers. Some magazines have merchandising staffs that will call on trade intermediaries such as retailers to let them know that a product is being advertised in their publication and to encourage them to display or promote the item. Another service offered by magazines (usually the larger ones) is the availability of research studies that they conduct on consumers and make available to advertisers. These studies may deal with general consumer trends, changing purchase patterns, and media usage or may be relevant to a specific product or industry.

An important service offered by some magazines is the availability of **split runs** whereby two or more versions of an advertisement are printed in alternate copies of a particular issue of a magazine. This service is used to conduct a "split-run test," where some offer or inquiry inducing a way of prompting responses is included in each ad. This allows the advertiser to determine which ad generates the most responses or inquiries and thus provides some evidence as to their effectiveness.

Disadvantages of Magazines

Although the advantages offered by magazines are considerable, they do have certain drawbacks. These include the costs of advertising, their limited reach and frequency, the long lead time required in placing an ad, and the problem of clutter and heavy advertising competition.

Costs   The costs of advertising in magazines obviously vary according to the size of the audience they reach and their selectivity. Advertising in large, mass circulation magazines such as *TV Guide, Reader's Digest,* or *Time* can be very expensive. For example, a full-page, four-color ad in *Time* magazine's national edition cost $120,130 in 1989. Popular positions such as back cover will cost even more. The costs of ad space in more specialized publications with smaller circulation would obviously be less. A full-page, four-color ad in *Tennis* magazine (circulation of 531,701) cost $23,340 in 1989.

Like any medium, the expense of using magazines must be considered not only from an absolute cost perspective but also in terms of relative costs. Most magazines tend to emphasize their effectiveness in reaching specific target audiences and their ability to do so on a low cost per thousand basis. Also, as discussed above, an increasing number of magazines are offering demographic and geographic editions, which helps lower their costs. Media planners generally focus on the relative costs of a publication in reaching the advertiser's target audience. However, they may recommend a magazine with a high cost per thousand because of its ability to reach a small, specialized market segment. Of course, advertisers with limited budgets will be interested in the absolute costs of space in a magazine and the costs of producing quality ads for these publications.

Limited Reach and Frequency   Magazines are generally not as effective as other media in offering reach and frequency. Studies of magazine audiences have revealed that nearly 90 percent of adults in the United States read one or more consumer magazines each month. However, the percentage of adults reading any individual publication tends to be much smaller, and magazines are thus often described as having thin penetration of households. For example, the circulation of *TV Guide,* which is the third highest of any magazine, is just over 16 million. This represents only 20 percent of the 91 million households in the United States.

As can be seen in Table 12–4, only 27 magazines had a paid circulation of greater than 2 million at the end of 1988. Thus, advertisers seeking broad reach must make media buys in a number of magazines, which means more negotiations, transactions, and the like. Magazines are generally not used as the sole basis of a broad reach strategy but rather are used in conjunction with other media.

The frequency level available through magazines can also be a problem since most are monthly—or at best, weekly—publications. Thus, the opportunity for building frequency through the use of the same publication is limited. Using multiple ads in the same issue of a publication is generally viewed as an inefficient way of building frequency. Most advertisers attempt to achieve frequency by adding additional magazines with a similar audience to the media schedule.

Long Lead Time   Another drawback of magazines is the long lead time needed to place an ad. Most major publications have anywhere from a 30- to a 90-day lead

Table 12—4   **Magazines with Paid Circulations of More Than $2 Million**

	Tops in Circulation—Six months ending December 31, 1988
Modern Maturity	19.30
Reader's Digest	16.45
TV Guide	16.30
National Geographic	10.57
Better Homes & Gardens	8.14
Family Circle	5.92
Woman's Day	5.57
Good Housekeeping	5.22
McCall's	5.14
Ladies' Home Journal	5.09
Time	4.65
National Enquirer	4.28
Guideposts	4.26
Redbook	3.95
Star	3.68
Playboy	3.56
People	3.35
Sports Illustrated	3.33
Newsweek	3.23
Prevention	3.14
American Legion	2.82
Cosmopolitan	2.76
U.S. News & World Report	2.30
Southern Living	2.29
Smithsonian	2.26
Glamour	2.19
Penthouse	2.11

Note: Scholastic Inc. did not file a publisher's statement by the Audit Bureau's press time.
Source: Audit Bureau of Circulations FAS-FAX report.

time, which means that space must be purchased and the ad must be prepared well in advance of the actual publication date. Once the closing date for advertising is reached, no changes in the art or copy of the ad can be made. The long lead time required by magazines means that magazine ads cannot be as timely as other media, such as radio or newspapers, in responding to current events or changing market conditions.

Clutter and Competition   While the problem of advertising clutter is generally discussed in reference to the broadcast media, magazines also have this drawback. The clutter problem for magazines is really somewhat of a paradox, as the more successful a magazine becomes, the more advertising pages it attracts, which leads to greater clutter. In fact, magazines generally gauge their success in terms of the number of advertising pages they attract.

Magazine publishers do attempt to control the clutter problem by maintaining a reasonable balance of editorial pages to advertising. However, many magazines today contain ads on more than half of their pages. According to the Magazine Publishers Association, the average ratio of advertising to editorial lineage among the top 50 or so magazines is 51.4 to 48.6 percent.[15] This clutter makes it difficult for the advertiser to gain the attention of the readers and draw them into the advertisement. Thus, many ads use strong visual images, headlines, or some of the creative techniques discussed earlier, to get the attention of readers.

While clutter is a problem for magazines, it is not viewed as serious an issue with the print media as for radio or television since, as noted earlier, consumers tend to be more receptive and tolerant of print advertising. Also, while they can control their exposure to a magazine ad simply by turning the page, broadcast advertisements are much more intrusive and difficult to ignore.

Magazine Circulation and Readership

Two of the most important considerations in deciding whether to utilize a magazine in the advertising media plan are the size and characteristics of the audience reached by the publication. Media buyers will evaluate magazines on the basis of the vehicle's ability to deliver the advertiser's message to as many people as possible in the target audience. To do this they must consider the circulation of the publication as well as its total readership and match these figures against the audience they are attempting to reach.

Circulation   Circulation figures represent the number of individuals that receive a publication, either through subscription or store purchase. The number of copies distributed to these original subscribers or purchasers is known as **primary circulation** and is used as the basis for the magazine's rate structure. The circulation for any particular issue of a magazine tends to fluctuate, particularly if it relies heavily on retail or newsstand sales. Thus, many publications base their rates on *guaranteed circulation* and provide advertisers with a rebate if the number of delivered magazines falls below the guarantee. To minimize the likelihood of rebating, most guaranteed-circulation figures are conservative; that is, they are set safely below the average actual delivered circulation, and advertisers are not charged for any excess circulation.

Many publishers have become discontented with the guaranteed-circulation concept since it requires them to provide refunds if guarantees are not met, but excesses in circulation result in a bonus for the advertiser. Thus, many publications have gone to a circulation rate base system whereby rates are based on a set average circulation. This figure is nearly always below the actual circulation delivered by a given issue, but there is no guarantee of circulation. However, it is unlikely that circulations will fall below the rate base since this would reflect negatively on the publication and make it difficult to attract advertisers at prevailing rates.

Circulation verification   Given that circulation figures are the basis for a magazine's advertising rates and one of the primary considerations in selecting a publication, the credibility of circulation figures is very important. To ensure that the circulation figures for a magazine are accurate, most major publications are audited by one of the circulation verification services. Consumer magazine and farm publication circulations are audited by the Audit Bureau of Circulations (ABC). This organization, which was organized in 1914 and is sponsored by advertisers, agencies, and publishers, collects and evaluates information regarding the subscriptions and sales of magazines and newspapers to verify their circulation figures. Only publications with 70 percent or more paid circulation (which means that the magazine was purchased at not less than half the magazine's established base price) are eligible for verification audits by ABC. Certain business publications are audited by the Business Publications Audit (BPA) of Circulation. Many of these are published on a **controlled-circulation basis,** meaning that copies are sent (usually free) to individuals the publisher feels are important and able to influence sales to a company.

Circulation verification services play an important role in providing the media planner with reliable figures regarding the size and distribution of a magazine's circulation and helping them evaluate its worth as a media vehicle. In addition to the circulation figures, the ABC statement provides other important information.[16] It shows how a magazine is distributed by state and county size as well as the percentage of the circulation sold at less than full value and the percentage arrears, which indicates how many subscriptions are being given away. This information is important since many advertisers feel that subscribers who pay for a magazine are more likely to read it than are those who get it at a discount or receive free copies.

Media buyers are generally skeptical over publications with circulation figures not audited by one of the verification services, and some companies will not advertise

Figure 12–11 **This Ad Uses Proof of Circulation to Compare One Publication to Another**

in unaudited publications. Circulation data, along with the auditing source, are available in Standard Rate and Data Service or from the publication itself. Figure 12–11 shows how *San Diego Magazine* uses ABC figures to make a favorable rate comparison against *San Diego Home/Garden Magazine,* one of its competitors.

Readership and Total Audience   In addition to considering the primary circulation figures for a magazine, advertisers may also be interested in the number of people that a publication reaches as a result of secondary or pass-along readership. **Pass-along readership** can occur when the primary subscriber or purchaser gives a magazine to another person to read or when the publication is read in places such as waiting rooms of doctor's offices or beauty salons, on airplanes, and so forth.

Advertisers generally attach greater value to the primary in-home reader versus the pass-along reader and the out-of-home reader, as the former generally spends more time with the publication, picks it up more often, and receives greater satisfaction from it than the out-of-home reader. Thus, this reader is more likely to be attentive and responsive to ads. However, pass-along circulation can be very important to a publication, and the value of these readers should not be totally discounted. Pass-along readers are an important part of the audience of many publications and can greatly expand the magazine's readership. *People* magazine, which has a high number of pass-on and out-of-home readers, commissioned a media research study to determine that its out-of-home audience spends as much time reading the publication as do its primary in-home readers because of the nature and layout of the publication.[17]

The **total audience,** or **readership,** of a magazine can be determined by taking the readers per copy, which is the total number of primary and pass-along readers, and multiplying this figure by the circulation of an average issue. For example, a magazine that has a circulation of 1 million and 3.5 readers per copy has a total audience of 3.5 million. However, it should be emphasized that rate structures are generally based on the more verifiable circulation figures of a publication, and many media planners devalue a pass-along reader by as much as 50 percent. While total readership estimates are reported by major syndicated magazine research services, which are discussed below, these numbers are often viewed with suspicion by media buyers. As was discussed in Chapter 10, a controversy has developed over the estimates of magazine readership used by the two major research firms.

Audience Research for Magazines

While the circulation and total audience size of a magazine are important in selecting a media vehicle, the media planner is also interested in the match between the magazine's readers and the advertiser's target audience. The obvious question here is whether the magazine reaches the type of reader to whom the company is trying to sell its product or service. Information relevant to this question is available from several sources including the publication's own research and syndicated research studies.

Most magazines provide media planners with reports and information detailing readers' demographics, financial profile, lifestyle, and product usage characteristics. The larger the publication, the more detailed and comprehensive the information it usually can supply about its readers. For example, the profile of the *San Diego Magazine* reader that was shown in Figure 12–6 comes from a study that was commissioned by the publication.

In addition to studies conducted by the magazines themselves, syndicated research studies are also available. For consumer magazines primary sources of information concerning magazine audiences are Simmons Market Research Bureau's Study of Media and Markets and the studies of Mediamark Research, Inc. (MRI). These studies provide the media planner with a broad range of information on the audiences of major national and regional magazines, including demographics, lifestyle characteristics, and product purchase and usage data. Most large advertising agencies and media buying services also conduct ongoing research that either focuses on or includes the media habits of consumers. This information can be used along with the above-mentioned sources in determining the value of various magazines in reaching particular types of product users.

Audience information for business publications is generally more limited than for consumer magazines. The widely dispersed readership and nature of business publication readers make audience research more difficult for these magazines. The media planner generally relies on information provided by the publication itself or by sources such as Standard Rate and Data Service. SRDS contains a business analysis of circulation for various publications that provides information on the title of the individual who receives the publication and the type of industry in which he or she works. This information can be of value in understanding the audience reached by various business magazines.

Purchasing Magazine Advertising Space

Cost Elements As noted earlier, magazine rates are primarily a function of the circulation of the publication. However, a magazine's advertising rates will vary in response to a number of other variables including the size of the ad, its position in the publication, the particular editions (geographic, demographic) chosen, any special mechanical or production requirements, and the number and frequency of insertions.

Advertising space is generally sold on the basis of space units such as full page, half page, and quarter page, although some publications quote rates on the basis of column inches. Obviously the larger the ad, the greater the cost. However, many advertisers use full-page ads since they result in more attention and readership. Several studies have found that full-page ads generated 36 percent more readership than half-page ads.[18,19]

Advertisements can be produced or run using black and white, black and white

Table 12–5   *Newsweek* **National Edition Space Rates**

	B&W	B&1C	4C
Full page	$59,850	$78,530	$ 95,715
2 columns	46,865	61,530	79,755
Half page	37,410	49,075	62,205
1 column or square third	23,945	31,400	41,475
Half column	12,450	16,380	—
4th cover	—	—	122,695
2nd & 3rd cover	59,850	78,530	95,715
Line rate*	190	—	—

*14 line minimum

Source: Newsweek 1989 Rates & Data.

plus one color, or four colors. The more color used in the ad, the greater the expense because of the increased printing costs. As can be seen in Table 12–5, a full-page black and white ad in *Newsweek* cost $59,850 in 1989, whereas a four-color ad was over $95,715. On average a four-color ad will cost 30 percent more than a black and white advertisement. Advertisers generally prefer using color because of the greater visual impact it makes, plus the fact that color ads have been found to be superior for attracting and holding attention.[20] Ads requiring special mechanical production such as bleed pages or special inserts may also result in extra charges.

The rates for magazine advertising space can also vary according to the number of insertions and amount of money spent during a specific period. The more often an advertiser contracts to run an ad, the less the space charges. Volume discounts are based on the total space purchased within a contract year, as measured in dollars. Advertisers can also save money by purchasing advertising in magazine combinations or networks.

Magazine networks offer the advertiser the opportunity to buy space in a group of publications as a package deal. These networks may be offered by publishers who have a variety of magazines that reach audiences with similar characteristics. The ad for the Petersen Magazine Network shown in Figure 12–12 promotes the coverage its leisure-time–enthusiasts publications provide of the 18- to 34-year-old male market. There are also networks offered by publishers of a group of magazines with diversified audiences as well as independent networks that sell space in groups of magazines published by a variety of companies. For example, the News Network sells space in a group of news-oriented publications such as *Time, Newsweek,* and *U.S. News & World Report.*

Comparing Rates   As discussed in Chapter 10, rate comparisons for magazines are made on the basis of the cost per thousand (CPM) criterion. The CPM formula is repeated here to refresh your memory:

$$CPM = \frac{\text{Page rate} \times 1,000}{\text{Circulation}}$$

A cost per thousand figure for a magazine reflects the cost of reaching 1,000 readers with a publication and thus having the opportunity to expose them to an advertisement. Please keep in mind that media planners often make adjustments in the way the CPM figure is calculated in evaluating a magazine. For example, they may use total audience rather than circulation if they feel comfortable about pass-along figures. A more likely adjustment is to substitute a specific target audience figure reached by the publication rather than using the aggregate circulation figure. Figure 12–13 shows an example of a promotional piece for *Business Week* magazine touting its lower CPM than *Forbes, Fortune,* or *Inc.* for reaching various groups of executives.

Cost per thousand comparisons among magazines may be calculated using various types of page sizes and ad formats. For example, the page rate for a full-page, black

and white ad in one magazine may be compared against the page rate for a half-page, four-color ad in another publication. Thus, the appropriate page rate figures would be used in making the CPM comparison of the different ad formats for each publication.

While the CPM figures are used by the media planner in evaluating and selecting magazines, they are not the only basis for choosing a publication. Other factors such as the editorial environment of the publication and its ability to focus on a specific target audience are also important considerations. Media buyers may decide to use a magazine with a higher CPM if they feel that it does the best overall job of communicating the message and meeting media objectives.

The Future of Magazines

The magazine industry continues to grow in the areas of both consumer and business publications. Many advertisers are increasingly turning to magazines as a cost-efficient way of reaching specialized audiences. A continuation in the trend toward greater market segmentation, market niche strategies, and regional marketing may result in more advertisers using magazines because of their high selectivity and ability to avoid wasted coverage or circulation.

An important development in magazines is the trend toward even more selectivity and specific target marketing. Many publications are expected to begin using **selective binding,** which is a computerized production process that allows the creation of hundreds of copies of a magazine in one continuous sequence, and **inkjet imaging,**

Figure 12–13 *Business Week* **Promotes Its Lower CPM Rates for Reaching Various Executives**

BusinessWeek

IF YOUR TARGET IS EXECUTIVES IN SMALL COMPANIES, BUSINESS WEEK IS THE REACH AND EFFICIENCY LEADER

1988/1989 SMRB

TOP MANAGEMENT

COMPANY SIZE	BUSINESS WEEK	FORBES	FORTUNE	INC
LESS THAN 100				
AUDIENCE (000)	**446**	300	303	265
4/C CPM	**$118.79**	$142.73	$152.48	$165.92
LESS THAN 50				
AUDIENCE (000)	**433**	272	282	235
4/C CPM	**$122.36**	$157.43	$163.83	$187.11
LESS THAN 25				
AUDIENCE (000)	**337**	227	237	212
4/C CPM	**$157.21**	$188.63	$194.94	$207.41
LESS THAN 10				
AUDIENCE (000)	**240**	162	191	147
4/C CPM	**$220.75**	$264.32	$241.88	$299.12

which makes it possible to personalize an advertisement, to offer ultranarrow targeting of readers.[21] Specialty publications such as *American Baby, Farm Journal,* and *Modern Maturity* have been using these processes to insert ad pages only into issues going to specific subscriber segments. However, in early 1990, three Time Inc. weeklies—*Time, Sports Illustrated,* and *People*—will begin offering these services. Many publishers feel that selective binding and inkjet imaging will allow advertisers the opportunity to target their messages more finely and will make magazines more competitive against direct mail.

The magazine industry does face some problems. The major factors driving magazine publishing costs are postage rates and paper costs. Increases in these areas along with increasing personnel costs can lead to economic problems for many publications. To increase revenue, they will have to raise their prices to readers or charge more for their advertising space. As was noted earlier, the rates consumers pay for magazines have increased significantly over the past decade, which will make it difficult to raise them further. It may also be difficult to raise the rates advertisers pay for space, as magazines are facing considerable competition, not only from one another but from other advertising media such as radio and television. Moreover, some publishers have begun negotiating rates with advertisers. This practice may become more commonplace as competition intensifies and may make it difficult for magazines to implement and sustain rate increases. Thus, magazine publishers will not only have to promote the inherent advantages of magazines as an advertising medium but will also have to refine further their publications and the services they offer to retain current users and attract new advertisers to the medium.

Newspapers

Newspapers are the second major form of print media and represent the largest of all advertising media in terms of total advertising dollar volume. In 1988 more than $31 billion was spent on newspaper advertising, which represents about 27 percent of the total advertising expenditures in the United States.[22] Newspapers are an especially important advertising medium to local advertisers and particularly to retailers who account for a large amount of newspaper advertising. However, newspapers also have characteristics that make them valuable to national advertisers. In fact, many of the advertising dollars spent by local retailers are actually provided by national advertisers through cooperative advertising programs (which are discussed in Chapter 16). Like magazines, there are different classifications or types of newspapers; they vary in terms of their characteristics and their role as an advertising medium. We will begin by examining the various ways by which newspapers can be classified.

Types of Newspapers

The traditional role of newspapers as a communication medium has been to deliver a prompt and detailed coverage of news as well as supplying other information and features that appeal to readers. The vast majority of newspapers are daily publications serving a local community. However, there are other types of newspapers that have special characteristics that can be valuable to advertisers including weekly, national, and special-audience newspapers.

Daily Newspapers Daily newspapers, which are published each weekday, are found in cities and larger towns across the country, with many areas having more than one daily paper. Daily newspapers are read by nearly 107 million adults each weekday.[23] They provide detailed coverage of news, events, and issues concerning the local area as well as business, sports, and other relevant information and entertainment. Daily newspapers can further be classified as morning, evening, or Sunday publications. In 1987 there were 1,655 daily newspapers in the United States, of which 70 percent were evening papers and 30 percent morning. There were also 830 Sunday newspapers, most of which were published by daily newspapers. Since 1965 the total circulation of daily newspapers has been between 60 and 63 million. However, the total number of dailies has been declining over the past 10 years, although the number of Sunday editions has been increasing.[24]

Weekly Newspapers Most weekly newspapers originate in small towns or suburbs where the volume of news and advertising is not adequate to support a daily newspaper. These papers focus primarily on news, sports, and events relevant to the local area and usually ignore national and world news, sports, and financial and business news. Weeklies are the fastest-growing class of newspapers, and in 1989 there were 7,606 such papers in the United States. Weeklies appeal primarily to local advertisers in the community because of their geographic focus and lower absolute cost. Most national advertisers avoid weekly newspapers because of their duplicate circulation with daily or Sunday papers in the large metropolitan areas and problems in contracting for and placing ads in these publications. However, the contracting and scheduling problems associated with using these papers have been reduced somewhat by the emergence of syndicates that publish the daily papers in a number of areas and sell ad space in all of their publications through one office.

National Newspapers While national newspapers are very common in Europe as well as many other foreign countries, there are but a handful in the United States. Newspapers in this country with national circulation include *The Wall Street Journal, The Christian Science Monitor,* and *USA TODAY*. All three are daily publications and have editorial content that has a nationwide appeal. *The Wall Street Journal* has the largest circulation of any newspaper in the country, selling over 2 million copies a day. *USA TODAY* represents the most recent national newspaper and has successfully positioned itself as "the nation's newspaper," as discussed in Promotional Perspective 12–3.

National newspapers appeal primarily to large national advertisers and to regional advertisers who use specific geographic editions of these publications, if available. For

Promotional Perspective 12–3

USA TODAY—The Nation's Newspaper

In 1982 the Gannet Company, Inc., one of the nation's leading newspaper publishers, caught the attention of the media world with its decision to publish a daily national newspaper called *USA TODAY*. The paper was launched in September 1982 amid considerable skepticism by the advertising industry and the media community. Some critics called it the fast food of journalism and nicknamed it "McPaper." The paper was criticized for its lack of in-depth coverage of stories and guidelines such as that no lead paragraphs should contain more than 25 words.

In the first few months of its existence, *USA TODAY* used greatly reduced advertising rates to get advertisers to use and become familiar with the paper. At the end of the first year the paper was averaging only three paid advertising pages per day and by the end of 1984 had reached only about 10 pages per issue. Losses were estimated to have reached as much as $150 million by the end of 1984. However, Gannet stuck to its five-year plan, which called for the paper to become profitable by 1987. The company was encouraged by the fact that the paper had exceeded circulation projections, and because of multiple readership of the average copy, the paper's total readership was estimated at over 4 million.

Despite the slow acceptance of *USA TODAY* by advertisers, consumers became increasingly interested in a full-color, upscale national newspaper that offered particularly good coverage of areas such as sports, entertainment, and business news. The paper's approach of marketing itself along the lines of a daily general interest magazine was beginning to catch on with readers. A Simmons Market Research Bureau survey in 1986 showed that *USA TODAY* had the most readers of any daily newspaper in the country and was second only to *The Wall Street Journal* in the important category of paid circulation. In 1985 the paper had a 44 percent increase in advertising lineage and by 1986 became the number-one print vehicle for automotive advertising, the leading category of newspaper advertising. Advertisers became increasingly attracted to the paper because of its high-quality graphics, full-color reproduction capabilities, and large audience.

As a national newspaper, *USA TODAY* appeals more to large national advertisers than to companies and retailers in the local advertising markets, which account for nearly 60 percent of all newspaper ad revenues. However, the paper now publishes a number of regional editions that have been succfessful in attracting local as well as large national advertisers. In addition to automobile companies, *USA TODAY* has attracted considerable ad pages from computer-, tobacco-, and travel-related companies. The paper has become particularly popular among airline travelers, many of whom are business executives who have input into their company's advertising decisions. The *USA TODAY* reader is somewhat younger,

Exhibit 12–3   ***USA TODAY* Has Become a Very Successful National Newspaper**

more affluent, and upscale than the reader of the average news weekly.

USA TODAY celebrated its fifth anniversary in September 1987 not only as the leading national newspaper in terms of total readership but also with a record number of ad pages (Exhibit 12–3). The Gannet Company, Inc. also has one other accomplishment worth noting: *USA TODAY* had its first profitable quarter in 1987, just as planned five years prior. In September 1988, "USA Today," a nightly television show based on the nation's newspaper, began airing on stations across the country. Many stations are betting the brevity, brightness, and soft-news approach that inspired the paper will be successful on television as well.

Sources: "*USA TODAY*'s Struggle to Snag More Advertisers," *Business Week*, October 15, 1984, p. 80; "*USA TODAY*, Yesterday and Tomorrow," *Madison Avenue*, January 1986, p. 62; Dennis Kneale, "TV Version of *USA TODAY* May Be Financial—If Not Critical—Success," *The Wall Street Journal*, February 4, 1988, p. 23.

Figure 12–14 **Ad Promoting a Paper Targeted to Hispanics**

example, *The Wall Street Journal* has six geographic editions in which ads can be placed.

Special-Audience Newspapers There are a variety of papers that offer specialized editorial content and are published for particular groups including labor unions, various professional organizations, industries, and hobbyists. For example, many individuals working in advertising and marketing read *Advertising Age,* which is the leading trade publication for these industries. Specialized newspapers are also published in areas with large foreign language–speaking ethnic groups such as Hispanics, Vietnamese, and Filipinos. Figure 12–14 shows an ad promoting *Diario Las Américas,* which is a paper targeted to Hispanics in the Greater Miami area.

Newspapers targeted at various religious groups compose another large class of special-interest papers. For example, there are more than 140 Catholic newspapers published across the United States. Another type of special-audience newspaper is one most of you probably read regularly during the school year—the college newspaper. Over 1300 colleges and universities publish a newspaper and offer advertisers an excellent medium for reaching college students.

Newspaper Supplements Although not a category of newspapers per se, many papers include magazine-type supplements, primarily in their Sunday editions. Sunday supplements, as they are often called, have been a part of most newspapers for many years and come in various forms. One type is the syndicated Sunday magazine such as *Parade* or *USA Weekend* that is distributed in hundreds of papers throughout the country. *Parade* has a circulation of over 32 million, whereas *USA Weekend* is carried by newspapers with a combined circulation of more than 13 million. These publications are very similar in nature to national magazines and carry both national and regional advertising.

Figure 12–15 **The *Los Angeles Times* Promotes Its Sunday Magazine**

YOU'RE ALWAYS IN GOOD COMPANY WITH LOS ANGELES TIMES MAGAZINE.

Whether we're profiling Michael Jackson, spotlighting Shirley MacLaine, or visiting Tommy Lasorda, Los Angeles Times Magazine always keeps its readers in good company. With probing, provocative stories on some of the world's most intriguing people. Delivered by some of the nation's top writing talents.

What's more, we cover a diverse spectrum of timely topics. From casual clothes to formal gardens. Broadcast News, L.A. to Main Street, Managua. And it's this eclectic, first-rate editorial and color photography that keeps bringing the West's top magazine audience back for more. Sunday after Sunday after Sunday.

Los Angeles Times Magazine. The perfect companion for the selective Southern Californian. And the ideal vehicle for the quality-conscious, profit-minded advertiser.

No matter how you look at it, you're always in good company with Los Angeles Times Magazine.

Los Angeles Times Magazine

(For advertising information call (213) 237-3000 or 1-800-528-4637, ext. 73025.)

Some large papers publish local Sunday supplements that are distributed by the parent paper. These supplements contain stories that are of more local interest, and ad space may be used by either local or national advertisers. While the *New York Times Sunday Magazine* is the best known of the local supplements, several other papers such as the *Washington Post, San Francisco Examiner,* and *Los Angeles Times* have their own Sunday magazines (Figure 12–15). In some areas, papers have begun carrying regional supplements as well as specialized weekday supplements that cover specific topics or interests such as food, sports, and entertainment. Supplements are valuable to advertisers who want to use the newspaper yet get four-color reproduction quality in their ads.

Types of Newspaper Advertising

In addition to there being several different types of newspapers, the advertisements appearing in these papers can also be divided into different categories. The major classifications of newspaper advertising are display and classified. In addition to these two dominant categories, other special types of ad and preprinted inserts also appear in newspapers.

Display Advertising **Display advertising** is found throughout the newspaper and generally uses illustrations, headlines, white space, and other visual devices in addition to the copy text. Display ads account for approximately 70 percent of the advertising revenue of the average newspaper. There are two types of display advertising that appear in newspapers—local and national (general).

Local advertising refers to ads placed by local organizations, businesses, and individuals who want to communicate with consumers in the market area served by the newspaper. Local advertising comes primarily from retailers. Supermarkets and department stores are among the leading local display advertisers along with the numerous other retailers and service operations such as banks and travel agents. Local advertising is sometimes referred to as *retail advertising* because retailers account for so much of the local ads found in a newspaper. However, it should be noted that local advertising does include other forms of advertising. Local advertisers account for approximately 85 percent of newspaper display advertising.

National or *general newspaper advertising* refers to display advertising done by marketers of branded products or services that are sold on a national or regional level. These ads are designed to create and maintain demand for a company's particular product or service and to complement the efforts of local retailers who stock and promote the advertiser's products. Automobile and tobacco companies along with airlines are heavy users of newspaper advertising, as shown in Table 12–6.

Classified Advertising **Classified advertising** also provides newspapers with a substantial amount of advertising revenue. These ads are arranged under subheads according to the product, service, or offering being advertised. Employment, real estate, and automotive are the three major categories of classified advertising. While most classified ads include only text set in uniform type, some newspapers also accept classified display advertising. These ads are run in the classified section of the paper but use illustrations, larger type sizes, white space, borders, and even color to enhance their appearance.

Special Ads and Inserts Special advertisements in newspapers include a variety of governmental and financial reports and notices and public notices of changes in business and personal relationships. There are also other types of advertising that ap-

Table 12–6 **Top 25 Newspaper Advertisers**

| Rank | Advertiser | Newspaper Expenditures | | | As % of Co.'s '88 Ad Total |
		1988	1987	% Chg	
1	May Department Stores Co.	$224,282	$230,174	(2.6)	56.1
2	Macy Acquiring Corp.	182,212	176,033	3.5	59.0
3	Sears, Roebuck & Co.	160,969	175,052	(8.0)	15.4
4	Campeau Corp.	124,488	134,833	(7.7)	47.8
5	Dayton-Hudson Corp.	90,630	81,062	11.8	39.4
6	General Motors Corp.	86,835	83,841	3.6	6.7
7	Texas Air Corp.	82,441	66,647	23.7	64.0
8	Philip Morris Cos.	76,711	46,048	66.6	3.7
9	Carter Hawley Hale Stores	75,554	52,353	44.3	47.3
10	J.C. Penney Co.	74,568	90,721	(17.8)	17.5
11	K Mart Corp.	73,073	82,033	(10.9)	11.6
12	Montgomery Ward & Co.	63,500	67,176	(5.5)	40.9
13	American Stores Co.	61,803	65,659	(5.9)	24.7
14	Time Warner	42,037	36,748	14.4	10.3
15	Woodward & Lothrop	38,856	36,625	6.1	48.7
16	RJR Nabisco	37,704	12,934	191.5	4.6
17	B.A.T. Industries PLC	35,915	61,875	(42.0)	19.5
18	Tandy Corp.	32,911	38,900	(15.4)	14.2
19	American Telephone & Telegraph	32,690	32,610	0.2	6.0
20	Dillard Department Stores	32,073	29,057	10.4	43.4
21	American Express Co.	30,251	29,286	3.3	12.2
22	Circuit City Stores	29,654	25,124	18.0	29.4
23	General Electric Co.	29,357	33,121	(11.4)	10.6
24	Safeway Stores	28,738	34,403	(16.5)	28.5
25	AMR Corp.	28,671	36,654	(21.8)	23.8

Note: Dollars are in thousands.
Source: Leading National Advertisers/Media Records, *Advertising Age,* September 27, 1989, p. 40.

pear in newspapers such as political or special-interest ads promoting a particular candidate, issue, or cause. **Preprinted inserts** are another type of advertising distributed through newspapers. These ads do not appear in the paper itself but rather are printed by the advertiser and then taken to the newspaper to be inserted before delivery. Many retailers use inserts such as circulars, catalogs, or brochures in specific circulation zones of the newspaper to reach shoppers in their particular trade area.

Advantages of Newspapers

Newspapers have a number of characteristics that make them popular among both local and national advertisers. These include their extensive penetration of local markets, flexibility, geographic selectivity, reader involvement, and the special services newspapers offer.

Extensive Penetration

One of the primary advantages of newspapers is the high degree of market coverage, or penetration, they offer an advertiser. In most areas 70 percent or more of households read a daily newspaper, and the reach figure may exceed 90 percent among some groups such as higher-income and -education-level households. Most areas are served by one or two daily newspapers, and often the same company owns both, publishing both a morning and an evening edition. Thus, by making one space buy the advertiser can achieve a high level of overall reach in a particular market.

The extensive penetration of newspapers makes them a truly mass medium and provides advertisers with an excellent opportunity for reaching all segments of the population with their advertising message. Also, since many newspapers are published and read daily, the advertiser can build a high level of frequency into a media schedule with newspapers.

Flexibility

Another advantage of newspapers is the flexibility they offer the advertiser. Newspapers provide flexibility in several ways. First, they are flexible in terms of requirements for producing and running the advertisements. Newspaper ads can be written, laid out, and prepared in a matter of hours, and for most dailies the closing time by which the ad must be received is usually no more than 24 hours (although closing dates for special ads such as those using color and Sunday supplements will be longer). The short production time and closing dates make newspapers an excellent medium for responding to current events or presenting timely information to consumers. For example, both national and local advertisers run ads each year congratulating the winning team in the Super Bowl, NBA Championships, World Series, and other popular contests. Promotional Perspective 12–4 discusses how Merrill Lynch, the financial services firm, took advantage of the timeliness of newspapers to respond to the "Black Monday" stock market crash in 1987.

A second dimension of newspapers' flexibility stems from the creative options they make available to advertisers. Newspaper ads can be produced and run in various sizes, shapes, and formats or make use of color or special inserts as a way of gaining the attention and interest of the readers. Ads can be run in Sunday magazines or other supplements, and a variety of scheduling options are possible, depending on the advertiser's purpose.

Geographic Selectivity

Newspapers generally offer advertisers more geographic or territorial selectivity than any other medium except direct mail. Advertisers can vary their coverage for various areas by choosing a paper—or combination of papers—that reaches the areas with the greatest sales potential. National advertisers take advantage of the geographic selectivity of newspapers to concentrate their advertising in specific areas they have problems reaching with other media or to take advantage of strong sales potential in a particular area. For example, automobile advertisers such as BMW,

Promotional Perspective 12—4

Using Newspaper Advertising to Respond to "Black Monday"

On October 19, 1987, individuals investing in the stock market experienced a very traumatic event when, after five years of unprecedented growth, the Dow Jones industrial average dropped 508 points. The crash was the worst in the history of the market in terms of point and percentage decline as well as dollar losses. Nearly all investors were affected by the event, which became known in the financial world as "Black Monday."

In the aftermath of Black Monday, the financial community was faced with an extraordinarily difficult marketing and communications problem. While there was uncertainty over what to tell investors, they knew that they must react quickly or face a further erosion in investor confidence. The situation called for not only an immediate response but also detailed and thoughtful information and advice to reassure worried investors. To deal with this crisis, many financial services companies turned to the advertising medium of newspapers to reach their clients and offer them some reassuring words.

Merrill Lynch, one of the largest financial services companies, reacted to Black Monday by creating an ad headlined "After October 19: A perspective" on Tuesday morning and placing it in newspapers on Wednesday (see Exhibit 12—4). The full-page ad ran in 10 local newspapers in addition to two national newspapers, *The Wall Street Journal* and *USA TODAY*. Merrill Lynch followed the first ad with a second one on Friday, October 23, headlined "Now, What about Next Week?" which updated the company's clients and the country as well as informing them about extended weekend hours when brokers would be available. Subsequent ads ran in 150 local newspapers as well as in international publications. A number of key people were involved in the creation of the ads including not only the advertising agency but also the chairman, the director of global services, and the director of financial market research at Merrill Lynch.

Merrill Lynch's director of advertising indicated that newspapers were a natural choice for the reassurance campaign, as the medium gave the company the ability to turn information around quickly and to go into detail to deliver as much information as possible. He noted

Exhibit 12—4   Merrill Lynch Reacted Quickly to Black Monday with Newspaper Ads

After October 19: A perspective.

On October 19, investor uncertainty abruptly turned into an unprecedented market decline. In one day the Dow Jones Industrial Average fell 22½ percent.

But the selling was not caused by any particular bad news, and there is no evidence that it was justified by the fundamental values of the stocks being sold.

Buy, sell, hold?

The worst thing to do right now would be to sell at distressed prices.

It's crucial at this point to get your bearings in this totally new environment, and decide upon a rational and prudent course of action.

Without minimizing the seriousness of a market decline of some 40 percent since its high last August, it is also correct to say that for investors who remain steady under fire this new market is studded with values. But before seeking them out, it makes sense to take a good, careful look around.

What will happen next?

Some historical perspective: One of the reasons for our optimism is the magnitude of the decline we've just been through. Some of the worst declines in history have not exceeded 50 percent in the initial selloff. Even those that were followed by poor economic fundamentals recovered as much as 50 percent of the losses in subsequent months.

One of the concerns in the bond market, and the barrier to long-term economic growth, was the fear of resurging inflation. The dangers on the inflation front seem very limited at this juncture.

A better environment ahead.

The fundamentals of the economy may be called into question, but we believe the markets are overreacting to events, and that the economic outlook is sound.

It cannot be said too strongly or too often: however severe this shock has been, this is no time to sell.

In fact, it is a time to take advantage of opportunities in financial assets.

Reducing risks with bonds.

The bond market has been at best unkind to investors for the past few months, but our fixed-income analysts point out that this week's big equity selloff was accompanied by some strengthening in the bond market.

We feel that long-term Treasury bonds currently yielding in the neighborhood of 10 percent offer a very satisfying return with relatively little risk.

Partly because of the stock market decline, the Federal Reserve Board is no longer so likely to pursue a tighter monetary course, which would tend to push interest rates upward.

The Industrial Renaissance.

In the stock market, the quest for value should focus on the major long-term resurgence of the industrial sector of the economy. For investors who want to make a move now, and who have the patience to hold on through short-term volatility, we are recommending a small group of companies in the heavy industrial and closely-related sectors that we believe have the potential to lead the recovery in the stock market.

We also see opportunities in utilities and certain insurance companies.

It's no time to go it alone.

At times like these, it's more important than ever to have continuing access to the kind of information and insight that can help you exploit the opportunities that uncertainty creates.

For our part, we continue offering our clients the reassurance of our financial strength, our proud tradition of trustworthiness and our leadership in providing professional guidance and service.

At Merrill Lynch, we remain confident in the financial markets, and in the underlying value of financial assets in this climate.

We recognize that emotions run high during times like these; however, it is critical that reason and objectivity prevail now more than ever.

We urge all investors to take no action out of fear, and to make careful and thoughtful decisions before taking any action at all.

Whatever volatility we face in the days ahead, we are committed to demonstrate to you the highest degree of professionalism and service. We urge you to take a long-term view and prepare yourself to participate in the opportunities we see ahead in a fundamentally sound economy.

 **Merrill Lynch**

© 1987 Merrill Lynch & Co., Inc.

that "getting the message out in a timely manner was as important as the message itself." Thus, the newspaper's ability to produce detailed and timely information made it the appropriate medium for this situation.

Source: Tamara Goldman, "Big Spenders Develop Newspaper Strategies," *Marketing Communications*, June 1988, pp. 24—29.

Mercedes, and Volvo use heavy newspaper media schedules in California and the New York/New Jersey areas to capitalize on the high sales potential for luxury import cars in these markets.

A number of companies such as General Motors, AT&T, and Campbell are using newspapers as part of their regional marketing strategies. Newspaper advertising provides them with more flexibility to feature products on a market-by-market basis, to respond and adapt campaigns to local market conditions, and to tie into more retailer promotions and thus foster more support from the trade.[25]

Local advertisers such as retailers are, of course, interested in geographic selectivity or flexibility within a specific market or trade area. Their media goal is to concentrate their advertising on the area from which they draw most of their customers.

Figure 12–16 **The *Los Angeles Times* Publishes Eight Zone Editions**

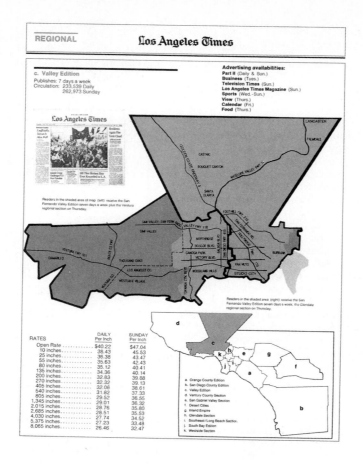

Many newspapers are now publishing several geographic or zone editions that provide local advertisers with the opportunity to do this. For example, the *Los Angeles Times* publishes eight geographic or zone editions. Figure 12–16 shows a description of the San Fernando Valley edition of the *Los Angeles Times* along with a map of the other seven zones.

Reader Involvement and Acceptance Another important feature of newspapers is the level of involvement and acceptance consumers have with newspapers and the advertisements they contain. The typical daily newspaper reader spends an average of 45 minutes a day reading the weekday newspaper and 62 minutes reading the Sunday paper.[26] Most consumers rely heavily on newspapers not only for news, information, and entertainment but also for information for making consumption decisions.

Many consumers actually purchase a newspaper *because* of the advertising it contains rather than in spite of it. Consumers use retail ads in particular to determine product prices and availability and to see who is having a sale. One aspect of newspapers that is helpful to advertisers is the readers' knowledge and involvement with particular sections of the paper. Most of us know that ads for automotive products and sporting goods are generally found in the sports section of most papers, whereas ads for financial services are found in the business section. The weekly food section found in many newspapers is popular for recipe and menu ideas as well as for the grocery store ads and coupons offered therein by many stores and companies. Table 12–7 shows readership figures for various sections of newspapers for adult men and women.

The value of newspaper advertising as a source of information has been shown in several studies. One study found that consumers look forward to newspaper ads more than for other media, whereas another showed that 80 percent of consumers indicated that newspaper ads were most helpful to them in doing their weekly shopping.[27,28]

Table 12–7   **Daily Newspaper Pages or Sections Usually Read (total adult readers, by sex)**

	Percentage of Weekday Audience		
	Adults	Men	Women
Usually read every page	61	62	61
Read certain pages or sections	39	38	39
Business, finance	76	78	74
Classified	76	76	77
Comics	75	75	76
Editorial page	80	78	81
Entertainment	81	78	85
Food, cooking	76	71	83
General news	94	94	95
Home furnishings, gardening	74	71	79
Sports	79	88	71
TV, radio listings	76	74	78
Projected base: average weekday audience (in 000s)	(113,337)	(56,018)	(57,319)

Source: Simmons Market Research Bureau, *1989 Study of Media & Markets.* This table appeared in "Key Facts 1989," Newspaper Advertising Bureau.

Newspaper advertising has also been rated the most believable of all forms of advertising in numerous studies.

Services Offered   While newspapers have numerous advantages as an advertising medium for reaching and communicating with consumers, they also can be valuable to the advertiser in terms of the special services they offer. For example, many newspapers offer merchandising services and programs to manufacturers that help convince local retailers that they should stock, display, and promote the company's product and make the trade aware of newspaper ads being run for the item.

Many newspapers are also an excellent source of local market information through their knowledge of market conditions and research they conduct such as readership studies and consumer surveys. Figure 12–17 shows a list of studies available from the Union-Tribune Publishing Company, publisher of the two major newspapers in San Diego.

Newspapers can also be of assistance to small companies through the free copy writing and art services they provide. Small advertisers without an agency or advertising department often rely on the newspaper to assist them in the writing and production of their ads.

Limitations of Newspapers

While newspapers have a considerable number of advantages, like all media they also have disadvantages and limitations that must be considered in evaluating and using them as media vehicles. The limitations of newspapers include their reproduction problems, short life span, lack of selectivity, and clutter.

Poor Reproduction   One of the greatest limitations of newspapers as an advertising medium is their poor reproduction quality. The coarse paper stock used for newspapers, the absence of color, and the lack of time papers have available for high-quality reproduction limits the quality of most newspaper ads. Newspapers have improved their reproduction quality in recent years, and color reproduction has become more readily available. Also, advertisers desiring high-quality color in newspaper ads can turn to several alternatives such as using free-standing inserts or Sunday supplements. However, these are more costly and may not be desirable to many advertisers. As a general rule, if the visual appearance of the product is important, the advertiser will not rely on newspaper ads. For example, ads for food products or fashions generally use magazines so as to capitalize on their superior reproduction quality and color.

Figure 12–17 Newspaper Publishers Such as the Union-Tribune Conduct Numerous Studies on Local Markets

Investigate the strength of the San Diego market

The Union-Tribune's portfolio of publications gives you a complete stock of information for your business.

■ **Continuing Analysis of Shopping Habits in San Diego (CASH)** — Measures purchase patterns for the last three years in 75 merchandise categories. CASH shows how a category performs and how individual retailers are doing, along with consumer profiles.

■ **San Diego Regional Shopping Center Report** — Spotlights the preferences and characteristics of regional center shoppers and defines each center's trade area.

■ **Shopping Center Locations in San Diego County Map** — Locates super-regional, regional, theme/specialty and community centers.

■ **Restaurant Customers of San Diego County** — Surveys local dining-out habits and profiles the typical restaurant customer.

■ **San Diego Travel Market Book** — Focuses on airline and cruise ship travel in San Diego County. Includes destinations, trends and traveler profiles.

■ **Financial Market Book** — Profiles San Diego County households with retail accounts at banks, credit unions and savings and loans.

■ **Automotive Dealers in San Diego County Map** — Locates all domestic and import car dealers in the county.

■ **Automotive Market Book** — Features share of market for cars and trucks, along with registration statistics for domestic and import cars and the leaders of the local automotive scene.

■ **The Annual Review of San Diego Business** — Studies economic trends through the decades and looks at current statistics and projections for the future. Breaks out data by county, sub-county and zip codes.

■ **Ad Performance Study** — Presents the performance of ads in the Union-Tribune for various product categories. The study measures ad exposure levels, reader preferences, cost efficiencies and the overall effectiveness of reaching your target market through advertising in The San Diego Union and The Tribune.

■ **Quick Market Stats** — Offers a one-page review of the San Diego market, media and Union-Tribune circulation and readership.

■ **Co-op: Good as Gold** — A Retailers' Guide to Co-op Advertising — Demonstrates how retailers can move branded merchandise through effective use of co-op newspaper advertising.

■ **Regional Media & Market Study** — Breaks down San Diego's population, housing statistics, consumer expenditures and media use in the county's North, South, East and Central zones.

■ **Median Family Income Map** — Shows San Diego County's median family incomes by zip codes.

■ **Major Daily Newspaper Penetration in Southern California** — Compares household coverage and circulation of newspapers in Southern California counties.

■ **The San Diego Movie and Video Market Book** — Features the preferences and characteristics of San Diego moviegoers, VCR owners and cable TV subscribers.

■ **How to Show a House, 24 Hours a Day** — Demonstrates the effectiveness of regular and display classified advertising for real estate accounts.

■ **You *Can* Take the San Diegan Out of San Diego** — Profiles the San Diego job market for recruitment advertisers. Includes comparisons of salaries, occupations, cost of living and job trends.

■ **Preprint Zone and Zip Code Map** — Outlines preprint zones and zip codes within the Union-Tribune's circulation area.

■ **Zoned Market Stats** — Presents market information, demographics, and newspaper coverage in separate North, South, East and Central zone booklets.

■ **More Ways to Make Your Business Strong** — Describes the Union-Tribune's complete selection of advertising products, rates and services.

Short Life Span Unlike magazines that may be retained around the house for several weeks, the life span of a daily newspaper is generally less than a day. In most homes the daily paper is read and discarded within a 24-hour period. Thus, an advertisement is unlikely to have any impact beyond the day of publication, and repeat exposure to an ad is very unlikely. Further compounding this problem is the short amount of time many consumers may spend with the newspaper and the possibility they may not even open certain sections of the paper. These problems can be offset somewhat by using high frequency in the newspaper schedule and by advertising in a section of the paper where consumers are likely to look for ads if they are in the market for a particular product or service.

Lack of Selectivity While newspapers do have the advantage of offering advertisers geographic selectivity, they are not a selective medium in terms of demographics or lifestyle characteristics. As noted earlier, most newspapers have extensive penetration and reach broad and very diverse groups of consumers. This makes it difficult for marketers to focus specifically on narrowly defined market segments through the newspaper. For example, a manufacturer of fishing rods and reels will find newspapers to be very inefficient because of the wasted circulation that results from reaching all the nonfishermen who purchase a newspaper. Thus, they are more likely to use special-interest magazines such as *Field & Stream* or *Fishing World* to advertise their equipment. Any newspaper ads for their products will be done through cooperative plans whereby retailers share the costs or spread them over a number of sporting goods featured in the newspaper ad.

Clutter Newspapers, like most other advertising media, suffer from a clutter problem since there are so many advertisements competing for the reader's attention. Sixty-four percent of the average daily paper in the United States is devoted to advertising. Thus, the advertiser's message must compete with numerous other ads for consumers' attention and interest. Moreover, the creative options in newspapers are somewhat limited by the fact that nearly every ad is in black and white. Thus, it can be very difficult for the newspaper advertiser to break through the clutter unless more costly measures such as large space buys or color are used. Some advertisers use creative techniques such as "island ads," whereby the advertisement is completely surrounded by editorial material. Island ads are often found in the middle of the stock market quotes on the financial pages of many newspapers.[29]

The Newspaper Audience

As with any medium, the media planner must understand the nature and size of the audience reached by a newspaper in considering its value in the media plan. As was noted above, newspapers as a general class of media do an excellent job of penetrating most households. Thus, the typical daily newspaper provides advertisers the opportunity to reach most of the households in a market with their advertising message. However, while local advertisers are interested in the ability of a newspaper to cover a particular market or trade area, national advertisers are concerned with reaching broad regions or even the entire country with their ads. Thus, they must purchase space in a number of papers to achieve the desired level of coverage.

The basic sources of information concerning the audience size of newspapers come from the circulation figures that are available through rate cards, on publisher's statements, or through Standard Rate and Data Service's *Newspaper Rates and Data*. Circulation figures for many newspapers are verified by one of the auditing services such as Audit Bureau of Circulations (discussed previously). While the rate cards or publisher's statements are used by local advertisers to get information concerning circulation figures and advertising rates, advertisers using a number of papers in their media plan generally find SRDS a convenient source.

Newspaper circulation figures are generally reported for three categories in addition to total circulation. These categories include city zone, the retail trading zone, and all other areas. The **city zone** is a market area composed of the city where the paper is published and contiguous areas similar in character to the city. The **retail trading zone** is the market outside the city zone whose residents regularly trade with merchants within the city zone. The "all other" category refers to all circulation not included in the city or retail trade zone.

In some instances circulation figures are provided only for the primary market, which is the city and retail trade zones, and the other area. The circulation patterns across the various categories are taken into consideration by both local and national advertisers in evaluating and selecting newspapers.

National advertisers who use newspapers often buy them based on the size of the market area they cover. For example, a large advertiser such as General Motors may decide to purchase advertising in the "first 10 markets," "first 50 markets," "first 100 markets," and so on. The national advertiser gets different levels of market coverage depending on the number of market areas purchased.

Audience Information Circulation figures provide the media planner with the basic data for assessing the value of newspapers and their ability to cover various market areas. However, the media planner is also interested in the characteristics of a newspaper's readers so as to match them against those of the advertiser's target audience. Data on newspaper audience size and characteristics are available from commercial research services and from studies conducted by the papers themselves.

Commercial studies providing readership information for the top 100 or so major markets are supplied by the Simmons-Scarbough Syndicated Research Associates. These studies cover more than 150 daily newspapers and provide reach and frequency estimates for various demographic groups. The audience information available from these studies is valuable to the media planner for comparing newspapers with other media vehicles that generally have similar data available. Many advertising executives and media planners feel that the newspaper industry must expand the amount of audience research data available or risk losing more advertising dollars to magazines and television.

Many newspapers commission and publish their own audience studies so as to provide current and potential advertisers with information on readership and characteristics of readers such as demographics, shopping habits, and lifestyles. These studies are often designed to provide information to advertisers as well as to help promote the effectiveness of the newspaper in reaching various types of consumers. Since they are sponsored by the paper itself, many advertisers are somewhat skeptical over the results of these studies. Careful attention must be given to the research methods and conclusions drawn by these studies when using them to make media decisions.

Purchasing Newspaper Space

Advertisers are faced with a number of options and pricing structures when purchasing newspaper space. The cost of advertising space depends not only on the newspaper's circulation but also on factors such as premium charges for color or special sections as well as discounts available. Also, the purchase process and the rates paid for newspaper space differ for national versus local advertisers. We will first consider the rate differential for national versus local advertisers.

National versus Local Rates
According to the American Association of Advertising Agencies, national advertising rates are, on average, 66 percent higher than those paid by local advertisers. Newspapers attribute the higher national rates to the added costs they incur in serving national advertisers, along with several other factors.

National and local advertisers differ in the method by which they purchase newspaper space. National advertisers are represented by an advertising agency and purchase space through a sales agent or "rep" representing the newspaper. The sales agents work for organizations representing a number of independent newspapers and/or newspaper chains. Their job is to supply the media buyer with information regarding the newspaper they represent and to promote the advantages of the newspaper in reaching specific markets and other services they offer to advertisers and their agencies. The representatives are paid commissions by the individual newspapers on the space they sell. The advertising agency also receives a 15 percent commission on any space purchased for their clients.

Local advertisers, on the other hand, usually deal directly with the newspaper's advertising department through the local representatives or reps working in the advertising sales department of the newspaper. These reps work with the local advertisers by making them aware of information and services provided by the newspapers and sometimes (for small advertisers) helping them plan and prepare their ads. While local sales reps receive a commission on the space they sell, the 15 percent agency commission or discount is not granted to local advertisers. However, the space rate for local advertisers is generally much lower than the rate charged national advertisers.

The differential rate structure for national versus local advertisers has been the source of considerable controversy. Newspaper publishers claim the rate differential is justified for several reasons. First, they argue that it costs more to handle national advertising since a 15 percent commission must be granted to advertising agencies and commissions must also be paid to the independent sales representatives who solicit nonlocal advertising. National advertising is also less dependable than local advertising since the national advertiser usually does not advertise in newspapers on a continual basis like a local advertiser. Thus, they argue that the costs of handling their business will be higher than for a local advertiser.

They also argue that national advertisers often request considerable merchandising assistance from newspapers to assist in implementing special promotions. Finally, newspaper publishers contend that demand for national advertising is inelastic and thus will not increase if rates are lowered or decrease if rates are higher. Thus, there is no incentive to lower the rates charged the national advertiser.

National advertisers do not view these arguments as valid justification for the rate differential charged by newspapers. They argue that the costs of handling national advertising are not greater than for local business. They point out that many national advertisers use newspapers on a regular basis, and since they use an agency to prepare their ads, they are less likely to request special services. National advertisers also note that the large and costly staff maintained by many newspapers to assist in the design and preparation of advertising is used mostly by local advertisers.

Some newspapers are making efforts to narrow the rate differential for national and local advertisers to a more reasonable level (Figure 12–18).[30] National advertisers will still pay higher rates in order to cover the agency commission that is paid by the newspapers, but the rates they pay will be more in line with those paid by local advertisers. However, the rate differential still remains for many papers. A survey by *News-Inc.* in 1989 of national and local rates for 22 newspapers in large and small markets found that the premiums paid by national advertisers ranged from 9 to 109 percent.[31] Many marketers sidestep the national advertiser label and the higher rates by channeling their newspaper ads through special category plans, cooperative advertising deals with retailers, and local dealers and distributors who pay local rates. However, the rate differential does limit many national advertisers from making newspapers a larger part of their media mix.[32]

Newspaper Rates

Traditionally newspaper space for national advertisers has been sold by the agate line system. And **agate line** measures $\frac{1}{14}$ inch in depth and one column wide; thus, there are 14 lines per inch. The size of an ad would generally be specified in terms of total agate lines, or "lineage," which is determined by the number of lines and columns the ad covered. For example, an ad that is 10 inches deep by 2 columns wide would contain 280 agate lines ($2 \times 10 \times 14$). Thus, the total cost for the ad would depend on the newspaper per-line rate. If the paper charged $3.00 per agate line, the ad would cost $840.

The problem with this system is that newspapers use page formats of varying width, as some have six columns per page, whereas others have eight or nine. Thus, the size, shape, and costs of an ad would vary depending on the column format used by the paper. This results in a complicated production and buying process for national advertisers purchasing space in a number of newspapers across the country.

To address this problem and make newspapers more comparable to other media who sell space and time in standard units, the newspaper industry developed **standard advertising units (SAUs)** and switched to this system in 1984. Under this system all newspapers will use column widths 2 $\frac{1}{16}$ inches wide, with tabloid-size papers having five columns per page and standard or broadcast papers being six columns in width. The *column inch* is used as the unit of measurement to create the 57 standard-size units or format sizes, as shown in Figure 12–19.

The national advertiser can prepare one advertisement in a particular SAU, and it would fit every newspaper in the country that accepts SAUs and rates would be quoted on that basis. Since over 1,400 or about 90 percent of the daily newspapers use the SAU system, the purchase and production process has been simplified tremendously for national advertisers.

Newspaper rates for local advertisers continue to be based on the column inch, which is one inch deep by one column wide. Advertising rates for the local advertiser are quoted per column inch, and total space costs are calculated by multiplying the number of column inches by the cost per inch.

Figure 12—19 **Standard Advertising Units**

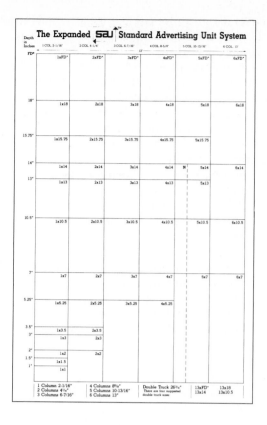

Rate Structures While the column inch and standard advertising unit are used for determining basic newspaper advertising rates, there are other options and factors the media planner must consider. Many newspapers charge **flat rates,** which means they offer no discount for large quantity or repeated space buys. Others may have an **open-rate structure,** which means that various discounts are available. These discounts are generally based on frequency or bulk purchases of space and are dependent on the number of column inches purchased in a year.

Newspaper space rates will also depend on any special requests the advertiser has such as preferred position or the use of color. The basic rates quoted by a newspaper are **run of paper,** or **ROP,** which means that the paper can place the ad on any page or in any position it desires. While most newspapers make an effort to place an ad in a position requested, the advertiser can ensure a specific section and/or position on a page by paying a higher **preferred position rate.** Color advertising is also available in many newspapers on a ROP basis or can be utilized through the use of preprinted inserts or Sunday supplements.

Advertisers can also buy newspaper space based on **combination rates** whereby a discount is offered for using several newspapers as a group. The most frequently used combination rate occurs when a publisher owns both a morning and an evening newspaper in a market and offers a reduced single rate for using the same ad in both newspapers, generally within a 24-hour period.

Combination discounts are also available when the advertiser buys space in several newspapers owned by the publisher in a number of markets or in multiple newspapers affiliated in a syndicate or newspaper group. Figure 12—20 shows an ad for the Network of City Business Journals. Advertisers can place their messages in business journals in 50 different cities with one media buy through this group.

Comparing Newspaper Rates As with other media, advertisers are interested in comparing the rates of newspapers with different rates and circulation on some common basis. The traditional standard for comparing newspapers has been to compute

Figure 12–20   The Network of City Business Journals Is an Example of a Newspaper Group

their **milline rate,** which is the cost per line of space per million circulation. The formula for this calculation is

$$\text{Milline} = \frac{1,000,000 \times \text{Rate per line}}{\text{Circulation}}$$

Thus, a newspaper with a circulation of 500,000 and a rate of $1.50 per line would have a milline rate of

$$\frac{1,000,000 \times 1.50}{500,000} = \$3.00$$

Since most newspapers have switched away from the agate line- to the column inch-based rate method, the cost per thousand method (CPM) is now used to make cost comparisons among newspapers. The CPM comparison uses the space unit the advertiser is buying (i.e., the particular SAU) in the numerator of the formula to compare newspapers with different circulation bases. For example, a full-page or 6 × FD SAU ad (6 columns wide by full depth [FD]—see Figure 12–19) in Newspaper A may cost $5,400 and $3,300 in Newspaper B. If the circulations of the two papers are 165,000 and 116,000, respectively, the CPM for this particular SAU in each paper would be calculated as follows:

$$\text{Newspaper A} = \frac{\$5,400 \times 1,000}{165,000} = \$32.73$$

$$\text{Newspaper B} = \frac{\$3,300 \times 1,000}{116,000} = \$28.45$$

The use of the CPM criterion as a comparison basis is more convenient than using the agate line method. It also allows the media planner to make intermedia comparisons between newspapers and other media that could not be done with the milline rate. Thus, the milline rate comparison method is rarely used by media planners in comparing the relative costs of newspapers.

The Future of Newspapers

Newspapers remain the largest advertising medium in terms of total advertising volume, despite the tremendous growth of the broadcast media. Newspapers' major strength lies in their role as a medium that can be used effectively by local advertisers on a continual basis. It is unlikely that newspapers' importance as a local advertising medium will change in the near future. However, newspapers have fallen behind television and magazines as a medium for national advertisers; newspapers accounted for only 6 percent of the $60 billion spent by national advertisers in 1987.

Newspapers' battle to increase their share of national advertising volume has proven to be very difficult. Not only is there the problem of reproduction quality and rate differentials, but newspapers are also facing competition from other media that are competing for the national advertisers' budgets in specific market areas.

The newspaper industry is particularly concerned about the "bypass," or loss of advertisers to direct marketing and telemarketing.[33] Many consumer products companies are making more use of direct marketing methods. Some firms, such as Kimberly-Clark, are developing large data bases that identify their best prospects and targeting telephone and direct mail promotions directly to them. Much of the money spent on these programs is coming at the expense of newspaper advertising budgets.

The intermedia battle that newspapers find themselves involved in is no longer limited to national advertising. Local radio and television stations (particularly cable television stations), as well as the expanded market for yellow pages advertising, are aggressively pursuing local advertisers.

The growth of newspapers as an advertising medium may also be limited by a decline in the popularity of the medium itself. Newspaper readership has been on a steady decline for the past two decades. In 1970 nearly 70 percent of the adult population read a newspaper on the average weekday. By 1987 this percentage had fallen to only 63 percent. Additionally, the percentage of U.S. households receiving a daily newspaper declined from 77 percent in 1980 to only 68 percent in 1988.

The decline in newspaper readership can be attributed to several factors including the fast-paced, time-poor lifestyle of the modern, dual-income household along with the continued growth and popularity of television. However, the trend may continue, as the current generation of young people in this country is even more dependent on the broadcast media and less likely to read a newspaper on a regular basis.

The newspaper industry faces a serious challenge in the future if it is to increase circulation and readership and attract advertising revenue. This means making newspapers more interesting and appealing to readers as well as expanding services and efforts to advertisers to encourage them to continue using the newspaper as an advertising medium.

Summary

Magazines and newspapers, the two major forms of print media, play an important role in the media plans and strategy of many advertisers. Magazines are a very selective medium and are very valuable to the advertiser for reaching specific types of customers and market segments. There are three broad categories or classes of magazines including consumer, farm, and business publications. Each of these three categories can be further classified according to the editorial content and audience appeal of the publication.

In addition to their high selectivity, the advantages of magazines include their excellent reproduction quality, long life, prestige, flexibility, and readers' high receptivity to magazine advertising. Disadvantages of magazines include their high cost, limited reach and frequency, the long lead time they require, and the advertising clutter in most publications.

Two of the most important considerations of the media planner in deciding whether to use a magazine are size and characteristics of the audience reached by the publication. Media buyers consider the circulation of a publication as well as its total readership and compare these figures against the audience the advertiser is attempting to reach. Circulation figures are used as the basis for a magazine's advertising space rate structure. For most major publications these figures are audited by a circulation verification service such as the Audit Bureau of Circulations.

Advertising space rates in magazines vary according to a number of factors such as the size of the ad, position in the publication, particular editions purchased, the use of color, and the number and frequency of insertions. Rate comparisons for magazines are made on the basis of the cost per thousand criterion, although other factors such as the editorial content of the publication and its ability to reach specific target audiences must also be considered.

Newspapers represent the largest advertising medium in terms of total volume, with over a fourth of all advertising dollars going to them. Newspapers are an especially important medium to local advertisers, particularly retailers. Newspapers are also used by national advertisers, with automobile, tobacco, and airline companies being among the heaviest users.

Newspapers are a broad-based medium and reach a large cross section of households in a particular area. In addition to their broad reach or penetration, newspapers have other advantages including flexibility, geographic selectivity, reader involvement, and special services they provide. Drawbacks of newspapers include their lack of high-quality ad reproduction, short life span, clutter, and lack of class selectivity.

The rates newspapers charge national advertisers are, on the average, 66 percent higher than those paid by a local advertiser. This differential rate structure for national versus local advertisers has been the source of considerable controversy, and some papers are beginning to reduce the rates paid by national advertisers. The buying and selling of newspaper ad space have undergone significant changes in recent years in order to simplify the use of the medium by national advertisers.

Trends toward market segmentation and regional marketing are prompting many advertisers to make more use of newspapers and magazines. However, both magazines and newspapers are facing increasing competition from other media such as radio, cable television stations, and direct marketing. Rising costs are presenting problems for magazines, whereas declining readership is a problem for newspapers.

Key Terms

High-involvement media
Selectivity
Gatefolds
Bleed pages
Split runs
Primary circulation
Controlled-circulation basis
Pass-along readership
Total audience/readership
Magazine networks
Selective binding
Inkjet imaging
Display advertising

Classified advertising
Preprinted inserts
City zone
Retail trading zone
Agate line
Standard advertising units (SAUs)
Flat rates
Open-rate structure
Run of paper (ROP)
Preferred position rate
Combination rates
Milline rate

Discussion Questions

1. Discuss how the role of magazines and newspapers as advertising media differs from that of television and radio.
2. Discuss the specific advantages and limitations of magazines.
3. What are some of the ways advertisers can increase the selectivity of their magazine ads?
4. What are the differences between magazine circulation and total audience or readership? If you were a media buyer, which of the two would you use in making your magazine buys?
5. If you were buying magazine advertising space for a golf club manufacturer, what factors would you take into account? Would your magazine selections be limited to golfing publications? Why or why not?
6. What are the specific advantages and disadvantages of newspapers as an advertising medium?
7. Do you agree with the policy of most newspapers whereby national advertisers are charged a higher rate than local advertisers? Support your position.
8. How might newspapers attract more business from national advertisers, aside from reducing the rate differential?
9. Discuss how advertisers deal with the clutter problem in both magazines and newspapers.
10. Discuss the future of both newspapers and magazines as advertising media.

Notes

1. Linda Williams, "You Can Tell—and Sell—a Magazine By Its Cover," *Los Angeles Times,* January 29, 1989, pt. IV, pp. 1, 6.
2. Betsy Sharkey, "Magazines Catch Celebrity Fever," *Adweek Special Report—Magazine World 1989,* February 13, 1989, pp. 4–5.
3. Amy Alson, "Making Ends Meet," *Marketing & Media Decisions,* August 1988, pp. 67–75.
4. Fred Pfaff, "Trading Up," *Marketing & Media Decisions,* August 1988, pp. 77–83.
5. Herbert E. Krugman, "The Measurement of Advertising Involvement," *Public Opinion Quarterly* 30 (Winter 1966/67), pp. 583–96.
6. From "Total U.S. Advertising Volume" (Newspaper Advertising Bureau, New York, N.Y., June 1989).
7. Pfaff, "Trading Up."
8. Jerry Schlosberg, "The Glittering City Magazines," *American Demographics,* July 1986, pp. 22–25.
9. *Magazine Audiences 2* (New York: Mediamark Research Inc., Spring 1982).
10. Ibid.
11. Steve Fajen, "Numbers Aren't Everything," *Media Decisions* 10 (June 1975), pp. 65–69.
12. "Study of Media Involvement," *Audits & Surveys,* November 1986.
13. Alson, "Making Ends Meet."
14. "Newsletter of Research," *Magazine Publishers Association,* no. 53 (November 1986).
15. Magazine Publishers Association, 1987.
16. Garfield Ricketts, "The ABCs of ABC Statements," *Marketing & Media Decisions,* November 1988, p. 84.
17. Study cited in Jim Surmanek, *Media Planning: A Practical Guide* (Lincolnwood, Ill.: Crain Books, 1985).
18. Cahners Publishing Company, "How Advertising Readership Is Influenced By Ad Size," (Cahners Advertising Research Report no. 110.1).
19. McGraw-Hill Research, "Larger Advertisements Get Higher Readership," LAP Report no. 3102.
20. McGraw-Hill Research, "Effect of Size, Color and Position Number of Responses to Recruitment Advertising," LAP Report no. 3116.
21. John Motavolli, "Toward An Age of Customized Magazines," *Adweek Special Report—Magazine World 1989,* February 13, 1989, pp. 36–37.

22. From "Total U.S. Advertising Volume," (Newspaper Advertising Bureau, New York, N.Y., June 1989).

23. "Key Facts 1988: Newspapers, Consumers, Advertising," (Newspaper Advertising Bureau, New York, N.Y., 1988).

24. Patrick Reilly, "Publishers Proudly Trot Out Their Sunday Best," *Advertising Age,* March 6, 1989, pp. S-1, 2.

25. Tamara Goldman, "Big Spenders Develop Newspaper Strategies," *Marketing Communications,* June 1988, pp. 24–29.

26. Survey by Newspaper Advertising Bureau, October 1988.

27. From a study reported in "Key Facts about Newspapers and Advertising" (Newspaper Advertising Bureau, New York: New York, 1982).

28. "Mom Still Reads Dailies for Food Ads: Burgoyne," *Advertising Age,* December 8, 1969, p. 32.

29. Ira Teinowitz, "Advertisers Harbor Island Ad Skepticism," *Advertising Age,* July 18, 1988, p. S-4.

30. "Newspapers Cut National Ad Rate," *Advertising Age,* June 8, 1987, p. 1.

31. Survey reported in *NewsInc.,* May/June 1989, p. 81.

32. Amy Alson, "The Search for National Ad Dollars," *Marketing & Media Decisions,* February 1989, pp. 29–31.

33. Thomas B. Rosenstiel, "Newspapers Fear Being Bypassed by Advertisers," *Los Angeles Times,* April 27, 1989, pt. IV, p.1.

13

Support Media and Direct Marketing

CHAPTER OBJECTIVES

1. To introduce the various support media available to the marketer in developing a promotional program

2. To introduce the area of direct marketing and direct marketing media

3. To provide an understanding of the advantages and disadvantages of support media and direct marketing

4. To illustrate some of the sources of information available on support media and direct marketing

A New Breed of Movie Commercials

A commercial in the middle of a movie? Yes, it was pulled off by Adidas in the 1988 film *Johnny Be Good,* and the viewers did not mind. How could they not mind seeing a commercial in the middle of a movie, you ask? The answer is what the advertising and promotions director for Adidas called "a dream of promotion."

In the film former Chicago Bears quarterback Jim McMahon actually appears in a commercial that becomes part of the movie script. So while the commercial is actually being seen by all of those in the audience, it is not perceived as a commercial at all but rather as part of the movie. The movie is about a young football star (Anthony Michael Hall) who gets to meet the pro player on the set of an Adidas commercial when taken there by his agent. The agent tells Johnny that "if he plays his cards right, he could be the Adidas man someday."

The innovative use of the Adidas commercial was the idea of Angelo Anastasio, the advertising and promotions director for Adidas, who heard that the movie needed a big-name football star but could not afford to pay the going rate of $200,000 for an appearance. Anastasio suggested the use of Adidas spokesperson McMahon for free if the scene with the commercial was worked in. It was, and the rest is history. The filmmakers saved approximately $200,000 and got their star. Adidas saved somewhere between $50,000 and $100,000—the price of a product placement—and both parties were happy. And the viewers probably never knew![1]

Introduction

The preceding story from *The Wall Street Journal* is just one example of the increasing number of alternative media that are becoming available to the marketer. Advertisements seem to be popping up everywhere—in places you never expect them to be and in situations like the one above in which you may not even realize that you are seeing one.

In this chapter we will review a number of support media—some of which are very new to the marketplace, others that have been around for quite some time—discussing the relative advantages and disadvantages, cost information, and audience measurement of each. We refer to these media as **support media** owing to the fact that for large advertisers—particularly national advertisers—the media reviewed in the previous chapters dominate their media strategies. Support media are used to reach those persons in the target market that these media may not have reached and to reinforce, or support, the message that has been communicated therein.

In addition to these support media, we will review the role of direct marketing. As you will see, direct marketing is a rapidly evolving area of marketing considered by many to be a field all of its own. Because direct marketing employs a number of media that are used to communicate the product/service offering to the potential buyers, we have included it in this text as a form of support media.

Having read this chapter, you may be surprised at just how many different ways there are to deliver the message and how often you are exposed to them. Let us begin our discussion with some of the more established, and perhaps more commonly known, alternatives.

Out-of-Home Media

Out-of-home advertising will be used here to refer to a variety of advertising forms including outdoor (billboards and signs), transit (both inside and outside the vehicle), skywriting, and a variety of other media. While outdoor advertising no doubt is one of the more commonly employed media—as shown in Figure 13–1—you will see that the others have also been increasing in use.

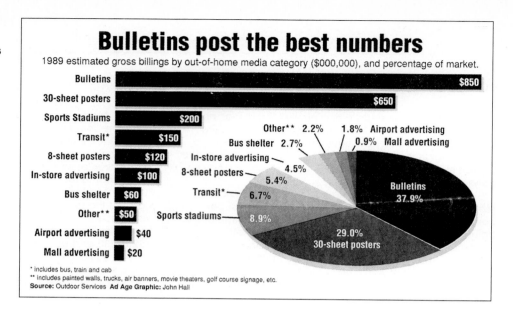

Bulletins post the best numbers

1989 estimated gross billings by out-of-home media category ($000,000), and percentage of market.

Bulletins	$850
30-sheet posters	$650
Sports Stadiums	$200
Transit*	$150
8-sheet posters	$120
In-store advertising	$100
Bus shelter	$60
Other**	$50
Airport advertising	$40
Mall advertising	$20

Other** 2.2%   1.8% Airport advertising
Bus shelter 2.7%   0.9% Mall advertising
In-store advertising 4.5%
8-sheet posters 5.4%
Transit* 6.7%
Sports stadiums 8.9%
Bulletins 37.9%
29.0% 30-sheet posters

* includes bus, train and cab
** includes painted walls, trucks, air banners, movie theaters, golf course signage, etc.
Source: Outdoor Services **Ad Age Graphic:** John Hall

Outdoor Advertising

It is believed that outdoor advertising has been in existence since the days of cave dwellers, and it is a known fact that both the Egyptians and Greeks employed this form of communication as early as 5,000 years ago. Outdoor certainly is one of the more pervasive communication forms—particularly if you live in an urban or suburban area.

Even though outdoor accounts for only about 1 percent of all advertising expenditures, and the number of billboards has decreased, it has been a steadily growing medium in terms of dollars billed. In 1982, approximately $888 million were spent in this area, whereas in 1988 this figure had risen to an estimated $1.4 billion.[2] Much of this continued growth can be attributed to the long-time users such as tobacco and spirits advertisers, but a number of new product categories have also increased expenditures in outdoor. For example, the increase in the number of females in the work force has led to more advertising of products targeted to this segment, whereas travel companies, entertainment and amusement attractions, insurance companies, and automotive companies have also seemingly "discovered" this medium, as demonstrated in Table 13—1.

A major reason for the continued success of outdoor is the result of the ability of this medium to remain innovative through technology. As can be seen in Figure 13—2, billboards no longer are limited to standard two-dimensional boards, as three-dimensional forms and extensions are now utilized to attract attention. In addition, electronic billboards and inflatables, like the one shown in Figure 13—3 that was used to promote the movie *King Kong,* have also opened new markets. In fact, if you think about it for a moment, you probably have been exposed to either sign boards or electronic billboards at sports stadiums, in supermarkets, in the campus bookstore and dining halls, in shopping malls, on the freeways, or on the sides of buildings from skyscrapers in New York City to Mailpouch Tobacco signs on the sides of barns in the Midwest. There should be little doubt that this is truly a pervasive medium.

At the same time, outdoor is not without its critics. Ever since President Lyndon Johnson's wife, Lady Bird, instigated a campaign to rid the interstate highways of billboard advertising—the Highway Beautification Act of 1965—there has been a controversy regarding its use. A number of cities and states have passed, or currently have pending, legislation limiting the use of this advertising form, considering it unsightly and obtrusive. In addition, a study conducted by the University of Michigan Survey Research Center showed that as many as 19 percent of those polled favored doing away with outdoor advertising, and 64.5 percent favored "reasonable" regulation.[3]

Table 13-1   1988 Outdoor Spending by Category

Category	Total Amount Spent (000)
Cigarettes, tobacco, and accessories	$358,874.6
Retail	163,513.8
Business and consumer services	127,481.9
Automotive, auto accessories/equipment	116,553.0
Beer/wine/liquor	112,617.3
Travel, hotels, and resorts	109,251.7
Publishing and media	95,373.0
Entertainment and amusements	88,643.5
Insurance and real estate	66,551.7
Food and food products	26,475.5
Drugs and remedies	23,552.0
Confectionary, snacks, and soft drinks	14,436.7
Apparel, footwear, and accessories	13,832.4
Mail order	10,405.8
Gasoline lubricants and fuel	9,262.3
Toiletries and cosmetics	7,244.9
Jewelry, optical goods, cameras	4,456.5
Computers/office equipment and stationery	4,442.3
Horticulture and farming	4,209.7
Building materials, equipment, and fixtures	3,413.0
Electronic entertainment, equipment, and supplies	2,575.9
Industrial materials	2,098.6
Soaps, cleaners, and polishes	1976.3
Household furnishing, supplies, and materials	1,901.6
Household equipment and supplies	1,313.4
Business propositions and employment recruitment	810.7
Sporting goods, toys, and games	768.3
Freight, industrial, and agricultural development	453.6
Pets, pet foods, supplies, and organizations	353.6
Airplanes, aviation equipment	157.3
Miscellaneous	43,666.8

Source: Institute of Outdoor Advertising, New York, 1989.

In addition, media buyers have not completely adopted the medium, partially because of image problems and because of the belief that outdoor is difficult to buy. (Approximately 80 percent of outdoor advertising is purchased by local merchants and companies.) Let us examine some of the advantages and disadvantages of the medium in more detail.

Figure 13-2   Outdoor Advertising Goes Beyond Two Dimensions

Figure 13–3   Inflatables Bring New Meaning to Outdoor Advertising

Advantages and Disadvantages of Outdoor   Outdoor offers the advertiser a number of advantages, including:

1. *Wide coverage of local markets* With proper placement a broad base of exposure is possible in local markets, with both day and night presence. A 100 GRP **showing** (the percentage of duplicated audience exposed to an outdoor poster daily) could yield possible exposure to an equivalent of 100 percent of the marketplace on a daily basis, or the equivalent of 3,000 GRPs over a month. This level of coverage is likely to yield high levels of reach.
2. *Frequency* Because purchase cycles are typically for 30-day periods, those persons reached are usually exposed a number of times, resulting in high levels of frequency.
3. *Geographic flexibility* Outdoor can provide a great deal of flexibility, given possibilities of placement along highways, near store locations, or via mobile billboards—almost anywhere that laws permit. Local, regional, or even national markets may be covered.
4. *Creativity* As shown in Figures 13–2 and 13–3, outdoor ads can be very creative and, as a result, attract attention. The use of large print, colors, and other elements allows for a high degree of creativity.
5. *Ability to create awareness* Because of its impact (and the requirement of a simple message), outdoor can lead to a high level of awareness.

At the same time, however, there are some limitations to outdoor, many of which are related to the advantages cited earlier:

1. *Waste circulation* While it is possible to reach very specific audiences, in many cases the purchase of outdoor will result in a high degree of waste circulation. It is not likely that all persons driving by a billboard or all persons within an area are likely to be part of the target market.

Table 13—2   **Companies Using the New Point-of-Purchase Media**

Company	Media Used
Thomas J. Lipton	Ads on supermarket aisle directories (Aisle Vision)
Campbell Soup	Interactive video kiosks
Kraft, Inc.	Do-it-yourself checkout with computerized special promotions and deals (Check Robot)
Procter & Gamble	In-store radio ads; Aisle Vision; Check Robot
Lever Brothers	Shopping cart ads (Actmedia)

Source: Adapted from David Kalish, "Supermarket Sweepstakes," *Marketing & Media Decisions*, November 1988, pp. 33–38.

2. *Limited message capabilities* Because of the speed with which most persons pass by outdoor ads, exposure time is limited. As a result, messages are limited to a few words and/or an illustration. Lengthy appeals are not possible.

3. *Wearout* Because of the high level of frequency of exposures mentioned earlier, outdoor may also lead to a quick wearout. Because peoples' daily routines do not vary much, they are likely to see the same ad numerous times and get tired of seeing it.

4. *Cost* Because of the decreasing signage available, and the higher cost associated with inflatables, the cost of outdoor advertising is high in both an absolute and a relative sense.

5. *Measurement problems* One of the more difficult problems regarding outdoor advertising lies in the accuracy of measuring reach, frequency, and other effects. (As will be seen in the measurement discussion, this problem is currently being addressed, though it has not been resolved.)

In sum, outdoor advertising has both advantages and disadvantages for the marketer. At the same time, some of these problems may not be inherent in some of the other forms of outdoor advertising. As such, they may offer alternatives for consideration. A brief discussion of some of these alternatives follows.

Additional Outdoor Media   A variety of other forms of outdoor advertising are also available. As you read about these, keep in mind the advantages and disadvantages of outdoor in general mentioned earlier and consider whether these alternatives have the same advantages and/or provide a possible solution to the disadvantages.

Aerial advertising   Airplanes pulling banners, skywriting (in letters as high as 1,200 feet), and blimps all constitute another form of outdoor advertising, **aerial advertising,** available to the marketer. Generally these media are not expensive in absolute terms and can be useful for reaching specific target markets. For example, Coppertone has often made use of skywriting over the beach areas to promote its tanning lotions, Gallo used skywriting to promote its wine coolers (Bartles & Jaymes), whereas local advertisers have promoted special events, sales, and the like.

Rolling boards   Another outdoor medium that is being successfully employed is that of **rolling boards**—one example of which is discussed in Promotional Perspective 13–1. Companies have painted Volkswagen Beetles with advertisements called Beetleboards, and others have painted trucks and vans. Still others have advertised on small billboards, mounted them on trailers, and driven around and/or parked in the geographic areas being targeted.

Point-of-purchase media   Advertisers are spending billions of dollars to promote their products in supermarkets and other types of stores with media beyond those typically used, such as displays, banners, and shelf signs. These point-of-purchase materials now include over 20 different types of media including video displays on shopping carts,

Figure 13−4 Campbell Soup Employs a Variety of Advertising Media

kiosks that provide recipes and coupons at the ends of counters and at cash registers, LED (light-emitting diode) boards and ads that broadcast over in-house screens. Spending on these new point-of-purchase media has increased 14 percent from 1987 to 1988, totaling over $13.4 billion.[4]

Much of the attraction of the point-of-purchase media is based on figures provided by the Point of Purchase Advertising Institute (POPAI) that state that approximately two thirds of consumers' purchases are made in the store, with some impulse categories demonstrating an 80 percent rate.[5] As a result, many advertisers have decided to spend more of their dollars closer to the place where decisions are made, as is reflected in the examples provided in Table 13–2.

Miscellaneous outdoor media Advertisements on parking meters, automatic teller machines, trash cans, ski lift poles, and even restroom walls have all added to the pervasiveness of this medium. Figure 13–4 shows an example of how Campbell Soup uses ads on chairlift poles at ski resorts to reach potential customers. The next time you are out, take a few moments to observe just how many different forms of outdoor advertising you are exposed to. We are sure you will be surprised!

Audience Measurement in Outdoor Advertising A number of sources of audience measurement are available to someone considering the use of outdoor advertising:

* Simmons Market Research Bureau conducts research annually for the Institute of Outdoor Advertising, providing demographic data, exposures, and the like.
* Audience Measurement by Market for Outdoor (AMMO) are audience estimates provided by Marketmath, Inc. for outdoor showings in over 500 different markets. Published annually, the reports are based on a series of local market travel studies and circulation audits and provide demographic characteristics of audiences.
* The Institute of Outdoor Advertising is a trade organization of the outdoor advertising industry. This organization gathers cost data and statistical information for outdoor advertising space purchases.
* The Point of Purchase Advertising Institute is a trade organization of point-of-purchase advertisers collecting statistical and other market information on point-of-purchasing advertising.

Promotional Perspective **13—1**

Rolling Boards Provide a Unique Advertising Medium

Within the past few years at least three new companies have started to market a new advertising medium that stretches polyvinyl chloride material over an aluminum frame on the side of tractor trailer trucks. The signage, of course, carries someone's advertising message. Who would see an ad on the side of a moving truck, you ask? So did 3M Corporation. What they found out was interesting, to say the least.

Ads on over-the-road trucks are estimated to generate 101 visual impressions per mile, or 10.1 million impressions per 100,000 yearly miles. Local trucks do even better, generating 16 million visual impressions per 100,000 yearly miles.

With so many impressions, you would almost have to assume that this form of advertising is effective. Unfortunately, this may not necessarily be the case. While the agency for Hiram Walker's Royal Canadian brand notes that follow-up surveys indicated that brand recognition increased 314 percent through the use of this medium, others are skeptical. Ford Motor Company is one of these skeptics. When Ford used 1,552 mobile boards in 10 test markets to introduce the Ford Tiempo, their objective was to get 20 to 30 percent awareness. Follow-up surveys indicated that the results achieved somewhere in the range of 4 to 10 percent—far less than sought.

Source: "Rolling Boards Shift into Gear," *Advertising Age,* December 12, 1985, p. 17.

- The Outdoor Advertising Association of America (OAAA) is the primary trade association of the industry, providing members assistance in respect to research, creative ideas, and more effective use of the medium.
- The Media Market Guide (MMG) provides physical dimensions, population characteristics, and media opportunities for the top 100 media markets.
- The Traffic Audit Bureau (TAB) is the auditing arm of the industry. TAB conducts traffic counts upon which the published rates are based.
- The Traffic Audit Bureau for Media Measurement is a new organization that will be functioning in 1990 to provide outdoor advertisers with data regarding exposures to a variety of outdoor media including bus shelters, aerial banners, in-store media, billboards, and the like. This organization was formed in response to complaints that the current methodologies employed might be outdated and overstating the reach provided by these media.

One of the weaknesses associated with outdoor advertising was stated as that of audience measurement. Space rates have typically been published on the basis of the number of desired showings, as shown in Table 13–3. For example, a 100 showing would theoretically provide coverage to the entire market. In Birmingham, Alabama, this would mean coverage of approximately 915,700 persons for a monthly rate of $23,361. Along with the rate information provided, the companies offering outdoor billboards will also provide reach and frequency estimates associated with the showings. Unfortunately, there is no valid way to determine whether the showings promised are actually performing as they are said to be. As such the buyer is somewhat at the mercy of the selling agent when making a purchase.

Because of criticism evolving about this problem, the industry has implemented a gross ratings point system similar to that employed in the television industry. While the system has helped to some degree, problems associated with the use of GRPs discussed earlier in this text are also present here and as such limit the usefulness of this information.

Transit Advertising

A second form of out-of-home advertising is **transit advertising.** While similar to outdoor in the sense that billboards and electronic messages may be employed, transit is targeted to the millions of people who are exposed to commercial transportation facil-

Table 13–3 Posting Space Rates and Allotments

Markets	Population (000)	100 GRP Showing Allotment Unilluminated	Illuminated	Total	Monthly Rate	50 GRP Showing Allotment Unilluminated	Illuminated	Total	Monthly Rate	25 GRP Showing Allotment Unilluminated	Illuminated	Total	Monthly Rate	10 GRP Showing Allotment Unilluminated	Illuminated	Total	Monthly Rate
Alabama																	
Birmingham Metro	915.7	16	52	68	$23,361	8	26	34	$11,811	4	13	17	$5,957	2	5	7	$2,408
Gadsden Metro	319.7	28	16	44	11,720	14	8	22	5,917	7	4	11	2,987	3	2	5	1,376
Huntsville Metro	446.2	20	28	48	15,299	10	14	24	7,732	5	7	12	3,900	2	3	5	1,636
The Shoals Metro	245.5	12	6	18	4,846	6	3	9	2,446	3	2	5	1,409	1	1	2	586
Tuscaloosa Metro	335.3	24	8	32	8,127	12	4	16	4,098	6	2	8	2,069	2	1	3	792
California/north																	
N. California Metro Plex	6,803.3	32	270	302	152,748	16	135	151	77,032	9	68	77	39,578	3	27	30	15,483
Sacramento Metro	1,217.5	10	50	60	29,899	5	25	30	15,080	3	13	16	8,082	1	5	6	3,047
San Francisco/Oakland/ San Jose Metro	5,585.8	22	220	242	122,850	11	110	121	61,952	6	55	61	31,496	2	22	24	12,437
California/south																	
Los Angeles Metro	11,837.9	52	448	500	248,373	26	224	250	125,256	13	112	125	63,269	5	44	49	24,813
San Diego Metro	2,085.3	12	68	80	39,295	6	34	40	19,819	3	17	20	10,010	1	7	8	4,029
S. California Metro Plex	13,923.2	64	516	580	287,667	32	258	290	145,075	16	129	145	73,279	6	51	57	28,842
Ventura/Oxnard Metro	596.9	8	6	14	6,944	4	3	7	3,490	2	2	4	2,033	1	1	2	1,026
Connecticut																	
Hartford Metro	611.0	20	28	48	17,527	10	14	24	10,634	5	7	12	5,477	2	3	5	2,284
Florida																	
Sarasota/Bradenton Metro	425.2	0	10	10	3,499	0	5	5	1,782	0	3	3	1,079	0	1	1	360
Tampa/St. Petersburg/ Clearwater	1,870.0	6	144	150	51,771	3	72	75	26,361	2	37	39	13,777	0	14	14	5,033
Georgia																	
Atlanta Metro	2,320.0	24	96	120	48,370	12	48	60	24,669	6	24	30	12,433	2	10	12	5,036
Brunswick/Hinesville/St. Marys	128.2	6	6	12	2,675	3	3	6	1,351	2	2	4	909	1	1	2	455
Savannah Metro	234.1	12	14	26	6,806	6	7	13	3,432	3	4	7	1,888	1	1	2	524
Illinois																	
Chicago Metro	6,353.0	44	284	328	161,232	22	142	164	81,294	11	71	82	41,062	4	28	32	16,076
Maryland																	
Baltimore Metro	1,540.0	28	108	136	53,284	14	54	68	26,923	7	27	34	13,594	3	11	14	5,581
New York																	
Rochester Metro	974.0	72	60	132	41,385	36	30	66	20,869	18	15	33	10,542	7	7	14	4,555
Ohio																	
Canton Metro	378.8	8	32	40	13,882	4	16	20	7,002	2	8	10	3,540	1	3	4	1,392
Cincinnati Metro	1,104.4	4	80	84	38,935	2	40	42	19,648	1	20	21	9,914	0	8	8	3,837
Cleveland Metro Plex	2,658.8	20	192	212	96,731	10	96	106	48,817	5	48	53	24,629	2	19	21	9,756
Pennsylvania																	
New Castle Metro	234.0	20	22	42	11,593	10	11	21	5,854	5	6	11	3,122	2	2	4	1,116
Pittsburgh Metro	2,500.0	74	126	200	80,405	37	63	100	40,598	18	32	50	20,575	7	13	20	8,261
Scranton/Wilkes-Barre	643.2	27	57	84	29,728	13	29	42	15,628	6	15	21	8,251	1	2	3	1,323
Texas																	
Austin Metro	581.1	12	32	44	13,332	6	16	22	6,726	3	8	11	3,393	1	3	4	1,244
Dallas/Ft. Worth Metro*	3,112.4	24	176	200	63,416	12	88	100	31,996	6	44	50	16,142	3	17	20	6,386
Dallas Metro*	2,026.9	16	112	128	40,512	8	56	64	20,440	4	28	32	10,312	2	11	13	4,145
Ft. Worth Metro*	1,085.5	8	64	72	22,904	4	32	36	11,556	2	16	18	5,830	1	6	7	2,241
Houston Metro	3,564.2	24	212	236	75,332	12	106	118	38,008	6	53	59	19,175	2	21	23	7,515
San Antonio Metro	1,106.9	0	72	72	23,832	0	36	36	12,024	0	18	18	6,066	0	7	7	2,359
Waco Metro	256.5	22	14	36	7,468	11	7	18	3,759	6	4	10	2,122	2	1	3	619
Wisconsin																	
Milwaukee Metro	1,390.9	30	98	128	54,343	15	49	64	27,429	8	25	33	14,261	3	10	13	5,642

*Liquor control ordinances in market require special alcoholic beverage coverage. See separate rate catalog.

Source: Gannet Outdoor Advertising.

ities, including buses, taxis, commuter trains, elevators, trolleys, airplanes, and sub-ways.

Types of Transit Advertising   There are actually three types, or forms, of transit advertising: (1) **inside cards** (2) **outside posters;** and (3) station, platform, or **terminal posters.** A brief description of each of these follows.

Inside cards   If you have ever ridden a commuter bus, you have probably noticed the cards placed above the seats and luggage area advertising restaurants, television or ra-dio stations, or a myriad of other products and services. A more recent innovation is the use of electronic message boards that carry current advertising information. While these message boards fulfill the same functions as inside cards, the ability to change the message and the visibility provide the advertiser with a more attention-getting me-dium.

A variation on inside transit advertising is shown in Figure 13–5. The airline ticket holder has been shown to be a very effective form of advertising communica-tion. We are sure that if you have ever taken a long trip—or even a short one—on a plane, you have probably read everything in sight. This form of advertising takes ad-vantage of a captive audience as well as a medium that keeps the message in front of the passenger during the time that he or she is holding the ticket—and sometimes that seems like forever!

Outside posters   Various forms of outdoor transit posters are used by advertisers to promote products and services. These posters may appear on the sides, back, and/or roofs of buses, taxis, trains, and subway and trolley cars. Some examples are shown in the ad for Transportation Displays, Inc., a leading outdoor and transit advertising com-pany (Figure 13–6).

Station, platform, and terminal posters   Floor displays, island showcases, electronic signs, and other forms of advertisements that appear in train or subway stations, air-line terminals, and the like, are all forms of transit advertising. As can be seen in Fig-ure 13–7, these advertisements can be very attractive and attention getting.

Advantages and Disadvantages of Transit Advertising   Some of the advan-tages of using transit advertising include:

1. *Exposure* Long length of exposure to an ad is one advantage that is particu-larly true with indoor forms. It is estimated that the average ride on mass transit is approximately 30 to 44 minutes, allowing for plenty of exposure time.[6] Likewise, as was noted in the airline ticket jacket example discussed earlier, the audience is essen-tially a captive one, with nowhere else to go and nothing much to do. As a result they may be more likely to read the ads—and read them more than once.

A second form of exposure provided is that regarding the absolute number of persons exposed. It was estimated that in 1987 approximately 8 million people rode mass bus transportation, providing a very substantial number of potential viewers.[7]

2. *Frequency* Because our daily routines are very standard, those who ride buses, subways, and the like, will be exposed to the advertisements a repeated number of times over the course of the time they are present. Consider the fact that if you rode the same subway to work and back every day, in a one-month period of time you would have the opportunity to see the ad approximately 20 to 40 times.

3. *Timeliness* Many shoppers use mass transit to reach their destinations. An advertisement promoting a product or service at a particular shopping area could re-sult in a very timely communication.

4. *Geographic selectivity* For local advertisers in particular, transit advertising provides an opportunity to reach a very select segment of the population. A purchase of a location in a particular neighborhood or area of the city would lead to exposure to those persons of specific ethnic backgrounds, demographic characteristics, and so on.

Figure 13–5   Airplane Ticket Holders Are Used to Promote a Variety of Products

Figure 13—6 **Outside Transit Posters Are Used on a Variety of Vehicles**

Figure 13—7 **Terminal Posters Can Be Used to Attract Attention**

5. *Cost* Transit advertising tends to be one of the least expensive media in terms of both absolute and relative costs. An advertisement on the side of a bus in Washington, D.C., for example, can be purchased for as low as $110 a month, whereas the estimated cost per thousand of transit advertising in the nation's 22 largest metropolitan areas is only approximately 14 cents.[8]

There are also some disadvantages associated with transit. These include the following.

1. *Image factors* To many advertisers, transit advertising does not carry the image that they would like to use to represent their products or services. Some advertisers may feel that having their firm's name on the side of a bus or on a bus stop bench may not reflect well on the image of the firm.

2. *Reach* While it was earlier stated that an advantage of transit advertising was the ability to provide exposure to a large number of persons, it must be kept in mind that these persons may have certain lifestyles and/or behavioral characteristics that may not be true of the target market as a whole. For example, in rural or suburban areas, mass transit is very limited or nonexistent. As a result the media would not be as effective for reaching these persons as it might be in inner-city and metropolitan areas.

3. *Waste circulation* Once again, while we discussed geographic selectivity as a possible advantage, it must be remembered that not everyone who rides a transportation vehicle or is exposed to transit advertising is a potential customer. For many products that may not have specific geographic segments, this form of advertising will incur a good deal of waste circulation.

Another problem with respect to an inability to target a specific group is related to the routes assigned to buses. For example, the same bus may not run the same route every day. To save wear and tear on the bus, some companies will alternate city routes—with much stop and go—with longer suburban routes to attempt to reduce strain on the vehicle. Thus, if this is the case in your city, a bus that goes downtown one day—and reaches the desired target group—may be in the suburbs the next, where there may be little market potential.

4. *Copy and creative limitations* Because of the nature of transit advertising, the marketer is limited in respect to both the creativity and copy he or she can use. With respect to the former, it may be very difficult to place colorful and attractive advertisements on cards or benches. With respect to the latter, while much copy might be provided on inside cards, on the outside of vehicles like buses and taxis the message will be much more fleeting, and short-copy points will be necessary.

5. *Mood of the audience* If you have ever ridden mass transportation at rush hour, or if you have flown coach recently, little needs to be said about the effects of mood. Sitting or standing on a crowded subway may not be conducive to reading advertising at all, let alone creating the mood that the advertiser would like for you to be in. Likewise, hurrying through an airport, whether crowded or not, may create anxieties that limit the effectiveness of the advertisements placed there.

In summary, transit advertising has its obvious advantages as well as disadvantages, and—as you now know—an advantage for one product or service advertiser may be a disadvantage to another. The point to be made here is that transit advertising can be an effective medium. However, one must understand the strengths and weaknesses associated with this form of advertising in order to use it properly.

Audience Measurement in Transit Advertising As with outdoor advertising, the cost basis for transit is the number of showings. In transit advertising, a 100 showing means that one ad would appear on or in *each vehicle* in the system, whereas a showing of 50 would mean that half of the vehicles would carry the ad. As you can imagine, if you are placing such ads on taxicabs, it may be extremely difficult—if not impossible—to determine who is being exposed to them.

Rate information is available from the sellers of transit advertising, and audience

Figure 13—8   **Examples of Specialty Advertising Items**

information is very limited. As a result, practically the only information that can be used in the purchase of transit ads may not be coming from purely objective sources.

Specialty Advertising

According to the Specialty Advertising Association International, **specialty advertising** is

> an advertising, sales promotion and motivational communications medium which employs useful articles of merchandise imprinted with an advertiser's name message or logo. Unlike premiums, with which they are sometimes confused, these articles (called advertising specialties) are always distributed free—recipients don't have to earn the specialty by making a purchase or contribution.[9]

As can be seen by this description, specialty advertising is often considered both an advertising medium as well as a sales promotions medium. For purposes of our discussion, we will treat it as a supportive advertising medium.

There are over 15,000 different **advertising specialties** items including ballpoint pens, coffee mugs, keytags, calendars, T-shirts, and matchbooks. In addition, such nonconventional specialties such as plant holders, wall plaques, and gloves with the advertiser's name printed on them have also been used to promote a company or its product, as have glassware, trophies, awards, and vinyl products, as shown in Figure 13—8. In fact, advertisers spend over $4 billion per year in specialty advertising items. The growth of this medium (342 percent) during the 1970s makes this the fastest growing of all advertising or sales promotions media.[10]

If you stop reading for a moment and take a look around your desk (or bed or beach blanket), you probably have some specialty advertising item around you. It may be the pen you are using, a matchbook, or even a book cover with the campus bookstore name on it. Specialty items are used for a variety of promotional purposes. They may be used to thank a customer for his or her patronage, to keep the name of the company in front of the person, to introduce new products, or to reinforce the name of an existing company, product, or service. Advertising specialties are also very often used to support other forms of product promotions.

Advantages and Disadvantages of Specialty Advertising

Like any other advertising medium, specialty advertising has both advantages and disadvantages that it offers to the marketer. Some of the advantages include the following.

1. *Selectivity* Because specialty advertising items are generally distributed directly to ones's target customers, the medium offers a high degree of *selectivity*. Selectivity, of course, reduces waste circulation, and the communication is distributed to the desired recipient.

2. *Flexibility* As the variety of specialty items included in Figure 13–8 demonstrates, this medium provides for a high degree of *flexibility*. A message as simple as a logo or as long as is necessary can be distributed through a variety of means. In addition, both small and large companies may employ this medium and are limited seemingly only by their own creativity.

3. *Frequency* Most forms of specialty advertising are designed for *retention*. As a result, items such as key chains, calendars, and pens remain with the potential customer for a long period of time, providing the opportunity for repeat exposures to the advertisng message at no additional cost.

4. *Cost* While the cost of some specialty items may be rather expensive (leather items, etc.), most of them are very inexpensively priced, making them affordable to almost any size organization or firm. With the high number of repeat exposures, on a cost per exposure basis, the relative cost of this advertising medium is even less.

5. *Supplementing other media* One of the major advantages of specialty advertising is its ability to supplement other media. Because of its low cost and repeat exposures the simplest message can act as a reinforcement of the appeal or information provided through other forms. For example, Saab-Scandia of North America presented new car buyers with a series of advertising specialties to support their "dedicated delivery" program promoted through print media. Document organizers, tire gauges, and tape deck cleaning kits were just some of the items used to reinforce the point that Saab wanted its customers to be satisfied.

Disadvantages of specialty advertising include the following.

1. *Image* While most forms of specialty advertising are received as friendly reminders of the store or company name, the firm must be careful in the specialty item chosen. The potential for "cheapening" the company image exists if a very inexpensive or improperly designed advertising form is utilized.

2. *Saturation* With so many firms and organizations now using this advertising medium, the potential exists for saturation of the marketplace. While one might argue that we can always use another ballpoint pen or book of matches, the value to the receiver declines if replacement is too easy, and the likelihood of retention of the item and even notice of the message is reduced. The more unique the specialty, the more value it is likely to have to the receiver.

Audience Measurement in Specialty Advertising

Owing to the nature of the industry, specialty advertising has no established ongoing audience measurement system similar to those discussed with other media. Research has been conducted in an attempt to determine the impact of this medium, however, including the following reports.

A 1982 study by Schreiber and Associates indicated that 39 percent of people receiving advertising specialties could recall the name of the company as long as 6 months after receiving the message, whereas a second study conducted by A. C. Nielsen found that 31 percent of respondents were still using at least one specialty that they had received at least 12 months earlier.[11,12]

A study by Gould/Pace University indicated that the inclusion of a specialty item in a direct-mail piece generated a greater response rate and that dollar purchases per sale were 321 percent greater than mail pieces without such items.[13] Finally, a report by Richard Manville Research, Inc. reported that the average household had almost four calendars and that if they had not been given such items free of charge, two thirds stated that they would purchase one—an indication of the desirability of this particular specialty item.[14]

The trade organization of this field is the Specialty Advertising Association (SAA) International. The SAA assists users in the development and utilization of specialty advertising forms. The organization also provides promotional and public relations support for specialty advertising and disseminates statistical and educational information.

Other Media

In addition to some of the more commonly thought of media, there are numerous other ways to promote products that may not come directly to mind. Some of these are reviewed here.

Advertising in Movie Theaters and on Videotapes

Two methods of delivering the message that are quickly increasing—to the dismay of many—is the use of movie theaters and videotape rentals to promote products and/or services. Commercials shown prior to the film and previews have seemingly replaced cartoons, with both local and national sponsorships. On videotapes, companies have placed ads prior to the movies as well as on the cartons containing the rentals. For example, Pepsi filmed a commercial for use on television that was a take-off on the hit movie *Top Gun*. This same commercial later appeared at the beginning of the videotape.

Advantages of Movie Theater and Videotape Advertising Both of these media provide a number of advantages to the advertiser, including the following.

1. *Exposure* The number of persons attending movies is rapidly on the increase, as is shown in Figure 13–9. At the same time, the number of households using VCRs is also increasing. The result of these growth figures is that there are an increased number of persons likely to be exposed to the ads. In addition, these viewers constitute a "captured audience," who also are known to watch less television than the average.[15]

2. *Mood* Assuming the movie is well liked, the mood can carry over to the product advertised. For example, in the *Top Gun* ad just mentioned, the setting was identical to that in the movie, and a carryover of the mood was very likely.

3. *Cost* The cost of advertising in a theater varies from one setting to the next. However, both in terms of absolute and relative costs per exposure the costs are low.

4. *Recall* Research indicates that approximately 87 percent of viewers can recall the ads that they saw in a movie theater the next day. This compares with an approximately 20 percent recall rate for television.[16]

5. *Clutter* Actually, the *lack* of clutter is another advantage offered by advertising in movie theaters. Most theaters limit the number of ads to only a few, and as long as this remains the rule, less clutter will occur than does in other media.

Figure 13-9 **More People Are Enjoying Movies**

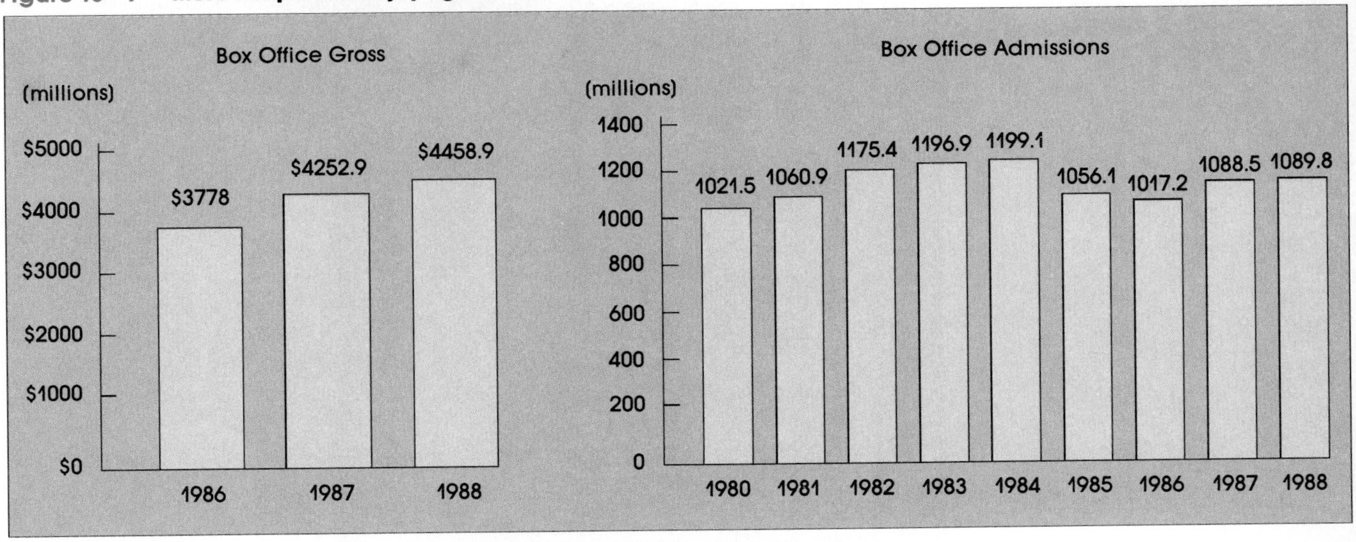

Box Office Gross

(millions)

$5000 —
$4000 — $3778 | $4252.9 | $4458.9
$3000 —
$2000 —
$1000 —
$0 —
     1986   1987   1988

Box Office Admissions

(millions)

1400
1200
1000
800
600
400
200
0

1021.5 | 1060.9 | 1175.4 | 1196.9 | 1199.1 | 1056.1 | 1017.2 | 1088.5 | 1089.8
1980 | 1981 | 1982 | 1983 | 1984 | 1985 | 1986 | 1987 | 1988

Source: *U.S. Economic Review* (New York: Motion Picture Association of America, Inc., 1989), p. 2.

Disadvantages of Movie and Videotape Advertising Some of the disadvantages associated with these advertising media are given below.

1. *Irritation* Perhaps the major disadvantage of this form of advertising is the fact that many people do not wish to see advertising in these media. One study indicated that a high degree of *irritability* may be created by these ads.[17] This dissatisfaction could also carry over to the product itself.

2. *Cost* While the cost of advertising in local theaters has been cited as an advantage because of the low rates charged, ads exposed on a national basis cost as much as $425,000 per minute to reach 25 million viewers.[18] This cost reflects a rate 20 percent higher than an equal exposure on television.

While only two disadvantages of theater advertising have been mentioned, the first of these is indeed a strong one. Many persons feel that because they have paid to see a movie (or rent a videotape) that advertising is an intrusion. In the Michael Belch and Don Sciglimpaglia study, many moviegoers stated that not only would they not buy the product advertised, but they would also consider boycotting it. Given that this is the case, advertisers should be very cautious in their use of this medium. Should the use of movies be desired, a different alternative—placing products in the movies—might be considered as an alternative. Let us discuss this approach.

Product Placements in Movies and Television

At the outset of this chapter, you read a brief report on the effectiveness of promoting a product through the movies. While this form of advertising does not constitute a major segment of the advertising and promotions business of firms, it, nevertheless, is a mode of delivery that has been proven to be effective for some companies. (Note: Like specialty advertising, some persons consider **product placement** as a promotion rather than as an advertising form. This distinction is not a critical one, and we have therefore decided to treat it as a form of advertising.)

A number of companies have paid to have their products used in movies and music videos. For example, Figure 13-10 shows OshKosh used a clever product placement in the movie *Big Top Pee Wee* by dressing an elephant in a pair of its jeans. Essentially, this form of advertising is sort of advertising without an advertising medium in the sense that the realism provided does not lead the audience member to

Figure 13–10 Many Companies Use Movies to Promote Their Products

realize that the product promotion is going on, yet the impact is real. For example, when Reese's Pieces candies were used in the movie *ET*, sales rose 70 percent and were added to the concessions of 800 movie theaters where they had previously not been sold.[19]

Likewise, the move to place products on television programs is also on the increase. In 1988 CBS broke its long-standing tradition of not mentioning brand names in its programs. Companies such as Coca-Cola (a Coke machine on "TV 101") and Pine Sol (a sweepstakes on the soap "All My Children") are just a few of the companies employing product tie-ins.

Advantages of Product Placements A number of advantages of product tie-ins have been suggested.

1. *Exposure* A large number of people see movies each year (over 1 billion admissions in 1988). The average film is estimated to have a life span of three and one-half years (with 75 million exposures), and most, if not all, of these moviegoers are very attentive audience members. Coupling this with the increasing home video rental market, and network and cable television (for example, HBO, Showtime, Movie Channel), the potential for exposure for a product placed in a movie is enormous. In addition, this form of exposure is not subject to zapping—at least not in the theater.

High exposure numbers are also offered for television tie-ins, based on the ratings and (at least in the case of soaps) the possibility to direct the ad to a defined target market.

2. *Frequency* Depending on how the product is used in the movie (or program),

there may be ample opportunity for *repeated exposures* (or even more if you are among the many people who like to watch a program or movie more than once). For example, in promoting Honda scooters, the advertising agency, Dailey and Associates, had the product used in movies as well as in the television program "Knight Rider." In the latter, the scooter was in front of the viewer in a series of different scenes, with total airtime of over five minutes!

3. *Support for other media* In the Honda advertising example just cited, the other media advertising the product included an appeal consistent with that in the television show. Coors has used the character E.T.—from the film of the same name in which Coors had placed their product—to support their public relations efforts by asking people not to drive when drinking. Kimberly-Clark Corporation created a sweepstakes, coupon offer, and TV-based ad around their Huggies Diapers product featured in the movie *Baby Boom*.

4. *Source association* In an earlier chapter in this book we discussed the advantages of source identification. When many potential consumers see their favorite movie star riding a Honda, wearing Adidas, or eating Reese's Pieces, this association may lead to a favorable product image. For example, when the star of the movie *Risky Business* (Tom Cruise) appeared in a pair of Ray-Ban sunglasses, the sales of Ray-Bans immediately increased from 18,000 to over 360,000 units.[20]

5. *Cost* While the cost of placing a product may range from as little as providing free samples to as much as a million dollars, these are extremes. As shown in Table 13–4, the CPM for this form of advertising can be very low, owing to the high volume of exposures that this medium generates. Of course, if the movie or program is seen more than once, the cost goes down again!

6. *Recall* A number of firms have measured the impact of product placements on next-day recall. Results ranged from Johnson's Baby Shampoo registering 20 percent to Kellogg's Corn Flakes registering 67 percent (on the movie *Raising Arizona*). Average recall is approximately 38 percent.[21] Again, you can see that these scores are better than those reported for television viewing.

Disadvantages of Product Placements
Some disadvantages are also associated with product placements.

1. *High absolute cost* While we have just stated that the CPM may be very low for product placement in movies, the absolute cost of placing the product may be very high, precluding some advertisers from its use. For example, in 1987 the cost of placing a product in the movies averaged $7,500.00, with many placements being substantially higher.[22]

2. *Time of exposure* While the method by which Ray-Bans and Reese's candy were exposed to the audience led to an obvious impact, the viewer's noticing the product is not a guarantee. Some product placements are more conspicuous than others and thus have a greater chance of being seen by viewers. However, other placements may not result in a prominent featuring of the product. In such a case, the advertiser

Table 13–4 **CPM for Motion Picture Advertising**

Title of Film	Theater Box Office	Audience[1]	Week in Wide Release	Cost per Thousand[2]
Big	$88,904,983	22,737,847	10	$0.32
Crocodile Dundee II	104,573,161	26,745,054	12	0.28
The Dead Pool	35,149,935	8,989,753	5	0.83
Who Framed Roger Rabbit	113,041,981	28,910,993	8	0.26
Bull Durham	43,575,439	11,144,614	9	0.67

[1] Audience is based on an average ticket price of $3.91 (Motion Picture Association, 1987).
[2] CPM is the cost for reaching 1,000 consumers with an advertisement multiplied by 1,000 divided by the total audience. (The average cost of a product placement is $7,500.)

Source: Creative Film Productions, Burbank, Calif., 1988. Statistics provided by the Motion Picture Association of America, New York, 1987.

runs the risk of not being seen—although it must be remembered that he or she runs the same risk through other forms of media advertising.

3. *Limited appeal* The advertisement of the product in this media form is limited in respect to the appeal that can be made. There is no potential for discussing product benefits or providing detailed information. Rather, appeals are limited to source association, use, and enjoyment. The endorsement of the product is in itself an indirect one, and the flexibility for product demonstration is subject to its use in the film.

4. *Lack of control* In many movies the advertiser has no say over how often and when the product will be shown. Miller beer, for example, found that its placement on the movie *Dragnet* did not work as well as expected, whereas Fabergé developed an entire Christmas campaign around its Brut cologne and its movie placement, only to find that the movie was delayed until February.

5. *Public reaction* Many television viewers and moviegoers are incensed at the idea of placing ads in the programs (movies). These viewers maintain that the barrier between program content and commercials should remain and have vowed to fight future efforts.[23]

Audience Measurement for Product Placements To date, no form of audience measurement other than that available from the providers is available. As a result, the potential advertiser may often have to make a decision based on his or her own creative insights as to potential effectiveness and/or rely on the credibility of the source. At the same time, however, at least one study has demonstrated the potential effectiveness beyond those examples just cited. As noted in a study by Eva Steortz, product placements have an average recall of 38 percent.[24]

Direct Marketing

One of the fastest-growing forms of promotions in terms of dollar expenditures is that of direct marketing. Were you to go back and read a text as recently as the 1970s, you would see that this medium was then referred to as *direct mail*. But as shown in Figure 13–11, direct marketing constitutes much more than just mail, and now direct mail is only the second most popular of the direct-response media after telephones.

In fact, before proceeding any further, it is necessary to make a distinction at this point between **direct marketing** and **direct-marketing media.** As you can see in Figure 13–11, *direct marketing* refers to an aspect of total marketing—that is, it involves marketing research, segmentation, evaluation, and the like, just as our planning model in Chapter 1 did. Likewise, direct marketing makes use of a set of direct-response media, including direct mail, telemarketing, interactive television, and other media. Books on direct marketing are available, and entire courses are taught on the subject. While we consider this form of marketing an extremely important one, for purposes of this text we will consider it as another method for promoting a product. Thus, while we will not devote an entire chapter to this topic, we will give it its justified consideration.

As stated, direct marketing involves much more than the standard practice of direct mail. Direct marketing is now used to refer to "an interactive system of marketing which uses one or more advertising media to effect a measurable response and/or transaction at any location."[25] This new definition demonstrates the broader perspective assumed and reflects the extension of this form of promotion to additional media. There is a reason why direct marketing has caught the attention of marketers and has grown so rapidly as a marketing and promotions tool: Direct marketing requires a *direct response,* and that means sales. It has been estimated that purchases of products and services through direct-response advertising exceeded $34 billion in 1988.[26] The types of firms currently (and that expect to in the future) employing this sales method

Figure 13—11 **Direct Marketing—An Aspect of Total Marketing**

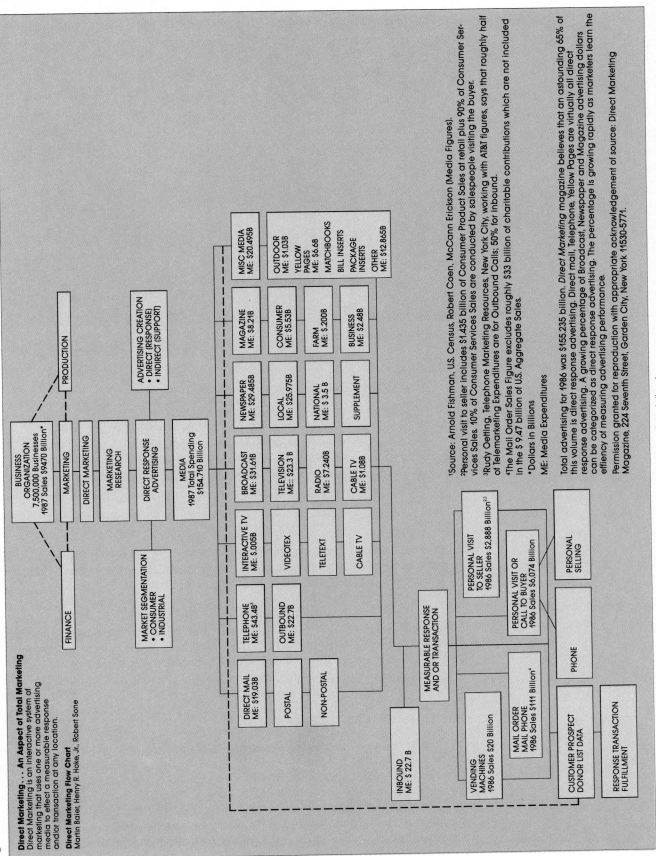

Direct Marketing . . . An Aspect of Total Marketing
Direct Marketing is an interactive system of marketing that uses one or more advertising media to effect a measurable response and/or transaction at any location.

Direct Marketing Flow Chart
Martin Baier, Henry R. Hoke, Jr., Robert Sone

¹Source: Arnold Fishman, U.S. Census, Robert Coen, McCann Erickson (Media Figures).

²Personal visit to seller includes $1,435 billion of Consumer Product Sales at retail plus 90% of Consumer Services Sales. 10% of Consumer Services Sales are conducted by salespeople visiting the buyer.

³Rudy Oetting, Telephone Marketing Resources, New York City, working with AT&T figures, says that roughly half of Telemarketing Expenditures are for Outbound Calls; 50% for inbound.

⁴The Mail Order Sales Figure excludes roughly $33 billion of charitable contributions which are not included in the $ 9.47 billion of U.S. Aggregate Sales.

*Dollars in Billions
ME: Media Expenditures

Total advertising for 1986 was $155.235 billion. *Direct Marketing* magazine believes that an astounding 65% of this volume is direct response advertising. Direct mail, Telephone, Yellow Pages are virtually all direct response advertising. A growing percentage of Broadcast, Newspaper and Magazine advertising dollars can be categorized as direct response advertising. The percentage is growing rapidly as marketers learn the efficiency of measuring advertising performance.

Permission granted for reproduction with appropriate acknowledgement of source: Direct Marketing Magazine, 224 Seventh Street, Garden City, New York 11530-5771.

Source: Direct Marketing (November 1988), p. 27. Reprinted with permission of the Direct Marketing Association, Inc.

Figure 13–12 **Involvement in Direct Marketing by Type of Industry**

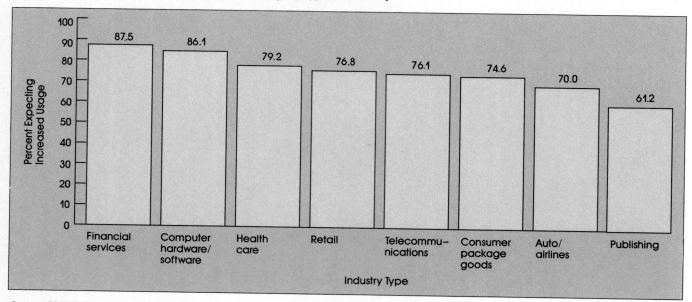

Source: DMA Research Department, Marketing Council, 1986, *DMA 1989 Statistical Fact Book.* Reprinted with permission of the Direct Marketing Association, Inc.

range from consumer products companies such as Wards and Sears to publishing companies to computers to financial services, as shown in Figure 13–12.

In addition to those industries noted above, and numerous others who sell their products through home shopping channels, direct marketing has been employed successfully in business-to-business markets and continues to show strong growth in that area as well.

The Growth of Direct Marketing

Direct marketing has been in existence since the invention of the printing press in the fifteenth century. Ben Franklin was a very successful direct marketer in the early 1700s, and Warren Sears and Montgomery Ward (you may have heard of these guys!) were employing this medium in the 1880s.

The major impetus behind the growth of direct marketing may have been the development and expansion of the U.S. Postal Service, as the catalog was now available to both urban and rural dwellers. The impact of the catalog, as is described in Promotional Perspective 13–2, literally revolutionized America's buying habits.

The catalog alone, of course, does not account for the rapid growth that is reflected in Table 13–5. Much of this growth has been attributed to a number of factors in American society, each of which has led to the increased attractiveness of this medium—both to the buyer and to the seller.

- *The use of consumer credit cards* The adoption of credit cards (there are now an estimated 194 million MasterCard and Visa cards in circulation in the United States and Canada) made it feasible to purchase both low- and high-ticket items through direct-response channels and also assured the seller that he or she would be paid. The combined result of these two factors is that since the 1950s credit card sales have increased to the point where $143.4 billion was purchased via credit cards in 1986. Of course, not all of this was through direct marketing; but needless to say, a high percentage of direct purchases do use this method of payment, and companies such as

Table 13-5   **Estimated Annual Direct Response Advertising Expenditures 1980-1988 (in millions of dollars)**

	1980	1981	1982	1983	1984	1985	1986	1987	1988
Newspapers									
Total	14,794	16,528	17,694	20,582	23,522	25,170	26,990	29,412	31,197
National	1,963	2,259	2,452	2,734	3,081	3,352	3,376	3,494	3,586
Local	12,831	14,269	15,242	17,848	20,441	21,818	23,614	25,918	27,611
Magazines	3,149	3,533	3,710	4,233	4,932	5,155	5,317	5,607	6,072
Farm publications	130	146	148	163	181	186	192	196	196
Television									
Total	11,474	12,847	14,706	16,789	19,900	20,770	22,881	23,904	25,686
Network	5,130	5,575	6,210	7,017	8,526	8,285	8,342	8,500	9,172
Spot	3,319	3,805	4,510	5,096	5,773	6,004	6,570	6,846	7,147
Cable (national)	50	105	195	303	466	637	676	760	942
Local TV	2,967	3,345	3,759	4,323	5,055	5,714	6,514	6,833	7,270
Cable (local)	8	17	32	50	80	130	179	203	254
Radio									
Total	3,702	4,230	4,670	5,210	5,813	6,490	6,949	7,206	7,798
Network	183	230	255	296	316	365	423	413	425
Spot	779	879	923	1,038	1,197	1,335	1,348	1,330	1,418
Local	2,740	3,121	3,492	3,876	4,300	4,790	5,178	5,463	5,955
Direct Mail	7,596	8,944	10,319	11,795	13,800	15,500	17,145	19,111	21,115
Business Publications	1,674	1,841	1,876	1,990	2,270	2,375	2,382	2,458	2,610
Outdoor									
Total	578	650	721	794	872	945	985	1,025	1,064
National	364	419	465	512	562	610	600	615	628
Local	214	231	256	282	310	335	385	410	436
Miscellaneous									
Total	10,453	11,711	12,736	14,294	16,530	18,159	19,299	20,731	22,312
National	5,478	6,154	6,722	7,348	8,586	9,551	9,879	10,533	11,398
Local	4,975	5,557	6,014	6,946	7,944	8,608	9,420	10,198	10,914
Total									
National	29,815	33,890	37,785	42,525	49,690	53,355	56,850	60,625	65,610
Local	23,735	26,540	28,795	33,325	38,130	41,395	45,290	49,025	52,440
Grand total	53,550	60,430	66,580	75,850	87,820	94,750	102,140	109,650	118,050

Source: Robert J. Coen, McCann-Erickson, Inc., 1989. Reprinted with permission of the Direct Marketing Association, Inc.

American Express, Diners Club, MasterCard, and Visa are themselves among some of the heaviest direct advertisers.

• *Direct-marketing syndicates*   Companies specializing in list development, statement inserts, catalogs, and sweepstakes opened many new opportunities to companies that previously had not explored this method of marketing. The number of these companies continues to expand, creating even more new users.

• *The changing structure of American society and the market*   Perhaps one of the major factors contributing to the success of direct marketing is that America is now a land of "money-rich and time-poor" persons.[27] The rapid increase of dual-income families (in 1988 an estimated 56.7 percent of women were in the work force) has meant more income. At the same time, trends toward physical fitness, do-it-yourself, and home entertainment have reduced the time available for shopping and have increased the attractiveness of direct purchases.

• *Technological advances*   The rapid technological advancement of the electronic media (to be discussed later in this chapter) and of computers has made it easier for the consumer to shop and for the marketer to be successful in reaching his or her desired target markets. As of the writing of this text, there were no less than 56 million television homes receiving home shopping programs, and home channel purchases totaled over $2.55 billion per year.[28] By 1992 over 79 million households will have access to a home shopping channel.[29]

• *Miscellaneous factors*   A number of other factors have contributed to the increased effectiveness of direct marketing including changing values, more sophisticated marketing techniques, improved image of the industry, and so on. Without beating

Promotional Perspective 13–2

The Sociocultural Impact of Catalogs

No one has expressed more vividly the sociocultural impact of catalogs than Daniel Boorstin, the Pulitzer Prize winning—historian and Chief Librarian of Congress.

It was not merely facetious to say that many farmers came to live more intimately with the good Big Book of Ward's or Sears, Roebuck than with the Good Book. The farmer kept his Bible in the frigid parlor, but, as Edna Ferber remarked in *Fanny Herself* (1917), her novel of the mail-order business, the mail-order catalogue was kept in the cozy kitchen. That was where the farm family ate, and where they really lived. For many such families, the catalogue probably expressed their most vivid hopes for salvation. It was no accident that pious rural customers without embarrassment called the catalogue "the Farmer's Bible." There was a familiar story of the little boy who was asked by his Sunday School teacher where the Ten Commandments came from, and who unhesitatingly replied that they came from Sears, Roebuck. . . .

Farm children now learned from the new Bible of their con-

sumption community. In rural schoolhouses, children were drilled in reading and spelling from the catalogue. They practiced arithmetic by filling out orders and adding up items. They tried their hand at drawing by copying the catalogue models, and acquired geography by studying the postal-zone maps. In schoolrooms that had no other encyclopedia, a Ward's or Sears catalogue handily served the purpose; it was illustrated, it told you what something was made of and what it was good for, how long it would last, and even what it cost. Many a mother in a household with few children's books pacified her child with the pictures in the catalogue. When the new book arrived, the pictures in the old catalogue were indelibly fixed in the memory of girls who cut them up for paper dolls. . . . The children of rural America thought of the big books from Sears and Ward's as exhaustive catalogues of the material world.

Source: Nat Ross, "A History of Direct Marketing," in *Direct Marketing Fact Book* (Direct Marketing Association, New York, 1985), p. 5. Reprinted with permission of the Direct Marketing Association, Inc.

this to death, suffice it to say that those factors that have contributed to the growth of this direct marketing will also assure its success in the future. The degree of success of those companies discussed in Table 13–6 demonstrates the potential offered by this approach.

Direct-Marketing Media

As shown in Figure 13–11, direct marketing employs a number of media including direct mail, telemarketing, direct-response broadcasting, and print. Each of these media is used to perform specific functions, although they generally follow what direct marketers refer to as a one- or two-step approach.

In the **one-step approach** the medium is used directly to obtain an order. For example, you probably have seen commercials on television for products like wrench sets, work-out equipment, or magazine subscriptions in which the viewer is urged to phone in using an 800 number to place an order immediately. Usually these ads allow for the use of a credit card or C.O.D., as well as a mail-in address. Their goal is to generate an immediate sale when the ad is shown.

The **two-step approach** may actually involve the use of more than one medium. In this strategy the first effort is designed to screen or qualify potential buyers. The second effort has the responsibility of generating the response. For example, many companies use telemarketing to screen on the basis of interest, then follow up to interested parties with more information designed to achieve an order or use personal selling to close the sale.

Direct Mail This direct-marketing medium constitutes what has been commonly referred to as "junk mail"—the unsolicited mail that you find in your mailbox. The amount of advertising dollars spent in direct mail continues to be one of the highest of all advertising media, with an estimated $19.03 billion spent in this area in 1986.[29] While we may often think of direct mail as junk mail, of course, all of it is not restricted to small companies seeking our business in an unsolicited manner. Well-known and -respected companies such as General Electric, American Express, and Citicorp have increased their expenditures in this area, as has Audi.

Table 13—6   **Direct Marketing Success Stories**

The following are just a few of the many examples of success stories from direct marketing.

Spiegel, Inc.
While becoming one of the most successful catalogs in the United States owing to a large degree to a willingness to sell price items to people who needed credit, Spiegel repositioned itself in 1982. The new Spiegel catalog includes a focus on designer clothes and is targeted at working women 25 to 54 years old. A new glossy cover, sections on fashions and the home, and a more defined target market led to a 20 percent increase in sales the first year to an estimated $500 million.

Bloomingdale's
A well-known retail store for many years, Bloomingdale's decided to enter the direct-response business in the late 1970s. The new operation, Bloomingdale's by Mail, has discovered that 60 to 70 percent of its catalog business is coming from areas without Bloomingdale's stores.

Hanover House
Started as a single retail dress shop in Hanover, Pennsylvania, in 1934, Hanover House found its direct-mail sales revenues far exceeding its retail operation by 1946. By 1972 the company was offering household gadgets, novelty items, and garden nursery products. The direct-response business was so successful that in 1977 the original retail shops were closed. In 1977 sales volume was an estimated $30 million, with total catalog circulation at 30 million. By 1983 over 200 million catalogs were mailed, with sales volume in excess of $215 million.

The Sharper Image
Richard Thalheimer parlayed a $100 mail-order ad into a $60 million catalog business in six years by selling fascinating and unusual gift items. The catalog business expanded into a cable business in 1982 and by 1983 reached over 600 cable communities.

Edmund Scientific Company
In 1942 Norman W. Edmund—an amateur photographer—needed a special lens. After locating 10 of the lenses, he placed a $9.00 magazine ad to sell the other 9. By 1983 the company occupied a 78,000 foot facility and distributed 8 million catalogs offering 4,000 science-related items including telescopes, weather monitoring and lab equipment, and science implements. Prices of these products ranged from a few dollars to over $2,000, and total sales exceeded $13 million.

Tobacco Companies
Banned from advertising their products on television in 1971, tobacco companies turned to direct marketing. In 1988 these companies spent over $450 million in this medium—more than magazines and newspapers combined.
Philip Morris USA was able to gain more than a one-point share of the cigarette market (each point is worth $300 million) by using direct marketing for its new Merit brand. R. J. Reynolds has built a data base of over 25 million smokers to target with its direct-marketing efforts.

Packaged-Goods Companies
Both General Foods and Procter & Gamble successfully employ direct marketing. General Foods has a data base of over 20 million households, whereas Procter & Gamble spent $25 million in the United States alone and is now expending its efforts internationally.

Sources: Fact Book on Direct Marketing (New York: New York Direct Marketing Association, 1987). Reprinted with permission of the Direct Marketing Association, Inc.; Jim Cobs, "Action Blends with Image Building," *Advertising Age*, November 9, 1988, p. 78.

While many advertisers would have shied away from the direct-mail medium in the past, fearful of the image that might be created, or harboring the belief that direct mail was a medium useful only for low-cost products, this is no longer the case. As shown in Figure 13—13, Porsche Motor Cars of North America ran a campaign targeted at very upscale buyers in an attempt to sell their most expensive automobile—a car that costs in excess of $50,000. Porsche management stated that the campaign was quite successful.

Keys to the success of direct mail are the **mailing list** from which names are generated and the ability to segment markets. Lists have now become more current and more selective, eliminating waste circulation. Segmentation on the basis of geography (usually through zip codes), demographics, and lifestyles has led to increased effectiveness. In fact, the most commonly employed lists are those individuals who are past purchasers of direct-mail products!

The importance of the list has in itself led to a business of its own. In 1987 there were an estimated 100,000 lists, and many companies have found it profitable to sell

Figure 13–13 **Porsche Used Direct Mail to Market a Very High Priced Item**

The 911/928 S 4 direct mail program.

We are pleased to introduce the 911/928 S 4 Direct Mail Program. A program that's as well engineered as our cars.

Direct Mail is a proven medium for getting high buy rate prospects into dealerships for test drives. Continuation of yearly direct mail activity also allows us to add potential customers to your database. Those potential customers can afford a Porsche and have demographics which make them likely prospects.

The objective of this year's mailing program is to stimulate floor traffic on the 911 or the 928 S 4. At the outset, you determine which vehicle you would like to select for the direct mail program.

The mailings have been developed to emphasize performance and heritage by utilizing the 911 and 928 S 4 inserts.

This mail program has been specifically designed to:

- Draw high buy rate prospects
- Offer prospects a "personalized dealer" test-drive invitation
- Provide quality stories utilizing our inserts to emphasize performance and heritage
- Offer you a second opportunity to contact each prospect

- Insure a high rate of response from the list provided you — and these will be qualified responses, people who have the money and the inclination to purchase a Porsche

In addition, this year's Program incorporates features based on suggestions from Dealers to make Direct Mail even more effective.

1. A program that you, the Dealer, can modify, tailor and customize while still maintaining a sophisticated Porsche look.

2. Strong performance and heritage stories developed to reinforce the exclusivity of Porsche.

3. Your own personalized Dealer introduction and offer to test drive.

4. An exciting video option that can be utilized in a variety of ways.

5. A *total* mailing list of prospects provided to you with Dealer sign-up. This allows a *complete* review of all names and zip codes.

6. Additional Dealership prospect names can be added to the list prior to mail-out.

7. A 95% deliverability guarantee on all mailings.

the names of purchasers of their products and/or services to such firms (see Promotional Perspective 13–3). Companies such as A. B. Zeller and Metromail provide such lists on a national level, whereas in almost any metropolitan area there are firms providing the same service on a local basis.

Broadcast Media   The success of direct marketing in the broadcast industry is truly remarkable. For example, one company in California sold almost $50,000 a day in a diet program at $19.95 per order, whereas others have sold products costing into the hundreds of dollars successfully. Perhaps the most amazing thing about these sales figures is that the advertising time purchased to sell these products was among the least expensive available in the medium. (Direct advertisers often employ a strategy of purchasing advertising time at the last moment to obtain a discount from the published rates. They also often purchase time on programs with low ratings or reruns, as the consumer is less likely to leave an interesting show or event to place the phone order!)

There are, of course, two broadcast media available to the direct marketer—television and radio. While radio was used quite extensively in the 1950s, its use and effectiveness have dwindled substantially in recent years. Thus, the majority of direct-marketing broadcast advertising now takes place on television and, accordingly, will receive the bulk of our attention here.

Direct marketing in the broadcast industry involves two forms of advertising—**direct-response advertising** and **support advertising.** In direct-response advertising, the product or service is offered and a sales response is solicited, either through the one- or two-step approach previously discussed. Examples include the ones cited earlier and ads for Ronco products, Whopper Choppers, and/or tips on football or basketball betting. Support advertising is designed to do exactly that—support other forms of advertising. Ads for Publishers Clearing House or Reader's Digest or other companies informing you to look in your mailbox for a coming sweepstakes entry are examples of this use of broadcast medium.

Promotional Perspective **13–3**

Melinda Gets on Mailing Lists

Melinda Guiles saved her "junk mail" for four years to write her story about mailing lists. More specifically, she wanted to attempt to track where (to whom) her name went when it got on someone's list. What she found was quite interesting.

To find out, Melinda used 24 different aliases when she subscribed to magazines or catalogs. Each one attracted a whole new group of junk mailers. For example:

Melinda F., who subscribed to *Fortune*, received offers of unsecured loans, gold MasterCards, investment guides, and invitations to test-drive a turbo Porsche.

Melinda S., a reader of *Savvy* magazine, is offered slightly imperfect panty hose and self-improvement courses.

Melinda O. gets offers of backyard tillers and letters from the American Association of Retired Persons—she subscribed to *Organic Gardening*.

Melinda R. joined the Book-of-the-Month Club's Cooking and Crafts Club and received quilt templates, fliers for doll-making kits, and free cake baking instructions, whereas Melisa M., who subscribed to *Ms*, was solicited by NOW, the American Civil Liberties Union, and Planned Parenthood.

The list goes on, along with all of Melinda's other names, but we figure that you get the picture. What you subscribe to is usually taken as an indication as to your interests, and everyone wants a piece of your action!

Source: Adapted from "Why Melinda S. Gets Ads for Panty Hose, Melinda F., Porsches," *The Wall Street Journal*, June 6, 1988, p. 1.

Print Media One of the more difficult media to employ for direct-marketing purposes is that of print—that is, magazines and newspapers. While catalogs might generally be considered an exception to this rule, having achieved a great deal of success (particularly with lower socioeconomic groups), direct marketing through newspapers and magazines has not worked as well. This does not mean that these media are not used (as is evidenced by the fact that expenditures totaled over $37 billion in 1986), only that the returns may not have been as great. Figure 13–14 provides an example of a direct ad that appeared in a daily newspaper. You can find many more in specific interest areas, whether it be financial newspapers, sports, sex, or hobby magazines.

Figure 13–14 Direct Advertising in a Print Vehicle

Telemarketing   If you have a telephone, you probably do not have to be told about the rapid increase in the use of **telemarketing.** Again, both profit and charitable organizations have employed this medium effectively in both one- and two-step approaches.

One of the more recent innovations in the use of telemarketing is the use of computers to "do the talking." The computer is hooked to a telephone, dials numbers that have been programmed in or at random, and records the receiver's comments for future consideration. While a cost-saving and -efficient method for phone soliciting, this approach has been considered offensive to many people and has therefore not achieved the success once expected.

The New Electronic Media   Over the past few years technological advances have opened up a number of new media for marketers. While these alternatives vary in many respects, a summary classification that might best describe these new media is that of electronic media. A review of some of these follows.

Teleshopping   The development of the toll-free 800 telephone number, combined with the widespread use of credit cards, has led to a dramatic increase in the number of persons who shop via their television sets (we have briefly mentioned home shopping channels earlier). Jewelry, kitchenware, insurance, and a variety of other products have now employed this medium to promote (and sell!) their products.

An even more recent innovation is the 900 number. Unlike the 800 prefix, 900 prefixes cost the phone caller at least 50 cents per call. To date, 900 numbers have been used to promote services such as football scores, talks with Santa Claus, friendship clubs, and opinion polls (among others) in a very successful fashion.

Infomercials   The lower cost of commercials on cable and satellite channels has led advertisers to a new form of advertising—the infomercial—which was discussed in Chapter 11. The originator of the infomercial was Warner-Amex, which launched the first interactive television system—QUBE. While QUBE never fulfilled expectations (it was abandoned in 1984), it was essentially the precursor of the home shopping channels described earlier, as many of these channels use this format.

Videotext (electronic teleshopping)   Unlike infomercials and home shopping channels, which rely on broadcast or cable video channels, **videotext** is an information retrieval service that takes place through one's personal computer. Videotext uses a telephone, television, and hand-held keyboard and allows subscribers to request electronic pages of text stored miles away in a computer, as shown in Figure 13–15.

With only a minimal knowledge of computers, home shoppers can select the information they want as though they were using an index of a book. Shoppers can purchase products, services such as airline tickets, play games, get stock market reports, view the latest headlines, and pay bills. Advertisers may provide their messages in the forms of logos or names or in longer segments, depending on the costs they wish to assume and the message they wish to convey.

The country's leading information retrieval services companies—CompuServe, Dow Jones, Prodigy (a joint venture between Sears and IBM), and the Source—have increased their information offerings over the years, making this medium more attractive to marketers. Advertisers who have participated in Videotex America services— a now-abandoned venture of the Times Mirror Corporation, the objectives they sought, and some of the reasons for doing so are shown in Table 13–7.

While videotext in theory offers a great new method of shopping and a completely new avenue for advertisers, the truth is that at this time the system has met with only limited success. While the number of subscribers and advertisers have both been on the increase, some of the major providers such as Times Mirror's Gateway system have abandoned their efforts. Until personal computers have made a much greater penetration of the home market—as forecasts had predicted—the value of this medium will likewise not reach its potential in the consumer market.

Figure 13–15   **How Videotex Works**

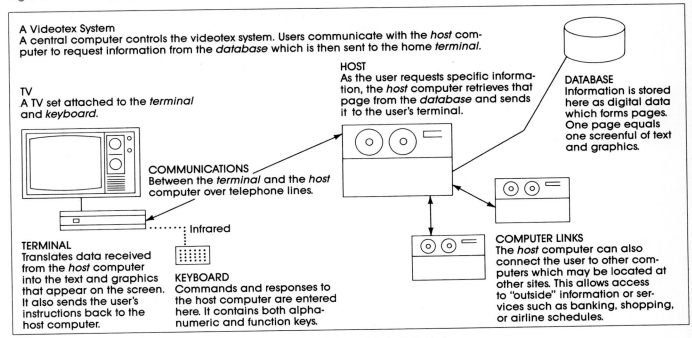

A Videotex System
A central computer controls the videotex system. Users communicate with the *host* computer to request information from the *database* which is then sent to the home *terminal*.

HOST
As the user requests specific information, the *host* computer retrieves that page from the *database* and sends it to the user's terminal.

DATABASE
Information is stored here as digital data which forms pages. One page equals one screenful of text and graphics.

TV
A TV set attached to the *terminal* and *keyboard*.

COMMUNICATIONS
Between the *terminal* and the *host* computer over telephone lines.

COMPUTER LINKS
The *host* computer can also connect the user to other computers which may be located at other sites. This allows access to "outside" information or services such as banking, shopping, or airline schedules.

Infrared

TERMINAL
Translates data received from the *host* computer into the text and graphics that appear on the screen. It also sends the user's instructions back to the host computer.

KEYBOARD
Commands and responses to the host computer are entered here. It contains both alphanumeric and function keys.

Note: This Times Mirror system uses the term *videotex.* However, we use the term *videotext* in the text.
Source: Videotex America—Gateway—Times Mirror Corporation, 1985.

Advantages and disadvantages of the new electronic media   Given the lack of time experienced by so many dual working families, the ability of the new electronic media to offer an alternative shopping medium holds great potential. The visual aspects of television allow for demonstrations and product representations not available through catalogs and as such provide the potential consumer with much more information upon

Table 13–7   **Why Marketers Chose Videotex**

Service Providers	Marketing Objective	Reason for Participating
Sears	Reach affluent homeowners	Subscriber demographics; interactive advertising
Buffums The Broadway Robinson's	Reach affluent department store customers	Targeted advertising; new distribution channel; electronic catalog
Williams-Sonoma Crabtree & Evelyn	Reach an affluent segment accustomed to mail-order shopping	Targeted advertising, with ordering capability
Ticketron Waldenbooks	Market a product with a limited shelf life, where inspection isn't necessary for purchase	Complex ad message, with frequent updating
Hallmark	Develop an electronic version of current product	New distribution channel, offered with electronic mail
Bache	Market time-sensitive information (The Wachtel Report)	"Instant" distribution
The Grocer	Build repeat business	Ease of reordering through videotex
Computerland	Reach electronics consumers	Receptivity of videotex subscribers to electronic products

Source: Videotex America - Gateway - Times Mirror Corporation, 1985, p. 7.

which to make a decision. The information retrieval systems such as videotex offer an almost unlimited opportunity for marketers.

At the same time, as noted, the success that was expected for these media has not been achieved. A number of reasons have been hypothesized, including:

- The fact that computers have not been adopted at the rate expected for home use.
- The fact that many people are still not comfortable with shopping without being able to handle the merchandise; that is, they prefer to feel the material, see the colors, try on the product, and so on, and not just buy it.
- The fact that shopping may, in itself, be a form of relaxation. To many people, a day in the shopping mall or downtown is a form of entertainment. It gets them out of the house, takes their mind off work, and provides them with an opportunity to interact socially. Some people feel that since they work hard to enjoy their money, at least they can take the time to enjoy spending it!

One area in which the use of videotex has been adopted, and continues to increase in use, is the *industrial sector.* In those situations where companies are bidding on government or private industry contracts that require specifications that must be met, the electronic media offer a distinct advantage over existing methods. For example, where specifications previously had to be mailed to prospective bidders, these specs are now available immediately through the video screen. When changes in specifications are required—which is very common—they are noted almost immediately, saving valuable time and effort to all parties involved.

In sum, while the electronic media may not be the answer for all marketers, or for all shoppers, they do satisfy the needs of a particular segment of society. The commitment made by the companies offering such services, as well as the success experienced by many of those who have advertised in these media, suggests that there is a bright future for advertisers in this area.

Advantages and Disadvantages of Direct Marketing

Many of the advantages of direct marketing have already been presented. A review of these and some additions follow.

1. *Selective reach* Direct marketing provides the advertiser the opportunity to reach a large number of persons as well as a more effective reach through the elimination or reduction of waste circulation. With respect to the former, intensive coverage may be obtained through broadcast advertising or through the mail. While everyone may not drive on highways where there are billboards, or pay attention to television commercials, virtually everyone receives mail. In the latter case, a good list will allow for a minimal amount of waste, as only those offering the highest potential are targeted. For example, a political candidate can direct a message at a very select group of people (those living in a certain zip code or members of the Sierra Club), whereas compact disc companies might target recent purchasers of compact disc players.

2. *Segmentation capabilities* As just mentioned, it is possible to purchase lists of recent product purchasers, bank card holders, recent automobile buyers, or a variety of others. As shown in Table 13–8, these lists may allow segmentation on the basis of geographic area, occupation, demographics, and job titles, to mention a few. When combining this information with that of the geo-coding capabilities of PRIZM or VISION (discussed in Chapter 7), effective segmentation strategies can be developed.

3. *Frequency* Depending on the medium utilized, it may be possible to build *frequency* levels. As noted, the program vehicles used for television advertising are usually some of the more inexpensive available; thus, the cost of purchasing repeat times is not prohibitive. At the same time, this may not be so easily accomplished through the mail, as an irritation factor may be associated with receiving the same mail repeatedly.

4. *Flexibility* As can easily be seen in Figure 13–16 direct marketing can take

Table 13—8 **An Example of the Variety of Lists Available**

MAIL RESPONSE LISTS

QUANTITY		PRICE
AUTOMOTIVE		
15,000,000	American Car Buyers/Foreign/or USA Models	Inquire
208,000	AutoWeek Subscribers	$60/M
146,000	Babcox Business Leaders	$65/M
160,000	Beverly Hills Motoring Accessories Buyers	$95/M
165,000	4 Wheel & Off Road Subs	$60/M
48,000	Hearst Motor Bookbuyers	$50/M
49,500	Hot Rod Magazine	$60/M
328,000	Classic Motor Books	$55/M
218,000	Auto/Truck Do-It-Yourselfers	$60/M
74,000	Cars & Parts Magazine	$70/M
BEAUTY/HEALTH/DIET		
800,000	American Health Magazine	$65/M
1,000,000	Bio-Energetics Research Buyers	$70/M
339,000	Comfortably Yours	$85/M
1,700,000	Cosmetique Beauty Buyers	$55/M
32,000	Cardiac Alert Subs	$85/M
33,000	Executive Fitness Letter	$75/M
912,000	Health Magazine	$60/M
480,000	Health Conscious Americans	$50/M
224,000	Tufts University Newsletter	$65/M
550,000	University of California—Berkeley Wellness Letter	$70/M
135,000	Vegetarian Times	$65/M
200,000	Weider Health and Fitness	$65/M
2,400,000	Prevention Magazine	$60/M
821,000	Weight Watchers Magazine	$65/M
BOOKBUYERS		
2,200,000	Better Homes & Gardens	$60/M
642,000	Barnes & Noble	$70/M
840,000	Boardroom Bookbuyers	$85/M
330,000	Warren, Gorham & Lamont	$90/M
	Bantam Bookbuyers	Inquire
	Book of the Month Club	Inquire
	CMG (College Bookbuyers)	Inquire
	Doubleday Bookbuyers	Inquire
	Literary Guild	Inquire
	MacMillan Bookbuyers	Inquire
	Prentice Hall, Inc.	Inquire
	Time-Life—INQUIRE BY SUBJECT	Inquire
BUSINESS MAGAZINES		
25,000	American Banker	$110/M
36,000	Apartment Management	$60/M
1,161,000	Boardroom Reports	$85/M
236,000	Business Week Subs at Business	$98/M
377,000	Business Month	$70/M
36,000	Cash Flow	$95/M
115,000	The Economist	$125/M
731,000	Forbes	$95/M
67,000	Government Executive	$85/M
74,060	High Technology	$80/M
560,000	Inc. Magazine	$90/M
57,000	Industrial Safety Hygiene News	$70/M
389,000	Kiplinger Washington Letter	$85/M
129,000	Plant Engineering	$65/M
	Cahners Magazines	Inquire
	Chilton Magazines	Inquire
	Gralla Publications	Inquire
	Hayden Publications	Inquire
	Hitchcock Magazines	Inquire
	Hunter Publications	Inquire
	McGraw Hill Publications	Inquire
	Penton/IPC Magazines	Inquire
	Technical Publishing	Inquire

Many types of **privately owned** specialty lists of people are also available, such as:

- **MAIL ORDER BUYERS** of various direct mail, TV or magazine products.
- **SUBSCRIBERS** to magazines, newsletters
- **CONTRIBUTORS** to fund-raising campaigns
- **CREDIT CARD HOLDERS,** charge customers

These lists can be related to your specific product or purpose. If your offer is not in competitive conflict with such lists, the owner will authorize use of his names for your mailing. **A SAMPLE MAILING PIECE MUST BE SUBMITTED WITH YOUR ORDER FOR APPROVAL.** These **RESPONSE LISTS** are an additional tool to target specific segments of your direct mail market.

PRICES, QUANTITIES, AND MINIMUMS (usually 5,000 — Inquire) for such lists are completely at the discretion of the list owner, and are subject to change. *Please inquire for details and current prices before placing your order.* Orders for RESPONSE LISTS are not commissionable and cannot be charged on credit cards.

These two pages are a *representative* group of such private response lists. Many, many more are available.

QUANTITY		PRICE
BUSINESS PRODUCT BUYERS		
110,000	Amsterdam Business	$80/M
64,060	Atlas Pen & Pencil	$75/M
112,000	Baldwin Cooke Co	$80/M
2,000,000	Day Timers	$85/M
240,000	Drawing Board	$70/M
75,000	Grayarc	$55/M
244,000	Delmart	$50/M
CHILDREN		
203,000	American Baby	$60/M
52,000	Baby Talk	$60/M
55,000	Bear Necessities	$80/M
500,000	Child Color Portraits	$50/M
715,000	Children's Reading Institute	$55/M
611,000	Childcraft	$75/M
280,000	Electric Company	$60/M
818,000	Encyclopedia Britannica Buyers	$55/M
43,000	Gifted Children Monthly	$75/M
630,000	Grolier Enterprises	$65/M
280,000	Humpty Dumpty Magazine	$60/M
308,000	Jack & Jill Magazine	$60/M
63,000	Muppet Magazine	$60/M
1,600,000	Field Publications	$60/M
86,000	Teen Beat	$50/M
645,000	Young Miss Magazine	$50/M
CONTRIBUTORS		

QUANTITY		PRICE
435,000	American Museum Natural History	$75/M
400,000	Animal Welfare Donors	$65/M
437,000	Greenpeace	$65/M
4,000,000	Health	$65/M
1,313,000	Humanitarian	$65/M
226,000	National Foundation Cancer Research	$60/M
148,000	National Glaucoma Research	$75/M
1,497,000	Political	$65/M
248,000	Political/Conservative	$65/M
162,000	Political/Liberal	$65/M
4,000,000	Religious	$65/M
586,000	Hands Across America Donors	$55/M
COMPUTERS/DATA/PROCESSING		
2,800,000	Personal Computer Owners/ Type of Brand	Inquire
700,000	Business Computer Owners/ Type of Brand	Inquire
260,000	Professionals Using Computers	Inquire
665,000	Brandon Computer Professionals	$75/M
255,000	Byte Magazine	$100/M
113,000	Computerworld Magazine	$125/M
70,000	Computer Systems News	$87/M
137,580	Compute! Magazine	$80/M
160,000	Datamation	$80/M
400,000	Family and Home Office Computing	$80/M
135,000	MIS Week	$110/M
453,000	PC Magazine	$100/M
CONSUMER MAGAZINES		
250,000	Americana Magazine	$65/M
93,000	Art & Antiques Magazine	$80/M
380,000	Atlantic Monthly	$80/M
148,000	American History Illustrated	$70/M
73,000	Birdwatchers Digest	$60/M
110,000	Collectors Mart	$60/M
1,160,000	Contest Newsletter	$70/M
1,100,000	Davis Publications	$55/M
295,000	Early American Life	$70/M
110,000	Fate Magazine	$65/M
919,000	Insight Magazine	$55/M
1,000,000	Life Magazine	$70/M
112,000	New Age Journal	$75/M
346,000	National Audubon Society	$70/M
2,700,000	Newsweek	$60/M
1,613,000	Popular Science	$55/M
59,000	Spy Magazine	$75/M
335,000	Success Magazine	$75/M
12,000,000	TV Guide Subscribers	$55/M
852,000	TV Guide Cable Subscribers	$65/M
2,100,000	U.S. News & World Report	$70/M
	Regional Magazines (By City)	Inquire
CREDIT CARD HOLDERS		
10,200,000	American Express Co	$95/M
113,000	Carte Blanche	$80/M
670,000	Diners Club	$80/M
388,000	Diners—Mail Order Buyers	$85/M
382,000	Diners—Airline Ticket Buyers	$90/M
200,000	Syndicated Bank Cardholders (Purchased in monthly VISA and MASTERCARD statements)	$65/M
4,480,000	Credit Card Service Bureau	$65/M
1,395,000	Bloomingdales	$65/M
175,000	Chargit—Credit Card Holders	$65/M
390,000	First Travel Club Cardholders	$70/M
	INQUIRE-MISCELLANEOUS PRODUCT BUYERS W/CARDS	
CULTURAL		

on a variety of creative forms. The direct-mail pieces shown here provide the advertiser with eye-catching and attention-getting capabilities. At the same time, the more involved direct-mail pieces shown also allow for the possibility of much copy and the ability to provide a great deal of information.

Figure 13–16 **Examples of Direct-Mail Pieces**

5. *Timing* While many media may require long-range planning and long closing dates, direct-response advertising can be much more *timely*. Direct mail, for example, can be put together very quickly and distributed to the target population. As noted earlier, the television programs typically used for direct-response advertising are older, less sought programs and, as a result, are much more likely to appear on the station's "list of available spots." In addition, a common strategy is to purchase available time at the last possible moment to get the best price.

6. *Personalization* No other advertising medium can provide the ability to personalize the message as well as direct marketing—specifically direct mail. Parents with children at different age levels can be approached with their child's name included in the appeal. Porsche owners will be mailed letters directly congratulating them on their new auto purchase and offering them accessories. Recent computer purchasers will be sent software solicitations. Graduating college students—as you will see—receive very personalized information, some of which recognizes their specific needs and offers solutions (such as credit cards!).

7. *Costs* While the CPM for direct mail may be very high on an absolute and a relative basis, one must keep in mind a previous discussion we have presented. Given the ability of direct mail to specifically target the audience, and eliminate waste circulation, the actual CPMs are reduced. The cost of the ads used on television are often among the lowest available.

A second factor contributing to the cost effectiveness of direct-response advertising is the **cost per customer purchasing.** Because of the low cost of media, it is possible—in fact, necessary—to have a very low cost associated with each sale generated.

8. *Measures of effectiveness* No other medium can measure the effectiveness of

its advertising efforts as well as can direct-response advertisers. Utilizing an effectiveness measure known as **cost per order (CPO),** advertisers can evaluate the relative effectiveness of an ad in as little as eight minutes based on the number of calls generated. Simply stated, if the advertiser targets a $5.00 return per order, and a broadcast commercial costs $250.00, the ad is considered effective if at least 50 orders are generated. Similar measures can be developed for print and direct-mail ads.

Disadvantages of direct marketing include the following.

1. *Image factors* As we noted at the outset of our discussion of direct marketing, the mail segment of this industry is often referred to as "junk mail." The reason for this terminology is very simple: Many people feel that the unsolicited mail they receive is promoting junk, whereas others dislike the idea that they are being solicited. This problem is particularly relevant given the increased volume of mail that is being sent. Likewise, the advertisements on television are often low-budget ads and are often for lower-priced products. The combination of these two elements contributes to the image that something less than the best products are marketed in this way. (Note: Some of this image is being overcome by the home shopper channels, in which very expensive products are being promoted.)

2. *Selectivity* One of the advantages cited earlier was that of being able to target potential customers specifically. While this is certainly true, this ability is most characteristic of direct mail and telephone marketing. The effectiveness of both of these methods is, however, directly related to the accuracy of the lists utilized. Lists must be kept current, as many people move, change occupations, and so on, and if the lists do not keep pace with these moves, the result may be a decrease in selectivity. The rapid advancement of the computerized list has greatly improved the capabilities to keep current and has reduced the incidence of bad names being included.

3. *Content support* In our discussion of the objectives to be accomplished in developing a media strategy in Chapter 10, we discussed mood and content of the medium. Magazines, for example, were cited as mood creating, and it was argued that this would contribute to the overall effectiveness of the ad placed therein. In direct-response advertising, the ability to create mood is limited to broadcast and print methods (those surrounded by program and/or editorial content), with direct mail being unlikely to do so.

Audience Measurement in Direct Marketing

A substantial number of sources of information for the purchase of direct marketing/advertising are available; however, for the measurement of audiences the list is much shorter. These include the following.

- *List services* A variety of providers of lists are available (an example of one such provider was shown in Table 13–8). These providers will vary in quality depending on the accuracy of the list and its currency.
- *Standard Rates and Data Service* The SRDS provides information regarding two types of lists—consumer lists and business lists. These lists are provided in two volumes of information entitled *Direct Mail List Rates and Data* and provide over 50,000 list selections in hundreds of classifications.
- *Simmons Market Research Bureau* In 1984 SMRB conducted the first ever study of customers who buy at home through the mail or via telephone (see Table 13–9). Information is provided in respect to total orders placed, type of products purchased, demographics, and purchase satisfaction, among others.
- *Direct Marketing Association, Inc.* The trade organization of the Direct Marketing Association is responsible for promoting direct marketing and providing statistical information on direct marketing use. The organization publishes a *Fact Book of Direct Marketing* containing information regarding use, attitudes toward direct marketing, rules and regulations, and so forth.

Table 13–9   **Ordered Merchandise by Mail or Phone in Last 12 Months (Adults)**

	Total U.S. '000	Ordered by Mail or Phone				Ordered by Mail				Ordered by Phone			
		A '000	B % Down	C Across %	D Index	A '000	B % Down	C Across %	D Index	A '000	B % Down	C Across %	D Index
Total adults	176250	88534	100.0	50.2	100	57177	100.0	32.4	100	20896	100.0	11.9	100
Males	84066	37142	42.0	44.2	88	23831	41.7	28.3	87	8792	42.1	10.5	88
Females	92184	51392	58.0	55.7	111	33346	58.3	36.2	112	12104	57.9	13.1	111
18–24	26535	11178	12.6	42.1	84	7035	12.3	26.5	82	2589	12.4	9.8	82
25–34	42634	21857	24.7	51.3	102	14615	25.6	34.3	106	5858	28.0	13.7	116
35–44	33688	19457	22.0	57.8	115	12599	22.0	37.4	115	5298	25.4	15.7	133
45–54	23361	12769	14.4	54.7	109	8239	14.4	35.3	109	3175	15.2	13.6	115
55–64	22021	11202	12.7	50.9	101	7267	12.7	33.0	102	2181	10.4	9.9	84
65 or older	28011	12072	13.6	43.1	86	7423	13.0	26.5	82	1796	8.6	6.4	54
18–34	69169	33034	37.3	47.8	95	21650	37.9	31.3	96	8447	40.4	12.2	103
18–49	115355	59329	67.0	51.4	102	38818	67.9	33.7	104	15521	74.3	13.5	113
25–54	99683	54083	61.1	54.3	108	35453	62.0	35.6	110	14330	68.6	14.4	121
35–49	46186	26294	29.7	56.9	113	17168	30.0	37.2	115	7075	33.9	15.3	129
50 or older	60895	29205	33.0	48.0	95	18359	32.1	30.1	93	5375	25.7	8.8	74
Graduated college	31644	19362	21.9	61.2	122	12852	22.5	40.6	125	5296	25.3	16.7	141
Attended college	32702	17875	20.2	54.7	109	11145	19.5	34.1	105	4568	21.9	14.0	118
Graduated high school	69681	36250	40.9	52.0	104	23814	41.6	34.2	105	8346	39.9	12.0	101
Did not graduate high school	42223	15047	17.0	35.6	71	9367	16.4	22.2	68	2686	12.9	6.4	54
Employed males	60414	28087	31.7	46.5	93	18274	32.0	30.2	93	7204	34.5	11.9	101
Employed females	51321	31076	35.1	60.6	121	20401	35.7	39.8	123	7897	37.8	15.4	130
Employed full-time	97700	51719	58.4	52.9	105	33687	58.9	34.5	106	13249	63.4	13.6	114
Employed part-time	14034	7445	8.4	53.0	106	4988	8.7	35.5	110	1852	8.9	13.2	111
Not employed	64516	29370	33.2	45.5	91	18503	32.4	28.7	88	5794	27.7	9.0	76
Professional manager	28104	17252	19.5	61.4	122	11485	20.1	40.9	126	4537	21.7	16.1	136
Tech/clerical/sales	35802	20383	23.0	56.9	113	13253	23.2	37.0	114	5550	26.6	15.5	131
Precision/craft	14098	6413	7.2	45.5	91	4085	7.1	29.0	89	1604	7.7	11.4	96
Other employed	33730	15116	17.1	44.8	89	9853	17.2	29.2	90	3411	16.3	10.1	85
Single	37865	15956	18.0	42.1	84	10267	18.0	27.1	84	3733	17.9	9.9	83
Married	106963	58840	66.5	55.0	110	37973	66.4	35.5	109	14659	70.2	13.7	116
Divorced/separated/widowed	31422	13739	15.5	43.7	87	8937	15.6	28.4	88	2504	12.0	8.0	67
Parents	67328	36330	41.0	54.0	107	23605	41.3	35.1	108	9813	47.0	14.6	123
White	152234	79230	89.5	52.0	104	51620	90.3	33.9	105	19026	91.1	12.5	105
Black	19434	7475	8.4	38.5	77	4358	7.6	22.4	69	1436	6.9	7.4	62
Other	4582	1829	2.1	39.9	79	1200	2.1	26.2	81	434	2.1	9.5	80
Northeast–census	37366	18442	20.8	49.4	98	11751	20.6	31.4	97	4981	23.8	13.3	112
Midwest	43426	24756	28.0	57.0	113	16640	29.1	38.3	118	6091	29.1	14.0	118
South	60402	28951	32.7	47.9	95	17881	31.3	29.6	91	6240	29.9	10.3	87
West	35057	16386	18.5	46.7	93	10905	19.1	31.1	96	3584	17.2	10.2	86
Northeast–mktg.	39212	19843	22.4	50.6	101	12880	22.5	32.8	101	5081	24.3	13.0	109
East central	25018	13017	14.7	52.0	104	8583	15.0	34.3	106	3125	15.0	12.5	105
West central	29350	16823	19.0	57.3	114	11379	19.9	38.8	120	4121	19.7	14.0	118
South	52142	24557	27.7	47.1	94	14782	25.9	28.3	87	5404	25.9	10.4	87
Pacific	30528	14295	16.1	46.8	93	9554	16.7	31.3	96	3164	15.1	10.4	87
County size A	73211	35143	39.7	48.0	96	22920	40.1	31.3	97	8089	38.7	11.0	93
County size B	52831	26895	30.4	50.9	101	16853	29.5	31.9	98	6178	29.6	11.7	99
County size C	26575	14007	15.8	52.7	105	8982	15.7	33.8	104	3229	15.5	12.2	102
County size D	23633	12488	14.1	52.8	105	8422	14.7	35.6	110	3400	16.3	14.4	121
Metro central city	53736	23560	26.6	43.8	87	14798	25.9	27.5	85	4687	22.4	8.7	74
Metro suburban	81523	43366	49.0	53.2	106	28303	49.5	34.7	107	11017	52.7	13.5	114
Non metro	40991	21608	24.4	52.7	105	14076	24.6	34.3	106	5192	24.8	12.7	107
Top 5 ADIs	40121	18875	21.3	47.0	94	12233	21.4	30.5	94	4790	22.9	11.9	101
Top 10 ADIs	55858	26884	30.4	48.1	96	17592	30.8	31.5	97	6514	31.2	11.7	98
Top 20 ADIs	80357	39408	44.5	49.0	98	25619	44.8	31.9	98	9625	46.1	12.0	101
Hshld inc. $60,000 or more	20289	12111	13.7	59.7	119	7527	13.2	37.1	114	3609	17.3	17.8	150
$50,000 or more	31340	18225	20.6	58.2	116	11600	20.3	37.0	114	5284	25.3	16.9	142
$40,000 or more	53108	30886	34.9	58.2	116	19862	34.7	37.4	115	8545	40.9	16.1	136
$30,000 or more	82233	46887	53.0	57.0	114	30534	53.4	37.1	114	12409	59.4	15.1	127
$30,000–$39,999	29126	16001	18.1	54.9	109	10672	18.7	36.6	113	3864	18.5	13.3	112
$20,000–$29,999	34891	18755	21.2	53.8	107	12203	21.3	35.0	108	4181	20.0	12.0	101
$10,000–$19,999	37097	16074	18.2	43.3	86	9917	17.3	26.7	82	3280	15.7	8.8	75
Under $10,000	22029	6818	7.7	31.0	62	4523	7.9	20.5	63	1026	4.9	4.7	39

Table 13–9 (concluded)

	Total U.S. '000	Ordered by Mail or Phone				Ordered by Mail				Ordered by Phone			
		A '000	B % Down	C Across %	D Index	A '000	B % Down	C Across %	D Index	A '000	B % Down	C Across %	D Index
Household of 1 person	21267	8812	10.0	41.4	82	5651	9.9	26.6	82	1780	8.5	8.4	71
2 people	55771	28049	31.7	50.3	100	18626	32.6	33.4	103	6048	28.9	10.8	91
3 or 4 people	71810	38267	43.2	53.3	106	24562	43.0	34.2	105	9436	45.2	13.1	111
5 or more people	27402	13406	15.1	48.9	97	8338	14.6	30.4	94	3632	17.4	13.3	112
No child in hshld	104468	50156	56.7	48.0	96	32472	56.8	31.1	96	10595	50.7	10.1	86
Child(ren) under 2 yrs	14095	6903	7.8	49.0	97	4470	7.8	31.7	98	1615	7.7	11.5	97
2–5 years	25865	13163	14.9	50.9	101	8770	15.3	33.9	105	3514	16.8	13.6	115
6–11 years	33171	17780	20.1	53.6	107	11690	20.4	35.2	109	4929	23.6	14.9	125
12–17 years	33224	18081	20.4	54.4	108	11319	19.8	34.1	105	4995	23.9	15.0	127
Residence owned	123262	67976	76.8	55.1	110	43571	76.2	35.3	109	16476	78.8	13.4	113
Value: $60,000 or more	70282	39998	45.2	56.9	113	25273	44.2	36.0	111	10347	49.5	14.7	124
Value: under $60,000	52980	27978	31.6	52.8	105	18298	32.0	34.5	106	6129	29.3	11.6	98

Summary

The purpose of this chapter has been to familiarize you with a number of alternative media that are available to the marketer in his or her advertising efforts. These include outdoor and transit advertising, advertising in movie theaters and on videotapes, and product placements. In addition, the rapidly emerging area of direct marketing was discussed. Some of these media are very conventional in nature and as such have developed methods of audience measurement, source books, and trade organizations. Others are less conventional, and the reliance for audience measures and effectiveness has to come from the providers themselves.

Each of these various media forms has its own advantages and disadvantages. While one form may be better for accomplishing certain objectives, it may be less useful for the attainment of others. Cost factors and other limitations may preclude the use of some. An inability to measure the effectiveness directly may limit the attractiveness of others. At the same time, the relative effectiveness of some of these less conventional forms of advertising may make them worthy of consideration to the marketer and open a previously unconsidered advertising alternative.

It is important that the marketer be knowledgeable of each alternative and weigh each in the determination of its ability to achieve the sought objectives at the best cost. While many of these media may be used to support other forms of advertising and promotion, direct marketing may constitute the sole promotional method used by many companies.

Key Terms

Support media
Out-of-home advertising
Showings
Aerial advertising
Rolling boards
Transit advertising
Inside cards
Outside posters
Terminal posters
Specialty advertising
Advertising specialties
Product placement

Direct marketing
Direct-marketing media
One-step approach
Two-step approach
Mailing list
Direct-response advertising
Support advertising
Telemarketing
Videotext
Cost per customer purchasing
Cost per order (CPO)

Discussion Questions

1. Discuss some of the advantages and disadvantages of outdoor advertising.
2. The text notes that users of transit advertising must rely on audience information provided by companies selling transit advertising space. Discuss some of the problems that might occur from this situation.
3. What is meant by a 100 GRP showing? Give examples of how GRPs are used in outdoor advertising. In transit.
4. Give examples of some of the new out-of-home media. Why have these become so popular?
5. What is videotext? Why has this concept not caught on as rapidly as expected?
6. Discuss some of the reasons why direct marketing has been receiving more and more attention from marketers.
7. What is the difference between the one-step and two-step approaches used in direct marketing?
8. What are some of the problems associated with direct marketing?
9. Discuss some of the advantages associated with specialty advertising. Some of the disadvantages.
10. Give examples of products that might best benefit from each of the media discussed in this chapter.

Notes

1. Adapted from "Consumer Products Become Movie Stars," *The Wall Street Journal,* February 29, 1988, p. 24.
2. "Top Spending Categories in Outdoor Advertising 1988," Institute of Outdoor Advertising, May 1989.
3. "Outdoor Advertising: Special Report," *Advertising Age,* December 12, 1985, p. 20.
4. David Kalish, "Supermarket Sweepstakes," *Marketing & Media Decisions,* November 1988, p. 34.
5. Ibid.
6. *Advertisers Take the City Bus to Work* (New York: Winston Network, 1988), p. 13.
7. Ibid.
8. "Transit Advertising," Winston Network, New York.
9. *Preference Building: The Dynamic World of Specialty Advertising* (Irving, Tex.: Specialty Advertising Association, 1988).
10. Ibid.
11. George L. Herpel and Steve Slack, *Specialty Advertising: New Dimensions in Creative Marketing* (Irving, Tex.: Specialty Advertising Association, 1983), pp. 79–80.
12. Ibid., p. 76.
13. Ibid., p. 78.
14. Ibid., p. 75.
15. Betsy Bauer, "New Quick Flicks: Ads at the Movies," *USA TODAY,* March 13, 1986, p. D1.
16. Ibid.
17. Michael A. Belch and Don Sciglimpaglia, "Viewers' Evaluations of Cinema Advertising" (Proceedings of the American Institute for Decision Sciences, March 1979).
18. "Hershey Befriends Extra-terrestrial," *Advertising Age,* July 19, 1982, p. 1.
19. Colin Leinster, "A Tale of Mice and Lens," *Fortune,* September 28, 1987, p. 8.
20. "Consumer Products Become Movie Stars," *The Wall Street Journal,* February 29, 1988, p. 23.
21. Ibid.
22. Ibid.
23. Joanne Lipman, "Movie Audiences Panning Shopworn TV Commercials," *The Wall Street Journal,* August 18, 1989, p. B1.
24. "Consumer Products."
25. *Fact Book on Direct Marketing* (New York: Direct Marketing Association, 1987), p. viii.

26. Direct Marketing Association, 1989.
27. Jagdish N. Sheth, "Marketing Megatrends," *Journal of Consumer Marketing* 1, no. 1 (June 1983), pp. 5–13.
28. Joanne Cleaver, "Consumers at Home with Shopping," *Advertising Age,* January 18, 1988, pp. S16–18.
29. Ibid.
30. *Direct Marketing Magazine,* November 1988, p. 27.

14

Creative Strategy

CHAPTER OBJECTIVES

1. To discuss what is meant by advertising creativity and examine the role of creative strategy in advertising

2. To examine the process that guides the creation of advertising messages and the various inputs to the stages of the creative process

3. To examine creative strategy development and the various appeals and execution styles used in advertising

4. To consider how clients evaluate the creative work of their agencies and guidelines for the evaluation and approval process

Consumers' Favorite Commercials

Before reading this page, stop for a moment and think about the ads you have seen recently. Which ones have caught your attention and really made an impression? Which television commercial would you rate as the "most outstanding" one you have seen? How do you think your list of top commercials compares against that of other consumers? Every year Video Storyboard Tests Inc., a New York ad-testing company, surveys more than 25,000 consumers across the country and asks them to name the most outstanding TV commercial they have seen. Table 14–1 lists the 25 most popular television campaigns of 1988, along with their 1987 ranking and the size of their television budget.

In 1988, for the second straight year, the most popular campaign was that for the California Raisin Advisory Board that featured the clay-animated California Raisins singing and dancing in high-top sneakers to tunes such as the Motown Classic "I Heard It Through the Grapevine." Just behind the popular Raisins were the campaigns for Pepsi/Diet Pepsi, McDonald's, and Bud Light beer featuring America's newest advertising celebrity: Spuds MacKenzie. Bud Light actually used a dual campaign featuring not only the Spuds commercials but its "Funny Lights" ads as well.

1988 was viewed as one of the driest years of the decade for advertising creativity as there were no new, really memorable or blockbuster campaigns or ad characters developed. Nearly all the commercials consumers cited as their favorites were holdover campaigns from prior years. The president of Video Storyboard Tests noted that "we seem to be moving away from risk-taking advertising and going back to formula advertising with an unprecedented number of the top 25 campaigns showing children, dogs and celebrities." One writer suggested that the unwillingness of advertisers to take creative risks is particularly dangerous in an era when viewers routinely zap commercials with their remote-control devices if they are not entertaining.

Four of the television campaigns in Video Storyboard's top 10 list in 1988 have been there for 10 years running, including those for McDonald's, Pepsi-Cola, Coca-Cola, and Miller Lite. McDonald's and Pepsi have used a variety of ad themes and campaigns over the past decade to generate entertaining and informative ads that keep attracting consumers' attention and interest. McDonald's has described its basic advertising strategy as consisting of "food, folks, and fun" and has used commercials featuring children and senior citizens as well as its trendy "Mac tonight" spot to create consistently popular advertising. Pepsi has aimed most of its ads at the "Pepsi Generation," which consists of the younger market, and has used people-oriented ads such as the extravagant (and expensive) Michael Jackson spots as well as hard-hitting comparative messages claiming taste superiority over Coke.

Coca-Cola has used a variety of theme-oriented ads over the years including the "Coke is it" campaign featuring the popular actor Bill Cosby as spokesperson. Coke has also used a number of celebrities in its ads for Diet Coke. Miller Lite has retained the same basic advertising concept for 15 years using former athletes and other celebrities such as Bob Uecker, Rodney Dangerfield, and more recently, Joe Piscopo to promote the "Great taste/less filling" theme. However, Miller is expected to phase out this long-running campaign in favor of one that repositions the brand against other light beers.

Most of the ads on Video Storyboard's top 25 list tend to be entertaining in nature and are for pleasure products such as fast food, soft drinks, beer, and pet foods. One advertising executive noted that "it is generally easier to get pleasure products into Video Storyboard Tests' top ranking because people are watching TV for entertainment." Another noted that since these are primarily image products, "the advertiser can spend 30 seconds entertaining the viewer since we're not forced to put information into the advertising."

Most of these ads are also for heavily advertised brands in product categories where a great deal of money is spent on advertising. It is not surprising that many of these campaigns are cited as the most outstanding since they are seen so often and thus have a greater chance of being mentioned in a recall test. However, it is interesting to note that not only was the California Raisin campaign ranked first in popularity, but it also had the *lowest* advertising budget, which is an indication of consumers' affection for the ads.

Some advertising and marketing executives are somewhat skeptical about the Video Storyboard popularity contest and question whether popular advertising really translates into sales. However, one advertising executive perhaps best summarized many marketers' opinions when he noted, "It's good to know people are at least paying attention to your message."[1,2,3,4]

Introduction

For most students, and marketing practitioners as well, the most interesting aspect of advertising and promotion is the creative side. We have all at one time or another been intrigued by an advertisement and admired the creative insight and thinking that went into it. A great ad is a joy to behold and often an epic to create, as the cost of producing many television commercials can reach several hundred thousand dollars. The creative strategy and process constitute an integral part of the promotional pro-

Table 14—1 **Most Popular Television Commercials of 1988**

1988 Rank	1987 Rank	Brand (Agency)	Estimated 1988 TV Spending (in millions)
1	1	California raisins (Foote, Cone & Belding)	$ 6.8
2	3	Pepsi/Diet Pepsi (BBDO)	106.4
3	5	McDonald's (Leo Burnett)	385.9
4	2	Bud Light (DDB Needham)	57.4
5	8	Isuzu (Della, Femina, McNamee WCRS)	30.0
6	4	Miller Lite (Backer Spielvogel Bates)	64.5
7	7	Coca-Cola (McCann-Erickson)	68.0
8	—	Stroh's (Lowe Marschalk)[1]	18.0
9	12	Wendy's (Backer Spielvogel Bates)	83.5
10	13	Levi's (Foote, Cone & Belding)	37.4
11	18	Partnership for a Drug-Free America (various agencies)	82.5[2]
12	—	AT&T (N.W. Ayer, Ogilvy & Mather)	216.1
13	—	Johnson's Baby Shampoo (Lintas)	10.0
14	—	Huggies (Ogilvy & Mather)	22.7
15	6	Bartles & Jaymes (Crawford Wu Films)	26.2
16	—	7-Up (Leo Burnett)	38.5
17	9	Du Pont Stainmaster carpet (BBDO)	29.0
18	11	Jell-O (Young & Rubicam)	30.0
19	—	Nike (Wieder & Kennedy)	16.7
20	—	Michelin (DDB Needham)	11.8
21	—	Gravy Train (Chiat Day)[1]	6.3
22	—	National Dairy Board (McCann-Erickson)	16.0
23	—	Little Caesar (Cliff Freeman & Partners)	9.9
24	—	Ragu (Waring & LaRosa)	19.1
25	—	King Kuts (J. Walter Thompson)	5.5

[1]Stroh's account has been moved to the Hal Riney & Partners ad agency, and Gravy Train account has been switched to the Bayer Bess Vanderwarker agency.
[2]Estimated value of TV time donated for these public-service spots.
Source: Video Storyboard Test Commercial Break newsletter and Arbitron's Broadcast Advertisers Reports. The table appeared in *The Wall Street Journal*, February 23, 1989, p. B1.

gram, as the manner in which the advertising message is developed and executed is often critical to the success or failure of the campaign.

A good creative strategy can often be the primary factor in determining the success of a product or service or reversing the fortunes of a troubled or struggling brand. For example, Marlboro cigarettes became the number-one-selling brand and has held that position for over two decades on the strength of its "Marlboro Country" advertising campaign. As was noted in the first chapter, Life Cereal was a struggling brand until it was rescued by the famous "Mikey likes it" ad, whereas the ad shown in Figure 14—1 was part of a very successful campaign that helped make Hennessy Cognac one of the leading liqueurs.

Creative advertising can also help create interest and excitement in a mundane and otherwise ordinary product. For example, carpeting has been traditionally viewed as a very dull product to advertise. However, when Du Pont introduced its revolutionary new Stainmaster carpet fibers, its agency used a humorous appeal featuring a cute little boy launching his dinner onto the floor to demonstrate the product's stain resistance (Figure 14—2). The Stainmaster commercial has been one of the most popular on television, reaching the top 10 in Video Storyboard's 1987 survey. More important, the ads were very effective in getting consumers to request specifically the Stainmaster brand when purchasing carpeting.[5]

While creative advertising can be a tremendous asset to a promotional program, a weak or poorly conceived ad can inhibit the effectiveness of a campaign, despite a solid promotional plan or a substantial budget. For example, Burger King changed ad campaigns five times in two years and ended up changing agencies twice in search of an advertising approach that would work, as discussed in Promotional Perspective 14—1.

Figure 14—1 This Ad Was Part of a Very Successful Campaign for Hennessy Cognac

Figure 14—2 This Humorous Commercial Was Very Effective in Getting Consumers to Request Stainmaster Carpeting

Promotional Perspective 14-1

Hungry for the Right Campaign

In the late 1970s and early 1980s Burger King, which was then a subsidiary of the Pillsbury Company, used successful advertising—such as the "Have it your way" theme and a hard-hitting "Battle of the burgers" campaign touting the superiority of its flame broiling to McDonald's frying process—to become the second largest fast-food chain in the country. However, by 1986 Burger King's 13 percent increase in sales came primarily from new restaurants, as sales in existing stores were up less than 1 percent.

Burger King's problems were due in part to the fact that the $13 billion hamburger market is no longer growing, and the entire fast-food industry has become very competitive. Burger King's main competitor, McDonald's, outspends it 3:1 on advertising and spent nearly $100 million introducing the McD.L.T. sandwich alone. However, many analysts felt that one of the company's biggest problems over the past few years has been its inability to come up with an effective and memorable advertising campaign that gives Burger King a strong image and position in the marketplace.

In a three-year period, Burger King had gone through five major ad campaigns. After abandoning the "Battle of the burgers" campaign, which was effective in gaining market share against McDonalds, the company launched a six-week promotion of its meatier Whopper using celebrities such as Mr T. in the ads. While this campaign did sell more Whoppers, it failed to attract new customers to the restaurants. In 1986 Burger King introduced Herb, the nerd in horn-rim glasses, white socks, and gaudy plaid clothes, who was supposedly the only person in America never to have tasted a Whopper. The Herb campaign was successful in generating a great deal of publicity; however, much of it was negative, as the campaign was criticized as being stupid, silly, and gimmicky. Herb was not successful in creating a strong image for Burger King or attracting customers—sales dropped 2 percent during the campaign.

After putting Herb to rest, the company tried a theme aimed at middle America with its "This is a Burger King town" campaign, featuring scenes of backyard barbecues and family snapshots. However, consumer awareness of the campaign was minimal, and in early 1987 a new ad campaign using the theme "The best food for fast times" was launched. This campaign attempted to position Burger King as the restaurant for people on the go and included fast-paced shots of young people living a very busy life and eating on the run. When this campaign began, one marketing consultant predicted that it would last only three months because the ad would do little to distinguish Burger King, as most people assume that a fast-food restaurant *is* convenient.

At about the same time this campaign began, Burger King management decided to put its $200 million account up for review. After a five-month agency review process, the company left J. Walter Thompson, its agency of 11 years, and awarded its advertising business to N. W. Ayer Inc. The new ad campaign developed by Ayer used the theme "We do it the way you do it" and emphasized the personal contact customers get at Burger King as well as three selling points: flame broiling, have it your way, and quality food.

It was hoped that the new approach would satisfy Burger King's appetite for a successful campaign and a strong identity in the market. However, after a few months, the new campaign was also falling flat, as Burger King's sales for the first quarter were at least 2 percent below previous year levels, and top executives at Pillsbury were critical of the campaign. Concern over the ineffectiveness of the advertising theme was evident by fall 1988 when Burger King turned to the use of a heavily advertised promotional game to help revive sales.

In early 1989 Pillsbury sold Burger King to Grand Metropolitan, a British company, and a new marketing team was hired. As you might have guessed by now, one of the first moves made by the new marketing vice president was to fire N. W. Ayer and begin searching for a new agency. Perhaps by the time you are reading this book, Burger King will have found the right campaign theme—or a new agency.

Sources: "Burger King Is Hungry—For the Right Ad Campaign," *Business Week*, March 16, 1987, pp. 82–84; "Burger King Shifts $200 Million Account to N. W. Ayer from J. Walter Thompson," *The Wall Street Journal*, September 29, 1987, p. 2; Scott Hume, "Pillsbury Puts Heat on Ayer," *Advertising Age*, June 27, 1988, p. 2; idem, "Burger King Play! 140M Promo Game," *Advertising Age*, September 19, 1988, p. 1; Scott Hume and Gary Levin, "Burger King Axes Ayer," *Advertising Age*, April 24, 1989, p. 1.

It should also be noted that just because an ad is creative or popular does not mean that it will increase sales or revive a declining brand. There are many examples in the annals of advertising of ads that have won awards for creativity but have failed to increase sales of the brand, and in some instances the failure to generate sales has cost the agency the account. Many advertising and marketing people have become very ambivalent toward—and in some cases, even critical of—advertising awards.[6,7] As was discussed in earlier chapters, the success of an advertising campaign cannot always be judged in terms of sales. The problem of finding a balance between creative advertising and effective advertising is a difficult one.

In this chapter we focus our attention on the area of creative strategy in advertising and promotion. We will examine creativity and the process that guides the creation of the advertising message as well as inputs into the creative process. Attention will also be given to various creative approaches, appeals, and executions that are available to the advertiser and considerations involved in using them. We will conclude with a discussion of some guidelines for evaluating the work of the creative specialists.

Advertising Creativity

The Creative Challenge

Those individuals who work on the creative side of advertising have the responsibility of developing an effecitve way of communicating the marketer's message to the customer. By the time the creative person or team sits down to develop an advertising message, a great deal of time, effort, and money has often been spent on identifying the target audience, conducting research to understand their needs and motives, and determining specific communications objectives. Despite all the input and background information, however, the creative development of the advertisement is usually the most difficult part of the campaign process.

Every marketing situation is somewhat unique, and each campaign or advertisement usually requires a different creative approach. One could find numerous lists of rules or guidelines that successful advertising copywriters have developed and offered for consideration in developing effective advertising.[8,9] However, most advertising people would probably argue that there is no magic formula, pattern, or recipe to follow for developing effective advertising. As advertising copywriter Hank Sneiden noted in his book *Advertising Pure and Simple:*

> Rules lead to dull stereotyped advertising, and they stifle creativity, inspiration, experimentation, initiative and progress. The only hard and fast rule I know of in advertising is that there are no rules. No formulas. No right way. Given the same problem, a dozen creative talents would solve it a dozen different ways. If there were a sure fire formula for successful advertising, everyone would use it. Then there'd be no need for creative people. We would simply program robots to create our ads and commercials and they'd sell loads of products—to other robots.[10]

As we saw in Chapter 3, marketers usually turn to advertising agencies to develop, prepare, and implement their creative strategy and programs. Agencies are used because they are specialists in the creative function of advertising. In areas where agencies are not used as often such as retailing, advertising tends to be more informational in nature, and less emphasis is placed on creativity.

Some of you may not be directly involved in the design and creation of advertisements, as you may choose to work in another department or may work on the client side of the business. However, because creative strategy is so crucial to the success of the firm's promotional effort, it is important that everyone involved with the promotional process have some understanding of the creative process that underlies the development of advertising messages, as well as the creative options available to the advertiser. Also, individuals on both the client and agency sides must interact and work with the creative specialists in developing the advertising campaign, implementing it, and evaluating its effectiveness. Thus, it is important that marketing and product managers, account representatives, researchers, and media personnel have an appreciation for the creative area and develop a productive relationship with creative personnel.

What Is Creativity?

Creativity is probably one of the most commonly used terms in advertising. Advertisements are often described as being creative, the people who come up with the ads are

Figure 14–3 D'Arcy Masius Benton & Bowle's Universal Advertising Standards

1. Does this advertising position the product simply and with unmistakable clarity?

The target audience for the advertised product or service must be able to see and sense in a flash *what* the product is for, *whom* it is for, and *why* they should be interested in it.

Creating this clear vision of how the product or service fits into their lives is the first job of advertising. Without a simple, clear, focused positioning, no creative work can begin.

2. Does this advertising bolt the brand to a clinching benefit?

Our advertising should be built on *the most compelling and persuasive* consumer benefit—not some unique-but-insignificant peripheral feature.

Before you worry about how to say it, you must be sure you are saying *the right thing*. If you don't know what the most compelling benefit is, you've got to find out before you do anything else.

3. Does this advertising contain a Power Idea?

The Power Idea is the vehicle that transforms the strategy into a dynamic, creative communications concept. It is the core creative idea that sets the stage for brilliant executions to come.

The ideal Power Idea should:
—Be describable in a simple word, phrase, or sentence without reference to any final execution.
—Be likely to attract the prospect's attention.
—Revolve around the clinching benefit.
—Allow you to brand the advertising.
—Make it easy for the prospect to vividly experience our client's product or service.

4. Does this advertising design in Brand Personality?

The great brands tend to have something in common: the extra edge of having a Brand Personality. This is something beyond merely identifying what the brand *does* for the consumer; all brands *do* something, but the great brands also *are* something.

A brand can be whatever its designers want it to be—and it can be so from day one.

5. Is this advertising unexpected?

Why should our clients pay good money to wind up with advertising that looks and sounds like everybody else's in the category? They shouldn't.

We must dare to be different, because sameness is suicide. We can't be outstanding unless we first stand out.

The thing is not to *emulate* the competition but to *annihilate* them.

6. Is this advertising single-minded?

If you have determined the right thing to say and have created a way to say it uncommonly well, why waste time saying anything else?

If we want people to remember one big thing from a given piece of advertising, let's not make it more difficult than it already is in an overcommunicated world.

The advertising should be all about that *one big thing*.

7. Does this advertising reward the prospect?

Let's give our audience something that makes it easy—even pleasurable—for our message to penetrate: a tear, a smile, a laugh. An emotional stimulus is that special something that makes them want to see the advertising again and again.

8. Is this advertising visually arresting?

Great advertising you remember—and can play back in your mind—is unusual to look at: compelling, riveting, a nourishing feast for the eyes.

If you need a reason to strive for *arresting* work, go no further than Webster: "Catching or holding the attention, thought or feelings. Gripping. Striking. Interesting."

9. Does this advertising exhibit painstaking craftsmanship?

You want writing that is really *written*. Visuals that are *designed*. Music that is *composed*.

Lighting, casting, wardrobe, direction—all the components of the *art* of advertising are every bit as important as the *science* of it. It is a sin to nickel-and-dime a great advertising idea to death.

Why settle for good, when there's great? We should go for the absolute best in concept, design and execution.

This is our craft—the work should sparkle.

"Our creative standards are not a gimmick," Steve emphasizes. "They're not even revolutionary. Instead, they are an explicit articulation of a fundamental re-focusing on our company's only reason for being.

"DMB&B's Universal Advertising Standards are the operating link between our vision today—and its coming reality."

---

known as "creative types," and ad agencies develop reputations for their creativity. Perhaps the reason why so much attention and discussion are focused on the concept of creativity in advertising is because the specific challenge given to those who develop ads is to be creative. It is their job to turn advertising objectives and selling premises into a creative concept that will bring the message to life. Of course, this begs the question, What is meant by *creativity?*

The Creative Education Foundation defines **creativity** as "a quality possessed by persons that enables them to generate novel approaches in situations, generally reflected in new and improved solutions to problems."[11] Some scientists have described creativity as "a feat of mental gymnastics engaging the conscious and subconscious parts of the brain. It draws on everything from knowledge, logic, imagination and intuition to the ability to see connections and distinctions between ideas and things."[12] **Advertising creativity** deals with the ability to generate fresh, unique, and appropriate ideas that can be used as solutions to communications problems.

The copywriters, artists, creative directors, and other personnel who are involved in the creative process have the responsibility of developing an advertising message that will attract the attention of, and hopefully persuade, an audience that is often uninterested and may even be resisting or defending itself from what the advertiser has to say. Their job is not only to write copy, design layouts, and produce commercials but also to find a central idea or approach around which the advertising campaign can be developed. Rather than simply stating what a product's or service's at-

WOMAN: Oh, Paul I like this haircut. It really shows off my . . .

PAUL: Ring around the collar.

You've got ring around the collar!

WOMAN: Those dirty rings.

Sprays and powders weren't good enough. So I tried Wisk.

Wisk does a better job

on ring around the collar.

And Wisk goes on

to get your whole wash clean.

WOMAN: Hi, Paul!
PAUL: Hi, Hey! Does everybody like your new look?

WOMAN: Yep, It's called. . .no more ring around the collar.

Wisk gets ring around the collar and your whole wash clean.

tributes or benefits are, they must put the advertising message into some "embellished form" that will engage the attention and interest of the audience and make the advertisement memorable.[13] They must take the research, concepts, ideas, and objectives that lead to the creative strategy and transform them into an advertisement that will effectively communicate the advertiser's message.

Figure 14—3 shows the D'Arcy Masius Benton & Bowles agency's "Universal Advertising Standards." These nine principles were developed by the agency to guide its creative efforts and help achieve superior creativity on a consistent basis. The agency defines a creative ad as one that meets all nine of these standards.

The ability to develop novel, yet appropriate, approaches to communicating with consumers is what makes the creative specialist in advertising so valuable—and often so hard to find. Creative personnel use a variety of approaches, signs, symbols, and the like, to communicate a product's benefits to consumers. For example, a number of years ago Lever Brothers wanted to communicate to housewives that Wisk laundry detergent is a powerful cleaner that attacks difficult-to-clean spots. The company used several straightforward ad themes such as "The liquid miracle for family wash" and "Wisk puts its strength where the dirt is" to attempt to accomplish this objective. Neither approach worked very well, and Wisk's share of the detergent market fell from 4.7 percent to 2.8 percent.

Wisk came up with a more creative way of expressing the brand's key benefit, however, after an executive at the brand's ad agency noted that research identified dirty shirt collars as a laundry problem frequently cited by women. He came up with the slogan "Ring around the collar" and made it the basis of Wisk's advertising campaign. This campaign theme lasted for more than 20 years and helped Wisk become one of the leading brands of liquid detergent and increase its overall market share to 8 percent (Figure 14—4).[14] The ads for Wisk were changed somewhat so as not to offend the modern-day woman, but the same theme was still used. However, in 1989 Wisk finally dropped the "Ring around the collar" theme in favor of a new creative approach.

Ironically, the copywriter responsible for the new theme—"Tsk, tsk, tsk, Wisk, Wisk, Wisk"—is the son of the person who developed the original "Ring" theme.

Creative Personnel

Many advertising professionals feel that those individuals who work on the creative side of advertising tend to be somewhat unique and different from those on the managerial side. The educational background of creative personnel is often in nonbusiness areas such as art, literature, music, humanities, or journalism, and thus their interests and perspectives tend to be different. Creative personnel tend to be more abstract and less logical, organized, and conventional in their approach to, and solution of, a problem. One study examined the personality characteristics of highly creative writers and architects, which are two types of professionals similar to creative people working in advertising. Highly creative people were found to be significantly more open to experience, more flexible, more unconventional, more playful, more aggressive, more independent, and more inner directed. They were also found to be more intuitive and perceptual in their orientation.[15]

There is a tendency sometimes to describe the creative person in advertising as "strange" or "odd." This may stem from the fact that creative personnel have often been viewed as nonconformists who dress differently and do not always work the conventional 9-to-5 schedule. However, in many agencies it is unlikely that you could tell the creative personnel from the account representatives by their dress or demeanor. Yet there are differences in the creative and managerial personalities and perspectives that must be recognized and tolerated for creative people to do their best work and to ensure successful interaction and cooperation among the creative and noncreative personnel.

Most advertising agencies thrive on creativity, as it is the major component in the product they produce. Thus, they must create an environment that fosters, and is conducive to, the development of creative advertising. The client must also learn to recognize and understand the differences in the perspectives of the creative personnel versus those of the marketing and product managers. While the client has the ultimate responsibility for approving the advertising, the opinions and work of the creative specialist must be considered and respected when evaluating advertising ideas and content.

The Creative Process

A number of advertising people have argued that creativity in advertising is best viewed as a process and that creative success is most likely when some organized approach is followed. This is not to say that there is an infallible blueprint or formula to follow to create effective advertising. As was noted earlier, many advertising people reject and resist attempts to standardize creativity or develop rules or guidelines to follow. However, most advertising creative professionals do follow a process when approaching the task of developing an advertisement.

One of the most popular and well-known approaches to creativity in advertising was developed by James Webb Young, a former creative vice president at the J. Walter Thompson agency. Young stated that

> the production of ideas is just as definite a process as the production of Fords; that the production of ideas, too, runs an assembly line; that in this production the mind follows an operative technique which can be learned and controlled; and that its effective use is just as much a matter of practice in the technique as in the effective use of any tool.[16]

Young's model of the creative process contained five steps or stages that included:

1. *Immersion* Gathering raw material and information through background research and immersing yourself in the problem

2. *Digestion* Taking the information, working it over, and wrestling with it in the mind
3. *Incubation* Putting the problems out of your conscious mind and turning the information over to the subconscious and letting it do the work
4. *Illumination* The appearance or birth of an idea—the "Eureka! I have it!" phenomenon
5. *Reality or verification* Looking back at the idea to see if it still looks good or solves the problem, then shaping and developing the idea to practical usefulness

Young's process of creativity is very similar to an approach outlined much earlier by English sociologist Graham Wallas who suggested that creative thought involved four stages:

1. *Preparation* Gathering background information needed to solve the problem through research and study
2. *Incubation* Getting away and letting ideas develop
3. *Illumination* Seeing the light or solution
4. *Verification* Refining and polishing the idea and seeing if it is an appropriate solution[17]

These models of the creative process are valuable to those working in the creative area of advertising, as they offer an organized way of approaching an advertising problem. It should be noted that these approaches stress the need for preparation or gathering of background information that is relevant to the problem as the first step in the creative process. As we have seen in earlier chapters, the advertiser and agency start by developing a thorough understanding of the product or service, the target market of interest, and the competition. Attention is also focused on the role of advertising in the marketing and promotional program.

One aspect of the creative process that these models do not say much about is how this information will be synthesized and used by the creative specialist. This part of the process is unique to the individual and, in many ways, is what sets apart the great creative minds and strategists in advertising. In the following section we will examine how various types of research and information can provide input to the creative process of advertising.

Inputs to the Creative Process

Preparation/Incubation/Illumination   Only the most foolish creative person or team would approach an assignment without first learning as much as they can about the client's product or service, the target market, the competition, and any other relevant background information. The creative specialist should also be knowledgeable of and open to information about the general trends, conditions, and developments in the marketplace as well as research on specific advertising approaches or techniques that might be effective in this situation. There are numerous ways by which the creative specialist can acquire background information that is relevant to the advertising problem. Some of these informal fact-finding techniques have been noted by Sandra Moriarty and include:

- Reading anything related to the product or market such as books, trade publications, or general interest articles, research reports, and the like.
- Asking everyone involved with the product for information such as designers, engineers, sales personnel, and consumers.
- Listening to what people are saying or talking about among themselves. Visits to stores, malls, restaurants, or even the agency cafeteria can be informative. Listening to the client can be particularly valuable since he or she often knows the product and market the best.
- Using the product or service and becoming familiar with it. This is imperative if the creative person is going to develop ads for it. The more you use a product, the more you know and can say about it.

Figure 14-5 This Ad Describes One Agency's Perspective on the Value of Fact-Finding

---

"Looking for the Capo d'astro bar."
By Bud Robbins

Back in the sixties, I was hired by an ad agency to write copy on the Aeolian Piano Company account. My first assignment was for an ad to be placed in The New York Times for one of their grand pianos. The only background information I received was some previous ads and a few faded close-up shots...and of course, the due date.

The Account Executive was slightly put out by my request for additional information and his response to my suggestion that I sit down with the client was, "Jesus Christ, are you one of *those*? Can't you just create something? We're up against a closing date!"

I acknowledged his perception that I *was* one of those, which got us an immediate audience with the head of our agency.

I volunteered I couldn't even play a piano let alone write about why anyone would spend $5,000 for *this* piano when they could purchase a Baldwin or Steinway for the same amount.

Both allowed the fact they would gladly resign the Aeolian business for either of the others, however, while waiting for that call, suppose we make our deadline.

I persisted and reluctantly, a tour of the Aeolian factory in Upstate New York was arranged. I was assured that "we don't do this with all our clients" and my knowledge as to the value of company time was greatly reinforced.

The tour of the plant lasted two days and although the care and construction appeared meticulous, $5,000 still seemed to be a lot of money.

Just before leaving, I was escorted into the showroom by the National Sales Manager. In an elegant setting sat their piano alongside the comparably priced Steinway and Baldwin.

"They sure do look alike," I commented.

"They sure do. About the only real difference is the shipping weight—ours is heavier."

"Heavier?" I asked. "What makes ours heavier?"

"The Capo d'astro bar."

"What's a Capo d'astro bar?"

"Here, I'll show you. Get down on your knees."

Once under the piano, he pointed to a metallic bar fixed across the harp and bearing down on the highest octaves. "It takes 50 years before the harp in the piano warps. That's when the Capo d'astro bar goes to work. It prevents that warping."

I left the National Sales Manager under his piano and dove under the Baldwin to find a Tinkertoy Capo d'astro bar at best. Same with the Steinway.

"You mean the Capo d'astro bar really doesn't go to work for 50 years?" I asked.

"Well, there's got to be some reason why the Met uses it," he casually added.

I froze. "Are you telling me that the Metropolitan Opera House in New York City uses this piano?"

"Sure. And their Capo d'astro bar should be working by now."

Upstate New York looks nothing like the front of the Metropolitan Opera House where I met the legendary Carmen, Risë Stevens. She was now in charge of moving the Metropolitan Opera House to the Lincoln Center.

Ms. Stevens told me, "About the only thing the Met is taking with them is their piano."

That quote was the headline of our first ad.

The result created a six year wait between order and delivery.

My point is this. No matter what the account, your Capo d'astro bar is there.

Everyone employed at Kresser & Robbins is dedicated to that proposition. No one works here because advertising beats heavy lifting.

That's why, if you allow us to unearth *your* Capo d'astro bar, I promise you this.

You'll feel something strange happening — maybe for the first time.

You'll view your advertising as a profitable investment rather than a questionable expense.

It's a very small difference. Like between night and day.

All it takes is a phone call.

(213) 553-8254

Kresser & Robbins, Inc.
2049 Century Park East / Los Angeles, California 90067 / Advertising & Public Relations

Home of the Capo d'astro bar.

- Working in and learning about the client's business. This is another way of gathering relevant background information. A creative person may want to work in a client's business to understand better the person they are trying to reach.[18]

Moriarty notes that the goal of these fact-finding techniques is to find an elusive, unrecognized fact or remark that will spark a creative theme or bring the creative strategy together. She cites an interesting example of how one advertising copywriter used his fact-finding for a piano account in an ad promoting his agency and its approach to advertising. The "Looking for the Capo d'astro bar" ad in Figure 14–5 describes the value of fact-finding by creative personnel. We encourage you to read it closely.

To assist in the preparation, incubation, and illumination stages, many agencies provide creative people with both general and product-specific preplanning input. **General preplanning input** can include books, periodicals, trade publications, scholarly journals, pictures, and clipping services, which gather and organize magazine and newspaper articles on the product, the market, and the competition, including the latter's advertisements. General preplanning input can also come from research studies conducted by the client, agency, media, or other services on trends, developments, and conditions in the marketplace.

For example, within a few weeks after the Black Monday stockmarket crash of October 19, 1987, there were several studies reported in *Advertising Age* and other publications on consumers' reactions to the crash and how it would affect their spending plans.[19] This type of information was very useful to creative specialists working on ads for products that might have been affected by the crash. The Porsche ad shown in Figure 14–6 is an example of a clever creative response to Black Monday.

In addition to general preplanning input, creative people are also provided with **product- (or service-) specific preplanning input.** This generally comes in the form of specific studies conducted on the product or service, the target audience, or a combi-

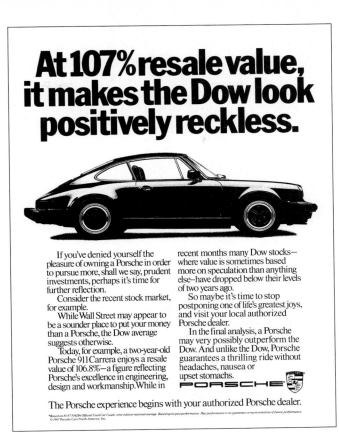

Figure 14—6 **Porsche Used a Clever Ad in Response to a Decline in the Stock Market**

nation of the two. Usage and attitude studies; market structure studies such as perceptual mapping, lifestyle, or psychographic research; market profile; and demographic studies are examples of product-specific preplanning input that can be provided to creative personnel.

A number of years ago the BBDO advertising agency developed an interesting approach for finding ideas around which creative strategies could be based called **problem detection.**[20] This research technique involves asking consumers familiar with a product (or service) to generate an exhaustive list of things that bother them or problems they encounter when using it. These problems are then rated by consumers for their importance, and various brands can be evaluated in terms of their association with each problem. The outcome of a problem detection study can provide valuable input for product improvements, for reformulations, or for new products. This process can also provide ideas for the advertising creative strategy regarding attributes or features to emphasize as well as guidelines for positioning or repositioning new or existing brands.

Some of this preplanning input may be available from studies performed by syndicated research firms. For example, Simmons and Mediamark Research, Inc. (MRI) conduct product usage studies that provide information on the demographic characteristics of users of various products and/or brands. These studies also break users down into categories based on intensity of usage of the product such as heavy, medium, and light users. This information can be used to develop a profile of the various user groups, such as the heavy user, and provide the creative specialist with a better understanding of the demographic characteristics of the audience for which he or she is creating the advertisement.

Other types of product-specific preplanning studies are conducted by the client or agency. Some agencies conduct large-scale psychographic studies on an annual basis and use these studies to construct psychographic or lifestyle profiles of users of a

Table 14—2   **Psychographics of Male Beer Drinkers**

	Percent Agreement		
	Non-users	Light Users	Heavy Users
He is self-indulgent, enjoys himself, and likes risks.			
I like to play poker.	18	37	41
I like to take chances.	27	32	44
I would rather spend a quiet evening at home than go out to a party.	67	53	44
If I had my way, I would own a convertible.	7	11	15
I smoke too much.	29	40	42
If I had to choose, I would rather have a color TV than a new refrigerator.	25	33	38
He rejects responsibility and is a bit impulsive.			
I like to work on community projects.	24	18	14
I have helped collect money for the Red Cross or United Fund.	41	32	24
I'm not very good at saving money.	20	29	38
I find myself checking prices, even for small items.	51	42	40
He likes sports and a physical orientation.			
I would like to be a pro football player.	10	15	21
I like bowling.	32	36	42
I usually read the sports page.	47	48	59
I would do better than average in a fist fight.	17	26	32
I like war stories.	33	37	45
He rejects old-fashioned institutions and moral guidelines.			
I go to church regularly.	57	37	31
Movies should be censored.	67	46	43
I have old-fashioned tastes and habits.	69	56	48
There is too much emphasis on sex today.	71	59	53
Beer is a real man's drink.	9	16	44
Playboy is one of my favorite magazines.	11	21	28
I am a girl-watcher.	33	47	54
Men should not do the dishes.	18	26	38
Men are smarter than women.	22	27	31

Source: Joseph T. Plummer, "Life Style and Advertising: Case Studies" (Paper presented at the 54th Annual International Marketing Conference, American Marketing Association, 1966).

product or service. Table 14—2 shows the psychographic profile of the heavy beer drinker developed from a study conducted by the Leo Burnett Advertising Agency. Close examination of this table shows that the heavy user of beer at the time of this study tended to be more of a risk taker, more self-indulgent, and more interested in sports than the light user or nonbeer drinker. The heavy beer drinker also appears to have been less concerned about responsibilities and had a stronger preference for physical, male-oriented activities.

The Leo Burnett agency used the findings of this psychographic study to develop a very successful ad campaign for Schlitz beer: "You only go around once in life, so go for the gusto." The ads featured virile models engaging in adventuresome activities and living a very exciting and enjoyable lifestyle. The campaign was very successful and helped make Schlitz one of the leading brands of beer in the country in the late 1960s and early 1970s. Unfortunately, the company encountered numerous problems a few years later (including an ineffective new ad campaign) and ended up being acquired by the Stroh Brewery Company.

Qualitative research studies such as focus-group interviews are also used at this stage to gain insight and understanding as to why and how consumers use a product, what is important to them in choosing a product, reactions to various brands and advertising appeals, or any other relevant issues. The information gained from focus-group studies can provide creative personnel with insight into consumers and often gives them valuable ideas that can be used as the basis for a creative approach.

Generally, creative personnel are quite open to any research or information that will help them understand the client's target market and assist in the generation of

Promotional Perspective   **14—2**

People Watching Helps Advertisers Better Understand Consumers

Suppose that you work for an advertising agency and have been assigned to work on an ice cream account the agency just acquired. Your assignment is to try and determine what ice cream really means to the typical consumer. Think for a moment about how you might approach this problem. You might propose a quantitative survey to ask consumers what attributes are important to them in choosing a brand of ice cream, what flavors they prefer, when they like to eat it, and the like. Or you could propose doing qualitative research such as focus-group interviews to let consumers tell you in their own words what ice cream means to them, why they eat it, and how they go about buying it. Quantitative studies such as surveys and qualitative research such as focus groups are very commonly used to answer this type of question. However, some marketers and ad agencies are going beyond surveys and focus groups and are studying consumers by observing them and becoming involved in their everyday lives.

Researchers at Young & Rubicam, the country's largest agency, call their research approach "ethnography," which is an anthropological term that refers to the study of cultures by living with a family and observing how they go about their lives. Young & Rubicam researchers used this approach to address the question posed above—what does ice cream mean to American consumers?—for its Breyer's ice cream account. The agency's researchers visited six families at home to observe their ice cream indulgence. They photographed people eating ice cream and taking that first lick. They looked in freezers, inspected bowls and utensils, and watched people put various toppings on America's favorite dessert. The director of marketing research at Kraft Inc., which owns the brand, noted that "we learned about people's response to ice cream and found that it is a very sensual, inner-directed experience." He noted that the research would hopefully guide the agency in developing more effective advertising.

Young & Rubicam conducts ethnographic research for a number of other clients such as General Foods, Johnson & Johnson, and Colgate, studying things such as how parents and kids interact, which brands are in the pantry or refrigerator, how the home is decorated, and how consumers go about using various products and brands, particularly those of the client. The director of research at the agency feels that "ethnography eliminates some of the distance between us and consumers and brings them alive for our creative staff. . . . The biggest mistake ad-agencies make is to presume they know people just because they have a lot of quantitative data."

Other marketers and consultants are using observational research to get a more realistic picture of consumers and their behavior than can be obtained from interviews. Some feel that techniques such as focus groups result in consumers portraying themselves as they would like to be rather than as they really are and that observational research is more helpful for areas where people have trouble putting things into words and for very routine or matter-of-fact behaviors.

Source: Ron Alsop, "People Watchers Seek Clues to Consumers' True Behavior," *The Wall Street Journal*, September 4, 1986, p. 29.

---

creative ideas. Promotional Perspective 14—2 describes how some agencies use observational studies of consumers to understand consumers better and to develop more effective advertising.

Once the creative specialist has acquired a sufficient amount of background research and information, he or she must blend it all together and generate imaginative and original ideas that form the basis of the campaign. There is little understanding or agreement as to how the incubation and illumination stage of the creative process occurs. However, one area where there is agreement is that not every idea that pops into the creative person's mind is necessarily a good one. Many creatives in advertising often end up looking back at what they thought were great ideas at the time and recognizing how bad they were.

Verification/Revision   The purpose of the verification/revision stage of the creative process is to evaluate the resultant ideas from the illumination stage, reject any that may be inappropriate, and refine and polish those that remain and give them final expression. Some of the techniques used at this stage include directed focus groups to evaluate creative concepts, ideas, or themes; message communication studies; portfolio tests; and the administration of viewer reaction profiles such as that shown in Figure 14—7 to provide evaluations of commercials on various dimensions.

At this stage of the creative process, members of the target audience may be asked to evaluate rough creative layouts and to indicate what message or meaning they get

Figure 14–7   Viewer Reaction Profiles Are Often Used to Measure Consumers' Evaluations of Proposed Ads

Commercial_____   Respondent I.D._____

TELEVISION COMMERCIAL REACTION PROFILE

HOW WELL DO YOU THINK EACH OF THE WORDS BELOW DESCRIBES THE
AD YOU HAVE JUST SEEN?

Extremely well. 5
Very well 4
Fairly well 3
Not very well 2
Not well at all 1

___meaningful to me   ___energetic

___tender   ___ingenious

___exhilarated   ___phony

___worth remembering   ___original

___vigorous   ___lovely

___irritating   ___imaginative

___novel   ___jolly

___humorous   ___enthusiastic

___amusing   ___stupid

___soothing   ___gentle

___ridiculous   ___exciting

___unique   ___for me

___serene   ___valuable

___playful   ___terrible

___merry   ___important to me

Figure 14–8   Ads Can Be Evaluated in Storyboard Form

from the ad or what they think of the execution style, reactions to a slogan or theme, and so on. Television commercials may be evaluated in storyboard form. A **storyboard** is a series of drawings used to present the visual plan or layout of a proposed commercial. It contains a series of sketches of the visual for key frames or scenes along with a description of the audio that will accompany each scene (Figure 14–8). To make the creative layout even more realistic, an **aniamatic** may be produced whereby a videotape of the storyboard is produced along with an audio soundtrack. Storyboards and aniamatics are useful not only for research purposes but also for presenting the creative idea to other agency personnel or to the client for discussion and approval.

At this stage of the process the creative team is attempting to find the best creative approach or execution style before moving ahead with the campaign theme and going into actual production of the ad. The verification/revision process may include more formal and extensive pretesting of the ad before a final decision is made to use this creative approach. Pretesting and other related procedures are examined in detail in Chapter 18.

Creative Strategy Development

Just like any other area of the marketing and promotional process, the creative aspect of advertising is guided by specific goals and objectives and requires the development of a creative strategy. A strategy is a plan of action or design for achieving a goal or end and is an essential first step in the development of any advertising campaign. As we have stressed in previous chapters (you may want to refer to Chapters 1 and 8 in particular) and in the examination of the creative process, the development of creative strategy begins with a thorough assessment of the marketing and promotional situation and a determination of what needs to be communicated to the marketer's target audience.

Creative strategy should be based on the consideration of a number of factors including the target audience, what basic problem or issue the advertising must address, what objectives the message seeks to accomplish, what major selling idea or key benefit the message needs to communicate, and any other supportive information that needs to be included in the advertisement. Once these factors are determined, a creative strategy statement that describes the message appeal and execution style that will be used in the advertisement should be developed. Many advertising agencies have the creative specialist or team state these elements in a document known as the copy or creative platform.

Copy Platform

A **copy platform** provides a work plan or checklist that is very useful in guiding the development of the advertising message. This document is prepared by the agency team or group assigned to the account and may include creative personnel as well as the account coordinator and representatives from media and research. The advertising manager and/or the marketing and product manager from the client side will also be involved in the process and must ultimately approve the copy platform. Table 14–3 provides an example of a copy platform outline that can be used to guide the creative process. It should be noted that there are several variations of the copy platform outline, and agencies are likely to vary in terms of the information and level of detail they include in this document.

Several components of the copy platform have already been discussed in earlier chapters. For example, in Chapter 8 we examined the DAGMAR model and saw how the setting of advertising objectives requires the specification of a well-defined target audience as well as development of a communications task statement regarding what message needs to be communicated to this audience. Defining the target audience is

Table 14—3   **Copy Platform Outline**

1. Basic problem or issue the advertising must address
2. Advertising and communications objectives
3. Major selling idea or key benefits to communicate
4. Target audience
5. Supportive information
6. Creative strategy statement (campaign theme, appeal, and execution technique to be used)

important in the development of creative strategy since the message approach or execution style used in the message may vary depending on the characteristics of the audience. The determination of what problem the product or service will solve or what issue must be addressed in the ad helps in establishing communications objectives for the message to accomplish. The final two components of the copy platform, the development of the major selling idea and creative strategy development, are primarily the responsibility of the creative team or specialist and are the crux of the creative strategy since they form the basis for the advertising campaign.

Advertising Campaigns

Most advertisements are part of a series of messages that make up an advertising campaign. The **advertising campaign** often consists of multiple messages in a variety of media that center on a single theme or idea. The determination of the central theme, idea, position, or image is a critical part of the creative process, as it sets the tone or direction for the development of the individual ads that make up the campaign. Some campaigns last only a short time, usually because they are ineffective or market conditions change, as was discussed in the Burger King example in Promotional Perspective 14—1. However, a successful campaign theme and creative strategy may last for several years or even longer. Philip Morris has been using the "Marlboro Country" campaign for over 25 years, while the "Man in the Hathaway shirt" campaign featuring the model with the distinctive eyepatch first appeared in 1951. The latter campaign has been modified by using celebrities in the ads such as Ted Turner and sports broadcaster Bob Costas (see Figure 14—9). Table 14—4 lists some of the more successful and enduring advertising campaign themes.

Once the creative theme or idea is established and approved, attention can then turn to the type of appeal and creative execution style or approach that will be used. However, before considering these parts of creative strategy, we will examine how major selling ideas are determined that can be used as the basis for the campaign.

The Search for the Major Selling Idea

As noted above, an important part of creative strategy is determining the central theme that will become the **major selling idea** of the ad campaign. As A. Jerome Jeweler states in his book *Creative Strategy in Advertising:*

> The major selling idea should emerge as the strongest singular thing you can say about your product or service. This should be the claim with the broadest and most meaningful appeal to your target audience. Once you determine this message, be certain you can live with it; be sure it stands strong enough to remain the central issue in every ad and commercial in the campaign.[21]

Some advertising experts argue that for an advertising campaign to be effective it must contain a "big idea" that attracts the consumer's attention, gets a reaction, and sets the advertiser's product or service apart from the competitions'. Well-known ad man John O'Toole describes the **big idea** as

> that flash of insight that synthesizes the purpose of the strategy, joins the product ben-

Figure 14—9   **Hathaway Has Run Its "Man in the Hathaway Shirt" Campaign for Nearly 40 Years**

efit with consumer desire in a fresh, involving way, brings the subject to life and makes the reader or audience stop, look, and listen.[22]

Of course, the real challenge to the copywriter is coming up with the big idea to use in the advertisement, as many products and services offer virtually nothing unique, and it can be quite difficult to find something interesting to say about them. David Ogilvy, who is generally considered one of the most creative advertising copywriters ever to work in the business, has stated:

> I doubt if more than one campaign in a hundred contains a big idea. I am supposed to be one of the more fertile inventors of big ideas, but in my long career as a copywriter I have not had more than 20, if that.[23]

While really great ideas in advertising are difficult to come by, there are several approaches that can be used for developing major selling ideas and as the basis of cre-

Table 14—4   **Examples of Some Successful and Long-Running Advertising Campaigns**

Company or Brand	Campaign Theme
Marlboro cigarettes	"Marlboro Country"
Hathaway shirts	"The man in the Hathaway shirt"
Allstate Insurance	"You're in good hands with Allstate"
Hallmark cards	"When you care enough to send the very best"
Budweiser beer	"This Bud's for you"
United Airlines	"Fly the friendly skies"
BMW automobiles	"The ultimate driving machine"
Miller Lite beer	"Great taste/less filling"
State Farm Insurance	"Like a good neighbor, State Farm is there"
AT&T	"Reach out and touch someone"

Figure 14–10 This Ad for Mobil 1 Uses a Unique Selling Proposition

Only one kind of oil can take this kind of heat.

Temperatures inside a car's engine can reach 570°F. Only synthetic motor oil can effectively take this heat.

Tests show that Mobil 1® Synthetic Motor Oil protects vital engine parts under these extreme conditions better than any

conventional motor oil. Mobil 1 costs more. But more people use it every day—because it doesn't pay to play with fire.

Mobil 1. Isn't your car worth the extra protection?

ative strategy. Some of the best known and most discussed approaches to developing selling premises include:

- The unique selling proposition
- Creation of a brand image
- Looking for the inherent drama
- Positioning

Unique Selling Proposition The concept of the **unique selling proposition (USP)** was developed by Rosser Reeves, former chairman of the Ted Bates agency, and is described in his influential book *Reality in Advertising.* Reeves noted that there are three characteristics of unique selling propositions:

1. Each advertisement must make a proposition to the consumer. Not just words, not just product puffery, not just show window advertising. Each advertisement must say to each reader: 'Buy this product and you will get this benefit.'

2. The proposition must be one that the competition either cannot or does not offer. It must be unique either in the brand or in the claim.

3. The proposition must be strong enough to move the mass millions, that is, to pull over new customers to your brand.[24]

Reeves claimed that the attribute claim or benefit that formed the basis of the USP should dominate the ad and should be emphasized through repetitive advertising. The ad shown in Figure 14–10 for Mobil 1 synthetic motor oil is an example of a message that uses a unique selling proposition.

An important consideration in the use of Reeves's approach to developing the major selling idea is, of course, finding a truly unique product or service attribute, benefit, or inherent advantage that can be used in the claim. This may require considerable research on the product and consumers not only to determine the USP but to document or substantiate the claim. As we shall see in Chapter 21, the Federal Trade Commission has become concerned with advertisers making claims of superiority or uniqueness without supporting data. Also, some companies have sued their competitors for making unsubstantiated uniqueness claims.[25] The Ted Bates agency that Rosser Reeves helped organize and that is now a part of Saatchi & Saatchi Advertising Worldwide was known for its "hard-sell" approach to advertising and was often the target of controversy and legal action over uniqueness claims made for its clients' products.

Creating a Brand Image In many product and service categories, competing brands are often so similar that it is very difficult to find or create a unique attribute or benefit to use as the major selling idea. Many of the packaged-goods products that account for much of the advertising dollars spent in the United States are difficult to differentiate on a functional or performance basis. Thus, the creative strategy used to sell these products is based on the development of a strong, memorable identity or meaning for the brand through **image advertising.** Sandra Moriarty has described the brand image approach as follows:

> Image advertising tries to wrap up all the pieces of the perception into a tight, simple concept or symbol. It emphasizes psychological association rather than physical product differences. Image advertising is indirect and long term. It develops a "reputation platform" for the brand or company rather than immediate sales.[26]

The advertising person most associated with image advertising is David Ogilvy, who popularized the idea of brand image in his famous book *Confessions of an Advertising Man.* Ogilvy noted that with image advertising "every advertisement should be thought of as a contribution to the complex symbol which is the brand image." He argued that the image or personality of the brand is particularly important when brands are similar:

> The greater the similarity between brands, the less part reason plays in brand selection. There isn't any significant difference between the various brands of whiskey, or cigarettes, or beer. They are all about the same. And so are the cake mixes and the detergents, and the margarines. The manufacturer who dedicates his advertising to building the most sharply defined personality for his brand will get the largest share of the market at the highest profit. By the same token, the manufacturers who will find themselves up the creek are those shortsighted opportunists who siphon off their advertising funds for promotions.[27]

Image advertising has been used as the main selling idea for a variety of products and services including soft drinks, liquor, cigarettes, automobiles, airlines, financial services, perfumes/colognes, and clothing, to name a few. Many consumers wear designer jeans, Ralph Lauren polo shirts, and Swatch watches or drink certain brands of beer or soft drinks because of the image of these brands. The key to successful image advertising is determining and developing an image that will appeal to product users. The ads for Lawman denim and The Baron cologne show examples of advertisements that have been successful in developing brand images (Figures 14–11 and 14–12).

Inherent Drama A somewhat different approach to determining the major selling idea is by finding the **inherent drama** or characteristic of the product that makes the consumer purchase it. The inherent drama approach expresses the advertising philosophy of Leo Burnett, the founder of the Leo Burnett agency in Chicago. Burnett argued that the inherent drama "is often hard to find but it is always there, and once found it is the most interesting and believable of all advertising appeals."[28] He felt that advertising should be based on a foundation of consumer benefits with an emphasis on the dramatic element in expressing these benefits.

Figure 14–11 **Designer Jeans Often Use Image Advertising**

JEANS BY LAWMAN

NO ONE HAS THE RIGHT TO PRESSURE YOU INTO ANYTHING THAT HURTS YOUR BODY, CLOUDS YOUR FUTURE, OR ROBS YOU OF YOUR SELF RESPECT.

WORLD CLASS DENIM

Figure 14–12 **Colognes and Fragrances Rely Heavily on Image Advertising**

IT'S ALL A MATTER OF STYLE.

The Baron

A distinctive fragrance for men. At fine department stores and Evyan Shops.

Burnett was an advocate of a down-home type of advertising that presents the idea or message in a warm and realistic way. Some of the more famous advertisements developed by the Leo Burnett agency using the inherent drama approach include those for Maytag appliances and Kellogg's cereals. Notice how the ad shown in Figure 14–13 uses this approach to dramatize the fact that Kellogg's Raisin Bran cereal contains more raisins than ever before.

Positioning The concept of **positioning** as a basis for advertising strategy was introduced by Jack Trout and Al Ries in the early 1970s and has become a popular basis of creative development.[29] From an advertising perspective, the basic idea of positioning is that advertising is used to establish or "position" the product or service in a particular place in the mind of the consumer.

Trout and Ries originally described positioning as the image consumers had of the brand in relationship to competing brands in the product or service category. However, the concept of positioning has been expanded beyond direct competitive positioning and, as was discussed in Chapter 7, can be done on the basis of product attributes, price/quality, usage or application, product users, or product class. Any of these can be used as the basis of a major selling idea that becomes the basis of the creative strategy and results in the brand occupying a particular place or position in the minds of the target audience. Actually, positioning can be done on the basis of a unique or distinctive attribute, which shows that the positioning and unique selling proposition approaches can overlap.

Positioning approaches have been used as the foundation of a number of successful creative strategies (as was shown in numerous examples in Chapter 7) and continues to be important as a basis for creative strategy. Figure 14–14 shows an exam-

Figure 14–13   This Ad Uses an Inherent Drama Approach

Figure 14–14   Avia Positions Its Footwear for the Serious Athlete

If this is what an afternoon of mixed doubles means to you, don't buy our shoes.

Avia 770's: use only as directed.

Avia® has taken a curious stance toward part of the tennis shoe market. We don't want it. It's not that we have anything against people whose only regular workout is tossing down cocktails. We'd just prefer that they bought somebody else's tennis shoes. Our shoes are for players at or near the fanatic level.

That's why Avia's patented Cantilever® sole has such a remarkable cushioning effect. It's why we developed lateral/medial forefoot straps, to help control side-to-side movement.

It's why we use Infinity 3000™ compound, to make these shoes last after others have deteriorated into mere sneakers. But those who will use Avia 770's only for marathon drinking sessions should save their money. And to be honest, being seen too often in bars could damage our reputation.

AVIA
FOR ATHLETIC USE ONLY.

Figure 14—15   **Procter & Gamble Has Effectively Positioned Dawn as Being Effective at Cutting Through Grease**

ple of an advertisement from Avia's "For athletic use only" campaign, which attempts to position its shoes for those interested in serious athletics and exercise.[30]

Positioning is often the basis of a firm's creative strategy when it has multiple brands competing in the same market. For example, Procter & Gamble markets three lines of dishwashing detergents—Ivory Liquid, Joy, and Dawn—and positions each one differently. Ivory is positioned on the basis of its mildness, and Joy for its ability to deliver "shiny dishes," whereas Dawn is positioned as being the most effective at cutting through grease (Figure 14—15).

The approaches to determining the major selling ideas discussed above are very popular and are often used as the basis of the creative strategy for advertising campaigns. These approaches represent specific "creative styles" that have become associated with some of the most famous and successful advertising creative minds and their agencies.[31] It should be noted, however, that there are many other creative approaches and styles that are available and are often used in advertising.

Also, agencies are by no means limited to any one creative approach. For example, the famous Marlboro Country campaign, which is a classic example of image advertising, was developed by the Leo Burnett agency, which is known more for the inherent drama approach, whereas many different agencies have followed the unique selling proposition approach advocated by Rosser Reeves and the former Ted Bates agency. The challenge to the creative specialist or team is to find a major selling idea, whether it be based on a unique selling proposition, brand image, inherent drama, position in the market, or some other approach, and use it as a guide to the development of an effective creative strategy. We now turn our attention to the specific appeal and ways of executing the creative idea.

Appeals and Execution Styles

Once the major selling idea has been agreed upon, the creative team then turns its attention to determining the specific type of appeal and execution style that will be used to carry out or develop the creative concept. The **advertising appeal** refers to the basis or approach used in the advertisement to elicit some consumer response or to influence consumer feelings toward the product, service, or cause. The **creative execution style** refers to the way in which a particular appeal is turned into an advertising message that is presented to the consumer. According to William Weilbacher:

> The appeal can be said to form the underlying content of the advertisement, and the execution the way in which that content is presented. Advertising appeals and executions are usually independent of each other; that is, a particular appeal can be executed in a variety of ways and a particular means of execution can be applied to a variety of

Figure 14–16   **This Ad for Geo Prizm Uses a Rational Logical Appeal**

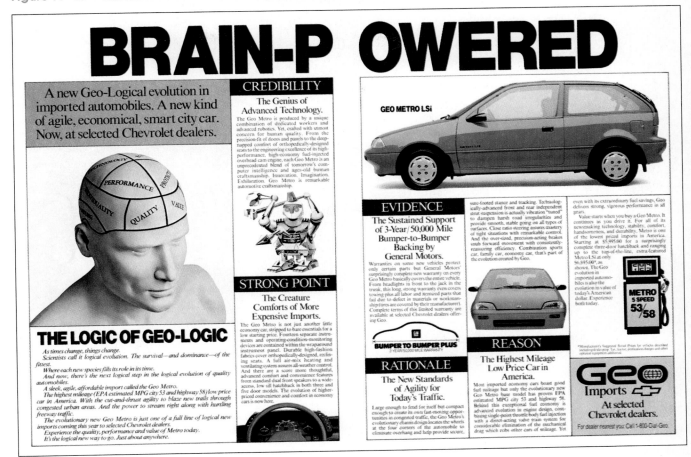

advertising appeals. Advertising appeals tend to adapt themselves to all media, whereas some kinds of executional devices are more adaptable to some media than others.[32]

Advertising Appeals

There are literally hundreds of different appeals that can be used as the basis for an advertising message. At the broadest level, these approaches are generally broken into two categories or classes, which are informational/rational appeals and emotional appeals. The use of rational versus emotional appeals was introduced in Chapter 6 in discussing message aspects of communication. Particular attention was given to the rational appeal of comparative advertising and the emotional appeals of fear and humor. In this section we will focus on some additional ways of using rational and emotional appeals as part of creative strategy. We will also consider how rational and emotional appeals can be combined in developing the advertising message.

Informational/Rational Appeals   **Informational/rational appeals** focus on the consumer's practical, functional, or utilitarian need for the product or service and emphasize features of a product or service and/or specific benefits or reasons for owning or using a particular brand. The content of these types of messages emphasizes facts, learning, and the logic of persuasion.[33] The ad for the new Geo Prizm automobile is an excellent example of this approach (Figure 14–16).

There are many rational motives that can be used as the basis for advertising appeals, including comfort, convenience, economy, health, and sensory benefits such

Figure 14—17   Goodyear Focuses on Customer Needs in This Ad

as touch, taste, and smell. In addition to these appeals, there are a number of other rational benefits or factors that are commonly used in advertising, such as quality, dependability, durability, efficiency, efficacy, and performance.

The particular features or benefits that are important to consumers and can serve as the basis of an informational/rational appeal message will vary from one product or service category to another as well as among various market segments. An important aspect of the preparation stage of the creative process is determining the particular features or benefits of the brand that should be emphasized in the advertising. For example, in recent years many automotive advertisers have been emphasizing attributes such as performance, warranties, and resale value. Research has shown that these are the most important criteria to many consumers in choosing a car, replacing economy and gasoline mileage.

Rational-based appeals tend to be informative in nature, and advertisers using this approach generally attempt to convince consumers that their product or service has a particular attribute or provides a specific benefit that is important to them or shows how the brand satisfies their needs. Their objective is to convince the target audience that they should buy the brand because it is the best available or does a better job of meeting their needs. The ad shown in Figure 14—17 for Goodyear tires is an example of such an appeal. The ad was part of Goodyear's "Nobody fits you like Goodyear" ad campaign, which sought to differentiate the company by showing that Goodyear's approach to selling tires is finding out more about a customer's needs.

Weilbacher identifies a number of product- or service-related appeals that would

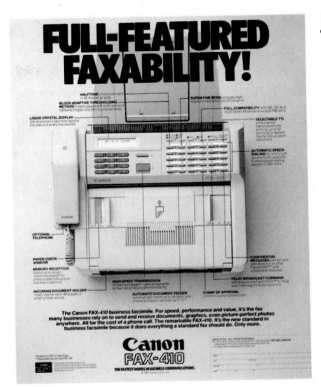

Figure 14–18   **An Example of a Feature Appeal Ad**

fall under the category of rational approaches, as they tend to be informative in nature and focus primarily on utilitarian benefits. His listing of product- or service-related appeals is shown in Table 14–5, and each is discussed briefly.

Ads that use a *feature appeal* focus on the dominant attributes or characteristics of the product or service. These types of ads tend to be highly informative in nature and attempt to present the customer with a number of product characteristics or benefits that can be used as the basis for a rational purchase decision. Technical and high-involvement products and services often use this type of approach. For example, the ad shown in Figure 14–18 for the Canon Fax-410 machine is an example of a feature appeal ad. Many feature appeal ads are based on the unique selling proposition approach that was discussed earlier and focus on a specific attribute.

When a *competitive advantage appeal* is used, the advertiser makes either a direct or an indirect comparison to another brand (or brands) and usually makes a claim of superiority on one or more attributes. This type of appeal was discussed in Chapter 6 under comparative advertising.

A *favorable price appeal* advertisement is one that makes the price offer the dominant point or focus of the message. Price appeal advertising is used most often by retailers for announcing sales, special offers, or low everyday prices (see Figure 14–19). However, this type of advertising is also used to sell products or services when the price offer becomes the dominant message of the ad, as shown in the ad for the Subaru Justy in Figure 14–20.

News appeals are those where some type of news about the product or service dominates the advertisement. This type of appeal can be used for a new product or service or to inform consumers of some change in the product/service such as a modification or improvement. The ad for American Airlines announcing a triple mileage offer for members of their frequent flier program is an example of this type of appeal (Figure 14–21).

Product/service popularity appeals stress the wide use or popularity of the product or service by pointing out factors such as the number of consumers who use the

Table 14–5   **Product- or Service-Related Appeals**

| Feature appeals |
| Competitive advantage appeals |
| Favorable price appeals |
| News appeals |
| Popularity appeals |
| Generic appeals |

Source: William M. Weilbacher, *Advertising*, 2nd ed. (New York: Macmillan, 1984), p. 198.

Figure 14–19   **A Retail Ad for Everyday Low Prices**

Figure 14–20 **Price Is a Dominant Appeal in This Subaru Ad**

Figure 14–21 **American Announces Its Triple Mileage Offer in This News Appeal Ad**

brand or have switched to it or its leadership position in the market. The main point of this type of appeal is that the widespread use or popularity of the brand is evidence that the product or service is good and liked by consumers and that others should consider using it. The ad for Salomon ski bindings, shown in Figure 14–22, is an example of this type of appeal.

The final type of product/service appeal noted by Weilbacher is the *generic appeal*. This type of appeal is used to promote the product or service class in general, rather than an individual brand. This type of appeal was discussed in Chapter 2 under primary demand advertising.

Emotional Appeals   **Emotional appeals** relate to the consumer's social and/or psychological needs for purchasing a product or service. Many of the motives consumers have for their purchase decisions are emotional in nature, and the "feelings" one has about a brand are often just as important as, if not more so than, knowledge of its features or attributes. Rational, informative-based appeals are viewed by advertisers for many products and services as very dull and as making it difficult to attract and hold the consumer's attention.

As was noted in Chapter 6, emotional appeals have become very popular in advertising, as marketers recognize that many purchase decisions are made on the basis of feelings and emotions and since many brands do not differ markedly from their competitors', making rational-based differentiation very difficult. To understand the importance of emotional appeals in advertising, it is only necessary to consider the 25 favorite TV campaigns that were presented at the beginning of the chapter. Nearly all

Figure 14—22 **This Ad for Salomon ski bindings Uses a Product Popularity Appeal**

these campaigns are based on emotional appeals and are characterized by strong entertainment value in their commercials.

There are many feelings or needs that can serve as the basis for an advertising appeal designed to reach and influence consumers on an emotional level, as shown in Table 14—6. These appeals are based on psychological states or feelings that are directed to the self such as pleasure or excitement as well as those that have more of a social orientation such as status or recognition.

There are many ways advertisers can use emotional appeals in their creative strategy. Appeals such as humor or sentiment can be used to put the consumer in a favor-

Table 14—6 **Bases for Emotional Appeals**

Personal States or Feelings	Social-Based Feelings
Safety	Recognition
Security	Status
Love	Respect
Affection	Involvement
Happiness	Embarrassment
Joy	Affiliation/belonging
Nostalgia	Rejection
Sentiment	Acceptance
Excitement	Approval
Arousal/stimulation	
Sorrow/grief	
Pride	
Achievement/accomplishment	
Self-esteem	
Actualization	
Pleasure	
Ambition	
Comfort	

Promotional Perspective **14-3**

Using Nostalgia to Sell Automobiles

The use of emotion in advertising is generally associated with products such as cosmetics, greeting cards, pictures, phone calls, and other products and services where feelings are very important. However, a campaign developed by the Young & Rubicam agency for Mercury automobiles a few years ago showed that an emotional appeal can be very successful in selling more practical items as well. Research by the agency found that awareness of the Mercury brand among the target audience of people aged 22 to 44 was very low. The agency's research also found a strong loyalty and emotional bond among this audience to music from the 1960s.

Rather than bombarding this audience with a litany of facts and information about the cars, Young & Rubicam decided to establish an emotional bond between the consumers and the Mercury brand. A series of ads were developed that became know as the "Big Chill" campaign (after the popular movie that featured a reunion of friends who had gone to college together in the 1960s). The campaign kicked off in 1984 with a television spot called "Reunion." The story line of this commercial was a college reunion set to the music of "Ain't No Mountain High Enough" and featured friends coming from various places, in their Mercurys of course, to the gathering.

The ad had a very strong emotional effect on viewers, as research conducted after it was aired showed that they were reading a variety of positive things into the commercial. The audience recalled all kinds of wonderful moments from their college days and attributed these moments to the Mercury brand. Subsequent spots in the campaign attempted to reinforce the feelings of identification with Mercury by acknowledging the changes these grown-up baby boomers have gone through, including marriage, children, careers, and so on.

Featuring the Mercury cars and brand name with well-liked music and nostalgic scenes apparently worked very well, as sales rose steadily from the beginning of the campaign, and Mercury's market share increased from 4.3 percent in 1983 to 5.1 percent in 1985. Moreover, the age of Mercury buyers decreased by nearly 10 years from 48 to 38.

Other advertisers have tried using 1960s music in advertising campaigns but have not gotten the same results. According to the advertising manager of the Lincoln-Mercury division, the campaign succeeded because it was successful at integrating the market's past with lifestyles of the present. He noted that "emotion is really understanding—a subtle way of touching your audience. And, if you're skilled enough and lucky enough and daring enough to create advertising that touches people, you will ultimately sell them."

Source: "Emotion Sells More Than Perfume: It Sells Cars Too," *Marketing News,* November 22, 1985, p. 4.

able frame of mind or mood state in anticipation that these positive feelings will transfer to the brand itself. It has been shown that positive mood states created by an ad can have a favorable effect on consumers' evaluation of a product.[34] Promotional Perspective 14–3 discusses how Lincoln-Mercury used nostalgia and music as the basis of a very effective advertising campaign. Advertisers can also use appeals to specific emotions such as security as the basis of their creative strategy (Figure 14–23).

Another reason for using emotional appeals is to influence consumers' interpretations of their product usage experience. One way of doing this is through the use of what is known as transformational advertising. A **transformational ad** is defined as

> one which associates the experience of using (consuming) the advertised brand with a unique set of psychological characteristics which would not typically be associated with the brand experience to the same degree without exposure to the advertisement.[35]

Transformational ads create feelings, images, meanings, and beliefs about the product or service that may be activated when consumers use it and thus "transforms" their interpretation of the usage experience. Christopher Puto and William Wells note that for an advertisement to be judged transformational, it must have two characteristics:

1. It must make the experience of using the product richer, warmer, more exciting, and/or more enjoyable than that obtained solely from an objective description of the advertised brand.
2. It must connect the experience of the advertisement so tightly with the experience of using the brand that consumers cannot remember the brand without recalling the experience generated by the advertisement.[36]

Figure 14-23 **This Sure Deodorant Ad Appeals to Emotional Security**

The "Reach out and touch someone" campaign used by AT&T over the past decade to encourage consumers to keep in touch with family and friends via the telephone is an example of a campaign that has made effective use of transformational advertising. The success of this campaign has been cited as one of the reasons for the growth of emotion and sentimentality in advertising.[37]

While emotional appeals have become very popular in advertising in recent years, advertisers must recognize that they will not always be effective. For example, a few years ago Bayer aspirin attempted to use a sentimental appeal featuring a family-run Italian restaurant where "Momma" had a headache. The ad bombed, and Bayer switched to a hard-sell approach whereby a stone-faced announcer made the unemotional statement: "Nothing works better than Bayer—nothing." As the president of McCann-Erickson-Worldwide noted concerning the use of emotional appeals:

> You're playing with something that can be absolute garbage, sentimental slop. Everyone will start throwing up if it's overdone.[38]

Combining Rational and Emotional Appeals In many advertising situations the decision facing the creative specialist is not one of choosing between an emotional versus a rational appeal but rather determining how to combine the two approaches. Consumer purchase decisions are often made on the basis of both emotional and rational motives, and copywriters must give attention to both elements in developing effective advertising. As noted copywriters David Ogilvy and Joel Raphaelson have stated:

> Few purchases of any kind are made for entirely rational reasons. Even a purely functional product such as laundry detergent may offer what is now called an emotional benefit—say the satisfaction of seeing one's children in bright clean clothes. In some product categories the rational element is small. These include soft drinks, beer, cos-

Figure 14—24 Saab Combines Both Rational and Emotional Appeals in This Ad

21 LOGICAL REASONS TO BUY A SAAB.

ONE EMOTIONAL REASON.

In each of us, there is a tough, cold, logical side that wants to have hard facts, data and empirical evidence before it will assent to anything.

So when your impulsive, emotional side saw the exciting photograph on the facing page and yelled "Hey, look at this!," your logical side immediately asked to see some solid and relevant information about the Saab.

Here, then, are some of the more significant hard facts about Saabs, facts that make a strong logical argument in favor of owning a Saab:

1) Front-wheel drive. Once, Saab was one of the few cars in the U.S. that offered this. Since then, most other carmakers have discovered the superior handling and safety of front-wheel drive and have followed Saab's lead.

2) Turbocharging. More power without more engine displacement. Saab's third generation of turbocharging, incorporating an intercooler and Saab's Automatic Performance Control system, is still a generation or two ahead of any competition.

3) Four-valve technology. Doubling the number of valves per cylinder improves engine efficiency enormously. Yet another group of manufacturers is beginning to line up behind Saab.

4) Advanced ergonomics. That's just a way of saying that all instruments, controls and functional elements are designed so that they will be easy and natural to use. A legacy of Saab's aerospace heritage. Saab is the only car manufacturer which also builds supersonic military jets.

5) Special steel underpanel. The Saab's smooth underside improves its aerodynamics and helps shed water to prevent rust.

6) Balance. 60% of the car's weight is borne by the front wheels, to maintain a consistent slight understeer and superior traction.

7) Rustproofing. A 16-step process that's designed to protect the car from the wetness and saltiness of Sweden's long winters.

8) Climate control. Your Saab is going to be comfortable inside, whatever is happening outside. Air conditioning is standard on all models, and effective insulation helps to control the temperature as well as the noise level inside.

9) High capacity electrical system. For reliable starts in subarctic cold.

10) Advanced Sound System. When you're in the Saab, the AM/FM cassette system sounds wonderful. When you get out, it can come with you, to provide the most theft deterrent possible.

11) One of the world's safest steering wheels. Heavily padded and designed to collapse in a controlled manner in case of heavy impact.

12) Safety cage construction. Last year, the U.S. Highway Loss Data Institute ranked the safety of cars based on actual damage and injury claims. Saab 900's were safer than any other midsize sedans.

13) Fold-down rear seats. This makes Saab the only performance sedan in the world that can provide up to 56 cubic feet of cargo space.

14) Large, 15-inch wheels. They permit good high-speed control with a very comfortable ride. They also permit larger disc brakes all around.

15) Price. It's modest, particularly when you see it against comparable Audi, BMW, Mercedes or Volvo models.

16) Side-cornering lights. These show you what you're getting into when you signal for a turn at night.

17) Front seats. Firmly supportive, orthopedically shaped and adjustable in practically every dimension you can imagine. They're even heated.

18) Saab dealers. They're all over the country, waiting to help you with specially trained mechanics and comprehensive stocks of Saab parts, and...

19) Saab accessories. These may be a bit too much fun for your logical side. They let you customize your Saab with factory-approved performance wheels, floor mats, fog lights and so on. And on. And on.

20) Saab's aircraft heritage. The first Saab automobile was designed by aircraft engineers who established a company tradition of carefully rethinking problems rather than just adopting the conventional solution.

21) The Saab driving experience. Best expressed on the facing page.

SAAB
The most intelligent cars ever built.

metics, certain personal care products and most old fashion products. And who hasn't experienced the surge of joy that accompanies the purchase of a new car?[39]

Well-known advertising copywriter Hal Riney has suggested that the balance of emotion and rationality in advertising depends on several factors, including

- The importance of what you have to say—more importance leads to more rationality.
- How familiar your message is—more familiarity leads to more emotion.
- The number of times the consumer will be exposed to your message—more repetition allows for more emotion.[40]

The need to appeal to both rational and emotional purchase motives has been recognized by many advertisers and agencies. The ad shown for Saab automobiles is an example of how the company has attempted to address directly both the rational and emotional considerations that are involved in the purchase of an automobile (Figure 14—24). Promotional Perspective 14—4 discusses how the Foote, Cone & Belding advertising agency has strived to combine rational and emotional approaches to advertising into a philosophy known as "whole brain thinking."

The majority of advertising for products and services could probably be placed in one of the categories of rational or emotional appeals discussed above. Of course, not every advertisement will fit neatly into these categories. For example, some ads such as the one shown in Figure 14—25 can simply be classified as *reminder advertising*. This type of ad does not rely on any specific type of appeal, and its only objective is to keep the brand name in the mind of the consumer. Well-known brands and market

Promotional Perspective 14-4

Whole Brain Thinking Works for Foote, Cone & Belding

Although the Foote, Cone & Belding agency (FCB) enjoyed a reputation for steady growth and consistent profits, for many years the agency was not known for its creative advertising. When Norman W. Brown took over as chief executive in 1982, one of his priorities was to have the agency develop more innovative advertising and improve its creativity image. Brown developed his own version of several well-known "whole brain" theories by stressing that people can be more imaginative if they get the rational, organized, left half of the brain working in tandem with the emotional, intuitive right side. He dubbed FCB's account executives "left brains" who look for rational thought, explicit truths, and what amounts to a hard-sell pitch as the main approach to advertising, whereas the creative people were called "right brains" and seen as focusing on holistic, emotional appeals. Brown encouraged a reconciliation of these two opposite approaches and a dominance of one over the other, depending on the product category and which appeal strikes the most responsive cord among consumers.

Brown's system has been viewed as being more important as a symbol than a system, although it has been credited with helping change the agency's "corporate culture" by stressing that teamwork, cooperation, and innovation are important and valued. Brown's whole brain approach is credited with reducing the waste in creative ideas and improving the agency's creative work and rep-

utation. An example of the whole brain approach was shown to work in a campaign FCB did for Sara Lee in introducing a line of new bagels. According to the creative director, the account team was tempted to make a "low-involvement-pitch" type of commercial listing the fine ingredients in the bagels. However, after using a little right brain thinking, they developed a more emotional pitch based on the fact that consumers said they eat Sara Lee products to indulge themselves. The creative team ended up with a commercial showing a woman savoring a bagel to the accompaniment of bump-and-grind music.

As evidence of how well Brown's whole brain approach is working, between 1983 and 1985 the agency gained $400 million in new billings. The agency had a record year in 1986, as its worldwide billings surpassed the $2 billion mark. FCB was named Agency of the Year for 1986 by *Advertising Age,* an award given for excellence in creativity. The agency also won six other awards including the Best TV Commercial of 1986, earned for the dancing raisins claymation spot the agency developed for the California Raisin Advisory Board. Brown's whole brain theory appears to be working at FCB—particularly the right half.

Sources: "For Foote Cone, the Answer Is Still 'Whole Brain Thinking,'" *Business Week,* March 3, 1986, p. 120; "FCB Is Tops," *Advertising Age,* July 6, 1987, p. 1; "Hot Raisins and More—FCB Turns on Its Creative Brainpower," *Advertising Age,* July 6, 1987, p. 24.

Three cheers for the holidays.

——————— HERSHEY'S KISSES ———————

Figure 14-25 **This Ad Serves as a Reminder for HERSHEY'S KISSES**

Figure 14—26   **This Ad Was Part of a Campaign Designed to Increase Awareness of Absolut Vodka**

Figure 14—26   **This Ad Was Part of a Campaign Designed to Increase Awareness of Absolut Vodka**

leaders often use reminder advertising. Some ads are also used primarily to gain attention and register the product name. The ad in Figure 14—26 was part of a campaign designed to build awareness of the brand name of Absolut Vodka in a market dominated by two strongly entrenched brands.

In addition to these categories, many ads are not designed to sell a product or service but rather to enhance the image of the company or meet other corporate goals such as soliciting investment or employee recruitment. This type of advertising is generally known as corporate image advertising and is discussed in more detail in Chapter 17.

Advertising Execution

Once the specific advertising appeal that will be used as the basis for the advertising message has been determined, the creative specialist or team must then turn its attention to its execution. *Creative execution* refers to the way in which an advertising appeal is carried out or presented. While it is obviously important for an advertisement to have a meaningful appeal or message to communicate to the consumer, the manner in which the ad is executed is also important.

One of the best known advocates of the importance of creative execution in advertising was William Bernbach, founder of the Doyle Dane Bernbach agency. Bernbach's philosophy stressed that how you say something in advertising is very important. In his famous book on the advertising industry, *Madison Avenue,* Martin Mayer notes Bernbach's reply to David Ogilvy's Rule 2 for copywriter's that "what you say in advertising is more important than how you say it." Bernbach replied that

> execution can *become* content, it can be just as important as what you say. . . . A sick guy can utter some words and nothing happens; a healthy vital guy says them and they rock the world.[41]

Figure 14—27   **Puritan Vegetable Oil Uses a Straightforward Factual Claim**

There are numerous ways that an advertising message or appeal can be presented. Table 14—7 presents a list of some of the more commonly used execution techniques. We will now turn our attention to a closer examination of some of these techniques and considerations involved in their use.

Straight-Sell or Factual Message   One of the most basic types of creative executions is the *straight-sell* or *factual message*. This type of ad relies on a straightforward presentation of information concerning the product or service. This type of execution is often used with informational/rational appeals where the focus of the message is the product or service and its specific attributes and/or benefits. This type of appeal may list only one product claim such as the Puritan vegetable oil ad shown in Figure 14—27 or can provide a great deal of product information such as done in many automotive ads.

This type of appeal is often used in print ads, with a picture of the product or service occupying part of the ad, whereas the straightforward factual copy takes up the remainder of the ad space. Straight-sell or factual executions are also used in television advertising, with an announcer generally delivering the sales message while the product/service is shown on the screen. Ads for high-involvement consumer products as well as industrial and other business-to-business products generally use this type of execution format (see Figure 14—28).

Scientific/Technical Evidence   A variation of the straight-sell or announcement execution is where scientific or technical evidence or information is presented in the advertisement. Advertisers will often cite technical information in their ads, results of scientific or laboratory studies, or endorsements by scientific bodies or agencies as sup-

Table 14—7   **Advertising Execution Techniques**

Straight-sell or factual message
Scientific/technical evidence
Demonstration
Comparison
Slice of life
Testimonial
Animation
Personality symbol
Fantasy
Dramatization
Humor
Combinations

Figure 14—28   **Ads for High-Involvement Products Such as Personal Computers Use a Straight-Sell Format**

Figure 14—29   **This Ad for a Yamaha CD Player Relies on Technical Information**

Figure 14–30   This Ad Demonstrates the Ease of Use of a Drug Delivery System

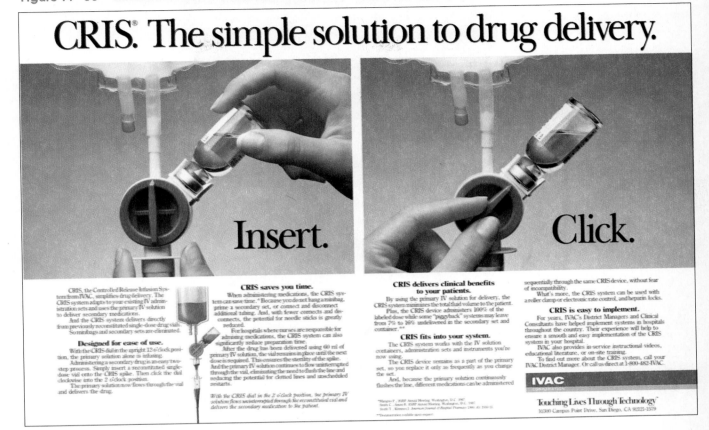

portive evidence for their advertising claims. For example, Procter & Gamble used the endorsement it received from the American Council on Dental Therapeutics concerning the value of fluoride in helping prevent cavities as the basis of the advertising campaign that made Crest the leading brand on the market. The Yamaha ad shown in Figure 14–29 uses technical information to explain how the CDX-910U compact disc (CD) player solves the problem of unwanted noise and distortion.

Demonstration   *Demonstration* advertising is designed to illustrate the key advantages or benefits of the product/service by showing it in actual use or in some contrived or staged situation. Demonstration executions can be very effective for convincing consumers of a product's utility or quality and for convincing them of the value or advantages of owning or using the brand. Television is a particularly well-suited medium for demonstration executions since the benefits or advantages of the product can be shown or performed right on the screen for the viewer to see. Although perhaps a little less dramatic than TV, demonstration ads can also be used as the basis for a print ad execution, as shown in the ad for IVAC's Controlled Release Infusion System (CRIS) (Figure 14–30).

Comparison   While comparative advertising was discussed in Chapter 6 as a type of advertising appeal, brand comparisons can also be the basis for the advertising execution. The *comparison* execution approach has become increasingly popular in recent years among advertisers since it offers a direct way of communicating a particular advantage a brand may have over its competitors or positioning a new or lesser known brand with industry leaders. The southern California Acura dealers used a comparative execution approach to introduce the Legend model and position it against BMW and Mercedes (Figure 14–31).

Figure 14–31   Acura Dealers Make Effective Use of a Comparative Execution

Slice of Life   A widely used advertising format, particularly for package-goods products, is what is known as the **slice-of-life execution,** which is generally based on a problem/solution–type approach. This type of advertisement attempts to portray a real-life situation involving a problem or conflict that consumers might face in their daily lives. The ad then focuses on showing how the advertiser's product or service can be used as a solution or way of resolving the problem. An example of a slice-of-life execution for Dawn dishwashing detergent was presented in Chapter 6 (Figure 6–10).

Slice-of-life executions are often criticized for being unrealistic and irritating to watch. This stems from the fact that this technique is often used to remind consumers of problems of a more personal nature such as dandruff, bad breath, body odor, and laundry problems. Very often these ads come across as very contrived, silly, phony, or even offensive to consumers. However, many advertisers still prefer this execution style because they feel it is effective at presenting a situation or problem to which most consumers can relate and at registering the product feature or benefit that helps sell the brand. Thus, companies such as Procter & Gamble and many others continue to use this execution approach.[42]

Slice-of-life or problem/solution execution approaches are not limited to consumer products advertising. A number of business products marketers have begun using this approach to demonstrate how their products and services can be used as solutions to business problems. Promotional Perspective 14–5 discusses AT&T's use of

Promotional Perspective   **14—5**

Business Advertisers Turn to "Slice-of-Death" Ads

Emotional advertising appeals using fear and anxiety have been commonplace in consumer product marketing for many years. However, recently these emotions are also being elicited in some business advertising through a new advertising genre one ad critic terms "slice-of-death." Perhaps the best known of this genre are ads for AT&T Business Systems (see Exhibit 14—5). In its "business realities" campaign, AT&T targets businesspeople in the process of purchasing a phone system for their company. In one ad a switchboard operator is shown telling a shaky cameraman that she is not taking the blame for the rotten phone system that was purchased by someone else. In another ad, two young businessmen meet in the washroom, and one confides his anxiety over selecting a phone system that has already become obsolete and expresses concern over his future.

While AT&T could have taken a more positive advertising approach that focused on the attributes of its phone system, the company felt that the anxiety ads offered a more powerful appeal. The director of advertising at AT&T noted that "business people are not always nice and polite to one another. They operate under a great deal of confusion and decisions are critical to their careers. What we're saying is don't make a mistake." He also indicated that the ads have attracted a lot of attention (as well as some controversy) and have had a positive effect on the sales force as well as AT&T sales.

The AT&T campaign has also inspired other business advertisers such as Wang and Apple to use the anxiety-inducing slice-of-death approach in their messages. The ads for Wang Computers show people walking in and out of the camera mumbling computer jargon and target managers who do not understand how to use computers. The ads have been described as having an "execustress" quality certain to create paranoia in aspiring top executives who are computer illiterate.

Source: Lynn Coleman, "Advertisers Put Fear into the Hearts of Their Prospects," *Marketing News*, August 15, 1988, p. 1.

Exhibit 14—5   **Slice-of-Death Ads Remind Executives of the Consequences of Making Bad Decisions**

what has been referred to as a "slice-of-death" execution technique that utilizes a fear/anxiety type of appeal.

Testimonials   Many advertisers prefer to have their messages presented by way of a **testimonial** whereby a person speaks on the behalf of the product or service based on his or her personal use of and/or experiences with it. Testimonial executions can use ordinary people such as satisfied customers discussing their own experiences with the brand and the benefits of using it. This approach can be very effective when the spokesperson delivering the testimonial is someone with whom the target audience can identify or the person has a particularly interesting experience or story to tell. It is important that the testimonial be based on actual use of the product or service to avoid any legal problems and that the spokesperson be credible.

A somewhat related but different execution technique from the testimonial is that of the **endorsement** whereby a well-known or respected individual such as a celebrity or expert in the product or service area is used to speak on behalf of the company or brand.

Animation   An advertising execution approach that has increased in popularity in recent years is that of using *animation.* With this technique, animated scenes are drawn by artists or created on the computer, and cartoon, puppet, or some other type of fictional character may be used in the advertisement. The use of cartoon animation is a particularly popular execution technique for creating commercials targeted at children, as anyone who has ever watched Saturday morning television has surely noticed.

Animated cartoon–type characters and commercials have also been used very successfully by the Leo Burnett agency in campaigns for Green Giant vegetables (valley of the Jolly Green Giant) and Keebler cookies (the Keebler elves). Another example of a very successful use of animation execution is the advertising campaign developed for the California Raisin Advisory Board, which—as noted at the beginning of the chapter—has been the most popular campaign on television for two consecutive years. A technique called "claymation" was used to create the dancing raisin characters used in these ads.

The use of animation as an execution style will probably increase as creative specialists discover the advanced animation techniques available using computer-generated graphics and other high-tech innovations.

Personality Symbol   Another type of advertising execution that many companies have found successful is that of developing a central character or *personality symbol* to deliver the advertising message and with which the product or service can be identified. This character can take the form of a person who is used as a spokesperson such as Mr. Whipple for Charmin toilet tissue or invented characters such as Frank and Ed who helped make Bartles & Jaymes one of the leading brands of wine coolers (Figure 14–32).

Personality symbols can also be based on fantasy characters developed by the creative team. As was discussed in Chapter 5, the use of VIPs, or visual image personalities, such as Charlie the Tuna, Morris the Cat, Tony the Tiger, or Max Headroom is a popular way of creating interest in advertising for low-involvement products. One of the most successful advertising personality symbols in recent years, particularly with college students, is Spuds MacKenzie, who is used to promote Anheuser-Busch's Bud Light beer. Promotional Perspective 14–6 discusses Anheuser-Busch's success in using Spuds as a personality symbol for Bud Light.

Fantasy   An execution technique that is very popular for emotional types of appeals such as image advertising is that of *fantasy.* Fantasy executions are particularly well suited for television, as the commercial can become a 30-second escape for the viewer

into another realm or lifestyle. When fantasy executions are used, the product or service becomes a central part of the situation created by the advertiser. Cosmetics ads often use fantasy appeals to create images and symbolism that become associated with the brand.

Dramatization   Another execution technique that is particularly well suited to television is that of *dramatization* where the focus is on telling a short story with the product or service as the star or hero. Dramatization is somewhat akin to the slice-of-life execution technique in that it often relies on the problem/solution approach. However, rather than just using a typical situation or vignette as the setting for the ad, the drama technique uses more excitement or suspense in telling the story. According to Sandra Moriarty, there are five basic steps to a dramatic commercial:

> First is exposition, where the stage is set for the upcoming action. Next comes conflict, which is a technique for identifying the problem. The middle of the dramatic form is a period of rising action where the story builds, the conflict intensifies, the suspense thickens. The fourth step is the climax, where the problem is solved. The last part of a drama is the resolution, where the wrapup is presented. In advertising that includes product identification and call to action.[43]

Of course the real challenge facing the creative team is how to encompass all these elements into a 30-second commercial. A good example of the dramatization execution technique is the ad for American Express Travelers Cheques shown in Figure 14—33.

Humor   Like comparisons, *humor* has been discussed as a type of advertising appeal, but this technique can also be used as a way of presenting other advertising appeals. Humorous executions are particularly well suited to television or radio, although some

Promotional Perspective 14—6

The Original Party Animal

The use of animals as personality symbols for advertising products and services has been around for several decades. Quantas Airlines has used Sydney the Koala bear, who hates Quantas for bringing too many tourists to Australia, for 25 years, whereas Morris, the finicky feline in 9-Lives cat food commercials, has been appearing on television since 1969. Some advertisers have had success with animated creatures such as Charlie the Tuna, who first started trying to trick fishermen into catching him in Star-Kist tuna commercials in 1961, whereas Tony the Tiger has been saying Kellogg's Frosted Flakes are GRRReat for over two decades.

While all these creatures have been around a while, none has had the popularity and impact of the latest personality symbol Spuds MacKenzie, the bullterrier who has been appearing in commercials for Anheuser-Busch's Bud Light beer (Exhibit 14—6). Spuds began his commercial career by appearing on Bud Light posters designed by DDB Needham, the Chicago agency that handles the brand's advertising. Spuds became a cult figure on college campuses, and Anheuser-Busch decided to make him a key part of the 1987 advertising program for Bud Light. He was introduced to national audiences during the 1987 Super Bowl—wearing a white tuxedo, strutting across the dance floor, and hailed as "the Original Party Animal."

Since first appearing in national advertising, Spuds's popularity has soared and created a whole industry of T-shirts and other Spuds paraphernalia. In New York 22 Spuds MacKenzie boutiques have been opened in Macy's Department stores featuring more than 200 items licensed to use his name and image. Spuds has been a guest on "Late Night with David Letterman" and also appeared in a movie with Martin Mull. Like any big star, he has also been the subject of rumors and controversy. First there was some flap over his gender as, although he has been given a masculine persona, Spuds is really a female. There have also been rumors that Spuds was pregnant, that he was really a pit bull, and that he died in an airline crash in Texas, a limo accident in New York, or a hot tub mishap in Los Angeles.

The public's reactions to and interest in Spuds has astonished advertising executives, and there are different theories as to why he is so popular. The creative director of the Ogilvy & Mather agency has theorized that Spuds's appeal stems from the fact that he looks like a real dog. He states that "most of the dogs and cats in commercials come from the same breeding factories, the same test tubes. They're all perfect Irish setters or Golden retrievers. He looks like a dog who's known lady dogs. He's a scrapper. You know he spent his childhood in pool halls." Another advertising executive suspects that Spuds's unconventional looks account for his success: "You've got this animal that's sort of ugly and sort of cute, yet he's surrounded by these sexy women. It's like every postpubescent male's dream. It's packed in enough fantasy that it allows people's lives to be uplifted."

Exhibit 14—6   **Spuds MacKenzie Has Been a Popular Personality Symbol for Bud Light**

Anheuser-Busch was late entering the light-beer market and ranks third in national sales behind Miller Lite and Coors Light. While Bud Light sales increased 20 percent in 1987, Anheuser-Busch executives are not sure of how much Spuds has affected sales since the bulk of the advertising for the brand uses another campaign that does not include him (the "I asked for a Bud Light" campaign). The company has expressed concern that the Spuds phenomenon might be a fad and burn itself out.

Anheuser-Busch has also had to deal with complaints that they are using Spuds to sell beer to minors. MADD (Mothers against Drunk Drivers) and other groups have complained about stuffed Spuds dolls being sold in toy stores and teenagers wearing Spuds T-shirts. The company attributed the blame for this on merchandising pirates and noted that licensed Spuds products are not intended to be marketed to people under the legal drinking age. Anheuser-Busch claims it generally does not show the Spuds spots in prime time so as to avoid exposing him to the under-21 audiences. However, antidrinking forces are not buying the company's arguments, and the National Association of State Alcohol and Drug Abuse directors called for an end to the Spuds campaign. It will be interesting to see how long the Original Party Animal's own party can last.

Sources: Beth Ann Krier, "Spuds MacKenzie: An Underdog's Triumph," *Los Angeles Times*, July 16, 1987, pt. V, p. 1.

Figure 14—33   **This American Express Ad Uses a Dramatization Approach**

print ads attempt to use this execution style. The pros and cons of using humor as an executional technique are similar to those associated with its use as an advertising appeal and were discussed in Chapter 6.

Combinations   It should be noted that many of the execution techniques discussed above can be *combined* in order to present the advertising message. For example, animation is often used to create personality symbols or to present a fantasy execution. Slice-of-life ads often are used to make a demonstration of a product or service, whereas comparisons are sometimes made using a humorous approach. It is the responsibility of the creative specialist(s) to determine whether more than one execution style can or should be used in creating the advertisement.

Client Evaluation and Approval of Creative Work

While the creative specialists have the responsibility of determining the advertising appeal and execution style that will be used in the ads that compose the campaign, the client must evaluate and approve the creative approach before any ads are actually produced. A number of different people on the client side may be involved in evaluating and approving the creative work of the agency, including the advertising manager, product or brand managers, the marketing vice president, representatives from the legal department, and sometimes even the president or chief executive officer (CEO) of the company or the board of directors.

The amount of input and influence each of these individuals has in the creative evaluation and approval process will vary depending on the company's policies, the importance of the product to the company, the role of advertising in the marketing program, and the nature of the advertising approach being recommended. For exam-

Figure 14–34 **Model of the Creation and Production Process**

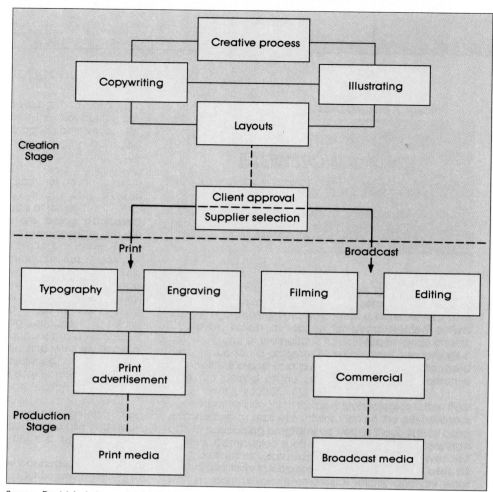

Source: David A. Aaker and John G. Myers, *Advertising Management,* 3rd ed. (Englewood Cliffs, N.J.: Prentice-Hall, 1987), p. 368.

ple, when the Chiat Day agency developed the controversial 1984 commercial to introduce the Macintosh personal computer (which was shown in Figure 3–9 in Chapter 3), the agency had to sell the ad to Apple's top management and board of directors, who expressed some concern over the way viewers might interpret and react to the commercial. Evaluation of the advertising by the company's, as well as the agency's, legal department is very important so that it can be determined whether the ad might be interpreted as being deceptive or breaking any laws or regulatory codes (this is discussed in more detail in Chapter 21).

In many cases top management will be involved in the selection of an advertising agency and must give approval to the particular campaign theme that will be used in the ads. Evaluation and approval of the individual ads proposed by the agency often lie with the advertising and product managers with primary responsibility for the brand. The account executive and a member of the creative team will present the creative concept to the client's advertising and product and/or marketing managers for their approval before beginning actual production of the ad.

As can be seen in Figure 14–34, there are two basic stages in the development of advertising—creation and production. Most of our discussion in this chapter has focused on the creation stage and the creative process whereby ideas, appeals, and execution styles are generated and developed. However, once the creative approach has been determined and approved, the attention then turns to the production process, which involves a variety of functions actually needed to produce the ad or commercial and put it into a finished form suitable for use by the media.

The client will have the opportunity to review and approve the final version of the advertisement after the production stage. However, it is important that a careful evaluation be made before the ad actually enters production, since this stage requires a considerable amount of time and money, as suppliers are hired to perform the various functions required to produce the actual ad. The client's evaluation of the print layout or commercial storyboard can be difficult since the advertising or product manager is generally not a creative expert and must be careful not to reject viable creative approaches or to accept ideas that will result in inferior advertising. There are certain guidelines that personnel on the client side can use to judge the efficacy of creative approaches suggested by the agency.

Guidelines for Evaluating Creative Output

There are numerous criteria advertisers might use to evaluate the creative approach suggested by the agency. In some instances the client may actually want to have the rough layout or storyboard pretested to get some quantitative information to assist in making the evaluation. However, in most instances the evaluation process will be done on more of a subjective basis whereby the advertising or product manager relies on qualitative considerations to make a judgment. Some of the most important and basic criteria or guidelines that might be used in evaluating creative approaches are discussed below.

• *Is the creative approach consistent with the brand's marketing and advertising objectives?* One of the most important factors the client must consider is whether the creative appeal and execution style being recommended by the agency are consistent with the marketing strategy for the brand and the role advertising and promotion has been assigned in the overall marketing program. This means that the creative approach must be compatible with the image of the brand and the way it is positioned in the marketplace and should contribute to the marketing and advertising objectives set forth.

• *Is the creative approach consistent with the creative strategy and objectives and does it communicate what it is supposed to?* It is important that the advertising appeal and execution meet the communications objectives laid out in the copy platform and that the ad says what the advertising strategy calls for it to say. Often, creative specialists will lose sight of what the advertising message is supposed to be communicating and come up with an approach that fails to execute the advertising strategy. Individuals responsible for reviewing and approving the approach under consideration should ask the creative specialists to explain how the appeal or execution meets the advertising strategy and contributes to the meeting of objectives.

• *Is the creative approach appropriate for the target audience?* Generally, a great deal of time has been spent defining, locating, and attempting to understand the target audience for the advertiser's product or service. Careful consideration should be given to whether the ad appeal or execution being recommended will appeal to, be understood by, and communicate effectively with the target audience. This will involve a careful consideration of all elements of the ad and how the audience will respond to them. The advertiser does not want to approve advertising that he or she feels will receive a negative reaction from the target audience. For example, it has been suggested that advertising targeted to older consumers should use models that are 10 years younger than the average age of the target audience since most people feel that they are younger than their actual chronological age.[44] Thus, the client may not want to approve an ad that contains a model that appears too old to the target audience.

• *Does the creative approach communicate a clear and convincing message to the customer?* Most advertisements are supposed to communicate a sales message to the customer. This means that the ad must be designed to tell the audience about the attributes, features, benefits, and so forth, of the product or service and provide them with a reason (or reasons) to buy the brand. Advertising for some products, such as automobiles, often is quite detailed and attempts to provide a great deal of information to the consumer for use in making a decision. However, advertisers must be careful not to try to put too much information and detail into an ad, as it is unlikely that most consumers will have the capacity or interest to attend to it all. The key factor is that the main selling points and supportive information be in the ad and come through to the audience and that extraneous ideas, words, and information be eliminated.

• *Does the creative execution overwhelm the message?* A very common criticism of advertising, and television commercials in particular, is that so much attention and emphasis are put on creative execution that the advertiser's message gets overshadowed. There are many examples of commercials that have been very creative and entertaining for viewers but have failed to register the brand name and/or selling points effectively.

With the increasing amount of clutter in most advertising media, it may be necessary to use a unique or novel creative approach to gain the viewer's or reader's attention. However, care must be taken to ensure that too much emphasis is not put on the execution of the message and that the consumer can remember who the advertiser is and what it is attempting to sell. The primary function of an advertisement is to communicate information that can influence the sale of a product or service. While clients want to make sure that the sales message is not lost at the expense of creative execution, they must also be careful not to stifle the efforts of the creative specialists and force them into producing dull and boring advertising.

• *Is the creative approach appropriate for the media environment in which it is likely to be seen?* As was discussed in earlier chapters, each media vehicle has its own particular climate or environment that results from the nature of its editorial content, the type of reader or viewer it attracts, and the nature of the advertisements it contains. Consideration should be given to how well the advertisement fits into the media environment in which it will be shown. For example, the Super Bowl not only has become the most popular sporting event in the country in terms of viewership but also has become a showcase for commercials. People who know or care very little about advertising know how much a 30-second commercial will cost an advertiser, and many pay as much attention to the ads as the game itself. Thus, many advertisers feel compelled to develop new ads for the Super Bowl or to save new commercials for the game so as to be noticed by the scrutinizing eye of the consumer.

• *Is the advertisement truthful and tasteful?* The ultimate responsibility for determining whether an advertisement deceives or offends the target audience really lies with the client. Most companies have standards regarding factors such as deceptive and/or offensive advertising, and it is the job of the advertising or product manager to evaluate the approach suggested by the creative specialists against these standards. If necessary, the firms's legal department may be asked to review the ad to determine whether the creative appeal, message content, or execution could cause any problems for the company. It is much better to catch and correct any potential legal problems before the ad is prepared and shown to the public than after the fact.

The factors discussed above are basic criteria the advertising manager, product manager, or other personnel on the client side can use in reviewing, evaluating, and approving the ideas offered by the creative specialists. There may be other factors specific to the firm's advertising and marketing situation that must be considered in evaluating the work of the creative team. Also, there may be situations where it is acceptable to deviate from the rules or standards that the firm usually uses in judging creative output. As we shall see in Chapter 18, the client may want to move beyond these subjective criteria and use more sophisticated pretesting methods to make a final determination as to the value of a particular approach suggested by the creative specialist or team.

The creative development and execution of the advertising message constitute an integral part of a firm's promotional program and are often the key to the success or failure of a marketing campaign. Marketers generally turn to advertising agencies to develop, prepare, and implement their creative strategy since they are specialists in the creative function of advertising. The specialist or team working on the creative side of advertising has the responsibility of developing an effective way of communicating the marketer's message to the customer. However, other individuals on both the client and agency sides must work with the creative specialists in developing the creative strategy, implementing it, and evaluating its effectiveness.

A great deal of attention is focused on the concept of creativity in advertising, as the challenge facing the writers, artists, and others who develop the ads is to be creative and come up with fresh, unique, and appropriate ideas that can be used as solutions to communications problems. Creativity in advertising is best viewed as a process that contains several steps or stages, including preparation, incubation, illumination, and verification. Various sources of information and assistance are available to provide input and assistance during this process and help the creative specialists determine the best campaign theme, appeal, or execution style.

Creative strategy development is guided by specific goals and objectives and is based on a number of factors including the target audience, the basic problem or issue the advertising must address, the objectives the message seeks to accomplish, and the major selling idea or key benefit the advertiser wants to communicate. These factors are generally stated in a copy platform, which is a work plan that is used to guide the development of the advertising campaign. An important part of creative strategy is determining the major selling idea that will become the central theme of the campaign. There are several approaches to doing this, including using a unique selling proposition, creating a brand image, looking for inherent drama in the brand, and using positioning.

Once a major selling idea is determined, attention is focused on the specific type of appeal and execution type that will be used to carry out the creative strategy. The appeal refers to the central message used in the ad to elicit some response from consumers or influence their feelings. Appeals can be broken into two broad categories of rational and emotional. Rational appeals focus on the consumers' practical, functional, or utilitarian need for the product or service, whereas emotional appeals relate to social and/or psychological reasons for purchasing a product. There are numerous types of appeals available to advertisers under each category. Creative execution refers to the way an advertising appeal is carried out or presented. A number of commonly used execution techniques were examined in the chapter, along with considerations for their use.

Creative specialists have the responsibility of determining the advertising appeal and execution style that make up the creative strategy. However, the client must review, evaluate, and approve the creative approach before any ads are actually produced. A number of criteria were examined that advertising, product, or brand managers and others involved with the promotional process might use to evaluate the approach suggested by the creative specialist before approving final production.

Key Terms

Creativity
Advertising creativity
General preplanning input
Product-specific preplanning input
Problem detection

Storyboard
Aniamatic
Copy platform
Advertising campaign
Major selling idea

Big idea
Unique selling proposition (USP)
Image advertising
Inherent drama
Positioning
Advertising appeal
Creative execution style

Informational/rational appeals
Emotional appeals
Transformational ad
Slice-of-life execution
Testimonial
Endorsement

Discussion Questions

1. Discuss the meaning of advertising creativity. Choose a print advertisement and a television or radio commercial you like and analyze them in terms of creativity.
2. How should advertising creativity be judged and who should be responsible for judging it—clients or agency creative specialists?
3. What is your opinion of advertising awards such as the Clios that are based solely on creativity? Should agencies pride themselves on their creative awards? Why or why not?
4. What are the various stages of the creative process? Do you agree with the notion that advertising creativity can or should follow a definitive process?
5. Assume that you have been assigned to work on the development of an advertising campaign for a new brand of cereal. Discuss the various types of general and product-specific preplanning input you might provide for the creative team.
6. What is meant by a major selling or "big idea"? What are some of the approaches to developing major selling ideas? Provide examples of each approach.
7. Discuss the difference between an advertising appeal versus a creative execution style. Choose several ads and analyze the particular appeal and execution style used in each.
8. What are the differences between informational/rational and emotional appeals? For what types of products and services would each type of appeal be most appropriate?
9. Choose an example of an advertisement that you feel uses an inappropriate appeal and/or execution style. What type of appeal or creative execution do you feel would be more appropriate?
10. Choose a current advertising campaign and analyze it with respect to the creative guidelines discussed in the last section of the chapter.

Notes

1. Ron Alsop, "In TV Viewers' Favorite 1987 Ads, Offbeat Characters Were the Stars," *The Wall Street Journal,* March 3, 1988, p. 19.
2. Janet Neiman, "Secrets of Long-Lasting Popularity," *Adweek,* March 7, 1988, F.C. 14–17.
3. Ron Alsop, "In '88, There Were No Ads Like Old Ads," *The Wall Street Journal,* February 23, 1989, p. B1.
4. Ira Teinowitz, "Miller to Bench Longtime Theme," *Advertising Age,* December 19, 1988, p. 1.
5. Ron Alsop, "Don Rickles, Devilish Kid Brings Dull Carpet Ads to Life," *The Wall Street Journal,* July 9, 1987, p. 31.
6. Bill Abrams, "What Do Effie, Clio, Addy, Andy and Ace Have in Common?" *The Wall Street Journal,* July 16, 1983, p. 1.
7. Jennifer Pendleton, "Awards—Creatives Defend Pursuit of Prizes," *Advertising Age,* April 25, 1988, p. 1.

8. David Ogilvy, *Confessions of an Advertising Man* (New York: Atheneum Publishers, 1963).

9. Hanley Norins, *The Compleat Copywriter* (New York: McGraw-Hill, 1966).

10. Hank Sneiden, *Advertising Pure and Simple* (New York: ANACOM, 1977).

11. David Mars, "Organizational Climate for Creativity" (Occasional Paper no. 4, Creative Education Foundation, Buffalo, 1969).

12. Emily T. Smith, "Are You Creative?" *Business Week,* September 30, 1985, pp. 81–82.

13. For an interesting discussion on the embellishment of advertising messages, see William M. Weilbacher, *Advertising,* 2nd ed. (New York: Macmillan, 1984), pp. 180–82.

14. Ron Alsop, "Ring around the Collar Ads Irritate Many Yet Get Results," *The Wall Street Journal,* November 4, 1982, p. 33.

15. Frank Barron, *Creative Person and Creative Process* (New York: Holt, Rinehart and Winston, 1969).

16. James Webb Young, *A Technique for Producing Ideas,* 3rd ed. (Chicago: Crain Books, 1975), p. 42.

17. Graham Wallas, *The Art of Thought* (New York: Harcourt, Brace and World, 1926).

18. Sandra E. Moriarty, *Creative Advertising: Theory and Practice* (Englewood Cliffs, N.J.: Prentice-Hall, 1986).

19. "Good News: Consumers Bounce Back," *Advertising Age,* November 9, 1987, p. 1.

20. E. E. Norris, "Seek Out the Consumer's Problem," *Advertising Age,* March 17, 1975, pp. 43–44.

21. A. Jerome Jeweler, *Creative Strategy in Advertising* (Belmont, Calif.: Wadsworth, 1981).

22. John O'Toole, *The Trouble with Advertising,* 2nd ed. (New York: Random House, 1985), p. 131.

23. David Ogilvy, *Ogilvy on Advertising* (New York: Crown, 1983), p. 16.

24. Rosser Reeves, *Reality in Advertising* (New York: Knopf, 1961), pp. 47, 48.

25. Bill Abrams, "Ad Constraints Could Persist Even If the FTC Loosens Up," *The Wall Street Journal,* December 10, 1981, p. 33.

26. Moriarty, *Creative Advertising,* p. 63.

27. Ogilvy, *Confessions.*

28. Martin Mayer, *Madison Avenue, U.S.A.* (New York: Pocket Books, 1958).

29. Jack Trout and Al Ries, "The Positioning Era Cometh," *Advertising Age,* April 24, 1972, pp. 35–38; May 1, 1972, pp. 51–54; May 8, 1972, pp. 114–16.

30. Marcy Magiera, "Avia Gets Nasty," *Advertising Age,* February 13, 1989, p. 4.

31. David A. Aaker and John G. Myers, *Advertising Management,* 3rd ed. (Englewood Cliffs, N.J.: Prentice-Hall, 1987).

32. Weilbacher, *Advertising,* p. 197.

33. William Wells, John Burnett, and Sandra Moriarty, *Advertising* (Englewood Cliffs, N.J.: Prentice-Hall, 1989), p. 330.

34. For a review of research on the effect of mood states on consumer behavior, see Meryl Paula Gardner, "Mood States and Consumer Behavior: A Critical Review," *Journal of Consumer Research* 12, no. 3 (December 1985), pp. 281–300.

35. Christopher P. Puto and William D. Wells, "Informational and Transformational Advertising: The Differential Effects of Time," in *Advances in Consumer Research,* vol. 11, ed. Thomas C. Kinnear (Ann Arbor: Association for Consumer Research, 1984), p. 638.

36. Ibid.

37. Bill Abrams, "If Logic Doesn't Sell, Try a Tug on the Heartstrings," *The Wall Street Journal,* April 8, 1982, p. 27.

38. Quote by John Bergin cited in ibid.

39. David Ogilvy and Joel Raphaelson, "Research on Advertising Techniques That Work and Don't Work," *Harvard Business Review,* July–August 1982, p. 18.

40. Hal Riney, "Emotion in Advertising," *Viewpoint: By, for and about Ogilvy and Mather* 1 (1981), pp. 5–13.

41. Mayer, *Madison Avenue,* p. 64.

42. Harry McMahan and Mack Kile, "Slice Sells with Drama," *Advertising Age,* September 14, 1982, p. 68.

43. Moriarty, *Creative Advertising,* p. 77.

44. Eva Pomice, "Madison Avenue's Blind Spot," *U.S. News & World Report,* October 3, 1988, p. 49.

15

Consumer-Oriented Sales Promotion

CHAPTER OBJECTIVES

1. To understand the role of sales promotion in a company's marketing and promotional program and to examine reasons for the increasing importance of sales promotion

2. To examine the various objectives of sales promotion programs

3. To examine the various types of consumer-oriented sales promotion tools and factors to consider in using them

4. To understand how sales promotion is coordinated with advertising

5. To consider potential problems and abuse by companies in their use of sales promotion

Wisk Bright Nights

For a number of years Wisk has been the leading brand of liquid laundry detergent with much of its success being attributed to its well-known "Ring around the collar" ad theme which was used for more than 20 years (see again Figure 14–4). However, in recent years, Wisk has been challenged by a number of new entrants into the liquid detergent market including a liquid version of Procter & Gamble's well-known Tide brand.

To help Wisk retain its number-one position, despite the increased competition, and to celebrate the product's new, improved formula and thirtieth anniversary, Lever Brothers decided to use an integrated consumer and trade promotion/public relations program built around the sponsorship of a 23-city national fireworks tour. The promotional objectives were not only to maintain Wisk's sales leadership but also to develop in-store support from retailers and community goodwill in local markets. (See Figure 15–1.)

The "Wisk Bright Nights '87" promotion was the first national fireworks tour ever held in the United States. The fireworks show was tied in with established local festivals, fairs, or special events such as Philadelphia's "We Are the People 200 Constitution" celebration. Each show consisted of a 24-minute fireworks display with a special "Ring around the sky" fireworks effect that symbolized the "Ring around the collar" ad theme. The fireworks were choreographed to 30 years of rock and roll music to commemorate Wisk's thirtieth anniversary. Publicity was generated by having the famous Grucci family, who executed the fireworks, serve as Wisk spokespersons for television, radio, and print interviews.

In addition to the fireworks shows, other consumer promotions activities included radio simulcasts, local radio and newspaper advertising, high-value coupons, and a sweepstakes offering the winner a trip to the International Fireworks Competition in Monte Carlo. The publicity and consumer promotions were backed up by a number of trade promotion elements including increased allowances to retailers for displaying Wisk, point-of-purchase material, and ad slicks for local retailer promotion of the fireworks events. Lever Brothers also held VIP parties for supermarket buyers and their families at the site of each show.

The Wisk Bright Nights '87 program was the most successful event promotion in Lever Brothers' history, as it registered more than 175 million impressions via national and local TV, print, and radio, and an estimated 3 million people attended the fireworks shows. Not only did Wisk retain its leadership in the liquid detergent market; it also set new sales records. Although liquid detergent sales increased by only 1.5 percent in 1987, Wisk's volume increased by more than 5 percent, and despite the continued introduction of new brands, Wisk's share of detergent displays increased by 10 percent. The promotion also won a "Reggie" award from the Promotional Marketing Association of America as one of the five best promotions of 1987.[1,2]

Figure 15–1   **Wisk Bright Nights '87 Was a Very Successful Promotion**

Figure 15–2   Kix Uses a T-Shirt Offer as a Premium Incentive

Introduction

For many years advertising was the major component in the promotional budget of most consumer product firms. Most companies would concentrate their promotional efforts on the development of advertising campaigns that would create or reinforce brand awareness and image and build long-term consumer loyalty to their products. Over the past decade, however, many marketers have come to the realization that heavy spending on advertising is often not enough to move their products off store shelves and into the hands of consumers. Companies are increasingly turning to sales promotion methods targeted at both consumers and the wholesalers and retailers who distribute their products and services. As was shown in the opening vignette, companies are developing fully integrated marketing programs that include consumer promotions, trade promotions, and dealer-incentive programs that are coordinated with advertising and publicity/public relations campaigns as well as sales force efforts.

The Scope and Role of Sales Promotion

Sales promotion has been defined as "a direct inducement that offers an extra value or incentive for the product to the sales force, distributors or the ultimate consumer with the primary objective of creating an immediate sale."[3] There are several important aspects to sales promotion that should be kept in mind as you read this chapter.

First, sales promotion involves some type of inducement that provides an *extra incentive* to buy. This incentive is usually the key element in a promotional program

and can include a coupon or price reduction, the opportunity to enter a contest or sweepstakes, a money-back refund or rebate, or an extra amount of a product. The incentive may also be a free sample of the product, which is given in hopes of generating a future purchase, or a premium, which also serves as a reminder of the brand name and reinforces its image, such as the Kix T-shirt offer (Figure 15–2). Most sales promotion offers attempt to add some value to the product or service. While advertising appeals to the consumer's mind and emotions in hopes of giving the individual a reason to buy, sales promotion appeals more to the pocketbook and provides an extra incentive for purchasing a brand.

A second point regarding sales promotion is that it is essentially an **acceleration tool** that is designed to speed up the selling process and is often used to maximize sales volume.[4] By providing an extra incentive, sales promotion techniques can motivate consumers to purchase a larger quantity of a brand or shorten the purchase cycle of the trade or consumers by encouraging them to take more immediate action.

Companies may also use limited time offers such as price-off deals to retailers or a coupon with an expiration date (Figure 15–3) to accelerate the purchase process. Sales promotion attempts to maximize sales volume by motivating customers who have not been responsive to advertising or other efforts to purchase a brand. The ideal sales promotion program is one that generates sales that would not otherwise be achieved by other means such as advertising. However, as we shall see later, many sales promotion programs end up being used more by current users of a brand rather than attracting new users.

A final point regarding sales promotion activities is that they can be targeted to different parties in the marketing channel. As shown in Figure 15–4, sales promotion can be broken into two major categories: consumer-oriented promotions and trade-oriented promotions. The various activities involved in **consumer-oriented sales promotion** include couponing, sampling, premiums, bonus packs, price-offs, rebates, contests, sweepstakes, and event sponsorship. These promotions are directed at the consumers who purchase goods and services and are designed to provide them with an inducement to purchase the marketer's brand.

As was discussed in Chapter 2, consumer-oriented promotions are part of a promotional "pull strategy" and work along with advertising to encourage consumers to

Figure 15—4   **Types of Sales Promotion Activities**

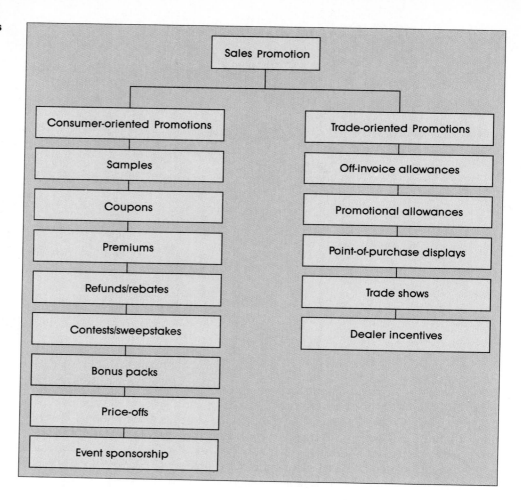

purchase a particular brand and thus create demand for it. It should also be noted that consumer-oriented promotions can also be used by retailers as a way of encouraging consumers to shop in their particular stores. For example, many grocery stores use their own coupons or sponsor contests and other promotions as ways of increasing store patronage.

Trade-oriented sales promotion includes activities such as promotional allowances, dealer incentives, point-of-purchase displays, sales contests and sweepstakes, trade shows, and other programs designed to motivate distributors and retailers to carry a product and make an extra effort to promote or "push" it to their customers. Approximately 60 percent of all sales promotional dollars are spent on trade promotions, with the remaining 40 percent going to consumer-oriented promotions. Many marketing programs include both trade- and consumer-oriented sales promotion programs, as it is important to stimulate both groups in order to maximize the effectiveness of the marketing and promotional program.

In this chapter we will focus on consumer-oriented sales promotions and the role they play in a firm's marketing and promotional program. Attention will be given to the objectives of sales promotional programs as well as the various sales promotion techniques and the considerations involved in using them. We will also examine how sales promotion can be integrated into the overall marketing and advertising program, as well as the problem of potential overuse—or even abuse—of sales promotion tools by many companies. Trade-oriented promotions are covered under the topic of reseller support in Chapter 16.

Figure 15-5 **Advertising and Promotion Spending in the '80s**

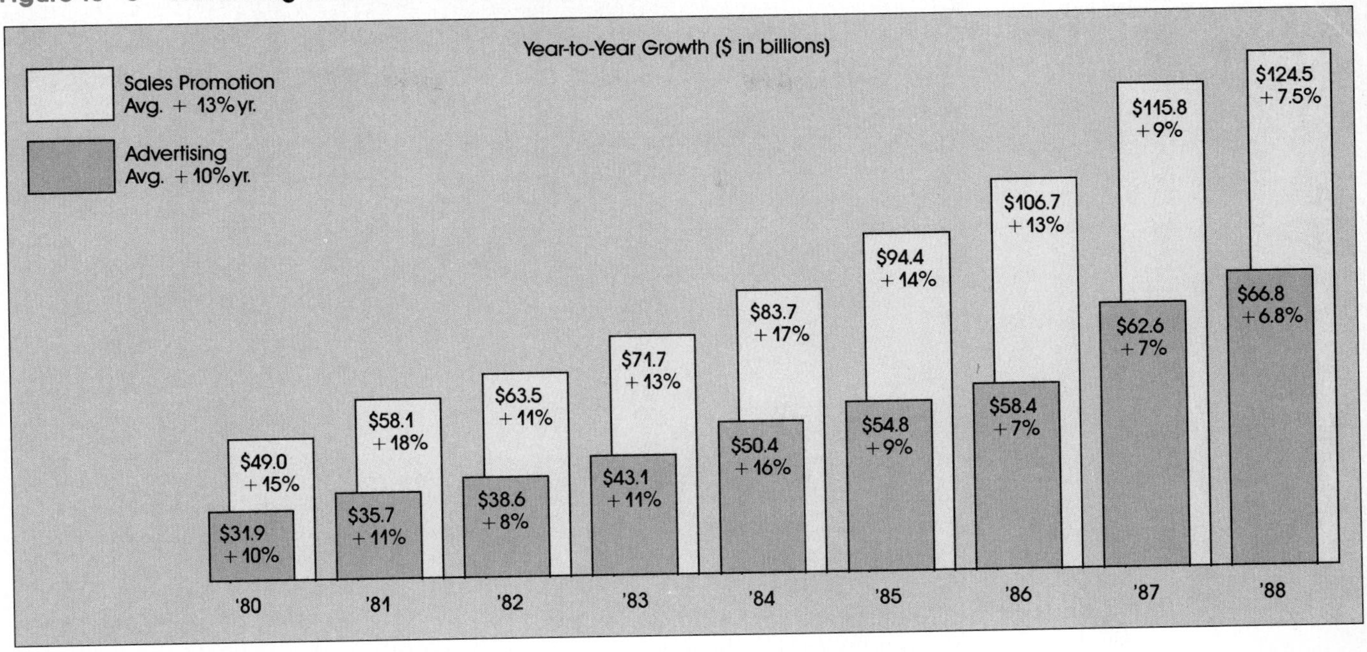

Source: *Marketing & Media Decisions*, July 1989, p. 124.

The Increasing Importance of Sales Promotion

The Growth of Sales Promotion

While the use of sales promotion techniques for consumers, as well as the trade, has been around for a long time, their role and importance in the marketing program have increased dramatically. As can be seen in Figure 15–5, over the past 10 years, total estimated expenditures on sales promotion have increased at an average annual rate of 13 percent, from $49 billion in 1980 to more than $124.5 billion in 1988. During this same time period, spending on national advertising increased 10 percent per year from $31.9 billion to $66.8 billion.

Not only has the total amount of money spent on sales promotion increased, but the percentage of marketers' budgets allocated to promotion has also been increasing. Annual studies by Donnelley Marketing track promotional spending of major packaged-goods companies in three categories: trade promotion, consumer promotion, and advertising. Figure 15–6 shows the long-term trend of allocations to each of the three categories and reveals that the percentage of the marketing budget spent on consumer and trade promotions has increased over the past decade, whereas the advertising portion has declined. The shift of marketing dollars to sales promotion among major packaged-goods companies is expected to continue. It has been predicted that the marketing mix of many packaged-goods companies will eventually reach 70 percent sales promotion and 30 percent advertising.[5]

Reasons for Increases in Consumer Sales Promotion

Declining Brand Loyalty/Increasing Promotional Sensitivity A major reason for the increase in consumer-oriented sales promotions is that consumers are becoming less brand loyal and purchasing more on the basis of value and convenience.

Figure 15—6 **Changes in Allocation of Promotional Dollars**

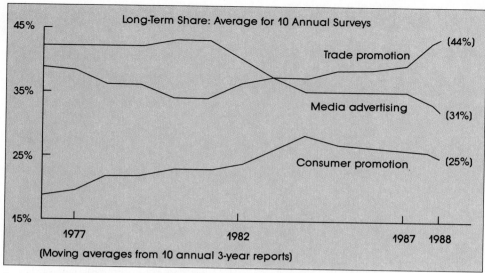

Source: Donnelley Marketing 11th Annual Survey of Promotional Practices (Stamford, Conn.: Donnelley Marketing, 1989).

Consumers are more willing than ever to switch back and forth among brands. It has been estimated that the percentage of consumers who are brand loyal is under 50 percent for most product categories.[6] This decrease in brand loyalty is due to a number of factors including the fact that consumers have become increasingly "promotion sensitive" and often choose to buy a brand only if it is on special, if it offers a premium, or if they have a coupon for it.

A study analyzing 50 supermarket brands in 23 product categories found that the percentage of purchases made with some sort of promotional offer increased from 23 percent in 1975 to 40 percent less than a decade later.[7] The results of a more recent study found consumers indicating that 54 percent of their purchases were made under some promotional inducement, with price promotions, coupons, and point-of-purchase displays being the most important.[8] In many product categories consumers have developed divided or multibrand loyalty whereby they make purchases from among a set of two or more preferred brands. These brands are all perceived as being satisfactory and interchangeable, and consumers will purchase whatever brand is on sale or for which they have a coupon.

Another reason for increased promotional sensitivity is the fact that many purchase decisions are being made in the store by consumers who are increasingly time poor and facing "hyperchoice," or too many choice options. One study found that there are 2.6 times as many choices of brands than consumers want in moderate-sized supermarkets.[9] When consumers make purchase decisions in the store, they are very likely to be attentive and responsive to promotional deals. Buying a brand that is on special or being displayed can also be a way of simplifying the decision-making process and dealing with the problem of overchoice. Leigh McAlister has described the consumers' declining loyalty and increasing promotional sensitivity as follows:

> As consumers go down the supermarket aisle they spend three to ten seconds in each product category. They often don't know the regular price of the chosen product. However, they do have a sense of whether or not that product is on promotion. As they go down the aisle, they are trying to pensively fill their baskets with good products without tiresome calculations. They see a "good deal" and it goes in the cart.[10]

The net effect of declining loyalty and increasing promotional sensitivity is that marketers are finding it increasingly necessary to use sales promotion techniques to attract and maintain customers. In many product categories, promotions are becoming very commonplace, which encourages increasingly sophisticated and price-sensitive consumers to use them.

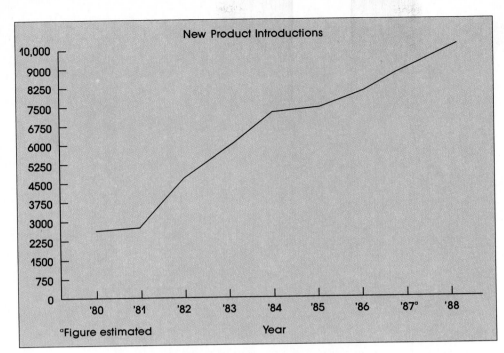

Figure 15–7   **Increase in New Product Introductions**

Sources: "Grocer 'Fee' Hampers New Product Launches," *Advertising Age,* August 3, 1987, p. 1; Rebecca Famin, "Where Are the New Brands?" *Marketing & Media Decisions,* July 1989, pp. 22–27.

Brand Proliferation   A major aspect of many firms' marketing strategies over the past decade has been the development of new products. As can be seen in Figure 15–7, over 10,000 new products were introduced to the marketplace in 1988, as compared with only 2,689 in 1980. The market has become saturated with new brands that often lack any significant advantages that can be used as the basis of an advertising campaign. Thus, companies have become increasingly dependent on sales promotion to encourage consumers to try these brands. In Chapter 4 we saw how sales promotion techniques can be used as part of the "shaping process" to lead the consumer from initial trial to repeat purchase at full price. Marketers are relying more on promotional tools such as samples, coupons, rebates, premiums, and other innovative promotions as ways of achieving trial usage of their new brands and encouraging repeat purchase.

Promotions are also important in getting retailers to allocate some of their precious shelf space to new brands. The competition for shelf space allocation for new products in supermarkets and other stores is enormous. Retailers will be more open to new brands with strong sales promotion support that will bring in more customers and thus help boost their sales and profits.[11]

Fragmentation of the Consumer Market   Many companies are finding that the consumer market has become increasingly fragmented and difficult to market to. A myriad of media options are available to consumers, with the growth of cable television, radio, and special-interest magazines making it difficult to find efficiencies in mass media. As traditional mass media–based strategies such as advertising become less effective, marketers are turning to more segmented, highly targeted approaches. For example, with the increasing focus on regional marketing, more major companies are tailoring their promotional efforts to specific geographic markets and even to certain retail chains.[12,13] Sales promotion tools have become one of the primary vehicles for doing this through programs tied into local flavor, themes, or events (Figure 15–8).

Short-term Focus   Some analysts have suggested that the increase in consumer-oriented sales promotions is motivated by marketing plans and reward systems that

Figure 15–8   Many Promotions Are Targeted to a Local Market

are geared to short-term performance and focus on the immediate generation of sales volume.[14] Consumer promotions are viewed by many firms as the most dependable tool for producing immediate sales, since they generally provide faster results than advertising, particularly when they are price related. This, of course, has led to considerable concern that managers may be becoming too dependent on the "quick sales fix" that can result from a promotion and that the brand franchise may be eroded by too many deals.

Increased Accountability   In addition to putting pressure on their marketing managers to produce short-term sales results, many companies are demanding to know just what they are getting from their promotional expenditures. It has been noted that many companies are shifting their promotional dollars from advertising sales promotion as a result of a new emphasis on economic accountability and sales performance.[15] Top management in many firms is demanding more measurable and accountable methods of relating promotional activities to sales, which is easier to do for sales promotion than for advertising.

Manufacturers are also facing increasing pressure from the trade as growth and consolidation of retail chains have led to increased retailer power. Not only are these more powerful retailers demanding sales performance from manufacturers' brands, but scanner data and new space management systems have resulted in improved ability for retailers to track sales results. Thus, many companies are developing creative marketing partnerships with retailers that include both trade and consumer promotional programs.

Clutter   The increasing problem of advertising clutter, which was discussed in previous chapters, has led many advertisers to turn to consumer promotions as a way of attracting consumers' attention and interest to their advertisements. The use of a promotional offer in an ad will often attract the interest of the consumer and thus may be a useful way of breaking through the clutter that is prevalent in most media today. For example, a study by the A. C. Nielsen Company has shown that ad readership scores are 25 to 40 percent higher for advertisements with coupons than for ads without them (Figure 15–9).[16]

Sales Promotion Objectives

As the use of sales promotion techniques continues to increase, companies must give consideration to what they hope to accomplish through their promotions and how they interact with other marketing activities such as advertising. As noted earlier, marketers often implement sales promotion programs to gain short-term sales increases with little attention given to the long-term, cumulative effect promotions may have on the brand's image and position in the marketplace. This often leads to ill-conceived programs that do little more than create short-term spikes in the sales curve.

Not all sales promotion activities are designed to achieve the same objectives. Attention must be given to just what the promotion is designed to accomplish and among what target audience. By having clearly defined objectives and measurable goals for their sales promotion programs, managers are forced to think beyond the short-term sale fix and consider the specific role the sales promotion should play in their overall marketing plan. Before examining some of the specific objectives for sales promotion, it is important to make the distinction between consumer-franchise-building sales promotion efforts and non-franchise-building efforts.

Consumer-Franchise-Building and Non-Franchise-Building Promotions

Sales promotion activities that are effective in communicating distinctive brand attributes and that contribute to the development and reinforcement of brand identity are often referred to as **consumer-franchise-building (CFB) promotions.**[17] Consumer sales promotion efforts cannot make consumers loyal to a brand that is of little value or that does not provide them with a specific benefit. However, some promotional activities can assist in making consumers aware of a brand and, by communicating its specific features and benefits, contribute to the development of a favorable brand image. Consumer-franchise-building promotions are designed to build long-term brand preference and help the company achieve the ultimate goal of full-price purchases that are not dependent on a promotional offer.

For many years, franchise or image building was viewed as the exclusive realm of advertising, whereas the role of sales promotion was viewed as generating short-term sales increases. However, many marketers have recognized the image building potential of sales promotion and are paying attention to the CFB value of their promotional programs. One sales promotion expert describes the acceptance of the image building potential of sales promotion as follows:

> Today's marketers who appreciate the potential of sales promotion as an ongoing strategy that works to build a brand's franchise recognize that promotion's potential goes well beyond mere quick-fix, price-off tactics. The promotion professional is familiar with a variety of approaches to generating consumer involvement—i.e., sweepstakes, special events, premiums, or rebates—and understands that the given campaign must work in harmony with long-term goals and brand positioning.[18]

There are a number of ways companies can use sales promotion techniques to contribute to their franchise building efforts. Rather than using a "one-time offer," many companies are developing promotional programs that encourage repeat purchases and long-term patronage. For example, many credit cards have developed promotional programs where consumers earn bonus points every time they use their card to charge a purchase. These points can then be redeemed for various items. Most airlines, as as well as many hotel chains, have developed frequent flyer or guest programs to encourage loyalty and repeat patronage.

Figure 15–9 The Use of a Coupon Helps Draw Consumers' Attention to an Ad

Figure 15–10   Häagen-Dazs Ties a Cents-Off Offer to Pledges for Public Television

Other ways of developing image building promotions include incorporating value-added elements into the promotional offer or reinforcing established images or positioning in the promotional support program.[19] For example, in its "Sweet Charity" campaign, Häagen-Dazs ice cream linked its cents-off coupon offer to an automatic contribution to Public Television. This "cause-related" promotion not only offered consumers a price reduction but also allowed them to support a cause that is consistent with the product's upscale positioning in the market (Figure 15–10).

Figure 15–11   This Promotion for Chunky Soups Helped Reinforce the Brand's Masculine Image

Campbell Soup used a multifaceted promotional program that was tied to the National Football League to reinforce the hearty, masculine positioning of its Chunky line of soups (Figure 15–11). The promotion included television, print, and outdoor advertising, in-store displays, special packaging, and a "Win Big" instant-winner game. The game prizes included a trip to the 1989 NFC-AFC Pro Bowl game in Hawaii, a very appropriate prize for the predominantly male target audience for Chunky soup.

Non-consumer-franchise-building promotions are those that are designed to accelerate the purchase decision process and generate an immediate increase in sales. These activities do little or nothing to communicate information about a brand's unique features or the benefits of using it and thus contribute very little to the building of brand identity and image. Price-off deals, bonus packs, and rebates or refunds are examples of non-CFB sales promotion techniques.

Many specialists in the promotional area have stressed the need for marketers to use sales promotion tools as a franchise builder and to create long-term continuity in their promotional programs.[20] Whereas non-CFB promotions merely borrow customers from other brands, well-planned CFB activities can convert consumers to loyal customers. Short-term non-CFB promotions do have their place in a firm's promotional mix, particularly when competitive developments warrant such activities. However, the limitations of non-CFB activities must be recognized in the development of a long-term marketing strategy for a brand.

Specific Promotional Objectives

While the basic goal of most sales promotion activities is to induce purchase of the brand, there are a number of different objectives the marketer might have for both new and established brands. Some of the specific objectives of sales promotion programs are examined in this section.

Obtaining Trial and Repurchase

One of the most important uses of sales promotion techniques is to encourage consumers to try a new product or service. While thousands of new products are introduced to the market every year, estimates are that as many as 90 percent of them fail within the first year of introduction.[21] Many of these failures are due to the fact that the new product or brand lacks the promotional support needed either to encourage initial trial by a sufficient number of consumers or to induce enough of those trying the brand to repurchase it.

Many new brands that are introduced are merely new versions of an existing product and usually do not offer benefits that are so unique that advertising alone can induce trial. Sales promotion tools have become an important part of new brand introduction strategies, as the level of initial trial can be increased through the use of techniques such as sampling, couponing, and refund offers.

The success of a new brand depends not only on getting initial trial but also on inducing a reasonable percentage of those who try the brand to repurchase it and establish ongoing purchase patterns. Promotional incentives such as coupons or refund offers are often included with a sample to encourage repeat purchase after trial. For example, when Clorox Super Detergent was introduced to the market, millions of free samples were distributed along with a 75-cent coupon (Figure 15–12). The samples allowed consumers to try the new detergent, while the coupon provided an incentive to purchase it.

Increasing Consumption of an Established Brand

While sales promotion is very important in the introduction of a new product or brand, many marketing managers are responsible for established brands that are competing in mature markets, against established competitors, and where consumer purchase patterns are often well set. Awareness of an established brand is generally high as a result of cumulative advertising effects, and many consumers may have tried the brand at one time or an-

Figure 15–12   Samples and Coupons Were Used to Help Introduce Clorox Super Detergent to the Market

other. These factors can create a very challenging situation for the brand manager who hopes to increase sales of the product or defend its market share against a competitor. Sales promotion can be an effective way to generate some new interest in or excitement for an established brand or to help increase sales or to defend market share against competitive threats.

There are several ways by which marketers can attempt to increase sales for an established brand, and sales promotion can play an important role in each. One way of increasing product consumption is by identifying new or additional uses for the brand. Sales promotion techniques such as the provision of recipe books or calendars that show various ways of using the product are often used to accomplish this (Figure 15–13).

Another strategy for increasing sales of an established brand is to use promotions that attract nonusers of the product category or users of a competitive brand. Attracting nonusers of the product category can be a very difficult task, as consumers may not see a need for the product or have an interest in using it. However, sales promotions can be designed to appeal to nonusers. For example, THE TORO COMPANY developed a very successful promotion called "Snow Insurance" to attract consumers who questioned whether they might have a need for a snowthrower because of the mild winters experienced by many areas of the country in 1986 and 1987.

Toro's sales promotion agency developed a "S'no Risk®" program whereby Toro offered a refund of from 50 percent to 100 percent of the purchase price if snowfalls were 20 percent to 50 percent less than the average for a given community (Figure 15–14). Toro underwrote the program through an insurance policy with premiums based on the number of sales. The promotion ran from June until December, and by December 10, sales exceeded season projections by 20 percent and promotion projections by 30 percent.[22]

A more common strategy for increasing sales of an established brand is to attract consumers who use a competitive brand. This is usually done by providing users of a competetive brand with an incentive to switch. One of the most successful promotions ever used for attracting users of a competitive brand was the Pepsi Challenge, which is discussed in Promotional Perspective 15–1.

AMERICAN BEAUTY
1990 Calendar
International Pasta Dishes
FREE*
AMERICAN BEAUTY® 1990 Calendar
PLUS $4.85 In Coupon Savings.
• 14 Delicious International Pasta Recipes, beautifully photographed.
• Plenty of room to write important dates.
* Free With 4 UPC Symbols.
To get your free pasta calendar, send this form and four (4) UPC symbols from any AMERICAN BEAUTY® pasta products. Or you can buy your calendar with no proofs of purchase for only $2.00. Send form to:
AMERICAN BEAUTY® PASTA CALENDAR OFFER
P.O. BOX 127, EMIGSVILLE, PA 17318-0127
I have included with this offer form (check one box):
4 UPC symbols for my free calendar
$2.00 in check or money order (no cash, please) to purchase my calendar
Make check payable to: AMERICAN BEAUTY® PASTA CALENDAR OFFER.
NAME
Please print legibly.
ADDRESS
CITY
STATE
ZIP
Please allow 6-8 weeks for delivery. Quantities are limited. Order now while supplies last. Limit one calendar per name or street address. Proofs of purchase, where required, submitted without this offer form will not be honored. Void where prohibited. Offer expires 11/30/89. © Hershey Foods Corporation 1989.
SAVE 25¢
Make a date for profitability with AMERICAN BEAUTY®.
Attractive Calendar Designed for 1990 Which Your Customers Will Enjoy Throughout the Year.
• Our third annual AMERICAN BEAUTY® calendar promotion themed "International Pasta Dishes" will keep your customers coming back for more.
• This promotion is a proven winner–recording increased consumer requests of +38% 1988 vs. 1987.
• Coupon savings worth $4.85 offered to generate future sales of AMERICAN BEAUTY® pasta and other related items.
• 14 beautifully photographed recipes are included to increase usage of pasta and other favorite foods.
Heavy Advertising Support to Generate Sales and Profits.
• Calendar offered FREE with 4 UPC Symbols from AMERICAN BEAUTY® pasta.
• Half-Page FSI support appearing 8/27/89 with a circulation of 10,080,000.
• Additional support via tear pads for on-display visibility.
So Stock Up Now and Watch Your Profits Build All Year Long.

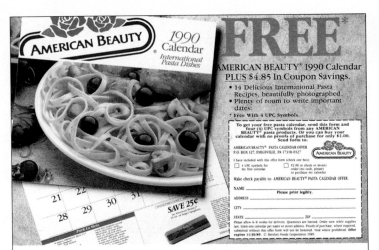

Figure 15–13 Calendars Showing Various Uses for a Product Can Help Increase Sales

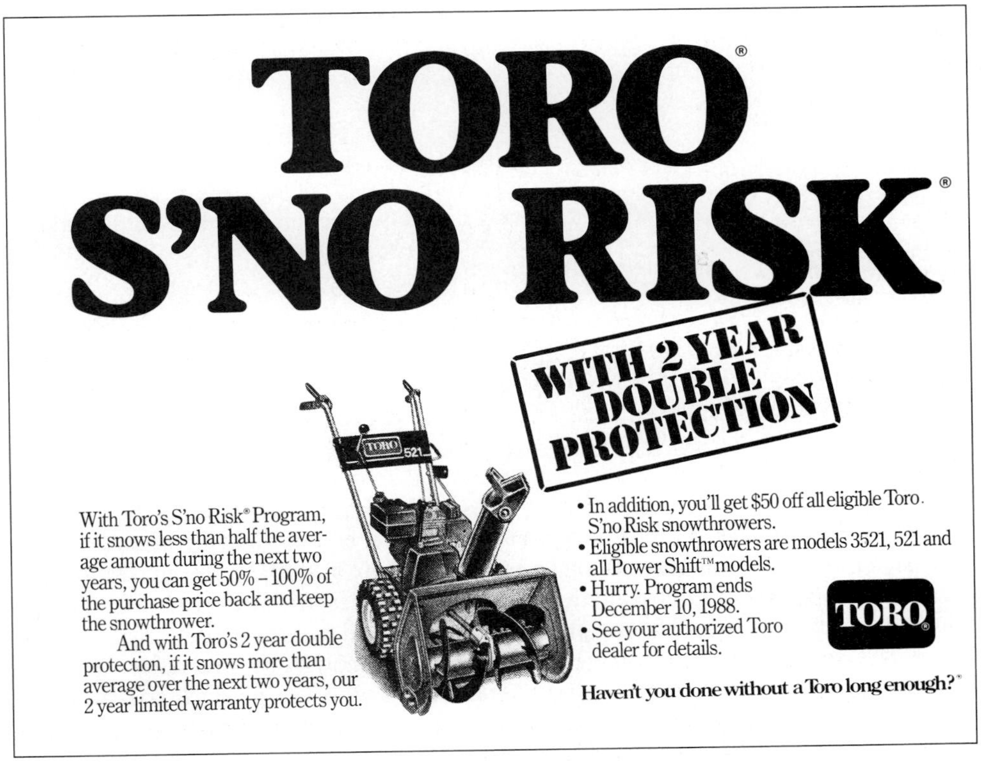

TORO®
S'NO RISK®
WITH 2 YEAR DOUBLE PROTECTION
With Toro's S'no Risk® Program, if it snows less than half the average amount during the next two years, you can get 50%–100% of the purchase price back and keep the snowthrower.
And with Toro's 2 year double protection, if it snows more than average over the next two years, our 2 year limited warranty protects you.
• In addition, you'll get $50 off all eligible Toro. S'no Risk snowthrowers.
• Eligible snowthrowers are models 3521, 521 and all Power Shift™ models.
• Hurry. Program ends December 10, 1988.
• See your authorized Toro dealer for details.
TORO
Haven't you done without a Toro long enough?®

Figure 15–14 Toro's S'no Risk® Promotion Helped Attract New Users

Promotional Perspective 15—1

The Pepsi Challenge

In the opinion of many marketing and advertising experts, one of the most successful promotional programs ever run may have been the famous "Pepsi Challenge" (Exhibit 15—1). In this campaign, Pepsi took on its arch rival, and industry leader, Coca-Cola in a hard-hitting comparative promotion that challenged consumers to taste the two brands in blind taste tests and let their taste decide which cola soft drink was the best. However, Pepsi did not enter the challenge promotion blindly.

Before beginning the challenge campaign on a nationwide basis, Pepsi had successfully tested the promotion in Dallas, where it resulted in as much as 75 percent increases in the brand's market share. Encouraged by these results, Pepsi decided to conduct a nationwide consumer research study to determine if the preference for Pepsi could be projected nationally. Over 3,000 in-home taste tests were conducted in more than 100 cities and towns across the country. On the basis of supportive research results and the favorable outcome of the Dallas test campaign, Pepsi management decided to use the "Pepsi Challenge" theme in a national advertising and promotional campaign.

A major part of the campaign was the consumer sales promotion program in which Pepsi Challenge booths were set up in high-traffic stores and shopping malls. Consumers were invited to re-create the challenge test by tasting the two brands without knowing which was which and then indicating their preference. The booths also included a scorecard, so the results could be tallied and seen by shoppers. The sales promotion campaign was designed to build on the excitement of the Pepsi Challenge advertising campaign and to reinforce the preference claim that was used as the theme for national and local advertising efforts. The promotional campaign also included Pepsi Challenge displays in retail outlets along with newspaper advertising carrying price-off coupons to help encourage consumer trial.

The Pepsi Challenge campaign is an example of a well-integrated promotion that coordinated all the elements of the promotional program including national and local advertising, consumer sales promotion, and trade support. The campaign was used for several years by Pepsi and was instrumental in helping Pepsi move ahead of Coke and become the market share leader in terms of supermarket sales. As a result of Pepsi's success, Coca-

Exhibit 15—1   **The Pepsi Challenge Was a Very Successful Promotion**

Cola launched a variety of counterattacks including the controversial decision to change its formula and launch New Coke in 1986.

Sources: John A. Quelch and Paul W. Farris, Case: Pepsi-Cola (A), *Cases in Advertising and Promotion Management,* 2nd ed. (Plano, Tex.: Business Publications, 1987); John Kotten, "Coca-Cola Executives Believe 1980 Is Critical in Battle with Pepsi," *The Wall Street Journal,* March 6, 1980, p. 1.

Defending Current Customers   With more new brands entering the market every day and competitors attempting to take away their customers through aggressive advertising and sales promotion efforts, many companies are turning to sales promotion programs as a way of holding present customers and defending their market share. There are several ways a company can use sales promotion techniques to retain its current customer base. One way is to "load" them with the product and thus take them out of the market for a certain period of time. Special price promotions, coupons, or bonus packs can be used to encourage the consumer to stock up on the brand.

This not only keeps consumers using the company's brand but also reduces the likelihood that they would switch brands in response to a competitor's promotion.

Enhancing Advertising and Marketing Efforts   A final objective for consumer trade promotions is to enhance or support the advertising and marketing effort for the brand. Sales promotion techniques such as contests or sweepstakes are often used to help draw attention to an advertisement and increase the consumer's level of interest or involvement with the message and the product. Sales promotion programs also can help encourage retailers to stock, display, and promote a brand during the promotional period. Cooperation from the trade is important to the success of a promotional program. Table 15–1 summarizes the various promotional objectives that have been discussed.

Consumer-Oriented Sales Promotion Techniques

In this section we turn our attention to examining the various sales promotional techniques used by marketers and the role they play in meeting the various objectives discussed above. Table 15–2 shows the extent to which these various consumer promotions are used by the largest as well as by the smaller packaged-goods companies. The Donnelley Marketing survey of promotional practices found that on average the largest packaged-goods firms use 7.8 of the 10 types of promotions, whereas the smaller firms use 6.3.[23]

Sampling

Sampling involves a variety of procedures whereby consumers are given some quantity of a product for no charge to induce trial. Sampling is generally considered to be the most effective way of generating trial, although it is also the most expensive. As a sales promotion technique, sampling is often used as a way of introducing a new product or brand to the market. However, as can be seen in Table 15–2, sampling is also used for established products—particularly by large companies. Some companies do not use sampling for established products since samples may be ineffective in inducing a satisfied user of a competitive brand to switch and may result in giving the product away to the firm's current customers—who would buy it anyway. There may be an exception to this when significant changes or modifications (new and improved) are made in a brand.

Manufacturers of packaged-goods products such as food, health, cosmetics, and

Table 15–1   Summary of Sales Promotion Objectives ✓

Encouraging trial of new product or brand
Encouraging repurchase of new product or brand
Increasing consumption of established brand
Identifying new or additional use
Attracting nonusers of brand or product
Attracting users of competitive product
Encouraging repeat purchase
Encouraging multiple or larger-size purchases
Defending market share or position
Enhancing advertising and marketing efforts

Table 15–2   Types of Consumer Promotions Used, 1988

Types of Promotion	Largest Firms*	Smaller Firms*
1. Couponing consumer direct	88%	95%
2. Money-back offers/cash refunds	96	78
3. Cents-off promotions	80	70
4. Sweepstakes	96	58
5. Premium offers	96	50
6. Sampling new products	72	65
7. Sampling established products	72	58
8. Couponing in retailers' ads	64	63
9. Prepriced shippers	64	45
10. Contests	52	43
Average number of types used	(7.8)	(6.3)

*Denotes annual sales volume. Largest firms = $1 billion+; smaller firms = less than $1 billion.

Source: Donnelley Marketing 11th Annual Survey of Promotional Practices (Stamford, Conn.: Donnelley Marketing, 1989), p. 23.

toiletries are heavy users of sampling since their products meet the three criteria that are important for an effective sampling program:

1. The products are of relatively low unit value, so samples do not cost too much.
2. The products are divisible, which means that they can be broken into small sample sizes that are adequate for demonstrating the brand's features and benefits to the user.
3. The purchase cycle for these products is relatively short, so the consumer will consider making an immediate purchase or will not forget about the brand when the next purchase occasion for the product does occur.

Benefits and Limitations of Sampling   There are several important benefits of using a sampling program. First, samples are an excellent way of inducing a prospective buyer to try a product or service. One expert estimates that approximately 75 percent of the households receiving a sample will try it.[24] The trial rates generated by a sampling program are much higher than those produced by advertising or other sales promotion techniques.

Getting the consumer to try a product leads to a second benefit of sampling, which is that a sample allows the consumer to experience the brand directly and thus gain a greater appreciation for its benefits. This can be particularly important when a product's features and benefits are difficult to describe through other means such as advertising. Many products such as foods, beverages, and cosmetics are examples of products where subtle features are most appreciated when experienced directly. Promotional Perspective 15–2 discusses how Apple Computer used a form of sampling to allow prospective buyers the opportunity to experience the Macintosh personal computer firsthand.

Obviously the marketer must feel that the brand has some unique or superior benefits for a sampling program to be worthwhile. If this is not the case, the sampled consumers will revert back to other brands and will not become repeat purchasers. The costs of a sampling program can only be recovered by getting a sufficient number of consumers to become regular users of the brand at full retail price.

Another possible limitation to sampling is the fact that the benefits of some products are difficult to gauge immediately, and the learning period required to appreciate the brand may require supplying the consumer with larger amounts of the brand than is affordable. For example, a product such as an expensive skin cream that is promoted as being effective at preventing or reducing wrinkles would have to be used over an extended time period before any effects might be noticed.

Sampling Methods   One of the basic decisions that the sales promotion or brand manager must make concerns the method by which the sample will be distributed. The sampling method chosen is important not only in terms of costs but also in terms of influencing the type of consumer who receives the sample. The goal in choosing a sampling method is to find an effective, cost-efficient method that gets the product to the best prospects for trial and subsequent repurchase. Some of the more widely used sampling methods, along with the pros and cons of each, are shown in Table 15–3. Some of the basic distribution methods include door-to-door, direct-mail, in-store, and on-package approaches.

Door-to-door sampling, whereby the sample is delivered directly to the prospect's residence, is sometimes used, particularly if it is important to control where the samples are delivered. While virtually any type of product samples can be delivered this way, this method is on the decline because of the expenses involved. Some companies may have their samples delivered directly as part of a cooperative effort where several product samples are sent at once to a household or through services such as Welcome Wagon, which calls on new residents in an area.

Sampling through the mail is common for small, lightweight products that are nonperishable such as the sample of Fab 1 Shot detergent shown in Figure 15–15. A

Promotional Perspective 15—2

Test-Drive a Macintosh

The use of sampling programs is commonplace in the packaged-goods area where products can be broken into small sampling units that are distributed to consumers. However, this is difficult to do for durable products, and consumers are often forced to make a purchase decision without having the opportunity to experience a product and determine its value.

When Apple Computer introduced the Macintosh, it was reputed to be one of the most innovative personal computers ever developed and also one of the most user-friendly. However, before Apple could expect consumers to pay several thousand dollars for a Mac, it had to convince them that the product was worth the money. To address this problem, Apple and its advertising agency, Chiat Day, borrowed a concept from the automobile industry by challenging consumers to "test-drive" a Macintosh (Exhibit 15—2). Apple was confident that once users had the chance to try its new computer, it would be difficult for them to resist purchasing it.

Under the test-drive program, interested consumers were actually permitted to take one of the computers home and use it for 24 hours. Apple developed software specifically for the trial that explained the unique benefits of the Mac. The promotion was supported with a television and print advertising campaign, and a variety of point-of-purchase material was developed to call attention to the promotion in computer stores. Also, to encourage retail support of the promotion, a 12-region sweepstakes was run awarding winners the use of a Porsche automobile for a year. The promotion was very successful, as more than 200,000 Macintoshes were "test-driven," and 40 percent of store sales were attributed to the promotion.

Source: Based on Jeffrey K. McElnea and Michael J. Enzer, "Building Brand Franchises," *Marketing Communications*, April 1986, p. 42.

Exhibit 15—2   Apple's "Test-Drive a Mac" Promotion Allowed Consumers to Sample a Macintosh

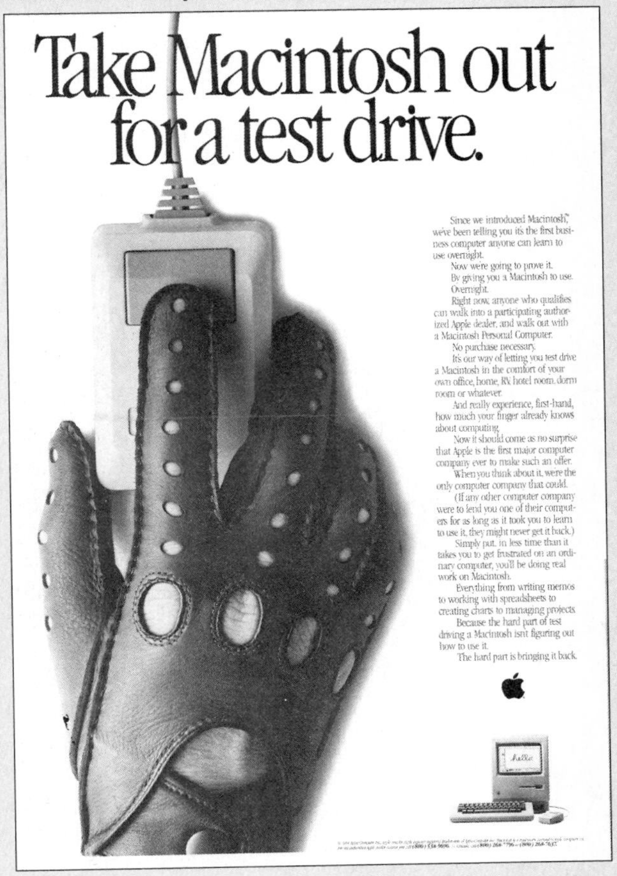

major advantage of this method is that the marketer has more control over where and when the product will be distributed and can target the sample to specific market areas. Many marketers are making increased use of information from companies such as Claritas' PRIZM-target marketing programs or National Decision Systems Vision to better target their sample mailings. The main drawbacks to through-the-mail sampling are postal restrictions and increasing postal rates.

In-store sampling has become an increasingly popular method of distributing samples, particularly for food products. This method is usually carried out by hiring temporary workers or "demonstrators" who set up a table or booth, prepare small samples of the product, and pass them out to shoppers. The in-store sampling approach can be very effective for food products, since consumers have an opportunity to taste the item and the demonstrator can give the consumer additional information about the product while it is being sampled. Demonstrators also will often give consumers a cents-off coupon for the sampled item to encourage immediate trial purchase. While this sampling method can be very effective, it can also be expensive and requires a great deal of planning, as well as the cooperation of the retailers.

Table 15–3 **Summary of Sampling Methods**

Eight Basic Sampling Media	Uses	Limitations
1. Door-to-door	Virtually any product can be delivered in this way	Most expensive means of sampling Problem with leaving perishables if occupant absent Illegal in some areas
2. Direct-mail	Best for small, light products that are nonperishable	Rising postal costs
3. Central location	Best for perishables such as food or when personal demonstration is required	If in-store, same offer must be made to all retailers (Robinson-Patman Act) Usually involves cost of sales training If in public place, may be illegal in some areas
4. Sample pack in stores	Best method for attracting retail support, because retailers sell the packs at a premium unit price	Requires retail acceptance like any other new product May necessitate special production for trial sizes
5. Cross-product sampling in or on pack	Good for low-cost sampling of a manufacturer's other products	Trial limited to users of "carrier" product Restricted for large products
6. Co-op package distribution	Good for narrow audiences such as college students, military personnel, brides	Little appeal to trade
7. Newspaper or magazine distribution	Relatively low-cost method of sample distribution for flat or pouchable products	Seem to be regarded by media vehicle recipients as "cheap" and are often disregarded, resulting in less trial than with other sampling methods Obviously limited to certain product types
8. Any of above with coupon	Increases postsample trial rate by using purchase incentive	Additional cost of coupon handling

Source: John R. Rossiter and Larry Percy, *Advertising & Promotion Management* (New York: McGraw-Hill, 1987), p. 343.

Figure 15–15 **A Product Sample Sent Through the Mail**

On-package sampling, whereby a sample of a product is attached to another item, is another common sampling method. This procedure can be very cost-effective, particularly for multiproduct firms that can attach a sample of a new product to an existing brand. However, its main limitation is that the sample is distributed only to consumers who purchase the item to which the sample is attached. Thus, the sample will not reach nonusers of the "carrier" brand.

This sampling method can be expanded by attaching the sample to multiple carrier brands and by including samples with products not made by the company. For example, WD-40 distributed samples of its lubricant/cleaner to purchasers of the Wagner Power Painter through an agreement with the manufacturer of the latter product (see Figure 15–16). The promotion was beneficial to both companies since the product helped in the cleaning and maintenance of the paint sprayer and allowed WD-40 to expose its product and its various uses to another important target market.

Figure 15–16   A Sample Distributed Along with a Related Product

Other Methods   The four sampling methods discussed above are the most common ways of distributing product samples. There are, however, a number of other methods used to distribute samples such as inserting packets in magazines or newspapers (particularly Sunday supplements). Some firms such as tobacco and cereal companies make samples available to consumers who call free numbers to request them or mail in sample request forms.

Many companies also make use of specialized sample distribution services such as Gift Pax, Inc., Ruben H. Donnley Corporation, and D. L. Blair. These companies will help the company identify consumers who are nonusers of a product or users of a competitive brand and develop appropriate procedures for distributing a sample to them. As college students, many of you probably receive sample packs at the beginning of the semester that contain trial sizes of a variety of products such as mouthwash, toothpaste, headache remedies, and deodorant.

Couponing

The oldest, yet most widely used and effective sales promotion tool is the *cents-off coupon.* Coupons have been around since 1895 when the C. W. Post Company started using the penny-off coupon to sell its new Grape-Nuts cereal. In recent years, coupons have become increasingly popular with consumers, which may explain their explosive growth among the manufacturers and retailers who use them as sales promotion incentives. As can be seen in Table 15–2, coupons are the most popular sales promotion technique and are used by nearly all the packaged-goods firms.

Over the past two decades, the number of coupons distributed by marketers has increased 1,243 percent from 16.5 billion in 1968 to 221.7 billion in 1988.[25] As can be seen in Figure 15–17, coupon distribution has increased by 36 percent since 1984 alone. Total coupon redemption declined 1 percent in 1988 to 7.05 billion, which was the first drop in five years. This decline was attributed in part to busier consumer lifestyles but primarily to a use of shorter coupon expiration dates by most marketers.[26]

According to the Manufacturers Coupon Control Center (MCCC), 77 percent of U.S. households clipped coupons in 1988, and more than 22 percent used five or more coupons weekly. The average face value of coupons has increased from just over 21 cents in 1981 to nearly 40 cents in 1988. A study by the MCCC found that a minimum of 23 cents is needed to get consumers to use a coupon, whereas for brands the consumer has never purchased, the value required jumps to 44 cents.[27]

Adding additional fuel to the coupon explosion are the vast numbers of coupons distributed through retailers that are not even included in aforementioned figures. In some markets retailers will double the face value of manufacturers' coupons, a practice that has led to coupon wars, as discussed in Promotional Perspective 15–3.

Figure 15–17 **Coupon Distribution Trends**

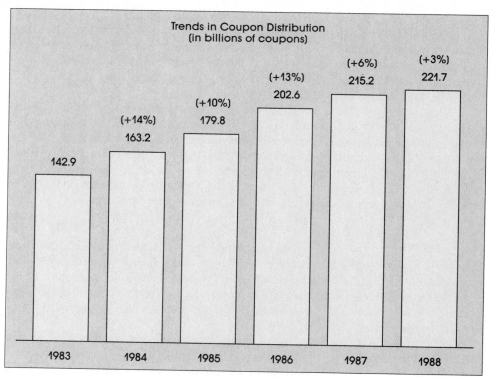

Source: *Coupon Distribution and Redemption Patterns, 1988* (Clinton, Iowa: Manufacturers Coupon Control Center, 1989), p. 1.

Advantages and Limitations of Coupons Coupons have a number of advantages that make them popular sales promotional tools for both new and established products. First, coupons make it possible to offer a price reduction to those consumers who are price sensitive without having to reduce the price for everyone. Price-sensitive consumers will generally seek out or purchase *because* of coupons, whereas those who are not as concerned about price will buy the brand at full value. Coupons also make it possible to reduce the retail price of a product without having to rely on retailers for cooperation, which can often be a problem.

Coupons are generally regarded as being second only to sampling as a promotional technique for generating trial. Since a coupon lowers the price of a product, the consumer's level of perceived risk associated with trial of a new brand is reduced. Coupons can be an effective way of encouraging repurchase after initial trial. As was shown earlier, many new products include a cents-off coupon inside the package to encourage repeat purchase.

Coupons can also be useful promotional devices for established products. They can be used to encourage nonusers to try a brand, to encourage repeat purchase among current users, and to get users to try a new and improved version of a brand. Coupons may also be helpful in getting users of a product to trade up to more expensive brands.

There are, of course, a number of problems associated with the use of coupons. First, it can be difficult to estimate how many consumers will use a coupon and when. Response to a coupon is rarely immediate, as the average amount of time taken to redeem a coupon is anywhere from two to six months. While redemption may be expedited through the use of an expiration date, coupons are generally not as effective as sampling for inducing initial product trial in a short time period. A number of factors can influence the redemption of a coupon, as shown in Table 15–4.

A problem associated with using coupons to attract new users to an established brand is that it is very difficult to prevent the coupons from being received and used by consumers who already use the brand. For example, General Foods decided to re-

Promotional Perspective **15—3**

The Coupon Wars—Double Trouble

One of the most competitive retail markets in the country is the southern California area, particularly in the supermarket industry where seven major chains compete for the consumer's food dollar. A popular marketing tool frequently used by some of the retailers is the "unlimited double coupons" offer whereby the store will double the face value of an unlimited number of manufacturers' cents-off coupons.

While a number of chains instituted double coupons as a major part of their marketing strategy, some have resisted the couponing fray and emphasized lower overall prices as the way to attract shoppers. These stores argued that double couponing is a foolish idea that ends up being paid for by all consumers in the form of higher shelf prices. Still others, such as market leader Ralphs, would allow customers to redeem a limited number of coupons for double credit (usually, two or three per trip).

In the first few months of 1987, however, Ralphs saw how effective the use of unlimited double coupons promotions can be, as shopper traffic at the chain dropped over 2.5 percent and the chain lost its leadership position. So how did Ralphs respond? With its own unlimited double couponing promotion, of course (Exhibit 15—3). According to the executive vice president (VP) of marketing for Ralphs, their research indicated that many of the chain's customers might be going somewhere else because of the unlimited double coupons. The marketing VP noted, "So we decided, if that's what they want, we'll offer them that to get them back." He indicated that Ralphs' strategy was to offer unlimited double coupons and at the same time maintain lower prices and higher standards. He also noted that "the only way a chain can offer unlimited double coupons and not raise prices is if they experience a significant increase in sales. If we don't get the increase in business to justify the program, we'll discontinue it."

Analysts and supermarket consultants note that grocery store chains go back and forth with unlimited double coupon promotions. They know that these promotions are very expensive and nobody really wins the coupon wars, except perhaps the consumer who is a heavy coupon user. However, as Ralphs learned, sometimes a move to meet these coupon promotions is a necessary defen-

Exhibit 15—3   **Double Couponing Is Common in the Supermarket Industry**

This Week At Ralphs... **Unlimited Double Coupons!***

Now There Is No Reason To Shop Anywhere Else!

Over the past two years thousands of shoppers have switched to Ralphs. Some switched for **Ralphs Verified Lower Prices**, which price surveys consistently place Ralphs among the lowest.

Other switched for **Ralphs Higher Standards.** Standards backed by our unconditional **Double-Your-Money-Back Guarantee** on all Ralphs meat and produce.

But because there are still some shoppers who haven't yet discovered the advantages

of shopping at Ralphs, we've added one more big reason to make you switch—**Ralphs Unlimited Double Coupons.**

We want to win you over, and if **Unlimited Double Coupons** is what it takes, that's what we'll do!

Ralphs Verified Lower Prices, Higher Standards and, this week, Unlimited Double Coupons.

Now there's no reason to shop anywhere else!

Ralphs

Lower Prices. Higher Standards.

sive strategy. The question is, How long will the coupon wars last, and if they stop, when will they start again?

Source: Based on Martha Graves, "The Coupon Gamble: Double or Nothing," *Los Angeles Times*, July 29, 1987, pt. IV, p. 1.

---

duce its use of coupons for Maxwell House coffee when research revealed that the coupons were being redeemed primarily by current users.[28] Thus, rather than attracting new users, the coupons end up reducing the company's profit margins among consumers who would probably purchase the product anyway.

Another problem associated with the use of coupons is the cost factor. Couponing program expenses are comprised not only of the face value of the coupon redeemed but also of costs for production, distribution, and handling of the coupons. Table 15—5 shows the calculations used by one company in determining the costs of a couponing program. The costs of a couponing program should be tracked very closely by the marketer to ensure that the promotion is economically feasible.

Yet another concern in the use of coupon promotions is the problem of misre-

Table 15–4   Factors Affecting Coupon Redemptions

1. Method of distribution
2. Product class size
3. Audience reached by coupon
4. Consumer's "need" for product
5. Brand's consumer franchise/market share
6. Degree of brand loyalty
7. Brand's retail availability/distribution
8. Face (monetary) value of coupon
9. Whether new or old (established) brand
10. Design and appeal of coupon ad
11. Discount offered by coupon
12. Area of country
13. Competitive activity
14. Size of coupon drop
15. Size of purchase required for redemption
16. Level of general support for advertising and promotion
17. Consumer attitude and product usage/number of potential users
18. Period of time since the coupons were distributed
19. Growth trend
20. Timing, if brand is subject to seasonal influences
21. Demographics, such as age, family size, annual income, and expenditures
22. General level of misredemption in the couponed area

Source: David J. Reibstein and Phyllis A. Traver, "Factors Affecting Coupon Redemption Rates," *Journal of Marketing* 46 (Fall 1982), p. 104.

demption or the cashing of a coupon without the purchase of the brand. Coupon misredemption or fraud occurs in a number of ways, including:

- Redemption of coupons by consumers for brands not actually purchased
- Redemption of coupons by sales clerks in exchange for cash
- The gathering and redemption of coupons by store managers or owners without the accompanying sale of the product
- The gathering or printing of coupons by criminals who sell them to unethical merchants, who in turn redeem them

A study by the Grocery Manufacturers of America and the Food Marketing Institute estimated coupon misredemption at 7.1 percent and reported that it is costing marketers nearly $273 million a year.[29] While efforts are being made to solve this problem, marketers must still allow a certain percentage for misredemption when estimating the costs of a couponing program. Ways of dealing with the coupon misredemption, such as improved coding, are being developed, but it still remains a problem.

Coupon Distribution   There are a number of ways coupons can be disseminated to consumers, including distribution in newspapers and magazines, through direct mail,

Table 15–5   Calculation of Couponing Costs

1. Distribution cost— 10,000,000 circulation × $4/M	$ 40,000
2. Redemptions @ 3.1%	310,000
3. Redemption cost— 310,000 redemptions × $0.15 face value	$ 46,500
4. Handling cost— 310,000 redemptions × $0.07	$ 21,700
5. Total program cost—1 + 3 + 4	$108,200
6. Cost per coupon redeemed— cost divided by redemptions	34.9¢
7. Actual product sold on redemption (misredemption estimated at 20%)—310,000 × 80%	$248,000
8. Cost per product moved— program cost divided by product sold	43.6¢

Source: Louis J. Haugh, "How Coupons Measure Up," *Advertising Age*, June 8, 1981, p. 56.

Table 15–6 **Coupon Distribution by Media**

Medium	1985	1986	1987	1988
Free-standing insert	59.9%	68.0%	72.7%	77.3%
Newspaper/ROP	12.2	7.4	5.9	5.4
Newspaper/co-op	8.0	7.1	4.6	2.4
Direct mail	4.4	4.0	5.3	5.0
In/on pack	4.8	5.8	5.3	5.2
Magazines	8.6	6.5	3.7	2.4
Other	2.1	1.2	2.5	2.3

ROP = Run-of-Paper
Source: Manufacturers Coupon Control Center.

and in or on packages. Distribution of coupons through newspaper free-standing inserts (FSIs) is by far the most popular method for delivering coupons to consumers. As can be seen in Table 15–6, FSIs accounted for 77.3 percent of all coupons distributed in 1988, which represents a 17 percent increase in their share of total distribution over 1985. The growth in coupon distribution through FSIs has come at the expense of vehicles such as manufacturers' ads in newspapers (newspaper ROP), newspaper co-op ads, and magazines.

A major advantage of media-delivered coupons is the brand exposure that results, particularly from newspapers. Also, many consumers actively search the newspaper for coupons, especially on Sundays or "food days" (when grocery stores advertise their specials). Thus, the likelihood of the consumer at least noticing the coupon is enhanced. Distribution of coupons through magazines can take advantage of the high selectivity of the publication for reaching specific target audiences. Finally, distribution of coupons through the media can be done at reasonable costs, particularly through the free-standing inserts.

While the distribution of coupons through FSIs has been increasing, this growth has resulted in a clutter problem. Consumers are being bombarded with too many coupons, and although each FSI publisher offers product exclusivity in its insert, this advantage may be negated when there are three inserts in a Sunday paper. Redemption rates of FSI coupons have declined from the 7 percent range to only 3.2 percent and are even lower for some products (Figure 15–18). In addition to the clutter problem and low redemption rates, the costs of using FSIs have increased substantially over the past few years, as the cost per thousand circulation has gone from an average of $3.00 to nearly $6.00.

These problems with FSIs are leading many marketers to look at alternative ways of delivering coupons that will result in less clutter and higher redemption rates, such as direct mail. Over the long term, it is expected that many marketers will switch out of FSIs and into other coupon delivery methods.[30]

The direct-mail method of distributing coupons has been increasing over the past few years and now accounts for 5 percent of all coupons distributed. The bulk of coupons disseminated via direct mail are sent by local retailers or through co-op mailings whereby a packet of coupons for a number of different products is sent to a household. These include couponing programs such as Donnelley Marketing's Carol Wright, Metromail's Red Letter Day, and Advo Systems' Mailbox Values.

Direct-mail couponing has several advantages. First, the mailing can be sent to a broad audience or targeted to specific geographic or demographic segments. Some co-op coupon programs such as Donnelley's Carol Wright have several special-market mailings to groups such as teenagers, senior citizens, Hispanics, and other segments. The firm that mails out its own coupons can be particularly selective in its selection of recipients. Another important advantage of direct-mail couponing is their higher redemption rate. Direct-mail couponing is a more effective way of gaining the attention of consumers and results in redemption rates of nearly 6 percent, which is much higher than that of FSIs.

Figure 15-18   **Grocery Products—Coupon Redemption Rates by Media**

Media		Average Redemption Rate (percent)	Middle–Half Range (percent)
Daily newspaper	ROP solo	2.1	0.8–3.3
	Co-op (all)	1.9	0.7–3.2
Sunday paper	FSI	3.6	2.1–5.5
	Supplement	1.2	0.6–1.8
Magazines	On-page	1.8	0.8–2.6
	Pop-up insert	3.6	2.0–5.4
Direct mail		5.8	3.4–9.6
In/on-pack	Regular in pack	14.0	5.8–22.9
	Regular on pack	12.9	6.0–23.7
	In pack cross-ruff	4.6	2.2–6.9
	On pack cross-ruff	3.8	1.9–6.0
Instant on pack		31.0	15.4–52.3

Source: *Coupon Distribution and Redemption Patterns, 1988* (Clinton, Iowa: Manufacturers Coupon Control Center, 1989), p. 11.

The major disadvantage of the direct-mail method of coupon delivery is the expense relative to other distribution methods. The cost per thousand figure for distributing coupons through co-op mailings ranges from $10 to $15, and a solo mailing can have a CPM as high as $100. Also, the higher redemption rate of mail-delivered coupons may in large part result from the fact that many of the coupon recipients are already users of the brand who take advantage of the coupons sent directly to them.

Placing coupons either inside or on the outside of a package is another method for distributing them. The in/on package coupon has the advantages of virtually no distribution costs and a much higher redemption rate than other couponing methods. There are several types of in/on package coupons. An in/on pack coupon that is redeemable for the next purchase of the same brand is known as a **bounce-back coupon.** The logic of using this type of coupon is to provide consumers with an inducement to repurchase the brand.

Bounce-back coupons are often used with product samples to encourage the consumer to purchase the product after trying a sample. They may also be included in or on the package during the early phases of a brand's life cycle to encourage repeat purchase or to act as a defensive maneuver for a mature brand that is facing competitive pressure and wants to retain its current users. The main limitation of bounce-back coupons is that they go only to purchasers of the brand and thus are not effective for attracting nonusers. Figure 15-19 shows a bounce-back coupon that was placed on the package for HERSHEY'S Chocolate Fudge Topping.

Another type of in/on pack coupon is the **cross-ruff coupon,** which is redeemable on the purchase of a different product, usually one made by the same company but occasionally through a tie-in with another manufacturer. Cross-ruff coupons have a redemption rate of 3.8 to 4.6 percent and can be effective in encouraging consumers to try other products or brands. Companies with wide product lines such as cereal manufacturers are common users of these coupons.

Yet another type of package coupon that some companies use is the **instant coupon.** This coupon is attached to the outside of the package, and the consumer rips it

Figure 15–19   **An Example of a Bounce-Back Coupon**

Source: Hershey Foods Corporation.

off and redeems it at the checkout stand. Instant coupons have redemption levels of around 30 percent and provide the consumer with an immediate point-of-purchase incentive. Some companies prefer to use instant coupons rather than price-off deals since the latter require more cooperation from retailers and can be more expensive since every package must be reduced in price.

Couponing Trends   Marketers are continually searching for new and more effective couponing techniques. The enormous increase in the number of coupons distributed by manufacturers has led to what might be called "coupon clutter." Households are receiving more coupons than they can possibly notice, clip, save, and remember to use. Some companies are introducing in-store coupon distribution techniques through vending machines, electronic dispensers, or personal distributors whereby consumers can request and receive coupons right in the store.[31] These distribution methods are preferred by some companies that feel coupons are most effective if they are given to consumers when they are ready to make a purchase. These techniques allow consumers to choose coupons they are interested in, removing the need to clip coupons from print ads and then remembering to bring them to the store.

Companies are also seeking ways of using coupons to attract the customers of their competitors. Estimates are that 65 percent to 85 percent of a manufacturer's coupons are used by current customers. Thus, marketers are attempting to target their coupons to users of competitive brands through marketing research and telemarketing. Even though precise targeting of coupons is expensive in terms of distribution costs, it can be more cost-effective than newspaper couponing for attracting new users. Promotional Perspective 15–4 discusses how technological advances are leading to more effective ways of using coupons and assessing their impact.

Premiums

Premiums are another type of sales promotion device used by many marketers. A **premium** is an offer of an item of merchandise or service either free or at a low price that is used as an extra incentive for purchasers. Nearly $4 billion was spent on consumer premiums in 1988, including direct premiums and mail-in offers. Marketers' use of premium offers is changing, as many are eliminating toys and gimmicks in favor of "value-added" premiums that reflect the quality of the product and are consistent with its image and positioning in the market. The two basic types of premium offers are those that are offered free and the self-liquidating premium.

Free Premiums   Free premiums are usually inexpensive gifts or merchandise that are included in the product package or are sent to consumers who make mail-in requests along with a proof of purchase. In/on package premiums are examples of commonly used free premium offers. These include towels or glasses packed in detergent

Promotional Perspective 15–4

Getting More Out of Coupons

While the use of coupons is increasing, companies are still facing enormous inefficiencies in their couponing programs. Problems such as misredemption and fraud, high processing costs, and difficulty in targeting coupons and tracking their effectiveness have made it hard for companies to get their money's worth out of their couponing promotions. Moreover, it is estimated that as many as 80 percent of coupons are used by loyal customers who would buy the company's products at full price.

Many of these problems are being addressed through technological advances made possible through the use of bar-coded coupons. While bar codes have been used for several years on products, many companies realize that they can be useful on coupons as well. More than 70 percent of U.S. supermarkets are equipped with scanning devices to read the bar codes, and a number of companies have evolved to use the bar coding and provide services to firms using coupons.

The use of bar codes on coupons has a number of advantages to both manufacturers and retailers. First, the costs of handling coupons are reduced, as processing that used to be done by hand is now handled automatically by the scanner. The scannable coupons make for faster checkouts and help reduce fraud and misredemption since scanning prevents an item from being substituted for the product on the coupon or the use of a coupon for a large-package size when a smaller size is actually purchased.

Another major benefit of the bar-coded coupons is the potential they offer companies for improving the distribution of their coupons to specific market segments rather than using relatively untargeted distribution methods. For example, one company developed a method for distributing coupons at supermarkets by identifying a customer's purchases through bar codes and printing coupons for a competitor's product for use on a future shopping trip. This system makes it possible for marketers to reach users of competitive brands with their coupons rather than people who already use their brand. For example, J. M. Smucker Co. ran a promotion whereby anyone who purchased arch rival's Sorrell Ridge's All-Fruit Jam automatically received a coupon good for a free jar of Smucker's jam from a smart cash register.

Exhibit 15–4   **Safeway's Checkout Coupons Program**

Here's a Great Savings Idea from Safeway
Introducing
Checkout Coupons™
Coupons for the products you use, actually printed as you check out!
(See Details on Reverse Side)

Companies are also using this system to link purchases of products that are in some sense related. For example, a consumer who purchases a caffeine-free cola would be issued a coupon for decaffeinated coffee. Safeway, one of the nation's largest supermarket chains, recently began a program whereby store coupons for a competitive brand or a product related to a purchased item are printed at the check stand as the consumer checks out (Exhibit 15–4).

Another benefit of the new technologies is that they provide companies with information on the effectiveness of their couponing programs as well as those of their competitors. Companies such as Burke Marketing Research Services track coupon redemption at the brand level and offer subscribers the opportunity to monitor their own, as well as competitors' promotional efforts, analyze what type of household is making a purchase, and determine what brand lost sales owing to a coupon-induced switch. Also, by tracking the timing of coupon redemptions, a company can gauge the effectiveness of its media plan.

With more and more coupons being dispensed by companies every year, marketers must find ways to improve the efficiency and effectiveness of their couponing programs. These new technologies offer companies greater opportunities to get their money's worth from their couponing dollars.

Sources: Merri Rosenberg, "Using High Tech to Make Coupons Pay," *Adweek*, November 11, 1985, p. 6; "Stealing the Right Shoppers," *Forbes*, July 10, 1989, pp. 104–5.

boxes; toys, balls, trading cards, or other items included in cereal packages; or samples of one product included with another (Figure 15–20). A 1988 survey found that in/on package premiums are consumers' most preferred type of promotion.[32]

Package-carried premiums are used because they have high impulse value and can provide an extra incentive to the consumer to use the product. There are, however, several problems associated with the use of in/on pack premiums. First, there is the cost factor, which results from the premium itself as well as from extra packaging efforts that are sometimes needed. Finding desirable premiums at reasonable costs can be difficult, particularly for adult markets. Using a poor premium may actually have a negative effect on sales.

Another problem with these premiums is the possible restrictions the firm may face from regulatory agencies such as the Federal Trade Commission, and the Food and Drug Administration or from industry codes regarding the type of premium used. Strict guidelines have been developed by the National Association of Broadcasters regarding the advertising of premium offers to children. Concern has been expressed over the potential for premium offers to entice children to request a brand to get the promoted item and then never consume the product. Marketers must also pay attention to the safety of the premiums they use. For example, General Mills used a premium offer of a small superball in packages of Cheerios and encountered problems when some young children ended up swallowing them. Millions of packages containing the premium had to be recalled.

Mail-in premium offers usually require the consumer to send in one or more proof-of-purchase symbols in order to receive premium items. Since most free mail-in premium offers require more than one proof of purchase, they can be effective ways of encouraging repeat purchase and rewarding brand loyalty. However, a major drawback of mail-in premiums is that they do not offer immediate reinforcement or reward to the purchaser and thus may not be effective in providing an extra incentive to purchase the brand. Very few consumers actually take advantage of mail-in premium offers as the average redemption rate is estimated to be between 2 and 4 percent.[33]

Self-Liquidating Premiums **Self-liquidating premiums** are those that require the consumer to pay some or all of the cost of the premium plus handling and mailing

Figure 15–21 **Example of a Premium Offer That Is Supportive of Brand Image and Positioning**

costs. The items used as self-liquidating premiums are usually purchased in large quantities by the company and offered to consumers at prices that are lower than would be paid at retail. The marketer usually does not attempt to make a profit on the premium item but only wants to cover his or her costs and offer a value to the consumer.

In addition to the cost savings, self-liquidating premiums offer several advantages to marketers. By offering values to consumers through the premium products, the advertiser can create interest in the brand and goodwill that may enhance the brand's image. These premiums can also be an effective way to encourage trade support and gain in-store displays for the brand and the premium offer. Also, self-liquidating premiums are often tied in directly to the advertising campaign and may be an effective way of extending an advertising message and contributing to the consumer-franchise-building effort for a brand. For example, the merchandise available in the Grape-Nuts Sporty Accessories Offer shown in Figure 15–21 is consistent with the image and positioning of the brand as a natural cereal for those interested in nature and the outdoors. The Michelob Night Hits tape offer helped reinforce the "Night belongs to Michelob" campaign theme used for the brand (Figure 15–22).

In some instances marketers have used product containers and packages to develop self-liquidating premiums. Fast-food restaurants often sell beverages in containers with logos of local sports teams, movie, television, or cartoon characters on them. Some companies will offer attractive packages for their products that can be saved and reused such as decorative cannisters for the kitchen, wine decanters, or jars for nuts and candy. Package premium offers can also have a functional relationship to the product such as the Gatorade squeeze-bottle premium shown in Figure 15–23.

Self-liquidating premium offers have the same basic limitations as mail-in premiums in that they have a very low redemption rate. It is estimated that fewer than 10 percent of U.S. households have ever sent for a premium, and less than 1 percent of

Figure 15—22 **Another Example of a Premium Offer That Is Supportive of Brand Image and Position**

self-liquidating offers are actually redeemed.[34] Low redemption rates can result in leaving the marketer with a large supply of items with a logo or some other brand identification that may make them very hard to dispose of. Thus, it is important to test consumers' reaction to a premium incentive and to determine whether they perceive the offer as a value. Another option is to use premiums with no brand identification. However, this can detract from the consumer-franchise-building value of a premium.

Contests and Sweepstakes

Contests and sweepstakes have become an increasingly popular consumer-oriented promotion. The number of nationally advertised contests and sweepstakes has increased from about 300 in 1975 to more than 1,000 in 1989 as companies look for ways to generate interest and excitement among consumers for their products and services. Many marketers view these types of promotions as having an appeal and glamour that tools such as cents-off coupons lack. Contests and sweepstakes are exciting to consumers because, as one expert has noted, consumers have a "pot-of-gold at the end of the rainbow mentality" and think they can win the big prizes being offered.[35]

There are differences between contests and sweepstakes. A **contest** is a promotion whereby consumers compete for prizes or money on the basis of skills or ability and winners are determined by judging the entries or ascertaining which entry comes closest to some predetermined critera (e.g., picking the winning teams and number of total points in the Super Bowl or NCAA Basketball Tournament). Contests usually provide a purchase incentive by requiring a proof of purchase to enter or an entry form that is available from a dealer or advertisement.

A **sweepstakes** is a promotion whereby winners are determined purely by chance and cannot require a proof of purchase as a condition for entry. Sweepstakes only re-

Figure 15—23 **A Premium Offer That Has a Functional Relationship to the Product**

FREE GATORADE® SQUEEZE BOTTLE
(plus postage and handling)
32-oz. plastic Squeeze Bottle with official Gatorade® logo.

SEND:
- Four (4) UPC/Purchase Seals from any size, any flavor of Gatorade® Thirst Quencher.
- 60¢ for postage and handling. (Send check or money order made payable to: Gatorade® Sports Item Offer.) DO NOT SEND CASH OR STAMPS.
- Mail-in Order Form.

SQUEEZE BOTTLE OFFER GOOD WHILE SUPPLIES LAST.

Figure 15—24   This Miller Lite Promotion Helped Increase Consumer Involvement

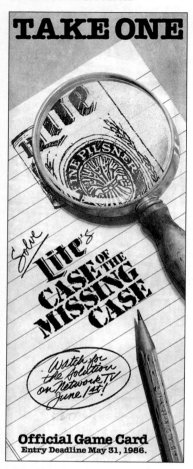

quire that the entrant submit his or her name for consideration in the drawing or selection of the prize or prizes. While this is often done on an official entry form, handwritten facsimile entries must also be permitted. Another form of a sweepstakes is a **game,** whick also has a chance element or odds of winning associated. The use of scratch-off cards with instant winners is a popular promotional tool. Some games take place over a longer time period and require more involvement by consumers. Games such as bingo are popular among retailers and fast-food chains as a way of building store traffic and repeat purchase.

Because they are easier to enter, sweepstakes attract more entries than contests and have become a more widely used sales promotion technique (refer to Table 15—2). Also, they are easier and less expensive to administer since every entry does not have to be checked or judged. Choosing the winning entry in a sweepstakes requires only the random selection of a winner from the pool of entries or generation of a number to match against those held by sweepstakes entrants.

Contests and sweepstakes can be an effective way of getting the consumer involved with a brand by making the promotion product relevant. For example, contests that ask consumers to suggest a name for a product or to submit recipes that make use of the brand can increase involvement levels. Some contests require consumers to read an advertisement or package or visit a store display to gather information needed to enter. Figure 15—24 shows a very successful promotion for Miller Lite beer that required consumers to gather point-of-purchase clue cards at bars and in stores to find out who stole the case of Lite beer. The promotion was very effective and generated record sales during the promotional period.[36] Of course, marketers must be careful not to make their contests too difficult to enter, as this may discourage participation among key prospects in the target audience and the contest may end up attracting only habitual or professional contests entrants.

Sweepstakes can also be used as a way of generating interest in or excitement over a brand. In an increasingly cluttered media environment, sweepstakes can provide consumers with an extra incentive for attending to an advertisement. As the president of one of the leading sweepstakes consulting firms has noted:

> Sweepstakes are the insurance policy for an ad campaign. It's a way to get attention in a world where everyone else is trying to get attention too. They also generate a sense of immediacy since there's always a deadline for entries.[37]

Contest and sweepstakes promotions can sometimes be an effective way of dealing with specific problems. For example, British Airways was faced with the problem of attracting American tourists to Europe in the middle of the wave of terrorist violence in summer 1986. The company used a six-month-long promotion whereby passengers were eligible to participate in an in-flight skill game as well as an instant-win sweepstakes with free roundtrip tickets on the Concorde, a shopping spree at Harrods, the famous London department store, and a Rolls Royce Silver Spirit among the prizes. The promotion drew 1 million entries in one week, and within 60 days of the start of the promotion, the airline was back to the load factor of the previous year.[38] (See Figure 15—25.)

As with other sales promotion techniques, sweepstakes can be particularly effective at franchise building when they are directly tied to the creative theme being used in the advertising campaign. For example, the Quaker Oats Microwave Sweepstakes was an effective way to promote the new microwave preparation feature of the product (Figure 15—26).

Problems with Contests and Sweepstakes   While the use of contests and sweepstakes continues to increase, there are a number of disadvantages and problems associated with these types of promotions that should be noted. One problem with many sweepstakes and/or contest promotions is that they often do little to contribute to the consumer-franchise-building effort for a product or service and may even detract from

Figure 15—25   **British Airways Used a Game and Sweepstakes to Overcome a Difficult Situation**

Figure 15—26   **This Sweepstakes Helped Promote a New Product Feature**

it. The sweepstakes or contest often becomes the dominant focus and completely over-shadows the brand. Thus, little has been accomplished other than to give out substantial amounts of money and/or prizes. Many promotional experts question the effectiveness of contests and sweepstakes, and some companies have even stopped using them. For example, companies such as Land O'Lakes, McDonald's, and Procter & Gamble cut back on their use of sweepstakes because of concern over their effectiveness and fears that consumers might become overdependent on them.[39]

There are also numerous legal problems and considerations that impact the design and administration of contests and sweepstakes. These promotions are regulated by a number of different federal agencies, and each of the 50 states has its own rules to follow. The regulation of contests and sweepstakes has been beneficial as it has helped clean up the abuses that plagued the industry in the late 1960s and has resulted in more favorable perceptions of these promotions among consumers. Companies still must be careful, however, in designing a contest or sweepstakes and awarding prizes. Most firms use consultants or firms specializing in the design and administration of contests and sweepstakes to avoid any legal problems.

A final problem that continues to detract from the effectiveness of contests and sweepstakes is the presence of professionals or hobbyists who submit large numbers of entries but have no interest in or intention to purchase the product or service. Because most states make it illegal to require a purchase as a qualification for a sweepstakes entry, consumers can enter as many times as they wish. Professional players will enter as many as several hundred entries per sweepstakes, depending on the nature of the prizes and the number of entries the promotion attracts. There are even newsletters available that inform them of all the contests and sweepstakes being held, the entry dates, estimated probabilities of winning for various numbers of entries, information on how to enter, and solutions to any puzzles or other information that might be needed to enter a contest. The presence of these professional entrants not only defeats the purpose of the promotion but may also deter entries from consumers who feel that their chance of winning is limited.

Refunds and Rebates

Refunds or rebates are offers to return some portion of the product purchase price, usually after supplying some sort of proof of purchase. Consumers are generally very responsive to refund or rebate offers, particularly as the size of the savings increases. Thus, refunds and rebates are used by all types of companies ranging from packaged-goods companies to manufacturers of major appliances and automobiles. The use of money-back offers/cash refunds ranks second to coupons among packaged-goods companies.

Refund offers are often used by packaged-goods marketers as a way to induce trial of a new product or to encourage users of another brand to switch. The savings offered through a cash refund offer may be perceived by the consumer as an immediate value that lowers the cost of the item. Of course the savings are realized only if the refund or rebate offer is redeemed by the consumer. Redemption rates for refund offers typically range from 1 to 3 percent for print and point-of-purchase offers to 5 percent for in/on package offers.[40]

Refund offers can also be an effective way to encourage repeat purchase. Many offers require consumers to send in multiple proofs of purchase as a condition for receiving the refund. In some cases the size of the refund offer may even increase as the number of purchases gets larger. Many packaged-goods companies are switching away from cash refund offers only to the use of coupons or cash/coupon combinations (see Figure 15–27). By using coupons in the refund offer, the marketer enhances the likelihood of repeat purchase of the brand.

The use of refunds—or as they are more commonly referred to, rebates—has become a widely used form of promotion for consumer durables. Products such as cameras, sporting goods, appliances, televisions, audio and video equipment, computers,

Figure 15–27 **A Cash/ Coupon Combination Refund Offer**

and automobiles frequently use rebate offers to appeal to price-conscious consumers. The use of rebates for expensive items such as automobiles was begun by Chrysler Corporation in 1981 as a way of boosting sales and generating cash for the struggling company. Rebates have since become a very common promotional technique not only in the auto industry and other durable products but for packaged-goods products as well.

Evaluating Refunds and Rebates As noted earlier, refunds and rebates can be effective sales promotional tools for creating new users and for encouraging brand switching or repeat purchase behavior or as a way of offering a temporary price reduction. In many instances, the refund or rebate offer may be perceived as an immediate savings or value even though the money is not received until the offer is redeemed, and many consumers will never follow through on the refund or rebate offer. Thus, a perception of a price reduction is operating and can influence purchase even though the consumer may fail to realize the savings. This means that the marketer can in effect reduce price for much less than if a direct price-off deal were utilized.

There are, of course, some problems associated with refunds and rebates. Many consumers are not motivated by a refund offer because of the delay in receiving the reward and the effort required to obtain the savings. Many consumers view the refund or rebate process of saving cash register receipts and proofs of purchase, filling out forms, and mailing in the offer as a complete hassle and do not want to be bothered by it.[41] Moreover, the terms of some rebate offers are often inconvenient or even unrealistic. For example, one well-known motor oil company offered a $2.40 rebate with the purchase of 12 quarts of motor oil but required consumers to send in the rebate form along with the emblems from seven cans. However, for most cars an oil change requires only four to five quarts of oil.[42]

Figure 15—28 **Bonus Packs Provide More Value for Consumers**

A study of consumers' perceptions of rebates found a negative relationship between the use of rebates and the perceived efforts and difficulties associated with the redemption process.[43] It was also found that consumers perceive manufacturers as offering rebates to sell products that are not faring well. Nonusers of rebates were particularly likely to perceive the rebate redemption process as too complicated and to have negative perceptions of manufacturers' motives for offering rebates. Thus, it is important that companies using rebates simplify the redemption process and use other promotional elements such as advertising to retain consumer confidence in the brand.

When small refunds are being offered, marketers might find other promotional incentives such as coupons or bonus packs more appropriate and effective. Marketers must be careful not to overuse refund or rebate offers and thus confuse consumers over the real price and value of a product or service. Also, consumers can become dependent on rebates and delay their purchases or only purchase brands for which a rebate is available. Many retailers have become disenchanted with rebates and the burden and expense of administering these programs. Promotional Perspective 15—5 discusses how these problems have led many marketers of small appliances to eliminate rebating programs entirely.

Bonus Packs

Bonus packs offer the consumer an extra amount of a product at the regular price by providing larger containers or extra units (Figure 15—28). Bonus packs result in a lower cost per unit for the consumer and thus provide extra value, as well as more of the product, for the money. There are several advantages to using bonus pack promotions. First, the bonus pack gives marketers a direct way of providing extra value to the consumer without having to get involved with things such as coupons or refund offers. The additional value of a bonus pack is generally obvious to the consumer and can have a strong impact on the purchase decision right at the time of purchase.

Bonus packs can also be an effective defensive maneuver against a competitor's promotion or introduction of a new brand. By loading current users with large amounts of their product, a marketer can often remove these consumers from the market and make them less susceptible to a competitor's promotional efforts. Bonus packs often receive favorable response from retailers and may result in larger purchase orders and favorable display space in the store as well.

Bonus pack promotions can be particularly effective when cooperation and relationships with retailers are favorable. It should be noted, however, that bonus packs often require additional shelf space and generally do not provide any extra profit margins for the retailer. Thus, the marketer can encounter problems with these promotions if trade relationships are not favorable. Another problem with bonus packs is that they may appeal primarily to current users who probably would have purchased the brand anyway or to promotion-sensitive consumers who may not become loyal to the brand.

Figure 15—29 **Examples of Price-Off Packages**

Price-Off Deals

Another type of consumer-oriented promotion technique is the direct **price-off deal,** which provides the consumer with a reduction in the regular price of the brand. Price-off reductions are typically offered right on the package itself through specially marked price packs, as shown in Figure 15—29. Typically price-offs range from 10 to 25 percent off the regular price, with the reduction coming out of the manufacturer's profit margin, not the retailer's. It is very important to maintain the retailer's margin during a price-off promotion in order to maintain its support and cooperation.

There are several reasons why marketers use price-off promotions. First, price-offs are controlled by the manufacturer, which enables them to ensure that the promotional discount does reach the consumer rather than being kept by the trade. As with a bonus pack, price-off deals usually present a readily apparent value to the shop-

Promotional Perspective   **15—5**

Pulling the Plug on Rebates

In many industries, rebating has become a standard marketing practice that is relied on to provide the consumer with a little extra incentive to purchase a product and to motivate retailers to stock and promote the item. However, a number of marketers in the small-appliance industry feel that rebates have outlived their usefulness as a marketing strategy and have decided either to cut back or to eliminate rebating programs. The decision by companies such as Sunbeam, Conair, National Presto, and Hamilton Beach to drop rebates stems from declining consumer response to rebate programs and waning consumer interest in and acceptance of rebate promotions by retailers.

Many marketing managers in the industry feel that consumers have been "rebated to death" and note that rebate redemption rates have fallen to only 10 percent. Moreover, many retailers began resisting rebates because of the burden and expense involved in administering these programs. For example, Target stores, which stopped handling rebates at the beginning of 1989, said that its out-of-pocket expense for maintaining rebate programs was more than $1 million a year. This figure did not include the time of workers who had to maintain the rebate bulletin boards and process complaints.

Some retailers, such as K mart and Best Products, even threatened to stop advertising products of manufacturers who continue to use rebates. They cited the hassles of handling rebate cards, which must be administered by the retailer instead of inserted with the product, and the administrative problems this poses. They also argue that rebates create more work for their advertising departments, which must keep track of when rebate promotions are run and write extra ad copy to explain them.

As rebates are phased out, many small-appliance marketers are taking the monies saved from these programs and channeling the funds into increased advertising, product development, and creative pricing. For example, Black & Decker was spending millions of dollars on rebating programs for many of its 175 products. The shifting of rebate money allowed the company to raise its advertising budget by 20 percent in 1988, invest more in new products, and improve its marketing image and profitability. Windemere Corporation, a manufacturer of hair dryers and other small appliances, eliminated rebates at the beginning of 1988 and increased its ad budget by 50 percent to $12 million.

Not all small-appliance companies have terminated rebates. North American Systems' Mr. Coffee was one of the first marketers to adopt rebates as a consistent marketing strategy and continues to use them despite the pressure from the trade to cut back. Many retailers continue to accept rebate offers, citing the fact that, despite the hassles, consumers still like to use them. They are also concerned that consumers may change to stores that are willing to accept rebate offers.

Sources: David Kiley, "Appliance Marketers Pull Plug on Rebates," *Adweek's Marketing Week,* November 9, 1987, p. 1; Martha Groves, "Mail-In Rebates Stirring Shopper, Retailer Backlash," *Los Angeles Times,* January 11, 1989, pt. IV, p. 1.

per, particularly when he or she has a "reference price point" for the brand and thus recognizes the value of the discount.[44] Thus, price-offs can provide a strong influence at the point of purchase when price comparisons are being made. Price-off promotions can also be useful in encouraging consumers to purchase larger quantities and thus preempt competitors' promotions and assist in obtaining trade support.

Price-off promotions may not be favorably received by retailers since they can create pricing and inventory problems. Most retailers will not accept packages with a specific price shown on the package. Thus, the familiar X amount off the regular price must be used. Also, as with bonus packs, price-off deals often appeal primarily to regular users rather than attracting nonusers. Finally, it should be noted that the Federal Trade Commission has a set of specific regulations regarding the conditions that price-off labels must meet and the frequency and timing of their use.

Event Sponsorship

Another type of consumer-oriented promotion that has become increasingly popular in recent years is that of **event sponsorship** whereby a company develops sponsorship relations with a particular event. The Wisk Bright Lights '87 promotion discussed at the beginning of this chapter showed how Lever Brothers made very successful use of the sponsorship of fireworks shows to promote Wisk detergent.

Many companies are turning increasingly to sponsorship of spectator sports. For example, it is estimated that more than 3,400 companies spent $1.35 billion to sponsor sporting events in 1987.[45] Among the more popular events for sponsorship are golf and tennis tournaments, auto racing, and running events. Bicycle racing, beach volleyball, skiing, and various water sports are also attracting corporate sponsorship. Traditionally, cigarette-, beer-, and automobile-related companies have been among the largest sports event sponsors. However, a number of other companies have become involved in event sponsorship such as Procter & Gamble, which spends over $30 million a year in this area and has begun using the services of events-marketing agencies.[46]

Many marketers are attracted to event sponsorship because it offers them a way of getting their company and/or product names in front of consumers. Moreover, by choosing the right events for sponsorship, companies can get visibility among consumers who constitute their target market. For example, RJR Nabisco, which spent nearly $100 million sponsoring sporting events in 1988, is heavily involved in sponsorship of automobile racing under its Winston and Camel cigarette brands. The company's market research indicated that racing fans fit the demographic profile of users of these brands very well and that consumers would purchase a product that was instrumental in sponsoring their favorite sport.[47] For tobacco companies, which are prohibited from advertising on radio and television, event sponsorship also provides them with a way to have their brand names seen on television.

Marketers also are attracted to event sponsorship because of the opportunities it offers for promotional tie-ins to regional markets. Events such as stock car races are very popular in southern states and are an effective way of reaching consumers in this region. Hanes Hosiery spent more than a million dollars in 1987 to put its Underalls panty hose logos on race cars and sponsor races as a way of reaching women in the southern states where its sales are weak.[48] As traditional media advertising becomes more crowded and expensive and regional marketing trends increase, it is likely that more companies will turn to the use of event sponsorship.

Coordinating Sales Promotion and Advertising

It is important that those individuals involved in the promotional process recognize and understand that sales promotion techniques usually work best when used in conjunction with advertising and that the effectiveness of an ad campaign can be enhanced by consumer-oriented sales promotion efforts. Rather than viewing advertising and sales promotion as separate activities competing for a firm's promotional budget, they should be viewed as complementary tools. It has been noted that when properly planned and executed to work together, advertising and sales promotion can provide a **synergistic effect** that is much greater than the response that would be generated from either promotional mix element being used alone.

Evidence of this synergistic effect comes from a study conducted over an 18-month period for a packaged-goods company. The results of this study, which are shown in Figure 15–30, showed that while advertising was able to increase sales a certain amount and sales promotion another amount, the combination of the two forms of promotion generated an additional level of sales.[49]

Proper coordination of the advertising and sales promotion efforts is essential if the firm wants to take advantage of the opportunities offered by each tool and get the most out of its promotional budget. Successful integration of advertising and sales promotion requires decisions concerning not only the allocation of the budget to each area but also the coordination of the ad and sales promotional themes, the target audience reached, and the timing of the various promotional activities.

Budget Coordination   As was noted at the beginning of this chapter, many companies are spending more money on sales promotion than on media advertising (this includes trade- as well as consumer-oriented promotions). It is difficult to say just what percentage of a firm's overall promotional budget should be allocated to advertising-versus consumer-oriented promotions. This allocation depends on a number of factors

Figure 15-30   **Interaction Effect of Advertising and Sales Promotion**

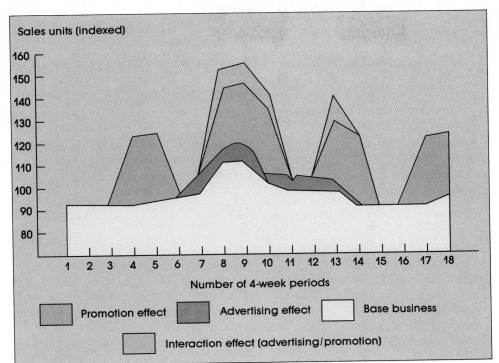

Source: Don Sunoo and Lynn Y. S. Lin, "Sales Effects of Promotion and Advertising," *Journal of Advertising Research* 18, no. 5 (October 1978), p. 37.

including the specific promotional objectives of the campaign, the market and competitive situation, and the stage of the brand in its life cycle.

Consider, for example, the way allocation of the promotional budget may vary according to the stage of a brand in the product life cycle. In the introductory stage a large amount of the budget may be allocated to sales promotion techniques such as sampling and couponing to induce trial. In the growth stage, however, promotional dollars may be used primarily for advertising to stress brand differences and keep the brand name in the minds of consumers.

When a brand moves to the maturity stage, advertising plays primarily a reminder role to keep consumers aware of the brand. Consumer-oriented sales promotions such as coupons, price-offs, premiums, and bonus packs may be needed periodically to maintain consumer loyalty, attract new users, and protect against competition. The study cited above on the synergistic effects of advertising and promotion examined a brand in the mature phase of its life cycle and found that 80 percent of its sales at this stage were due to sales promotions. When a brand enters the decline stage of the product life cycle, it is likely that most of the promotional support will be removed and expenditures on sales promotion are very unlikely.

Coordinating Ad and Promotional Themes   To integrate the advertising and sales promotional programs successfully, the theme of consumer promotions should be tied in with the advertising and positioning theme wherever possible. As was noted in evaluating the various sales promotion techniques, these tools should attempt to communicate a brand's unique attributes or benefits and to reinforce the sales message or campaign theme. In this way the sales promotion effort contributes to the consumer-franchise-building effort for the brand.

Media Support and Timing   Media support for a sales promotion program is also critical and should be coordinated with the media program for the advertising cam-

Table 15–7   **Shifting Role of the Promotion Agency**

Traditional	New Improved
1. Primarily used to develop short-term tactics or concepts 2. Hired/compensated on a project-by-project basis 3. Many promotion agencies used a mix—each one hired for best task and/or specialty 4. One or two contact people from agency 5. Promotion agency never equal to ad agency—doesn't work up front in annual planning process 6. Not directly accountable for results	1. Used to develop long- and short-term promotional strategies, as well as tactics 2. Contracted on annual retainer, following formal agency reviews 3. One or two exclusive promotion agencies for each division or brand group 4. Full team or "core group" on the account 5. Promotion agency works on equal basis with ad agency—sits at planning table up front 6. Very much accountable—goes through a rigorous evaluation process

Source: Russ Bowman, "The Envelope, Please," *Marketing & Media Decisions*, April 1988, p. 130.

paign. Media advertising is often needed to deliver the sales promotional materials such as coupons, sweepstakes, contest entry forms, premium offers, and even samples. However, media support is also needed to inform consumers of a promotional offer as well as to create prior awareness, interest, and favorable attitudes toward the brand. By using advertising prior to a sales promotion program, the marketer can make consumers aware of the brand and its benefits and thus increase their responsiveness to the promotion. Consumers are more likely to redeem a coupon or respond to a price-off deal for a brand they are familiar with or have favorable feelings toward than for a brand they have never heard of or know nothing about.

A marketer running a promotion without prior or concurrent advertising not only may be limiting its effectiveness but also may be damaging the image of the brand. Consumers may perceive the brand as being "promotion dependent" or a cheap brand. This can result in a lower likelihood of consumers developing favorable attitudes and long-term loyalty. Conversely, the effectiveness of an advertisement can be enhanced by a consumer promotion. As noted earlier, consumers may be more likely to attend to an advertisement that contains a coupon, premium offer, or an opportunity to enter a sweepstakes or contest.

In order to coordinate their advertising and sales promotion programs more effectively, many companies are having their sales promotion agencies become more involved in the advertising and promotional planning process. Rather than hiring agencies to develop individual, non-franchise-building types of promotions with short-term goals and tactics, many firms are having their sales promotion and advertising agencies work together to develop more fully integrated promotional strategies and programs. Table 15–7 shows how the role of sales promotional agencies is changing.

Table 15–8   **Sales Promotion Dilemma**

		OUR FIRM	
		Cut back promotions	Maintain promotions
ALL OTHER FIRMS	Cut back promotions	Higher profits for all	Market share goes to our firm
	Maintain promotions	Market share goes to all other firms	Market share stays constant; profits stay low

Source: Michael L. Rothschild, *Marketing Communications* (Lexington, Mass.: D. C. Heath, 1987), p. 436.

Sales Promotion Abuse

The increasing use of sales promotion in the marketing program is more than a passing fad and has been characterized as a change in the fundamental, strategic decisions regarding how companies market their products and services. However, the value of this increased emphasis on sales promotion has been questioned by several writers, particularly with regard to the lack of adequate planning and management of sales promotional programs.[50,51]

As the use of consumer-oriented sales promotion techniques increases, an important factor to consider is whether marketers are becoming too dependent on and possibly even abusing this element of the marketing program. Consumer promotions can be a very effective tool for generating short-term increases in sales. As was discussed at the beginning of this chapter, many brand managers would rather use some type of promotion to produce immediate sales rather than invest in advertising and build the brand's image over an extended time period. As the director of sales promotion services at one large advertising agency noted:

> There's a great temptation for quick sales fixes through promotions. It's a lot easier to offer the consumer an immediate price savings than to differentiate your product from a competitor's.[52]

Overuse of sales promotion can be detrimental to a brand in several ways. A brand that is constantly promoted may lose perceived value from the perspective of the consumer. Consumers often end up purchasing a brand because it is on sale, they get a premium, or they have a coupon, rather than basing their decision on a favorable attitude they have developed. However, when the extra promotional incentive is not available, they may switch to another brand.

Alan Sawyer and Peter Dickson have used the concept of *attribution theory* to examine how the use of sales promotion may affect consumer attitude formation.[53] According to this theory, people acquire attitudes by observing their own behavior and considering why they acted in a certain manner. Consumers who consistently purchase a brand using a promotional tool such as a coupon or because of a price-off deal may "attribute" their behavior to the external promotional incentive rather than to a favorable attitude toward the brand. However, when no external incentive is available, consumers should be more likely to attribute their purchase behavior to favorable underlying feelings about the brand.

Another potential problem with consumer-oriented promotions is that a **sales promotion trap** or spiral can result when a number of competitors are making extensive use of promotions.[54] Very often a firm begins using sales promotions as a way of differentiating its product or service from the competition. If the promotion is successful and leads to a differential advantage (or even appears to be doing so), competitors may quickly copy the promotional program. When all the competitors are using sales promotions extensively, it not only lowers profit margins for each firm but also may make it difficult for any one firm to hop off the promotional bandwagon.[55] This promotional dilemma is shown in Table 15–8.

A number of industries such as cosmetics and airlines have fallen into this promotional trap. In the cosmetics industry, gift-with-purchase and purchase-with-purchase promotional offers, which were originally developed as a tactic for getting buyers to sample new products, have become a very common, and costly, way of doing business.[56] In the airline industry, frequent flyer programs were begun several years ago as a way of encouraging loyalty to a particular carrier. However, nearly all the competitors quickly developed mileage-award programs out of fear of losing customers to airlines who offered them.

These programs have become very costly to administer and are costing the airlines millions of dollars every year. The problem became even more acute in 1988 when

Delta Airlines began its triple-mileage promotion as a way of generating business during the slow winter months. However, other airlines quickly matched the triple-mileage offer, and all the carriers found themselves accumulating large frequent flyer liabilities without the benefit of any differential advantage.[57] Many airline executives long for the day when they can eliminate these programs.

The effective use of consumer-oriented sales promotions requires that marketers carefully consider both the short-term impact of a promotion as well as the long-term effect it may have on the brand. Consideration should also be given to the ease with which competitors can develop a retaliatory promotion and the likelihood of their doing so. Marketers must be careful not to damage the brand franchise with sales promotions or to get the firm involved in a promotional war that erodes the brand's profit margins and often threatens its long-term existence. Marketers are often tempted to resort to sales promotions to deal with declining sales and other problems rather than examining other aspects of the marketing program such as channel relations, price, packaging, product quality, or advertising.

Summary

For many years advertising was the major promotional mix element of most consumer product companies. Over the past decade, however, marketers have been allocating more of their promotional dollars to sales promotion. Sales promotion programs can be classified as either being trade or consumer oriented.

The focus of this chapter has been on consumer-oriented sales promotions and the role they play in a firm's marketing and promotional program. There has been a steady increase in the use of sales promotion techniques to influence and motivate consumers' purchase behavior. The erosion of brand loyalty, increase in new product introductions, fragmentation of the consumer market, short-term focus of marketing and product managers, and increase in advertising clutter are some of the reasons for this increase.

Consumer-oriented promotions can be characterized as being either franchise-building or non-franchise-building promotions. The former contribute to the development and reinforcement of brand identity and image, whereas the latter are designed to accelerate the purchase process and generate immediate increases in sales.

A number of consumer-oriented sales promotion techniques were examined in this chapter, including sampling, couponing, premiums, contests and sweepstakes, rebates and refunds, bonus packs, price-off deals, and event sponsorship. The characteristics of these promotional tools were examined, along with their specific advantages and limitations.

Advertising and sales promotion should not be viewed as separate activities but rather as complementary tools. When planned and executed properly, advertising and sales promotion can produce a synergistic effect that is greater than the response generated from either promotional mix element alone. To accomplish this, there must be coordination of advertising and promotional themes, target audiences, and media scheduling and timing.

Consideration must also be given to the potential for sales promotional abuse. This can result when marketers become too dependent on the use of sales promotion techniques and sacrifice long-term brand position and image for short-term sales increases. In many industries, sales promotion traps or spirals develop when a number of competitors make extensive use of promotions and it becomes difficult for any single firm to cut back on promotion without risking a potential loss in sales. Overuse of sales promotion tools can not only result in lower profit margins but can also threaten the image and viability of a brand.

Key Terms

Sales promotion
Acceleration tool
Consumer-oriented sales promotion
Trade-oriented sales promotion
Consumer-franchise-building (CFB)
    promotions
Non-consumer-franchise-building
    promotions
Sampling
Bounce-back coupon
Cross-ruff coupon

Instant coupon
Premium
Self-liquidating premiums
Contest
Sweepstakes
Game
Bonus packs
Price-off deal
Event sponsorship
Synergistic effect
Sales promotion trap

Discussion Questions

1. What are the differences between consumer-oriented and trade-oriented sales promotions? Discuss the importance and role of each in a firm's marketing program.
2. Discuss the various reasons why sales promotion has become so important and is receiving an increasing portion of marketers' promotional budgets.
3. What are the differences between consumer-franchise-building and non-franchise-building promotions? Cite current examples of each.
4. Provide an example of current sales promotion efforts that correspond to the objectives shown in Table 15–1.
5. Discuss the various methods that can be used for delivering product samples, along with their advantages and limitations.
6. Discuss the advantages and disadvantages of coupons. What factors will influence consumers' use of coupons?
7. What are the basic types of premium offers? Discuss how a premium can add value to a brand.
8. Why do you think contests and sweepstakes have become so popular in recent years? Are you in favor of these types of promotions? Why or why not?
9. How might marketers measure the effectiveness of an event sponsorship promotion such as a golf or tennis tournament or an automobile race?
10. What is meant by a sales promotion trap or spiral? What are the options for a company involved in such a situation?

Notes

1. Russ Bowman, "The Envelope, Please," *Marketing & Media Decisions,* April 1988, pp. 131–34.
2. Nathaniel Frey, "Ninth Annual Advertising & Sales Promotion Report," *Marketing Communications,* August 1988, pp. 9–19.
3. Louis J. Haugh, "Defining and Redefining," *Advertising Age,* February 14, 1983, p. m-44.
4. Scott A. Neslin, John Quelch, and Caroline Henderson, "Consumer Promotions and the Acceleration of Product Purchases," in *Research on Sales Promotion: Collected Papers,* ed. Katherine E. Jocz (Cambridge, Mass.: Marketing Science Institute, 1984).
5. Julie Liesse Erickson and Judann Dagnoli, "The Party's Over," *Advertising Age,* February 27, 1989, p. 1.
6. *The Wall Street Journal Centennial Survey,* cited in Ron Alsop, "Brand Loyalty Is Rarely Blind Loyalty," *The Wall Street Journal,* October 19, 1989, p. B1.

7. Todd Johnson, NPD Research Inc., "Declining Brand Loyalty Trends: Fact or Fiction?" (Paper presented at the Fourth Annual AMA Marketing Research Conference, October 5, 1983).

8. Bob Schmitz and Keith Jones, "The New Retailer/Marketer: Friend or Foe?" in *Looking at the Retail Kaleidoscope, Forum IX* (Stamford, Conn.: Donnelley Marketing, 1988).

9. Robert B. Settle and Pamela L. Alreck, "Hyperchoice in the Marketplace," *Marketing Communications,* May 1988, p. 15.

10. Leigh McAlister, "A Model of Consumer Behavior," *Marketing Communications,* April 1987, p. 27.

11. Ruth M. McMath, "Winning the Space Wars," *Marketing Communications,* May 1988, pp. 55–58.

12. Lynn G. Coleman, "Marketers Advised to Go Regional," *Marketing News,* May 8, 1989, p. 1.

13. Lisa Petrison, "Aiming the Pitch at the Corner Store," *Adweek's Marketing Week—Promote,* September 21, 1987, p. 6.

14. F. Kent Mitchel, "Strategic Use of Advertising and Promotion," *Marketing Communications,* April 1986, pp. 34–36.

15. Frey, "Ninth."

16. Nielsen Clearing House, *NCH Reporter,* no. 1, 1983.

17. R. M. Prentice, "How to Split Your Marketing Funds Between Advertising and Promotion Dollars," *Advertising Age,* January 10, 1977, pp. 41–42, 44.

18. Quote by Vincent Sottosanti, president of Council of Sales Promotion Agencies, in "Promotions That Build Brand Image," *Marketing Communications,* April 1988, p. 54.

19. Examples cited in "Promotions That Build Brand Image," p. 55.

20. Jeffrey K. McElenea and Michael J. Enzer, "Building Brand Franchises," *Marketing Communications,* April 1986, pp. 42–64.

21. "Study of New Product Failure Refutes Basic Premise of Growth," *The Wall Street Journal,* June 26, 1980, p. 29.

22. McElenea and Enzer, "Building Brand Franchises."

23. *Donnelley Marketing 11th Annual Survey of Promotional Practices* (Stamford, Conn.: Donnelley Marketing, 1989).

24. Reference cited in John P. Rossiter and Larry Percy, *Advertising and Promotion Management* (New York: McGraw-Hill, 1987), p. 360.

25. "Coupon Distribution and Redemption Patterns," *Manufacturers Coupon Control Center (MCCC),* 1989.

26. "Coupon Redemptions Declined in 1988," *Adweek's Promote,* May 1, 1989, p. 4.

27. *MCCC,* "Coupon Distribution."

28. N. Giges, "GF Trims Its Use of Coupons," *Advertising Age,* December 7, 1981, p. 22.

29. Amy E. Gross, "Curing the Misredemption Malady," *Adweek's Promote,* May 1, 1989, p. 32.

30. Julie Liesse Erickson, "FSI Boom to Go Bust?" *Advertising Age,* May 1, 1989, pp. 1, 82.

31. "In-Store Pioneers Clip Coupon Competition," *Advertising Age,* January 24, 1985, p. 6.

32. Survey by Oxtoby-Smith, Inc. cited in "Many Consumers View Rebates as a Bother," *The Wall Street Journal,* April 13, 1989, p. B1.

33. William R. Dean, "Irresistible But Not Free of Problems," *Advertising Age,* October 6, 1980, pp. S1–S12.

34. William A. Robinson, "What Are Promos' Weak and Strong Points?" *Advertising Age,* April 7, 1980, p. 54.

35. "Sweepstakes Fever," *Forbes,* October 3, 1988, pp. 164–66.

36. Example from William A. Robinson, "Best Promotions of 1986–1987," *Marketing Communications,* October 1987, p. 43.

37. Quote by Richard Kane, president of Marden-Kane Sweepstakes Consulting firm, cited in "Catching Consumers with Sweepstakes," *Fortune,* February 8, 1982, p. 87.

38. Robinson, "Best Promotions."

39. "Catching Consumers."

40. Russell D. Bowman, *Couponing and Rebates: Profits on the Dotted Line* (New York: Lebhar-Friedman Books, 1980).

41. "Many Consumers View Rebates."

42. "The Rebate That Isn't," *Consumer Reports,* January 1986.

43. Peter Tat, William A. Cunningham III, and Emin Babakus, "Consumer Perceptions of Rebates," *Journal of Advertising Research,* August/September 1988, pp. 45–50.

44. Edward A. Blair and E. Laird Landon, "The Effects of Reference Prices in Retail Advertisements," *Journal of Marketing* 45, no. 2 (Spring 1981), pp. 61–69.
45. "Nothing Sells Like Sports," *Business Week,* August 31, 1987, pp. 48–53.
46. Laurie Freeman, "P&G Has Event-ful Plans," *Advertising Age,* June 22, 1987, p. 41.
47. Shav Glick, "Takeovers, Mergers Take Their Toll, Too," *Los Angeles Times,* March 27, 1989, pt. III, p. 14.
48. Ronald Alsop, "Laundry Soap and Pantyhose Hitch a Ride on Racing Cars," *The Wall Street Journal,* December 13, 1987, p. 21.
49. Don Sunoo and Lynn Y. S. Lin, "Sales Effect of Advertising and Promotion," *Journal of Advertising Research* 18, no. 5 (October 1978), p. 37.
50. Benson P. Shapiro, "Improved Distribution with Your Promotional Mix," *Harvard Business Review,* March/April 1977, p. 116.
51. Roger A. Strang, "Sales Promotion—Fast Growth, Faulty Management," *Harvard Business Review,* July/August 1976, p. 119.
52. Quote by Thomas E. Hamilton, director of Sales Promotion Service—William Esty Advertising, cited in Felix Kessler, "The Costly Couponing Craze," *Fortune,* June 9, 1986, p. 84.
53. Alan G. Sawyer and Peter H. Dickson, "Psychological Perspectives on Consumer Response to Sales Promotion," in *Research on Sales Promotion: Collected Papers,* ed. Katherine E. Jocz (Cambridge, Mass.: Marketing Science Institute, 1984).
54. William E. Myers, "Trying to Get Out of the Discounting Box," *Adweek,* November 11, 1985, p. 2.
55. Leigh McAlister, "Managing the Dynamics of Promotional Change," in *Looking at the Retail Kaleidoscope, Forum IX* (Stamford, Conn.: Donnelley Marketing, April 1988).
56. "Promotions Blemish Cosmetic Industry," *Advertising Age,* May 10, 1984, pp. 22–23, 26.
57. "Triple-Mileage Plans: How High a Price?" *The Wall Street Journal,* January 28, 1988, p. 17.

16

The Role of Personal Selling and Reseller Support in the Promotional Program

CHAPTER OBJECTIVES

1. To understand the promotional mix programs targeted to resellers
2. To examine the role of personal selling in the promotional mix
3. To examine the advantages and disadvantages of personal selling as a promotional program element
4. To demonstrate how personal selling is combined with other program elements in the design of a promotional program

Slotting Gives Retailers Muscle

The "hot" thing in the retail industry right now is something called the *slotting allowance*. Also called *stocking allowances, introductory allowances,* or *street money,* slotting allowances are the fees that often must be paid to retailers to gain admission into their stores and are considered by manufacturers to be little more than blackmail. For example, a Utah ice cream maker had to abandon his plans to enter the California market when two chain operations demanded $20,000 each to carry the product. Northeastern grocery stores often require $15,000 to $40,000 slotting allowances, whereas American Beauty pasta paid $750 an item for its 26-item line to a West Coast buyer.

The retail operator has a different view. These buyers cite statistics that show that new product introductions climbed from 2,689 in 1980 to over 9,000 by 1987. They cite rising costs of entering new data into their computers, finding warehouse space, redesigning shelves, and informing employees of each new entry as justification for the charges. In addition, they say, retailers were always at the mercy of the large manufacturers for product success rates or failures, but now that they have their own data, they cherish the independence. It is their turn to be in power!

The final decision as to the validity of slotting allowances may not end up being decided by either party, however. Late in 1988 the Federal Trade Commission began to gather data on slotting fees in an attempt to determine their legality.

Regardless of who is correct, two things are certain: Slotting allowances have certainly shifted the power to the retailers, and they are not going to give it up too soon![¹]

Introduction

Throughout this text, we have been discussing promotional programs and strategies that involve the consumer either directly or indirectly. Of course, not all distribution channels are manufacturer-to-consumer direct, as many involve the use of intermediaries. These intermediaries—wholesalers and retailers—provide a vital link in the marketing process, and in the communications process, and can exert a great deal of influence on customers as well as the manufacturers themselves (as is evidenced in the lead-in to this chapter). An effective promotions program must include efforts targeted to these intermediaries—or **resellers**—as well as the consumer. These programs should be designed to assist the reseller in the communication of information about the manufacturer's products and to motivate the reseller to stock, promote, and sell them.

In addition to using advertising and promotions to reach resellers, manufacturers usually will employ a sales force. The job responsibilities of the sales staff will, of course, be to sell the product or service but will also include many of the tasks necessary to attain communications objectives. Sales persons may become involved in assisting in the development and implementation of advertising and promotions efforts targeted to intermediaries and will, in turn, be the target of their own organization's promotional efforts.

In this chapter we will discuss promotional program efforts that are targeted to these "indirect" channel members. As you will see, most firms will need to develop a separate promotional mix with specific objectives that are designed to assist in the goal of moving the product through these channels.

Reseller Involvement in the Promotional Program

The degree to which the reseller will become a part of a firm's advertising and promotions program is a function of a number of factors including the distribution strategy employed by the manufacturer, the nature of the product, and the stage of the product life cycle.

Figure 16–1 **Push versus Pull Promotional Strategies**

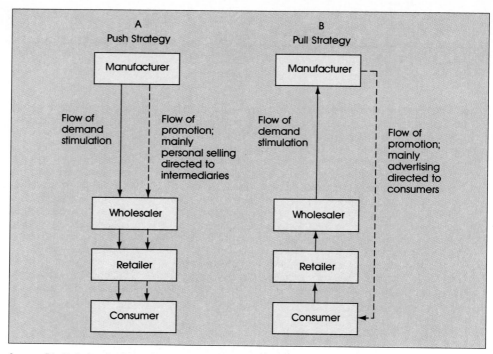

Source: Eric N. Berkowitz, Roger A. Kerin, and William Rudelius, *Marketing,* 2nd ed. (Homewood, Ill.: Richard D. Irwin, 1988), p. 445.

The Distribution Strategy

As shown in Figure 16–1 (and discussed in Chapter 2), marketers may employ either a **pull promotional strategy** or a **push promotional strategy.** In the former the target of advertising and promotions efforts is the ultimate consumer. Thus, for products such as aspirin, toothpaste, shampoo, or other consumer products, ads will be placed in consumer magazines, television, radio, or other media that the consumer will be involved with. Promotions will include samples, coupons, and/or sweepstakes that the consumer will receive directly. In these instances the reseller will have minimal involvement, usually only stocking and, of course, selling and servicing.

In a push strategy, however, advertising and promotions efforts are targeted to the resellers in an attempt to have these intermediaries more involved in the promotions and selling process. Thus, advertising will be directed to trade journals, and sales promotions, contests, and sweepstakes will also be reseller oriented.

The Nature of the Product

The specific nature of the product will often dictate whether a push or a pull strategy is employed. Products with rapid turnover rates, significant profit margins, high demand, and/or a highly differentiated character may typically support a pull strategy. Others such as industrial products, component parts, and those characterized by a derived demand may require a push approach. Still others may demand both push and pull strategies—such as autos and appliances.

Stage of the Product Life Cycle

As the product progresses through its life cycle, promotional strategies will change. In the early stages (introduction and growth) promotions will involve both push and pull strategies, with the primary objectives being to create awareness of the product and to gain distribution. As more competitors enter (late growth and maturity), the advertis-

Figure 16—2   This Pine-Sol Trade Ad Encourages Retailers to Feature the Brand During a Sweepstakes Promotion

ing and promotions will emphasize differentiation, with dealer incentives for stocking and pushing the specific brand. Finally, in the latter stages (late maturity and decline) promotions may give way to price reductions and/or other marketing mix strategies considered to be more effective. Advertising and promotions—while still employed— may play a much less important role.

Having determined the strategy to be pursued, marketers need to develop a promotional mix targeted to resellers, just as they would to consumers. Let us examine this process.

Developing the Promotional Mix for Resellers

All of the promotional mix elements used to communicate to consumers might also be used to reach resellers. For the most part, however, advertising, sales promotions, and personal selling constitute the bulk of these efforts.

Advertising to Resellers

While advertising to resellers will be designed to accomplish many of the same communications objectives as other advertising—for example, creating awareness, interest, and so on—both the message and the media employed for this purpose will differ. For example, the ads shown in Figures 16–2 and 16–3 have very different messages to convey. In the first ad, the objective is to encourage retailers to feature and display Pine-Sol products during the "Whole House" Sweepstakes promotion. The ad informs retailers of the company's plans for attracting customers to their stores during the promotion. In Figure 16–3 the message is slightly different, as the objective here is to

Figure 16–3   Trade Advertising Designed to Demonstrate Reseller Benefits

demonstrate the benefits derived by resellers when they carry the manufacturer's brand. In these examples, the messages are designed to elicit resellers' support, as well as to demonstrate that these intermediaries are being supported by the manufacturer.

The media used to reach resellers will also be different from those used in the consumer market. General interest magazines such as *Time* or *Newsweek,* television, radio, and other consumer-oriented media are seldom employed. Rather, trade media—magazines, newsletters, trade shows, and so on—such as those shown in Figure 16–4 are more likely to be used.

In addition to the different message and media strategies employed, advertising programs themselves may be different. For example, many manufacturers offer programs that are designed to share the costs and efforts of advertising with retailers.

Cooperative Advertising   One program used to foster reseller involvement is that in which the sponsorship and cost of the communications are shared by more than one party. This form of advertising is known as **cooperative advertising,** and, as shown in Table 16–1, assumes more or less significant roles, depending on the relationship between the manufacturer and reseller.

As shown in Table 16–1, cooperative advertising takes on a more significant role in those situations in which the manufacturer is dependent on the reseller. In those situations in which the manufacturer is more dominant, cooperative advertising is less likely to play a significant role in the marketing mix.

Three distinct types of cooperative advertising relationships exist[2]

1. **Horizontal cooperative advertising** refers to advertising sponsored in common by a group of retailers or other organizations providing products or services to the mar-

Figure 16–4   Trade Magazines Reach Those with Special Interests

ket. Figure 16–5 shows an example of an ad representing a cooperative effort among ski resorts in Summit County, Colorado.

2. **Vertical cooperative advertising** is advertising initiated and implemented by retailers and paid for (at least in part) by a manufacturer or manufacturers, as demonstrated in Figure 16–6 in which San Diego Carpet Co. and Du Pont have combined efforts.

3. **Ingredient-producer cooperative advertising** is that supported by raw materials manufacturers with the objective being to help establish end products that include materials and/or ingredients supplied by the company. Figure 16–7 shows an example of a cooperative ad run by Metal-Cladding, Inc., promoting the application of Du Pont's Teflon® finishes to the coating of food processing equipment.

Table 16–1   Conditions Defining the Relative Importance of Cooperative Advertising

Cooperative Advertising Plays a Significant Role in the Marketing Mix: Retailer-Dependent Marketing	Cooperative Advertising Plays a Lesser Role in the Marketing Mix: Manufacturer-Dominated Marketing
Shopping goods	Convenience goods
Infrequently purchased goods	Frequently purchased goods
Relatively expensive	Relatively inexpensive
Considered purchase	Impulse purchase
Purchase for ego enhancement	Utilitarian purchase
Hidden attributes	Easily observed product attributes
Brand loyalty low	Brand loyalty high
Personal service retailing	Self-service retailing
Selective distribution	Broad distribution

Source: Robert F. Young and Stephen A. Greyser, *Managing Co-operative Advertising: A Strategic Approach* (Lexington, Mass.: D. C. Heath, 1983), p. 22.

Figure 16—5   Horizontal Cooperative Advertising Is Reflected in This Ad for Colorado Ski Resorts

Figure 16—6   Du Pont Engages in Vertical Cooperative Advertising

Figure 16—7   This Ad by Metal-Cladding, Inc., Is an Example of Ingredient-Sponsored Cooperative Advertising

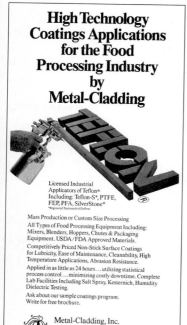

The most common form of cooperative advertising is that of vertical cooperative advertising, which is placed by a retailer and paid for in part (or in whole) by the manufacturer, with both the manufacturer's and the retailer's names appearing on the advertisement. The most common arrangement is for the ad format to be prepared either by the retailer or by the manufacturer and placed in the local media by the retailer. After the ad has been run, the retailer requests reimbursement from the manufacturer, usually for a percentage of the media costs. Specific requirements for the ad format must be met (if the retailer uses his or her own ad), and verification in the form of a tear sheet (for print) or an affidavit from the station (in broadcast) is necessary. While the program sounds simple enough, you will see in the next section that it may not provide all the advantages expected.

Advantages and Disadvantages of Cooperative Advertising   Cooperative advertising provides the manufacturer and resellers with a number of potential benefits, including:

- The capability of extending advertising resources through the purchase of local media at local rates
- The ability to tailor the advertising to local market conditions—for example, increasing and decreasing expenditures as demand warrants
- Specifically indicating to potential customers where the product can be purchased
- Assisting local resellers in their promotional efforts, thereby enhancing the position of both the manufacturer and the reseller in the marketplace
- Controlling the advertising message to ensure that the message conveyed is that intended and is consistent throughout each market
- Gaining preferential treatment from the trade in stocking
- Creating goodwill among resellers and between resellers and manufacturers
- Stretching the advertising dollar by having more than one party contributing to the promotional budget

Along with these benefits, however, may come problems. Unless the program is tightly controlled, the following disadvantages may accrue:

- Control of the message may not always be possible. In those instances where the reseller is responsible for putting the ad together, the message control has now shifted hands. (This may be a particularly acute problem in a situation where the reseller is a powerful force in the marketplace and is able to exert its independence.) In other instances different retailers may have their own objectives in mind and may not agree with others as to the message to be communicated.
- Legal problems may result from discrimination. The Federal Trade Commission (the regulator of advertising) in the form of the Robinson-Patman Act requires that there be equal availability of cooperative advertising funds. Manufacturers must be careful not to violate this law.
- Administrative problems are often common. This is particularly true in those instances in which the manufacturer has a large number of retailers (imagine for a moment the administration of a Black & Decker co-op program in hardware stores!). It may also be complicated in horizontal efforts when each party is used to operating independently.
- Claims disputes may arise both in respect to the amount of the allowance and in respect to verification of the placement.
- The effect on the image of the manufacturer is at risk in those situations where the reseller is responsible for the ad design. An unprofessional advertisement will not reflect favorably on the reseller or the manufacturer.
- Control over the program is often difficult at all levels.

In addition to these problems, determination as to who shall be allowed to participate, refund amounts, and so on, are all possible sources of problems.

In summary, it can be seen that cooperative advertising has the potential to provide the marketer with an effective promotional tool that works with the reseller as well as the ultimate consumer of the product or service. At the same time, it is obvious that this advertising practice is not without its possible pitfalls.

Promotions to Resellers

As noted at the outset of our discussion of resellers, intermediaries consist of wholesalers and retailers—both of whom may be target markets. Manufacturers' promotions will generally involve both groups, as these **trade promotions** are targeted to distributors, wholesalers, and retailers. Trade promotions may take on a variety of objectives and forms, including the following.

Special incentive payments and contests One important target of promotional efforts is the sales force of the reseller. These salespeople are likely to be much more familiar with the market, more frequently in touch with the consumer (whether it be another reseller or the ultimate consumer), and larger in number than the manufacturer's own sales organization. As such, they are an important link in the distribution chain.

Knowing this, manufacturers have developed promotional programs targeted directly to these persons. These programs may involve cash payments directly to the sales force—known as **pm's**, or **push monies**—in which the manufacturer rewards the salesperson directly for promoting and selling its product. When actual cash payments are not made directly, contests or sweepstakes may be employed, in which the performance of the sales force may win them a trip, prizes, or both. As can be seen in Table 16–2, these incentives and awards may be tied to product sales, new account placements, or merchandising efforts. While they may require the approval of the intermediaries themselves, these promotions are generally targeted directly to the sales staffs.

Because of the direct manufacturer–sales staff connection, these incentives are

Table 16–2 **Three Forms of Promotion Targeted to Reseller Salespersons**

Product or program sales
Awards are tied to the selling of a product; for example,
Selling a specified number of cases
Selling a specified number of units
Selling a specified number of promotional programs
New account placements
Awards are tied to:
The number of new accounts opened
The number of new accounts ordering a minimum number of cases or units
Promotional programs placed in new accounts
Merchandising efforts
Awards are tied to:
Establishing promotional programs (such as theme programs, etc.)
Placement of display racks, counter displays, and the like

often the source of conflicts between resellers and manufacturers. In many cases the intermediaries resent being bypassed by the manufacturers, who feel that a conflict of interest may be being created. Their concern is that the sales force may devote an undue amount of effort to the attainment of the manufacturer's objectives to the exclusion of their own. In these instances, participation in such programs may be forbidden.

From another perspective, intermediaries may believe that they can offer less compensation to their sales force, as the balance will be made available by participation in manufacturer-sponsored incentive programs. This often results in a displeased sales force. In both of these instances the desired effect of the program is not being realized.

Promotional allowances   In some situations the manufacturer will offer **promotional allowances,** or payments, to resellers for merchandising its products and/or running in-store promotional programs. These payments extend beyond those offered for media advertising and might include the use of special displays, in-store advertising, and/or other special programs designed to promote the product.

Sales training programs   Another form of manufacturer-sponsored promotions is that in which the employees of the reseller participate in **sales training programs** designed to increase their skills. These programs may involve training devoted to increasing product knowledge; for example, most major computer companies provide schools for retail companies' employees—or they may include sales techniques and motivational components. In both instances the objective is to develop a more informed salesperson, which ultimately will lead to more sales success.

Selling aids   Many selling aids are made available to resellers and their sales staffs. For example, in-store demonstrations, reference manuals, product brochures, or other materials such as those shown in Figure 16–8 are often employed both as a selling tool and as a source of information available to the sales staff.

Displays and point-of-purchase materials   The next time you are in a store, take a moment to examine the multitude of promotional materials being employed. These materials are designed to draw the consumer's attention to the product through effective merchandising. As shown in Figure 16–9, these tools may include end-of-counter displays, banners, posters, or a variety of other materials designed to gain attention and interest. Promotional Perspective 16–1 provides one example of how manufacturers are helping store managers increase sales through more efficient shelf space planning.

Slotting allowances   The lead-in to this chapter discussed the very common—and very controversial—practice of **slotting allowances.** As noted, opinions as to the pur-

Figure 16—8 **Brochures with Product Information Aid the Selling Effort**

pose of slotting fees differ. The position of retailers is that increased competition, a proliferation of new products, and small profit margins require them to ask for these fees. They argue that the monies will be spent to promote the products, redesign shelves, and reprogram computers.

Manufacturers have their own opinion as to how these monies are used. One food industry source estimated that 70 percent of all slotting fees go directly to the retailers' bottom line. The same source also estimated that approximately 55 percent of all manufacturers' trade promotions dollars are now going to slotting fees.[3] If these numbers are correct, and the monies are not used for the purpose for which they are intended, the manufacturers may have a legitimate argument in their cry of "blackmail."

Failure fees   Some retailers have demanded—and manufacturers have complied with—a **failure fee**. If a product does not hit a minimum sales target within three months, this fee is designed to cover the costs associated with stocking, maintaining inventories, and then pulling the product.[4]

Pricing promotions   Usually when we think of **pricing promotions** we think about those discussed in Chapter 15 on consumer sales promotions—that is, cents-off deals; buy-one, get-one-free programs; and so on. There are pricing promotions that are tar-

Figure 16—9 Merchandising Tools Are Used to Support Resellers' Efforts

geted to resellers also. Like consumer pricing promotions, these may involve cash discounts, free merchandise, or special terms.

A variety of objectives may be sought when pricing promotions are used, but in most cases, the manufacturer wishes to have the cost savings accrued by the reseller passed on to the ultimate consumer. As you might well expect, this pass-along does not always take place, as the resellers keep the gains for themselves. The net result is that the ultimate purpose of the promotion is not realized, and in many cases bad relations may be created between the manufacturer and the reseller. Since manufacturers have no way to insist that the promotions be conducted as desired, they must ultimately decide whether or not the implementation of such a strategy is in their best interest.

Public Relations to Resellers

A third element of the promotional mix—public relations—is also employed to provide reseller support. As you will see in Chapter 17, intermediaries may be targets of public relations efforts, and/or the manufacturer may work together with local retail operations to cosponsor events, special programs, and the like.

Personal Selling to Resellers

The final promotional mix element—personal selling—is used extensively in promoting to resellers. While the extent of the use of personal selling will vary by industry, and by firm, in almost every case, it constitutes a major communications link between the manufacturer and the reseller. Later in this chapter we will go into detail as to how this program element is used to sell to resellers as well as to support them.

Promotional Perspective **16—1**

Retail Stores Are Using Planograms to Improve Sales

Some of the biggest names in corporate America are becoming involved in the grocery store shelf management system. Owing to the increasing competition for shelf space, manufacturers have been forced to become partners with retailers by helping them maximize the use of their shelf space.

The shelf management system—or planogram—is a computer-based program that (at the marketer's expense) allows the retailer to input sales information from its own scanner data. The analysis helps the retailer achieve the best design for store shelves by stocking the most lucrative brands. The manufacturer also gains, as the best-selling brands are rarely allowed to run out of stock.

Some people do not believe that these planograms work so ideally, however. For example, they ask, what happens if a store gets three different planograms from three different competitors in a product category? How will they decide which one to take? Or, what happens as new products are introduced or when advertising levels change? Also, they ask, how often do the planogram schematics need to be updated and changed?

Running a planogram program is not inexpensive. Most reports cost the manufacturer between $25,000 and $30,000 (though some are offered at $7,000). Despite this high price, companies such as Frito-Lay, Procter & Gamble, Kraft, Coors, Lever Brothers, and Dannon Yogurt are promoting the systems.

Many supermarket chains are not impressed by these big names, however. They feel that they can still do their own planning and want to see what the manufacturers can do for them—without their being involved to a great degree. Their position is that planograms are leading to fights between manufacturers and that as long as they are in the driver's seat, they'll let them fight it out—just so long as they continue to bring in profits for their stores!

Source: Adapted from Rebecca Fannin, "Planograms: Friend or Foe?" *Marketing & Media Decisions*, May 1988, pp. 48—54.

Control and Evaluation of the Reseller Support Program

As with the other promotional program elements, the marketing manager must consider the relative effectiveness of the reseller support programs if he or she is to be able to develop the most appropriate promotional mix. In the evaluation of these programs, the marketing and communications objectives established in Chapter 8 should constitute the evaluative criteria for determining the relative effectiveness of the efforts. Given that sales figures may not always be a realistic measure, the manager must keep in mind the objectives of the promotions: Are they to introduce new products, thereby necessitating awareness and trial, or are they designed to create a more informed reseller sales force that can comprehend and respond more effectively to the needs of its customers? Obviously the efforts involved and the measures of relative effectiveness will differ in each situation. The fact remains, however, that specific communications objectives are being sought and that these programs are part of the promotional mix that will be designed to attain them. Thus, the basis for evaluation will remain the same: Is the program strategy accomplishing what it set out to do, that is, achieving the communications goal?

Unfortunately, the ability to measure the effectiveness of the programs targeted to resellers is difficult. The process becomes even more complicated when you realize that much of the implementation is out of the control of the manufacturer and that the firm must rely on the participation and cooperation of outside agents—for example, wholesalers and retailers and their sales staffs. While in many cases it may be possible to exert some controls—the performance criteria established for cooperative advertising constitute one example—in many other instances it is not as easy.

One method often employed for the collection of information is that of reports provided by the company's own sales staff. These reports may involve details on the number of programs implemented, the perceived success (both from the firm's and the reseller's perspectives), and an overall evaluation of the merits of the program. While this would seem at face value to be a very useful way to gather information as well as to exert control to see that the programs are used as intended, the reality is that it may not be so. While, as an employee of the manufacturer, the salesperson's ultimate responsibilities should be to the employer, managers must also recognize that representatives must deal with their customers on a day-to-day basis. To be effective, they must be mindful of the needs of these customers as well as those of the employer. Some programs may not be as beneficial to the reseller as marketing would think they are. In addition, many of the competitive brands carried by the reseller may also be offering promotional programs—some of which may be better than their own.

In these instances it is the responsibility of the sales force to report such information to the marketing staff so that more useful and effective programs may be established. For the sales staff to provide such a critical function, however, two factors are required:

1. The sales staff must understand the program and its intended objectives (this is particularly true if the objectives are communications objectives, as salespeople often think in sales-objectives terms).
2. The marketing staff must be open-minded in evaluating the feedback provided by the sales force.

While in theory these factors seem obvious and simple enough, in reality this is not often the case.

In conclusion, the efforts of resellers are not always under the control of the marketer. As a result the best designed programs may never fulfill their expectations. At the same time, the more control that can be attained, the more effective promotional programs are likely to be. Encouraging the participation of resellers and the company's own sales force in providing information on the design, implementation, and effectiveness of such programs will go far in ensuring that appropriate promotional plans are set in force.

Personal Selling

In Chapter 1 we stated that while we recognized the importance of personal selling, and the role that it plays in the overall marketing and promotions effort, this topic would not constitute a major emphasis in this text. While we do not wish to downplay the importance of this promotional mix element, we noted that personal selling is not typically under the control of the advertising and promotions department—usually being the responsibility of the sales manager. At the same time, this does not mean that the personal selling effort does not provide a valuable contribution to the promotional program. To develop a promotional plan effectively, the roles and responsibilities of the company's sales force must be considered and integrated into the communications program. A strong cooperative effort between the departments is necessary.

The remainder of this chapter will focus on the role that personal selling assumes in the promotional mix, the advantages and disadvantages associated with this program element, and the basis for evaluating its contributions to the attainment of communications objectives. In addition, we will explore the ways in which personal selling is combined with other program elements—both to lend support to them as well as to receive support from them.

The Role of Personal Selling in the Promotional Mix

As noted, manufacturers may promote their products *directly* to consumers through advertising and promotions and/or direct-marketing efforts or *indirectly* through resellers and salespersons. (In many situations the sales force may call on customers directly—for example, in the insurance industry or real estate business. However, in this chapter we will focus most of our attention on the personal selling function as it exists in most large corporations—that is, as a link to resellers.) Depending on the role defined by the organization, the responsibilities and specific tasks of salespersons may differ, but ultimately these tasks are designed to lead to the attainment of communications and marketing objectives.

Personal selling is different from the other forms of communication presented thus far in that messages flow from a sender (or group of senders) to a receiver (or group of receivers) directly (and usually face to face). Because of this *direct* and *interpersonal communication,* the sender is able to immediately receive and evaluate feedback from the receiver. This communications process—known as **dyadic communication** (between two persons or groups)—allows for more specific tailoring of the message and more personal communications than are available in many of the other media discussed. As a result the message itself can be changed to address specific needs and wants of the receiver—a capability not available through nonpersonal media.

In some situations this ability to focus on specific problems is mandatory, as a standard communication would not be sufficient. For example, consider an industrial buying situation in which the salesperson is an engineer. In promoting the company's products and/or services, the salesperson must be able to understand the specific needs of the client. This may mean understanding the tensile strength of materials or being able to read blueprints or plans to understand the requirements. Or consider a salesperson representing a computer graphics firm. Part of his or her responsibility for making a sale may involve the design of a software program to solve a problem unique only to this customer. You can see that in these instances mass communications are not capable of accomplishing these tasks.

While the examples just given are both from industrial settings, personal selling is not restricted only to this market; it plays a critical role in the consumer market as well. As noted by the great entrepreneur Marshall Field: "The distance between the salesperson and the potential buyer is the most important three feet in business."[5] While Field was referring to the consumer as the buyer, we already have seen that resellers must be considered as well. Personal selling plays an important role in consumer products companies as they must secure distribution, motivate resellers to stock and promote the product, and so on.

Why is personal selling so important? Let us examine its role with respect to other promotional program elements.

Determining the Role of Personal Selling

One of the first questions that the manager will need to ask when preparing the promotional program is, What will the specific responsibilities of personal selling be, and what role will it assume relative to the other promotional mix elements? To determine what this role should be, management should be guided by four specific questions:

1. What specific information must be exchanged between the firm and potential customers?
2. What are the alternative ways of carrying out these communications objectives?
3. How effective is each alternative in carrying out the needed exchange?
4. What is the cost-effectiveness of each alternative?[6]

Let us examine these in more detail.

• *Determining the information to be exchanged*   In keeping with the objectives established by the communications models presented in Chapter 6, you can see that the salesperson may have a variety of messages to communicate, for example, creating awareness of the product or service offering, demonstrating product benefits for evaluation, initiating trial, and/or closing the sale. In addition, answering questions, countering misconceptions, and discovering potentially unmet needs may also be necessary.

• *Examining promotional mix alternatives*   In previous chapters, we discussed the roles of advertising and sales promotions, and in Chapter 17 we will examine the

Table 16–3   **Market Logic Grid Demonstrating the Role of Personal Selling versus Nonpersonal Communication Elements in the Selling Process**

Steps Required to Complete a Sale	Percent of Marketing Effort	Percent of Marketing Responsibility	
		Personal (tell)	Nonpersonal (read)
Build basic awareness	20	30	70
Demonstrate competitive advantages	35	40	60
Make specific recommendations	25	90	10
Get the order	15	100	0
Customer follow-up and service	5	50	50
Total	100	60	40

Source: Tom Wotruba and Edwin K. Simpson, *Sales Management* (Boston: Kent Publishing, 1979), p. 74.

responsibilities of public relations and publicity. Each of these program elements offers specific advantages and disadvantages, and each needs to be considered in development of the promotions mix. Likewise, personal selling is an alternative that must be considered, offering distinct advantages in some situations, while less appropriate in others.

• *Evaluating the relative effectiveness of alternatives*   Depending on the target market and the objectives sought, each of the program elements must be evaluated in respect to its relative effectiveness. As noted, personal selling provides a number of characteristics that will make it more effective in many situations. At the same time, advantages are provided by other program elements that may increase their attractiveness. For example, the ability to reach a large number of persons with one distinct and consistent message or the opportunity to repeat messages may be accomplished more effectively and more cost efficiently by advertising.

• *Determining cost-effectiveness*   One of the major disadvantages associated with personal selling is often considered to be the costs involved. (In 1988 McGraw-Hill estimated that the average cost per sales call was $251.00.)[7] In evaluating program elements, their effectiveness must also be considered in terms of the costs associated with their use. While the cost of a personal sales call may not be prohibitive in industrial settings where a single purchase may be in the millions of dollars, the same cost may be unfeasible in a consumer market. Other media may be capable of communicating the required message at a much lower cost.

Table 16–3 presents a **market logic grid** that compares the role of personal selling to nonpersonal forms of communication with respect to their use in the various steps in the selling process. While the numbers presented in Table 16–3 will vary for different companies or industries, they do provide an example of the role that each element might assume. This role may be altered as the selling task requires and for different market situations, as shown in Table 16–4. (Later in this chapter you will see that the role that other promotional elements play in support of the selling effort may also alter these figures.)

Table 16—4   **When the Sales Force Is a Major Part of the Communications Mix**

Mix Area	Characteristics
Product or service	Complex products requiring customer application assistance (e.g., computers, pollution control systems, steam turbines)
	Major purchase decisions, such as food items purchased by supermarket chains
	Features and performance of the product requiring personal demonstration and trial by the customer (e.g., private aircraft)
Channels	Channel system relatively short and direct to end users
	Product and service training and assistance needed by channel intermediaries
	Personal selling is needed in "pushing" product through channel
	Channel intermediaries available to perform personal selling function for supplier with limited resources and experience (e.g., brokers or manufacturer's agents)
Price	Final price negotiated between buyer and seller (e.g., appliances, automobiles, real estate)
	Selling price and or quantity purchased enable an adequate margin to support selling expenses (traditional department store compared to discount house)
Advertising	Advertising media do not provide effective link with market targets
	Information needed by buyer cannot be provided entirely through advertising and sales promotion (e.g., life insurance)
	Number and dispersion of customers will not enable acceptable advertising economies

Source: David W. Cravens, Gerald E. Hills, and Robert B. Woodruff, *Marketing Decision Making: Concepts and Strategy* (Homewood Ill.: Richard D. Irwin, 1980), p. 384. Reprinted by permission of Richard D. Irwin, Inc.

The Nature of Personal Selling

To integrate the personal selling effort into the overall promotional program properly, it is necessary to understand the nature of this tool. Let us examine some of the characteristics of personal selling.

The Costs of Personal Selling   In some industries personal selling constitutes a substantial portion of the communications effort and may account for most of the promotional budget. The reasons for this are twofold: First, much attention is devoted to this function because of the advantages it offers over other communication methods; and second, it is, in itself, an expensive form of communication. As demonstrated by Figure 16–10, the average cost per sales call varies by industry—ranging from a low of $155 to as high as $301 in the industrial sector. In both instances the cost of a communication does not come cheap!

When the cost per sales call is compared with the cost per message delivered through other media (we saw in other chapters that these costs could be as low as 3 cents), this figure seems outrageous. At the same time, you must keep in mind that to take these numbers at face value may lead to an unfair comparison. In considering the costs of personal selling it is necessary to consider the nature of the call, the objectives sought, and a determination as to whether other program elements could deliver the message as effectively. It may be that the higher costs cannot be avoided.

The costs associated with personal selling are even higher when you consider the fact that one sales call is not likely to be enough to close a deal. This is particularly true in the industrial market, as shown in Table 16–5, where multiple calls may be required. The costs per closing a sale now appear even more intimidating (though in industrial markets the returns, as stated, may easily warrant the expense).

Overall, it can be seen that personal selling is an expensive way of communicating. At the same time, however, you should also recognize that personal selling usually involves more than just communicating and that the returns (more direct sales) may be greater than those offered by the other program elements.

Figure 16–10   **Average Cost per Sales Call by Industry**

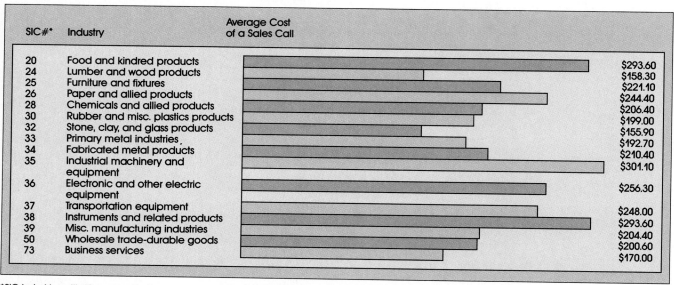

SIC#*	Industry	Average Cost of a Sales Call
20	Food and kindred products	$293.60
24	Lumber and wood products	$158.30
25	Furniture and fixtures	$221.10
26	Paper and allied products	$244.40
28	Chemicals and allied products	$206.40
30	Rubber and misc. plastics products	$199.00
32	Stone, clay, and glass products	$155.90
33	Primary metal industries	$192.70
34	Fabricated metal products	$210.40
35	Industrial machinery and equipment	$301.10
36	Electronic and other electric equipment	$256.30
37	Transportation equipment	$248.00
38	Instruments and related products	$293.60
39	Misc. manufacturing industries	$204.40
50	Wholesale trade–durable goods	$200.60
73	Business services	$170.00

*SIC industries with 10 or more business-to-business companies reporting are shown in this figure.
Source: McGraw-Hill Research 1987, "Cost of a Business-to-Business Sales Call." Survey based on an *n*th sample of vice presidents of sales and sales managers in business-to-business companies drawn from the circulation list of *Business Marketing* magazine.

Personal Selling Responsibilities   *Sales and Marketing Magazine* uses three categories to classify salespersons including **order taking, creative selling,** and **missionary sales.**[8] Of course, all firms do not treat each of these responsibilities the same, nor

Table 16–5   **Costs to Close a Sales Call**

SIC	Industry	No. of Cases	Average Number of Calls to Close a Sale	Average Cost per Sales Call	Average Cost to Close a Sale[a]
25	Furniture and fixtures	9	3.3	$239.90	$ 791.67
26	Paper and allied products	13	4.8	106.20	509.76
27	Printing, publishing, and allied industries	7	5.1	66.10	337.11
28	Chemicals and allied products	45	4.9	133.00	651.70
29	Petroleum/refining and related industries	7	5.0	142.00	710.00
30	Rubber and misc. plastic products	12	5.6	98.80	553.28
32	Stone, clay, glass, and concrete products	16	4.5	95.30	428.85
33	Primary metal industries	19	3.7	117.90	436.23
34	Fabricated metal products	58	5.0	126.10	630.50
35	Machinery (except electrical)	155	5.9	182.10	1,074.39
36	Electrical and electronic machinery equipment	83	4.9	210.90	1,033.41
37	Transportation equipment	30	6.7	367.20	2,460.24
38	Instruments; photographic and optical goods	31	4.5	150.60	677.70
45	Transportation by air	6	3.0	83.80	251.40
49	Utilities and sanitary services	6	3.5	170.20	595.70
63	Insurance	5	3.6	64.40	231.84
73	Business services	8	4.6	195.00	897.00
75	Automotive repair services	5	4.8	93.80	450.24

[a]This is determined by multiplying the average number of calls to close a sale by the average cost per sales call for each SIC.
Source: McGraw-Hill, LAP Report no. 8052.1. McGraw-Hill Laboratory of Advertising Research, 1988.

Table 16—6   **Types of Sales Jobs**

Creative Selling

Creative selling jobs may require the most skill and preparation of any of the selling positions. In addition to prospecting, the salesperson must assess the situation, determine the needs to be met, present the capabilities for satisfying these needs, and get an order. In many instances the salesperson is the "point man" who has established the initial contact on behalf of the firm and who has the major responsibility for completing the exchange. He or she is, in fact, the "order-getter."

Order Taking

Once the initial sale has taken place, the creative seller may be replaced (not physically!) by an order-taker. The role of the order-taker is much more casual. In many instances it may involve what is referred to as a *straight rebuy*—that is, the order does not change much (soft water or bottled water delivery persons are examples). In those instances where a slight change is considered, the order-taker may be involved in a modified rebuy, which may require some creative selling (for example, a salesperson calling on a wholesale food company may have a list of products to sell). Should a major purchase decision be required, however, the role of making the sale may again be turned over to the creative seller.

Missionary Sales Reps

The missionary representative is essentially a support role. While performing many of the tasks assumed in creative selling, the missionary rep may not actually take the order. Rather he or she will introduce new products, new promotions, and/or new programs, with the actual order to be taken by the company's order-taker or by a distributor representing the company's goods. In addition, the missionary sales rep may have additional account service responsibilities. Missionary reps are most often employed in industries where a middleperson is employed by the manufacturer for product distribution purposes (food products, pharmaceuticals, etc.).

are their salespersons limited to only these tasks. For example, with respect to the above tasks, job requirements may include: (1) locating prospective customers; (2) determining customers' needs and wants that are not being satisfied; (3) recommending a means of satisfying these needs and/or wants; (4) demonstrating the capabilities of the firm and/or the firm's products for providing this satisfaction; (5) closing the sale and taking the order; and (6) following up and servicing the account. Table 16–6 provides a general description of these job classifications and some of the responsibilities assigned to each.

It is important to remember that one of the advantages that the salesperson offers is the opportunity to assess the situation firsthand and to adapt the sales message accordingly (hence, this is a **direct feedback** network). No other promotional element provides this opportunity. As a result the successful salesperson is one who is constantly analyzing the situation, reading the feedback provided by the receiver, and presenting the message in a way that specifically meets the customer's needs.

While you might expect that this is an easy task, this may not always be the case. Sometimes buyers will not or cannot accurately express their needs. At other times the salesperson may be required to become more of a problem solver for the client. More and more, successful salespeople are being asked to assist in the decision-making process of the buyers. The more that salespeople can become entrenched in the planning and decision making, the more confidence and reliance the buyer will place in them.

In other instances the true motivation for purchasing may not be the one that is offered. While you might expect that buyers are basing their decisions on rational and objective factors, this may not always be the case. Even in industrial markets (where product specifications may be critical) or in reseller markets (where product movements and/or profits are important), many purchase decisions are made on what might be considered nonrational criteria. (Not irrational, but involving other than purely cost or other product benefits.) Since it is generally believed that these purchase situations involve less emotion and more rational thinking than many consumer purchases, this is an important insight.

Consider the dilemma that faces the marketer. If he or she provides advertising and promotions that speak only to the rational purchase motives—which is what one

Promotional Perspective 16–2

Confessions of a Few Salespeople

Often we think that the sales process involves the art or science of conducting a needs assessment, providing the product or service that best satisfies that need, and offering follow-up support. In particular in industrial settings, it is often assumed that decision makers are evaluating their suppliers on the most rational of criteria such as product quality, price, and delivery time. Sometimes this rational thinking may not be the case. Rather, in both consumer and industrial markets, other factors may really be the true reason for the decision. In these situations, only a personal selling role will be able to make the sale. Consider these examples of sales that were made, as revealed by salespeople in both market settings:

- *Case I* The creative salesperson and a client—as a result of calling on the same buyer for a number of years (even though the salesperson was not able to sell the company anything)—became personal friends. They would spend weekend evenings together having drinks or attending parties or other social events, played golf and tennis together, and often double dated. The very first time the incumbent supplier was late on an order, the friend had the business.

- *Case II* A supplier in the Southeast would take his best buyers on the company's private plane to attend a major college football game every season. Even though his price was not the best nor his service outstanding, he seldom lost an account.
- *Case III* For years, an industrial salesperson was unable to get in the door at a particular company because the buyer was reportedly satisfied with his existing suppliers. Then one day the salesperson attended a high school wrestling match and noticed that one of the wrestlers had the same last name as the buyer he had been unable to see. On Monday, upon calling on the account, he asked the buyer if that was his son he had watched wrestling. After about 1.5 hours of conversation, about 15 minutes of which were not about wrestling and the son's skills, the salesperson left with a sizable order.
- *Case IV* Each Christmas a buyer from a local company would throw a party for his neighbors without spending a dime. All the provisions were donated to him as presents from existing suppliers as well as those trying to gain his business.

might expect that one should do—he or she may be unable to make the sale. On the other hand, how could an advertiser possibly know all the emotional or nonrational criteria influencing the decision, let alone integrate this information into its messages? Once again, you can see the importance of the personal sales effort, as this may be the only way to uncover the many motivations for purchasing, and addressing them.

In Promotional Perspective 16–2 a number of alternative reasons why buyers purchased are presented based on actual sales force experiences. While we would not suggest that these examples reflect the way that sales are always made, they are provided to demonstrate that the salespersons' role and what they bring to the marketing program often go beyond those tangible factors previously listed.

Based on the information just provided, the importance that personal selling plays in the promotional mix should now be more obvious. This program element provides for opportunities that are not offered by any other form of message delivery. While the variety of tasks performed by salespeople offers some distinct advantages to the marketing program, these same tasks may also constitute disadvantages, as you will now see.

Advantages and Disadvantages of Personal Selling

The nature of personal selling positions this promotional tool uniquely among those available to the marketer, offering some very distinct advantages, including the following.

- *Allowing for two-way interaction* The ability to interact with the receiver allows the sender to determine the impact of the message. As such, problems in comprehension, objections, or more in-depth discussions of certain selling points can be provided immediately. In other forms of mass communications, this direct feedback is not available, and such information cannot be immediately obtained—if it can be obtained at all.

- *Tailoring of the message*   Because of the direct interaction, messages can be tailored specifically to the receiver. Because of this more precise message content, the sender is better able to address specific concerns, problems, and needs of the consumer. In addition, he or she is able to determine when to move on to the next selling point, ask for the sale, or close the deal.
- *Lack of distraction*   In many personal selling situations, a one-to-one presentation is conducted. In these situations the likelihood of distractions is minimized, and the buyer is generally paying more attention to the sales message. Even in those situations in which the presentation is made by a gr. / of salespersons, or in which more than one decision maker is present, the setting may be less distracting than those in which nonpersonal mass media are employed.
- *Involvement in the decision process*   Through the process of consultative selling, the seller has become more of a partner in the buying decision process, acting in conjunction with the buyer to solve problems. The net result of this is more involvement and more reliance on the salesperson and his or her products and services.

As you can see, the advantages of personal selling focus primarily on the dyadic communications process, the ability to alter the message, and the opportunity for direct feedback. Sometimes, however, these potential advantages are not always realized. In fact, they may in themselves become disadvantages.

Some of the disadvantages associated with personal selling include the following.

- *Inconsistent messages*   Earlier we stated that the ability to adapt the message to the receiver was a distinct advantage of personal selling. At the same time, the lack of a standardized message can become a disadvantage. The message to be communicated is generally well thought out, planned, and designed by the marketing staff with a particular communications objective in mind. Once the determination has been made as to what this message will be, it is communicated to all receivers. The salesperson may alter this message—sometimes not in the way the marketer intended. Thus, the marketing staff may be at the mercy of the sales force with respect to what exactly will be communicated. (Sales communications aids may offset this problem to some degree, as you will see later in this chapter.)
- *Sales force–management conflict*   Unfortunately, there are situations in even the best of marketing companies in which one has to wonder if the sales staff and marketing staff know that they work for the same company and for the same goals. Because of failures to communicate, corporate politics, and a myriad of other reasons, the sales force and marketing managers may not be working as a team. As a result the marketing staff may not understand the problems faced by the sales staff, or the salespeople may not understand why marketing people do things the way they do. The result is that the sales force may not use materials provided from marketing, that marketing may not be responsive to the field's assessment of customer needs, and so forth. The bottom line is that the communications process is not as effective as it could be primarily because of a lack of internal communications and/or conflicts.
- *High cost*   We discussed earlier the high cost involved in personal selling. As the cost per sales call continues to climb, the marketer may often find that mass communications may be a more cost-effective alternative.
- *Poor reach*   Even if you ignore the costs of a personal sales communication, it is still easy to see that this program element will not be as effective for reaching as many members of the target audience as are other elements. Even if money were no object (not a very likely scenario!), the sales force has only so many hours and so many people that they are able to reach in a given period of time. Further, the frequency with which these accounts are reached will also be low.

Combining Personal Selling with Other Promotional Tools

As with the other program elements, personal selling is usually used as one component of the promotional mix. In fact, very rarely—if ever—is personal selling used alone. Rather, this promotional tool both supports and is supported by other program elements.

Combining Personal Selling and Advertising

When considering specific market situations and communications objectives, the advantages of advertising would make this program element more effective in the early stages of the response hierarchy (for example, in creating awareness and interest), whereas personal selling would be more likely to be used in the later stages (for example, stimulating trial, getting the order, etc.). Thus, each may be more or less appropriate depending on the objectives sought. In developing a promotional mix, these elements can be combined in such a way as to compensate for the weaknesses of the other, thus creating a situation where these elements complement each other.

For example, consider the situation involved in a new product introduction. Given an adequate budget, the initial objective might be to reach as many persons in the target market as quickly and as cost effectively as possible. Since the primary objective is awareness, and a simple message is all that is required, advertising would likely be the most appropriate medium.

Now suppose there were specific benefits that needed to be communicated that were not very obvious or easy to comprehend, and a product demonstration would be useful. Or consider a situation in which the objective is to ask for the sale. In these situations advertising is not likely to be sufficient, and personal selling would be a more appropriate tool. In common marketing situations such as these, you can see how well the combination of advertising and personal selling would work together to attain the objectives sought.

A number of studies bear out this complementary relationship. A study by Theodore Levitt showed that sales reps from well-known companies are better received than those from companies that did not spend advertising dollars to create awareness.[9] (Once they were in the door, however, the buyer expected the salesperson to perform better than those from lesser known companies.) Once a salesperson from a less well known company was able to get in to see the buyer—if he or she were able—the salesperson would have an approximately equal likelihood of making the sale. In risky situations the well-advertised company representative would again have the advantage.

In other studies John Morrill found that selling costs were as much as 2 percent to 28 percent lower if the buyer had received an advertising message prior to the salesperson's arrival.[10] McGraw-Hill Corporation, in a review of 54 studies, concluded that the combination of advertising and personal selling was important given that "less than 10 percent of industrial decision makers had been called upon by a salesperson from a specific company about a specific product in the previous two months."[11]

These studies suggest that by combining advertising and personal selling, the company is likely to improve reach, reduce costs, and improve the probability of a sale. As you can see, this certainly leads to a complementary relationship.

Combining Personal Selling and Public Relations

The job descriptions presented in Table 16–6 demonstrate the fact that personal selling involves much more than just selling products and/or services. In many situations the personal selling agent may be the best source of public relations available to the firm. In their day-to-day duties salespersons are representing the firm and the products of that firm. Their personalities, servicing of the account, cooperation, and empathy not only influence the sales potential but at the same time reflect on the organizations they represent.

Table 16–7 **The Growth of Telemarketing as a Sales Function: Reasons for Growth (in percent)**

	Telephone Sales and Service	Field Sales
Total growth related	58.0	61.8
Overall business growth or expansion	44.7	43.1
Adding product lines	10.2	8.0
Adding territories	3.1	10.7
Total system related	20.8	7.5
Added centralized telemarketing dept.	11.5	1.8
Added/changed computer system	6.2	4.4
Centralized sales and marketing	3.1	1.3
Customer demand	10.5	10.2
Cost efficiencies	1.4	0
Other	2.0	2.2
Can't tell/no response	9.8	18.2

Note: Adds to more than 100 percent owing to multiple mentions.
Source: Kate Bertrand, "The Inside Story," *Business Marketing,* September 1987, p. 62.

The salesperson may also be used directly in a public relations role. For example, in many firms the salesperson is encouraged to participate in community activities, such as the Jaycees, Little League, or other social organizations. In other instances the sales force, in conjunction with the company, has sacrificed time from their daily duties to assist persons in time of need. For example, following a catastrophic flood, a beer company in the Northeast distributed water in its cans to flood victims, using the sales force to make the deliveries. During the Los Angeles earthquake in 1987, local companies donated food and their sales forces' time to aid quake victims, whereas Coors provided free water in its cans to residents of Pittsburgh when a barge break contaminated the drinking water. As you might expect, these actions do not go unnoticed and result in goodwill toward both the company and its products while at the same time serving a benefit to society.

Combining Personal Selling and Direct Marketing

Companies have found that by integrating direct marketing—specifically telemarketing—into their field sales operations, they are becoming more effective in their sales efforts. Remember that we said earlier that the cost of a sales call and the cost associated with closing the sale are already very high and on the increase. Many marketers have been able to reduce these costs by combining the telemarketing and sales efforts. The telemarketing department is used to screen leads and—after qualifying potential buyers on the basis of interest credit ratings, and the like—pass on the leads to the sales force. The net result is a higher percentage of sales closings, less wasted time by the sales force, and a lower cost per sale average.

As shown in Table 16–7, there has been a rapid growth in the use of the telemarketing-sales combination for many firms, as they have determined that the phone can be used effectively for service and follow-up functions as well as for growth-related activities. Supplementing personal selling efforts with the phone calls in turn frees the sales force and allows them to spend more time selling.

The telemarketing staff, in addition to selling and supporting the sales efforts, has been able to provide a public relations dimension. By being able to communicate more often with the buyer, goodwill is created, enhancing the likelihood of customer satisfaction and loyalty.

In addition to telemarketing, other forms of direct marketing have been employed successfully. For example, many companies send out lead cards to screen prospective customers on their level of interest. The salesperson then follows up on those expressing a genuine interest, saving valuable time and increasing the potential for a sale.

Combining Personal Selling and Sales Promotions

The program elements of sales promotions and personal selling are also used to support each other. For example, many of the sales promotions targeted to resellers are presented and distributed by the sales force, who will ultimately be responsible for removing them or replacing them as well.

While trade sales promotions are designed to support the reseller, and are often targeted to the ultimate consumer, many other promotional tools are designed to assist the sales staff. Flip charts, leave-behinds, and specialty advertisements may be designed to assist salespersons in their presentations, to serve as reminders, or just to create goodwill. The number of materials available may range from just a few to hundreds, depending on the company. (If you ever get the chance, look into the trunk of a car of a consumer products salesperson. You will find everything from pens to calendars to flip charts to samples to lost baseball mitts—all but the last of which are provided to assist in the selling effort.)

Likewise, many sales promotions are targeted at the sales force itself. Sales incentives such as free trips, cash bonuses, or gifts are often used to stimulate sales efforts. And—as we saw with resellers—contests and sweepstakes may also be employed.

It is important that the elements of the promotional program work together, as each has its specific advantages and disadvantages. While personal selling is valuable in efforts to accomplish certain objectives, and in its support of other promotional tools, it must likewise be supported by the other elements. Advertisements, sales promotions, and the like may be targeted to the ultimate user, resellers, or to the organization's sales force itself.

Evaluating the Personal Selling Effort

Like all other elements of the promotional mix, the personal selling function must be evaluated with respect to its contribution to the overall promotional effort. As we stated earlier, the costs of personal selling are often high, but the returns may be just as high.

Because the sales force is under the control and supervision of the sales manager, evaluations are typically based on sales criteria. Sales analyses may be performed with respect to total sales volume, by territories, by product line, by customer type, or by sales representative.[12] In addition, other sales-related criteria such as new account openings, customer contacts, and/or service records can be used. Customer relations and personal characteristics are also sometimes considered, as shown in Table 16–8.

From a promotional perspective, sales performances are important, as are the contributions of individuals in generating these sales. On the other hand, the promotions manager is charged with evaluating the performance of the personal selling effort as one program element contributing to the overall promotional program. As such, he or she will need to use different criteria in determining its effectiveness.

Criteria for Evaluating Personal Selling Contributions to the Promotional Program

A number of criteria may be used to evaluate the contribution of the personal selling effort. These include:

- *Providing marketing intelligence*—the ability of the sales force to feed back information regarding competitive programs, customer reactions, market trends, and other factors that may be important in the development of the promotional program
- *Follow-up activities*—the use and dissemination of promotional brochures and correspondences with new and existing customers; providing feedback as to the effectiveness of various promotional programs

Table 16—8   **Criteria Used to Evaluate Sales Forces**

Sales Results	Sales Efforts
Quantitative Measures	

Sales Results	Sales Efforts

Orders
  Number of orders obtained
  Average order size (units or dollars)
  Batting average (orders ÷ sales calls)
  Number of orders canceled by customers
	Sales calls
	  Number made on current customers
	  Number made on potential new accounts
	  Average time spent per call
	  Number of sales presentations
	  Selling time versus nonselling time
	  Call frequency ratio per customer type

Sales volume
  Dollar sales volume
  Unit sales volume
  By customer type
  By product category
  Translated into market share
  Percentage of sales quota achieved
	Selling expenses
	  Average per sales call
	  As percentage of sales volume
	  As percentage of sales quota
	  By customer type
	  By product category
	  Direct selling expense ratios
	  Indirect selling expense ratios

Margins
  Gross margin
  Net profit
  By customer type
  By product category
	Customer service
	  Number of service calls
	  Displays set up
	  Delivery cost per unit sold
	  Months of inventory held by customer type
	  Number of customer complaints
	  Percentage of goods returned

Customer accounts
  Number of new accounts
  Number of lost accounts
  Percentage of accounts sold
  Number of overdue accounts
  Dollar amount of accounts receivable
  Collections made of accounts receivable	

Qualitative Measures

Sales-related activities
  Territory management: sales call preparation, scheduling, routing, and time utilization
  Marketing intelligence: new-product ideas, competitive activities, new customer
    preferences
  Follow-ups: use of promotional brochures and correspondence with current and potential
    accounts
  Customer relations
  Report preparation and timely submission

Selling skills
  Knowing the company and its policies
  Knowing competitors' products and sales
    strategies
  Use of marketing and technical backup
    teams
  Understanding of selling techniques
  Customer feedback (positive and
    negative)
  Product knowledge
  Customer knowledge
  Execution of selling techniques
  Quality of sales presentations
  Communication skills

Personal characteristics
  Cooperation, human relations, enthusiasm, motivation, judgment, care of company
    property, appearance, self-improvement efforts, patience, punctuality, initiative,
    resourcefulness, health, sales management potential, ethical and moral behavior

Source: Rolph E. Anderson, Joseph F. Hair, and Alan J. Bush, *Professional Sales Management* (New York: Mc-Graw Hill, 1988), p. 519.

- *Program implementations*—the number of promotional programs implemented; the number of shelf and/or counter displays used and so forth; the implementation and assessment of cooperative advertising programs
- *Attainment of communications objectives*—the number of accounts to whom presentations were made (awareness, evaluation); the number of trial offers accepted (trial), and the like

When combining these criteria with those used by the sales department, the promotions manager should be able to gain an accurate assessment of the effectiveness of the personal selling program. On the other hand, the ability to make these evaluations will require a great deal of cooperation between the departments.

Summary

The ultimate consumer of the product or service is not the only target market at which promotional efforts must be expended. Intermediaries—wholesalers and retailers—may often be recipients of promotional efforts.

Advertising programs and strategies will need to be designed to move resellers through the response hierarchy and to motivate them to promote and sell the manufacturer's products. In addition, a distinct set of media will be used to deliver these programs.

A number of promotions and special programs are targeted to the trade. In addition to cooperative advertising programs, price-off deals, slotting allowances, and training programs are just a few of the promotional tools manufacturers may offer.

Evaluating the effectiveness of reseller support programs is often a difficult task given the fact that resellers may deal with more than one manufacturer of the same product and that the company's own sales force must answer to both the employer as well as the customer. Thus, much of the promotional effort is not under as tight a control of the marketing department as might be desired.

An even lesser amount of control can be exerted on the reseller. While the strength of the manufacturer may allow them to exert both positive and negative sanctions, the fact remains that the reseller is usually operating independently of the manufacturer and in fact may be dealing with competitors with similar products and promotional programs. As was noted in the discussion of slotting fees, the control may actually be in the hands of the reseller.

This chapter also discussed the nature of personal selling and the role that this program element plays in the promotional mix. Personal selling offers the marketer the opportunity for a dyadic communications process—that is, a two-way exchange of information. As a result, it is possible for the salesperson to instantaneously assess the situation and the effects of the communication and adapt the message if necessary.

While this exchange offers the opportunity to tailor the message to the needs and wants of the receiver specifically, it also offers the disadvantage of an unstandardized message, as the final message communicated will be under the control of the salesperson. In an attempt to develop a standard communication, marketers provide their reps with flip charts, leave-behinds, and other promotional pieces to assist them in their presentations and to provide information to the prospective buyer.

Evaluation of the personal selling effort is usually under the control of the sales department, as sales is the most commonly used criterion. At the same time, the promotions manager must assess the contribution that personal selling is providing by using non-sales-oriented criteria.

Key Terms

Resellers

Pull promotional strategy

Push promotional strategy

Cooperative advertising

Horizontal cooperative advertising

Vertical cooperative advertising

Ingredient-producer cooperative
advertising

Trade promotions

Push monies (pm's)

Promotional allowances

Sales training programs

Slotting allowances

Failure fees

Pricing promotions

Personal selling

Dyadic communication
Market logic grid
Order taking

Creative selling
Missionary sales
Direct feedback

Discussion Questions

1. Discuss some of the advantages and disadvantages of using personal selling as part of the promotional program.
2. Explain the differences in promotional strategies that would be involved in pull versus push efforts.
3. Describe the three types of cooperative advertising arrangements. Give examples of each.
4. Describe some of the recent changes in technology that might affect how personal selling activities are conducted.
5. Explain why both intermediaries and manufacturers may fail to gain from the use of pm's (push monies).
6. What are some of the criteria typically used by marketers to evaluate personal selling's contribution to the promotional program?
7. Discuss some of the problems inherent in the evaluation of reseller support programs.
8. In what situations, and for what types of products, might personal selling be effective? Give examples.
9. Discuss the concept of slotting fees. How might manufacturers best deal with these fees?
10. Discuss how the buying motives of resellers might differ from those of users of the product. How might advertising address these motives differently?

Notes

1. "Grocer Fee Hampers New Product Launches," *Advertising Age,* August 3, 1987.
2. Robert F. Young and Stephen A. Greyser, *Cooperative Advertising Practices and Problems* (Cambridge, Mass.: Marketing Science Institute, 1982).
3. Judann Dagnoli and Laurie Freeman, "Marketers Seek Slotting-Fee Truce," *Advertising Age,* February 22, 1988, p. 12.
4. "Want Shelf Space at the Supermarket? Ante-up," *Business Week,* August 7, 1989, pp. 60–61.
5. Carl G. Stevens and David P. Keane, "How to Become a Better Sales Manager: Give Sales-people How to Not Rah Rah," *Marketing News,* May 30, 1980, p. 1.
6. Tom Wotruba and Edwin K. Simpson, *Sales Management* (Boston: Kent Publishing, 1989).
7. McGraw-Hill LAP Report no. 8013.9 (New York: McGraw-Hill Corporation, 1988).
8. Thayer C. Taylor, "A Letup in the Rise of Sales Call Costs," *Sales and Marketing Management,* February 25, 1980, p. 24.
9. Theodore Levitt, "Communications and Industrial Selling," *Journal of Marketing* 31 (April 1967), pp. 15–21.
10. John E. Morrill, "Industrial Advertising Pays Off," *Harvard Business Review,* March/April 1970, p. 4.
11. "Salespeople Contact Fewer Than 10% of Purchase Decision-Makers Over a Two-Month Period," McGraw-Hill LAP Report no. 1029.3 (New York: McGraw-Hill, 1987).
12. Rolph E. Anderson, Joseph F. Hair, and Alan J. Bush, *Professional Sales Management* (New York: McGraw-Hill, 1988).

17

Public Relations, Publicity, and Corporate Advertising

CHAPTER OBJECTIVES

1. To demonstrate the roles of public relations, publicity, and corporate advertising in the promotional mix

2. To differentiate between public relations and publicity and to demonstrate the advantages and disadvantages of each

3. To examine the reasons for corporate advertising and the advantages and disadvantages associated with this form of communication

4. To examine methods for measuring the effects of public relations, publicity, and corporate advertising

Oprah's Loss Is Optifast's Gain

"When talk show host Oprah Winfrey announced on TV that she'd lost more than 60 pounds on the Optifast meal replacement program, executives at Sandoz Nutrition Corp. must have thought they'd died and gone to heaven."

The preceding quote from *Advertising Age* magazine pretty well sums up what Oprah's announcement did for Sandoz. Without paying Oprah a cent, Sandoz had a celebrity endorser with her own television show. Even better (or as a direct result!) Sandoz's Optifast sales grew an estimated 25 to 30 percent during the next six weeks.

While sales had been slowly increasing prior to Winfrey's announcement, after she announced her weight loss, the phones began ringing off the hook. This is despite the fact that the company has never run—and has no intentions of running—consumer advertising (a print ad is scheduled for professional journals), for fear that doctors might be alienated and that consumers might become confused.

While Sandoz may decide not to take advantage of the publicity by running consumer advertising, other companies may. A spokesperson for Optifast noted concern that competitors might increase their advertising efforts in an attempt to confuse consumers about the differences between Optifast and their products to increase their own sales. One competitor's—Thompson Medical's Slim-Fast—sales were also riding the wave of the liquid diet popularity, and the company emerged as a prime candidate for increased promotional efforts. [1]

Introduction

The Optifast example demonstrates the power of publicity and its effects on the marketability of a product or service. As noted, Sandoz neither paid nor solicited Oprah to plug its product. Fortunately for Sandoz, in this case the communication was a positive one. Because publicity may sometimes be beyond the control of the marketer, it may pose more of a threat than an opportunity—for example, in the past products and brand names have been destroyed by adverse publicity (remember the Suzuki Samurai discussion in Chapter 1?), whereas others have achieved incredible success as a result of favorable publicity (for example, Cabbage Patch dolls.)

Publicity, like public relations and corporate advertising, consists of promotional program elements that may be of great benefit to the marketer. As such, publicity constitutes an integral part of the overall promotional effort that must be managed and coordinated with the other elements of the promotions mix. However, as you will see in this chapter, these three tools do not always have the specific goals of product and service promotion as objectives, nor do they always involve the same methods as you have become accustomed to as you have read this text. Typically, these activities are more involved in changing attitudes toward an organization or issue rather than in promoting specific products or affecting behaviors directly (though you will see that this role is changing in some firms). In this chapter we will explore the roles of public relations, publicity, and corporate advertising, the advantages and disadvantages of each, and the process by which these elements are employed. Some very interesting examples of such efforts—both successful and unsuccessful—are also included.

Public Relations

What is public relations? How does it differ from other elements discussed thus far? Perhaps a good starting point would be to define what the term **public relations** has traditionally meant and then to introduce its "new" role.

The Traditional Definition of Public Relations

While a variety of books define *public relations,* perhaps the most comprehensive is that offered by the *Public Relations News* (the weekly newsletter of the industry):

Figure 17–1 **Four Classes of Marketing and Public Relations Use**

		PUBLIC RELATIONS	
		Weak	Strong
MARKETING	Weak	1 Example: Small social service agencies	2 Example: Hospitals and colleges
	Strong	3 Example: Small manufacturing companies	4 Example: Fortune 500 companies

Source: Philip Kotler and William Mindak, "Marketing and Public Relations," *Journal of Marketing* 42 (October 1978), p. 14.

the management function which evaluates public attitudes, identifies the policies and procedures of an organization with the public interest, and executes a program of action (and communication) to earn public understanding and acceptance.[2]

As this definition indicates, public relations is a management function. It should be noted at this point that the term *management* should be used in its broadest sense, in that it is not limited only to business managements but includes other types of organizations as well and extends to profit as well as nonprofit institutions and organizations.

Second, it should be noted that this definition of public relations defines a process that requires a series of stages including

1. The determination and evaluation of public attitudes
2. The identification of policies and procedures of an organization with a public interest
3. The development and execution of a communications program designed to bring about public understanding and acceptance

This process does not take place at just one point in time. To have an effective public relations program, an *ongoing* effort must be established and continued over months or even years.

Finally, this definition indicates that public relations involves much more than activities designed to sell a product or service. In fact, the public relations program may involve some of the promotional program elements previously discussed but may use them in a different way and for a different purpose. For example, press releases may be mailed to announce new products or changes in the organization. Special events may be organized to create goodwill in the community, and advertising may be used to demonstrate the firm's position on a controversial issue.

The New Role of Public Relations

While the traditional definition of public relations described its role in the organization for many years, in an increasing number of marketing-oriented companies a new set of responsibilities has been established for this function. Under its new role, public relations takes on a much broader—and more marketing-oriented—perspective, designed to promote the organization as well as its products and/or services.

Figure 17–1 demonstrates four different relationships that marketing and public relations have assumed in an organization. As can be seen, these relationships are defined by the degree of use of each function.

Class 1 relationships are those characterized by a minimal use of either function. Organizations with this design typically have very small marketing and/or public relations budgets and devote little time and effort in this regard.

Those organizations characterized by a *class 2* relationship have a well-established public relations function but do very little in the way of formalized marketing activities. As indicated in Figure 17–1, colleges and hospitals typically have such a design, although in both cases the marketing activities are increasing.

Many small companies are typified by a *class 3* organization in which marketing tends to dominate, whereas the public relations function is minimal. Private companies (without stockholders) and small manufacturers with little or no publics to appease tend to employ this design.

Class 4 enterprises have both a strong marketing and a strong public relations department. In many of these organizations these two departments operate independently. For example, public relations may be responsible for the more traditional responsibilities described earlier, whereas marketing is responsible for promoting specific products and/or services. At times, both groups may work together, and both report to top management.

The new role of public relations might best be characterized by the class 4 categorization noted above, although with a slightly different relationship. Rather than each department operating independently, the two now work much more closely together, blending their talents to provide the best overall image of the firm and its product or service offerings. Public relations departments increasingly position themselves as a tool both to supplant and to support the traditional advertising and marketing efforts. Examples of how the public relations department may operate in this respect and some of the results are demonstrated in Promotional Perspective 17–1.

Integrating Public Relations into the Promotional Mix

Given the broader responsibilities of public relations, the issue now becomes one of integrating this element into the promotional mix. Philip Kotler and William Mindak suggest that a number of alternative organizational designs are possible, with either marketing or public relations being the dominant function, both being equal but separate functions, or the two performing the same roles.[3] While each of these designs has its merits, in this text we will consider public relations as a promotional program element. This means that while a broader role will be defined, traditional responsibilities must still be assumed.

Whether a traditional role or a more marketing-oriented one is assumed, public relations activities will still be tied to specific communications objectives. The need to assess public attitudes and to create a favorable corporate image is of no less importance than strategies designed to promote products or services directly.

The Process of Conducting Public Relations

The actual process of conducting public relations and integrating it into the promotional mix involves a series of tasks. As you will see, these tasks involve both traditional and marketing-oriented activities.

The Determination and Evaluation of Public Attitudes

Given that public relations is concerned with attitudes toward the firm or specific issues beyond those directed at a product or service, the very first question that you may ask is, Why? Why is the firm so concerned with the public's attitudes?

One reason is that these attitudes may impact sales of the firm's products themselves. For example, sales of Coors beer have been very directly influenced by the boycotts against the company initiated by union members and minorities—both of whom

Promotional Perspective 17–1

Combining the Effects of Marketing and Public Relations

In recent years many companies have been combining their marketing and public relations efforts. The following examples demonstrate ways that publicity and public relations have been used to support marketing efforts.

Wendy Ewald—a photography teacher in Appalachia—recently published a collection of photos of preteens based on her five years of work in the area. When Ewald went on television talk shows to promote the collection, she took her Canon Sure Shot Supreme camera with her. When asked how she got the children to sit still for the shots, Ewald replied, "The first thing is that kids have to have a camera that they're comfortable with . . . like the Canon Sure Shot Supreme." She continued to describe the camera as the talk show's own cameras zoomed in to focus on the product she was touting. In fact, Canon was actually sponsoring Ewald's tour to the tune of $500 to $2,000 per appearance.

After Hurricane Gilbert swept over Jamaica in 1988, two Jamaican groups had different public relations needs. The Jamaican government wanted to play up the damage so as to receive international aid, whereas the Jamaica Tourist Board needed to show that the island was recovering quickly—to attract tourists.

GCI International (the public relations arm of Grey Advertising) brought in 1,000 leading tour operators to visit the reconstituted Jamaica to show that the country was still an attractive tourist location. Since only a few television network crews made the trip, GCI prepared its own five-minute video—paid for by the tourist board and broadcast over satellite news services. GCI estimates that 60 to 70 stations used some form of the material in their newscasts—some showing the damages, but others indicating how well the island was recovering—nearly all with no acknowledgment that the tourist board had paid for the hookups and images provided.

Remember "Mikey" in the Life cereal example from Chapter 1? More than a decade after Quaker Oats had stopped using the commericals featuring him, rumors started to flow about his whereabouts. Quaker's public relations firm found the now-grown actor, hid him from the press, and instigated the "search for the grown Mikey" campaign. The results? Even though the sweepstakes to find Mikey generated the smallest prizes ever (only 100 awards of $100 each), over 75,000 persons sent in guesses as to who the real Mikey was—the largest sweepstakes response Quaker has ever had.

Source: Adapted from Art Kleiner, "The Public Relations Coup," *Adweek's Marketing Week*, January 16, 1989, pp. 20–23.

---

have developed negative attitudes toward the brewer. The oil spill that occurred in Prince William Sound, Alaska, in 1989 when the tanker, Exxon Valdez, hit a submerged reef resulted in very unfavorable attitudes toward Exxon (the owner of the oil ship), which led to a number of protests and the return of thousands of the company's credit cards. Figure 17–2 shows an ad run by Exxon in response to this public relations problem.

Second, no one wants to be perceived as a "bad citizen." Corporations exist in communities, and their employees may both live and work there. Negative attitudes will carry over to employee morale and may result in a less-than-optimal working environment internally and/or in the community.

As a result of this concern with the perceptions of the public, many firms engage in research designed to keep the firm abreast of the public's attitudes. Surveys of public attitudes are commonplace among privately held corporations, utilities, and/or publicly held companies. The advertisement shown in Figure 17–3 is one way of collecting such information, whereas other, more standard research techniques are also used. The reasons for conducting this research are many, including the following.

1. It provides input into the planning process. Once the firm has determined the attitudes of the public, these attitudes serve as the starting point in the development of programs designed to maintain favorable positions or change unfavorable ones.

2. It serves as an "early warning system." Once a problem exists, it may require substantial efforts in time and money to correct it. By conducting research, the firm may be able to identify potential problems and handle them effectively before they become an issue.

3. It secures support internally. Should research indicate that a problem or potential

AN OPEN LETTER TO THE PUBLIC

On March 24, in the early morning hours, a disastrous accident happened in the waters of Prince William Sound, Alaska. By now you all know that our tanker, the Exxon Valdez, hit a submerged reef and lost 240,000 barrels of oil into the waters of the Sound.

We believe that Exxon has moved swiftly and competently to minimize the effect this oil will have on the environment, fish and other wildlife. Further, I hope that you know we have already committed several hundred people to work on the cleanup. We also will meet our obligations to all those who have suffered damage from the spill.

Finally, and most importantly, I want to tell you how sorry I am that this accident took place. We at Exxon are especially sympathetic to the residents of Valdez and the people of the State of Alaska. We cannot, of course, undo what has been done. But I can assure you that since March 24, the accident has been receiving our full attention and will continue to do so.

L. G. Rawl
Chairman

Figure 17–2   Exxon Apologizes for the Alaskan Oil Spill

Figure 17–3   Times Mirror Ad Designed to Gain Readers' Views

Table 17–1   **Ten Questions to Evaluate Marketing Public Relations Plans**

1. Does the plan reflect a thorough understanding of the company's business situation?
2. Has the PR (public relations) program made good use of research and background sources?
3. Does the plan include analysis of recent editorial coverage?
4. Do the PR people fully understand the product—its strengths and weaknesses?
5. Does the PR program describe several cogent, relevant conclusions from the research?
6. Are the program objectives specific and measurable?
7. Does the program clearly describe what the PR activity will be and its benefits to the company?
8. Does the program describe how its results will be measured?
9. Do the research, objectives, activities, and evaluations tie together?
10. Has the PR department communicated to marketing throughout the development of the program?

Source: Adapted from Hugh M. Ryan, "Public Relations Is More Than Publicity: Ten Questions to Evaluate Your Marketing PR Plan," *Marketing News,* March 13, 1989, pp. 8–9.

problem exists, then it will be much easier for the public relations arm to gain the support that it needs to address this problem.

4. It increases the effectiveness of the communication. By better understanding the problems and/or potential problems, the firm is better able to design communications that will effectively deal with them in the proper manner.[4]

Establishing a Public Relations Plan

In a survey of 100 top and middle managers in the communications field regarding their public relations programs, over 60 percent indicated that their "programs" involved little more than the use of press releases, press kits for trade shows, and new product announcements.[5] Further, these tools were not formulated into a formal public relations effort but rather were used only as they felt they were needed. In other words, no structured program was evident in well over half of those companies surveyed! As we noted earlier, the public relations process is an ongoing one, requiring formalized policies and procedures for dealing with problems and opportunities. Just as you would not develop an advertising and/or promotions program without policies and procedures and a plan, you should not institute public relations efforts this way. Moreover, this plan needs to be integrated into the overall marketing communications program. Table 17–1 provides just some of the questions that marketers need to ask to determine whether the public relations plan is an appropriate one. As you can see, these questions tie in very well with the promotional planning process stressed throughout this text.

Developing and Executing the Public Relations Program

Because of the broad role that public relations may be asked to perform, the public relations (PR) program may need to extend beyond that of the promotional program itself. A broader definition of the target market, additional communications objectives, and different messages and delivery systems may be employed. Let us examine this process.

Determining Relevant Target Audiences   The targets of public relations efforts may be varied, with different objectives established for each. Some may be directly involved in the product purchase, whereas others may affect the firm in a different way (for example, stockholders, legislators, etc.). In addition, these audiences may include persons both internal or external to the firm.

Internal audiences may include the employees of the firm, investors and stockholders, suppliers, members of the local community, and of course, current customers. You may be wondering at this point why members of the local community or customers of the firm are considered internal rather than external. According to John

Figure 17—4   An Example of a Newsletter Used for Internal Corporate Communication

Figure 17—5   Annual Reports Serve a Variety of Purposes

Marston, these groups should be considered internal owing to the fact that they are already connected with the organization in some way and constitute the group the firm would normally communicate with in the ordinary routine of work.[6] **External audiences,** on the other hand, are those people who are not necessarily closely connected with the organization, for example, the public at large.

It may be necessary to communicate with these groups on an ongoing basis for a variety of reasons ranging from ensuring goodwill to introducing new policies, procedures, or even products. A few examples might help.

Employees of the firm   The goals of maintaining morale and providing employees with an indication of the results of their efforts are often prime objectives of the public relations program. Organizational newsletters, notices on bulletin boards, paycheck envelope stuffers, direct mail, and annual reports are just some of the methods used to communicate with these groups. Figure 17—4 shows an example of one such internal organization communication used by AT&T.

Personal methods of communicating may be as formal as an established grievance committee or as informal as an office Christmas party. Other social events such as corporate softball and/or bowling teams are also employed to create goodwill.

Stockholders and investors   You may typically think of an annual report such as that shown in Figure 17—5 as serving the purpose of providing stockholders and investors with financial information regarding the firm. While this is certainly one purpose, annual reports will also provide a communications channel in which this audience may be informed as to why the firm is or is not doing well, future plans, or other information that goes beyond just that of numbers. In addition to the annual report, shareholders meetings, video presentations, or other forms of direct mail may be employed

Figure 17–6 Chevron Demonstrates Public Concern

for this purpose. Companies have used these approaches to generate additional investments, to bring more of their stocks "back home" (that is, become more locally controlled and managed), and to produce funding to solve specific problems, as well as to promote goodwill.

Community members   Those persons who live and work in the community in which a firm is located or doing business are often the target of public relations efforts. Such efforts may involve advertisements informing the community of activities that the organization is engaged in, for example, reducing air pollution, cleaning up water supplies, or as shown in Figure 17–6, protecting endangered species. (As you can also tell from Figure 17–6, the community can be defined very broadly!) Demonstrating to the public that the organization is a good citizen, and has their welfare in mind, may also be a reason for communicating to these groups.

Suppliers and customers   An organization, of course, wishes to maintain a level of *goodwill* with its suppliers as well as its consuming public. It is obvious that consumers are less likely to wish to buy from a company that they do not feel is socially conscious and might take their loyalties elsewhere. Likewise, suppliers may be inclined to exhibit the same behaviors.

Sometimes sponsoring a public relations effort will result in direct evidence of success. For example, the "Say no to drugs" campaign resulted in a boon to companies manufacturing drug testing kits, hospitals offering drug rehabilitation programs, and television news programs' ratings.[7] At the same time, indirect indications of the success of these efforts may include more customer loyalty, less antagonism, or greater cooperation between the firm and its suppliers or consumers.

Sometimes a public relations effort may be targeted to more than one of the groups cited above. For example, San Diego Gas & Electric (SDGE), the public utility company for the San Diego area, has, over time, suffered from extreme negative atti-

To our customers:

SDG&E management believes it's important to have the benefit of public participation in our company's customer policies and practices. Decisions about gas and electric service affect everyone. Therefore, we want to involve a broad-based representation of customers in examining SDG&E's operations.

That's what our Consumer Outreach Program is all about—community involvement. The success of the program so far is due in large measure to the interest of those community representatives who have given their time and effort.

What has emerged is a growing consensus of customer attitudes, concerns and expectations relating to our company and its operations. I am much encouraged by the positive and constructive recommendations produced thus far.

Clearly, the Consumer Outreach Program is an important two-way means of communication on energy, a subject that touches the lives of every one of us. Please read the report that follows, and I believe you will share my optimism about the value of this program.

Jack E. Thomas

Jack E. Thomas,
Executive Vice President,
Utility Operations
San Diego Gas & Electric

tudes among its customers, brought about by their high utility rates. This problem was aggravated when a series of management blunders resulted in even higher rates, and plans were announced to build a nuclear plant in one of the lagoons near the ocean, resulting in protests from consumers and environmentalists. Stockholders and potential investors lacked trust, and employee morale was at a low. (Company cars with the SDGE logo on the doors were vandalized and drivers were threatened to the point where the identifying logos had to be removed.)

The public relations plan developed to deal with these problems targeted a variety of publics and employed a number of channels. Television spots were used to show consumers how to save energy. Print ads were utilized to explain the reasons for the energy purchases made by management, and public relations programs such as the Consumer Outreach Program shown in Figure 17–7 were developed. The outcome of these programs has been shown to have led to much more favorable attitudes among all the publics targeted (at least employees can put the SDGE logo back on their cars!).

Relevant audiences may also include those persons not directly involved with the firm. External audiences may include the press, educators, civic and business groups, governments, potential customers and the financial community.

The press   Perhaps one of the most critical of the external publics is that of the press. It is the press that determines what you will read in your newspapers or see on television, what is news, and how this news will be presented. Because of the press's extreme power, there is a need to keep the press informed of the actions of the firm. Thus, companies issue press releases and communicate through conferences, interviews, and special events as a means of disseminating information. The press is generally receptive to such information, as news people are interested in good stories so long as the communications are handled professionally.

One person who has mastered this task quite well is Steven Jobs—the founder

Figure 17–8   The Yellow Pages Distribute Information to College Professors

of Apple Computer. Jobs was able to achieve extensive press coverage of his introduction of the Macintosh, and later the NeXT computers, by establishing a well-staged event in which the media were the first to see the new innovations. These events were very well attended and got both products off to an excellent start.

Educators   A number of organizations provide educators with information regarding their activities. Organizations such as the Direct Marketing Association, the Specialty Advertising Association, and the American Association of Yellow Pages Publishers (as shown in Figure 17–8), among others, keep educators informed in an attempt to generate goodwill as well as exposure for their causes. These groups, as well as major corporations, provide information regarding new innovations, state-of-the-art research, or other items of interest.

Much of the reason underlying the release of this information is that educators are, to a degree, like the press—that is, they control the flow of information to certain parties—in this case, people like you.

Civic and business organizations   The local Jaycees, Kiwanis, and other nonprofit civic organizations also serve as gatekeepers of information to those in their sphere of influence. Speeches made at organization functions, financial contributions, or sponsorships are all designed to create goodwill. Likewise, memberships of corporate executives on the board of directors of nonprofit organizations are also ways of generating positive public relations.

Governments   Direct efforts to influence government bodies at both a local and a national level are often employed as a public relations effort. Successful *lobbying* may mean immediate success for a product, whereas laws or regulations passed that may be detrimental to the firm may cost it millions. Imagine for a moment what the ap-

Table 17–2   **Getting the Public Relations Story Told**

Jonathan Schenker of Ketchum Public Relations, New York, suggests four new technological methods to make life easier for the press and to increase the likelihood of getting one's story told:

1. *Telephone press conferences* Since reporters cannot always get to a press conference, use the telephone to call them for coverage.
2. *In-studio media tours* Satellite communications providing a story, and a chance to interview, from a central location such as a television studio will save broadcast journalists time and money by eliminating their need to travel.
3. *Multicomponent video news releases (VNR)* A five-component package consisting of a complete script in print and on tape, a video release with a live reporter, a local contact source at which to target the video, and a silent video news release that allows the station to fill in with its own news reporter will lend an advantage owing to their budget-savings capabilities.
4. *Targeted newswire stories* By targeting the public relations message, reporters are spared the need to read through volumes of news stories, selecting only those of interest to them and their target audiences.

Source: "Want the Story Told? Then Make Life Easy for Reporters," *Marketing News,* October 9, 1987, p. 7.

proval of NutraSweet meant to Searle or what could happen to the beer and wine industries should television advertising be banned.

Financial groups   In addition to current shareholders, potential shareholders and investors may be relevant target markets. Financial advisers, lending institutions, and others must be kept abreast of new developments as well as the financial information typically provided, as they offer the potential for new sources of funding. Press releases and corporate reports have played an important role in providing information to these publics.

Implementing the Public Relations Program   Once the research has been conducted and the target audiences have been identified, the public relations program must be developed and delivered to the receivers. A number of public relations tools are available for this purpose.

The press release   As previously noted, one of the most important publics is that of the press. To have information used by the press, it must be factual, true, and/or of interest to the medium as well as its audience. As shown in Table 17–2, there are certain things that the source of the **press release** can do to improve the likelihood that the "news" will be disseminated.

In addition to those methods shown in Table 17–2, the information will need to be of interest to the readers of that medium. For example, financial institutions may issue press releases to business trade media and/or to the editor of the business section of a common-interest medium such as the newspaper. Information on the release of a new rock album will be of more interest to radio disk jockeys than to television newscasters, whereas sports news will also have its interested audiences.

Press conferences   By now we are all familiar with press conferences held by political figures. While used less often by organizations and corporations, this form of delivery can be very effective. Of course, the topic must be of major interest to a specific group before it is likely to gain coverage. Usually major accomplishments such as the awarding of the next Super Bowl or Olympics location or major breakthroughs, such as medical cures, emergencies, or catastrophies, are topics warranting a national press conference, whereas on a local level community events, local developments, and the like may receive coverage. Press conferences are often used by companies when they have significant news to announce, such as the introduction of a new product or advertising campaign. For instance, L. A. Gear received considerable media attention when it held a press conference in September 1989 to announce that singer Michael Jackson would serve as the company's advertising spokesperson (for $20 million!).

Figure 17–9 **This Bayer Aspirin Ad Capitalized on Favorable Publicity**

Exclusives   Although most public relations efforts may seek a variety of channels for distribution, an alternative strategy may be to offer one particular medium exclusive rights to the story. Should this medium or group reach a substantial number of persons interested in that area, the offering of an **exclusive** may enhance the likelihood of acceptance. As you watch television over the next few weeks, watch for the various networks' and local stations' offerings of exclusives. Notice the attention they pay to these exclusives and how the media actually use them to promote themselves.

Interviews   While you are watching television, or when you are reading magazines, pay close attention to the personal interviews being conducted. Usually, someone will have some specific questions or issues to be raised, and a spokesperson is provided by the firm for answering them. For example, when the *Challenger* space shuttle accident occurred, a spokesperson for Morton Thiokol—the company responsible for the manufacturing of the O-rings that contributed to the explosion—was interviewed to provide the company's perspective. When Chrysler was accused of selling cars used by employees as new, Lee Iacocca, the president of Chrysler, himself served as the interviewee to give the company's response to the charges.

Other methods of distributing information include photo kits, by-lined articles (articles written by the firm, signed, and offered for publication), speeches, and trade shows. Of course, the specific mode of distribution to be used will be determined by the nature of the story and the interest of the media and its publics.

Advantages and Disadvantages of Public Relations

Like the other program elements, there are both advantages and disadvantages to be accrued through the use of public relations.

Some of the advantages are:

• *Credibility*   Because public relations communications are not perceived in the same light as advertising—that is, the public does not realize that the organization either directly or indirectly paid for the communications—they tend to have more credibility among the receivers. The fact that the medium is not being compensated for providing the information may lead the receiver to consider the news as more truthful and credible.

For example, an article that appears in newspapers or magazines discussing the virtues of aspirin may be perceived as much more credible than an advertisement for the same product. Or as was shown in Promotional Perspective 17–1, the consumer may not know that the source of the communication was the sponsoring organization.

Sometimes, news about a product may in itself serve as the subject of an ad. Figure 17–9 demonstrates how Sterling Drug, Inc. developed an effective advertising campaign using information that appeared in press articles about the ability of aspirin to reduce the risk of heart attacks.

• *Cost* Both in absolute and relative terms, the cost of public relations is very low—particularly when considering the possible effects. While many firms employ public relations agencies and spend millions of dollars in this area, for smaller companies this form of communication may be the most affordable of the alternatives available. Many public relations programs require little more than the time and expenses associated with putting the program together and getting it distributed and yet are still able to accomplish their objectives.

• *The avoidance of clutter* Because of the nature of the communication—that it may be typically perceived as a *news item*—public relations messages are not subject to the clutter of advertisements. A story regarding a new product introduction or breakthrough is perceived as a news item and is likely to receive more attention. Referring back to Steven Job's introduction of the NeXT computer, all the major networks covered the story, as did major newspapers and magazines. Some (like CNN) devoted two to three-minute segments to the introduction.

• *Lead generation* Information provided about a technological innovation, a medical breakthrough, and the like, will almost immediately result in a multitude of inquiries. These inquiries may provide the firm with the potential of some quality sales leads. For example, Vend-a-Video, a manufacturer of a videocassette vending machine, received dozens of inquiries regarding its product from one article that appeared in a trade magazine discussing the product's development. Leads from as far away as Germany and Brazil offered the company a potential source of sales.

• *Ability to reach specific groups* Because some products may have appeal to only a small segment, it is not feasible to engage in advertising and/or promotions to reach this group. In addition, the firm or organization may not have the financial capabilities to engage in promotional expenditures. One of the best—and only—ways to communicate to these groups is that of public relations, through any of the delivery channels discussed.

• *Image building* Effective public relations will lead to the development of a positive image for the organization or firm. A strong image is, in turn, insurance against later misfortunes. For example, in 1982 seven people in the Chicago area died after taking Extra Strength Tylenol capsules that had been laced with cyanide (by an as-yet-unidentified person). Within one week of the news of the poisonings, Tylenol's market share fell from 35 to only 6.5 percent. Strong public relations efforts combined with an already strong product and corporate image made it possible for the product to rebound (despite the opinions of many experts that the product had no chance of recovering!). A brand or firm with a lesser image would never have been able to come back.

Perhaps the major disadvantage of using public relations is the potential for not completing the communications process. While it was mentioned earlier that public relations sometimes offers the advantage of being able to break through the clutter of commercials, it is also possible that while the message may be noted by the receiver, the connection to the source is not achieved. For example, many firms' public relations efforts are never associated with their sponsors.

One of the potential ways that public relations may misfire is through mismanagement and a lack of coordination with the marketing department. As was stated earlier in this chapter, some organizations have separate marketing and public relations departments. When these departments operate independently, there exists the potential for inconsistent communications, redundancies in efforts, and so on.

While there may be other disadvantages associated with public relations, the two discussed here are the most commonly occurring. The key to effective public relations is to establish a good program, worthy of public interest, and manage it properly. To determine if this program is working, it is necessary to measure the effectiveness of the public relations effort.

Measuring the Effectiveness of Public Relations

As with the other promotional program elements, it is important to evaluate the effectiveness of the public relations efforts. In addition to determining the contribution of this program element on the attainment of communications objectives, the evaluation offers additional advantages:

1. It tells management what has been achieved through public relations activities and actions.
2. It provides management with a quantitative means of measuring public relations achievements.
3. It provides management with a means of judging the quality of public relations achievements and activities.[8]

As shown in Table 17–3, a number of criteria may be used to measure the effects of such programs. In addition to the methods provided in Table 17–3, Raymond Simon suggests additional means for accomplishing this evaluation process, including:

- *Personal observation and reaction*   One method suggested is that of personal observation by one's superiors. This observation and evaluation should take place at all levels of the organization.
- *Matching objectives and results*   Specific objectives designed to attain the overall communications objectives may be established. Relating these objectives to actions, activities, or media coverage is suggested. For example, an objective of placing a feature story in a specific number of media may serve as an objective, quantitative, and measurable goal.
- *The team approach*   Harold Mendelsohn suggests that one way to achieve attitude and behavior modification through public information campaigns is to use the **team approach** whereby evaluators are actually involved in the campaign.[9] By using research principles and working together, actual rather than assumed intents and efforts will be developed—and potentially accomplished.

Table 17–3   **Criteria for Measuring the Effectiveness of Public Relations**

A system for measuring the effectiveness of the public relations program has been developed by Lotus HAL. The criteria used in the evaluation process include:
- The total number of impressions over time
- The total number of impressions on the target audience
- The total number of impressions on specific target audiences
- Percentage of positive articles over time
- Percentage of negative articles over time
- Ratio of positive to negative articles
- Percentage of positive/negative articles by subject
- Percentage of positive/negative articles by publication or reporter
- Percentage of positive/negative articles by target audience

Source: Katharine D. Gaine, "There Is a Method for Measuring PR," *Marketing News*, November 6, 1987, p. 5.

- *Management by objectives*   In this method the executives and their managers act together to identify goals to be attained and the responsibilities of the managers in this endeavor. These goals are then used as a standard to measure accomplishments.
- *Public opinions and surveys*   Research in the form of public opinion surveys may be used to gather data to evaluate program goal attainment.
- *Audits*   Both internal and external audits might be used. **Internal audits** involve evaluations by one's superiors or peers within the firm to determine how well one (or one's programs) has (have) been performing. **External audits** are conducted by outside parties, including consultants, the client (in the case of a public relations agency), or others not within the organization itself.

In summary, the role that public relations is assuming in the promotional mix is changing. As public relations become more marketing oriented, the criteria by which they are evaluated will also need to change. At the same time, other—nonspecifically marketing-oriented—activities will continue to be the responsibility of the public relations department and will also serve as a basis for evaluation.

Publicity

The various definitions attached to the word **publicity** by *Webster* include the following:

> an act or public device designed to attract public interest; information with news value issued as a means of gaining public attention or support; the dissemination of information or promotional materials.[10]

As you can see by this definition, there is no clear distinction between publicity and what we have just been discussing under the heading of public relations.

There are, however, several major differences between publicity and public relations. First, the former is typically a *short-term* strategy, whereas public relations is a concerted program extending over a period of time. Second, public relations is designed to provide positive information about the firm and usually is controlled by the firm or an agent of the same. Publicity, on the other hand, is not always positive and is not always under the control of, or paid for by, the organization. In many cases, publicity—both positive and negative—originates from sources other than the firm.

In most organizations control and dissemination of publicity constitute one of the functions to be performed by the public relations department. While part of the public relations effort, publicity is at the same time an element that requires special attention and effort. In this section we will discuss the role that publicity plays in the promotional program and some of the ways that marketers will both use and react to these communications.

The Power of Publicity

Perhaps one of the factors that most sets off publicity from the other program elements is the sheer *power* that this form of communication can generate. Unfortunately for the marketer, as can be seen in Promotional Perspective 17–2, this power is not always realized in the way he or she would like it to be. In no uncertain terms, publicity can make or break a product or even a company, as is evidenced by the success of Cabbage Patch dolls (which used very little in the way of promotions other than publicity and public relations and still became one of the most successful products ever released by Coleco). Or, on the negative side, you may (if you are not too young) remember General Motor's first compact, the Corvair.

The Corvair was cruising along (no pun intended!) with some success until consumer advocate Ralph Nader released his report entitled "Unsafe at Any Speed," which essentially claimed that the car was unsafe to drive. After this information spread, the

Promotional Perspective 17–2

The Power of Publicity

The following are just a few examples reflecting the power that publicity can render. As you can see by these examples, the result is sometimes extremely beneficial to the firm—and at other times extremely detrimental.

Osborne Computers—A Disaster

In 1981 Osborne made history with the introduction of the Osborne I personal computer. Annual sales quickly reached $70 million, a public stock offering was made, and the company was lavishing in a wealth of venture capital.

In 1983 news was leaked that a new Osborne computer—the Executive model—would soon be released. The Executive was to be an even more advanced version than the Osborne I and would be available some time around May or June. Unfortunately, the information leak occurred in January. Upon hearing that the Executive would soon be available (at a price not significantly higher than the Osborne I), those interested in purchasing the Osborne I decided to wait for the new model and delayed their purchase. At the same time, production problems led to a later-than-expected introduction date, leading many to get tired of waiting and to purchase a competitive model. Dealers could generate no sales of Osborne I's and, unable to obtain Executives, took on other competitive models—the snowball gained momentum.

By September, Osborne Computers had filed for bankruptcy. The darling of the computer industry only a year earlier was now a major loser—owing to the poor timing of publicity.

AUDI—Alleged Acceleration Problems

In 1978 Audi of America, Inc., a subsidiary of West German automaker Volkswagen AG, introduced the Audi 5000 model to spearhead its efforts to gain market share in the lucrative U.S. market. The 5000 model became a popular car in the United States, accounting for 47,766 of the 74,241 cars Audi sold in this country in 1985. However, in 1987 the Audi 5000 received very damaging publicity when news reports began circulating that a flaw in the design of the vehicle could result in "sudden acceleration," whereby the car would accelerate out of control. By

1987 sales of the 5000 model declined to only 25,946 units. Audi blamed the reversal in sales on the negative publicity surrounding the 5000's alleged acceleration problems. The company could not revive sales of the 5000 and decided to discontinue the model.

The negative publicity Audi received from the sudden acceleration problem not only affected the 5000 models but also carried over to Audi's entire product line. Audi was cleared by the federal government of any blame for faulty engineering in relation to the sudden acceleration problem. However, despite attractive rebates and three years of free maintenance for buyers, as well as generous dealer incentive programs, Audi sales for 1989 were projected to reach only 21,000. Some sources have indicated that Audi may soon pull out of the U.S. market if it cannot reverse the sales decline. Once again, negative publicity may have caused insurmountable problems for a company.

Michael Jackson and Pepsi—A Great Marriage

In 1984 Pepsi-Cola signed pop singer Michael Jackson to a multimillion dollar contract to appear in advertisements and promotional events designed to promote Pepsi. Because of his popularity, the agreement received immense publicity in almost every major media. The television networks carried the news as well as the first commercial spot, newspapers regularly reported the events, and radio—of course—provided much airtime.

The net result was that in addition to the exposure that would normally occur from media purchases, Pepsi received millions of dollars worth of free exposure, not to mention the word-of-mouth advertising among Michael Jackson fans and the media in general!

Was the money well spent? Apparently Pepsi thought so: They signed Jackson to a $10 million renewal contract in 1987!

Sources: "Television News Coverage of PepsiCo's New Ad Campaign with Pop Superstar Michael Jackson Got the Soft Drink Maker $2.75 Million Free Air Time," *The Wall Street Journal*, March 8, 1989, p. 33; Bradley A. Stertz, "Audi Rebate Plan on 5000 Model Has the Look of Bait and Switch," *The Wall Street Journal*, June 21, 1988, p. 35; David Kiley, "Audi's Defense Plan Has Not Stopped Slump in Sales," *Adweek's Marketing Week*, October 9, 1989, p. 27.

Corvair was doomed to failure and, as a result of falling sales and other mechanical problems, was soon removed from the market. As has been discussed, the same fate nearly befell the Suzuki Samurai and the Audi 5000, both of which received negative publicity regarding product safety and experienced sharp declines in sales.

Earlier we discussed the substantial drop in Tylenol sales resulting from extensive media coverage of the tampering of its products while on store shelves. The Johnson & Johnson marketing efforts (including a strong public relations emphasis) designed to aid recovery were a model in proficiency that will be studied by students of marketing (both in the classroom and in the boardroom) for many years to come. By January 1983, almost 100 percent of the original brand share had been regained.

The point of all these examples—and we are sure that you can add many more to both sides of this list—is to demonstrate the impact of publicity and the potential for success and/or failure that it carries. But why? Why is publicity so potentially more powerful than advertising or sales promotions—or even other forms of public relations? A number of reasons are offered. The first is that publicity is highly *credible*.

Why is publicity credible? Unlike advertising and sales promotions, publicity is not usually perceived as being sponsored by the company (and, of course, in the negative instances never is!). As a result the consumer perceives this information as more objective and places more confidence in it. In fact, *Consumer Reports*—the medium responsible for at least one of the examples previously cited—recently ran an advertising campaign designed to promote its credibility by specifically noting that it does not accept advertising and therefore can be more objective in its evaluations.

In other instances the information may be perceived as akin to an endorsement by the medium in which it appears. For example, publicity regarding a breakthrough in the durability of golf balls and reported by *Golf* magazine will go far in the promotion of this product. *Car & Driver's* "Car of the Year" reflects that magazine's perception of the quality of the auto selected.

Still another reason is the *news value* of publicity and the frequency of exposure that it is able to generate. The Michael Jackson Pepsi commercial discussed in Promotional Perspective 17–2 appeared on every major television network—both as paid commercials and free, as each of the national news programs discussed the magnitude of the contractual agreement and aired the ads.

A similar effect was achieved by Big Boy Restaurants when the chain ran a national campaign asking consumers whether it should do away with the "Big Boy" holding a burger outside the front of each of its stores. All the major networks reported the results in the form of news, and thousands of letters were sent to the company asking them not to do away with the "kid."

The bottom line is that publicity is *news,* and as much research has shown, people like to pass on information that has news value. Publicity thus results in a significant amount of word-of-mouth communication—free and credible information regarding the firm and its products.

The Control and Dissemination of Publicity

In some of the examples cited earlier, the control of publicity was not always in the hands of the company. While the Osborne Computer example demonstrated the firm's own blunder in allowing the information to leak out, in the case of Suzuki and Audi the firms could do little or nothing to stop the media from releasing the information. When publicity becomes news, it will be reported on and carried by the media, sometimes despite the efforts of the firm. In these instances the organization will need to react to the potential threat created by the news.

A good example of one company's efforts to respond to adverse publicity is shown in Figure 17–10. In 1989 all the major news media carried stories relating the fact that the chemical Alar, which was used by some growers to regulate the growth of apples, was a potential cause of cancer in children. Despite published denials by reliable scientific and medical authorities, including the Surgeon General, that Alar does not cause cancer, a few special interest groups were able to generate an extraordinary amount of adverse publicity, causing concern among consumers and purchasing agents. A few school districts took apples off their menus, and even applesauce and juice were implicated. To state their position, Tree Top ran the ad shown in Figure 17–10 to help alleviate consumers' fears. In addition, a direct mailing was sent to nutritionists and daycare operators to further clarify Tree Top's position.

In other instances, however, publicity can be controlled and must be managed like any other promotional tool. In the Osborne Computer case, a few months' delay of the information regarding the new computer may have meant the difference between complete success and total failure.

Likewise, publicity can also be used to work for the marketer. For example, New Retail Concepts, Inc., the marketer of No Excuses jeans, took advantage of the publicity surrounding the Donna Rice-Gary Hart scandal in 1987 by using Ms. Rice in its

Figure 17–10   **Tree Top Responds to the Threat of Negative Publicity**

Figure 17–11   **No Excuses Jeans Effectively Makes Use of Publicity**

At Tree Top, 100% Pure Means 100% Safe.

Our business is children. And nobody goes to greater lengths to protect their health.

That's why Tree Top instituted strict safety procedures years ago to keep Alar out of our products.

Right from the start, we require growers to certify their fruit is *not* treated with Alar. Then we sample and test the fruit before it's processed. Over 8,000 of these tests have been conducted in the last year alone. Fact is, we've rejected tons of apples because they haven't measured up to Tree Top's high standards.

As a final safety check, the finished product is continuously sampled throughout the day, everyday.

As a result, we can assure you that all Tree Top juices and applesauce are 100% safe to consume.

There's been a lot said about Alar lately. But no matter what you've heard, they weren't talking about Tree Top.

We Always Give You 100%®

"I have no excuses. I just wear them."

—Donna Rice

no **excuses.**

advertisements (Figure 17–11). The company scheduled a press conference with Rice to announce the affiliation the night after Gary Hart went on "Nightline" to say he would not reenter the presidential race.

When Hart later decided to return to the race, the commercial was aired on a number of national news programs, as the ads were the only existing footage that anyone had of Rice. Thus, the ads were shown in prime time at virtually no cost to the company—the company was able to introduce their product with a very small advertising budget ($500,000).[11]

To the degree that they are able, marketers will like to have control over the time and place in which information is released. Courses are offered, and books have been written regarding the role of publicity in the public relations process and how to manage this function. Without going into details, suffice it to say that these books involve such issues as how to make a presentation, whom to contact, how to issue a press release, and specific information for each medium addressed—including television, radio, newspapers, magazines, and direct-response advertising. In addition, they offer alternative media that may be used such as news conferences, seminars, events, and personal letters, as well as insights as to how to deal with government and other legislative bodies. Because this information is too extensive to include as a single chapter in this text, we suggest that you pursue one of the many texts available on this subject for additional insights.

Advantages and Disadvantages of Publicity

Beyond the potential impact of negative publicity discussed earlier, you may be wondering if there is anything that can be said about this form of communication that is not entirely positive. As noted previously, publicity offers the advantages of credibility, news value, significant word-of-mouth communications, and a perception of being endorsed by the media. For the most part two major problems arising from the use of publicity must be addressed.

Timing   The Osborne example demonstrates the importance of properly timing the publicity release. This timing is not always completely under the control of the marketer, however. Unless the information to be conveyed is perceived as having very high news value by the press, the timing of the communication release will be entirely up to the media—if it gets released at all. Thus, the information may be released earlier than desired or too late to make much of an impact.

Accuracy   One of the major methods for getting publicity is the press release. Unfortunately, the information sometimes "gets lost in the translation"—that is, it is not always reported the way that the provider wishes it to be. As a result, inaccurate information, omissions, or other errors may result. Sometimes when you see a publicity piece that has been written based on a press release, you wonder if they are even talking about the same topic!

Measuring the Effectiveness of Publicity

The methods employed for measuring the effects of publicity are essentially the same as those discussed earlier under the broader topic of public relations. Rather than to reiterate these methods here, we thought it might be more interesting to show you an actual example. Promotional Perspective 17–3 discusses a model developed by Ketchum Public Relations for tracking the effects of publicity. (I guess we just provided Ketchum with some free publicity!)

Corporate Advertising

One of the more controversial forms of advertising employed by firms is that of **corporate advertising.** Actually an extension of the public relations function, corporate advertising does not promote any one specific product or service. Rather, it is designed to promote the firm overall—either by enhancing its image, assuming a position on a social issue or cause, or seeking direct involvement in something. Why is corporate advertising considered controversial? A number of reasons are offered:

1. *Consumers are not interested in this form of advertising* A Gallup and Robinson study reported in *Ad Age* in 1983 indicated that consumers were as much as 35 percent less interested in corporate ads than they were in product-oriented advertising.[12] Much of this disinterest may be due to the fact that the consumer may not understand the reasons behind such ads. Of course, much of this confusion results from the fact that the ads themselves may not be very good from a communications standpoint.

2. *A costly form of self-indulgence* Firms have been accused of engaging in corporate image advertising only to satisfy the egos of top management. While this may or may not be true, the impetus for this argument stems from the fact that corporate ads are not easy to write. That is, the message that is to be communicated is not as precise and specific as one that is designed to position a product, for example. As a result the top managers often will dictate the content of the ad, with the copy then reflecting their ideas and images of the corporation.

3. *A belief that the firm must be in trouble* Some critics believe that the only reason that firms engage in this form of advertising is because the company is in trouble—either in a financial sense or in the public's eye—and is advertising to attempt to remedy the problem.

Promotional Perspective 17-3

The Ketchum Publicity Tracking Model

Paul H. Alvarez, chairman and chief executive officer of Ketchum Public Relations, describes his firm's publicity tracking model as follows:

We have done a pretty good job in educating clients on what publicity programs can and cannot do, and what can be realistically expected. But true accountability requires *measured* results. Is publicity *measurable*?

Up to now, perhaps not. But Ketchum Public Relations has been working for three years on "The Ketchum Publicity Tracking Model," the first computer-based measurement system designed specifically to evaluate publicity programs. It goes beyond traditional accounting methods such as reporting to the client the number of column inches or the amount of broadcast time obtained, and total audiences reached. . . . It evaluates, via a publicity exposure index and a publicity value index, the amount of target audience exposure received and the degree to which planned messages were delivered to the target audience.

In planning a campaign to be evaluated by the model, the client and the firm agree upon standards of performance in two areas: the number of gross impressions to be achieved within the target audience, and the key messages to be delivered to that audience. The firm's computer is programmed with audience statistics from media in 120 top national markets. Performance standards for a given program are also programmed into the computer along with campaign results.

Results are printed out by media category, target audience reached and the quality (based on numerical values assigned to various 'selling' points in the copy) of the message delivered to the audience. It then produces two evaluative numbers: an overall exposure index and an overall value

index. Taking 1.00 as a standard index for the campaign, the degree to which the index is above or below this figure shows to what extent performance was above or below the norm.

In the accompanying "Sample Tracking Report," based on a campaign in Orlando, Florida, the exposure index (1.08) and the value index (1.48) indicate that the program overall met expectations and exceeded the established norms.

The first column of figures in the report shows media exposure among designated market area (DMA) audiences. The second column records average size/length of exposure for each medium, which is translated into average media units (based on a norm of 1.00) and publicity exposure units.

The columns for average impact factor and publicity value units indicate the degree to which key "selling" points in the copy were mentioned in the exposures. Note that the average impact factor for network television is low (0.81). The reason is that although the subject of the campaign (a special event) was mentioned fairly often (1.93 average media units), mention of specific dates and other key copy points did not meet expectations.

The tracking model also demonstrates in advance what a publicity program will do. Thus it is a tool for deciding whether or not a program is worth carrying out. If the decision is "go," it then reports how well objectives were met. Instead of guesswork, we now have a method for placing accountability to the client on a factual basis.

Source: Reprinted with permission from the July 1983 issue of *Public Relations Journal*, p. 29. Copyright Public Relations Journal, 1983.

Sample Tracking Report

Placement Type	DMA Target Audience (thousands)	Average Size/ Length	Average Media Units	Publicity Exposure Units (thousands)	Average Impact Factor	Publicity Value Units (thousands)
Newspapers	4,552	1/9 page	0.93	4,233	1.26	5,334
Magazines	268	1/2 page	1.66	455	1.47	656
Television (network)	95	5:10 min	1.93	183	0.81	149
Television (local)	504	6:05 min	2.13	1,073	1.81	1,946
Radio (local)	200	10:00 min	2.60	520	1.40	728
Totals	5,619		1.15	6,454	1.37	8,813

Publicity exposure norm = 5,960,000
Publicity exposure index (6,454/5,960) = 1.08
Publicity value index (8,813/5,960) = 1.48

Notes:
The publicity exposure norm is established by estimating the target audiences (adults 18–49, weighted 60 percent male, 40 percent female) and exposure of a "good" hypothetical placement schedule.
The publicity exposure index suggests that the campaign's exposure was 1.08, as good as expected on a normal (= 1.00) basis.
The publicity value index suggests that the impact value of the campaign was 1.48 times as good as expected on a normal (= 1.00) basis.

As you will see in the following pages of this chapter, there are a number of forms of corporate advertising, each with its own objectives in mind. The argument of these critics is that these objectives have become important only because the firm is not, or has not been, managing itself properly.

4. *Corporate advertising is a waste of money* Given that the ads do not directly appeal to anyone, are not understood, and do not promote anything specific, critics argue that the monies could be better spent in other areas. Again, much of this argument has its foundation in the fact that the corporate image ads are often intangible. They typically do not ask directly for a purchase; they do not ask for investors; rather, they present a position or try to create an image. Because they are not specific, many critics feel that their purpose is lost on the audience, and therefore these ads are not a wise investment of the firm's resources.

Despite these criticisms, and others, corporate advertising has become increasingly more prevalent since the 1970s. It has been estimated that more than 7 percent of all advertising dollars spent are for corporate advertising, meaning that billions of dollars are spent on this form of communication.[13]

While corporate advertising has generally been regarded as the domain of companies such as USX, Kaiser Aluminum, and Boise Cascade—that is, companies with no products to sell directly to the consumer market—this is no longer the case. Procter & Gamble ran its first corporate spot in 1987, and other consumer products companies such as IBM and AT&T have also increased expenditures in this area.

As noted above, one of the criticisms leveled at the users of corporate advertising stems from the fact that so many people are not sure exactly what corporate advertising is or what its purpose is. This form of advertising has been used as a catchall for any type of advertising run for the direct benefit of the corporation rather than its products or services—obviously, a lot of advertising falls into this categorization.[14] For purposes of this text (and to attempt to bring some perspective to the term) we will use the broader-based term of *corporate advertising* to describe various types of advertising that are designed to promote the organization itself rather than its products or services.

Objectives of Corporate Advertising

There are a number of objectives corporate advertising may attempt to accomplish. This form of advertising may be designed with two goals in mind: (1) creating a positive image for the firm and (2) communicating the organization's views on social, business, and environmental issues. More specific applications include:

1. Boosting employee morale and smoothing labor relations
2. Helping newly deregulated industries ease consumer uncertainty and answer investor questions
3. Helping diversified companies establish an identity for the parent firm, rather than relying solely on brand names[15]

As these objectives indicate, corporate advertising is targeted at both internal and external audiences and involves the promotion of the organization as well as its ideas.

Types of Corporate Advertising

Attainment of the objectives is sought through the implementation of the various forms of corporate advertising. As you will see, each form is designed to achieve specific goals.

Image Advertising   One form of corporate advertising is that devoted to the promotion of the organization's overall *image*. Such advertising may accomplish a number of objectives including that of creating *goodwill* both internally and externally, creating a position for the company, and generating resources—both human and financial. A number of methods are used.

1. *General image or positioning ads* As shown in Figure 17–12, ads are often designed to create an image of the firm in the mind of the public. As can be seen in

Figure 17—12   Allstate Positions Itself as "The Good Hands People"

THE SHORTEST DISTANCE BETWEEN TWO POINTS IS OFTEN ONE INDIVIDUAL.

Compassion. You can't teach it. Or place too great a value on it. But you could measure it, down this very road on June 23rd, in the actions of Allstate Claims Adjuster Don Molder, who left his house at five a.m. to drive to the scene of a fire sixty miles away. All just to shorten the distance between a man's loss and his recovery. In times of need, people like Don Molder understand that just one person can make the difference between feelings of despair and feelings of hope. Just one more reason to leave it to The Good Hands People.

A member of the Sears Financial Network

Allstate
You're in good hands.

the figure, Allstate is attempting to create the image of itself as a company that cares for its customers and places them in the security of "the good hands people."

2. *Sponsorships* Often a firm will run corporate image advertising on programs or television "specials." For example, the Hallmark or IBM specials and documentaries on network television and Mobil and Gulf Oil program sponsorships on Public Service Broadcasting are designed to promote the corporation as a good citizen. By associating itself with high-quality and/or educational programming, the firm hopes that there will be a carryover effect that benefits its own image.

Other examples of sponsorships include those run by American Express and Chrysler to support the refurbishing of the Statue of Liberty. In both of these instances, the sponsoring organizations benefited from the association, as did the charity that received the funds. American Express card usage during the campaign increased by 25 percent, whereas $1.7 million was raised for refurbishing the statue.[16] Certainly, a favorable corporate image was created!

3. *Recruiting* The promotional piece for Deloitte & Touche presented in Figure 17—13 is a good example of corporate image advertising designed to attract college graduates. While not appearing in the media, the brochure is nevertheless designed to promote a corporate image for the company. Thus, if you are a graduating senior considering a career in accounting this brochure would be of interest to you.

The Sunday employment section of most major metropolitan newspapers is an excellent place to see this form of corporate image advertising at work. The next time you have a chance, notice the ads contained in these papers and consider the image that the firms are presenting.

4. *Generating financial support* Some corporate advertising is designed specifically to generate investments in the corporation. By creating a more favorable image, the firm will look attractive to potential stock purchasers and investors. More investments mean more working capital, more monies for research and development, and

Figure 17—13   **Deloitte & Touche Creates an Image for Recruitment**

so on. Thus, in this instance, corporate image advertising is almost attempting to make a sale—the product is the firm itself.

While there is no concrete evidence that corporate image advertising will lead directly to increased investment, at least one study does show that a correlation does exist between the price of stock and the amount of corporate advertising done.[16] That is, that those firms with higher dollars spent in corporate advertising also tend to have higher-priced stocks.

Before leaving this discussion of image advertising, it may be interesting to examine some of the factors that have been shown to affect corporate image. Promotional Perspective 17—4 reveals the results of a survey conducted by *Fortune* magazine. As you can see, this thing called image is not unidimensional! The most admired firms represented in *Fortune's* survey did not gain their positions merely by publicity and word of mouth.

It should be recognized that creating a positive corporate image is also not likely to be accomplished just by running a few advertisements. Quality of products and services, innovativeness, sound financial practices, being a good corporate citizen, and engaging in sound marketing practices are just a few of the many factors that will contribute to overall image.

Social, Business, and Environmental Issue Advertising   A second major form of corporate advertising is that of issue-oriented advertising, or as it is often called, **advocacy advertising.** Advocacy advertising has been defined as

Promotional Perspective 17–4

Factors That Affect Corporate Image

While a myriad of factors may contribute to the image of a company, what is interesting is that companies that have very positive images tend to do well on many factors rather than just one. For example, in a recent *Fortune* study, eight different corporate attributes were used for evaluation (Exhibit 17–4). The results of this study provide some interesting insights. For example, Merck—the number-one most respected firm overall—ranked first in seven of the eight attributes under consideration. Likewise, the Financial Corporation of America ranked as one of the least admired firms on eight of the eight factors. While you could argue that changing the attributes might result in different ratings, the fact is that those items under consideration do reflect important criteria for evaluation, covering marketing and financial and social issues.

Source: Adapted from Ellen Schultz, "America's Most Admired Corporations," *Fortune*, January 18, 1988, p. 36.

Exhibit 17–4   *Fortune's* Eight Attributes of Reputation

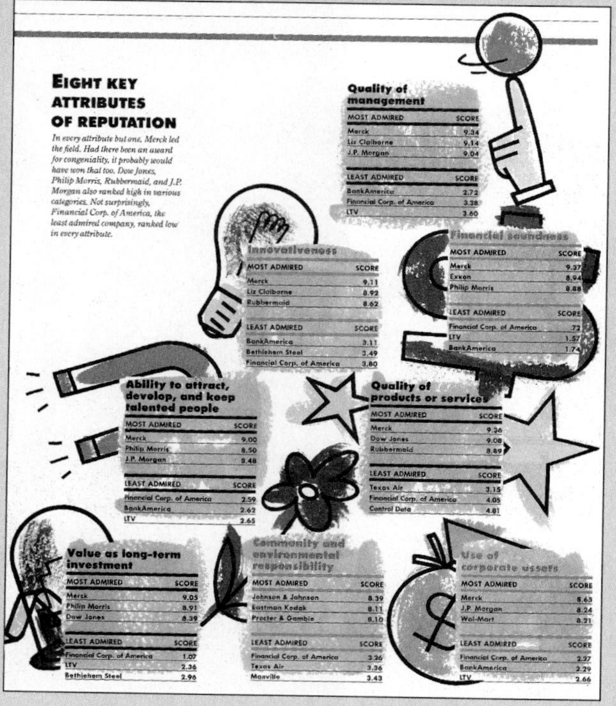

concerned with the propagation of ideas and elucidation of controversial social issues of public importance in a manner that supports the position and interest of the sponsor.[18]

While still seeking the objective of portraying an image for the company or organization, advocacy advertising does so in a much more indirect manner—that is, by adopting a position on a particular issue rather than promoting the organization itself.

Advocacy advertising—an example of which is shown in Figure 17–14—has increased in use over the past few years and has also met with increased criticism. The ads may be sponsored by a firm itself or by an industry association and are designed to provide the readers with insight as to how the firm operates or management's position on a particular issue.

Sometimes the advertising will result as a response to negative publicity or because the firm was unable to place the message through public relations channels and felt that its position warranted the expenditures. In other situations, the firm may just wish to have certain ideas accepted or have society understand its concerns.

While advocacy advertising has recently fallen under criticism from a number of sources—including consumer advocate Ralph Nader—as you can see in Figure 17–15, this form of communication has been around for quite some time. AT&T engaged in the practice of issues-oriented advertising as early as 1908 and continued to employ this form of communication throughout the twentieth century. While critics

Heroes

A coffin draped in the American flag...surviving officers in dress uniforms, mourning their fallen comrade...families in black, quietly sobbing, trying to understand what cannot be understood.

We have seen it too many times, the final rites for our defenders—fallen not in foreign wars, but today, right here at home in hundreds of American cities and towns. Another kind of war—against crime—is killing one American law-enforcement officer in the line of duty every 57 hours.

Like those fallen in other wars, these men and women wear the many faces of America. They are black and they are white; they trace their roots back to Asia and Africa and Europe and the Americas. They are young and old, they are commanders, detectives, and foot soldiers in the battle against lawlessness.

Consider these numbers:
- 30,000 law-enforcement officers have been killed on duty in the history of the U.S.
- In 1987 (the most recent data available), 155 officers were killed, 21,273 were wounded and 63,842 were assaulted with a weapon.
- In the past 10 years, 1,525 police officers have been killed, 204,584 have been injured and 590,822 have been assaulted.

- Every day, 500,000 American law-enforcement officers subject themselves to these risks, on our behalf.

How do we honor them? And how do we keep their sacrifices vivid in the public consciousness? One way is through the construction of the National Law Enforcement Officers Memorial. Congress has declared that the memorial will be built on three acres of open space at Washington, D.C.'s Judiciary Square. Groundbreaking is planned for Spring 1989, and the memorial should be ready for dedication by Peace Officers' Memorial Day, May 15, 1990.

Apart from donating the land, Congress purposely allocated no money for the construction. That is to come from corporations, organizations and individual donors. The fund-raising goal for the memorial is $7.5 million; more than $1.2 million has been raised to date.

Join us in contributing to the National Law Enforcement Officers Memorial Fund, 1360 Beverly Road, Suite 305, McLean, VA 22101. Contributions are tax deductible. Your contribution also is a symbol of support for our hometown heroes, for their service and sacrifice. They deserve it. They've earned it.

Mobil®

©1988 Mobil Corporation

contend that those with large advertising dollars may be able to purchase more ad space and time, and that the advocacy ads may be misleading, the checks and balances inherent in the system that control for regular product advertising also are operating in this area. The ultimate judge, of course, will always be the reader.

Advantages and Disadvantages of Corporate Advertising

A number of reasons for the increased popularity of corporate advertising become evident when you examine the advantages of this form of communication. Some of these advantages are provided below.

1. It is an excellent vehicle for positioning the firm. Firms—like products—need to establish an image or position in the marketplace. Corporate image ads are one vehicle for accomplishing this objective. As we noted much earlier in this text, a well-positioned product will be much more likely to achieve success than will one without an image or a vague one. The same holds true of the firm. Stop and think for a moment about the image that comes to mind when you hear of IBM, Apple, Johnson & Johnson, or Procter & Gamble. Now what comes to mind when you hear the words Unisys, USX, or Navistar? While we are not saying that these latter three companies are not successful—because they most certainly are—we are suggesting that their corporate identity (or position) is not as well entrenched as those first cited. What is

Figure 17–15 Advocacy Ads Have Been Used for Years

SHE'S A PARTNER IN A GREAT AMERICAN BUSINESS

She is one of 850,000 owners of Bell System securities. They are typical Americans—some young, some middle age, some old. They live in every part of the nation.

One may be a housewife in Pennsylvania. Another a physician in Oregon—a clerk in Illinois—an engineer in Texas—a merchant in Massachusetts—a miner in Nevada—a stenographer in Missouri—a teacher in California—or a telephone employee in Michigan.

For the most part, Bell System stockholders are men and women who have put aside small sums for saving. More than half of them have held their shares for five years or longer. More than 650,000 of these 850,000 security holders own stock in the American Telephone and Telegraph Company—the parent company of the Bell System. More than 225,000 own five shares or less. Over fifty per cent are women. No one owns as much as one per cent of the stock of A. T. & T. In a very real sense, the Bell System is a democracy in business—owned by the people it serves.

More than 270,000 men and women work for the Bell System. One person out of every 150 in this country owns A. T. & T. securities or stock and bonds of associated companies in the Bell System.

BELL TELEPHONE SYSTEM

Democracy

"—of the people, by the people, for the people"

People of every walk of life, in every state in the Union, are represented in the ownership of the Bell Telephone System. People from every class of telephone users, members of every trade, profession and business, as well as thousands of trust funds, are partners in this greatest investment democracy which is made up of the more than 175,000 stockholders of the American Telephone and Telegraph Company.

If this great body of people clasped hands they would form a line more than 150 miles long. Marching by your door, it would take more than 48 hours of ceaseless tramping for the line to pass.

This democracy of Bell telephone owners is greater in number than the entire population of one of our states; and more than half of its owners are women.

There is one Bell telephone shareholder for every 34 telephone subscribers. No other great industry has so democratic a distribution of its shares; no other industry is so completely owned by the people it serves. In the truest sense, the Bell System is an organization "of the people, by the people, for the people."

It is, therefore, not surprising that the Bell System gives the best and cheapest telephone service to be found anywhere in the world.

"BELL SYSTEM"
AMERICAN TELEPHONE AND TELEGRAPH COMPANY
AND ASSOCIATED COMPANIES
One Policy, One System, Universal Service, and all directed toward Better Service

158

important is the fact that those companies with strong positive corporate images may have an advantage over competitors that may be enhanced by promoting the company overall.

2. Corporate image advertising takes advantage of the benefits to be derived from engaging in public relations. As the public relations efforts of firms have increased, the attention paid to these events by the media has lessened. (Not because they are of any less value, but rather because there are more events to cover.) The net result is that when a company engages in a public relations effort, there is no guarantee that it will receive press coverage and publicity. Corporate image advertising will get the message out, and though it may not be exactly the same as reading it from an objective source, the fact remains that what has been done can be communicated.

3. Corporate image advertising reaches a very different target market. Corporate image advertising is not—and should not always be—targeted to the general public. It is a special form of communication that may be targeted to a select group or target market. Quite often, corporate image advertising is targeted to investors and managers of other firms rather than to the general public. As such, it is not critical if everyone does not like or appreciate this form of communication, so long as the target market does. In this respect, this form of advertising may very well be accomplishing its objectives.

Some of the disadvantages of corporate advertising were alluded to earlier in this chapter. To these criticisms, we can add the following.

1. *Questionable effectiveness* There is no strong evidence to support the fact that corporate advertising works. Despite the data cited earlier that demonstrated a corre-

lation between stock prices and corporate image advertising, many believe that this correlation may have little meaning. For example, a study by Bozell & Jacobs Advertising of 16,000 ads concluded that corporate advertising contributed to only 4 percent of the variability in the company's stock price, compared with a 55 percent effect attributable to financial factors.[19] A second study also casts doubts on earlier studies that concluded that corporate advertising worked.[20]

2. *The constitutionality and/or ethics*   Some critics contend that since larger firms have more monies, they can control public opinion and that this is unfair and unethical. This point was briefly mentioned earlier and in fact was resolved in the courts in favor of the advertisers. Nevertheless, there are many who still see such advertising as unfair and immediately take a negative view of the sponsor.

As you can see, a number of valid points have been offered in support of arguments for and against corporate advertising. Two things are certain: (1) There is no definite conclusion as to who is right in this instance, and (2) the fact remains that this communications form continues to be on the increase.

Measuring the Effectiveness of Corporate Advertising

As you no doubt can tell from our discussion on the controversy and conflicting opinions surrounding corporate advertising, there needs to be some method for determining whether or not such advertising is effective. In this section we will focus our attention on how such evaluations might be made.

• *Attitude surveys*   One method of determining the effectiveness of corporate advertising is conducting attitude surveys to gain insights into both the public's and investors' reactions to ads. The "Phase II" study conducted by Yankelovitch, Skelly & White (a market research firm in New York) is perhaps one of the best known applications of this measurement method.[21] In this study the firm measured recall and attitudes toward corporate advertisers, and reported that corporate advertising is more efficient in building recall for a company name than is product advertising alone. In addition, frequent corporate advertisers rated better than those with low corporate ad budgets on virtually all attitude measures.

• *Studies relating corporate advertising and stock prices*   The Bozell & Jacobs study reported on earlier is one of a number of studies that have examined the effect of various elements of corporate advertising (for example, position in the magazine, source effects, etc.) on stock prices. As we reported earlier, there have been conflicting conclusions resulting from these studies, indicating that while the model for such measures seems logical, methodological problems may be accounting for at least some of the discrepancies.

• *Focus group research*   Focus groups have been used both before and after the development of corporate advertisements to gain insights into what investors want to see in ads and their reactions after such ads have been developed. As with product-oriented advertising, this method also has its limitations, although it does allow for some effective measurements.

In sum, measuring the effectiveness of corporate advertising has employed some of the methods used to measure product-specific advertising. At the same time, research in this area has not kept pace with that of the consumer market (one study reported that only 35 of the Fortune 500 companies ever attempted to measure performance of their annual reports).[22] While a number of reasons have been cited for this lack of effort, the most commonly offered is the fact that corporate ads are often the responsibility of those in the highest management positions in the firm, and these parties do not wish to be held accountable. Interestingly, those who should be most concerned with accountability are the ones most likely to shun this responsibility!

Summary

Throughout this chapter, we have examined the role of the promotional elements of public relations, publicity, and corporate image advertising. In each case we noted that these areas are all of significant importance to the marketing and communications effort and that they are usually considered in a different way than the other promotional elements. The reasons for this special treatment stem from the fact that, first, they are typically not designed to promote a specific product or service and, second, because in many instances it may be harder for the consumer to make the association between the communication and its intent.

Public relations was shown to be useful in respect to traditional responsibilities, as well as in a more marketing-oriented role. In many firms, public relations is a separate department operating independently of marketing, whereas in others it is considered a support system. Many large firms may have an external public relations agency, just as they have an outside advertising agency.

In the case of publicity, another factor enters the equation—the lack of control as to the communication that the public will receive. In the areas of public relations and corporate image advertising, the source remains the organization, and much more control is afforded. Dealing with publicity is often more of a reactive than a proactive approach. The effects of publicity may be more instrumental or detrimental to the success of a product or organization than all other forms of promotion combined.

While all publicity cannot be managed, the marketer must nevertheless recognize its potential impact. Publicity releases and the management of information are just two of the factors under the control of management. At the same time, proper reaction and strategy relating to uncontrollable events are also responsibilities that must be dealt with.

Corporate advertising was described as being controversial. Much of this stems from the fact that because the source of the message in this form of communication is top management, the rules that are applied to other advertising and promotion forms are often not used. This element of communication definitely has its place in the promotional mix. However, to be effective it must be used with each of the other elements, with specific communications objectives in mind.

Finally, it was noted that measures of evaluation and control are required for each of these program elements as they are for all others in the promotional mix. We have presented some methods for taking such measurements and some evidence as to why it is important to use them. As long as the elements of public relations, publicity, and corporate image advertising are considered an integral component of the overall communications strategy, they must respect the same rules as the other elements to ensure success.

Key Terms

Public relations
Internal audiences
External audiences
Press release
Exclusive
Team approach

Internal audits
External audits
Publicity
Corporate advertising
Advocacy advertising

Discussion Questions

1. Discuss the role of public relations in the promotional mix.
2. Discuss the difference between the "traditional" role of public relations and the "new" role.

3. Explain the difference between public relations and publicity. In what ways are they the same?
4. Why is publicity so powerful? Give examples of how publicity has worked for and against companies.
5. How can a manager manage publicity? What are some of the things that can be done in response to negative publicity?
6. What is corporate advertising? How does it differ from product-oriented advertising?
7. What are the various forms that corporate advertising might assume? Give examples of each.
8. What can be done to measure the effects of public relations programs?
9. Why is corporate advertising controversial?
10. In the chapter, we mentioned Exxon's reaction to the Alaskan oil spill. Using the concepts presented in this chapter, discuss some of the things that Exxon might have done to remedy the negative publicity generated.

Notes

1. Adapted from Patricia Winters, "Oprah's Loss Is Optifast's Gain as Sales Soar," *Advertising Age,* December 12, 1988, p. 62.
2. Raymond Simon, *Public Relations, Concept and Practices,* 2nd ed. (Columbus, Ohio: Grid Publishing, 1980), p. 8.
3. Philip Kotler and William Mindak, "Marketing and Public Relations," *Journal of Marketing* 42 (October 1978), pp. 13–20.
4. Simon, *Public Relations,* p. 164.
5. Bob Donath, "Corporate Communications," *Industrial Marketing,* July 1980, pp. 53–57.
6. John E. Marston, *Modern Public Relations* (New York: McGraw-Hill, 1979).
7. Joe Agnew, "Marketers Find the Antidrug Campaign Addictive," *Marketing News,* October 9, 1987, p. 12.
8. Raymond Simon, *Public Relations, Concepts and Practices,* 3rd ed. (New York: John Wiley & Sons, 1984), p. 291.
9. Harold Mendelsohn, "Some Reasons Why Information Campaigns Can Succeed," *Public Opinion Quarterly,* Spring 1973, p. 55.
10. *Webster's Collegiate Dictionary,* 1989, p. 690.
11. Neil Cole, "How Scandal Helped No Excuses Sell Jeans," *Adweek,* January 16, 1989, pp. 52–53.
12. Joseph Bruillard, "Timely Messages," *Advertising Age,* August 29, 1983, p. M-30.
13. Jaye S. Niefeld, "Corporate Advertising," *Industrial Marketing,* July 1980, pp. 64–74.
14. Tom Garbett, "What Companies Project to Public," *Advertising Age,* July 6, 1981, p. 51.
15. Francis Houghton, "How Ads Can Sell More Than Products," *Nations Business,* March 1984, pp. 61–62.
16. *Adweek,* June 16, 1986, p. 39.
17. Ed Zotti, "An Expert Weighs the Prose and Yawns," *Advertising Age,* January 24, 1983, p. M-11.
18. Prakash Sethi, *Advertising and Large Corporations* (Lexington, Mass.: Lexington Books, 1977), pp. 7–8.
19. Niefeld, "Corporate Advertising," p. 64.
20. Donath, "Corporate Communications," p. 52.
21. Ibid., p. 53.
22. Ibid., p. 52.

18

Measuring the Effectiveness of the Promotional Program

CHAPTER OBJECTIVES

1. To discuss reasons for measuring advertising effectiveness

2. To examine the various dependent measures that are used in assessing advertising effectiveness

3. To evaluate alternative methods for conducting measures of advertising effectiveness

4. To review the requirements of conducting proper effectiveness research

Creatives versus Researchers—The Battlelines Are Drawn

All is not peaceful in the advertising community. The reason? The creative department blames it on the researchers. The researchers say the creatives have overenlarged egos. The basis for the argument is whether or not to conduct advertising research to guide development and measure the effectiveness of ads. Following are some of the opinions offered by both sides.

> Copy research stifles creativity and worse yet kills good ideas.

> Copy research protects our investment in advertising.

> Testing is forcing mediocrity because everyone is afraid to take risks.

> Business-school-ism has invaded not only the client offices but the research firms and agencies themselves. . . . The MBAs are in part responsible for the current analytical process that is sweeping away the creative people in their efforts to get down to the lowest common denominator.

The test commercial may cost $50,000, but if it is not a good commercial, we can save a firm millions.

We in the creative department don't want to be tested—we did that in high school and college. We want ideas, and we want research to bring us ideas.

Seventy-five percent of our research is "up-front" [input] and that's where it should be.

Seventy-five to 80 percent of ads never have any effect on sales. But clients are afraid of numbers and they don't want to know this. So we don't push it [measurements of effectiveness].

Look, we all know we should measure effectiveness. All of us except our clients. They think the money is better spent on media or creative. What am I to tell them?

Who will win this battle? It's difficult to say because arguments in support of both positions have merit. However, it is important that this issue be resolved so that more effective advertising can result.

Introduction

The quotations offered above demonstrate the controversy surrounding the measurement of the effectiveness of the promotional program. The source of these opinions is varied, coming from representatives of large and small firms and agencies from across the United States. As these quotes indicate, the camps have been formed—the creatives versus the researchers, the copywriters versus the marketers. Yet even though this controversy exists, both sides will agree that there is a value—even a necessity—to conducting research. The disagreement is not the need for advertising research; rather, it lies in the way such research is conducted and in how the results are used.

Measuring the effectiveness of the promotional program is a critical element in the promotional planning process. Research allows the marketing manager to evaluate the performance of specific program elements and provides input into the next period's situation analysis. It is a necessary ingredient to a continuing planning process and yet is a task that often is not carried out.

In this chapter we will discuss some reasons why firms should measure the effectiveness of their advertising and promotional programs and why many decide not to. In addition, we will examine how, when, and where such measurements can be conducted. Prior to beginning this discussion, however, it is important to understand that in this chapter we are concerned with research that is conducted in an evaluative role—that is, to measure the effectiveness of advertising and promotion and/or to assess various strategies prior to implementing them. This is not to be confused with research discussed earlier in this text that served as input into the development of the promotional program. While evaluative research may take place at various times throughout the promotional process (including the development stage), it is carried out with the specific purpose of assessing the effects of various strategies. Let us begin our discussion with the reasons why research to measure effectiveness should be conducted as well as some of the reasons why firms do not do so.

Arguments for and against Measuring Effectiveness

Almost any time one engages in a project or activity—whether for work or fun—some measure of performance takes place. For example, in sports you may compare your golf score against par, or when skiing, you may compare your time on a race course to others. In business, employees are generally given objectives to accomplish, and their job evaluations are based on their ability to achieve these objectives. Advertising and promotion should not be an exception to this rule. That is, it is important to determine how well the communications program is working and to measure this performance against some standards. Some of the reasons for taking such measures follow.

Reasons for Measuring Effectiveness

Assessing the effectiveness of advertisements both before they are implemented and after the final versions have been completed and fielded offers a number of advantages:

1. *Avoiding costly mistakes* The top three advertisers in the United States spent over $4 billion in advertising and promotion in 1989. The top 100 spent a total of over $30 billion. Obviously this is a lot of money to be throwing around without some understanding as to how well it is being spent. If the program is not achieving its objectives, the marketing manager would want to know so as not to continue to spend (waste!) money on it.

Just as important as the out-of-pocket costs discussed in the previous paragraph is the *opportunity* loss that accrues from a poor communications effort. If the advertising and promotions program is not accomplishing its objectives, not only is the money spent lost but so too is the potential gain that could result from an effective program. Thus, the value of measuring the effects of advertising might not be considered so much a savings of money as it is an opportunity to make money, as is so well demonstrated by Promotional Perspective 18–1.

2. *Evaluating alternative strategies* Typically a firm may have a number of alternative strategies under consideration. For example, there may be some question as to which medium should be used or whether one message is more effective than another. In another instance the decision may be between the use of two alternative promotional program elements. Research may be designed to assist the manager in determining which strategy is most likely to be effective and should be employed. For example, Coors often tests alternate versions of its advertising in different cities to determine which ad communicates most effectively.

3. *Increasing the efficiency of advertising in general* You may have heard the expression "Can't see the forest for the trees!" Sometimes advertisers get so close to the project that they lose sight of what it is they are seeking, and because they know what they are trying to say, they expect that their audience will also understand. They may use technical terms or jargon that they feel everyone is familiar with, when they are not. At other times the creative department may get too creative, or too sophisticated, losing the meaning that they need to communicate in the process. An added benefit of conducting research is the opportunity to develop more efficient and effective communications. As you can see, the reasons for evaluating communications are valid and somewhat obvious. But as you also saw in the lead-in to this chapter, not everyone agrees with the need to evaluate. The next section examines some of the reasons why.

Reasons Why Effectiveness Measures Are Not Used

A number of reasons for not measuring the effectiveness of advertising and promotions strategies are also offered.

1. *Cost* Perhaps the most commonly cited reason for not testing (particularly among smaller firms) is the expense associated with such efforts. To conduct good

Promotional Perspective 18–1

How Testing Saved a Bank Program

Recently, a bank with assets of over $1 billion and a strong community image of conservatism decided to initiate an innovative and somewhat risky checking and savings program. Because it would be the first in the market with this program, the bank would stand to gain a sizable market share, as well as enhance its image as the most innovative financial institution in the market. At the same time, because the program had the potential to be confusing to customers, the bank also was threatened with the potential for failure, not only with the program itself but also as a reflection on the bank's image.

After much planning and discussion, the marketing manager and program director decided on a program that they considered profitable to the bank and also attractive to the customer. The program was developed, and preliminary print advertisements and statement stuffers were developed.

In discussing the program with the institution's marketing consultants, some questions arose—both with the program itself and in the way that it was to be communicated. After much deliberation, all parties involved agreed to a pretest of both the communications prior to implementation.

To make a long story short, the decision to test was the correct one. While it cost the bank approximately $14,000 and delayed initiation by one month, the results demonstrated two important facts:

1. The advertisements and statement stuffers designed to communicate the program were difficult to understand and would not have accomplished the objectives intended.
2. Not only was the advertising flawed, but the program as it was designed was virtually unattractive to the target market and would have attracted few investors.

The initial month's newspaper advertising alone would have cost the bank approximately $62,000, and the program—had it failed initially—would not have been recoverable. As you can see, both out-of-pocket and opportunity costs warranted the investment in research (and may have saved a few jobs in the process!).

---

research can be expensive, both in terms of time and money. As a result, many managers decide that time is critical and they must implement the program while the opportunity is available. Second, many managers will explain that they feel that the monies spent on research could be better spent on improved production of the ad, additional media buys, and the like, and elect to allocate their budgets to these priorities rather than testing and evaluation.

The fact is that while the former of these arguments may have some merit, there is very little in the second. Imagine what would happen if a poor campaign were developed, or if the incentive program did not motivate the targeted audience. Not only would you be spending money without the desired effects, but the effort could possibly do more harm than good. Spending more money to buy media will not remedy a poor message nor substitute for an improper promotional mix. For example, one of the nation's leading brewers watched its test-market sales for a new brand of beer fall short of expectations and decided that more media time was the answer. The solution, it thought, was to buy all the television time available in the market for December and January so long as it matched its target audience. At the end of January, sales had not improved at all. Upon final analysis—the product was abandoned in the test market—it was determined that the problem was not in the media at all but rather in the message, as no reason to buy was communicated. In this case, research would have identified the problem, and millions of dollars and a brand might have been saved. The moral of this story is that spending monies that might have been used for research to gain increased exposure to the wrong message is not a sound management decision.

2. *Research problems* A second reason cited for not measuring effectiveness is that it is very difficult to isolate the effects of advertising. As you know, each of the marketing mix variables will impact the success of a product or service. Because it is not always possible to measure the contribution of each marketing element directly, some managers become frustrated and decide not to test at all. Their argument is one of, "If I can't determine the specific effects, why spend the money?"

Figure 18–1 Chiat Day Expresses Its Feelings toward Testing

This argument also suffers from weak logic. While we agree that it may not always be possible to determine that the contribution made by promotions is an exact dollar or sales amount, proper employment of research can provide useful results.

3. *Disagreement as to what to test* The objectives sought in the promotional program may differ by industry, by stage of the product life cycle, or even for different people within the firm. The sales manager may want to see the impact that promotions has on sales, top management may wish to know the impact on corporate image, whereas those involved in the creative process may wish to assess recall and/or recognition of the advertisement. The lack of agreement as to what to test often results in no testing at all.

Again, there is little rationale for this position. With the proper design, many, if not all, of the above might be measured. Since every promotional element is designed to accomplish its own objectives, there is no reason why research cannot be used to measure their effectiveness in doing so.

4. *The objections of creative* It has been argued by many—and denied by others—that the creative department does not want its work to be tested and that many agencies are reluctant to have their work submitted for testing. The fact is that this is both true and false. Members of advertising agencies' creative departments will often agree that they do not wish to be evaluated on the creative aspects of ads. Their arguments are that the tests are not true measures of the creativity and effectiveness of the ads; that applying measures will stifle their creativity; and that the more creative the ad, the more likely it is to be successful. They argue that they should be allowed to be creative and not subject to the limiting guidelines that marketing may impose. The advertisement run by the Chiat Day Advertising Agency shown in Figure 18–1 reflects how many of those in the advertising business feel about this subject.

At the same time, the marketing manager is ultimately responsible for the success of the product or brand. Given the substantial dollar amounts being allocated to advertising and promotion, the burden for the proper use of these monies is part of the job requirements he or she is expected to perform. It is the manager's right, and responsibility, to know how well a specific program—or a specific advertisement—will perform in the market. As such he or she is ultimately responsible to ensure that measures of effectiveness are employed.

Conducting Research to Measure Effectiveness

We will now turn our discussion to the examination of how to measure communications effects. More specifically, this section will consider what elements to evaluate, as well as where and how such evaluations should take place.

What to Test

In Chapter 5 we discussed the components of the communications model (source, message, media, receiver) and the importance of understanding the role of each in the promotional program. Given the importance placed on the understanding of these factors, it follows that it is necessary to determine how each is impacting the communications process. In addition, other decisions that must be made in the promotional planning process must also be evaluated.

Source Factors   An important question to be asked is whether or not the spokesperson who is being used is effective and how the target market will respond to him or her. For example, John McEnroe, considered by many to be the obnoxious "bad boy" of tennis because of his sometimes abrasive on-court antics, proved to be an extremely successful spokesperson for Dunlop, Nike, and Bic. Or, as often happens, a product spokesperson may be an excellent source initially but, owing to a variety of reasons, may lose impact over time. For example, as you can see in Figure 18–2, Bill Cosby is a spokesperson for the city of Reno. At one time or another, he has also been a representative for Ford, Jell-O, Kodak, and E. F. Hutton, among others—which might bring his credibility into question (as discussed in Chapter 6). In other instances, characteristics of the source (changes in attractiveness or likability) or other external factors may lead to changes in source effectiveness.

Message Variables   Both the message and the means by which this message is being communicated constitute bases for evaluation. For example, in the brewery's new product entry example discussed earlier, it was stated that the message never provided a reason for the consumer to try the new product. In other instances, the message may not be strong enough to "pull readers into the ad" by attracting their attention, or clear enough to be used to make an evaluation. A number of factors regarding the message and its delivery may have an impact on its effectiveness, including the headline, illustrations, text, and layout.

Many ads are made that never get to be seen by the public because of the message they convey. For example, a Susan Anton ad in which she was eating a piece of Pizza Hut pizza was considered too erotic for the company's small-town image. Likewise, an ad created for General Electric (GE) in which Uncle Sam gets slapped in the face (to demonstrate our growing trade imbalance) was killed by the company's chairman.[1]

Media Strategies   Just as there are a number of media decisions to be made, there is also a need to evaluate these decisions. Research may need to be designed to determine which media class (for example, broadcast versus print), subclass (newspaper ver-

Figure 18—2 **Bill Cosby Is Spokesperson for a Number of Companies**

sus magazines), or specific vehicles (which newspapers or magazines) generate the most effective results. In addition, the location within a particular medium (front page versus back page) and size or length of time of the ad or commercial merit examination. For example, Figure 18–3 demonstrates that by choosing a larger ad, reader attention to that ad will increase. Similarly, those involved in direct-response advertising on television have found that it is more effective to advertise on some programs than on others. As noted by one successful direct-marketing advertiser who found that old television shows yield more responses than first runs:

> The fifth rerun of "Leave It to Beaver" will generate much more response than will the first run of a prime-time television program. Who cares if you miss something you have seen four times before? But you do care when it's the first time you've seen it.[2]

Another factor that must be considered is that of the **vehicle option source effect.** The vehicle option source effect is "the differential impact that the advertising exposure will have on the same audience member if the exposure occurs in one media option rather than another."[3] There are differences in the way persons perceive ads that result from the context in which the ad appears.[4,5]

A final factor to be considered with respect to media decisions is that involving scheduling. The evaluation of flighting versus pulsing or continuous schedules is an important one to consider, particularly given the increasing costs of media time. Likewise, there may be opportunities associated with increasing advertising weights in periods of downward sales cycles or recessions. The manager experimenting with these alternative schedules and/or budget outlays should attempt to measure the differential impact that may result.[6]

Budgeting Decisions A number of studies have been conducted that have examined the effects of budget size on advertising effectiveness and the effects of various ad

Figure 18–3 **The Relationship between Ad Size and Reader Attention**

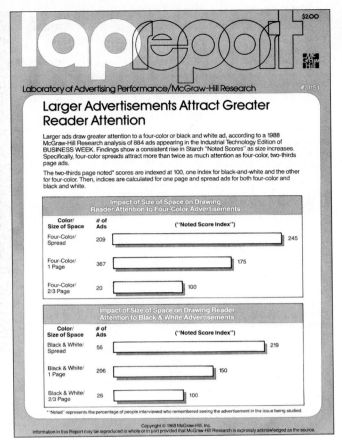

expenditures on sales. For example, a number of companies have attempted to determine if increasing their ad budget will directly impact sales. The results of these studies have shown that this relationship is often hard to determine. Much of this difficulty may be due to the fact that sales is often used as an indicator of effectiveness. More definitive conclusions may be possible if other dependent variables—such as the communications objectives stated earlier—are used.

When to Test

Virtually all test measures can be classified according to the time in which they are conducted. **Pretests** are those measures taken prior to the implementation of the campaign, whereas **posttests,** of course, take place after the ad or commercial has been in the field. A variety of pretests and posttests are available to the marketer, each with its own methodology designed to measure some aspect of the advertising program. Figure 18–4 provides a good classification scheme and categorization of these various testing methods.

Pretesting Pretests may take place at a number of points of time, from as early on as idea generation to rough execution to testing the final version prior to implementing it. In addition, more than one type of pretest may be used. For example, concept testing (which will be discussed later in this chapter) may take place at the very earliest development of the ad or commercial. At this point, little more than an idea, basic concept, or positioning statement may be under consideration. In other instances, layouts of the ad campaign including headlines, some body copy, and rough illustra-

Figure 18–4 Classification of Testing Methods

	Advertising-Related Test (reception or response to the message itself and its contents)	**Product-Related Test** (impact of message on product awareness, liking, intention to buy, or use)

Laboratory Measures (respondent aware of testing and measurement process)	**Cell I**
	
	Pretesting procedures
	
	1. Consumer jury
	2. Portfolio tests
	3. Readability tests
	4. Physiological measures
	    Eye Camera
	    Tachistoscope
	    GSR/PDR
		Cell II
		
		Pretesting procedures
		
		1. Theater tests
		2. Trailer tests
		3. Laboratory stores

Real-World Measures (respondent unaware of testing and measurement process)	**Cell III** Pretesting procedures 1. Dummy advertising vehicles 2. Inquiry tests 3. On-the-air tests Posttesting procedures 1. Recognition tests 2. Recall tests 3. Association measures 4. Combination measures	**Cell IV** Pretesting and posttesting procedures 1. Prepost tests 2. Sales tests 3. Minimarket tests

Source: Adapted from the classification schema utilized by Ivan Ross at the University of Minnesota, in Engel, Warshaw, and Kinnear, *Promotional Strategy,* 6th ed. (Homewood, Ill.: Richard D. Irwin, 1987), p. 407.

tions may be used. For television commercials, storyboards and animatics may be tested.

The methodologies employed to conduct pretests may vary. Focus groups are often employed in which participants freely discuss the meanings they get from the ads, consider the relative advantages of alternatives, and even suggest improvements or additional themes. Sometimes in addition to the focus groups—or as an alternative—participants are asked to evaluate the ad on a series of rating scales. Different agencies may use their own set of measures, and in-home interviews, mall intercept, or laboratory methods may be used to gather the data.

The advantage of pretesting at this stage is to gain feedback at a relatively inexpensive cost. Thus, any problems with the concept or the way it is to be delivered are identified, without having spent large amounts of money in development. Sometimes, more than one version of the ad is evaluated to determine which is most likely to be effective.

The disadvantage, of course, is that the final product may be much more effective in communicating than are the mock-ups, storyboards, or animatics. The mood-enhancing and/or emotional aspects of the message will be very difficult to communicate in this format. Another disadvantage often cited is that of time delays. Many marketers feel that to be first in the market offers them a distinct advantage over competitors. Thus, they will forego research in order to save time and ensure this position.

Posttesting   Posttesting is also a common practice among both advertisers and ad agencies (with the exception of testing commercials for wearout). Table 18–1 presents the results of a study that examined ad agency and advertisers' use of various advertising research methods. As can be seen, the percentage of organizations that evaluate

Table 18–1   **General Findings Regarding Copy Research**

	Total		Agencies		Advertisers	
	No.	%	No.	%	No.	%
Total respondents	*112*	*100.0*	*39*	*100.0*	*73*	*100.0*
Undertake preliminary, background, or strategic research in preparation for advertising campaigns	104	92.9	39	100.0	65	89.0
Evaluate copy ideas, storyboards, other formats prior to rough commercial	85	75.9	34	87.2	51	69.9
Evaluate rough commercial execution of other formats prior to finished commercial	102	91.1	38	97.4	64	87.7
Evaluate finished commercials	105	93.8	35	89.7	70	95.9
Evaluation of television campaigns	98	87.5	37	94.9	61	83.6
Test competitive commercials	73	65.2	27	69.2	46	63.0
Test commercials for wearout	29	25.9	9	23.1	20	27.4

Source: Benjamin Lipstein and James P. Neelankavil, "Television Advertising Copy Research: A Critical Review of the State of the Art," *Journal of Advertising Research* 24, no. 2 (April/May 1984), p. 21.

finished commercials and TV campaigns is very high. Posttesting is designed to perform two roles: (1) to determine if the campaign is accomplishing the objectives sought; and (2) to serve as input into the next period's situation analysis. As with pretests, a variety of posttest measures are available, most of which involve survey research methods.

Where to Test

In addition to considering when to test, decisions must be made with respect to *where* these tests should take place. As was shown in Figure 18–4, these tests may take place in either laboratory or field settings.

Laboratory Tests   **Laboratory tests** are those in which persons are brought to a particular location where they are shown ads and/or commercials and either asked questions about them or have their responses measured by other methods—for example, pupil dilation, eye tracking, or galvanic response measures.

    The major advantage of the lab setting is the *control* that it affords the researcher. Changes in copy, illustration, formats, colors, and the like, can easily be manipulated at a small cost, with the differential impact of each assessed. Thus, it becomes much easier for the researcher to isolate the contribution that each factor makes.

    The major disadvantage is the lack of *realism*. Perhaps the greatest effect of this lack of realism is a **testing bias.** When people are brought into a lab—even if it has been designed to look like a living room—they know they are to be tested. As a result, they may feel that they have to be sensitive to the ads and scrutinize them to a much greater degree than they typically might, given a more natural setting. In this case, "everyone becomes an expert." A second problem with this lack of realism is the fact that the *natural viewing situation*—complete with distractions or comforts of the home—is not duplicated. Sitting in a lab setting may not be the same as viewing at home on the couch, with the wife/husband and kids, dog, cat, and parakeet chirping in the background. (A bit later you will see that some testing techniques have made substantial progress in correcting this deficiency—no, they did not bring in the dogs and the parakeets!) Overall, however, the control offered by this method probably outweighs the disadvantages, which accounts for the frequent use of lab methods.

Field Tests   **Field tests** are tests of the ad or commercial under natural viewing situations. In this testing format the realism that is not present with lab methods is available, as are all the factors cited above (distractions, comforts, noise). In addition, the effects of repetition, program content, and even the presence of competitive messages are brought into consideration.

Table 18—2   **Positioning Advertising Copy Testing (PACT)**

1. Provide measurements that are relevant to the objectives of the advertising
2. Require agreement about how the results will be used in advance of each specific test
3. Provide multiple measurements (because single measurements are not adequate to assess ad performance)
4. Be based on a model of human response to communications—the reception of a stimulus, the comprehension of the stimulus, and the response to the stimulus
5. Allow for consideration of whether the advertising stimulus should be exposed more than once
6. Recognize that the more finished a piece of copy is, the more soundly it can be evaluated and requires, as a minimum, that alternative executions be tested in the same degree of finish
7. Provide controls to avoid the biasing effects of the exposure context
8. Take into account basic considerations of sample definition
9. Demonstrate reliability and validity

Source: "Ad Agencies Endorse Copy Testing Principles," *Marketing News,* vol. xv, 17, February 19, 1982, p. 1.

The major disadvantage of field tests is the lack of control, as it may be difficult or impossible to isolate causes of viewers' evaluations. Events that might not normally be operating may be present during the test, biasing the results. Competitors may learn of the research and attempt to sabotage it, and field tests usually take more time and money to conduct, so the results are not as quickly available to be acted upon. Thus, while realism is gained, it is gained at the expense of other important factors. It is up to the researcher to determine which trade-offs will be required.

How to Test

To this point we have discussed some of the factors that should be tested, as well as where and when this testing would take place. This discussion was very general in nature and was designed to establish a basic understanding of the overall process as well as some key terms. In this section we will be more specific in discussing some of the more commonly used methods employed at each stage. Prior to engaging in this discussion, however, it is important to establish some criteria upon which advertisements and commercials should be judged.

Conducting evaluative research is not an easy process. Nevertheless, some standards are considered necessary, and in 1982, 21 of the United States' largest advertising agencies endorsed a set of principles aimed at "improving the research used in preparing and testing ads, providing a better creative product for clients, and controlling the cost of TV commercials."[7] This set of nine principles, called **PACT (Positioning Advertising Copy Testing),** defines *copy testing* as research "which is undertaken when a decision is to be made about whether advertising should run in the marketplace. Whether this stage utilizes a single test or a combination of tests, its purpose is to aid in the judgment of specific advertising executions."[8] The nine principles determined to define a good copy testing are shown in Table 18—2.

As you can see by this list of principles, advertisers and their clients have expressed a concern for developing *appropriate* testing methods. Adherence to the principles included here might not make for perfect testing methods, but it would go a long way toward improving the state of the art and would help alleviate at least one of the arguments cited earlier for not testing. Having established the guidelines for good testing procedures, let us now turn our attention to how such testing takes place.

The Testing Process

Testing may take place at various points throughout the development of the advertisement or advertising campaign. This research may be of the following types: (1) con-

Table 18–3   **Concept Testing**

Objective:	A concept test is designed to explore consumers' responses to various ad concepts as expressed in words, pictures, or symbols.
Method:	Alternative concepts are exposed to consumers who match the characteristics of the target audience. Reactions and evaluations of each are sought through a variety of methods including focus groups, direct questioning, and survey completion. Sample sizes will vary depending on the number of concepts to be presented and the consensus of responses.
Output:	Output consists of qualitative and/or quantitative data evaluating and comparing alternative concepts.

cept generation research, (2) rough, prefinished art, copy, and/or commercial testing, (3) finished art or commercial pretesting, and (4) market testing of ads or commercials (posttesting).

Concept Generation and Testing

Table 18–3 describes the process involved in advertising **concept testing.** Concept testing is conducted at a very early stage in the campaign development process, with the primary objective of exploring the targeted consumer's response to a potential ad or campaign to having the consumer evaluate advertising alternatives. Positioning statements, copy, headlines, and/or illustrations may all be under scrutiny. The material to be evaluated may be as simple as a single headline or may involve a rough drawing or sketch of the advertisement. In addition, elements such as the colors used, print type, package designs, and even p-o-p materials may be evaluated.

The methods employed for concept testing may vary. One of the more commonly used is that of focus groups. These focus groups usually consist of 8 to 10 persons considered to be in the target market for the product. For example, in testing new concepts for Jell-O gelatin, Young & Rubicam assessed reactions of mothers and children (the mothers being the buyers; the children, the ultimate consumers). The number of groups to be used will vary, depending on group consensus, strength of response, and/or the degree to which participants like or dislike the concepts. It is not at all unusual for a number of groups to be employed (some companies report using as many as 50 or more to develop the campaign), although usually less than 10 are required to test a concept sufficiently.

While focus groups continue to be a favorite methodology used by marketers, the fact is that they are often overused. Weaknesses with focus groups—as shown in Table 18–4—demonstrate that there are appropriate and inappropriate circumstances in which this methodology should be employed.

Another way of gathering consumers' opinions of concepts is the use of mall intercepts in which consumers in shopping malls are approached and asked to evaluate rough ads and/or copy. Rather than participating in a group discussion, individual assessments are gathered through the use of questionnaires, rating scales, and/or rankings.

Table 18–4   **Weaknesses Associated with Focus Group Research**

- The results are not quantifiable.
- Sample sizes are too small to generalize to larger populations.
- Group influences may bias participants' responses.
- One or two members of the group may steer the conversation or dominate the discussion.
- Consumers become instant "experts."
- Members may not represent the target market (are focus group participants a certain type of person?).
- Results may be taken to be more representative and/or definitive than they really are.

Table 18−5   **Rough Testing Terminology**

A rough commercial is an unfinished execution that may fall into three broad categories:

Animatic roughs
  Succession of drawings/cartoons
  Rendered artwork
  Still-frames
  Simulated movement:
    Panning/zooming of frame/rapid
      sequence
	Live-action rough
	  Live motion
	  Stand-in/nonunion talent
	  Nonunion crew
	  Limited props/minimal opticals
	  Location settings

Photomatic roughs
  Succession of photographs
  Real people/scenery
  Still-frames
  Simulated movements:
    Panning/zooming of frame/rapid
      sequence
	Finished
	  Live motion/animation
	  Highly paid union talent
	  Full union crew
	  Exotic props/studio sets/special effects

Source: "Burke Rough Commercial Recall Testing," Burke Market Research, 1988.

Rough, Prefinished Art, Copy, and/or Commercial Testing

Because of the high cost associated with the production of an ad or commercial (many network commercials cost in the hundreds of thousands of dollars to produce), advertisers are increasingly spending more monies testing at early stages where only a rendering of the final ad is evaluated. Slide photographs of the art work posted on a screen, kinematics (video tapes of commercial storyboards), and animatics have all been used to test at this stage. (See Table 18−5 for an explanation of terminology.) Because such tests can be conducted for about $3,000, the use of research at this stage is becoming ever more popular.

The cost of the test, of course, is only one factor to be considered. The test is of little or no value—regardless of how inexpensive it is—if it does not provide relevant and accurate information. Thus, rough tests must provide an indication of how the finished commercial would perform. Some studies have demonstrated that the *reliability* of these testing methods is favorable and that the results do typically correlate very well with the finished ad.[9,10]

Most of the tests conducted at the prefinished stage involve lab settings, although some on-air field tests are also available. Some of those more commonly employed include:

1. *Comprehension and reaction tests* One of the key factors of concern to the advertiser is whether or not the ad or commercial conveys the meaning intended. The second item of concern is the reaction that the advertisement generates. Obviously, the advertiser does not wish to put forth an advertisement that evokes a negative reaction or is offensive to someone. **Tests of comprehension and reaction** are designed to assess these responses. (Which makes you wonder why some ads are ever brought to the marketplace!)

Tests of comprehension and reaction employ no one standard procedure. Personal interviews, group interviews, and focus groups have all been used for this purpose, and sample sizes have varied according to the needs of the client, although it is very rare for less than 50 or more than 200 respondents to be tested.

2. *Consumer juries* Using consumers representative of the target market to evaluate the probable success of an ad is the basis of this method. Members of the group may be asked to rate or rank order a selection of layouts or copy versions presented in paste ups on separate sheets. (The verdict is the final outcome!) The objectives sought and methods employed in **consumer juries** are shown in Table 18−6, whereas an example of some questions asked of jurists is shown in Table 18−7.[11]

While the jury method offers the advantages of *control* and *cost-effectiveness*, there are some serious flaws in the methodology that limit its usefulness. For example:

Table 18–6   **Consumer Juries**

Objective:	Potential viewers (consumers) are asked to evaluate ads and to give their reactions to and evaluation of them. When two or more ads are tested, viewers will usually be asked to rate or rank order the ads according to their preferences.
Method:	Respondents are asked to view ads and rate or rank them according to two methods: (1) the order of merit method or (2) the paired comparisons method. In the former, the respondent is asked to view the ads, then rank them from one to *n* according to their perceived merit. In the latter, ads are compared only two at a time, with each ad being compared to every other ad in the group, and the winner listed. The best ad is that which wins the most times. Consumer juries typically employ 50 to 100 participants.
Output:	An overall reaction to each ad under consideration as well as a rank ordering of the ads based on the viewers' perceptions.

- *The consumer may become a self-appointed expert.* One of the benefits sought from the jury method is the *objectivity* and *involvement* in the product or service that the targeted consumer can bring into the evaluation process. It is possible, however, that knowing that they are being asked to critique advertisements the participants try to become more *expert* in their evaluations—paying more attention and being more critical than they might typically be. The result may be a less-than-objective evaluation and/or a potential for evaluation on other elements than those sought.

- *The number of ads that can be evaluated is limited.* Whether *order of merit* or *paired comparison methods* are used, the ranking procedure becomes very involving and tedious as the number of alternatives under consideration increases. For example, consider the ranking of 10 ads. While the top two and the bottom two ranked may very well reveal differences, those ranked in the middle may not really yield much discriminating information. In the paired comparison method, the number of evaluations required can easily be calculated by the formula

$$\frac{n(n-1)}{2}$$

So in a situation where six alternatives were to be considered, a total of 15 evaluations would have to be made. As the number of ads increases, the task would become even more unmanageable.

- *A halo effect is possible.* Sometimes participants may rate an ad good on all characteristics because they like a few and overlook specific weaknesses or bad attributes. This tendency, called the **halo effect,** distorts the rankings or ratings and defeats one of the values offered—the ability to control for specific components. (Of course, the reverse may also occur, that is, rating an ad bad overall due to only a few bad attributes.)

- *Preferences for specific types of advertising may overshadow objectivity.* Ads that involve emotions or pictures may receive higher ratings or rankings than those employing copy, facts, and/or rational criteria. Thus, even though the latter form may prove to be more effective in the marketplace, they may be judged less favorably by the jurists if these persons prefer the former types of ads.

Table 18–7   **Questions Asked in a Consumer Jury Test**

1. Which of these advertisements would you most likely read if you saw it in a magazine?
2. Which of these headlines would interest you the most in reading the ad further?
3. Which advertisement convinces you most of the quality or superiority of the product?
4. Which layout do you think would be most effective in causing you to buy?
5. Which advertisement did you like best?
6. Which advertisement did you find most interesting?

Table 18−8   **Reflections: Burke Marketing Research's Print Test**

Objective:	A test designed to measure recall and reader's impressions of print advertisements.
Method:	Mall intercepts in two or more cities are used to screen respondents and have them take home "test magazines" for reading. Participants are phoned the next day to determine opinions of the ads, recall of ad contents, and other questions of interest to the sponsor. Approximately 225 persons constitute the sample.
Output:	Scores reported include related recall of copy and visual elements, sales messages, and other nonspecific elements. Both quantitative (table) scores and verbatim responses are reported.

Some of the problems noted here can be remedied by the use of *ratings scales* versus rankings. However, ratings are also not always valid, suffering from many of the problems noted above. Thus, while consumer juries have been used for a number of years, and are still frequently employed, questions of bias have led researchers to question the validity of this method. As a result a variety of other methods (to be discussed later in this chapter) are more commonly employed.

Pretesting Finished Ads

As shown in Table 18−1, this stage of testing has received the most attention and participation among marketing researchers and their agencies. At this stage a finished advertisement or commercial is used; however, it has not been presented to the market. As a result, it is still possible to make changes prior to fielding.

Many researchers prefer to test at this stage since the ad is in final form—which they feel provides a better test—and yet still has not been seen by the target market. A variety of test procedures are available for both print and broadcast ads, including both laboratory and field methodologies.

Print methods include the use of portfolio tests, analyses of readability, and the use of dummy advertising vehicles. Broadcast tests include theater tests and on-air tests, whereas both print and broadcast may use physiological measures. A discussion of each and identification of some of the firms providing such services follow.

Pretesting Finished Print Messages A number of methods for pretesting finished print ads are available, one of which is **Burke's Reflections test** described in Table 18−8. While a number of different measures may be used, only the most commonly employed of these methods are discussed here.

Portfolio tests This laboratory methodology is designed to expose a group of respondents to a portfolio consisting of both control and test advertisements. Having viewed the portfolio, respondents are asked to indicate what information they recall from the ads. The assumption is that the ads that yield the *highest recall* will be the most effective.

While **portfolio tests** offer the opportunity to compare the alternative ads under consideration directly, a number of weaknesses with this method may limit its applicability. These include the following.

1. Factors other than advertising creativity and/or presentation may be affecting recall. Interest in the product or product category, the fact that respondents know that they are participating in a test, or interviewer instructions (among others) may account for more differences than the ad itself.
2. Recall may not be the best test. Some researchers argue that for certain types of products—those of low involvement—recognition (ability to recognize the ad

when shown) may be a better measure than recall. Thus, by using recall erroneous results might occur.

One way of determining the validity of this method would be to correlate results obtained by the portfolio method with readership scores obtained once the product has been placed in the field. Whether such validity tests are being conducted or not is not readily known, although the use of portfolio methods does continue to remain popular in the industry.

Readability tests   A test of the communications efficiency of the copy in a print ad is possible without ever actually conducting an interview with a potential reader. This test uses a formula known as the **Flesch formula,** named after its developer, Rudolph Flesch. In the formula, readability of the copy is assessed by determining the average number of syllables per 100 words. Human interest appeal in the material, length of sentences, and familiarity with certain words are also taken into consideration and correlated with the educational background of targeted audiences. Previously established norms for various target audiences have been established and serve as a basis for comparison. The test suggests that copy is most comprehended when sentences are short, words are concrete and familiar, and personal references are drawn.

The advantage of this method, of course, is the fact that many of the interviewee biases associated with other tests are eliminated. Second, gross errors in understanding can be avoided. Finally, the fact that norms have been established offer an attractive standard for comparison.

Disadvantages are also inherent, however. The copy may become too mechanical, and the direct input of the receiver is not available. Without this input, other contributing elements, such as creativity, cannot be addressed. To be effective, therefore, this test should only be used in conjunction with other pretesting methods. (Did we use short sentences, concrete and familiar words, and frequent personal references?)

Dummy advertising vehicles   An improvement on the portfolio test is a methodology in which ads are placed in "dummy" magazines developed by an agency or research firm. The magazines contain regular editorial features of interest to the reader, as well as the test ads, and are distributed to a *random sample* of homes in predetermined geographic areas. Readers are instructed that the magazine publisher is interested in evaluations of editorial contents and that they are to read the magazines as they normally would. Having completed this task, readers are interviewed on both the editorial contents and their reactions to the ads. Recall, readership, and interest-generating capabilities of the advertisement are assessed.

The advantage of this method is that it provides a more natural setting than does the portfolio test. Readership takes place in the participant's own home, the test more closely approximates a natural reading situation, and the reader may go back to the magazine—as they might typically do.

At the same time, the same disadvantages associated with portfolio tests are inherent here. The testing effect is not completely eliminated, and product interest may still bias the results. Thus, while this test methodology offers some advantages over the portfolio method, it is not a guaranteed measure of determining the advertising's impact.

Pretesting Finished Broadcast Ads

While a variety of methods for pretesting broadcast ads are available, we will again focus our attention on the most popular of these.

Theater tests   One of the most popular laboratory methods for pretesting finished commercials has been that of **theater testing.** A number of variations in the methodologies employed exist, but prior to discussing these, it will be helpful to understand the basic theater testing concept.

Table 18–9   **Alternative Theater Methodologies**

Advertising Research Services (ARS) runs theater tests in four different cities, on a total sample of 400 to 600 persons. Precommercial brand preferences are taken, and in this test, respondents are asked to choose from pictures of packages of brands—thus resulting in a recognition test rather than recall.

Viewers then watch a 30-minute television program with three sets of two commercials embedded in the program. Questions are then asked about the program. A second program of 30 minutes is then shown, with six additional commercials included. Any of the 12 commercials might be the test commercial. The measure of brand preference change is taken after the second program.

After approximately 72 hours, one half of the sample is phoned to obtain a measure of recall. These results are compared against norms established from previous tests.

Advertising Control for Television (ACT)—a lab procedure of the McCollum/Spielman Co.—uses approximately 400 respondents representing four different cities. The initial brand preference measure is taken by asking participants which brands they most recently purchased. Respondents are then divided into groups of 25 to view a 30-minute program with seven commercials inserted in the middle. Four are test commercials; the other three are control commercials with established viewing norms. After viewing the program, respondents are given a recall test of the commercials.

After completing the recall test, a second 30-minute program is shown, with each test commercial shown again. The second measure of brand preference is taken at this time, with persuasion measured by the percentage of persons who switched preferences from their most recently purchased brand to one shown in the test commercials.

Participants in theater tests are recruited by telephone, mall intercepts, and/or the mailing of tickets. In the recruitment procedure, those sought are invited to view pilot films of proposed new television programs. In some instances the show is actually being tested, but more commonly a standard program is used so that audience responses can be compared with normative responses established by previous viewers. Sample sizes range from 250 to 600 total participants.

When first entering the theater, viewers are informed that a drawing will be held for gifts and are asked to complete a product preference questionnaire asking which products they would prefer, should they win. This form also requests demographic data from the respondent. Participants may be seated in specific locations in the theater to allow observation by age, sex, and so on. The program and commercials are viewed, and a form asking for the viewer's evaluations is distributed. Participants are then asked to complete a second form for a drawing, so that changes in product preference can be noted. In addition to product/brand preference information, additional information regarding responses to the commercials may be obtained, including

1. Interest in, and reaction to, the commercial
2. Overall reaction to the commercial as measured by an adjective check list
3. Recall of various aspects of the commercial
4. Interest in the brand under consideration
5. Continuous (frame-by-frame) reactions throughout the commercial

As noted, there are variations in the methods of the various theater testing operations. While all measure brand preference changes, each has its own way of conducting the tests. Some may not take all the measures listed above. Others may ask the consumers to turn dials or push buttons on a keypad to provide the continual responses, and so on. An example of some of these methodologies is shown in Table 18–9.

Theater tests have both proponents and opponents. Those opposed to this methodology cite a number of disadvantages associated with this form of pretesting. First, they argue that the environment is too *artificial*—the lab setting is in itself bad enough, but to ask respondents to turn dials or, as one service does, to wire people for physiological responses takes one too far from a natural viewing setting. Second, the contrived measure of brand preference change seems too simple and too phony to believe. Critics contend that participants will see through it and make changes because they

Table 18–10   ASI Market Research—Recall Plus Test

Objective:	Allows for the testing of finished or rough commercials to allow day-after recall and verbatim reactions.
Method:	One control and four test commercials are inserted into new 30-minute family television programs. The commercials and program are sent to two geographically dispersed cities and aired on CATV during prime-time viewing hours. Approximately 200 female viewers between the ages of 18 and 65 are randomly selected from all homes on the CATV system in the area. Commercials are then reexposed to viewers who recalled the ad, with more diagnostic questions then administered.
Output:	Day-after recall scores, verbatim responses to the commercials, and test-retest reliability scores are provided. Scores on competitive commercials (if used) are also provided.

think they are supposed to since they are being tested. Finally, the *group effects* of having others present and overtly exhibiting their reactions may have an effect on the viewers, who may not have had any reactions themselves.

Proponents, on the other hand, argue that such tests offer some distinct advantages. In addition to the control offered, they cite the value of established norms (averages of commercials' performances) as an indication of how one's commercial will fare against others in the same product class that have been tested previously. Further, they argue that the brand preference measure has been supported by actual sales results in the past.

Despite the limitations of theater testing, most major consumer product companies use, or have used, them to evaluate their commercials. They argue that despite its shortcomings this method allows for the identification of strong or weak commercials and a comparison to norms of other ads.

On-air tests   Some of the firms conducting theater tests also provide a second form of commercial testing in which the commercials are inserted into actual television programs in certain test markets. Typically, the commercials are in finished form, although the testing of ads earlier in the developmental process is becoming more common. This form of testing is referred to as an **on-air test** and often includes single-source ad research (which will be discussed later in this chapter). In addition to Information Resources, Burke Marketing Research, ASI Market Research, Inc., and Nielsen are well-known providers of on-air tests. Table 18–10 describes one of these services—that of ASI's Recall Plus Test.

On-air testing techniques offer all the advantages of field methodologies, as well as all the disadvantages. In addition, negative aspects of the specific measures taken through the on-air systems have been cited. One concern that has been expressed is a problem associated with the use of **day-after recall scores**—the primary measure used in these tests. Lyman Ostlund notes that measurement errors created by the "natural environment" may result from the position of the ad in the series of commercials shown, the adjacent program content, and/or the number of commercials being shown.[12] While the testing services feel that their methods overcome many of these criticisms, each still uses recall as a primary measure of effectiveness. Since recall tests may best reflect the degree of attention, and interest in an ad, attempts to claim that the tests may indicate the ad's impact on sales may be going too far. (In 28 studies reviewed by Jack Haskins, only 2 were able to demonstrate that factual recall could be related to sales.)[13]

On the plus side, most of the testing services have offered evidence of both validity and reliability of the on-air pretesting of commercials. Both ASI and Burke claim that their pretest and posttest results yield the same recall scores 9 out of 10 times— a strong indication of reliability and a good predictor of the effect the ad is likely to have when shown to the population as a whole.

Table 18–11   **Eye Movement Research**

Objective:	To track viewers' eye movements to determine what viewers read or view in print ads and what attention is focused on in television commercials or billboards.
Method:	Fiber optics, digital data processing, and advanced electronics are used to follow eye movements of viewers and/or readers as they view an ad.
Output:	Relationship between what readers see, recall, and comprehend. Scan paths on print ads, billboards, commercials, and print materials. (Can also be used to evaluate package designs.)

In summary, on-air pretesting of finished or rough commercials offers some distinct advantages over lab methods and some indications as to the likelihood of success of the advertisement. Whether or not the measures used provide as much of an indication as the providers say they will still remains in question.

Physiological measures   A less commonly used method of pretesting finished commercials is that involving a laboratory setting in which physiological response variables are measured. These measures indicate the receiver's *involuntary* response to the ad and, as such, theoretically alleviate biases associated with voluntary measures reviewed to this point. (Involuntary responses are those over which the individual has no control. For example, heartbeat, reflexes, etc.) A variety of physiological measures have been used to test both print and broadcast ads.

1. *Pupil dilation* Research in the area of **pupillometrics** is designed to measure dilation and constriction of the pupils of the eye in response to stimuli. *Dilation* is an activity most closely associated with action, whereas *constriction* involves the body's conservation of energy.

Advertisers have used pupillometrics to evaluate product and package design as well as to test ads, believing that the interest value of the ad or preference for two ads could be determined. A stronger interest in (or preference for) an ad would be indicated by pupil dilation, as would arousal or attention-getting capabilities. Other attempts to determine the affective (liking or disliking) responses created by advertisements have met with less success.

Because of the high costs associated with this testing method, and some methodological problems, the use of pupillometrics has waned over the past decade. However, these methods can be useful in evaluating certain aspects of advertising.

2. *GSR/EDR* Galvanic skin response—also know as **electrodermal response**—measures the *resistance* or *conductance* the skin offers to a small amount of current passed between two electrodes. Response to a stimulus will activate sweat glands, which in turn will increase the conductance of the electrical current. Thus, reaction to advertising might be reflected in GSR/EDR activity. In their review of the research in this area, Paul Watson and Robert Gatchel have concluded that GSR/EDR (1) is sensitive to affective stimuli, (2) may present a picture of attention, (3) may be useful as measures of long-term advertising recall, and (4) is useful in measuring ad effectiveness.[14]

While a number of companies have (and many still do) offered skin response measures, this research methodology is not commonly employed at this time.

3. *Eye tracking* A methodology that is more commonly employed is that of **eye tracking** (see Table 18–11). In eye tracking tests, viewers are asked to view an ad while a sensor aims a beam of infrared light at the eye. The beam follows the movement of the eye as it views the ad or commercial and provides information as to the exact spot upon which the viewer is focusing. A *continuous* reading of responses is obtained, demonstrating what elements may be attracting attention, how long the viewer is focusing on specific elements of the ad, and the sequence in which these elements are being viewed.

By using eye tracking, researchers can identify strengths and weaknesses in an advertisement. For example, certain elements of an ad—such as attractive models or background occurrences—may distract the viewer's attention away from the brand or product being advertised. In such a case, steps may be taken to remedy this distraction prior to fielding the ad. In other instances, colors or illustrations may attract attention and create viewer interest in the ad.

4. *Brain waves* **Electroencephalographic (EEG) measures** can be taken from the skull to determine electrical frequencies in the brain. These electrical impulses are used in two areas of research:

- **Hemispheric lateralization** involves the determination of alpha activity in the left and right sides of the brain. It has been hypothesized that the left and right sides of the brain perform separate functions, with the right side processing visual stimuli, whereas the left processes verbal stimuli. The right hemisphere is thought to respond more to *emotional* stimuli, whereas the left responds to logical reason; and the left is responsible for recall, whereas the right determines recognition.[15] If these hypotheses are correct, the implications would be that advertisers could design the ads to increase learning and memory by creating stimuli to appeal to each hemisphere. However, at this time, there are researchers who believe that lateralization is not a valid explanation of how the brain functions and that to design an ad to appeal to one side or the other would be highly implausible.

- **Alpha activity** refers to the degree of brain activation, with people being referred to as in an alpha state when they are inactive, resting, and/or sleeping. The theory is that a person in an alpha state is less likely to be processing information (recall correlates negatively with alpha levels) and that attention and processing will require moving one from this state. By measuring one's alpha level while viewing a commercial, it would be possible to assess the degree to which attention and processing are likely to take place.

While EEG research has attracted the attention of academic researchers, it has been much less successful in attracting the interest of practitioners.

Market Testing of Advertisements

Because the advertisement and/or campaign has been implemented does not mean that there is no longer a need for testing. The fact that pretests have been conducted on smaller samples and may in some instances have questionable merit necessitates an examination of how the ad is doing in the field. In this section we will discuss some of the measures of posttesting an advertisement. You will quickly see that some of the tests are similar to those discussed in the previous section and that many of the same companies provide these services.

Posttests of Print Ads   A variety of print posttests are available, including inquiry tests, recognition tests, and recall tests.

Inquiry tests   Used both in consumer- and business-to-business market testing, **inquiry tests** are designed to measure advertising effectiveness on the basis of *inquiries* generated from advertisements appearing in various print media. The inquiry may take the form of the number of coupons returned, the number of times a phone call is generated by the ad, or direct inquiries through reader cards. For example, you may have recently called in response to an ad in a local medium and found that you were asked where you found out about the company or product or where you saw the ad. In essence, this is a very simple and easily employed measure of the advertisement or media effectiveness. More complex methodologies of measuring effectiveness through inquiries are also used. These methods may involve (1) running the ad in successive issues of the same medium, (2) running **split-run tests** in which variations of the ad are run in alternative copies of the same newspaper or magazine, and/or (3) running

Table 18–12   **The Starch Readership Report**

Objective:	To determine recognition of print advertisements as well as a comparison to other ads of the same variety or in the same magazine.
Method:	Samples are drawn from 20 to 30 urban areas reflecting the geographical circulation of the magazine. Personal interviewers are used to screen readers for qualifications and to determine exposure and readership. Samples include a minimum of 200 males and females, as well as specific audiences where required. Participants are asked to go through the magazines, looking at the ads, and provide specific responses.
Output:	Starch Readership Reports generate three recognition scores: • A Noted Score—the percentage of readers who remember seeing the ad • A Seen-Associated Score—the percentage of readers who recall seeing or reading any part of the ad identifying the product or brand • A Read-Most Score—the percentage of readers who reported reading at least one half of the copy portion of the ad

the same ad in different media. The measures taken by each of these methods will yield information on different aspects of the strategy. For example, in the first instance, one would be measuring the *cumulative* effects of the campaign, whereas in the second, specific elements of an ad or different versions of the ad would be under examination. In the final method, the medium rather than the ad itself is the focus of the effectiveness measure.

While inquiry tests may yield some useful information, weaknesses in this methodology limit its effectiveness. For example, inquiries may not necessarily be a true measure of the attention-getting or information-providing aspects of the ad. It is possible that the reader may be attracted to an ad, read it, and even store the memory provided therein but not be motivated to inquire at that particular time. Other factors such as time constraints, lack of a need for the product or service at the time the ad is run, or other factors may limit the number of inquiries. To conclude that the ad was not effective—or was less effective—may be erroneous, as attention-getting qualities, attitude change, awareness, and recall of copy points may all have been affected, although this might not be reflected. At the other extreme, a person with a particular need for the product may respond to the ad, regardless of specific elements of the ad itself. This person would then be considered as having responded to the ad for reasons associated with the ad, when in actuality he or she would have responded to any version.

The major advantages of inquiry tests may be the fact that they are very inexpensive to implement and that some feedback with respect to the general effectiveness of the ad or media used is possible. However, comparisons of alternative versions of an ad or specific creative aspects are usually not very effective.

Recognition tests   Perhaps the most commonly employed form of posttesting of print ads is the **recognition method**—most closely associated with Starch INRA Hooper. The *Starch Readership Report* allows the advertiser to assess the impact of an ad in a single issue of a magazine, over time and/or across alternative magazines (see Table 18–12). Starch measurements are taken for over 75,000 advertisements in over 1,000 issues representing over 100 consumer, farm, and business magazines and newspapers per year. As can be seen in Figure 18–5, a number of measures of the ad's effectiveness are provided.

In addition to the Starch Readership Report described in Table 18–12, Starch also offers the *Starch Impression Study* and the *Starch Ballot Readership Study*. The Starch Impression Study provides consumers' qualitative impressions of ads—for example, company image, important features, and so on—whereas the latter measures readership in business magazines.

The advantages claimed by the Starch methods are (1) that the pulling power of various aspects of the ad can be assessed through the control offered, (2) that a comparison to the effectiveness of competitors' ads can be determined through the use of

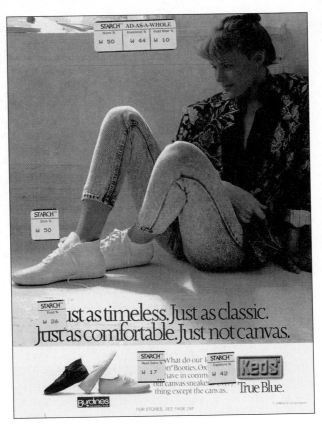

Figure 18—5 **Example of a Starch Scored Advertisement**

the norms provided, (3) that alternative ad executions can be tested, and (4) that readership scores are a useful indication of the consumers' *involvement* in the ad or campaign. (With respect to this last statement, it is argued that the reader must read and become involved in the ad before the ad will have an opportunity to communicate. To the degree that this readership can be shown, a direct indication of effectiveness is possible.)

Of the advantages cited above, perhaps the most valid is that of the ability to judge specific aspects of the ad. Many researchers have criticized other aspects of the Starch recognition method (as well as other recognition measures) based on the following:

1. *The problem of false claiming* Research has indicated that in recognition tests respondents may claim to have seen an ad when in fact they have not. False claims may be a result of having seen similar ads elsewhere, expectations that such an ad would appear in the medium, or the personality of the respondent. In addition, interest in the product category has been shown to increase reporting of ad readership. Whether this false claiming is deliberate or not, the problem remains that such claims lead to an overreporting of effectiveness. On the flip side, factors such as interview fatigue may lead to an underreporting bias—that is, not reporting an ad that may have been seen.

2. *Interviewer sensitivities* Anytime research involves interviewers, there is a potential for bias. Respondents may feel that they need to impress the interviewer or that they might appear unknowledgeable if they continuously claim not to recognize an ad. In addition, there also exists the possibility of variance associated with interviewer instructions, recordings, and so on, regardless of the amount of training and sophistication involved.

3. *Reliability of recognition scores* By their own admission, Starch notes that the reliability and validity of their readership scores increase with the number of in-

Table 18–13   **Gallup & Robinson Magazine Impact Research Service**

Objective:	To track recall of advertising (and client's advertisements) appearing in magazines to assess performance and effectiveness.
Method:	Test magazines are placed in participants' homes and respondents are asked to read the magazine that day. A telephone interview is conducted the second day to assess recall of ads, recall of copy points, and consumers' impressions of the ads. Sample size is 150 persons.
Output:	Three measurement scores are provided: • Proven Name Registration—the percentage of respondents who can accurately recall the ad • Idea Communication—the number of sales points the respondents can recall • Favorable Buying Attitude—the extent of favorable purchase reaction to the brand or corporation

sertions tested. Essentially they are saying that to test just one ad on a single exposure may not produce valid or reliable results.

In sum, despite its critics, the Starch Readership studies continue to dominate the posttesting of print advertisements. The value provided by norms and the fact that reliability and validity can be improved with multiple exposures may underlie the decisions to employ this methodology.

Recall tests   A number of tests to measure recall of print ads are available. Perhaps the most well known of these are the *SAMI-Burke Standard Print Test* and the *Gallup and Robinson Impact Test*—the latter of which is described in Table 18–13. These **recall tests** are similar to those described earlier under the section on pretesting of broadcast ads in that they attempt to measure recall of specific ads.

In addition to the interviewer problems discussed in the section on recognition tests, other factors have been cited as disadvantages associated with recall tests. The reader's degree of involvement with the product and/or the distinctiveness of the appeals and visuals may lead to higher recall scores, although in general the method may actually lead to lower levels of recall than actually exist (though the advertiser would be happy with an error in this direction). Since critics contend that the test is not strong enough to reflect recall accurately, many ads may be considered less effective than they really are and will be abandoned or modified without cause.

On the plus side, it is felt that recall can assess the impression on memory created by the ad. Proponents of recall tests contend that the major concern may not be the score results themselves but rather how these scores are interpreted.

Posttests of Broadcast Commercials
A number of methods exist for the posttesting of broadcast commercials. Again, the most commonly used will be discussed here.

Day-after recall tests   As noted earlier in this chapter the most popular method of posttesting employed in the broadcast industry is that of the **Burke Test** (Table

Table 18–14   **Burke DAR Test**

Objective:	To determine the ability of the commercial to gain viewer attention, communicate an intended message, associate the brand name with the message, and affect purchase behavior.
Method:	Interviews take place the day after the commercial airs in numerous cities throughout the United States. A sample of 200 persons who confirmed that they watched the program in which the ad was placed are used. All individuals are asked if they remember a commercial, then all that they can remember about it.
Output:	Scores reflecting unaided and aided recall, indicating that they remember the commercial and whether they can relate details about it.

18–14). While the Burke Test actually refers to a specific test provided by SAMI-Burke, Inc.—the *day-after recall (DAR)* test (Burke also offers a "selector" test, which adds additional measures to DAR)—the name *Burke Test* has almost become generic for all recall tests. It is important to recognize, however, that the methodology employed is the recall test and that other firms such as Gallup & Robinson and ASI Market Research, Inc. provide the same services. In addition, variations and extensions on the basic DAR test are available.

While different organizations offer their own methodologies, the effectiveness measure is still the number of persons able to *recall* the ad. For example, in comparing the Burke and Gallup & Robinson tests, differences in the markets used, the number of respondents, and the selection of respondents (Burke calls the day after the ad until 200 persons are found who have seen a program, whereas Gallup & Robinson prerecruits viewers) are evident. At the same time, both tests provide scores reporting two basic factors:

1. *Unaided recall* No aids are provided to the respondent. Rather, they are asked a simple question such as, "While watching [program] last night, did you see a commercial for [product category]?" Thus, the unaided recall score would reflect the percentage of respondents who recalled a particular commercial—a strong measure of memory.

2. *Aided recall* In the aided test, "aids" are given, such as, "While watching [program] last night, did you see a commercial for [brand name]?" The percentage of respondents who can then recall the commercial is then reported as an "aided" score.

As demonstrated in Promotional Perspective 18–2, the Burke Score may make or break an ad—sometimes erroneously—as you will see in the following section.

As with the other methodologies discussed, recall tests are not without their critics. In addition to those problems cited earlier, the following disadvantages have been suggested:

1. DAR tests may favor *nonemotional* appeals. Because the respondent is asked to verbalize the message, thinking messages may be easier to recall than are emotional communications. Thus, the recall scores for emotional ads may be lower.[16]

2. Program content may influence recall. The surrounding program content in which the ad appears may lead to different recall scores for the same brand. The net result is a potential inaccuracy in the recall score and in the norms used to establish comparisons.[17]

3. The use of a prerecruited sample (Gallup & Robinson) may increase attention to the program and the ads contained therein because the respondents know that they will be "tested" the next day. This effect would lead to a *higher* level of recall than really exists.

The major advantage of the day-after recall tests is that they are field tests. Thus, the natural setting is supposed to provide a more realistic response profile. Also a major reason for the high use of these tests is the fact that norms are provided that give the advertisers a standard for comparison for how well their ads are performing.

Test marketing of broadcast ads   Many companies conduct tests designed to measure their advertising effects in specific test markets prior to releasing them nationally. In test marketing the markets are chosen on the basis of their representativeness of the target market. For example, a company may test its ads in Portland, Oregon, San Antonio, Texas, or Buffalo, New York, if the demographic and socioeconomic profiles of these cities matches the product's market. A variety of factors might be tested, including reactions to the ads themselves (for example, alternative copy points), the effects of various budget sizes, or special offers. The ads are in finished form and are placed in the media in which they might normally appear, with measures of effectiveness taken after the ads have been run.

The advantage of test marketing of ads is the realism provided, in that regular viewing environments are used and the testing effects are minimized. In addition, it

Promotional Perspective 18-2

To Burke or Not to Burke?

It is not at all unusual to be sitting in an advertising agency and hear someone running down the hall yelling, "We Burked at 32!" In fact, a Burke Score of 32 might get a number of persons in the agency—as well as the client—excited. What is a Burke Score?

Burke Marketing Research in Cincinnati, Ohio, is one of the most well known companies in the business of testing television commercials through a methodology known as DAR—day-after recall. The company tests commercials by calling local television watchers at random to determine whether or not they can recall a commercial shown on television the previous night. This related recall score reflects the number of persons who could recall at least one substantial element of the advertisement.

An average Burke Score is 24. One of the highest ever recorded (for Meow Mix cat food) was 75. Some ads have scored as poorly as 0. Of course advertisers are elated when they exceed the norms and have been known to lose accounts when they are below average. To a degree both the advertisers and their clients live by the Burke Score.

Yet Burke is not always an excellent predictor of advertising effectiveness. One of the most successful advertising campaigns ever—Mikey for Life Cereal—flunked its Burke test. Others have scored over 50 and the products have failed miserably. Still, Burke seems to remain the standard in television commercial testing.

Source: Adapted from Max Gunther, "To Burke or Not to Burke?" *TV Guide*, February 7, 1981, pp. 3–8.

has also been shown that a high degree of control can be attained if the test is designed successfully. For example, an extensive test market study was designed and conducted by Seagram and Time, Inc. to measure the effects of advertising frequency on consumers' buying habits. The results of this research—detailed in Promotional Perspective 18–3—provide some interesting insights. In addition to those insights, this study demonstrated just how much could be learned from research conducted in a field setting but with some experimental controls. It also demonstrates quite effectively that with proper research it may be possible to gain strong insights into the impact of advertising campaigns.

The Seagram's study also reveals some of the disadvantages associated with test market measures—not the least of these of which are the cost and time factors. Few firms have the luxury to spend three years and thousands of dollars to conduct such a test. In addition, as noted earlier, there is always the fear that competitors may discover and intervene in the research process.

Given both the advantages and disadvantages of test marketing, however, it is safe to conclude that this testing methodology offers the possibility to provide substantial insight into the effectiveness of advertising. If care is taken to minimize the negative aspects of such tests, the results can be quite useful.

Single-source tracking studies **Single-source methods** track the behaviors of consumers from the television set to the supermarket checkout counter. Participants with cable TV in a designated area who agree to participate in the studies are provided with a card (similar to a credit card) that identifies their household and provides the research company with their demographics. The households are split into matched groups, with one group receiving an ad, whereas the other does not, and/or alternate ads are sent to each. Their purchases are then recorded from the bar codes of the products bought. Commercial exposures are then correlated with purchase behaviors.

Earlier in this chapter, we briefly mentioned the use of single-source ad research in pretesting broadcast commercials. A recent study demonstrates that the single-source methodology can also be used effectively to posttest ads, allowing for a variety of dependent measures and tracking the effects of increased ad budgets, alternative versions of ad copy, and even ad effects on *sales*.[18] As shown in Table 18–15, three

Promotional Perspective 18—3

Major Study Details Ads' Effect on Sales

A major test market study of advertising effectiveness was conducted by Jos. E. Seagram & Sons, and Time, Inc. exploring the effects of advertising on awareness, recall, attitudes, and sales. Because it is extremely difficult to measure the impact of advertising on sales—with the exception of the direct-response variety—advertising researchers have argued for the inclusion of other mediating variables, noting that these factors would lead to the ultimate behavior—sales. This study has gone a step further and attempted to ascertain this relationship directly.

The most expensive advertising study ever commissioned by Time was conducted over a three-year period in two test markets—Milwaukee and the state of Missouri—and employed two Time, Inc. magazines (Time and Sports Illustrated) and eight Seagram's liquor brands. The only media carrying the ads for the eight brands over this time were the two test vehicles. Over 20,000 persons participated, 80 percent of whom drank liquor.

The results of the study yielded some very interesting findings, including:

- Recall is a poor indicator of advertising effectiveness.
- Even a single ad can have a major impact on brand awareness.

- It is harder to increase a well-known product's favorability rating among consumers through an extended ad campaign than it is to increase dramatically a favorable rating for a little-known product.
- The impact of advertising continues to grow during an extended advertising campaign and does not necessarily level off or drop during the later weeks of the campaign.
- Consumption increased 35 percent for those persons who had seen one or two ads in the previous four weeks, and 72 percent for those who had seen four ads during that period.
- When exposed to the ad four times in a month, 170 percent more people said that they had purchased the advertised brand in that period.

While essentially a field test, the study has been hailed in the advertising industry as a "landmark" experiment owing to the institution of rigid controls. Many advertisers feel that this study is one of the most conclusive ever conducted in an attempt to demonstrate the effect of advertising and advertising/frequency on sales.

Source: Adapted from Stuart Emmrich, "Major Study Details Ads' Effect on Sales," Advertising Age, June 21, 1982, p. 1.

single-source methods have been used for this purpose—BehaviorScan (Information Resources, Inc.), AdTel (SAMI-Burke), and ERIM (A. C. Nielsen).

Many advertisers believe that these single-source measures will change the way that research is conducted, as the advantages of control and the ability to measure the effects of the ads on sales directly are possible. As shown in Promotional Perspective 18–4, a number of major corporations are now employing this method.

While single-source testing is certainly a valuable tool, it still has some problems. As one researcher working with these data notes, "Scanner data focuses on short term sales effects, and as a result captures only 10–30% of what advertising does."[19] Others have complained that the data are too complicated to deal with, as an overabundance of information is available. Still another disadvantage is the high cost of collecting single-source data.

Table 18–15   **Single-Source Ad Tracking Systems**

BehaviorScan	1. Ten geographically dispersed test communities. Four examples: Pittsfield, MA; Rome, GA; Eau Claire, WI; and Visalia, CA 2. About 30,000 panel households 3. Requires cable television system
AdTel	1. Five geographically dispersed test communities. Three examples: Portland, ME; the Quad Cities (Davenport, IA; Moline, IL; etc.); and Boise, ID 2. About 12,000 panel households 3. Requires cable television system
ERIM	1. Two test communities: Sioux Falls, SD; and Springfield, MO 2. About 6,000 panel households 3. No requirement for cable television

Source: Dave Kruegel, "Television Advertising Effectiveness and Research Innovation," Journal of Consumer Marketing 5, no. 3 (Summer 1988), p. 45.

Promotional Perspective 18–4

Wired Consumers: Market Researchers Go High-Tech

Remember the book and movie *1984* in which electronic eavesdropping was so prevalent in the United States? Well, some people think that some of the testing techniques employed in the ad industry are right out of the movie!

Information Resources, Inc. (IRI) offers its advertising clients an electronic testing service that allows them to test participating consumers without their even knowing when they are being tested. (Of course, the participants are willing subjects who have earlier volunteered to be involved for the opportunity to win prizes ranging from small appliances to trips to Hawaii.)

The system works like this: Households agree to participate and provide IRI with extensive demographic and socioeconomic information about themselves. A microprocessor is placed in their CATV converter, and a "Shoppers Hotline" card is given to them to give to the cashier at the local grocery store when they make purchases.

Inside an electronic control room at the local ca-

ble TV franchise, test commercials are sent to the various households—not all receiving each ad and none knowing which are test ads and which are real. At night, a computer connects with the participating household microprocessor to determine what they watch each day and to see if they watch complete programs or flip channels.

Product purchases are then correlated with ad tests (sometimes employing coupons) to determine whether ad pitches had any effect. At other times, only viewing behaviors are observed. Companies like Campbell Soup, General Foods, Procter & Gamble, and Dart & Kraft have all used the system. Tylenol used it to determine consumers' reactions to safety-sealed capsules after the 1982 poison scare. All of this, and you never even know when you are being tested!

Source: Adapted from "Wired Consumers: Market Researchers Go High-Tech to Hone Ads, Weed Out Flops," *The Wall Street Journal*, January 23, 1986, p. 33.

Tracking print broadcast ads   One of the more useful and adaptable forms of posttesting involves tracking the effects of the advertising campaign by taking measurements at regular intervals. **Tracking studies** have been used to measure the effects of advertising on awareness, recall, interest, and attitudes toward the ad and/or brand as well as purchase intentions. (Ad tracking may be applied to both print and broadcast ads but is much more commonly employed with the latter.) Personal interviews, telephone surveys, mall intercepts, and even mail surveys have been used for this purpose. Sample sizes typically range from 250 to 500 cases per period, with quarterly or semiannual surveys being most common. The results of tracking studies yield perhaps the most valuable information available to the marketing manager for assessment of the current programs and planning for the future.

The major advantage of tracking studies is the fact that the study can be tailored to each specific campaign and/or situation. By maintaining a standard set of questions, effects of the campaign can be tracked over time. In addition, the effects of various media can also be determined—although with a much lesser degree of effectiveness. Tracking studies have also been used to measure the differential impact of alternative budget sizes, the effects of flighting, brand or corporate image, and recall of specific copy points. Finally, when designed properly, as shown in Table 18–16, tracking studies also offer the advantages of a high degree of reliability and validity.[20]

Some of the problems cited with the recall and recognition measures are inherent with tracking studies, as many other factors may be affecting both brand and advertising recall. Despite these limitations, however, tracking studies have been shown to be a very effective method for assessing the effects of advertising campaigns.

In summary, you can see that each of the testing methods considered in this chapter has its limitations. The question that may come to your mind, then, is probably, Can we actually conduct testing of advertising effectiveness? or What can be done to ensure that we have a valid and reliable test? Promotional Perspective 18–5 provides an affirmative answer to the first of these questions, whereas the final section of this chapter will suggest some answers to the latter.

Table 18–16   **Factors Making or Breaking Tracking Studies**

1. Properly defined objectives
2. Alignment with sales objectives
3. Properly designed measures (e.g., adequate sample size, maximum control over interviewing process, adequate time between tracking periods)
4. Consistency through replication of the sampling plan
5. Random samples
6. Continuous interviewing (that is, not seasonal)
7. Evaluative measures must be related to behavior (attitudes have met this criterion; recall of ads does not)
8. Asking critical evaluative questions early to eliminate bias
9. Measure competitors' performance
10. Questions that ask where the advertising was seen or heard often provide misleading results (television always wins)
11. Building news value into the study
12. Using "moving averages" to spot long-term trends and avoid seasonality
13. Reporting data in terms of relationships rather than as isolated facts
14. Integrating key marketplace events with tracking results (for example, advertising expenditures of self and competitors, promotional activities associated with price changes in ad campaigns, introductions of new brands, government announcements, changes in economic conditions)

Source: Adapted from Fred Cuba, "Fourteen Things That Make or Break Tracking Studies," *Journal of Advertising Research* 25, no. 1 (February/March 1985), pp. 21–23.

Establishing a Program for Measuring Advertising Effects

Having carefully read the preceding sections, you are certainly now aware that there is no sure-fire method of testing advertising effectiveness. However, you should also be aware that pressures to determine the contribution that these ads are making to the overall marketing effort are also on the increase. While there is no one simple solution to this problem, there are certain things that can be done to help improve this measurement task. Let us first begin by reviewing the major problems with some existing methods and then examine some possible improvements that can be made.

Problems with Current Research Methods

In evaluating current testing methods against the criteria established by PACT, it becomes obvious that some of the principles important to good copy testing can be accomplished rather readily, whereas others will require substantially more effort. For example, principle 6—providing equivalent test ads—should require a minimum of effort. The researcher can easily control the state of completion of the test communications. Also of relative ease are principles 1 and 2—providing measurements relative to the objectives sought and determining a priori how the results will be used.

We have seen throughout this text that each promotional medium, the message, and the formulation of the budget are all established with consideration of the marketing and communications objectives sought. By following the decision sequence model as it has been designed, the roles of each of these elements will have been established. Thus, by the time one gets to the measurement phase, the criteria by which these programs will be evaluated should simply fall into place.

Of slightly more difficulty are principles 3, 5, and 8, although, once again, these factors are pretty much in the control of the researcher. For example, providing multiple measurements (principle 3) may require little more than budgeting accordingly to ensure that more than one test is conducted. At the most, it may require considering two alternative, but similar, measures to ensure reliability. Likewise, principle 5—exposing the test ad more than once—can be accomplished with a proper research design. Finally, sample definition (principle 8) requires little more than sound research methodology, as any test should employ those consumers in the market targeted to

Promotional Perspective 18—5

How AT&T Tested the "Slice of Death" Ads

When AT&T startled the advertising community with its "slice of death" ads (which were previously discussed in Chapter 14), it was not just the result of good luck or an effective creative director. The ads—which portray angry, frightened businesspeople coping with major telephone and computer problems—were developed using strong research methods.

From the start, research played a critical role. Participation in focus groups with small-businesspersons played a key role in establishing the original concept, as AT&T managers and ad agency personnel generated ideas from listening to years of problems being expressed. The promise that AT&T would offer these businesses would be "peace of mind."

To determine how to deliver the message, three alternative approaches were created in animatic form. Each was shown to a new set of focus groups, primarily to gain additional insights. Based on these results, the most serious "deadly confessions" version was selected.

Once the creative direction was established, the company used its in-house test/control persuasion and recall methodology to test it further. This test consisted of three components—a measure of day-after recall, attitude change, and extensive diagnostics. Target audience executives were chosen as respondents. The results of this testing indicated above-average levels of persuadability, criticism, and annoyance.

Focus groups were used in the next phase, primarily to determine if the quantitative results could be supported. They were. The company had to weigh the trade-offs between the criticisms and annoyances against the high attention-getting and persuadability factors. They decided to go with the campaign.

When the campaign broke nationally in March 1987, tracking results demonstrated that consumers responded almost immediately—and in a generally positive manner. Criteria such as "leadership in telephone systems" and "the company to call for telephone systems" and "dependable products" were the common evaluations.

But AT&T was not done yet. In an unusual move for advertisers, the company conducted research among its salespeople, asking them to provide their impressions of how the campaign affected them and their customers. Again, an enthusiastic "thumbs up" evaluation was shown.

The rest is history. The award-winning campaign was continued and even expanded. Three agencies were used to develop a cooperative effort that looked like only one shop was used. The results were—and continue to be—impressive.

Source: Adapted from Thornton C. Lockwood, "Behind the Emotion in 'Slice of Death' Advertising," *Business Marketing,* September 1988, pp. 87–93.

---

assess its effectiveness. You would not use a sample of nondrinkers to evaluate potential new liquor commercials!

The more difficult factors to control—and the principles that perhaps may best differentiate between good and bad testing procedures—are those contained in the PACT requirements 4, 7, and 9. Fortunately, however, addressing each of these will contribute to the attainment of the others.

The best starting point is principle 4, which states that the research should be guided by and based on a model of human response to communications and that this model must consider a number of responses including reception, comprehension, and behavioral response. The reason it is the best, in our opinion, is that it is the one least addressed by practicing researchers at this time. If you recall, the material covered in Chapter 5 proposed a number of such models that might be used for the purpose of fulfilling this principle's requirements. Yet even though these models have existed for quite some time, very few—if any—of the research methods commonly employed attempt to integrate this information into their methodologies. Most of these methods discussed here do little more than provide recall scores—in spite of the fact that many researchers have shown that recall is a poor measure of effectiveness. Those that do claim to measure such factors as attitude change or brand preference change are often fraught with problems that severely limit their reliability. To have an effective measure, some relationship to the communications process must be included.

It might seem at first glance that principle 7—provide a nonbiasing exposure— might fall into one of the categories of being easier to accomplish. A review of both lab and field measures would indicate that this will not be that easy to do. Lab measures, while offering control, are artificial and lend themselves to testing effects. Field measures, while more realistic, often lose control. The Seagram and Time, Inc. study—while perhaps having the best of both worlds—is perhaps too large a task for most firms to undertake. While not perfect, some of the improvements associated with the single-source systems will help to solve this problem. In addition, properly designed ad tracking studies will provide truer measures of the impact of the communication. As technology develops, and more attention is paid to this principle, we should expect to see improvements in methodologies in the near future.

Last—but in no way least—is principle 9, the concern for reliability and validity. Most of those measures discussed have been shown to be lacking in one of these criteria, if not both, yet these are two of the most critical factors discriminating between good and bad research. The most basic of research classes always insists that research designs provide evidence of reliability and validity. If the study is properly designed, and by that we mean that it addresses principles 1 through 8, it should result in meeting these requirements.

Essentials of Effective Testing

Most simply put, good tests of advertising effectiveness must address the nine principles established by PACT. One of the easiest ways to accomplish this is by following the decision sequence model in formulating promotional plans. For example:

- *Establish communications objectives* We have stated that except for a few instances—most specifically, direct-response advertising—it is extremely difficult if not impossible to show the direct impact of advertising on sales. Given this fact, the marketing objectives established for the promotional program do not typically serve as good measures of communication effectiveness. For example, it will be very difficult (or too expensive) to demonstrate the effect of an advertisement on brand share or on sales. On the other hand, the attainment of communications objectives will help lead to the accomplishment of these marketing objectives and can be measured. As such they serve as viable dependent measures.

- *Employ a consumer response model* Early in this text we reviewed hierarchy of effects models and cognitive response models. Either or both of these lend themselves to providing an understanding of the effects of communications and as such lend themselves to serving as the communications goals we said are required.

- *Employ both pretests and posttests* From a cost standpoint—both actual cost outlays and opportunity costs—pretesting makes sense. As seen throughout this chapter, it may mean the difference between success and/or failure of the campaign or even the product itself. At the same time, the use of posttesting drops off dramatically. Given some of the limitations of pretests, the much larger samples, and more natural setting of posttesting, this information may be required to determine the true effectiveness of the ad or campaign.

- *Understand and implement proper research* It is critical to understand research methodology. What constitutes a good design? Does it have validity and reliability? Does it measure what we want it to and what we need it to? There is no shortcut to this criterion, and there is no way to avoid it if you truly want to measure the effects of advertising.

Summary

The purpose of this chapter was to introduce you to issues involved in measuring the effects of advertising and promotions. These issues included reasons for testing, reasons why companies do not test, and the review and evaluation of various research methodologies. Having done this, we arrived at a number of conclusions including: (1) advertising research to measure effectiveness is important to the promotional program, (2) not enough companies test their ads, and (3) problems exist with current research methodologies. In addition, we reviewed the criteria for sound research and suggested some things to do to accomplish effective studies.

There is no doubt that all marketing managers want to know how well their promotional programs are working. This information is critical to planning for the next period, as program adjustments and/or maintenance will be based on the results of the evaluation of the existing strategies. The problems often lie in the fact that the measures taken to determine such effects are either inaccurate or improperly used.

This chapter demonstrated that testing must meet a number of criteria to be successful—as defined by PACT. In addition, these evaluations should take place both before and after the campaigns have been implemented.

A variety of research methods were discussed, many of which are provided by syndicated research firms such as SAMI-Burke, Arbitron, and A. C. Nielsen. In addition, it was noted that companies have also developed their own testing systems.

Single-source research data such as BehaviorScan, ERIM, and AdTel were discussed and noted as a source of data for measuring the effects of advertising. These single-source systems offer strong potential for improving the effectiveness of ad measures in the future, as commercial exposures and reactions may be correlated to actual purchase behaviors.

Key Terms

Vehicle option source effect
Pretests
Posttests
Laboratory tests
Testing bias
Field tests
PACT (Positioning Advertising Copy Testing)
Concept testing
Tests of comprehension and reaction
Consumer juries
Halo effect
Burke's Reflections Test
Portfolio tests
Flesch formula
Theater testing

On-air tests
Day-after recall scores
Pupillometrics
Electrodermal response
Eye tracking
Electroencephalographic (EEG) measures
Hemispheric lateralization
Alpha activity
Inquiry tests
Split-run tests
Recognition method
Recall test
Burke Test
Single-source tracking methods
Tracking studies

Discussion Questions

1. Discuss some of the reasons why agencies and firms do not take measures of advertising effectiveness and why they should do so.
2. Should creativity be subject to testing? Give reasons why it should and should not.
3. Explain the differences between pretests and posttests. Give examples of each.
4. Discuss the advantages of lab tests. Of field tests.
5. Explain what is involved in concept testing. Give some examples of what might be tested at this stage.
6. What is a Burke Score? How can it make or break an ad?
7. Discuss how tracking studies might be tied into the hierarchy-of-effects models.
8. Discuss the elements necessary to conduct good advertising testing research.

9. Why is it important to test source factors? Give some examples to support your position.
10. Discuss the concept of single-source research. What advantages does it offer the marketer?

Notes

1. Bruce Horowitz, "TV Ads That Public Will Never See," *Los Angeles Times,* August 3, 1988, p. 1.
2. Personal interview with Jay Khoulos, president of World Communications, Inc., 1988.
3. David A. Aaker and John G. Myers, *Advertising Management,* 3rd ed. (Englewood Cliffs, N.J.: Prentice-Hall, 1987), p. 474.
4. Joel N. Axelrod, "Induced Moods and Attitudes toward Products," *Journal of Advertising Research* 3 (June 1963), pp. 19–24.
5. Lauren E. Crane, "How Product, Appeal, and Program Affect Attitudes toward Commercials," *Journal of Advertising Research* 4 (March 1964), p. 15.
6. Robert Settle, "Marketing in Tight Times," *Marketing Communications* 13, no. 1 (January 1988), pp. 19–23.
7. "21 Ad Agencies Endorse Copy Testing Principles," *Marketing News* 15, no. 17 (February 19, 1982), p. 1.
8. Ibid.
9. John M. Caffyn, "Telepex Testing of TV Commercials," *Journal of Advertising Research* 5,. no. 2 (June 1965), pp. 29–37.
10. Nigel A. Brown and Ronald Gatty, "Rough V Finished TV Commercials in Telepex Tests," *Journal of Advertising Research* 7, no. 4 (December 1967), p. 21.
11. Charles H. Sandage, Vernon Fryburger, and Kim Rotzoll, *Advertising Theory and Practice,* 10th ed. (Homewood, Ill.: Irwin, 1979).
12. Lymund E. Ostlund, "Advertising Copy Testing: A Review of Current Practices, Problems and Prospects," *Current Issues and Research in Advertising,* 1978, pp. 87–105.
13. Jack B. Haskins, "Factual Recall as a Measure of Advertising Effectiveness," *Journal of Advertising Research* 4, no. 1 (March 1964), pp. 2–7.
14. Paul J. Watson and Robert J. Gatchel, "Autonomic Measures of Advertising," *Journal of Advertising Research* 19 (June 1979), pp. 15–26.
15. Flemming Hansen, "Hemispheric Lateralization: Implications for Understanding Consumer Behavior," *Journal of Consumer Research* 8 (1988), pp. 23–36.
16. Hubert A. Zielske, "Does Day-After Recall Penalize 'Feeling Ads'?" *Journal of Advertising Research* 22, no. 1 (1982), pp. 19–22.
17. Terry Haller, "Day After Recall to Persist Despite JWT Study; Other Criteria Looming," *Marketing News,* May 18, 1979, p. 4.
18. Dave Kruegel, "Television Advertising Effectiveness and Research Innovations," *Journal of Consumer Marketing* 5, no. 3 (Summer 1988), pp. 43–52.
19. Jeffrey L. Seglin, "The New Era of Ad Measurement," *Adweek's Marketing Week,* January 23, 1988, p. 24.
20. James F. Donius, "Marketing Tracking: A Strategic Reassessment and Planning Tool," *Journal of Advertising Research* 25, no. 1 (February/March 1985), pp. 15–19.

19

Business-to-Business Communications

CHAPTER OBJECTIVES

1. To understand the differences between business-to-business and consumer product advertising and promotions

2. To understand the objectives of business-to-business communications

3. To recognize the role that various program elements play in the business-to-business promotional program

4. To examine the methods for evaluating promotional program effectiveness in business-to-business communications

Business-to-Business Advertising No Longer Means Grade B

The scene is a meeting of the creative department of a typical New York ad agency on a Monday morning. The discussion involves the development of an all-trade advertising campaign for a new computer account.

The first suggestion is to have a sexy model—representing a female executive—laying across the computer. "No sex," says the creative director. "This is serious stuff."

Suggestion two is a humor ad in which a young executive male searches club to club, bar to bar in search of the meaning of life—and finds it was in his computer all along. This suggestion is also rejected. "No humor," says the creative director. "We need something new and dynamic—like a guy in a suit and tie."

After much deliberation the group develops a campaign—34 lines of copy, explaining what the computer does, accompanied by a small black and white photograph of a man in a gray suit and tie working at a terminal. . . .

While this is not the way that all business-to-business advertising campaigns develop, it is not an uncommon scenario. For years business-to-business and industrial advertising have been considered by many to be synonymous with dull.

Things are changing, however. The use of sexy models, fear and humor appeals, and an increased emphasis on creativity are revolutionizing the advertising of this industry. Who knows—someday we may see ads without men in gray suits and a product orientation![1]

Introduction

Often when we think of advertising and promotions, it is in regard to consumer products or—as shown in Chapter 16—resellers of these products. In fact, approximately $100 billion a year is spent in the advertising of products used in business and industrial markets.[2] As you will see, the objectives sought in these communications and the strategies designed to achieve them are often very different from those we have discussed in earlier chapters.

The lead-in to this chapter reflects what many advertisers feel business-to-business advertising is all about: boring, factual, and plain. While this may have been the case for many years, the fact is that business-to-business advertising is becoming more creative, more emotional, and more interesting. The "slice of death" ads discussed in the previous chapter as well as the creative chapter are but one example of how communications to this industry are changing, and as you will see as this chapter progresses, business-to-business advertising is becoming more sophisticated and, in many ways, more similar to the consumer market.

Business-to-Business Communications

Before we discuss how business-to-business communications are used, it is important to establish an understanding of exactly what it is that we are referring to when we use this term. Had you opened an advertising and/or promotions text just a few years ago, you probably would not have found a chapter titled "Business-to-Business Advertising." Rather, you would have noted titles such as "Industrial Marketing" or "Industrial Advertising." Much of the material would have dealt with topics such as advertising in the industrial sector and advertising to manufacturers.

As the United States has moved from an industrial to a service economy (approximately two thirds of the national economy is now accounted for by the latter), a new and different target market has evolved. This market still includes those involved in the industrial sector but has been broadened to include a "nation of office workers."

Along with this new market came the need to broaden the title given to advertising and promotions used to communicate with this new segment. Many of those involved in business communications felt that the title of *industrial advertising* was somewhat misleading, that it did not represent the true nature of the industry, and

Figure 19–1 **Participants in a Buying Center**

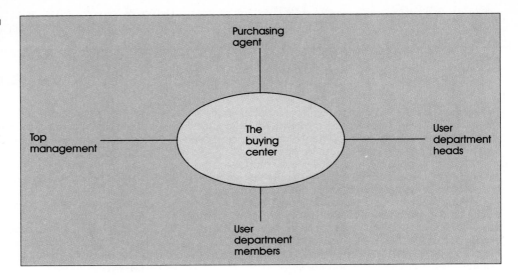

that it was not current with the profession. Thus, a few years ago the industry began to refer to itself as *business-to-business.* For purposes of this text we will use the term **business-to-business advertising,** although we want you to recognize that this term still includes communications targeted to the industrial sector. (When it is important to make a distinction between industrial and service sectors, we will specifically cite the market we are referring to.)

Differences between Business-to-Business and Consumer Communications

The primary difference between business-to-business and consumer-oriented communications is that the latter is generally targeted at those consumers who will *actually use* the product or service in its final form, whereas business-to-business communications are directed to companies involved in the production of goods or services that are designed to facilitate the operation of the enterprise. These products are typically thought of as having a **derived demand**—that is, their demand is generated or driven by the need for other goods or services.

To understand the role of business-to-business communications consider what is involved in the manufacturing of an automobile. While the auto is the final consumer product, the materials that are used to manufacture the car—steel, rubber, leather, plastic, and so on—must be purchased, as do the building, equipment, and the products used to market it. You can be sure that there will be competition among suppliers to attempt to gain the auto manufacturer's business. Goodyear and Firestone may compete for the tire business, USX and Wheeling-Pittsburgh may want to sell the steel, and so on. As you can imagine, all the elements of the promotional mix will be employed in an attempt to sell these products.

While there are a number of differences between business-to-business and consumer communications, perhaps nine key characteristics best differentiate the areas:[3]

1. *The decision maker* While in consumer markets the consumer and decision maker may be the same person—or persons in those products/services characterized by joint decision making—this may not be the case in the business-to-business setting. In the latter market, one person may perform both roles, but it is more typically the case that the buying decision is made by a **buying center** or committee. The buying center is often formalized and includes individuals from throughout the organization, as shown in Figure 19–1.

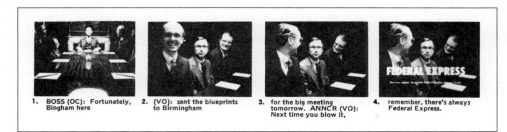

Figure 19–2 **Federal Express Ads Show Consequences of the Wrong Decision**

1. BOSS (OC): Fortunately, Bingham here
2. (VO): sent the blueprints to Birmingham
3. for the big meeting tomorrow. ANNCR (VO): Next time you blow it,
4. remember, there's always Federal Express.

In this case, all those involved must be reached and influenced, with different message and media strategies possibly required for each. Sometimes the decision maker is not readily apparent to the marketer.

2. *Communications* Communications are designed to support the sales effort. As elements of the promotional mix, advertising and promotions may take on a major role or a supportive one. In business-to-business marketing, the latter of these roles is typically assumed by advertising. Thus, communications tend to be much more information based, rational, and designed to generate leads or inquiries in support of the sales staff. As noted by one business-to-business agency:

> Each ad should make it desirable for the potential customer to contact the manufacturer, all inquiries should be responded to in the same day, and all information should help the customer sell the product or service to their management.[4]

3. *Purchase decisions* Whereas purchase decisions may be very quick in the consumer market, the more common case in the business-to-business setting is a *long-range* time perspective. Immediate sales are rare, as committee decisions, budgetary considerations, and buying formulas may need to be addressed before the actual purchase is made. In some industrial situations, it is not at all uncommon to be operating on three- to five-year purchase cycles. Since many of the products have long life cycles, decisions are much less frequent and much more involved.

4. *Buyer involvement* The buyer generally is involved in the decision to purchase a consumer product. In business-to-business settings this involvement may take on a different dimension. If a consumer product does not live up to expectations, the buyer is unhappy and suffers the consequences. If a poor decision is made in an industrial setting, the entire organization may suffer—and more than the buyer's personal satisfaction is at stake. He or she may lose his or her job or experience other consequences, as is so well demonstrated in the Federal Express commercial shown in Figure 19–2.

5. *Integration of communications elements* While business-to-business marketing efforts are rapidly improving, many marketers have considered this sector to be less sophisticated than those involved in consumer marketing. One of the prime reasons for this opinion is the fact that the advertising and marketing programs had commonly not been integrated in the industrial firms, with each seemingly going its own direction.

In a survey conducted by *Business Marketing* magazine, 40 percent of the top marketers in industrial companies regarded their ad agency's planning expertise to be only fair to poor (see Figure 19–3) and complete service even worse. Some of this performance evaluation can be attributed to the lack of industry experience of the agency, whereas high costs and other factors were also cited, as shown in Figure 19–4.

Some of the factors cited in Figures 19–3 and 19–4 are being overcome as business-to-business marketers become more sophisticated and begin to apply many of the same methods employed in the consumer market. One example of this can be

Figure 19–3   The Performance Ratings Top Marketers Give Advertising Agencies

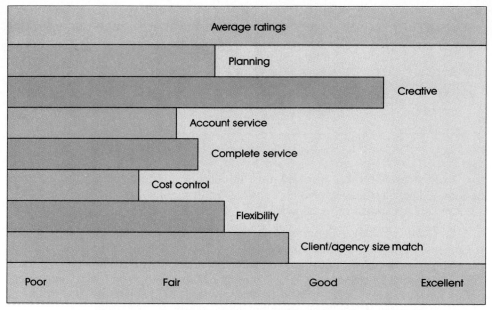

Figure 19–3   The Performance Ratings Top Marketers Give Advertising Agencies

Source: Starmark Report I, 1988, p. 7. Reprinted with permission from Business Marketing Magazine. Copyright Crain Communications, Inc.

seen in the area of market segmentation. Just as the consumer market previously relied mainly on demographic segmentation, so too (until even more recently!) did business-to-business marketers. Now, as demonstrated by Promotional Perspective 19–1, the use of psychographics is becoming more commonplace in segmenting business markets. Behavioral models such as the **Social Style Model**—a model suggesting that businesspersons' "social styles" will influence how they react on the job—and the **CUBE Model** (Comprehensive Understanding of Business Environments)—in which values and lifestyles of corporate buying groups are detailed—are being used to assist in the segmentation process.[5]

6. *Budget allocations* The bulk of marketing monies in business-to-business sectors has traditionally been allocated to support of the sales organization. As a result,

Figure 19–4   Top Business Marketers' Most Common Complaints about Agencies

	Percent responding
Lack of industry experience	20%
High Costs/lack of structure	15%
Inability to listen	8%
Tendency to overact	6%
Slow response	4%
Unqualified employees	2%
Undefined objectives	1%

Source: Starmark Report I, 1988, p. 7. Reprinted with permission from Business Marketing Magazine. Copyright Crain Communications, Inc.

Promotional Perspective 19–1

Segmenting by Corporate Cultures

While consumer products companies have employed psychographics in their market segmentation analyses for years, the same has not been true of business-to-business marketers. Just as consumer companies have considered the effects of cultures on the purchase decision process, so now do business-to-business companies—only the focus is on the culture of the organization, or corporate culture. As noted by Philip Monchar of Total Research Corporation of Princeton, New Jersey, knowing the psychological profile of members of an organization is important because they will have adopted the corporate culture and will know what is and is not acceptable behavior. Monchar's research on corporate executives of 303 large and middle-size firms has led to the identification of three corporate culture segments: the "happy doers," "middle of the roads," and "satisfaction seekers."

Happy doers constitute approximately 36 percent of the sample, according to the study. These persons are more interested in maintaining a smooth operation than they are in their customers' satisfaction. They are least likely to change vendors, they are satisfied with their current suppliers, and purchase decisions are usually made by a single top-level manager relying on little input.

Middle of the road cultures (about 33 percent of the sample) are characterized by a willingness to work with multiple vendors. However, all vendors must meet the company's model of the "personalized service caterer" that handles specific orders and unusual circumstances. Decisions are made after long studies of the issues, and formal evaluations are conducted frequently.

Satisfaction seekers (30 percent of the sample) are considered by Monchar as the most promising targets. They are the most customer oriented, are frequently dissatisfied with current vendors' prices and performances, and are most likely to conduct formal evaluations. As a result they are most likely to switch suppliers. At the same time, however, they are the most cautious about making decisions, making them much slower than the other groups and involving more persons.

Advertising strategies can be developed to appeal to each segment, according to Monchar. For example, he notes that to reach "satisfaction seekers," ads should stress a company's ability to provide services quickly and accurately. To reach the "middle of the roaders," suggestions that the provider can offer tailored services in a given time frame are likely to work. He does not say how to reach the "happy doers"!

Source: Adapted from "Segmenting Markets by Corporate Culture," *Business Marketing*, July 1988, pp. 50–51.

advertising and promotions expenditures often receive less of the marketing budget. Likewise, marketing research—used extensively by consumer products firms—receives much less support in the industrial sector (constituting only about 6 percent of the overall advertising budget).[6]

7. *Evaluation measures* In Chapter 18, we discussed the variety of measures of advertising effectiveness employed by consumer products firms. Later in this chapter you will see that the industrial sector has its own measures that it employs, some of which are similar to those of consumer products companies but most of which assume their own orientation. Usually, these measures are tied directly to sales rather than communications objectives.

8. *Message content* The content of the communications message of consumer products advertisers may be designed to create awareness, interest, or other communications objectives and may employ both rational and emotional approaches. While there has recently been an increase in the use of emotional appeals, business-to-business communications tend to focus on the use of information presented in a logical and rational format, as can be seen in Figure 19–5. Humor, sex, and other forms of emotional appeals have been used in relatively few instances, as most ads tend to be very technical, information laden, and factual. The use of testimonials is also a very common business-to-business approach.

9. *Media use* As you should expect, the media used by those involved in business-to-business advertising are often very different than the media employed in the consumer products sector. Since the media employed is the topic of a later section of this chapter, we will not go into this in depth at this time. Suffice it to say at this point that the media tend to be more specifically targeted, whereas in the consumer products market, mass media such as television and radio are more commonly used.

Figure 19–5 **Rational Appeals Are Dominant in Business-to-Business Ads**

In summary, there are obviously many differences between the communications strategies of industrial and consumer products–oriented companies. Much of this can be attributed to the nature of the industries, whereas some may be a result of marketing sophistication. Still others can be attributed to the fact that business-to-business marketers may define the objectives of advertising and promotions differently than their consumer market counterparts.

Establishing Business-to-Business Communications Objectives

The objectives that have been established earlier in this text are just as relevant for business-to-business marketers as they are for consumer products firms. Obviously, business-to-business advertisers will have marketing objectives that they wish to accomplish, and they should establish communications objectives as a means for attaining these goals. Likewise, establishing a *corporate image* is no less important for industrial firms than it is for their consumer counterparts.

However, as we have stated, business-to-business marketers have often concentrated their efforts directly on the attainment of sales. To this end the emphasis in advertising and promotions has been to support sales efforts, and sales have been used as the measure of their success. In this text, we take the position that communications and sales objectives need not be independent. That is, in business-to-business markets there is a need to achieve the same objectives as those sought in consumer markets to reach sales goals. These objectives include creating awareness; establishing a favorable image or position in the marketplace; and generating consumer interest, knowledge, and trial of the product, among others.

Figure 19–6 **Business-to-Business Ads Are Becoming More Exciting**

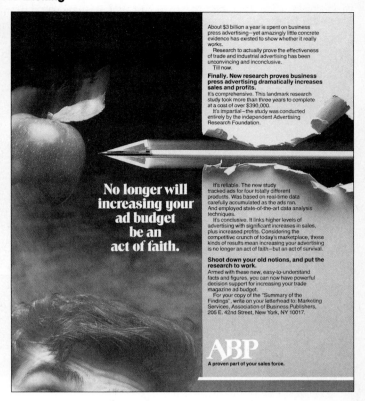

Developing and Implementing the Business-to-Business Program

Just as the objectives of business-to-business programs have been different from those of consumer markets, so too have the strategies employed to achieve these objectives. These differences are becoming less distinct, however, as you will see.

Developing Business-to-Business Promotional Strategies

In the past personal selling has been the primary promotional tool used by business-to-business marketers. As a result, much less emphasis has been focused on the development of advertising and promotional programs. Advertising was used almost exclusively to create awareness of products, and the messages were typically very rational, information laden, and somewhat "unexciting." Recently the role of advertising in the business-to-business promotional program has changed. For example, the use of color, illustrations, models, and emotional appeals has become more commonplace, as the role ascribed to this promotional element has expanded. As demonstrated in the ads for SPS Technologies and ABP shown Figure 19–6, exciting ads are no longer only the domain of consumer products marketers.

At the same time, this change in advertising strategy does not reflect a reduced emphasis on providing information and knowledge. Rather, it stems from the realization that to be seen and read the advertisement must gain the attention of the receiver. These ads must be designed to cut through the clutter of other competing ads and to assist in the attainment of communications objectives such as knowledge, evaluation, and attitude formation. Thus, more attractive and creative advertising is designed to accomplish these objectives.

Figure 19–7 This Business-to-Business Ad Is Designed to Stimulate Trial

Likewise, advertising strategies designed to achieve trial have increased. As you can see in the Nomadic Structures, Inc. ad shown in Figure 19–7, the ad goes beyond just providing product information and actually attempts to move the reader to action—in this case, asking for more information or (hopefully!) a trial demonstration.

In addition to advertising and promotions programs, business-to-business marketers have realized the importance of other promotional program elements. While personal selling continues to play a significant role in the promotional mix, public relations and direct-marketing efforts have also increased. The use of direct mail and telemarketing have been instrumental in reducing selling costs by screening prospects, determining interest levels and qualifications, and serving as a more cost-effective means of disseminating information to prospective customers. Public relations programs designed to achieve better customer relations and the use and management of publicity have also increased.

Sales promotions, like advertising, have become more creative and, along with the other promotional elements, have taken on a support role. An excellent example of this is provided in the materials shown in Figure 19–8. Notice that in addition to the ad a direct-mail brochure, a leave-behind promotional piece, and a demo disk are all used to promote the product. (These promotional materials generated the best response the Tektronics Division has had in years!)

Given the high costs of personal sales calls, support provided by advertising and promotional efforts is a direct benefit to be realized by industrial firms. Studies conducted by McGraw-Hill estimate that business publication advertising enhances personal selling efforts at only 21 cents per contact—far less than the $251.63 cost per sales call.[7] In addition, sales inquiries occurring through these activities may result in the generation of leads from sources the sales force previously had no knowledge of or time to explore on their own, increasing market coverage.

Figure 19–8   Tektronics Uses a Variety of Promotional Materials

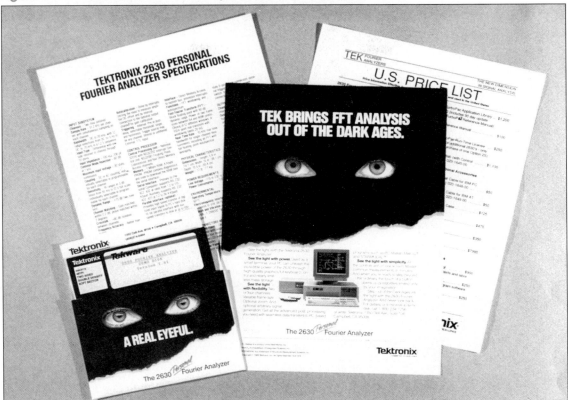

Implementing the Business-to-Business Program

As was noted earlier, nearly $100 billion was spent by the largest business-to-business marketers in the advertising and promotion of their products, services, and corporate image in 1988. Table 19–1 yields some interesting insights into the allocation of the business-to-business promotional budget. Those program elements that have the closest contact with the prospective buyer (direct marketing, trade shows, and incentives) generally receive the most emphasis, whereas those that seem to be more indirectly related to sales objectives receive much less attention. Let us examine these expenditures in more detail.

Advertising   Because of the broad reach of advertising, many of the media used to reach the consumer market receive less of the budget in the business-to-business sector. Advertising tends to be concentrated in business publications that reach specific

Table 19–1   Promotional Allocations of Business-to-Business Marketer

Advertising	$ 8,589,371,000
Direct marketing	30,850,000,000
Trade shows	21,000,000,000
Sales promotion	7,616,900,000
Incentives	15,065,871,000
Sales force management	5,920,000,000
Public relations	2,405,300,000
Research	2,190,200,000
Total	$93,637,642,000

Source: Bob Donath, "The $100 Billion Marketing Mix," *Business Marketing*, July 1986, p. 4. Reprinted with permission from Business Marketing Magazine. Copyright Crain Communications, Inc.

Table 19-2   Top 100 Specialized Business Publication Advertisers

Company	Ad Expenditures (in millions of dollars)	Company	Ad Expenditures (in millions of dollars)
1. AT&T Co.	16.507	51. BASF Corp.	3.175
2. Du Pont Co.	12.537	52. Pfizer Inc.	3.165
3. Hewlett-Packard Co.	11.594	53. Matsushita Electric Industrial Co.	3.128
4. General Electric Co.	10.936	54. Eaton Corp.	3.100
5. General Motors Corp.	9.658	55. Wyse Technology	3.092
6. NEC Corp.	9.446	56. Staley Continental Inc.	3.090
7. IBM Corp.	8.926	57. Tenneco Inc.	3.071
8. 3M Co.	8.886	58. GTE Corp.	3.065
9. Tektronix Inc.	7.754	59. Dow Jones & Co.	2.956
10. Motorola Inc.	7.071	60. United Technologies Corp.	2.951
11. Compaq Computer Corp.	7.001	61. Square D Co.	2.945
12. ITT Corp.	6.898	62. Monsanto Co.	2.908
13. Honeywell Inc.	6.543	63. TeleVideo Systems Inc.	2.898
14. Eastman Kodak Co.	5.997	64. Philip Morris Cos.	2.893
15. Caterpillar Tractor Co.	5.669	65. AST Research	2.888
16. NCR Corp.	5.474	66. Gould Inc.	2.882
17. Ford Motor Co.	5.448	67. Hitachi Ltd.	2.865
18. Toshiba Corp.	5.321	68. USG Corp.	2.861
19. Emerson Electric Co.	5.309	69. National Semiconductor Corp.	2.847
20. McGraw-Hill Publications Co.*	5.189	70. Conde Nast Publications Inc.*	2.829
21. Tyson Foods Inc.	5.148	71. W.R. Grace & Co.	2.809
22. Parker Hannifin Corp.	4.938	72. PCS Ltd.	2.781
23. Time Inc.	4.875	73. McDonnell Douglas Corp.	2.773
24. Texas Instruments Inc.	4.709	74. Clorox Co.	2.740
25. Premark International Inc.	4.649	75. Pierce Foods	2.735
26. Hearst Corp.*	4.584	76. Dover Corp.	2.734
27. American Dairy Association	4.573	77. Masco Corp.	2.718
28. Harris Corp.	4.547	78. LH Research	2.704
29. Rockwell International Corp.	4.466	79. SGS Semiconductor	2.699
30. Digital Equipment Corp.	4.459	80. Lotus Development Corp.	2.687
31. Philips N.V.	4.385	81. Raytheon Co.	2.646
32. RJR Nabisco Inc.	4.338	82. Andersen Corp.	2.642
33. Allied-Signal Inc.	4.265	83. Merck & Co.	2.618
34. Fujitsu America	4.214	84. Canon Inc.	2.594
35. BCI Holdings Corp.	4.038	85. Hayes Microcomputer	2.569
36. American Gas Association	4.024	86. AMR Corp.	2.533
37. Mars Inc.	3.977	87. American Express Co.	2.489
38. Dow Chemical Co.	3.974	88. Westinghouse Electric Corp.	2.461
39. Siemens AG	3.955	89. Tandy Corp.	2.453
40. AMP Inc.	3.756	90. Ciba-Geigy Ltd.	2.414
41. Nestle S.A.	3.685	91. General Signal Corp.	2.408
42. Cooper Industries Inc.	3.636	92. Imperial Chemical Industries PLC	2.383
43. Procter & Gamble Co.	3.579	93. Bristol-Myers Co.	2.375
44. Bell Canada	3.513	94. Trinova Corp.	2.372
45. The Stanley Works	3.475	95. Bayer AG	2.353
46. Xerox Corp.	3.447	96. Control Data Corp.	2.339
47. Avis Inc.	3.356	97. Alto-Shaam Inc.	2.325
48. Pittway Corp.*	3.285	98. Bell Atlantic Corp.	2.321
49. H.J. Heinz Co.	3.265	99. SAS Institute	2.312
50. Scientific Components Corp.	3.195	100. Park Ridge Corp.	2.274

*Free or discounted house ads may be included in the ad pages attributed to publishing company expenditures.

Note: Data drawn by counting ad pages in 580 specialized business publications. Advertiser expenditures are determined by applying the one-time rate to the space run. Although color and cover premiums are considered, agency discounts, bleed premiums, bulk discounts, etcetera, are not.

Source: Business Marketing, July 1988, p. 69. Reprinted with permission from Business Marketing Magazine. Copyright Crain Communications, Inc.

markets and the yellow pages. Table 19-2 shows the hundred leading advertisers in specialized business publications. (A poll of business marketers showed that 98 percent had advertised in one of the many trade publications available.)[8] Much less of the advertising dollar is spent on broadcast, outdoor, or other media that do not allow for specific targeting.

While broadcast media have not been used extensively in the past, this trend is changing. As Table 19-3 demonstrates, when used properly, even the broadest-reaching medium—television—may be used effectively.

Table 19–3   **Using Television in Business-to-Business Advertising**

While most business-to-business advertisers make little or no use of television in their promotional plans, Jeffrey W. Kaumeyer, of Hammond Farrell, Inc.—a New York advertising agency specializing in industrial marketing—notes that given three essential conditions, a number of possibilities for television exist:

The Essential Conditions

1. The prospects must be concentrated geographically.
2. The sales pitch must be boiled down to one simple, compelling human message.
3. Television must be complemented by the other, more basic components in a complete marketing communications plan.

The Possibilities
Ten other situations when television should be considered:

1. A first-class memorable spot can be produced for less than $197,000.
2. Purchase patterns are cyclical or heavily seasonal.
3. Buying influences are large in number and growing.
4. The most important buying influencers are hard to get in to see.
5. Speed of communication is essential.
6. The objective is to breathe life into a tired product and/or sales force.
7. Competitors' spending is "drowning out" your message.
8. You can continue to maintain at least a modest national presence.
9. Your marketing effort could use the support of indirect influences.
10. Your agency is making a good profit on your business (spot TV buying is not lucrative to the agency!).

Source: Jeffrey Kaumeyer, "When Should Business/Industrial Advertising Use Broadcast TV?" *Business Marketing,* April 1985, pp. 106–15. Reprinted with permission from Business Marketing Magazine. Copyright Crain Communications, Inc.

In fact, many of the mass media are experiencing an increase in business-to-business advertisements, owing to an increase in the business-to-business mass market. With such a large number of persons employed in the service business, marketers have often found that their advertising may now employ the use of mass media, with significantly less waste circulation than previously expected. (Notice the increasing number of ads for copy machines, computers, or other office equipment now being shown on prime-time television, an example of which is shown in Figure 19–9.)

Direct Marketing   Just as the consumer market has discovered the advantages of direct marketing, so too has the business-to-business marketer—particularly the benefits associated with telemarketing. Of the $31 billion estimated yearly expenditures in direct marketing, almost $28 million, or 90 percent, was allocated to telemarketing. An additional $3.1 billion was allocated to direct mail.

The reasons for the attractiveness of telemarketing include:

1. *Coverage* Telemarketing efforts can lead to significantly more contact with customers and potential customers. Thus, more persons can be exposed to the marketing communication and reached in much less time.
2. *Costs* We have already discussed the high cost per sales call of field salespersons. Add in the benefits offered as a prescreening device, and as a follow-up strategy, and telemarketing becomes an even more attractive alternative.
3. *Sales* Business-to-business sales account for approximately 80 percent of the sales generated through telemarketing. At an average sale of $1500, this effort is well spent (Figure 19–10).
4. *Market research* The telephone allows the business-to-business marketer to engage in instant market research. The direct contact this medium provides between the marketer and his or her customer allows the marketer to gain the customer's insights almost immediately while at the same time being able to gauge the response and follow up or probe.

As can be seen in Table 19–4, the use of direct-marketing methods—particularly telemarketing—is being applied to a number of sales and marketing functions.

Figure 19—9 **Business-to-Business Ads Are Becoming More Commonplace on Television**

All indications are that this trend is likely to continue and probably increase as personal selling and other media costs continue to climb.

Trade Shows As shown in Table 19—1, after direct marketing, the business-to-business marketer is most likely to utilize trade shows as a means of communica-

Figure 19—10 **Value of Average Business-to-Business Telemarketing Sale**

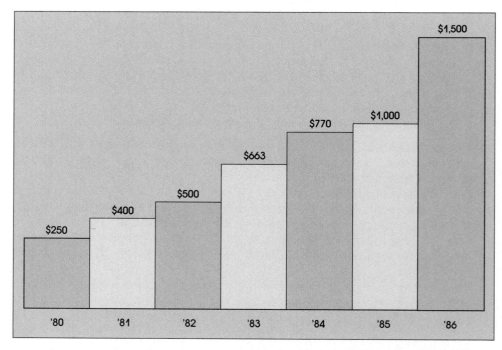

Source: National Telemarketing Association estimates, 1985. Adapted from *Business Marketing,* 1985 Survey, p. 7. Reprinted with permission from Business Marketing Magazine. Copyright Crain Communications, Inc.

Table 19–4 **Applications of Telemarketing in Business-to-Business Communications**

Application/Integration Through	Percentage
Customer service	83.5
Customer discretion or whoever is available to the customer at the time.	31.5
Telephone representatives refer service requests to the field.	24.7
Field representatives refer service requests to telephone representatives.	23.2
Separate field and telephone accounts/territories.	4.1
Order taking	88.8
Field representatives refer orders to telephone representatives.	30.7
Customer discretion or whoever is available to the customer at the time.	28.3
Telephone representatives refer orders to the field.	26.7
Separate field and telephone accounts/territories.	3.1
Handling complaints	84.7
Field representatives refer complaints to telephone representatives.	31.1
Customer discretion or whoever is available to the customer at the time.	24.5
Telephone representatives refer complaints to the field.	21.1
Separate field and telephone accounts/territories.	7.8
Product prepurchase information	87.4
Field representatives refer inquiries to telephone representatives.	32.9
Customer discretion or whoever is available to the customer at the time.	26.6
Telephone representatives refer inquiries to the field.	24.1
Separate field and telephone accounts/territories.	3.8
Lead generation	99.9
Telephone representatives refer leads to the field for follow-up.	40.0
Marketing/advertising services assigns leads to both.	37.7
Field representatives refer leads to telephone representatives for follow-up.	22.2
Lead qualification	75.0
Telephone representatives qualify leads then hand them off to the field for follow-up.	34.4
Field representatives qualify leads, then hand them off to telephone representatives for follow-up.	28.1
Marketing/advertising services assigns lead follow-up to both.	12.5
Prospecting	78.6
Telephone representatives refer prospects to the field for follow-up.	38.5
Field representatives refer orders to telephone representatives for follow-up.	29.3
Marketing/advertising services assigns prospects to both.	10.8
Full account management	97.6
Shared accounts: Telephone and field representatives exchange information on sales/service activity by phone, fax, mail, and electronic mail.	92.4
Separate telephone and field accounts/territories.	5.2
Dealer locator	79.3
Customer discretion or whoever is available to the customer at the time.	29.2
Telephone representatives refer inquiries to the field.	25.0
Field representatives refer inquiries to telephone representatives.	20.9
Separate field and telephone accounts/territories.	4.2

Note: Only integration methods mentioned by a significant number of respondents are mentioned above.

Source: Business Marketing, September 1987, p. 70. Reprinted with permission from Business Marketing Magazine. Copyright Crain Communications, Inc.

tion. In 1987 an estimated $21 billion was spent on this medium, with an estimated 87 percent of business magazine readers (or 40 million persons) stating that they had attended a trade show.

The reasons for the extensive use of this medium are many. First, the *cost per contact* is significantly lower when one uses trade shows than it would be through the field sales force. Equally important is the quality of the sales contact, as the majority of those attending trade shows have some influence in the purchase decision process, and most of those in attendance are there specifically to seek out new ideas or suppliers. The net result of this cost/contact combination is that the estimate to close a sale at a trade show is approximately $72 versus the over $1000 cost we cited earlier to do the same through the sales force.[9] Given these numbers, you can see why approximately 94 percent of industrial firms state that they use this communications medium.

Figure 19–11 **Percentage of Companies Spending Money on Sales Promotion**

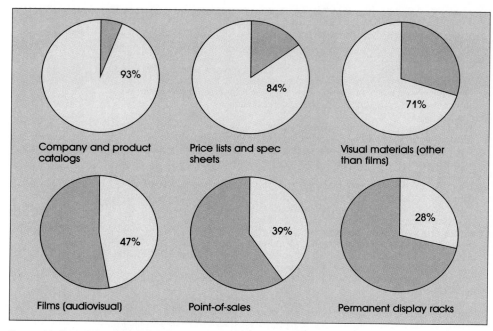

Source: McGraw-Hill Research, 1984. Adapted from Business Marketing Survey Research, 1985. Reprinted with permission from Business Marketing Magazine. Copyright Crain Communications, Inc.

Sales Promotions Approximately $7.6 billion was spent on sales promotions by industrial firms in 1987. As shown in Figure 19–11, these monies were allocated to a number of items ranging from company catalogs to point-of-sales materials to display racks. The role of these materials is to provide the sales force with aids to assist him or her in the selling effort and to be used as leave-behinds to serve as a reinforcement to the selling effort.

Incentives The use of incentives constitutes a substantial portion of the business-to-business communications budget (approximately 16 percent).[10] The majority of that money is spent on merchandise incentives provided to the company's sales force, dealers, distributors, and customers. This merchandise includes the use of specialty advertising materials, whereas others may be televisions, VCRs, radios, and even computers that are given as motivational tools. Another category not specifically mentioned in this category is cash incentives—most of which are provided directly to one's own sales force.

Public Relations While constituting only about 3 percent of the budget, 8 out of 10 industrial companies report that they have a formalized public relations function.[11] Because the public relations media typically used include business paper articles, trade magazines, and journals, the use of public relations has been used in much more of a marketing role than for other reasons mentioned in Chapter 17—as demonstrated in Figure 19–12.

Videotext Earlier in this book we discussed the medium known as videotext and at that time noted that the consumer use had not reached its expectations. It was stated that the consumer market for videotext was still a few years away. This is not the case in the business-to-business market. Some well-known companies such as IBM, Digital Equipment Corp., AT&T, and Honeywell are already employing this means of communication and have found it to be very successful. Given the large volumes of specific information that are often required by industrial firms, the capabilities of videotext make this medium a viable tool.

One of the markets in which videotext has been most useful is that of the gov-

Figure 19–12   **The Major Emphasis Top Marketers Place on Public Relations Programs**

	Percent responding*
Marketing/product support	85%
Corporate image building	19%
Employee communications	11%
Community relations	6%
Special events	6%
Financial/investor tours	5%
*Response adds to more than 100% due to multiple mentions.	

Source: Starmark Report 1, 1988, p. 12. Reprinted with permission from Business Marketing Magazine. Copyright Crain Communications, Inc.

ernment sector. Information regarding new laws, changes in product specifications, or contracts open for bid is very quickly and effectively communicated through this method. Since government decisions are typically (at least in theory!) based on comparative bids for products or services provided, communication of information relevant to the structuring of the bid is important, and timing is critical.

In summary, the relative use of each of the program elements discussed here will vary from one firm to the next. The use of each of these tools will be dictated by the objectives to be accomplished as well as the budgets provided, just as was the case in consumer products–oriented companies. Also, as was the case in consumer products companies, there is a need to employ marketing research as an input into the promotional program and for the purpose of evaluating the effectiveness of these programs. This topic of the use of research constitutes the basis of our discussion in the next section.

The Role of Research in the Business-to-Business Promotional Program

Throughout this text, we have discussed the contribution of research to the promotional process—both as an *input* into decision making as well as a *measure of the effectiveness* of various programs. Of course, the business-to-business market is no exception to this rule. In this section we will examine the business-to-business marketers' use of research as an aid to identification and entry into various markets. In the final section we will examine the use of research as a measure for evaluating the effectiveness of the promotional effort.

Research Input into the Decision Process

One of the factors that makes business-to-business marketing different is the fact that there often may be **multiple buying influences.** The roles of influencer, decision maker, purchaser, and user may not always be assumed by the same individuals. In this case the marketing manager must identify all those involved in the purchase decision process. This may mean that the manager may have to identify prospects by industry, by size of plant, and by title or job function. Otherwise, the advantages to be gained from specialized business media are lost, as the message will go unseen. To assist in this task, the manager has a number of secondary sources available.

Standard Industrial Classification (SIC) Data **SIC data** are provided by the U.S. Bureau of the Budget and provide a numerical description of a company based on the product it produces. Companies carry a three- or four-digit code, with each additional identifying code number more specifically identifying the manufactured product or service. Most major libraries contain SIC classification data, or the same can be acquired from the U.S. Government Printing Office in Washington, D.C.

Dun & Bradstreet **Dun & Bradstreet** publishes a plant list index based on SIC codes. While the government codes list the products made by plants, it does not carry the reverse information—that is, the names and number of plants manufacturing SIC code products. This information is provided by Dun & Bradstreet.

MCC Media Data Form The **MCC Media Data Form** provides information regarding an industry publication's circulation as well as its universe, or number of companies engaged in the business that this medium is addressing.

Census of Manufacturers The **Census of Manufacturers** provides reports on 452 SIC manufacturing industries in the United States, including number of establishments, employment, payrolls, hours worked, value added by manufacturing, quantity and value of products shipped, materials consumed, and capital expenditures.

U.S. Industrial Outlook **U.S. Industrial Outlook** is a yearly report provided by the U.S. government detailing sales, shipments, and forecasts for selected industries. The report also identifies key trends, innovations, and foreign impacts on the market.

Trade Publications In addition to those sources cited above, business-to-business marketers also rely on an estimated 3,000 trade publications. Certainly not all of these are relevant to each industry, as each provides specific information of interest and relevance to its own audience, as shown in Table 19–5. Still other trade magazines have a more general appeal, creating a broader base of interest.

Of course, business-to-business marketers also engage in *primary* research. This research may serve as input to the planning process or as a measure of effectiveness.

Evaluating Promotional Efforts

While 9 out of 10 business-to-business marketers consider marketing research to be important in their communications programs, Figure 19–13 seems to indicate that this importance is attributed more to research input rather than to evaluation. As can be seen, of the top 10 research studies used, none of these is specifically oriented to

Table 19–5 **A Sampling of Trade Publications**

Publication		Industry
	Industry Specific	
Banking Industry		Banking
Beverage Industry		Bottling
American Cemetery		Cemetery and monuments
Interior Textiles		Drapery
Dairy Field		Dairy
Library Journal		Education
Product Marketing		Cosmetics
Executive Jeweler		Jewelry
Coal Age		Coal mining
	General Industry	
Advertising Age		Advertising
Sales & Marketing Management		Sales/marketing
Forbes		Financial/business
Computer World		Computers

Figure 19—13 **Top 10 Research Studies Used by Business-to-Business Marketers**

	Percent responding*
Market position studies	56%
Readership studies	46%
Customer attitude studies	42%
Focus groups	37%
New product feasibility studies	37%
Competitive environment analyses	35%
Brand preference studies	33%
Market potential studies	31%
Company image studies	27%
Prospect feedback studies	20%
*Response adds to more than 100% due to multiple mentions.	

Source: Starmark Report I, 1988, p. 10. Reprinted with permission from Business Marketing Magazine. Copyright Crain Communications, Inc.

measuring the effects of advertising and promotions. (While focus groups are also cited, these groups are primarily used to "provide in-depth views of sales prospect attitudes" rather than to evaluate ads.) Of the monies that are spent specifically on advertising research, approximately 23 percent is used to pretest the effectiveness of ads or to follow up the effects once the ad campaign has been implemented.[12] The remaining 77 percent is again used as input into the advertising program.

Interestingly, even though the number of dollars spent on evaluative research appears low, there are a number of research services available to the business-to-business advertiser, as shown in Table 19–6. These services provide a variety of effectiveness measures.

Throughout this chapter we have repeatedly mentioned the fact (probably to the point where you cannot wait to see it again!) that business-to-business marketers tend to place a very strong emphasis on the use of advertising and promotional tools to assist in the sales support effort. It should come as no surprise, then, that the measures most commonly employed to determine the relative effectiveness of these programs also employ the criterion of assessing contribution to the selling effort. Examination of the measures of advertising effectiveness that are employed by business-to-business advertisers reflects the emphasis placed on these efforts.

In addition to some of the more commonly employed criteria used in the general-interest and/or consumer market (read most, awareness, attention, recall), more behavioral (and sales-oriented) items such as readership by purchase decision, built preference, kept customers sold, referred ad to someone else, and specified or purchased product, among others, are offered. In Table 19–7 the criteria used by *Copy Chasers*—a panel of business-to-business experts who evaluate ads for *Business Marketing* magazine—provides insight into what is considered necessary to communicate effectively in this market.

As you can see, in the business-to-business market the expectations of the role

Table 19-6   A Sampling of Effectiveness Measures Available to Business-to-Business Advertisers

Ad-Sell Performance Study	McGraw-Hill telephone survey of 100 magazine readers. Scores: established contact; created awareness; aroused interest; built preference; kept customers sold
Ad-Chart	Chilton Marketing Research Co. survey of 100 readers. Scores: % noticed ad; % started to read; % read half or more; total readership index; informativeness index; cost-effectiveness index
Beta Research	Conducts studies in health care field. Scores: likelihood of reading; changes in opinion of product as a result of ad; informativeness of ad; believability of ad
Fosdick Ad Evaluation	Surveys 100 respondents. Scores: buyers who read ad; buyers who did not read ad; nonbuyers who read ad; nonbuyers who did not read ad
Gallup and Robinson	Reports on 150 respondents. Scores: proved name registration; idea communication; favorable attitude
Starch Readership Reports	Readership of ads. Scores: noted; associated; read most
Advalue	Readership by 100 persons. Scores: recall seeing; readership; ad effect; action taken; future purchase; salesperson contact; ad comparisons
Ad Lab	Mail survey sent to 750 to 1,500 subscribers. Scores: total sample noting; total sample who started to read; total sample reading more than half; total finding ad informative/useful; buyers noting/specified; buyers/specifiers starting to read; buyers/specifiers reading more than half; buyers/specifiers finding ad or editorial informative/useful

Source: Adapted from *Advertising Research* (New York: Business Professional Advertising Association, 1983), pp. 37–60.

to be performed by advertising are somewhat different than what might be expected in the consumer market. The question to be asked here is, Should advertising be expected to generate such results? Or, perhaps even more interestingly, is this also a potential reason as to why so little is spent on measuring advertising effectiveness in the business-to-business market?

In sum, marketing and advertising research in business markets tends to be more oriented to that conducted for the purpose of providing input into the marketing and promotional programs. As the role of advertising continues to change in this area, the amount and types of research used may follow.

Table 19-7   The Copy Chasers Criteria

1. The successful ad has a high degree of visual magnetism.
2. The successful ad selects the right audience.
3. The successful ad promises a reward.
4. The successful ad backs up the promise.
5. The successful ad talks person to person.
6. The successful ad presents the selling proposition in logical sequence.
7. The successful ad invites the reader into the scene.
8. Successful advertising is easy to read.
9. Successful advertising has been purged of nonessentials.
10. Successful advertising emphasizes the service, not the source.

Source: Business Marketing, January 1989, p. 75. Reprinted with permission from Business Marketing Magazine. Copyright Crain Communications, Inc.

Summary

This chapter has presented a slightly different perspective of the use of advertising and promotion. It was noted that the business-to-business advertiser views the role of advertising and promotions somewhat differently than those in the consumer products industries. Whereas the latter may perceive the role of advertising and promotions to be designed to impact communications objectives, in the business-to-business sector it is generally considered to be a sales support aid.

Because of the role that advertising and promotions are asked to assume, the message and media strategies designed to accomplish the sales support objectives are again different than those that might be more commonly employed in the consumer products market. Messages tend to be more information laden, more straight to the point, and designed to elicit inquiries or answer questions. The use of illustrations, humor, and/or sex are much less commonly employed.

The media employed by industrial advertisers are also different. It was noted that no less than 3,000 trade journals exist in the area, with the vast majority of firms reporting that they make use of these. Trade shows and sales incentives were also commonly employed. Videotext—somewhat of a disappointment in the consumer products market—has found a great reception in the industrial sector.

Finally, the measures used to determine the effectiveness of business-to-business strategies were also shown to be sales support oriented. Criteria such as number of inquiries generated, referrals, and actual purchases are often employed to determine the relative effectiveness of alternative strategies.

Key Terms

Business-to-business advertising
Derived demand
Buying center
Social Style Model
CUBE Model
Multiple buying influences

SIC data
Dun & Bradstreet
MCC Media Data Form
Census of Manufacturers
U.S. Industrial Outlook

Discussion Questions

1. Explain why *business-to-business advertising* has replaced the use of the term *industrial advertising.*
2. What are some of the reasons why business-to-business advertising has tended to be more rational and product specific in its appeals?
3. Explain some of the differences in media strategies employed by business-to-business and consumer products marketers.
4. Discuss some of the criteria used to evaluate business-to-business ads. How do they differ from those used in the consumer products market?
5. Find examples of business-to-business ads that reflect service sector and industrial sector products. Discuss the appeals used in each.
6. Why has the use of mass media such as television and consumer magazines for advertising business-to-business products and services been on the increase?
7. Why are trade shows such an important medium for the business-to-business advertiser?

Notes

1. Adapted from "Business to Business No Longer Means Grade B," *Adweek,* December 9, 1985, p. 28.
2. "We're All Consumers, Right?" *Business Marketing,* New York, 1988.
3. Yolanda Brugaletta, "What Business to Business Advertisers Can Learn from Consumer Advertisers," *Journal of Advertising Research* 25, no. 3 (June/July 1985), pp. 8–9.
4. Anderson & Lembke, Inc., Stamford, CT, 1985 sales promotion literature.
5. Tom Eisenhart, "How to Really Excite Your Prospects," *Business Marketing,* July 1988, pp. 44–55.
6. *The Starmark Report I, Business Marketing,* 1988, p. 10. Reprinted with permission from Business Marketing Magazine. Copyright Crain Communications, Inc.
7. LAP Report no. 70208 (New York: McGraw-Hill, 1988).
8. *Advertising Research* (New York: Business/Professional Advertising Association Report, 1983), p. V.
9. *1986 Starmark Report, Business Marketing,* p. 9.
10. Bob Donath, "The $100 Billion Marketing Mix," *Business Marketing,* July 1986, p. 4.
11. *1986 Starmark Report,* p. 17.
12. Ibid.
13. Ibid.

20

International Advertising and Promotion

CHAPTER OBJECTIVES

1. To examine the importance of international marketing and the role of international advertising and promotion

2. To examine the various factors in the international environment and how they influence advertising and promotion decisions

3. To consider the issue of global versus localized marketing and advertising and the pros and cons of each

4. To examine the various decision areas of international advertising

5. To examine the role of other promotional mix elements in the international marketing program

Parker Tries Global Advertising

In the early 1980s the Parker Pen Company sold one of the world's best-known brands of writing instruments. More than 500 styles of pens were manufactured in 18 plants and marketed from local offices in more than 150 countries, all of which created their own packaging and advertising. However, the market was changing rapidly, as the Japanese were flooding the United States and many other countries with inexpensive, disposable pens, and distribution patterns were moving from department and stationery stores to mass market outlets.

In 1982 Parker hired a new president and CEO who decided that the company must pursue the low-end market and developed a new strategy that called for vigorous marketing of low-priced pens. An integral part of the new strategy was the decision to launch a global marketing effort whereby Parker would centralize and standardize everything connected with the selling effort, including packaging, pricing, promotional materials, and especially advertising. A formidable team of international marketing executives was assembled, and everything was brought under the global marketing umbrella. The product line was reduced to 100 pen styles made at only eight plants, and Parker's advertising, which had been handled by more than 40 different agencies around the world, was turned over to a single agency to handle on a worldwide basis.

The global marketing and advertising strategy was implemented in early 1984. Parker management insisted that the advertising for Parker pens, regardless of model, be based on a common creative strategy and positioning. A worldwide advertising theme—"Make your mark with a Parker"—was adopted, and the ads used similar graphics, layout, and photography, despite strong resistance from the agency, which was opposed to the "one world, one brand, one look" global advertising idea (see Figure 20–1). Parker also encountered resistance and displeasure from local managers in its overseas markets who resented the home office mandating what the advertising should be and what agency they had to use.

In 1985 Parker suffered a $12 million loss, and by 1986 the pen business was sold to a group of local British managers who forced out the executives who had implemented the global approach. Parker returned to its customized strategy whereby local managers choose their own agencies and develop their own ads, which are once again tailored to local markets. The company went from the verge of bankruptcy to once again being profitable.

The global advertising strategy was not the sole cause of Parker's problems, as the company also experienced serious production problems, an increase in the value of the dollar, and the difficulty of attempting to pursue a low-end market that ran against its tradition and image. However, Parker's failed attempt at global marketing shows the problems a firm can encounter when it tries to standardize its advertising, ignore market differences, and take decisions out of the hands of the local managers who must implement them.[1,2]

Introduction

Throughout this book attention has been focused on the development of promotional programs for products and services sold to the U.S. market. One of the reasons for this orientation is that U.S. companies have traditionally devoted most of their marketing efforts to the domestic market, since they often lack the resources, skills, or incentive to go abroad. This is changing very rapidly, however, as U.S. corporations recognize not only the opportunities that foreign markets offer for new sources of sales and profits but also the necessity of marketing their products internationally.

Many firms are finding that the U.S. market offers them limited opportunity for expansion owing to slow population growth, saturated markets, and intense competition. For example, U.S. tobacco companies are faced with a declining domestic consumption as a result of restrictions on their marketing and advertising efforts and the growing antismoking sentiment in this country. Thus, companies such as R. J. Reynolds and Philip Morris are turning to foreign markets in Asian, European, and South American countries where there are less restrictions and cigarette consumption is increasing.[3,4]

It has also become increasingly important for U.S. companies to adopt an international marketing orientation since imports are taking a larger and larger share of the domestic market for many products and are likely to continue to do so in the future. Japanese companies, which have captured significant portions of the U.S. consumer electronic and automobile markets, are now beginning to move into other prod-

Figure 20–1 **Parker's Global Advertising Strategy Called for Nearly Identical Ads in Each Foreign Market**

uct areas such as soft drinks, cosmetics, laundry detergents, and clothing.[5,6] The United States has been running a continuing **balance-of-trade deficit** whereby the monetary value of our imports exceeds that of our exports. American companies are realizing that we are shifting from being an isolated, self-sufficient, national economy to being part of an interdependent **global economy.**[7] This means that U.S. corporations not only must take steps to defend against foreign inroads into the domestic market but also must learn how to market their products and services to other countries.

The importance, as well as the potential profitability, of international marketing has long been realized by a number of U.S. companies such as IBM, Ford, General Motors, Exxon, Dow Chemical, Du Pont, and Colgate-Palmolive, which generate a great deal of their sales and profits from foreign markets. Gillette sells over 800 products in more than 200 countries, whereas Procter & Gamble markets 165 products in 11 product categories overseas and had international sales of $6.5 billion in 1988.[8] Coke, Pepsi, McDonald's, and many other U.S. brands are known all over the world (Figure 20–2).

While many U.S. companies are becoming more aggressive in their pursuit of

Figure 20—2 **McDonald's Is Familiar to Consumers around the World**

international markets, some of the largest multinational corporations, and most formidable marketers, are European companies such as Unilever, Nestlé, Seemens, Philips NV, and Renault as well as the various Japanese automobile and electronic manufacturers and packaged-goods companies such as Suntory, Shiseido, and Kao.

Table 20—1 shows the top 50 advertisers in terms of advertising spending outside the United States. While U.S.-based Procter & Gamble is ranked number one in terms of worldwide spending, the Anglo-Dutch consumer products conglomerate Unilever emerged as the top advertising spender outside the United States in 1988. Of the top 50 spenders on advertising outside this country, only 10 are headquartered in the United States, whereas 29 are based in Japan and 11 in Europe. These figures indicate the importance that foreign-based multinational corporations place on the international marketplace (including the United States) in their corporate strategies.

Role of International Advertising and Promotion

Advertising and promotion are crucial parts of the international marketing program of firms competing in the world marketplace as evidenced by the more than $19 billion spent on advertising in 1988 by the top 50 firms alone. More and more companies are recognizing that an effective promotional program is particularly important for competing in foreign markets. As Vern Terpstra notes in his book *International Marketing:*

> Promotion is the most visible as well as the most culture bound of the firm's marketing functions. Marketing includes the whole collection of activities the firm performs in relating to its market, but in other functions the firm relates to the market in a quieter, more passive way. With the promotional function, however, the firm is standing up and speaking out, wanting to be seen and heard.[9]

However, in addition to its importance, many companies are realizing the challenge and difficulties they face in developing and implementing advertising and promotion programs for international markets. Companies planning on marketing and advertising their products or services abroad are faced with an unfamiliar marketing environment and customers with a different set of values, customs, consumption patterns and habits, as well as differing purchase motives and abilities. Not only may the language vary from country to country, but several may be spoken within a country,

Table 20–1   **Fifty Leading Advertisers in Spending Outside the United States**

Rank	Advertiser	Headquarters	Primary business	Countries in which spending was reported for 1988	Non-U.S. spending ($000)	'88-'87 % chg	U.S. spending ($000)	W'wide spending ($000)	Non-U.S. as % of w'wide
1	Unilever NV/PLC	Rotterdam/London	Soaps	Argentina, Australia, Austria, Bahrain, Belgium, Brazil, Britain, Canada, Chile, France, Germany (West), India, Italy, Japan, Malaysia, Mexico, Netherlands, New Zealand, Puerto Rico, Qatar, South Africa, Spain, Switzerland, Thailand	$1,207,509	42.6%	$607,500	$1,815,009	66.5%
2	Procter & Gamble Co.	Cincinnati	Soaps	Australia, Austria, Bahrain, Belgium, Britain, Canada, France, Germany (West), Italy, Japan, Mexico, Netherlands, New Zealand, Oman, Philippines, Puerto Rico, Qatar, Saudi Arabia, United Arab Emirates	932,724	39.3%	1,506,900	2,439,624	38.2%
3	Nestle SA	Vevey, Switzerland	Food	Argentina, Australia, Austria, Belgium, Brazil, Britain, Canada, Chile, France, Germany (West), Japan, Jordan, Mexico, Netherlands, New Zealand, Philippines, Spain, Taiwan, Thailand	600,586	35.8%	573,800	1,174,386	51.1%
4	Renault SA	Paris	Automotive	Argentina, Austria, Belgium, Britain, France, Germany (West), Italy, Netherlands, Spain, Thailand	370,056	30.7%	NA	370,056	100.0%
5	Matsushita Electric Industrial Co.	Osaka, Japan	Electronics	Britain, Hong Kong, Japan, Taiwan, Thailand	365,252	53.6%	61,754	427,007	85.5%
6	Fiat SpA	Turin, Italy	Automotive	Belgium, Britain, France, Germany (West), Italy, Netherlands, Spain	354,568	35.6%	458*	355,026	99.9%
7	Mars Inc.	McLean, Va.	Food	Australia, Austria, Belgium, Britain, Canada, France, Germany (West), Japan, Netherlands, New Zealand	352,983	45.1%	339,700	692,683	51.0%
8	Kao Corp.	Tokyo	Soaps	Japan, Taiwan, Thailand	344,233	19.2%	12,022*	356,255	96.6%
9	Nissan Motor Co.	Tokyo	Automotive	Australia, Britain, Canada, Germany (West), Japan, Mexico, Netherlands, New Zealand, Thailand	333,215	17.9%	224,900	558,115	59.7%
10	Toyota Motor Co.	Toyota City, Japan	Automotive	Australia, Belgium, Canada, Germany (West), Japan, Netherlands, New Zealand, Norway, Oman, Saudi Arabia, Switzerland, Thailand, United Arab Emirates	322,598	16.5%	272,900	595,498	54.2%
11	Henkel	Duesseldorf	Soaps	Austria, Belgium, France, Germany (West), Italy, Netherlands, Spain	318,647	35.6%	NA	318,647	100.0%
12	Philip Morris Cos.	New York	Food	Argentina, Australia, Bahrain, Britain, Canada, France, Germany (West), Hong Kong, Italy, Japan, Kuwait, Malaysia, Mexico, Netherlands, Oman, Qatar, Saudi Arabia, Switzerland, United Arab Emirates	318,065	32.1%	2,058,200	2,376,265	13.4%
13	Peugeot SA	Paris	Automotive	Austria, Belgium, Britain, France, Germany (West), Netherlands, Spain, Thailand	292,341	41.1%	24,342*	316,683	92.3%
14	General Motors Corp.	Detroit	Automotive	Austria, Belgium, Brazil, Britain, Canada, France, Germany (West), Mexico, Netherlands, Norway, Switzerland, Thailand	274,061	41.5%	1,294,000	1,568,061	17.5%
15	Honda Motor Co.	Tokyo	Automotive	Australia, Canada, Germany (West), Japan, Mexico, New Zealand, Thailand	272,599	NA	243,300	515,899	52.8%
16	Mitsubishi Motors Corp.	Tokyo	Automotive	Australia, Japan, New Zealand	266,256	NA	68,931	335,187	79.4%
17	Hitachi Ltd.	Tokyo	Electronics	Japan, Thailand	257,620	52.0%	14,069*	271,689	94.8%
18	Colgate-Palmolive Co.	New York	Soaps	Australia, France, Germany (West), India, Italy, Malaysia, Mexico, Netherlands, New Zealand, Philippines, Puerto Rico, South Africa, Thailand	253,532	10.2%	306,600	560,132	45.3%
19	Coca-Cola Co.	Atlanta	Food	Argentina, Australia, Austria, Brazil, Britain, Canada, Chile, France, Germany (West), Israel, Japan, Mexico, Netherlands, New Zealand, Philippines, Thailand	236,603	21.3%	385,100	621,703	38.1%
20	Ford Motor Co.	Dearborn, Mich.	Automotive	Argentina, Australia, Austria, Belgium, Brazil, Britain, Canada, France, Germany (West), Mexico, Netherlands, New Zealand, Norway, Switzerland, Thailand	234,914	7.0%	569,800	804,714	29.2%
21	NEC Corp.	Tokyo	Electronics	Japan, Mexico, New Zealand, Thailand	232,735	25.2%	10,886*	243,620	95.5%
22	Volkswagen AG	Wolfsburg, W. Germany	Automotive	Argentina, Belgium, Britain, France, Germany (West), Mexico, Norway, South Africa, Spain, Sweden, Thailand	230,313	27.0%	140,300	370,613	62.1%
23	Suntory	Tokyo	Beer	Japan	210,568	11.7%	2,238*	212,806	98.9%
24	Toshiba Corp.	Tokyo	Electronics	Japan, Thailand	199,829	37.2%	19,210*	219,039	91.2%
25	Asahi Breweries	Tokyo	Beer	Japan	197,456	55.9%	138*	197,594	99.9%
26	Ferrero SpA	Perugia, Italy	Food	Italy, Germany (West)	191,420	86.4%	5,521*	196,942	97.2%
27	Philips NV	Eindhoven, Netherlands	Electronics	Argentina, Austria, Brazil, Chile, France, Germany (West), India, Italy, Japan, Mexico, Netherlands, New Zealand, Thailand	187,498	39.2%	144,311	331,809	56.5%
28	Kirin Brewery Co.	Tokyo	Beer	Japan, Thailand	186,992	51.9%	1,080*	188,072	99.4%
29	Daiei	Kobe, Japan	Retail	Japan	181,023	28.5%	NA	181,023	100.0%
30	Kellogg Co.	Battle Creek, Mich.	Food	Argentina, Australia, Britain, Canada, France, Germany (West), Japan, Mexico, New Zealand	179,831	25.7%	683,100	862,931	20.8%
31	Lion Corp.	Tokyo	Soaps	Japan	177,993	6.4%	NA	177,993	100.0%
32	Nippon Telephone & Telegraph	Tokyo	Telecommunications	Japan	177,039	36.4%	NA	177,039	100.0%
33	Sapporo Beer	Tokyo	Beer	Japan	173,079	71.0%	NA	173,079	100.0%
34	Fujitsu Ltd.	Tokyo	Computers	Japan, Thailand	155,976	58.4%	30*	156,005	100.0%
35	Sharp Corp.	Osaka, Japan	Electronics	Japan, Thailand	153,617	44.2%	12,140*	165,757	92.7%
36	Takashimaya	Osaka, Japan	Retail	Japan	153,208	32.8%	NA	153,208	100.0%
37	Fuji Photo Film Co.	Tokyo	Photography	Japan, Mexico, Thailand	152,691	31.3%	11,735*	164,426	92.9%
38	C&A NV	Amsterdam	Retail	Austria, Germany (West), Netherlands	145,481	6.6%	NA	145,481	100.0%
39	PepsiCo	Purchase, N.Y.	Food	Argentina, Australia, Britain, Canada, Japan, Mexico, Netherlands, New Zealand, Puerto Rico, Qatar, Saudi Arabia, Singapore	138,911	45.8%	712,300	851,211	16.3%
40	British Government	London	NA	Britain	134,887	-2.9%	48,063	182,950	73.7%
41	BMW AG	Munich, West Germany	Automotive	Britain, France, Germany (West), Japan, Netherlands	109,879	27.3%	91,090	200,969	54.7%
42	Barilla SpA	Parma, Italy	Food	Italy	106,260	40.3%	NA	106,260	100.0%
43	McDonald's Corp.	Oak Brook, Ill.	Food	Australia, Canada, Hong Kong, Japan, Mexico, Netherlands, New Zealand, Singapore	99,761	33.0%	728,300	828,061	12.0%
44	Gervais Danone	Levallois-Perret, France	Food	Belgium, France, Italy, Japan	96,857	14.7%	NA	96,857	100.0%
45	RJR Nabisco	New York	Food	Canada, France, Hong Kong, Japan, Malaysia, New Zealand	96,758	60.5%	814,500	911,258	10.6%
46	Jacobs Suchard	Zurich	Food	Argentina, Austria, Germany (West)	90,196	6.8%	4,254*	94,450	95.5%
47	BAT Industries	London	Retail	Argentina, Brazil, Hong Kong, Japan, Malaysia, Netherlands, South Africa	89,465	70.9%	184,100	273,565	32.7%
48	British Telecom	London	Telecommunications	Britain	82,659	74.9%	786*	83,445	99.1%
49	Kingfisher	London	Retail	Britain	82,425	37.5%	NA	82,425	100.0%
50	Cole Myer	Sydney	Retail	Australia	80,107	15.6%	NA	80,107	100.0%

Notes and sources: Advertising expenditures are in thousands of U.S. dollars for year-end 1988. In many countries, ad spending figures are estimates and/or gross figures. * indicates that U.S. spending figures include measured media only as reported by LNA/Arbitron Multi-Media reports. All other U.S. spending figures include estimated unmeasured expenditures, from AA's 100 Leading National Advertisers, Sept. 27, 1989. Non-US ad spending includes only countries in the column headed "Countries in which spending was reported." See also "How to read this ranking." Page S-14. Peugeot SA includes spending for Citroen and Talbot.

Source: Advertising Age, December 19, 1988, p. 26.

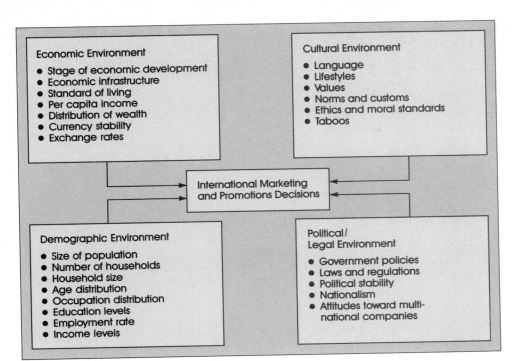

Figure 20-3   **Forces in the International Marketing Environment**

such as in India or Switzerland. Many U.S. companies also find that media options are much more limited in many foreign countries owing to lack of availability or limited effectiveness. As a result of all these factors, different creative and media strategies as well as changes in other elements of the advertising and promotional program are often required for foreign markets.

In this chapter the focus is on the role of advertising and promotion in a company's international marketing program. We will examine the environment of international marketing and how companies must adapt their promotional programs to conditions in each country. Attention will be given to the issue of whether a company should use a global marketing and advertising approach or whether it needs to develop customized campaigns for each market. We will also examine how firms organize for international advertising, select agencies, and consider various decision areas such as research, creative strategy, and media selection. While the primary focus of this chapter will be on international advertising, we will also consider issues involved in using other promotional mix elements in international marketing, including sales promotion, personal selling, and publicity.

The International Environment

Just as with domestic marketing, companies engaging in international marketing must carefully analyze and consider the major environmental factors of each market in which they compete. The major environmental factors affecting international marketing include economic, demographic, cultural, and political/legal variables. Figure 20-3 shows some of the factors marketers must consider in each category when analyzing the environment of each country or market. Consideration of these factors is important not only in evaluating the viability and/or potential of each country as a market but also in designing and implementing a marketing and promotional program.

Economic Environment

A country's economic conditions indicate its present and future potential for consuming, as products and services can only be sold to countries where there is enough in-

Table 20–2   **Advertising Expenditures by Country, 1987**

Country	Total Reported 1987 Advertising Expenditures (in millions of U.S. $)	
United States	109,650.00	
Japan	27,273.20	
United Kingdom	10,266.00	
Germany, Fed. Rep.	9,985.80	
Canada	5,479.90	
France	6,723.00	
Italy	4,380.10	
Spain	4,372.20	
Australia	3,033.10	
Brazil	1,991.00	
Netherlands	3,193.00	
Switzerland	2,976.80	
Finland	1,471.50	
Sweden	1,416.80	
South Korea	1,182.20	

Source: "Twenty-Second Survey of World Advertising Expenditures," Starch INRA Hooper, Inc. in cooperation with International Advertising Association, 1988.

come to buy them. This is generally not a problem in developed countries such as the United States, Canada, Japan, and most of Western Europe, as consumers in these industrialized nations generally have higher income levels and standards of living. Thus, they have the capability and an interest in purchasing a variety of products and services. It is also important to note that developed countries have the **economic infrastructure** in terms of the communications, transportation, financial, and distribution networks that are needed to conduct business in these markets effectively. Not only do many developing countries lack purchasing power, but there are also limited communications networks available to firms that might want to promote their products or services to these markets.

For most companies, industrialized nations represent the greatest marketing and advertising opportunities for the reasons cited above. A report by Starch INRA Hooper and the International Advertising Association showed that the United States spends more money on advertising than do all other nations combined.[10] Per capita spending on advertising was also the highest in the United States at $424.07, compared with an average of $51.43 for the other 66 countries. Table 20–2 lists the countries with more than $1 billion in advertising expenditures in 1987.

As can be seen in this table, advertising expenditures are greatest in the more highly developed countries of the world. However, as was noted earlier, most of these countries have stable population bases, and their markets for many products and services may already be saturated. Thus, companies are turning their attention to some of the developing nations that have expanding populations and present greater growth opportunities. For example, Swiss-based Nestlé, which is the world's largest food company, estimates that 20 percent of the world's population in Europe and North America consumes 80 percent of its products. While Nestlé continues to target the European and American markets with ads such as the one shown in Figure 20–4, the company is also focusing attention on Third World nations as the "market of tomorrow".[11]

Demographic Environment

In addition to considering the economic environment of a country, international marketers must also examine its various demographic characteristics. Major demographic differences exist between various countries as well as within them. Marketers must consider a variety of demographic factors including income levels and distribution, age and occupation distributions of the population, household size, education, and employment rates. In some countries, factors such as literacy rates must be considered,

as many people cannot read and thus they would not respond well to print ads. Demographic data can provide insight into the living standards and lifestyles in a particular country that can be helpful in planning an advertising campaign.

Demographic data provide marketers with insight into the market potential of various foreign markets. For example, China already has over 1 billion people, and by the year 2000 the population of India is expected to reach nearly 1 billion. Promotional Perspective 20–1 discusses how American companies are beginning to turn their attention to China, a country that is being touted as the "last marketing frontier."

Latin America remains one of the world's largest potential markets.[12] Brazil, which has the largest consumer market in South America, is expected to have a population of over 200 million by the year 2000 and will be a growth market for many products and services. In 1988 the Brazilian government passed legislation permitting the sale of diet soft drinks, which had been kept out of the $2 billion soft-drink market by the country's powerful sugar cane growers. Coca-Cola and Pepsi-Cola both quickly entered the market with their diet products.[13]

Cultural Environment

Another extremely important aspect of the international marketing environment is the culture of each country. Among the most important cultural variables for marketers to consider are the language, the customs, the tastes, the attitudes, the lifestyle, the values, and the ethical/moral standards of each society. Nearly every country exhibits cultural differences that influence both the needs and wants of consumers and also how they go about satisfying them.

Marketers must be sensitive to foreign cultures not only in determining what products and services they can be sold but also in communicating with them. Advertising is often the most effective method of communicating with potential buyers and

Promotional Perspective 20-1

Advertising Returns to China

For many years marketers could only dream of selling their products to China's more than 1 billion people. However, companies such as Coca-Cola, Pepsi, General Foods, Kodak, Sony, and Nike are now marketing their products to the world's largest potential mass market. And advertising, once banned as a capitalist scourge, has not only returned but is being encouraged both internationally and by foreign companies. The Chinese government has hailed advertising as a great economic force that can boost developing nations through the role it plays in linking consumption to production.

The rebirth of advertising in China actually began in 1979 with the end of the cultural revolution and the country's massive remodernization drive, which has resulted in unprecedented surges in wages, prices, production, and retail sales. The country's leaders say advertising fits into the reawakening of the country's economy, because it not only stimulates sales but also teaches Chinese consumers and business leaders about developments in the rest of the world during the past 30 years.

Underlying the advertising boom is a new spirit of consumption. Young couples in the country aspire for what they call the "eight big things"—a color TV, a refrigerator, a stereo, a camera, a motorcycle, a modern furniture suite, a washing machine, and an electric fan. Of course, advertisers do not want them to stop there and hope to sell them a host of other products. China is said to be a brand-conscious society, and although most of the brands are local, anything American is in high demand.

Advertisers have a variety of media to choose from in China, including major daily newspapers, popular magazines, television, and billboards—the last of which are the most popular medium. The *People's Daily* newspaper has the largest circulation in the world (5 million), but only 10 percent of the paper is devoted to advertising, and rates are very high. Foreign firms will often pay much more than the standard rates to avoid the three- to six-month wait to advertise in the paper. Television is the newest medium in China and the fastest growing. There are an estimated 80 million TV sets in the country, and 200 to 600 million people tune to CCTV, China's national television network.

While the size of the Chinese market makes it very appealing to foreign companies, there are still many limitations and obstacles advertisers must deal with. For example, the average annual per capita income in China is about Y300 (Y = yuan) or U.S.$100. Even in major cities, where the standard of living is relatively high, incomes average only about U.S.$50 per month. Thus, a large part of a family's income goes to food and basic necessities. Savings are designated for purchase of special items such as one of the eight big things, for which consumers demand high quality.

Foreign companies also face tremendous cultural barriers and political/legal restrictions when marketing to China. The government urges that advertising not affect the political, moral, or social climate in that country. To protect consumers and raise the standards of advertising, tough new regulations have been enacted that crack down on advertisers that misrepresent products or make wildly exaggerated claims. Cigarette advertising is prohibited on radio and TV and in magazines, whereas ads for alcohol are permitted but require government approval. Advertising in China is very basic, and agencies encourage their clients to keep the ads straightforward, factual, and single-minded. Emphasis should be given to performance, quality, and durability. Because of Japan's dominance among foreign advertisers in China, many Western companies look to the Japanese to see what they are doing. China represents a market of tremendous potential to many companies that are willing to take a long-term strategy, go through the learning process, and remain committed to building relationships in this country.

The civil unrest and violence that occurred in China in June 1989 has led many Western companies and advertising agencies to reassess their plans for the Chinese market. Many ad agencies, marketers, and media closed offices and canceled advertising campaigns, and the future of the operations has become uncertain. Some industry experts feel that China may become less open to Westernization and foreign products, which would reduce the need for advertising. Others, however, feel that China's move toward commercialism will continue and that business will soon return to normal.

Sources: Marian Katz, "Knowing Chinese Ways Keys Access to Rich New Markets," *International Advertiser*, December 1985, p. 16; Lynne Reaves, "China: A New Frontier for Advertisers," *Advertising Age*, September 16, 1985, p. 74; Anetta Miller "Advertisers Take on China," *Newsweek*, December 1, 1986, p. 65; Lynne Curry, "China Fights Wild Ad Claims," *Advertising Age*, December 21, 1987, p. 15; Julie Skarr Hill, "China Quake," *Advertising Age*, June 12, 1989, pp. 1, 76.

creating markets in other countries. However, advertising can also be one of the most difficult aspects of the international marketing program because of the problems involved in attempting to develop messages that will be received and properly interpreted and understood in various countries.

Language is an area where international advertisers often have problems. The advertiser must know not only the native tongue of the country but also the nuances, idioms, and subtleties of the language. International marketers must be aware of the connotation of words and symbols used in their messages and understand how advertising copy and slogans are translated. An example of a failure of an advertiser to understand the local translation of its message was when Coca-Cola first introduced its soda to the Asian market: The Chinese translated the name with Chinese characters that sounded like "Coca-Cola," but read as "Bite the wax tadpole."[14] The company changed the characters to mean "Tasty, evoking happiness," which is the Oriental equivalent of "Have a Coke and a smile." An American airline competing in Brazil advertised the "rendezvous lounges" in its jets until it found out that in the Brazilian dialect of Portugese this meant a place to make love.[15]

In addition to language, advertisers can encounter problems with the connotative meaning of signs and symbols used in their messages. For example, Pepsodent toothpaste was unsuccessful in Southeast Asia because it promised white teeth to a culture where black or yellow teeth are symbols of prestige. An American ad campaign using various shades of green in the ads was a disaster in Malaysia where the color symbolizes death and disease.

Problems arising from language diversity and differences in the signs and symbols can usually be best solved with the help of local expertise. Marketers should consult local employees or use an ad agency that is very knowledgeable in the local language and can help verify that the advertiser is in fact saying what it wants to say. Many companies also turn to agencies specializing in the translation of advertising slogans and copy into foreign languages to assist in the development of their messages for different countries.

Tastes, traditions, and customs also are an important part of cultural considerations for advertising in other countries. The customs of a society affect not only what products and services are sold to a country but also the way they must be sold. For example, in France, cosmetics are used heavily by men as well as by women and advertising to the male market is very commonplace.

One of the more difficult markets for many American advertisers to understand is Japan because of its unique values and customs. For example, the Japanese have a very strong commitment to the group, and social interdependence and collectivism are as important to the Japanese as individualism is to most Americans. While ads stressing individuality and nonconformity have traditionally not been prevalent advertising appeals in Japan, one study did find that these Westernized values are becoming more commonplace in Japanese advertising.[16] The Japanese also have a strong distaste for ads that confront or disparage the competition and tend to prefer soft-, rather than hard-sell, appeals. Table 20–3 shows a list of advertising appeals that one copywriter suggests would not work well in Japan, along with some appeals that would help sell a product.

Moral and ethical standards are another aspect of culture that advertisers must consider. For example, in many Arab countries such as Saudi Arabia, advertisers must be aware of various taboos originating from conservative applications of the Islamic religion. Alcohol and pork are forbidden in the country and cannot be advertised. The ban is so strict that even images of pigs as stuffed toys cannot appear in ads. Human nudity is forbidden, as are pictures of anything sacred such as images in the shape of a cross or photographs of Mecca. The faces of women may not be shown in photographs, and for items such as cosmetics, drawings of women's faces are used.[17]

Political/Legal Environment

The political and legal environment in a country is one of the most important factors influencing the advertising and promotional programs of international marketers. Regulations differ in every country owing to economic and national sovereignty considerations, nationalistic and cultural factors, and the goal of protecting consumers not only from false or misleading advertising but in some cases, from advertising in general. It is difficult to make generalized statements regarding advertising regulation at the in-

Table 20–3   **Advertising Appeals for the Japanese Market**

The Appeals That Do Not Work in Japan	The Art of Selling—Japanese Style

A copywriter who wishes to appeal to a Japanese audience would be wise to forget the following fundamental American appeals:
 	
Be the first person in your neighborhood to own the Frammis washing machine . . .
 	
(Japanese buyers would never want to be out of step with their neighbors. Nor would they wish to appear to be superior. This is considered to be very bad taste.)
 	
FREE . . . this $4.96 volume . . . no strings attached . . .
 	
(The average Japanese buyer would simply not believe that something is given for nothing.)
 	
Less work for mother . . .
 	
(The Japanese housewife wants her family to know that she has personally prepared every bite of food. TV dinners are virtually unknown in Japan. Several years ago, food processors were introduced in Japan. They were a dismal failure. Why? Because Japanese housewives want to do all that chopping and blending by hand. Anything less would be considered an insult to the family.)
 	
Act today—and save 10 percent off this price of this brand-new model hi-fi phonograph . . .
 	
(Price is not considered a significant appeal to the Japanese buyer. They are more concerned with the dependability and reliability of the company.)
 	
Here's a great way to express your individuality and set yourself apart from the crowd . . .
 	
(The Japanese consider individuality to be a bad thing. There is a saying that Japanese children learn—almost from the first day of school: The nail that stands the highest is the nail that gets hit by the hammer.)
 	
Now . . . for the very first time . . .
 	
(In America, a phrase like this would be very appealing. In Japan, it is guaranteed to lose customers. The Japanese buyer simply does not want to be first to own something.)
	So what appeals does a copywriter use when attempting to sell something to a Japanese audience?
	    I discussed this matter with Bruce Guilfoile, who is a Japanese-American account executive at McCann Erickson Hakuhodo, Inc.—one of Tokyo's major advertising agencies. (They are also one of the major agencies specializing in Japanese direct response.)
	    Guilfoile told me which appeals I must use—as a copywriter in Japan.
	
	Our company has been in business for over 35 years . . .
	
	(Stability is considered a great virtue in Japan—and this appeal is viewed as very important to the people of Japan.)
	
	Our TV set is guaranteed to last longer than any other TV set on the market . . .
	
	(Reliability is the major value that the Japanese look for when buying a product.)
	
	Our company has the strength of the Rock of Gibralter . . .
	
	(Image is very important to the Japanese.)
	
	This is an idea whose time has come . . .
	
	(The Japanese are great believers in timing. Even if an idea seems incredibly "hot," they will wait—until the time is right. Once they are committed to a course of action, it would take wild horses to get them to change.)
	
	Buy this product . . . it will help bring greater harmony to your life . . . at home and at the office . . .
	
	(Beyond a doubt, this is the most appealing thing you could be saying to a Japanese. They are intensely concerned about their human relations. Any product that claims to improve human relations is guaranteed to sell in Japan.)

Source: Milton Pierce, "Direct Response in Japan," *Direct Marketing,* November 1986, p. 160.

ternational level, as some countries are increasing government regulation and control of advertising, whereas others are decreasing them. Government regulations and restrictions can affect various aspects of a company's advertising program, including:

- The type of products that may be advertised
- The content or creative approach that may be employed in advertising
- The media that all advertisers (or different classes of advertisers) are permitted to employ
- The amount of advertising that a single advertiser may employ in total or in a specific medium
- The use of foreign languages in advertisements

- The use of advertising material prepared outside the country
- The use of local versus international advertising agencies
- The specific taxes that may be levied against advertising[18]

A number of countries have bans or restrictions on the advertising of various products. Cigarette advertising is banned in some or all media in numerous countries besides the United States including Argentina, Canada, England, France, Italy, Norway, Sweden, and Switzerland. In China, tobacco and liquor advertising are banned except in hotels where only foreigners can stay and shop. In Sweden, advertising for alcoholic beverages is banned except for light beer. While international marketers are accustomed to restrictions on the advertising of products such as cigarettes, liquor, or pharmaceuticals, they often are surprised by some countries' restrictions on other products or services. For example, margarine cannot be advertised in France. The French government has also restricted the advertising of tourism because it encourages the French to spend their francs outside the country.[19]

Many countries have restrictions on the media that advertisers can use. For example, Sweden and Norway do not permit television or radio advertising, whereas Denmark finally began phasing in advertising on a limited basis in 1987. Media availability in Saudi Arabia is very limited, as television and radio advertising is banned, and the limited number of magazines and newspapers are subject to government and religious restrictions.[20] While tobacco and alcohol are officially banned from Spanish television, advertisers of low-tar cigarettes and wine and beer may buy television time after 9:30 P.M. if they pay a 100 percent surcharge.

In addition to the restrictions on the type of products that can be advertised and the media that can be used, many governments have rules and regulations that affect the advertising message. France does not permit comparative advertising, whereas Germany frowns upon it and requires a rigorous fairness test before making comparative claims. Many countries have restrictions on the types of claims advertisers can make, the words they can use, and the way products can be represented in ads. In addition, there are copyright and other legal restrictions that make it difficult to maintain the same name from market to market. For example, Diet Coke is known as Coca-Cola Light in Germany, France, and other countries because of legal constrictions prohibiting the use of the word *diet* (Figure 20–5). Promotional Perspective 20–2 discusses some of the problems advertisers face in creating ads for various countries.

Government regulations and restrictions can also influence the use of foreign languages in advertising as well as the production of the ad. A study conducted for the International Advertising Association in 1985 revealed that of the 46 countries surveyed, more than 90 percent permitted the use of foreign languages in print ads and direct mail.[21] However, only 72 percent allowed foreign-language commercials on television, on radio, or in cinema ads, and 25 percent of the countries restricted foreign-language ads to media targeted to foreigners in their country. The study also found that 22 percent of the countries prohibited the use of foreign-produced ads and foreign talent, whereas 38 percent had partial restrictions. For example, Revlon had to spend an extra $100,000 to film nearly identical versions of a Jontue perfume commercial in Australia and Columbia since both countries refused to accept the version of the ad produced in the United States.[22]

These restrictions are motivated primarily by economic considerations, as many countries require local production of at least a portion of television commercials to help build local film industries and create more jobs for local producers of print and audio visual materials. However, nationalistic and cultural factors also contribute to these restrictions, along with a desire to prevent large foreign ad agencies from dominating the advertising business in a country and thus hampering its development.

Constraints on the Advertising and Promotional Program

As shown in Figure 20–6, the international environment of advertising and promotion poses a set of constraints on a company's international marketing communica-

Figure 20–5 **Diet Coke Must Use a Different Name in France**

tions program. One of the problems created by differences in the marketing environment of foreign countries is that companies cannot do any advertising on a global or even regional basis. The challenge facing the international marketer is to examine these environmental constraints and restrictions and find ways to overcome or accommodate them. In some countries, steps are being taken to ease some of the legal restrictions and other barriers facing international advertisers. Promotional Perspective 20–3 discusses how the advertising environment in Europe will be changing with the implementation of the "1992" plan, which is designed to remove trade barriers among the 12 nations in the European Community.

Figure 20–6 **Constraints on International Communications**

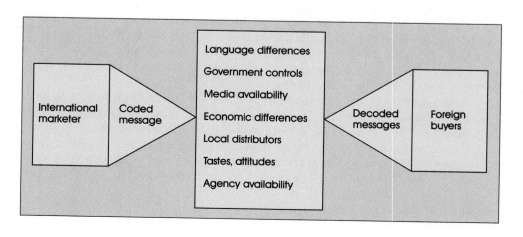

Promotional Perspective   20–2

Different Rules Create Problems for Global Advertisers

As companies increase their international marketing efforts, they are finding themselves besieged by a maze of different rules, restrictions, and regulations that various countries have concerning advertising. For example, the legendary Marlboro cowboy has been banned from advertising in Britain on the grounds that heroic figures in cigarette ads might have special appeal and encourage people to start smoking. The People's Republic of China once banned the Marlboro cowboy's blue jeans because they represent "Western decadence," whereas in Malaysia the Marlboro man had to be a local model.

Restrictions and regulations have made it very difficult to create global ad campaigns that can be used in various countries. For example, ad executives at the J. Walter Thompson agency point to a Kellogg's cereal commercial produced for British television to demonstrate how varying regulations can affect an ad. References to iron and vitamins would have to be deleted in the Netherlands, whereas a child wearing a Kellogg's T-shirt would have to be edited out in France where children are forbidden from endorsing products on television. In Germany the line "Kellogg's makes their cornflakes the best they've ever been" would have to be deleted because of rules against making competitive claims.

Austria is another country where children cannot be used in commercials. To deal with this restriction, companies have resorted to hiring dwarfs or using animated drawings of kids instead. Many countries also are careful to protect children from exploitation. In the Netherlands candy companies must show a toothbrush in their ads, whereas in France there is a limit on how much money a company can spend on advertising children's products such as toys, and premiums cannot be worth more than 1 percent of a product's sales price. In Belgium no reference to dieting is permitted in commercials, and in Denmark, ads cannot make nutritional claims.

To deal with these problems, the various chapters of the New York–based International Advertising Association (IAA) have been developing some form of self-regulation that will hopefully deter more government rules and restrictions. In 1986 the IAA's global media commission recommended that advertising be allowed to support the growth of global media and that advertising controls and restrictions should be relaxed. However, the growing influence of consumer advocacy and protectionist groups, along with ideological objections to advertising in some countries, will mean that varying rules, regulations, and restrictions will continue. Thus, advertisers will have to continue to adjust their ads to rules and regulations in each country.

Sources: Ronald Alsop, "Countries' Different Ad Rules Are Problem for Global Firms," *The Wall Street Journal,* September 27, 1984, p. 33; "Curbs on Ads Increase Abroad as Nations Apply Standards of Fairness and Decency," *The Wall Street Journal,* November 25, 1980, p. 48; Valerie Mackie, "Relax Ad Bans: IAA," *Advertising Age,* December 9, 1985, p. 40; Laurel Wentz, "Pan-European Ad Faces Regulatory Gymnastics," *Advertising Age,* April 24, 1989, p. 44.

Global versus Localized Advertising

The discussion of differences in the marketing environment of various countries suggests that each market is different and requires a distinct marketing and advertising program. However, in recent years a great deal of attention has been focused on the concept of **global marketing** whereby a company utilizes a common marketing plan for all countries in which it operates, thus selling the product in essentially the same way everywhere in the world. **Global advertising** would fall under the umbrella of global marketing as a means of implementing this strategy by using the same basic advertising approach in all markets. The ads for Rolex watches shown in Figure 20–7 were part of a global print campaign run in 25 countries, featuring international achievers such as singer Placido Domingo, tennis star Chris Evert, and golfer Seve Ballesteros.

The concept of global marketing is not new, as debate over standardization versus localization of marketing and advertising programs was begun over a decade ago.[23,24] However, the idea of global marketing has become popularized in recent years by the theorizing of Theodore Levitt, who suggests that the worldwide marketplace has become homogenized and that the basic needs, wants, and expectations transcend geographic, national, and cultural boundaries.[25,26] One writer has described Levitt's position on global marketing as follows:

> Levitt's vision of total worldwide standardization is global marketing at the extreme. He argues that, thanks to cheap air travel and new telecommunications technology, con-

Promotional Perspective **20–3**

Europe "1992"

In 1992 the 12 nations of the European Community (EC) will begin implementing their plan to remove physical, fiscal, and technical boundaries to trade among themselves. The plan, which is generally referred to as "1992," is designed to create a single European market of more than 300 million consumers that will rival the United States and Japan in world trade power. It will hopefully mean that people, products, and services will be able to move among EC nations with the same ease they move across U.S. state borders. Health, safety, and other technical requirements will be standardized, making it possible for a product approved for sale in one country to be accepted automatically in another.

The 1992 plan is expected to make the marketing of many products in Europe much easier. For example, part of the plan envisions uniform standards for television commercials. Currently, multinational companies must prepare several versions of their commercials to comply with different regulations for broadcast advertising in various countries. Although commercials would carry different voice-overs, the savings in production costs would be substantial. The availability of precious advertising time, which is still very limited in many countries, should increase dramatically. Competition from advertising-funded pan-European satellite channels is forcing governments to allow new, privately owned television channels, and in 1992 the state broadcasting monopolies in EC countries will be deregulated.

It is expected that the 1992 plan will significantly transform the market and revolutionize the selling of products and services in Europe. Multinational marketers and advertising agencies are already making changes and restructuring their organizations in anticipation of changes in the competitive environment in European Community countries. Many companies are making plans to approach Europe as a single market, rather than as a group of distinct countries, by realigning their product lines and developing advertising strategies that can be used on a pan-European basis. Some are choosing to consolidate their advertising with one large agency rather than using different agencies in each country. In turn, many agencies are merging their foreign offices to strengthen their capability to serve the entire EC.

The 1992 program will have significant consequences for European consumers and the advertisers and agencies attempting to market products and services there. However, many experts still feel that in the near future the majority of consumer products will still be marketed on a national basis, taking into account cultural differences, perspectives, and tastes. Others argue that a single European market will be an important step toward not just pan-European brands but true global brands.

Sources: Kevin Cote, "1992: Europe Becomes One," *Advertising Age*, July 11, 1988, p. 46; Laurel Wentz, "1992 to Breed Global Brands," *Advertising Age*, April 24, 1989, p. 44.

sumers the world over are thinking—and shopping—increasingly alike. According to Levitt, "The New Republic of Technology homogenizes world tastes, wants and possibilities into global marketing proportions, which allows for world standardized products."[27]

Not everyone, however, agrees with Levitt's global marketing theory, particularly with respect to advertising, as they argue that products and advertising messages must be designed and/or adapted to meet the differing needs of consumers in various countries.[28,29] We will consider the advantages and problems of global marketing—and advertising in particular.

Advantages of Global Marketing and Advertising

The idea of a global marketing strategy and advertising program does offer certain advantages to a company, including:

- Economies of scale in production and distribution
- Lower marketing and advertising costs as a result of reductions in planning and control
- Lower advertising production costs
- Abilities to exploit good ideas on a worldwide basis and introduce products quickly into various world markets
- A consistent international brand and/or company image
- Simplification of coordination and control of marketing and promotional programs

Advocates of global marketing and advertising contend that standardized products are possible in all countries if marketers emphasize quality, reliability, and low prices. They argue that people everywhere want to buy the same products and live the same way. The results of product standardization are lower design and production costs as well as greater marketing efficiency, which translates into lower prices for consumers. Additionally, product standardization and global marketing enable companies to roll out products faster into world markets, which is becoming increasingly important as product life cycles become shorter and competition increases.

There are several examples of the effective use of global advertising. Coca-Cola often uses the same image-oriented advertising approach all over the world, and the company estimates that it saves more than $8 million a year because it does not have to develop new imagery for each market. In 1989, Coke began using its first new international advertising appeal in six years when it made "You can't beat the feeling" (which was already in use in the United States—see Figure 20–8) its worldwide advertising theme replacing "Coke is it!"[30] Figure 20–9 shows an example of a Coke ad from this global campaign used in Spain.

Another example of cost savings through the use of a global campaign was the approach Colgate-Palmolive used to introduce its tartar control toothpaste in over 40 countries. By standardizing the packaging and providing only two different ads that local executives could choose between, the company estimated that it saved $1 to $2 million in advertising production costs.[31] Figure 20–10 shows the storyboard for "The Wall" commercial, which was adapted to foreign markets by changing the voice-over to the appropriate language. Many other companies also use global advertising approaches. For example, Victor Kiam, chairman of Remington products, makes the same commercial pitch for the company's electric razors in 15 languages.

Figure 20—8   Coke Uses the "You Can't Beat the Feeling" Theme in the United States

Figure 20—9   Coke Also Uses "You Can't Beat the Feeling" as Its Global Theme

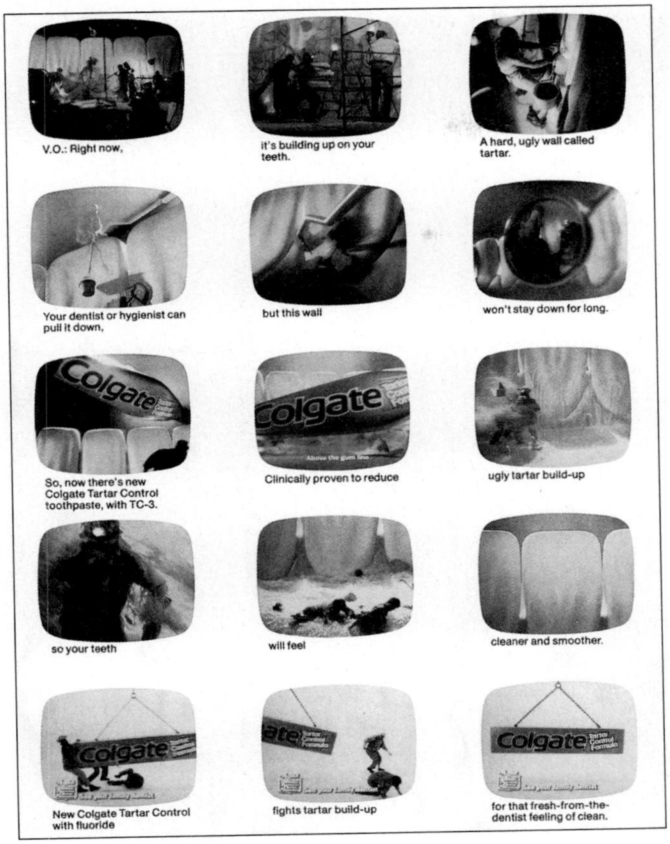

Figure 20–10 **Colgate Used This Commercial in More Than 40 Countries**

Problems with Global Advertising

While the concepts of global marketing and advertising have received a great deal of attention recently, not everyone agrees with the strategy. Opponents of the standardized, global approach argue that differences in culture, market, and economic development; consumer needs and usage patterns; media availabilities; and legal restrictions make it extremely difficult to develop an effective universal approach to marketing and advertising. They argue that advertising is particularly difficult to standardize because of cultural differences in circumstances, language, traditions, values, beliefs, lifestyle, music, and so on. Moreover, some experts argue that cultural change is occurring not necessarily in the direction of commonality of culture but rather in the direction of cultural diversity. Thus, advertising's job of informing and persuading consumers and moving them toward favoring and using a particular brand can only be done within a given culture.

Another problem marketers face when attempting to use a global campaign is that consumer usage patterns and perceptions of a product may vary from one country to another. Thus, advertisers must adjust their marketing and advertising approaches to different problems or situations they may be facing in various markets. For example, when Nestlé Corporation introduced its Nescafe Instant Coffee brand, the company was faced with at least five different situations in various parts of the world, including:

1. In the United States, where the idea of instant coffee had great penetration but where Nescafe had the minor share
2. In continental Europe, where Nescafe had the major share of the market, but the idea of instant coffee was in the early stages
3. In the tea-drinking countries, such as the United Kingdom and Japan, where tea drinkers had to be converted not just to coffee but to instant coffee

Figure 20–11   **Nescafe Instant Coffee Ad Used in Japan**

4. In Latin America, where the preferred coffee was a heavy one that could not be duplicated with an instant version
5. In Scandinavia, where Nestlé had to deal with the ingrained custom of keeping a pot of coffee on the stove from early morning until late at night

Nestlé had to use different advertising strategies for each market with varying executions, as a global campaign would not have been able to address the varying situations adequately.[32] Figures 20–11, 20–12, and 20–13 show examples of Nescafe ads used in Japan, Sweden, and Norway.

Many experts feel that it is very difficult to standardize products and advertising messages. They argue not only that there is the problem of cultural differences but that marketing a standardized product the same way all over the world can turn off consumers, alienate employees, and blind a company to diversities in customer needs. For example, when McDonald's expanded to Puerto Rico it alienated consumers by using American TV ads dubbed in Spanish and then by using Hispanic ads that were brought in from New York, which subsequent research showed looked too Mexican.[33] The vignette at the beginning of this chapter discussed the problems Parker Pen encountered when it attempted to develop a global campaign and ignore differences in local markets. The strategy failed in part because local marketing managers resented the standardization of ads and advertising agencies.

Some marketing experts argue that all the attention being focused on the concept of global advertising stems from large agencies trying to get more business by encouraging companies to use one mega-agency to handle their advertising worldwide. For example, Philip Kotler argues that

> there are only a few products, if any, that you can safely standardize. I really think the whole global marketing craze is just a ploy by advertising agencies to get new business.[34]

Figure 20—12   **Nescafe Instant Coffee Ad Used in Sweden**

Upptäck Nescafé Lyx. De finaste kaffesorter i förädlad form.

Gott, nybryggt kaffe har i all sin enkelhet en förunderlig förmåga att skapa stämning.
Bjud på Nescafé Lyx. Gjort på högklassiga kaffebönor. Blandat, rostat och malt med närmast petnoga omsorg. Men framför allt är det förädlat genom frystorkning, världens

hittills bästa metod att bevara ett kaffes känsliga smakämnen.
Slå sjudande vatten över de gyllenbruna Nescafé-kornen så blommar den utsökt rika kaffesmaken och aromen upp igen.
Brygg det i kopp eller kanna och låt det gärna dra någon minut innan du serverar så framträder den fylliga smaken ännu bättre.

Figure 20—13   **Nescafe Instant Coffee Ad Used in Norway**

Nescafé Gull - like god kaffe hver gang

Figure 20–14   **The Saatchi & Saatchi Advertising Agency Is a Proponent of Global Brands and Advertising**

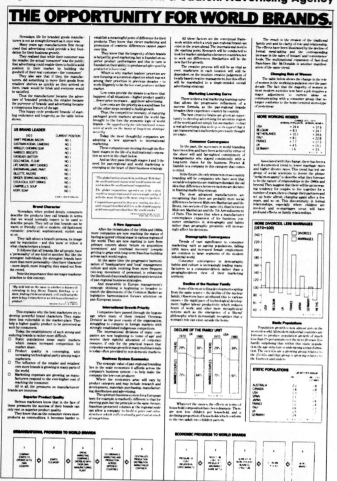

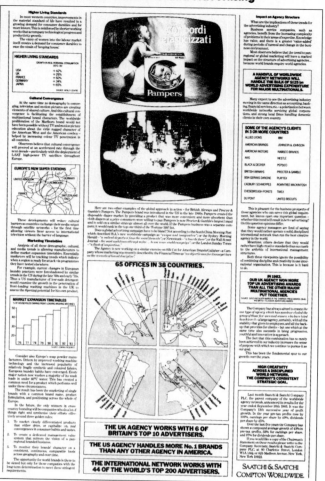

Indeed, some agencies such as London-based Saatchi & Saatchi, which is one of the world's largest agencies with offices in 58 countries, are strong proponents of global marketing and have developed global campaigns for a number of clients including British Airways and Procter & Gamble. Saatchi & Saatchi views the opportunity for global brands and advertising as very plausible for a number of reasons including, (1) convergence in demographic and cultural trends, and (2) an increasing spillover of media across national borders, fueled by the growth and development of satellite television (Figure 20–14).

When Is Globalization Appropriate?

While globalization of advertising is viewed by many in the advertising industry as a difficult task, some progress has been made in learning what products and services are best suited to worldwide appeals. Products that can take advantage of global marketing and advertising opportunities include

1. Brands that can be adapted for a visual appeal that avoid the problems of trying to translate words into dozens of languages
2. Brands that are promoted with image campaigns that lend themselves to themes that play up to universal appeals such as sex or wealth
3. High-tech products coming to the world for the first time; new technology prod-

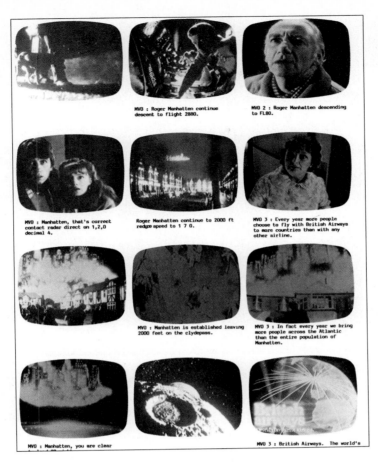

Figure 20–15 **British Airways' Manhattan Landing Commercial Was Used in 40 Countries**

ucts coming on the world at once and not steeped in the cultural heritage of the country

4. Products with nationalistic flavor if the country has a reputation in the field[35]

A global advertising campaign used by British Airways to promote its brand name and image as "The world's favorite airline" is an example of a service in the first category. The company used its famous "Manhattan landing" television commercial, which featured a flying saucerlike replica of the island of Manhattan rotating across the sky and cruising in for a landing at London's Heathrow airport. The commercial relied primarily on visual effects to communicate the message and was used in 40 countries with only the language in the voice-overs changing (Figure 20–15).

Products such as jewelry, liquor, and cigarettes are examples of items in the second category that can be promoted using image advertising. Marlboro uses its "Marlboro Country" theme featuring the cowboy around the world, whereas many cosmetic companies use the similar image campaigns in many countries. Figure 20–16 shows an ad for Chanel N° 19 perfume used to advertise the brand in the United States as well as in numerous other countries.

Levitt, as well as many advertisers, feels that consumers are very similar with regard to emotional desires and motives and that emotions such as joy, sentiment, excitement, and many others are universal.[36] Thus, it is very common to find global advertising campaigns making use of emotional and image appeals. One advertising executive summarized this point very well:

> What it all boils down to is that we are all human. We share the gift of emotional response. We feel things. And we feel them in remarkably similar ways. We speak different languages, we observe different customs, but we are wired to each other and to an ulti-

Figure 20–16 An Image Advertising Appeal Is Used to Advertise Chanel Perfume in the United States and Many Other Countries

Witty. Confident. Devastatingly feminine.

CHANEL N°19

The Outspoken Chanel.

mate power source that transcends us in a way that makes us subject to a common emotional spectrum.[37]

High-tech products such as personal computers, calculators, and consumer electronic items such as VCRs, televisions, or audio equipment are examples of products in the third category. Products in the fourth category would include French wine and cheeses or German beer or automobiles. For example, Volkswagen emphasizes its "German engineering" in ads throughout the world and particularly in the United States where consumers have very favorable opinions toward German-made cars (Figure 20–17).

Global Products, Local Messages

While the pros and cons of globalized marketing and advertising continue to be debated, many companies are taking what might be called an in-between approach by standardizing their products and basic marketing strategy but localizing their advertising messages. This approach suggests that similar desires, goals, needs, and uses for products and services exist but that advertising must be tailored to the local realities and conditions in each market. This approach has been described by agencies as "Think global, act local" and by Grey Advertising as "Global vision with a local touch."[38] Rather than using a global advertising message that will be seen by diverse markets, advertisers are tailoring their ad executions to local cultures and situations.

An excellent example of this concept is a campaign used by the Coca-Cola Company. A few years ago, Coke's agency, McCann-Erickson Worldwide, created an award-winning commercial showing American football hero "Mean Joe Greene" giving his jersey to a young boy who had given him a bottle of Coke after a tough game. However, the ad could not be used outside the United States because not only was Greene unknown but so too is the American game of football. Rather than abandon the con-

Figure 20–17   **Volkswagen Emphasizes the Strong Reputation of German Engineering in Its Advertising**

cept, the agency adapted it to other countries by creating ads featuring stars of the more popular international sport of soccer. Ads in South America used the popular Argentine star Mardonna, and those in Asia used Thailand star Niwat as the heroes in the commercial (Figure 20–18).

A recent study examined the international advertising strategies of successful U.S. multinational corporations and found that only 9 percent used totally standardized or global advertising for all foreign markets, 37 percent used all localized advertising, and the remaining 54 percent used a combination strategy of standardizing some portions of their advertising for local markets.[39] A major risk of the global or standardized approach was felt to be a lack of communication owing to cultural differences. Thus, the "Think global, act local" approach appears to be the dominant strategy used by many international advertisers, as they feel that it is important to adapt advertising components such as language, models, scenic backgrounds, product attributes, and other elements to blend with the culture.

Decision Areas in International Advertising

As is the case with domestic marketing, certain organizational and functional decisions must be made by companies developing advertising and promotional programs for international markets. These decisions include organization, agency selection, advertising research, creative strategy and execution, and media strategy and selection.

Organizing for International Advertising

One of the first decisions a company must make when it decides to market its products to other countries is how to organize the international advertising and promotion function. This decision is likely to depend on how the company is organized overall

Figure 20–18   Coke Used International Sports Stars for Commercials in Various Countries

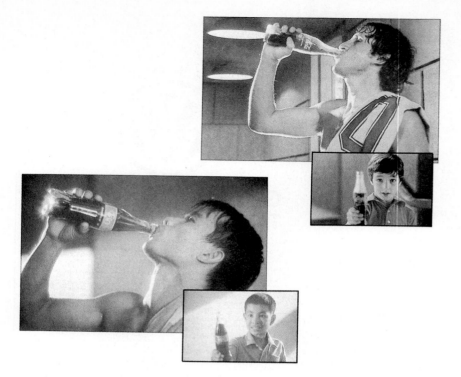

for international marketing and business. There are three basic options for organizing the international advertising and promotion function including centralization at the home office or headquarters, decentralization of decision making to local foreign markets or a combination of the two alternatives.

Centralization   Many companies prefer centralization of the international advertising and promotional function whereby all decisions such as agency selection, research, creative strategy and campaign development, media strategy, and budgeting are done at the firm's home office. Complete centralization is likely when market and media conditions are similar from one country to another, when the company has only one or a few international agencies handling all of its advertising, when the company can use standardized advertising, or when it desires a consistent image worldwide. Centralization might also be used when a company's international business is small and it operates through foreign distributors or licensees who do not become involved in the marketing and promotional process.

Many companies also prefer the **centralized organizational structure** as a way of protecting their foreign investments and keeping control of the marketing effort and corporate and/or brand image. For example, Delta Airlines has a highly centralized structure for international advertising, with all creative work and media placement controlled out of the company's headquarters in Atlanta. According to the company's advertising and sales promotion director, Delta is very concerned about how its name and image are presented in various markets, as "What Delta is in America, Delta is in Europe."[40]

The centralized approach can result in considerable cost savings, as it reduces the need for staff and administration at the local subsidiary level. As the trend toward globalized marketing and advertising strategies continues, companies are likely to move more toward centralization of the advertising function to maintain a unified world brand image rather than presenting a different image in each market. Some foreign managers may actually prefer centralized decision making, as it removes them from the burden and responsibility of advertising and promotional decisions and means that they do not have to defend local decisions to the home office. However, many marketing and advertising managers in foreign markets oppose centralized control, as they argue that such a structure is too rigid and makes it difficult to adapt the advertising and promotional program to local needs and market conditions. As noted earlier, Parker Pen encountered such resistance when it attempted to implement a global advertising strategy.

Decentralization   Under a **decentralized organizational structure,** marketing and advertising managers in each market have the authority to make their own advertising and promotional decisions. Local managers can select advertising agencies, develop budgets, conduct research, approve creative themes and executions, and select advertising media. Companies using a decentralized approach are obviously putting a great deal of trust and faith in the judgment and decision-making ability of personnel in local markets. This approach is often used when companies feel that local managers know the marketing situation in foreign countries the best. It is also felt that they are more effective and highly motivated when given control and responsibility for the advertising and promotional program in their markets. Decentralization also may be needed in small or highly unique markets where it is not worthwhile for headquarter's involvement or advertising tailored to the local market is needed.

Combination   While there is an increasing trend toward centralizing the international advertising function, many companies actually use a combination of the two approaches. With the combination approach, the home office or headquarters will have the most control over advertising policy, guidelines, and operations in all markets. The international advertising manager will work closely with the representatives from the international agency (or agencies) and will set advertising and promotional objectives, have budgetary authority, be responsible for approving all creative themes and executions, and approve media selection decisions, particularly when they are made on a regional basis or overlap with other markets.

Advertising managers in regional or local offices are responsible for submitting advertising plans and budgets for their markets, which are reviewed and considered by the international advertising manager. Local managers will play a major role in working with the agency in adapting appeals to their particular markets and making media selection decisions.

The combination approach allows for consistency and uniformity in a company's international advertising, yet still permits local input and adaptation of the promotion program. Most consumer product companies find that local adaptation of the advertising is necessary for foreign markets yet desire control of the overall worldwide image they project. One company that uses a combination approach is Eastman Kodak. Kodak provides central strategy and support to local offices and acts as consultants to them. Although each country is autonomous, the main offices controls the quality of advertising and advertising policy. Media buying is done on a local level. However, the main office becomes involved in special media opportunities and overall strategy for events such as Olympic sponsorship and regionalized campaigns.[41]

Agency Selection

One of the most important decisions a firm engaged in international marketing must make is the selection of an advertising agency. There are three basic alternatives the company has in selecting an agency to handle its international advertising. First, the company can choose a major agency with both domestic and overseas offices. Many U.S. agencies have offices all over the world and have become truly international agencies. Table 20–4 shows the top 10 U.S. agencies in 1988 by worldwide, U.S., and non-U.S. billings. As can be seen in this table, these agencies derive a substantial portion of their income from foreign business.

Table 20—4 *AA's Top 10 U.S. Agencies by Billings in 1988*

\ Top 10 Agencies by Worldwide Billings			Top 10 Agencies by U.S. Billings			Top 10 Agencies by Non-U.S. Billings		
Rank	Agency	World-wide Billings	% Chg	Rank	Agency	U.S. Billings	% Chg	Rank	Agency	Non-U.S. Billings	% Chg

Rank	Agency	World-wide Billings	% Chg	Rank	Agency	U.S. Billings	% Chg	Rank	Agency	Non-U.S. Billings	% Chg
1	Young & Rubicam	$5,390	9.9	1	Young & Rubicam	$2,792	8.5	1	McCann-Erickson Worldwide	$3,067	31.0
2	Saatchi & Saatchi Advertising	5,054	11.1	2	BBDO Worldwide	2,414	7.6	2	Saatchi & Saatchi Advertising	2,844	17.4
3	Backer Spielvogel Bates Worldwide	4,678	15.0	3	Saatchi & Saatchi Advertising	2,210	3.9	3	Backer Spielvogel Bates Worldwide	2,714	20.0
4	McCann-Erickson Worldwide	4,381	28.2	4	Backer Spielvogel Bates Worldwide	1,964	8.6	4	Young & Rubicam	2,598	11.4
5	FCB-Publicis	4,358	26.0	5	DDB Needham Worldwide	1,929	17.8	5	FCB-Publicis	2,532	37.6
6	Ogilvy & Mather Worldwide	4,110	12.2	6	Ogilvy & Mather Worldwide	1,875	7.4	6	Lintas:Worldwide	2,240	33.4
7	BBDO Worldwide	4,051	8.0	7	FCB-Publicis	1,826	12.8	7	Ogilvy & Mather Worldwide	2,235	16.5
8	J. Walter Thompson Co.	3,858	18.6	8	D'Arcy Masius Benton & Bowles	1,794	14.6	8	J. Walter Thompson Co.	2,070	26.8
9	Lintas:Worldwide	3,586	28.6	9	J. Walter Thompson Co.	1,788	10.4	9	HDM	1,709	45.1
10	D'Arcy Masius Benton & Bowles	3,361	23.2	10	Leo Burnett Co.	1,765	13.9	10	BBDO Worldwide	1,637	8.6

Notes: Dollars are in millions. Only U.S.-based agencies are ranked in these tables. Agencies are consolidated to include subsidiaries.
Source: Advertising Age, March 29, 1989, p. 2.

Many companies prefer to use a U.S.-based international agency, as this gives them greater control and convenience and also facilitates coordination of overseas advertising. In many cases, companies will use the same agency to handle its international as well as its domestic advertising. For example, Texas Instruments had 28 different agencies handling its advertising around the world before hiring one agency to handle both its foreign and domestic business. Eastman Kodak cut a 50-agency international roster down to 2 large international agencies.

As was discussed in Chapter 3, there has been a flurry of mergers and acquisitions in the advertising agency business in the United States in recent years. Many agencies have been merging or making acquisitions, both at home and in other countries, in order to be able to offer full-service global marketing and advertising operations to clients seeking more business in foreign markets. For example, Ogilvy & Mather acquired Euramerica, a small New York–based firm that specializes in the translation of ads into foreign languages.[42] Euramerica was developed into a full-service agency and operates as an independently operated member of the Ogilvy Group, specializing in international advertising (Figure 20–19).

Large agencies are subject to acquisition as well, as Ogilvy & Mather was acquired in a hostile takeover by the London-based WPP Group in 1989.[43] The WPP Group also purchased another large New York agency, J. Walter Thompson, in 1987 on the same premise that large mega-agencies can offer clients greater global marketing strengths and service synergies.

A second alternative for the international marketer is to choose a domestic agency that—rather than having its own foreign offices or branches—is affiliated with agencies in other countries or belongs to a network of foreign agencies. An agency may acquire a small minority interest in several foreign agencies or become part of an organization of international agencies. This allows the agency to remain independent yet sell itself as an international agency offering multinational coverage and contacts.

The advantage of this arrangement is that the client can use a domestic-based agency yet still have access to foreign agencies that have a detailed knowledge and understanding of market conditions, media, and so on, in each local market. There

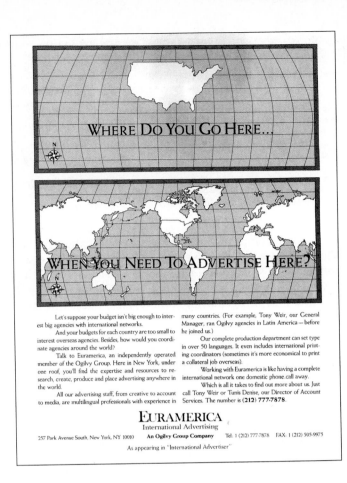

Figure 20—19   **An Ad Promoting an Agency's International Subsidiary**

may be several problems with this approach, however, as the local agency may have trouble coordinating and controlling the efforts of independent agencies and/or there may be variations in the quality of work of network members. Thus, companies considering this option must ask the local agency questions regarding its ability to coordinate and control the activities of its affiliates and the quality of their work in specific areas such as creative and media.

The third alternative the international marketer has is to select a local agency for each national market in which it sells its products or services. As noted earlier, local agencies often have the best knowledge and understanding of the marketing and advertising environment in a country or region and thus may be able to develop the most effective advertising.

Some companies like to choose local agencies because it gives them the flexibility to choose the best local talent in each market. In many countries smaller, independent agencies may be doing the best creative work and, because of their independence, may be more willing to take risks and thus develop the most effective ads. Another reason for choosing local agencies is to increase the involvement and morale of foreign subsidiary managers by giving them responsibility for managing the promotion function in their markets. Some companies have their subsidiaries choose a local agency, as they are often in the best position to evaluate local agencies and will be the ones who must work closely with them.

Criteria for Agency Selection   The selection of an agency to handle a company's international advertising depends on how the firm is organized for international marketing and the type of assistance it needs to meet its goals and objectives in foreign markets. Table 20–5 lists some of the criteria that a company might use in making the agency selection decision.

Table 20–5   Criteria for Selecting an Agency to Handle International Advertising

- Ability of agency to cover relevant markets
- Quality of agency work
- Market research, public relations, and other services offered by agency
- Relative roles of company advertising department and agency
- Level of communication and control desired by company
- Ability of agency to coordinate international campaign
- Size of company's international business
- Company's desire for local versus international image
- Company organizational structure for international business and marketing (centralized versus decentralized)
- Level of involvement of company with international operations

Source: Adapted from Vern Terpstra, *International Marketing*, 4th ed. (New York: Dryden Press, 1987), pp. 432–33.

Some companies may choose a combination of the three alternatives discussed above because their involvement in each market differs, as does the advertising environment and situation in each country. Several experts in international marketing and advertising advocate the use of international agencies by international companies, particularly those firms moving toward global marketing and striving for a consistent corporate or brand image around the world.[44,45] The trend toward mergers and acquisitions and the formation of mega-agencies with global marketing and advertising capabilities suggests that the international agency approach will become the preferred arrangement among large companies.

Advertising Research

Research plays the same important role in the development of international advertising and promotion programs that it does domestically, as its purpose is to help managers make more informed and better decisions. However, many companies do not conduct advertising research in international markets. Probably the main reason for this is the high cost of conducting research in foreign markets, coupled with the limited budgets many firms have for international advertising and promotion. For many companies, international markets have not represented a large percentage of their overall sales, and thus investments in research have been difficult to justify. Thus, rather than making advertising decisions on the basis of quality marketing information, generalizations based on casual observations of foreign markets have guided the promotional process.

As companies increase their emphasis and investment in international marketing, they are recognizing the importance of conducting marketing and advertising research to better understand the characteristics and subtleties of consumers in foreign markets. There are a number of areas where information from research on foreign markets can help firms make better advertising decisions, including:

- Information on demographic characteristics of markets
- Information on cultural differences such as norms, lifestyles, and values
- Information on consumers' product usage, brand attitudes, and media usage and preferences
- Copy testing to determine reactions to different types of advertising appeals and executions
- Research on the effectiveness of advertising and promotional programs in foreign markets

Some of this information is available through secondary sources. For example, the United Nations and other international agencies are sources of international demographic information.[46] Table 20–6 lists some of the sources of international demographic and economic data. It should be noted, however, that the reliability of United Nations data has been questioned because member countries often provide inaccurate or unsubstantiated information.[47]

Table 20—6 **Selected Sources of International Demographic and Economic Data Available from the United Nations and Other Sources**

Compendium of Social Statistics
Published sporadically by the United Nations. Includes basic statistical indicators describing the social situation in the world and in particular regions, as well as changes and trends in standards of living. For instance, information is provided on population size, vital statistics, health conditions, food consumption and nutrition, housing, education and cultural activities, labor forces and conditions of employment, incomes and expenditures, and consumer prices. The most recent edition was published in 1980.

Demographic Yearbook
Published annually by the United Nations, this text is a primary source of demographic data regarding approximately 220 countries. The data describe population changes such as rate of increase, birth rates and death rates, migration, and marriages and divorces.

Index to International Public Opinion 1985-86
Published annually by Survey Research Consulting International, Inc. Contains data collected in over 100 countries. This information is obtained by the firm's own surveys as well as other surveys. Respondents are categorized by such factors as age, sex, education, and income.

Monthly Bulletin of Statistics
A monthly publication of the United Nations reporting on population, human resources, transportation, trade, income, and finance. Provides current economic and social data for many of the tables published in the *United Nations Statistical Yearbook*.

Production Yearbook
This annual publication contains about 225 tables of data on important aspects of food and agriculture, including index numbers of agriculture and food production, food supplies, means of production, prices, freight rates, and wages throughout the world. If no official or semiofficial figures are available from a country, estimates are made by the U.N. Food and Agriculture Organization on its production of major crops, livestock, and other food products. These data are available on computer tape.

UNESCO Statistical Yearbook
Contains information on population, education, science and technology, libraries, museums, newspapers and other periodicals, book production, paper consumption, film and cinema, television and radio broadcasting, and cultural expenditures. Information is provided for over 200 countries. Published by the U.N. Educational, Scientific, and Cultural Organization.

United Nations Statistical Yearbook
Published annually by the United Nations since 1949, this publication provides statistics about the world regarding population, human resources, agriculture, forestry, fishing, industrial production, mining and quarrying, manufacturing, construction, energy, internal trade, external trade, transportation, communication, consumption, wages and prices, balance of payments, finance, housing, health, education, and science. *World Statistics in Brief*, available since 1976, is an annual summary of some of the most frequently used data in the *Yearbook*. Yearbooks are also available for particular world regions, such as Latin America and Asia.

World Economic Survey
This annual publication is a comprehensive review and analysis of world economic conditions and trends. Separate data are presented for developing countries, centrally planned economies, and developed market economics. Published by the United Nations.

World Health Statistics Annual
Published by the World Health Organization and the Statistical Office of the United Nations, this publication provides information on vital statistics, causes of death, infectious diseases, health personnel, and hospital establishments.

Source: Kenneth E. Runyoh and David W. Stewart, *Consumer Behavior*, 3rd ed. (Columbus, Ohio: Merrill Publishing Company, 1987), p. 72.

Information related to specific aspects of consumer needs and decision making in foreign markets such as product and brand attitudes, usage patterns, and media habits are generally more difficult to find, particularly in developing countries. However, more information is becoming available to international advertisers. For example, A. C. Nielsen has developed a large international data base that tracks purchase patterns of over 2,000 product classes in 25 countries, whereas Predicast has a foreign intelligence syndicated service. Information on media usage in European countries has increased tremendously in the past decade also.[48]

Much of the information advertisers need to make informed decisions must be gathered from research generated by the company and/or agency. Companies often find

Table 20–7   **Cross-Cultural Attitudes and Opinions (% agreement)**

"Everyone Should Use a Deodorant"	"A House Should Be Dusted and Polished Three Times a Week"	"I Attend Church Regularly"
U.S.A.: 89	Italy: 86	Spain: 77
French Canada: 81	Germany: 70	Italy: 75
English Canada: 77	U.K.: 59	French Canada: 73
U.K.: 71	France: 55	Germany: 70
Italy: 69	Spain: 53	U.S.A.: 65
France: 59	Australia: 33	English Canada: 44
Australia: 53	U.S.A.: 25	U.K.: 36
		France: 23
		Australia: 16

Source: Joseph Plummer, "Consumer Focus in Cross-National Research," *Journal of Advertising,* Spring 1977, pp. 10, 11.

that consumer needs and wants, purchase motives, and usage patterns vary from one country to another, and research is needed to understand these differences. Some companies and their advertising agencies conduct psychographic research in foreign markets to determine differences in lifestyles and product usage patterns. Table 20–7 shows differences in cross-cultural attitudes and opinions from an agency's psychographic study.

It is also important for advertisers to conduct research on consumers' reactions to the advertising appeal and execution style they plan to use in foreign markets. One agency researcher recommends testing the basic premise and/or selling idea to be used in a global campaign first to be sure that it has some relevance to the target audience in the various markets where it will appear:

> The logic behind this is that if the basic premise or selling idea has little relevance or appeal in a significant number of the markets, there is no value, at this time, of proceeding further by testing executions. If the premise or selling idea "works" either via testing, or you conclude from other upfront research and market analysis that it could work, you would then move to the second phase—executional testing. Here the primary focus should be on comprehension of the strategic message and its explicit or implicit support. . . . The test at this phase should also focus on the central cross-cultural emotional or symbolic issue through a custom-designed research methodology.[49]

Creative Decisions

Another decision facing the international advertiser is the determination of the appropriate advertising messages for each market. Creative strategy development for international advertising is basically similar in process and procedure to domestic advertising. Advertising and communications objectives should be formulated based on the marketing strategy and market conditions in foreign markets. Major selling ideas must be developed, and specific appeals and execution styles must be chosen.

An important factor that influences the development of creative strategy for international marketers is the issue of global versus localized advertising. As was noted earlier in the discussion of the two approaches, global advertising uses the same basic appeal and execution style, with perhaps minor variations, in all countries. If the standardized approach is taken, the challenge facing the creative team is to develop advertising that will transcend cultural differences and communicate effectively in every country.

When companies follow a **localized advertising strategy,** the creative team must determine what type of selling idea, ad appeal, and execution style will work in each market. A product may have to be positioned differently in each market depending on consumers' usage patterns and habits. For example, General Foods found that in France people drink very little orange juice and almost none at breakfast. Thus, when the company decided to market its Tang instant breakfast drink in France, the agency developed ads positioning the brand as a refreshment for any time of day rather than as a substitute for orange juice, which was the approach used in the U.S. market.[50]

Attention must also be given to what type of advertising appeal or execution style will be most effective in each market. Emotional appeals such as humor may work well in one country but not another because of differences in cultural backgrounds and consumer perceptions of what is or is not funny. While humorous appeals are quite common in the United States and Britain, they are not used often in Germany, where consumers tend to be more serious and do not respond favorably to humor in advertising.

Some countries such as France, Italy, and Brazil are more tolerant of and receptive to sexual appeal and nudity in advertising than are other societies. The Grey Advertising Agency found that an ad it developed for Camay soap in the United States, which featured a man touching a woman's skin while she bathed, would be a disaster in Japan. Even the idea of a man being in the bathroom with a female in Japan would be considered taboo.[51]

Media Selection

One of the most difficult decision areas for the international advertiser is that of media strategy and selection. U.S. firms generally find that there are major differences in the media outside the United States and that media conditions may vary considerably from one area to another, particularly in developing countries. Media planners face a number of problems in attempting to communicate advertising messages to consumers in foreign countries.

First, the types of media available in each country are different. Many homes in developing countries do not have television sets, whereas in some countries television advertising is not accepted or the amount of commercial time is severely limited. For example, in West Germany, TV restrictions include limiting advertising time to 20 minutes a day on each of the government-owned channels, restricting commercials to four five minute breaks and banning them on Sundays and holidays. Germany's two privately owned television stations, however, are permitted to devote up to 20 percent of airtime to commercials.

In the Netherlands, television spots on the Dutch networks are limited to 5 percent of airtime and must be booked up to a year in advance. Programs also do not have fixed time slots for ads, making it impossible to plan commercial buys around desired programs. Some countries such as Denmark just began accepting television commercials in 1987 by allowing a daily five-minute block of advertising time on regional channels.[52]

The number of television sets in other parts of the world such as India and China is increasing tremendously. However, there is still controversy over television advertising in many countries. Promotional Perspective 20–4 discusses the controversy over television advertising that has occurred in India.

The characteristics of media may differ from country to country in terms of their coverage, cost, quality of reproduction, restrictions, and the like. Another problem international advertisers face is obtaining reliable media information such as circulation figures, audience profiles, and costs. In some countries media rates are negotiable and/or may fluctuate owing to unstable currencies and economic conditions. Thus, there are a number of factors and concerns facing advertisers when putting together their international media plans and schedules.

The goal of international advertisers in choosing media is to select those vehicles that reach their target audience most effectively and efficiently. This means that attention must be given to the various media options regarding their ability to reach the appropriate people in each market and their costs. Media selection is often done on a localized basis, even when a centrally planned, globalized campaign is used. Many advertisers do this because they feel that local agencies or media buyers have more

Promotional Perspective 20–4

Television Advertising Increase Creates Controversy in India

With over 730 million people, India is second only to China in terms of population and is potentially one of the world's most promising markets. Television first aired in India in 1959 but did not spread outside the major cities until 1982 when the government-run network, Doordarshan, began to transmit via its own satellite. Today there are an estimated 5.2 million TV sets in India reaching 50 million people at peak times, compared with only 450,000 sets 10 years ago. With sales of new TV sets rising each year, programming on Doordarshan is expected to reach 30 million sets and 300 million people in the next five years.

For years the Indian government viewed television primarily as an educational tool. However, TV has caught on as an entertainment medium, and in 1985 Doordarshan began accepting privately sponsored and produced programs such as serials. The dramatic growth in the size of the viewing audience and popularity of television has triggered intense competition for prime-time commercial spots. Television advertising revenue increased from $575,000 in 1976 to $100 million in 1987.

As the frequency of commercials increases, the long-standing debate over TV advertising continues. Many people in India feel that commercials have an adverse effect on programming and hurt viewers. An Indian sociologist concluded after an extensive study that broadcast advertising was promoting consumerism, aggravating tension between rich and poor, and creating unrealistic expectations for many Indians. However, Prime Minister Rajiv Gandhi has focused attention on the middle class and is encouraging consumption.

Even so, Doordarshan officials are taking a cautious approach to advertising, as current guidelines restrict commercials to only 10 percent of programming time. TV advertising has also failed to gain complete acceptance among viewers, as there has been so much controversy over commercial interruptions that the network is considering limiting ads to the beginning and end of a program.

Advertisers in India also must deal with what may be the world's most difficult communications problem, as there are 14 major languages in India and many more dialects. The most common language used for advertising is English, even though it is spoken by only 10 percent of the Indian population. Many advertisers favor English ads because they target opinion leaders and the small, but affluent, upper class of Indian society. Some experts feel that the language problem may limit the growth of television as an advertising medium in the country. Advertising agencies are working on ways of overcoming the language barrier such as using primarily visual messages or using voice-overs in the various languages.

Sources: Sheila Tefft, "TV Advertising Booming in India Despite Controversy," *Advertising Age*, March 31, 1986, p. 59; idem, "India Advertising Flourishes," *Advertising Age*, December 7, 1987, p. 52.

knowledge of local media and better opportunities to negotiate rates, and its gives subsidiary operations more control and ability to adapt to media conditions and options in their market. Media planners have two options available, which are using national or local media or international media.

Local Media   Many advertisers choose to use the local media of a country to reach its consumers. Print is the most used medium on a worldwide basis, since television commercial time is limited in many countries, as is the number of homes with TV sets. Many foreign countries not only have magazines that are circulated on a countrywide basis but also have national and regional newspapers as well. While newspapers are primarily a medium for local retail advertising in the United States, in many countries they contain advertising directed to a national audience. Also, as in the United States, most countries have magazines appealing to special interests or activities and thus allow for targeting and selectivity in media selection.

As discussed earlier, restrictions and regulations have limited the development of television as a dominant advertising medium in many countries. However, TV is a primary medium for obtaining nationwide coverage in most developed countries and is an important medium because of the tremendous creative opportunities it offers. Restrictions on television may be lessening in some countries, and time availability may increase. For example, in 1986 the French government awarded the first fully commercial TV channel license. The number of TV stations and television advertising in Italy exploded in the past decade since government restrictions against private broadcasting were lifted.[53] Advertising groups are using economic, legal, and political pressure to get more television commercial time from reluctant European governments.

Figure 20—20 *Newsweek* **Advertises Its International Magazine Network**

The increase in TV channels through direct broadcasting by satellite to many European households, which is discussed below, may hasten this process.[54]

In addition to print and television, there are many other local media available to advertisers including radio, direct mail, billboards, cinema, and transit advertising. These media provide international advertisers with greater flexibility and the opportunity to reach specific market segments and local markets within a country. Most international advertisers will rely heavily on national and local media in their media plans for foreign markets.

International Media The other way for the international advertiser to reach audiences in various countries is through the use of **international media** that have multimarket coverage. The primary focus of international media has traditionally been magazines and newspapers. A number of U.S.-based, consumer-oriented publications have international editions including *Time, Newsweek, Reader's Digest,* and *National Geographic* and the newspaper *USA TODAY.* Figure 20—20 shows an ad for *Newsweek*'s international magazine network. U.S.-based business publications with foreign editions include *Business Week, Fortune, Harvard Business Review,* and *The Wall Street Journal.*

Table 20—8 lists the 16 major global media with their North American, foreign, and worldwide circulation, ad rates, global cost per thousand, and top worldwide advertisers in each publication. As can be seen in this table, the most frequently advertised products in these international publications include airlines, automobiles, consumer electronics, computers, financial services, and tobacco. The top advertisers include AT&T, N. V. Philips, IBM, General Mills, and Singapore Airlines.

Table 20—8 **Advertising Age's Global Media Lineup**

Title/ Publisher/ Headquarters	Paid North American Circulation/ % chg	Paid Foreign Circulation by Region/ % chg	Worldwide Circulation/ % chg	B&W Pg Cost/ % chg/ 4/c Pg Cost in 1989	B&W Pg Cost/ 4/c Pg Cost Projected for 1990	Global CPM B&W Pg in 1989/ % chg	Top Worldwide Advertisers in 1989
Dailies							
Financial Times of London Financial Times Ltd. London	20,760 10.8	Europe: 257,133 (1.1) Middle East/ Africa: 3,369 (1.0) Asia/Pacific: 3,800 (0.4) Latin America: 302 49.5 Caribbean: 415 (43.5)	285,779 (0.3)	$34,944 1.3 $56,100	NA NA	$122.28 1.7	British Airways British Gas Toshiba Daimler-Benz Renault
International Herald Tribune New York Times & Washington Post Neuilly, France	4,754 16.7	Europe: 133,343 0.1[1] Middle East/ Africa: 6,809 (16.5)[1] Asia/Pacific: 34,953 10.0[1] Latin America: 2,334 13.3[1]	182,193[1] 3.0	39,432 5.1 74,920	$41,160 $78,204	216.43 3.4	Republic Bank of N.Y. Lufthansa Airlines Thai Airlines AT&T Co. Carrera
People's Daily Gao Di Beijing	52,000 NA	Europe: 15,000 NA Middle East/ Africa: 7,000 NA Asia/Pacific: 63,000 NA Latin America: 13,000 NA China: 3,850,000 NA	4,000,000 NA	105 NA NA	NA NA	0.26 NA	Panasonic Sharp Electronics Sanyo Boeing Co. Toyota
USA Today Gannett Co. Arlington, Va.	1,755,000 6.4	Europe: 40,100 17.7[2] Asia/Pacific: 13,000 8.2[2]	1,808,100 6.6	52,113[3] 4.5 69,083[3]	NA NA	28.82[3] 8.5	AT&T Co. TWA Stouffer Hotels Thai Airlines American Airlines
Wall Street Journal Dow Jones & Co. New York	1,835,713[4] (1.8)	Europe: 44,758 3.7 Asia/Pacific: 37,093 4.2	1,917,564 (1.6)	117,394 7.4 NA	123,041 NA	61.22 9.2	American Express IBM Corp. Merrill Lynch AT&T Co. General Motors Corp.
Weeklies							
Business Week McGraw Hill New York	900,989 1.0	Europe: 46,331 5.8 Middle East/ Africa: 7,470 15.3 Asia/Pacific: 28,527 12.2 Latin America: 21,410 7.3	1,004,727 1.7	41,895 9.3 63,680	45,205 68,715	41.70 7.5	AT&T Co. General Motors Corp. IBM Corp. Digital Canon
The Economist The Economist Newspaper London	161,166 13.0	Europe: 158,716 7.1 Middle East/ Africa:	380,924 9.1	9,000 11.8 29,000	10,000 32,000	23.63 2.5	Singapore Airlines Lufthansa Airlines

Title/ Publisher/ Headquarters	Paid North American Circulation/ % chg	Paid Foreign Circulation by Region/ % chg	Worldwide Circulation/ % chg	B&W Pg Cost/ % chg/ 4/c Pg Cost in 1989	B&W Pg Cost/ 4/c Pg Cost Projected for 1990	Global CPM B&W Pg in 1989/ % chg	Top Worldwide Advertisers in 1989
		13,502 (1.4) Asia/Pacific: 41,056 7.6 Latin America: 6,484 3.4					Bank of America Nynex Morgan Guaranty Trust
Guardian Weekly Guardian Publications Manchester, England	25,260[5] (1.3)	Europe: 19,102 5.8 Middle East/ Africa: 5,701 (1.4) Asia/Pacific: 14,084 2.3 Latin America: 1,584 10.9 West Indies: 397 (10.2)	66,128 1.6	2,369[6] (12.2) NA	NA NA	35.82 (13.6)	Abbey National Standard Chartered Bank Halifax Hill Samuel Nat. Westminster Bank
Newsweek Newsweek Ltd. New York	3,288,453 (0.8)	Atlantic: 310,293 2.8 Asia: 209,432 0.8 Latin America: 55,471 2.3 Australia: 109,200 0.1[7]	3,972,849 (0.4)	95,615 4.7 156,100	NA NA	24.07 5.1	Singapore Airlines Rothmans International Rolex Thai Airlines KLM
Paris Match International Publications Filipacchi Paris	35,045 (11.6)	Europe: 136,506 (3.0) Middle East/ Africa: 34,022 (9.1) Asia/Pacific: 1,979 3.6 Latin America: 3,434 (20.6) Other: 25,182 29.5	236,167[11] 0.0	8,561 6.0 12,532	8,989 13,158	36.25 6.0	Philip Morris Cos. B.A.T. Tobacco S.M.H. Group watches Peugeot Citroen
Time Time Inc. New York	4,746,417 (6.7)	Europe: 441,147 0.7 Middle East/ Africa: 72,397 (6.4) Asia/Pacific: 422,000 6.8 Latin America: 88,000 0.0	5,769,961 (5.2)	144,741 6.7 225,680	NA NA	25.09 10.0	Singapore Airlines Rothmans International Philip Morris Cos. Daimler-Benz IBM Corp.

Monthlies

Title/ Publisher/ Headquarters	Paid North American Circulation/ % chg	Paid Foreign Circulation by Region/ % chg	Worldwide Circulation/ % chg	B&W Pg Cost/ % chg/ 4/c Pg Cost in 1989	B&W Pg Cost/ 4/c Pg Cost Projected for 1990	Global CPM B&W Pg in 1989/ % chg	Top Worldwide Advertisers in 1989
National Geographic National Geographic Society Washington	9,456,510 1.7	Europe: 723,356 11.1 Middle East/ Africa: 67,776 6.4 Pacific: 382,357 8.1 Latin America: 98,515 3.9	10,728,514 2.6	136,725 7.1 180,480	143,505 186,555	12.74 4.3	Canon Inc. Iberia Airlines Spanish Tourist Board Olympus Optical Co. Mazda Corp.
Reader's Digest	18,280,470 (1.5)	Atlantic: 7,190,342	28,403,377 (0.7)	254,170 5.7	265,125 353,875	9.12 5.4	Franklin Mint Nestle SA

Table 20–8 **(concluded)**

Title/ Publisher/ Headquarters	Paid North American Circulation/ % chg	Paid Foreign Circulation by Region/ % chg	Worldwide Circulation/ % chg	B&W Pg Cost/ % chg/ 4/c Pg Cost in 1989	B&W Pg Cost/ 4/c Pg Cost Projected for 1990	Global CPM B&W Pg in 1989/ % chg	Top Worldwide Advertisers in 1989
Reader's Digest Assn. Pleasantville, N.Y.		(0.3) Asia/Pacific: 1,728,995 5.7 Latin America: 1,203,570 2.1		340,275			Unilever NV NV Philips Kraft Co.
Scientific American Scientific American Inc. New York	531,634 0.9	Europe: 75,118 6.5 Middle East/ Africa: 3,789 16.1 Asia/Pacific: 21,855 3.7 Latin America: 5,840 7.0	638,216 1.8	20,400 6.9 30,600	20,400[8] 30,600[8]	31.96 5.1	General Motors Corp. Hughes Aircraft Questar McDonnell- Douglas Amoco
South South Publications London	5,120 (17.8)	Europe: 8,723 (24.6) Middle East/ Africa: 26,909 (7.3) Asia/Pacific: 24,506 25.7 Latin America: 11,500 (11.8)	76,758 (3.3)	4,283 5.0 6,845	4,997 7,187	55.80 8.6	NV Philips Boeing Co. Lufthansa Airlines Airbus Rothmans International
WorldPaper[9] World Times Boston	3,000 (87.5)	Middle East/ Africa: 29,000 (58.3) Asia/Pacific: 236,500 (21.9) Latin America: 568,000 136.7 Iceland: 10,000 NA Soviet Union: 270,000 NA	1,116,500 75.4	38,090 22.4 NA	NA NA	34.12 (30.2)	AT&T Co. Lufthansa Airlines Hertz Sheaffer Eaton Federal Express
Fortune Time Inc. New York	672,134[10] 2.4	Europe: 51,157 2.6 Middle East/ Africa: 7,953 (17.1) Asia/Pacific: 40,146 2.5 Latin America: 11,600 (7.1)	782,990 2.0	33,200 6.5 50,800	NA NA	43.97 6.5	Boeing Corp. Samsung Group ICEX Daimler-Benz J.P. Morgan & Co.

Notes: [1]Average daily circulation, audited by OJD, Paris. [2]Second half '89 projection. [3]Figures given are for Monday–Thursday. Friday rate differential effective in '89 due to ABC measured circulation bonus in weekend edition. [4]Sept. 30, 1989 ABC figure. [5]Feb. '89 figure. [6]Full page b&w figure of £1,500 is converted to dollars using Nov. '89 exchange rate of 1.579. [7]Oct. '88–March '89. [8]No change in b&w and 4/c page cost anticipated through Sept. '90. [9]Distributed as a newspaper/magazine supplement. [10]North America-national equivalent pages. All other regions actual pages. [11]Calendar year 1989 and 1988. Figures do not include circulation in France, which in 1989 came to 775,758.

Source: Advertising Age, December 4, 1989, p. S-4.

The international publications offer advertisers a way of reaching large audiences on a regional or worldwide basis. Readers of these publications are usually upscale, high-income individuals who are desirable target markets for many of the products and services listed in Table 20–8. There are, however, several problems with these international media that can limit their attractiveness to many advertisers. Their reach in any one foreign country may be low, particularly for specific segments of a market. Also, while the audiences of these publications are desirable to companies selling business or upscale consumer products and services, they do not cover the mass consumer markets or specialized market segments very well. There are other U.S.-based publications in foreign markets that offer advertisers ways of reaching specific market segments.

While print remains the dominant medium for international advertising, many companies are turning their attention to international commercial television. Packaged-goods companies in particular, such as Gillette, McDonald's, Pepsi, and Coca-Cola, view television advertising as the best way to reach mass markets and effectively communicate their advertising messages. Satellite technology has assisted and helped spread the development and growth of cable television in other countries as well as making global television networks a reality.

There are already five satellite networks operating in Europe that beam entertainment programming across a number of countries, including media magnate Rupert Murdoch's SKY Television; ITV's Super Channel, which is based in England; and Music Television. In 1989 Murdoch launched SKY Television, which absorbed his existing general entertainment SKY channel and includes three new channels: SKY News, SKY Movies, and SKY Sports. All but the movie channel will be advertising supported.[55]

The main incentive to the growth of these satellite networks has been the severely limited program choices and advertising opportunities on government-controlled stations in most of Europe. However, many European countries are planning new channels as governments move to preserve cultural values and protect advertising revenues from going to foreign-based networks. The next major development in European broadcasting is **direct broadcast by satellite (DBS)** to homes and communities equipped with small, low-cost receiving dishes. The first DBS satellite was launched by West Germany in 1987, and Britain and Scandinavian countries are expected to have DBS satellites by 1990.

While European advertising expenditures for television have increased by over 60 percent since 1985 to over $7 billion, many experts question the extent to which the satellite channels will share in this growth. Not only do satellite channels face increasing competition from national channels, but they must also deal with individual governments' attempts to restrict advertising to their country over foreign satellite channels.[56] However, in 1988 the European court ruled that the Dutch government could not stop advertisements on pan-European satellite TV channels from airing their spots at Dutch viewers by subtitling them in English.[57]

Despite these problems, advances in satellite and communications technology, the expansion of multinational companies with global marketing perspectives, and the development of global advertising agencies mean that the use of television as a global medium by advertisers is likely to increase. Promotional Perspective 20–5 discusses the growth of MTV as a global station.

The Role of Other Promotional Mix Elements

The focus of this chapter has been on advertising, since it is usually the primary element in the promotional mix of the international marketer. However, as in domestic marketing, promotional programs for foreign markets will generally include other elements such as personal selling, sales promotion, and public relations. The role of these other promotional mix elements will vary depending on the firm's marketing and promotional strategy in foreign markets.

Promotional elements such as sales promotion and public relations may be used to support and enhance advertising efforts, whereas the latter may also be used to create or maintain favorable images for companies in foreign markets. For some firms, personal selling may be the most important promotional element, and advertising may

Promotional Perspective 20—5

MTV Goes International

MTV (Music Television) Network was launched in the United States in 1981 as a pioneering 24-hour rock video channel on cable television. The New York—based company, which is a unit of Viacom International, Inc., is seen in 49 percent or approximately 45 million American homes, and its growth parallels that of cable TV at 7 to 8 percent a year. However, MTV is seeking an audience far beyond the U.S. shores, as it has expanded into 24 countries including Australia, Japan, and many European and South American nations (Exhibit 20—5).

The president of MTV argues that the station has an edge in attracting its target audience of 12- to 34-year-olds around the world and delivering them to advertisers. He notes that this is the first international generation and that despite cultural differences, teenagers from various countries are much more similar to each other than they are to their parents as "they wear Levi's, shop at Benetton, wear Swatch watches and drink Coca-Cola." Rock 'n' roll music is the greatest common denominator of young people around the world, and music is a global language that crosses borders very easily.

MTV has entered into a number of joint ventures to finance its overseas expansion. In Europe, the station broadcasts 24 hours a day, seven days a week, whereas in Australia it airs just 6 hours a week on Friday and Saturday nights. MTV Japan was launched in July of 1988 and airs five hours a week in early morning hours on Tuesdays and Fridays, since there are only a few stations and time slots available.

A number of major advertisers have signed long-term agreements with MTV Europe including Levi, Toyota, Coca-Cola, Pepsi-Cola, JVC Stereo, and all the major American record and movie companies. While the network is currently operating at a loss in most foreign markets, MTV sees itself as being on the ground floor of the coming global communications network. One company executive stated that the company's goal is "to be the global rock 'n' roll village where we talk to the youth worldwide."

Source: William K. Knoedelseder, Jr., "MTV Goes Global," *Los Angeles Times*, December 18, 1988, pt. IV, pp. 1,4.

Exhibit 20—5   **MTV Has Expanded Into Many Foreign Countries**

play more of a supportive role. In this final section, we will briefly consider the role these other promotional mix elements play in the international marketing program.

Personal Selling

Personal selling is an important promotional tool for many companies engaged in international marketing. As you no doubt know by now, companies selling industrial and high-technology products generally rely heavily on personal selling as the primary method for communicating with their customers. The same emphasis on personal selling will occur when these companies market their products on an international basis. Consumer products firms may also use personal selling to call on distributors, wholesalers, or major retailing operations in foreign markets. Because of low wages in many developing countries, some companies will hire large sales staffs to perform missionary activities and support selling and advertising efforts.

Because it involves personal contact and communication, personal selling is generally even more culture bound than advertising. Thus, most companies use sales representatives from the host country to staff their sales force, and personal selling activities and sales programs are adapted to each market. Management of the sales force is usually decentralized to the local subsidiaries; however, the international marketer will set the general sales policy and offer advice to foreign managers on the role personal selling should play in their market, the development of the sales program, and various aspects of sales management.

Sales Promotion

As we saw in Chapter 15, sales promotion is one of the fastest-growing areas of marketing in the United States. Many companies are also relying on sales promotion tools and techniques to help sell their products in foreign markets as well. Promotional tools that are effective in the United States such as free samples, premiums, contests, and gifts generally work well in other markets.

One form of sales promotion that has become very popular among many U.S. firms for use in foreign markets is event sponsorship. Many customer products firms sponsor sporting events, concerts, and other music-oriented radio and TV programs in foreign countries to help promote their products and enhance the image of the company around the world. For example, Pepsi has sponsored Michael Jackson and Tina Turner concert tours in numerous foreign countries, whereas Coca-Cola set up a pan-European sponsorship department to oversee its music-related marketing efforts.[58]

There are several problems marketers may encounter in their use of sales promotion in foreign countries. First, promotions that rely heavily on retailer involvement and cooperation may not be effective, as distribution channels in foreign markets are usually different from those in the United States. Retailers tend to be smaller in size and larger in number in some markets, making it difficult to contact them. They may also lack the facilities or interest to participate in promotion programs. Marketers may also find that the media needed to distribute sales promotional materials are not as readily available in foreign countries as in the United States.

Other considerations in the design of sales promotion are the cultural differences and constraints of each market. Companies must have sales promotional incentives that are attractive and of interest to consumers in local markets if they are to have an impact on behavior. For example, Japanese women are less likely to take advantage of contests, coupons, or other promotions than are women in this country.[59] Premium offers in particular must be adapted to the tastes and interests of local consumers.

One of the most important factors affecting the use of sales promotion in foreign countries is the presence of legal restrictions and regulations. Laws affecting sales promotion are generally more restrictive in other countries than they are in this country. Some countries have outright bans on some sales promotion techniques such as contests, games, or lotteries, whereas other countries restrict the size or amount of a sam-

Table 20–9 Which European Countries Allow These Promotions?

Promotion	U.K.	Spain	West Germany	France	Italy
In-pack premiums	●	●	○	▲	●
Multiple-purchase offers	●	●	▲	●	●
Extra product	●	●	▲	●	●
Free product	●	●	●	●	●
Mail-in offers	●	●	○	●	●
Purchase-with-purchase	●	●	○	●	●
Cross-promotions	●	●	○	●	●
Contests	●	●	▲	●	●
Sell-liquidating premiums	●	●	●	●	●
Sweepstakes	▲	▲	○	▲	▲
Money-off coupons	●	●	○	●	▲
Next-purchase coupons	●	●	○	●	▲
Cash rebates	●	●	▲	●	○
In-store demos	●	●	●	●	●

● Permitted ○ Not permitted ▲ May be permitted

Source: "Europe Remains Mixed Bag," *Advertising Age,* August 7, 1989, p. 45.

ple, premium offer, or prize. Certain countries also have strict rules regarding the nature of a sales promotion offer. For example, the government of Finland took McDonald's to court for a commercial using a promotion offering customers a toy plastic boat with the purchase of a hamburger. They said the ads offered children boats, not hamburgers, and thus contravened strict national promotional rules.[60] Table 20–9 shows how restrictions on promotions vary among five European countries.

These restrictions often mean that marketers must develop separate promotions for each country. For example, a marketing manager at Levi Strauss noted that the company has found it impossible to do any promotions on a pan-European basis because sales promotions rules vary so much from one country to another.[61] Marketers must be aware of regulations and restrictions regarding the use of sales promotion tools in each country and take them into account in designing their programs. To deal with many of the problems and decision areas in the design of sales promotion programs for foreign markets, many companies use local agencies to develop them or turn to international sales promotion companies.

Public Relations

Many companies involved in international marketing are recognizing the importance of using public relations to support and enhance their marketing and advertising efforts.[62] Public relations activities are needed to deal with local governments, media, trade associations, and the general public, as all these groups may feel threatened by the presence of a foreign multinational in their country. The job of public relations agencies in foreign markets is not only to help the company sell its products or services but also to present the firm as a "good corporate citizen" who is involved with and concerned about the future of the country.

Companies generally must have a favorable reputation and image if they are to be successful in foreign markets. Those with negative reputations or images may face pressure from the media and local governments or ultimately even boycotts by consumers. For example, Nestlé has been a target of consumer boycotts in several countries, including the United States, for its aggressive marketing of infant formula to mothers in Third World countries. To deal with this problem the company stopped the advertising of the product and the distribution of free samples and set up a commission to monitor its compliance.[63]

Often, public relations efforts are needed to deal with specific problems a company faces in international markets. For example, the G. D. Searle company had problems getting its NutraSweet low-calorie sweetener into some markets because of strong sugar lobbies in Australia, Canada, and Europe who were fighting to retain sugar as the only sweetener in beverages. These lobbies encouraged the foreign press to pick up on some of the unfavorable news about the product that was published in the U.S. media.

To deal with this problem, Searle retained Burson-Marsteller, the second largest PR company in the world, to help design factual ads about the product, and to conduct other public relations activities to counter the problems and get the facts out about it.

Like advertising, public relations is becoming more and more of a global activity and, like ad agencies, public relations firms are merging with and/or acquiring overseas offices so that companies can use one firm to communicate with appropriate parties all over the world.

Summary

Many U.S. companies are recognizing not only the opportunities but also the necessity of marketing their products and services internationally because of the saturated markets and intense competition from both domestic and foreign competitors. Advertising and promotion are important parts of the international marketing program of a multinational corporation. Advertising is generally the most cost-effective way of communicating with buyers and creating a market in other countries.

Companies engaging in international marketing must carefully analyze the major environmental forces in each market in which they compete, including economic, demographic, cultural, and political/legal factors. These factors are important not only in assessing the potential of each country as a market but also in designing and implementing advertising and promotional programs.

There are two basic approaches a company can take toward international marketing—a global marketing strategy or a localized approach. In recent years a great deal of attention has been focused on global marketing whereby a standard marketing program is used in all markets. Global advertising falls under this strategy, as the same basic advertising approach is used in all markets. Opponents of the standardized or global approach argue that differences in culture, market, and economic conditions, and consumer needs and wants make it impractical to develop a universal approach to marketing and advertising. Many companies use an in-between approach by standardizing their basic marketing strategy but localizing advertising messages to fit each market.

There are a number of important decision areas in the development of advertising and promotional programs for international markets. These include organization, agency selection, advertising research, creative strategy and execution, and media strategy and selection. Companies can use either a centralized or a decentralized organizational structure for their international advertising operations or a combination of the two. Many American companies use a U.S.-based international agency to handle their international advertising or use a domestic agency that has affiliates in other countries. A third alternative is to select a local agency for each market.

In addition to advertising, personal selling, sales promotion, and public relations are also part of the promotional mix of the international advertiser. Personal selling may be the most important element of some companies' international marketing programs, whereas sales promotions and public relations are generally used to support and enhance advertising efforts.

Key Terms

Balance-of-trade-deficit	Centralized organizational structure
Global economy	Decentralized organizational structure
Economic infrastructure	Localized advertising strategy
Global marketing	International media
Global advertising	Direct broadcasting by satellite (DBS)

Discussion Questions

1. Discuss some of the reasons why international markets are becoming so important to U.S. companies.
2. Discuss the role advertising and promotion play in a firm's international marketing program. Choose two countries and discuss the problems a U.S. company might encounter in advertising its products in these foreign markets.
3. What are the various environmental factors that must be considered in developing an international marketing program? Discuss how these environmental forces would influence a firm's advertising in foreign markets.
4. What are the pros and cons of global advertising? Do you favor a global or a localized strategy? Defend your position.
5. What types of products and services lend themselves to global advertising? For which types of products or services would global advertising be inappropriate?

6. What are the three ways a company can organize for international advertising and promotion?

7. What are the three basic alternatives a company has in selecting an agency to handle its international advertising? Under what conditions might each alternative be used?

8. Evaluate the argument of Martin Sorrell, chairman of the London-based WPP Group, which has purchased several large U.S. agencies, that mega-agencies best serve the global marketing and advertising needs of multinational companies.

9. Discuss the role research plays in the development of international advertising and promotional programs. How would information gained from research help in the creation of advertising messages for foreign markets?

10. Discuss the role of nonadvertising promotional mix elements such as sales promotion, personal selling, and publicity/public relations in international marketing. How might these promotional mix elements differ outside the United States?

Notes

1. Joseph M. Winski and Laurel Wentz, "Parker Pens: What Went Wrong?" *Advertising Age,* June 2, 1986, p. 1.

2. Joanne Lipman, "Marketers Turn Sour on Global Sales Pitch," *The Wall Street Journal,* May 12, 1988, p. 1.

3. George White, "Marlboro Man Passes Japanese Cigarette Maker on Ride to Asia," *Los Angeles Times,* June 20, 1988, pt. IV, p. 3.

4. "PM on Right Track Overseas," *Advertising Age,* November 21, 1988, p. 37.

5. Brian Dumaine, "Japan's Next Push into U.S. Markets," *Fortune,* September 26, 1988, pp. 135–42.

6. David Killburn, "Kao Angles Its Way onto the U.S. Stage," *Advertising Age,* April 10, 1989, p. 54.

7. John Naisbitt, *Megatrends* (New York: Warner Books, 1982).

8. Laurie Freeman and Laurel Wentz, "P&G on a Roll Overseas," *Advertising Age,* June 27, 1988, p. 30.

9. Vern Terpstra, *International Marketing,* 4th ed. (New York: Holt, Rinehart and Winston— Dryden Press, 1987), p. 427.

10. Lera Vanier, "US Ad Spending Doubles All Other Nations," *Advertising Age,* May 16, 1988, p. 36.

11. Shawn Tully, "Nestlé Shows How to Gobble Markets," *Fortune,* January 16, 1989, pp. 74– 78.

12. Irene Lawrence, "Latin America Still Offers Great Marketing Opportunities," *International Advertiser,* October 1985, pp. 12–13.

13. Julia Michaels, "Coke, Pepsi Map Battle in Brazil," *Advertising Age,* August 22, 1988, p. 67.

14. Annette Miller, "Advertisers Take on China," *Newsweek,* December 1, 1986, p. 65.

15. Jonathan R. Slater, "The Hazards of Cross-Cultural Advertising," *Business America,* no. 7, April 2, 1984, pp. 20–23.

16. Barbara Mueller, "Reflections on Culture. An Analysis of Japanese and American Advertising Appeals," *Journal of Advertising Research,* June/July 1987, pp. 51–59.

17. Marian Katz, "No Women, No Alcohol, Learn Saudi Taboos Before Placing Ads," *International Advertiser,* February 1986, pp. 11–12.

18. Dean M. Peebles and John K. Ryans, *Management of International Advertising* (Newton, Mass.: Allyn and Bacon, 1984).

19. Laurel Wentz, "Local Laws Keep International Marketers Hopping," *Advertising Age,* July 11, 1985, p. 20.

20. Katz, "No Women, No Alcohol."

21. J. J. Boddewyn and Iris Mohr, "International Advertisers Face Government Hurdles," *Marketing News,* May 8, 1987, pp. 21–22.

22. Ron Alsop, "Countries' Different Ad Rules Are Problem for Global Firms," *The Wall Street Journal,* September 17, 1984, p. 33.

23. Robert D. Buzzell, "Can You Standardize Multinational Marketing?" *Harvard Business Review,* November/December 1968, pp. 102–13.

24. Ralph Z. Sorenson and Ulrich E. Wiechmann, "How Multinationals View Marketing," *Harvard Business Review,* May/June 1975, p. 38.
25. Theodore Levitt, "The Globalization of Markets," *Harvard Business Review,* May/June 1983, pp. 92–102.
26. Theodore Levitt, *The Marketing Imagination* (New York: Free Press, 1986).
27. Anne B. Fisher, "The Ad Biz Gloms onto Global," *Fortune,* November 12, 1984, p. 78.
28. Keith Reinhard and W. E. Phillips, "Global Marketing: Experts Look at Both Sides," *Advertising Age,* April 15, 1988, p. 47.
29. Anthony Rutigliano, "The Debate Goes On: Global vs. Local Advertising," *Management Review,* June 1986, pp. 27–31.
30. Michael J. McCarthy, "Coke to Use 'Can't Beat the Feeling' as World-Wide Marketing Theme," *The Wall Street Journal,* December 12, 1988, p. B5.
31. Lipman, "Marketers Turn Sour."
32. Example from speech by Eugene H. Kummel, chairman emeritus, McCann-Erickson Worldwide, and Koji Oshita, president and CEO, McCann-Erickson, Hakuhodo, Japan, in San Diego, California, October 19, 1988.
33. Lipman, "Marketers Turn Sour."
34. Quote cited in Fisher, "The Ad Biz," p. 80.
35. Criteria cited by Edward Meyer, CEO, Grey Advertising, in Rebecca Fannin, "What Agencies Really Think of Global Theory," *Marketing & Media Decisions,* December 1984, p. 74.
36. Levitt, "The Globalization of Markets."
37. Quote cited in Reinhard and Phillips, "Global Marketing," p. 47.
38. Fannin, "What Agencies Really Think," p. 75.
39. Robert E. Hite and Cynthia L. Fraser, "International Advertising Strategies of Multinational Corporations," *Journal of Advertising Research,* August/September 1988, pp. 9–17.
40. Sherri Shamoon, "Centralized International Advertising," *International Advertiser,* September 1986, pp. 35–36.
41. Ibid.
42. "Translator Takes a Creative Turn," *International Advertiser,* June 1986, p. 47.
43. Gary Levin, "Ogilvy Under WPP Wing," *Advertising Age,* May 22, 1989, pp. 1, 72.
44. Terpstra, *International Marketing.*
45. Peebles and Ryans, *Management of International Advertising.*
46. Doris Walsh, "Demographics for Advertisers," *International Advertiser,* June 1986, p. 47.
47. Peebles and Ryans, *Management of International Advertising.*
48. John D. Furniss, "Germany Leads the Way in Special Audience Research," *International Advertiser,* October 1985, p. 30.
49. Joseph T. Plummer, "The Role of Copy Research in Multinational Advertising," *Journal of Advertising Research,* October/November 1986, p. 15.
50. Ron Alsop, "Efficacy of Global Ad Projects Is Questioned in Firm's Survey," *The Wall Street Journal,* September 13, 1984, p. 31.
51. Fannin, "What Agencies Really Think."
52. David Bartal and Laurel Wentz, "Danes Phase in TV Spots," *Advertising Age,* November 23, 1987, p. 42.
53. James H. Rosenfield, "The Explosion of Worldwide Media," *Marketing Communications,* September 1987, p. 65.
54. Laurel Wentz, "All Eyes on Europe TV Time," *Advertising Age,* May 23, 1988, p. 71.
55. Laurel Wentz, "Murdoch's Vision: The Sky's the Limit," *Advertising Age,* August 22, 1988, p. 66.
56. Laurel Wentz, "TV Nationalism Clouds Sky Gains," *Advertising Age,* December 14, 1987, p. 56.
57. Wentz, "All Eyes on Europe TV Time."
58. Marina Specht and Anika Michalowska, "Coke Tunes in Music Events," *Advertising Age,* August 15, 1988, p. 43.
59. Media Update, "What You Should Know About Advertising in Japan," *Advertising World,* April 1985, pp. 18, 42.
60. Wentz, "TV Nationalism."
61. Wentz, "Local Laws."
62. "Foreign Ads Go Further with PR," *International Advertiser,* December 1986, p. 30.
63. Tully, "Nestlé Shows How."

21

Advertising Regulation

CHAPTER OBJECTIVES

1. To examine how advertising is regulated including the role and function of various regulatory agencies

2. To examine how self-regulation of advertising takes place and to evaluate this regulatory mechanism

3. To examine how advertising is regulated by various federal and state governmental agencies

4. To examine the operation, procedures, and programs of the Federal Trade Commission in regulating advertising

There Is More to It Than Creating the Ad

Suppose for a moment that you are the advertising manager for a consumer products company and have just reviewed a new commercial your advertising agency has created. You are very excited about the ad, as it presents some new claims regarding the superiority of your brand that should help differentiate it from the competition. However, before you can consider approving the commercial for use, there are a number of questions to which you must have answers such as: Are the claims verifiable? If research was done, were proper procedures used in collecting the data and analyzing and presenting the findings? Do we have the proper research results to support our claims? Did we have the right people in the study and/or were there any conditions that might have biased the results? Are the claims made in the ad consistent with the research data?

Before approving the commercial, you decide to have it reviewed by the company's legal department and also ask your agency to have their attorneys examine it. Assuming that the internal and agency reviews are acceptable, the ad will then be sent to the major networks, who will have their censors examine it. If they have any problems with the commercial, they may ask for more information or send it back for modification. None of the networks will run the commercial until it has received approval from its Standards and Practices Department.

Once the ad is approved and aired, it is subject to close scrutiny from a number of state and federal regulatory agencies, such as the state attorney general's office and the Federal Trade Commission. Individual consumers or competitors who find the ad misleading or have some other concern may file a complaint with the National Advertising Division of the Council of Better Business Bureaus. You must also consider the fact that disparaged competitors may sue you if they feel your ad has distorted the facts and misleads consumers. If you lose the litigation, your company may have to retract the claims and pay the competitor for damages, which may run into millions of dollars.

After considering all these regulatory issues, you must ask yourself if the new ad can meet all these challenges and whether it is worth the risk. Maybe you ought just to continue with the old approach that made no specific claims and simply said that your brand was great.

Introduction

As can be seen from the scenario presented above, regulatory concerns can play a major role in the advertising decision-making process. Advertisers operate in a complex environment of local, state, and federal rules and regulations. Additionally, there are a number of advertising and business-sponsored associations, consumer groups and organizations, and the media that attempt to promote honest, truthful, and tasteful advertising through their own self-regulatory programs and guidelines. The legal and regulatory aspects of advertising are very complex areas, as there are a number of parties who are concerned over the nature and content of advertising and its potential to offend, exploit, mislead, and/or deceive consumers. There are numerous guidelines, rules, regulations, and laws that have been enacted that constrain and restrict advertising.

While in most situations these rules and regulations primarily influence individual advertising messages, there are situations where advertising for an entire industry can be affected. For example, cigarette advertising was banned from the broadcast media in 1970, and currently there is strong sentiment to impose severe restrictions on the advertising and promotion of alcoholic beverages. In May 1989 the surgeon general endorsed recommendations of the Workshop on Drunk Driving, which suggested placing conspicuous warning labels in all alcohol ads, banning the use of celebrities with strong "youth appeal" in alcohol ads and promotions, prohibiting alcoholic beverage companies from sponsoring sporting events, prohibiting alcohol ads and promotions on college campuses, and requiring dissemination of health and safety messages to the public.[1,2] While both the alcohol manufacturers and the advertising industry have voiced strong opposition to these recommendations and are prepared to fight any restrictions, it is likely that some changes in alcohol advertising will occur.

Regulation and control over advertising come from internal or self-regulation by various groups within the advertising industry as well as from external state and federal regulatory agencies such as the Federal Trade Commission (FTC), the Federal Communications Commission (FCC), the Food and Drug Administration, and the U.S. Post Office. While only the governmental agencies (federal, state, and local) have the force of law, most advertisers will also abide by the guidelines and decisions of internal regulatory bodies. In fact, internal or self-regulation from various groups such as the media probably has more of an influence on the day-to-day operations and decision making of advertisers than do governmental rules and regulations.

It is important for all of those involved in the advertising decision-making process, both on the client side and the agency side, to have an understanding of various regulatory bodies and the general intent of their regulatory efforts, how they operate, and how they influence and affect advertising. In this chapter we will examine the major sources of advertising regulation including efforts by the industry at self-regulation and external regulation by governmental agencies.

Self-Regulation

For many years the advertising industry has practiced and promoted the use of voluntary **self-regulation** as a means of regulating and controlling advertising. Most advertisers and their respective agencies, as well as the media, recognize the importance of maintaining consumer trust and confidence and for advertising to be perceived as truthful and nonoffensive. Self-regulation has also been viewed by advertisers as a way of limiting interference with and control over advertising by the government, as this may result in more stringent and troublesome regulations. Self-regulation and control of advertising emanate from all segments of the advertising industry including individual advertisers and their agencies, business and advertising associations, and the media themselves. Let us examine some of these.

Self-Regulation by Advertisers and Agencies

The self-regulatory process actually begins with the interaction of the client and the agency when creative ideas are generated and submitted for consideration. Most companies have specific guidelines, standards, and policies to which advertising for their products or service must adhere. Advertisers recognize that their ads are a reflection of the company, and thus they will carefully scrutinize every message to ensure that they are consistent with the image the firm wishes to project to the general public. Companies will also carefully review their ads to be sure that any claims they make are reasonable and verifiable and do not mislead or deceive consumers. Ads are usually examined by corporate attorneys to avoid any potential legal problems, which not only could be time-consuming and expensive to the firm but also could result in negative publicity and embarrassment.

Internal control and regulation also come from the advertising agency, as most agencies have standards regarding the type of advertising they either want or are willing to produce. Most reputable agencies attempt to avoid ads that might offend consumers or that they feel may be misleading. Agencies are responsible for verifying all product claims made by the advertiser and ensuring that there is adequate documentation or substantiation available. As such, they can be held legally responsible for fraudulent or deceptive claims and in some cases have been fined when their clients have been found guilty of engaging in deceptive advertising.

Many agencies have a creative review board or panel composed of experienced personnel who examine ads for content and execution as well as their potential to be perceived as offensive, misleading, and/or deceptive. Additionally, most agencies either employ or retain lawyers who also review the ads and determine whether they might pose any potential legal problems for the agency and the client.

Self-Regulation by Trade Associations

While many advertisers and their agencies have internal policies and standards that they follow in developing their advertising, many industries have also developed self-

Figure 21-1 Wine Institute Code of Advertising Standards

GUIDELINES. These guidelines shall apply only to voluntary subscribers of this Code of Advertising Standards.

1. Wine and wine cooler advertising should encourage the proper use of wine. Therefore subscribers to this code shall not depict or describe in their advertising:

   a. The consumption of wine or wine coolers for the effects their alcohol content may produce.
   b. Direct or indirect reference to alcohol content or extra strength, except as otherwise required by law or regulation.
   c. Excessive drinking or persons who appear to have lost control or to be inappropriately uninhibited.
   d. Any suggestion that excessive drinking or loss of control is amusing or a proper subject for amusement.
   e. Any persons engaged in activities not normally associated with the moderate use of wine or wine coolers and a responsible life style. Association of wine use in conjunction with feats of daring or activities requiring unusual skill is specifically prohibited.
   f. Wine or wine coolers in quantities inappropriate to the situation or inappropriate for moderate and responsible use.
   g. The image of wine and wine coolers in advertising and promotion shall be adult-oriented and socially responsible. Comparative or competitor-derogatory advertising is inappropriate.

2. Advertising of wine has traditionally depicted wholesome persons enjoying their lives and illustrating the role of wine in a mature life style. Any attempt to suggest that wine directly contributes to success or achievement is unacceptable. Therefore, the following restrictions shall apply to subscribers of this code:

   a. Wine and wine coolers shall not be presented as being essential to personal performance, social attainment, achievement, success or wealth.
   b. The use of wine and wine coolers shall not be directly associated with social, physical or personal problem solving.
   c. Wine and wine coolers whall not be presented as vital to social acceptability and popularity.
   d. It shall not be suggested that wine or wine coolers are crucial for successful entertaining.

3. Any advertisement which has particular appeal to persons below the legal drinking age is unacceptable. Therefore, wine and wine cooler advertising by code subscribers shall not:

   a. Show models and personalities in advertisements who are under the legal drinking age. Models should appear to be 25 years of age or older.
   b. Use music, language, gestures or cartoon characters specifically associated with or directed toward those below the legal drinking age.
   c. Appear in children or juvenile magazines, newspapers, television programs, radio programs or other mdeia specifically oriented to persons below the legal drinking age.
   d. Be presented as being related to the attainment of adulthood or associated with "rites of passage" to adulthood.
   e. Suggest that wine or a wine cooler product resembles or is similar to another type of beverage of product (milk, soda, candy) having particular appeal to persons below the legal drinking age.
   f. Use current or traditional heroes of the young such as those engaged in pastimes and occupations having a particular appeal to persons below the legal drinking age.
   g. Use amateur or professional sports celebrities, past or present.

4. Code subscribers shall not show motor vehicles in such a way as to suggest that they are to be operated in conjunction with wine or wine cooler use.

   Advertising should in no way suggest that wine or wine coolers be used in connection with driving motorized vehicles such as automobiles, motorcycles, boats, snowmobiles, or airplanes.

5. Wine and wine cooler advertising shall not appear in or directly adjacent to television or radio programs or print media which dramatize or glamorize over-consumption or inappropriate use of alcoholic beverages.

6. Wine and wine cooler advertising by code subscribers shall make no reference to wine's medicinal or caloric values.

7. Wine and wine cooler advertising by code subscribers shall not degrade the image or status of any ethnic, minority or other group.

8. Wine and wine cooler advertising shall not be directed to underage drinkers or pregnant women. Wine and wine cooler advertising will not portray excessive drinking.

9. Wine and wine cooler advertising by code subscribers shall not exploit the human form, feature provocative or enticing poses, nor be demeaning to any individual.

10. A distinguishing and unique feature of wine is that it is traditionally served with meals or immediately before or following a meal.

    Therefore, when subscribers to this code use wine advertising which visually depicts a scene or setting where wine is to be served, such advertising shall include foods and show that they are available and are being used or are intended to be used.

    This guideline shall not apply to the depiction of a bottle of wine, vineyard, label, professional tasting etc. where emphasis is on the product.

    All advertising—including, but not limited to direct mail, point-of-sale, outdoor, displays, radio, television and print media—should adhere to both the letter and the spirit of the above code.

regulatory programs. This is particularly true in industries where advertising is prone to controversy such as liquor and alcoholic beverages, drugs, and various products marketed to children. These trade and industry associations have developed their own advertising guidelines or codes that member companies are expected to abide by. For example, the Wine Institute (Figure 21–1), the U.S. Brewers Association, and the Distilled Spirits Council of the United States Inc. all have guidelines that member companies are supposed to follow in advertising alcoholic beverages. Other industry trade associations with advertising guidelines and programs include the Toy Manufacturers Association, Motion Picture Association of America, the Pharmaceutical Manufactur-

Promotional Perspective 21–1

The Liquor Industry Changes Advertising Codes to Get Products on Television

Although there is no specific law prohibiting advertising of hard liquor on radio or television, ads for spirit products are rarely seen or heard over the airways. Ads for liquor have been effectively banned for over five decades as a result of code provision of the National Association of Broadcasters and by agreements of liquor manufacturers and their self-governing body, the Distilled Spirits Council, not to broadcast advertising for spirits of any kind. However, in November 1987 members of the Distilled Spirits Council revised their "Code of Good Practice," with one of the key changes being a decision by the industry to permit television advertising for "spirits coolers" that contain no more than 7 percent alcohol by volume. Spirit coolers have the same alcohol content as a wine cooler but are made from rum, a distilled spirit, rather than wine. The council also amended its code to allow spirits ads on closed-circuit TV in hotels and restaurants and on airline movie screens.

One of the reasons for the decision by the council was to help manufacturers of hard liquor remain competitive. Sales of distilled spirits declined for three consecutive years, and television advertising is viewed as a way of reversing the sales slide. Bacardi Imports Inc. is one of the companies planning on using television ads for its new product Bacardi Breezer, a rum-based fruit drink. However, the company will have to air its ads on independent stations, as all the major networks have rejected the commercials. The director of broadcast standards of

ABC noted, "If we're not responsible self-regulators, the government will step in," whereas another network executive noted that any erosion in current standards could lead to a backlash that would result in a complete ban of alcoholic beverage advertising on television. Bacardi and the council have argued that the product has the same amount of alcohol as any other cooler, and the company has supplied documentation of this to the independent stations that have agreed to accept the ads.

Consumer health groups are very upset over the incursion of liquor marketers into television in any form. The National Council on Alcoholism has expressed concern over the precedents being set by the video ads, as have groups concerned about drunk driving. The Center for Science in the Public Interest has called the acceptance of spirit ads "back door advertising" and argues that it could lead to the advertising of other forms of distilled spirits on television.

Despite the criticism, liquor marketers, faced with steadily eroding sales for many brands, plan to continue the use of video advertising, as they say a splashy video sales pitch can have much more impact than print and billboard ads.

Sources: Bruce Horowitz, "Liquor Industry Plan for 'Spirits Coolers' Ads on TV Gets Icy Reception," *Los Angeles Times*, April 5, 1988, p. 10; Ron Alsop, "Despite Ban, Liquor Marketers Finding New Ways to Get Products on Television, *The Wall Street Journal*, March 14, 1988, p. 27.

ers Association, and the Proprietary Association (the trade association for nonprescription drug makers), among others.[3] Promotional Perspective 21–1 demonstrates how the Distilled Spirits Council recently revised its Code of Good Practice in an effort to help liquor manufacturers remain competitive in a declining market.

Many professions also maintain advertising guidelines through local, state, and national organizations. Professional associations such as the American Medical Association and the American Bar Association for years restricted advertising by their members on the basis that promotional activities such as advertising would lower the status of the professional in the eyes of the public and would lead to unethical and fraudulent claims. However, professional codes that restrict advertising have been the target of attack from governmental regulatory agencies as well as various consumer groups that argue that the public has a right to be informed about the services provided by the professional and his or her qualifications and background. They also argue that advertising by professionals will lead to improvements in professional services, as consumers become better informed and are better able to shop around for these services.[4]

In 1977 the Supreme Court held that state bar associations' restrictions on advertising are unconstitutional and that attorneys have First Amendment freedom of speech rights to advertise.[5] Following this ruling, many restrictions on advertising were removed by a number of professional associations, and advertising by lawyers and other professionals has become commonplace.[6] (See Figure 21–2.) In 1982 the Supreme Court upheld an order by the FTC permitting advertising by dentists and physicians,

Figure 21–2   Advertising by Lawyers Has Become Commonplace as a Result of a 1977 Supreme Court Ruling

Man:
We were being strangled by our debts. We couldn't sleep, our work suffered . . . We'd heard about bankruptcy, but didn't know much about it.

Lawyer:
By the time the Brill's came to Jacoby & Meyers, they were being harrassed by their creditors, their wages were attached and their home was in foreclosure. We stopped all that.

Man:
We figured, our creditors were using lawyers to protect their rights. Why shouldn't we?

Lawyer: The Brill's just needed a chance to get a fresh start.

Jacoby & Meyers
When it's time to call a lawyer about a bankruptcy.

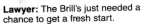

which has resulted in ads by medical and dental organizations as well as by individual practitioners.[7]

Research has shown that consumers generally favor increased use of professional advertising. However, the professionals themselves continue to have reservations about its use, as they are concerned that advertising will have a negative impact on their image, credibility, and dignity and see benefits to consumers as unlikely.[8] Advertising by professionals is likely to gain in popularity, particularly by individuals entering the profession. Associations such as the American Bar Association and the American Medical Association have developed guidelines for advertising by their members to help maintain standards and guard against misleading, deceptive, or offensive ads.

While industry associations' guidelines are meant to show that member firms and individuals are concerned with the impact and consequences of their advertising, their effectiveness is limited to the ability of the particular association or profession to enforce the code or restrictions. Associations have no legal basis for enforcing these guidelines and must usually rely on peer pressure from members or other nonbinding sanctions as a way of getting advertisers to comply with these standards.

Self-Regulation by Businesses

A number of self-regulatory mechanisms have been established by the business community in an effort to control advertising practices. The largest and best known of these is through the **Better Business Bureau** (BBB). The BBB is not limited to one particular industry but rather promotes fair advertising and selling practices in all industries. Established in 1916 to handle consumer complaints about local business practices and particularly advertising, there are local BBBs located in principal cities throughout the United States, supported entirely by dues of the more than 100,000 member firms.

The local BBBs receive and investigate complaints from consumers and other companies regarding the advertising and selling tactics of businesses in their area. Each local office has its own individual operating procedures for handling these complaints; however, the general procedure is to contact the violator and, if the complaint proves true, to request that the practice be stopped or changed. If the violator does not respond, negative publicity may be used against them or the case may be referred to appropriate governmental agencies for further action.

While the BBBs provide effective control over advertising practices at the local level, the parent organization of the local offices, the **Council of Better Business Bureaus,** plays a major role in the monitoring and control of advertising at a national level. The council will often assist new industries in the development of codes and standards for ethical and responsible advertising practices and also provides ongoing information concerning advertising regulations and legal rulings to advertisers, agen-

Table 21–1 **Sources of NAD Cases, 1988**

NAD monitoring	37
Competitor challenges	41
Local BBBs	9
Consumer complaints	9
Other	7
Total	**103**

Source: NAD Report 18, no. 12, January 16, 1989, p. 43.

cies, and the media. The council also plays an important self-regulatory role through its National Advertising Division (NAD) and Children's Advertising Unit. The NAD works closely with the **National Advertising Review Board** (NARB) to sustain truth, accuracy, and decency in national advertising. The NAD/NARB has become the advertising industry's primary self-regulatory mechanism and, as such, warrants additional discussion.

NAD/NARB In 1971 four associations—the American Advertising Federation (AAF), the American Association of Advertising Agencies (AAAA), the Association of National Advertisers (ANA), and the Council of Better Business Bureaus—joined forces to establish the **National Advertising Review Council** (NARC). The NARC was established to sustain high standards of truth, accuracy, morality, and social responsibility in national advertising. The council has two operating arms: the National Advertising Division of the Council of Better Business Bureaus and the National Advertising Review Board. The NAD/NARB constitutes the advertising industry's most effective self-regulatory mechanism.

The NAD maintains an advertising monitoring program that is the source of many of the cases it reviews along with complaints received from consumers and consumer groups, local BBBs, and competitors' challenges (Table 21–1). The NAD acts as the investigative arm of the NARC and, after initiating or receiving a complaint, determines the issue, collects and evaluates data, and makes the initial decision on whether the advertiser's claims are substantiated. The NAD may ask the advertiser to supply appropriate substantiation for the claim in question. If this is done, the case is dismissed. If the NAD does not find the substantiation to be satisfactory, it negotiates with the advertiser to secure modification or permanent discontinuance of the advertising.

If the NAD and the advertiser fail to resolve the controversy, an appeal can be made by either party to have a review by a five-person panel from the National Advertising Review Board. The NARB is composed of 50 executives including 30 national advertisers, 10 advertising agency representatives, and 10 representatives from the public sector. If the NARB panel agrees with the NAD and rules against the advertiser, the advertiser must discontinue the advertising in accordance with the panel decision. If the advertiser refuses to comply, the NARB will refer the matter to the appropriate government agency and indicate the fact in its public record. Figure 21–3 shows a flowchart of the steps in the NAD/NARB review process.

Although the NARB has no power to order an advertiser to stop running an ad or sanctions it can impose, no advertiser who participated in the full process of an NAD investigation and NARB appeal has refused to abide by the panel's decision.[9] Most cases do not even make it to the NARB panel. For example, in 1988, of the 103 NAD investigations, 27 ad claims were substantiated, 75 were modified or discontinued, and only 1 was referred to the NARB for resolution.

The NAD/NARB is a valuable and effective self-regulatory body. Cases brought to the NAD/NARB are handled at a fraction of the cost (and there is much less publicity) than if they were processed through a governmental agency such as the FTC. The system also works because judgments are made by the advertiser's peers, and most companies feel compelled to comply with their decision. Former FTC chairman Robert Pitofsky noted that the success of the NARB is one of the major reasons for a decline in the number of deceptive advertising cases filed by the FTC.[10] It has been suggested that firms may prefer self-regulation rather than government intervention, as many companies will challenge competitor's unsubstantiated claims through self-regulatory groups such as the NARB.[11]

Advertising Associations Various groups in the advertising industry have also been proponents of self-regulation. The two major national organizations, the AAAA and the AAF, actively monitor and police industrywide advertising practices. The AAAA,

Figure 21–3   Steps in the NAD/NARB Review Process

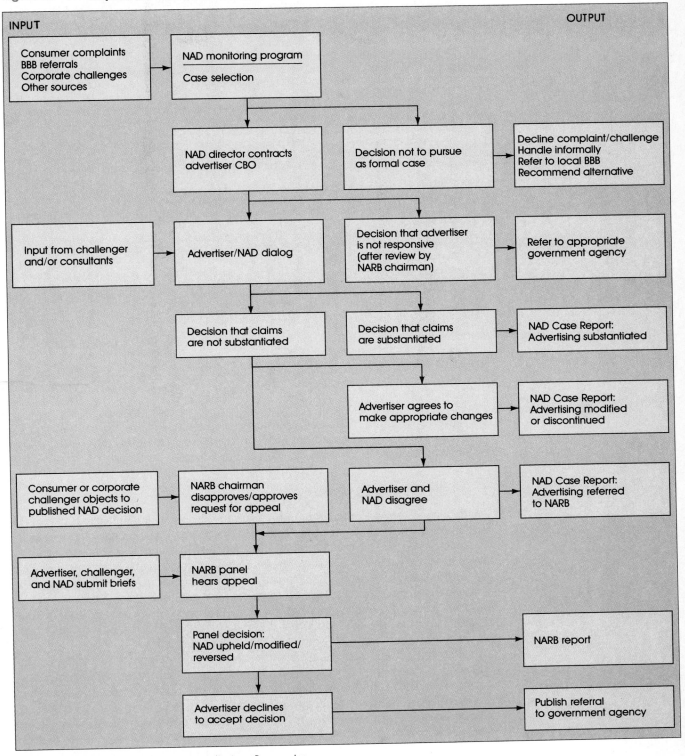

INPUT   OUTPUT

Consumer complaints
BBB referrals
Corporate challenges
Other sources
→ NAD monitoring program
Case selection

NAD director contracts
advertiser CBO

Decision not to pursue
as formal case
→ Decline complaint/challenge
Handle informally
Refer to local BBB
Recommend alternative

Input from challenger
and/or consultants
→ Advertiser/NAD dialog

Decision that advertiser
is not responsive
(after review by
NARB chairman)
→ Refer to appropriate
government agency

Decision that claims
are not substantiated

Decision that claims
are substantiated
→ NAD Case Report:
Advertising substantiated

Advertiser agrees to
make appropriate changes
→ NAD Case Report:
Advertising modified
or discontinued

Consumer or corporate
challenger objects to
published NAD decision
→ NARB chairman
disapproves/approves
request for appeal

Advertiser and
NAD disagree
→ NAD Case Report:
Advertising referred
to NARB

Advertiser, challenger,
and NAD submit briefs
→ NARB panel
hears appeal

Panel decision:
NAD upheld/modified/
reversed
→ NARB report

Advertiser declines
to accept decision
→ Publish referral
to government agency

National Advertising Division, Council of Better Business Bureaus, Inc.

which is the major trade association of the advertising agency business in the United States, has established standards of practice and has its own creative code. The organization also will issue guidelines for specific types of advertising such as comparative messages (Figure 21–4). The AAF consists of advertisers, agencies, media, and numer-

Figure 21–4   American Association of Advertising Agencies Policy Statement and Guidelines for Comparative Advertising

The Board of Directors of the American Association of Advertising Agencies recognizes that when used truthfully and fairly, comparative advertising provides the consumer with needed and useful information.

However, extreme caution should be exercised. The use of comparative advertising, by its very nature, can distort facts and, by implication, convey to the consumer information that misrepresents the truth.

Therefore, the Board believes that comparative advertising should follow certain guidelines:

1. The intent and connotation of the ad should be to inform and never to discredit or unfairly attack competitors, competing products, or services.
2. When a competitive product is named, it should be one that exists in the marketplace as significant competition.
3. The competition should be fairly and properly identified but never in a manner or tone of voice that degrades the competitive product or service.
4. The advertising should compare related or similar properties or ingredients of the product, dimension to dimension, feature to feature.
5. The identification should be for honest comparison purposes and not simply to upgrade by association.
6. If a competitive test is conducted, it should be done by an objective testing source, preferably an independent one, so that there will be no doubt as to the veracity of the test.
7. In all cases the test should be supportive of all claims made in the advertising that are based on the test.
8. The advertising should never use partial results or stress insignificant differences to cause the consumer to draw an improper conclusion.
9. The property being compared should be significant in terms of value or usefulness of the product to the consumer.
10. Comparatives delivered through the use of testimonials should not imply that the testimonial is more than one individual's thought unless that individual represents a sample of the majority viewpoint.

Source: Policy Statement and Guidelines for Comparative Advertising (New York: AAAA, 1974).

ous advertising clubs. The association has established standards for truthful and responsible advertising and has been active in the legislative area of advertising and in influencing agencies to abide by its code and principles.

Self-Regulation by Media

Another important self-regulatory mechanism in the advertising industry is that of the media. Most media maintain some form of advertising review process and, except in the case of political advertising, may reject any ads they regard as objectionable. As was noted in earlier chapters, some media exclude the advertising of an entire product class, whereas others may ban individual ads that they feel are offensive or objectionable. For example, *Reader's Digest* does not accept advertising for tobacco or liquor products, whereas for many years *Ms.* magazine refused to accept ads for Virginia Slims cigarettes because the editors felt that the slogan "You've come a long way baby" overstated the advances made by women in their fight for equality.

Newspapers and magazines have their own set of advertising requirements and restrictions that will often vary depending on the size and nature of the publication. Large, established publications such as major newspapers or magazines often have strict standards regarding the type of advertising they will accept. As noted in Chapter 12, some magazines such as *Parents* or *Good Housekeeping* regularly test products advertised therein and offer a "Seal of Approval" and refund offers for products that are later found to be defective. Such policies are designed to enhance the credibility of the publication and increase the reader's confidence in the products advertised in these magazines.

Advertising on television and radio has been regulated for years through codes developed by the industry trade association—the National Association of Broadcasters (NAB). Both the radio code (established in 1937) and the television code (1952) pro-

Promotional Perspective 21–2

Network Censors Decide Whether Ads Are Okay

Reviewers—or as many refer to them, censors—in the broadcast standards and practices division of the three major networks sift through nearly 1,000 commercials per week to determine if the ads are in good taste, are too aggressive, and/or are deceptive. What these editors find displeasing will never make it on the air. Considering that advertising pays the way for the television networks, the network censors are surprisingly tough. For example, ABC has been known to find problems with as many as 4 of every 10 ads they review. Many advertisers think that the networks are too tough, which has resulted in some heated arguments.

Advertisers and network censors may argue vehemently about how much of the toilet can be shown in a commercial for a toilet cleaner, whether a mother can talk to her daughter about "murdering her clothes," or if it is okay to say "jock itch" before 11:30 P.M. Sometimes only subtle changes are required to make a commercial acceptable, whereas in some cases an ad may be completely rejected. For example, ethnic stereotypes such as sleepy Mexicans or Orientals mixing up their l's and r's usually do not make it. The networks contend that they are protecting the public from unacceptable, offensive, or potentially deceptive ads by establishing rigid standards, and that they carry the responsibility of entering people's homes with appropriate and tasteful messages.

Source: Bill Abrams, "The Networks Censor TV Ads for Taste and Deceptiveness," *The Wall Street Journal*, September 30, 1982, p. 33.

vided the standards for broadcast advertising for many years. Both codes prohibit the advertising of certain products such as hard liquor and also have standards regarding the manner in which products can be advertised. However, in 1982 the NAB suspended all of its code provisions after portions dealing with time standards and required length of commercials in the television code were found to be in restraint of trade by the courts. While the NAB codes are no longer in force, many individual broadcasters, such as the major television networks, have adopted major portions of the code provisions into their own standards.[12]

Probably the most stringent review process of any media is that of the three major television networks. All three networks maintain "Standards and Practices" divisions, which carefully review all commercials submitted to the network or individual affiliate stations. Advertisers are required to submit all commercials intended for airing on the network or an affiliate station for review by the network's broadcast standards department.

Commercials at various stages of the production process are submitted for review by sending a script, storyboard, animatic, or finished commercial (when the advertiser feels there is little chance of objection). The network reviewers will consider whether the proposed commercial meets acceptable standards and is appropriate for certain audiences. For example, different standards will be used for ads designated for prime-time versus late night spots or for children's versus adults' programs. An example of the three networks' guidelines for children's advertising is shown in Table 21–2.

It is estimated that each of the three major networks receives over 50,000 commercials a year for review, with nearly two thirds being accepted and only 3 percent rejected. The remaining 30 percent are revised and resubmitted for review, with most problems being resolved through negotiation.[13] Promotional Perspective 21–2 discusses how the networks censor television ads for taste and deception.

Network standards regarding acceptable advertising are constantly changing. In 1987 the networks began to allow advertisers of lingerie products to use live models rather than mannequins, and advertising for contraceptives has recently been appearing on some stations. It is likely that network standards will continue to change as society's values and attitudes toward certain issues and products change. It is also likely that the networks may relax some of their standards and restrictions in response to competition from independent and cable stations, which tend to be much less strin-

Table 21—2   **A Sampling of the TV Networks' Guidelines for Children's Advertising**

Each of the major television networks has its own set of guidelines for children's advertising, although the basics are very similar. A few rules, such as the requirement of a static "island" shot at the end, are written in stone; others however, occasionally can be negotiated.
  Many of the rules below apply specifically to toys. The networks also have special guidelines for kids' food commercials and for kids' commercials that offer premiums.

	ABC	CBS	NBC
Must not overglamorize product	✓	✓	✓
No exhortative language, such as "Ask Mom to buy. . ."	✓	✓	✓
No realistic war settings	✓		✓
Generally no celebrity endorsements	✓	Case-by-case	✓
Can't use "only" or "just" in regard to price	✓	✓	
Show only two toys per child or maximum of six per commercial	✓		✓
Five-second "island" showing product against plain background at end of spot	✓	✓	✓ (4 to 5)
Animation restricted to one third of a commercial	✓		✓
Generally no comparative or superiority claims	Case-by-case	Handle w/care	✓
No costumes or props not available with the toy	✓		
No child or toy can appear in animated segments	✓		✓
Three-second establishing shot of toy in relation to child	✓	✓ (2.5 to 3)	✓
No shots under one second in length		✓	
Must show distance a toy can travel before stopping on its own		✓	

Source: "Double Standard for Kids' TV Ads," *The Wall Street Journal,* June 10, 1988, p. 25.

gent in their requirements for commercials. However, television is probably the most carefully scrutinized and frequently criticized of all forms of advertising, and the networks must be careful not to offend their viewers and detract from the credibility of advertising.

Appraising Self-Regulation

As can be seen from the preceding discussion, there are a number of sources of internal regulation or self-regulation in advertising. The three major participants in the advertising process—the advertisers, the agencies, and the media—all work both individually and collectively to encourage truthful, ethical, and responsible advertising. The advertising industry views self-regulation as an effective mechanism for controlling abuses in advertising and avoiding the use of offensive, misleading, or deceptive practices and prefers this form of regulation to government intervention. Self-regulation of advertising has undoubtedly been effective and in many instances has probably led to the development of standards and practices that are higher than those imposed by law and beyond the proper scope of legislation.

It should be noted, however, that there are limitations to self-regulation, and this process has been criticized in a number of areas. For example, concern has been expressed over the fact that it often takes the NAD six months to a year to resolve a complaint, during which time a company has often stopped using a commercial anyway. Concern has also been expressed over budgeting and staffing constraints, which limit the NAD/NARB system's ability to investigate more cases and complete them more rapidly.[14] Self-regulation has also been criticized for being self-serving to the advertisers and advertising industry and lacking the power or authority to be a viable alternative to federal or state regulation.

Many critics do not feel that advertising can, or should be, controlled solely by self-regulation. They argue that regulation by governmental agencies is necessary in many instances to ensure that advertising provides consumers with accurate information and does not mislead or deceive them. Negative perceptions of self-regulation have prompted many parties to turn to the federal and state government for control and regulation of advertising. We will now focus our discussion on governmental regulation of advertising.

Federal Regulation of Advertising

Governmental control and regulation of advertising stem from various federal, state, and local laws and regulations, with enforcement being the task of various government agencies. The most important source of external regulation comes from the federal government, particularly through the **Federal Trade Commission** (FTC). Thus, while we will examine other governmental agencies that regulate advertising, we will focus most of our attention on federal regulation of advertising and the operation and policies of the FTC.

Background on Federal Regulation of Advertising

Federal regulation of advertising actually originated in 1914 with the passage of the **Federal Trade Commission Act** (FTC Act), which created the FTC, the agency that is today the most active in, and has the primary responsibility for, the control and regulation of advertising. The FTC Act was originally passed to help enforce antitrust laws—such as the Sherman and Clayton acts—by helping to restrain unfair methods of competition. The main focus of the five-member commission given the power to enforce the act was in protecting competitors from one another, as the issue of false or misleading advertising was not even mentioned. In 1922 the Supreme Court upheld an FTC interpretation that false advertising was an unfair method of competition, but in the 1931 Raladam case (*FTC* v. *Raladam Co.*), the Court ruled that the commission could not prohibit false advertising unless there was evidence of injury to a competitor by the ads.[15] This ruling limited the power of the FTC to protect consumers from false or deceptive advertising and led to a consumer movement that resulted in an important amendment to the FTC Act.

In 1938 the **Wheeler-Lea Amendment** was passed, which amended section 5 of the FTC Act to read:

> Unfair methods of competition in commerce and unfair or deceptive acts or practices in commerce are hereby declared to be unlawful.

A very important aspect of the amendment was the fact that the FTC was empowered to act against advertising if there were evidence of injury to the public, and proof of injury to competition was not necessary. The Wheeler-Lea Amendment also gave the FTC the power to issue cease and desist orders and levy fines on violators and extended its jurisdiction over false advertising of foods, drugs, cosmetics, and therapeutic devices. This amendment also provided the FTC with access to the injunctive power of the federal courts. Initially this pertained only to the marketing of food and drug products but was expanded in 1972 to include all products where there is a threat to the public's health and safety.

In addition to the FTC, there are numerous other federal agencies that are responsible for, or involved in, the regulation of advertising. The authority of these agencies is limited, however, to a particular product area or service, and these agencies often rely on the FTC to assist in the handling of false or deceptive advertising cases. Thus, we will examine the FTC and its operations in more detail prior to discussing these other federal agencies.

The Federal Trade Commission

The FTC is charged with the responsibility of protecting both consumers and businesses from anticompetitive behavior and unfair and deceptive practices. The major divisions of the FTC include the Bureaus of Competition, Economics, and Consumer Protection. The Bureau of Competition is responsible for enforcing antitrust laws, whereas the Bureau of Economics aids and advises the commission on the economic aspects of its activities and prepares economic reports and surveys. The Bureau of Consumer Protection investigates and litigates cases involving acts or practices alleged to be deceptive or unfair to consumers. The National Advertising Division of the Bureau of Consumer Protection is responsible for enforcing those provisions of the FTC Act that forbid misrepresentation, unfairness, and deception in national advertising.

As noted, the FTC has had the power to regulate advertising since the passage of the Wheeler-Lea Amendment. However, it was not until the early 1970s—following criticism of the commission in a book by "Nader's Raiders" and a special report by the American Bar Association for its lack of action against deceptive promotional practices—that the FTC became active in the regulation of advertising.[16,17]

The authority of the FTC was increased considerably throughout the 1970s. A particularly important piece of legislation affecting the commission was the Magnuson-Moss Act of 1975, which resulted in dramatic broadening of the FTC's powers and a substantial increase in its budget. The first section of this act dealt with consumers' rights regarding product warranties and allowed the commission to require restitution for deceptively written warranties where the consumer lost more than $5. The second section, the FTC Improvements Act, gave the FTC the power to establish **trade regulation rules** (TRRs), which are industrywide rules that defined unfair practices before they occurred.

During the decade of the 1970s the FTC made enforcement of laws regarding false and misleading advertising a top priority, as several new programs were instituted, budgets were increased, and the commission became a very powerful regulatory agency. However, many of these programs, as well as the expanded powers of the FTC to develop regulations on the basis of "unfairness," became the source of considerable controversy. At the source of this controversy has been the fundamental issue of what constitutes unfair or deceptive advertising. We will now turn our attention to this important issue.

What Is Deceptive or Unfair Advertising?   Advertising has a responsibility in most economic systems of providing consumers with information that they can use as a basis for making consumption decisions. However, if this information is untrue or misleads the consumer, then the advertising is not fulfilling this basic function. The problem that arises, however, concerns just what constitutes an untruthful or deceptive advertisement. Deceptive advertising can take a number of forms, ranging from an intentional false or misleading claim by the advertiser to ads that may be true in a literal sense but may leave some consumers with a false or misleading impression.

The issue of deception, including its definition and measurement, has received considerable attention from the FTC and other regulatory agencies. One of the problems regulatory agencies must deal with in determining deception is making the distinction between false or misleading messages and those that, rather than relying on verifiable or substantiated objective information about a product, rely on subjective claims or statements about a product, a practice known as puffery.

Puffery has been legally defined as

> advertising or other sales presentations which praise the item to be sold with subjective opinions, superlatives, or exaggerations, vaguely and generally, stating no specific facts.[18]

The use of puffery in advertising is very common. For example, Bayer aspirin calls itself the "Wonder drug that works wonders," whereas Nestlé claims that "Nestlé makes the very best chocolate." Superlatives such as the "greatest," "best," and/or "finest" are puffs frequently used in advertising.

Puffery has generally been viewed as a form of "poetic license" or allowable exaggeration for the advertiser. The FTC has taken the position that consumers expect exaggeration or inflated claims in advertising and that puffery is recognizable by consumers and will not lead to deception since it is not believed. However, some studies have shown that consumers may believe puffery claims and may perceive them as literally true.[19,20] One study found that consumers could not distinguish between a verifiable fact-based claim and puffery and were just as likely to believe both types of claims.[21] Ivan Preston has argued that puffery has a detrimental effect on consumers' purchase decisions by burdening them with untrue beliefs and refers to it as "soft core deception" that should be considered illegal.[22]

While unfair and deceptive acts or practices in advertising are the primary focus of the FTC, these terms have never really been precisely defined, and the FTC has continually developed and refined a "working definition" used in its attempts to regulate advertising. The traditional standard used in determining if an advertising claim is deceptive was whether it had the "tendency or capacity to deceive." However, this standard was criticized for being vague and all-encompassing.

Efforts by the FTC to develop trade regulation rules, whereby the commission could establish industrywide rules that would define unfair practices and have the force and effect of law, were limited by Congress in 1980 with the passage of the FTC Improvements Act. The trade regulation rules were the source of considerable controversy since they were based on the concept of "unfairness," which critics argued was very difficult to define and received overly broad use by the FTC.

In 1983 the FTC, under Chairman James Miller III, put forth a new working definition of **deception,** which is as follows:

> The commission will find deception if there is a misrepresentation, omission or practice that is likely to mislead the consumer acting reasonably in the circumstances to the consumer's detriment.[23]

The commissioners' statement briefly explained the three essential elements of the definition:

> First, there must be a representation, omission or practice that is likely to mislead the consumer.
>
> Second, we examine the practice from the perspective of a consumer acting reasonably in the circumstances
>
> Third, the representation, omission or practice must be a "material" one. The basic question is whether the act is likely to affect the consumer's conduct or decision with regard to a product or service. If so, the practice is material, and consumer injury is likely because consumers are likely to have chosen differently but for the deception.[24]

The goal of then Chairman Miller, who drafted this definition, was to help the commission determine which cases were worth pursuing and to prevent the FTC from dealing with those considered trivial. Miller argued that for an advertisement to be considered worthy of challenge by the FTC, it should be seen by a substantial number of consumers, it should lead to significant injury, and the problem should be one that market forces are not likely to remedy. However, concern has been expressed that this revised definition will put a greater burden on the FTC to prove that deception has taken place and to prove that a deceptive act influenced the consumers' decision-making process in a detrimental way.

What constitutes unfairness remains a controversial issue. However, two of the factors the FTC takes into consideration in evaluating an ad for deception are (1) whether there are significant omissions of important information and (2) whether advertisers can substantiate the claims made for the product or service. The FTC has developed several programs that address these issues.

Affirmative Disclosure   A problem in determining deception is that an ad can be literally true, yet leave the consumer with a false or misleading impression if the claim is true only under certain conditions or circumstances or if there are limitations to what the product can do. Thus, the FTC may require advertisers to include certain types of information in their advertisements so that consumers will be aware of all the consequences, conditions, and limitations associated with use of the product or service. The requirement that cigarette advertisements contain a warning concerning the health risks associated with smoking is an example of an **affirmative disclosure** requirement.

The goal of affirmative disclosure is for consumers to have sufficient information to make an informed decision. An ad may be required to define the testing situation, conditions, or criteria used in making a claim. For example, fuel mileage claims in automobile ads are based on Environmental Protection Agency (EPA) ratings since they offer a uniform standard for making comparisons.

Advertising Substantiation   A major area of concern to regulatory agencies in protecting consumers and promoting fair competition is whether advertisers can support or substantiate the claims made in their advertisements. For many years there were no formal requirements concerning substantiation of advertising claims. Many companies would make specific claims in their ads without having any documentation or support such as laboratory tests and clinical studies available. In 1971 the FTC adopted an **advertising substantiation** program that required advertisers to have documentation to support the claims made in their ads and to prove they are truthful.[25] This program was broadened in 1972 to include the requirement that advertisers must substantiate their claims before the ad appears. The program requires substantiation of claims made with respect to safety, performance, efficacy, quality, or comparative price of a product.

The FTC's substantiation program has had a major effect on the advertising industry, as it has shifted the burden of proof from the commission to the advertiser. Prior to the substantiation program, the FTC was required to prove that an advertiser's claims were unfair or deceptive when challenging a case. There have been a number of cases where advertisers have been ordered by the FTC to cease making inadequately substantiated claims. For example, General Motors was told to discontinue claims that its Vega automobile "handles better," whereas Firestone was ordered to stop ads claiming that its tires "stop 25 percent faster."

The goals of ad substantiation are to provide consumers with a basis for believing advertising claims such that they can make rational and informed decisions and to deter companies from making claims that they cannot adequately support. The FTC has taken the perspective that it is illegal and unfair to consumers for a firm to make a claim for a product without having a "reasonable basis" for making the claim. In their decision to require advertising substantiation the commissioners made the following statement:

> Given the imbalance of knowledge and resources between a business enterprise and each of its customers, economically it is more rational and imposes far less cost on society, to require a manufacturer to confirm his affirmative product claims rather than impose a burden on each individual consumer to test, investigate, or experiment for himself. The manufacturer has the ability, the know-how, the equipment, the time and resources to undertake such information, by testing or otherwise, . . . the consumer usually does not.[26]

Many advertisers have expressed considerable concern and responded negatively to the FTC's advertising substantiation program. They argue that it is too expensive to document all their claims and that most consumers either would not understand or would not be interested in the technical data and information used to substantiate the same. Some advertisers have argued that they might choose to avoid the substantiation issue entirely by using puffery claims, which do not require substantiation.

Generally, advertisers making claims covered by the substantiation program should have available prior substantiation of all claims. However, in 1984 the FTC issued a new policy statement that suggested that after-the-fact substantiation might be acceptable in some cases and that it would only solicit documentation of claims from advertisers that are under investigation for deceptive practices.

The FTC's Handling of Deceptive Advertising Cases

Consent and Cease and Desist Orders
Allegations that a firm is engaging in unfair or deceptive advertising come to the attention of the FTC from a variety of sources including complaints from competitors, from consumers, from other governmental agencies, or from the commission's own monitoring and investigations. Once the FTC decides that a complaint is justified and warrants further action, it notifies the offender, who then has 30 days to respond to the complaint. The advertiser can agree to negotiate a settlement with the FTC by signing a **consent order,** which is an agreement to stop the practice or advertising in question. This agreement is for settlement purposes only and does not constitute an admission of guilt by the advertiser. Most FTC inquiries are settled by consent orders, as this saves the advertiser the cost and possible adverse publicity that might result if the case were to go further.

If the advertiser chooses not to sign the consent decree and contests the complaint, a hearing can be requested before an administrative law judge employed by the FTC but not under its influence. The judge's decision may be appealed to the full five-member commission by either side. The commission will either affirm or modify the order or may choose to dismiss the case. If the complaint has been upheld by the administrative law judge and the commission, the advertiser can appeal the case to the federal courts.

The appeal process described above may take some time, and the FTC may want to stop the advertiser from engaging in the deceptive practice. One instrument the FTC has at its disposal as a result of the Wheeler-Lea Amendment is the power to issue **cease and desist orders.** The cease and desist order requires that the advertiser stop the specified advertising claim within 30 days and prohibits the advertiser from engaging in the objectionable practice until after the hearing is held. Violation of a cease and desist order is punishable by a fine of up to $10,000 a day. A number of firms have violated the terms of a cease and desist order and have had to pay substantial fines, although most firms usually comply. The FTC complaint procedure is summarized in Figure 21–5.

Corrective Advertising
By using consent and cease and desist orders the FTC is usually able to put a stop to a particular advertising practice it feels is unfair or deceptive. However, a problem may still exist even if an advertiser ceases using a deceptive ad, since consumers can still retain some or all of the deceptive claim in memory. To address this problem of residual effects of prior deceptive advertising, in the 1970s the FTC developed a program known as **corrective advertising.** Under this program, an advertiser found guilty of deceptive advertising can be required to run additional advertising designed to remedy the deception or misinformation contained in previous ads.

The impetus for corrective advertising was a case involving the Campbell Soup Company in which marbles were placed in the bottom of a bowl of vegetable soup to force the solid ingredients to the surface. This created a false impression that the soup contained more vegetables than it really did (although Campbell Soup argued that if the marbles were not used, all the ingredients would settle to the bottom, leaving an impression of fewer ingredients than actually existed!). While Campbell Soup agreed to stop the practice, a group of law students calling themselves SOUP (Students Opposed to Unfair Practices) argued to the FTC that this would not remedy false impressions created by prior advertising and contended that Campbell Soup should be required to run advertising to rectify the problem.

Although the FTC did not order corrective advertising in the Campbell case, it has been required in a number of subsequent cases. For example, Profile Bread ran

Figure 21–5 **FTC Complaint Procedure**

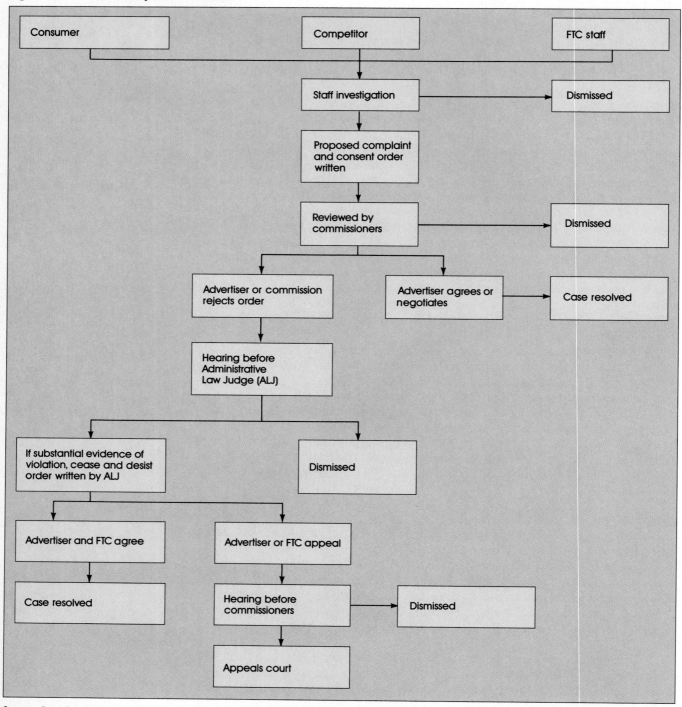

Source: Gary Armstrong and Julie Ozanne, "An Evaluation of NAD/NARB Purpose and Performance," *Journal of Advertising* 12, no. 3 (1983), p. 24. Reprinted with permission.

ads stating that each slice contained fewer calories than other brands. However, the ad did not mention that this was because slices of Profile Bread were thinner than those of other brands. Ocean Spray Cranberry Juice was found guilty of deceptive advertising because it claimed to have more "food energy" than orange or tomato juice but failed to note that it was referring to the technical definition of food energy, which is calories. The texts of the corrective messages required in each of these cases are shown

Table 21—3   Examples of Corrective Advertising Messages

Profile Bread	Ocean Spray	STP
"Hi, (celebrity's name) for Profile Bread. Like all mothers, I'm concerned about nutrition and balanced meals. So, I'd like to clear up any misunderstanding you may have about Profile Bread from its advertising or even its name. "Does Profile have fewer calories than any other breads? No. Profile has about the same per ounce as other breads. To be exact, Profile has seven fewer calories per slice. That's because Profile is sliced thinner. But eating Profile will not cause you to lose weight. A reduction of seven calories is insignificant. It's total calories and balanced nutrition that count. And Profile can help you achieve a balanced meal because it provides protein and B vitamins as well as other nutrients. "How does my family feel about Profile? Well, my husband likes Profile toast, the children love Profile sandwiches, and I prefer Profile to any other bread. So you see, at our house, delicious taste makes Profile a family affair." (To be run in 25 percent of brand's advertising, for one year.)	"If you've wondered what some of our earlier advertising meant when we said Ocean Spray Cranberry Juice Cocktail has more food energy than orange juice or tomato juice, let us make it clear: we didn't mean vitamins and minerals. Food energy means calories. Nothing more. "Food energy is important at breakfast since many of us may not get enough calories, or food energy, to get off to a good start. Ocean Spray Cranberry Juice Cocktail helps because it contains more food energy than most other breakfast drinks. "And Ocean Spray Cranberry Juice Cocktail gives you and your family Vitamin C plus a great wake-up taste. It's . . . the other breakfast drink." (To be run in one of every four ads for one year.)	As a result of an investigation by the Federal Trade Commission into certain allegedly inaccurate past advertisements for STP's oil additive, STP Corporation has agreed to a $700,000 settlement. With regard to that settlement, STP is making the following statement: "It is the policy of STP to support its advertising with objective information and test data. In 1974 and 1975 an independent laboratory ran tests of the company's oil additive which led to claims of reduced oil consumption. However, these tests cannot be relied on to support the oil consumption reduction claim made by STP. "The FTC has taken the position that, in making the claim, the company violated the terms of a consent order. When STP learned that the test did not support the claim, it stopped advertising containing that claim. New tests have been undertaken to determine the extent to which the oil additive affects oil consumption. Agreement to this settlement does not constitute an admission by STP that the law has been violated. Rather, STP has agreed to resolve the dispute with the FTC to avoid protracted and prohibitively expensive litigation."

Source: William W. Wilkie, Dennis L. McNeill, and Michael B. Mazis, "Marketing's 'Scarlet Letter': The Theory and Practice of Corrective Advertising," *Journal of Marketing* 48 (Spring 1984), pp. 13, 25.

in Table 21—3. In each case the advertisers were ordered to spend 25 percent of their annual media budget to run corrective ads.

Another case where corrective advertising was required involved the STP Corporation for claims regarding the ability of its oil additive to reduce oil consumption. STP was required to run corrective ads stating that independent laboratory tests it had made could not be relied upon to support its oil consumption reduction claims. The text of this corrective ad is also shown in Table 21—3. Many of the corrective ads run in the STP case appeared in business publications to serve as a notice to other advertisers that the FTC was enforcing the corrective advertising program.

One of the most publicized corrective advertising cases involved Listerine mouthwash. In 1975 the FTC charged that since 1921 the Warner-Lambert Company had run ads promoting Listerine as being effective in the prevention of colds and sore throats. However, the FTC ruled that the company had no valid support for this claim. In addition to ordering the company to stop using it, Warner-Lambert was required to run $10 million worth of corrective ads over a 16-month period stating that "Listerine will not help prevent colds or sore throats or lessen their severity." Listerine appealed the FTC decision all the way to the Supreme Court, which rejected the argument that corrective advertising violates advertisers' First Amendment rights; thus the order was upheld; forcing Warner-Lambert to run corrective messages.

Corrective advertising is probably the most controversial of all the FTC programs. Advertisers have argued that corrective advertising infringes on First Amendment rights of freedom of speech. The effectiveness of corrective advertising campaigns has also been questioned, as has the FTC's involvement in the business of creating advertisements through the requirement of particular content in corrective messages.[27] Propo-

Table 21–4   **Summary Conclusions on Corrective Advertising**

1. The FTC is empowered to order corrective advertising as a remedy against deceptive advertising campaigns.
2. There are important legal constraints as to when and in what manner the FTC can employ this remedy form.
3. Corrective advertising holds the potential to yield beneficial effects for consumers.
4. Corrective advertising appears to hold the potential to affect the sales and/or image of the advertised brand.
5. There is little evidence of a systematic FTC program for corrective advertising:

   - Bursts of case activity have been followed by long periods of inactivity.
   - Philosophical and personnel changes occurred throughout the 1970s and early 1980s at both the staff and commissioner levels.
   - Past orders have used a wide range of requirements for corrective advertising.

6. Consent negotiations between FTC staff members and company representatives have played a key role in the exact requirements in almost every case to date.
7. Consumer effectiveness of corrective advertising has not been the primary concern of the orders issued to date.
8. In communication terms, past corrective advertising orders against major advertisers appear to have been weak.
9. In terms of consumer impacts, the major corrective advertising orders appear *not* to have been successful in remedying consumer misimpressions across the marketplace.
10. If corrective advertising is to continue as an FTC remedy, some changes in the form of the orders will be required.

Source: William L. Wilkie, Dennis L. McNeill, and Michael B. Mazis, "Marketing's 'Scarlet Letter': The Theory and Practice of Corrective Advertising," *Journal of Marketing* 48 (Spring 1984), p. 26.

nents and opponents of corrective advertising continue to argue the benefits and pitfalls of this program. Table 21–4 presents 10 summary conclusions on corrective advertising made by William Wilkie, Dennis McNeill, and Michael Mazis after studying over a decade of corrective advertising cases and research.

Current Status of Federal Regulation by the FTC

During the decade of the 1970s the FTC became a very powerful and active regulator of advertising in the United States. However, by 1980 Congress had become very concerned over the FTC's broad interpretation of unfairness, which led to the restrictive legislation of the 1980 FTC Improvements Act. Concern over the meaning of "unfair" advertising remains on the grounds that it is vague and subject to whatever meaning an individual wants to assign to it.[28]

During the 1980s the FTC became less active and cut back its regulatory efforts. This change was in large part due to the laissez-faire attitude of the Reagan administration toward the regulation of business in general. The FTC's focus changed to handling only the most blatant cases of deception and to pursuing cases involving true eccentrics and charlatans, such as a company that sold "muscle building" pills and frauds involving diamond investment scams and oil-land lotteries.[29] Some concern has been expressed that the FTC has become too narrow in its regulation of national advertising, forcing companies and consumer groups to seek relief from other sources such as state and federal courts or through self-regulatory groups such as the NAD/NARB.[30]

In 1988/89 an 18–member panel chosen by the American Bar Association undertook a study of the FTC as a 20-year follow-up to the 1969 report used by President Richard Nixon to overhaul the commission. The report filed by the commission expressed strong concern over the FTC's lack of sufficient resources and staff to regulate national advertising effectively and called for more funding to be provided to the commission. The committee suggested that the FTC should retain its authority to use "unfairness" as the basis for issuing industrywide rules as well as complaints against individual advertisers.[31] The report called on the Bush administration to become more involved in the enforcement of advertising regulations. It is generally expected that the FTC will take more of an activist role under the Bush administration than during the Reagan years.[32]

An indication that the FTC may resume more of an activist role occurred in early 1989 when the commission charged Campbell Soup Company with making deceptive claims in its soup advertising. The ads in question claimed that the company's soups are low in fat and cholesterol and thus helpful in fighting heart disease. However, the FTC argued that the ads failed to disclose that Campbell's soups are high in sodium, which may increase the risk of heart disease. The director of the FTC's Bureau of Consumer Protection noted that this case would serve as a warning to the food industry that the commission takes deceptive health claims seriously and will police the advertising of such claims.[33]

While most advertisers have relied on self-regulatory mechanisms and the FTC to deal with the problem of deceptive or misleading advertising by their competitors, many companies are becoming more active by filing lawsuits against competitors who they feel are making false claims. One piece of legislation that has become increasingly important in this regard is the Lanham Act, which warrants further discussion.

The Lanham Act

This act was originally written in 1947 as the Lanham Trade-Mark Act to protect words, names, symbols, or other devices adopted to identify and distinguish a manufacturer's products. The **Lanham Act** was amended to encompass false advertising by prohibiting "any false description or representation including words or other symbols tending falsely to describe or represent the same." While the FTC Act did not provide individual advertisers with the opportunity to sue a competitor for deceptive advertising, civil suits are permitted under the Lanham Act.

More and more companies are using the Lanham Act to sue competitors for their advertising claims, particularly since comparative advertising has become so common. For example, the act was used against Bristol-Myers's Body on Tap Shampoo to stop the company from using TV ads showing tests indicating the product's superiority. It was argued that the tests were not valid and that the use of a slinky model in the ad distracted from the presentation of the results in the message.[34]

American Home Products (AHP) sued Johnson & Johnson for claims in Tylenol ads that ibuprofen-based analgesics, including AHP's Advil brand, cause stomach irritation. A U.S. district court fined Jartran Inc. a record $20 million in punitive damages on top of the $20 million awarded to U-Haul International to compensate for losses resulting from ads comparing the companies' prices and equipment that were ruled deceptive.

One legal expert has noted that "the ability of one business to challenge another's advertising under section 43(a) of the Lanham Act is the most significant development in advertising regulation in the past ten years."[35] The ease of suing competitors for making false claims was facilitated even more with the passage of the Trademark Law Revision Act of 1988. According to this law, anyone is vulnerable to civil action who "misrepresents the nature, characteristics, qualities or geographical origin of his or her or another person's goods, services or commercial activities." This wording closed a loophole in the Lanham Act, which made no mention of another person's goods, as it had prohibited only false claims about one's own goods or services. While many disputes over comparative claims are never contested or are resolved through the NAD, it is likely that more companies will take rivals to court under the Lanham Act for several reasons, including the broad information discovery powers available under federal civil procedure rule, the speed with which a competitor can stop the offending ad through a preliminary injunction, and the possibility of collecting damages.[36]

Even though the Federal Trade Commission has become less active and aggressive in its regulation and control of unfair and deceptive advertising practices, advertisers are unlikely to find it any easier to make false or misleading claims. Private sector regulators, the courts, and competitors will continue to police advertising claims and practices.

Additional Federal Regulatory Agencies

The Federal Communications Commission
The FCC was founded in 1934 to regulate broadcast communication and has jurisdiction over the radio, television, telephone, and telegraph industries. The FCC has the authority to license broadcast stations as well as to remove a license or deny renewal to stations not operating in the public's interest. The FCC's authority over the airways gives it the power to control advertising content and to restrict what products and services can be advertised on radio and television. The FCC controls the airways of obscene and profane programs and/or messages and can eliminate those that it finds in poor taste. While the FCC can eliminate ads that are deceptive or misleading, it generally works closely with the FTC in the regulation of advertising.

Many of the FCC's rules and regulations for television and radio stations have been eliminated or modified. As noted in Chapter 11, the FCC no longer limits the amount of television time that can be devoted to commercials. Under the Reagan administration, the controversial **Fairness Doctrine,** which required broadcasters to provide time for opposing viewpoints on important issues, was also repealed on the grounds that it was counterproductive. It was argued that the Fairness Doctrine resulted in a reduction in the amount of discussion of important issues because a broadcaster might be afraid to take on a paid controversial message on the grounds that it might subsequently be required to provide equal free exposure for opposing viewpoints.

It was under this doctrine that the FCC required stations to run commercials about the harmful effects of smoking prior to the passage of the Public Health Cigarette Smoking Act of 1970 (which banned broadcast advertising of cigarettes). Many stations still do provide time for opposing viewpoints on controversial issues on the basis that this is consistent with the station's public service requirement and not necessarily directly related to fairness.

The Food and Drug Administration
Now under the jurisdiction of the Department of Health and Human Services, the FDA has authority over the labeling, packaging, branding, ingredient listing, and advertising of packaged foods and drug products. The FDA is authorized to require caution and warning labels on potentially hazardous products and also has limited authority over nutritional claims made in food advertising. This agency has the authority to set rules for promoting these products and also has the power to seize food and drugs on charges of false and misleading advertising.

The U.S. Postal Service
The U.S. mail is essentially a major advertising medium, as a large number of marketers use the mail to deliver advertising and promotional messages. The Post Office Department has control over advertising involving the use of the mail and ads involved with lotteries, fraud, and obscenity regulations. The postmaster general has the power to impose legal sanctions for violations of these statutes as well as fraudulent use of the mail. The fraud order under U.S. Postal Service regulations has been used frequently to control deceptive advertising by numerous direct-response advertisers. These firms advertise on television or radio or in magazines and newspapers and use the U.S. mail to receive orders and payment. Many have been prosecuted by the Post Office Department for use of the mail in conjunction with the sale of a fraudulent or deceptive offer.

Bureau of Alcohol, Tobacco, and Firearms
The Bureau of Alcohol, Tobacco, and Firearms (BATF) is an agency within the Treasury Department that enforces laws, develops regulations, and is responsible for tax collection for the liquor industry. The BATF is the governmental agency that regulates and controls the advertising of alco-

Promotional Perspective 21-3

Sears and New York City Battle Over Ads

Sears, Roebuck and Company and the New York City Department of Consumer Affairs are currently waging a battle over what the agency called advertising that attempts to deceive the consumer. According to the Consumer Affairs department, Sears ran a number of ads that it considered deceptive, including:

- Promoting a discounted price, such as 30 percent off, without explaining whether the markdown is based on the regular price of the merchandise
- Advertising clothing prices without stating where the prices started
- Promoting a tire sale without stating how much its more expensive tires sell for
- Stating that a carpet cleaning bargain was about to end when the promotion was going to continue for months

Sears, arguing that it has never been found in violation of New York consumer laws, believes that the ads are not deceptive or harmful to the general public. Thus, instead of changing its ads, the retail giant is fighting back in the courts, contending that it should be able to advertise as it sees fit. Sears has argued that if the city wins, it will have no alternative but to suspend all advertising in New York City. While no one except Sears knows what this would amount to, the company spends $1.17 billion a year to advertise its products nationally.

Should Sears lose the case, the city is asking for $500 for each violation and is also asking the courts to issue a permanent injunction against Sears to prohibit future violations of the sorts alleged. Sears is asking the federal court to declare New York City's laws regarding false advertising unconstitutional.

Source: "Sears Has Everything Including a Messy Fight over Ads in New York," *The Wall Street Journal*, June 28, 1988, p. 13.

---

holic beverages. The agency determines what information will be provided in ads as well as determines what constitutes false and misleading advertising. It is also responsible for the inclusion of warning labels on alcohol advertising and the banning of the use of active athletes in beer commercials. The BATF can impose strong sanctions for violators of its regulations.

State Regulation

In addition to the various federal rules and regulations, advertisers must also concern themselves with numerous state and local controls over advertising. An important development in state regulation of advertising was the adoption, in 44 states, of the Printers' Ink Model Statutes as a basis for advertising regulation. These statutes were drawn up in 1911 by *Printers Ink,* which for many years was the major trade publication of the advertising industry. Many states have since modified the original statutes and adopted laws similar to those of the Federal Trade Commission Act that serve as a basis for false and misleading advertising.

In addition to recognizing decisions by the federal courts regarding false or deceptive practices, many states have special controls and regulations governing the advertising of specific industries or practices. As the federal government became less involved in the regulation of national advertising during the 1980s, many state attorneys general began to enforce state laws regarding false or deceptive advertising. For example, the attorneys general in New York and Texas initiated investigations of advertising by Kraft Inc. regarding claims in ads saying that the pasteurized cheese used in Cheez Whiz was real cheese.[37] McDonald's was asked by attorneys general in three states to stop running ads claiming that its food is high in nutrition on the basis that the ads were deceptive.[38] Promotional Perspective 21-3 discusses a battle by the city of New York and Sears over deceptive advertising.

The **National Association of Attorneys General** (NAAG) has made concerted moves against a number of national advertisers as a result of inactivity by the FTC during the Reagan administration. In 1987 the NAAG developed enforcement guidelines on airfare advertising that were adopted by more than 40 states. The NAAG also has become involved in other regulatory areas including car rental price advertising, and in 1989 it began studying automobile manufacturer and dealer ads as well as advertising dealing with nutrition and health claims in food ads.[39]

The foray of the NAAG into regulation of national advertising has raised the issue of whether the states working together can create and implement uniform national advertising standards that would, in effect, supersede federal authority. However, the American Bar Association panel that examined the FTC concluded that the Federal Trade Commission is the proper regulator of national advertising and recommended that the state attorneys focus their attention on practices that harm consumers within a single state.[40] This report also called for cooperation between the FTC and the state attorneys general. It remains to be seen how the NAAG will fare in its efforts to regulate national advertising. However, it has become evident that states will become involved in the policing of national, as well as local, advertising.

Advertisers have become increasingly concerned over the trend toward increased regulation of advertising at the state and local levels, as this could have a severe impact on national advertising campaigns if they had to be modified for various states or municipalities. Thus, the advertising industry is keeping a watchful eye on changes in advertising rules, regulations, and policies at these levels.

Summary

Regulation and control of advertising stem from internal or self-regulation, as well as from external control from federal, state, and local regulatory agencies. For many years the advertising industry has promoted the use of voluntary self-regulation as a way of regulating advertising and limiting interference with, and control over, advertising by the government. Self-regulation of advertising emanates from all segments of the advertising industry, including advertisers and their agencies, business and advertising associations, and the media.

The NAD/NARB has become the primary self-regulatory mechanism for national advertising and has been very effective in achieving its goal of voluntary regulation of advertising. The various media also have their own set of advertising guidelines, with the major television networks maintaining the most stringent review process and restrictions.

Traditionally the federal government has been the most important source of external regulation, with the Federal Trade Commission serving as the major watchdog of advertising in the United States. The FTC has the responsibility of protecting both consumers and businesses from unfair and deceptive practices and anticompetitive behavior. The FTC became very active in the regulation of advertising during the 1970s when several new programs and policies were initiated, including affirmative disclosure, advertising substantiation, and corrective advertising. In 1983 the FTC developed a new working definition of deceptive advertising.

Over the past decade the commission has become less active in the area of advertising regulation, focusing its attention on the pursuit of individual violators rather than emphasizing the regulation of entire industries. However, it is likely that the FTC will become more active in the policing of false and deceptive advertising. Many companies have taken their own initiative in regard to deceptive advertising by filing lawsuits under the Lanham Act against competitors who make false claims. Many states, as well as the National Association of Attorneys General, have also become very active in exercising their jurisdiction over false and misleading advertising.

Key Terms

Self-regulation
Better Business Bureau
Council of Better Business Bureaus

National Advertising Review Board
National Advertising Review Council
Federal Trade Commission

Federal Trade Commission Act
Wheeler-Lea Amendment
Trade regulation rules
Puffery
Deception
Affirmative disclosure
Advertising substantiation

Consent order
Cease and desist orders
Corrective advertising
Lanham Act
Fairness Doctrine
National Association of Attorneys
   General

Discussion Questions

1. Evaluate the proposed restrictions on alcohol advertising that are discussed at the beginning of the chapter. Do you agree with the proposed limitations? Do you feel they will be effective in curbing alcohol consumption? Support your position.

2. Many marketing and advertising executives are opposed to any type of restrictions on the advertising of a legal product such as cigarettes or alcohol on the grounds that this is a violation of First Amendment rights to freedom of speech. Do you agree or disagree with this argument?

3. Evaluate the role of self-regulation of advertising through organizations such as the NAD/NARB. What are the incentives of advertisers to cooperate with self-regulatory bodies?

4. Discuss the role of the Federal Trade Commission in regulating advertising. Do you feel that the FTC should play a more active role in the regulation of advertising? Why or why not?

5. What is meant by deceptive advertising? Evaluate the new definition of *deception* written by former FTC Chairman Miller.

6. Campbell Soup was accused of running deceptive ads recently, not because of any claims it made for the product but rather because its advertising did not warn consumers that Campbell soups are high in sodium. Do you feel that advertisers should be found guilty of deceptive advertising for what they do not say, or should their responsibility be limited to the claims they do make?

7. What is meant by puffery? Find examples of several ads that use puffery. Do you think advertisers should be permitted to use puffery? Why or why not?

8. Do you feel that advertisers should be required to substantiate their claims before running an ad, or is it acceptable to provide documentation in response to a challenge of their advertising claims?

9. What is the purpose of corrective advertising? How should the FTC determine the extent of the corrective advertising effort required of an advertiser and the media in which it should appear? How would you determine whether corrective advertising has accomplished its purpose?

10. Discuss the importance of the Lanham Act. What types of advertising are most likely to be affected by this piece of legislation?

Notes

1. Cyndee Miller, "Proposed Alcohol Ad Restrictions Cause Big Brew-haha," *Marketing News,* February 13, 1989, p. 2.
2. Alex M. Freedman, "Koop Urges Alcoholic-Beverage Curbs, Including Ad Restrictions and Tax Rise," *The Wall Street Journal,* June 1, 1989, p. B6.
3. Priscilla A. LaBarbera, "Analyzing and Advancing the State of the Art of Advertising Self-Regulation," *Journal of Advertising* 9, no. 4 (1980), p. 30.
4. John F. Archer, "Advertising of Professional Fees: Does the Consumer Have a Right to Know?" *South Dakota Law Review* 21 (Spring 1976), p. 330.
5. *Bates* v. *State of Arizona,* 97 S.Ct. 2691. 45 *U.S. Law Week* 4895 (1977).
6. "Lawyers Learn the Hard Sell—And Companies Shudder," *Business Week,* June 10, 1985, p. 70.

7. Bruce H. Allen, Richard A. Wright, and Louis E. Raho, "Physicians and Advertising," *Journal of Health Care Marketing* 5 (Fall 1985), pp. 39–49.

8. Robert E. Hite and Cynthia Fraser, "Meta-Analyses of Attitudes toward Advertising by Professionals," *Journal of Marketing* 52, no. 3 (July 1988), pp. 95–105.

9. Gary M. Armstrong and Julie L. Ozanne, "An Evaluation of NAD/NARB Purpose and Performance," *Journal of Advertising* 12, no. 3 (1983), pp. 15–26.

10. Trade Regulation Reports, "National Advertising Review Board Congratulated by FTC Member," no. 390, June 19, 1979, p. 1.

11. Dorothy Cohen, "The FTC's Advertising Substantiation Program," *Journal of Marketing* 44, no. 1 (Winter 1980), pp. 26–35.

12. Lynda M. Maddox and Eric J. Zanot, "The Suspension of the National Association of Broadcasters' Code and Its Effects on the Regulation of Advertising," *Journalism Quarterly* 61 (Summer 1984), pp. 125–30, 156.

13. Eric Zanot, "Unseen But Effective Advertising Regulation: The Clearance Process," *Journal of Advertising* 14, no. 4 (1985), p. 48.

14. Steven W. Colford, "Speed Up the NAD, Industry Unit Told," *Advertising Age,* May 1, 1989, p. 3.

15. *FTC* v. *Raladam Co.*, 258, U.S. 643 (1931).

16. Edward Cox, R. Fellmeth, and J. Schultz, *The Consumer and the Federal Trade Commission* (Washington, D.C.: American Bar Association, 1969).

17. American Bar Association, *Report of the American Bar Association to Study the Federal Trade Commission* (Washington, D.C.: The Association, 1969).

18. Ivan L. Preston, *The Great American Blow-Up: Puffery in Advertising and Selling,* (Madison: University of Wisconsin Press, 1975), p. 3.

19. Isabella C. M. Cunningham and William H. Cunningham, "Standards for Advertising Regulation," *Journal of Marketing* 41 (October 1977), pp. 91–97.

20. Herbert J. Rotfeld and Kim B. Rotzell, "Is Advertising Puffery Believed?" *Journal of Advertising* 9, no. 3 (1980), pp. 16–20.

21. Herbert J. Rotfeld and Kim B. Rotzell, "Puffery vs. Fact Claims—Really Different?" in *Current Issues and Research in Advertising,* ed. James H. Leigh and Claude R. Martin, Jr. (Ann Arbor: University of Michigan, 1981), pp. 85–104.

22. Preston, *The Great American Blow-Up.*

23. Federal Trade Commission, "Policy Statement on Deception," 45 ATRR 689 (October 27, 1983), at 690.

24. Gary T. Ford and John E. Calfee, "Recent Developments in FTC Policy on Deception," *Journal of Marketing* 50, no. 3 (July 1986), pp. 86–87.

25. Cohen, "The FTC's Advertising Substantiation Program."

26. *Trade Regulation Reporter,* Par. 20,056 at 22,033, 1970–1973 Transfer Binder, Federal Trade Commission, July 1972.

27. William L. Wilkie, Dennis L. McNeill, and Michael B. Mazis, "Marketing's 'Scarlet Letter': The Theory and Practice of Corrective Advertising," *Journal of Marketing* 48 (Spring 1984), pp. 11–31.

28. Steven W. Colford, "ABA Panel Backs FTC Over States," *Advertising Age,* April 10, 1989, p. 1.

29. Jeanne Saddler, "FTC's New Case-by-Case Policy Irks Those Favoring Broader Tack," *The Wall Street Journal,* July 3, 1985, p. 17.

30. "Deceptive Ads: The FTC's Lassez-Faire Approach Is Backfiring," *Business Week,* December 2, 1985, p. 136.

31. Colford, "ABA Panel."

32. Steven W. Colford, "Bush FTC May Clamp Down on Ads," *Advertising Age,* April 17, 1989, p. 63.

33. Alex M. Freedman, "FTC Alleges Campbell Ad Is Deceptive," *The Wall Street Journal,* January 27, 1989, pp. B1, 7.

34. Bill Abrams, "Ad Constraints Could Persist Even If the FTC Loosens Up," *The Wall Street Journal,* December 10, 1981, p. 33.

35. Bruce P. Keller, "How Do You Spell Relief? Private Regulation of Advertising under Section 43(a) of the Lanham Act," *Trademark Reporter* 75 (1986), p. 227.

36. Bruce Buchanan and Doron Goldman, "Us vs. Them: The Minefield of Comparative Ads," *Harvard Business Review,* May/June 1989, pp. 38–50.

37. "Deceptive Ads."
38. Robert Johnson, "3 States Charge McDonald's Ads on Its Foods' Nutrition Are Deceptive," *The Wall Street Journal,* April 27, 1987, p. 14.
39. Jennifer Lawrence, "State Ad Rules Face Showdown," *Advertising Age,* November 28, 1988, p. 4.
40. Colford, "ABA Panel."

22

Evaluating the Social and Economic Aspects of Advertising

CHAPTER OBJECTIVES

1. To consider various perspectives concerning the social and economic aspects of advertising
2. To examine and evaluate the social criticisms of advertising
3. To examine the economic role of advertising and its effects on consumer choice, competition, and product costs and prices
4. To examine and evaluate perspectives regarding the economic effects of advertising

What They Are Writing About Advertising

For years the advertising industry has been a favorite topic for many writers. Authors of both novels and supposed nonfiction "exposés" of the inner workings of Madison Avenue have found success by writing about the advertising industry. In the 1946 novel *The Hucksters*, by Fredric Wakeman, who wrote the book while working as a copywriter at Foote, Cone & Belding, an account executive confesses, "We're all a bunch of hustlers and connivers in this industry." The book was a best-seller and was later made into a motion picture. In 1947 Herman Wouk wrote *Aurora Dawn*, which centered around an agency and its soup company client. A classic line from this book has an advertising executive pointing out, "Advertising blasts everything that is good and beautiful in this land with a horrid spreading mildew."

There have also been a number of nonfiction books that have made the best-seller lists by exposing the supposedly secret and manipulative techniques advertisers use on consumers. Vance Packard's 1957 book *The Hidden Persuaders* provided readers with notions about advertisers' ability to "biocontrol" the mind of consumers by using motivation research and other techniques to dig deeply into their psyches. And, of course, there is every college student's favorite, *Subliminal Seduction* by Wilson Bryan Key, which deals with advertisers' purported use of subliminal embedding that operates below the conscious level of perception and awareness. Key has written several other books including *Media Sexploitation, The Clam Plate Orgy*, and most recently, *The Age of Manipulation*. He is a favorite on the lecture circuit with his uncanny ability to analyze ads and find subliminal messages embedded in them such as sexual and phallic symbols, death warning ghosts, and other anxiety-inducing elements.

Not everyone who writes about advertising bashes or criticizes it. There are a number of "like-it-is books" written by successful real-world advertising executives such as Rosser Reeves (*The Reality of Advertising*), David Ogilvy (*Confessions of An Advertising Man* and *Ogilvy on Advertising*), John O'Toole (*The Trouble with Advertising*), and Jerry Della Femina (*From Those Wonderful Folks Who Gave You Pearl Harbor: Front-Line Dispatches from the Advertising War*). There is also the book written by Martin Mayer, *Madison Avenue*, which was first published in 1957 but is still regarded as a classic "basics" book about the industry and is recommended by many agencies for their new employees.

While these books are well known and respected by most people with knowledge and insight into the industry, it is unfortunately the more sensational, and what Fred Danzig calls the "steamy-cum-sleazy," writings that get most of the attention and shape the public's perceptions and image of the advertising industry and profession.[1]

Introduction

> If I were to name the deadliest subversive force within capitalism, the single greatest source of its waning morality—I would without hesitation name advertising. How else should one identify a force that debases language, drains thought, and undoes dignity?[2]

The primary focus of this text has been on the role of advertising and other promotional variables as marketing activities used to convey information to, and influence the behavior of, consumers. We have been concerned with examining the advertising and promotion function in the context of a business and marketing environment and from a perspective that basically assumes that these activities are appropriate. However, as can be seen in the quote shown above from noted economist Robert Heilbroner, not everyone shares this viewpoint. Advertising is the most visible of all business activities and is prone to close scrutiny by those who are concerned over the methods and approaches used by advertisers to sell their products and services.

Because of its high visibility and pervasiveness, along with its persuasive character, advertising has been the subject of a great deal of controversy and criticism. As noted in the opening vignette, numerous books have been written that are critical of advertising, including not only its methods and techniques but also the social consequences that result from it. Various parties and scholars including economists, politicians, sociologists, government agencies, social critics, special-interest groups, and consumers themselves have attacked advertising for a variety of reasons including its excessiveness, the way it influences society, the methods used by advertisers, its supposed exploitation of consumers, and its effect on our economic system.

The role of advertising in society is a controversial one and at various times has

Figure 22–1   Ads by Calvin Klein Have Been the Target of Criticism by Women's Groups and Others

led to actions to attempt to control or limit advertisers' ability to influence consumers. For example, in the late 1970s the Federal Trade Commission held hearings to consider a proposal to restrict severely—and in some cases, ban—all advertising to children. Recently there has been a movement started by special-interest groups such as MADD (Mothers against Drunk Driving) and SMART (Stop Marketing Alcohol on Radio and TV) to ban all alcoholic beverage advertising from television and radio. As noted in the previous chapter, the surgeon general endorsed recommendations by these groups to impose severe restrictions on alcohol advertising and promotions.

The actions of specific advertisers have been criticized as well. Groups such as NOW (National Organization for Women) and Women against Pornography have been critical of advertisers such as Guess? for depicting women as sex objects in their advertisements and of Calvin Klein for promoting sexual permissiveness and using erotic ads (Figure 22–1). However, Klein, who creates his own advertising, argues that the ads are not meant to offend anyone but rather to gain attention and interest in a very cluttered media environment.

Advertising is a very powerful force in our society, and our discussion would not be complete without considering the various criticisms regarding its social and economic effects as well as some of the defenses against these charges. We will first consider the various criticisms of advertising from a societal perspective and then turn our attention to appraising its effect on the economy. It should be noted that the primary focus in this chapter will be on social and economic aspects of advertising, as this is the promotional mix variable that is the subject of the most concern, controversy, and regulation.

Social Criticisms of Advertising

Much of the controversy over advertising stems from the ways it is used by many companies as a selling tool and because of the impact advertising has on society's tastes, values, and lifestyles. Criticism of the specific techniques used by advertisers include arguments that it is deceptive or untruthful, that it is offensive or in bad taste, and that it exploits certain groups such as children. Each of these criticisms will be discussed along with responses of advertisers to these attacks. We will then turn our attention to criticisms concerning the influence of advertising on values and lifestyles, as well as charges that it perpetuates stereotyping and that advertisers can exert influence and control over the media.

Advertising as Untruthful or Deceptive

One of the major attacks against advertising is that many ads are misleading or untruthful and end up deceiving the consumer. The issue of deceptive advertising and attempts by industry and government to regulate and control it were discussed in the previous chapter. As was noted in that discussion, advertisers should have a reasonable basis for making a claim about product performance and, in many instances, may be required to provide substantiating evidence to support their claims. There is still the problem, however, that deception can occur in a more subtle way as a result of how the consumer perceives the ad and the resulting impact on beliefs.[3] The difficulty of determining just what constitutes deception, along with the fact that advertisers have the right to use puffery and thus make subjective claims about their products, tends to complicate the issue of whether an ad is untruthful or misleading. However, a concern of many critics is the extent to which advertisers are deliberately untruthful or misleading in their advertising.

While there are occasionally situations where advertisers have made overtly false or misleading claims, these cases usually have involved smaller companies and represent an extremely small portion of the $110 billion spent on advertising each year. Most advertisers do not design their messages with the intention of misleading or deceiving consumers. Not only would such practices be considered unethical by most firms, but they would also be risking their reputation and subjecting themselves to prosecution by various regulatory groups or government agencies. National advertisers in particular invest large sums of money to develop loyalty to, and enhance the image of, their brands. Thus, these companies are not likely to risk the consumer trust and confidence they enjoy by intentionally deceiving consumers.

The problem of untruthful or fraudulent advertising may exist more at the local level and in specific areas such as direct mail and other forms of direct-response advertising. However, there have been a number of deceptive and misleading advertising cases involving large national advertisers as well. National advertisers will often test the limits of various industry and governmental rules and regulations to make claims that will give their brands an advantage in highly competitive markets.

While many critics of advertising would probably accept the argument that most advertisers are not out to deceive or mislead consumers deliberately, they are still concerned over whether consumers are receiving proper information to make an informed choice. They argue that advertisers usually present only information that is favorable to their position and thus do not always tell consumers the "whole truth" about a product or service. An example of this is the Federal Trade Commission's charge of deceptive advertising against Campbell Soup for failure to disclose that its soups are high in sodium and may increase the risk of heart disease. The director of the FTC's Bureau of Consumer Protection has noted that

> this case stands for the proposition that when you advertise a particular quality or characteristic of your product, you should disclose facts that tend to undermine or refute the specific claims you have made.[4]

Table 22–1 "Advertising Principles of American Business" of the American Advertising Federation (AAF)

1. *Truth* Advertising shall reveal the truth, and shall reveal significant facts, the omission of which would mislead the public.
2. *Substantiation* Advertising claims shall be substantiated by evidence in possession of the advertiser and the advertising agency prior to making such claims.
3. *Comparisons* Advertising shall refrain from making false, misleading, or unsubstantiated statements or claims about a competitor or his products or service.
4. *Bait advertising* Advertising shall not offer products or services for sale unless such offer constitutes a bona fide effort to sell the advertised products or services and is not a device to switch consumers to other goods or services, usually higher priced.
5. *Guarantees and warranties* Advertising of guarantees and warranties shall be explicit, with sufficient information to apprise consumers of their principal terms and limitations or, when space or time restrictions preclude such disclosures, the advertisement shall clearly reveal where the full text of the guarantee or warranty can be examined before purchase.
6. *Price claims* Advertising shall avoid price claims that are false or misleading, or savings claims that do not offer provable savings.
7. *Testimonials* Advertising containing testimonials shall be limited to those of competent witnesses who are reflecting a real and honest opinion or experience.
8. *Taste and decency* Advertising shall be free of statements, illustrations, or implications that are offensive to good taste or public decency.

Source: Courtesy of the *American Advertising Federation.*

Many feel that advertising should be primarily informative in nature and should not be permitted to use puffery or embellished messages. Others argue that advertisers have the right to present the most favorable case for their products and services and should not be restricted to just the provision of objective, verifiable information.[5] They note that consumers can protect themselves from being persuaded against their will and that the various industry and governmental regulatory bodies and mechanisms are sufficient to keep advertisers from deceiving or misleading consumers. Table 22–1 shows the Advertising Principles of the American Advertising Federation which many advertisers use as a guideline in preparing and evaluating their ads.

Advertising as Offensive or in Bad Taste

Another common criticism of advertising, particularly by consumers, is that ads are offensive, tasteless, irritating, boring, obnoxious, and so on. In a 1987 survey, the Ogilvy & Mather advertising agency found that only 59 percent of people like advertising, compared to 68 percent in a 1985 study. Half of the consumers surveyed considered most ads as being in poor taste versus 43 percent two years prior, and the percentage who believe advertising provides useful information slipped from 76 percent to 71 percent.[6]

Sources of Distaste Consumers can be offended or irritated by advertising in a number of ways. Some are offended by the fact that a product or service, such as contraceptives or personal hygiene products, is advertised at all. It is only in the last few years that publications began accepting ads for condoms, as the AIDS crisis forced them to reconsider their restrictions on advertising for the product (Figure 22–2). The major television networks gave their affiliates permission to accept condom advertising in 1987.[7]

A study of prime-time television commercials found that there is a strong product class effect with respect to the type of ads consumers perceived as distasteful or irritating. The most irritating commercials were ads for feminine hygiene products, whereas commercials for women's undergarments and hemorrhoid products were close behind.[8] Another study found that consumers are more likely to dislike advertisements for products they do not use and for brands they would not buy.[9] Despite the fact that people may find them offensive, ads for personal products such as herpes medication,

douches, home pregnancy tests, and colon cancer detection kits have become more commonplace on television and in print and the public more accepting of them.[10] However, advertisers still must be careful as to how these products are presented and the language and terminology used in the ads. Promotional Perspective 22–1 discusses some of the rules, regulations, and taboos advertisers must deal with to have their TV commercials approved by the networks.

Another way advertising can offend consumers is by the type of appeal or the manner of presentation. For example, many people take offense to the use of appeals that exploit consumer anxieties. Fear appeal ads, particularly for products such as deodorants, mouthwash, and dandruff shampoos, have often been criticized for attempting to create anxiety and using a fear of social rejection as a way of selling these products. Some ads for home computers were also criticized for attempting to create anxiety in parents over the need for their young children to be able to use a computer or fail in school.

Sexual Appeals The type of advertising appeals that have received the most criticism for being offensive or in poor taste are those using sexual appeals and/or nudity. These techniques are often used as ways of gaining consumers' attention and in some cases may not even be appropriate to the product being advertised. Even if the sexual appeal is appropriate for the product, many people may be offended by it. Concern has been expressed over both the use of nudity in advertising and also by sexually provocative and suggestive ads. For example, in 1987, Playtex broke new ground in advertising when its television commercials for bras began using models instead of mannequins. Playtex's major competitor, Maidenform, did not take long to react and made the first commercial showing a woman removing her bra—albeit while remaining fully attired in a sweater.[11] Maidenform also developed what some felt was a rather risqué

Promotional Perspective 22–1

Things You Do Not See in Television Ads

In recent years the major networks have loosened their standards regarding the advertising of certain products on television. They now allow their stations to show ads for feminine hygiene products and condoms and recently began allowing actresses to model bras in commercials. However, the networks still have detailed regulations concerning what is and is not allowed in the commercials they will air. Advertisers must submit storyboards of planned commercials to the networks, which are examined very carefully and often sent back for changes or rejected all together. The various rules, regulations, and standards that the networks have for commercials affect the way many products can be advertised. Some of these include:

- *Pills* The networks refuse to show people putting aspirin, cold tablets, or even antacids into their mouths. Network censors argue that the cumulative effects of seeing people popping pills in all those commercials for over-the-counter drug products is potentially harmful to consumers.
- *Passionate kissing* Even though very commonplace on television programs, the networks either do not allow open mouth or lingering kissing in commercials or put the ads on a restricted schedule, allowing them to air only after 10 P.M. or during daytime programs. Even though the networks do not demand it, most couples shown in commercials wear wedding rings, even if they are not kissing.
- *Toilet paper* Ads show it rolling down the stairs or being squeezed by Mr. Whipple but never hanging in a bathroom, as toilet paper cannot be shown next to a

toilet. Direct or indirect references to the product's function are also not acceptable. Toilet bowls, banned for many years, can now be shown, although the word *toilet* can only be used once and the bowl cannot be shown being flushed.
- *Liquor* Not only is hard-liquor advertising forbidden but so too is the use of any props that look like mixed drinks in commercials for other products. While beer ads are permitted, only CBS allows them to show people actually drinking it.
- *Feminine hygiene* Advertising for products such as douches is acceptable as long as no mention is made of what they are used for. Tampons and feminine napkin ads cannot show the actual product. The networks do now allow the word *period* but usually only once in 30 seconds.
- *Deodorants* While deodorant ads are commonplace, advertisers cannot depict wetness, odor, or where or how you use the product.

The networks are also sensitive to commercials that show consumers eating to excess or depict gastrointestinal matters such as burping. Humorous appeals are also scrutinized very carefully. For example, a humorous frozen pizza ad in which a woman opens a freezer and a chef hands her a pizza pie was rejected because censors were afraid a child would see it and lock himself or herself into a refrigerator.

Source: Joanne Lipman, "Censored Scenes: Why You Rarely See Some Things in Television Ads," *The Wall Street Journal*, August 17, 1987, p. 17.

campaign featuring famous celebrities such as actors Michael York, Omar Sharif, Christopher Reeves, and Corbin Bernsen discussing their feelings about women and lingerie (Figure 22–3).

Many critics of advertising are concerned that sexually suggestive ads are being used not only by those advertisers who use them as a product-relevant selling tool but also increasingly by companies with nonsexual products such as laundry detergents and athletic shoes. For example, an ad for Fab laundry detergent that the agency titled "reverse strip" shows an attractive man suggestively jumping out of bed and hopping into his "sinfully soft" clothes (Figure 22–4). Borateem Bleach ran a print ad showing the arms of six men reaching out to grab a woman dressed in skin-tight, zebra-striped shorts and wearing a bracelet that looked like handcuffs. The president of the agency that created the ad noted that "the company had to find a way to grab attention for a product in a pretty dull category."[12] Promotional Perspective 22–2 discusses how a small shoe company used sexual imagery in its advertising to increase sales.

Advertisers who use nudity and sexual suggestiveness argue that their ads are not offensive and are consistent with contemporary values and lifestyles that are more tolerant and accepting of this type of advertising. Some argue that their ads are appropriate for the target audiences they are trying to reach, as they are generally younger and less likely to be offended.

Figure 22–3   Maidenform Uses Celebrities to Discuss Women's Lingerie

"Lingerie does a lot for a woman. Not to mention what it does for a man. I love a woman who says how she feels. But I also love a woman who has secrets. In fact, it's what she keeps to herself that says the most about her. Lingerie. That's a secret she doesn't share with the world. So sometimes you don't find out. But, then again, sometimes you do."
Maidenform offers women over 150 ways to express themselves. Obviously, people are listening.

MAIDENFORM

Advertisers also complain about the double standard that exists for TV programs and commercials, noting that even the most suggestive commercials are bland compared with what is shown in many television programs. The networks argue, however, that they have to scrutinize commercials more carefully because ads encourage people to imitate behaviors, whereas programs are merely meant to entertain. Network executives also note the complaints of parents who are concerned about their children see-

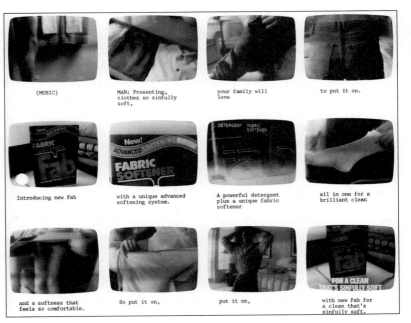

Figure 22–4   A Sexy Ad Is Used to Sell a Laundry Detergent

(MUSIC)

MAN: Presenting, clothes so sinfully soft,

your family will love

to put it on.

Introducing new Fab

with a unique advanced softening system.

A powerful detergent plus a unique fabric softener

all in one for a brilliant clean

and a softness that feels so comfortable.

So put it on,

put it on,

with new Fab for a clean that's sinfully soft.

Promotional Perspective **22–2**

Using Sex to Sell Sneakers

How does a small sports shoe company compete against larger firms that have marketing and advertising budgets 20 to 30 times larger than theirs? This was the problem facing the Swedish advertising agency of Hall and Cederquist when they were hired to design an ad campaign for Travel Fox, a small footwear company trying to compete against industry giants Reebok and Nike in the casual footwear market. To make an impact and gain consumers' attention, the agency decided to use sexual imagery and developed an ad campaign that sent the industry abuzz. The print ads, whose only product information was that the shoes were made of leather, featured various permutations of two intertwined nude bodies, just sexually distinguishable, each sporting a pair of Travel Fox sneakers (Exhibit 22–2). The company spent 20 percent of their $5 million in total sales in 1986 on the campaign, and sales in the New York area, where the advertising was concentrated, tripled in one year.

Although successful, the ad created some very negative reactions among many people, and many magazines refused to run it. While Travel Fox did modify the ad, the company's marketing director stated, "We had no idea the ad would create this controversy. . . . If we've offended anyone we apologize, but as far as our company is concerned, there is nothing distasteful about the ad." However, a few months later the company fired its agency and decided to alter its advertising approach. While the company president noted that "the shock appeal absolutely worked," he indicated that the company would no longer use sex to advertise its shoes.

Exhibit 22–2   **Travel Fox Used a Sexual Appeal to Sell Shoes**

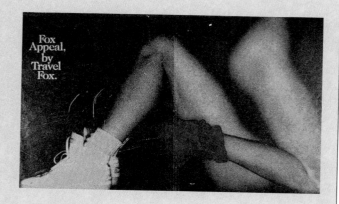

The use of a sexual advertising appeal such as this reflects how far advertisers feel they must sometimes go to break through all of the advertising clutter and gain consumers' attention. For Travel Fox, sexual imagery appears to have been an effective way of not only doing this but for selling their shoes as well.

Sources: Andrew Sullivan, "Flogging Underwear: The New Raunchiness of American Advertising," *New Republic,* January 18, 1988, pp. 20–24; Laurie P. Cohen, "Sex in Ads Becomes Less Explicit as Firms Turn to Romantic Images," *The Wall Street Journal,* February 11, 1988, p. 25.

ing these ads, since they cannot always be there to change the channel or turn off the set when a suggestive or provocative ad comes on TV.

Because of the increasing clutter in the advertising environment, it is likely that advertisers will continue to use sexual appeals and other techniques that many people find offensive but catch the attention of consumers in their target audience. How far the advertisers can go with these appeals, however, will probably depend on the public's reactions to the ads. When the public feels that they have gone too far, they are likely to put pressure on the advertisers to change their ads and on the media to no longer accept ads that are too explicit or offensive. It has been suggested that a return to sexual conservatism in this country, sparked by the fear of AIDS, has led many advertisers to tone down the use of explicit sexual appeals and imagery in their ads.[13]

Advertising and Children

One of the most controversial topics advertisers must deal with is the issue of advertising to children. The advent and growth of television have provided advertisers with a vehicle through which children can be readily and easily reached. Sources have estimated that children between the ages of 2 and 11 watch an average of 26 hours of television a week and may see between 22,000 and 25,000 commercials a year.[14] Studies have also shown that television is an important source of information for children about products.[15] Concern has also been expressed over marketers' use of other promotional vehicles and techniques such as radio ads, point-of-purchase displays, premiums in packages, and the use of commercial characters such as the Smurfs as the basis for television shows.

Critics argue that children, particularly young ones, are especially vulnerable to advertising because they lack the necessary experience and knowledge to understand and evaluate critically the purpose of persuasive advertising appeals. Research has shown that preschool children cannot differentiate between commercials and television programs, do not perceive the selling intent of commercials, and cannot distinguish between reality and fantasy.[16,17] Research has also shown that children need more than a skeptical or critical attitude toward advertising, as they must understand how advertising works in order to use their cognitive defenses against it effectively.[18] Because of their limited ability to interpret the selling intent of a message or tell the difference between the program and a commercial, critics charge that advertising to children is inherently unfair and deceptive and thus should be banned or severely restricted.

At the other extreme are those who argue that advertising is a part of life and children must learn to deal with it as part of the **consumer socialization process** of acquiring the skills needed to function in the marketplace.[19] They argue that existing rules' restrictions are adequate for controlling children's advertising.

This issue received a great deal of attention in 1979 when the Federal Trade Commission held hearings to examine proposed changes in regulations regarding advertising to children. An FTC staff report recommended:

- All television advertising be banned for any product that is directed to or seen by audiences composed of a significant proportion of children who are under age 8 because they are too young to understand the selling intent of advertising
- The banning of advertising for sugary products that pose a dental health risk from TV shows seen by significant numbers of children between ages 8 and 11
- Allowing continued TV advertising of less hazardous sugared foods to the 8- to 11-year-old group but only if individual food advertisers fund "balancing" nutritional and/or health disclosures.[20]

The FTC proposal was intensely debated with the advertising industry and a number of companies arguing strongly against it. Their opposition was based on several factors including advertisers' right of free speech under the First Amendment to communicate with those consumers who make up their primary target audience.[21] They also argued that studies have shown that children are more capable of perceiving persuasive intent than was originally believed, that inability to perceive such intent does not necessarily lead to incorrect beliefs about products, and that there was no evidence of a relationship between television advertising of sugared foods and incidence of tooth decay.[22] Opponents of the ban also argued that parents should generally be involved in helping children interpret advertising and can refuse to purchase products they feel are undesirable for their children.

The FTC proposal was defeated, and changes in the political environment that resulted in less emphasis on government regulation of advertising have ended much of the debate over this issue. However, concern over advertising to children remains, and parent and consumer groups such as the Center for Science in the Public Interest and Action for Children's Television are still active in putting pressure on advertisers regarding what they feel are inappropriate or misleading ads for children. Promotional Perspective 22–3 discusses a recent effort by Congress to limit the amount of commercial time on children's programs.

Children are also protected from the potential influences of television commercials by network censors and industry self-regulatory groups such as the Council of Better Business Bureau's Children's Advertising Review Unit (CARU). The CARU has strict self-regulatory guidelines for children's advertising regarding the type of appeals, product presentation and claims, disclosures and disclaimers, the use of premiums,

Promotional Perspective 22–3

Limiting Advertising to Children

In June 1988 Congress overwhelmingly enacted a law requiring the Federal Communications Commission to enforce new commercial time limits for television programming targeted to children. The Senate likewise approved the measure by a voice vote with no objections. The measure aimed at reimposing limits dropped by the FCC in 1984 that would restrict commercials to 12 minutes per hour on weekday kids' shows and to 10½ minutes on weekends. It also required broadcasters to air educational programs for children. The measure was passed as a result of concern that too many commercials could have a negative effect on children. A cosponsor of the House bill said that 20 percent of TV stations exceed the proposed time limit for commercials.

Opponents to the bill argued that it would violate free speech guarantees and stated that sponsors had no idea how many commercials, if any, would be harmful. They also contended that if commercials are so bad, the ban should be extended to adult programming as well. FCC officials argued that the broadcast industry should police itself and that government should not intrude in the regulatory process.

All the arguments for and against the bill appeared to be for naught, however, as President Ronald Reagan refused to sign the bill when it reached his desk in November 1988. He stated that the bill "cannot be reconciled" with constitutional guarantees of freedom of speech. His pocket veto infuriated lobbyists and members of Congress. The president of Action for Children's Television, a strong supporter of the bill, termed the veto a form of "ideological child abuse." Congressmen and Senators vowed to reintroduce the measure. It is expected that the Bush administration will have a more cooperative relationship with the FCC and that the new president will sign the bill if it comes before him.

Sources: "House Votes to Limit Ads in Kids' TV," *Los Angeles Times*, June 9, 1988, p. 1; "Babes in Adland," *Time*, November 21, 1988, p. 17; "Bush May OK Bill on Kids' TV Ads," *Marketing News*, March 27, 1989, p. 7.

safety, and use of techniques such as special effects and animation. The five basic principles underlying the CARU guidelines for all advertising addressed to children under 12 years of age are presented in Table 22–2.

The major networks also have strict guidelines for ads targeted to children. For example, in network TV ads, only 10 seconds can be devoted to animation and special effects, whereas the final 5 seconds are reserved for displaying all the toys shown earlier in the ad, disclosing whether they are sold separately and whether accessories such as batteries are included. Networks also require 3 seconds of every 30-second cereal ad to portray a balanced breakfast, usually by showing a picture of toast, orange juice, and milk.[23]

Advertising to children has been, and will remain, a controversial topic. A recent study found that marketers of products targeted to children feel that advertising to them is beneficial because it provides useful information on new products and does not disrupt the parent-child relationship. However, the general public did not have such a favorable opinion, as older consumers and those from households with children had particularly negative attitudes toward children's advertising.[24]

It is important to many companies that they be able to communicate directly with children. However, only by being sensitive to the naiveté of children as consumers will they be able to do so freely and avoid potential conflict with those who feel that children should be protected from advertising.

Social and Cultural Consequences

Concern is often expressed over the impact of advertising on society, particularly with respect to its influence on values and lifestyles. While there are a number of factors that influence the cultural values, lifestyles, and behavior of a society, the overwhelming amount of advertising and its prevalence in the mass media lead many critics to argue that advertising plays a major role in influencing and transmitting social values. In his book *Advertising and Social Change*, Ronald Berman notes the major role advertising is playing relative to other institutions:

Table 22–2   Children's Advertising Review Unit Guidelines for Children's Advertising

PRINCIPLES

Five basic principles underlie these guidelines for advertising directed to children:

1. Advertisers should always take into account the level of knowledge, sophistication, and maturity of the audience to which their message is primarily directed. Younger children have a limited capability for evaluating the credibility of what they watch. Advertisers, therefore, have a special responsibility to protect children from their own susceptibilities.

2. Realizing that children are imaginative and that make-believe play constitutes an important part of the growing up process, advertisers should exercise care not to exploit that imaginative quality of children. Unreasonable expectations of product quality or performance should not be stimulated either directly or indirectly by advertising.

3. Recognizing that advertising may play an important part in educating the child, information should be communicated in a truthful and accurate manner with full recognition by the advertiser that the child may learn practices from advertising that can affect his or her health and well-being.

4. Advertisers are urged to capitalize on the potential of advertising to influence social behavior by developing advertising that, wherever possible, addresses itself to social standards generally regarded as positive and beneficial, such as friendship, kindness, honesty, justice, generosity and respect for others.

5. Although many influences affect a child's personal and social development, it remains the prime responsibility of the parents to provide guidance for children. Advertisers should contribute to this parent-child relationship in a constructive manner.

Source: Children's Advertising Review Unit, *Self-Regulatory Guidelines for Children's Advertising,* 3rd ed., 1988, National Advertising Division, Council of Better Business Bureaus, Inc., pp. 4–5.

The institutions of family, religion, and education have grown noticeably weaker over each of the past three generations. The world itself seems to have grown more complex. In the absence of traditional authority, advertising has become a kind of social guide. It depicts us in all the myriad situations possible to a life of free choice. It provides ideas about style, morality, behavior.[25]

While there is general agreement that advertising is an important social influence agent, opinions as to the value of its contribution are often quite negative. Advertising is criticized for a number of reasons including charges that it encourages materialism, that it manipulates consumers to buy things they do not really need, that it perpetuates stereotyping, and that advertisers control the media. Each of these criticisms is discussed below.

Advertising Encourages Materialism   Many critics claim that advertising has an adverse effect on consumer values by encouraging **materialism,** which is defined as a preoccupation with material things rather than intellectual or spiritual concerns. The United States is undoubtedly the most materialistic society in the world, which many critics attribute to advertising that

- Seeks to create needs rather than merely showing how a product or service fulfills them
- Surrounds consumers with images of the good life and suggests that the acquisition of material possessions leads to contentment and happiness and adds to the joy of living
- Suggests that material possessions are symbols of status, success, and accomplishment and/or will lead to greater social acceptance, popularity, sexual appeal, and so on

The ad shown in Figure 22–5 for Rolls Royce automobiles is an example of how advertising might promote materialistic values.

The criticism of advertising on the grounds that it encourages materialistic values assumes several things. First, it assumes that materialism is undesirable and is sought at the expense of nonmaterialistic goals. Many feel that materialism is an acceptable part of the **Protestant ethic,** which stresses hard work and individual effort

Figure 22–5 **Rolls Royce Appeals to Consumers' Materialism**

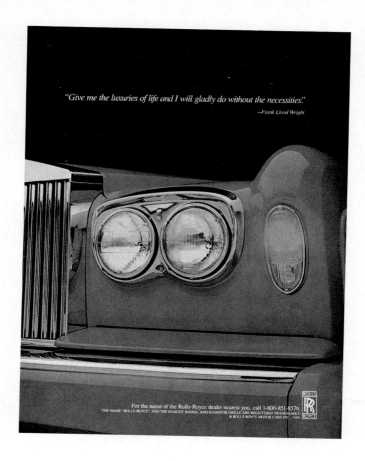

"Give me the luxuries of life and I will gladly do without the necessities."
—Frank Lloyd Wright

and initiative and views the accumulation of material possessions as evidence of success. There are also those who argue that the acquisition of material possessions is not necessarily bad and, in fact, has an important economic impact by encouraging consumers to keep consuming even though their basic needs may well be met. Most Americans believe that economic growth is essential and that materialism is both a necessity and an inevitable part of this progress.

Economist John Kenneth Galbraith, often a very vocal critic of advertising, has noted the role advertising plays in industrialized economies by encouraging consumption:

> Advertising and its related arts thus help develop the kind of man the goals of the industrial system require—one that reliably spends his income and works reliably because he is always in need of more. . . . In the absence of the massive and artful persuasion that accompanies the management of demand, increasing abundance might well have reduced the interest of people in acquiring more goods. . . . Being not pressed by the need for these things, they would have spent less reliably to get more. The consequence—a lower and less reliable propensity to consume—would have been awkward for the industrial system.[26]

It has also been argued that an emphasis on material possessions does not rule out consumers being interested in intellectual or spiritual cultural values. Defenders of advertising argue that interest in higher-order goals is more likely when basic needs have been met. Also, Raymond Bauer and Stephen Greyser have argued that consumers may purchase material things in the pursuit of nonmaterial goals.[27] For example, the purchase of an expensive stereo system may be made to enjoy music rather than simply to impress someone or acquire a material possession.

Even if one assumes that materialism is undesirable, there is still the issue of whether advertising is responsible for creating and encouraging these values. While

Figure 22–6   **The Advertising Industry Argues That Advertising Is a Reflection of Society**

many critics argue that advertising is a major contributing force to materialistic values, others argue that advertising merely reflects or mirrors the values of society rather than molding or shaping them.[28,29] They argue that consumers' values are defined by the society in which they live. Moreover, they argue that these value systems are the results of extensive long-time socialization or acculturation.

The argument that advertising is responsible for creating a materialistic and hedonistic society has also been addressed by Stephen Fox in his book *The Mirror Makers: A History of American Advertising and Its Creators*. Fox concludes that advertising has become a prime scapegoat for our times and that advertising merely reflects society on itself. In discussing the effect of advertising on cultural values, he notes:

> To blame advertising now for those most basic tendencies in American history is to miss the point. It is too obvious, too easy, a matter of killing the messenger instead of dealing with the bad news. The people who have created modern advertising are not hidden persuaders pushing our buttons in the service of some malevolent purpose. They are just producing an especially visible manifestation, good and bad, of the American way of life.[30]

Figure 22–6 shows an ad developed by the American Association of Advertising Agencies (AAAA) that suggests that advertising is a reflection of society's tastes and values and not vice versa. This ad was part of a campaign that addressed some of the common criticisms of advertising.

While it is probably unrealistic to hold advertising as solely accountable for our materialism, it should be recognized that it does play a contributing role by portraying products and services as symbols of status, success, and achievement and by encouraging consumption. As Richard Pollay has noted:

> While it may be true that advertising reflects cultural values, it does so on a very selective basis, echoing and reinforcing certain attitudes, behaviors, and values far more frequently than others.[31]

The extent to which advertising is responsible for materialism, as well as the desirability of such values, are deep philosophical issues that will continue to be part of the debate over the societal value and consequences of advertising.

Advertising Makes People Buy Things They Do Not Need A common criticism of advertising is that it has the power to manipulate consumers and make them buy things they do not need. Many critics argue that advertising should be limited to the provision of information that can be useful in making purchase decisions and not be persuasive in nature. Information advertising—which reports factual, functional information such as price, performance, and other objective criteria—is viewed as acceptable and desirable. Persuasive advertising, however, which plays on consumers' emotions, anxieties, and psychological needs and desires such as status, self-esteem, and attractiveness, is viewed as undesirable and unacceptable. Persuasive advertising is criticized for fostering dissatisfaction and/or discontent among consumers and encouraging them to purchase products and services to solve these problems. It is charged that advertising exploits consumers and persuades them to go beyond basic needs or necessities, as was noted in discussing materialism.

Defenders of advertising offer a number of rebuttals to these criticisms. First, in response to the argument that only informational advertising is acceptable, they point out that a substantial amount of advertising is essentially informational in nature.[32] Also, it is difficult to separate desirable informational advertising from undesirable persuasive advertising. For example, Shelby Hunt, in examining the *information-persuasion dichotomy*, points out that even advertising that most observers would categorize as very informative is often very persuasive.[33] He argues that the basic purpose of advertising is to persuade and that highly informative ads are often very effective in persuading consumers to purchase a product. Hunt notes that

> if advertising critics really believe that persuasive advertising should not be permitted, they are actually proposing that no advertising be allowed, since the purpose of all advertising is to persuade.[34]

Defenders of advertising also take issue with the argument that advertising should limit itself to dealing with basic functional needs. In our society most lower-level needs recognized in Maslow's hierarchy such as the need for food, clothing, and shelter are satisfied, and it is natural for people to move from basic needs to higher-order ones such as self-esteem and status or self-actualization. Consumers are free to choose the degree to which they want to attempt to satisfy their desires, and advertisers should associate their products and services with the satisfaction of higher-order needs.

There are two other important defenses proponents of advertising offer against the charge that advertising makes people buy things they do not really need. First, this criticism attributes too much power to the ability of advertising to make consumers do things against their will and assumes that consumers have no ability to defend themselves against advertising. Second, it ignores the fact that consumers have the freedom to make their own choices when confronted with persuasive advertising. While they will readily admit the persuasive intent of their business, advertisers also are quick to note that it is extremely difficult to make a consumer purchase a product he or she really does not want or need, as Coca-Cola discovered when it attempted to reformulate Coke in 1985.

If advertising were as effective and as powerful as the critics claimed, we should not see products with multimillion dollar advertising budgets failing in the marketplace. The reality of the situation is that consumers do have a choice, and they are not being forced to buy. Persuasion, it can be argued, is very much a part of our lives, and consumers have the ability to ignore ads for products and services that they do not really need or that fail to interest them. Figure 22–7 shows an ad from the campaign by the American Association of Advertising Agencies that refutes the argument that advertising makes consumers buy something they do not need.

Figure 22—7 The AAAA Responds to the Claim That Advertising Makes Consumers Buy Things They Do Not Need

Advertising and Stereotyping Advertising is often accused of creating and perpetuating stereotypes through its portrayal of certain groups including women and ethnic minorities such as blacks and Hispanics.

Women One area where advertising has received a particularly large amount of criticism is for its stereotyping of women. Critics have charged that advertising generally depicts women as housewives or mothers and has failed to acknowledge the changing role of women in our society. Concern has also been expressed over women being shown as decorative objects or sexually provocative figures. A number of studies have been conducted through the years that have examined advertising's portrayal of women and the problem of female stereotyping. A decade ago, Alice Courtney and Thomas Whipple conducted an extensive review of the findings of nearly 70 studies in this area and concluded that

> advertising portrays the typical woman in a limited and traditional role, that woman's place in advertising is seen to be in the home, and that her labor force roles are underrepresented. Women are typically portrayed as housewives and mothers, as dependent upon men, and sometimes subservient. Women are often "used" as sexual or decorative objects in advertising but are seldom shown or heard in authoritative roles, such as announcers or voice overs. On the other hand, men are depicted as the voices of authority, the older and wiser advice-givers and demonstrators. They are shown in a wider range of occupations and roles in their working and leisure lives or as beneficiaries of women's work in the home.[35]

While sexism and stereotyping of women still exist, advertising's portrayal of women is improving in many areas.[36] Many advertisers have begun to recognize the

Figure 22–8 Many Advertisers Are Changing the Way Women Are Portrayed in Their Ads

changing role of women in our society and the importance of portraying them realistically. The increase in the number of working women has resulted not only in women having more influence in the family decision-making process but also in more single-female households, which means more independent choice decisions. Thus, many advertisers are making special efforts to depict women in a favorable manner by showing them in a diversity of roles reflecting their changing place in society and avoiding stereotyping. The ad shown in Figure 22–8 is an example of how advertisers are changing their portrayals of women.

Feminist groups such as the National Organization for Women (NOW) continually attack advertising that portrays women in traditional sexist roles. NOW has also been critical of advertising for portraying women as sex objects and has argued that such advertising contributes to the problem of violence against women. NOW and other groups often protest to advertisers and their agencies against advertisements that they feel are insulting to women and have even called for boycotts against offending advertisers.

Blacks/Hispanics Blacks and Hispanics are two ethnic groups that have also been the target of stereotyping in advertising. For many years, advertisers virtually ignored blacks and Hispanics as identifiable subcultures and viable markets. Thus, advertisements were often not targeted to these ethnic groups, and the utilization of blacks and Hispanics as spokespersons, communicators, models, or actors in advertisements was very limited. For example, in a 1973 review of the role of blacks in advertising, Waltrud Kassarjian noted an increase in the sheer number of blacks appearing in print ads but not to a point proportional to their number in the general population.[37] A 1983 study examining the portrayal of Hispanics in general-interest magazines found a very

Figure 22–9   **Coors Appeals to Black Consumers in This Ad**

WE WON'T LET THE DOORS CLOSE ON CALVIN'S FUTURE.

To someone without a good education, the future can look like a door that's closed to opportunity. Saddest of all are the staggering numbers of promising minority students to whom the doors to education are closed for lack of available funds.

We at the Adolph Coors Company are getting together with minority students. Because we believe that no deserving youth should be denied an education just because there isn't enough money. So we've helped by making several desperately needed contributions—to numerous Black colleges and universities as

well as to the United Negro College Fund.

Because if we have anything to say about it, the day will come when school doors will be wide open to every student who wants an education.

Coors

We Believe Open Minds Open Doors.

low incidence of use of Hispanic models (of 206 ads containing models, only 3 were Hispanic) despite the fact that Hispanics composed nearly 10 percent of the readership of these publications.[38]

In recent years not only has the use of blacks in advertising increased, but so has the depiction of their social and role status.[39,40] The use of Hispanics in ads is also increasing, and the manner in which they are depicted is changing as marketers recognize that they represent a very viable and expanding market.[41] Not only are advertisers being careful to avoid ethnic stereotyping, but they are also striving to develop advertising that has specific appeal to various ethnic groups (Figure 22–9). However, recently some advertisers have been criticized for cutting back on marketing programs aimed at black consumers, as discussed in Promotional Perspective 22–4.

Advertisers must be sensitive to the portrayal of specific groups of people in their ads. There is little question that advertising has been guilty of stereotyping women and ethnic groups in the past and, to a certain extent, still does so today. Advertisers might argue that in some cases this has been justified. For example, some women are content as homemakers and housewives and have no problem with ads depicting them as such. However, as the role of women changes, advertisers must change their portrayal of them and avoid demeaning stereotypes. Advertising must also take into ac-

Promotional Perspective 22–4

Marketers' Interest in Blacks as Separate Market Declining

During the 1970s and early 1980s marketing and advertising programs targeted at black consumers increased sharply. However, as the decade of the 1980s came to a close, many companies were showing a declining interest in marketing to blacks as a separate market. Some advertisers cite budget cuts as one reason why they have eliminated their black marketing and advertising programs. For example, sagging sales forced Wendy's to eliminate a marketing program aimed at black consumers coupled with management feelings that the program was dispensable because black actors were used in its regular ads anyway.

Another reason for the cutbacks is that many companies feel that the $200 billion black consumer market can be reached just as easily through general marketing. They argue that specialized advertising to some subcultures such as Hispanics is necessary because of language and cultural differences. However, many marketers feel that blacks are not that different from whites so as to warrant specialized ads. They argue that black consumers have similar media habits to whites and can be reached in the same way.

Black media executives, however, maintain that blacks are sufficiently distinct and have different preferences and customs that warrant specialized advertising

programs. Some argue that many marketers neglect black advertising to avoid having their products or brands identified as black products. The declining interest in marketing to blacks has caused problems for several black-owned advertising agencies and media specializing in reaching this market. Many companies are expanding to the Hispanic market, which is growing rapidly and receiving considerable attention and ad spending from advertisers.

Some companies such as McDonald's, Anheuser-Busch, and Seven-Up still have black marketing programs, whereas others such as Kinney Shoes, Chrysler, and Sony have hired ad agencies to develop special ad campaigns for black consumers. Procter & Gamble, Toyota, and other companies have been pressured to spend more money in black-owned media. However, many advertisers note that spending money on black advertising and in black media outlets are not necessarily the same thing. They argue that many black-owned media are not necessarily the best way to reach the black consumer and prefer to use other media vehicles.

Source: Laurie P. Cohen, "Slowdown in Advertising to Blacks Strains Black Ad Firms and Media," *The Wall Street Journal*, March 3, 1988, p. 29.

count the increasing importance of minority groups in our society and not only increase the incidence of their use in ads but also avoid stereotyping or negative role portrayals.

Advertising and the Media The fact that advertising plays such an important role in financing the media has led to concern on the part of many people that advertisers can influence or even control the media. We will consider arguments on both sides of this controversial issue.

Arguments supporting advertiser control Some critics charge that the media's dependence on advertisers' support makes them susceptible to various forms of influence, including exerting control over the editorial content of magazines and newspapers; biasing editorial opinions to favor the position of an advertiser; limiting coverage of a controversial topic, issue, or story that might reflect negatively on a company; and influencing the program content of television.

Newspapers and magazines receive nearly 70 percent of their total revenue from advertising, whereas commercial television and radio derive virtually all their income from their advertisers. Small, financially insecure newspapers, magazines, or broadcast stations are the most prone to influence and pressure from advertisers, particularly companies who account for a large amount of the medium's advertising revenue. A local newspaper may be reluctant to print an unfavorable story about a local automobile dealer or grocery store chain upon whose advertising it depends heavily.

While larger, more financially stable media should be less susceptible to an advertiser's influence, they may also be reluctant to carry stories detrimental to companies who purchase large amounts of advertising time or space. For example, since cigarette commercials were taken off radio and TV in 1970, tobacco companies have allocated most of their budgets to the print media. The tobacco industry outspends all other national advertisers in newspapers, and cigarettes constitute the second largest category of magazine advertising behind transportation. This has led to charges that magazines and newspapers avoid printing articles on the hazards of smoking to protect this important source of ad revenue. Promotional Perspective 22–5 discusses the charge of selective inattention by the print media to the smoking controversy.

Individual television stations as well as the major networks also can be influenced by advertisers. Programming decisions are obviously made largely on the basis of what shows will attract the largest number of viewers and thus be most desirable to the advertiser. Critics of television argue that this often results in a reduction in the quality of television, as educational, cultural, and informative programming is usually sacrificed for shows that get high ratings and appeal to the mass markets. Advertisers have also been accused of putting pressure on the networks to change their programming. Many advertisers have begun withdrawing their commercials from programs that contain too much sex and violence, often in response to threatened boycotts of their products by consumers if they advertise on these shows.

There have been several situations where the networks have had difficulty attracting sponsors for controversial programs. In 1981 ABC had difficulty attracting sponsors for its movie *The Day After,* which depicted life in the United States following a nuclear war. Many advertisers did not want to be associated with the program because they felt that sponsorship might result in their being perceived as antinuclear. In 1989 NBC had trouble getting advertisers for the movie *Roe vs. Wade,* which was the story of the woman whose case led to the 1973 Supreme Court ruling legalizing abortion. Several companies withdrew their sponsorship as a result of threats from antiabortion groups to boycott advertisers that bought time in the movie.[42]

Arguments against advertiser control   There is little doubt that the commercial media's dependence on advertising means that advertisers can exert influence on its character, content, and coverage of certain issues. However, there are several reasons offered by media executives as to why it is incorrect to assume that advertisers control or exert undue influence over the media.

First, they point out that it is in the best self-interest of the media that they not be influenced too much by advertisers. To retain public confidence, they must report the news fairly and accurately and not be perceived as biased or attempting to avoid controversial issues. Media executives point to the vast amount of topics they cover and the investigative reporting they often do as evidence of their objectivity. It is in their best interest to build a large audience for their publications or stations so that they can make their medium more valuable to advertisers and charge more for advertising space and time.

Media executives also note the fact that an advertiser needs the media more than they need any individual advertiser, particularly when the medium has a large audience or does a good job of reaching a specific market segment. Many publications and stations have a very broad base of advertising support and can afford to lose an advertiser who might attempt to exert too much influence or control over them. This is particularly true for the larger, more established and financially secure media. For example, a consumer products company would find it difficult to reach its target audience effectively and efficiently without network television and could not afford to boycott them because of disagreement over editorial policy or program content. Likewise, even the local advertiser in a small community may be very dependent on the local media such as the newspaper, as it may be the most cost-effective media option available.

The media in the United States are basically supported by advertising, and this support means that we can enjoy them for free or for a fraction of what it would cost

Promotional Perspective 22–5

Protecting Advertising Dollars?

Ever since cigarette commercials were banned from radio and television in 1971, tobacco companies have bought a disproportionate amount of print media advertising. Tobacco firms spend nearly $2 billion a year advertising their products, with much of this money being allocated to newspapers and magazines. The vast sums of money tobacco firms spend on print advertising have led to accusations that advertising revenues inhibit some publications' coverage of the health hazards associated with cigarette smoking. Although tobacco companies are not accused of using heavy-handed, direct pressure, critics contend that some publications, particularly the smaller and weaker ones, may engage in self-censorship when covering the smoking controversy by toning down stories or avoiding the issue altogether.

Spokespersons for the Tobacco Institute, the cigarette manufacturers' lobbying group, and various cigarette companies generally deny these charges, as do most newspapers and magazine editors and publishers. Cigarette industry executives claim that they try not to get involved in the editorial content of publications in which they advertise, and many magazine editors are outraged by the allegations. However, studies that have examined magazine coverage of the smoking and health controversy suggest otherwise. In 1983 the American Council for Science and Public Health examined the content of 18 magazines published between 1965 and 1981 and found that with the exception of publications such as *Reader's Digest* and *Good Housekeeping*, which refuse to accept cigarette advertising, coverage of the health hazards of smoking was minimal or nonexistent.

In 1983 and 1984 both *Newsweek* and *Time*, the nation's leading newsweeklies, carried special advertising sections on physical fitness, nutrition, and healthier lifestyles that were intended to promote preventive medicine. However, both gave little or no attention to the potential health risks associated with smoking. Both publications were generating more than $750,000 a week from cigarette advertising at the time.

Several women's magazines such as *Cosmopolitan, Redbook, Ms.,* and *Harper's Bazaar,* which cover many issues related to women's health, have been taken to task for ignoring the health hazards of smoking in their publications. The editor and publishers of *Ms.* stated that the magazine's policy is to let its largely college-educated readers decide for themselves whether or not to smoke. Publishers of many smaller publications acknowledge their dependence on cigarette advertising revenue and their reluctance to carry editorial content that might offend cigarette makers. The editor of a weekly newspaper in Minnesota noted that the job of his paper is to cover local news and events and not to become involved in controversial social issues.

Cigarette makers, like liquor companies, are very concerned over the editorial environment in which their ads appear. Tobacco companies stipulate that their ads cannot appear near obituaries or stories antithetical to smoking or tobacco. For many years the R. J. Reynolds Tobacco Co. asked to be notified in advance if a publication planned to run a negative story on smoking so that it could avoid advertising in that issue. Although the company dropped its policy after critical scrutiny from the *Columbia Journalism Review* and *The Wall Street Journal,* publishing and advertising executives note that big advertisers are still informally alerted about stories that could be detrimental to their business.

With the growing tide of antismoking sentiment in the United States, many publications will find it difficult to ignore running stories on the smoking controversy. In April 1988, *Time* ran a cover story dealing with the battle between smokers and nonsmokers that did address health issues and contained a cigarette ad. However, the pressure from tobacco companies found a new target around the same time when RJR Nabisco Inc. fired one of its agencies, Saatchi & Saatchi DFS Inc., over an ad the agency produced for another client, Northwest Airlines, that promoted the carrier's smoking ban. The spot showed a plane full of people applauding after the voice-over announced Northwest's plans to ban smoking on all domestic flights. The agency, which had been with Nabisco for 18 years and handled $90 million worth of billings for Nabisco products, was not responsible for any cigarette advertising for RJR.

Sources: Janet Guyon, "Do Publications Avoid Anti-Cigarette Stories to Protect Ad Dollars?" *The Wall Street Journal,* November 22, 1982, pp. 1, 20; Elizabeth M. Whelan, "When *Newsweek* and *Time* Filtered Cigarette Copy," *The Wall Street Journal,* November 1, 1984, p. 3; "RJR Swears Off Saatchi and Nabisco Is in a Sweat," *Business Week,* April 18, 1988, p. 36.

without advertising. The alternative to an advertiser-supported media system is support by users through higher subscription costs for the print media and with television, a fee or some type of pay-per-view system. Another alternative is government-supported media such as that used in many other countries for television and even newspapers. However, this would raise the problem of government control and runs counter to most people's desire for freedom of the press. Although not perfect, a system of advertising-supported media provides us with the best option for receiving information and entertainment. The ad in Figure 22–10, which was part of the AAAA campaign, notes how advertising contributes to lowering the cost of magazines for consumers.

Figure 22–10 **This Ad Points Out How Advertising Lowers the Cost of Magazines for Consumers**

THIS AD HAS ALREADY SAVED YOU MONEY.

If you paid for this magazine, we have something in common.
We paid for it, too.
In fact, every advertiser you see in these pages paid handsomely for the privilege of being here.
And what we paid went toward the cost of producing the magazine. Which made it a lot cheaper for you to buy.
How much cheaper? Well, if you took all the advertising away, the average magazine would cost you about twice as much.
And offer you about half as much.
After all, advertising informs you about new products. It helps you make smarter decisions about what to buy. Often it enlightens you. Sometimes it entertains you.
And yes, occasionally it annoys you. But if it does, you can take advantage of one of advertising's nicest features.
You can simply ignore it.
It might hurt our feelings. But we'll still chip in for your magazine.

ADVERTISING.
ANOTHER WORD FOR FREEDOM OF CHOICE.
American Association of Advertising Agencies

Summarizing the Social Effects of Advertising

We have examined a number of issues and criticisms that are often made of advertising and have attempted to analyze the arguments both for and against these concerns. By now it should be obvious to you that many people do not have a high opinion of advertising and have serious concerns over its impact on society. While there are numerous rules, regulations, policies, and guidelines that advertisers are expected to comply with and follow, they do not cover every advertising situation. Moreover, what one individual views as distasteful or unethical may be quite acceptable to another.

Negative opinions regarding advertising have been around just about as long as the field itself, and it is very unlikely that they will ever disappear. However, it is important that the advertising industry remain cognizant of, and address the various issues and concerns over, the effects of advertising on society. Advertising is a very powerful institution, but it will only remain so as long as consumers have faith and trust in the ads they see and hear every day. Many of the problems and controversies discussed here can be avoided if individual decision makers are willing to make ethical considerations an important element of the advertising planning process.[43] As the famous adman David Ogilvy once noted in discussing the social responsibility of advertisers: "The consumer is not a moron; she is your wife."

Economic Effects of Advertising

In addition to being scrutinized from a social perspective, considerable attention has been given to examining the economic impact of advertising. Advertising plays an important role in a free market system such as ours by making consumers aware of products and services and providing them with information that can be used for decision making. Advertising's economic role goes beyond this basic function of information provision, however, as it is viewed as a powerful force that can affect the functioning of our entire economic system.

Advertising is viewed by many as a positive force that encourages consumption and fosters economic growth. Proponents of advertising note that it has very positive economic consequences, as it not only informs customers of available goods and services but also facilitates entry into markets for a firm or a new product or brand; leads to economies of scale in production, marketing, and distribution, which in turn leads to lower prices; and accelerates the acceptance of new products and hastens the rejection of inferior or unacceptable products.

On the other hand, critics of advertising are much less favorable in their assessment of advertising's role and effect on our economic system. They view advertising as a detrimental force that not only fails to perform its basic function of information provision adequately but also adds to the cost of products and services and discourages competition and market entry, which leads to industrial concentration and results in overall higher prices for consumers.

In their analysis of advertising, economists generally take a macroeconomic perspective whereby they consider the general economic impact of advertising on an entire industry or on the economy as a whole rather than its effect on an individual company or brand. Our examination of the economic impact of advertising will focus on these broader macrolevel issues. We will consider a number of the major issues regarding the role and impact of advertising on our economy including its effect on consumer choice, competition, and product costs and prices.

Effects on Consumer Choice

Some critics argue that advertising has a detrimental effect on consumer choice, as large advertisers use their power to limit our options to a few well-advertised brands. Economists argue that advertising is used to achieve (1) **differentiation,** whereby their products or services are perceived as unique or better than competitors', and (2) brand loyalty, which enables large national advertisers to gain control of the market, usually at the expense of smaller brands.

Larger companies often end up charging a higher price and are able to achieve a more dominant position in the market than smaller firms that either cannot or do not compete against them and their large advertising budgets. When this occurs, advertising not only restricts the choice alternatives to a few well-known and heavily advertised brands but also becomes a substitute for competition based on price or product improvements.

There are certain product categories such as soft drinks, beer, and cereals where heavily advertised brands dominate the market.[44] However, advertising generally does not create brand monopolies and reduce the opportunities for new products to be introduced to consumers. The fact is that in most product categories, there are a number of different brands on the store shelves and new products are being introduced all the time. As was noted in Chapter 15, over 10,000 new products were introduced in 1988, and the number of new products continues to increase every year.

The opportunity to advertise new brands gives companies the incentive to develop new brands and improve their existing ones. When a successful new product such as a personal computer or wine cooler is introduced, competitors quickly follow and use advertising to inform consumers about their brand and to attempt to convince them that it is superior to that of the original manufacturer. Companies such as Compaq, a personal computer manufacturer, have used advertising to compete against older, more established computer companies (Figure 22–11).

Effects on Competition

One of the most common criticisms economists have with advertising concerns its effects on competition. They argue that it is the power in the hands of the large firms

Figure 22–11   Advertising Helped Compaq Achieve Rapid Sales Growth

with the huge advertising budgets that creates a **barrier to entry,** which is a condition that makes it difficult for other firms to enter the market. This in return results in less competition and higher prices. Economists note that smaller firms already in the market find it difficult to compete against the large advertising budgets of the industry leaders and are often driven out of business. For example, in the U.S. beer industry the number of brewers has declined from 170 in 1970 to less than 50 in 1989. In their battle for market share, industry giants Anheuser-Busch and Miller, who have over 60 percent of the market, have increased their ad budgets substantially. Anheuser-Busch alone spent $634 million on advertising in 1988. However, on a per barrel basis, these companies are spending much less than smaller firms, making it very difficult for the latter to compete.

Large advertisers clearly enjoy certain competitive advantages. First, there are certain **economies of scale** in advertising, particularly with respect to factors such as media costs. Firms such as Procter & Gamble and Philip Morris Companies, which spend close to $2 billion a year on advertising and promotion, are able to make large media buys at a reduced rate, which can then be allocated to their various products at a lower cost.

Large advertisers usually sell more of a product or service, which means that they may have lower costs and can afford to allocate more monies to advertising and thus use the costly but more efficient media such as network television. Their large advertising outlays also give them greater opportunity to differentiate their products and develop brand loyalty. To the extent that these factors occur, smaller competitors are placed at a disadvantage, and new competitors are deterred from entering the market.

Figure 22–12 Advertising Has Helped Hyundai Enter the Automobile Market in the United States

While advertising may have an anticompetitive effect on a market, there is no clear evidence that advertising alone reduces competition, creates barriers to entry and thus increases market concentration. Lester Telser has noted that high levels of advertising are not always found in industries where firms have a large market share. He found an inverse relationship between product class advertising intensity and market share stability of the leading brands.[45] These findings run contrary to many economists' position that industries controlled by a small number of firms have high advertising expenditures and that high advertising budgets result in stable brand shares for market leaders.

Defenders of advertising also note that it is unrealistic to attribute a firm's market dominance and barriers to entry solely to advertising. There are a number of other factors to consider such as price, product quality, distribution effectiveness, production efficiencies, and competitive strategies. For many years products such as Coors beer and Hershey chocolate bars were dominant brands even though these companies spent very little on advertising. Hershey did not begin advertising until 1970, 66 years after the company was founded. The company relied on the quality of its products, its favorable reputation and image among consumers, and its extensive channels of distribution to market its brands. Industry leaders often tend to dominate markets because of their superior product quality and the fact that they have the best management and competitive strategies, not simply because of the size of their advertising budgets.[46]

While market entry against large established competitors is difficult, companies with a quality product at a reasonable price will often find a way to break into a market. Moreover, they usually find that rather than impeding their entry into the market, advertising actually facilitates their market entry by making it possible to communicate the benefits and features of their new product or brand to consumers. For example, Hyundai introduced its Korean-made cars to the U.S. market in 1986 and by 1988 was selling more than 200,000 vehicles a year. Hyundai has captured a significant portion of the U.S. automobile market by offering quality and reliable cars at a low price and spending nearly $25 million each year to tell consumers about them through advertisements such as the one shown in Figure 22–12.

Effects on Product Costs and Prices

A major area of debate among economists, advertisers, and consumer advocates and policymakers concerns the effects of advertising on product costs and prices. Critics argue that advertising results in increases in the prices consumers pay for products and services, citing a number of reasons for this. First, they note that the large sums of money spent on advertising a brand constitute an expense that must be covered, and thus the consumer ends up paying for it in the form of higher prices. This basic "somebody must pay for it" argument is a common criticism made by consumer advocates. Several studies have shown that firms with higher relative prices advertise their products more intensely than do those with lower relative prices.[47,48]

A second way advertising can result in higher prices is by increasing product differentiation and by adding to the perceived value of the product in the mind of the consumer. As noted by Paul Farris and Mark Albion, product differentiation occupies a central position in theories of advertising's economic effects.[49] The fundamental premise here is that advertising is able to increase the perceived differentiation of physically homogeneous products and to enable advertised brands to command a premium price. Albion and Farris offer some ways advertising can increase product differentiation, which are shown in Table 22–3.

Critics of advertising generally point to the differences in prices between national brands and private label brands that are physically similar, such as aspirin or tea bags, as evidence of the added value created by advertising. The consumers' willingness to pay a higher price for heavily advertised national brands rather than purchasing the lower-priced, nonadvertised brand because of this added value is seen as wasteful and irrational. However, it should be noted that consumers do not always buy for rational, functional reasons, as the emotional, psychological, and social benefits derived from purchasing a national brand can be important to many people. Moreover, as noted by Albion and Farris,

> Unfortunately there seems to be no single way to measure product differentiation, let alone determine how much is excessive or attributable to the effects of advertising.
> . . . Both price insensitivity and brand loyalty could be created by a number of factors such as higher product quality, better packaging, favorable use experience and market position. They are probably related to each other but need not be the result of advertising.[50]

Proponents of advertising offer several other counterarguments to the claim that advertising increases prices. They will acknowledge that advertising costs are, at least in part, paid for by consumers. However, this does not mean that consumers are paying more because of advertising, as it may actually help lower the overall cost of a product. For example, it has been argued that advertising helps firms achieve economies of scale in production and distribution by providing information to, and stimulating demand among, mass markets. These economies of scale help cut the cost of producing and marketing a product, which can in turn lead to lower prices—if the advertiser chooses to pass the cost savings on to the consumer. The ad shown in Figure 22–13, from the AAAA campaign, emphasizes this point. (Of course it is important to recognize that the decline in calculator prices was also due to improvements in technology and lower costs resulting from the development of microchips.)

Another way advertising can lower prices is by making a market more competitive, which usually leads to greater price competition. A study by Lee Benham found that prices of eyeglasses were 25 to 30 percent higher in states banning eyeglass ad-

Table 22–3   Some Views on How Advertising Increases Product Differentiation

Common Assumptions About Products and Consumers

A. Products can be described according to various product attributes or benefits provided to the consumer.
B. Different brands possess varying amounts of these attributes.
C. Consumers differ according to their desire for various attributes (preference functions).
D. Consumers do not perceive all brands as perfect substitutes for each other; therefore, "product differentiation" is said to exist. Price is not the sole criterion for selecting a brand to purchase.

Central Underlying Concepts

Market segmentation:
　　Certain groups of consumers with similar preference functions may perceive a subset of the total number of brands as being closer substitutes than the other brands.
Brand loyalty:
　　Brands perceived by a group of consumers to offer the "best" combination of attributes will be purchased more often by that group of consumers.
Price inelasticity:
　　Consumers will be willing to pay more for the brands that come closest to offering a combination of attributes that corresponds with their "ideal" brand.

Effects of Advertising

Advertising further differentiates products, increases brand loyalty, and increases price elasticity of demand.

A1. Introducing new attributes into the choice decision ("polyunsaturated fats are better for your health").
B1. Influencing consumers' assessment of the product's performance on a given attribute. (Although experience may play an important role, many qualities may be unmeasurable or impossible for consumers to judge from inspection and use—Crest has fluoride; Anacin dissolves faster.)
C1. Influencing the combination of attributes regarded as "ideal" (preference function)— for example, fewer preservatives are preferred.

Source: Paul W. Farris and Mark S. Albion, "The Impact of Advertising on the Price of Consumer Products," *Journal of Marketing* 44, no. 3 (Summer 1980), p. 19.

Figure 22–13   This Ad Suggests That Advertising Can Lead To Lower Product Costs

A SIMPLE LESSON IN ECONOMICS FOR ANYONE WHO BELIEVES ADVERTISING RAISES PRICES.

1965 Calculator—Over $2,000.00   1984 Calculator—Under $10.00

In the beginning there was the calculator.

It was a new idea. It had never been advertised. And it cost a fortune.

Then the people who sold calculators started to advertise them. That was hardly a new idea. But it, too, cost a fortune.

Now, you might think all that expensive advertising would drive the price of a calculator to incalculable heights.

But no. What happened was exactly the opposite.

It doesn't make sense. How can something as costly as advertising end up saving you money?

It's really quite simple. Advertising spreads news. When it spread the news of the calculator, people started to buy.

As more calculators were sold, more were produced. As more were produced, the cost of producing them came down. And because advertising creates competition, their quality and sophistication went up.

So today, using an electronic calculator is almost cheaper than counting on your fingers. And advertising helped make it happen—just as it has for countless other products.

In fact, with a little effort you could probably figure out precisely how much money advertising has saved you over the years.

But don't try it without a calculator.

ADVERTISING.
ANOTHER WORD FOR FREEDOM OF CHOICE.
American Association of Advertising Agencies

vertising versus those that permitted eyeglass advertising.[51] Robert Steiner analyzed the toy industry and concluded that advertising resulted in lower consumer prices. He argued that a curtailment or removal of TV advertising would be very detrimental to the level of consumer prices for toys.[52] Finally, as was noted in discussing the effects of advertising on choice, advertising is a means to market entry rather than a deterrent and helps stimulate product innovation, which makes markets more competitive and helps keep prices down.

Overall, it is difficult to reach any firm conclusions regarding the relationship between advertising and prices. After conducting an extensive review of this area, Farris and Albion concluded that

> the evidence connecting manufacturer advertising to prices is neither complete nor definitive . . . . consequently, we cannot say whether advertising is a tool of market efficiency or market power without further research.[53]

However, some economists disagree with this conclusion. For example, James Ferguson argues that economic theory indicates that advertising cannot increase the cost per unit of quality to consumers because if it did, consumers would not continue to respond positively to advertising.[54] He notes that advertising lowers the costs of information about brand qualities, leads to increases in brand quality, and lowers the average price per unit of quality.

Summarizing Economic Effects

Albion and Farris suggest that economists' perspectives regarding the effects of advertising can be divided into two principal models or schools of thought, each of which makes very different assumptions regarding the influence of advertising on the economy. Table 22−4 summarizes the main points of the Advertising = Market Power and the Advertising = Information perspectives.

Advertising = Market Power This model reflects traditional economic thinking and views advertising as a way of changing consumers' tastes, lowering their sensitivity to price, and building brand loyalty among buyers of advertised brands. This results in higher profits and market power for the large advertiser, reduces competition in the market, and leads to higher prices and fewer choice alternatives for consumers. Proponents of this viewpoint are generally negative in their assumptions regarding the economic impact of advertising.

Advertising = Information This model takes a more positive viewpoint of advertising's economic effects, as it views advertising as providing consumers with useful information, increasing their price sensitivity, which moves them toward lower-priced products, and increasing competition in the market. Advertising is viewed as a means of communicating with consumers and telling them about a product and its major features and attributes. More informed and knowledgeable consumers result in pressure on companies to provide high-quality products at lower prices, and efficient firms remain in the market, whereas inefficient firms leave as new entrants appear. Proponents of this model assume that the economic effects of advertising are favorable and view it as contributing to more efficient and competitive markets.

These two perspectives take very divergent views regarding the economic impact and value of advertising. We have considered arguments on both sides regarding the effect of advertising on consumer choice, competition, and product costs and prices. It is unlikely that the debate over the economic effects and value of advertising will be resolved soon. Many economists will continue to take a negative view of advertising and the effects it has on the functioning of the economy, whereas advertisers will continue to view it as an efficient way for companies to communicate with their customers and as an essential component of our economic system.

Table 22—4   Two Schools of Thought on Advertising's Role in the Economy

Advertising = Market Power		Advertising = Information
Advertising affects consumer preferences and tastes, changes product attributes, and differentiates the product from competitive offerings.	Advertising	Advertising informs consumers about product attributes and does not change the way they value those attributes.
Consumers become brand loyal and less price sensitive and perceive fewer substitutes for advertised brands.	Consumer Buying Behavior	Consumers become more price sensitive and buy best "value." Only the relationship between price and quality affects elasticity for a given product.
Potential entrants must overcome established brand loyalty and spend relatively more on advertising.	Barriers to Entry	Advertising makes entry possible for new brands because it can communicate product attributes to consumers.
Firms are insulated from market competition and potential rivals; concentration increases, leaving firms with more discretionary power.	Industry Structure and Market Power	Consumers can compare competitive offerings easily and competitive rivalry is increased. Efficient firms remain, and as the inefficient leave, new entrants appear; the effect on concentration is ambiguous.
Firms can charge higher prices and are not as likely to compete on quality or price dimensions. Innovation may be reduced.	Market Conduct	More informed consumers put pressures on firms to lower prices and improve quality. Innovation is facilitated via new entrants.
High prices and excessive profits accrue to advertisers and give them even more incentive to advertise their products. Output is restricted compared with conditions of perfect competition.	Market Performance	Industry prices are decreased. The effect on profits due to increased competition and increased efficiency is ambiguous.

Source: Paul W. Farris and Mark S. Albion, "The Impact of Advertising on the Price of Consumer Products," *Journal of Marketing* 44, no. 3 (Summer 1980), p. 18.

Figure 22—14   This Message Summarizes the Viewpoint of Proponents of the Advertising Industry Regarding Its Economic Effects

<u>Now, what does advertising mean?</u>

To me it means that if we believe to any degree whatsoever in the economic system under which we live, in a high standard of living and in high employment, advertising is the most efficient known way of moving goods in practically every product class.

My proof is that millions of businessmen have chosen advertising over and over again in the operations of their business.

Some of their decisions may have been wrong, but they must have thought they were right or they wouldn't go back to be stung twice by the same kind of bee.

It's a pretty safe bet that in the next ten years many Americans will be using products and devices that no one in this room has even heard of. Judging purely by past performance, American advertising can be relied on to make them known and accepted overnight at the lowest possible prices.

Advertising, of course, makes possible our unparalleled variety of magazines, newspapers, business publications, and radio and television stations.

It must be said that without advertising we would have a far different nation, and one that would be much the poorer—not merely in material commodities, but in the life of the spirit.

Leo Burnett

This excerpt is from a speech given by Leo Burnett on the occasion of the American Association of Advertising Agencies' 50th Anniversary, April 20th, 1967.

The ad shown in Figure 22—14, which is an excerpt from a speech given by famous adman Leo Burnett, summarizes the perspective of most advertising people on the economic effects of advertising. Perhaps the only area of agreement will be that advertising is indeed a major economic force that has both positive and negative effects on the functioning of our economy.

Summary

Advertising is a very powerful institution and has been the target of considerable criticism regarding its social and economic impact. Much of the criticism of advertising concerns the specific techniques and methods used by advertisers, as well as advertising's effect on societal values, tastes, lifestyles, and behavior. Critics argue that advertising is deceptive and untruthful; that it is often offensive, irritating, or in poor taste; and that it exploits certain groups such as children. Many people feel that advertising should be informative only in nature and that advertisers should not use subjective claims, puffery, embellishment, or persuasive techniques.

Advertising often offends consumers by the type of appeal or manner of presentation used, with sexually suggestive ads and the use of nudity receiving the most criticism. Advertisers argue that their ads are consistent with contemporary values and lifestyles and are appropriate for the target audiences they are attempting to reach. The issue of advertising to children is an area of particular concern, as critics argue that children lack the experience, knowledge, and ability to process and evaluate persuasive advertising messages rationally. Although an FTC proposal to severely restrict advertising to children was defeated, advertising to children remains a controversial issue.

The pervasiveness of advertising and its prevalence in the mass media have led critics to argue that it plays a major role in influencing and transmitting social values. Opinions as to the value of advertising's contribution to values are often very negative. Advertising has been charged with encouraging materialism, manipulating consumers to buy things they do not really want or need, perpetuating stereotyping through its portrayal of certain groups such as women and minorities, and controlling the media.

Advertising has also been scrutinized very carefully with regard to its economic effects. The basic economic role of advertising is to provide consumers with information to assist them in making consumption decisions. Advertising is viewed by some as a detrimental force that has a negative effect on competition, product costs, and consumer prices. Economists' perspectives regarding the economic effects of advertising follow two basic schools of thought: the Advertising = Market Power model and the Advertising = Information model. Arguments consistent with each perspective were considered in analyzing the economic effects of advertising.

Key Terms

Consumer socialization process
Materialism
Protestant ethic

Differentiation
Barrier to entry
Economies of scale

Discussion Questions

1. Evaluate the argument that advertising should be primarily informative in nature. Do you agree or disagree with this argument? Defend your position.
2. Find examples of three ads that you find irritating, offensive, or in bad taste. Discuss the basis of your displeasure with these ads.
3. Many advertisers complain that a double standard exists for television programs versus commercials, as the networks scrutinize commercials more closely than the shows. Do you agree with the networks' position that commercials should be held to higher standards than programs? Why or why not?
4. Evaluate the arguments for and against advertising to children. Do you agree with the proposal the FTC put forth in 1979 to ban or limit severely children's advertising?
5. With which position do you agree?
    - "Advertising determines American consumers' tastes and values and is responsible for creating a materialistic society."
    - "Advertising is a reflection of society and mirrors its tastes and values."
6. Discuss the arguments for and against the claim that advertising exerts too much influence or even controls the media.
7. Discuss the role of advertising as an economic force, giving attention to arguments for and against its effects on the economy.
8. Do you feel that advertising increases or decreases the costs of products and services? Defend your position.
9. Compare the Advertising = Market Power and Advertising = Information perspectives regarding the economic effects of advertising.

Notes

1. Fred Danzig, "The Good, the Bad, the Ugly," *Advertising Age,* November 9, 1988, p. 107.
2. Robert L. Heilbroner, "Demand for the Supply Side," *New York Review of Books* 38 (June 11, 1981), p. 40.
3. J. Edward Russo, Barbara L. Metcalf, and Debra Stephens, "Identifying Misleading Advertising," *Journal of Consumer Research* 8 (September 1981), pp. 119–31.
4. Quote cited in Alex M. Freedman, "FTC Alleges Campbell Ad Is Deceptive," *The Wall Street Journal,* January 27, 1989, pp. B1, 4.
5. Shelby D. Hunt, "Informational vs. Persuasive Advertising: An Appraisal," *Journal of Advertising,* Summer 1976, pp. 5–8.
6. Study cited in Ron Alsop, "Advertisers Find the Climate Less Hostile Outside the U.S.," *The Wall Street Journal,* December 10, 1987, p. 29.
7. "More Stations Accepting Condom Spots," *Broadcasting,* February 23, 1987, p. 41.
8. David A. Aaker and Donald E. Bruzzone, "Causes of Irritation in Advertising," *Journal of Marketing* 5, Spring 1985, pp. 47–57.
9. Stephen A. Greyser, "Irritation in Advertising," *Journal of Advertising Research* 13 (February 1973), pp. 3–10.
10. Ron Alsop, "Personal Product Ads Abound as Public Gets More Tolerant," *The Wall Street Journal,* April 14, 1986, p. 19.
11. "Maidenform Is Going Braless in Its Sexy New Ad Campaign," *The Wall Street Journal,* April 23, 1987, p. 31.
12. Bruce Horowitz, "Sex in Ads: It Can Even Sell Detergent," *Los Angeles Times,* July 8, 1987, p. 1.
13. Laurie P. Cohen, "Sex in Ads Becomes Less Explicit as Firms Turn to Romantic Images," *The Wall Street Journal,* February 11, 1988, p. 25.
14. Rita Weisskoff, "Current Trends in Children's Advertising," *Journal of Advertising Research* 25, no. 1 (1985), pp. RC 12–14.
15. Scott Ward, Daniel B. Wackman, and Ellen Wartella, *How Children Learn to Buy: The Development of Consumer Information Processing Skills* (Beverly Hills, Calif.: Sage, 1979).
16. Thomas S. Robertson and John R. Rossiter, "Children and Commercial Persuasion: An Attribution Theory Analysis," *Journal of Consumer Research* 1, no. 1 (June 1974), pp. 13–20.
17. Scott Ward and Daniel B. Wackman, "Children's Information Processing of Television Advertising," in *New Models for Communications Research,* ed. G. Kline and P. Clark (Beverly Hills, Calif.: Sage, 1974), pp. 81–119.
18. Merrie Brucks, Gary M. Armstrong, and Marvin E. Goldberg, "Children's Use of Cognitive Defenses against Television Advertising: A Cognitive Response Approach," *Journal of Consumer Research* 14, no. 4 (March 1988), pp. 471–82.
19. For a discussion of consumer socialization see Scott Ward, "Consumer Socialization," *Journal of Consumer Research* 1, no. 2 (September 1974), pp. 1–14.
20. *FTC Staff Report on Advertising to Children* (Washington, D.C.: Government Printing Office, 1978).
21. Ben M. Enis, Dale R. Spencer, and Don R. Webb, "Television Advertising and Children: Regulatory vs. Competitive Perspectives," *Journal of Advertising* 9, no. 1 (1980), pp. 19–25.
22. Daniel B. Wackman, Scott Ward, and Emily Wartella, "Comments on FTC Staff Report," *Public Policy Issues in Marketing,* 1979, pp. 81–97.
23. Ronald Alsop, "Watchdogs Zealously Censor Advertising Targeted to Kids," *The Wall Street Journal,* September 5, 1985, p. 35.
24. Robert E. Hite and Randy Eck, "Advertising to Children: Attitudes of Business vs. Consumers," *Journal of Advertising Research,* October/November 1987, pp. 40–53.
25. Ronald Berman, *Advertising and Social Change* (Beverly Hills, Calif.: Sage, 1981), p. 13.
26. John K. Galbraith, *The New Industrial State* (Boston: Houghton Mifflin, 1967), cited in Richard W. Pollay, "The Distorted Mirror: Reflections on the Unintended Consequences of Advertising," *Journal of Marketing,* August 1986, p. 25.
27. Raymond A. Bauer and Stephen A. Greyser, "The Dialogue That Never Happens," *Harvard Business Review* 50 (January/February 1969), pp. 122–28.
28. Morris B. Holbrook, "Mirror Mirror on the Wall, What's Unfair in the Reflections on Advertising," *Journal of Marketing* 5 (July 1987), pp. 95–103.

29. Theodore Levitt, "The Morality of Advertising," *Harvard Business Review,* July/August 1970, pp. 84–92.

30. Stephen Fox, *The Mirror Makers: A History of American Advertising and Its Creators* (New York: Morrow, 1984), p. 330.

31. Richard W. Pollay, "The Distorted Mirror: Reflections on the Unintended Consequences of Advertising," *Journal of Marketing* 50 (April 1986), p. 33.

32. Jules Backman, "Is Advertising Wasteful?" *Journal of Marketing* 32, January 1968, pp. 2–8.

33. Hunt, "Informational."

34. Ibid., p. 6.

35. Alice E. Courtney and Thomas W. Whipple, "Sex Stereotyping in America: An Annotated Bibliography," *Marketing Science Institute,* Report no. 80–100, February 1980, p. v.

36. "Women's Image in Ads Changing, But Shape Isn't," *Marketing News,* February 15, 1988, p. 6.

37. Waltrud M. Kassarjian, "Blacks as Communicators and Interpreters of Mass Communication," *Journalism Quarterly,* Summer 1973, pp. 285–91.

38. Helen Czepic and J. Steven Kelly, "Analyzing Hispanic Roles in Advertising," in *Current Issues and Research in Advertising,* ed. James H. Leigh and Claude Martin (Ann Arbor: University of Michigan, 1983), pp. 219–40.

39. R. F. Busch, Allan S. Resnik, and Bruce L. Stern, "A Content Analysis of the Portrayal of Black Models in Magazine Advertising," in *American Marketing Association Proceedings: Marketing in the 1980s,* ed. Richard P. Bagozzi (Chicago: AMA, 1980).

40. R. F. Busch, Allan S. Resnik, and Bruce L. Stern, "There Are More Blacks in TV Commercials," *Journal of Advertising Research* 17 (1977), pp. 21–25.

41. Robert Mack, "Tapping into the Hispanic Market," *Marketing Communications,* March 1988, pp. 54–61.

42. Judith Graham, " 'Roe' Advertisers Risk Boycotts," *Advertising Age,* May 15, 1989, p. 2.

43. For a discussion of ethics in advertising see John Crichton, "Morals and Ethics in Advertising," in *Ethics, Morality & the Media,* ed. Lee Thayer (New York: Hastings House, 1980), pp. 105–15.

44. For a discussion of monopolies in the cereal industry see Paul N. Bloom, "The Cereal Industry: Monopolists or Super Marketers?" *MSU Business Topics,* Summer 1978, pp. 41–49.

45. Lester G. Telser, "Advertising and Competition," *Journal of Political Economy,* December 1964, pp. 537–62.

46. Robert D. Buzzell, Bradley T. Gale, and Ralph G. M. Sultan, "Market Share—A Key to Profitability," *Harvard Business Review,* January/February 1975, pp. 97–106.

47. Robert D. Buzzell and Paul W. Farris, "Advertising Cost in Consumer Goods Industries," *Marketing Science Institute,* Report no. 76–111, August 1976.

48. Paul W. Farris and David J. Reibstein, "How Prices, Ad Expenditures, and Profits Are Linked," *Harvard Business Review* 57 (November/December 1979), pp. 173–84.

49. Paul W. Farris and Mark S. Albion, "The Impact of Advertising on the Price of Consumer Products," *Journal of Marketing* 44, no. 3 (Summer 1980), pp. 17–35.

50. Ibid., p. 19.

51. Lee Benham, "The Effect of Advertising on the Price of Eyeglasses," *Journal of Law and Economics* 15 (October 1972), pp. 337–52.

52. Robert L. Steiner, "Does Advertising Lower Consumer Price?" *Journal of Marketing* 37, no. 4 (October 1973), pp. 19–26.

53. Farris and Albion, "The Impact," p. 30.

54. James M. Ferguson, "Comments on the Impact of Advertising on the Price of Consumer Products," *Journal of Marketing* 46, no. 1 (Winter 1982), pp. 102–05.

Index

Credits

p. 185: © 1987 DDB Worldwide Inc. Used by permission DDB Needham Worldwide Inc. and Partnership for a Drug Free America.   Fig. 6–20, p. 185: Reprinted from *Journal of Marketing,* published by the American Marketing Association.   Fig. 6–21, p. 187: Used by permission of Miller Brewing Company.   Fig. 6–23, p. 190. Copyright Apple Computer, Inc., 1984.   Fig. 6–24, p. 191: Used by permission of Chrysler Motors.

Chapter 7

Fig. 7–2, p. 201: Coca-Cola, diet Coke, and Sprite are trademarks of The Coca-Cola Company and are used with permission.   Fig. 7–4, p. 204: Courtesy of Blue Cross of California.   Fig. 7–5, p. 206: © The Procter & Gamble Company. Used with permission.   Fig. 7–6, p. 209: SRI International.   Fig. 7–7, p. 210: Used by permission of McCann Erickson, McCann Health Care.   Fig. 7–8, p. 212: Courtesy National Decision Systems, Inc., Encinitas, CA.   Fig. 7–9, p. 212: Schenley Industries Inc.   Fig. 7–10, p. 214: Used by permission of Scott Tinley PerformanceWear.   Fig. 7–11, p. 215: Reprint permission by Timex Corporation.   Fig. 7–12, p. 215: Used by permission of Movado Watch Corporation, Lyndhurst, NJ.   Fig. 7–13, p. 215: Young & Rubicam Advertising Agency.   Fig. 7–14, p. 216: Used by permission of Colgate-Palmolive Company.   Fig. 7–15, p. 217: Used by permission of Matsushita Electric Corporation of America.   Fig. 7–16, p. 218: Used by permission of Tyco Industries, Inc.   Fig. 7–17A, p. 218: Used by permission of L.A. Gear CA Inc.   Fig. 7–17B, p. 219: Used by permission of Pete Stone Photography & NIKE, Inc.   Fig. 7–17C, p. 219: Used by permission of New Balance Athletic Shoe, Inc.   Fig. 7–18, p. 220: Used by permission of WD-40 Company.   Fig. 7–19, p. 220: Used by permission of The Potato Board, Denver, CO.   Fig. 7–20, p. 221: Used by permission of DMB&B and General Motors Corp., Pontiac Division.   Fig. 7–21, p. 221: Courtesy of Domecq Importers, Larchmont, NY.   Fig. 7–22, p. 222: Courtesy of the Museum of Modern Mythology.   Fig. 7–23, p. 223: From Rolling Stone Magazine 1988. By Straight Arrow Publishers, Inc. © 1988. All Rights Reserved. Reprinted by permission. Advertising firm: Fallon McElligot.   Exhibit 7–3B, p. 224: Courtesy Pontiac Division of General Motors.

Chapter 8

Fig. 8–1, p. 229: Photos courtesy of NCR Corporation. Materials courtesy of NCR Corporation.   Fig. 8–2, p. 230: Courtesy The Dow Chemical Company.   Fig. 8–3, p. 231: Reprinted with permission of Hoffman LaRoche, Inc.   Exhibit 8–1, p. 236: Oldsmobile Division, General Motors Corporation.   Fig. 8–5, p. 237: Cincinnati Microwave, Inc.   Fig. 8–6, p. 238: *L.A. Times* and Pat's Ski & Sports.   Fig. 8–7, p. 239: RCA Brand. Thomson Consumer Electronics, Inc.   Fig. 8–10, p. 247: Copyright 1989 McDonald's Corporation. Re-

printed with permission.   Fig. 8–11, p. 249: Reprinted from *Journal of Advertising Research,* Copyright 1980 by the Advertising Research Foundation.

Chapter 10

Fig. 10–5, p. 296: *Channels.* C. C. Publishing L. P.

Chapter 11

Fig. 11–2, p. 331: Radio Advertising Bureau.   Fig. 11–3, p. 332: Courtesy Mazda Motor of America, Inc.   Fig. 11–5, p. 334: Fred/Alan Inc.   Fig. 11–6, p. 336: Used by permission of Federal Express.   Table 11–2, p. 339: Reprinted by permission of Variety, Inc. *Variety* is a registered trademark of Variety, Inc. Fig. 11–7, p. 342: Eisaman, Johns & Laws, Inc. Advertising.   Fig. 11–9, p. 349: Nielsen Media Research.   Fig. 11–10, p. 352: The Arbitron Company.   Fig. 11–11, p. 355: The Arbitron Company.   Fig. 11–12, p. 358: © 1989 ESPN, Inc.   Fig. 11–13, p. 359: Courtesy of Turner Broadcasting System, Inc. Exhibit 11–6, p. 364: Hugh Thrasher, Executive Vice President, Motel 6, L.P.   Fig. 11–15, p. 365: Radio Advertising Bureau.   Fig. 11–16, p. 366: Used by permission of Martlet Importing Company.   Fig. 11–17, p. 369: Rodger M. Seelert, Califormula Radio Group. Fig. 11–18, p. 369: Standard Rate and Data Service, Spot Radio Rates and Data.   Fig. 11–19, p. 370: The Arbitron Company.

Chapter 12

Fig. 12–1, p. 378: "The Best and Worst Selling Covers of 1988," by Linda Williams. Copyright, 1989, *Los Angeles Times.* Reprinted by permission.   Fig. 12–2, p. 383: Courtesy *Runner's World* magazine.   Fig. 12–3, p. 383: Reprinted with permission of BEEF magazine.   Fig. 12–4, p. 384: Courtesy of *Newsweek.*   Exhibit 12–1, p. 385: Courtesy of Architectural Digest Publishing Corp./Warren Psaff, Inc.   Fig. 12–5, p. 386: San Diego Magazine Publishing Company.   Fig. 12–6, p. 387: Courtesy of *Newsweek.*   Fig. 12–7, p. 388: © 1988 McDonald's Corporation, used with permission.   Exhibit 12–2A, p. 389: Used by permission of Honeywell, Inc. Exhibit 12–2B, p. 389: Transamerica Corporation.   Fig. 12–8, p. 390: Used by permission of WD-40 Company.   Fig. 12–9, p. 391: Copyright 1989 The Hearst Corporation. Fig. 12–10, p. 392: Photographed for MPA by Stephen Wilkes.   Fig. 12–11, p. 396: San Diego Magazine Publishing Company.   Fig. 12–12, p. 399: Promotion Director, Petersen Publishing Company.   Fig. 12–13, p. 400: *Business Week* Magazine.   Exhibit 12–3, p. 402: Created by Lois/GGK Advertising.   Fig. 12–14, p. 403: Diario Las Americas.   Fig. 12–15, p. 404: *Los Angeles Times.*   Exhibit 12–4, p. 407: Merrill Lynch & Co., Inc.   Fig. 12–16, p. 408: *Los Angeles Times* Marketing Research Department.   Fig. 12–17, p. 410: Services provided by the Union-Tribune Publishing Company.   Fig. 12–18, p. 413:

The Columbus Dispatch, 34 S. Third St., Columbus, OH 43215.   Fig. 12–19, p. 414: Newspaper Advertising Bureau, Inc.   Fig. 12–20, p. 415: Frank Della Sala, Marketing Manager—The Network of City Business Journals; Jim Aylward, Creative Director—Barkley & Evergreen Advertising; Powell Michael, Art Director—Barkley & Evergreen Advertising.

Chapter 13

Fig. 13–1, p. 422: Reprinted with permission from *Advertising Age.* © Crain Communications, Inc. All Rights Reserved.   Fig. 13–2, p. 423: © 1989, Bijan Fragrances, Inc.   Fig. 13–3, p. 424: Photo courtesy of Robert Keith & Co., San Diego, CA.   Fig. 13–4, p. 426: Copyright by Ken Kerbs Photography, 1989.   Fig. 13–5, p. 429: Used by permission of American Airlines.   Fig. 13–6, p. 430: TDI (Transportation Displays, Inc.)   Fig. 13–7, p. 430: TDI (Transportation Displays, Inc.)   Fig. 13–8, p. 432: Specialty Advertising Association International.   Fig. 13–10, p. 436: Courtesy of Paramount Pictures Corporation.   Fig. 13–13, p. 444: Courtesy Porsche Cars North America.   Fig. 13–14, p. 445: Used by permission of The ESOT Group, Inc.   Fig. 13–15, p. 447: Courtesy of the Times Mirror Company, Los Angeles, CA.   Table 13–8, p. 449: Courtesy of Alvin B. Zeller, Mailing Lists.   Fig. 13–16 (left), p. 450: CRS Advertising, c/o Charles Schwab & Co., Inc.   Fig. 13–16 (right), p. 450: Used by permission of Cadillac Motor Car Division.   Table 13–9, pp. 452–53: Simmons Market Research Bureau, Inc.

Chapter 14

Fig. 14-1, p. 459: © 1986 Schieffelin & Company.   Fig. 14-2, p. 459: DuPont Flooring Systems—Stainmaster™ Carpet. Fig. 14-3, p. 462: D'Arcy Masius Benton & Bowles.   Fig. 14-4, p. 463: Courtesy of Lever Brothers Company.   Fig. 14-5, p. 466: Used by permission of Kresser & Robbins Inc.   Fig. 14-6, p. 467: Courtesy Porsche Cars North America. Fig. 14-8, p. 470: Courtesy of San Diego Trust & Savings Bank.   Fig. 14-9, p. 473: Courtesy of Hathaway.   Fig. 14-10, p.474 Reprinted with permission of Mobil Corporation.   Fig. 14-11, p. 476: Used by permission of Lawman Sportswear, Inc. and Banks-Shand & Associates.   Fig. 14-12, p. 476: Evyan Perfumes, New York, NY 10016. Fig. 14-13, p. 477: ® Kellogg Company. ©1988 Kellogg Company, all rights reserved. Actor: Alfred Dennis.   Fig. 14-14, p. 477: Avia Athletic Footwear.   Fig. 14-15, p. 478: © The Procter & Gamble Company. Used with permission. Fig. 14-16, p. 479: Chevrolet Motor Division, General Motors Corporation.   Fig. 14-17, p. 480: The Goodyear Tire & Rubber Company. Fig. 14-18, p. 481: Used by permission of Canon USA, Inc.   Fig. 14-19, p. 481: Used by permission of Lucky Stores, Inc.   Fig. 14-20, p. 482: Used by permission of Subaru of America.   Fig. 14-21, p. 482: Used by permission of American Airlines.